PERU

ROSS WEHNER & RENÉE DEL GAUDIO

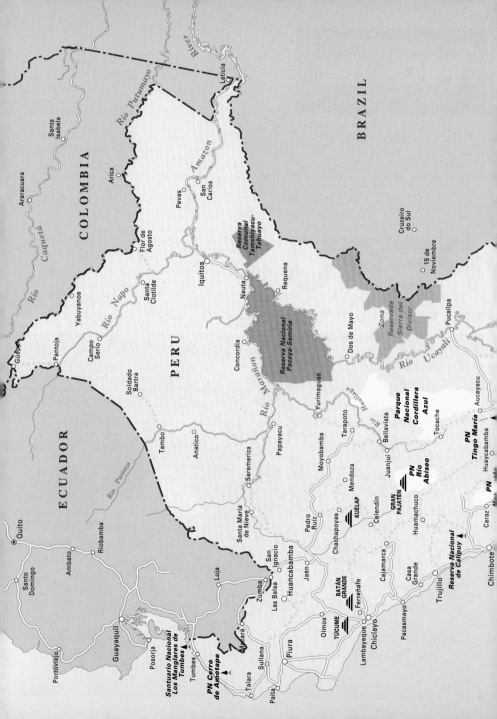

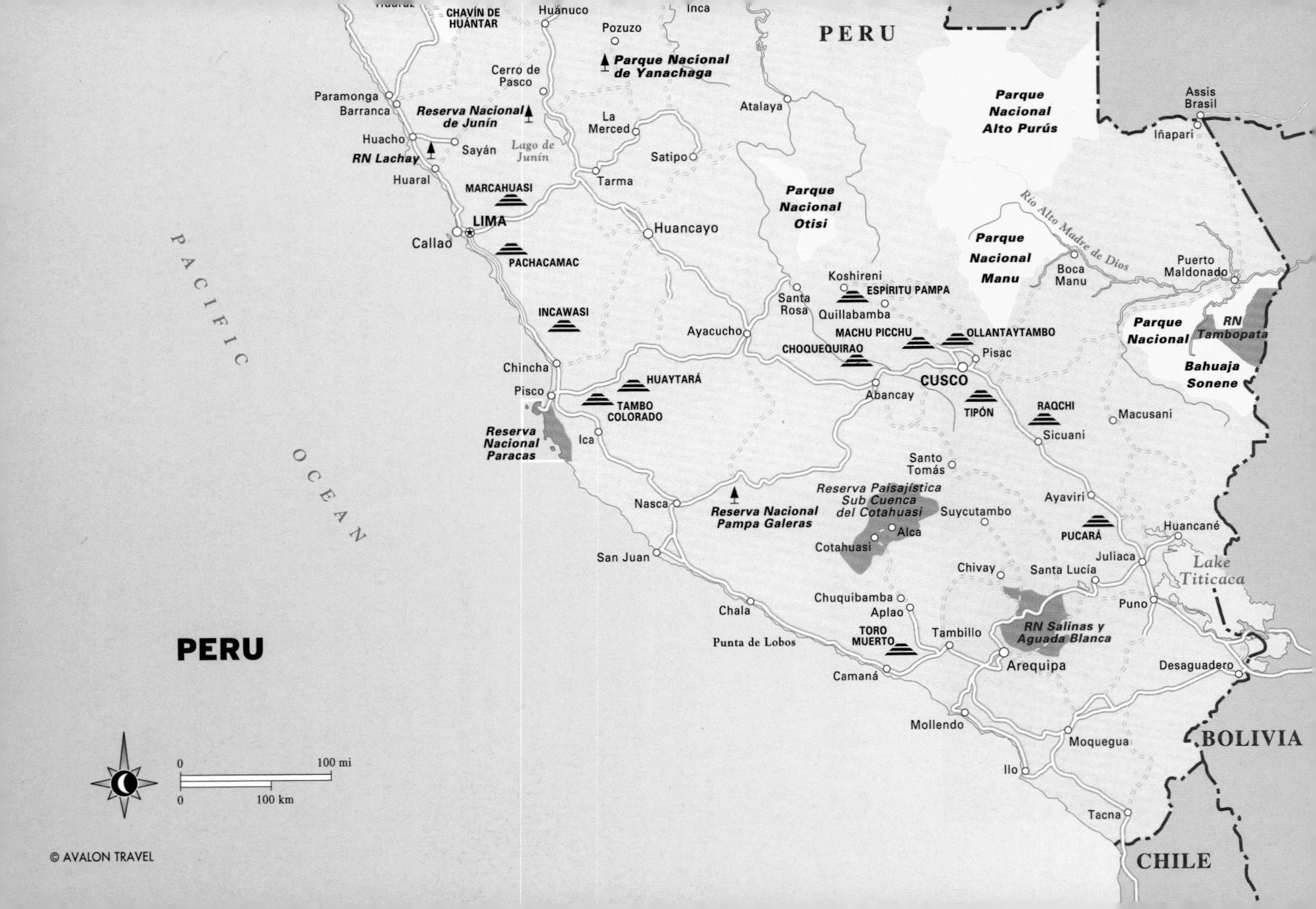

PERU

0 100 km
0 100 mi

PACIFIC OCEAN

PERU

CHILE

BOLIVIA

Paramonga
Barranca
RN Lachay
Huacho
Sayán
Huaral
Callao
LIMA
MARCAHUASI
PACHACAMAC
Reserva Nacional
de Junín
CHAVÍN DE
HUANTAR
Huánuco
Cerro de
Pasco
Pozuzo
La Merced
Lago de
Junín
Parque Nacional
de Yanachaga
Inca
INCAWASI
Chincha
Pisco
Reserva
Nacional
Paracas
Ica
TAMBO
COLORADO
HUAYTARÁ
Tarma
Huancayo
Satipo
Atalaya
San Juan
Nasca
Ayacucho
Santa
Rosa
Quillabamba
Koshireni
ESPIRITU PAMPA
Parque
Nacional
Otisi
Punta de Lobos
Chala
Reserva Nacional
Pampa Galeras
Reserva Paisajística
Sub Cuenca
del Cotahuasi
CHOQUEQUIRAO
MACHU PICCHU
Parque
Nacional
Manu
Parque
Nacional
Alto Purús
Chuquibamba
Cotahuasi
Alca
Santo
Tomás
Abancay
CUSCO
OLLANTAYTAMBO
Boca
Manu
Assis
Brasil
Iñapari
Camaná
TORO
MUERTO
Aplao
Tambillo
Chivay
Suycutambo
TIPÓN
Pisac
Puerto
Maldonado
Mollendo
Arequipa
RN Salinas y
Aguada Blanca
Santa Lucía
Ayaviri
Sicuani
RACCHI
PUCARÁ
Macusani
Parque
Nacional
Bahuaja
Sonene
RN
Tambopata
Ilo
Moquegua
Tacna
Desaguadero
Puno
Huancané
Juliaca
Lake
Titicaca
Río Madre de Dios

Contents

Discover Peru

The Spaniards' first assumptions about Peru, when they sailed down its coast in 1528, involved barren beaches and man-eating savages. It was not until they journeyed through ochre desert and lush river valleys, up and over snowy passes, and into the sublime, magical realm of the altiplano that they realized the importance of the Inca. This empire, the New World's most advanced, had temples and highways rivaling those of Renaissance Europe and an abundance of what the Spaniards most wanted, gold. In Cusco, the Inca capital, the Spaniards found finely crafted gold figurines, four-inch-thick temple walls, shields and vases, and even hand plows — all made of gold.

Today Cusco remains the primary draw for travelers to Peru. People come to wander the cobblestone streets, marvel at the Spanish churches built atop massive Inca walls, eat alpaca steaks and sweet corn, and party until dawn at the city's nightclubs. Those who stumble off the beaten path in Peru's altiplano, or high plains, will journey back in time to the stone huts, the fields of quinoa, and the brightly clothed Quechuan people first encountered by the Spaniards. In the nearby cloud forest, reachable only by train or trek, is one of the world's greatest wonders: Machu Picchu, a city of stone literally carved into a massive jungle ridge.

Yet Cusco and Machu Picchu are just the beginning of what Peru

offers. There are at least a dozen archaeological sites around Peru that rival the historical significance of Machu Picchu; perfect breaks to surf and heaping bowls of ceviche to eat in the northern beach towns; snow-covered mountains to climb; freeze-dried-potato soup to eat in stone huts with Quechuan families; and miles of Amazon to float with nothing more than a hammock and a bunch of bananas.

Of special interest is Peru's desert coast, which is rubbing shoulders with India and Egypt as a must-see destination for those drawn to the ancient and mysterious. A series of advanced cultures such as the Nasca, Moche, Chimú, and Sicán flourished here thousands of years before the Inca. They left behind huge adobe pyramids, tombs, stone carvings, brightly painted murals, and, most importantly, tombs. Of special interest are the Nasca Lines, an enigmatic collection of hummingbirds, monkeys, and mythical beings etched into the desert.

But perhaps the most impressive aspect of Peru is the people and the depth of their culture, which continues to maintain its unique identity today.

Planning Your Trip

▶ WHERE TO GO

The Sacred Valley

Begin your trip to the Cusco area with the Sacred Valley, which the Inca considered paradise for its fertile earth. Up and down the valley, the Inca built a string of the Inca's most sacred sites, including temples and fortresses in Pisac and Ollantaytambo. This charming valley is a destination in its own right with a great range of lodging and restaurants, day hikes, horseback rides, mountain biking, and more.

Machu Picchu

The Sacred Valley is cut by the Río Urubamba, which rushes toward the most fabled achievement of the Inca: Machu Picchu. The fabled lost city is a breathtaking citadel arranged along a jungle-covered ridge. Hiking either the Salcantay route or the Inca Trail, a paved stone highway that culminates in a bird's-eye view of the ruins, is a memorable way to arrive. The train ride in and out also affords incredible views of the area's scenery.

Cusco

After visiting the Sacred Valley and Machu Picchu, travelers are acclimatized to Cusco's high altitude. They are also primed for Cusco's complex culture, which remains today an antagonistic mixture of Inca and Spanish cultures. The Spanish erected more than a dozen baroque churches atop flawless Inca walls. Cusco must-visits are the artisan barrio of San Blas, the fortress of Sacsayhuamán, and the Inca sun temple Coricancha.

Lake Titicaca and Canyon Country

The highlight of a visit to Lake Titicaca, the world's highest navigable lake, is an overnight

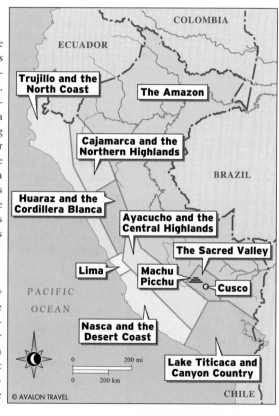

IF YOU HAVE...

- **ONE WEEK:** Visit the Sacred Valley, Cusco, and Machu Picchu.

- **TWO WEEKS:** Visit all of the above but extend your time in the Sacred Valley to hike, mountain bike, and go horseback riding. Add on a hike along the Inca Trail or the Salcantay trek to Machu Picchu, or experience the Amazon around Puerto Maldonado or the Manu Biosphere Reserve.

- **THREE WEEKS:** Add an overland adventure from the Moche, Sicán, and Sipán archaeological monuments of Peru's northern coast up into the Chachapoya cloud forest. This remote corner of Peru is rich in exotic birds, lost cities such as Kuélap, and off-the-beaten-path treks.

the sacred mountain of Salcantay near Cusco

with a family on islands where villagers cultivate potatoes and quinoa on rock terraces. Arequipa, near Peru's southern coast, is a sophisticated colonial city known for its European feel, world-renowned cuisine, and its 16th-century convents and churches built of *sillar*, a sparkling white volcanic stone. Stone villages dot the rim of nearby Colca Canyon, where Cruz del Cóndor is a guarantee for spotting the world's largest flying bird.

The Amazon

If you fly above the Amazon, you will see clouds and an endless emerald blanket of vegetation, interrupted only by the muddy squiggles of jungle rivers. Here travel is by motorized dugout canoe, which is one of the best ways to see toucans, tanagers, and other rainforest birds. Near Iquitos it is common to see pink river dolphins and lily pads the size of dinner tables. Around Puerto Maldonado or Parque Nacional Manu you have a good chance of seeing giant otters and other Amazon mega fauna.

Nasca and the Desert Coast

Dug into the landscape a thousand years ago and preserved by the arid climate, the unexplained Nasca Lines form hummingbirds, whales, and also trapezoids. Nearby is the Ica Desert, an unexplored area of sand dunes and an astounding variety of marine fossils. On the way to Lima, stop at the Reserva Nacional de Paracas, a coastal reserve for sea lions, 200 bird species, and the endangered Humboldt penguin. Farther on is Chincha, where there is a small, outspoken Afro-Peruvian culture.

Lima

Traditionally avoided by travelers because of its gray weather and grimy downtown, Lima is making a roaring comeback. On the Plaza Mayor, upscale restaurants and cafés now neighbor the country's most important colonial *catedral* and the presidential and archbishop's palaces. The outlying districts of San Isidro and Miraflores offer the greatest range of lodging, bars, and Peruvian cuisine. Bohemian Barranco is the nightlife district and favored backpackers' den.

Hiking through the Cordillera Vilcanota east of Cusco, trekkers approach the massive Nevado Ausangate (20,900 feet).

Ayacucho and the Central Highlands

Nowhere is Peru's colonial past more palpable than Ayacucho. The most stunning city of Peru's Andes, Ayacucho has a gorgeous *catedral* and two dozen other colonial churches and is surrounded by ruins from the pre-Inca Huari culture. Farther north the mountains give way to the rammed earth villages of the

Río Urubamba in the Sacred Valley

Mantaro Valley, which is the best place in Peru to buy weavings, carved gourds, and other handicrafts.

Huaraz and the Cordillera Blanca

Trekkers who make it over Punta Unión, a pass at 4,750 meters in the Cordillera Blanca, rub their eyes in disbelief when they first see Alpamayo. This pyramid of fluted snow lures climbers from around the world. It is but one of dozens of majestic snow giants that spring from Peru's high grasslands to form a spectacular tumble of broken glaciers, jagged peaks, and emerald lakes such as Lagunas Llanganuco. Farther south, and separated by an area of high-altitude grasslands, the Cordillera Huayhuash rises in even more dramatic shapes.

Trujillo and the North Coast

Huaca de la Luna, an adobe pyramid, was built by the ancient Moche culture and is now surrounded by the colonial city of Trujillo. The most famous of the Moche rulers were the Lords of Sipán, whose tombs were unearthed in 1987 near Chiclayo. The gold masks, huge turquoise-studded earrings, scepters, and other items from the tombs are on display at Chiclayo's excellent Museo Tumbas Reales de Sipán. The cultures that succeeded the Moche left a string of impressive cities on the north coast, including Chan Chan, near Trujillo, and Túcume and Batán Grande, near Chiclayo.

Cajamarca and the Northern Highlands

The gorgeous countryside around Cajamarca is laid with Inca paths, or Qhapaq Ñan, and the enigmatic irrigation canals of Cumbemayo. One of the country's best baroque churches is in Cajamarca's Complejo Belén, which also houses Atahualpa's famous ransom room, or Cuarto de Rescate. Up in the cloud forests farther inland, the Chachapoya culture built a series of stone cities. The crowning achievement was Kuélap, a fortress perched on a limestone cliff. Massive defense walls protected the city's 400 round stone homes.

squirrel monkey at Pilpintuwasi Butterfly Farm and Animal Orphanage outside Iquitos

▶ WHEN TO GO

The traditional time to visit Peru is in the South American winter, June–August, when dry, sunny weather opens up over the mountains and the Amazon. Because Peru's dry months coincide perfectly with summer vacation in North America and Europe, this is also when most travelers visit Peru. Prices for lodging tend to go up during these months, and hot spots like Machu Picchu can be crowded. Especially crowded times are Inti Raymi, the June 24 sun festival in Cusco, and Fiestas Patrias, the national Peruvian holiday at the end of July.

The bulk of the rainy season is December–April, when trekking and other outdoor activities are hampered by muddy paths and soggy skies. To avoid crowds, we heartily recommend squeezing your trip in between the rainy season and the high tourist months. April, May, September, October, and even November are excellent times to visit Peru. The weather is usually fine and prices for lodging tend to be lower.

There are some dry spots in the country, however, even during the wettest months. Peru's largest jungle city, Iquitos, is far enough down the Amazon basin to have a less-pronounced wet season. Clouds move in most afternoons throughout the year, drop a load of water, and then shuffle away again to reveal sun. The only thing that fluctuates in Iquitos year-round is the Amazon River itself, which

Inti Raymi, Cusco's Inca sun festival, is held each year on June 24 in Cusco.

heaves up and down in tune with highland rains. So Iquitos is a year-round option for visiting the Amazon, and Peru's desert coast can also be visited year-round because hardly any rain falls here. Ironically, the sunniest months on the coast are the wettest in the highlands, December–March. The weather is especially bright and sunny in Peru's extreme north coast, where surfers congregate for the white-sand beaches and huge seasonal breaks.

► BEFORE YOU GO

Vaccinations
Most travelers to Peru do get the vaccinations recommended by the Centers for Disease Control (www.cdc.gov), which include hepatitis A and B and typhoid for the Andean areas, and yellow fever and malaria for certain jungle areas.

Passports and Visas
Citizens of the United States, Canada, United Kingdom, South Africa, New Zealand, and Australia and residents of any other European or Latin American country do not require visas to enter Peru as tourists at present time, but they will need to pay departure taxes of $31 for international flights and $7 for domestic flights. Visitors entering the country can get anything from 30 to 180 days stamped into both a passport and an embarkation card that travelers must keep until they exit the country. If you require more than 30 days, be ready to support your argument by explaining your travel plans and showing your return ticket. Extensions can be arranged at Peru's immigration offices in Lima, Arequipa, Cusco, Iquitos, Puno, and Trujillo for US$21.

Transportation
Most travelers arrive in Peru by plane, and all international flights into Peru arrive in Lima. Travel to Cusco or the jungle is an additional plane ride. Because of flight patterns, most travelers end up spending a night or a day in Lima either coming or going. We recommend travelers spend at least a day in Lima, preferably on the way home, to take in this amazing city. Peru's new buses, with luxurious onboard service, are a great option for domestic travel.

Explore Peru

▶ THE 21-DAY BEST OF PERU

This 21-day tour brings together most of the main travel routes throughout Peru, and travelers can easily take one part (for instance the journey from Lima to Cusco) and take out another (the tour of northern Peru). More than anything, it is proof of all that Peru has to offer—and it still leaves out a lot. The odyssey unfolds chronologically among Peru's ancient ruins and colonial cities, with a dab of Amazon and a dash through the desert for balance. Getting around is accomplished via a straightforward combination of planes, trains, buses, and *combis*.

Day 1

Begin by flying into Lima and catching a connecting flight to Peru's north, where you will spend two nights at Huanchaco, a coastal town near Trujillo.

Day 2

During the day you can see colonial Trujillo, the Moche pyramid of Huaca de la Luna, and the Chimú city of Chan Chan.

Day 3

In the morning see Trujillo's Museo Cassinelli, then hop on a bus for Chiclayo (three hours). Hire a private car and head to a country inn at Túcume (45 minutes), where you will stay two nights sleeping in the bucolic countryside near the pyramids.

Day 4

After seeing the Lords of Sipán treasures at the Museo Tumbas Reales de Sipán, visit the Sicán pyramids at Batán Grande and the new Museo Sicán.

Day 5

Fly from Chiclayo to Lima. Here you begin the time-honored backpacker's route to Cusco. Take a bus to Pisco (three hours) and a short *combi* ride to the beach town of Paracas, where you stay two nights.

Day 6

Explore Reserva Nacional de Paracas. Watch sea lions and perhaps endangered Humboldt penguins, picnic on a wilderness beach, and return to your hotel for sunset over the Pacific Ocean.

Day 7

Take a bus to Nasca (2.5 hours) to visit Museo Antonini and aqueducts and stay the night. Or take a bus to Ica (one hour) for a tour of pisco bodegas and sandboarding on

EXPERIENTIAL TOURISM

a volunteer and children at an elementary school in Ollantaytambo

Experiential tourism, where travelers go beyond mere sightseeing and engage with local communities in a meaningful way, is a fast-growing global movement with many forms in Peru. The best experiential tourism operators have built long-term relationships that benefit communities in concrete ways, such as improving quality of local schools or health clinics. Here are some great opportunities for homestays, volunteering, and cultural immersion in Peru, broken down by region.

CUSCO AND THE SACRED VALLEY

Peru's most reputable trekking agencies have forged long-term bonds with Andean communities and offer cultural treks and other well-designed, off-the-beaten-path experiences. These agencies include **Peruvian Andean Treks** (www.andeantreks.com), **ExplorAndes** (www.explorandes.com), and **Tambo Treks** (www.tambotreks.net). In Ollantaytambo, an NGO we recommend is **Awamaki,** which helps weavers in the highlands community of Patacancha recover ancient weaving techniques and bring their weavings to overseas markets. Awamaki sets up a range of volunteer placements and homestays in both Ollantaytambo and Patacancha.

THE AMAZON

There are many experiential travel opportunities in Puerto Maldonado and Manu, where most agencies and lodges have built relationships with local communities. In Puerto Maldonado, **Rainforest Expeditions** operates the gorgeous **Posada Amazonas** lodge in conjunction with the mestizo Ese Eja community of Infierno. The award-winning lodge is designed to offer guests an intimate experience with Ese Eja culture. In Manu, **Pantiacolla Tours** operates the **Yine Project,** a lodge built and operated with the Yine Indians in the community of Diamante. Guests spend time with villagers, participate in traditional art workshops, and learn how to canoe with the expert Yine boatsmen.

HUARAZ AND CORDILLERA BLANCA

We highly recommend **Respons Sustainable Tourism Center** (www.respons.org), which can arrange homestays and work experiences in Vicos and other communities around Huaraz. This organization also offers treks on a remote and recently restored section of the Inca Trail, the Inka Naani, near the central highlands town of Huánuco. Another option in Huaraz is **Andean Alliance** (www.thelazydoginn.com), a nonprofit run by the Canadian owners of the Lazy Dog Inn. They can match your skills with local work projects and also set up homestays.

Host mothers wait for their homestay guests on Islas Amantaní.

the dunes above Lago Huacachina, where you stay the night. You choose.

Day 8

Enjoy a morning overflight of the Nasca Lines from either Nasca or Ica. Take the bus to Arequipa from Ica (eight hours) or Nasca (6.5 hours). Check in for a two-night stay in Arequipa.

Day 9

Tour sophisticated Arequipa, a sparkling white city best known for the 17th-century Monasterio de Santa Catalina.

Day 10

Take a flight or bus trip from Arequipa to Puno (seven hours by bus).

Days 11-12

Explore Lake Titicaca with a day tour of Islas Amantaní and Islas Uros. Return to Puno for the night, or consider a stay with a family on Amantaní.

Day 13

Continue onward to Cusco. From Puno you can fly, take a direct nonstop train, or ride a tour bus that allows you to see the ruins along the way (nine hours). Upon arrival, grab a 1.5-hour taxi or *combi* ride from Cusco to

a sacred *chacana* symbol below Ollantaytambo's Temple of the Sun

Machu Picchu

Ollantaytambo, a living Inca village in the heart of Peru's Sacred Valley.

Days 14-15

Recharge in the lush surroundings of the Sacred Valley. Options include touring Ollantaytambo's old Inca city and the Temple of the Sun, rafting the Río Urubamba, and going horseback riding or day hiking on one of the area's many Inca trails. On the second day, walk or mountain bike from the Inca ruins of Moray down a steep valley past the Salineras, or salt mines, and back to Ollantaytambo.

terraces on the Island of Taquile, Lake Titicaca

Day 16

Take an early morning train to Machu Picchu from the Sacred Valley and cruise to the ruins as early as you can. Spend a full day at Machu Picchu, then hop on the afternoon train-and-bus combination back to Cusco.

Days 17-18

Tour the Cusco area, where you will have two days to soak in the churches, the artisan neighborhood of San Blas, and the fortress of Sacsayhuamán.

Days 19-20

As a final treat, take a morning flight (30 minutes) to Puerto Maldonado in the Amazon for a two-night stay at a jungle lodge.

Day 21

From Puerto Maldonado catch a morning flight to Lima's airport, where you can leave your bags, and then take a quick peek at the city center and enjoy a gourmet dinner in Miraflores. Then hop a red-eye for home.

BEST ECOLODGES

a visit to the El Chino village from Tahuayo Lodge near Iquitos

The top tier of Peru's ecolodges, both in the Andes and the Amazon, have a well-developed philosophy and strategy for caring for the environment and providing an organic, natural experience for guests. These lodges also typically train and hire local people, serve organic food produced by local communities, and provide eco-friendly services such as natural spa treatments and healing ceremonies. Here are some of our favorite ecolodges in Peru:

- **Los Horcones de Túcume** is in the backyard of the 26 massive pyramids of Túcume, one of Peru's most sacred healing centers outside of the northern Peruvian city of Chiclayo. This rural lodge, built according to the building techniques of the ancient Moche culture, features rooms made of adobe and *algarrobo* beams, which open up to covered terraces and views of the surrounding fields. The food here is as organic as it gets, and Don Víctor, a reputed shaman in the area, lives nearby the lodge and works with visitors upon request.

- **Reserva Amazónica** is the brainchild of leading Peruvian eco-pioneers José and Denise Koechlin, who also own the similarly eco-minded and elegant **Machu Picchu Pueblo Hotel** at the base of Machu Picchu. Reserva Amazónica offers 41 private wooden bungalows, organic food, canopy walks, visits to local communities supported by the lodge, and its own line of organic shampoo and conditioner. Both lodges have extraordinary on-staff nature guides and other resources to explore and understand the surrounding environment.

- **Casa de Pocha** is a working organic farm perched in the hills above Carhuaz, in the Cordillera Blanca. The adobe lodge has rustic rooms with eucalyptus beams, a sauna, and a yoga studio. Meals are organic and mostly vegetarian and cooked in a solar stove or over an open fire.

- **Tahuayo Lodge,** a four-hour boat ride from Iquitos, is next door to the world-class Amazon biodiversity of the Tamshiyacu Tahuayo communal reserve. Founded by U.S. naturalist Paul Beaver, Tahyauo Lodge has been featured in *Outside* magazine and other publications for its off-the-beaten-path jungle adventures. This lodge, with 15 wooden rooms, hammock hall, and laboratory/library complex, has access to both dry and flooded forest as well as a zip line that sends guest soaring 35 meters above the jungle floor.

► FROM THE INCA TO THE AMAZON

Because both Cusco and Machu Picchu are near the Amazon, we have designed this trip to encompass all three experiences. This 10-day trip takes you to Peru's most important cultural ruins and allows you to see highlands, cloud forest, and rainforest. We recommend five days on your own to explore Cusco and the Sacred Valley and then a five-day jungle tour with the operator of your choice in either the Manu or Puerto Maldonado area.

Depending on your interests or travel dates, you might want to consider modifications to this itinerary. Between October and April when the jungle near Puerto Maldonado is rainy and many of its lodges are closed, fly from Lima to Iquitos instead and visit the Reserva Nacional Pacaya Samiria. Pacaya Samiria, like Manu Biosphere Reserve, is a huge tract of virgin rainforest where you have excellent chances of seeing a wide range of wildlife. Rains in the lowland Amazon

of northern Peru are spread more evenly throughout the year.

If you are looking to minimize travel time and maximize hotel luxury, consider replacing the five-day Manu trip with a shorter trip to Puerto Maldonado. Keep in mind that human development around Iquitos and Puerto Maldonado has had an impact on the jungle within a one- or two-hour boat ride, and jungle trips in these regions present less biodiversity than if you travel a bit farther in. An option in the Puerto Maldonado region that offers a chance to see biodiversity similar to that of Manu and Pacaya Samiria is the Tambopata Research Center, a seven-hour boat ride from Puerto Maldonado.

Day 1

Arrive in Lima and catch an early morning connecting flight to Cusco. In Cusco, take a taxi to Ollantaytambo, a living Inca village

Nevado Ausangate (20,900 feet) is the main peak of the Cordillera Vilcanota outside of Cusco.

ARCHAEOLOGY INTENSIVE

Peru is the New World's cradle of civilization and has enough archaeological sites for a lifetime of study. From the birth of Peru's first city states five millennia ago to the spectacular conquest of the Inca five centuries ago, Peru's history is well-documented via a series of ruins, artifacts, legends, and written chronicles.

Nearly all visitors to Peru see Machu Picchu and Cusco, but here are some history and archaeology suggestions, broken down by region, for those who want to explore farther afield. Specialty operators like **Far Horizons Archaeological & Cultural Trips** arrange tours to all these places with archaeologist guides and a series of exclusive lectures.

Nasca Lines

SACRED VALLEY

In **Ollantaytambo,** visit the **Temple of the Sun** or take the daylong hike to the **Inti Punku,** or Sun Gate. This sacred stone portal features spectacular views of the Sacred Valley and its snow-covered peaks.

Other archaeological must-sees in the Sacred Valley include the fortress and sun temple at **Pisac,** Inca walls at **Chinchero,** and the concentric agricultural terraces at **Moray.**

MACHU PICCHU

Once at Machu Picchu, hike farther afield to the **Inca bridge,** on the edge of the Machu Picchu complex, and the **Temple of the Moon,** a beautifully sculpted cave. Note that Temple of the Moon is done together with an ascent of **Huayna Picchu,** the peak above Machu Picchu. Arrive early to visit these sites, which close after the daily quota of visitors is reached.

CUSCO

In the Cusco area, do not miss the spectacular hike from **Q'enqo** to the fortress of **Sacsayhuamán.** We also recommend a half-day tour from Cusco to see pre-Inca ruins at **Pikillacta,** the Inca ruins at **Tipón,** and the magnificent Spanish colonial church at **Andahuaylillas.**

NASCA

See the **Nasca Lines** (giant renderings of monkeys, spiders, and other water-related symbols dug into the desert floor by pre-Inca groups) by air. Round-trip overflights leave each day from Lima.

Check out the elaborate aqueducts and other waterways that allowed the Nasca to transport water from miles away under the desert floor. Spiral staircases, which descend into the underground aqueducts, can be explored on foot.

LIMA

For an introduction to Peru's archaeology, visit the **Museo Nacional de Arqueología. Pachacámac,** an adobe ceremonial center 31 kilometers south of Lima, functioned as a temple and oracle for at least a thousand years before it was desecrated by the Spanish.

CHICLAYO AND THE NORTH COAST

Peru's pre-Inca cultures included the **Moche, Chimú,** and **Sicán,** which all flourished in the coastal valleys of Peru's north coast. These cultures built giant adobe pyramids, which today are vast, eroding mud hills. They also left behind a variety of artifacts and gold treasures.

In **Trujillo,** view the Moche murals at the **Huaca de la Luna,** the expansive Chimú citadel of **Chan Chan,** the erotic ceramics at **Museo Cassinelli,** and the city's well-preserved colonial mansions.

In and around **Chiclayo,** visit the Moche site of **El Brujo,** the impressive gold- and silverwork in the **Lords of Sipán** exhibit at the **Museo Tumbas Reales de Sipán,** the Sicán pyramids of **Batán Grande,** and the new multimedia **Museo Sicán.**

colorful herbal dyes at the Pisac market near Cusco

in the Sacred Valley, where you can rest and acclimatize.

Days 2-3

Tour the Sacred Valley, with stops at the Ollantaytambo Temple of the Sun and the market and ruins of Pisac. On day two, explore the village of Chinchero before hiking or mountain biking from the enigmatic circular Inca terraces at Moray past the crystallized salt mines known as Salineras and back to Ollantaytambo.

Day 4

Take the early morning train to Machu Picchu and spend the day touring the ruins and bird-watching in the cloud forest. Return on the afternoon train-and-bus combination to Cusco, where you will spend two nights.

Day 5

Experience Cusco's unique combination of Inca ruins, colonial architecture and museums, markets, and cafés.

Day 6

If you choose to go to the Manu Biosphere Reserve, you will fly from Cusco into Boca Manu. Upon arrival, you will take a motorboat ride into the Manu Biosphere Reserve and settle into your jungle lodge or tented camp.

one of Chinchero's weavers

ADRENALINE RUSH

Whether it's climbing ice, rock, or mountains, surfing point breaks, mountain biking, sandboarding, trekking, kayaking, or rafting, Peru has it. From the snowcapped Cordillera Blanca and the sand dunes in the Ica Desert to the brilliant green waters of Lake Titicaca and the rivers of the Amazon, Peru has something for every adrenaline junkie.

Amazon River bank, Iquitos

CUSCO AND THE SACRED VALLEY

- **Kayak** and **raft** on the **Río Apurímac.**
- **Parapent** off the rim of the Sacred Valley with Wayra, an outfitter near Urubamba.
- Take a **horseback ride** to **Maras** and **Moray.**
- **Rock climb** outside Cusco at the **Via Ferrata,** a system of ropes on a 300-meter rock face.
- **Trek** around **Ausangate.**
- **Climb** the highly technical glaciers and peaks of the **Cordillera Vilcanota.**
- **Mountain bike** in the high plains around **Paucartambo,** through cloud forests, and into the **Manu basin.**

LAKE TITICACA AND CANYON COUNTRY

- **Sea kayak** across Lake Titicaca, the world's highest navigable lake.
- **Trek, mountain bike, hike,** and **raft** in the **Colca and Cotahuasi Canyons,** twice the depth of the Grand Canyon.
- Break the 6,000-meter mark by climbing the snow-covered **Chachani** volcano outside **Arequipa.**

THE AMAZON

- **Raft** and **kayak** down the **Río Tambopata,** a 10-day journey from the high Andes to the Amazon.
- Ride a **zip line** through the jungle canopy at the **Tahuayo Lodge** near **Iquitos.**
- **Mountain bike** from the **high Andes** into the **Manu basin.**

NASCA AND THE DESERT COAST

- **Sandboard** down 100-meter sand dunes at **Lago Huacachina.**
- **Trek** through the **Ica Desert** in search of fossils, mummies, and wilderness beaches.

LIMA

- **Paraglide** along the seaside bluffs of **Miraflores,** the coastal suburb of Lima.
- Hit **world-class breaks Punta Rocas** and **Punta Hermosa.**
- **Ride Peruvian** *paso* **horses** near Mamacona, on excursions around the ceremonial center of **Pachacámac.**
- Hit the **rock climbing wall** at **Millennium Gym.**
- Explore the **Pacific Ocean** between Ancón and Cerro Azul aboard a **sea kayak.**

HUARAZ AND THE CORDILLERA BLANCA

- **Climb** perfect granite fissures and summit out on **Huascarán,** Latin America's second-highest peak
- **Kayak** and **raft** the **Río Santa.**
- **Mountain bike** the **Cordillera Negra.**
- **Trek** past **Alpamayo,** voted the world's most beautiful mountain.

TRUJILLO AND THE NORTH COAST

- **Surf** the pipeline at **Cabo Blanco** and the breaks at **Máncora.**

red and green macaws at the Manu Biosphere Reserve

Day 7-9

Tour an oxbow lake on a platform boat equipped with a spotting scope. Manu's oxbow lakes host a huge range of wildlife, including giant otters, 13 species of monkeys, and large mammals like tapirs. Hike through different areas of local rainforest with a guide who along the way points out wildlife that you would otherwise miss. Explore the jungle canopy by climbing up to a lookout tower 20 meters above the forest floor.

Day 10

Return to Boca Manu by boat. Catch the 35-minute flight from Boca Manu back to Cusco, flying over jungle, highlands, and glacier-capped mountains along the way. Catch a connecting flight into Lima and arrive in the early afternoon. Head to central Lima to see the Catedral and Palacio del Gobierno, and have lunch at T'anta, all on the Plaza Mayor. Return to the airport for a night flight home.

► GETTING OFF THE TOURIST TRACK

This odyssey through Peru's northern highlands and Amazon is for those who want to get off the beaten path to experience an awesome cross-section of Peru's geography.

If you have a few extra days, there are several exciting side trips you could tag on to the base trip to fill out your travels. Consider starting in either Trujillo or Chiclayo. These cities are close to an array of pre-Inca ruins and their corresponding museums. The most ambitious idea is to fly to Chiclayo first to visit Museo Tumbas Reales de Sipán and Túcume. Then take a three-hour bus ride to visit Trujillo, along with the ruins of Huaca de la Luna and Chan Chan. From there you would head to Cajamarca and follow the trip described here.

However, if you want to spend extra time in virgin rainforest, you should explore the Reserva Nacional Pacaya Samiria. Get off the Yurimaguas–Iquitos cargo boat in the middle of the first night at the town of Lagunas. From here, you can head out with a dugout canoe and a guide for a week of camping in the reserve.

Day 1

Arrive in Lima and then fly to Cajamarca, where Francisco Pizarro captured Inca emperor Atahualpa and ransomed him for a room of gold. Besides Atahualpa's chamber (called the Cuarto de Rescate), Cajamarca offers baroque churches, the carved aqueducts at Cumbemayo, and a stunning pastoral setting.

Day 2

After a morning visit to Cumbemayo, begin the rough overland journey to the cloud forest of the Chachapoya. The first leg of the trip involves an afternoon bus from Cajamarca to the charming country town of Celendín (four hours). There you will spend the night before heading to Leymebamba in the morning.

Day 3

Take a bus to Leymebamba. This is a spectacular, eight-hour journey down and up the Marañón Canyon, which is deeper than Arizona's Grand Canyon and ranges from high-altitude grasslands to the subtropical valley floor. Overnight in a hotel near Leymebamba's quiet central plaza.

Day 4

Explore Leymebamba with a visit to the Museo Leymebamba and a hike to the lost city of La Congona. That afternoon, take a *colectivo* down the Utcubamba Valley to Chillo or Tingo (1.5 hours). Plan on a two-night stay at one of the charming country lodges at the foot of Kuélap.

Day 5

Hike to the Chachapoya citadel of Kuélap.

Day 6

Take a *colectivo* to Pedro Ruiz (one hour) to

Gocta Falls, Chachapoya cloud forest

sunset over the Río Huallaga, Tingo María

get back on paved highway, and hop on a bus for Tarapoto (eight hours).

Day 7

Relax in Tarapoto by visiting Laguna Sauce or hiking to the local waterfalls. Spend another night in Tarapoto.

Day 8

The most adventurous part of this trip begins

This canopy walkway threads its way through bromeliads and bird nests at the Explorama Lodge in Iquitos.

with an early-morning *colectivo* ride over the muddy, potholed road to Yurimaguas (6–8 hours). That afternoon, board a cargo boat down the Río Huallaga for a 36-hour ride bound for Iquitos.

Day 9

Rest up on the boat by swinging on a hammock, eating bananas, and watching the Amazon float by.

Day 10

Disembark in Iquitos in the morning or beforehand for a visit to the Amazon lodge of your choice, such as Tahuayo Lodge or Explorama Lodge.

Days 11-12

Rise early both days to catch sight of hoatzins and river otters at their early morning feeding. In the afternoon, wander the terra firma in search of tiny frogs or fish for pirañas.

Day 13

Return to Iquitos for a celebratory dinner— or keep floating on into Brazil!

Day 14

Fly to Lima and return home.

THE SACRED VALLEY

The river that runs past Machu Picchu is the Río Urubamba, which the Inca considered a sacred reflection of the Milky Way. Before reaching Machu Picchu, the Río Urubamba flows through the Sacred Valley, a breathtaking landscape of snowcapped mountains, red granite cliffs, and lush green terraces. The Sacred Valley runs roughly from Pisac to Ollantaytambo and a bit beyond to Piscacucho, a highly fertile region that was the Inca breadbasket and still produces much of the grains and vegetables consumed in Cusco. Compared to the chilly, thin air of Cusco, the Sacred Valley is lush and sunny. For the Inca the Sacred Valley was literally paradise on earth, a vision of Eden made incarnate. Inca palaces, fortresses, and sun temples dot this valley, along with charming Andean villages that produce and sell some of

the country's finest handicrafts. Along with Machu Picchu and Cusco, the Sacred Valley is at the top of Peru's must-see list.

Two of the most interesting towns in the Sacred Valley are the Inca villages of Ollantaytambo and Pisac. Ollantaytambo is Peru's best example of a living Inca village, where people still live in the graceful Inca homes and use the same waterways that were used by their ancestors 500 years ago. Ollantaytambo's sun temple towers above town and contains Inca stonework as impressive as that found in Cusco and Machu Picchu. Pisac is best known for its daily handicrafts market, which draws large crowds of travelers each day. But Pisac also has an interesting variety of Inca architecture in town, along with important Inca ruins in the hills above. Pisac's

© RENÉE DEL GAUDIO AND ROSS WEHNER

THE SACRED VALLEY

HIGHLIGHTS

◖ **Pisac Market:** Peru's most famous crafts market takes place in Pisac daily. This ancient Inca village is nestled in the shadow of an imposing Inca fortress and temple (page 29).

◖ **Pisac Ruins:** What's unique about Pisac's ruins, apart from their extraordinary beauty, is their range. Here you will find not only religious Inca architecture, but also residential, agricultural, and military (page 30).

◖ **Moray and Salineras:** This six-hour downhill hike is a gorgeous introduction to the Sacred Valley. Start at Moray, a complex of concentric agricultural terraces, and then head downhill past Salineras, a centuries-old salt mine still in operation today (page 37).

◖ **Ollantaytambo Temple:** Second in importance only to Machu Picchu, Ollantaytambo includes some of the Inca's best stonework, including a series of ceremonial baths, elegant trapezoidal doorways, and a sun temple that faces the rising sun (page 48).

◖ **Inca Granaries (Pinkuylluna):** This moderate, 1.5-hour hike will give you a spectacular view of Ollantaytambo, its gleaming sun temple, and interesting grain storehouses, known in Quechua as *colcas* (page 51).

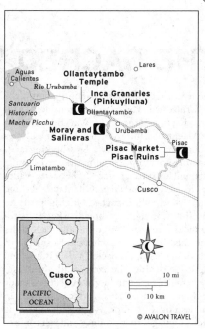

LOOK FOR ◖ TO FIND RECOMMENDED SIGHTS, ACTIVITIES, DINING, AND LODGING.

ruins offer an interesting window into Inca life because they combine religious, civilian, and military architecture in a single location.

A growing body of research proves that much of Inca architecture, especially in the Sacred Valley, was built with the movements of the sun and stars in mind. The temple-fortresses of Pisac and Ollantaytambo both correspond very precisely to lunar and solar events. Moray, an area of terraced natural depressions, was probably designed to use sun and shade to work as an agricultural laboratory. The Inca went to great effort to redirect the Río Urubamba into a stone channel—to maximize farming land, but also probably to reflect the straight shape of the Milky Way. The great care the Inca took in aligning buildings

with the sun, moon, and stars reflects their vision of the Sacred Valley as a sacred, celestial landscape.

Heavy rains in January 2010 caused significant flooding in the Sacred Valley, including the displacement of about 10,000 people in the valley alone. The village of Taray, near Pisac, was nearly completely destroyed.

PLANNING YOUR TIME

The traditional way to visit Cusco, Machu Picchu, and the Sacred Valley is all wrong. Most travelers arrive in Cusco and spend a night or two seeing Cusco. Then they take a whirlwind day tour of the Sacred Valley and then take the train from Cusco to Machu Picchu in one day.

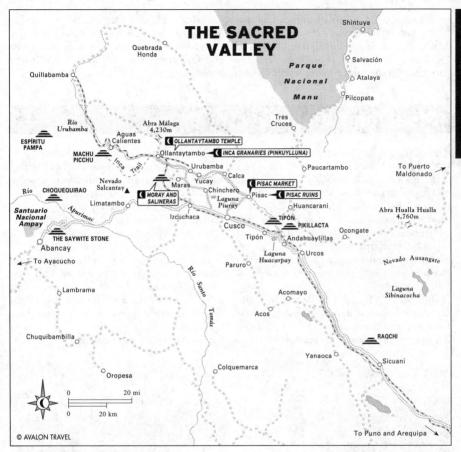

THE SACRED VALLEY

Shintuya

Quebrada
Honda

Quillabamba

Salvación

Parque

Nacional

Atalaya

Manu

Pilcopata

Río
Urubamba

Abra Málaga
4,230m

Tres
Cruces

ESPÍRITU
PAMPA

Aguas
Calientes

☾ OLLANTAYTAMBO TEMPLE

MACHU
PICCHU

Ollantaytambo ← ☾ INCA GRANARIES (PINKUYLLUNA)

Inca Trail

Urubamba

Paucartambo

To Puerto
Maldonado

Nevado
Salcantay

Maras

Yucay

Calca

☾ PISAC MARKET

CHOQUEQUIRAO

Río

☾ MORAY AND
SALINERAS

Chinchero

Laguna
Piuray

Pisac   ☾ PISAC RUINS

Apurímac

Limatambo

Abra Hualla Hualla
4,760m

Santuario
Nacional
Ampay

Izcuchaca

Cusco

Huancarani

☾ TIPÓN PIKILLACTA

Ocongate

THE SAYWITE STONE

Tipón

Andahuaylillas

Abancay

Laguna
Huacarpay

Urcos

Nevado Ausangate

To Ayacucho

Paruro

Lambrama

Río Santo

Acomayo

Laguna
Sibinacocha

Tomás

Acos

Chuquibambilla

RAQCHI

Colquemarca

Yanaoca

Sicuani

Oropesa

0   20 mi

0   20 km

© AVALON TRAVEL

To Puno and Arequipa

The first thing wrong with this plan is that Cusco is at 3,400 meters (11,150 feet). Most people feel at least some discomfort from altitude sickness, which can feel like the flu and is a heck of a way to start a vacation. A much better plan is to head first for the Sacred Valley, a pastoral paradise with Southern California–like weather that is, most important, 500 meters lower. Few people get altitude sickness here.

Visiting the Sacred Valley first makes sense from a chronological perspective as well. The ruins of Ollantaytambo and Pisac are a good introduction to Machu Picchu. After understanding the Inca side of the equation, travelers

then can return by train to Cusco, which is a Jerusalem-like blend of two opposing cultures—Spanish colonial and Inca imperial.

The standard one-day Sacred Valley tour from Cusco is a mistake. This tour whisks visitors through the Pisac market, lunch in Urubamba, and a visit to the Ollantaytambo ruins. Visitors usually miss the Pisac ruins, some of the finest in Peru, and also get shortchanged on Ollantaytambo.

The best plan is to start your Peru trip with 2–3 days in the Sacred Valley and then take a train from the Sacred Valley to Machu Picchu. Return can be from Machu Picchu directly

THE SACRED VALLEY

back to Cusco. As of 2010, floods had disrupted normal rail service between Cusco and Machu Picchu. As a result, all trains to Machu Picchu are now starting from Piscacucho, the last village in the Sacred Valley before the Río Urubamba plunges into the narrow gorges leading to Machu Picchu. Normal rail service from Sacred Valley towns such as Urubamba and Ollantaytambo will be restored in the near future.

Pisac and Vicinity

This quaint Andean town, nestled near the top of the Sacred Valley, is best known for a huge crafts market that is probably Peru's number two tourist draw behind Machu Picchu. Every day is market day, with the biggest days being Tuesday, Thursday, and Sunday. Hundreds of travelers descend upon this village as part of a whirlwind day tour from Cusco that begins here in the morning and continues on for lunch at Urubamba and a tour of the ruins at Ollantaytambo.

But there is a lot more to Pisac, and an increasing number of travelers are staying here for a night or two to explore farther afield. There are plans to move the market just out of the plaza, allowing visitors to enjoy the beautiful pisonay trees and colonial church with a backdrop of the ruins. The Inca fortress above town represents the most important Inca ruins in the valley besides Ollantaytambo. The ruins contain a rare combination of residential, military, and religious construction that sheds a deep light onto the daily life of the Inca.

In the high plains beyond the fortress, there are remote villages that can be reached only on foot. Roman and Fielding Vizcarra, owners of Hotel Pisaq, lead recommended trips into the surrounding countryside to visit these Quechuan villages and the remote ruins of Cuyo Chico and Cuyo Grande.

© CARLOS SALA, PROMPERU

Intihuatana, the main sun temple

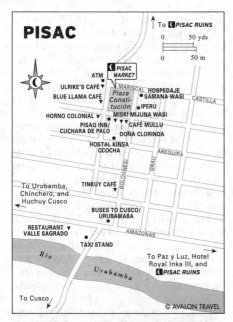

PISAC

To **(** PISAC RUINS

0   50 yds

0   50 m

(PISAC MARKET

ATM

ULRIKE'S CAFÉ ▾

BLUE LLAMA CAFÉ ▾

MARISCAL   HOSPEDAJE

Plaza   ● SAMANA WASI

Consti-   CASTILLA

tución   ● IPERU

HORNO COLONIAL ▾   MISKI MIJUNA WASI

PISAQ INN/   ▾▾ CAFÉ MULLU

CUCHARA DE PALO   DOÑA CLORINDA

HOSTAL KINSA

CCOCHA   AREQUIPA

To Urubamba,   TINKUY CAFÉ

Chinchero, and

Huchuy Cusco

BUSES TO CUSCO/

URUBAMABA

RESTAURANT ▾   AMAZONAS

VALLE SAGRADO

TAXI STAND

Río   To Paz y Luz, Hotel

Royal Inka III, and

Urubamba   **(** PISAC RUINS

To Cusco

© AVALON TRAVEL

BOLOGNESI   GRAU

© KAZIA JANKOWSKI

wool on display at Pisac's colorful market

SIGHTS

(Pisac Market

Pisac has evolved into one of the biggest, certainly the most famous, *artesanía* markets in all of South America. It begins every day at 9 A.M. when the first tour buses arrive from Cusco and winds down around 5 P.M. when the last tourists leave. The town's main square is filled wall-to-wall with stalls selling the full range of Peruvian *artesanía:* carved gourds (*mates burilados*), ceramics, felt hats, alpaca sweaters and mittens, musical instruments, paintings, antiques, a huge variety of trinkets, and, most of all, weavings and jewelry. Even if you are not buying, the café balconies overlooking the market offer superb people-watching: Hundreds of camera-toting tourists, from every conceivable country on earth, haggle with Quechuan-speaking merchants. Quality tends to be in the low to middle range—the good stuff is found in the homes of the *artesanos* themselves or in upscale city galleries—but, after a bit of bargaining, prices can be very reasonable, especially if buying in quantity.

Though touristy beyond belief, the Pisac market has a remarkably deeper side that is rooted in its colonial past and has proven resilient to mass tourism. On Sunday only, campesinos from surrounding villages set up a barter market, or *mercado de treque,* which is an ancient Peruvian custom and an interesting example of the informal economies upon which highlanders depend. Quechuan-speaking Indians sit behind huge piles of potatoes, carrots, herbs, and other vegetables in one corner of the square. They sell these products to buy essentials (salt, sugar, kerosene, matches, medicines) but also trade to acquire other foods, such as oranges from the Quillabamba Valley. It exists side-by-side with the Pisac market but ends by 3 P.M. so that villagers can walk home before dark.

Also on Sunday only, masses in Quechua are held at 6 and 11 A.M. in **San Pedro Apóstol de Pisac,** the colonial church on the main square that was rebuilt after the 1950 earthquake. The early mass is held for townspeople, and the later one is reserved for the *varayocs* and *regidores* (elected mayors and their appointed deputies) of the 13 villages that are a two- to five-hour walk away through the mountains. After mass, the officials proceed around the square in their Sunday best before baptisms, and sometimes a wedding, are held in the church. Between services, it is possible to enter the church for a glimpse at the Inca foundations and an interesting collection of colonial paintings.

Pisac Ruins

Pisac is one of Cusco's few great Inca ruins that feature all types of architecture—agricultural, hydraulic, military, residential, and religious. It probably began as a military garrison to guard against incursion from the Anti Indians, who occupied the easternmost corner of the empire known as **Antisuyo** (present-day Paucartambo and the Manu jungle). Pachacútec probably built Pisac's imperial architecture, though oddly there is no mention of Pisac in the Spanish chronicles.

There are several ways to see the Pisac ruins (7 A.M.–3 P.M., admission with Cusco ruins ticket), but the best is to take a US$3–4 taxi up the eight-kilometer highway to the ruins. Instead of going to the main entrance, tell your taxi to go right on the switchback and head farther up to the Pisac ruins of Qanchisracay. From here a trail leads along a ridge, through a tunnel, and down into the **Intihuatana,** or the main sun temple. The walk is steep and exposed to heights, but safe. Or arrive at the Intihuatana via the main path from the main entrance. Allow for one or two hours for Pisac (return to town via taxi) and another two hours for walking downhill all the way to town.

Qanchisracay is one of three residential areas in Pisac. It is composed of rough stone buildings, walls with niches, and small squares. These were probably military garrisons and, in the style of a medieval castle, shelter for villagers in times of war. An easier residential area to visit, below the Intihuatana, is named after the Andean partridge *p'isaqa*—the namesake of Pisac itself.

From Qanchisracay an Inca trail traverses the hillside, arrives at a small pass, then heads

terraces above the Pisac ruins

© BETH FUCHS

up and over a rocky summit to the sun temple, behind and out of sight. At the pass, four purification baths flow with water brought down from a lake at 4,500 meters. Below are five agricultural terraces, once planted with potatoes and *olluco,* the Andean tuber. On the opposing cliff wall, thousands of holes left by grave robbers are all that is left of what was once the Inca's largest cemetery. On the other side of the pass to the left, a 10-minute detour around the corner reveals Inca buttresses, which were once spanned by a hanging bridge made of plant fibers. This is an alternative trail to the Intihuatana and passes a series of fine irrigation canals.

The main path from the pass crosses through a military wall with a perfect trapezoidal door, known as the **Door of the Serpent.** Above is the second residential area, **Hanam P'isaq** (upper Pisac). The path now climbs up steep staircases and niches carved out of the rock itself, alongside a cliff and through the **Q'alla Q'asa** (Split Rock) tunnel. Faced with a vertical rock face, Inca engineers decided to enlarge a rock fissure and bore through the entire cliff—how they did this, with no iron or steel implements, boggles the mind.

The best view of the Intihuatana is from above. Like the sun temple at Machu Picchu, the Intihuatana is an oval building of perfect masonry encasing a votive rock. The pillar atop the rock was used to track the sun's movements. (Most of the finely carved pillar was recently chopped off by thieves—not long before the one in Machu Picchu was chipped during the filming of a beer commercial.) The walls of five other temples surround the temple, including one that was probably devoted to the moon. To the right is a series of restored baths that flow into an underground canal. In front of the Intihuatana is a sacred *chacana* symbol.

Off the easier trail back to the main entrance of the ruins is **P'isaqa,** the third and finest residential area, with its own ritual bath. These were probably homes for the elite, as opposed to the military garrisons closer to the pass. Most people head back at this point to

the main entrance, though there are two trails from here that make for pleasant two-hour walks back to Pisac. One descends directly to the Río Quitamayo, with spectacular views, while the other drops through the lookout towers of Coriwayrachina and an area of steep terracing. Both trails merge on the other side of the river for the final descent into town.

ENTERTAINMENT AND EVENTS

There are no discos in Pisac, but the cafés around the square serve beer and cocktails.

Pisac's big festival is **La Virgen del Carmen,** which begins on July 15 and runs for five days. The first day includes a horse-riding contest followed by a series of religious processions and dances.

SHOPPING

Apart from the Pisac market, there are crafts shops open all week long (10 A.M.–9 P.M. daily) on all the main streets leading from the square, especially **Mariscal Castilla, San Francisco,** and **Bolognesi.** Contemporary art is sold in the first floor of the **Café Art Gallery Mullu** (Plaza Constitución 352) and in a related gallery a block from the square on San Francisco.

ACCOMMODATIONS
Under US$10

The best budget option is **Hostel Kinsa Ccocha** (Arequipa 307, tel. 084/20-3101, US$10 pp), which has several plain, clean rooms a block from the Plaza Constitución. Ask for a newer room, which has higher ceilings. Private baths are an additional US$5.

Hospedaje Samana Wasi (Plaza Constitución 509, tel. 084/20-3018, US$5 s, US$10 d) offers shoebox-size rooms overlooking the plaza, shared bathrooms, and a restaurant (7 A.M.–9 P.M.). Private baths are an extra US$3 per person. **El Artesano** (Calle Vigil s/n, US$8 s, US$11 d) is a family home that has a few rooms for tourists. Luckily, the guest rooms are big and clean, which makes up for having to share the bathroom with the family.

US$25-50

◖ **Pisac Inn,** formerly Hotel Pisaq (Plaza Constitución, tel. 084/20-3062, www.pisacinn.com, US$45 s, US$55–65 d with breakfast) is a labor of love for Roman Vizcarra and Fielding Wood-Vizcarra, a Peruvian-American couple who founded the hotel in 1993. The adobe building, covered in bright murals, includes the excellent Cuchara de Palo restaurant, with balconies overlooking the market square. Past the building's threshold is a hushed, contemplative atmosphere that recalls Fielding's hometown of Taos, New Mexico. Friezes of turquoise and scarlet fringe the sand-colored walls, and the atmosphere—neither Inca nor Navajo—is billed as a "celebration of indigenous culture all over the Americas." Additional perks include a US$25 Cusco airport pickup, rock-heated sauna, laundry, and a constant supply of water from the hotel's own well—a big advantage, given Pisac's sporadic water supply. Rooms with shared baths are only US$35 for a single to US$55 for a triple. Roman speaks English, Spanish, Quechua, Italian, and German and leads tours throughout the area that combine culture with a bit of spirituality. They have a range of trips described on their related website, www.peruculturaljourneys.com.

New Yorker Diane Dunn's pride and joy ◖ **Paz y Luz** (off the road to the ruins 2 km outside of town, tel. 084/20-3204, www.pazyluzperu.com, US$35 s, US$55 d with breakfast, cash only) is her collection of earth-colored lodges on the edge of the Río Urubamba above Pisac. The base of her healing center, the inspiration of her book *Cusco: Gateway to Inner Wisdom,* and the starting point of many long walks in the surrounding fields, the lodge truly offers all the peace and light that its name promises. The rooms are comfortable and tastefully decorated, with brand-new bathrooms. A central area has a woodstove, dining table, and polished wood staircase. In the back, in a separate building, is a one-bedroom apartment with its own kitchen. The growing complex includes a restaurant, conference room, meditation room, and rooms for long-term residents.

Prices for long-term guests and descriptions of massage services, spiritual workshops, and other offerings are on the website.

US$50-100

On the outskirts of town, **Hotel Royal Inka III Pisac** (on road to the ruins 1 km outside of town, tel. 084/20-3064, www.royalinkahotel.com, US$53 s, US$80 d) is a charming, converted hacienda with a mid-19th-century chapel. Unfortunately, most of the rooms are in a cold and charmless modern addition. Some rooms have woodstoves, however, and the second and third floors offer views out over the fields. There is a range of services, mostly included in the price, such as an Olympic-size pool (available to nonguests), private whirlpool tub, sauna, tennis court with rented rackets, horses, bikes, game room, restaurant, bar, and videos. There is also a spa, where you can get a massage for US$25 and other treatments. Without a deep discount, this hotel can seem overpriced, especially when compared to other, more charming and considerably cheaper options nearby.

Also outside town is **Melissa Wasi** (on road to the ruins 1 km outside of town, tel. 084/79-7589, www.melissa-wasi.com, US$120 for a bungalow), a charming hotel with separate bungalows built into the hillside. Owners Joyce and Chito have created a beautiful house to accommodate people for a breakfast of homemade bread, eggs, and fresh coffee before sitting in the colorful gardens. Bungalows sleep up to four people, and all have WiFi and a complete kitchen.

FOOD
Cafés, Bakeries, and Ice Cream

◖ **Ulrike's Café** (Plaza Constitución, tel. 084/20-3195, 7 A.M.–9 P.M. daily, US$4). Ulrike Simic, the classy German owner of this playful establishment, offers a lunch menu (US$7, including vegetarian options) and makes a delectable array of cheesecakes, including chocolate chip, coffee, and lemon. The walls are painted in yellows, greens, and pinks, and a mixture of music drifts through the air, making every sitting nook a perfect respite from the bustling world of commerce outside.

Café Art Gallery Mullu (Plaza Constitución 352, 9 A.M.–8 P.M. daily, US$4) has an interesting collection of contemporary art on the first floor and a café, with nice market views, on the second.

Blue Llama Café (Plaza Constitución, tel. 084/20-3135, www.bluellamacafe.com, 7 A.M.–9 P.M. daily, US$4) is one of the newest additions to Pisac, offering excellent food and service in its funky restaurant. Great coffee, brownies, and pancakes, along with traditional cuisine, are available all day long. This is a comfy place to hang out with a book or good friends.

Tinkuy Café is another fun place in Pisac, where owners Alfredo and Nancy with their sheep Meli offer a good range of juices, coffee, and vegetarian food. They have a daily menu for US$3. Alfredo speaks excellent English and can help with tours of the area.

If you are in the mood for something quick, tasty, and cheap, try the empanadas made in a few old, wood-fired *hornos coloniales* (colonial ovens) around town. The flaky empanadas—dough filled with cheese, sliced onion, tomato, olives, and oregano—can be had for US$0.50 each on the corner of the main square near the Pisac Inn or on Mariscal Castilla 372, one block away on the other end of the square.

Peruvian

The best place for trout in Pisac, and maybe the whole Cusco area, is **Restaurant Valle Sagrado** (Amazonas 116, tel. 084/43-6915, 8 A.M.–11 P.M. daily, US$2–5), operated over the last 15 years by the motherly Carmen Luz. During lunch, this place is packed with locals who come not only for the trout but for chicken, soups, sandwiches, and lamb ribs. Restaurant Valle Sagrado is right on the main drag, along with many other lesser restaurants; look for its faux-Inca walls.

Despite its humble entrance, **Doña Clorinda** (Plaza Constitución, tel. 084/20-3051, 7 A.M.–7 P.M. daily, US$2–5) serves up safe, flavorful *comida típica*. Highlights are *lomo*

saltado and *rocoto relleno*. There is a basic lunch menu for US$2 or a more luxurious version for US$5.

The gourmet option in town is **Cuchara de Palo** (Plaza Constitución, tel. 084/20-3062, www.pisacinn.com, 11:30 A.M.–8:30 P.M. daily, US$5–15), inside Pisac Inn. With bright green walls and tree-trunk tables, the atmosphere and the food are all natural. Vegetarians should try the *quinoa chaufa* (fried quinoa), and meat-eaters should go for the duck in elderberry sauce or *lomo saltado*.

For dessert, stop by **Miski Mijuna Wasi** (Plaza Constitución 345, tel. 084/20-3266, 7 A.M.–8:30 P.M. daily), where the *crocante de lúcuma* is the house specialty.

Markets

The best supermarkets are **Sofis Market** (Bolognesi s/n, tel. 084/20-3017, 6:30 A.M.–10 P.M. daily) and **La Baratura** (Manuel Prado 105, 6 A.M.–10 P.M. daily).

© PROMPERU

The fertile Sacred Valley produces much of the grains, vegetables, and fruit consumed in nearby Cusco.

INFORMATION AND SERVICES

The best info about Pisac is available from **Tinkuy Café, Ulrike's Café, Paz y Luz,** or **Pisac Inn,** which also offers laundry, money exchange, and fax services.

There is a clinic and pharmacy above the plaza near the public parking area. Other pharmacies are on Bolognesi and are generally open 8 A.M.–9 P.M. daily, with a midday closure for lunch.

There is a **Global Net ATM** on the corner of the main square, next to Ulrike's Café, and a store that changes foreign currency and travelers checks on the square near the church.

Tourist information is found on the corner of Bolognesi and San Francisco (tel. 084/20-3026).

A **mailbox** is on the main square inside the Restaurant Samana Wasi, which also sells stamps. There are **phone booths** at Sofis Market on Bolognesi and near the municipality on the main square. **Internet** is available in several sites around the Plaza de Armas. Hours are usually 9 A.M.–11 P.M. daily.

GETTING THERE AND AROUND

Buses for Pisac leave Cusco from below Tullumayo and Garcilaso every 20 minutes and charge US$1 for the one-hour journey. There are also buses available on Puputi street. For a 45-minute ride, hire a taxi in Cusco's Plaza de Armas for US$10. Buses drop passengers off at the bridge on the main highway, from which it is a three-block walk uphill to the market and main square. Return buses to Cusco leave from the same spot every 15 minutes up until 7 P.M. Buses heading the opposite direction also stop here on the way to Yucay and then Urubamba (US$0.50, 30–40 minutes). Once in Pisac, taxis can be taken eight kilometers to the main Pisac ruins entrance (US$3) or the upper level (US$4).

SIDE TRIPS
Huchuy Cusco

After Ollantaytambo and Pisac, Huchuy Cusco is the next most important Inca ruin in the Sacred Valley. This site features a two-story *kallanka,* or Inca hall, that is nearly

trail at the Pisac ruins

© RENÉE DEL GAUDIO AND ROSS WEHNER

drinking *chicha* at the Sunday market in Chinchero

Urubamba is marked with a large blue sign from the National Institute of Culture.

Another highly recommended option is to approach Huchuy Cusco from the opposite direction in a two-day hike across the high plains from Cusco. The trip starts at Sacsayhuamán in Cusco and follows the original Inca Trail to Calca, heading past finely wrought canals, villages, and several 4,000-meter passes. The total trip is 17 miles, including the final descent to Lamay, where you can catch a bus back to Cusco via Pisac. Both trips are described in detail in Peter Frost's *Exploring Cusco.* For either route, bring plenty of water and food as there is little along the way.

Chinchero

Chinchero is a small Andean village, off the beaten tourist track, that lies along the shortest driving route between Cusco and the Sacred Valley. Chinchero is perched on the high plains at 3,800 meters above sea level and has great views over the snowcapped Urubamba range. It is nearly 400 meters above Cusco, so visitors should be aware of altitude sickness.

Past Chinchero's less-than-appealing street front is the main square, where a handicrafts market is held on Tuesday, Thursday, and Sunday. A number of talented weavers in Chinchero exhibit their wares at this market, which is smaller and less touristy than Pisac. The highlight of the square is an Inca wall with huge niches, which probably formed part of an Inca palace. Above the square is a 17th-century adobe church that was built on Inca foundations, which has deteriorated floral designs painted on its interior. It is open for visitors on market days only.

On market days, you can also catch a weaving demonstration at one of the local workshops. Starting as young as age 5, girls learn to wash wool; a couple of years later they are spinning the wool into thread, and finally by 12 or 15, they are weaving actual pieces. To understand the complexity and incredible skill that goes into creating these pieces, we recommend stopping by **Exposición de Artesanías**

40 meters long and topped off by a well-preserved third story of adobe—it is easy to imagine this adobe painted, as were the buildings in Cusco, and topped off with a pyramid of thick thatch. There are also terraces, a square, an Inca gate, and many other rougher buildings within a few hundred meters of the hall. The whole site commands a small plateau, 800 meters above the Sacred Valley, with spectacular views.

This was probably the royal estate once known as Caquia Jaquijahuana, where, according to myth, Inca Viracocha hid when the Chancas threatened to invade Cusco in 1438. One of his sons, who later renamed himself Pachacútec, rose up and defeated the Chancas, thus beginning the meteoric rise of the Inca. After the conquest, the Spaniards found a mummy at this site—said to be that of Viracocha.

Reaching Huchuy Cusco is not easy, but it's worth the effort. The shortest way to get there is a three-hour, uphill hike from Lamay, a village between Pisac and Urubamba. The entrance to the footbridge that crosses the Río

Mink'a Chinchero (Albergue 22, tel. 084/30-6035, minka@hotmail.com, hours vary).

If you're looking for a more active day, and you can leave Chinchero by noon, you'll have time for a nice four-hour hike that drops along an old Inca trail into this valley and ends at Huayllabamba, where *combis* pass in the late afternoon for Urubamba or Pisac. From the church, a wide trail leads up the opposite side of the valley and then gradually descends into the Sacred Valley. Once you arrive at the Río Urubamba, the Sacred Valley's main river, head right (downstream) toward the bridge at Huayllabamba.

There's a hostel or two in Chinchero, but they are very basic and the town's high altitude and bone-chilling nights make the Sacred Valley—almost 1,000 meters lower—a much better option. In Cusco, *colectivos* for Chinchero can be taken from the first block of Grau near the bridge (US$0.75, 45 minutes).

YUCAY

This quiet town, a few kilometers east of Urubamba, consists of a large, grassy plaza where soccer games are played in the shade of two massive pisonay trees reputed to be 450 years old. Various colonial homes, now hotels, front the square along with the restored colonial church of Santiago Apóstol. On the far end of the square, near the highway, lies the adobe palace of Sayri Túpac, who settled here after emerging from Vilcabamba in 1558. Away from the main square lie quiet, dusty streets and extensive Inca terracing on the hillsides near town. There are few services outside the hotels clustered around the square.

Accommodations

The unpretentious **Hostel Y'llary** (Plaza Manco II 107, tel. 084/20-1112, US$27 s, US$33 d with breakfast) has rustic, large rooms with high ceilings and comfortable beds. The views from the flower garden are amazing, and it is also possible to pitch a tent in the yard (US$5 pp).

The luxurious **Sonesta Posadas del Inca** (Plaza Manco II, Yucay 123, tel. 084/20-1107, www.sonesta.com, US$94–170 s, US$99–180 d, prices depend on season and come with breakfast) is like a small village with rooms spread out among plazas and gardens, courtyard fountains, a miniature crafts market, and a chapel. The hotel is built around the charming 16th-century Santa Catalina de Sena monastery, where 21 rooms are located. The modern though colonial-style building next door has another 40 rooms or so with high ceilings, cable TV, lock boxes, and bathrooms with tubs. Amenities include a nice restaurant (US$15 lunch buffet), jewelry shop, ATM, and a full spa. Even if you don't stay here, stop in and see the excellent museum, which has a range of ceramics, *quipus,* and weavings from most of Peru's cultures, from the Chavín to the Inca.

The well-decorated **La Casona de Yucay** (Plaza Manco II 104, tel. 084/20-1116, www.hotelcasonayucay.com, US$85 s, US$105 d with breakfast) is a colonial hacienda that has been converted into a hotel with large rooms and great views. The colonial sitting room is elegant, though the gardens need some work.

Food

The Sacred Valley's best-kept gastronomical secret is ◖ **Huayoccari Hacienda Restaurant** (Km 64 Pisac–Ollantaytambo highway, call for directions beforehand, tel. 084/22-6241 or cell 084/962-2224, hsilabrador@latinmail.com, US$45 pp). This elegant gourmet retreat, two kilometers up a dirt road near Yucay, is a converted country manor perched high on a ridge overlooking the Sacred Valley. Past a rustic courtyard, the restaurant's walls are lined with colonial paintings, altars, and ceramics collected by José Ignacio Lambarri, whose family has owned the land and nearby hacienda for more than three centuries. The garden terraces offer dazzling views and digestive walks past roses and fuchsias to Inca terraces and some of the most fertile farmland in Peru.

Apart from its privileged location, Huayoccari has the most sophisticated cuisine in all of Cusco. It is completely organic and, best of all, based on the hacienda's original recipes. Lunch begins with *sara lagua,* a cream soup made of local white corn, fresh cheese, and the herb *huacatay.* Main courses include steamed river trout with a sauce of herbs and fresh capers, or chicken rolled with fresh cheese and country bacon and covered with *sauco*berry sauce. The whole meal builds toward the desserts, made of delectable fruits found only in Peru: cheesecake with *aguaymanto* marmalade, chirimoya meringue, or a *sacha*tomate compote. Though off the beaten path, Huayoccari is well worth the trek for the food, the country setting, and the private collection of art. There are only a handful of tables, so make reservations well in advance. Huayoccari

is between Pisac and Urubamba and can be reached via taxi from either town.

A more conventional option, but with a diverse menu, is **Allpa Manka** (St. Martin 300, tel. 084/20-1258, www.cuscofood.com, 11 A.M.–3:30 P.M. and 6–9:30 P.M. daily, US$12–15). The US$12 buffet lunch, taken in the sunny patio with live music, can be a restful break from the go-go tourist grind.

Getting There and Around

From Cusco, buses leave for Yucay from the first block of Grau. Frequent buses pass Yucay's main square going one direction to Pisac (30 minutes) or to Urubamba (10 minutes) in the other.

Urubamba and Vicinity

Urubamba lies smack in the center of the Sacred Valley and thus makes a good base for exploring the valley. Ollantaytambo is 20 minutes down the valley one way and Pisac is 40 minutes the other way. From here, another highway climbs onto the high plains toward Chinchero, a weaving center with a Sunday market and Inca ruins, and Cusco.

Despite its location on an atrocious highway strip, Urubamba is a relaxed and friendly town that grows on people who spend time here. The massive flow of tourism through the Sacred Valley—especially strong on the biggest Pisac market days (Sunday, Tuesday, and Thursday)—mostly bypasses Urubamba, which has just one good ruin and little else to attract tourists besides its pleasant square and a colonial cathedral. Other towns, like Ollantaytambo or even Pisac, have more of a Quechua flavor, but none are as mellow as Urubamba. Recently, several hip bars and cafés have sprung up in response to a stream of college students brought here by ProPeru and other student organizations.

The plains above Urubamba are spectacular: The snow-covered Cordillera Urubamba rises over a patchwork of russet and chocolate-brown fields. In the middle is Maras, a dense

cluster of red tile roofs, and two other startling visual anomalies. Moray is a set of huge natural depressions in the earth that were elaborately terraced by the Inca. Salineras is a blinding-white salt mine that sprawls across the mountain slope.

With these sights plus mountain biking, rafting, and horseback riding, it is no surprise that Urubamba is home to the valley's best hotels. Because the day tours through the valley stop here for lunch, Urubamba also has the greatest concentration of good restaurants. A final Urubamba highlight worth mentioning is the Seminario Ceramics studio.

SIGHTS
◖ Moray and Salineras

If you want to soak in the Sacred Valley's spectacular scenery, spend time wandering around the high plains above Urubamba. First stop is **Maras,** a dusty town with a few colonial churches and *chicherías,* fermented corn-beer shops advertised by red plastic bags tied to the end of wooden poles. There is also an ancient hatmaker named Teodosio Argandaño Caviedes—his shop is near the corner of Leguía and Jesús. About five kilometers farther, or a half hour along a good dirt road, lie the four natural depressions of Moray (7:30 A.M.–5:15 P.M. daily, US$3). These sinkholes, 150 meters deep, were caused by rain eroding the calcium-rich soil.

With its perfect terracing, Moray appears at first glance to be a ceremonial center or a Greek-style amphitheater. But researchers have discovered that the pits harbor a cluster of microclimates. Gradations of sun, shade, and elevation among the terraces create dramatic differences in temperature. Irrigation canals and the discovery of different seeds on the terraces are additional clues that Moray was once a gigantic crops laboratory. It was here, perhaps, that the Inca learned to grow corn and potatoes in a variety of elevations, fueling the expansion of the empire.

On the nearby hills that lead down to the Urubamba Valley, the Inca once again transformed nature: A spring of warm, salty water was diverted into thousands of pools, where sunlight evaporates the water and leaves a thin

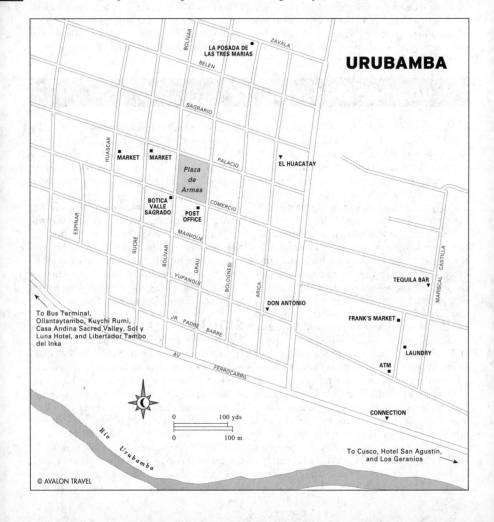

URUBAMBA

To Bus Terminal,
Ollantaytambo, Kuychi Rumi,
Casa Andina Sacred Valley, Sol y
Luna Hotel, and Libertador Tambo
del Inka

To Cusco, Hotel San Agustín,
and Los Geranios

© AVALON TRAVEL

© JORGE RIVEROS CAYO

The concentric circles at Moray are believed to have been an Inca agricultural laboratory.

crust of salt. The salt mines, or *salineras,* continue to be worked by a collective of 260 salt miners from the nearby villages of Maras and Pichinjoto. (You may see this salt marketed overseas as "Peruvian pink salt.") Today there are 5,740 pools, or *pocitos,* each of which yields 150 kilograms of unrefined salt per month. There is a dazzling, and oft-photographed, contrast between the barren hillsides and the snow-white salt pools, which visitors can explore along narrow, crunchy paths.

To reach Moray, take a Cusco–Urubamba bus and get off at the Maras turnoff (say *"ramal a Maras, por favor"*). *Colectivos* wait here and charge US$6–9 for a half-day tour of Maras, Moray, and Salinas. A recommended company is **Empresa Transporte Moray.** To get from Moray to Salinas, car-bound travelers must return to Maras and then proceed another five kilometers downhill to the salt mines. Another option is to get a ride to Maras (four kilometers) and then walk the remaining seven kilometers to Moray (two hours, mostly uphill), through a patchwork of fields. From Moray, it is a two-hour walk—ask for directions along

the way—to the salt mines. A steep but beautiful path continues for another kilometer or two from Salinas to the Urubamba Valley, ending five kilometers down from Urubamba and at the doorstep of the recommended Tunupa Restaurant. This whole circuit makes for an excellent full-day tour on horse, bike, or foot, though many travelers elect to be dropped off at Salineras and take the scenic, one-hour walk to Urubamba.

ENTERTAINMENT AND EVENTS

Urubamba's nightlife has improved with the influx of students. The best way to begin an evening is with an empanada and a beer at **La Esquina** (Comercio 407, tel. 084/20-1554), on the main square. The owner of this pizza-and-empanada bar, a Lima transplant named Lucy, sings whenever the spirit moves her (and her musician friends show up).

Late night, your options are twofold: **Connection** (Mariscal Castilla, 6 P.M.–close) is a laid-back bar with a bit of art on the walls and an owner-DJ who spent the last eight years

WHERE FIESTAS ARE SERIOUS BUSINESS

With a final burst of drinking, dancing, and eating this past weekend we have at last wound up our annual participation in the fiesta of Our Lady of the Nativity, at Huayllabamba, a pueblo just upstream from Urubamba.

It's serious business. We had to scour our section of the Sacred Valley for guinea pigs and barnyard fowl, because the tasteless supermarket chicken is not acceptable to Our Lady. We had been fattening up a flock of ducks and a handful of free-range pigs and earmarked suckling piglets for the fiesta. A steer was dispatched, and many of our guests undertook to bring along sheep, more piglets, maize, and the scores of other items that go into endless days and nights of jolly breakfasts, lunches, suppers, and nonstop Andean music and dancing. Each of the meals is a banquet, some attended by hundreds of guests.

We were *mayordomos*, or sponsors, for one of the dozen groups that, each with its own elaborate costume, its own music, its own ancient tradition, danced for Our Lady. Her dressed-up statue was paraded round town, up the hill to a chapel, all in a tradition-ridden timetable organized by no one. There's no coordinating committee, and if anyone owns an electronic watch, they don't spend much time looking at it.

It would be misleading to say, though, that it's a clockwork operation. When my 12-year-old boy goes along for the rehearsals for the Capac Negro (*Millionaire Slaves of the Virgin*) dance group, in the weeks leading up to the fiesta, he has to wait till everyone else, including the fellow with the taped practice music, arrives. But on the day, you saw a score or so of lads each in elaborate uniform, dancing with military precision to ancient Quechua tunes and rhythms, with dirges and chants that reach back thousands of years. Our Lady is just the latest in a long line of *apus*, the Andean gods who reside on the snow peaks, some of them visible from Huayllabamba.

A dozen more dance groups come along, with colorful costumes representing jungle Indians fighting the Inca, or the Inca fighting the Spaniards, or even – rather boring this one – barbers in top hats and morning coats, foot-long noses and scissors going snip-snip in time to weird Andean-medieval flute music.

One wonders what the contribution of these fiestas is to the gross domestic product. What do the World Bank people who drift by from time to time in their chauffeur-driven, laptopped Toyota 4x4s think of all this? What say the Inter-American Development Bank, USAID, and the European Union development people with their tax-free incomes and diplomatic passports?

We can be pretty sure that they switch off their satellite-feed cell phones and join in. They may not be having much luck solving our poverty, but that doesn't mean they can't spot the kind of party that, as they would be the first to recognize, none of them could begin to organize for themselves. Huayllabamba's **Virgen de la Natividad** is held September 7–10.

(Contributed by Nicholas Asheshov, M.A., a British journalist who has covered Peru for decades. Asheshov is the Planning Director for Andean Railways Corp. in Urubamba.)

in the United States. **Tequila Bar** (third block of Mariscal Castilla, tel. 084/80-1646, tequilaclub@hotmail.com, noon onwards), however, is the wild dance spot. Within the course of a night, this Jekyll and Hyde place can swing from mellow artist pub to Wild West bar, with fists (and beer bottles!) flying.

Urubamba erupts in bullfights, dancing, and partying during the Pentecostal celebration of Señor Torrechayoc in late May or early June and then once again for Urubamba Day on November 9. An even better party, however, is Huayllabamba's Virgen de la Natividad, held September 7–10.

SHOPPING

When in Urubamba, do not miss **Seminario Ceramics** (Barriózabal 111, tel. 084/20-1002, www.ceramicaseminario.com, 8 A.M.–5 P.M. daily). With Pablo Seminario focusing on form and Marilú Behar on color, this husband-and-wife team began to crank out ceramics out of a small home in Urubamba over two decades ago. Thanks to international recognition and lucrative contracts (including a deal with Pier 1 Imports), their original adobe workshop has blossomed into an expansive, garden-filled complex where visitors can pet llamas, watch an educational video, and see the whole ceramics-making process. The couple's workshop produces a range of objects from compotes and coffee cups to sculptures and large painting frames adorned with delicate touches of silver. Everything is handmade, painted with natural mineral oxides, and kiln fired.

For upscale shopping, head to an outlet of **Artenesia Mon Repos** (Cabo Conchatupa s/n, tel. 084/20-1174, www.monrepos-peru.com, 9 A.M.–6 P.M. daily), a Lima-based clothing store with classic designs.

RECREATION
Hiking, Biking, and Horseback Riding
Urubamba is a fast-growing center of adventure sports, including horseback riding, mountain biking, rafting, trekking, and paragliding. There are some highly recommended horseback rides—that can also be done on foot or mountain bike—on both sides of the Urubamba Valley. The sun in the Sacred Valley is intensely bright, so bring a sun hat and sunscreen. It is best to get an early start to avoid the often cloudy (sometimes rainy) afternoons.

To the north (snow-covered mountain side), several mule tracks lead up valleys to high passes on the Cordillera Vilcabamba. On the other side are remote Quechuan villages in the Lares Valley, a journey of several days with an option of returning by car at the end.

One of these valleys, the **Pumahuanca,** is a pleasant half-day trip that combines streams glinting in the morning sun; a series of microclimes, including forests of rhododendrons and native quenua trees; and, at the turnaround point, ruins of several two-story Inca buildings. The other valley above Urubamba

dead-ends at Chicón, the glaciated peak (5,530 meters) that looms above the village. This peak is rarely climbed, even though it is one of the easier summits in the Cusco area.

For those who can take a full day on a horse or on a bike, there is a breathtaking circuit on the south side of the valley that traverses the high plains around Maras and Moray and then descends via the salt mines to Urubamba. The scenery is spectacular.

Wayra (part of the Sol y Luna Hotel outside Urubamba, tel. 084/20-1620, www.wayrasacredvalley.com) rents mountain bikes and has the best selection of *paso* horses in the valley. Another great option for *paso* horses is **Perol Chico** (Carretera Urubamba–Ollantaytambo, tel. 084/974-79-8890, www.perolchico.com). These elegant animals, which kick their feet out to one side for a smooth ride, are best for the Maras–Moray–Salinas loop or a flat loop around the valley (they are not well suited, however, for the steep Pumahuanca ride).

Rafting
All of the Cusco rafting agencies descend the Río Urubamba, which is at its wildest during the high-water months December–May. Day trips run US$40–55. Some trips include one night of camping near Ollantaytambo, mountain biking, and a chance to see ruins the next day.

As the river drops between June and November, the agencies run the steeper, lower section that ends just past Ollantaytambo, though the rapids rarely exceed Class III. The water itself, unfortunately, is somewhat polluted, with plastic festooning the banks.

One of the most professional rafting companies in Peru is **Amazonas Explorer** (Collasuyo 910, Urb. Miravalle, Cusco, tel. 084/25-2846, www.amazonas-explorer.com). **ExplorAndes** (Av. Garcilaso 316-A, Cusco tel. 084/23-8380 or Lima tel. 01/715-2323, www.explorandes. com) also offers high-end rafting trips.

Some less expensive but also experienced agencies are recommended for easier trips. **Apumayo Expediciones** (Jr. Ricardo Palma N-5, Santa Monica, tel. 084/24-6018, www.apumayo.com) is run by Pepe López, a kayaker with a lot of experience on Peru's rivers. He recently built an adventure center on the banks of the Río Urubamba, downstream of Ollantaytambo.

Mayuc (Portal Confituras 211, Plaza de Armas, Cusco, tel. 084/24-2824, www.mayuc.com) is one of the pioneering rafting companies and operates an excellent day trip on Río Urubamba.

Loreto Tours (Calle del Medio 111, Cusco, tel. 084/22-8264, loretotours@planet.com.pe) provides varied rafting itineraries and good-quality equipment.

Terra Explorer Peru (Santa Ursula D-4, Huanchac, tel. 084/23-7352, www.terraexplorerperu.com) is owned by Piero, the youngest of the Vellutino brothers, all dedicated and well known adventure sportsmen and white-water rafters. **Munaycha** (based in the Sacred Valley, tel. 084/984-770-108 or 084/984-770-381, www.munaycha.com) belongs to Duilio, the oldest Vellutino brother, and also offers rafting on Peru's best known rivers.

Climbing

A new adventure in the Sacred Valley is the **Via Ferrata** (tel. 084/98-974-360-260, viaferrata@naturavive.com, www.naturavive.com, US$60 pp), a system of ropes and pulleys that allows you to climb a 300-meter cliff and then rappel, or descend, about 100 meters. The whole experience lasts three–five hours and can even be done by small children. Reservations must be made in advance by emailing or calling Natura Vive.

Paragliding

The best place to get parapenting lessons in the Cusco area is Wayra (part of the Sol y Luna Hotel outside Urubamba, tel. 084/20-1620, www.wayrasacredvalley.com), where owners Marie-Hélène Miribel and Franz Schilter offer paragliding lessons. They are the only internationally certified instructors in Cusco. They charge US$150 for a tandem one-hour flight, taking off from a nearby mountain and landing in the valley itself.

ACCOMMODATIONS
Under US$10

Hotels in Urubamba tend toward upscale, and finding a budget hotel can be tricky. A good option is the shared room at **La Posada de las Tres Marias** (Zavala 307, tel. 084/20-1006, posada3marias@yahoo.com, US$10 pp with breakfast). This converted house has a large dining room, which opens onto a huge garden complete with a patio and tables for an afternoon beer and card playing. The hotel also has private rooms, but they are overpriced for their value.

US$10-25

Los Geranios Hostel (Cabo Conchatupa s/n, tel. 084/20-1093, US$14 s, US$21 d), best known for its lunch buffets, has a few rooms with lots of sunlight, private baths, and hot water. The backyard spills onto the Urubamba riverbanks.

US$25-50

If you've ever wanted to live in a tree house, **⟨ Las Chullpas** (Gonzalo Muñoz, tel. 084/20-1568, www.chullpas.uhupi.com, US$45 s/d) is your chance. Chalo, a Chilean, and his German wife, Leonie, have created a lovely set of 10 bungalows, interlaced with gardens, whose tree-trunk floors, tile mosaics, and adobe walls remind you that nature is very playful. One room has a slide in the bathroom, and all beds are covered with homemade alpaca duvets. Sitting in the gardens and watching the hummingbirds is a real treat.

US$100-150

The **Hotel San Agustín Monasterio de la Recoleta** (Recoleta s/n, tel. 084/20-1004, www.hotelessanagustin.com.pe, US$120 s, US$144 d) occupies a stunning, 16th-century Franciscan monastery, though erratic service continues to keep guests away. There is a modern addition with a few spectacular rooms upstairs, outfitted with exposed beams, stone showers, and sun windows. Rooms in the old section are surrounded by a stone courtyard and cannot be renovated because of historical restrictions—they are nicer than the bland modern rooms. All rooms have private baths.

Over US$150

Mexican owner Claudia calls her flower-lined, central walkway the hummingbird corridor. She's right. Walking down it, you're almost guaranteed to see the world's largest hummingbirds. But even better is when the birds flit around your private house, which is what Claudia and her architect husband rent to their lucky guests. 🄲 **Kuychi Rumi Lodging** (Km 74.5 Urubamba-Ollantaytambo Highway, tel. 084/20-1169, www.urubamba.com, US$154 s or d) offers six fully-equipped houses with two bedrooms, a sitting room, and a kitchenette. Tastefully designed and decorated, the houses are meant for a several-day stay, but even if you only have a night, they are worth the privacy and comfort.

Our vote for the most elegant, luxurious hotel in the Sacred Valley goes to the **Sol y Luna Hotel** (tel. 084/20-1620, www.hotel-solyluna.com, US$200 s/d to US$750 for a new deluxe suite, with breakfast), opened in 2000 by Marie-Hélène Miribel and Franz Schilter. This French-Swiss couple have carefully designed every last detail of their 43 bungalows, including terra-cotta tiles, exposed beams, marble bathrooms, and king-size beds. Stay at the newly created luxury bungalows, which include a hot tub on your patio. The US$27 poolside buffet is exquisite, using local produce from the valley. It also has a dessert spread that includes cake made from *lúcuma,* the intoxicatingly tasty fruit. Groups are often treated to *pachamanca* cooking with *marinera* dance demonstrations. Plan on spending time here to stroll through the hotel's gardens, lounge by the pool, work out at the gym, or check into the spa, which includes a whirlpool tub and massage. There are 20 Peruvian horses (*caballos de paso*) lodged in elegant stables in the back and available for half- and full-day rides. If that is not enough, the hotel also rents mountain bikes, coordinates cultural trips to a local school and orphanage, and offers paragliding outings with the owners, Cusco's only internationally certified instructors. Through an associated nonprofit organization, the hotel has also recently created a local school and engaged in other philanthropic efforts.

Another new upscale option is the **Libertador Tambo del Inka** (Av. Ferrocarril, tel. 84/58-1777, www.luxurycollection.com/vallesagrado, US$455 to US$565 s), designed by Bernard Fort on the banks of the Urubamba. The elegant lobby, with 12-meter ceilings, mixed international standards with Peruvian decor. The 128 rooms and suites all have either a balcony or a terrace, and all come with WiFi, cable TV, and iPod docks. This luxury hotel has a 1,800-square-meter spa offering massages, pool and Jacuzzi. At night, hit the Bar Kiri, with its outstanding back-lit onyx wall.

Outside Urubamba

In Yanahuara, just 15 minutes outside of Urubamba on the road to Ollantaytambo, the hotel chain **Casa Andina** has constructed one of its **Private Collection** hotels (5th Paradero, tel. 084/976-5501, www.casa-andina.com, US$200 s d with breakfast). The result is a labyrinth of glassed lobbies, gardens, spa center, and planetarium. You might just have to spend two nights to take advantage of it all. There's so much to do, you'll have to make sure you don't spend all your energy sightseeing. It's also very child friendly with a small playground, llamas, and lots of open space.

In Huayllabamba, the **Aranwa** (tel. 01/434-1452, www.aranwahotels.com, US$160 s/d) chain of hotels has opened a new 100-bedroom, 15-suite complex that includes one of the largest spas in the Sacred Valley. The luxury hotel includes a business center, three restaurants, a sushi bar, and even a cinema. The newer buildings are built around a historic hacienda. There is no formal address for this hotel, but you will find it on the main road between Huayllabamba and Urubamba.

Rio Sagrado (Km 75.8 Cusco–Urubamba Highway, tel. 084/20-1631, www.riosagrado. com, US$205 s) is the latest in the Orient-

PERU'S BATTLE WITH THE BOTTLE

Every time travelers buy a plastic water bottle, they are contributing to a solid waste problem that is reaching epic proportions not only in Cusco but all over Peru. The best way to understand the problem is to raft along Cusco's Río Urubamba, where tree roots are blanketed in thick gobs of plastic bags and beaches are completely covered with plastic bottles.

What resources Peru's municipal governments have are used to fight poverty, not improve the environment. There is no plastic recycling in Peru, so everything ends up in open landfills or, as is the case with the Urubamba, floating downstream to the Amazon. Nearly 200 million plastic bottles are produced every month in Peru alone, and a good chunk of these are consumed by tourists – who need a few liters of purified water for each day in Peru.

Recently a boycott campaign has been initiated by longtime Ollantaytambo resident Joaquín Randall, who manages his family's El Albergue Hotel in Ollantaytambo.

Here's how travelers can do their part to resolve Peru's plastic addiction:

- Carry a reusable hard plastic or other water bottle and fill it with treated or boiled water.

- Buy sodas and water in refillable glass bottles.

- Demand that your hotel provide water tanks (*bidones*) or at the very least boiled water for refilling bottles.

- Reuse plastic bags over and over and do not accept new ones.

- Spread the word.

Express line of hotels, located on the outskirts of Urubamba. It's a newly built hotel with a mixture of high-quality rooms, suites, and two-story bungalows. As seems to be the fashion in the valley, they have also created a spa.

FOOD
Peruvian
The Sacred Valley day tours use Urubamba as a lunch spot, so there are a half dozen restaurants that offer good lunch buffets. The best, and newest, of these is **Alhambra** (Km 74 Urubamba–Ollantaytambo Highway, tel. 084/20-1200, www.alhambrarestaurant.com, noon–3:30 P.M. and 7 P.M.–close daily, US$12–14). The buffet table, full of colors and flavors, is a work of art! Another excellent buffet is available at **Killa Wasi,** the restaurant connected to Sol y Luna Hotel (tel. 084/20-1620, www.hotelsolyluna.com, noon–7 P.M. Tues., Thurs., and Sun., US$27).

If you're looking for a more informal atmosphere, try **3 Keros** (Sr. de Torrechayoc, tel. 084/20-1701, noon–3:45 P.M. and 6–9:30 P.M. Wed.–Mon., US$12–15). Ricardo, the owner of this laid-back restaurant, dishes up *cuy* specials and Quillabamba mangos while his patrons catch the Michigan game.

Los Geranios (Cabo Conchatupa s/n, tel. 084/20-1093, noon–5 P.M. daily, US$9 buffet) is the least pretentious and most authentic of a group of restaurants on Urubamba's main drag. **Finestra** (Mariscal Castilla 107, tel. 084/20-1005, 8:30 A.M.–4:30 P.M. and 6–10 P.M. Mon.–Sat., US$2–5) is the place to go for a filling midday lunch menu. The service is fast and the decor pleasant.

International
After years of working abroad, first in Spain, then Germany, chef Pio Vasquez has finally returned to his home country, Peru. With the help of his German wife, Iris, they have created an elegant restaurant and garden. Have your passion fruit pisco sour on the patio of

El Huacatay (Arica 620, tel. 084/20-1790, www.elhuacatay.com, 1–10 P.M. Mon.–Sat., US$10–15) before moving into the intimate dining room for a main course based on local produce from arugula to fresh trout. Dessert is Pío's passion, so leave room for the chocolate mousse. Child-friendly.

Another new option is **Don Antonio** (corner of Jr Yupanqui and Arica, tel. 084/20-1501, noon–7 P.M. daily), offering a small menu with pasta, fish, and meat, set in a beautiful garden with fountain.

Markets

For the basics—fruit, cheese, cold cuts, and wine—there's **Frank's Market** (Mariscal Castilla 1032, 7:30 A.M.–2 P.M. and 3–10:30 P.M. daily).

INFORMATION AND SERVICES

There's a **police station** on Palacio (s/n, tel. 084/20-1012). The **town clinic** is on 9 de Noviembre (s/n, tel. 084/20-1032, lab open 8 A.M.–1 P.M.), or visit Dr. Hugo Chavez (Palacios 133, tel. 084/965-5386). There are now a number of tourist clinics in Urubamba, including **SOS Urgent Medical** (Mariscal Castilla, tel. 084/20-5059), which is a modern facility that works with different insurance companies. There are pharmacies all over town, but a good option is **Botica Valle Sagrado** (Bolivar 469, tel. 084/20-1830, 8 A.M.–10 P.M. daily).

On the highway in front of Urubamba, there is a **Banco de Crédito** ATM, and in the Pesca gas station there is a **Global Net** ATM.

The **post office** is on the main square, along with several pay phones under the municipality awning. There are several **Internet** locales, which are generally open 9 A.M.–10 P.M. daily.

Do your laundry at **Clean Wash Laundry** (Mariscal Castilla 100, 8 A.M.–7 P.M. Mon.–Sat.).

Volunteering

ProPeru (Apartado 70, tel. 084/20-1562, www.proworldsc.org) is a highly recommended organization, run by a Peruvian named Richard Webb. The organization arranges homestays for college students (and older folks, too) in Urubamba, Cusco, and other areas in Peru. Students take classes in art, history, anthropology, and Spanish, and work on service projects that range from reforestation to setting up a women's shelter or the town's first Internet café. ProPeru receives rave reviews from its students and is surely one of the better foreign study programs in Peru. Other volunteer organizations in Urubamba include **Casa de los Milagros** (casademilagros@yahoo.com, www.chandlersky.org, U.S. tel. 408/532-0644), which works with children with disabilities.

GETTING THERE AND AROUND

From Cusco, *combis* for Urubamba leave from the first block of Grau near the bridge (US$1.25, 1.5 hours). *Combis* drop passengers at Urubamba's bus station on the main drag, where frequent transport continues for the 20-minute ride to Ollantaytambo and Pisac (40 minutes).

Motocars are ubiquitous in Urubamba and can be contracted cheaply to arrive at the Chicón or Pumahuanca road or for getting to Yucay. **Sol y Luna Hotel** offers a full-day valley tour to Ollantaytambo and Pisac, in a private car with lunch included. Another option is to contract a private driver and car—Ollantaytambo and Pisac together is US$40, while one or the other is US$25. Ask your hotel for recommendations.

Ollantaytambo and Vicinity

Ollantaytambo is the last town in the Sacred Valley before the Río Urubamba plunges through steep gorges toward Machu Picchu. It is the best-preserved Inca village in Peru, with its narrow alleys, street water canals, and trapezoidal doorways. The Inca temple and fortress above town is second in beauty only to Machu Picchu. In the terraced fields above town, men still use foot plows, or *chaquitacllas,* to till fields and plant potatoes. There are endless things to explore in and around Ollantaytambo, which is framed by snowcapped Verónica mountain and surrounded on all sides by Inca ruins, highways, and terraces. Whisking through Ollantaytambo, as most travelers do, is a great shame. Stay and get to know the place.

Ollantaytambo is also in the throes of a tremendous struggle to save its way of life against the mass forces of tourism and development. Trinket sellers have crowded the areas in front of the Inca temple and the train station. Nondescript pizzerias are creeping onto the main square, which is continually shaken by the passing of massive trucks bound for the Camisea pipeline in the jungle around Quillabamba. One solution to these problems, as resident Wendy Weeks suggests, is to move the train station outside of town and have visitors enter as the Inca did—through the main gate and *on foot.*

The town's saving grace, and what should carry it through its present crisis, is the tremendous sense of community that is palpable to anyone who pauses here. A cadre of researchers, led by English archaeologist Anne Kendall, have spent considerable time researching Inca farming technology and have restored hundreds of farming terraces and aqueducts.

HISTORY

Ollantaytambo was occupied long before the Inca by the Quillques, who built some of the rougher buildings at Pumamarca and on the ridge near the Ollantaytambo temple itself. After Inca emperor Pachacútec conquered this area around 1440, construction began on a ceremonial center and royal estate that housed an estimated 1,000 workers year-round. What Ollantaytambo is most famous for, however, is a 1537 battle in which the Inca defeated a Spanish army—and nearly massacred it altogether.

The battle happened during the 1536–1537 Inca rebellion, when Manco Inca was forced to withdraw his troops to Ollantaytambo after being defeated by the Spanish at Sacsayhuamán. Hernando Pizarro arrived at Ollantaytambo one morning at dawn with 70 cavalry and 30 foot soldiers. But Manco Inca's men were waiting on the terraces of the sun temple, which had been hastily converted into a fort. Pedro Pizarro wrote afterward, "We found it so well fortified that it was a thing of horror." Conquistadors Juan, Francisco, and Hernando Pizarro were brothers, and Pedro Pizarro was their cousin.

© AMBER DAVIS COLLINS, WWW.LIFEUNSCRIPTEDPHOTOGRAPHY.COM

Río Urubamba outside Ollantaytambo

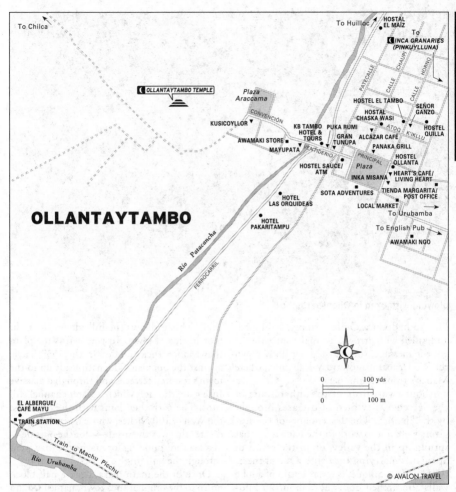

To Chilca

To Huilloc

HOSTAL
EL MAÍZ

To
INCA GRANARIES
(PINKUYLLUNA)

PATECALLE

CHAUPI

CALLE

HORNO

OLLANTAYTAMBO TEMPLE

Plaza
Araccama

CONVENCIÓN

KUSICOYLLOR

HOSTEL EL TAMBO

CALLE

SEÑOR
GANZO

HOSTAL
CHASKA WASI

ATOQ

HOSTEL
QUILLA

AWAMAKI STORE

KB TAMBO
HOTEL &
TOURS

PUKA RUMI

GRAN
TUNUPA

ALCÁZAR CAFÉ

K'IKLLU

MAYUPATA

VENTIDERIO

PANAKA GRILL

HOSTEL SAUCE/
ATM

PRINCIPAL

Plaza

INKA MISANA

HOSTEL
OLLANTA

HEART'S CAFÉ/
LIVING HEART

OLLANTAYTAMBO

SOTA ADVENTURES

TIENDA MARGARITA/
POST OFFICE

HOTEL
LAS ORQUIDEAS

LOCAL MARKET

To Urubamba

HOTEL
PAKARITAMPU

To English Pub

AWAMAKI NGO

Río Patacancha

FERROCARRIL

0   100 yds

0   100 m

EL ALBERGUE/
CAFÉ MAYU

TRAIN STATION

Train to Machu Picchu

Río Urubamba

© AVALON TRAVEL

From high on the upper terraces, Manco Inca commanded his troops from horseback—co-opting the symbol of Spanish strength—as jungle archers shot volleys of arrows and Inca soldiers fired off slingshots and rolled boulders. Sensing defeat, the Spaniards retreated, but Manco Inca pulled a final surprise. On cue, he diverted the Río Urubamba and flooded the plains below Ollantaytambo, causing the Spaniards' horses to founder in the mud. Manco's forces fought the Spanish all the way to Cusco, where Pizarro waited for Diego de Almagro to return from his Chile campaign with reinforcements. Manco Inca, meanwhile, recognized the growing strength of the Spaniards and withdrew to Vilcabamba.

After Manco's departure, the whole valley became an *encomienda* for Hernando Pizarro, who pursued Manco deep into Vilcabamba and raided his camp in 1539. Manco narrowly escaped, but his wife and sister, Cura Ocllo, was captured and brought to Ollantaytambo. After Manco refused to surrender, Francisco

plowing with oxen in Ollantaytambo

© BETH FUCHS

Pizarro had Cura Ocllo stripped, whipped, and killed with arrows. To make sure Manco got the message, they floated her body down the Río Urubamba toward Vilcabamba, where Manco's troops found her.

About two-thirds of the inhabitants of the Sacred Valley died of diseases brought by the Spanish. The descendants of the survivors were put to work in the haciendas that sprung up in the valley, often the result of Spaniards marrying Inca elite. One of these, the Hacienda Sillque, is today a ruin of adobe walls and arched doorways, about 20 kilometers west of Ollantaytambo. A road down the Urubamba Valley to Quillabamba was begun in 1895. It was this road that Hiram Bingham took to "discover" Machu Picchu in 1911. In the 1920s, the road was converted into the rail line that now carries travelers to Machu Picchu.

SIGHTS
City Tour

Ask your bus driver to let you off one kilometer before Ollantaytambo at the original Inca Trail, which follows the hillside on the right (north) side of town. To your left is the plain that Manco Inca flooded in the 1537 battle against the Spanish. The path leads up to the town's restored terraces and through a massive Inca gate, through which a water channel still runs. The path then joins with the road past the Wall of 100 Niches, whose inward slant indicates this was the inside—not the outside—of a roadside building (or maybe the road went through the building).

Once in the main plaza, head a half block north to the original Inca town, named **Qozqo Ayllu,** which is laid out in the form of a trapezoid and bisected by narrow, irrigated alleys. Oversized trapezoidal doorways open in the courtyards of homes, or *kanchas,* occupied continuously ever since Pachacútec's time.

◖ Ollantaytambo Temple

The other half of Ollantaytambo, **Araqama Ayllu,** is across the Río Patacancha. The main square is fronted with a series of monumental buildings, and above is the temple that was being constructed when the Spaniards

perfect stonework at Ollantaytambo's Temple of the Sun

arrived—and was later converted into a fortress by Manco Inca.

Two hundred steps lead up terraces to a double-jamb gateway and the **Temple of Ten Niches,** a long wall with odd protuberances. Some say these bumps draw heat away from the slabs, preventing them from expanding. Others say they somehow served in the transport of the blocks. Or perhaps the Inca valued them as we do today, for the graceful shadows they cast across the stone.

Above is the unfinished **Temple of the Sun,** considered one of the masterpieces of Inca stonework. Six giant monoliths of pink rhyolite are perfectly slotted together with thin slices of stone and oriented to glow with the rising sun. Traces of the *chacana* symbols and pumas that once decorated the walls can still be seen. What is unusual about the wall is the long straight lines—and the molten bronze that was poured in the T-joints to hold the wall together. These features indicate the wall was probably the handiwork of Lake Titicaca's Colla Indians, who were brought to work here by Pachacútec as part of the forced labor

system known as *mitimayo*. According to J. P. Protzen, the wall was probably intended to be one side of a great platform, which seems likely with the unfinished blocks, rough walls, and plaza nearby. It is uncertain why the construction stopped—perhaps it was Pachacútec's death, a rebellion of the Colla Indians, the smallpox epidemic of 1527, or the arrival of the Spaniards.

To the left of the plaza, the **Cachicata quarry** appears high on the hillside. The Inca dragged boulders weighing up to 52 tons down the mountain, across the Río Urubamba and the valley floor, and then up a steep ramp—the top of which is at a 25-degree angle, three times that allowed on most U.S. highways! Ollantaytambo expert Vincent Lee used sleds and levers to show how the Inca moved such blocks up the ramp, which still leads up the hillside to the temple. On the ridge above the temple are rougher buildings and the **Incahuatana,** the hitching place of the Inca, where prisoners may have been lashed into the human-sized portals.

At the base of the ruins are the **Princess**

Baths, a half dozen fountains adorned with *chacana* symbols. Some of the fountains are engineered in such a way as to cause a whirlpool that allows sediment to drop before the water continues over a delicately shaped spout. On the steep flanks of Pinculluna, the sacred hill that rises above the Inca town, are the ruins of several granaries, which glow in the afternoon sun.

ENTERTAINMENT AND EVENTS

Ollantaytambo has a small but lively nightlife scene, due mainly to a community of expats who live in town year-round. Be sure to patronize places that seem respectful of surrounding residents and do not encourage use of drugs, which is an increasing problem in town. **Señor Ganso** (Horno Calle, 1.5 blocks from the square, 9 A.M.–11 P.M. daily) has a great second floor lounge. Bars and clubs change often in Ollantaytambo.

During the **Fiesta de Reyes** (the Celebration of the Kings) on January 6, a revered image of Jesus is brought down to Ollantaytambo from Marcacocha, a town high up in the Patacancha Valley. The event includes a solemn procession around Ollantaytambo's main square, which involves even more images of baby Jesus.

On January 6, over 200 Wallta dancers come down from the hills of Mount Pinkuylluna. These Quechua-speaking communities, dressed in the traditional red outfits, dance and lead processions until the following day.

During the eight-day **Carnaval** season in late January and early February, the upper Patacancha Valley explodes into a series of traditions: cow branding, offerings to mountain *apus* by local priests, *wallata* (the dance of the condor), and ritual battles between towns that are now fought with mature fruit instead of rocks.

The town's most important celebration is the **Señor de Choquequilca,** which happens during the Pentecost at the end of May or early June. The festival dates back to the miraculous appearance of a wooden cross near the town's Inca bridge. A chapel dedicated to El Señor de Choquequilca was completed in the main square in 1995.

SHOPPING

To find authentic, all-natural weavings and handicrafts, head to **Awamaki** (Calle Convención s/n, across from the temple, www.awamaki-us.org). All proceeds go to the people of the communities with which Awamaki works.

RECREATION

Several agencies operate trips, including horseback riding, rafting, biking, etc. in this area. One that is highly recommended is **KB Tambo Tours** (Ventiderio s/n, tel. 084/20-4091, www.kbperu.com), run by a long-time resident originally from the United States. **Sota Adventures** (Plaza de Armas s/n, tel. 084/984-080-718), operated by two local brothers; **KB Tours** (Plaza de Armas s/n, tel. 084/20-4133, kbtours_2@hotmail.com); and the NGO **Awamaki** (Calle Convención s/n, across from the temple, www.awamaki-us.org) also organize excursions to the communities outside Ollantaytambo.

© CARLOS SALA, PROMPERU

the terraces at the temple in Ollantaytambo

Hikes

Ollantaytambo is a great base for a number of excellent hikes, treks, and community visits in the area. A detailed map of a dozen local hikes is available from the NGO Awamaki (Calle Convención s/n, across from the temple, www.awamaki-us.org) for about US$5. Summaries of these hikes, taken from the Awamaki guide with permission, are listed here. Before setting out on these hikes, check with Awamaki for updated directions.

◖ Inca Granaries (Pinkuylluna)

This moderate, 1.5-hour hike explores the Inca ruins that can be seen from town on the hillside opposite the Ollantaytambo fortress. The larger buildings were used for agricultural storehouses called *colcas*. Along with the multiple Inca sites, this steep hike offers great elevated views of Ollantaytambo and the fortress.

To reach the trailhead from the plaza, take Calle Principal toward Cusco. Take your first left after leaving the plaza completely on Calle Lares. After a few blocks, you will see a stone staircase on your right with a sign for Pinkuylluna. The stone staircase continues up the mountain for 10 to 15 minutes before the trail forks. The trail to the right (with the wooden handrail) will lead you around the corner to the first Inca ruins.

After exploring these, the best option is to descend back down to the fork in the trail and take the trail uphill in the other direction. The trail passes another Inca site and arrives at the large four-tiered storehouse in about 20–30 minutes. From here you can continue up the trail to the four towers that mark the crown of the head of the Tunupa, the god of abundance. If you continue up the mountain from here the views improve but the trail becomes unclear.

Pumamarca

The round-trip hike to the ruins of Pumamarca takes about 4–6 hours from Ollantaytambo on a moderate, steadily climbing trail. The ruins of Pumamarca sit on a hillside overlooking the convergence of the Río Patacancha and the Yuracmayo (White River). The well-preserved site was thought to be a checkpoint to control access to Ollantaytambo.

To reach Pumamarca, follow Patacalle out of town. Shortly after the first bridge, a large path leaves the main road to the right and follows the river. Follow this path for about 15 minutes until it rejoins the main road at the small town of Munaypata. Just up the road you will see an electrical pole on the left labeled 2224 and a path leading behind the adjacent house. Follow this path uphill for 15 more minutes to a blue archaeological marker for the Media Luna terraces in front of you. At this point, follow the switchback up the hill to your right (and not the path in front of you toward the terraces). The trail continues to climb steeply but will soon become more gradual.

After another hour or so of hiking, the trail comes to a clearing with small waterfalls and the beginning of ancient aqueducts. The trail follows an aqueduct and in 20–30 more minutes the ruins of Pumamarca will become apparent on the hillside in front of you. The trail becomes less clear at this point, but you can take multiple routes through the terraced fields up to the ruins (the main entrance is on the right side of the complex). At times there is someone working at the ruins who can provide information, but if not there is currently no entrance fee or hours when the ruins are closed. After exploring the ruins, you can return to Ollantaytambo by the same path or you can descend the hillside to the town of Pallata and take the road down from there.

Inca Quarries (Canteras) and Sun Gate (Inti Punku)

This round-trip walk, which takes 4–6 hours and a few more to reach the Sun Gate, begins at the Inca bridge near Ollantaytambo and along the banks of the Río Urubamba. It follows a fairly well-preserved Inca trail to Cachicata, the stone quarry 700–900 meters above the valley floor that is visible from the Ollantaytambo sun temple. It was here that the great stone blocks were slid down the hillside and hauled across the river to Ollantaytambo. There are three separate stone quarries, within half a kilometer of one another, littered with massive chiseled blocks and small *chullpas,* or burial towers. The western and highest quarry contains mysterious needle-shaped blocks that are up to seven meters long.

From Cachicata, it is possible to see that the terraces below the Ollantaytambo ruins form a pyramid shape, with one 750-meter-long wall aligning with the rays of the winter solstice. New Age theorists Fernando and Edgar Elorieta believe this is the original Pakaritampu, where the four Inca brothers emerged to found Cusco. A few hours' walk above the Cachicata is a perfect Inca gate that frames Salcantay in the background. On the trail approaching the quarries, numerous *piedras cansadas* (tired stones) that never made it to their final destination can be observed. The trail climbs high on the hillside, offering great views of Ollantaytambo and the surrounding peaks. Be prepared; the majority of the hike is fully exposed to the sun, and the only available water is near the beginning of the hike.

Begin by taking a right after the Inca bridge. After about 15–20 minutes take a left at the fork up the hill (a boulder at the fork is labeled "Canteras"). Continue to stay left, following the main path when other trails diverge. In about 20–30 minutes you will reach agricultural terraces and stone building foundations. Follow the trail straight past the foundations, not the smaller trail uphill. You will arrive at the first quarry 1.5–2 hours after starting. Look for small stone buildings built on top of large boulders beneath you. Just after passing through the quarry, look for a smaller path to the left leading uphill from the large trail. If you choose to filter water, a small switchback to the left immediately after this turn will lead to the last water source.

Follow switchbacks up the hillside past the first quarry for one hour. As the grassy trail starts to level out, watch out for a rounded stone resembling a primitive wheel off the trail to your left. As the trail plateaus you will see a much larger quarry to your left and several small fields. These flat fields are a great

place to camp if you plan to spend the night. A large boulder in the middle of the quarry has "Instituto National de Cultura" painted in white. Before and to the left of this boulder, a path made of smaller stones leads up though the quarry. Exploring this path, you can find a burial site with skeletons under a large boulder, along with many quarried stones that never made it to Ollantaytambo.

Looking further ahead on the same trail, you can see Inti Punku, or the Sun Gate, on the ridge ahead. To continue to Inti Punku, pass the large boulder with "I.N.C." painted on it and head toward the largest boulder you see. Find the trail on the left side of the boulder and follow it uphill, crossing a scree field. After 30–45 minutes the trail comes to a grass field with Inca ruins (another good campsite). The trail continues just beyond and uphill from these. The trail forks once at a small ravine about 10 minutes from the Sun Gate; take a right through the ravine. About 30–45 minutes from the ruins you will reach Inti Punku. From Inti Punku, return along same path to the last quarry (about 1 hour).

The return route from Las Canteras should take 1.5–2 hours. Follow the trail down switchbacks to the first quarry. Take a left just past the first quarry on a small path and circle back under the quarry. From here you can see two houses with metal roofs on the left hillside. Continue to descend along this ridge toward the houses and the trail improves. From the houses, continue along the trail downhill into the valley. The trail improves and continues downhill through more houses and finally to a bridge. Cross the bridge and follow the railroad tracks on your right. Turn left at a set of stone stairs after 10–15 minutes on tracks and follow the path back to town.

ACCOMMODATIONS
Under US$10
Unlike Urubamba, Ollantaytambo has plenty of good budget options for backpackers taking the morning or afternoon train to Machu Picchu. **Hostel Quilla** (Calle Quiswar s/n,

tel. 084/79-5432, US$5 shared bathroom, US$16.50 private bathroom) is the town's best budget option. Rooms are simple and cozy and there is a communal kitchen, equipped with an oven. The shared bathrooms have hot water. Just down the street is another cheap option, **Hostel El Tambo** (Calle Horno, 1.5 blocks from the plaza, tel. 084/77-3262, US$5 pp) The baths are also shared with hot water. According to the owner, Hiram Bingham stayed at this hostel back in 1911.

In the old Inca town, **Hostal Chaska Wasi** (Calle del Medio s/n, tel. 084/20-4045, www. hostalchaskawasi.com, US$5 dorm, US$9 d) has several clean rooms, with wooden floors, arranged around a tiny courtyard. The terrace on the top of the building is a good place to drink tea and look at the Inca granaries. Walking through town, and following the road left (toward the ruins) to the San Isidro neighborhood, you'll find a few families that have turned their homes into hostels under a now-defunct government program. Rooms here cost around US$5 for dorm rooms and shared bathrooms. Private rooms are also available.

US$10-50

An excellent option in this price range is the new **Hostel Iskay** (Patacalle s/n, tel. 084/20-4180, www.hosteliskay.com, US$10–15 s, US$25–30 d with continental breakfast), a small and lovely hostel with a beautiful garden and an astounding view of the ruins. The rooms are clean and simple (the family room on the other end of the garden has a beautiful kapuli tree that grows into the wall of the room). The common living/dining area with sofas, television, books, and board games has real Inca walls and an open kitchen. The friendly Spanish owners are long-time residents of Ollantaytambo. Another comfortable option is **KB Tambo** (Ventiderio s/n, tel. 084/20-4091, www.kbperu.com, US$20 s, US$30 d), which has cozy, unpretentious modern rooms with private bathrooms from singles and doubles to family suites. It has a beautiful small garden and a rooftop with amazing views of the ruins, a Jacuzzi, full bar, and pizza oven.

Hostel Las Orquideas (Ferrocarril s/n, tel. 084/20-4032, lasorquideas3@hotmail.com, US$20 s, US$30 d with breakfast) has small, plain rooms with private baths around a courtyard and garden. Spend your afternoon relaxing in the grassy courtyard.

US$50-100

Ollantaytambo's most charming and best-known hotel is **El Albergue** (Ferrocarril s/n, tel. 084/20-4014, www.elalbergue.com, US$58 s, US$74 d with breakfast). The lodge was opened by Wendy Weeks, a painter from Seattle, who arrived here in 1976 after an overland journey with her husband, writer Robert Randall. After her husband's death in 1990, Wendy stayed to raise her two sons here—Joaquín, who now runs the lodge, and Ishmael, who is an internationally recognized sculptor. Wendy Weeks is a beloved member of the community and a passionate spokeswoman for its preservation.

To reach El Albergue, head to the train station, through the gate, and down the tracks in the direction of an arrow and large sign for El Albergue painted on a wall. Or if you are arriving by train, simply disembark, and you'll be there. Compared to the mayhem of the station, El Albergue is a hushed paradise. Blue-and-yellow tanagers flit among datura flowers and a huge Canary Island palm that was planted in the 1920s. The rooms are huge, with whitewashed walls, wood tables and beds, and an uncluttered grace. This year, eight new upscale rooms, which cost US$94 per night, have been built in the back. They have floor heating and bathtubs. Decorations include local weavings, Wendy's paintings, a vase of flowers, and a river stone or two. After a breakfast of coffee and French toast, guests browse through the eclectic store, which sells books, weavings, bottles of Matacuy (a homemade *digestif*), and sundry hard-to-find objects—Ekeko dolls, Waq'ullu dance masks, and all the metal fittings for a *sapo* table, the colonial game that is like horseshoes with a twist. Days end with a book on the wood balconies above the garden, followed by an evening steam in the wood-fired sauna. Bottled water, and pisco sours on the house during happy hour, come with the rooms.

Hostel Sauce (Ventiderio s/n, tel. 084/20-4044, www.hostelsauce.com.pe, US$89 s, US$98 d with breakfast) is a serene, upscale establishment with eight sun-filled rooms overlooking the Ollantaytambo ruins. The restaurant, serving salads, meats, and pastas, has a cozy sitting area with a fireplace and couches.

US$100-150

Built in 2000, the luxury **Hotel Pakaritampu** (Ferrocarril s/n, tel. 084/20-4020, www.pakaritampu.com, US$127 s, US$132 d with breakfast) seems a bit out of place in Ollantaytambo. The modern two-story buildings appear overly grand for this humble town and its ruins. But if this doesn't bother you, the hotel does have pleasant gardens and large rooms with wood floors, spring mattresses, goose down duvets, telephones, and small balconies. The nice couches and a fireplace are good for having a drink by, and there is an interesting library. The restaurant is not recommended. Other services include laundry, Internet, and luggage storage.

FOOD
Peruvian and International
For an excellent meal, head down to the train station to the restaurant **◖ El Albergue** (Ferrocarril s/n, tel. 084/20-4077, reservations@elalbergue.com, 5 A.M.–9:30 P.M. daily, US$6–10). Using organic vegetables from the Sacred Valley, the menu is inventive and has great vegetarian options. Try the alpaca with *huacatay* mash or the lamb tenderloin with chimichurri and quinoa risotto. Pasta lovers can order a plate of homemade fettuccini with their favorite sauce. Reservations are recommended. The best coffee in Ollantaytambo is also found at the train station, at the El Albergue's **Café Mayu** (Ferrocarril s/n, tel. 084/20-4014, 5 A.M.–9:30 P.M. daily, US$2–15). Order your favorite coffee, be it an espresso, latte, or cappuccino, and drink it to wash down a delicious chocolate chip cookie

or brownie. Coffees are also available in the hotel's restaurant.

Kusicoyllor Café-Bar (Calle Convención across from the temple, tel. 084/20-4114, 8 A.M.–10 P.M. daily, US$5–8), located directly in front of the ruins, serves a variety of traditional dishes with a modern flair, as well as croissants, espresso, and homemade ice cream.

◖ Pachamama Grill (Convención s/n, 11:30 A.M.–10 P.M. daily, US$7–10) has amazing trout, pizza, and *lomo saltado*. Local NGO Awamaki can even arrange cooking classes with Zenayda, the charismatic and accomplished chef at Pachamama Grill!

Another good bet is the **Panaka Grill Restaurant** (Plaza de Armas s/n, 7 A.M.–10 P.M. daily, US$7–10), whose second floor tables look down on the plaza, and whose clean kitchen sends out flavorful plates of grilled alpaca, *lomo saltado,* and pizza.

A favorite in town is **Puka Rumi** (Ventiderio s/n, tel. 084/20-4091, 7:30 A.M.–8:30 P.M. daily, US$4–10). The Chilean owner has brought over the traditions from his home country and offers everything from enormous and delicious sandwiches to local dishes including the town's best *lomo saltado.* The menu is extremely varied and has options for all budgets. For dessert, try the brownies.

Vegetarian
Heart's Café (Plaza de Armas s/n, tel. 084/20-4078, www.heartscafe.org, 7 A.M.–9 P.M. daily, US$5–18) was founded by Sonia Newhouse and is about the only place in Ollantaytambo that has a book exchange. This place serves home-cooked meals using mainly organic ingredients and has everything from soups, salads, and sandwiches to main dishes and even afternoon tea with scones. Profits go to Sonia Newhouse's NGO, Living Heart.

Markets
The best minimarket for snacks or a picnic is **Inka Misana** on the Plaza de Armas. But head to the local market for fresh fruit and produce.

INFORMATION AND SERVICES

The best source for information on Ollantaytambo is the information office at **KB Tambo** (tel. 084/20-4091, www.kbperu.com) or the NGO Awamaki (Calle Convención s/n, across from the temple, www.awamaki-us. org). Awamaki's new U.S. website, www. awamaki-us.org, has tons of great information about Ollantaytambo, as does www.ollantaytambo.org.

The **police** and the **Botica Drugstore** (tel. 084/20-4015, 8 A.M.–9 P.M. daily), which has public phones, are both located on the main square. For medical needs, **Centro de Salud** (Ferrocarril s/n, tel. 084/20-4090) is open 24 hours. Banco de Crédito has an **ATM** in Hotel Sauce, and there is another ATM on the Plaza de Armas.

The **post office** (Principal, 7 A.M.–6 P.M. Mon.–Sat.) is in Tienda Margarita, but there are several places in town to buy stamps and postcards. There are several Internet places on and around the main plaza for about US$2/hour.

Volunteer Opportunities and NGOs

There are several NGOs in Ollantaytambo that you may contact if you're looking for volunteer opportunities and homestay options.

Based in Ollantaytambo, **Awamaki** (Calle Convención s/n, across from the temple, www.awamaki-us.org), founded by American Kennedy Leavens, is a Peruvian NGO partnered with a U.S. NGO of the same name that administers a weaving project with Quechua women and promotes health, education, and sustainable tourism. They have been instrumental in helping weavers in Patacancha and other communities restore their ancient weaving techniques and find sustainable ways to market their products. Awamaki can arrange all kinds of volunteer experiences, Spanish language immersion programs, homestays, excursions to the communities outside of Ollantaytambo, and classes in ceramics, basket weaving, and cooking. A highly recommended experience is Awamaki's weaving class in Patacancha.

Another NGO is **Living Heart** (www.livingheartperu.org), founded by Sonia Newhouse, who also owns **Heart's Cafe** on the Plaza de Armas. Living Heart aims to improve the quality of life for disadvantaged Andean children.

Ollantaytambo's elementary school has a **Tierra de Niños** (Children's Land) organized by **Ania** (www.mundodeania.org), a Lima-based NGO that helps inculcate the love of nature in children. The main force behind Ollantaytambo's Children's Land is Aima Molinari, who can be reached at aimamolinari@gmail.com. More information about the project can be found at www.tiniollantaytambo.blogspot.com

GETTING THERE AND AROUND

To get to Ollantaytambo from Cusco by bus, take the bus from the first block of Grau near the bridge (US$1.50, 90 minutes) to Urubamba and then hop another *combi* for the 20-minute, US$1 ride to Ollantaytambo. However, the most convenient option to get to Ollantaytambo from Cusco is to take a car or *colectivo* from the Paradero Pavitos (US$3.50, 90 minutes) to Ollantaytambo.

The station where you catch the train from Ollantaytambo to Aguas Calientes is a 10- or 15-minute walk from the main square along the Río Patacancha. From Ollantaytambo, various trains leave for Machu Picchu. For up-to-date prices and times, see www.perurail.com. Two new train companies started in 2010 and will be operating from Ollantaytambo—**Inca Rail** (www.inkarail.com) and **Andean Rail** (www.andeanrailways.com). Visit the websites for updated schedules and prices.

Reaching Cusco from Ollantaytambo is easy. *Combis* leave Ollantaytambo's main square for Urubamba, where another *combi* can be taken to Cusco. Direct buses for Cusco (US$1.75, 80 minutes) leave from Ollantaytambo when the evening trains arrive. The most convenient option is taking a car or *colectivo* from the train station or the main plaza (US$3.50).

Buses from Cusco also pass through Ollantaytambo on their way up-and-over the high pass at Abra Málaga and on to the jungle city of Quillabamba, which is the gateway to the biodiverse lower Urubamba basin. Trucks and a few buses headed in this direction stop in Ollantaytambo's main square in the morning and at 8 P.M. Ask local *combi* drivers for more details.

Taxis can be rented for quick trips to Urubamba (US$10) or to the town of Huilloq for a day hike.

PATACANCHA

Patacancha is a traditional Quechua community about an hour's drive above Ollantaytambo on a dirt road. People in Patacancha live much as they have for centuries, weaving, farming, and raising animals.

While in Patacancha please be aware that tourism can be harmful. Be sensitive and discreet in shooting your photos, avoid gaping into people's doorways, and don't go visit the school, as this is very disruptive to classes. Be aware that you will probably be flocked by women trying to sell you things, much of it junk purchased in Cusco. Look for the naturally dyed, hand-woven textiles for which the community is known.

Patacancha is difficult to visit independently, as very little Spanish is spoken and there is no daily public transportation. *Combis* do leave the plaza of Ollantaytambo Wednesday and Friday very early in the morning (6-ish). Or, just head up Patacalle. It's a 4–5 hour walk to the community, and most drivers, if you see any, are willing to pick you up for a few *soles*.

For a deeper understanding of life in Patacancha, the Ollantaytambo-based NGO **Awamaki** (Calle Convención s/n, across from the temple, www.awamaki-us.org) offers alternative community visits. The half-day tour, in English, includes transport, a visit to the Awamaki cooperative's weaving center, a demonstration of the weaving process, and the opportunity to buy top-quality, authentic weavings directly from the women. The tour also includes a visit to a Quechua house with permission, a respectful environment for photo-taking and nutritious snacks and a small tip for the women who participate. All proceeds benefit the project. US$10–30 depending on group size; contact tours@awamaki.org for information. Awamaki can also arrange weaving lessons and home stays in Patacancha.

MACHU PICCHU

Though many photographers have tried, no glossy postcard can capture the sweep and majesty of Machu Picchu. Viewed from above, the city's streets, temples, and stairways sprawl across a jungle ridge that drops more than 300 meters into the Río Urubamba below. Andean peaks, including the horn-shaped Huayna Picchu, rise in the background and frame this mist-drenched island in the sky.

A visit to Machu Picchu is many visitors' main motivation for coming to Peru. The place has a vibrant, spiritual feel and is probably the world's best example of architecture integrating with the landscape. It is in some respects the Inca's lesson to the western world, teaching us how to build our world around nature, not against it.

There is not a stone out of place at Machu Picchu. Terraces, gardens, temples, staircases, and aqueducts all have purpose and grace. Shapes mimic the silhouettes of surrounding mountains. Windows and instruments track the sun during the June and December solstices. At sunrise, rows of ruins are illuminated one by one as the sun creeps over the mountain peaks. The sun, moon, water, and earth were revered by the Inca, and they drive the city's layout.

Adding to Machu Picchu's mystery is the fact that archaeologists still do not know when or why it was built. The ruins of Machu Picchu were known to locals, who led Yale archaeologist Hiram Bingham to the site in 1911. Bingham cleared the site, understood its importance, and announced Machu Picchu to the world.

© GABRIELLA HOLLAND

MACHU PICCHU

HIGHLIGHTS

◖ Royal Tomb and Temple of the Sun: This semicircular Temple of the Sun aligns perfectly with the movement of the sun and sits on top of a cave, which the Inca transformed into a sinuous mastery of stone. This cave may have once contained the revered mummy of Inca Pachacútec, the Inca's most powerful and famed ruler (page 64).

◖ Intihuatana: Experts continue to debate over the meaning of this carved stone. There are theories that it's a sun dial, sacrificial altar, or a temple to the surrounding mountain gods. There is no question that it is a profoundly beautiful and spiritual stone sculpture, perhaps the first example of truly abstract sculpture in world history (page 65).

◖ Temple of the Moon and Huayna Picchu: Towering above Machu Picchu is the summit of Huayna Picchu, a sacred summit reached via a two-hour hike up stairs, switchbacks, and, for the final bit, a ladder. Nearby is the enigmatic Temple of the Moon. This nat-

ural cave, sculpted with curving stone walls, is the energetic counterpart to Machu Picchu (page 67).

◖ Inca Trail: For those who hike it, this sacred path is part trek, part religious pilgrimage. It winds down from the windswept mountains to lush cloud forest, passing 30 ruins along the way, then reaching Machu Picchu (page 72).

◖ Two-Day Inca Trail: A great option for those short on time, or not wanting to camp, is the two-day version of the Inca Trail. This hike includes some spectacular ruins and the glorious entry to Machu Picchu via the Inti Punku, or Sun Gate (page 75).

◖ Salcantay Trek to Machu Picchu: This five-day option does not have the stone paths or Inca ruins of the Inca Trail, but does offer stunning views of snow-covered mountains and a true wilderness appeal. This is the way to arrive at Machu Picchu for hard-core trekkers wanting to get a taste of the high Andes (page 76).

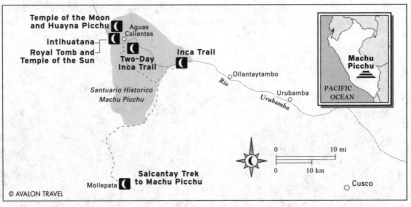

LOOK FOR ◖ TO FIND RECOMMENDED SIGHTS, ACTIVITIES, DINING, AND LODGING.

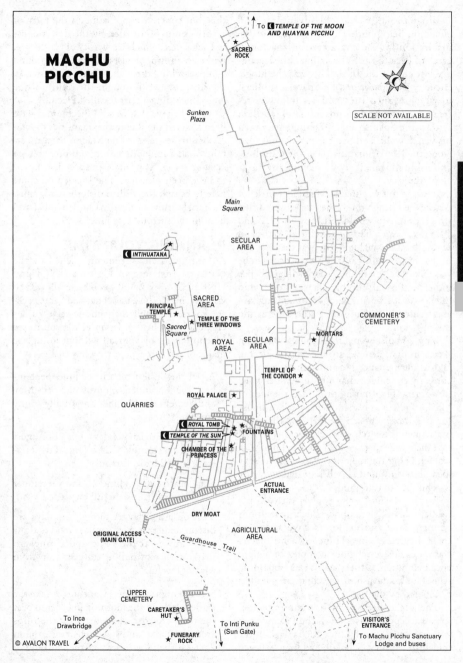

MACHU PICCHU

To ☾ *TEMPLE OF THE MOON AND HUAYNA PICCHU*

SACRED ROCK

Sunken Plaza

SCALE NOT AVAILABLE

Main Square

SECULAR AREA

☾ INTIHUATANA ★

SACRED AREA

COMMONER'S CEMETERY

PRINCIPAL TEMPLE ★   ★ TEMPLE OF THE THREE WINDOWS

Sacred Square

ROYAL AREA

SECULAR AREA

MORTARS ★

TEMPLE OF THE CONDOR ★

ROYAL PALACE ★

QUARRIES

☾ ROYAL TOMB ★
☾ TEMPLE OF THE SUN ★   ★ FOUNTAINS

CHAMBER OF THE PRINCESS ★

ACTUAL ENTRANCE

DRY MOAT

AGRICULTURAL AREA

ORIGINAL ACCESS (MAIN GATE)   *Guardhouse Trail*

UPPER CEMETERY

CARETAKER'S HUT ★

To Inca Drawbridge

FUNERARY ROCK ★

To Inti Punku (Sun Gate)

VISITOR'S ENTRANCE

↓ To Machu Picchu Sanctuary Lodge and buses

© AVALON TRAVEL

Bingham, a 36-year-old adventurer who ended up being both a U.S. Senator and the inspiration for the character Indiana Jones, came to Peru to find Vilcabamba, the legendary lost city of the Inca. This was the jungle enclave, well-described by Spanish soldiers, to which Manco Inca and his followers retreated following their unsuccessful rebellion against the Spanish in 1537. Bingham began his search walking down the newly built road along the Río Urubamba (now the train line) and asking locals if they knew of any ruins along the way.

It was in this way that local resident Melchor Arteaga led Bingham to the vine-covered site, which Bingham would return to in 1912 and 1915 to excavate. He was convinced, to the end of his life, that Machu Picchu was the "lost city of the Inca." But historians are now certain he was incorrect. A wealth of supporting evidence indicates the real Vilcabamba was farther into the jungle at Espíritu Pampa, which Bingham also visited but dismissed at the time as too insignificant.

Bingham discovered more than 100 human skeletons in cemeteries around Machu Picchu, and an inexperienced scientist on his team incorrectly concluded that 80 of them belonged to women. The finding prompted the idea of Machu Picchu as a giant *acllahuasi,* or house for the Inca's chosen "virgins of the sun." Subsequent research on the skeletons proved that there were men, women, and children with women being the majority; however, the sexy idea blazes on (and is still repeated today by Machu Picchu tour guides).

Part of Machu Picchu's power is that it is a riddle, a blank slate upon which generations of historians and explorers have scribbled their theories. Some claimed Machu Picchu was an exclusive religious complex or a giant coca plantation. Others said it was a boarding school for brainwashing the children of leaders conquered by the Inca.

The latest theory, which is gaining widespread acceptance, is that Machu Picchu was a winter retreat built by Inca Pachacútec in the mid-15th century. Scholars had long believed this, but concrete proof came in the form of a 16th-century suit filed by the descendants of Pachacútec, which University of California, Berkeley, anthropologist Dr. John Rowe found while searching through archives in Cusco. In the suit, the family sought the return of the lands, including a retreat called Picchu.

Many believe that Machu Picchu may have been a sacred site due to the quantities of *huacas* or shrines, and while Machu Picchu certainly had a religious sector, and probably an *acllahuasi* too, its primary purpose is believed to have been pleasure. The Inca could come here to escape the chill rains of Cusco, enjoy the jungle fruits of nearby Quillabamba, and hunt in the surrounding jungle.

PLANNING YOUR TIME

According to an agreement reached by the National Institute of Culture (INC) and UNESCO, only 2,500 people are allowed to visit Machu Picchu a day. That said, large package tours and their megaphone-style guides create a lot of hustle. In order for you to see Machu Picchu by yourself without losing the magic of the ruins, here are a few tips:

- Avoid the busiest months of June–September. The "shoulder" months of April–May and September–October are usually sunny as well.

- Avoid the Peruvian holidays, July 28–August 10. The days around Cusco's Inti Raymi festival, June 24, are also busy.

- Skip solstice days (June 21 and December 21), when the ruins are full by 6 A.M.

- Visit on a Sunday. Although Sundays are discounted for locals, Sundays tend to draw large crowds at the Pisac and Chinchero markets, thereby pulling travelers away from Machu Picchu.

- Stay the night at Aguas Calientes or take the earliest train in the morning in order to beat the train crowds, which arrive at the ruins around 10 A.M. and start departing around 2 P.M. Either arrive early in the morning or linger in the late afternoon. During midday, when Machu Picchu is most crowded, you can hike to Huayna Picchu, the Temple of the Moon, and the Inca bridge.

Machu Picchu admission is expensive by Peruvian standards and only lasts one day, though a second day is half price. Foreigners pay US$46, and nationals and students under 26 with an ISIC card pay US$22. There are no ticket sales on-site. Tickets must be bought in advance in *soles* at the **INC** office in Cusco (Av. el Sol) or in Aguas Calientes at **Centro Cultura Machu Picchu** (Pachacútec s/n, tel. 084/21-1196). A passport is necessary to complete the transaction. The ruins are open 6 A.M.–5:30 P.M. daily.

Shuttle
Buses to Machu Picchu leave every 5–15 minutes from just below Agua Caliente's second bridge. **Consettur Machupicchu** (Hermanos Hayar s/n, tel. 084/21-1134) sells the tickets, US$7 one-way and US$14 round-trip, with the first bus leaving at 5:30 A.M. and the last

at 5:30 P.M. If you want to catch the first bus up to Machu Picchu, which is a good idea, arrive at least 45 minutes early as morning lines form. The bus takes about a half hour to wind its way up the switchbacks to the ruins. It is also possible to following the footpath to the ruins, which cuts the switchback. This arduous, all-uphill hike in the moist cloud forest takes about 90 minutes.

Facilities
Outside the gate of the ruins, there are bathrooms and, usually, piles of free walking sticks. **El Mirador Snack Bar** (US$4) sells bottled water, sandwiches, and hamburgers that you can take away or eat at picnic tables overlooking the ruins. The gourmet **Sanctuary Lodge Restaurant** (tel. 084/21-1039, 11:30 A.M.–3 P.M. daily, US$35) serves an extraordinary buffet lunch open to the public that is worth the price if you have a good appetite and want to spoil yourself. There is also a separate dining room with an à la carte menu (US$40–50) serving international and Peruvian food (the ginger-iced

young boy chasing the shuttle bus to Machu Picchu

MACHU PICCHU

parfait is especially good). If you plan on eating at Machu Picchu, bring cash with you as you will need it. However, it is advisable to bring snacks and plenty of water with you, as it can be a long day out. There are no ATMs at Machu Picchu so bring cash!

Guides and Tours

During the day there are always guides, of varying quality, waiting at the entrance. A highly recommended guide with 22 years of experience in Machu Picchu is Fernando Luque (hatunchaka@hotmail.com, tel. 084/984-755-200). He can be contacted in advance. Another option is the Machu Picchu Sanctuary Lodge (tel. 084/21-1039, http://machupicchu.orient-express.com), where expensive, top-notch guides can be hired.

Ruins Tour

GUARDS' QUARTERS

From the ticket booth, the path enters the south side of Machu Picchu through the Guards' Quarters, which are two-story storehouses orientated to the June solstice. These buildings now form the modern-day entrance. Instead of going through these buildings, we suggest taking the path, usually marked with white arrows, which you will find on your left just after walking through the ticket area and

before arriving at the Guards' Quarters. This 10-minute hike switchbacks up into the forest alongside the terraces and arrives at a lookout offering the oft-photographed view over Machu Picchu. From here, it is easy to understand Machu Picchu's basic layout: A large grassy square divides the city in three areas. To the left are the **Royal and Sacred Areas,** which were probably reserved for the Inca emperor and his court. To the right is the **Secular Area,**

ruins at Machu Picchu

© BETH FUCHS

where the workers lived, and below the lookout itself is the **Agricultural Area.** Running near the lookout area is the main Inca Trail, which comes all the way from Cusco. Looking left, it's possible to see the Inca Trail coming down the terraced hillsides from the **Inti Punku,** or Sun Gate, the ceremonial entrance to Machu Picchu. On the other side of the Inca Trail are smaller paths that lead uphill to the Caretaker's Hut and another that leads across the terraces to the **Inca drawbridge.**

AGRICULTURAL AREA

Beneath the lookout and above the Guards' Quarters are agricultural terraces that face the sun year-round and were used to grow multiple crops. In 2002, Cusqueñan archaeologist Elva Torres took samples from different terraces to determine what crops the Inca cultivated in Machu Picchu. The results showed that they cultivated pumpkins, squash, tomatoes, peppers, and other indigenous tubers, such as *yacon,* which is used to treat diabetes.

CARETAKER'S HUT

This hut is one of the highest points in Machu Picchu, which allowed a caretaker to see a large stretch of the the Río Urubamba in addition to the main entrance from the Inti Punku, or Sun Gate. The Caretaker's House is built in the *wayrana* style, whereby one of the four walls is left completely open to promote ventilation.

FUNERARY ROCK

A carved slab is situated on the left-hand side of the Caretaker's Hut. It is a large, white, granite altar with carvings of three steps and a large flat bed on top. There is also a ring pointing in the direction of the solstice; its significance remains unknown. The Funerary Rock is surrounded by many other foreign rocks such as limestone, which is found in Sacsayhuamán and other quarries far from Machu Picchu. These rocks are believed to have been left over from Inca offerings. Above the rock is a small, four-sided building whose function also remains unknown.

MAIN GATE

Continuing from the Caretaker's Hut, follow the Inca Trail downhill to the Main Gate to Machu Picchu. A gigantic entrance door with locks on the inner part of the door was used to close Machu Picchu. Passing the Main Gate, continue on for about 40 meters, where, to your right, you will find a building with many doors on the first floor. The ground floor of this building was probably used as a meeting area, while the second floor was a storage room where produce was dried by ventilation. Below these storehouses, there are more than 15 constructions on different levels that were used as housing. Going back up to the main trail, continue three minutes until you arrive at an open area with numerous rocks. This area is the quarry of Machu Picchu.

QUARRIES

The main quarry of Machu Picchu lies on the hillside just past the Main Gate. However, there are two more quarries beside the **Sacred Rock** and another below the **Secular Area.**

Some houses are found in the Main Gate quarry, and they probably belonged to the workers. Returning to the main path, walk down the main stairway of the citadel, which has 16 different fountains that are all interconnected. The first fountain is on the right hand side before arriving at the rest hut. From this first fountain, walk downhill following the water into the **Royal Tomb** and **Temple of the Sun,** the most sacred of Machu Picchu's religious areas.

FOUNTAINS

There are two different theories behind the fountains. Some say they were used to supply drinking water to the people of Machu Picchu, and others say that they were ritual baths.

The fountains have two very distinct styles. The first three fountains are constructed in fine stone, and the rest are built in a more rustic style using stone and mortar. Walk down 10 steps, where you will see a small entrance to the right that will take you to the impressive natural cave, which the Inca fashioned into the Royal Tomb.

◖ ROYAL TOMB AND TEMPLE OF THE SUN

Here you will find a beautiful chamber where the mummy of Inca Pachacútec may have been stored, although no remains were ever found. The stonework and overall design of the building make it one of the Inca's most famed and elaborate constructions. The rocks are elegantly fitted into the contours of the natural cave, a perfect example of the Inca using carved stone to enhance the beauty of natural stone. The tomb contains three long niches and one smaller one, which has its own altar. At the entrance of the cave, there is bedrock with three long steps believed to have been used to give offerings to the dead. Inside the tomb, you will see a chalk grid, which has been drawn by the INC to determine any seismic movement in Machu Picchu.

Machu Picchu features a series of beautifully sculpted caves, such as the Royal Tomb.

Straight ahead is a wooden stairway next to an Inca stairway; both lead to the Temple of the Sun. Please note: It is forbidden to use the Inca stairway.

The Temple of the Sun, also called El Torreón or The Tower in Spanish, is above the Royal Tomb and is unmistakable thanks to its perfect circular walls, which lean inwards for stability and recall the Coricancha in Cusco. The temple has two windows. One faces the sunrise at Inti Punku, the Sun Gate, on the December solstice and the other is orientated to the June solstice. These windows created rays of light inside the temple during these sacred days.

The temple was recently excavated to strengthen the walls. During this process, three niches were discovered, of which the middle niche has the distinctive double jamb. They have covered this new discovery with glass. On the left side of the temple is a small two-story building that is believed to have been the house of either a princess or a high priest. Near the sun temple is an exquisite fountain that unifies the sacred elements of Inca cosmology (sun, rocks, water, and wind).

ROYAL PALACE

The buildings on the other side of the main staircase are known as the Royal Palace, because it is here that the Inca and his family lived while visiting Machu Picchu. There are a few beautiful trapezoidal doorways and perfect Inca stonework, both tell-tale signs of royal architecture. Follow the doorways and staircases to a large stone patio.

On the right-hand side of the patio there is a large fine door that is presumed to be the entrance to an area where the Inca slept. There are a few other rooms that the Inca and his family used for different purposes.

Climb to the top of the main staircase and turn right before the quarry. Continue about 60 meters to the botanical garden, where you may see various species of native flora. There are orchids, passion fruit trees, and a coca plant.

Beyond the garden to the left is the Sacred Square, containing both the Temple of the Three Windows and the Principal Temple.

SACRED SQUARE AND TEMPLE OF THE THREE WINDOWS

This square has major buildings on three sides, making it one of the more important ceremonial areas of Machu Picchu. As you enter the plaza, the first building on the left is somewhat crude. It probably served a specific utilitarian function and was plastered over to give it a finished look. The temple on the right, which overlooks the main square of Machu Picchu, is known as the Temple of the Three Windows and is built of gigantic stones like the structures in Sacsayhuamán. The three giant trapezoidal windows were perfectly fitted, and there are two additional windows, which were later filled to make niches. Although the exact purpose of this building is unknown, ritual ceramics such as *keros* (drinking cups) were found in the foundations in the 1980s.

The construction here was never completed. We know this because a marker that indicates where a rock should have been chiseled is still visible on the northwestern wall. To the west of this plaza is a circular wall similar to Cusco's Coricancha (sun temple).

PRINCIPAL TEMPLE

This building forms the third corner of the Sacred Square and is composed of enormous horizontal stones hewn from bedrock. The temple faces Cerro Machu Picchu and has an enormous altar on the back wall. Above the altar are very high niches where ceremonial items were placed. The damage sustained to the stonework is due to insufficient foundations (an uncommon problem at Machu Picchu, where an estimate 80 percent of all stonework is underground and used to shore up the buildings on extremely steep and uneven ground).

Directly in front of the temple is a rustic house, believed to have been the house of the priest. Leaving the main square, going west behind the Principal Temple, you will come to a small construction on the right-hand side known as the **Sacristy.**

The Sacristy is the only room within the city

that has the Inca imperial style but that is not a temple or a palace. If you look carefully, you may notice the anti-seismic construction using bedrock, keystones, and the famous 32-sided stone. Also note the unfinished polishing on the rocks.

Leaving the Sacristy, go to your right and climb up the impressive stairway to the top. On your right-hand side, there is a rock that represents the mountains of Putucusi and Yanantin, having the same exact form. Continue upwards to the home of the Intihuatana.

◖ INTIHUATANA

This exquisite four-sided sculpture was likely considered the most sacred place in Machu Picchu because of its unusual form and the three elements of sacred Inca architecture: bedrock to represent mother earth or Pachamama, fine Inca imperial architecture, and three-sided *wayrana* buildings. Without a doubt this was a highly sacred stone, or *huaca,* for

MACHU PICCHU

© JORGE ESQUIROZ, PROMPERU

Machu Picchu's Intihuatana is considered by some to be the world's first truly abstract piece of art.

the Inca. Scholars dispute the function of this stone and have largely dismissed its use as a sun dial. Theories of its use include a solar observatory, sacrificial altar, or a temple aligned with the surrounding mountains and their resident *apus* (gods). What is remarkable about the Intihuatana is that there is no logical explanation for its careful but bizarre shape. We believe the Intihuatana is a deeply sacred work of art, perhaps the world's first abstract sculpture.

In front of the Intihuatana there is a stone on the ground that looks like an arrow and points directly south, similar to a stone found on Huayna Picchu. This observatory is surrounded by two three-walled constructions, one of which is completely intact. Follow the white arrows down the stairs to the bottom. Turn right and cross the plaza. To the north, there are two more *wayrana* buildings that surround the Sacred Rock.

SACRED ROCK

The form of the Sacred Rock, which is flanked by sacred *wayrana* buildings, is identical to the form of the mountain Yanantin located in the foreground. Before this rock was protected a few years ago, hundreds of Machu Picchu visitors would spread their arms across this rock each day to feel its energy. Behind the Sacred Rock to the left is the entrance to Huayna Picchu and the Temple of the Moon, and to the right is a short trail that heads back in the direction of the Guards' Quarters (the entrance to Machu Picchu). This trail leads past a quarry to the Secular Area.

SECULAR AREA

The Secular Area is where the hundreds of workers and servants for Machu Picchu lived and worked. It is divided between *kanchas,* or living compounds, for the *ayllus,* or clans, or Inca elite. The design is broken up and chaotic, and it's difficult to follow a set route through the area. Think of this area as the bustling, populated part of the citadel where most people lived and worked. If you lose track of the directions, head to the general areas indicated by the map.

After the narrow entrance, there is a large open area with two enormous buildings that probably functioned as *kallancas* or great halls. These buildings were used by workers for celebrations, and doubled as large rain shelters.

Returning to the trail and heading in the direction of the Guards' Quarters, continue until you find a series of two-story *colcas* or storehouses. Continue along this trail for about 50 meters until you reach a corner. Head left on the steps and then head right, again in the direction of the Guards' Quarters. Continue ahead for about 60 meters until you reach an area known as the Mortars.

MORTARS

In the open space to the east, there is a large *wayrana*. Mortars that are sculpted in a circular shape with a concave base are found in the ground. While Bingham thought they were grinders, the modern-day hypothesis is that they were filled with water and used as earthquake detectors. Another speculation is that they were mirrors to view constellations.

This area is also the *acllahuasi,* or the "house of the chosen ones." If you explore the area, you will see that it has a large secure doorway. Exiting the principal door, head left to the corner and go down the stairs where you will see a tomb, known as **Intimachay** or Cave of the Sun. This was an important burial site in the citadel, and it contains a window that aligns perfectly with the first sunlight of the December solstice. Next to Intimachay is a large cave that contains a well-carved altar where many remains were found.

Back up the stairs and to your left is a large rock that has a slide on it. On top you will find an altar. From here, go down the stairs to the left, following the arrows to the Temple of the Condor.

TEMPLE OF THE CONDOR

At the entrance, there is an open area with a sculpted rock on the ground known as the head of the condor. Directly behind are the wings of this impressive Andean bird. Below the wings is a cave with stairs and niches on the wall believed to have been a tomb. In 1975, this cave was excavated by Alfredo Valencia, who found the bones of both llamas and guinea pigs. Experts believe the flat rock outside was used as a sacrificial table.

Above the condor, there are three very unusual niches that have two holes on either side. While Hiram Bingham thought this was the prison, it is now believed to have been a place to worship mummies.

To the left of the condor, there is a large two-story building. In order to enter the building, you must climb down the stairs, where you will find another tomb inside the house. Under the stairs, there are small holes in the base of the wall that were used to farm *cuy* or guinea pigs, a method still used in communities throughout the Andes. Returning to the Temple of the Condor and going to the far left, there is another cave. Go inside and you will find yet another tomb. To exit this chamber, duck under the small door, turn left, then go directly to the right, where you will find another secular area that offers a fabulous view of the Agricultural Area and the Temple of the Sun. Climb the stairs in the direction of the Temple of the Sun, but before arriving, turn left and follow the arrows to exit back to the Guards' Quarters, from where you started your walk.

Hikes and Treks

☾ TEMPLE OF THE MOON AND HUAYNA PICCHU

The hike from the Machu Picchu ruins to the summit of Huayna Picchu (elevation 2,740 meters, or 290 meters above Machu Picchu) is a moderate two-hour walk, and approximately 1.9 kilometers round-trip. It starts at the Sacred Rock and passes through a gate that is open 7 A.M.–1 P.M. Only 400 adults a day are allowed to do this climb (children are not allowed). Arrive early if you want to climb Huayna Picchu. It may make sense to climb Huayna Picchu in the morning and then see the ruins afternoon, in order to avoid missing

© BETH FUCHS

peak of Huayna Picchu

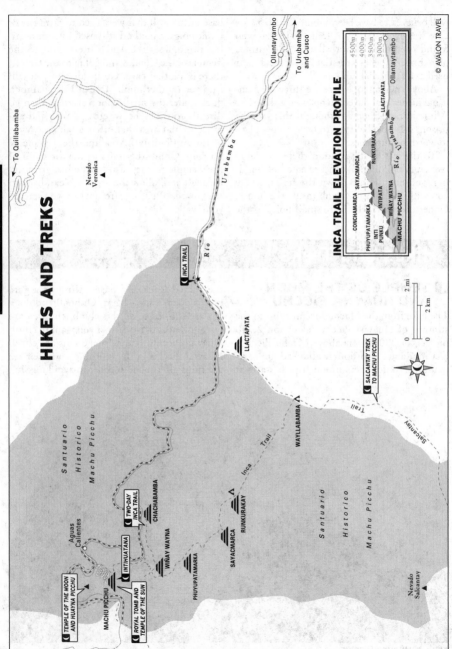

HIKES AND TREKS

INCA TRAIL ELEVATION PROFILE

© AVALON TRAVEL

this hike. While it is steep, the path is in excellent shape, though the last 20 meters include a steep rock slab that must be climbed with a ladder and a rope. The Inca built retaining terraces, buildings, tunnels, staircases, and a shrine on the top of the mountain. Human remains were also found in caves. The splendor of Huayna Picchu is the breathtaking view of the entire complex, which spreads out before the summit like a map.

Farther down on the slopes of Huayna Picchu is the Temple of the Moon, a construction equally as exquisite as the Temple of the Sun but with an entirely different mood. The easiest way to visit the Temple of the Moon is to retrace your steps down from Huayna Picchu and take the marked trail turnoff halfway down, which leads directly to the site. There is also a very steep and technically challenging trail that descends from behind the summit of Huayna Picchu itself. This trail, which can be hard to find, contains a short but near-vertical section climbed with a lashed wooden ladder. Visiting the Temple of the Moon adds about 1–2 hours onto the Huayna Picchu hike. If you

visit both Huayna Picchu and the Temple of the Moon, expect to spend about 3–4 hours, so take plenty of water and food.

The Temple of the Moon is a medium-sized natural cave where rocks have been fitted perfectly in flowing, gentle shapes. Instead of the tower and bright sunlight of the Temple of the Sun, everything here is recessed and dark, with sinuous lines. The Temple of the Moon itself is a wall of doors and windows sculpted perfectly into the space created by a giant overhanging rock. A bit below there is a doorway that leads to other structures, including a lower cave that is near to where the trail from Huayna Picchu descends. The Temple of the Moon is wonderful in part because few people ever visit it. The spiritual energy of the place is palpable.

INTI PUNKU AND INCA DRAWBRIDGE

If you have the time and the energy, head to the Caretaker's Hut and hike up the Inca Trail, which arcs across the mountain slope to a high pass. It is about a one-hour walk to this pass,

The Inca drawbridge, about a 20-minute hike from Machu Picchu, spans a gap in an Inca road built on a sheer cliff face.

TREKKING 101

Peru is one of the world's top trekking destinations, and the Inca Trail is Peru's number one trek. Beginning in the high Andes with vistas of sparkling glaciers, the Inca Trail passes a dozen major Inca ruins before plunging into the cloud forest towards Machu Picchu. Apart from the Inca Trail, there are dozens, even hundreds, of incredible treks in Peru's Andes, which are in the same league for trekking as the European Alps, the Alaska Range, or the Himalaya. Apart from the Cusco area, the other main trekking area in Peru is the Cordillera Blanca, the second-highest mountain range in the world, and its lesser-known but equally dramatic sister range, the Cordillera Huayhuash.

PLANNING THE INCA TRAIL

The Inca Trail is the only trek in Peru where all trekkers must hike with a licensed guide and where there is a limit of 500 people per day on the trail, including trekkers. These recent rules are a result of the Inca Trail's popularity and the resulting impact that tens of thousands of trekkers are having on its stone trail and the surrounding ecosystem. For the Inca Trail, your only option is to sign up with a licensed agency – and sign up early, as the Inca Trail fills up six months or more ahead of time.

As a result of these new rules, Inca Trail prices have increased from as low as US$90 in 2000 to a minimum of US$450 today. Walk-in-off-the-street agencies no longer offer last-minute Inca Trail trips. Inca Trail bookings are now done almost exclusively online as the trail's licensed operators have to confirm all reservations several months in advance. To check the official departure availability, visit the website www.nahui.gob.pe. If a date you want is already booked, it's still worth checking with agencies as they often have cancellations on certain days.

PLANNING OTHER TREKS

Any other trek in Peru, including the Salcantay alternative route to Machu Picchu, has a couple of planning options. The easiest, and most expensive, is to sign up with a reputable agency and let it take care of all the details. But you can also custom-design a trip and then hire an agency to take care of logistics such as transport, food, lodging, porters, *arrieros*, cooks, and certified guides. If you can find a reliable trekking or climbing guide, available for US$80-110 per day, he or she can organize all these details for you for an extra fee. Or you can do it all on your own, which is complicated to negotiate properly but possible if you speak Spanish.

WHEN TO GO

The traditional trekking season in Peru is May-August, but the best weather is June and July. Avoid the last week in July when Peru's hotels are often booked solid for the Fiestas Patrias celebration around July 28. If you are gunning for a main trekking route, you will encounter fewer people during the months of April, May, September, and October. These "shoulder months" are the best times to trek in Peru as they are outside of the rainiest months (November-March) and also the busiest tourist months (June-August). April and May, and even March if you don't mind an occasional rain storm, are especially gorgeous as the rainy season has just ended and the highlands are vibrant green.

AGENCIES AND GUIDES

The motto "you get what you pay for" is especially true when it comes to hiring a trekking agency or guide. Go with an established, well-recommended agency. If you skimp on an agency, you can be guaranteed the agency will either skimp on you (poor food, no bathroom tent), the porters (low wages, no health care), or the environment (pit latrines, no regard for Leave No Trace, or LNT, principles).

ACCLIMATIZATION

Plan for at least 3-4 days to acclimatize before heading out on a trek anywhere in Andean Peru. The Cordillera Blanca's most popular trek, the four- or five-day trek through the Santa Cruz Valley, involves at least one high pass, Punta Unión, at 4,760 meters. And the Inca Trail has two passes of approximately 4,000 meters.

Acclimatize by sleeping low and hiking high. A great way to acclimatize in the Cusco area is to spend your first few days in the Sacred Valley and then hike up out of valley floor in places like Pisac, Urubamba, and Ollantaytambo. In Huaraz, good options include day hikes in the Cordillera Negra and Quebrada Quilcayhuanca.

ON YOUR OWN
Because of the altitude, most parties end up hiring an *arriero*, who carries loads on burros, donkeys, or llamas. It's hard to enjoy the scenery while hiking with a full pack at Peru's altitudes, no matter how fit you are. There are other reasons to hire an *arriero* as well: It is a great cultural experience, helps the local economy, and makes your trip safer – *arrieros* often know the routes as well (or better) than a mountain guide, provide evacuation support, and can serve as camp guards.

Arrieros will expect you to pay their wages the day that they return to the main town, usually the day after the end of your trek. This means that for a four-day trek, you will pay the *arriero* five days of wages.

Groups usually hire a cook, too. Peru's cooks pack in fruit, vegetables, sacks of rice, and often a live chicken or two. Pay the people you hire fairly and treat them with respect. You are their employer, so you are ultimately responsible for their health and safety. These are some standard daily wages: US$10 for an *arriero* and US$8 for every mule, US$15 for camp guardian, US$25 for a porter, and US$25-30 for a cook. Also, you are expected to provide shelter and food for your *arriero*, cook, and porters.

If you are on your own, you will have to negotiate the entry and grazing fees that Andean communities increasingly charge trekking groups that pass through their lands. The fees change rapidly and are generally relatively minor. Grazing fees are generally around US$2-5 per horse. Inquire with an agency about fees ahead of time.

MAPS AND GEAR
The best place to get maps is the South American Explorers Club (www.saexplorers.org) in Cusco (Atoqsaykuchi 670, tel. 084/24-5484) or in the Miraflores neighborhood of Lima (Piura 135, tel. 084/445-3306).

Most people who are trekking or climbing on their own bring all their own gear, but high-quality equipment can be rented for affordable prices in Cusco and Huaraz. Email agencies ahead of time for reservations and prices.

Peru's tropical sun is intense, so bring strong sunscreen, a sun hat, dark glacier glasses, and a long-sleeved shirt. Most trekkers use trekking poles for descending the scree slopes and steep trails. The weather is cold, but extreme storms are rare in the dry months from May to September. On most Peru treks, sleeping bags rated for 0°F and thermal long underwear or fleece pants are fine.

Pretty much all supplies, with the exception of freeze-dried food, are available in markets in Cusco. You'll find pasta, powdered soup, cheese, powdered milk, beef jerky, dried fruit, and more. White gas *(bencina blanca)* is sold at hardware stores along Calle Plateros in Cusco and at numerous places in Huaraz and Caraz. Get a shop recommendation from an agency or gear store to ensure you find the highest quality gas, and fire up your stove before you go to make sure everything works. Remember that airlines sometimes reject travelers with camp stoves and fuel bottles that have been previously used. It's best to travel with a new stove and bottles, if at all possible.

HAZARDS AND PRECAUTIONS
While the vast majority of trekkers to the Cusco and Huaraz areas never encounter any safety threats, the more popular trekking areas have seen an increase in theft. If you leave your camp for a day hike, make sure to leave a camp guardian, such as an *arriero*, behind. Entire camps of tents have been stolen recently in the Cordillera Blanca while teams were on the mountain.

The main hazards of trekking in Peru, however, are straightforward: sun, altitude, and cold. If you protect yourself from the sun, acclimatize properly, and have the right gear, you will have a great time.

where there is a stone construction known as the Sun Gate or Inti Punku (2,720 meters).

After visiting Inti Punku, go back down the same trail to the path that branches off for the Caretaker's Hut. Instead of continuing uphill to the Caretaker's Hut continue along via the terraces along an alternative path that heads into the forest before arriving at a path with sheer cliff walls. At one point, it even passes over a man-made ledge, like that found on the upper route at the Pisac ruins. The trail ends near a gap at the stone ledge, where the Inca evidently placed a drawbridge or a series of logs that could be withdrawn if necessary. The path past the drawbridge is overgrown and washed out, but it was an alternative route for reaching the Inca Trail back to Cusco.

CERRO MACHU PICCHU

This moderate three-hour hike is a good alternative to climbing Huayna Picchu if Huayna Picchu has reached its daily quota or if you are afraid of heights (Huayna Picchu has one steep and exposed section). The hike up Cerro Machu Picchu (3,051 meters, or 601 meters above Machu Picchu) offers lots of fresh air, quiet natural surroundings, and a great view at the top. Cerro Machu Picchu is the mountain above Machu Picchu in the direction of the Inti Punku, or Sun Gate. To get there take the Inka Trail out of the Machu Picchu ruins past the Caretaker's Hut and towards Inti Punku. About 150 meters past the Caretaker's Hut, head right up a set of stairs with a sign that says "To Machu Picchu Mountain." Follow the trail for one hour through a habitat of exotic birds, orchids, lichen, moss, and trees, until arriving at the bottom of a set of Inca stairs. From here, it is a steep, 45-minute uphill walk. This is an excellent acclimatization hike for anyone preparing for a post-Machu Picchu trek. Various caves that contained skeletons when found by Hiram Bingham's expedition are located at the base of Cerro Machu Picchu. This area is therefore called **Upper Cemetery.**

◖ INCA TRAIL

Though at times crowded, the hike to Machu Picchu is an unforgettable experience—both a backpacking trip and a religious pilgrimage. There are lots of ways to do it, including walks

one of Machu Picchu's resident llamas

© AMBER DAVIS COLLINS, WWW.LIFEUNSCRIPTEDPHOTOGRAPHY.COM

of 1–4 days, with or without a pack on your back. All trail hikers must go with an agency, to ensure everyone's safety and keep trash off the trail. (The Inca Trail is part of the Machu Picchu Historical Sanctuary, administered by the National Institute of Culture.) There is a wide range in price and quality among Inca Trail agencies, and reservations should be made at least six months in advance.

The two- or even one-day option begins at Km 104 of the railroad line and includes a steep hike to reach the final stretch of the Inca Trail, including the ruins at Wiñay Wayna. Some agencies continue the same day to Machu Picchu and stay overnight in Aguas Calientes, while others camp near Wiñay Wayna to enter Machu Picchu the following morning.

We highly recommend the four-day trip, which passes more than 30 Inca sites along the way and includes the most spectacular scenery.

Trekking Agencies

Peruvian Andean Treks, ExplorAndes, and

Tambo Treks are the longest established trekking companies in Cusco; they pioneered the contemporary trekking culture. We recommend them, not only for their unsurpassed experience and professionalism, but also because they consistently recycle their trash, pack out all human waste, treat water carefully, and pay porters fair wages.

Among the more than 150 licensed agencies operating in Cusco, the standard of service and social and environmental responsibilities vary greatly. It is up to the client to be discerning and to research thoroughly before booking. All agencies listed here are recommended.

Peruvian Andean Treks (Pardo 705, tel. 084/22-5701, www.andeantreks.com) is owned by American and long-time Cusco resident Tom Hendrickson. This company was voted Cusco's best tour operator in 2006.

ExplorAndes (Av. Garcilaso 316-A, tel. 084/23-8380 or Lima tel. 01/715-2323, www.explorandes.com) is Peru's most established adventure sports agency. It offers the traditional Inca Trail hike, as well as variations that combine it with treks above the Sacred Valley or around Nevado Salcantay and Nevado Ausangate. ExplorAndes was voted Peru's best overall tour operator by the Ministry of Tourism in 2005.

Tambo Treks (Casilla 912, tel. 084/23-7718, www.tambotreks.net) is owned by Andreas Holland and has been operating for over 30 years. It offers diverse treks and tours with tailor-made itineraries (six people minimum), which accommodate group specifications and a wide range of special interests. The staff are very knowledgeable, and since its foundation Tambo Treks has had a profound commitment to helping local communities. Most importantly however, the welfare of all their staff has always been a priority as has working in an ecologically sustainable and responsible manner.

Auqui Mountain Spirit (José Gabriel 307, Urb. Magisterial, tel. 084/26-1517, www.auqui.com.pe), run by Roger Valencia, has been operating for over 20 years. This high-end agency has a very experienced team and specializes

in customized trips, especially for corporate clients.

Ecoinka (Saphy 456, tel. 084/22-4050, www.ecoinka.com) was founded by Ricky Schiller, who has been involved in the tourism industry for over 30 years. The expert staff provide excellent service.

Perú Sur Nativa (Magisterio 2da Etapa K-7-302, tel. 084/22-4156, www.perusurnativa.com) is owned by long-time Cusco adventurer extraordinaire Raúl Montes.

Enigma (Clorinda Matto de Turner 100, tel. 084/22-2155, www.enigmaperu.com) is one of the newer agencies; it has gourmet cooks. It offers Inca Trail treks combined with Nevado Salcantay, Vilcabamba, and the ruins of Choquequirao.

Inca Explorers (Ruinas 427, tel. 084/24-1070, www.incaexplorers.com) has a range of longer trips to Vilcabamba, Choquequirao, and the Cordillera Vilcanota.

Q'ente (Choquechaca 229, tel. 084/22-2535, www.qente.com) has been running since 1995 and provides a good service and trained staff.

hiking the Inca Trail

© RENÉE DEL GAUDIO AND ROSS WEHNER

MACHU PICCHU

The following Inca Trail operators are at the bottom of the price range but have been reported to be environmentally responsible.

United Mice (Plateros 351, tel. 084/22-1139, www.unitedmice.com) is probably the most recommended backpacker's choice. It also offers a seven-day Salcantay trek.

Peru Treks & Adventure (Garcilaso 265, Of. 11, 2nd Fl., tel. 084/50-5863, www.perutreks.com) is also responsible for the very informative website Andean Travel Web (www.andeantravelweb.com).

Andina Travel (Santa Catalina 219, tel. 084/25-1892, www.andinatravel.com) offers frequent departures for the Inca Trail and interesting sociocultural projects.

Four-Day Inca Trail

DAY ONE

This trip traditionally begins with an early-morning three-hour bus ride to Piscacucho, which is at Km 82 of the train line at 2,700 meters (some agencies use the train instead, which drops backpackers a bit farther down at Km 84). The trail begins in a subtropical ecosystem, with lots of agave plants and Spanish moss hanging from the trees. Many of the cacti along the trail have a parasite that turns crimson when you crush it in your fingers, a trick local woman use for lipstick. The first ruins you pass are **Patallacta,** meaning "city above terraces" in Quechua, a middle-class residential complex used as a staging ground for Machu Picchu. There is 12 kilometers of hiking this first day, with an elevation gain of 500 meters to Wayllabamba, where most groups camp the first night with stunning views of the Huayluro Valley.

DAY TWO

The 12 kilometers covered on this day are much more strenuous because you gain 1,200 meters in elevation and climb two mountain passes back to back. On the backside of the first pass, at 4,200 meters, you will pass by the ruins of **Runkurakay,** a round food storehouse strategically located at a lookout point. This site has an incredible view over a

© RENÉE DEL GAUDIO AND ROSS WEHNER

The ruins of Sayaqmarka are encountered on day two of the Inca Trail.

valley and nearby waterfall. The second pass, at 3,950 meters, is named Dead Woman's Pass after a mummy discovered there. In the late afternoon you will see the ruins of **Sayaqmarka** (3,625 meters), with good views of the Vilcabamba range. Sayaqmarka was probably used as a *tambo,* or resting spot, for priests and others journeying to Machu Picchu. The complex is divided into a rough lower section and a more elaborate upper area that was probably used for ceremonial purposes. Most trekkers camp this second night at **Pacaymayo,** with views of snow-covered peaks, including Humantay (5,850 meters) and Salcantay (6,271 meters), the highest peak in the area.

DAY THREE

This is a relatively easy day with plenty of time for meandering and lots of memorable sights. You enter the cloud forest, full of orchids, ferns, and bromeliads, to reach the ruins of **Phuyupatamarka,** a ceremonial site from where you first see the back of Machu Picchu,

The Inca Trail crosses steep hillsides at times and features dramatic drop offs.

marked with a flag. Look out for humming-birds, finches, parrots, and the crimson Andean cock of the rock. Most groups rest at a halfway lookout point that is often shrouded by clouds. From here, it is a two-hour hike straight down, dropping 1,000 meters to the third campsite at 2,650 meters, where there are hot showers, cold beers, and a restaurant. There is usually plenty of time in the afternoon to see the ruins of **Wiñay Wayna,** a spectacular ceremonial and agricultural site that is about a 10-minute walk away. We were lucky enough to see these ruins under the light of a full moon, which was truly mesmerizing. This complex is divided into two sectors, with religious temples at the top and rustic dwellings below. The hillside is carved into spectacular terraces and the Río Urubamba flows far below.

DAY FOUR

Most groups rise very early in the morning in an attempt to reach the sanctuary before sun-rise, and it can feel like walking in a herd of cattle. The walk is flat at the start and then inclines steeply up to **Inti Punku** (the Sun

Gate), from where you will be rewarded with a 180-degree view of Machu Picchu. Your guide will take you through the ruins, leaving you time to wander on your own and to climb Huayna Picchu if you haven't had enough.

☾ Two-Day Inca Trail

This two-day trip consists of one day of trek-king and one day of visiting Machu Picchu. It is a fairly easy hike, and for those who like to avoid camping, there's the advantage of stay-ing in a hotel.

A short train ride from Ollantaytambo brings you to Km 104 (altitude 2,100 meters) of the train tracks. Your trek begins across the river at the ruins of **Chachabamba,** where visits of the complex are usually offered by most trek-king agencies. From here, an eight-kilometer ascent through orchids, waterfalls, and hum-mingbirds in the cloud forest brings you to the impressive site of **Wiñay Wayna.** In Quechua this means "forever young" and it is home to the beautiful, bright purple forever young or-chids. Most people stop here for lunch before

Inca Trail porter

MACHU PICCHU

© FIONA CAMERON

the sacred peak of Salcantay

continuing along the Inca trail to Inti Punku, the Sun Gate, before arriving at Machu Picchu itself. Due to changes in regulations, everyone who does the short Inca Trail now hops on a bus and stays in a hotel in Aguas Calientes. The following day, you return early by bus for a full day to see Machu Picchu and surroundings.

◖ SALCANTAY TREK TO MACHU PICCHU

This five-day trek, which includes one day in Machu Picchu, is one of the latest alternatives in the area. As there are no restrictions, unlike on the Inca Trail, you can do this trek on your own or with a guide or agency. If you don't like camping, there are now high-quality lodges along the route operated by **Mountain Lodges of Peru** (Av. El Sol 948, Centro Commercial Cusco Sol Plaza, tel. 084/24-3636, www. mountainlodgesofperu.com).

Day One

Leaving Cusco, take the road heading towards Lima, to the town of Limatambo and the site of **Tarawasi,** named after the berry *tara,* which grows in the area. Continue on to **Soraypampa**

(3,869 meters), which is above the nearby herding village of Mollepata. At Soraypampa there is a campsite and a lodge operated by Mountain Lodges Peru. This company offers luxury high-altitude trekking, with four lodges located along the Salcantay route. Their lodges are all designed with elements of environmental sustainability in mind. With heating, hot showers, incredibly comfortable beds, and Jacuzzis, this is a great option for trekkers who either do not want to camp or don't want to carry the gear on the way to Machu Picchu.

In Soraypampa, you have wonderful views of both **Salcantay** (6,264 meters) and **Humantay** (5,917 meters) mountains. If you are staying in the lodge, you can hike to the beautiful multi-colored lake at the foot of Humantay glacier as an acclimatization tour. Some trekkers prefer to push on past Soraypampa to a campsite at **Soyroccocha** (4,206 meters). The campsite is at a very high altitude, so come acclimatized and bring plenty of warm clothing.

Day Two

This is the day of the high pass (4,600 meters)

and possible sightings of the intriguing Andean chinchilla, a furry rodent that resembles a baby bunny rabbit. Switchbacks take you up to the pass to spectacular snowy views of the mountain. From here, it is a steep 3.5-hour downhill walk through both barren high plains and cloud forest to the campsite of **Colpapampa** (2,682 meters).

Day Three

Colpapampa to **La Playa** is a breathtaking trek. You are now well into the cloud forest. This agricultural area is awash with coffee, avocados, citrus fruits, and wild strawberries. This day is the easiest, as it is only a slight descent to La Playa (2,042 meters).

Day Four

Today you get to Aguas Calientes. Follow an old trail for about two hours to the pass (2,743 meters) and down to the Inca town of **Llaqtapata.** Here there is a small archaeological site and a spectacular view of Machu Picchu. After Llaqtapata, the trail is hard, steep, downhill, and super slippery in the rainy season. The elevation decreases 914 meters in three hours to the train station at the hydroelectric plant. From here, to get to Aguas Calientes, most people take the 4:30 P.M. train (US$8); however, some people choose to walk along the train track to Aguas Calientes, which takes approximately three hours (eight kilometers). Almost all tours offer a night in a hotel in Aguas Calientes before going to Machu Picchu the next day.

INCA JUNGLE TRAIL

The latest route to Machu Picchu is locally known as the Inca Jungle Trail—Peru's version of planes, trains, and automobiles. This is a four-day trip that includes biking, hiking, and trains.

Day One

After 10 years, a decent road to Quillabamba has finally been made. A bus ride of about three hours passes Urubamba and Ollantaytambo to the new road, which leads you to the **Abra de Málaga** (4,350 meters). Most tours bike 80 kilometers down this road to the town of Santa María, which is a vertical drop of 3,000 meters. Be very careful and aware since this road is very busy with speeding minibuses and huge trucks.

Day Two

This day is a six- to seven-hour trek through high jungle. An old Inca trail has recently been discovered here and is currently being restored. The walk itself takes you through coffee plantations, coca fields, and fruit farms. This walk is a hiker's favorite as it takes you directly to the hot springs in Santa Teresa. Unfortunately, the floods in January 2010 washed the baths out completely, although there is talk of restoring them.

Day Three

This is another day of trekking; the geography is very similar to that of the previous day. After a morning of trekking, you will finally arrive at the hydroelectric plant, where a train will take you to Aguas Calientes. The following day is the normal day tour of Machu Picchu.

Getting There and Around

There are various ways to reach Aguas Calientes, the town at the base of Machu Picchu. You can take the Inca Trail or the Salcantay route, ride the train from Ollantaytambo (90 minutes) or Cusco (2.5 hours), or take the Inca Jungle Trail or bus journey through Santa Teresa. Once in Aguas Calientes, there are frequent bus shuttles to Machu Picchu, though some choose the two-hour forest hike that cuts across the road's switchbacks. There was a government plan some years back to build a Swiss-style tram, but that was, thankfully, rejected after much controversy. Once inside Machu Picchu, the only way to get around is by foot.

During the 1990s, a company named HeliCusco operated huge Russian helicopter

CAMISEA GAS FIELD: THE LAST PLACE ON EARTH

Up until the discovery of the Camisea Gas Field, few outsiders had ever entered the lower Urubamba basin, a vast swath of rainforest downriver from Machu Picchu. A treacherous river gorge deterred boat traffic, and the sheer flanks of the **Cordillera Vilcabamba** hindered would-be colonists.

Thanks to its geographic isolation, the lower Urubamba has evolved over millions of years into one of the world's top 25 megadiversity hot spots, according to Conservation International. Biologists continue to discover an unprecedented variety of endemic plant and animal species in the area.

This swath of mountains and jungles is also the last hiding place for several thousand semi-nomadic Indians who choose to live in complete isolation from the outside world. Some of these indigenous groups fled to these remote headwaters a century ago to escape the disease and slavery of the rubber boom, the last major Amazon bonanza. Their way of life was supposedly protected in the 1970s when the Peruvian government declared the area a cultural reserve for the Yine, Nahua, and Kirineri peoples.

That protection has been crumbling ever since engineers discovered an estimated 11 trillion cubic feet of gas under the jungle floor, now known as the Camisea Gas Field. After more than two decades of negotiations, the Peruvian government signed an agreement to develop Camisea in early 2000. The lower Urubamba has never been the same since.

Dynamite explosions replace the murmur of rivers and shrieking of parrots, as engineers map the contours of the vast gas deposit along a checkerboard of paths spaced a mere 300 yards apart. Chainsaws and bulldozers clear forest to make way for access roads, unloading zones, a processing plant, and drilling platforms, several of which are inside the cultural reserve. Helicopters routinely buzz the canopy. A 25-meter-wide corridor of cleared jungle snakes its way up and over the Cordillera Vilcabamba and down into the jungle below.

The lead Camisea players are Texas-based **Hunt Oil** and the Argentine companies **Plus-Petrol** and **Grupo Techint,** which are leading

---

trips to Machu Picchu, blowing many of Aguas Calientes's sheet-metal roofs off in the process. Thankfully, helicopters have been banned inside the Machu Picchu Historical Sanctuary, and condors are slowly returning to the area. We saw one cruising in the air underneath the ruins: Watch for fingerlike feathers at the ends of the wings, whitish upper wings, and a white neck.

TRAIN

Two major events have completely recast train service to Machu Picchu. The first was the floods in January 2010, which took out large areas of the train track between Ollantaytambo, in the Sacred Valley, and Aguas Calientes, at the foot of Machu Picchu. Until the tracks are repaired, trains will depart from Piscacucho, about an hour downstream from Ollantaytambo. After the repairs, normal service is expected to

be restored to Ollantaytambo, from which all trains to Machu Picchu typically depart.

The second major event is the breakup of the long-time PeruRail monopoly. Only time will tell whether the entry of two new train companies will result in lower prices and better service. Before booking train service to Machu Picchu, or asking your hotel to book trains for you, we recommend checking the websites of all three companies.

The first new Machu Picchu train service is the **Machu Picchu Train,** owned by Andean Railways (Av. El Sol 576, Cusco, across from the Coricancha, tel. 084/22-1199, www.machupicchutrain.com). This company is importing a series of fancy coaches and will be price competitive with PeruRail. Once tracks are repaired, the Machu Picchu Train will leave Ollantaytambo at 7:20 A.M. and 12:36 P.M. and arrive in Aguas Calientes 90 minutes

the US$1.6 billion effort to drill the gas and then ship it to the coast via two separate pipelines. Hunt is also building a US$2.1 billion liquefied natural gas plant on the coast south of Lima, which will soon be operational. Another Texas company, the KBR division of **Halliburton,** runs a Camisea gas plant next to **Paracas,** Peru's most important marine reserve. Conservationists opposed the project on the grounds that a single tanker spill could wipe out Paracas's already endangered marine life. The project went ahead regardless and began operation in 2004.

During the early stages of the project, U.S. media coverage focused on the behind-the-scenes lobbying, from both the Bush Administration and the Inter-American Development Bank, IDB, which helped make the project happen. The real story, however, is the destruction in the lower Urubamba. The service roads and test paths being built for the project are becoming highways for colonists, illegal loggers, and wildlife poachers – the same pattern of destruction that destroyed most of the Amazon in the 20th century.

Since December 2004, there have been five ruptures of the Camisea pipeline, which sent thousands of barrels of gas into the pristine Urubamba River and polluted local water supplies. Unchecked erosion from the pipeline has also muddied water supplies and decimated fish, the main food source, in some areas. A Peruvian government report estimated that 17 indigenous people have died of diseases brought to the area by oil workers.

The Peruvian government, for its part, says the Camisea project will produce valuable foreign revenue and help Lima make its transition to cleaner-burning fuels. The oil companies, meanwhile, have promised to minimize impact by using lateral drilling technology and oil platforms normally used for deep-sea drilling. And the IDB will also begin to monitor the environmental impacts of Camisea as part of the bank's latest US$800 million loan. "This is a mega project," said Peru president Alan García of Camisea's liquefied natural gas plant. "In the construction of this plant, it is estimated that Peru's economy will grow nearly one percent per year over the next three years."

---

later. The train returns from Aguas Calientes to Ollantaytambo at 10:30 A.M. and 4:15 P.M. Prices vary according to time but are approximately US$75 one-way.

The second new service is **Inca Rail** (Av. El Sol 611, Cusco, tel. 084/23-3030, www.incarail. com), which offers three daily departures from Ollantaytambo at 6:40 A.M., 11:35 A.M., and 4:36 P.M. and three daily departures from Aguas Calientes at 8:30 A.M., 2:02 P.M., and 7 P.M. The trains have an executive class (US$50 one-way) and a first class (US$75 one-way).

The traditional option is **PeruRail** (Av. Pachacútec, Cusco, tel. 084/22-8722, www. perurail.com), which offers three train services from Ollantaytambo and Poroy, near Cusco, to Aguas Calientes: the **Backpacker** (US$96 round-trip, US$48 one-way), the **Vistadome** (US$120 round-trip, US$60 one-way), and the luxury **Hiram Bingham service** (US$588

round-trip US$334 one-way). The Backpacker train is nearly as comfortable as the Vistadome, with large, soft seats and plenty of leg room. Food for sale includes sandwiches (US$4) and candy bars (US$2). The perks of the Vistadome include large viewing windows in the ceilings, shows put on by train attendants (including fashion walks to promote alpaca clothing), luxurious seats, lights snacks and beverages, and live Andean music.

The Hiram Bingham service is in a whole different league. A full brunch is served on the ride from Poroy (15 minutes outside Cusco) to Machu Picchu, where guests are treated to a deluxe ruins tour and a full tea at the Sanctuary Lodge. On the ride home, pre-dinner pisco sours are served in the elegant dark wood bar, accompanied by a live band and dancing. A gourmet four-course dinner follows at your private table, accompanied by a selection of wines. Afterwards, there is live music and dancing for those with energy. Hands down, this is the most luxurious train service in Latin America. If it feels like the Orient Express, it is—PeruRail has been operated by Orient-Express Ltd. since the late 1990s.

All trains now depart from Ollantaytambo except the Hiram Bingham service. The Hiram Bingham luxury train avoids the famous (or infamous) switchbacks out of Cusco by leaving from the Poroy station, which is a 15-minute drive from Cusco. It departs at 9 A.M. and arrives in Aguas Calientes at 12:30 P.M. On the return, the train departs Aguas Calientes at 6 P.M. and gets to Poroy at 9:25 P.M.

The Cusco–Machu Picchu train crosses high, desolate plains before descending to meet the Urubamba Valley. Once past Ollantaytambo, the rail enters a gorge that grows narrower and deeper as it continues its descent. Look for occasional glimpses of snow-covered Verónica (5,750 meters) to the right. At Km 88 there is a modern bridge built on Inca foundations.

As the vegetation and the air grow thicker, the train descends into what the Peruvians call the *ceja de selva,* or the eyebrow of the jungle, and the Río Urubamba starts crashing over house-sized boulders. The train continues until reaching the ramshackle town of Aguas Calientes.

BUS JOURNEY FROM SANTA TERESA

The elaborate bus ride to Machu Picchu via Santa Teresa is hardly worth it unless you are really counting your pennies. From the Terminal de Santiago in Cusco, take a bus to Santa María (six hours, US$3). From Santa María, it is a two-hour bus ride to Santa Teresa. From there, shared taxis called *colectivos* will take you across the river to Oroya, where you can take a 5:30 P.M. train to Aguas Calientes (US$8), or where you can walk three hours to the town. No matter what, if you choose this route, you will need to spend the night in Aguas Calientes, which may put another dent in your pocket.

Aguas Calientes

Ever since a landslide destroyed the train line past Machu Picchu to Quillabamba, Aguas Calientes is literally the end of the line for the Cusco–Machu Picchu train. Once a ramshackle town, Aguas Calientes's recent structural improvements have brought paved roads, a colorful crafts market, and a growth in business. New restaurants and hotels are wedging their way into what little available valley space there is. With an economy that lives entirely on tourism, it makes for an interesting stay for a couple of days. Staying overnight in Aguas Calientes will allow you to give Machu Picchu and the surrounding area the time it takes to truly absorb its magnitude. Two nights can be even better, allowing you the opportunity to visit other attractions in the area.

SIGHTS

The town spreads uphill from the tracks, past a square and up the main drag of Pachacútec

alongside the Río Aguas Calientes. On the other side of the river, the Orquideas neighborhood is becoming the new hotel zone and is also home to the new stadium.

At the top of Pachacútec are the town's **thermal baths** (US$4, with towels and even bathing suits for rent). The baths are cleanest in the morning and are usually quite grimy by evening. On an uphill dirt trail, past the baths are a few spectacular waterfalls for bathing. This path leads uphill for several hours to a string of remote waterfalls. The baths are actually quite attractive.

Follow the road toward Machu Picchu, and just before the uphill schlep to the ruins, you'll find the new **Museo del Sitio Machu Picchu** (highway to Machu Picchu at Puente Ruinas, 9 A.M.–4:30 P.M. daily, US$7.5). The English-Spanish signs in this small, modern museum lead you geographically, culturally, and historically through Machu Picchu. Dioramas explain

MACHU PICCHU

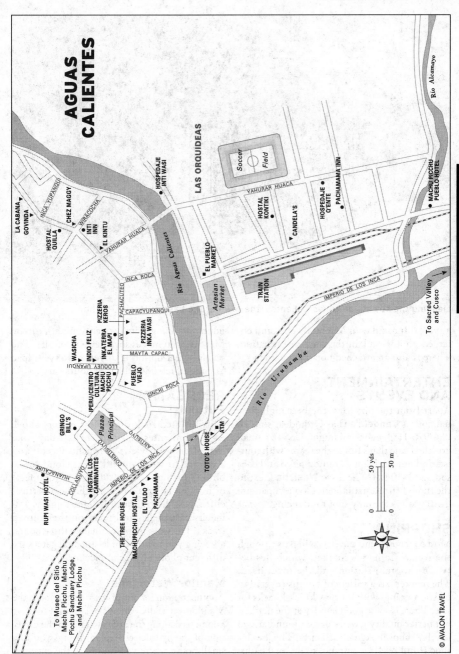

AGUAS CALIENTES

LAS ORQUIDEAS

LA CABANA
GOVINDA
CHEZ MAGGY
HOSTAL QUILLA
INTI INN
EL KINTU
WIRACOCHA
HOSPEDAJE INTI WASI

Río Aguas Calientes

HOSTAL KONTIKI
CANDELA'S
HOSPEDAJE Q'ENTE
PACHAMAMA INN

Soccer Field

YAHURAR HUACA

MACHU PICCHU PUEBLO HOTEL

Río Alcamayo

INCA ROCA
PACHACUTEC
CAPACYUPANQUI
PIZZERIA KEROS
PIZZERIA INKA WASI
INKATERRA EL MAPI
MAYTA CAPAC
SINCHI ROCA

WASICHA
INDIO FELIZ
IPERU/CENTRO CULTURA MACHU PICCHU
PUEBLO VIEJO
LLOQUEY UPANQUI

EL PUEBLO MARKET
Artesian Market
TRAIN STATION

IMPERIO DE LOS INCA

Río Urubamba

To Sacred Valley and Cusco

GRINGO BILL'S
Plaza Principal
ATM
TOTO'S HOUSE

RUPI WASI HOTEL
HUANACAURE
COLLASUYO
CONSISUYO
HOSTAL LOS CAMINANTES
ANTISUYO
IMPERIO DE LOS INCA
THE TREE HOUSE
MACHUPICCHU HOSTAL
EL TOLDO
PACHAMAMA

To Museo del Sitio Machu Picchu, Machu Picchu Sanctuary Lodge, and Machu Picchu

0   50 yds
0   50 m

N

© AVALON TRAVEL

© SERGIO SCHABELMAN

cleaning the streets of Aguas Calientes, the town at the base of Machu Picchu

a typical Incan day in Machu Picchu, and enlarged photos explain the site's investigation. There is also an attached botanical garden.

ENTERTAINMENT AND EVENTS

Apart from the pizzerias, the best nighttime hangout is **Candela's** (Las Orquideas s/n, tel. 084/976-1173, noon–midnight, US$4), a small art-filled café that's full to the seams with tourists and guides. Happy hour on pisco and coca sours is 8–10 P.M. The disco **Wasicha** (next to the Indio Feliz Restaurant on Lloqueyupanqui, 6–10 P.M.) is the only spot for dancing.

SHOPPING

Most Machu Picchu travelers will pass through the Aguas Caliente's market, which lies between the train station and the town itself. The market has a variety of booths covered in plastic awnings with touristy knick-knacks for sale. There is some good jewelry at the market, but better quality jewelry can be found at two jewelry shops in Aguas Calientes. The jewelry shop **Rumi Wasi** (at entrance to thermal baths,

hours vary but generally open at night), run by Marcus, who makes silver jewelry on site. The second great option is **Joyeria Maky** (Capac Yupanqui, tel. 084/21-1136, hours vary).

RECREATION
Putukusi

This forested rock dome 400 meters above Aguas Calientes is a superb half-day hike that offers great views of Machu Picchu and a chance to see many different cloud forest birds. The highlight is 200 meters (600 feet) of wooden ladders nailed to the near-vertical cliff face. The trailhead is signed and is 150 meters past the control point on the railroad tracks. The walk is approximately three hours, allowing you to arrive in leisure and get a very different photo of Machu Picchu.

Mandor Waterfalls

Another option for out-of-town recreation is the Mandor waterfalls. About a one-hour walk (five kilometers) along the railway track in the direction of the hydroelectric plant brings you to a small house where you must pay the entrance

© CYNTHIA BEAMS

Those with extra time in Aguas Calientes can try climbing the perilously steep wooden ladders to Putukusi, a peak that offers spectacular views of Machu Picchu.

fee (US$3.50). From here, it is a 45-minute hike through a banana plantation and jungle that starts from Km 115 off the tracks. Make sure to take the trail on the right-hand side.

Orchid Garden

Operated by four locals, this garden is truly a work in progress, with around 250 different species of orchids. In Las Orquideas, from the left entrance of the stadium, the garden is at the end of the street at the house of Leonardo Guttierez. He will gladly take you on a one-hour tour for a small donation towards the maintenance of the garden. Those interested in doing research here should email hatunchaca@ hotmail.com. Fernando, who speaks English, can assist you in organizing a field study on the endemic orchids for a month or longer.

Alccamayo Waterfall

This hike is perfect for those with little time on their hands. From the top right-hand corner outside the stadium in Las Orquideas, follow a small lane until you reach the chapel.

Continue on to the end of the street and take a left behind the last house. The walk takes you through the forest to a 25-meter cascade. If you are looking for a guided tour (in Spanish), ask around for a man named Edwin Escalante, the young owner of the property, who over the past four years has been improving the paths, flora, and fauna.

ACCOMMODATIONS

Compared to the rest of the country, lodging in Aguas Calientes is exorbitantly expensive. The cleanest budget places are in the Orquideas neighborhood, across from the Río Aguas Calientes, which flows from the hot baths and cleaves the town in two. In Aguas Calientes, forking over a bit more dough to be in the US$25–50 range buys a lot of extra comfort, hot water, and river views. The most upscale hotels are slightly outside of town. The Machu Picchu Pueblo Hotel is upstream from town, and the Machu Picchu Sanctuary Lodge is next to the ruins themselves.

Downstream from Machu Picchu, Santa

Teresa used to have a few backpacker lodges and a stunning river-side pool that was destroyed in the January 2010 floods. Before heading to Santa Teresa, check on whether these services are once again available.

Under US$10

Hospedaje Inti Wasi (Las Orquideas M-23, tel. 084/21-1036, jddggk@latinmail.com, US$5 pp) is the nicest budget place in terms of natural surroundings. To get there, walk from the train station all the way up the right side of the Río Aguas Calientes until it dead-ends at a point a few hundred meters below the hot baths. The main sitting area is a plant-filled courtyard, diffused with yellow light from a yellow, semitransparent roof and echoing with the sounds of the river nearby. The bunk rooms are small and sparse, with foam beds, and have a tendency to heat up in the sun. Bathrooms are clean, with water heated by electric showerheads.

US$10-25

In the Orquideas neighborhood is **Hospedaje Q'ente** (Las Orquideas near the soccer field, tel. 084/21-1110, US$9 s, US$12 d). Rooms here are basic but clean. Private baths are an additional US$1.50 per person. The main appeal is the neighborhood itself, which has a soccer field and a small-town feel that is a welcome respite from the hustle of Aguas Calientes.

Down by the train tracks, on the other side of town, is the decrepit but classic **Hostal Los Caminantes** (Imperio de los Incas 140, tel. 084/21-2007, US$9 pp). This old wooden building has been receiving backpackers for decades and has friendly management, even if the rooms have foam beds and are in need of renovation. Hot water and rooms with private baths are available (US$12 pp).

Hostal Pirwa (Pachacútec s/n, tel. 084/21-1170, reservaspirwa@gmail.com, US$10 dorm room) is part of the Pirwa chain of hostels found throughout Peru. It is simple, clean, and a good place to meet other backpackers.

Off the road to Machu Picchu, just before Puente Ruinas, there is a **municipal campground** (US$10 pp). If you opt to camp, make sure you have plenty of bug repellent. The campground is right next to the river.

US$25-50

Hostal Quilla (Pachacútec s/n, tel. 084/21-1009, US$25 s, US$35 d) is on Pachacútec between Wiracocha and Túpac Inca Yupanqui. Rooms are plain with tile floors but service is friendly.

Hostal Kontiki (Las Orquideas, MZ A-9, tel. 084/984-296-340, hostalkontiki@hotmail.com, US$20 s, US$30 d) is a clean and friendly hotel. Breakfast is included and English is spoken. For information on a guided tour of the areas and Machu Picchu, ask for Fernando, the hotel owner/manager.

A company named Sierra Andina operates three hotels in Aguas Calientes, all lined up next to one another on both sides of the tracks. We recommend two of them: the **Machupicchu Hostal** (Imperio de los Inca 313, tel. 084/21-1034, sierrandina@gmail.com, US$35 s, US$40 d with breakfast), where rooms are arranged around a plant-filled courtyard overlooking the river. There is a sitting area with a great river view, and the rooms themselves are plain, clean, and comfortable. Next door is the sister **Presidente Hostal** (Imperio de los Inca 135, tel. 084/21-1212, sierrandina@gmail.com, US$60 s, US$65 d), a similar production with carpeted, bigger rooms. This place has the look and feel of a real hotel; rooms are pleasant, with earth-colored walls—ask for one that overlooks the river.

US$50-100

A great option is the peaceful, clean and modern **Pachamama Inn** (Las Orquideas Chaskatika s/n, tel. 084/21-1141, hostalpachamamainn@hotmail.com, US$60 s, US$80 d, plus US$20 for a Jacuzzi in your room). This hotel comes with all the trimmings: 24-hour hot water, a money exchange, tourist information, and a restaurant. Strangely enough, all rooms are equipped with mirrors on the bathroom ceiling.

A more mediocre hostel in this price range is **HanaqPacha Orquideas** (Las Orquideas s/n, tel. 084/21-1027, US$70 s US$90 d). It is clean and simple, and breakfast is included. However, the bathrooms tend to be quite small.

US$100-150

The Limeño owner of **Rupa Wasi** (Huanacaure 180, tel. 084/21-1101, www.rupawasi.net, US$70 s, US$100 d) is also a tour guide, so he's quick to give you a tour of the surrounding orchids and point out the view up the gorge. If you strain, you might see Machu Picchu. But perhaps the best place to catch the view is from your room's private balcony. Rooms are rustic but comfortable with down duvet covers, and breakfast is served in the adjoining restaurant complete with yogurt, granola, and even focaccia bread.

The charming **(Gringo Bill's** (signed well off one corner of the main square, tel. 084/21-1046, www.gringobills.com, US$75–130 d with breakfast), one of the oldest hotels in Aguas Calientes, has a treehouse atmosphere and large rooms with balconies and great showers. The downside is that some rooms have overpowering New Age fluorescent paintings, and guests have to make an advance down payment at an office in Cusco. The newer suites on the top floors are the best.

Hostal Restaurant La Cabaña (Pachacútec M-20, tel. 084/21-1048, www.cabanahostal. com, US$110 s/d, with breakfast) is a friendly place at the top of the main street. Rooms have tile floors, textured walls, and wooden ceilings. The owners, Beto and Marta, take an ecosensitive approach. ("We're trying to return to what we've destroyed," Beto told us.) Additional services include guides for walks, security boxes, laundry, and a DVD player with more than 150 movies. They also offer better rates in the restaurant for guests of the hotel.

Over US$150

A formerly state-owned hotel has been taken over by the Inkaterra Group to create **El Mapi** (Pachacútec 109, tel. 084/21-1011, reservas@ byinkaterragroup.com, US$200 s or d with breakfast buffet). This hotel is by far the most modern looking of the Inkaterra range, with a beautiful bar, restaurant, and wooden fencing along the windows. To get there from the main square take the main road, Pachacútec, and it is on the right-hand side.

The owners of the Aguas Calientes restaurants Toto's House and Pueblo Viejo have various hotels: **Inti Inn** (Pachacútec s/n, tel. 084/21-1137, www.grupointi.com, US$140 s or d). Although the rooms are impressively small, the furnishings are pleasant, the beds firm and comfortable, and your towels come wrapped up like a Christmas package.

(The Machu Picchu Pueblo Hotel (Railroad Km 110, tel. 084/21-1132, www. inkaterra.com, US$394 s, US$500 d) is one of Peru's most elegant hotels and has been aptly described a "paradise at Machu Picchu's feet." A short walk from the hustle and bustle of Aguas Calientes, this peaceful patch of rainforest echoes the tumbling of the nearby Río Urubamba and the sounds of some 150 different tropical birds. Stone paths wind through the forest past fountains and pools and up to secluded bungalows. Large rooms feature rustic colonial-style furniture, rough tile floors, luxury bathrooms, recessed reading areas, and nice details like fluffy bathrobes, fruit, and the hotel's own line of organic shampoos, soaps, and conditioners. The hotel has grown since 1978 with an earth-friendly philosophy that includes building all of its furniture on-site. It received the Sustainable Travel award from *National Geographic Traveler* in 2002.

Pueblo Hotel is the only Machu Picchu hotel to give visitors a taste of the jungle, and it's the best substitute for those not planning to visit the Amazon. The biologist guides lead early-morning bird-watching walks (we saw a range of tanagers, hummingbirds, motmots, and the Andean cock of the rock in two hours). The hotel's nature walks include the biggest orchid collection in Peru (372 species), a butterfly house, and a miniature tea plantation. The hotel has reintroduced the *Oso anteojos* (Andean spectacled bear) to the area; three bears now live in the grounds of the hotel, and you can also take a tour to visit them. There is an excellent restaurant, a bar, a spa (US$60 for massage and sauna), and a spring-fed swimming pool. Guides lead a two-hour walk up into the forest to waterfalls and pre-Inca stone carvings as well as other day hikes in the area.

If you have deep pockets and want to stay within a stone's throw of the lost Inca city, check out the (**Machu Picchu Sanctuary Lodge** (next to the entrance to the ruins, tel. 084/21-1039, res-mapi@peruorienteexpress. com.pe, http://machupicchu.orient-express. com, US$825 s/d with full board). The lodge began as a state-owned hotel in the 1970s, but it was privatized in 1995 and ultimately acquired by Orient-Express Hotels, which also operates Cusco's finest hotel, Hotel Monasterio, and PeruRail. Orient-Express is not allowed to make any additions to the building, so it remains a small, modest hotel on the outside with an elegant interior. The 31 rooms have been outfitted with antiques, king-size beds, and cable TV, and the slightly more expensive rooms have views over the ruins. One advantage of staying here is a night excursion to the ruins, hosted by a local shaman, which is difficult to do from Aguas Calientes. There are two restaurants, one serving gourmet à la carte items (US$40–50) and the other offering an extraordinary buffet (US$29). The hotel also offers trekking, river rafting, and mountain-biking trips; walking paths behind the hotel lead through an orchid garden. In high season, this hotel is booked solid, so make reservations at least three months in advance.

The lastest five-star hotel in Machu Picchu, which took two years to build, is **Sumaq** (Av. Hermanos Ayar s/n, tel. 084/21-1059, reservas@sumaqhotelperu.com, US$480 s, US$600 d). This stunning hotel has been built in an Inca style with large, spacious rooms, each with its own range of amenities, beautiful king-size beds, and bathtubs. The hotel offers cooking classes, bird-watching tours, and access to a spa equipped with a sauna, massage service, and a Jacuzzi. Dinner is also included in the price.

Another option is the upscale **Hatuchay Towers** (Carretera Puente Ruinas MZ 4, tel.

084/21-1201, www.hatuchaytower.com, US$282 s, US$305 d), which is fully equipped with elevators. Breakfast and dinner are included, and family suites as well as regular rooms are available. While you shouldn't be put off by the garish mural in the lobby, the hotel restaurant, with its delicious buffet, is highly recommended, and fair-trade textiles from a community in Chinchero are for sale at the hotel shop.

FOOD

Along the railroad tracks and up on the main street, Pachacútec, Aguas Calientes is awash with pizzerias and their street salespeople. While quality has definitely risen in the last few years, you must still be cautious and choose carefully—many are not as good a bargain (nor as clean) as advertised.

International

For something different, try (**The Tree House** (Huanacaure 180, in the Rupa Wasi hotel, tel. 084/21-1101, www.rupawasitreehouse.com.pe, 5:30 A.M.–3 P.M. and 7–11 P.M. daily). The wooden ecological restaurant brings a fine selection of wines and pisco to accompany its high-quality but affordable food. Try the delicious trout coated in quinoa or the Thai chicken. They can also provide a yummy box lunch for your visit to Machu Picchu.

The strangely named **Paraquechayoc** (Pachacútec s/n, tel. 084/21-1278, 8 A.M.–10 P.M.) has a small trout farm out the back of the restaurant with over 5,000 trout at a time. Owners Victor and Rosemary prepare the fresh trout in an open kitchen overlooking the Río Aguas Calientes. Their specialty is a large, beautifully presented plate of oven-baked trout with bacon and spinach. Since Victor trained at the Hotel Monasterio in Cusco, you can sit back and expect something special.

The French-Peruvian–owned (**Indio Feliz** (Lloque Yupanqui Lote 4 M-12, tel. 084/21-1090, noon–4 P.M. and 6–10 P.M. Mon.–Sat., US$9) serves up some of the best food in town, best described as Peruvian cuisine with French touches, served in American portions. The two-story restaurant has a peaceful, homey feel, with tables in a sunny upstairs dining room. The four-course set menu is huge and, when we were there, included quiche lorraine, *sopa criolla*, lemon or garlic trout, ginger chicken, and apple pie. There is so much food, in fact, that a single meal can be divided for two people, something the kitchen is happy to do. There is real espresso, calla lilies on all the tables, and opera music in the background.

Pueblo Viejo (Pachacútec s/n, tel. 084/21-1193, www.grupointi.com, 10 A.M.–11 P.M., US$3–6) is at the bottom of the restaurant row and has a cozy atmosphere, including live music and a fireplace. There is a huge range of food here, from vegetarian and pizza to grilled meats. There are affordable lunchtime menus here as well. If you like this place, check out **Toto's House** (tel. 084/22-4179, www.grupointi.com, 9 A.M.–11 P.M.), a more upscale restaurant on the tracks nearby with an US$20 lunch buffet and river views.

Farther down the track, **El Toldo** (Av. Imperio de los Incas 147, tel. 084/21-1363, toldosrestaurant@yahoo.com, 10 A.M.–10 P.M., US$8–10) also specializes in pizzas and has a good breakfast for US$7.

Pachamama (Av. Imperio de los Incas 145, tel. 084/21-1141, 9 A.M.–9 P.M., US$8–10) has been part of Aguas Calientes for many years. It offers pizzas, main courses, good desserts, and is a great place for groups. And yet another restaurant on the tracks, **El Kintu** (Av. Pachacútec 150, tel. 084/21-1336, mapijose@gmail.com, 8 A.M.–10 P.M., US$6–10) is an interesting restaurant with an Inca decor, open kitchen, and barbecue. It has a very relaxed atmosphere and is a perfect place to hang out for a drink. There's also a small hostel attached to the restaurant.

Last but not least is the bar at the hot springs, **Paqcha Tarinakuy.** Carlos, the owner, has been here for 13 years and makes one of the best pisco sours in Peru. Hop into the relaxing baths; when you wish for a drink, signal by waving your hands in the air, and the waiters will come and serve you.

Pizza

Restaurant-Pizzeria Inka Wasi (Pachacútec 112, tel. 084/21-1010, www.inkawasirestaurant.com, 9 A.M.–10 P.M. Mon.–Sat., 1–10 P.M. Sun., US$10) offers a US$13 buffet but also serves trout, chicken brochettes, ceviche, pastas, pizzas, and their specialty dish—guinea pig. Along Pachacútec, other recommended places include **Pizzeria Keros** (Pachacútec 116, tel. 084/21-1374, 9 A.M.–11 P.M. daily), which also serves Peruvian dishes like guinea pig and grilled alpaca, and **Chez Maggy** (Pachacútec 156, tel. 084/21-1006, 11 A.M.–4 P.M. and 6–11 P.M. daily, US$7–10). Along with its sister restaurants throughout the country, Chez Maggy has an established reputation for great pastas and wood-fired pizzas. One place to avoid is the pizzeria **Big Brother,** as there have been several reports of food poisoning.

Vegetarian

Excellent vegetarian food is available at **Govinda** (Pachacútec 20, tel. 084/975-3993, 7 A.M.–10 P.M. daily), which has a variety of lunch menus for US$2–8.

Markets and Shops

The biggest minimarket is **El Pueblo,** next to the main market. With juices, yogurts, fresh bread, deli meats, and cheeses, it's a good place to put together a picnic.

Various hotels and restaurants prepare box lunches, including Gringo Bill's, Rupi Wasi, La Cabana, and Machu Picchu Pueblo Hotel.

INFORMATION AND SERVICES

There is a helpful **Iperú** office (Pachacútec s/n, tel. 084/21-1104) just up the main street from the square that hands out free maps. If you haven't bought your Machu Picchu entrance ticket, you can do it at **Centro Cultura Machu Picchu** (Pachacútec s/n, tel. 084/21-1196, US$37). Tickets must be purchased before heading to the ruins. However, at present, there is word from the INC that tickets will only be available via Internet; check www.inc-cusco.gob.pe for up-to-date information.

Police are located on the tracks right across from Hostal Presidente.

vista dome train from Ollantaytambo to Aguas Calientes

Where the tracks cross the Río Aguas Calientes is an **EsSalud** clinic (tel. 084/21-1037) with emergency 24-hour service, and on the other side is the **Ministerio de Salud clinic. Señor de Huanca drugstore** (8 A.M.–10 P.M. daily) is on the tracks across from the Hostal Presidente. If they don't have what you need, the **Pharmacy Popular** (Puputi s/n, tel. 084/22-8787, 8 A.M.–10 P.M. daily) is just off the plaza.

Banco de Crédito has an **ATM** on Imperio de los Incas, near Toto's House.

The **post office** is on the Plaza de Armas and open 10 A.M.–2 P.M. and 4–8 P.M. Monday–Saturday.

There are **Internet** places around the main square.

Laundry Angela (Pachacútec 150, tel. 084/21-2205, US$2/kg) will wash clothes the same day.

GETTING THERE AND AROUND

The only way to reach Aguas Calientes is by trekking or taking the **Inca Rail** (www.inkarail.com) or **Andean Rail** (www.andeanrailways.com). There are few vehicles and taxis in Aguas Calientes. The place is small enough that most visitors walk everywhere.

CUSCO

Along with the Aztec capital of Tenochtitlán (now swallowed by modern-day Mexico City), Cusco was the other imperial capital of the Americas at the start of the Spanish conquest. Cusco was a dazzling sight, with its temples of elegantly fitted stone, colossal plazas, royal palaces, and the hilltop fortress of Sacsayhuamán, which the Inca somehow built from house-sized stones. This was the capital of the New World's Roman empire and, as in Rome, paved highways fanned out from here through an empire that had stretched in a mere century between southern Chile and Colombia. As Francisco Pizarro marched wide-eyed through this kingdom in 1533, Cusco became the holy grail of his conquest. Two scouts he sent ahead told him the city was as elegant as a European city and

literally covered in gold. Before the scouts left Cusco, they used crowbars to pry 700 plates of gold off the walls of Coricancha, the sun temple.

Despite four centuries of Spanish domination, Cusco still seems to be in a tug-of-war between Spanish and Inca cultures. Though the Spaniards destroyed the Inca buildings in an act of domination, they had enough common sense to leave many of the bulging, seamless stone walls as foundations. These walls line many of Cusco's narrow cobblestone alleys, which thread among the many baroque churches and convents the Spaniards built here. Part of Cusco's power, and the reason visitors linger here, is the uneasy cultural tension evident in places like Coricancha and even hotel lobbies, where seamless Inca walls

© RENÉE DEL GAUDIO AND ROSS WEHNER

HIGHLIGHTS

◖ **Catedral:** Cusco's baroque cathedral, built atop a former Inca palace, dominates the town's Plaza de Armas and is filled with a huge range of paintings from the Cusco School, elegant carved choir stalls, and a gold-covered Renaissance altar (page 95).

◖ **San Blas:** This charming neighborhood is our favorite place to stay, eat, and shop in Cusco. Its narrow cobblestone streets, lined with gorgeous colonial architecture, are car-free and blissfully peaceful (page 99).

◖ **Coricancha and Santo Domingo:** Coricancha, the Inca sun temple, was once covered with thick plates of solid gold. After sacking it, the Spaniards built a Dominican church atop its seamless walls. The bizarre juxtaposition illustrates the religious conflict that agitates Cusco even today (page 100).

◖ **Sacsayhuamán:** This stone fortress of massive zigzag walls, fashioned from stone blocks weighing hundreds of tons, towers over Cusco and is the ultimate expression of the Inca's military strength (page 102).

◖ **The Center for Traditional Textiles of Cusco:** This pioneering center not only sells Cusco's finest textiles, but also supports local weavers and helps them recover their ancient weaving techniques in the process (page 107).

LOOK FOR ◖ TO FIND RECOMMENDED SIGHTS, ACTIVITIES, DINING, AND LODGING.

are nestled incongruously among arcades of Spanish arches.

With its proximity to the standout attractions of Machu Picchu and the Sacred Valley, Cusco is one of the top destinations in Latin America and the mecca of the Gringo Trail, the well-trod backpacker's route through Latin America. The sheer quantity of restaurants, hotels, and cafés indicates the city's dependence on tourism, which somehow has not diminished Cusco's charm. Schoolchildren run through the street yelling in Quechua, and villagers in the surrounding countryside retain their native dress,

festivals, and love of *chicha,* the local brew of fermented corn.

Cusco is at 3,400 meters (11,150 feet), and most people who arrive here feel some form of *soroche,* or altitude sickness, which can range from a headache and the chills to more serious ailments. The best plan is to visit the Sacred Valley and Machu Picchu first and return to Cusco after becoming used to the altitude.

The heart of Cusco is its Plaza de Armas, which stands out for its huge, 16th-century cathedral. Beyond the Plaza de Armas, and opposite the cathedral, are two charming squares, Plaza Regocijo and Plaza San Francisco.

Farther along in this direction lies the market of San Pedro. To the side of the cathedral, a narrow pedestrian street named Procuradores is lined wall-to-wall with restaurants, bars, and cafés. This is Cusco's Gringo Alley, which is crowded with aggressive salespeople. Behind the cathedral, steep alleys lead to San Blas, a bohemian neighborhood that contains most of our favorite hostels and bars.

HISTORY

As with most empires, the foundation of the Inca empire is shrouded in myth. The best-known version is that the empire began around A.D. 1100, when Manco Cápac and Mama Oclla, children of the sun and the moon, arose from the waters of Lake Titicaca and searched the land for a place to found their kingdom. When they reached the fertile valley of Cusco, Manco Cápac was able, for the first time, to plunge his golden staff into the ground. This was the divine sign that showed them where to found the Inca capital city, which was christened Q'osqo, or "navel of the world."

The seeds of truth in this legend are that the **Tiwanaku** (A.D. 200–1000), from the south shores of Lake Titicaca, were the first advanced culture to reach the Cusco area. Around A.D. 700 an even more potent culture, the **Huari** (A.D. 700–1100) from Ayacucho, spread here and built aqueducts, the large city of Pikillacta, and probably, as some archaeologists believe, the first water temple at Pisac. The Inca, sandwiched between these two advanced cultures, rose out of the vacuum created when both collapsed. The Inca combined the Tiwanaku stonework and farming techniques on one hand with the Huari highway system and mummy worship on the other. The result was a potent system of economic and political organization.

Little is known about Inca history, though it is believed Manco Cápac probably existed and was indeed the first Inca. There were 13 Inca emperors, though the empire for all practical purposes began with Inca Yupanqui, the ninth Inca leader and one of the younger sons of **Inca Viracocha.** Around 1440 the Chancas,

the tribe that toppled the Huari, had amassed a large army that was poised to overrun Cusco. Inca Viracocha fled, probably to his estate at Huchuy Cusco in the Sacred Valley, but Inca Yupanqui stayed on to defend Cusco. Of the ensuing battle, mestizo chronicler Inca Garcilaso de la Vega reports that even the stones of Cusco rose up and became soldiers. Against overwhelming odds, Inca Yupanqui and a team of seasoned generals beat back the Chancas.

After the battle, Inca Yupanqui changed his name to **Pachacútec** ("shaker of the earth" in Quechua), took over Cusco from his disgraced father, and launched the Inca's unprecedented period of expansion. Pachacútec created a vision of the Inca people as a people of power, ruled over by a class of elites who were allowed the privilege of chewing coca leaves and wearing large ear plugs. He used a stick-and-carrot strategy, learned from the Huari, of conquering territories peacefully by bearing down on them with overwhelmingly large armies on one hand, and by offering the rich benefits of being integrated into a well-functioning web of commerce on the other.

In the Cusco area, what is most obvious about Pachacútec is that he was a master builder. He fashioned the city of Cusco into the shape of a puma, a sacred animal admired for its grace and strength, with Sacsayhuamán as the head, the city as the body, and the Coricancha sun temple as the tail. He built a huge central plaza, which included both today's Plaza de Armas and the Plaza Regocijo, and also somehow devised a way to move the stones to begin construction of Sacsayhuamán. He is credited for building nearly all of the other major Inca monuments in the area, including Pisac, Ollantaytambo, and probably even Machu Picchu. Pachacútec's armies conquered the entire area between Cusco and Lake Titicaca and also spread north through the central highlands.

His son, **Túpac Yupanqui,** was less of a builder and even more of a warrior. He spent most of his life away from Cusco in long, brutal campaigns in northern Peru against the

CUSCO

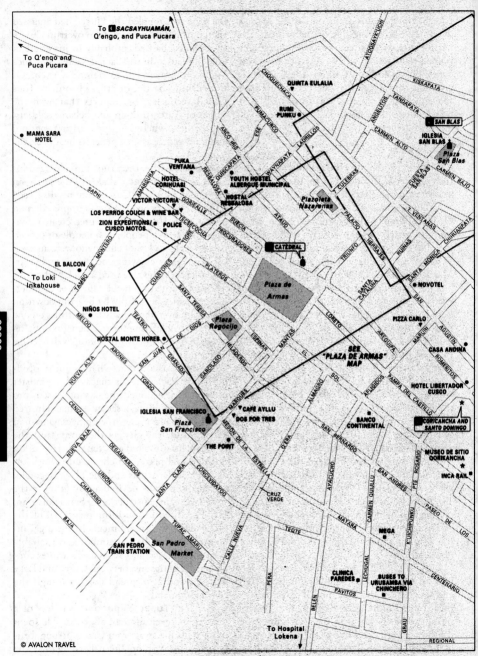

To ◪*SACSAYHUAMÁN*, Q'engo, and Puca Pucara

To Q'enqo and Puca Pucara

To Loki Inkahouse

MAMA SARA HOTEL

EL BALCON

NIÑOS HOTEL

HOSTAL MONTE HOREB

QUINTA EULALIA

RUMI PUNKU

PUKA VENTANA

HOTEL CORIHUASI

VICTOR VICTORIA

YOUTH HOSTEL ALBERGUE MUNICIPAL

HOSTAL REBALOSA

LOS PERROS COUCH & WINE BAR

ZION EXPEDITIONS/ CUSCO MOTOS

POLICE

Plazoleta Nazarenas

CATEDRAL

Plaza de Armas

Plaza Regocijo

◪ SAN BLAS

IGLESIA SAN BLAS

Plaza San Blas

NOVOTEL

PIZZA CARLO

CASA ANDINA

HOTEL LIBERTADOR CUSCO

SEE "PLAZA DE ARMAS" MAP

IGLESIA SAN FRANCISCO

Plaza San Francisco

CAFÉ AYLLU

DOS POR TRES

THE POINT

BANCO CONTINENTAL

CORICANCHA AND SANTO DOMINGO

MUSEO DE SITIO QORIKANCHA

INCA RAIL

SAN PEDRO TRAIN STATION

San Pedro Market

MEGA

CLINICA PAREDES

BUSES TO URUBAMBA VIA CHINCHERO

To Hospital Lorena

© AVALON TRAVEL

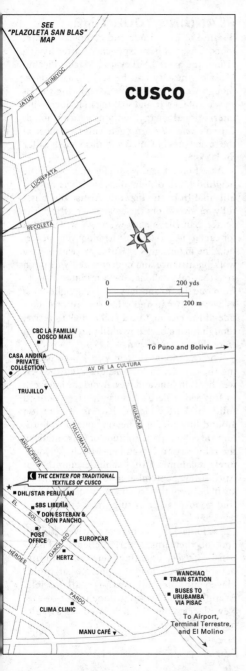

stubborn Chachapoyans. He dominated the entire coastline, including the Chimú empire based at Chan Chan, and pushed all the way to Quito, in present-day Ecuador.

His son, **Huayna Cápac,** the last Inca to rule over a unified empire, seemed to be ruling over a territory that had extended itself almost to the breaking point. Nevertheless he continued the campaign in the north, fathering a son named **Atahualpa** in Quito, and pushed the Inca empire to its last limits, up against what is now the Ecuador-Colombia border. After his death Atahualpa challenged **Huáscar,** the legitimate heir in Cusco, and a disastrous civil war broke out, killing thousands of Inca and badly damaging the empire's infrastructure.

In the end, Atahualpa was victorious. He might have been able to unify the empire again if it were not for the fact that **Francisco Pizarro** and a small Spanish army had begun their march across Peru. Pizarro and his men took Atahualpa hostage in November 1532 and held him until an entire room was filled with gold, much of which was taken from Cusco and carried by llama trains to Cajamarca. Then the Spaniards murdered Atahualpa anyway and continued their march to Cusco.

To maintain stability, Pizarro needed to find a new Inca ruler, and he befriended **Manco Inca,** another son of Huayna Cápac in Cusco, who was grateful to Pizarro for having routed Atahualpa's army of Quito-based Inca. Under the guise of liberators and with Manco Inca's blessing, Pizarro and his men entered Cusco and took full and peaceful possession of the city in November 1533.

It didn't take long, however, for Manco Inca to grow resentful. The Spaniards had sacked Cusco for all of its gold and silver in the first month, picking clean the gold-filled sun temple and even the sacred Inca mummies and melting everything into bars for shipping to Spain. They lived in the palaces of the former Inca emperors and forced Inca nobles to hand over their wives.

Manco Inca escaped from Cusco and by May 1536 had amassed an army estimated at 100,000–200,000 soldiers, who used slingshots

CUSCO

to throw red-hot coals onto Cusco's thatched roofs, burning their beloved city to the ground. Trapped, the Spaniards made a last-ditch effort against the Inca, who had occupied the fortress of Sacsayhuamán. During a battle that raged for more than a week, the Spaniards prevailed against overwhelming odds, causing Manco Inca to retreat to Ollantaytambo and then later to the jungle enclave of Vilcabamba. The Inca resisted for more than three decades until their last leader, Inca **Túpac Amaru,** was captured in the Amazon and executed in Cusco's main square in 1573.

By this time, Cusco had already faded from prominence. After its gold was gone, Francisco Pizarro left for the coast and made Lima the capital of the new viceroyalty. More than two centuries later, an Indian who claimed Inca descent and called himself Túpac Amaru II would rally Inca fervor once again and launch another siege of Cusco. But the Spaniards quickly captured him and hung him in Cusco's main square. His body was quartered and pieces of it were left in the squares of surrounding Inca villages as a warning for the future.

Cusco would have ended up another quiet Andean city like Cajamarca and Ayacucho were it not for Hiram Bingham's discovery of Machu Picchu in 1911. That discovery sparked an international interest in Cusco, which flourished in the 1920s with a glittering café society and a generation of intellectuals that included photographer Martín Chambi. During the 1920s the train line was built past Machu Picchu that still carries travelers today.

A **1950 earthquake,** the most severe in three centuries, destroyed the homes of 35,000 people in Cusco but had the unexpected benefit of clearing away colonial facades that had covered up Inca stonework for centuries. Much of the Inca stonework visible today around Cusco, including the long wall at Coricancha, was discovered thanks to the earthquake. Based on these ruins, and Cusco's colonial architecture, Cusco was declared a **UNESCO World Heritage Site** in 1983.

PLANNING YOUR TIME

Because of its altitude and complex cultural roots, Cusco is best experienced after having visited the Sacred Valley and Machu Picchu. Most of the city can be seen in two days, though we have spent weeks exploring the alleyways of Cusco, and soaking in its incredibly international energy, without getting bored. Cusco's *boleto turístico* gets you into most of the major sites of Cusco and the Sacred Valley for US$45.

As a home base, we prefer staying in the neighborhood of San Blas, which is an uphill hike from the Plaza de Armas but blissfully removed from the noise and traffic of the center. San Blas's narrow streets are difficult for cars to negotiate and therefore very peaceful. The main sights of Cusco are within easy walking distance and concentrated within an area that takes about 10–15 minutes to walk from one side to another. Outlying sights such as Sacsayhuamán and other ruins on the outside of the city require a taxi or bus to arrive, though hiking back downhill into Cusco is an enjoyable way to return.

The traditional time to visit Cusco is during the dry season May–August, but the best weather is in June and July. Avoid the last week in July when Peru's hotels are often booked solid for Peru's Fiestas Patrias celebration around July 28. An increasing number of visitors are enjoying the solitude of Cusco during the rainy season November–March. We definitely recommend the "shoulder months" of April, May, September, and October, which are in between the dry and rainy seasons. You'll find good weather during these months and few crowds.

Taxi hijackings, where taxi drivers kidnap and rob their unsuspecting clients, do happen in Cusco. Examine your taxi carefully before getting inside, especially at night. Have your hotel call a taxi, if at all possible. At night, avoid walking alone in out-of-the-way places or while inebriated, as assaults happen every week.

Sights

PLAZA DE ARMAS

Cusco's Plaza de Armas is surrounded by colonial stone arcades and graced with two extraordinary churches, the Catedral and the Jesuit Iglesia de la Compañía. Though a grove of native trees was unfortunately ripped out in the late 1990s, Cusco's main square is a lively place for locals and tourists alike—full of child shoe shiners, hand-holding schoolgirls, and old men sharing crossword puzzles. Two flags fly over the square, the red-and-white flag of Peru and the rainbow-colored flag of the Inca nation, which is nearly identical to the gay pride flag. It is much older, of course, and its eight colors represent the four corners of Tahuantinsuyo, the Inca empire.

◖ Catedral

Cusco's baroque Catedral (Plaza de Armas, 10 A.M.–6 P.M. daily, US$8.50 or *boleto religioso*) sits between the more recent church of **Jesús María** (1733) on its right and, on its left, **El Triunfo** (1539), the first Christian church in Cusco, built to celebrate the victory over Manco Inca. The cathedral was built on top of Inca Viracocha's palace using blocks of red granite taken from Sacsayhuamán and took more than a century to construct from 1560 onwards. At least four earthquakes from 1650 to 1986, along with damp and neglect, had taken a serious toll on the building. Fortunately, Cusco's archbishop acquired financial backing from Telefónica for a complete

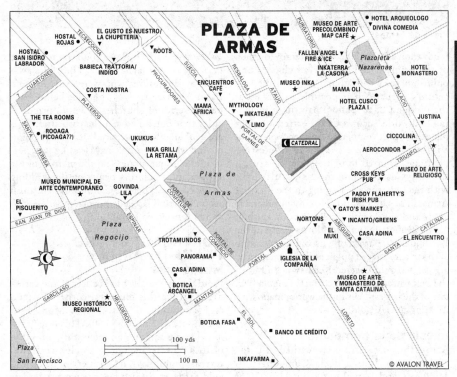

© AVALON TRAVEL

CUSCO

Plaza de Armas

renovation 1997–2002, which removed much of the grime that had covered chapels and paintings over time. For the first time in a century perhaps, it is possible to make out the unique **Cusco School** paintings, including odd works such as Christ eating a guinea pig at the Last Supper and a (very) pregnant Virgin Mary. There is also an interesting painting, reported to be the oldest in Cusco, showing Cusco during the 1650 earthquake with the townspeople praying in the Plaza de Armas. The church also contains considerable gold- and silverwork, including a silver bier for the **Señor de los Temblores** (Lord of the Earthquakes), patron of Cusco. It also holds a 17th-century carved pulpit and choir stalls and an original gold-covered Renaissance altar. In the bell tower is the huge María Angola bell, one of the largest bells in the world, made with 27 kilograms of gold.

Iglesia de la Compañía

Across the corner from the cathedral is the 17th-century Iglesia de la Compañía (9–11:30 A.M. and 1–5:30 P.M. daily, US$3.50 or *boleto religioso*), which was built on top of the palace of Inca Huayna Cápac. This church was built by the Jesuits, who were expelled from Latin America in 1767, but not before they built a series of churches in Peru's principal cities that outshine even the cathedral. This graceful, highly ornate facade is a case in point, behind which is a single nave leading to a spectacular baroque altar. Near the main door is a 17th-century painting depicting the wedding of Inca princess Beatriz Clara Coya to Spanish *captín* Martín García de Loyola, grandnephew of San Ignacio de Loyola.

NORTHEAST OF THE PLAZA DE ARMAS
Museo Inka

Head down the alley to the left of the cathedral to reach this museum (corner of Ataúd and Túcuman, 8 A.M.–7 P.M. Mon.–Fri., 9 A.M.–4 P.M. Sat., US$3.50). This ornate colonial home contains an interesting collection of Inca objects, including jewelry, ceramics, textiles, mummies, and a variety of metal and gold artifacts. It also has the world's largest

Iglesia de la Compañía

CUSCO

CUSCO'S TOURIST TICKET

You will go broke if you pay to get into each museum, church, and archaeological site around Cusco. Even if you are going to visit only a few places, buy a *boleto turístico* for US$45 (US$24 for students under age 26 with ISIC card). The ticket covers 16 sites in and around Cusco, including must-sees like Sacsayhuamán, Pisac, and Ollantaytambo, and you cannot actually get into a lot of the sites if you do not have the ticket. The tickets can be bought at the entrances to most major sites or at **COSITUC** (Av. El Sol 103, #102, www.boletoturisticocusco.com, 9 A.M.-5 P.M. Mon.-Fri.). Unfortunately, the pass only lasts 10 days. There is a process for extending expired passes, but − take it from us − it's not worth wasting a day navigating the halls of the Instituto Nacional de Cultura, which is a harrowing bureaucracy even by Peruvian standards.

The ticket covers these 16 sites: Museo Municipal de Arte Contemporáneo, Museo Histórico Regional, Museo de Arte Popular, Museo de Sitio Coricancha, Centro Qosqo de Arte Nativo, Monumento a Pachacútec, Sacsayhuamán, Q'enqo, Puca Pucara, Tambo Machay, Pisac, Ollantaytambo, Moray, Chinchero, Tipon, Pikillacta.

The Coricancha temple (US$3.50) and the Museo de Arte y Monasterio de Santa Catalina (US$2.50) are not included in the ticket, but if you go to both you only pay US$5. The Catedral (US$8.50), Iglesia de la Compañía (US$3.50), Iglesia San Blas (US$5), and the Museo de Arte Religioso (US$5) are not covered either, but if you plan to go to all four you can buy the *boleto religioso* at the entrance of any of these sites for US$17 (US$8.50 for students under age 26 with ISIC card). Other interesting sites not included are the Iglesia de La Merced (US$2), Museo Inka (US$3.50), and the Museo de Arte Precolombino (US$7).

COLONIAL PAINTING: THE CUSCO SCHOOL

The religious paintings that cover the walls of Peru's colonial churches are more than decoration. For centuries after the conquest, painting was the Catholic church's main tool for converting Peru's native peoples, who for the most part did not read or speak Spanish. The church's religious campaign produced thousands of now-priceless works and renowned schools of painting in Cusco and Quito, in present-day Ecuador.

Shortly after the conquest, the different orders of the Catholic church began importing paintings into Lima from well-known painters of the ongoing European Renaissance. The museum at Iglesia San Francisco in Lima contains works by European painters who influenced the American schools of painting, collectively known as the Spanish American baroque. These 16th-century European masters included the Spanish painters Francisco de Zurbarán and Bartolomé Esteban Murillo and Flemish master Peter Paul Rubens.

By 1580, demand for European paintings had so outstripped supply that European painters began arriving to Lima in search of lucrative commissions. One of these was Italian Jesuit Bernardo Bitti (1548–1610), who was a disciple of Caravaggio and the brightly colored, emotional works of the Italian baroque. He was probably the single most influential European painter to work in Peru, and his paintings can be seen at La Merced in Cusco, La Compañía in Arequipa, and Lima's San Francisco museum. With the guidance of Bitti and other European masters, the church orders set up convent studios around Peru where Indian and mestizo artisans cranked out a staggering quantity of paintings in serial fashion – one painter would specialize in clothing, another in landscape, and still another in face and hands.

Right from the start, the workshops in Cusco began developing a unique style that blended the European baroque with images from Peru, including local trees, plants, animals, and foods. Cusco's cathedral, for instance, contains a painting that shows the Last Supper served with roasted guinea pig and *chicha,* the local corn beer. In another painting nearby, there is a pregnant Virgin Mary with the lustrous, smooth hair of Andean women. Often the dress of the Virgin Mary has a triangular shape, which art scholars believe is a transformation of the ancient Andean practice of worshipping *apus,* or sacred mountains.

The painters of the Cusco School also used a lot of gold to highlight their paintings and create a richly decorated surface. Most paintings pictured the Virgin Mary, scenes from the life of a saint, or panoramas of devils and angels. An entirely unique invention of Cusco's painters was the archangels, flying through the air with ornate Spanish clothing and armed with muskets. Far from the tranquil realism of the Flemish baroque, these paintings portrayed a dazzling otherworld, filled with powerful spiritual beings, which were meant to awe, stun, and frighten Indian viewers into accepting Catholicism. The most famous painters of the Cusco School were Diego Quispe Tito, Juan Espinosa de los Monteros, and Antonio Sinchi Roca, though it is difficult to decipher who did what because paintings were rarely signed.

In Quito, new-world painters embarked on a different course. The founder of the Quito School was Father Bedón, who studied with Bitti in Lima but quickly dropped the Italian mannerist style upon returning to Quito. Instead he ushered in a type of religious painting that combined the gold decorations of the Cusco School with the colder colors and shadowy depths favored by Peter Paul Rubens and other Flemish painters. The cathedrals in northern Peru, including Cajamarca and Trujillo, often feature paintings from both schools side by side.

collection of *qeros,* wooden cups the Inca used for drinking.

Museo de Arte Precolombino

Farther down the alley to the left of the cathedral, toward the Plaza de las Nazarenas, is the fabulous private Museo de Arte Precolombino (MAP, Plaza de las Nazarenas 231, tel. 084/23-3210, www.map.museolarco.org, 9 A.M.–10 P.M. daily, US$7). MAP opened its doors in June 2003 and contains an exquisite array of ceramics, painting, jewelry, and objects made of silver and gold. Unlike at other archaeological museums, the pieces here are not meant to be viewed as artifacts representative of their cultures. They are ancient works of art, pieces of elaborate craftsmanship and beauty that were handpicked from the Museo Larco in Lima. The museum has an elegant layout designed by Fernando de Szyszlo, one of Peru's most respected contemporary painters, and in the courtyard is an interesting glass box containing the MAP café, one of Cusco's most upscale restaurants. Near the end of the plaza is the 400-year-old **Seminario San Antonio Abad,** which has been converted into the Hotel Monasterio, Cusco's first five-star hotel. Even if you are not a guest, sneak a peak at the courtyard and the 17th-century **Iglesia San Antonio Abad.**

Museo de Arte Religioso

Just one block downhill from Museo de Arte Precolombio along Palacio, this museum (Palacio and Hatun Rumiyoc, 8 A.M.–6 P.M. daily, US$5 or *boleto religioso*) resides in a colonial building that was built by the Marquis of Buenavista and later occupied by Cusco's archbishop. These days its handsome salons showcase religious paintings from the 17th and 18th centuries. Walk up the alleyway Hatun Rumiyoc and you will see that the entire museum is built upon a foundation of Inca stones that fit perfectly into one another. This was the foundation of an early ruler of Cusco, **Inca Roca,** and near the end of the street you will find the famous stone with 12 sides, all of which conform perfectly to their neighbors. Sadly, the stone was badly chipped and scarred by a group of unknown vandals in April 2004.

◖ San Blas

Walk away from the Plaza de Armas along Hatun Rumiyoc and continue walking straight until reaching Cuesta San Blas, which leads to Cusco's San Blas neighborhood. This square, known as **Plazoleta San Blas,** is home to several artisan families who have been operating here for decades. Its steep cobblestone alleys offer excellent views over Cusco.

Iglesia San Blas (Plazoleta San Blas, 8 A.M.–6 P.M. daily, US$5 or *boleto religioso*) is a small, whitewashed adobe church built in 1563. One of the New World's most famous works of art is found here, a carved pulpit made from the trunk of a single tree. There is also a gold-covered baroque altar.

Another interesting place to visit, on top of the fountain in the Plazoleta San Blas, is the family-run **Museo de la Coca** (Suytuk'atu 705, museodelacoca@hotmail.com, 8 A.M.–8 P.M.

© RENÉE DEL GAUDIO AND ROSS WEHNER

San Blas is a great place to stay, stroll, and eat in Cusco.

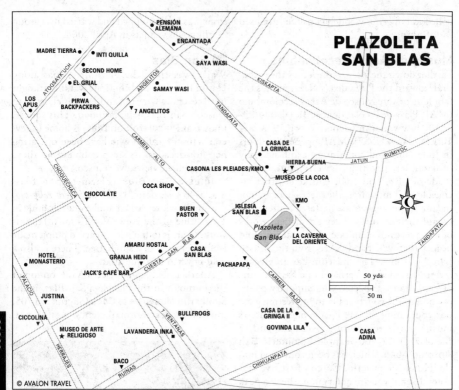

PLAZOLETA SAN BLAS

daily, US$3.50). This interesting exhibition demonstrates the history of the coca leaf through to the adulterated production of cocaine. It also has a boutique filled with a large selection of coca products. San Blas is a great neighborhood to find accommodations or just to wander around and have lunch.

EAST OF THE PLAZA DE ARMAS
Museo de Arte y Monasterio de Santa Catalina

From the Plaza de Armas, head down Arequipa to this museum (Arequipa, 8:30 A.M.–5:30 P.M. Mon.–Sat., US$2.50 or US$5 with entry to Coricancha), which was built on top of the enclosure where the chosen virgins of the Inca lived, known as the *acllahuasi,* or "house of the chosen ones." In a strange historical twist, the Spaniards converted the building into a convent, where 30 nuns remain cloistered to this day. Holy women have thus lived in this building for at least five centuries. The museum has a good collection of Cusco School paintings and an impressive Renaissance altar. A highlight is a trunk containing miniature figurines depicting the life of Christ, which was used by Catholic missionaries for proselytizing in far-flung regions of Peru.

Coricancha and Santo Domingo

The greatest prize in the Spaniards' 1533 sacking of Cusco was Coricancha (Plazoleta Santo Domingo, 8:30 A.M.–5:30 P.M. Mon.–Sat., 2–5 P.M. Sun., US$3.50 or US$5 with entry to Museo de Arte y Monasterio de Santa Catalina), the sun temple. For the Inca, the building had many functions. It was foremost a place where offerings were burnt in thanks to the sun, though there were also rooms devoted to the moon, stars, lightning, thunder, and rainbows. Like so much of Inca ceremonial architecture, the building also served as a solar observatory and mummy storehouse.

The south-facing walls of the temple were covered with gold in order to reflect the light of the sun and illuminate the temple. Inside was the **Punchaco,** a solid-gold disk inlaid with precious stones, which represented the sun and was probably the most sacred object in the Inca empire. Pizarro's scouts had already produced approximately a ton and a half of gold by stripping the inner walls of Coricancha. When the main Spanish force gained Cusco, they gathered hundreds of gold sculptures and objects from the temple, including an altar big enough to hold two men and an extraordinary artificial garden made of gold, including cornstalks with silver stems and ears of gold. Tragically, everything was melted down within a month—except for the Punchaco. It disappeared from the temple and its whereabouts are unknown to this day.

The Dominicans took over the Coricancha and dismantled most of it, using the polished ashlar to build their church and convent of Santa Domingo on top of the sun temple's walls. For centuries, many of the Coricancha's walls were hidden beneath the convent. But in 1950 an earthquake caused large sections of the convent to crumble, exposing Inca walls of the highest quality.

It requires considerable imagination today to picture how the Inca's most important temple must have once looked. The eight-sided sacrificial font, stripped of the 55 kilograms of gold that once covered it, stands in the middle of the Coricancha's main square. The rooms that surround it may once have been covered with silver and dedicated to the moon, stars, and thunder. The wall running along the temple's eastern side is 60 meters long and 5 meters high, and each block is perfectly interlocked with its neighbor. But the highlight is the curved retaining wall beneath the facade of the church, which has not budged an inch in all of Cusco's earthquakes.

Sharing the same entrance as the Coricancha is Cusco's most serious contemporary art gallery, **Galería del Convento de Santo Domingo** (Plazoleta Santo Domingo, 8:30 A.M.–5:30 P.M. Mon.–Sat., US$3.50). It is the best place to see young emerging local artists.

Museo de Sitio Coricancha

Reached through an underground entrance across the garden from the Coricancha is this rather unimpressive museum (Av. El Sol, 9 A.M.–6 P.M. Mon.–Sat., 8 A.M.–1 P.M. Sun., entry with *boleto turístico*), which exhibits a few artifacts from the excavation of Coricancha, a model of the sun temple, and blueprints of its floor plans. There are no guides available here, and explanations are in Spanish only.

On your way back to the Plaza de Armas, walk down the narrow alley of Loreto. To your right are the Inca walls of the *acllahuasi,* now the Santa Catalina convent. To the left are the walls of the palace of Huayna Cápac, now the Iglesia de la Compañía.

SOUTHWEST OF THE PLAZA DE ARMAS

From the Plaza de Armas, walk up Mantas one block to the **Iglesia de la Merced** (tel. 084/23-1821, 8 A.M.–12:30 P.M. and 2–5:30 P.M. Mon.–Sat., US$2), which was completely rebuilt following the 1650 earthquake. Inside the church lie two conquistadores, a father and a son who were executed by the Spanish shortly after the conquest. Diego de Almagro the Elder was hung after he rebelled against Francisco Pizarro's authority, and his son, Diego de Almagro the Younger, was executed four years later for murdering Francisco Pizarro in revenge. Hanging on the walls nearby the tombs are paintings by the 16th-century master Bernardo Bitti. The church's elegant cloisters contain a small museum, which showcases a magnificent monstrance made of gold, silver, and precious stones.

From the Iglesia de la Merced, head down Heladeros to the **Plaza Regocijo** and the

CUSCO

Museo Histórico Regional (Heladeros, tel. 084/22-5211, 8 A.M.–5 P.M. Tues.–Sun., entry with *boleto turístico* or US$4.50), which was once the home of one of colonial Peru's most famous and eloquent writers, mestizo Inca Garcilaso de la Vega. The museum provides a fine survey of Peru's pre-Inca cultures, starting with preceramic arrowheads and continuing with artifacts from the Chavín, Moche, Chimú, Chancay, and Inca cultures. The holdings include a Nasca mummy and, on the second floor, colonial furniture and paintings from the Cusco School. Across the Plaza Regocijo in the municipality is the **Museo Municipal de Arte Contemporáneo** (Plaza Regocijo, 9 A.M.–6 P.M. Mon.–Sat., entry with *boleto turístico* or US$4.50), which contains contemporary art of varying quality.

From Plaza Regocijo, walk down Garcilaso to **Iglesia San Francisco** (8 A.M.–noon and 3–5 P.M. daily), a convent and church that stands above the plaza of the same name. This church, with three naves and in the shape of a Latin cross, was built in 1572 and is one of the few churches in Cusco to survive the 1650 earthquake. As a result, its convent is one of the few remaining examples of the highly ornate 16th-century plateresque style, complemented here by *azulejo* tiles imported from Seville. There are two smaller colonial churches down Santa Clara from here toward the market and the train station: The first is **Iglesia Santa Clara** (8 A.M.–noon and 3–5 P.M. daily), which is open only for early-morning mass 6–7 A.M., and the second is **Iglesia San Pedro** (8 A.M.–noon and 3–5 P.M. daily).

OUTSIDE CUSCO

There are four highly recommended Inca ruins outside of Cusco, which many Cusco agencies offer as part of a rushed, half-day tour. The ruins all accept the *boleto turístico* or they charge US$5 per ruin and are open 7 A.M.–6 P.M.; after-hours visits are possible at Sacsayhuamán, the ruins closest to Cusco. Peter Frost's excellent guide to Cusco, *Exploring Cusco,* details some interesting walks around

this spectacular landscape between the four sites, which are littered with aqueducts, Inca roads, caves, shrines, and carvings.

All the ruins lie close to the road that runs between Cusco and Pisac. An enjoyable way to see the ruins is to take a Pisac bus or taxi to the farthest ruins, Tambomachay, and walk the eight kilometers back to Cusco, visiting all the ruins along the way (this walk can be shortened considerably by just walking between Q'enqo and Sacsayhuamán, a distance of one kilometer). Occasional robberies have been reported in this area, so it is better to walk in a group of two or more during the early part of the day.

◖ Sacsayhuamán

Looming over Cusco to the north are the ruins of Sacsayhuamán (7 A.M.–6 P.M. daily), a hilltop fortress with three ramparts of zigzag walls that run for nearly 300 meters on its north side. The largest stones—nearly 8.5 meters high and 361 tons, according to historian John Hemming—were placed at the apex of the walls to strengthen them. Every Inca citizen had to spend a few months of the year working on public works, and the Inca used this tremendous reserve of labor to move the stones, using log sleds and levers. But even engineers have a hard time understanding how the Inca fitted these huge stones so perfectly together.

Only the largest stones of Sacsayhuamán remain. Up until the 1930s, builders arrived at Sacsayhuamán to cart away the precut stone of this apparently limitless quarry, so it is difficult to appreciate how impregnable Sacsayhuamán must have been. Three towers once crowned the top of Sacsayhuamán, and two of their foundations are visible. During Manco Inca's great rebellion, the Spaniards managed to establish a base on the opposing hill and spent two days charging across the plain on horseback and attempting to scale the defensive walls. On the first day, one of the stones fired by the Inca slingshots struck Juan Pizarro, Francisco's younger brother, who died that night. On

where the Spaniards based themselves during their assault on Sacsayhuamán. There is a rock outcrop on top, beautifully carved with sacred steps. Sacsayhuamán is a steep, two-kilometer walk from Cusco or a 10-minute taxi ride (US$2). Taxis wait in the parking lot for the return trip to Cusco.

Q'enqo

One kilometer past Sacsayhuamán is the shrine of Q'enqo (7 A.M.–6 P.M. daily), which means "zigzag" in Quechua. It is a large limestone outcrop carved with enigmatic steps leading nowhere, a sacred motif that is found on nearly every *huaca,* the sacred stone revered by the Inca. On the top of the rock are faint carvings of a puma and a condor. Carved into the rock are perfect zigzag channels, which probably flowed with *chicha* or llama blood during ceremonial rituals, much like the Saywite Stone between Cusco and Abancay. Below the rock are caves carved with niches where mummies of lesser nobility may once have been kept. Nearby is an amphitheater with niches centered framing an upright stone, which was probably defaced long ago by Spanish extirpators of idolatry. Between Q'enqo and Sacsayhuamán is a series of soccer fields, where rather pitiful horses can be rented for quick rides in the area (US$5 per half hour, price negotiable).

Puca Pucara

The least significant of the ruins outside Cusco, Puca Pucara (7 A.M.–6 P.M. daily), meaning "red fort" in Quechua, was probably not a fort at all but rather a storage facility or an Inca *tambo,* or lodge. Perhaps when the Inca emperor came to visit the baths of Tambomachay, his court waited here. There are several chambers below and a platform on top with excellent views. The distance between Puca Pucara and Q'enqo is six kilometers along the road.

Tambomachay

Called the Inca's Bath, Tambomachay (7 A.M.–6 P.M. daily) lies about 300 meters off the Pisac road, though it is well marked

The Sacsayhuamán ruins, just above Cusco, are a monument to the Inca's most ferocious battle against the Spaniards.

CUSCO

the evening of the second day, the Spaniards launched a surprise attack with ladders and successfully forced the Inca into the three stone towers. As the Spaniards massacred the estimated 1,500 soldiers trapped inside, many Inca preferred to leap to their deaths from the high tower. The next morning, condors feasted on the dead bodies, and this grisly image is emblazoned on Cusco's coat-of-arms.

These days the flat fields outside of Sacsayhuamán, where the Inti Raymi culminates each June, is a peaceful place to stroll. In the mornings, Cusco residents come here to jog or do yoga on the grassy lawn, which is considerably larger than a soccer field. A huge trapezoidal door leads up a walkway to the top of the ruins, which is a marvelous place to bring wine and watch the sun setting over Cusco. Because many tourists come here in the evening, guards are posted to put visitors at ease as dusk falls. If you have time, visit the top of Rodadero hill,

with a sign. It is a well-preserved example of the sacred water fountains found at nearly every important Inca temple, including Pisac, Ollantaytambo, and Machu Picchu. The Inca took a natural spring and painstakingly channeled the water through three waterfalls, which continue to work perfectly today. There is a fine Inca wall above with ceremonial niches. The Inca worshiped water as a vital life element, and this site no doubt formed part of a water cult. From here, you can see Puca Pucara, on the other side of the road.

Entertainment and Events

FOLKLORIC MUSIC AND DANCE

The **Centro Qosqo de Arte Nativo** (El Sol 604, tel. 084/22-7901, US$5), founded in 1924, has a highly recommended music and dance show 6:45–7:45 P.M. on most evenings. The Centro was founded in 1924 as the first organized music and dance center in Cusco. Most of the Peruvian restaurants in the Plaza de Armas have live Andean music during dinner.

The once prestigious Garcilaso cinema and theater, has gone through many transformations since its opening in 1963, including housing a pornographic cinema, evangelical church, and arcade all at the same time. In 2007 it was converted into the **Teatro Kusikay** (Union 117, tel. 084/25-5414, www.kusikay. com, 9 A.M.–9 P.M. Mon.–Sat.), solely dedicated to the show **Paukartanpu**, which is a colorful spectacle based on a religious festival. The show starts at 7:30 P.M. Monday–Saturday and costs US$35. It is a modern and fun insight into Andean culture interpreted through impressive acrobatics, traditional dance, music, and folklore, as well as theater and circus.

CAFÉ BARS

A great place to hang out either at night or during the day is **Los Perros Couch & Wine Bar** (Tecsecocha 436, tel. 084/24-1447, 11 A.M.–midnight daily, US$5). The relaxed atmosphere and comfy couches make an inviting backdrop for a delicious light lunch, an afternoon smoothie over a game of backgammon, a cup of coffee perusing a magazine, or a nice glass of red wine in the evening.

Just up the road is **Indigo** (Tecsecocha 2, 2nd Fl., tel. 084/26-0271, 11 A.M.–2 A.M. daily, US$5), another nice place to slump into a couch in front of an open fire and unwind. Hookahs are available with an impressive selection of exotic tobaccos. The Thai dishes are not bad and reasonably priced.

Known for its raucous private parties, **Fallen Angel Fire & Ice** (Plazoleta Nazarenas 221, tel. 084/25-8184, 11 A.M.–11 P.M. daily, US$5) is the most outrageous place to get a drink. There are glass-covered bathtub fish tanks instead of tables, techno music, and multicolored

© AMBER DAVIS COLLINS, WWW.LIFEUNSCRIPTEDPHOTOGRAPHY.COM

indigenous parade in Cusco's Centro

daiquiris. The steaks are the specialty of the creative dinner menu. The owner, Andres Zuniga, has also set up a lavish and flamboyant guesthouse on the same property.

Despite the distracting decor, **The Tea Rooms** (Santa Teresa 364, 2nd Fl., tel.084/23-1317, noon–midnight daily, US$7) is spacious and bright and not a bad place for an evening martini or a classic, though overpriced, afternoon tea for two with sandwiches, scones, and cakes for US$17.

PUBS AND LIVE MUSIC

The English **Cross Keys Pub** (Triunfo 350, 2nd Fl., tel. 084/22-9227, 10 A.M.–2 A.M. daily) recently moved to a new location, but nevertheless continues to be a Cusco classic owned by Barry Walker, British consul and owner of Manu Expeditions. It has dartboards, typical pub fare including chili con carne, and English beer on tap. Happy hours run 6:30–7:30 P.M. and 9:30–10 P.M.

Another good pub in town with nice views over the Plaza de Armas and a great place to play a game of pool or darts is **Nortons** (Santa Catalina Angosta 116, 7 A.M.–2 A.M. daily). There is an impressive selection of imported beers from England, Belgium, and Mexico, including Old Speckled Hen and Abbot Ale on tap. For hangovers a classic English breakfast and a cheap Bloody Mary do the trick.

The atmosphere at **Paddy Flaherty's Irish Pub** (Triunfo 124, tel. 084/24-7719, 11 A.M.–2 A.M.) is a taste of home, at least for those of us who hang out at Irish pubs. It serves Guinness, among other beers, and has a two-for-one happy hour 7–8 P.M. The kitchen offers shepherd's pie, chicken wings, and stuffed potato skins.

For something a little different try **La Chupeteria Shot Bar** (Tecsecocha 400, 8 P.M.–late daily). The imposing picture of Che Guevara and the motto "revolutionary drinking theory" say it all. La Chupeteria adds an exciting twist to a night on the town with its huge array of creative shots. For an impressive spectacle of fire and sparks the Swiss Verbier shot is a must.

Another interesting drinking experience is **El Pisquerito** (San Juan de Dios 250, tel. 084/23-5223, www.elpisquerito.com, 11 A.M.–2 A.M. daily). Owned by one of Peru's most experienced bartenders, Hans Hilburg, this charming little bar specializes exclusively in pisco. There is an extensive menu of delicious designer cocktails and a nice selection of Spanish-style tapas and pizzas.

Hands down the best mojito in Cusco is at **Hierba Buena** (Suytuk'atu 715-B, San Blas, tel. 084/26-0685, 9 A.M.–12:30 A.M. Mon.–Sat.). Make sure to also try the *chicha tu madre,* a drink made with purple maize juice and pisco.

If you are up for some live music there are plenty of places in Cusco. Locals and foreigners head to **Ukukus** (Plateros 316, 8 P.M.–late daily, sometimes a small cover on weekends), a live music venue and bar that has been a classic of Cusco's nightlife scene since it was founded over a decade ago. Shows start at 10:30 P.M. and range from Afro-Peruvian to rock, with affordable drinks.

The hippest place for an evening out is **Bullfrogs** (Warankallki 185, tel. 084/22-1762, 3 P.M.–late daily), a large, two-story, gay-friendly bar with stone walls and colorful beanbags. It has a great atmosphere, the cocktails are good, entertainment options include a pool table, foosball, movies during the day, and live music nightly.

A local expat favorite and a good live music spot that has been around for years is **7 Angelitos** (Siete Angelitos 638, tel. 084/23-6373, 3 P.M.–late daily). Walter, the entertaining owner, prides himself on having some of the best mojitos in town. There are two-for-one happy hours 7:30 P.M.–9:30 P.M. and 11 P.M.–11:30 P.M. just as the bands start playing. If it is late and the door is closed just knock, as it is more than likely the party will still be going on inside.

Above the Plazoleta San Blas, **KMO** (Tandapata 100, tel. 084/23-6009, 3 P.M.–2 A.M. daily), Indigo's sister bar, has been a live music hot spot for years and has happy hour all night.

DISCOTHEQUES

If you still have energy after a pub warmup, there are many places to dance until dawn in Cusco. The Cusco nightclub scene is constantly changing. Clubs open and close monthly and the "in" place has no real criteria. Recently, however, the most frequented dance spot and therefore extremely crowded is **Inkateam** (Portal de Carnes 298, 9 P.M.–6 A.M. daily). Tourists and locals dance to the blasting sounds of techno, reggae, and electro. Happy hour is 9 P.M.–midnight, and there are also free salsa classes every night 9–11 P.M.

Mama África (Portal de Panes 109, 3rd Fl., www.mamaafricaclub.com, 9 P.M.–6 A.M. daily) has been around for a 15 years but is constantly moving and has at various times been the place to go. It still fills up, and every Wednesday at 2 A.M. they have electronic sessions.

Another of Cusco's frequented dance spots is **Roots** (Waynapata 194, 9 P.M.–6 A.M. daily), which also offers salsa classes at 9 P.M. Once you have perfected your salsa moves head to **El Muki** (Santa Catalina 114, 10 P.M.–6 A.M. weekends), the best salsa spot in Cusco, frequented almost exclusively by Cusqueños.

FESTIVALS

Celebrated continuously since the devastating quake of 1650, Cusco's procession of the **Señor de los Temblores** (Lord of the Earthquakes) traditionally begins at Cusco's cathedral on the Monday before Easter.

One of Peru's most enigmatic festivals is **Qoyllur R'itti,** which takes place in May or June before Corpus Christi on the slopes of the Nevado Ausangate at 4,800 meters. During the three-day festival, elaborately costumed men climb in the middle of the night to hew huge blocks of ice, which they carry on their backs down the mountain at dawn. Thousands of campesinos from neighboring communities come to this spot to bring ice down from the mountain or participate in the colorful masked dances. This festival, Christian only on the surface, grew out of the Andean tradition of worshipping mountains, or *apus,* to ensure rains

and good harvests. The pilgrims trek toward the mountain from the town of Tinki, which is several hours away from Cusco on the rough road to Puerto Maldonado. If you are in Cusco during this time, you can find agencies along Plateros in Cusco that sell transport and camping packages.

During Cusco's **Corpus Christi,** which usually happens in early June, elaborate processions fill the streets of Cusco as all the bells in the city ring. Each procession carries a different saint, which is treated as if it were a living person, in the same way the Inca paraded their ancestors' mummies around these same streets five centuries ago.

A country festival that is straightforward for travelers to attend is the June 15–17 festival of the **Virgen del Carmen** in Paucartambo, a pleasant colonial town that is a four-hour bus ride from Cusco on the way to the Manu. The festival includes an extraordinary range of dances and costumes. Many Cusco agencies offer inexpensive lodge-and-transport packages to the festival, which include a dawn trip to Tres Cruces, a fabulous place to watch the sun rise over the Amazon basin.

Cusco's biggest festival is **Inti Raymi,** the Inca celebration of the June 21 winter solstice. The festival, which lasts 10 days on either side of the solstice, was banned by the Spaniards in 1535. But in 1944, a group of Cusco intellectuals re-created the sacred ceremony by studying chronicles and historical documents. Each year, hundreds dress up as Inca priests, nobles, and chosen women, and one man, chosen by audition, gets to be Inca Pachacútec. The main day, June 24, begins at 10 A.M. at the Coricancha (the sun temple) and ends around 2 P.M. at Sacsayhuamán, where thousands of tourists sit on the fort's walls for a good view as Pachacútec speaks with a sun god through a microphone. It is a highly staged, touristy production, completely unlike the more down-to-earth countryside festivals.

Fiestas Patrias, the national Peruvian holiday at the end of July, is one of Peru's most important holidays. The festival honors Peru's independence on July 28 and Peru's armed forces on July 29. A large amount of Peruvians travel in the week that falls around these dates. Hotels, transport, and other services are often booked during this time.

Santuranticuy, on December 24, is one of the largest arts-and-crafts fairs in Peru. Nativity figures, miniature altars, and ceramics are laid out on stalls in the Plaza de Armas by hundreds of artists.

Shopping

Crafts shops are wall-to-wall along Triunfo, which leads from the Plaza de Armas and becomes Rumiyoc and Cuesta San Blas before dead-ending into Plazoleta San Blas, the center of Cusco's bohemian/art district. Several families who have been producing crafts for decades have their workshops here and can often be seen at work.

CERAMICS AND WEAVINGS

The family workshop **Artesania Mendivil** (Plazoleta San Blas 634, 9 A.M.–6 P.M. Mon.–Sat.) is known worldwide for its religious sculptures with long mannerist necks made of plaster cloth, rice paste, and wood. Hilario Mendivil began working as a craftsman at the age of 10 in 1939; though he has passed away, his sons continue the tradition.

World-acclaimed ceramicist Pablo Seminario, whose studio is in Urubamba, has a showroom on the Plaza de Armas. At **Seminario** (Portal de Carnes 244, tel. 084/24-6093, www.ceramicaseminario.com, 9 A.M.–9 P.M. Mon.–Sat., 5–9 P.M. Sun.) there are colonial-style ceramics all designed according to Pablo's unique style.

Another great association run by the altruistic Franco Negri is **Casa Ecológica** (Portal de Carnes 236, interior 2, tel. 084/25-5427, www.casaecologicacusco.com, 9 A.M.–9:30 P.M. daily), which was created to promote sustainable development in rural communities. The shop sells traditional handicrafts produced with natural fibers as well as organic cosmetics and food products.

Another shop whose revenue goes directly to the artists from the communities surrounding Cusco is **Chaska Handicrafts** (Garcilaso 265-1, tel. 084/23-5407, 9 A.M.–1 P.M. and 3–9 P.M. Mon.–Sat.). Just down the road is **Agua y Tierra** (Garcilaso 210, tel. 084/22-6951, 9 A.M.–1 P.M. and 3–9 P.M. Mon.–Sat.), which sells all kinds of jungle handicrafts.

For mainstream touristy products there are crafts markets in Cusco where bargaining is standard procedure. One is right on the Plaza de Armas next to Iglesia de la Compañía (10:30 A.M.–1 P.M. and 3:30–9 P.M. Mon.–Sat., 4–9 P.M. Sun.). A 10-minute walk down Avenida El Sol takes you past many more markets, but the biggest is **Centro Artesanal Cusco** (El Sol and Tullumayo, 8 A.M.–10 P.M. daily).

⟨ The Center for Traditional Textiles of Cusco

The highest-quality textiles for sale in all of Cusco are at The Center for Traditional Textiles of Cusco (Av. El Sol 603, tel. 084/22-8117, www.textilescusco.org, cttc@terra.com.pe, 7 A.M.–8 P.M. Mon.–Sat., 9 A.M.–8 P.M. Sun.). Nilda Callañaupa, a weaver and scholar from Chinchero, set up the center with the admirable goal of recovering ancient technologies, showcasing high-quality weaving, and sending revenue straight back to the remote, neglected villages that produce them. Local weavers give daily demonstrations, and there are displays that explain all the plants, minerals, and berries used for natural dyes. The textiles here are far better than those found elsewhere in Cusco and only slightly more expensive.

ALPACA PRODUCTS, CLOTHING, AND JEWELRY

For the finest alpaca clothing, head to **Kuna,** which has shops all over Cusco. The most central is on the Plaza de Armas (Portal de Panes 127, tel. 084/24-3191, www.kuna.com.pe, 9 A.M.–10 P.M. daily). Another reliable option is **Sol Alpaca** (Plaza Nazarenas 167, tel. 084/23-2687, www.solalpaca.com, 9 A.M.–9 P.M. Mon.–Sat.). For up-market, expensive llama products, including leather, **Casa de la Llama** (Palacio 121, tel. 084/24-0813, 9 A.M.–10 P.M.daily) is good.

Werner & Ana (Plaza San Francisco 295-A, tel. 084/23-1076, www.werner-ana.com, 9:30 A.M.–9 P.M. Mon.–Sat.) is a hip clothing boutique with styles in alpaca and other fine materials.

Hilo (Carmen Alto 260, tel. 084/25-4536, 10 A.M.–1 P.M. and 2–6 P.M. Mon.–Sat.) is a funky little shop with original clothes handmade by self-taught Irish designer Eibhlin Cassidy. Browse through her unique collection of dresses, blouses, and belts while sipping on a cup of tea. For other young new Peruvian designer clothes and jewelry pop into **Pulga** (Carmen Alto 227), **Maracuya** (Tecsecocha 424), or **Claudia Lira** (Choquechaca 162).

There are exclusive jewelry shops all around the Plaza de Armas and up Cuesta San Blas; they mostly sell works of silver. The most well-known and found everywhere is **Ilaria** (Portal Carrizos 258, tel. 084/24-6253, www.ilariainternational.com).

CONTEMPORARY ART AND HANDICRAFTS

Contemporary art can be found in several shops along Triunfo, between the Plaza de Armas and San Blas. **Primitiva** (Hatun Rumiyoc 495, tel. 084/26-0152, www.coscio.com, 10 A.M.–9 P.M. Mon.–Sat.) features the art of Argentine painter Federico Coscio, who captures the landscapes and people around Cusco.

If you are looking for something a little different, **Indigo** (Santa Teresa 317, www.galeriasindigo.com.pe, 9 A.M.–10 P.M. daily) has modern housewares and handicrafts inspired by traditional Andean designs.

There is nothing quite like **Pedazo de Arte**

(Plateros 334-B, tel. 084/24-2967, 9 A.M.–9:30 P.M. daily), a cute shop owned by Japanese artist Miki Suzuki, with unique miniature Peruvian handicrafts.

BOOKSTORES

SBS Bookshop (Av. El Sol 781-A, tel. 084/24-8106, www.sbs.com.pe, 8:30 A.M.–1:30 P.M. and 3:30–7:30 P.M. Mon.–Fri., 8 A.M.–1 P.M. Sat.) is Peru's foremost importer of English books and has a good collection at its small Cusco shop. With choices in English, French, German, Portuguese, Spanish, and Quechua, you'd be hard pressed not to find a book at **CBC La Familia** (Tullumayo 465, tel. 084/23-4073, 10 A.M.–2 P.M. and 4–8 P.M. Mon.–Sat.). Genres include novels, cookbooks, art, and even photography.

The largest book exchange in Cusco can be found at **Libreria Puro Peru** (Heladeros 167, tel. 084/22-1753, librarypuroperu@hotmail.com, 9 A.M.–10 P.M. daily).

If you are nostalgic for a magazine from home you may find it at **Febav Bookstore** (El Sol 106, Galeria La Merced, Stand 109, tel. 084/23-6967).

MUSIC STORES

Director Kike Pinto has collected more than 400 instruments for the **Taki Andean Music Museum** (Hatunrumiyoq 487-5, interior, tel. 084/22-6897, www.takimuseum.org, pinto.kike@gmail.com, 10 A.M.–8 P.M. Mon.–Sat.), some of which are for sale, along with CDs, books, and music lessons.

OUTDOOR AND TRAVEL GEAR

The best shops for getting high-end outdoor apparel and equipment, although expensive, are **Tatoo** (Triunfo 346, tel. 084/22-4797, 10 A.M.–9 P.M. Mon.–Sat., 2–9 P.M. Sun.), **Cordillera** (Garcilaso 210 shop 102, tel. 084/24-4133, 9 A.M.–9:30 P.M. daily), and **The North Face** (Plazoleta Espinar 188, tel. 084/23-2130, 9 A.M.–9 P.M. daily).

Recreation

Along with Huaraz in the Cordillera Blanca, Cusco is Peru's main adventure travel center. The variety of intriguing options and high-quality agencies spur adventurers into Herculean feats of back-to-back sports. One 21-year-old Israeli we met had trekked to Choquequirao, Salcantay, and the Inca Trail, rafted four days down the Class IV **Río Apurímac,** and mountain biked around Maras and Moray above the Sacred Valley. He had just returned from a guided trip down the Río Chilive, just outside the Manu park, where his group floated for 10 days on a homemade balsa raft. He wanted to ride in a hot-air balloon, paraglide over the Sacred Valley, and ride a Peruvian *paso* horse in Urubamba, but by that point he was broke.

For your safety, and for the environment, choose your agency carefully. If you choose to raft a serious river, like the Class IV Apurímac, go with accredited agencies and before departure check the equipment. An average of two tourists a year die on the Apurímac alone, and though not even the best agency can take away all the risk, a new raft, full safety equipment, and most importantly an experienced guide make a big difference.

Fly-by-night agencies, with which Cusco is crawling, offer incredibly cheap prices but usually at the expense of your comfort and safety—and, worst of all, at the expense of the environment. This is especially true on the Inca Trail, where trash and human waste is becoming a serious problem. These low-budget agencies do not tend to follow the principles of sustainable adventure travel, nor do they treat their staff fairly. The porters and cooks are not paid enough, they are not provided with acceptable standards of food and camp accommodation, and they do not receive proper training. Most agencies' websites claim to practice responsible tourism, but these claims are probably unfounded if their prices are low cost.

Dozens of these agencies are closed down

each year once the rangers in the Machu Picchu sanctuary catch on. However, the same agency can open again under a new name, which often mimics the high-quality leaders in the field. The excellent Trek Peru, for instance, is often confused with Peru Trek, Peruvian Trek, Trekking Peru, etc. The courts are so backlogged with copyright cases that rarely do agencies defend their name. So the confusion lingers. Travelers who spend a bit more money to go with reputable agencies are helping to push up the bar of quality for all of Cusco's agencies.

Most of the agencies offer a variety of activities, ranging from mountain biking to rafting, but we have organized them according to their main focus. Amazonas Explorer, for instance, is most famous for its rafting trips but does a good range of trekking, mountain-bike trips, and cultural tours as well.

TREKKING
The Inca Trail is by far the most popular trekking route in the Cusco area because of its spectacular route of ruins and varied ecosystems. But there are other excellent treks in the Cusco area worth considering. Though they do not have the Inca Trail's variety of ruins or the cachet of leading to Machu Picchu, they are less crowded and plunge into remote areas of Andean villages, tumbling jungle, and out-of-the-way archaeological sites. While all hikers on the Inca Trail must go with a licensed agency, the other routes described here can be done independently by those with enough Spanish to ask directions. The best time to trek in the Cusco area is during the dry winter months April–November; the most crowded months on the Inca Trail are June–August.

Make sure your agency is one of those licensed by INRENA, the government conservation agency. A list of approved agencies can be obtained through Iperú. Before scheduling your trip, ask your chosen agency pertinent questions: What is included in the price (e.g., train fares and entry fees), what type of tents and general equipment do they provide, what is the maximum number of trekkers in a group? Also very important is to confirm that your operator is bringing a bathroom tent. The most reputable and responsible agencies do not use the public bathrooms but instead carry PETT toilets, which use organic compounds to break human waste so that it can be packed out of the trail and disposed of properly. Groups are accompanied by porters and there is a legal limit of 20 kilograms (44 pounds) for group gear and 5 kilograms (11 pounds) for personal gear, per porter, which is checked at the beginning of the trail.

Nevado Salcantay, at 6,271 meters, is the sacred mountain that towers above the Inca Trail and eventually drops to Machu Picchu itself. Many agencies offer a four- to five-day trek starting from Mollepata, a town 3.5 hours from Cusco in the Limatambo Valley. If you are trekking on your own it can be reached by any bus heading from Cusco to Abancay. In Mollepata, you can hire mules and local guides. The route traverses part of the Cordillera Vilcabamba, including spectacular views of several snow-covered peaks. It crests the 4,700-meter Salcantayccasa Pass before descending between the stunning glaciers of Humantay and Salcantay. The trek then goes through the lovely Huyracmachaypampa and down through forested slopes to the hot springs at Colpapampa. From here the trail follows the Santa Teresa River to the humid lowlands with the option to trek a little farther to the Inca ruins of Patallacta. From here you descend to the hydroelectric station at Intihuatana, where you can board a train for the short journey to Machu Picchu. The alternative is to walk 2–3 hours along the train track to Aguas Calientes.

Choquequirao is a huge Inca complex perched on a ridge top in the Vilcabamba area that includes many fine Inca walls and double recessed doorways. It was probably built as a winter palace by Inca Túpac Yupanqui, in the same way that his father, Pachacútec, probably built Machu Picchu. It was discovered by

© RENZO UCCELLI, PROMPERU

It's a grueling climb to reach Choquequirao, but it is worth the effort.

Hiram Bingham in 1911, though it was lost again until the 1980s when a series of explorers trudged through this rugged territory to find this and other ruins in the area. The Peruvian government (INC), backed by UNESCO, launched a campaign to restore the ruins, and much of the work has been completed to a very high standard. It is worth spending a full day exploring this site as it has some unique features, such as the wonderful stylized white stone llamas.

The most common approach is from Cachora, where guides and mules can be rented, reached by taking a bus to Abancay and getting off at a road past the Sayhuite Stone. The first day is spent hiking down to the Río Apurímac, and the second continues straight up the other side, a long six-hour slog uphill onto the cloud forest ridge. Some agencies offer a combined 10-day trek that leads from Choquequirao all the way to Machu Picchu. Another option is to reach Choquequirao from Huancacalle, near the Inca ruins of Vitcos, a spectacular eight-day traverse of the Cordillera Vilcabamba.

There are various trekking routes through the **Cordillera Vilcanota,** the range to the east of Cusco that is dominated by the sacred **Nevado Ausangate** (6,384 meters). Trekking guides say that this is one of the more untouched and spectacular areas of Peru.

The classic route is a seven-day loop around the peak of Ausangate, which begins at the town of Tinqui in the high puna grasslands and crosses four passes between 4,300 and 5,500 meters. The views include the fluted faces and rolling glaciers of all the mountains of the range, including Colquecruz and Jampa, and the route passes through remote hamlets of llama herders and weavers. This area is famous for its **Qoyllur R'itti** moveable festival in May or June, when thousands of campesinos converge on the slopes of Ausangate.

The truly adventurous and fit may want to try reaching **Espíritu Pampa,** the true "Lost City of the Inca" that served as the base for the Inca's 35-year rebellion against the Spanish. Gene Savoy's discovery of the ruins in 1964 made world news, and several subsequent expeditions have tried, in vain, to keep the jungle from growing over the immense site.

The trip starts from the village of Huancacalle, which can be reached by taking a truck or bus from Cusco over the Abra Málaga to Quillabamba and hopping off at the Huancacalle turnoff. The Cobos family, which has guided all the Vilcabamba explorers since Gene Savoy, operates a small hostel in Huancacalle and rents mules for US$7 a day. From Huancacalle, a path leads to the Inca ruler's original exile at Vitcos, where Manco Inca was murdered by the Spanish, and the exquisite sacred rock of Chuquipalta (the subject, among others, of Hugh Thomson's book *White Rock*). The path heads to **New Vilcabamba,** a colonial-era mining town, and then ascends a 3,800-meter pass before plunging into the jungle below. The path includes sections of fine Inca staircases along a steep and tortuous

CUSCO

an Andean homestead on the trekking circuit around Ausangate Nevado, in Cusco's Cordillera Vilcanota

© JEFF TREBAC

valley to the ruins, which are in mosquito-ridden rainforest at 1,000 meters. Instead of walking back all the way to Huancacalle, it is possible to walk for a day or two alongside the river on good paths until you reach the town of Kiteni on the Río Urubamba. From here, a bus goes back to Quillabamba. This trip takes 7–10 days.

Trekking Agencies

Peruvian Andean Treks, ExplorAndes, and Tambo Treks are the longest established trekking companies in Cusco; they pioneered the contemporary trekking culture. We recommend them, not only for their unsurpassed experience and professionalism, but also because they consistently recycle their trash, pack out all human waste, treat water carefully, and pay porters fair wages. Over the last three decades, these operators have developed ties with a number of Quechua communities in the Cusco area, where they are embarking on a new brand of participatory cultural activities such as harvesting potatoes, building adobe homes, and even herding llamas.

Trekking prices vary greatly based on the season, the number of people in the group, the length of the trek, the trek itself, and other factors. Because of licensing requirements the four-night Machu Picchu trek now costs US$1,500, though most agencies charge US$500–600 for group bookings. The shorter two-day Inca Trail is around $200–250 for group bookings. The alternative five-day Salcantay Trek to Machu Picchu is in the US$300–850 range, though most operators offer group Salcantay treks for around US$500. Other treks in the Cusco area, such as in the Lares Valley, generally run about US$100 per day. Be careful to ask your agency whether the price includes all entry fees (an important consideration for Salcantay in particular).

Peruvian Andean Treks (Pardo 705, tel. 084/22-5701, www.andeantreks.com) is owned by American and long-time Cusco resident Tom Hendrickson. It operates on the Inca Trail and runs treks through jungle areas and the Lares Valley in the Cordillera. It is also the best

option for climbing expeditions in the snow-covered peaks around Cusco. This company was voted Cusco's best tour operator in 2006.

ExplorAndes (Av. Garcilaso 316-A, tel. 084/23-8380 or Lima tel. 01/715-2323, www.explorandes.com) is Peru's most established adventure sports agency. It offers the traditional Inca Trail hike, as well as variations that combine it with treks above the Sacred Valley or around Nevado Salcantay and Nevado Ausangate. Kayaking on Lake Titicaca, rafting down the Tambopata or Apurímac, and llama-supported treks around the Cordillera Blanca and Huayhuash near Huaraz are also offered. Recently it has operated a variety of special-interest tours around Peru, focusing on orchids, potatoes and maize, camelids, ceramics, cacti, textiles, coca, and other medicinal plants. ExplorAndes was voted Peru's best overall tour operator by the Ministry of Tourism in 2005.

Tambo Treks (Casilla 912, tel. 084/23-7718, www.tambotreks.net) is owned by Andreas Holland and has been operating for over 30 years. It offers diverse treks and tours with tailor-made itineraries (six people minimum), which accommodate group specifications and a wide range of special interests. The staff are very knowledgeable, and since its foundation Tambo Treks has had a profound commitment to helping local communities. Most importantly, however, the welfare of all their staff has always been a priority, as has working in an ecologically sustainable and responsible manner. Tambo Treks' sister company, Tambo Film (www.tambofilm.com), specializes in outfitting film and television productions throughout Peru.

Two long-standing, reputable and very professional trekking agencies are Auqui Mountain Spirit and Ecoinka.

Auqui Mountain Spirit (José Gabriel 307, Urb. Magisterial, tel. 084/26-1517, www.auqui.com.pe), run by Roger Valencia, has been operating for over 20 years. This high-end agency has a very experienced team and specializes in customized trips, especially for corporate clients.

© GABRIELLA HOLLAND

trekking camp high in the Andes

Ecoinka (Saphy 456, tel. 084/22-4050, www.ecoinka.com) was founded by Ricky Schiller, who has been involved in the tourism industry for over 30 years. The expert staff provide excellent service.

Among the more than 150 licensed agencies operating in Cusco, the standard of service and social and environmental responsibilities vary greatly. It is up to the client to be discerning and to research thoroughly before booking. The agencies listed here are all recommended.

Perú Sur Nativa (Magisterio 2da Etapa K-7-302, tel. 084/22-4156, www.perusurnativa.com) is owned by long-time Cusco adventurer extraordinaire Raúl Montes. Montes has a real eye for adventure and an unflappable sense of humor (we confirmed this after spending two weeks with him on a balsa raft in the Manu jungle eating only green bananas and red-bellied piraña!). Perú Sur Nativa also runs trips in other parts of South America as well as nearby Choquequirao, Carabaya, Vilcabamba, and to the Manu rainforest.

Enigma (Clorinda Matto de Turner 100, tel. 084/22-2155, www.enigmaperu.com) is one of the newer agencies; it has gourmet cooks. It offers Inca Trail treks combined with Nevado Salcantay, Vilcabamba, and the ruins of Choquequirao. Alternative adventures include horseback riding, ayahuasca therapy, and bird-watching.

Inca Explorers (Ruinas 427, tel. 084/24-1070, www.incaexplorers.com) has a range of longer trips to Vilcabamba, Choquequirao, and the Cordillera Vilcanota, as well as participative tourism such as weaving, farming, and traditional healing.

Q'ente (Choquechaca 229, tel. 084/22-2535, www.qente.com) has been running since 1995 and provides a good service and trained staff.

The following Inca Trail operators are at the bottom of the price range but have been reported to be environmentally responsible.

United Mice (Plateros 351, tel. 084/22-1139, www.unitedmice.com) is probably the most recommended backpacker's choice. It also offers a seven-day Salcantay trek.

Peru Treks & Adventure (Garcilaso 265, Of. 11, 2nd Fl., tel. 084/50-5863, www.perutreks.com) is also responsible for the very informative website Andean Travel Web (www.andeantravelweb.com).

Andina Travel (Santa Catalina 219, tel. 084/25-1892, www.andinatravel.com) offers frequent departures for the Inca Trail and interesting sociocultural projects.

RAFTING AND KAYAKING

There are many excellent rafting and kayaking options around Cusco. The easiest, and most common, are day trips along the Class III rapids of the Río Urubamba in the Sacred Valley (US$40–55). They often include one night of camping near Ollantaytambo, mountain biking, and a chance to see ruins the next day. December–May, when the river is swollen, agencies tend to raft the upper section above Pisac. When the water drops after June, they run the section of the river lower down between Ollantaytambo and Chilca. Farther downstream, the water rushes onward to Machu Picchu in great cataracts of unnavigable, Class VI water.

CUSCO

© CYNTHIA BEAMS

Rafting on the Río Apurímac or the Río Urubamba is an excellent day trip from Cusco.

Another day option is the easier stretch of the Río Apurímac below the Cusco–Abancay highway, a gentle stretch that passes the foundations of an Inca hanging bridge made famous by Thornton Wilder in his classic *The Bridge of San Luis Rey*. The Apurímac here is generally sunny and subtropical, so bring sunscreen, a hat, mosquito repellent, and swimwear because a quick dip in local hot springs is often included.

A popular three-day rafting trip is on the upper Apurímac (US$400–650), which can only be run between June and October. The Apurímac plunges through a steep and wild gorge and an endless series of Class III–V rapids. Agencies that operate this section of the river usually also offer trips on Cotahuasi (US$1,950 approximately), a similar though more exacting canyon near Arequipa that takes 10 days to navigate in a full-scale, supported expedition.

Our vote for most spectacular rafting expedition, though, goes to the Río Tambopata (US$1,500–2,500), which is a great way to combine a mountain rafting adventure with world-class Amazon biodiversity. This 10- to 12-day trip begins in cloud forest north of Lake Titicaca with a few days of Class III–V rapids and ends floating on torpid jungle waters through the pristine Parque Nacional Bahuajua Sonene. Participants usually stay at the Tambopata Research Center, a rustic lodge operated by Rainforest Expeditions that is minutes from the world's largest macaw clay lick. Floating silently through this untouched rainforest provides a good opportunity to spot a jaguar or tapir and a huge range of birds and more common animals such as capybara, turtles, and giant otters. The trip includes a flight back to Cusco from the jungle city of Puerto Maldonado.

If you want to go kayaking instead of rafting, agencies will often loan you a kayak on the easier rivers such as the Urubamba and lower Apurímac. Some agencies, such as Erik's Adventures, offer kayaking schools.

Rafting and Kayaking Agencies

Like trekking prices, rafting rates vary greatly based on the season, the number of people in the group, the difficulty of the rapids, and the section of the river. Prices for a daylong rafting trip on the Urubamba River are typically US$25–100 per person per day, including lunch. For the four-day Apurímac River trip, which includes Class III–IV rapids, prices are typically US$300–1,100. Most operators, however, charge US$500–600.

One of the most professional rafting companies in Peru is **Amazonas Explorer** (Collasuyo 910, Urb. Miravalle, tel. 084/25-2846, www.amazonas-explorer.com). It runs a variety of innovative trips in Peru, Chile, and Bolivia, including canoeing, mountain biking, trekking, and rafting. One of the best trips is a 16-day expedition that begins with sightseeing in Cusco and Lake Titicaca and ends in rafting down the Río Tambopata and two nights at the Tambopata Research Center.

ExplorAndes (Av. Garcilaso 316-A, tel. 084/23-8380 or Lima tel. 01/715-2323, www.explorandes.com) also offers high-end rafting trips.

The following are less expensive but also experienced agencies. They are recommended for easier trips. **Apumayo Expediciones** (Jr. Ricardo Palma N-5, Santa Monica, tel. 084/24-6018, www.apumayo.com) is run by Pepe López, a kayaker with a lot of experience on Peru's rivers. He recently built an adventure center on the banks of the Río Urubamba, downstream of Ollantaytambo. The center, which shares profits with the nearby community of Cachiccata, offers hikes and mountain biking for the rafters who arrive here after descending the Río Urubamba. Apumayo runs trips down the Apurímac, Tambopata, and Cotahuasi and offers reforestation cultural treks and the classic Inca Trail.

Mayuc (Portal Confituras 211, Plaza de Armas, tel. 084/24-2824, www.mayuc.com) is one of the pioneering rafting companies and operates an excellent day trip on Río Urubamba. It also does rafting trips on the Apurímac and in Tambopata.

Loreto Tours (Calle del Medio 111, tel. 084/22-8264, loretotours@planet.com.pe)

provides varied rafting itineraries and good quality equipment.

Terra Explorer Peru (Santa Ursula D-4, Huanchac, tel. 084/23-7352, www.terraexplorerperu.com) is owned by Piero, the youngest of the Vellutino brothers, all dedicated and well known adventure sportsmen and white-water rafters. Terra Explorer offers all kinds of rafting trips including Cotahuasi and Tambopata, mountain treks, and mountain biking. **Munaycha** (based in the Sacred Valley, tel. 084/984-77-0108 or 084/984770381, www.munaycha.com) belongs to Duilio, the oldest Vellutino brother, and also offers rafting on Peru's best known rivers as well as sea kayaking trips off the coast of Arequipa and on Lake Huyñaymarca, a rarely visited part of the Titicaca.

MOUNTAIN CLIMBING

Cusco is surrounded by majestic snow-covered peaks that offer outstanding mountaineering possibilities, though none should be tried by people without mountaineering experience—even with a good guide. Unlike many of the mountains in the Cordillera Blanca, these Andean routes are steep, icy, and complicated. Avalanches are common, especially on Salcantay. Several international climbing agencies operate in Peru.

Mountain Climbing Agencies

Licensed mountain guides in Peru, working on an independent basis, will charge US$100–150 per day. An agency that arranges a technical climb will generally charge twice or three times that rate on a daily basis. For climbing in Cusco, it's a good idea to inquire with agencies in Huaraz, Peru's climbing headquarters. Huaraz agencies are often able to lead climbing trips all over the country.

The best local mountaineering agency is **Peruvian Andean Treks** (Pardo 705, tel. 084/22-5701, www.andeantreks.com), owned by climber Tom Hendrickson. A highly recommended guide in Cusco is **Américo Serrano** (tel. 084/24-7299). Serrano has all the international climbing certifications and is one of the instructors who trains new Peruvian mountain guides in the Cordillera Blanca. In 2003, he assisted Lonnie Thompson, an internationally known glaciologist from Ohio State University, in an expedition to measure glacial recession in Peru's southern Andes.

There are six other internationally certified guides working in Peru. The best way to reach them is through **Camp Expedition** (Triunfo 392, of. 202, tel. 084/43-9859, www.campexpedition.net), which leads rappelling, climbing, and canyoneering adventures in the Cusco area.

BIKING

Nearly all of the rafting and kayaking agencies do bike tours and rent bikes. A highly recommended company is **Loreto Tours** (Calle del Medio 111, tel. 084/22-8264, loretotours@planet.com.pe, US$100 per day for guided tours). Peru's best-known mountain biker, Omar Zarzar Casis (omarzarzar@aventurarse.com), has written a book describing routes in Cusco and across the country. He is a good English-speaking contact for those planning a major ride in the area. **Gravity Assisted Mountain Biking** (Santa Catalina Ancha 398, tel. 084/22-8032, www.gravityperu.com, US$100 per day for guided tours) has great equipment and experienced guides for adventure mountain-biking tours.

Many of the Manu tour operators give clients the option to bike partway down the magnificent dirt-road descent from Acanaju Pass at 3,800 meters into the jungle. This route, which also passes through Pisac and Paucartambo provides a stunning glimpse of more than a dozen ecosystems.

Many agencies also offer mountain-biking in the Sacred Valley, especially on the Chinchero plateau around Moray and Maras, with a final descent past the salt mines (Salineras) to Urubamba. The Abra Málaga (4,600 meters), which lies along the highway between Ollantaytambo and Quillabamba, is another of Peru's spectacular mountain-to-jungle descents. This trip is now part of a bus/biking/walking alternative to the Inca Trail, which takes you past the pristine Colcamayo hot springs in Santa Teresa, from where you can either walk or catch the train to Machu Picchu.

BIRD-WATCHING

The Cusco area has one of the world's highest areas of bird biodiversity, particularly where the high Andes meet the Amazon rainforest. Particularly rich environments are the Abra Málaga (4,200 meters) area, en route to Quillabamba, and the Acanaju Pass (3,800 meters), en route to Parque Nacional Manu. Barry Walker, owner of Manu Expeditions and author of *A Field Guide to the Birds of Machu Picchu, Peru,* leads excellent birding. Barry can be reached through **Manu Expeditions** (Pardo 895, tel. 084/22-6671, birding@manuexpeditions.com, www.birdinginperu.com, US$250 per day for guided tours with more than six people).

The high-quality **InkaNatura** (Ricardo Palma J1, Urb. Santa Monica, tel. 084/25-5255, www.inkanatura.com, US$275 per day for guided tours with more than six people) and **Gran Peru** (www.granperu.com, US$175 per day for guided tours with more than six people) also run birding trips throughout the country. Leo Oblitas is an excellent birding guide and works for some of the leading bird-watching agencies.

HORSEBACK RIDING

Adventure Specialists (U.S. tel. 719/783-2076, www.adventurespecialists.org, prices vary, call ahead) leads highly recommended, custom horse-packing trips all over Peru and especially in the Cusco area. Founder and co-owner Gary Ziegler is a true adventurer, archaeologist, and noted Inca expert.

Manu Expeditions (Pardo 895, tel. 084/22-6671, www.manu-expeditions.com, prices vary, call ahead) offers a range of horse-riding expeditions that explore areas of the Vilcabamba and Choquequirao (17 days), as well as Machu Picchu and the surrounding cloud forest (15 days). Another of its itineraries is from the Andes to the Amazon (14 days). One- and two-day rides around Cusco are also offered.

The best options for riding Peruvian *paso* horses is **Wayra** (part of the Sol y Luna Hotel outside Urubamba, tel. 084/20-1620, info@wayrasacredvalley.com, www.wayrasacredvalley.com, US$195 per day) and **Perol Chico** (Carretera Urubamba–Ollantaytambo, tel. 084/974-79-8890, www.perolchico.com, prices vary, call ahead).

EXTREME SPORTS

A wacky adventure opportunity is **Action Valley** (Santa Teresa 352, tel. 084/24-0835, www.actionvalley.com, US$64 bungee jump, US$20 paint ball). This park, 11 kilometers from Cusco on the road to Chinchero, has a 107-meter bungee drop, a catapult that throws people 120 meters into the air with 3.2 g's of force, a 36-meter climbing pole, a 124-meter rappel wall, and a 10-meter climbing wall.

There are some beautiful paragliding spots in the Cusco area. **Leo Paragliding School** (Triunfo 392, of. 202, tel. 084/23-9477, www.cusco.net/leo-paragliding, US$75 pp) offers tandem flights as well as paragliding training courses. Another recommendable option for tandem paragliding flights over the Sacred Valley is **Viento Sur,** run by the European owners of Sol y Luna Hotel in Urubamba (tel. 084/20-1620, www.hotelsolyluna.com, US$195 pp).

Via Ferrata (tel. 084/984-11-2731, www.naturavive.com, US$45 pp, family rates available) is a 300-meter rock face located in Pacha between Urubamba and Ollantaytambo. It is equipped with wire cables and footholds to allow people with no previous experience to enjoy the adrenaline rush of rock with all the necessary safety equipment.

ESOTERIC EXPERIENCES

Cusco is a center for a range of spiritual and esoteric activities, though the main operators seem to change constantly. A good touchstone and longtime expert is José (Pepe) Altamirano, the owner of the agency **Gatur** (Puluchapata 140, tel. 084/22-3496 or 084/22-7829, www.gaturcusco.com, prices vary, call ahead). Tourists are shown traditional practices by native healers with **Back2Nature** (www.back2nature.no, prices vary, call ahead), owned by Norwegian Irene Kingswick and Peruvian Dennis Alejo.

Many Cusco agencies, including **Enigma,** offer sessions with the ayahuasca hallucinogen. Leslie Myburgh at **Another Planet** (Triunfo 120, tel. 084/22-9379, www.anotherplanet-peru.net, prices vary, call ahead) and Diane Dunn at **Paz y Luz** (tel. 084/20-3204, www.pazyluzperu.com, prices vary, call ahead) in Pisac are other good contacts for ayahuasca and San Pedro ceremonies.

SIGHTSEEING TOURS

There is fierce competition, along with frequent price wars, between Cusco's agencies for general sightseeing tours. Most of the agencies are clustered around the Plaza de Armas and offer competitive prices. There are also luxury tours.

The most popular tours include a half-day city tour and the full-day tour of the Sacred Valley, which includes Pisac market, lunch in Urubamba, Ollantaytambo, and sometimes Chinchero as well. There is also a half-day tour of the ruins outside of Cusco, which include Sacsayhuamán, Q'enqo, Puca Pucara, and Tambomachay. Another half-day tour explores the ruins heading toward Puno, including the magnificent church in Andahuaylillas, Pikillacta, and Tipón.

Several agencies in Cusco cater to groups and also reserve tickets and provide tours for independent travelers. **Condor Travel** (Saphy 848, tel. 084/24-8181, www.condortravel.com, US$35 daylong group tour) is one of the most established and professional operators of traditional tourism.

Gatur (Puluchapata 140, tel. 084/22-3496 or 084/22-7829, www.gaturcusco.com, US$35 daylong group tour) is operated by José Altamirano, one of the most respected authorities on local history.

Orellana Tours (Garcilaso 206, tel. 084/26-3455, orellanatours@terra.com.pe, US$20 daylong group tour) is an inexpensive agency with a good reputation. **Milla Turismo** (Pardo 689, tel. 084/23-1710, www.millaturismo.com, US$32 daylong group tour) is well established and very professional.

Americana de Turismo (Garcilaso 265, tel. 084/24-0999, www.americanadeturismo.net, US$28 daylong group tour) provides excellent sightseeing itineraries.

Attraction (Av. Baja 145, tel. 084/23-2143, www.attraction-voyages.com, price vary, call ahead) is a French-run agency whose main focus is luxury travel. The high-end company offers alternative options for seeing the traditional sites—for example, chauffeur-driven four-wheel drive trips to Lares and special interest travel (photography tours with internationally acclaimed photographer Carlos Nishyama and culinary tours with renowned chefs).

Franco Negri, owner of **Casa Ecológica** (Portal de Carnes 236, interior 2, tel. 084/25-5427, www.casaecologicacusco.com, US$85 per day, prices may vary depending on trip), also runs interesting and innovative community day trips such as visiting an organic farming association in Lamay and using traditional Andean agricultural tools. The day ends with a meal prepared using local ingredients. There are also weaving trips to the community of Amaru, where you can observe and partake in all processes of ancient weaving. The visits directly benefit the people from the communities and indirectly the conservation of their environment and traditional arts and techniques.

JUNGLE TRIPS

Many people who visit Cusco do not realize how close they are to the Amazon jungle. An half-hour plane ride and a few hours in a boat take you to a comfy lodge in Puerto Maldonado, with outstanding opportunities for seeing birds, mammals, and insects. A longer trip to Parque Nacional Manu offers a chance to see a greater variety of animals, especially predators such as the black caiman and the jaguar.

Accommodations

Our favorite neighborhood in all of Cusco is San Blas, the bohemian district above the Plaza de Armas that is crisscrossed with narrow alleys and teeming with cozy hostels, artisan galleries, and some of Cusco's best bars. San Blas has a relaxing, artsy vibe, and its narrow streets keep out the traffic and smog of central Cusco.

Traffic has made parts of Cusco unpleasant. These areas include the extension of Plateros and Avenida El Sol, where even the back rooms of hotels hum with the noise of taxis and amplified advertisements. Outside of San Blas, Cusco's nicest lodging is along out-of-the-way streets like Suecia, Choquechaca, or Siete Cuartones/Nueva Alta, where classy bed-and-breakfasts are lined up along charming cobblestone streets. Always make a reservation ahead of time in Cusco, and ask for the kind of room you want (e.g., with a view or double bed). Despite a steady increase in Cusco hotels, the best ones are increasingly booked solid May–November. If you arrive and don't like your room, you can usually wriggle out of your reservation after your first night and head elsewhere—there are lots of good options, especially among the newer, lesser-known hostels. It is best not to judge a hotel, especially the more economic accommodations, by the bedding, bathroom tiles, and decor in general.

UNDER US$10

For budget accommodations backpacker hostels are a good option, and there are now quite a few in Cusco. The most popular are **The Point** (Meson de la Estrella 172, tel. 084/25-2266, www.thepointhostels.com, US$8–11 dorm, US$12–15 d) and **LOKI Inkahouse** (Cuesta Santa Ana 601, tel. 084/24-3705, www.lokihostel.com, US$8–11 dorm, US$27 d private bath). Both have locations in Lima and Máncora, dorm rooms (and a few private rooms) that open onto TV rooms, Internet stations, shared kitchens, and bars. They have a reputation for their parties and you are bound to meet other travelers.

Youth Hostal Albergue Municipal (Quiscapata 240, San Cristóbal, tel. 084/25-2506, albergue@municusco.gob.pe, US$5 dorm, US$7 d), part of Hostelling International, has great views from the balcony, clean bunk rooms, and a shared kitchen. A discount is given to youth hostel members.

Pirwa Backpackers (Portal de Panes 151, tel. 084/24-4315, www.pirwahostelscusco.com, US$7.50–10 dorm, US$12.50 d) has four central locations: the Plaza de Armas, Suecia, San Blas, and San Francisco. They all have a variety of dorms and private rooms, most with shared kitchen, common rooms, and a tour/travel desk. **Samay Wasi** (Atocsaycuhi 416, tel. 084/25-3108, Siete Angelitos 675, tel. 084/23-6649, www.samaywasiperu.com, US$7–9 dorm, US$20 d) has two great locations in San Blas. Both offer shared and double rooms and nice gardens. At Siete Angelitos ask about their star room famous for its views.

Probably the best value for money is **Inti Quilla** (Atocsaycuhi 281, tel. 084/25-2659, www.intiquilla.8m.com, US$7 d shared bath, US$9 d private bath, breakfast not included). Also in San Blas, this very basic but clean hostel has two triple rooms and five double rooms around a nice, sunny courtyard. Some rooms have private bathrooms and there is 24-hour hot water. **El Balcón Colonial** (Choquechaca 350, tel. 084/23-8129, balconcolonial@hotmail.com, US$7 s, US$14 d) is a bed-and-breakfast with five clean rooms with firm beds. One has a private bath, and there's a small shared kitchen with breakfast tables, a computer with Internet, and a very friendly and accommodating owner.

US$10-25

The standout feature at **Hostal Resbalosa** (Resbalosa 494, tel. 084/22-4839, www.hostalresbalosa.com, US$16 d shared bath, US$22 d private bath) is the sweeping view over the city from various sunny terraces and common

rooms. The front rooms are older and noisier than the others, but all have hot water and cable TV. Prices are negotiable.

For a location one block from the Plaza de Armas, try **Hostal Rojas** (Tigre 129, tel. 084/22-8184, US$14 d shared bath, US$24 d with private bath), with clean, carpeted rooms around a sunny courtyard.

The charming **Sihuar** (Tandapata 351, tel. 084/22-7435, casasihuar@hotmail.com, US$25 d) is a two-level building that looks out over a nice patio and garden. The rooms are very pleasant and more tastefully decorated than most, with wood floors and woven rugs and gas-heated hot water. Sihuar is great value.

Also in San Blas but a little higher up is the Belgian/Peruvian-run **Hostal Sweet Daybreak** (Pasñapakana 133, tel. 084/22-5776, www.hostalsweetdaybreak.com, US$12 per person, US$24 d private bath, breakfast not included). This cute, family-owned hotel has a variety of rooms ranging from a six-bed dorm with shared bath to double rooms with private baths. Prices are negotiable, especially for groups. It has amazing panoramic views of the city, a lovely garden with rustic wooden tables, free WiFi, cable TV, and hot water 24 hours.

The newly inaugurated **Puca Ventana Hostel** (San Cristobal 109, tel. 084/24-3673, US$25 d) is a small, eight-room hostel all with private bathrooms, WiFi, cable TV, and breakfast. It has a simple rustic feel, a nice living room with great views of the city, and a very friendly atmosphere.

US$25-50

◖ Niños Hotel (Meloq 442, tel. 084/23-1424, www.ninoshotel.com, US$40 s or d) is a remarkable place with a cause. Its Dutch owner uses hotel revenue to feed, clothe, and provide medical assistance to needy street boys. And as if that isn't enough reason to stay here, just four blocks from the Plaza de Armas, the restored colonial home of Niños Hotel is absolutely lovely. With large, stylish rooms, hardwood floors, and a pleasant courtyard for taking breakfast, it's easy to make yourself at home. There is a second location at Fierro

476 (tel. 084/23-1424) and a Niños Hotel Hacienda in Huasao.

Just one block from the Plaza de Armas, **Hostal San Isidro Labrador** (Saphy 440, tel. 084/22-6241, labrador@qnet.com.pe, US$35 s, US$45 d) is a simple and elegant place with a handful of rooms, each with its own charm. It is right next to the police station and thus is one of the safer locations in Cusco. This hotel is operated by the Lambarri family, who also run the exclusive Huayoccari Hacienda Restaurant in Yucay.

In the center of San Blas are **Casa de la Gringa** (Tandapata 148) and **Casa de la Gringa II** (Carmen Bajo). The houses (tel. 084/24-1168, www.casadelagringa.com, US$28–31 d), owned by Lesley Myburgh, are recommended for their colorful rooms, friendly staff, and small gardens. There is a New Age, spiritual air about the place, and the dedication to such matters, including the imbibing of San Pedro and ayahuasca, is very sincere.

A lovely place in Tandapata is **《 Casona les Pleiades** (Tandapata 116, tel. 084/50-6430, www.casona-pleiades.com, US$50 d). Whether it be Melanie or Philip who opens the door for you, the welcome is bound to be warm and friendly. This young French couple have made their seven-room home into a guesthouse, and their aim is to make you feel right at home. That's why there are down comforters on the beds and eggs made to order for breakfast.

In lower San Blas, one of the nicer hotels in Cusco is **《 Amaru Hostal** (Cuesta San Blas 541, tel. 084/22-5933, www.cusco.net/amaru, US$33 s, US$43 d). The 27 rooms, with balconies, are spread around two sun-filled patios overflowing with geraniums and roses. The rooms have comfy beds and wood floors, and are small but nice. Rooms here vary dramatically—ask for the corner rooms with sun porches, wicker furniture, and vistas on both sides. For those on a budget there are cheaper rooms with shared bathrooms. The hostel has two more locations in San Blas at Chihuampata 642 (tel. 084/22-3521) and the private Hosteria Anita at Alavado 525 (tel. 084/22-5499).

The very sweet and good value European/ Peruvian hotel **Madre Tierra** (Atocsaycuchi 647-A, tel. 084/25-7358, www.hostalmadre-tierra.com, US$49 d) has seven comfortable carpeted rooms and cozy and inviting communal areas with white sofas, exposed beams, and open fireplaces.

Just down the street is **El Grial** (Carmen Alto 112, tel. 084/22-3012, www.hotelelgrial.com, US$30 s, US$45 d), a small, friendly hostel with basic but comfortable rooms and a sunny, pleasant dining area for breakfast. The **South American Spanish School** is right next door and run by the same owners.

The best value accommodation in San Blas and a great alternative to hotels is **《 Saya Wasi Apart Hotel** (Kiskapta 1000, San Blas, tel. 084/25-4160, www.sayawasi.com, US$25 pp). These three sunny, comfortable, and tastefully decorated self-catering apartments include a lounge area with cable TV, kitchenette, bathroom, and floor-to-ceiling windows with incredible views. There is also a lovely communal terrace with even more spectacular panoramic views of the entire city.

US$50-100

《 Hostal El Balcon (Tambo de Montero 222, tel. 084/23-6738, www.balconcusco.com, US$55 s, US$69 d) is a lovely restored colonial house with rustic charm and a pretty, flower-filled garden. This 16-room hostel is quaint and homely, and rooms are decorated simply with weavings on the beds.

Charming, German-owned **《 Pensión Alemana Bed and Breakfast** (Tandapata 260, tel. 084/22-6861, www.cuzco-stay.de, US$55 d) is the closest thing to a European pension in Cusco. There are 12 light and airy rooms, many with incredible views over the city, very comfortable beds, and great showers. A pleasant garden looks out over the red-tiled roofs of the city, and a nightly fire crackles in the dining room.

The unpretentious **Hostal Corihuasi** (Suecia 561, tel. 084/23-2233, www.corihuasi.com, US$44 s, US$55 d) is a quick, steep walk up from the Plaza de Armas and has old-world charm that befits Cusco. The rooms of this rambling, eclectic colonial house are connected by verandas and walkways. Some of the rooms are nicer with views over the city; others are dark, with porthole windows.

In Santiago, one of Cusco's oldest neighborhoods, is the charming ◖ **Panza del Artista** (Calle Jorge Ochoa 215 interior, tel. 084/26-2610, www.panzadelartista.com, US$40 s, US$60 d). The seven rooms, some with sweeping views of the center of Cusco from their balconies, are spacious and open with natural light. The terraced gardens are perched above the bustling city and provide respite with all-day sun, lush local plants, and a variety of birds. Owners Adam L. Weintraub (who has a good new photography book on the Cusco region called *Vista Andina*) and Xiomara Romero win over guests with their extended Cusqueñan family. Guests can sit for hours in the family kitchen, a welcome respite from the touristy center. The hotel is about a 10-minute walk from downtown, near the San Pedro market.

MamaSara Hotel (Saphy 875, tel. 084/24-5409, www.mamasarahotel.com, US$70 s, US$85 d) is very pleasant and comfortable. The rooms are heated, spacious, and immaculate and come with flat-screen TVs, good showers, and oxygen on request.

Encantada (Tandapata 354, tel. 084/24-2206, www.encantadaperu.com, US$70 s, US$90 d) is a pleasant new hotel in a modern building with great views. The minimalist decor and white comforters are a breath of fresh air. The hotel also doubles as a massage and spa center, and there are special packages: one night's accommodation with two hours of Jacuzzi and massage costs US$150. The owners also have **A Mi Manera,** a nice restaurant on Triunfo, and a recommendable tour agency— **Culturas Peru** (www.culturasperu.com).

An impressive, original Inca doorway, once the entrance to a sacred place, is now the way into the hotel **Rumi Punku** (Choquechaca 339, tel. 084/22-1102, www.rumipunku.com, US$70 s, US$90 d). Light-filled terraces, a garden with an original Inca wall, and a gym and spa make this a pleasant place to stay. The rooms have all the necessary amenities and the staff are friendly and helpful.

US$100-150

The national and reliable hotel chain ◖ **Casa Andina** (www.casa-andina.com) has three of its "classic" hotels at ideal locations in the center of Cusco. Two are within one block of the Plaza de Armas (Santa Catalina Angosta 149, tel. 084/23-3661, cac-catedral@casa-andina.com, and Portal Espinar 142, tel. 084/23-1733, cac-cuscoplaza@casa-andina.com, US$125 d), and one is near Coricancha (San Agustín 371, tel. 084/25-2633, cac-koricancha@casa-andina.com, US$125 d). These well-designed, comfortable hotels provide excellent service. The aim of the hotels is to reflect the local character of a place and give a genuine experience using local ideology and using local products where possible without sacrificing comfort and convenience. All rooms have down comforters, heating, and cable TV, and a generous breakfast buffet is included.

Guests are greeted by tuxedo-wearing doormen at the upscale, Swiss-managed **Los Apus** (Atocsaycuchi 515, tel. 084/26-4243, www.losapushotel.com, US$89 s, US$109 d). The rooms have wood floors, heating, comfortable beds, and cable TV. Breakfast is served in a nice glass-roofed courtyard.

The **Hotel Arqueologo** (Pumacurco 408, tel. 084/23-2569, www.hotelarqueologo.com, US$120 d standard, US$140 d superior) occupies an old colonial building. Rooms with high ceilings wrap around a rustic stone courtyard or overlook a grassy garden. The hotel tries to maintain a eco-friendly philosophy by having its own bio-veggie garden, recycling rubbish, providing a fountain with drinking water to refill bottles, and only providing TVs in rooms upon request. The first-floor café **Song Thé** has comfortable sofas, a fireplace, and French pastries.

The attractive boutique hotel **Casa San Blas** (Tocuyeros 566, tel. 084/23-7900, www.casasanblas.com, US$110 d, US$156 suite) prides itself on giving a personalized service. It is ideally located, set back off the Cuesta

CUSCO

San Blas, and has great views of the city from its sunny roof terrace. Rooms are comfortable, have all the necessary amenities, and are decorated simply with traditional weavings on the walls. There are also self-catering suite apartments with kitchenettes. Sustainability issues are addressed by giving guests the option to reuse bedding and towels and re-fill water bottles, light bulbs are energy-saving, and there are double curtains to reduce the need for heating.

As the name suggests, **《 Second Home Cusco** (Atocsaycuchi 616, tel. 084/23-5873, www.secondhomecusco.com, US$110 s, 120 d) in San Blas really is a home away from home. This highly recommended bed-and-breakfast, owned by artist Carlos Delfin, son of the famous sculptor Victor Delfin, has three very simple but nicely decorated, light-filled junior suites: the skylight suite, the patio suite, and the balcony suite. Each has its own special charm. There is another great Second Home located in Lima.

US$150-250

The finest of the Casa Andina Classic collection hotels is the **《 Casa Andina San Blas** (Chihuampata 278, tel. 084/26-3694, cac-sanblas@casa-andina.com, US$156 d standard, US$192 d superior), built around a colonial stone courtyard with some of the best views of Cusco's rooftops and mountains. The cozy sitting areas with wood-burning fires, the rustic bar, and the lovely terrace make this a great place to escape and relax. It has all attributes expected from Casa Andina and more. If you are after an even more luxurious Casa Andina experience you will find it at the **《 Casa Andina Private Collection** (Plazoleta Limacpampa Chico 473, tel. 084/23-2610, capc-cusco@casa-andina.com US$241 d standard, US$373 suite). Located in a beautiful 18th-century manor house, the hotel centers around three majestic interior patios. The sitting room with its plush red couches is the ideal place to unwind with a pisco sour. There is a nice gourmet restaurant that spills onto the main patio, where you can dine to the pleasant gurgling of the pretty fountain. The extensive and delicious breakfast buffet includes local, hearty dishes, as well as the standard breakfast fare, which will keep you going for most of the day.

The sophisticated **Novotel** (San Agustín 239, tel. 084/58-1030, www.novotel.com, US$240 d modern room, US$320 d colonial room) is in a restored colonial manor that has a delightful patio lined with stone arches, lamps, and wicker furniture for evening drinks. Undoubtedly the best rooms are those on the second floor around the stone courtyard, with wood floors, high ceilings, king-size beds, sitting areas, and all creature comforts (security box, minibar, cable TV, heating). The other 82 rooms are comfortable but bland, small, and sterile in an unfortunate five-story modern addition.

Equal in elegance and similar in layout, but cheaper and better value is **Picoaga Hotel** (Santa Teresa 344, tel. 084/22-7691, www.picoagahotel.com, US$160 d modern room, US$180 d colonial, US$200 junior suite), which is ideally located one block from Plaza Regocijo and a two-minute walk from the Plaza de Armas. This 17th-century colonial mansion, once belonging to the Spanish noble Marquis de Picoaga, has been well restored with stone archways and columns wrapping around a classic colonial patio. The colonial rooms are most definitely worth the extra US$20 as they are bigger, lighter, more comfortable, and aesthetically more pleasing than the rooms in the characterless modern part.

OVER US$250

The five-star **Hotel Libertador Palacio del Inka** (Plazoleta Santo Domingo 259, tel. 084/23-1961, www.libertador.com.pe, US$305 d standard, US$325 d junior suite, US$385 suite) has a great location next to Coricancha, the Inca sun temple. It occupies the Casa de los Cuatro Bustos, Francisco Pizarro's last home. It is built on the foundation of the *acllahuasi,* "the house of the chosen ones," where virgins picked by the Inca lived in seclusion from society.

The entrance to the Hotel Libertador is spectacular. A stone portal leads into a glass-roofed lobby, lined on one side by Spanish stone arches and on the other by exposed portions of stone Inca walls. There is an excellent buffet breakfast served alongside another large square, ringed with two stories of stone arcades. Throughout the hotel are examples of original colonial furniture, artifacts, and paintings—the owners are avid collectors. Ask for rooms in the colonial section, with views of the sun temple. The suites are larger with sitting areas and marble bathrooms, and are probably worth paying the extra for.

One of the more memorable places to stay in Cusco is (**Hotel Monasterio** (Palacio 136, Plazoleta Nazarenas, tel. 084/60-4000, www.monasterio.orient-express.com, US$634 basic d or US$806–2,232 suites), a 415-year-old monastery that has been converted into a most elegant five-star hotel. The stone lobby leads to a dramatic stone courtyard, graced with an ancient cedar tree and lined with two stories of stone archways. Colonial paintings line long hallways, which wrap around two other fabulous stone patios. The rooms are decked out in old-world Spanish decor, including carved wooden headboards and colonial paintings, and include all the plush five-star comforts. They can even be pumped with oxygen, simulating an altitude 900 meters lower that allows guests to sleep more soundly.

The hotel occupies the former Seminario San Antonio Abad, which was built in 1595 on top of the Inca Amaru Qhala Palace but was badly damaged in the 1650 earthquake. During the restoration, a colonial baroque chapel was added, which remains open to guests and has one of the most ornate altars in Cusco. After yet another damaging earthquake in 1950, the building was condemned and auctioned by the Peruvian government in 1995. It eventually landed in the hands of Orient-Express Hotels, which carefully restored the stonework, planted fabulous gardens, and converted the former cells into 126 plush rooms. These days, guests take lunch in the main square, which is shaded by a giant cedar, scented by a rose garden, and filled with the gurgling of a 17th-century stone fountain. The hotel hosts one of Cusco's three gourmet restaurants, and also includes a small massage room. It's a few minutes' walk from the Plaza de Armas.

Diagonally opposite the Monasterio on Plaza de las Nazarenas is undoubtedly the best hotel in Cusco, (**Inkaterra La Casona** (Plaza de las Nazarenas 113, tel. 084/23-4010, www.inkaterra.com, US$720 patio suite, US$924 balcony suite, US$1,128 plaza suite), the latest masterpiece of the Inkaterra group. This beautiful colonial mansion was first built in 1585 and following the Spanish conquest was possessed by Francisco Barrientos, lieutenant to Diego de Almagro. It has now been officially named a historical monument by the National Institute of Culture. La Casona has been exquisitely restored into 11 luxurious suites, retaining its original heritage right down to the minutest detail. The doors to La Casona are closed off to the outside world, ensuring the utmost privacy and creating a serene and relaxing oasis for guests. The philosophy of the hotel is to provide a personalized service; therefore there is no reception, just a butler and concierge who prioritize individuals' needs and tend to their every whim. Rooms are impeccably decorated with faded frescoes, colonial tapestries, Persian rugs, and antiques, ensuring the original feel of the home without sacrificing modern comfort and luxury. Every suite has thermostat controlled heated floors, flat-screen TV, DVD player, iPod speakers, WiFi, and mini bar. The bathrooms are superbly designed with the most contemporary amenities, including free-standing bathtubs, marble showers with two types of showerheads, lush towels, and handmade toiletries. Special touches such as bowls of fresh fruit, housekeeping service three times a day, and a private spa and massage room make a stay at La Casona truly exceptional. As if this were not enough La Casona prides itself on being one of Peru's first carbon-neutral hotels.

CUSCO

Food

CAFÉS, BAKERIES, AND ICE CREAM

The most popular café in Cusco is [C] **Jack's Café Bar** (Choquechaca/Cuesta San Blas, tel. 084/25-4606, 7:30 A.M.–11 P.M. daily, US$5), and with good reason. It is famous for big breakfasts, such as "El Gordo": a huge pile of eggs, home-made baked beans, fried potatoes, bacon, and sausages. For lunch there are great salads and sandwiches made with home-made bread. There is a fully stocked bar, as well as milk shakes, fruit juices, and coffees. In short—a real taste of home.

Along Cuesta San Blas, you'll eventually walk into the warm baking aromas of **Buen Pastor** (Cuesta San Blas 575, tel. 084/24-0586, 7 A.M.–8 P.M. Mon.–Sat.). This bakery run by nuns has warm empanadas and sweet pastries all at very affordable prices. For an authentic French bakery there is **Qosqo Maki** (Tullumayo 465, tel. 084/23-4035, www.qosqomaki.com, 8 A.M.–8 P.M. Mon.–Sat.), which has very good brown country loaves and tasty croissants. It is part of the long-standing and respected NGO Centro Bartolomé de la Casas, and proceeds go to the foundation.

To satisfy a chocolate craving, stop in the tiny [C] **Chocolate** (Choquechaca 162, tel. 084/25-8073, 7 A.M.–11 P.M. daily), a shop serving steaming mugs of hot chocolate and chocolates by the piece. If you fancy sampling some creative coca-flavored chocolate and baked goods head to the **Coca Shop** (Carmen Alto 115, 9 A.M.–8 P.M. Mon.–Fri.).

If you are after a hefty sandwich head to **Juanito's** (Qanchipata 596, tel. 01/994-170-852, 12–3 P.M. and 6–11 P.M. Mon.–Sat., Fri. and Sat. open until 3 A.M., US$4). There is a selection of 30 fillings both meaty and vegetarian, including alpaca and *lechon*.

For a lighter lunch on the lovely Plaza de las Nazarenas there is **Mama Oli** (Plaza

A red plastic flag means *chicha*, a fermented corn drink, is for sale.

© GABRIELLA HOLLAND

CUSCO

woman selling bread inside a *colectivo* station in Cusco

Nazarenas 199, 8 A.M.–8 P.M. Mon.–Sat. and 9 A.M.–4 P.M. Sun., US$4). This Peruvian–French–owned café has great juices, fresh soups, quiches, and desserts.

On the Plaza de Armas, the laid-back **❰ Trotamundos** (Portal Comercio 177, tel. 084/23-9590, 8 A.M.–11 P.M. daily, US$5) has balcony seating over the Plaza de Armas and is a great place to wile the day away. It serves some of the best french fries and *pie de limon* you'll find in Cusco.

The classic Cusqueño **Café Ayllu** (Marqués 263, 6:30 A.M.–10:30 P.M. Mon.–Sat., US$4) opened 35 years ago, and its glass display still cases pastries made from the age-old recipes. Be sure to try the *ponche de leche,* a pisco and milk cocktail, or a sliced roast suckling pig sandwich. **Dos Por Tres** (Marquez 271, tel. 084/23-2661, 9 A.M.–9 P.M. daily, US$2.50) is another Cusco classic and artist hangout. The coffee, almost always made by the owner, is cheap and delicious.

No café is better located for postcard-writing than **Don Esteban & Don Pancho** (Av. El Sol 765-A, tel. 084/25-2526, 8 A.M.–10 P.M. Mon.–Sat., 8 A.M.–8 P.M. Sun., US$5). Directly across from the post office, this café has a varied menu of sandwiches, empanadas (try the *aji de gallina* one), desserts, and bread made on the premises.

Dolce Vita (Santa Catalina Ancha 366, tel. 084/24-7611, 10 A.M.–9 P.M. daily, US$2) is the best place for homemade ice cream. Your only trouble will be deciding on a flavor: *chicha,* pisco sour, *lúcuma,* and coca are just a few of the exotic creations.

PERUVIAN

The area around the Plaza de Armas is overflowing with Peruvian restaurants. Here are some of the better quality ones. **La Retama** (Portal de Panes 123, 2nd Fl., tel. 084/22-6372, 11 A.M.–11 P.M. daily, US$10) has a great kitchen and wide-ranging Peruvian menu. A nightly buffet accompanied by a live folkloric music-and-dance show makes dinner into theater. On the ground floor of Portal de Panes is **Inka Grill** (Portal de Panes 115, tel. 084/26-2992, www.inkagrillcusco.com, 11 A.M.–11 P.M. daily, US$13), the first restaurant to bring Novoandino cuisine to Cusco and one of passionate restaurateur Rafael Casabonne's six restaurants (all excellent: www.cuscorestaurants.com). The *ensalada de langostinos* has quinoa-encrusted shrimp that literally melt in your mouth. The valley trout is fresh and tasty, and the pepper steak is also a popular choice.

Pucara (Plateros 309, tel. 084/22-2027) has a worthwhile daily US$3.50 lunch menu. The dishes are clean and simple, and the desserts and chocolate truffles are very good. **Café Restaurant Victor Victoria** (Tecsecocha 474, tel. 084/27-0049, 7:30 A.M.–10 P.M. daily) also has a reasonable lunch menu for US$5. The food is homey and there is an ample salad bar.

Pacha Papa (Plazoleta San Blas 120, tel. 084/24-1318, www.cuscorestaurants.com, 9:30 A.M.–10:30 P.M. daily, US$11) occupies a sunny courtyard across the street from the Iglesia San Blas. Peruvian specialties such as tamales, quinoa soup, and an acclaimed *lomo*

CUSCO

STREET FOOD

For the brave of heart and stomach, there are plenty of great street food options in Cusco.

- Start your street food tour with a mid-morning snack of *salteñas*, which are meat-, veggie-, and egg-filled pastries best eaten with a squeeze of lemon and a touch of *rocoto*. The best place for these is **Salteñas Copacabana** (Qeros 220), a small restaurant just off Avenida El Sol.

© GABRIELLA HOLLAND

Anticuchos, or roasted meat, is a favorite Cusco street food.

- At the Portal de Belen, and just outside the Gatos Market, is a lovely lady who sells the best tamales in town. Choose between the sweet *dulce* or savory *salado* option of these maize treats.

- For an evening degustation head to the intersection of Maruri and Loreto where you will find a stand, usually surrounded by people, that has the most tender and flavorful *anticuchos* (marinated meat skewers) in Cusco. The *anticucho de corazon* (heart meat) will melt in your mouth!

- For one of the best Peruvian desserts head to the Ruinas and Tullumayo intersection where you'll find a tiny little restaurant that is renowned for having the best *picarones* in town. These deep-fried sweet potato doughnuts, served hot and covered with syrup, are irresistible.

- To wash everything down, look out for a cart full of glass bottles with colorful liquids at Choquechac aand Cuesta San Blas. These are different herb concoctions that are mixed into a sweet tea called *emoliente*. The gooey texture comes from *linasa*, a gooey but healthy gelatinous linseed extract.

- If you still have room for a last midnight snack, head to Plazoleta San Blas to find a woman who sells rice pudding and *mazamorra morada*, a jelly-like dessert made from purple maize. She is there every day without fail into the wee hours of the night.

saltado are also served. A local favorite in San Blas is **Quinta Eulalia** (Choquechaca 384, 12:30–5 P.M. daily, US$6), which has been serving traditional Andean food since 1941. Prices are very reasonable and servings are massive. Dishes include *cuy, chicharrón,* and *rocoto relleno* (stuffed pepper). Besides the excellent food, this place has a great atmosphere, with tables in a sunny courtyard and live music.

A highly recommended, unpretentious restaurant that serves fantastic Peruvian food is **Trujillo** (Tullumayo 542, tel. 084/23-3465, restaurant_trujillo@speedy.com.pe, 9 A.M.–8 P.M. Mon.–Sat. and 9 A.M.–5 P.M. Sun., US$10–15). The menu is vast, servings are generous and everything is bound to be genuine and delicious. It is particularly famous for its *ají de gallina,* and the meat of the *asado a la olla* literally melts in your mouth.

INTERNATIONAL

One of Cusco's better Italian restaurants is **Cosa Nostra** (Plateros 358-A, 2nd Fl., tel. 084/23-2992, www.cosanostraristorante.com, noon–3:30 P.M. and 7–10:30 P.M. Mon.–Sat., US$10–15). The pasta is fresh and prepared in the authentic Italian way. The gnocchi, beef carpaccio, and beef filet in balsamic sauce are also good.

Another excellent Italian restaurant with a new and improved menu is (**Incanto** (Santa Catalina Angosta 135, tel. 084/25-4753, www. cuscorestaurants.com, 11 A.M.–11 P.M. daily, US$10–12). The minimalist decor shows off not only the Inca walls, but also the simple and flavorful food. Service is impeccable. The squid ink risotto is divine and the homemade fettuccini with seafood is light, spicy, and extremely tasty. Above Incanto and belonging to the same owner is **Greens** (Santa Catalina Angosta 135, 2nd Fl., tel. 084/24-3379, www. cuscorestaurants.com, 11 A.M.–11 P.M. daily, US$10), a creative organic restaurant. The concept is that the ingredients are separated into food groups for you to mix and match to your liking. The vegetables are prepared simply but well with nice touches such as mashed potatoes made from potatoes roasted in lamb juice. Every single ingredient used in the restaurant is 100 percent organic right down to the wholemeal flour.

If you are after Indian food, **Korma Sutra** (Tandapata 909, tel. 084/23-3023, 5 P.M.–midnight Tues.–Sun., US$8–12) is a good option. While the decorations are a little somber and plain, the curries, although overpriced, are colorful and tasty, especially the onion *bhaji* and the lamb *rogan josh.*

The German-owned (**Granja Heidi** (Cuesta San Blas 525, tel. 084/23-8383, 8:30 A.M.–9:30 P.M. Mon.–Sat.) has farm-fresh produce, including delicious natural yogurt, homemade granola, and a light and tasty midday lunch menu for US$7.50.

At the top of Cuesta San Blas by the fountain in the Plazoleta San Blas is another light, fresh option for lunch. The cute and charming French-owned **La Caverne del Oriente** (Plazoleta San Blas 646, tel. 084/984-609-045, 9 A.M.–9 P.M. daily, US$4) serves homemade French specialties such as hot goat's cheese salad, *flamenkuche,* and Mediterranean dishes such as couscous. The lunch menu is limited but great value (US$3.50). The Dutch/Argentinian-run **Encuentros Café** (Suecia 320, tel. 084/22-2703, www.encuentroscafe. com) also serves a worthwhile US$3.50 midday menu.

El Gusto Es Nuestro (Tecsecocha 420, tel. 084/25-5060, www.elgustoesnuestrorestaurant.com, 6–10:30 P.M. Mon.–Sat., US$10) is an unpretentious family run restaurant. The friendly Cordon Bleu–trained chef not only cooks the delicious meals but also waits and interacts with the clients. The food is international and ranges from Cobb salad to French onion soup to local favorites like *lomo saltado.*

Australian Tammy Gordon's (**Baco Wine Bar and Restaurant** (Ruinas 465, tel. 084/24-2808, bacorestaurante@yahoo.com, 6 P.M.–midnight Mon.–Sat., US$10–15) has a lovely, relaxing atmosphere. Thin-crust pizzas topped with such options as duck prosciutto and mushroom or blue cheese, marinated figs, and basil are simply delightful. Their organic salads and grilled meats are also delicious accompanied by a great wine from their extensive list.

FINE DINING

At the ambitious **MAP Café** (Plaza Nazarenas 231, tel. 084/24-2476, www.cuscorestaurants. com, mapcafe@cuscorestaurants.com, 11 A.M.–10 P.M. daily, US$16–24) dinner guests sit in a perfectly proportioned glass box, reminiscent of architect Philip Johnson's glass house, which seemingly floats in the stone courtyard of the Museo de Arte Precolombino. The food is a gourmet and sophisticated interpretation of traditional Andean cuisine. The glazed and deep fried *cuy* legs on a *choclo* foam with *tarwi* salad is a tasty and less confronting way to try guinea pig. A favorite dish on the menu is the *capchi de setas,* a mouthwatering creamy mushroom, potato, and broad bean casserole topped with a buttery pastry. The desserts are some of the most creative and delectable in Cusco. The

Many of Cusco's restaurants feature singing and dancing in the evenings.

© FIONA CAMERON

specialty is hot truffle balls with *aguaymanto* and pisco, served with vanilla ice cream and a surprise shot. If you're up for a full three-course meal then the US$50 menu is worth it.

Cicciolina (Triunfo 393, 2nd Fl., tel. 084/23-9510, cicciolinacuzco@yahoo.com, 8–11:30 A.M., 12:30–4 P.M., and 6–11 P.M. daily, US$12–15) is the most happening restaurant in town, popular with tourists and locals alike. A casual lunch here might be a sandwich, salad, and smoothie or their daily menu, but dinner should be taken in the deep red dining room. There, you can truly enjoy the cracked black pepper tagliatelli or grilled scallops in an oriental sauce over your choice of a glass of Peruvian, Argentine, Chilean, French, or Italian wine. For something sweet try the strawberries and port. If you leave satisfied, come back the following morning for breakfast and delicious croissants at the Cicciolina bakery. They also provide a picnic catering service, anywhere you wish, with tables, tablecloths, waiters, and all the trimmings.

For an evening meal with an entertaining operatic twist, **Divina Comedia** (Pumacurco 406, tel. 084/43-7640, info@restaurantcusco.com, 11:30–3 P.M., 6:30–11 P.M. Wed.–Mon., US$12–15) is a lot of fun. The Divine Comedy theme, medieval-influenced decor, and waiters dressed in period clothing are a fitting backdrop to the talented opera singers who entertain you while you dine. The beautifully presented modern and traditional dishes taste as good as they look.

For an all-around great dining experience, the best fusion restaurant in Cusco is **(Limo** (Portal de Carnes 236, 2nd Fl., tel. 084/24-0668, www.cuscorestaurants.com, 11 A.M.–3 P.M. and 6 P.M.–midnight daily, US$12–15). Rafael Casabonne's latest project is a tastefully decorated restaurant with a great view over the Plaza de Armas. The service is excellent but most importantly the food is superb. Start the evening with a plate of experimental Peruvian-influenced sushi rolls; the ceviche roll and the tuna rolls can hold their own anywhere in the world. The *tiraditos* and ceviches, especially the *ceviche oriental,* are delicious. As a main, the crab meat and breaded shrimp bathed in *leche de tigre* is a winner.

PIZZA

Pizza Carloía (Maruri 381, tel. 084/24-7777, midnight–3 P.M. and 5–11 P.M. Mon.–Sat., 5:30–11 P.M. Sun., US$10) has traditional Italian woodfire oven pizzas with thin smoky crusts. Those meat lovers who like a bit of spice should try the Diablo.

Babieca Trattoría (Tecsecocha 418-A, tel. 084/50-6940, 11 A.M.–midnight, US$12) has excellent dough, gourmet toppings such as alpaca and trout, and a seriously gigantic pizza called the Kilometriza for US$20.

A very cute, cozy, and affordable pizzeria is **Justina** (Palacio 100, interior, tel. 084/25-5475, 5–11 P.M. daily, US$10). The specialty of the house is the mushroomy and delicious Pizza Justina.

VEGETARIAN

Although most restaurants in Cusco have vegetarian options, there are a few places dedicated exclusively to vegetarian cuisine. A popular option is **Govinda** (Espaderos 128, 8 A.M.–10 P.M. daily, US$3–5), half a block from the Plaza de Armas. This small Indian-inspired restaurant has flavorsome dishes, but the US$8.50 midday menu is overpriced.

For some inexpensive vegetarian and vegan fare head to **Govinda Lila** (Carmen Bajo 228-A, 9 A.M.–9 P.M. daily, US$2–3.50). This cute little place is great value for money. The US$2 lunch menu includes a great salad buffet, a soup, a main, and a simple dessert. The US$3 breakfast buffet has everything you could possibly want except for eggs. The muesli and yogurt are homemade by the friendly owner,

Lojita. For a sweet finish make sure you try the Govinda pie.

A worthwhile and economic option is **El Encuentro** (Santa Catalina Ancha 384, tel. 084/24-7977, 9 A.M.–3 P.M. and 6–9 P.M. Mon.–Sat., US$3.50–5). It has a clean, simple midday menu for US$2, which also has a salad bar, with interesting options such as a vegetarian *ají de gallina*.

MARKETS

The **Mercado San Pedro** (Túpac Amaru, 6 A.M.–7 P.M.), near the San Pedro train station, has amazing fruit and vegetables. Come here to try the unique and delicious granadilla and chirimoya and cheap juices, but keep your eyes out for pickpockets and those who silently slice backpacks with razors to steal the goodies within.

Several blocks past Mercado San Pedro toward Avenida Ejercito is **El Baratillo,** which on Saturday morning is full of the most fascinating secondhand wares. If you have time to browse properly you can find some real treasures, but be careful with your valuables.

El Molino, just behind the central bus station, is Cusco's largest black market and has everything. It is a little out of the center of town, so it's best to catch a cab. Not many tourists come here, but as long as you hang onto your wallet you will be fine.

The largest supermarket is **Mega** (Plaza Túpac Amaru and Matara). **Gato's Market** (Portal Belen 115) and **Market** (Portal Mantas 120) are both on the Plaza de Armas; they're small and pricey but do stock hard-to-find imported products.

CUSCO

Information and Services

TOURIST INFORMATION

The **South American Explorers Club (SAE)** (Atocsaycuchi 670, tel. 084/24-5484, www. saexplorers.org, 9:30 A.M.–5 P.M. Mon.–Fri., 9:30 A.M.–1 P.M. Sat.) is a gold mine of information. It costs US$60 to join as an individual for a year, US$90 for a couple, though nonmembers are allowed to look around as well. This is definitely worth the cost if you will be in Peru for any length of time, and is a recommended first stop in Cusco. No matter how much research you have done, you will always learn something here and, at the very least, meet some interesting people. Club members can peruse trip reports for all over the Cusco area, use the well-stocked library, make free calls to the United States and Canada, and receive discounts at a wide range of restaurants, language schools, hotels, and agencies. It is also the only place in Cusco that sells topographical maps. The club hosts weekly events, and there is a new volunteer room that helps travelers become involved in children's, women's, and jungle projects.

If all you need is some basic tourist information and a map, services are free at the friendly **Iperú** (Portal Mantas 188, tel. 084/26-3176, www.peru.info, 8:30 A.M.–6:30 P.M. Mon.–Fri., 8 A.M.–2 P.M. Sat.) or in the airport (tel. 084/23-7364, 6 A.M. until the last flight).

POLICE

Travelers can contact the tourist police through the Iperú office, but a larger, **24-hour tourist police office** is on Saphi 510 (tel. 084/24-9654), where officers speak some English.

IMMIGRATION

Tourist visa enquiries can be made at the **Immigration Office** (Av. El Sol 314, tel. 084/22-2741, 8 A.M.–noon Mon.–Fri.).

HEALTH CARE

One of the major hospitals of Cusco is **Hospital Lorena** (Plazoleta Belén 1358, in the Santiago neighborhood, tel. 084/22-1581 or 084/22-6511).

A good reliable clinic that accepts international insurance, has adept doctors, and offers 24-hour service is **Clinica Paredes** (Lechugal 405, tel. 084/22-5265, www.clinicaparedes.com). Another recommendable clinic is **Cima Clinic** (Pardo 978, tel. 084/25-5550 or 084/984-651-085, www.cima-clinic.com), which specializes in altitude problems.

Dr. Américo Ortiz de Zevallos Olivera (Urb. El Hogar B-3, San Sebastian, tel. 084/984-743-054 or 084/27-0085, americo_odzo@hotmail.com) is a first-rate private doctor and surgeon who makes house and hotel calls 24 hours a day. He speaks English, has a great bed manner, and charges according to the patient's financial situation. He also works part-time at **SOS Medical Group** (Suecia 368, tel. 084/25-4492).

The best pharmacies are **InkaFarma** (Av. El Sol 210, tel. 084/24-2631, www.inkafarma.com.pe, 24 hours), **Boticas Arcangel** (Mantas 132, tel. 084/22-1421, 7 A.M.–11 P.M. daily), and **Boticas Fasa** (Av. El Sol 130, tel. 084/24-4528, www.boticasfasa.com.pe, 7 A.M.–11 P.M. Mon.–Sat., 8 A.M.–9 P.M. Sun.).

A recommended dental clinic is **Vivadent Clinica Odontologica** (El Sol 627-B, 2nd Fl., tel. 084/23-1558 or cell tel. 084/984-746-581, www.vivadentcusco.com). Dr. Virginia Valcarcel Velarde is expensive but very professional and experienced.

BANKS AND MONEY EXCHANGE

Getting money out of an ATM usually means a stroll down the first few blocks of Avenida El Sol, where **Banco de Crédito** is on the first block and **Banco Continental** and **Interbank** are on the third. The Banco de Crédito and Interbank are open all day 9 A.M.–6:30 P.M. (the others usually close 1–3 P.M.), with Saturday hours 9 A.M.–1 P.M. All the banks

CITY SAFETY

It is a common misconception that traveling through Peru's remote countryside is risky while spending time in a tourist town like Cusco is safe. In fact, the exact opposite is true. Taxi assaults, where cab drivers rob their passengers, are on the rise in Cusco. Most of these are simple robberies, though some have involved violence. Here are some tips for staying out of trouble:

- Take only authorized taxis; these can be easily recognized by a hexagonal yellow sticker on the windshield. Even better is to go with a radio taxi company – these have advertising and phone numbers on their roofs.

- Look at the taxi driver and decide whether you feel comfortable with him. If you feel nervous, wave the taxi on and choose another.

- Always take a taxi late at night, especially after drinking. Night taxis anywhere in town cost US$1.

- Walk in a group at night, and women should never walk alone.

- Carry your wallet in your front pocket and keep your backpack in front of you in a market or other crowded area. In markets, it is often better to leave most of your money and passport at home.

- Walk with purpose and confidence.

- When riding on a bus, store your luggage below or keep it on your lap. Do not put it on the racks above you where others can reach it as you sleep.

- Be wary of new friends at bars and on the street – many scams involve misplaced trust or the lure of drugs and sex and are hatched over the space of hours. Think twice before you go somewhere out of the way with someone you just met.

are closed on Sunday. For wire transfers, there is a **Western Union** (Av. El Sol 627-A, tel. 084/24-4167, 8:30 A.M.–7:30 P.M. Mon.–Fri., 8:30 A.M.–1:30 P.M. Sat.).

There is an overwhelming number of money exchange places, especially along the Avenida El Sol, and they are all much the same. A reliable option is **Panorama** (Portal de Comercio 149, 9 A.M.–10 P.M. daily). The rate is always fair and the bills brand new as they come directly from the bank.

COMMUNICATIONS

Cusco's main **post office** is the Serpost (Av. El Sol 800, tel. 084/22-4212, www.serpost.com.pe, 8 A.M.–8 P.M. Mon.–Sat. and 9:30 A.M.–1 P.M. Sun).

The city is crawling with different Internet places, all of which have cable connections and are generally good. In San Blas, a good place is **SanBlasNet** (Cuesta San Blas 106, 10 A.M.–10 P.M. daily). The owner, Jaime, is super friendly and will help you with just about everything.

Long-distance and international calls can be made at many Internet places, which are all similar in price.

LANGUAGE SCHOOLS

Cusco has more Spanish schools than any other city in Peru, though it is hard to be truly immersed in Spanish unless you can somehow isolate yourself from English speakers. Considering what they include, the school packages are considerably cheap: pre-arranged hostel or homestay with local family, breakfast, airline reservations, volunteer work options, city tour, dance and cooking classes, lectures, and movies. An intensive group class with all these perks runs around US$200–300 per week with 20 hours of classes, while a private package is around US$300–400. A private teacher, without lodging or food, is US$9–11 per hour. All prices quoted are for a week with 20 hours of classes.

Academia Latinoamericana de Español

CUSCO

(Plaza Limacpampa Grande 565, tel. 084/24-3364, www.latinoschools.com, US$190 private classes, US$160 group classes) is a professional, family-run business with schools in Peru, Ecuador, and Bolivia. They have great host families in Cusco and offer volunteer programs and also university credits through New Mexico State University. **Amigos Spanish School** (Zaguan del Cielo B-23, tel. 084/24-2292, www.spanishcusco.com, US$120 group) gives half of its income to children with disabilities and has highly recommended teachers.

Centro Tinku (Nueva Baja 560, tel. 084/24-9737, www.centrotinku.com, US$180 group, US$220 private) is a cultural institution that offers standard and custom-made Spanish and Quechua classes. All the teachers are fully certified. Off the Plazoleta San Blas is the affordable and quaint yet professional **Mundo Antiguo Spanish School** (Tandapata 649, tel. 084/22-5974, www.learnspanishinperu.net, US$55 group, US$190 private), run by a friendly Peruvian-Dutch couple. The main aim of this school is to keep it intimate, personal, and welcoming. **Maximo Nivel** (El Sol 612, tel. 084/25-7200, www.maximonivel.com, US$110 group, US$200 private) has schools all over North and South America.

LAUNDRY

Most Cusco hostels offer laundry service for the going rate of US$1.50/kilogram. Otherwise the best place for washing clothes (although a little more expensive) and especially for dry cleaning is **Lavandería Inka** (Ruinas 493, tel. 084/22-3421, 8 A.M.–1 P.M. and 3–8 P.M. Mon.–Sat.). For just regular washing **Lavandería Louis** (Choquechaca 264-A, tel. 084/24-3485, 8 A.M.–8 P.M. Mon.–Sat.) is a reliable and economic option at US$1/kilogram.

PHOTOGRAPHY

Digital photographers can download their full media cards to a CD in 20 minutes at many camera shops in Cusco. The catch is that you usually need the USB cord that works with your camera. An exception is **Foto Panorama** (Portal Comercio 149, in front of the cathedral, tel. 084/23-9800, 8:30 A.M.–10 P.M.), which accepts most different media cards. Another highly recommended place for developing or digital services and products is **Foto Nishiyama** (Triunfo 346, tel. 084/24-2922). It also has other locations around town, including on Avenida El Sol.

MASSAGES AND SPAS

There is no shortage of massage therapists (or people claiming to be) in Cusco desperately trying to get your business. Olga Huaman and her team at **Yin Yang** (El Sol 106, Galerías La Merced, Office 302, 3rd Fl., tel. 084/25-8201, cell 084/984-765-390, yinyang_masajes@hotmail.com, 9 A.M.–10 P.M. daily) give very professional massages as well as reiki and offer room service or sessions at their premises. **Angel Hands** (Heladeros 157, tel. 084/22-5159, 6 A.M.–10 P.M.) offers similar services. The **Siluet Sauna and Spa** (Quera 253, Interior 4, tel. 084/23-1504, 10 A.M.–10 P.M. daily) offers massages along with a whirlpool tub and hot and dry saunas.

If you really want to treat yourself to a day of luxurious pampering try **Samana Spa** (Tecsecocha 536, tel. 084/23-3721, cell 084/984-389-332, www.samana-spa.com), in a nicely renovated colonial house. They offer professional massages, steam and dry saunas, Jacuzzis in the lovely stone patio, and all sorts of beauty treatments including facials and manicures. There are special packages such as the Inka Trail Relief, which includes a deep tissue massage, steam/dry sauna, manicure/pedicure, and a Jacuzzi for US$110.

Getting There and Around

AIR

Cusco's airport (tel. 084/22-2611) is 10 minutes south of town and the taxi ride costs about US$2.50. Taxes for domestic flights are US$5.84 pp.

All Cusco-bound travelers must first arrive in Lima and then board another plane in Cusco, for which there are currently three main operators. To approach Cusco's airport, planes must fly at considerable altitude and down a narrow valley, passing ice-covered Nevado Salcantay en route. Because of the tricky approach and winds, afternoon flights are frequently cancelled. If possible, fly in and out of Cusco in the morning.

LAN (Av. El Sol 627-B, tel. 084/25-5552 or Lima tel. 01/213-8200, www.lan.com) is the most reliable airline and has more than 10 Cusco-bound flights a day. It often has very good offers if you book ahead of time. **Star Perú** (Av. El Sol 627, tel. 084/25-3791 or 084/23-4060, www.starperu.com) and **Taca** (Av. El Sol 602-B, tel. 084/24-9921 or 084/24-9922, Lima tel. 01/213-7000, www.taca.com) are also reliable and sometimes have cheaper flights.

In addition, LAN has daily flights from Lima and Cusco to Puerto Maldonado and Arequipa, as well as various other destinations around Peru. Star Perú also flies from Lima or Cusco to Puerto Maldonado and from Lima to other Peruvian destinations.

BUS

There is a new long-distance bus terminal, the **Terminal Terrestre,** on the way to the airport (Via de Evitamiento 429, tel. 084/22-4471). This huge building is busy, safe, and crammed with all of the long-distance bus companies, bathrooms, and a few stores selling snacks. Companies generally open 6 A.M.–9 P.M. and accept reservations over the phone, with payment on the day of departure (you have to speak Spanish, though).

A recommended way to get to **Puno** is with one of the tourist buses that visit the ruins on the way. These buses include a huge buffet lunch, English-speaking guide, and stops at most of the major ruins on the way. **Inka Express** (Plateros 320, tel. 084/24-7887, www.inkaexpress.com, US$50) makes stops in the exquisite colonial church of Andahuaylillas, the Inca ruins of Raqchi, and a buffet lunch stop in Sicuani. In the afternoon the bus stops at La Raya pass and the ruins of Pukará before arriving in Puno. The buses generally leave Cusco at 8 A.M. and arrive at 5 P.M. in Puno, include hotel pickup and drop-off, and even have oxygen tanks on board for altitude problems. There is a 10 percent discount for groups of more than four people.

For direct service to Puno, **Ormeño** (tel. 084/22-7501, www.grupo-ormeno.com) has a daily bus leaving at 9 A.M., which arrives in Juliaca at 1:30 P.M. and Puno at 2 P.M. (US$14 for Royal Class, which has onboard food service and plusher seats than even the Imperial buses). **Imexso** (tel. 084/22-9126, imexso@terra.com.pe), for the most part, has good service and new buses, with English-language videos. **Copacabana** has a bus service leaving at 8 A.M. for US$5.

Many of the above companies offer transfer buses leaving for **Bolivia,** though some go through Desaguadero and others through Copacabana (launching point for Isla del Sol). Ormeño (tel. 084/22-7501) has a direct business-class bus (no meals) through Desaguadero to La Paz, leaving daily at 9 P.M. To head through Copacabana, try Tour Peru, which leaves 10 P.M. daily (US$28). Another recommended company for getting to Bolivia is Litoral, though there are many more options in Puno's excellent Terminal Terrestre. The border crossing, which is open between 8 A.M. and 3 P.M., is quick and easy: Passengers need only get off the bus for a few minutes on each side of the border to have their passports stamped—remember to ask for the maximum number of days (usually 90).

Buses for the 20-hour haul to **Lima** now head to Abancay before crossing the mountains to the coast at Nazca and then heading north for Lima. Ormeño offers the extra-plush Royal Class service, which leaves at 10 A.M. and arrives in Lima the following day at 6 A.M. for US$50. There are also plain, one-story buses with a stop in Abancay. Another recommended company is **Expreso Wari** (tel. 084/24-7217, www.expresowari.com.pe), which has buses with seats that recline into beds. Trips including meals leave at 12:30 P.M. and 8 P.M. for US$52. They also have a less luxurious service leaving at 2 P.M. and 4 P.M. for US$28. **Cruz del Sur** (tel. 084/24-8255) has a good Imperial service leaving at 3:30 P.M. and 6:30 P.M. **Tepsa** (tel. 084/22-4534, www.tepsa.com.pe) is also a reliable option for Lima. The only company with transfer service through Abancay on to **Ayacucho** is **Expreso Los Chankas** (tel. 084/24-2249).

The journey to **Arequipa** via Juliaca takes 8.5 hours. **Cruz del Sur** (tel. 084/24-8255) has Imperial buses that include dinner and bingo leaving at 2 P.M. for US$34, and Ormeño offers a similar-quality service. **Enlaces** (tel. 084/25-5333) and **Cial** (tel. 804/22-1201) also have Imperial buses leaving daily.

Most people who visit Colca head to Arequipa first and then take the three-hour drive to Chivay, the Colca gateway, from there. There is an alternative, spectacular route on rocky roads that branches off from Sicuani and heads past Laguna Languilayo, the Tintaya copper and gold mine, and Condorama Dam on the Río Colca. This Cusco–Chivay route takes at least 11 hours, though more in rainy season, and it is best to do it on Saturday when buses are frequent. First head to Sicuani and scout for a Chivay direct bus or truck. If none is available, take local buses to El Descanso, Yauri, Chichas, and on to Chivay. (This 250-kilometer route between Sicuani and Chivay would also make an excellent mountain-bike journey.) Another option from Colca is provided by the company **Colca** (tel. 084/26-3254), which has daily buses to Arequipa. This bus takes the traditional route through Juliaca

and then stops at Pampa Cañaguas en route to Arequipa. The only direct option for Tacna, the border town for Chile, is **Cruz del Sur** (tel. 084/24-8255), which leaves at 4:30 P.M. and arrives at 8:30 A.M. the following day.

If you are a glutton for punishment you might want to consider the two-day bumpy but spectacular bus journey through Ocongate to **Puerto Maldonado,** the hardest of Cusco's three jungle destinations. The best way to do this is to head to Urcos and take a bus or truck onward from there. Atalaya, the gateway to the Parque Nacional Manu, is similarly hard to reach, but the journey can generally be made in a long day. Travelers must first head to Paucartambo. For Quillabamba, **Ampay** (tel. 084/24-9977) has buses leaving for the 8.5-hour journey for US$7 from the Terminal Terrestre.

Other options for Quillabamba and all other destinations in the Cusco region are the informal *terminales* where buses, *combis,* and *colectivos* leave when full. These are often located in places that are unsafe at night or early in the morning. They generally operate from 5 A.M. until as late as 7 P.M. Here is a list of *terminales* for destinations around Cusco. Most taxi drivers know where they are.

For **Quillabamba,** there is a roadside pickup spot, called a *terminal de paso,* at the last block of Avenida Antoñia Lorena, the principal exit road for the route that goes through the Sacred Valley before heading over Abra Málaga into the jungle (7 hours, US$6).

For **Urubamba,** there are two options. Buses for the shorter, 1.5-hour route, through Chinchero, leave from the first block of Grau near the bridge (45 minutes, US$0.75 for Chinchero; 1.25 hours, US$1.50 for Urubamba). Collective taxis at Pavitos do the same route but go all the way to Ollantaytambo (1.5 hours, US$3.50 pp).

Collective taxis and buses for **Pisac** and **Calca** via Urubamba leave from Puputi and the last block of Tullumayo (one hour, US$1.5 for Pisac; 1.5 hours, US$1.50 for Urubamba).

For **Andahuaylillas** and **Urcos,** on the way to Puno, buses leave from Avenida de la

Cultura in front of the regional hospital (1.5 hours, US$1).

For **Sicuani,** farther along this same route, buses also leave from Cultura but near Manuel Prado (3 hours, US$3.50).

For **Paucartambo,** buses leave from Cultura and Diagonal Angamos (3 hours, US$3).

Buses for **Paruro** leave from Belen and Grau (3 hours, US$3).

TRAINS

The train service between Cusco and Machu Picchu is being transformed by two events, so Peru visitors should check for the latest train information online. First, severe floods in the Sacred Valley in January 2010 destroyed miles of railroad track to Machu Picchu. While the track was being repaired, trains to Machu Picchu were departing only from Piscacucho, a village downstream from Ollantaytambo and at the end of the Sacred Valley.

The second, and very welcome, event is the breakup of the **PeruRail** monopoly and the emergence of two new train companies: **Inca Rail** and **Machu Picchu Train.** Hopefully, new competition will reduce prices and increase train availability to Machu Picchu.

These trains are the only nonstrenuous way to reach Machu Picchu, and a highly interesting way to reach Lake Titicaca as well. A major problem with trains from Cusco, especially during high season, is availability. The easiest way to get tickets is through a hotel or a travel agent. Otherwise visitors should make reservations online. The third, and least desirable option, is to head down to the Cusco train station, a process that, especially during high season, can take an hour or two.

PeruRail still operates trains from Cusco, but most Machu Picchu travelers now depart farther down the line at Ollantaytambo in the Sacred Valley. From Ollantaytambo the train enters the narrow Urubamba gorge, which offers spectacular views of snowcapped Verónica peak (5,710 meters or 18,865 feet) on the right (eastern) side of the train as the landscape transforms into the lush and humid *ceja de selva,* or "eyebrow of the jungle." By the time the train reaches Aguas Calientes, the ramshackle town closest to Machu Picchu, travelers have descended from the dry high plains to mountainous cloud forest.

PeruRail

ENAFER, the former state-owned railroad company, was privatized in the mid-1990s and has been operated since 1999 by **PeruRail** (www.perurail.com), a division of Orient-Express Hotels.

PeruRail offers many train services to Machu Picchu: the **Backpacker** (US$48 one-way, leaves Poroy 7:42 A.M., leaves Aguas Calientes 4:43 P.M.), the **Vistadome** (US$71 one-way, leaves Poroy 6:53 A.M., leaves Aguas Calientes 3:20 P.M.), and the luxury **Hiram Bingham service** (US$334 one-way to Machu Picchu, US$307 one-way from Machu Picchu, leaves Poroy 9:05 A.M., leaves Aguas Calientes 5:50 P.M.). These trains can also be caught from Ollantaytambo. The other services depart only from Ollantaytambo. These include the **Backpacker Cerrojo** (varies in price US$31–43 one-way depending on the departure time, six departures daily), the **Valley Especial** (US$43 one-way earlier train, leaves Ollantaytambo 5:10 A.M. and leaves Aguas Calientes 8:53 A.M., US$60 later train, leaves Ollantaytambo 8 A.M. and leaves Aguas Calientes 5:27 P.M.), and the **Vistadome Valley** (varies in price US$43–60 one-way depending on the departure time, five departures daily).

For trains to Puno, the PeruRail deluxe Andean Explorer (US$220 one-way)—departs on Monday, Wednesday, and Friday (and Saturday April–October) from Wanchaq Station (Av. El Sol s/n, tel. 084/23-3592) at 8 A.M. and arrives at 6 P.M. in Puno. This spectacular, nine-hour trip winds through the vast altiplano past snowcapped mountains.

Inca Rail

Inca Rail (Av. El Sol 611, tel. 084/23-3030, www.incarail.com) offers three daily departures from Ollantaytambo (6:40 A.M., 11:35 A.M., and 4:36 P.M.) and three daily departures from Aguas Calientes (8:30 A.M.,

CUSCO

2:02 P.M., and 7 P.M.). The trains have an Executive Class (US$50 one-way) and a First Class (US$75 one-way).

Machu Picchu Train

The Machu Picchu Train, owned by Andean Railways (Av. El Sol 576, across from the Coricancha, tel. 084/22-1199, www.machupic-chutrain.com) is importing a series of fancy coaches in a bid to shake up Machu Picchu train service. We like this outfit for a couple of reasons. First, Andean Railways battled PeruRail for years in a David-vs.-Goliath battle that ended in the collapse of PeruRail's monopoly. Second, one of the owners of Andean Railways is Nicholas Asheshov, a British journalist and entrepreneur who has lived in Peru for four decades. Nick knows Peru better than anyone and has also played an important role, along with adventurers Gary Ziegler, Hugh Thompson, and others, in unearthing recent important archaeological ruins in Peru's high Andes. Nick runs the new train service from his adobe electronic home on the grounds of the Libertador Tambo del Inca Hotel in Urubamba.

For the moment, the Machu Picchu Train leaves Ollantaytambo at 7:20 A.M. and 12:36 P.M. and arrives in Aguas Calientes 90 minutes later. The train returns from Aguas Calientes to Ollantaytambo at 10:30 A.M. and

4:15 P.M. Prices vary according to time but are approximately US$75 one-way.

CAR AND MOTORCYCLE RENTAL

Through its Cusco operator, at **Hertz** (Av. El Sol 808, tel. 084/24-8800, www.gygrentacar.com) you can rent a Toyota, be it a Corolla or a Land Cruiser. Rental rates include insurance, taxes, and 250 free kilometers per day. **Europcar** (Av. El Sol 809, tel. 084/22-1010, www.europcar.co.uk) also operates in Cusco. Motorcycles can be rented at **Cusco Moto** (Saphi 592, tel. 084/22-7025, www.cuscomototourperu.com), which has 125cc scooters (US$35 per day) and 250cc (US$60 per day) and 400cc (US$100 per day) Hondas. The price includes helmet, gloves, goggles, jacket, and medical and legal insurance. It also offers tours of the Sacred Valley, Maras and Moray, and even Colca Canyon.

LOCAL TRANSPORTATION

A taxi anywhere in Cusco's center costs US$0.85 or US$1 at night. Always be careful with taxis, especially at night. Because Cusco's center is so compact (and congested), few travelers find the need to take buses or *combis*—though the ones that head down Avenida El Sol toward the Terminal Terrestre and airport are useful.

Vicinity of Cusco

There are very interesting ruins along the road that heads south to Lake Titicaca. These cultural sites, from pre-Inca, Inca, and colonial times, form an interesting day tour from Cusco that an increasing number of agencies are offering. These landmarks can also be visited on the highly recommended special tourist buses between Cusco and Puno, which hit all the sights described, head over La Raya Pass, and then keep going to Puno and Lake Titicaca.

Tipón

One of the most elaborate and well-preserved examples of Inca agricultural terracing is Tipón (7 A.M.–5 P.M., US$1.50), which lies 22 kilometers south of Cusco and then another four kilometers up a valley via a switchbacking gravel road. The terraces, finely fitted and impossibly tall, run in straight lines to the head of a narrow valley. They are irrigated by an elaborate aqueduct that still runs from Pachatusan, the sacred mountain that looms over the site, whose name in Quechua means "cross beam of the universe." There are remains of a two-story house on the site and other ruins, possibly a fort, near the top of the aqueduct.

Rumicolca and Pikillacta

Though the Inca refused to admit it, much of their highway network and organizational know-how was based on the **Huari Empire,** which spread across Peru like a wildfire A.D. 500–1000. An example of Huari engineering is Rumicolca, a huge aqueduct that sits on a valley pass on the side of the highway about 32 kilometers from Cusco. The Inca altered the construction, added a few stones, and converted it into a giant gateway to Cusco, though the remains of the old water channels can still be seen.

Nearby is Pikillacta (6 A.M.–6 P.M., US$2), the largest provincial outpost ever built by the Ayacucho-based Huari. This curious walled compound, with nearly 47 hectares (116 acres) of repetitive two-story square buildings, sprawls across the rolling grasslands with little regard to topography. The floors and walls, which are made of mud and stacked stone, were plastered with white gypsum and must have gleamed in the sun. But the Inca so thoroughly erased evidence of the Huari that little about their empire is known today. For many years Pikillacta was thought to be a huge granary, like the Inca site of Raqchi. But excavations have revealed evidence of a large population that left behind refuse layers as deep as three meters. Part of the city caught fire between A.D. 850 and 900, and the Huari withdrew from the city around the same time, bricking up the doors as they went. Whether they abandoned the city because of the fire, or burnt it as they left, is unclear. Some historical information is available at the new museum at the entrance. In the valley below is Lago Sucre and, even farther on, Lago Huacarpay. On the far shores of this lake are the ruins of **Inca Huáscar's summer palace,** much of which continues to be enjoyed today by locals as the Centro Recreacional Urpicanca, the local country club. From the

The Inca converted the Huari aqueduct of Rumicolca into a gateway to Cusco.

© RENÉE DEL GAUDIO AND ROSS WEHNER

shoulder of the highway, it is possible to see ceremonial staircases the Inca built into the landscape above the lake.

Andahuaylillas

The colonial village of Andahuaylillas, 37 kilometers south of Cusco, has a charming plaza shaded with red-flowered pisonay trees and an adobe church, **San Pedro** (8:30 A.M.–noon and 2–5 P.M. Mon.–Sat., 8–10 A.M. and 3–5 P.M. Sun., free), which is built on the foundations from the early Inca empire. Though it's unremarkable on the outside, the doors open to a dazzling painted ceiling, frescoes, and wall-to-wall colonial paintings. This is the most finely decorated church in all of Cusco, probably in all of Peru, though calling it the "Sistine Chapel of the Americas," as some do, is going a bit far. One highlight is a mural by Luis de Riaño depicting the road to heaven and the road to hell, with a full-blown display of all the respective rewards and punishments.

There is a well-known natural healing

CUSCO

center just off the square, **Centro de Medicina Integral** (Garcilaso 514, tel. 084/25-1999, 9 A.M.–7 P.M. daily, medintegral@hotmail.com), with a charming stone courtyard with gardens and plain rooms for US$8 pp. The center attracts a considerable number of overseas visitors for massage, meditation, harmonizing energy therapy, and other treatments.

Urcos

Driving through the main square of this small village, 47 kilometers south of Cusco, it is hard not to notice Urcos's tidy colonial church with a public balcony on the second floor and stone steps in front. On the outskirts of town, there is the beautifully decorated chapel at Huaro, which is on a hilltop overlooking a small lake. According to legend, Inca Huáscar threw a huge gold necklace into these waters to protect the treasure from the Spaniards. The story seemed probable enough that *National Geographic* recently funded an exploration of the lake's bottom by scuba divers—though thick mud prevented them from finding anything.

Raqchi

Raqchi (119 km south of Cusco, 8 A.M.–6 P.M., US$3) is a ceremonial center built by **Inca Pachacútec** that offers a fascinating glimpse into the ambition and organization skills of his budding empire. Rising above the humble village of Raqchi, a wall of adobe nearly 15 meters high and 90 meters long sits on a carved Inca wall. This was once the center of a huge hall, the roof of which was supported by adobe columns—one of which has been restored—on either side. On the side are six identical squares, each with six stone buildings, which probably served as a soldiers' barracks. But the most impressive part of Raqchi is line after line of round stone houses—200 in all—that once were filled with a gargantuan amount of quinoa, freeze-dried potatoes, and corn.

Sicuani

There are several nice lunch spots in Sicuani, 138 kilometers south of Cusco. At the **Casa Hacienda Las Tunas** (J.C. Tello 100, tel. 084/35-2480, US$4), Sofia Vásquez serves up a huge, scrumptious buffet of Peruvian food from 11:30 A.M. onwards, when the Inka Express bus pulls in. Her sister, Edith, has good trout and meat dishes at the **Cebichería Acuarios** (Garcilazo de la Vega 141, 2nd Fl., tel. 084/80-9531, US$3) on the plaza.

LAKE TITICACA AND CANYON COUNTRY

Southern Peru, the country's second travel destination after Cusco and Machu Picchu, is full of contrasts. Breathtaking landscapes and geography, elegant and exquisite architecture, colorful people, and century-old traditions are all present in this vast region where the Colca Canyon, the deepest in the planet, and Lake Titicaca, the highest navigable lake in the world, attract thousands of nature-lovers and adventure-seekers every year.

Arequipa is Peru's most elegant city and seems at times more like southern Spain rather than South America. It's a wonderful place to come and enjoy the extraordinary cuisine, stroll the elegant streets, and soak in the romance of this city. Laid-back and sunny, Arequipa is known as the "white city" as it is constructed entirely of white volcanic stone.

Colonial churches and *casonas* line the street leading to the elegant Plaza de Armas, where a stately cathedral is flanked by palm trees and framed by three volcanoes: Chachani, Pichu Pichu, and Misti. The city's architectural highlight is the Monasterio de Santa Catalina, a maze of churches, plazas, and homes where cloistered nuns have lived since 1579.

Arequipa is surrounded by some of the country's most bizarre and remote landscapes: snowcapped volcanoes, lava fields, high-altitude deserts, and two of the deepest canyons on the planet. Stone villages, graced with colonial churches and elaborately carved altars, dot the rim of the Colca Canyon. The Río Colca leads into Colca Canyon, which is twice as deep as Arizona's Grand Canyon. Andean condors, the world's largest flying bird, can be

© JORGE RIVEROS CAYO

HIGHLIGHTS

◖ Plaza de Armas: Any tour of Arequipa should begin in Peru's most elegant urban square, with its neoclassical cathedral, arcades, palm trees, flowers, and fountains (page 143).

◖ Monasterio de Santa Catalina: Since the 16th century, nuns have lived cloistered amid the timeless archways and chapels of this miniature city, built entirely of white volcanic stone (page 147).

◖ Monasterio de las Carmelitas Descalzas de Santa Teresa de Arequipa: This 300-year-old Carmelite monastery, recently opened to the world, offers a rare collection of colonial art (page 148).

◖ La Cruz del Cóndor: Nowhere can the Andean condor, the world's largest flying bird, be seen so reliably as from this spot perched on the rim of the Colca Canyon (page 174).

◖ Folklore Festivals: Lake Titicaca is known as the Folklore Capital of Peru, so you shouldn't miss a chance to take in one of the local festivals. Puno's best known, Fiesta de Virgen de la Candelaria, reaches a fever pitch on February 2, when an image of the Virgin Mary is paraded through the streets amid hundreds of dancing devils, angels, and other extravagantly costumed characters (page 178).

◖ Kayaking Lake Titicaca: The only way to see the emerald waters and snow-covered mountains of the world's highest navigable lake is by boat – kayaking gives you the view from the water's edge (page 179).

◖ Islas Amantaní and Taquile: Staying with a family on one of Lake Titicaca's islands is a great way to immerse yourself in the lake's

natural beauty and the ancient lifestyles of its villagers (page 188).

◖ Isla Suasi: Lake Titicaca's only privately owned island boasts awesome views of Bolivia's Cordillera Real, a eucalyptus steam sauna, lakeside cottages, and gourmet cuisine (page 192).

LOOK FOR ◖ TO FIND RECOMMENDED SIGHTS, ACTIVITIES, DINING, AND LODGING.

watched soaring just meters away from those assembled at La Cruz del Cóndor, a morning lookout point on Colca Canyon.

In the southeast region of the country, Lake Titicaca, a massive expanse of water, sprawls across the middle of a Peruvian high plateau known as Meseta del Collao. While boating across the lake's sapphire waters, it is easy to understand why the Inca considered this their sacred, foundational landscape. Lake Titicaca is one of Peru's cradles of civilization, and staying with families—who speak either Quechua or Aymara—on the lake's islands or peninsulas is a good way to experience ways of life that extend back thousands of years. It is also the best way to see the lake's bucolic scenery of winding country lanes, transparent waters, and Mediterranean-like sunlight.

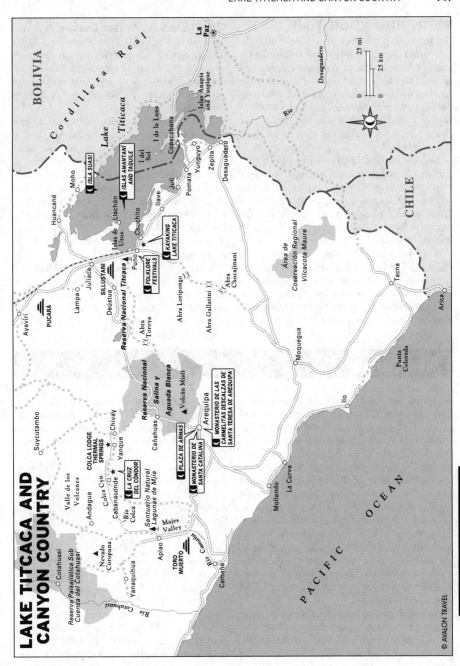

LAKE TITICACA AND CANYON COUNTRY

PLANNING YOUR TIME

An increasing number of travelers take the bus from Lima to Arequipa and stop along the coast at Paracas, Ica, or Nasca before heading up to Lake Titicaca and Cusco. Bus companies in Peru offer extremely comfortable double-decker buses with nonstop itineraries and VIP service including 180-degree reclinable seats, food, and WiFi. Traveling by bus on these routes is completely safe.

Because of the dramatic changes in altitude between Peru's coast and highlands, staying at least two days in Arequipa before continuing to Puno or Cusco is a must. At an elevation of 2,300 meters, Arequipa is a good place to acclimatize before heading to Lake Titicaca (3,800 meters) or Cusco (3,300 meters).

Travel options between Arequipa and Puno—a five-hour drive—include a wide variety of good buses too, with comfy seats on a very good highway with breathtaking views of the **Reserva Nacional Salinas y Aguada Blanca.** The travel options between Puno and Cusco include the **Andean Explorer,** a deluxe train service with excellent views, or a high-quality tourist bus that has the advantage of stopping at a string of interesting ruins along the way. Travelers with less time can also fly between Arequipa, Juliaca (an hour away from Puno), and Cusco.

Lake Titicaca has an increasingly fair share of tourist traps these days. Puno, the gateway city, though quite grimy, is the starting point for most of the off-the-beaten-path adventures, such as kayaking in the lake, arranging homestays on **Taquile** or **Amantaní** island, or the lesser-known **Anapia** and **Yuspique** islands or in the **Península de Capachica.** Traveling by bus on either shore of Lake Titicaca and stopping in towns along the way is another interesting option.

The best time to visit is between March and November, the sunny winter months. Bring lots of warm clothing for the freezing nights and a wide-brimmed hat and sunscreen for the intense sun.

Arequipa

Arequipa has a long tradition of producing Peru's presidents, laureate writers, poets, and artists. Like other great coastal cities such as Trujillo and Lima, Arequipa was founded shortly after the Spanish conquest and has a wealth of convents, churches, colonial homes, and fine art. But Arequipa is the most subdued and relaxed of Peru's coastal cities. Constructed entirely of white *sillar* stone, the city gleams in the sun and is home of the most stunning Plaza de Armas in all of Peru. Some blocks behind the main square, light shifts delicately across the arches, streets, and homes inside of the 400-year-old **Monasterio de Santa Catalina,** a citadel that could have been lifted right out of southern Spain.

Arequipa is for adventurers. One of the three volcanoes that tower above the city, **Chachani,** is the most attainable 6,000-meter mountain in Peru. A bit farther away lie some of the country's most extraordinary landscapes, including high-altitude deserts, a magical place called the **Valley of the Volcanoes,** and two of the world's deepest canyons: **Cotahuasi** and **Colca.**

The better known and more accessible of these two, the Colca Canyon, is five hours away. The canyon was only connected to the modern world in the late 1970s, and villagers living in the valley adhere to their centuries-old ways of life. This is one of the most spectacular and safe places in Peru for trekking and mountain biking. Rafting is also possible in the canyon and lower down on the Río Majes.

Arequipa is also for foodies, and Arequipeños are extremely proud of their culinary tradition. Products such as *cuy* (guinea pig), *rocoto* (a bell pepper–shaped chili), and *camarones* (freshwater prawns) are the foundation of a richly made, exquisite gastronomy that is one of the best in Peru.

© RENÉE DEL GAUDIO AND ROSS WEHNER

Arequipa street life

Each meal is a ritual that locals and foreigners enjoy thoroughly, tracing its recipes and cooking techniques back to pre-Hispanic times.

The Collagua people occupied the Arequipa area for millennia, as evidenced by the extensive terracing in the Colca valley, which was improved by the Inca. But the name for Arequipa apparently comes from Inca Mayta Cápac, who reportedly arrived at present-day Arequipa with his army and uttered the Quechua phrase *"ari, que pay"* meaning "yes, stay here." After conquering the area in the 15th century, the Inca began the practice of sacrificing children atop the area's highest volcanoes. **Juanita,** the mummy of a 13-year-old girl, captured worldwide attention in 1995 when she was discovered atop Volcano Ampato at 6,380 meters. Her mummy can now be seen in Arequipa's **Museo Santuarios Andinos** of the Santa María Catholic University.

The city of Arequipa was founded on August 15, 1540, by Captain Garcí Manuel de Carbajal after disease forced the Spaniards from an earlier settlement near Camaná, near the coast. Arequipa blossomed as a trade hub between Lima and southern Peru, including Cusco, Puno, and the rich silver mines in Potosí, in current Bolivia.

Arequipa has a long history of earthquakes. More than 300 buildings collapsed after a major earthquake in 1588, which prompted King Charles V to issue a royal order limiting building height. The city was covered with ash by erupting Huaynaputina a few decades later and leveled by earthquakes roughly once per century—in 1687, 1788, 1869, 1958, and 1960. The latest earthquake, in 2001, measured 7.5 on the Richter scale and knocked down one of the towers of the cathedral, which has since been repaired.

SIGHTS
☾ Plaza de Armas

The horizontal, white facade of the neoclassical cathedral is nearly as long as a football field and features pointed bell towers, ornate square windows, and huge columns. *Portales* or arches take up the other three sides of the square, which overflows with palm trees, flowers, and a fountain in the middle topped with

CANYON COUNTRY

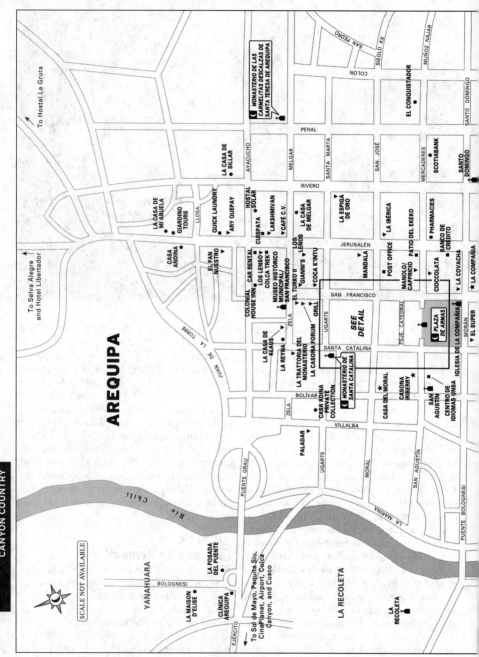

AREQUIPA

SCALE NOT AVAILABLE

To Hostal La Gruta

To Selva Alegre and Hotel Libertador

Río Chili

To Sol de Mayo, Paquita Siu, CinePlanet, Airport, Colca Canyon, and Cusco

YANAHUARA

LA MAISON D'ELISE
CLINICA AREQUIPA
LA POSADA DEL PUENTE

BOLOGNESI
EJÉRCITO

PUENTE GRAU
PUENTE BOLOGNESI

LA RECOLETA
LA RECOLETA

MONASTERIO DE LAS CARMELITAS DESCALZAS DE SANTA TERESA DE AREQUIPA

SAN PEDRO
COLON
SIGLO XX
MUÑOZ NAJAR

PERAL

EL CONQUISTADOR

SANTO DOMINGO

LA CASA DE SILLAR

AYACUCHO
MELGAR
SANTA MARTA
SAN JOSÉ
MERCADERES
SCOTIABANK
SANTO DOMINGO

RIVERO

LA CASA DE MI ABUELA
GIARDINO TOURS
LLOSA
QUICK LAUNDRY
ARY QUEPAY
HOSTAL SOLAR
CUSPATA
LAKSHMIVAN
CAFÉ C.V.
LA CASA DE MELGAR
LA ESPIGA DE ORO
LA IBÉRICA
PATIO DEL EKEKO
PHARMACIES
BANCO DE CRÉDITO

JERUSALÉN

CASA ANDINA
EL PAN NUESTRO
CAR RENTAL
LOS LENSO
COLCA TREK
MUSEO HISTÓRICO MUNICIPAL/ SAN FRANCISCO
EL TURKO II
GIANNI'S
COCA K'INTU
LOS LEÑOS
MANDALA
POST OFFICE
MANOLO/ CAPRICCIO
CIOCCOLATA
LA COVACHA

SAN FRANCISCO

COLONIAL HOUSE INN

LA TORRE
JUAN DE LA TORRE

LA CASA DE KLAUS
LA REYNA
LA TRATTORIA DEL MONASTERIO
LA CASONA FORUM

ZELA
ZELA

UGARTE
UGARTE

SANTA CATALINA

SEE DETAIL

PSJE. CATEDRAL
PLAZA DE ARMAS
IGLESIA DE LA COMPAÑIA
MORAN
EL SUPER
LA COMPAÑIA

CASA ANDINA PRIVATE COLLECTION
PALADAR

BOLÍVAR
VILLALBA

MONASTERIO DE SANTA CATALINA
CASA DEL MORAL
CASONA IRIBERRY
SAN AGUSTÍN
CENTRO DE IDIOMAS UNSA

MORAL
SAN AGUSTÍN
LA MARINA

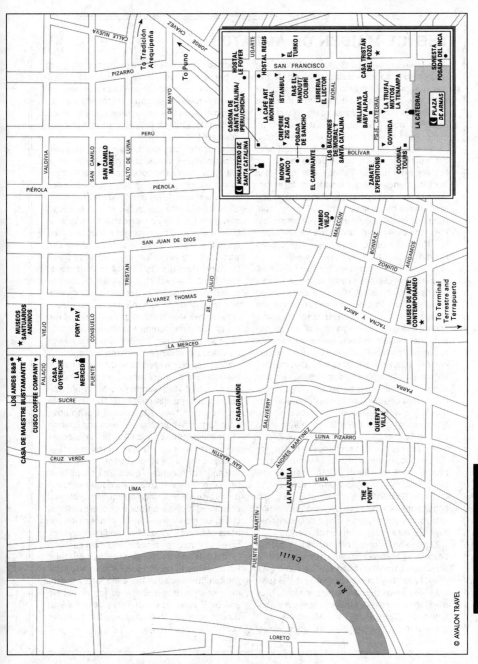

© AVALON TRAVEL

THE ICE MAIDEN OF AMPATO

Juanita was only 12 or 13 years old when she walked up a wooden staircase and onto the snowy summit of Ampato (6,380 meters), accompanied by Inca priests intent on making a sacrifice to the *apu*, or mountain god, of Ampato. She wore a feathered headdress and an elaborately woven shawl and skirt, decorated with pieces of gold jewelry. An Inca priest gave her a narcotic potion, which probably put her to sleep after days of fasting – and then killed her with a single, precise blow to her forehead. Juanita was wrapped in a fetal position and surrounded by ceramic pots containing food, figurines made of gold and carved wood, textiles, and other objects needed for the afterlife. Then the tomb was sealed with carved rocks and, over time, by snow as well.

After being frozen in ice for five centuries, Juanita's concealment came to an end when a neighboring volcano, Sabancaya, began showering ash onto Ampato's summit. The gray ash absorbed the sun's warmth and gradually melted snow, uncovering a trail of curious objects that would eventually lead archaeologists to Juanita's tomb. First there was a round ceremonial square, made of stones, that climber Miguel Zárate discovered in 1989 on a ridge at 5,000 meters. In a subsequent trip, Miguel discovered ceramics and bones at 5,800 meters, along with the remains of wooden stairs. Miguel knew that there was probably a tomb atop Ampato because his father, Carlos Zárate Sandoval, had run into similar evidence before discovering the tomb of an Inca princess atop Picchu volcano in 1964. Miguel went to see high-altitude archaeologist Johan Reinhard, of Chicago's Field Museum of Natural History, who had spent more than two decades uncovering Inca tombs atop Peru's highest peaks without ever finding a well-preserved mummy.

Zárate and Reinhard returned to Ampato in September 1995, accompanied only by a burro driver, and they retraced the path the Inca priests probably took on their way to the summit. They knew they were on the right track when they discovered bits of rope, ceramics, and wood. But the real breakthrough came in the thin air near the summit, when Miguel spotted a fan made of red feathers poking out of the snow. Juanita's stone tomb had melted out of the snow on the summit ridge and slid downhill toward the crater, scattering the fan, gold plates, and three figurines made of silver, gold, and spondylus shell. But the mummy was nowhere to be seen.

To locate Juanita, the climbers wrapped rocks in yellow plastic and rolled them downhill. Near where the rocks came to rest, they found Juanita, who was still wrapped in her Inca shawl even after her 60-meter roll down a snow slope into the crater. After a few days of work, Miguel and Johan carried the 36-kilogram mummy to the base of Ampato and then on to the village of Cabanaconde, where she was driven to Arequipa and eventually flown to John Hopkins University in Baltimore, Maryland. The fact that the Inca climbed to 6,380 meters, sacrificed children in the snow, and then buried them in bizarre and elaborate tombs made front-page news around the world. Juanita's mummy has allowed scientists to understand what she ate, what her health was like, and who her living relatives are.

Reinhard discovered three other mummies, though less well preserved, in subsequent trips to Ampato's summit (it turns out the stone platforms discovered by Miguel Zárate on the summit were the ceilings of tombs). Based on archaeological evidence and Spanish chronicles, Reinhard and other archaeologists believe the Inca sacrificed children as part of *capac-cocha,* a ceremony meant to appease the *apus,* or mountain gods. The purpose of this ceremony was to ensure good rains, but it was also used during earthquakes, volcanic eruptions, droughts, floods, or other times of crisis. Each child was carefully chosen (on the basis of beauty, innocence, and intelligence), taken to Cusco for a ritual, and then paraded through towns on the way to the mountain. Participation in *capac-cocha* was an honor for the families because the child, after death, became a spiritual go-between for the people and their *apus,* still venerated across Peru, though offerings these days consist mainly of coca leaves and *chicha.*

an usual character—some say it is a soldier, others an angel—known as *el tuturutu*.

La Catedral (tel. 054/23-2635, 7–11:30 A.M. and 4:30–7:30 P.M. Mon.–Sat., 6:30 A.M.–1:30 P.M. and 4:30–7:30 P.M. Sun., free, guides work for a tip) is most beautiful in the afternoon when its front is stained orange by the setting sun. It was begun in 1544, partially destroyed in the 17th century by earthquakes, and then completely burnt in an 1844 fire. Then it was built in its present neoclassical style and outfitted with one of the largest organs in South America (imported from Belgium) and a carved wooden pulpit that is supported by a swimming, serpent-tailed devil.

On an opposite corner of the plaza is the **Iglesia de la Compañía** (Álvarez Thomas and General Morán, tel. 054/21-2141, 9 A.M.–12:30 P.M. and 3–6 P.M. Mon.–Fri., 11:30 A.M.–12:30 P.M. and 3–6 P.M. Sat., 9 A.M.–12:30 P.M. and 5–6 P.M. Sun., US$2 for chapel), which was founded by the Jesuits in 1573, though the present building dates from 1650. The large church, with three naves and a cupola, is best known for its mestizo facade (church fronts in which stone sculptures blend traditional Jesuit or Catholic icons with Andean imagery and symbolism) and its **Chapel of San Ignacio de Loyola,** decorated with works from the mannerist master Bernardo Bitti (1550–1610). The nearby sacristy contains vivid murals of jungle plants and animals, a sort of visual introduction for missionaries being prepared for the Amazon. The Jesuits' minor cloisters—now a crafts market—lie a few doors down General Morán Street. There are gargoyles depicting figures from pre-Inca cultures and, in the adjacent major cloisters, elaborately carved columns with Mudejar (Muslim) designs.

◖ Monasterio de Santa Catalina

The architectural highlight of the historic center of Arequipa is the 425-year-old Monasterio de Santa Catalina (Santa Catalina 301, tel. 054/60-8282, www.santacatalina.org.pe, 9 A.M.–5 P.M. daily, 8 A.M.–8 P.M. Tues.–Thurs., US$11, guides work for a tip).

© NANCY CONNICK AND DAVE JANKOWSKI

CANYON COUNTRY

Monasterio de Santa Catalina in Arequipa is made entirely of *sillar*, a white volcanic rock.

THE REPUBLIC OF AREQUIPA

Arequipeños stick out in Peru, much in the same way that it is hard to miss a Texan in the United States. Arequipeños seem more Spanish, more confident, and have a fierce regional pride that manifests itself in passports for the "Republic of Arequipa." No one jokes, however, about the several revolutions that have been plotted here over the last two centuries. Nor about the fact that the mayor of Arequipa, as recently as 2001, publicly discussed secession and that two of Peru's most controversial recent historical figures – Shining Path head Abimael Guzmán and Fujimori henchman Vladimir Montesino – both hail from here.

One theory behind Arequipeñismo – as the local braggadocio is called – is population based. There have always been more Spaniards in Arequipa. In the mid-18th century, for instance, there were 22,000 Spaniards out of a total population of 37,000 (Lima, at the same time, had only 18,000 Spanish out of a total population of 62,000). Arequipa received even more European immigrants after independence, when numerous English families settled in Arequipa and set up trading houses for the area's alpaca wool.

Probably the main reason for Arequipa's distinct feel is its geographic and economic isolation from the rest of the country. It is far closer to Bolivia and Chile than to Lima, for instance, and Arequipeños have long complained that they are neglected by the centralized powers that be in Lima. The huge haciendas, which dominated other parts of Peru, have always been balanced by small landowners and merchants who have depended on an internal, southern economy between Tacna, Moguegua, Mollendo, and Puno – not to mention La Paz, Bolivia, and Arica, Chile.

The monastery is a citadel built in 1579 entirely of *sillar* with a hundred houses, 60 streets, three cloisters, main square, church, cemetery, and painting gallery. As many as 175 nuns lived here during the 17th and 18th centuries, including the daughters of wealthy families, who lived in private houses with up to four servants. More than 400 colonial paintings, mostly from the Cusco School, hang in a gallery that was once a shelter for widows, single mothers, and homeless women.

One of the most prominent nuns was **Sor Ana de los Ángeles Monteagudo** (1620–1686), who was elected Mother Prioress of the monastery. A series of miracles were attributed to this nun, even after her death, which made the nuns of the monastery write a petition to the Vatican to try to make her saint. The process continues.

Today, there are a few nuns living in modern quarters in the convent; they subsist on tourist entry fees. The nuns were shut off from the rest of the city until 1985, when they became half-cloistered, meaning they can now leave and shop for food or visit relatives (up until that year, they spoke with families only through screened windows). Photographers should visit late in the afternoon, when the light falls across the buildings at interesting angles.

◖ Monasterio de las Carmelitas Descalzas de Santa Teresa de Arequipa

The Monasterio de las Carmelitas Descalzas de Santa Teresa de Arequipa (Melgar 303, tel. 054/28-1188, 9 A.M.–5 P.M. Mon.–Sat., 9 A.M.–1 P.M. Sun., US$4, guides work for a tip), founded in 1673, is not as ostentatious as Santa Catalina but definitely is fascinating too. After the earthquake in 2001, the monastery suffered considerable damage. This is when, after 295 years of total seclusion, and after restoring the religious site, the Carmelite nuns decided to open part of the convent to the world as a museum. The nuns still keep partially cloistered.

More than 300 works of art are exhibited in the long *sillar*-built hallways with decoratively painted walls. Carmelite nuns still meander during certain hours of the day, and thus visitors can hear them crossing galleries behind closed

© JORGE RIVEROS CAYO

inside Arequipa's Monasterio de las Carmelitas Descalzas de Santa Teresa de Arequipa

doors. If you happen to be there around noon, you will hear, but never see, 21 cloister nuns and five novices singing the *Angelus* in Latin. A gallery exhibits techniques and materials used to make effigies, paintings, sculptures, murals, and metalwork during the 17th and 18th century.

Student tour guides, who deserved to be nicely tipped, are available and fluent in English, French, German, and Portuguese. A nice shop in the front patio sells delicious pastries and empanadas baked by the nuns, books about the monastery, and rose-scented soap also made by the Carmelites.

Other Churches

Iglesia de San Francisco (Zela 103, tel. 054/22-3048, 7–9 A.M. and 4–8 P.M. Mon.–Sat., 10 A.M.–noon Sun.) is a 16th-century Franciscan church with a Latin cross shape and an unusual brick entranceway. The next-door convent, also designed in 1569 by Gaspar Báez, is worth visiting if it's open, as is the adjacent **Chapel of the Third Order,** built in 1777.

Other convents and churches worth visiting include **Santo Domingo** (corner of Santo Domingo and Piérola, tel. 054/21-3511, 7 A.M.–noon and 3–7:30 P.M. Mon.–Fri., 7–9:30 A.M. and 3–7:30 P.M. Sat., 5:30 A.M.–12:30 P.M. and 6:30–7:30 P.M. Sun.), which was built around 1680 and has the oldest mestizo-style facade in the city. Another fine mestizo facade is to be found at **San Agustín** (corner of San Agustín and Sucre, tel. 054/20-0066, 7–9 A.M. and 4–8 P.M. Mon.–Sat., 7 A.M.–12:30 P.M. and 6–8 P.M. Sun.), for which construction began in 1576. **La Merced** (third block of La Merced, tel. 054/21-3233, 6:30–9:30 A.M. and 4–8 P.M. Mon.–Sat., 6:30 A.M.–8 P.M. Sun.) has fine carved wooden sculptures and a colonial library. **La Recoleta** (Recoleta 117, tel. 054/27-0966, 9 A.M.–noon and 3–5 P.M. Mon.–Sat., US$1.50) is a Franciscan convent built in 1648 with beautiful cloisters, a library, and a museum of Amazon artifacts collected by missionaries. It is located across the Río Chili, about a 10-minute walk east from the Plaza de Armas.

Museums

One of Peru's most interesting museums, dedicated to the high-altitude archaeology

CANYON COUNTRY

pioneered by U.S. anthropologist Johan Reinhard, is the **Museo Santuarios Andinos** (La Merced 110, tel. 054/21-5013, www.ucsm. edu.pe/santury, 9 A.M.–6 P.M. Mon.–Sat., 9 A.M.–3 P.M. Sun., US$4, US$1.50 students). The museum contains the mummy of 13-year-old Juanita, an Inca human sacrifice recovered from the summit of Ampato (6,312 meters). The discovery was chosen by *Time* magazine as one of the world's 10 most important scientific discoveries of 1995.

There are also 18 other mummies discovered on volcano tops in Peru, Chile, and Argentina, along with the textiles, gold, wood carvings, and ceramics found in their tombs—a rare chance to see Inca art overlooked by both the Spaniards and modern-day grave robbers. Included in the entry fee is an obligatory, excellent one-hour tour that includes a documentary made by *National Geographic.*

Near San Francisco Church is the **Museo Histórico Municipal** (Plaza San Francisco, 8 A.M.–5 P.M. Mon.–Fri., US$0.75), with a naval museum, portrait gallery of Arequipa's elites, historical photographs of the city, and a series of caricatures and paintings by local artist Jorge Vinatea Reynoso (1900–1931).

The **Museo de Arte Contemporáneo** (Arica 201, near Arequipa, tel. 054/22-1068, 10 A.M.–5 P.M. Tues.–Fri., 10 A.M.–2 P.M. Sat.–Sun., US$2.50) is situated across the old train station, housed in a 1900s mansion built for the manager of the Peruvian Corporation, the English train company that built most of Peru's rail lines from the 1870s onward. The museum has an interesting collection of 20th-century art, including photographs by the brothers Miguel and Carlos Vargas, who mentored Martín Chambi, the famed Cusco photographer. The museum showcases an interesting range of young local artists heavily influenced by the horrors of the Shining Path terrorist movement, along with a few paintings from Peru's most famous painters, such as Fernando de Szyszlo and Enrique Polanco, among others.

Colonial Mansions

Arequipa, like Trujillo and Lima, has several colonial mansions, or *casonas,* worth visiting. Many of them were expropriated by President Juan Velasco in the late 1960s and have subsequently been converted into banks. The best of the houses is the **Casa del Moral** (Moral 318, tel. 054/21-4907, 9 A.M.–5:30 P.M. Mon.–Sat., US$1.50, US$1 students), which was built around 1700 and receives its name from a graceful *moral* (mulberry tree) in a courtyard paved with *canto rodado* or river stones and lined with beautiful ochre walls. The elaborate and dense carving over the front door includes pumas spitting out serpents, and the rooms are restored and decorated with period art and furniture.

Casona Iriberry (San Agustín on the Plaza de Armas, tel. 054/20-4482, 9 A.M.–1 P.M. and 4–8 P.M., free), has a series of graceful stone patios and spacious rooms built in 1793 and recently converted into the Centro Cultural Chávez de la Rosa. Try to read the messages carved above the doorways—one says, in old Spanish, "This house was made in the year 1743. I ask God that he who would live in it, recite an Our Father."

Casa Tristán del Pozo (San Francisco 108, tel. 054/21-5060, 9 A.M.–1 P.M. and 3:45–6 P.M. Mon.–Fri., 9 A.M.–1 P.M. Sat., US$4) receives its name from General Domingo Tristán del Pozo—member of one of Arequipa's most prominent and powerful families—who commissioned it in 1738. The house has been converted into a cultural center and offices for the BBVA Banco Continental and includes a stately portico, entryway, and double patios.

Two other homes worth visiting are on La Merced, near the Plaza de Armas. The simple and elegant **Casa del Maestre Bustamante** (first block of La Merced), presently not open for visitors, was built in 1759. Over the door of **Casa Goyeneche** (La Merced 201, tel. 054/21-2251, 9:15 A.M.–3:15 P.M. Mon.–Fri., US$4) there is an ecclesiastical coat of arms of Arequipa's bishop José Sebastián Goyeneche (1784–1872). This home, with a large and graceful patio, is occupied by the Banco Central de Reserva del Perú and contains a good collection of paintings from the Cusco School.

Yanahuara

A jaunt across the Río Chili for lunch at La Nueva Palomino restaurant can easily be combined with a digestive stroll, a few blocks north, to the charming square of the Yanahuara neighborhood. It is graced with stone archways, views of Misti, and the 18th-century **Iglesia San Juan Bautista** (9 A.M.–noon and 4–8 P.M. Mon.–Fri., 7 A.M.–1 P.M. and 3–8 P.M. Sat.–Sun., free). The church's walls are nearly two meters thick, and the roof's arch was built with a flat shape to accommodate the relative weakness of *sillar* (this shape was found to be stronger than the perfect arch). The elaborately carved facade is considered to be one of Peru's masterpieces of religious art. Look closely to find a cherubim with feathered crowns, which is a pre-Hispanic symbol of power outlawed in Peru during colonial times.

About five minutes away by taxi (US$1.50) is the **Mirador de Carmen Alto,** which offers views of all the volcanoes, the city of Arequipa, and a *sillar* quarry used by the Spaniards. There are Collagua terraces nearby, a few resident alpacas and llamas, and a small snack bar.

La Mansión del Fundador

This restored church and home (Huasacache, 6.5 km from Arequipa, tel. 054/44-2460, 9 A.M.–5 P.M. daily, US$3), 20 minutes outside of town, was first owned by Garcí Manuel de Carbajal, who founded Arequipa in 1540. The house later became a Jesuit retreat before being bought and restored by the city's illustrious Archbishop José Sebastián de Goyeneche in the early 1800s. The church is plain, with an arching stone ceiling, and the home has a large patio flanked with rooms filled with original paintings and furniture. A taxi costs around US$4 for a one-way ride.

Sabandía

This pleasant country town has a 17th-century *molino* or flour mill (8 km southeast of Arequipa, 9 A.M.–6 P.M. daily, US$3), which still turns with the force of water. The hamlet of Paucarpata, surrounded by Collagua terracing, is a favorite weekend lunch spot with locals

and is a bit farther down the road. *Combis* head frequently to Sabandía from Jorge Chávez and Victor Lira (US$1), or a taxi charges around US$5 for the 15-minute trip.

ENTERTAINMENT AND EVENTS
Nightlife

Arequipa has great nightlife: San Francisco, Zela near Plaza San Francisco, and Santa Catalina streets are ground zero. Walk down these streets to survey the options, as bars open and close constantly and vary depending on the night of the week. **Déjà Vu** (San Francisco 319-B, tel. 054/934-7809, 9 A.M.–5 A.M. daily) is normally packed with people lured by its chic atmosphere of tables under *sillar* arches, live music Wednesday–Saturday nights, and great pizzas. Movies are shown every evening at 7:30 P.M.

Next door is **La Casona Forum** (San Francisco 317, tel. 054/20-2697, www.forumrockcafe.com, Mon.–Sat.), which is home to a variety of bars and discotheques, including **Zero Pub & Pool** (www.zeropub-pool.com, 6:30 P.M.–1 A.M.), on the second floor, which is a glitzy rock-and-roll pub with pool tables and live music on Thursdays. **Forum** (10 P.M.–2 A.M.), on the first floor, is Arequipa's best discotheque for salsa and other latin rhythms; it gets going after 11:30 P.M., offering different levels and even a waterfall, with live concerts on Friday and Saturday. **Retro** (6 P.M.–1 P.M.), for drinks and chatting, and **Terrase** (6:30 P.M.), a karaoke bar, round out the mix.

Nearby, there are several other bars, including **Istanbul** (San Francisco 231A, tel. 054/937-2264, 6 P.M.–4 A.M. daily), with charming sofas on the first floor and a nook upstairs, being the perfect place for an early-evening drink. Locals hang out at **Ad Libitum** (San Francisco 233, tel. 054/993-1034, 6 P.M.–4 A.M. daily), a dimly lit, laid-back place with a wide range of affordable cocktails. **Mono Blanco** (corner of Ugarte and Santa Catalina, 2nd floor) also is a relaxed place to go for a drink. Mojitos are especially good here.

A great live music and drinks place is **La Café Art Montréal** (Ugarte 210, tel. 054/931-2796, 3 P.M.–2 A.M. Mon.–Fri., 3 P.M.–4 A.M. Thurs.–Fri., 5 P.M.–4 A.M. Sat.). This swanky colonial space, built of *sillar* in the 19th century and divided up into rooms with vaulted ceilings, swings with Cuban protest, Latin rock, and other live music from Wednesday to Saturday. There is a light menu including burritos (US$3), guacamole, pizza and pastas, and crepes.

If you want to see a movie on a big screen go to the eight-theater **CinePlanet** (Ejército 793, 2 km west of center over Puente Grau, Mall Saga Falabella, tel. 054/27-1945, www. cineplanet.com.pe, US$5). Movie times and options can be found in *El Pueblo,* the local newspaper, or on CinePlanet's website.

Arequipa has a lean but worthwhile cultural calendar that is promoted in the newspaper *El Pueblo* and in *El Búho* (www.elbuho.com.pe), an extremely smart weekly publication that is a good source of information as well. **Teatro Municipal** (second block of Mercaderes, 7 P.M., free admission) has weekly concert listings at the door, with live string orchestras, big bands, guitar ensembles, and other Latin groups. Other exhibits and performances are held at **Instituto Cultural Peruano Alemán** (Ugarte 207, tel. 054/21-8567), **Centro Cultural Peruano Norteamericano** (Melgar 109, tel. 054/89-1020, www.cultural.edu.pe/mvia), and **Alianza Francesa** (Santa Catalina 208, tel. 054/21-5579, www.afarequipa.org.pe).

Festivals

Arequipa's main festival is **Founders Day,** August 15, which includes a week of fireworks, parades, dancing, and bullfights. One of Peru's more famous pilgrimages is the Virgen de Chapi on May 1. Pilgrims trek 45 kilometers, or about 15 hours, from Arequipa to the small town of Chapi, which is blanketed with flowers by day and lit by fireworks at night. Other local festivals include Virgen de la Candelaria in Cayma on February 2, the bullfighting festival in Characato on June 24, and the Virgen del Rosario in Yanahuara on October 8.

SHOPPING

Arequipa continues to thrive, as it has for centuries, as the center of Peru's wool industry. Wools and fine clothing shops are all over town and, for the real aficionados, the main wool producers can arrange visits to factories and highland ranches with alpacas and vicuñas. Apart from alpaca goods, the city produces high-quality jewelry and chocolates.

Shopping Centers

Across the street from the Monasterio de Santa Catalina is the newly remodeled **Casona Santa Catalina** (Santa Catalina 210, tel. 054/28-1334, www.santacatalina-sa.com.pe, 9 A.M.–9 P.M. daily). Once a colonial house, this building now houses a variety of upscale shops, a restaurant, an Internet café, and even an **Iperú** office. If you are looking to buy alpaca, chocolate, or pisco, this could be your one-stop shopping.

Patio de Ekeko (Mercaderes 141, tel. 054/21-5861, www.patiodelekeko.com, 10 A.M.–9 P.M. Mon.–Sat., 11 A.M.–8 P.M. Sun.) is a touristy complex near the square. Its multiple floors are filled with classy crafts, alpaca shops, a high-end jewelry store, an Internet café, a restaurant, and even a big-screen cinema showing documentaries on Arequipa.

Alpaca Wool

Millma's Baby Alpaca (Pasaje Catedral 117, tel. 054/20-5134, millmas@hotmail.com, 9 A.M.–9 P.M. daily) is one of the nicer shops in a narrow pedestrian street behind the cathedral, with a wide selection of men's and women's sweaters (US$40–120), coats, and scarves.

Michell & Cia is the world's leading producer and exporter of alpaca fiber. The company started in 1931 and now it has a top-end outlet chain named **Sol Alpaca** (Alameda San Lázaro 101, tel. 054/20-2525, www.michell.com.pe, 9:30 A.M.–1 P.M. and 2:30–7 P.M. Mon.–Fri., 11 A.M.–1:30 P.M. Sat.) with stores in Cusco, Lima, and Santiago de Chile. Sweaters, scarves, coats and even carpets are sold, with people on hand to demonstrate the hand sorting of alpaca

DON'T LOOK A CAMELID IN THE MOUTH

The most honored gift, and most common form of tribute, among the Inca was not gold, but finely woven garments of alpaca or, even better, vicuña wool. A relative of the camel, the llama was also the Inca's only beast of burden and their primary source of meat. These high-altitude camelids made the Inca empire possible.

Arequipa, surrounded by high-altitude grasslands, has been the center of Peru's lucrative wool industry since colonial times and even before. Now that alpaca ranches are spreading across the United States like wildfire, some of Arequipa's main wool exporters – such as Grupo Inca and Michell – occasionally lead tours up to highland alpaca ranches. Participants help round up and shear wild vicuñas and learn how to spin wool and loom-weave.

The finest fiber of any wool-producing animal comes from the **vicuña**, which was brought back from the verge of extinction in the 1960s. Each of these camelids is sheared every three or four years and only yields a mere 250 grams of wool. Shearing vicuñas was only made legal again in 1995, and the wool remains highly regulated. Clothing made from their wool, considered the world's most luxurious animal fiber, can cost several thousand dollars. The Inca would have been pleased – they only let nobles wear vicuña clothing.

The vicuña herds typically consist of one male who walks in front of a harem of up to six females, though it is not uncommon to see mixed herds of up to 50 vicuñas. A good place to see them in herds is Pampa Cañahuas, en route to Colca Canyon from Arequipa.

The largest camelid, with fiber nearly as fine as the vicuña's (around 16 microns), is the **guanaco**. Like the vicuña, it is difficult to domesticate and has a thin, orange-brown wool of incredible fineness. There are only 500,000 guanacos, mostly in the highlands of Chile and Argentina, and their wool is highly regulated on the international market.

The **alpaca** is a whole other animal. For starters, there are more than 10 million alpacas in the world – more than three-quarters of which are in Peru. Their wool has a delightful range of browns, blacks, whites, and grays. The wool fiber also has a dramatic range of fineness, which is carefully measured by merchants in determining the value of the wool.

All over Peru's highlands, women can be seen weaving in fields as they tend a flock of grazing alpacas, which have a sheeplike abundance of wool that fluffs up even around their eyes. The *suris* (long-haired alpacas) can produce over three kilograms of wool every two years! On the other hand, grilled alpaca meat has been popping up in restaurants around Peru, overtaking llama as the meat of choice.

Because **llamas** have much coarser wool than alpacas, they are generally used for their meat and as pack animals. Llamas and alpacas can intermingle – the result is called a *huarizo* – and can be difficult to tell apart. But llamas generally are larger, have much less hair, and have a small tail that sticks out in the back. Dried llama meat, a traditional Andean food, is called *charqui* – perhaps the only Quechuan word to make its way into the English lexicon (as beef "jerky").

A final word of caution: Llamas and alpacas, even the ones with pink tassels tied on their ears, are not friendly creatures. They have a well-deserved reputation for spitting grass loogies at anyone who comes too close. If the cheeks puff out, and the ears flatten, back off!

fiber and loom weaving. A tour of the factory, located in Parque Industrial, can be arranged here at the shop.

Grupo Inca (Miguel Forga 348, Parque Industrial, tel. 054/22-9998, www.grupoinca. com, 8 A.M.–12:30 P.M. and 2:30–6 P.M. Mon.–Fri.) groups a series of companies that also produce and export alpaca fiber. **Inca Tops** (sales@incatops.com) sells world-class tops and yarns of alpaca wool and cotton. **Incalpaca TPX** (Condor 100, Tahuaycani neighborhood, tel. 054/60-3000, www.incalpaca.com, 9:30 A.M.–7 P.M. Mon.–Fri., 11 A.M.–4 P.M. Sat.), on the other hand, produces the finest cloth, outerwear, knitwear, and home items. It is the only company in Peru licensed to sell vicuña wool, which costs US$600 a kilogram. It has shops named **Kuna** in Patio del Ekeko, Casona Santa Catalina, and at Libertador Hotel.

Alpaka Studio (Claustros de la Compañía, store 17, tel. 054/20-2486, www.prosur.com. pe, 9:30 A.M.–1:30 P.M. and 3:30–7:30 P.M. Mon.–Sat.), whose collections feature city and outdoor clothing. Organic products are also available at **Colca Trading Company** (Santa Catalina 300-B, tel. 054/24-2088, 9 A.M.–8 P.M. Mon.–Sat.), including cotton garments, organic alpaca sweaters, silver jewelry, rugs, and scarves.

Jewelry and Antiques

For jewelry, **Aqlla** (Pasaje Catedral 112, tel. 054/20-5088, 9 A.M.–8:30 P.M. daily) is a stylish shop and showroom of handmade silver jewelry. It also has artistic and modern scarves, sweaters, wool coats, and ceramics. **L. Paulet** (General Morán 118, Claustros de la Compañía, tel. 054/28-7786, 9 A.M.–1 P.M. and 3:30–8 P.M. daily) specializes in gold and silver handmade jewelry, as well as hand-knit and handwoven baby alpaca textiles.

There are several antiques shops clustered on Santa Catalina. **Antiguedades y Objetos de Arte** (Santa Catalina 406, tel. 054/22-9103, 9 A.M.–1 P.M. and 3–8 P.M. daily), **El Anticuario** (Santa Catalina 300, tel. 054/23-4474, 9 A.M.–1 P.M. and 3–7 P.M. daily), and **Arte Colonial** (Santa Catalina 312, tel. 054/21-4887, 10 A.M.–8 P.M. daily) all sell everything from small crafts to antique furniture. A wide range of inexpensive crafts can be found at the **Fundo de Fierro** handicraft market, on the corner of the Plaza San Francisco.

Chocolate

La Ibérica (Jerusalén 136, tel. 054/21-882, www.laiberica.com.pe), Arequipa's century-old chocolate company, produces the best bitter chocolate in the country. It has shops on Mercaderes, at the Saga Falabella Mall, and at the airport. The dark fondant bars are irresistible, and the small chewable toffees come in five flavors.

Bookstores

Along with Lima, Arequipa has the most bookstores in Peru, the best of which is **Librería el Lector** (San Francisco 221, tel. 054/28-8677, 9 A.M.–9 P.M. daily), with European charm. Owner Fernando Rosas has a great collection of books on Peruvian culture—including many in English—and on archaeology, politics, cooking, music, flowers, photography, and travel. The shop also has an English-language fiction section and book exchange. There are several other bookshops along San Francisco near the plaza.

RECREATION

Colca Canyon and other stunning areas near Arequipa, like the Majes Valley, are one big adventure playground. There is a huge range of options, including Class III–V rafting, mountain biking, trekking, climbing, and good agencies to make it happen. Before you go, remember the altitude: Acclimatize in Arequipa.

Climbing

The closest volcano to Arequipa is **Misti** (5,830 meters), and it is generally climbed in two days/one night. There are a few routes, but the easiest begins from a new road that reaches 3,400 meters. From here climbers ascend 6–7 hours to make base camp around 4,700 meters before climbing at dawn up Misti's snowy south side. It is possible to be back in Arequipa by the afternoon.

The easiest 6,000 meter peak—perhaps in all of Latin America, maybe in the whole world—is **Chachani** (6,095 meters). Three hours of driving from Arequipa brings climbers to 5,100 meters, from which they ascend two more hours to base camp. The summit is another 5–6 hours away the following morning, though a new road may put future climbers within four hours of the summit. Though it's possible to climb Chachani in a single day from Arequipa, it seems safer (and more enjoyable) to plan on at least two.

Another popular mountain, which can be combined with a trekking circuit through Colca Canyon, is **Ampato** (6,312 meters). A car can be driven to 4,900 meters, from where climbers ascend for two hours to base camp at 5,200 meters. Summit is then another six hours. Another route from Cabanaconde, in the Colca Canyon, begins at an Inca ceremonial center at 5,000 meters near the northeast side of the volcano. The summit is about seven hours away from here, and the neighboring volcanoes of **Sabancaya** (5,995 meters) and **Hualca Hualca** (6,095 meters) can also be climbed from this same camp. Colca is also the launching point for **Mismi** (5,597 meters), the source of the Amazon.

Coropuna (6,425 meters), Peru's second-highest peak, is rarely climbed because it is 10 hours from Arequipa. But its slopes are gentler than those of many of the other volcanoes, and it is sandwiched by and on the way to both Cotahuasi and Valley of the Volcanoes.

Most of Arequipa's volcanoes are gentle and relatively free of ice, so few climbers rope up, though crampons might be required for the summit push. Although not as technical as the mountains around Huaraz, any mountain near 6,000 meters demands caution and experience. Only go without a guide if you have climbing experience and have done your homework ahead of time.

Along Santa Catalina Street there are at least a dozen adventure agencies. We recommend **Zárate Expeditions** (Santa Catalina 115A, Window B, tel. 054/20-6314 or 054/997-1535), founded by the legendary mountain climber and guide Carlos Zárate Sandoval. It offers guided expeditions to all the local volcanoes, along with a range of treks, and its services include food and transport. The agency offers trips to Misti, Chachani, and Colca/Ampato. Miguel "Miki" Zárate, who discovered the Juanita mummy atop Ampato in 1995, is one of the guides.

Naturaleza Activa (Santa Catalina 211, tel. 054/959-822-436 or 958-681-486, naturactiva@yahoo.com) is a highly recommended option for Colca treks or mountain biking.

Owner and guide Lalo Sánchez Bendezú offers excellent treks in Colca for three days/two nights (US$75 pp) and a bigger loop of four days/three nights (US$95 pp) that include more sites than other agencies.

Another recommended agency that has been around for a while is **Colca Trek** (Jerusalén 401-B, www.colcatrek.com.pe). Traditional customized treks to Colca can be arranged, as well as part-biking, part-trekking expeditions or a biking countryside tour. The shop has the best range of camping gear (for sale and rent) in the area, and it also rents bikes and usually has white gas.

Trekking

The areas around Arequipa, such as Colca Canyon, offer fabulous trekking for those who like views of canyons and volcanoes and a hot, sunny climate. Unlike in the more popular Cordillera Blanca, trekkers have no problem getting off the beaten path and need not worry much about robbery or other safety issues. The views range from immense canyon rims to wide valleys studded with volcanoes. The villages, isolated during centuries, are friendly and unforgettable.

Zárate Expeditions (Santa Catalina 115A, Window B, tel. 054/20-6314 or 054/997-1535), **Naturaleza Activa** (Santa Catalina 211, tel. 054/959-822-436 or 958-681-486, naturactiva@yahoo.com), and **Colca Trek** (Jerusalén 401-B, www.colcatrek.com.pe) offer the best organized treks and are glad to answer questions for those going on their own. Topographical maps can be bought at the South American Explorers clubhouses in Cusco and Lima, or the Instituto Geográfico Militar in Lima (or, in a pinch, copied in Arequipa). Ask for detailed information—especially concerning the availability of water—at each village you pass. Apart from running out of water, the main things to watch for are sunburn and getting cold at night. Bring a wide-brimmed hat, sunscreen for the day, a warm sleeping bag, and a jacket.

Rafting and Kayaking

Expert boaters rank **Cotahuasi Canyon** up

IRON BOATS UP AND OVER THE ANDES

Peru is filled with stories about large iron boats lugged to improbable places. In 1890, rubber baron Carlos Fermín Fitzcarrald and an army of 1,000 Piro Indians lugged an entire steamship up and over a ridge, nearly 10 kilometers, to connect two river basins. This harebrained scheme became the subject of *Fitzcarraldo*, the 1982 movie directed by Werner Herzog.

An even crazier but less well-known scheme was concocted by the Peruvian navy in 1861, when it ordered not one but two huge iron gunboats – the *Yavarí* and the *Yapura* – for patrolling the waters of Lake Titicaca. Within two years, the Thames Iron Works and Ship Building in London had the gunboats shipped, in crates, around Cape Horn to Arica, the Peruvian port that would later be snatched by Chile in the War of the Pacific.

This is where the story becomes surreal. From the desert coast, with the Andes looming before them, porters hefted the crankshafts to their shoulders, while mules stood, knees quivering, under the weight of hull sections and crates containing more than 2,766 ship parts. The 466-kilometer journey, up and over the Andes, wound up steep and treacherous trails and included a final 4,700-meter pass. Not surprisingly, getting everything to the shores of Lake Titicaca took more than six years. With much fanfare, the *Yavarí* was launched on Christmas Day 1870 and the *Yapura* three years after.

Because of a lack of coal, the navy began shoveling a more abundant local fuel source into the ship's boilers: dried llama dung. But more space was needed to accommodate the manure piles. The *Yavarí* was cut in half in order to add 12 meters to her hold, bringing her to a total length of 50 meters. Finally, in 1914, her steam engine was replaced by a Swedish-made Bolinder, a four-cylinder diesel. Half a century later, the boats were decommissioned. The *Yapura* was sold for scrap metal, and the *Yavarí* was abandoned on the lake's shores, its instruments carted off to Arequipa's municipal museum.

The sight of the forgotten ship, whose hull had rusted little in the lake's fresh waters, moved Englishwoman Meriel Larken to action in the early 1980s. She launched the Yavarí Association to save the old ship and attracted the financial support of Britain's Prince Philip, who had visited Lake Titicaca in 1962. In 1999, more than 40 years after her last voyage, the *Yavarí* once again slipped her moors and began plying the waters of Lake Titicaca.

The *Yavarí* is, without a doubt, the most interesting thing to see in Puno, and one-of-a-kind in the whole world. The bunk, engine, and map rooms have been meticulously restored, and the bridge has all the ship's original navigation equipment, including an old-fashioned sextant and compass. The Bolinder engine, lovingly restored by Volvo engineers, is considered the oldest working ship engine in the world. When the association has more funds, it plans to build 10 cabins and offer what will surely be unforgettable overnight lake cruises – hopefully in 2011, when the *Yavarí* turns 150 years old.

with Cusco's Río Apurímac, another extraordinarily beautiful wilderness river with a steady stream of Class IV rapids. Colca, on the other hand, is a steeper and more closed canyon with unavoidable Class V rapids. Rafting guides prefer Cotahuasi over Colca because there are portages around all the Class V rapids, the hillsides offer more ruins and terracing, and the river is doable even for first-time rafters. That doesn't mean, however, that it's not hard.

The best rafting operator in Arequipa is **Cusipata** (Jerusalén 408A, tel. 054/20-3966, www.cusipata.com), run by Gian Marco Vellutino. From April to December, Cusipata has daily half-day trips down the Río Chili, which tumbles through Arequipa and includes one Class IV chute (US$30 pp). Another excellent option is a three-day kayaking school, the last two days of which include time on the Class III waters of the Río Majes, the large downstream section of the Río Colca. Cusipata's more serious endeavors include descents of the Cotahuasi Canyon twice a year in conjunction with Bio Bio Expeditions in the United States.

Biking

The standard Colca mountain-bike route begins at Patapampa, at 4,950 meters, and drops into the Colca Valley at Chivay at 3,650 meters. Bikers follow dirt roads along the north side of the river and cross the bridge to Yanque. The third day would include the Cruz del Condór and Maca, and end in Cabanaconde. **Cusipata** (Jerusalén 408A, tel. 054/20-3966, www.cusipata.com) can also design extraordinary routes in Cotahuasi and the Valley of the Volcanoes. Cusipata also rents bikes.

Another good option is **Naturaleza Activa** (Santa Catalina 211, tel. 054/959-822-436 or 958-681-486, naturactiva@yahoo.com), which also offers more mellow biking trips around Arequipa's countryside.

Tour Guides and Agencies

The standard Arequipa tours are the city tour and the countryside tour, both about three hours. The city tour includes Yanahuara church and lookout, the Compañía church, and the Santa Catalina Monastery—ask for your guide to visit colonial homes as well. The country tour includes the mill at Sabandía and the Mansión de Fundador. The most reputable agency is **Giardino Tours** (Jerusalén 604-A, tel. 054/22-1345, www.giardinotours.com), run by the same owners as La Casa de mi Abuela in Arequipa and La Casa de Mama Yacchi in Colca Canyon. Another agency with a good reputation is **Colonial Tours** (Santa Catalina 106, tel. 054/28-6868, colonialtours02@hotmail.com). A final option is **Ricketts Turismo** (Moral 229, tel. 054/22-2208, www.rickettsturismo.com).

ACCOMMODATIONS

As one of Peru's top business centers, Arequipa has dozens of hotels, including many charming options under US$50 for a double and more top-end options, including the beautiful *casona* of Casa Andina Private Collection

Arequipa and the outstanding five-star Hotel Libertador.

Under US$10

In a residential neighborhood, 10 minutes south of the center, **The Point** (Lima 515, tel. 054/28-6920, www.thepointhostels.com, US$8–11 dorm, US$15 d) in Arequipa is part of a backpacker hostel chain. On-site is everything to keep you entertained: Internet, TV and DVD player, a shared kitchen, and nightly parties that gather on the rooftop terrace. Bathrooms are shared but there is hot water. This is a great option to meet other backpackers and partiers.

US$10-25

Colonial House Inn (Puente Grau 114, tel. 054/22-3533, www.colonialhouseinn-arequipa.com, US$11 s, US$18 d with breakfast) has rooms with shared bathroom around a courtyard and a nice rooftop terrace with mountain views. This bed-and-breakfast is located on a busy street, but the thick colonial walls keep out the noise. Book early since the place is often full.

El Caminante Class (Santa Catalina 207-A, 2nd Fl., tel. 054/20-3444, www.elcaminanteclass.com, US$13 s, US$18) is a very good deal, conveniently located in an old 18th-century house between Plaza de Armas and Santa Catalina Monastery. Rooms are comfy, with private bathrooms. Amenities include a laundry and a book swap. There are also cheaper rooms with shared bathrooms.

Posada de Sancho (Santa Catalina 213-A, tel. 054/28-7797, inkarootshostel@hotmail.com, US$13 s, US$20 d with breakfast) is a simple colonial home with 15 large rooms and two tiled patios with sitting tables and potted geraniums. Rooms have wooden floors, high ceilings, and windows facing either the street or the patio. There is no Internet.

Los Andes Bed & Breakfast (La Merced 123, tel. 054/33-0015, www.losandesarequipa.com, US$13 s, US$24 d with breakfast) is quite a new and excellent option, with comfy, very clean single, double, or larger rooms for groups, with and without private bathrooms. Features include an open kitchen where you can cook meals, safe security boxes, luggage storage, laundry service, an impressive library and reading lounge, book exchange, cable TV, and WiFi.

La Casa de Sillar (Rivero 504, tel. 054/28-4249, US$16 s, US$25 d with breakfast) has nine rooms, some with private bathrooms, in a colonial house opening onto a sunny patio. Four rooms traditional *sillar* arches and construction. The rooms are simple, and the breakfast more than ample: yogurt, fruit, and hash browns. There is WiFi, along with a TV room and laundry service.

US$25-50

Six blocks from the Plaza de Armas, **La Casa de mi Abuela** (Jerusalén 606, tel. 054/24-1206, www.lacasademiabuela.com, US$29 s, US$39 d with breakfast) has a delightful oasis of gardens and lawns. Rooms, which wind around the gardens, are of varying quality and years. The newer rooms are bigger, with a modern hotel feel. Older rooms are darker, but with a more homey feeling. The hotel offers every conceivable traveler's service: excellent beds, cable TV, phones, laundry, massages, a library, a game room, Internet, a pool, and one of the best tour agencies in Arequipa—Giardino Tours. Because of all the activities, this is an especially good place for families.

La Casa de Melgar (Melgar 108, tel. 054/22-2459, www.lacasademelgar.com, US$30 s, US$40 d with breakfast) is worth it for a fascinating glimpse into 18th-century Arequipa. The house has 1.5-meter-thick *sillar* walls, vaulted ceilings, wood floors and shutters, and six interior patios. Each room is unique, with antique rocking chairs and armoires, vaulted stone showers, rotary phones, and funky stained-glass skylights. Room 104 is huge with a fireplace.

For those who prefer to be out of the city center, **Vallecito** is a quiet, relaxed neighborhood with homes built in the early 20th century, about a five-minute taxi ride south of town. **La Plazuela** (Plaza Juan Manuel Polar 105, Vallecito, tel. 054/22-2624, www.hostal-laplazuela.com, US$30 s, US$40 d with breakfast) is a large home from the early 1900s that has been converted into a bed-and-breakfast with a nice lawn, sitting area, and dining area. The rooms are all painted in light pastel colors and have individually controlled heating, a minibar, cable TV, and WiFi. Airport transfer is included if you stay three days or more.

Hostal Solar (Ayacucho 108, tel. 054/24-1793, www.hostalsolar.com, US$34 s, US$38 d with breakfast and airport transfer) is a charming hostel some blocks away from the center of town, with a small library, sitting room, and rooftop terraces. The 15 rooms have wood or carpeted floors, *sillar* walls, high ceilings, WiFi, and TV. The kitchen is available for guest use, and there is a 24-hour doctor on call.

A charming option in the upscale neighborhood of Selva Alegre, just north of the city center, is **Hostal La Gruta** (La Gruta, tel. 054/22-4631, www.lagrutahotel.com, US$35 s, US$45 d with breakfast). This cozy hostel offers 16 rooms in a discreet 1970s house. Each room is different, one with an interior garden, another with a fireplace. All have carpet, fridges, and cable TV and open up to a small garden. It doesn't really feel like a hotel here, more like staying in a guest room.

The entry to the **El Conquistador** (Mercaderes 409, tel. 054/21-2916, www.hostalelconquistador.com, US$37 s, US$49 d with breakfast) is quite stunning, crossing an elegant colonial patio and entering into the reception and dining area with vaulted *sillar* construction built in the 1770s. The actual rooms, however, are an unfortunate 1980s modern addition lacking charm. Rooms are a bit dark, but are comfortable with carpet, cable TV, and telephones. The original building is worth a visit even if you don't plan to stay here.

Los Balcones de Moral y Santa Catalina (Moral 217, tel. 054/20-1291, www.balconeshotel.com, US$38 s, US$49 d with breakfast) is an excellent choice, located in a beautiful and highly preserved colonial house on a corner. It has a quiet reception room, simple breakfast area, and a row of huge, comfortable rooms overlooking the cathedral bell towers and also the Chachani volcano. Apart from being large, the 17 rooms have gorgeous wood floors, nice beds and furniture, WiFi, cable TV, and a telephone.

US$50-100

In the Vallecito neighborhood is **Queen's Villa** (Luna Pizarro 512, Vallecito, tel. 054/28-3060, www.queensvillahotel.com, US$50 s, US$61 d with breakfast), with rooms and a handful of bungalows surrounded by pleasant gardens, sitting tables, palm trees, and a nice pool. The rooms vary in quality and have parquet, tile, or carpeted floors. The tranquil setting and amenities, such as inexpensive laundry, cable TV, WiFi, and kitchenettes in some bungalows, make the place worth your money.

Casa Andina Classic-Arequipa Jerusalén (Jerusalén 603, tel. 054/24-4481, www.casa-andina.com, US$76 s or d, US$131 suite with buffet breakfast) is a completely remodeled modern hotel that stands out for the bright red-and-orange blocks designing its facade. Its comfortable 94 rooms have security boxes, cable TV, WiFi, and comfy beds, and many have tubs.

On the other side of Río Chili is **Hotel La Maison D'Elise** (Bolognesi 104, tel. 054/25-6185, www.hotelmaisondelise.com, US$78 s, US$100 d, including breakfast). The modern, blocky exterior contrasts with the architecture of the rooms, which attempts to imitate the local colonial construction. All 43 rooms have cable TV, phones, WiFi, large bathrooms, and easy access to a grassy lawn with a small pool and good views of Misti. Amenities include a 24-hour free medical service, laundry, and a parking lot.

US$100-150

Sonesta Posada del Inca-Arequipa (Portal de Flores 116, tel. 054/21-5530, www.sonesta.com/Arequipa, US$100 s, US$120 d with breakfast) has a privileged location right on the Plaza de Armas. There is a rooftop terrace with a small pool, where you can be served lunch, overlooking the square. A handful of rooms

have private terraces over the square itself; the remaining rooms look into a modern, interior courtyard. Amenities include air-conditioning, minifridges, cable TV, WiFi, and a safety deposit box.

West of town is the charming **La Posada del Puente** (Esquina Puente Grau/Av. Bolognesi 101, tel. 054/25-3132, www.posadadelpuente.com, US$105 s, US$125 d with breakfast), across the Puente Grau. The landscaping is well done and the modern rooms with vaulted ceilings overlook the Misti volcano and Río Chili. All have cable TV and WiFi. The elegant dining room has a view of the river too.

Over US$150

Casa Andina Private Collection Arequipa (Ugarte 403, tel. 054/22-6907, www.casa-andina.com, US$208 s or d, US$263 suite, buffet breakfast and airport transfer included) is the finest hotel in Arequipa's historic center, and one of the best in the whole city. Declared a historic monument, this colonial mansion was Arequipa's Casa de Moneda, the old Mint House, in 1794. Restored and remodeled in 2008, the hotel features two ample colonial courtyards, original frescoes, and an exquisite chapel long hidden from view.

The hotel boasts five spectacular large suites with Peru's republican-era decor, a skylight shielding the main courtyard from Arequipa's intense sun, and 36 new spacious rooms, all with WiFi, flat screens, bathtubs, room service, and other amenities. Amenities include an Internet center, an ATM, a fourth-floor terrace, a handicrafts and gift shop, a colonial-style bar, and an excellent gourmet restaurant called Alma, with superb regional food. This hotel is three blocks away from the Plaza de Armas.

The grand **Hotel Libertador** (Plaza Bolívar s/n, Selva Alegre, tel. 054/21-5110, www.libertador.com.pe, US$220 s or d, US$395 junior suite with buffet breakfast) is the only five-star hotel in Arequipa. It sits next to one of the city's largest and prettiest parks, yet is still only a 15-minute walk to the Plaza de Armas. The rose-colored, republican-style building, built

CANYON COUNTRY

in the 1940s, has a grand lobby with elegant details carried throughout the building. The rooms and suites are decorated soberly with dark wood furniture, deep red carpets, and huge bathrooms with tubs, among all amenities for this kind of hotel. The big outdoor pool is surrounded by gardens and a playground. There is a Sunday buffet at the restaurant.

FOOD

Arequipeños are proud of their cuisine, and rightly so. But besides traditional food, there are innovative chefs whipping up Turkish, French, Japanese, Thai, Moroccan, and Italian food in the city. Additionally, Arequipa has a hidden culinary gem: *picanterías*, holes-in-the-wall, that can be very modest or more fancier, where the real Arequipeño cuisine is made and can be enjoyed.

Cafés, Bakeries, and Ice Cream

Arequipeños take their desserts very seriously, as is evident by the colorful window displays along the first block of Mercaderes or on Portal de Flores on the Plaza de Armas. The lineup on this street starts with **Manolo** (Mercaderes 107, tel. 054/21-9009, 7 A.M.–1 A.M. daily, US$5), a relaxed diner where locals come to indulge in inexpensive Peruvian meals and decadent desserts. **Cappricio** (Mercaderes 121, tel. 054/39-1000, 10 A.M.–10 P.M. Sun.–Thurs., 10 A.M.–11 P.M. Fri.–Sat., US$4) is the best, serving espresso, Italian food, and great pastries and desserts in a diner-like atmosphere.

Cafés on the Plaza de Armas are similar but with tourist prices. The exception is **La Covacha** (Portal de Flores 130, tel. 054/20-4991, 7 A.M.–10 P.M. Mon.–Sat., noon–8 P.M. Sun., US$1), serving espresso and desserts including tiramisu, chocolate mousse, and cheesecake. Next door to Librería el Lector is the charming **Colibri** (San Francisco 225, tel. 054/21-1120, 8 A.M.–11 P.M. Mon.–Fri., 5–11 P.M. Sat., 9 A.M.–11 P.M. Sun., US$1), with vaulted *sillar* ceilings, wood floors, and great espresso. It serves crepes, pies, salads, and brochettes.

On Jerusalén you can find delicious

having dessert on Arequipa's Plaza de Armas

© JORGE RIVEROS CAYO

empanadas at the tiny **El Pan Nuestro** (Jerusalén 515, tel. 054/28-1990, 6 A.M.–10 P.M. daily). For a coffee with a cause, head to **Café C.V.** (Jerusalén 406, tel. 054/22-6376, 8 A.M.–6 P.M., US$1). All proceeds go to **Casa Verde,** an orphanage for street kids. You can also buy handmade purses and backpacks to support the children. Missing an American latte? Head to **Cusco Coffee Company** (La Merced 135, tel. 054/28-1152, www.cuscocoffee.com, US$2). This is the closest you'll come to Starbucks in Arequipa.

Peruvian

Ary Quepay (Jerusalén 502, tel. 054/20-4583, www.aryquepay.com, 11 A.M.–11 P.M., US$5–13) is a good traditional Peruvian food restaurant in the historic center, despite being very touristy. The food is good and you have a varied menu with Arequipeñ cuisine as well as dishes from other regions in Peru. Live folkloric music starts 6:30 P.M.

You can find a more modern take on the same foods at **Coca K'intu** (San Francisco 302-

A, tel. 054/22-4360, 11 A.M.–midnight daily, US$7–9). This restaurant starts its meals with a marinated-olive amuse-bouche. Follow this with a pisco sour and a tender alpaca steak with passionfruit sauce, and you will have tried one of their best specialties. The best table in the house is tucked into a window nook, and one of its chairs is a big armchair.

International
Middle Eastern food is not easy to find in Peru. But in Arequipa you have it, due to a century-old tradition of immigrants; all the restaurants are clustered around San Francisco Street. **El Turko I** (San Francisco 216-A, tel. 054/20-3862, www.elturko.com.pe, US$3–5, open 24 hours) is the best place to go for a quick delicious bite at any time of the day and night. Whether it is a *dönner kebab* (US$2); a *cacik* salad, made with cucumber, yogurt, and garlic (US$3); *patlicanli urfa,* lamb meatballs with a veggie sauce and rice (US$4.60); or *yaztürlüzü,* a chicken and veggie stew (US$4.60), this place is worth every cent.

El Turko II (San Francisco 315, tel. 054/21-5729, www.elturko.com.pe, 8 A.M.–midnight daily, US$5–12) is the older sister of Turko I—a real gem. With a smart decor in the restaurant, hummus, falafel, eggplant dishes, and lamb are just a few items on the delicious Turkish menu. For dessert, the *baklava* with a scoop of vanilla ice cream (US$4.50) is just like heaven.

The Moroccan resto-lounge **Ras El Hanout y los 40 Sabores** (San Francisco 227, tel. 054/22-7779, www.raselhanout40.com, 9 A.M.–11 P.M. Mon.–Sat., US$7–12) is the creation of a Peruvian family with a Moroccan past. The restaurant serves traditional-style tagines, salads, *kemia,* lamb brochettes, *harira* soup, couscous, and mint tea, of course. It is the second Moroccan restaurant in South America.

Creperie Zig Zag (Santa Catalina 208, tel. 054/20-6620, www.zigzagrestaurant.com, US$3–5) is inside the colonial house of the Alliance Française. In this tiny café, with a definite French atmosphere, you can watch as your crepes are made. There is a menu of salty and sweet crepes.

◖ **Paquita Siu** (Calle Granada 102, Urb. Los Sauces, Cayma, tel. 054/25-1915, noon–4 P.M. and 6–11 P.M. Mon.–Sat., noon–5 P.M. Sun., US$5–20) is without doubt the best place to enjoy first-rate Chinese, Japanese, and Thai food. The one responsible for such an incredible culinary experience is Martín Ortiz Siu, an experienced chef who lived 10 years in London, son of legendary culinary figure Paquita Siu. The menu includes a spicy panang, Thai green curry (US$10), prawn tempura with teriyaki sauce (US$11), and an *arroz chaufa especial* (fried rice, US$4), among at least 60 dishes from these three different cuisines.

There are several restaurants with rooftop and sidewalk seating on Pasaje La Catedral, the charming pedestrian alley behind the cathedral. The best views are at **Mixto's** (Pasaje La Catedral 115, tel. 054/20-5343, 9 A.M.–10 P.M. daily, US$4–7). The menu offers everything from *cebiche* to pastas to pizzas. Next door, **La Trufa** (Pasaje La Catedral 111, tel. 054/40-5290, 9 A.M.–11 P.M. daily, US$3–7) has good pasta, chicken curry, seafood, and great service. Live folkloric music is featured Monday–Saturday from 7 P.M.

Picanterías
The name refers to a place where spicy food is sold (*picante* means spicy), even if all meals are not necessarily hot. The origin of these eateries can be traced back to at least 19th-century Arequipa, where artists, bohemians, and foodies would gather for a bite during the day—partying, or on a Sunday lunch. *Picanterías* still hold much of Arequipa's culinary essence. So, if you are a foodie and willing to dig into the real thing, you should consider going to, at least, a couple of places; they only open for lunch.

Sabor Caymeño (Plaza de Armas de Cayma 112, tel. 054/25-1362, 6 A.M.–6 P.M. Mon.–Fri., 4 A.M.–6 P.M. Sat., 3 A.M.–6 P.M. Sun., US$3–8) is probably one of the last genuine *picanterías* in the city, located in the upper district of Cayma. The unusual opening hours are because the featured dish of this place is *adobo*—macerated pieces of pork meat in corn beer, served in a soup-like sauce in which you dip fresh, crusty bread—a typical meal that people eat after a long night of partying and drinks, and this is one of the best places to try it. But this eatery, owned by friendly Doña María Meza, who is still in charge of the cooking, also has *caldo* (meat broth), *costillares* (fried ribs with potatoes), and smaller appetizers. As in any other *picantería,* the place is open as long as there is food.

La Lucila (Grau 147, Sachaca, tel. 054/20-5348, http://pincaterialalucial.com, US$3–6), located outside Arequipa in the rural town of Sachaca, is without doubt the most celebrated of all *picanterías,* due to her owner, Lucila Salas Valencia, a living legend of Arequipa's culinary heritage. Born in 1917, Doña Lucila was in charge of her business until just some years ago, cooking in a old, artisan-made kitchen, where you could still see guinea pigs running in between your legs, and food was cooked over a wood stove. Things have changed of course, and now, La Lucila is quite trendy but trying to preserve tradition in the food-making. Specialties include: *rocoto relleno* (baked, stuffed bell pepper–like chilis), duck, *camarones* (freshwater prawns) in different versions (fried, stewed, or in chowder), *cuy chactado* (deep-fried guinea pig), and a different soup for every day of the week.

La Nueva Palomino (Pasaje Leoncio Prado 122, Yanahuara, tel. 054/25-3500, 11 A.M.–5 P.M. Mon.–Sat., 11 A.M.–6 P.M. Sun., US$5–10) is a good example of a *picantería* that has been in business for three generations. The Palomino family, made up of savvy cooks—grandmother, mother, and granddaughter—has opened other restaurants with similar names (La Palomino, for example, is on the corner of Leoncio Prado and Misti; it is much more traditional and owned by a cousin). The menu includes boiled lima beans with mint, *choclo con queso* (boiled corn with chunks of cheese), *chupe de camarones* (freshwater prawn chowder), *pastel de papas* (baked potato cake),

and another 50 dishes with lamb, beef, duck and chicken. Portions are huge, so we highly suggest ordering a few dishes and sharing.

Tradición Arequipeña (Dolores 111, tel. 054/42-6467, noon–7 P.M. Sun.–Thurs., noon–8:30 P.M. Fri., noon–midnight Sat., US$5–10) is less traditional but still well reputed for its food. The menu includes *adobo,* 11 versions of *camarones,* and a range of *chupes* (soups). Food is served either indoors under bamboo ceilings or in a cactus-lined garden. On Saturday at 5 P.M., there is a live band, including an orchestra.

Last but not least, the more-than-hundred-year-old **Sol de Mayo** (Jerusalén 207, Yanahuara, tel. 054/25-4148, www.restaurant-soldemayo.com, 11 A.M.–10 P.M. Mon.–Sat., 11 A.M.–6 P.M. Sun., US$5–9) is the result of a long road of transformation from a hole-in-the-wall to a sophisticated restaurant. Still a *picantería* at heart (that's why it's included in this list), this eatery is probably the most popular with tourists. Highly recommended dishes are the *ocopa con queso frito, rocoto relleno,* and anything with *camarones.* The service here is excellent, with the waiters literally running from table to table!

Fine Dining

With a menu initially designed by Peru's iconic chef, Gastón Acurio, and a location in the Monasterio de Santa Catalina, **La Trattoria del Monasterio** (Santa Catalina 309, tel. 054/20-4062, noon–4 P.M. and 7–11 P.M. Mon.–Sat., noon–4 P.M. Sun., US$7–15) was bound for success. But the clean white tablecloths, attentive service, and precise dishes have closed the deal. Some suggested specialties are tagliolini with lamb ragu (US$10), prawn risotto with artichokes and saffron (US$12), and the extraordinary and emblematic *rocoto relleno de camarones,* with *pastel de papas* (US$9). Verónica Luque, the owner, also runs a café inside the Santa Catalina Monastery and owns Cappricio.

Zíngaro Restaurant (San Francisco 309, tel. 054/21-7662, www.zingaro-restaurante.com, US$5–12) is a highly acclaimed restaurant, based in a colonial house, that serves an interesting fusion of Peruvian and Mediterranean gastronomy. Order anything from Novoandino selections or a filet mignon to trout or a delicious *chupe de camarones* (prawn chowder). Don't miss the delicious coca or *rocoto* sours.

Zig Zag (Zela 210, tel. 054/20-6020, www. zigzagrestaurant.com, 6 P.M.–midnight, US$5–12) is a cozy place right across from Plaza San Francisco, with house specialties such as stone-cooked alpaca, ostrich, and lamb meat, which is served carpaccio-style or sizzling, on a stone slab. Its claim to fame is an iron spiral staircase supposedly built by Gustav Eiffel. Some diners have found this place a bit overrated. Try it and decide for yourself.

Chicha por Gastón Acurio (Santa Catalina 210, Int. 105, tel. 054/28-7360, www.chicha. com.pe, US$6–15) is the new go-to restaurant in town, with a very chic atmosphere and impeccable service. The food can be an explosion of flavors for the uninitiated in world cuisine, but the result of a fusion between Arequipeño, Mediterranean, and Asian flavors can be a blast. Cocktails are superb and desserts even better.

Pizza
The best pizza in town is at **Gianni's** (San Francisco 304, 6 P.M.–1 A.M. Mon.–Sat., US$5–6), an Italian-owned restaurant with the freshest of ingredients (the mushrooms aren't canned here, always the true test). Dinners are served with generous glasses of Chilean or Argentine wine or liters of sangria. A local favorite is **Marengo** (Santa Catalina 221, tel. 054/28-4883, 8 A.M.–midnight daily, US$5–10). This pizzeria has been in town for 13 years and has locations in Cusco and Cajamarca. The most laid-back of all the pizzerias is the cave-like **Los Leños** (Jerusalén 407, tel. 054/28-9197, 3–11 P.M. daily, US$4–6), serving great wood-fired pizzas for over a decade. The dim lighting and graffiti on the *sillar* walls give it a pub atmosphere.

Vegetarian
The strictly vegetarian **Lakshmivan** (Jerusalén 402, tel. 054/22-8768, 7 A.M.–10 P.M. daily, US$3.50) serves incredibly well-priced, creative dishes in a pleasant garden patio. The menu includes seven different soy meat dishes, vegetarian paella, spinach lasagna, tofu and soy hamburgers, pumpkin soup, and 16 different salads under US$3—including the hard-to-find Greek salad. This is also the best place around for a healthy breakfast of muesli, yogurt, and homemade bread.

Govinda (Santa Catalina 120, tel. 054/28-5540, 7 A.M.–9:30 P.M. daily, US$2.50) has one of its largest restaurants here, a half block from the Plaza de Armas, with both indoor and courtyard seating. The menu is a range of vegetarian, Italian, Hindu, and Peruvian plates. Natural yogurt can be bought by the liter or quaffed in the form of a mango shake along with the US$2.50 lunch menu.

Markets
Mercado San Camilo (on San Camilo between Nicolás de Piérola and Perú) is the main market in the city, where you can find meat, vegetables, fruits, good cheese, and anything you can think of. There are also *juguerías,* or juice stands, where you can drink any kind of mix for US$1.50. On the Plaza de Armas, **El Super** (Portal de la Municipalidad 130, tel. 054/28-6616, 9:15 A.M.–9:15 P.M. Mon.–Sat., 9:15 A.M.–1:30 P.M. Sun.) can fill in with dry goods, yogurt, tuna, beer, and wine.

INFORMATION AND SERVICES
Tourist Information and Police
The **Iperú** (Santa Catalina 210, tel. 054/22-1227, www.peru.info, 9 A.M.–7 P.M. daily) tourist information office is in the Casona de Santa Catalina. There is a second **Iperú** at the airport (tel. 054/44-4564). The **tourist police** are at Jerusalén 315 (tel. 054/20-1258).

Immigration Office
Tourist visas can be extended at the **Migraciones** (J.L. Bustamante and Rivero, Urb. Quinta Tristán, tel. 054/42-1759, 8 A.M.–1 P.M. Mon.–Sat.).

Health Care

For health care, **Clínica Arequipa** (Puente Grau and Bolognesi, tel. 054/25-3416, 24 hours) is a fully equipped hospital and pharmacy with some of the better doctors in town. **PAZ-Holandesa** (Jorge Chávez 527, tel. 054/20-6720, www.pazholandesa.com, 24 hours) is another well-equipped medical practice founded by a Dutch neurosurgeon from Rotterdam. It began as a children's hospital but is now seeing tourists and providing dental care as well. A specialized dental clinic in town is **Dental Care San José** (Quiñones B-5, Yanahuara, 9 A.M.–1 P.M. and 4–9 P.M. Mon.–Fri., 9 A.M.–7 P.M. Sat.).

At the corner of Jerusalén and Mercaderes, there are two reliable pharmacies: **Botica Fasa** (Mercaderes 145, www.boticasfasa.com.pe, 7 A.M.–midnight Mon.–Sat., 9 A.M.–11 P.M. Sun.) and **Boticas BTL** (Mercaderes 200, 24 hours).

Banks and Money Exchange

There are many money exchange offices around the first block of San Francisco, and most of the banks with ATMs are near the Plaza de Armas, including Interbank (Mercaderes 217, **Scotiabank** (Mercaderes 410), **Banco de Crédito** (Jerusalén 125), and **BBVA Banco Continental** (San Francisco 108). Money wires can be received at **Western Union** (Santa Catalina 115, 8:30 A.M.–7:30 P.M. Mon.–Sat., 9 A.M.–1 P.M. Sun.).

Communications

The **Serpost** mail office is at Moral 118 (www.serpost.com.pe, 8 A.M.–8 P.M. Mon.–Sat., 9 A.M.–2 P.M. Sun.). Although there is fast Internet on almost every corner, one of the quieter cafés is **CiberMarket** (Santa Catalina 115-B). For late-night Internet, try **Online** (Jerusalén 412, 9 A.M.–midnight). International Internet calls can be made at **Catedral Internet** (Pasaje La Catedral 101, tel. 054/22-0622, 8 A.M.–11 P.M. daily) and at the café at Jerusalén 301. In Vallecito, Internet is available at San Martin 222. There are private phone booths at the **Telefónica office** (Santa

Catalina 118), and **AQP Comunicaciones** in the Terminal Terrestre offers cheap long-distance telephone calls. **DHL** shipping service is at Santa Catalina 115 (tel. 054/23-4288).

Language Schools

There are many language schools in Arequipa. Some offer group lessons and other individual classes. If you are interested in a homestay, ask the school if it arranges them. Many do. A handful of recommended schools are listed here. Contact Carmen Cornejo at the **Centro de Intercambio Cultural** (Cercado, Urb. Universiteria, tel. 054/22-1165, www.ceicaperu.com). Besides Spanish, **Centro de Idiomas UNSA** (San Agustín 106, tel. 054/24-7524) offers English, French, Portuguese, and Chinese classes. **Rocio language classes** (Melgar 209, of. 22, tel. 054/22-4568, www.spanish-peru.com) is a more affordable option, and classes are catered to students' flexibility. The best is **Centro Cultural Peruano Norteamericano** (Melgar 109, tel. 054/80-1022), which offers Spanish and English courses and has offices throughout Peru.

Laundry

A good laundromat is **Quick Laundry** (Jerusalén 520, tel. 054/20-5503, 7 A.M.–8 P.M. daily, US$1.50/kg), which has same-day service. **Magic Laundry** (Jerusalén 404) is another good option.

Car Rental

You don't need a four-wheel drive for the bumpy but beautiful drive to Colca Canyon, but it's recommended. Companies include **Genesis Rent A Car** (Alcides Carrión 701, tel. 054/20-2356, no credit cards), **Hertz** (Palacio Viejo 214, tel. 054/28-2519, www.hertz.com, 24 hours, must be 24 or older), and **Carisa** (Pampita Zevallos 325, Yanahuara, tel. 054/25-5474, carisarent@terra.com).

GETTING THERE AND AROUND
Air

The **Alfredo Rodríguez Ballón International Airport** (Aviación s/n, tel. 054/44-3464) is seven kilometers northwest of the city, or about a US$3 cab ride.

LAN (Lima tel. 01/213-8200, www.lan.com) has at least 6–8 daily flights between Lima and Arequipa, and several other to/from Cusco (via Juliaca) and Lima. **Star Perú** doesn't fly to Arequipa, but Peruvian Airlines (www.peruvianairlines.pe) has four daily flights to/from Arequipa.

Bus

There are daily departures to Lima, Tacna, Cusco, and Puno from the two bus terminals Arequipa has—the rather empty **Terrapuerto** and the bustling **Terminal Terrestre**—right next to each other on Jacinto Ibañez, a five-minute, US$2 taxi ride outside of town. Most companies have offices in the Terminal Terrestre that are open 7 A.M.–9 P.M.

Most bus companies make the 15-hour direct trip to Lima overnight, with different services, including buses stopping along the way in Nasca and Ica. The best option is **Cruz del Sur** (Terminal Terrestre, tel. 054/42-7375, www.cruzdelsur.com.pe), with seven daily departures to Lima, which has nearly full beds on the first floor for US$47 and reclining seats on the second floor for US$30.

Oltursa (Terminal Terrestre, tel. 054/42-6566, www.oltursa.com.pe) is also a good option, with four daily departures. Prices range US$29–45, depending on the floor. **Ormeño** (Terrapuerto or Terminal Terrestre, tel. 054/42-3546 or 054/42-4187, www.grupo-ormeno.com.pe) has US$35 direct Royal Class buses, US$25 business class buses with video and bathroom, and a US$25 economy bus. Other Lima options include **Civa** (tel. 054/42-6563, www.civa.com.pe), with comfortable buses from US$18–34.

Direct buses also leave Arequipa for the five-hour journey to Tacna, Peru's border town with a duty-free port but few tourist attractions besides the heaps of imported, almost-new Toyota station wagons (US$3,000 each). From here a US$3 half-hour taxi ride can be taken across the border to Arica, Chile, where most travelers continue south in Chile by bus or by domestic flight. Ormeño buses leave for Tacna three times a day for US$5, and Cruz del Sur offers a US$8 Imperial service. Transportes Flores has buses that head south daily to Moquegua (3.5 hours), Ilo (five hours), and on to Tacna (six hours).

For the Colca Canyon, **Turismo Milagros** (Terminal Terrestre, tel. 054/42-3260) has buses leaving daily at 4 A.M. and 2:30 P.M. for the three-hour journey to Chivay. The buses wait there a half hour and then continue two hours onto Cabanaconde, arriving at 9:30 A.M. and 8 P.M. The morning bus drops travelers off at the Cruz del Cóndor, about 20 minutes before Cabanaconde. Return buses leave Cabanaconde at 11 A.M. and 10 P.M., and from Chivay at 1:30 A.M. and 2:30 P.M. Travelers looking for the wild overland route to Cusco should try **Carhuamayo** (tel. 054/42-6835), which has buses leaving Arequipa that pass by Pampa Cañahuas, Condorama Dam, Espinar, and Sicuani en route to Cusco, a 10-hour journey through beautiful, rugged highlands. The US$8 bus leaves at 7 A.M. and 7:30 P.M. daily.

Local Transportation

Arequipa is a safe city by Peruvian standards, so you can either call a taxi or flag one on the street. A recommended company is **Taxi 21** (tel. 054/21-2121). If they're busy, try the taxi company at 054/43-1313.

Colca Valley and Canyon

Road engineers could hardly believe their eyes when they visited the Colca Valley in the late 1970s to build the area's first road. Condors cruised through the brilliant blue skies. A river lay thousands of feet below at the bottom of an impenetrable canyon. Potatoes and corn overflowed from thousands of stone terraces. Stone-and-adobe villages, each with a small but elegant colonial church, were strung like pearls along the valley rim. Women herded alpacas while dressed in fantastically embroidered skirts and hats with ribbons and sequins.

Even with a spate of new roads and tourist hotels, Colca Valley and Colca Canyon are still an odd combination of historical time warp and geological anomaly. The Collagua and Cabana peoples who lived here for at least 2,000 years, from 800 B.C. onward, built an ingenious terracing system on the valley walls that collects snowmelt from nearby volcanoes. Inca Mayta Cápac arrived here with his army in the 15th

century and, according to Spanish chronicler Francisco Jerónimo de Oré, sealed the conquest by marrying Mama Tancaray Yacchi, daughter of a local Collagua chief. The Inca built for her a house of copper that, according to legend, was melted to make the gigantic bells that still hang in Coporaque's towers.

The Spaniards, a century after the Inca, were less kind: They herded villagers into *reducciones* (new settlements) and put them to work in plantations or the nearby Caylloma silver mine. All the while, the Collaguas absorbed Catholic imagery into their festivals. The women copied the petticoats of the Spanish women, adding their natural indigos and bright blues and their fine, paisley-like embroidery. And then Colca, with neither roads nor communications, was forgotten.

In 1979, shortly after the road was built for the Condorama Dam, a motley crew of six Polish adventurers led by Piotr Chmielinski

Collagua woman and a hawk in Colca Canyon

© JORGE RIVEROS CAYO

CANYON COUNTRY

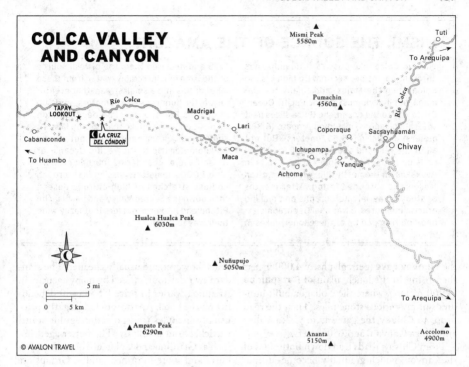

COLCA VALLEY AND CANYON

Mismi Peak
5580m

Tuti

To Arequipa

Río Colca

Pumachin
4560m

Río Colca

TAPAY
LOOKOUT

Madrigal

Lari

Coporaque

Sacsayhuamán

Cabanaconde

LA CRUZ
DEL CÓNDOR

Chivay

Ichupampa

To Huambo

Maca

Yanque

Achoma

Hualca Hualca Peak
6030m

Nuñupujo
5050m

0   5 mi

0   5 km

To Arequipa

Ampato Peak
6290m

Ananta
5150m

Accolomo
4900m

© AVALON TRAVEL

and Andrzej Pietowski, with Peruvian Antonio Vellutino (the owner of **Cusipata**), discovered another side of Colca: adventure. They made the first river descent of the Colca Canyon. In a grueling five-week journey, they navigated the Class V waters of the canyon and confirmed that the Colca Canyon was at least 3,400 meters deep—more than twice the depth of Arizona's Grand Canyon. Since that expedition, Colca Canyon has become, along with Cusco and Huaraz, a center for adventure sports. From Cabanaconde, near the end of the canyon road, climbers begin to climb Ampato, the 6,300-meter volcano where the Juanita mummy was discovered. Numerous other hikes and mountain-bike routes lead throughout the canyon and its spectacular villages.

PLANNING YOUR TRIP

The shortest way into Colca is a four-hour journey on bumpy, dusty roads from Arequipa.

After the first hour of smooth pavement outside Arequipa, the route veers into a lunar landscape, decorated only with rocks, *ichu* grass, and the blob-like *yareta* plant. The fluorescent green **yareta** appears to be a moss-covered boulder but is actually a plant that lives for centuries but only grows to about one meter. It requires a very specific climate: the dry, desolate tundra over 4,200 meters. The plant survives because of its hundreds of tightly bunched waxy leaves, which trap moisture inside and allow the plant to withstand temperatures down to -50°C.

This whole area is part of the **Reserva Nacional Salinas y Aguada Blanca,** which is devoid of humans but teems with animals: flamingos, geese, and black-faced Andean gulls congregate at salty lakes. Vicuñas graze the grasslands, and *vizcachas*—they look like rabbits but are actually a rodent—dart among the stony fields. The road in climbs high, passing

CANYON COUNTRY

MISMI, THE SOURCE OF THE AMAZON?

The Río Colca, like Cusco's Urubamba, has different names per section. Up high it's the Colca, then the Majes, and finally the Camaná, but it all dumps into the Pacific Ocean. On its way to the ocean, the Colca slices past several volcanoes, including Ampato (6,380 meters) and Mismi (5,597 meters). But not all of the rain and snow that falls on Mismi ends up in the Colca. Some of it collects in two lakes on the north side, which are often frozen and shrouded in fog. After months of studying aerial photographs and making precise measures, a National Geographic expedition tromped up to these lonely lakes in 1975 and declared them the official source of the Amazon. Incredibly, water from these lakes drains into a small stream that eventually, after hundreds of kilometers, ends up in Cusco's Río Apurímac. So depending on its position, a snowflake that falls on Mismi's summit can either have a brief but bumpy 75-kilometer trip to the Pacific Ocean – or it can have a meandering journey of more than 7,000 kilometers, passing first through endless stretches of high-altitude desert, then down the Sacred Valley and past Machu Picchu and into brown rivers that lazily wind their way to Brazil.

the **Sumbay cave** (petroglyphs) at 4,000 meters then rising to the lonely plain of **Patapampa** (4,900 meters), where the Collagua built hundreds of mysterious stone piles. Then the road drops to **Chivay** the gateway to Colca Valley and Colca Canyon, at 3,650 meters.

From Chivay, roads lead down both sides of the canyon, which gradually becomes deeper and more pronounced as it works its way from Chivay. The villages on the north side are less visited by tourists and have nice colonial churches. Starting from Chivay, a dirt road crosses the Río Colca and passes through Coporaque, Ichupampa, and Lari and dead-ends in Madrigal. Cars can return to the other side of the canyon via bridges near Ichupampa and Lari. The more often visited side of the canyon is the south side, leading to **Cruz del Cóndor,** where a 60-kilometer dirt road leads from Chivay to Yanque, Achoma, Maca, Pinchollo, and Cabanaconde.

Colca is spread out, and churches keep odd hours, so travelers who want to see a lot of Colca should consider renting a car or doing a two-day agency tour. If your budget can handle the US$100 daily car rental fee, we strongly recommend this option. The best way to experience Colca is simply by stopping, at whim, en route to take pictures, explore the valley and the canyon, and feel the crisp air. The agency

deals, however, are usually cheaper. The standard two-day tour, offered by many agencies in Arequipa, varies in price US$45–80 depending on the hotel. Apart from lodging, the price usually includes transportation, guide, tourist ticket, and breakfast. The better agencies, such as Giardino and Colonial Tours, have new buses and more informed guides. Groups are often just a few people.

Most two-day tours leave Arequipa and stop to see vicuñas and other archaeological remains in the Reserva Nacional Salinas y Aguada Blanca before exploring the Inca ruins and churches around Chivay. But the highlight is a starlit evening soak in thermal hot springs, either near Chivay or, better yet, at the Colca Lodge near Coporaque. Groups rise early the next morning to drive an hour or two down the canyon to the Cruz del Cóndor. Afterwards, groups visit the churches in Yanque, Maca, or Pinchollo and then head back to Arequipa. Because of road conditions, few agencies take the longer **Pulpera** return route, which takes a few more hours but passes through the interesting villages of Callali, Sibayo, and Tuti and tours the petroglyphs at Mollepunko Cave. Until the road improves, this last route is only recommended for people with an extra day on their hands.

If you are traveling on your own, it is easy to

take a bus to Chivay or Cabanaconde and travel around on foot or by *colectivo*. AUTOCOLCA, the Colca Canyon managing authority, requires a US$25 tourist ticket to access Cruz del Cóndor as well as the area's churches. Proceeds supposedly maintain the valley and canyon's historical sights.

Colca's skies are sunny and deep blue April–October, making a wide-brimmed hat and sunscreen essential. Make sure, too, to bring plenty of warm clothing, as temperatures can get below freezing at night. If you are not coming from Cusco, stay in Arequipa for a few days to avoid *soroche* or altitude sickness. Chivay itself is at 3,652 meters.

ENTERTAINMENT AND EVENTS
Festivals
The Colca Valley has a well-deserved reputation for beautiful festivals. **La Virgen de Candelaria** is celebrated in Chivay, Acoma, and Maca on February 2–3. Both **Carnaval,** in late February, and **Easter week,** in April, are lively in Colca. **La Fiesta de San Juan** is celebrated in Yanque and several other Colca towns on June 13.

The celebration of the **Virgen del Carmen** around July 16 is a huge event in Cabanaconde and Chivay, along with that of **Santiago Apóstol** in Coporaque and Madrigal on July 25. An interesting eight-day festival takes place in Chivay from August 15 on, in honor of the town's patron saint, **La Virgen de la Asunción,** with simultaneous celebrations taking place in Coporaque, Maca, and Yanque.

Yanque's **Spring Festival** happens September 23. **La Fiesta de la Virgen del Rosario** takes place October 7 in Chivay, Achoma, Ichupampa, Maca, and Yanque. **Todos Santos** (All Saints' Day) and **Los Fieles Difuntos** (All Souls' Day) can be enjoyed throughout Colca Valley on November 1–2. The final big event is a celebration for **La Virgen Inmaculada** in Chivay and Yanque, during which time the five-day Wititi dance is performed. The Wititi is also performed in Yanque from December 25 onward. PromPeru,

the government promotion agency, keeps an updated list of festivals at www.peru.info.

RECREATION
Trekking
Those who enjoy hiking in Arizona's Grand Canyon will love Colca Canyon, which has the added beauty of volcanoes and untouched villages.

A popular short trek drops 1,200 meters down into Colca Canyon from the village of Cabanaconde to **Sangalle,** a riverside oasis where three campgrounds with pools have sprung up since 2000. Their names—Paradise, Oasis, and Edén—play off the same theme and are easy to confuse. Sangalle, which feels subtropical even when Chivay is chilly, is a great place to read books and lounge by the pool. But don't expect any cross-cultural encounters. You can camp for a few dollars a night or rent cane huts with rickety beds, and they also sell beer and food. As they are close to one another, check out each campsite before you choose. You will need to pack out all solid waste, including organic waste, cans, glass, and plastic—a look at the riverbanks will show the area's trash management problems. Hiking down takes two or three hours, but returning to Cabanaconde, which most people do the second day, can take twice as long.

A longer, more interesting option is to cross a footbridge at Sangalle and hike up the other side of the Colca Canyon to the charming village of Tapay. Another path leads from here back to a good camping spot farther upstream on the Río Colca. From here the path winds uphill, approximately 1,200 meters, to the Cruz del Cóndor. This trip could be done in two or three days, though getting to the Cruz del Cóndor by 8 A.M. would mean breaking camp by 4 A.M.

Other interesting treks involve hiking along the canyon rim between various towns. Despite what your maps say, there are ancient Collagua paths connecting most villages together. Because most of the tourists travel along the Cruz del Cóndor side, the best trekking is on the north side of the canyon—though it

© RENÉE DEL GAUDIO AND ROSS WEHNER

resting at the base of Colca Canyon

CANYON COUNTRY

is easy to cross back and forth at the bridges near Maca and Yanque. Colca is a safe and easy place to improvise a route, as long as you have a few liters of water, a bit of Spanish, and a wide-brimmed hat.

A truly adventurous four- or five-day route leads from Cabanaconde to the Valley of the Volcanoes and retraces the steps of Robert Shippee and George Johnson, who flew over and mapped the entire area in 1929. They were so intrigued by the Valley of the Volcanoes that they forged out from Cabanaconde to find it. Their route drops west (downstream) into the Colca Canyon and then back up the other side to the village of Choco, at 2,473 meters. After camping here, hike up and over a 4,500-meter pass and then on to the village of Chacas, 3,100 meters. A road, with sparse traffic, leads from here to Andagua, at the head of the Valley of the Volcanoes, one day's hike away.

CHIVAY

The village of Chivay, at 3,652 meters, lies where the main road to Arequipa meets the Colca Valley. It is the traditional base for exploring either the valley or the canyon, though it has become a bit touristy in recent years. Many backpackers are now heading to Cabanaconde, closer to the Cruz del Cóndor, or to excellent new lodges near Coporaque or Yanque. Chivay has the best-equipped clinic (with a laboratory), and it's the police and mountain rescue headquarters.

Sights

Chivay has an interesting 18th-century church, **Nuestra Señora de la Asunción,** and a bridge with Inca foundations right outside of town that once supported a hanging bridge made of plant fibers. Immediately on the other side of the bridge is the Inca road to Cusco, marked by a path leading up to stone grain stores. On the hillside above are several round Inca storehouses.

Chivay's main draw, however, is **La Calera thermal baths** (4:30 A.M.–7 P.M., US$4 for foreigners), which lie two kilometers outside of town. There are five hot pools, including two new ones designed for tourists. The first is an outdoor pool at river's edge, and the second is round and enclosed with a domed ceiling. Both are clean and kept at a temperature of 40°C, though they can become quite packed with travelers during the evenings. Other hot baths in the area are the riverside tubs at **Colca Lodge.** They are a half-hour drive away (US$6–12 for round-trip taxi) and are free with the purchase of a lunch or dinner. Otherwise access is US$10–15.

After stargazing in the hot springs, why not head to **Casa Andina's Planetarium** (Huayna Cápac s/n, tel. 054/53-1020, www.casa-andina. com, hourly showings 6:30 P.M.–9:30 P.M., US$10) and learn what you were looking at? Nightly shows explain the ancient Andean culture's understanding of star-filled Colca sky. The presentation involves both an indoor and outdoor viewing through a telescope.

Accommodations

The best choice in town for those on a budget is the friendly **La Casa de Lucila** (Grau

© NANCY CONNICK AND DAVE JANKOWSKI

children in Chivay, in the Colca Canyon

folkloric show. A more peaceful option is **Pozo del Cielo** (tel. 054/53-1041, www.pozodelcielo. com.pe, US$47 s, US$58 d with breakfast). The hotel is right across the Inca bridge from Chivay, perched up on a bluff that is an easy walk to the nearby Inca ruins. The lodge is laid out like a small stone-and-adobe village, with rooms of whitewashed walls, exposed beams, and excellent canyon views. The cozy dining room serves typical Andean food.

Food

The locals' favorite lunch spot is the clean and well-run **Yavarí** (Plaza de Armas 604, tel. 054/48-9109, 7 A.M.–9 P.M. daily, US$3), serving spit-roasted chicken or a delicious daily US$3 menu with lots of options. The best meal in town is served up on the long wooden tables of **Witite** (Siglo XX 328, tel. 054/53-1154, 10 A.M.–4 P.M. daily, US$5–7). The English-speaking owner offers an excellent midday buffet for US$6, which includes trout caught in the nearby river and alpaca meat.

El Nido (Zarumilla 216, tel. 054/53-1010, 10 A.M.–11 P.M. daily, US$6–8) is probably the classiest choice in town. It serves alpaca seven different ways and has a good wine list. The most intriguing cocktail is El Inca Rabioso (The Pissed-Off Inca), a concoction of *maté de coca* and pisco. It also has a nightly *peña* (live *criollo* music) at 8 P.M. A simpler choice is **Killari** (Plaza de Armas 601, tel. 054/53-1225, 9 A.M.–9 P.M. daily, US$4–6), whose lunch menu often features the potato dish *causa* and trout. For pizza, **Lobo's Bar Pizzeria** (Plaza de Armas 101, tel. 054/53-1081, 9 A.M.–10 P.M. daily, US$4) is the trendiest place, with hip music, pizzas from a wood-fired oven, and three drinks for US$4 during happy hour.

For drinks try **McElroy's Irish Bar** (General Morán, Plaza de Armas, tel. 054/53-1086, 6 P.M.–midnight), with a pool table, Heineken, and two nightly happy hours. For local music and dancing, there is **Yllalkuy** (22 de Agosto 330, tel. 054/80-3353, 9 A.M.–11 P.M. daily, US$6). This odd sunken chamber is in need of a good scrubbing and, like most *peñas,* is best known for its drinks and dancing—not its food.

131, tel. 054/53-1109, www.vitatours.com. pe, US$23 s, US$29 d with breakfast). The comfortable, homelike hotel is very clean with carpeted rooms. Another option, near the market, is **Colca Wasi Kolping** (Siglo XX s/n, tel. 054/53-1076, www.hoteleskolping.net, US$26 s, US$35 d with breakfast). The seven bungalows of this small hotel open on to the canyon and are perfect for those who want to be near the town but close to nature. The **Colca Inn** (Salaverry 307, tel. 054/53-1111, www.hotelcolcainn.com, US$23 s, US$36 d with breakfast) is a reliable midrange choice with large rooms and good beds. The bathrooms and carpet are in need of an update, but the downstairs bar has a pool table. **Casa Andina** (Huayna Cápac s/n, tel. 054/53-1020, www.casa-andina.com, US$86 s or d with breakfast), part of a well-run national chain, is a charming complex of rooms and 30-odd bungalows connected by stone-lined walkways. The rooms are tastefully decorated, with modern bathrooms, beds with down comforters, and heaters. The large dining room serves buffet dinners with a nightly

Information and Services

The office of Colca's main **tourist police** (tel. 054/48-8623, 24 hours) and mountain rescue are on the main plaza. Just a block up from the plaza, on Siglo XX, is the **AUTOCOLCA** office (8 A.M.–1 P.M. and 4–7 P.M. Mon.–Fri., 8 A.M.–1 P.M. Sat.), which sells the Colca tourist ticket. There is a 24-hour **health center** (Puente Inca s/n, tel. 054/53-1074), and a good pharmacy is **Botica Rivera** (Salaverry 123, 9 A.M.–10 P.M. daily). There is a **Banco de la Nación** on the plaza, with ATM. The post office, **Serpost,** is also on the plaza.

Getting There and Around

Chivay's new bus station, with good bathrooms and snack shops, is a five-minute walk on the outskirts of town. **Empresa de Transportes Reyna** (tel. 054/53-1014) has US$7 buses leaving for Arequipa. **Turismo Milagros** (tel. 054/53-1115) offers a similar service at comparable prices. The final option is **Transportes Andalucia** (tel. 054/53-1106), whose US$7 buses leave for Arequipa five times daily.

Once in Chivay, *colectivos* for the thermal baths leave when full from the main square (US$1, 15 minutes)—or a taxi costs US$1. *Colectivos* also leave from the main square for the Cruz del Cóndor (US$25 round-trip); a private taxi for up to four people is US$30. From Chivay, *colectivos* also leave frequently for villages on both sides of the canyon.

YANQUE

Yanque, 10 kilometers west of Chivay, is a simple town with dirt streets and a baroque church, **Inmaculada Concepción,** which was rebuilt in 1702 and has a mestizo facade carved with various saints, including Santa Rosa de Lima. The main in-town attraction is the **Museo de Yanque** (Plaza de armas, 9 A.M.–6:30 P.M. daily, US$4), which illustrates the area's history through displays and videos. From the east side of the Plaza de Armas, a one-kilometer path leads to an ancient stone bridge over the Río Colca. From the bridge, the adobe walls of Inca hanging tombs are perched on the cliff face. Those with energy

and two free hours can cross the Colca and climb up to the ruins at **Uyu Uyu,** where the Collagua lived before the Spanish forced them to settle in present-day Coporaque. Return by walking over the car bridge just downstream of Yanque, where there are public hot springs (4 A.M.–7 P.M. daily, US$0.50). Or, if you can swing it, stop at the tubs of Colca Lodge near Coporaque (free access with lunch or dinner, or US$10–15.)

Accommodations and Food

The best backpacker hostel is the simple and clean **El Tambo** (San Antonio 602, Arequipa tel. 054/968-8125 or Yanque tel. 054/83-2174, hhostaltambo@hotmail.com, US$5 s, US$10 d), whose rooms face a grassy garden. Though a bit isolated on the road at the outskirts of town, **Tradicion Colca** (Colca s/n, tel. 054/42-4926, www.tradicioncolca.com, US$30 s, US$40 d with breakfast) has a charming feel, with comfortable rooms with large beds. The central stone building has a thatched roof, a fireplace, and a nice sitting area with games. **Eco Inn** (Lima 513, Puno tel. 051/36-5525, www.hotelecoinn.com, US$55 s, US$65 d with breakfast) is four blocks from Yanque's square and has views over the canyon. As of now, this choice is perfect for families, because the first floor has a king or queen bed and the upstairs loft has twins, but there are plans to remodel and make all the rooms doubles.

El Parador del Colca (Curiña s/n, tel. 084/24-1777, www.paradordelcolca.com, US$320 pp with full pension) is Colca's most elegant lodge. This Orient-Express hotel is a series of luxurious bungalows perched on a secluded bench above the Río Colca. Push open the door to your bungalow and you will be welcomed to a sitting area with a fireplace and a plush, poster bed. This room, in turn, opens up on one side to a patio, complete with whirlpool tub, and on the other side winds into a designer bathroom.

The four-station Wellness Center offers a range of massages and therapeutic treatments, making this the perfect place for travelers in need of a little pampering and relaxation.

You could easily spend a few days here, walking through the gardens, sipping Colca sours (made from the fruit of the Sancayo cactus), or gazing at the nighttime sky from your personal hot tub. César Torres, surely one of the friendliest and most professional hotel managers in Peru, can help arrange transport and other travel logistics.

COPORAQUE

Across the river from Chivay and about eight kilometers west is the tiny village of Coporaque. There are no services here, and the only phone in the area is the plaza's pay phone (the two hotels listed have radios only). Coporaque's church, **Santiago Apóstol,** was built in 1569 and is the oldest in the valley. Its false balconies seem almost medieval, and the towers contain bells said to be melted from the copper palace of a Collagua princess, Mama Yacchi. Inside there is a fascinating and primitive altar and a variety of 16th-century images. Around the corner is the facade of **La Capilla de San Sebastián.**

Accommodations and Food

Some of the best food in Colca Canyon is cooked at **La Casa de Mama Yacchi** (Arequipa tel. 054/24-1206, www.lacasademamayacchi.com, US$40 s, US$52 d with breakfast). This hotel is within walking distance from Coporaque's main square and is a great base for day hikes through the Colca Valley. The whitewashed rooms are comfortable and clean, with great valley views. The kitchen churns out a variety of fresh salads, perfectly cooked meat dishes, and homemade sauces—the US$5 lunch buffet is an excellent value. An unlikely staff member is Manchita, the pet llama who greets guests at the front door.

Colca Lodge (in Arequipa Jerusalén 212, tel. 054/20-2587, www.colca-lodge.com, US$82 s, US$92 d with breakfast) has the distinct advantage of being the only place in Colca to have world-class thermal baths. The hotel, owned by Grupo Inca, has a fabulous riverside location and hands out fishing poles and floatable duckies for guests who want to play. The rooms have

wood floors, lofts, and excellent river views. There are also suites with fireplaces and family cottages. The restaurant is overseen by Arequipa's acclaimed Zig Zag restaurant, and the buffet breakfast is sensational. Upstairs, the lounge, with a fireplace and a cozy bar, has a nightly informational slide show. The hotel can arrange horseback rides and walking tours to the ruins of Uyu Uyu, the Inca bridge, and Yanque. But its best feature lies down a stone trail near the river. There, boiling hot springs bubble into stone pools and steam into the cool river air. Nonguests have access to the baths, open 24 hours a day, if they buy a lunch or dinner or pay US$10–15.

MACA TO CABANACONDE

While there is no place to stay in Maca or anywhere along the road until Cabanaconde, this stretch of the canyon is the area that draws the most tourist attention. The dramatic views, the Cruz del Cóndor, and an impressive hike up to a steaming geyser are worth the haul from wherever happens to be your base point.

Maca and Pinchollo

Maca, 23 kilometers west of Chivay, was nearly destroyed by repeated eruptions of nearby Sabancaya Volcano in the late 1980s. Because it sits on a geological fault line, it is continually disturbed by earthquakes. The village's charming church, **Santa Ana,** is damaged but still standing. The facade is decorated with miniature false pillars, carved flowers, and a curious balcony that was used by missionaries to preach and present images to the natives. On the way outside of town, the **Choquetico Stone** is a carved Collagua model of nearly 10,000 hectares of terracing in the Colca Canyon. This rock was perhaps used for prophetic or rainmaking rituals, perhaps in conjunction with *chicha* or llama blood. On the surrounding hills are ancient *colcas,* adobe-and-stone granaries for which the canyon is named.

The 17th-century **San Sebastián** church in Pinchollo, 27 kilometers west of Chivay, is another church worth visiting, with a baroque

CANYON COUNTRY

altar and a baptistry with elaborately painted entrance.

Geyser

This nameless geyser lies up an incredibly bumpy road, which turns off the main road before reaching La Cruz del Cóndor. Pushing up the road is certainly worth it. Just make sure you have a guide.

Upon stepping out of the car, the walk to the geyser is about one hour. The skinny dirt trail winds through green and yellow brush, arriving first at small bubbling pools and finally at the geyser. However, the telltale steam gives away the gushing water long before your arrival. This is an excellent place to spot condors. The day we went we saw four!

La Cruz del Cóndor

Colca's main draw, the condor lookout, has become touristy beyond belief and, most mornings, teems with vendors and tour buses. Still, this spot, perched 360 meters above the Colca Canyon and about 60 kilometers (1.5 hours) from Chivay, commands a spectacular view over the canyon and is one of the best spots to see the Andean condor. An enormous vulture, with a silver collar and a wingspan of nearly 3.3 meters, zooms past the lookout nearly every morning—usually around 8 A.M., again at 10 A.M., and sometimes in the late afternoon. The birds sleep on the canyon walls at night and, after the sun heats the air, ride thermals up into the sky until they are nearly out of sight. At least a pair, but sometimes as many as a dozen, show up in the morning during the nonrainy months between April and December. Fewer show up during the September–October mating season. Farther up the road there is the less mobbed Tapay lookout, where condors fly but less frequently. Any bus headed to Cabanaconde will let travelers out at either of these spots.

Getting There and Around

If you do not come with an organized tour, your option for seeing this section of the canyon is a Chivay- or Cabanaconde-based bus company. There are three that run regularly: **Empresa de Transportes Reyna** (Chivay tel. 054/53-1014), **Turismo Milagros** (Chivay tel. 054/53-1115), and **Transportes Andalucia** (Chivay tel. 054/53-1106). Catch an early morning bus from one of the base towns, and ask to be let off at La Cruz del Cóndor. For the return, stand by the side of the road and flag down one of the same companies, whose buses make a return trip late morning.

CABANACONDE

Cabanaconde, at 3,287 meters elevation and 65 kilometers west of Chivay, is the last of the five villages strung out along the southern edge of the Colca Canyon. The road doesn't end here, but it does become rougher and heads away from the canyon, which becomes much deeper and more serpentine. (Buses do, however, travel the 12 hours to Arequipa along this road.) Cabanaconde is a great place to stay because it is quiet, has a few inexpensive hostels, and is only 15 minutes from La Cruz del Cóndor and adventure activities. The town's church, **San Pedro Alcántara,** was rebuilt after a 1784 earthquake and has sun, moon, and stars carved onto its imposing front.

Accommodations

One of the town's better known accommodations is **Valle del Fuego** (Grau and Bolívar, one block from the plaza, tel. 054/83-0032, valledelfuego@hotmail.com, US$5 s, US$10 d), which is basic and clean. The owner, Pablo Junco, is a great source of information, and he also operates the recommended Pablo Tours agency. The worthwhile hotel restaurant is **Rancho del Colca.** The other place is **La Posada del Conde** (San Pedro and Bolognesi, tel. 054/44-0197, pdelconde@yahoo.com, US$17 s, US$22 d), with private bathrooms. The nicest and most upscale place to stay is **Kuntur Wassi** (Cruz Blanca s/n, tel. 054/81-2166, www.kunturwassi.com, US$8 dorm, US$27 s, US$37 d with breakfast). This friendly, well-run hotel is one block uphill from the plaza and has adobe-and-stone rooms. The nice bathtubs feel great after a long walk out of the canyon. The restaurant is open 7 A.M.– 10 P.M. daily.

The best food in Cabanaconde is in hotel restaurants, even at the budget level.

Getting There and Around

For the six-hour journey from Arequipa, options include **Empresa de Transportes Reyna, Turismo Milagros,** and **Transportes Andalucia.** These companies have about four buses daily, most of which leave before noon. For the return trip, contact the same agencies, all of which have offices in the Arequipa bus stations and on Cabanaconde's main plaza.

COTAHUASI CANYON AND VICINITY

Cotahuasi Canyon, the deepest in the world at 3,354 meters, is more rugged than Colca. Since it was overlooked by the Spanish, there are few churches here. The Inca, however, built a highway along much of the canyon for transporting dried fish from Puerto Inca on the coast all the way to Cusco. Today, the ruins of these roads connect several villages that grow citrus fruits on thousand-year-old terraces.

The main town is Cotahuasi, which is a 12-hour bus ride from Arequipa at 2,680 meters. There are a few simple places to eat, sleep, and buy groceries here. The best is **Alojamiento Chavez** (Cabildo 125, tel. 054/21-0222), with a pleasant courtyard and friendly and knowledgeable owner.

The road continues up the canyon to the villages of Tomepampa, Lucha, and Alca. One good **trek** heads down the canyon from Cotahuasi along a path that crosses the river several times and leads, after a few hours, to the village of **Sipia.** Nearby is the thunderous 60-meter-high **Cataratas de Sipia.** Trekkers can continue downstream to more isolated villages and ruins—and, with enough time, all the way to the Pacific, as the Inca did. Agencies

in Arequipa offer four-day treks to these areas. Arequipa-based Cusipata and Cusco-based **rafting** agencies lead eight-day Cotahuasi Canyon trips.

Buses for Cotahuasi leave in the evening from Arequipa's bus terminal (12 hours) and arrive at dawn. Return buses to Arequipa leave Cotahuasi daily. If you can, travel this route during the day. The spectacular road passes over a 4,650-meter pass between Coropuna (6,425 meters) and Solimana (6,093 meters) before dropping into Cotahuasi.

VALLEY OF THE VOLCANOES

Partway along the Arequipa–Cotahuasi Canyon route, the road branches off for **Andagua,** a small village at the head of the Valley of the Volcanoes. The small valley, sandwiched between Colca and Cotahuasi and only 65 kilometers long, is a seemingly endless lava field, lorded over by the snowcapped Coropuna and Escribano and punctuated by more than 80 perfect volcanic cones. In the middle of it all is a lake and the gentle Río Andagua, which runs underground through much of the valley. Few people travel here, and those who **trek** along this valley need to carry a tremendous amount of water. Near the village of Ayo, a few days' trek away from Andagua, the valley leads to Lago Mamacocha. There is also an adventurous five-day route, which retraces the 1929 route of Shippee and Johnson and passes through Chacas to Cabanaconde in Colca Canyon. Andagua-bound buses leave several times a week from Arequipa's bus station.

For those with a four-wheel-drive vehicle, a fascinating circuit connects Cotahuasi and Andagua and then heads to the Colca Canyon via Cailloma. Except in Chivay, there is probably no gasoline along this route, and not even the best maps are completely accurate, but the scenery is legendary.

Puno

The first impression you get when you arrive this city is of a sprawling, somewhat unappealing city surrounded by an extraordinary landscape. It has a few colonial churches and an incredible number of religious festivals. Because it is Peru's only major city on the shores of Lake Titicaca, most travelers pass through here en route to more interesting destinations. As a result, there is a good range of hotels, restaurants, and agencies.

Great efforts have been made to improve Puno's attractiveness. The wooden lake boats, powered by converted car engines from the 1950s, are safer now that they are equipped with life jackets, fire extinguishers, and cell phones. They also float higher out of the water with an enforced limit on passengers. The terminal on the edge of town brings all of the major bus companies together and is just a few minutes' walk from the port, where boats leave for Amantaní and Taquile Islands.

During the early days of the Peruvian viceroyalty, Puno was a stopover for those traveling between Arequipa and the Potosí mine, in present-day Bolivia. But in 1688, a silver mine was discovered at nearby Laicota and the town was renamed San Carlos de Puno. During this time, important churches were built in Puno and around the shores of Lake Titicaca, with mestizo facades similar to those in Arequipa.

SIGHTS
City Tour

One of Puno's most interesting sights, just outside of town, is the **Yavari** (behind Sonesta Posada Hotel, tel. 051/36-9329, www.yavari.org, 8 A.M.–5 P.M. daily, free), one of the world's great antique ships. Sent in pieces from England in 1862, the *Yavari* took six years to arrive at its destination. First, it was sent around Cape Horn, then carried by porters and mules over the Andes, and finally assembled on Lake Titicaca.

If you have the time and the energy, start your tour three blocks from the Plaza de Armas at **Parque Huajsapata,** the mirador overlooking Puno with a huge sculpture of Manco Cápac, the first Inca. Take extra precaution here, as there have been recent reports of robbery assaults on single tourists.

In the Plaza de Armas is the city's **Catedral Basílica San Carlos Borromeo** (8 A.M.–noon and 3–5 P.M. daily), which was built in the 17th century by Peruvian master stonemason Simon de Asto. The interior is rather spartan in contrast to the carved facade but contains an interesting silver-plated altar. Next to the cathedral is the 17th-century **Casa del Corregidor,** built by Father Silvestre de Valdés, who was in charge of the cathedral construction. It has a pleasant courtyard, now occupied by Puno's most charming café.

At the corner of Conde de Lemos and Deústua is the **Balcony of the Conde de Lemos** (no tours) which is part of a building where Peru's viceroy lived when he first stopped in the city. It is now the headquarters of the Cultural Institute of Peru. Across the street from the balcony is the **Museo Dreyer Municipal** (Conde de Lemos 289, next to Plaza de Armas, 7:30 A.M.–3:30 P.M. Mon.–Fri., US$1), which has a collection of pre-Inca and Inca ceramics, gold, weavings, and stone sculptures, as well as stamps and documents on the history of the Spanish foundation of Puno.

Puno's **pedestrian street,** Lima, connects the Plaza de Armas to **Parque Pino** and has the city's best restaurants and cafés. The 18th-century church gracing Parque Pino is dedicated to San Juan Bautista and contains the Virgen de Candelaria, Puno's patroness and center of its most important festival. Past Parque Pino is the **Coca Museum & Customs** (Deza 301, www.cocamuseo.com, 9 A.M.–1 P.M. and 3–8 P.M. daily, US$5). This excellent family-run museum has two parts: Half the exhibits explain the history of the coca plant, and the other half, accompanied by a movie, displays the folkloric

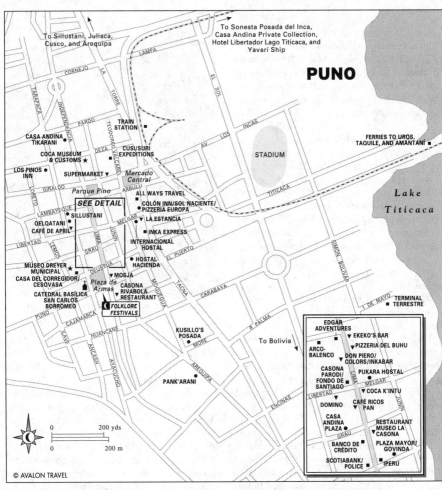

costumes used in traditional dances. Silva, the museum coordinator and director, speaks English and reads coca leaves. The street, which switches names to Independencia, leads to Arco Deústua, a huge stone arch dedicated to those killed in the battles for independence in Junín and Ayacucho. Another option from Parque Pino is to head a few blocks downhill, toward the lake, to Puno's huge central market, which is especially busy in the mornings. Puno visitors may also want to take a half day and see the ruins of Sillustani.

ENTERTAINMENT AND EVENTS
Nightlife

The second-floor lounge of **Colors Restaurant Lounge** (Lima 342, tel. 051/36-9254, 10 A.M.–midnight daily) is the best place for evening drinks and appetizers. The black sofas are showcased against white walls, the cocktails are varied, and some evenings there's a DJ. The best pub in Puno is **Kamikaze** (Grau 148, 5 P.M.–midnight Tues.–Sun.). For dancing, there's **Ekeko's Pub** (Lima 355, 5 P.M.–close daily), which ladles out free drinks 7:30–9:30 P.M. The best and one of the only discos in Puno is the salsa-influenced **Domino** (Libertad 437, 7 P.M.–3 A.M. Tues.–Sun.). **El Palacio del Folklore** (Lima 723, 7 P.M.–2 A.M.) is a *peña* that opens on Friday and Saturday nights with a wide range of regional dances, although the schedule is a bit unreliable.

◖ Folklore Festivals

A highlight of any visit to Lake Titicaca is seeing one of 300 traditional festivals that happen in this area each year. PromPeru, the government promotion agency, keeps an updated list of festivals at www.peru.info. Lake Titicaca has the richest and most vibrant dances and celebrations in all of Peru, and it is worth timing your trip to see one. With precision and endurance, entire towns participate in the orchestras, musical groups, and elaborately costumed dances. Though performed on Catholic holidays, most of the dances in Puno are rooted in pre-Columbian rituals of harvest, planting, herding, and magic.

Puno's Fiesta de la Virgen de la Candelaria

© PROMPERU

The most famous dance is **La Diablada,** performed yearly on February 2 during Puno's **Fiesta de la Virgen de la Candelaria.** The dance is essentially a struggle between dozens of elaborately costumed angels and bug-eyed, horned devils, along with an ever-growing cast of new characters: the Widow, the Skeleton, the Old Man, the Mexican, the Redskin, Batman, etc. Other dances include **Choq'elas,** which is performed before the roundup of the vicuñas, and **Q'ajelo,** which ends when the gun-toting shepherds steal the dancing maidens before they carry them off over their shoulders.

The **musical instruments** are a good example of the intermingling of Spanish with Inca and Aymara. The trumpets, tubas, saxophones, and stringed instruments are recent European contributions, but the flutes, panpipes, and drums have evolved over thousands of years. The flutes range from the tiny *quena,* which looks like a penny-whistle, to the huge *pincullo,* made out of a chunk of *algarrobo* wood. The panpipes range from the handheld *zampoñas* or *antaras* to the *sicus,* which are almost as tall

as their players. There is also a huge range of drums, rattles, and bells.

SHOPPING

Puno has three old buildings that have been renovated into small shopping centers with cafés. **Casa del Corregidor,** which houses **The Fair Trade Shop** (Deústua 576, tel. 051/36-5603, www.casadelcorregidor.ciap.org, 8 A.M.–11 P.M. daily) is near the plaza; **Casona Parodi** (Lima 394, 9 A.M.–10 P.M. daily) is on the main drag; and **Casa de Wiracocha** (Tarapacá 260, tel. 051/36-3542, 10 A.M.–10 P.M. daily) is tucked away on a side street.

Puno is a good place to buy alpaca wool clothing and weavings. Good spots include the **Casa del Artesano** (10 A.M.–10 P.M. daily) at Lima 549 and the **Arts & Crafts Center** (10 A.M.–10 P.M. daily) across the street, on the pedestrian mall near the main square, and the market on the railway between Los Incas and Lampa. The highest quality is found at **Alpaka's** (Lima 394, tel. 051/36-3551, 9 A.M.–noon and 4–10 P.M. Mon.–Sat., 4–8 P.M. Sun.), in Casona Parodi, and at the expensive **Alpaca 111** (Lima 343, www.alpaca111.com, 10 A.M.–10 P.M. daily), which both sell nice sweaters, scarves, and shawls.

RECREATION

The turquoise waters of Lake Titicaca are Puno's main draw, and there are two ways to get out on them: the traditional, large, motorized boats, or a kayak. We strongly encourage the latter. There are also opportunities for horseback riding, biking, and even birdwatching.

◖ Kayaking Lake Titicaca

There is no better way to see the beauty of Lake Titicaca than by sea kayak. We began our kayaking trip far from the hustle and bustle of Puno, in **Llachón,** a Quechuan village on the lake's shore. At dawn, with Bolivia's snow-covered mountains aglow, we launched brand-new sea kayaks onto black waters. I had been to Lake Titicaca several times before but never had I experienced it like this.

Instead of chugging across the lake on a diesel-powered boat, we glided on glassy waters past boulders covered with bright-green algae. We breathed in the musty air and watched waves fold onto the white-sand beaches. I would have sworn we were on an ocean were it not for the impossibly thin air—and the fact that our guide kept drinking the crystal-clear lake water from his cupped hands. We left the shoreline and began to paddle across the lake, as deep as 900 feet in some places, toward the rising hulk of **Isla Amantaní.** By evening, the lake was glassy calm and stained red by the setting sun.

Titikayak (Bolognesi 334, tel. 051/36-7747, www.titikayak.com), partly owned by the reputable ExplorAndes agency, offers a variety of safe and organized kayak trips leaving from Llachón. A half-day trip tours the shores of the peninsula, a full-day trip goes back and forth to Taquile or Amantaní, and a three-day trip that explores the island in detail. Longer 10-day trips to out-of-the-way places can be arranged. The company has excellent equipment and

kayaking on Lake Titicaca

provides everything needed. **Valentin Quispe** (tel. 051/982-1392, llachon@yahoo.com) in Llachón is the kayak caretaker, and trips can also be arranged directly through him.

Motorboat Tours

An early morning start of the day will find you, and 10–20 others, at the Puno port boarding a double-deck motorboat and throwing on a life jacket. In an hour, on the typical tour, you'll be at the **Islas Uros.** From there, it is another 2–3 hours on to **Islas Amantaní** and **Taquile.** The motorboat's enclosed first floor is often the DVD room, where educational films about the lake and its cultures are shown. The second floor is an open-air deck for sightseeing. Tours can be arranged as day trips or overnights. Some travel agencies now have high-speed boats, which greatly reduce travel time.

Horseback Riding

Horseback riding can be done at the recommended **Fundo Chincheros** (8 km north of Puno on Puno–Juliaca Highway, tel. 051/35-5694, www.fundochincheros.unlugar.com, $25 pp half-day tour), a country hacienda in the valley just north of Puno operated by the owners of the café Cecovasa in La Casa del Corregidor. Apart from trail rides, the day is spent hiking through cactus forest, seeing vicuñas, and having a garden picnic next to a rare 17th-century *capilla abierta,* or open chapel. The controversial constructions, which were banned after 1680, allowed Spanish priests to baptize Indians without having to let them in the church.

Tour Guides and Agencies

All Ways Travel (Tacna 234, tel. 051/35-5552, www.titicacaperu.com) can also arrange kayak trips, but its specialty is socially conscientious tourism. Managed by Victor Pauca and his entrepreneurial daughter Eliana, a grad of the International Development Policy School at Duke University, the agency offers slightly more expensive trips that are worth it for their quality and community benefits. A two-day trip to Uros, Amantaní, and Taquile, with an overnight on Amantaní, costs US$25 pp with

meals. Educational tours leave on the weekends so that tourists can help teach English, art, and reading to island schoolchildren. But the most exciting trip is the two- or three-day Anapia and Yuspique trip. These islands in southern Lake Titicaca are seldom visited. The agency has a second location in the Casa del Corregidor.

Run by a Peruvian husband-wife team, **Edgar Adventures** (Lima 328, tel. 051/35-3444, www.edgaradventures.com) focuses on activity. If you want to go visit Lake Titicaca, then Edgar will take you to the uncommercialized island of Ticunata, where you will spend the afternoon farming with locals. Or if you prefer horseback riding, Edgar will take you to Sillustani. Apart from these trips, the agency also offers mountain biking and bird-watching expeditions, as well as conventional tours.

Dozens of agencies offer the traditional day or overnight trips to the lake's islands and the surrounding sites of Sillustani and Chucuito. Be sure to use a recommended guide, and remember; you get what you pay for. One reliable agency is **Cusi Expeditions** (Teodoro Valcarcel 126, tel. 051/36-9072, 6:30 A.M.–8 P.M. daily). It offers trips to Uros; Uros and Taquile; Uros, Amantaní, and Taquile; and to Sillustani. **Suri Explorer** (Teodoro Valcarcel 136, tel. 051/36-8188, suriexplorer@hotmail.com) offers similar trips at comparable prices. Both of these companies also provide transfers for US$5 to the Juliaca airport. A final recommended agency is **Arcobaleno** (Lambayeque 175, tel. 051/36-36-4068, www.titicacalake.com), which works largely with big groups from abroad but can also accommodate individual travelers.

ACCOMMODATIONS
US$10-25

Kusillo's Posada (Federico More 162, tel. 051/36-4579, kusillosposada@yahoo.es, US$16 s, US$29 d with breakfast), a backpacker's hostel, has a very homey feeling. The first-floor living room, dining room, and kitchen are open to guest use, and the upstairs bedrooms are bright and clean with telephones and WiFi. This is a good place for a long-term stay.

US$25-50

Casa Panq'arani (Arequipa 1086, tel. 051/36-4892, www.casapanqarani.com, US$25 s, US$50 d with breakfast) "is not a restaurant, neither a hotel," the owners claim. "It is grandma's house for you to stay in." Nothing could be truer. Consuelo Giraldo and her family live in this beautiful dreamlike house, which has some extra rooms with private bathrooms, and a terrace, giving you the feeling that you are not staying at a bed-and-breakfast. You can order meals cooked by Doña Consuelo, including local traditional food or other dishes. This is probably one of the best places to stay in Puno.

Posada Don Giorgio (Tarapacá 238, tel. 051/36-3648, www.posadadongiorgio.com, US$29 s, US$43 with breakfast) is another cozy option some blocks away from downtown, with great service in a very relaxed and quiet atmosphere. Rooms are quite simple but with comfortable beds and very clean bathrooms. There is WiFi, a small business center, a good restaurant, and rent-a-car service too. This is a highly recommendable place to stay.

For a more traditional hotel, the quiet **Sillustani** (Tarapacá 305, tel. 051/35-1881, www.sillustani.com, US$40 s, US$56 d with breakfast) has comfortable, carpeted rooms with bathtubs and cable TV. Buffet breakfast is served in a formal dining room.

US$50-100

The most elegantly old-fashioned place in town is the Belgian-owned **Colón Inn** (Tacna 290, tel. 051/35-1432, www.coloninn.com, US$50 s, US$60 d with breakfast). This hotel's large rooms are arranged around a marble-floored lobby, sun-filled sitting rooms, and atrium. Rooms have cable TV and writing desks.

For some unknown reason Puno has four hotels named "plaza," very close to each other, and with almost exactly the same rates. They're all relatively new and comfortable, and have friendly staffs. **Plaza Mayor Hostal** (Deústua 342, tel. 051/36-6089, www.plazamayorhostal.com, US$55 s, US$70 d with breakfast) has king-size mattresses, feather pillows, bathtubs, and cable TV. Breakfasts are served in a window-lined dining room. The hotel has all major amenities, including WiFi and heaters in the rooms.

Casona Plaza Hotel (Arequipa 655, tel. 051/36-5614, www.casonaplazahotel.com, US$55 s, US$70 d with buffet breakfast) has 64 comfy and spacious rooms, with very nice bathrooms, hair dryer, room heating, cable TV, WiFi, and 24-hour room service. The hotel has a restaurant-bar, laundry service, free Internet, private garage, and medical assistance. It is conveniently located one block from Puno's Plaza de Armas.

Sol Plaza Puno (Puno 307, tel. 051/35-2658, www.solplazahotel.com, US$55 s, US$70 d with buffet breakfast), half a block from the Plaza de Armas, is another of these new options in town, with nice comfortable beds in the rooms, despite the decoration, which is quite cheesy. Services in this three-star hotel include bathrooms with showers and bathtubs, room heating, WiFi, cable TV, oxygen if requested, a bar, a restaurant, and massage service upon request.

Puno Plaza Hotel (Puno 419, tel. 051/35-1424, www.punoplazahotel.com, US$60 s, US$70 d with buffet breakfast) offers great views of Puno's Plaza de Armas and cathedral from its rooms on the third and fourth floors. This hotel also has two suites (US$100), which are quite fancy. Owner Humberto Béjar is also a skilled chef; he leads a very friendly staff.

Casa Andina has two hotels in the city. **Casa Andina Classic-Puno Plaza** (Grau 270, tel. 051/36-3712, www.casa-andina.com, US$76 s or d, US$109 superior room, with buffet breakfast) is a block away from the Plaza de Armas, with comfy rooms, cable TVs, elevator (very useful if you've just arrived to Puno), oxygen upon request, WiFi, and down comforters. **Casa Andina Classic-Puno Tikarani** (Independencia 143, tel. 051/36-7803, www.casa-andina.com, US$87 s or d, with buffet breakfast) is the better option of these two, away from downtown, with a quieter atmosphere. This hotel has a fireplace and a courtyard but most importantly more spacious bedrooms than her sister hotel. It also has all amenities, including an ATM and oxygen upon request.

US$100-150
An affordable luxury option, on the lake near Hotel Libertador Lago Titicaca, is **Sonesta Posada del Inca** (Sesqui Centenario 610, tel. 051/36-4112, www.sonesta.com, US$115 s, US$125 d). Rooms are cheerful with plaid bedspreads, warm colors, heaters, and all the amenities. An exquisite breakfast buffet (US$7) is served on a lakeside dining room or outdoors on an open porch. The hotel also has oxygen and Internet (US$4/hour). The *Yavari,* Puno's most interesting attraction, is docked a few meters away.

If it is a chilly day on the lake, you can slip down to the lobby of **Casa Andina Private Collection** (Sesqui Centenario 1970, tel. 051/36-3992, www.casa-andina.com, US$115 s, US$130 d) for a hot cup of tea. But if it is bright and sunny, throw open your windows and step out into your lakeside balcony. Half the rooms face the lake, and all have down comforters, cable TV, telephones, and writing tables. The bar serves an excellent *muña* sour, the local take on pisco sour, and the lakeside restaurant serves the flavorful Novoandino menu of U.S.-trained chef Teddy Bouroncle. There is also a business center with fast Internet, a jewelry shop, and a small gift store.

Over US$150
Of all the former state-owned hotels, the five-star **Hotel Libertador Lago Titicaca** (Isla Esteves s/n, tel. 051/36-7780, www.libertador.com.pe, US$195 s or d with breakfast) is one of the more stunning. It is like a huge alabaster cruise ship, perched on its own island jutting into Lake Titicaca. From the marble lobby, the rooms rise on both sides over a huge glass-enclosed courtyard and an expansive, elegant area with a bar and couches. Lying in the king-size beds, surrounded by five-star amenities, with the sun rising over Lake Titicaca, is truly deluxe—especially when you consider the spa and whirlpool tub awaiting you. The hotel even has its own dock, where tours leave for the islands.

FOOD
Most of Puno's best restaurants are along Lima, the upscale pedestrian street off the Plaza de Armas. A good local dish to try is *chairo,* a soup of beef or lamb, potatoes, beans, squash, cabbage, *chuño* (dried potato), wheat, and *chalona* (dried mutton). *Trucha* (trout), *pejerrey,* and *ishpi* are excellent local fish, and *sajta de pollo* is a chicken stew mixed with potatoes and peanuts.

Cafés, Bakeries, and Ice Cream
The most charming place to hang out is **Cecovasa** (Deústua 576, tel. 051/35-1921, 10 A.M.–10 P.M. Tues.–Fri., 10 A.M.–2:30 P.M. and 5–11 P.M. Sat.–Sun., US$1), set in the 17th-century Casa del Corregidor. The café is an NGO, whose 5,000 members work in the Puno coffee industry. All eight types of coffee are local and delicious. The menu also offers Greek salads, gourmet appetizers, and a range of teas. There is no place better to enjoy a snack than on the café's sun-filled patio. **Café Ricos Pan** (Lima 424 and Moquegua 326, tel. 051/35-1024, www.ricospan.com.pe, 6 A.M.–10 P.M. Mon.–Sat., 3–9 P.M. Sun., US$2) serves good milk shakes, quiche, and espresso drinks at incredibly cheap prices. Standouts include the apple pie, gooseberry cheesecake, and US$1.50 pisco sours.

Peruvian
Start with a coca sour at **Coca K'intu** (Lima 401, tel. 051/36-5566, 8 A.M.–10:30 P.M. Sun.–Fri., 4–10:30 P.M. Sat., US$7–14), and you'll be nicely warmed up for the forthcoming creative and sophisticated dinner. The *causa de trucha* is smooth and flavorful, and the *pejerrey* with tomatoes and olive sauce robust and delicious.

Famous for its antique iron collection, which hangs on its whitewashed walls, **Restaurant Museo La Casona** (Lima 517, tel. 051/35-1108, 9 A.M.–10 P.M. daily, US$5–7) is an institution in Puno. This is your chance to try guinea pig, garlic alpaca meat, and *anticuchos.* Its more elegant sister restaurant **La Casona Rivarola Restaurant** (Lima 775, tel. 051/36-9401, US$7–12) is on the same street, one block past the Plaza de Armas. A cheaper option for similar food is **Don Piero** (Lima 364, tel. 051/36-5943, 7:30 A.M.–10 P.M. daily, US$5–7), which has been around for more than 20 years and has especially good trout and a US$5 menu. Off Lima, **La Estancia** (Libertad 137, tel. 051/36-5469, 11 A.M.–10 P.M. daily, US$6–8) serves excellent *parrillas* (grilled meats) and trout, and has an unlimited salad bar.

Two recommended Novoandino restaurants that also make a good afternoon coffee stop are the friendly **Mojsa** (Lima 635, 2nd Fl., tel. 051/36-3182, www.mojsarestaurant.com, 7 A.M.–11 P.M. daily, US$3–7), with a view over the Plaza de Armas, and **Fondo de Santiago** (Lima 394, tel. 051/975-3188, 11 A.M.–midnight daily, US$6–8), in the Casona Parodi.

When in need of a filling, home-cooked meal, there's **Café de April** (Tarapacá 391, tel. 051/36-9261, 9 A.M.–9 P.M. Mon.–Sat., US$2–5), whose Argentine owner, Viviana, is full of energy.

International

Flip open the black-and-white, artsy menu of **Colors Restaurant Lounge** (Lima 342, tel. 051/36-9254, 10 A.M.–midnight Sun.–Fri., 4 P.M.–midnight Sat., US$7–10) and you'll quickly realize that the same artistic sensibilities have reached the food. A *lomo saltado* is whipped into a sandwich, and trout and beef are sliced thin into carpaccio. The most popular dish is the Andean cheese fondue, but the menu also offers Greek- and Thai-inspired dishes. A few doors down, and by the same owners, is **IncaBar** (Lima 348, tel. 051/36-8031, 8 A.M.–10 P.M. Sun.–Fri., 4–10 P.M. Sat., US$6), which has really good food. Greek salads; guacamole; pomadoro pasta with plum tomatoes, basil, and garlic; and chicken curry are just a few of the tempting dishes. Unfortunately, time has begun to wear on the restaurant and it is not as popular as it once was.

Located inside the Colón Inn is the tiny **Sol Naciente** (Tacna 290, tel. 051/35-1432, 10 A.M.–2 P.M. and 6–10 P.M. daily, US$7–9), with a menu of Peruvian, Belgian, French, Italian, and Hungarian dishes.

Pizza

Locals say the cozy **Machu Pizza** (Arequipa 409, tel. 051/992-1838, 4:30–11 P.M. daily, US$2) holds the honor for best pizza. It also delivers. **Del Buho Pizzería** (Lima 346 and Libertad 386, 4–11 P.M. daily, US$3–7) serves good pizza in town and becomes lively at night. More expensive than the others, but worth it for the atmosphere, is **Pizzería Europa** (Tacna 290, tel. 051/35-1432, 6–10 P.M. daily, US$5), inside the charming Colón Inn, whose pizzas are wood-fired.

Vegetarian

The reliable **Govinda** (Deústua 312, tel. 051/35-1283, noon–7 P.M. Mon.–Sat., US$2–3), found in nearly every Peruvian city, serves *torta de quinoa* and *saltado de broccoli* to four tables in a tiny café.

Markets

Near the **Mercado Central,** where you can buy produce, cheeses, and meats, there is a **Supermarket** (Oquendo 226, 8 A.M.–10 P.M. daily), which sells yogurts, cold cuts, and dry goods.

INFORMATION AND SERVICES

Free tourist information and maps are available at **Iperú** (Deústua with Lima, tel. 051/36-5088, www.peru.info, 8:30 A.M.–7:30 P.M. daily). For more detailed information, visit the **Regional Tourism Office** (Ayacucho 682, tel. 051/36-4976, 7:30 A.M.–5:15 P.M. Mon.–Fri.). A concise and interesting pamphlet that explains life on the islands and shore is Juan Palao Berastain's *Titikaka Lake: Children of the Sacred Lake,* available in bookstores and tour agencies.

The **national police** (Deústua 792, tel. 051/36-6271, 24 hours) are located on the Plaza de Armas, and the **tourist police** (Deústua 538, tel. 051/35-4774, 24 hours) are next door.

Peruvian Immigrations (Ayacucho 260, tel. 051/35-7103) can extend tourist visas, though expect a wait. North Americans, Britons, New Zealanders, and Australians do not need visas to enter Bolivia but can ask for information at the **Bolivian Consulate** (Arequipa 270, tel. 051/35-1251, 8 A.M.–2 P.M. Mon.–Fri.).

For health care, options include **Hospital Manuel Nuñez Butrón** (El Sol 1022, tel. 051/35-1021, 24 hours), **Clínica Los Pinos** (Los Alamos B-2, tel. 051/35-1071), and **Clínica Puno** (Ramón Castilla 178, tel. 051/36-8834). **Ricardo Roca Torres** (Moquegua 191, tel. 051/962-0937, www.touristhealth.com) is an English-speaking doctor who works especially with tourists. **Santa Cruz Botica,** at the corner of Lima and Libertad, is a good option for pharmacy needs.

For money matters, head to Lima, the pedestrian street, for **Interbank** (Lima 485) and **Banco Continental** (Lima 470), with **Scotiabank** on the Plaza de Armas. All have ATMs.

The post office is **Serpost** (Moquegua 269, tel. 051/35-1141, 8 A.M.–8 P.M. Mon.–Sat.).

There is fast **Internet** at several cafés along Lima. At many cafés, you can also make international calls. Laundry can be done at **Don Marcelo** (Lima 427, tel. 051/35-4247).

GETTING THERE AND AROUND
Air
Unfortunately, Puno does not have an airport. The closest is **Aeropuerto Manco Cápac** (tel. 051/32-2905) in Juliaca, about 45 minutes north of Puno. **LAN** (Tacna 299, tel. 051/36-7227, or Lima tel. 01/213-8200, www.lan.com) flies the routes Lima–Juliaca and Juliaca–Arequipa several times a day. LAN also has a Cusco–Juliaca flight.

Bus
Puno's **Terminal Terrestre** (1 de Mayo 703, intersection with Bolívar, tel. 051/36-4733 for schedule questions, US$0.30 entry), opened in 2001, has greatly improved the pleasure of busing into Puno. It is safe, with restaurants, snack bars, and even a clean, though noisy, hostel. From here buses arrive from and depart for Juliaca, Arequipa, Tacna, Cusco, Lima, and La Paz, Bolivia (through both Desaguadero and Copacabana). The travel times given here are correct; if a bus company promises you a dramatically shorter ride, do not believe it. We also do not recommend traveling at night.

If you're going to spend a day riding to Cusco, why not make a trip of it? There are two tourist buses that include a huge buffet lunch, English-speaking guide, and stops at most of the major ruins on the way. **Inka Express** (Tacna 255, tel. 051/36-5654, www.inkaexpress.com, US$25) makes stops in Pukará and La Raya before having a buffet lunch in Sicuani. The bus then continues to see the extraordinary Inca ruins at Raqchi and the exquisite colonial church at Andahuaylillas. The buses generally leave Puno at 8 A.M. and arrive at 5 P.M., and include hotel pickup and drop-off. Some buses even have onboard oxygen tanks for altitude problems. A similar service is offered by **First Class** (Lima 177, tel. 051/36-5192, or Sol 930 in Cusco, tel. 084/22-3102, firstclass@terra.com.pe, US$20).

Ormeño (tel. 051/36-8176, www.grupo-ormeno.com) has a direct, seven-hour bus to Cusco. Another recommended company is **Imexso** (tel. 051/36-9514), which has nice buses with TVs and bathrooms leaving at 8:30 A.M. (US$6, with snack) or 8:30 P.M. (US$4, without snack).

There are many options for the five-hour trip to Arequipa. Both Ormeño and **Cruz del Sur** (tel. 051/36-8524, www.cruzdelsur.com.pe) have buses that leave at 3 P.M. (US$5–6). Several buses stop briefly in Arequipa during the brutal, 20-hour push to Lima. Cruz del Sur's Lima bus costs US$35, and Ormeño has a bus that leaves at 3:30 P.M. or 7 P.M. **Cial** (tel. 051/36-7821, www.expresocial.com) also has decent buses that leave twice a day for Lima. To drive to Tacna, through Moquegua, your best option is **San Martin** (tel. 05/36-3631), which has a bus twice a day.

Train

One of the highest passenger trains in the world runs between Cusco and Puno. The views along this route are fantastic, though the train rolls right by a series of interesting ruins. It does stop briefly, however, at the high pass of La Raya, 4,314 meters, where a colonial chapel stands alone in the middle of the high plateau. One train per day leaves Cusco at 8 A.M., stops in La Raya at 12:15 P.M. and Juliaca at 3:50 P.M., and arrives in Puno at 5:50 P.M. Another train leaves each day from Puno at 8 A.M., stops in Juliaca at 9:05 P.M. and La Raya at 12:45 P.M., and arrives in Cusco at 5:50 P.M. This deluxe Andean Explorer is US$220 one-way, including lunch. This first-class service has elegant dining cars, an open-air bar car, and luxurious coaches (designed by James Parks and Associates, the same company that designed the first-class cabins for Singapore Airlines). Tickets can be bought at the station in Puno (La Torre 224, tel. 051/36-9179) or reserved online through **PeruRail** (www.perurail.com).

Boat

Two luxury boat companies offer interesting, though expensive, options for traveling between Puno and La Paz in a single day. The trips include a bus to **Copacabana**, boat rides and tours of **Islas del Sol y de la Luna,** and a final bus journey to **La Paz** (about 13 hours). It can also be done in the opposite direction for those who, for example, want to fly into La Paz and out of Cusco.

Crillon Tours (available in Puno through the Arcobaleno agency) takes passengers from Puno to Copacabana by bus, from Copacabana to Isla del Sol to Huatajata, Bolivia, by high-speed hydrofoil, and then on to La Paz (US$189). The total journey is about 13 hours. At Huatajata, Crillon also operates the five-star Inca Utama Hotel & Spa and La Posada del Inca, a restored colonial hacienda on Isla del Sol. Crillon has

offices in the United States (1450 S. Bayshore Dr., Suite 815, Miami, FL 33131, tel. 888/848-4222, daruis@titicaca.com) and in La Paz (Camacho 1223, tel. 591/233-7533, titicaca@gaoba.entelnet.bo) and an informative website at www.titicaca.com.

Transturin has buses and slightly slower mini-cruise ships, or catamarans, working the same basic route though docking at Chúa, Bolivia. This can either be a day tour or include a night aboard a catamaran docked at Isla del Sol. It has offices in Puno through **Leon Tours** (Libertad 176, tel. 051/35-2771, leontours@terra.com.pe), in Copacabana (6 de Agosto s/n, tel. 08/62-2284), and La Paz (Mariscal Santa Cruz 1295, 3rd Fl., tel. 912/31-0647, sales@turismo-bolivia.com); its website is www.transturin.com. Transturin also offers day trips from Puno to La Paz, visiting Isla del Sol (US$155), and a variety of all-inclusive package tours.

Local Transportation

Two recommended taxi companies are **Taxi Tours** (tel. 051/36-7000) and **Aguila Taxi** (tel. 051/36-9000).

To rent a motorcycle, contact **Mototitikaka** (José Moral 141, tel. 051/975-3400, titicacarent@yahoo.com), which also offers motorcycle tours to Sillustani, Punta Churo, and Juli.

Inexpensive, safe boats leave from Puno's public dock, at the end of Avenida Titicaca, for most of the surrounding islands. The dock facilities include police, clinic, bathrooms, and stalls that sell food, sweaters, hats, and more. Boats leave for a 2.5-hour tour of Uros between 7 A.M. and 4 P.M. (US$3). There are *colectivo* boats that leave for the 3.5-hour trip to Taquile at 7:30 A.M. (US$6). Those who want to overnight on Amantaní can take an 8:30 A.M. boat (US$9) that visits Uros en route to Amantaní. To travel from Amantaní onto Taquile the next day, you need to arrange transport with a travel agency. A private boat for a one-day trip to Taquile and back costs around US$90.

Lake Titicaca

Lake Titicaca seems more like an ocean than a lake. Bright-green algae blankets beach boulders and fills the air with a musty, seaside smell. Waves lap sand beaches. The intense blue waters, as deep as 270 meters, stretch endlessly in all directions. The only reminders, in fact, that Lake Titicaca is a lake are the impossibly thin air and a backdrop of snow-covered mountains—and the sight of islanders drinking the lake's clear waters out of their cupped hands.

The best way to experience Lake Titicaca is to leave behind the bustle of Puno and escape to the lake's placid shores and islands. Here you will find paths bordered by stone walls, a crystal-clear sky, and sweeping views of arid, sun-baked terraces. The land, shaded in places by groves of eucalyptus, plunges into waters below. On sunny days, the air is perfectly still and the sky blends with the water to form a single expanse of blue. The mood changes quickly, however, when squalls swoop in from the high plateaus, plunging temperatures and whipping the lake into a froth of gray waters. By evening, when the lake is calm again, the sunset appears as a line of fire around a half moon, the curvature of the earth plainly visible.

It is no coincidence that the Inca decided first to conquer this lake, nor that they formed a creation myth around it. The Inca contend that the sun sent his son, Manco Cápac, and the moon sent her daughter, Mamo Ocllo, to emerge from the waters of Lake Titicaca and found the Inca empire. It is also no coincidence that the Spaniards decided to bequeath this lake and its people directly to the king, and not to a conquistador as was usually the case. For despite its altitude and barren appearance, Lake Titicaca has been a cradle of civilization and a center of wealth. The dense populations of Quechua- and Aymara-speaking people around this lake have a unique place in Peruvian culture because their ways of life go back at least 3,000 years.

By 600 B.C., the Chiripa and Pukara populations were already building temples around the lake, which offered a perfect combination of grasslands for llamas and alpacas, an ample supply of fish, and good growing conditions for potatoes and quinoa. By A.D. 200 the carved, gold-covered stone blocks were being raised on the shores of Lake Titicaca to build Tiwanaku, a city in present-day Bolivia that lasted a thousand years. The Tiwanaku empire, along with the Ayacucho-based Huari, would later spread its deities and urban ways of life across Peru, laying the foundation for the Inca empire. The Tiwanaku empire collapsed around A.D. 1000, perhaps because of a drought, and the Lupaca and Colla emerged to build the tombs at Sillustani and other monuments. These proud cultures would become famous for their bloody rebellions against both the Inca and the Spanish.

ISLAS UROS

Visitors tend to find the bizarre sight of floating Islas Uros (Uros Islands), about a 20-minute boat ride from Puno, either depressing or highly interesting. The Uros, an ancient lake civilization who were harassed by the Spanish to near extinction, probably fled to these islands to escape forced labor in Spanish silver mines, though they may have come here earlier to isolate themselves from the Collas or Inca. Their way of life revolves around the *tótora*, or reed, which they cut and pile to form giant floating islands that are anchored to the shallow lake bottom.

The true Uros people, whom legends say were protected from cold by their thick, black blood, have long since intermingled with the Aymara, whose language they now speak. Nevertheless, the islanders preserve a way of life that is probably based on Uros traditions. They live in family units governed by a grandfather, and they prearrange marriages—sometimes right after the births of the future bride and groom. They fish, hunt birds, and move about the lake in huge *tótora* rafts that

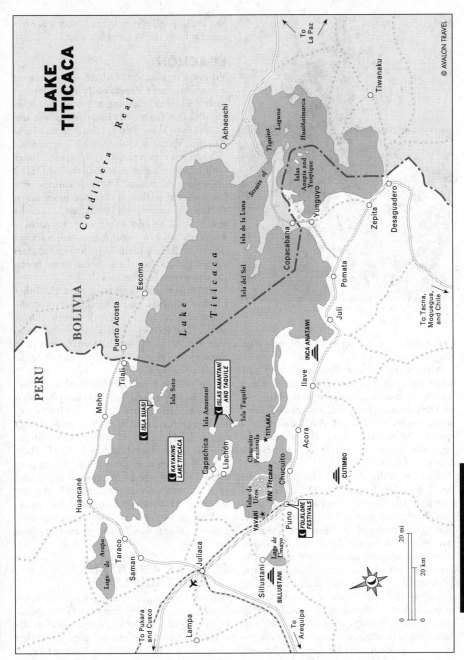

© AVALON TRAVEL

LAKE TITICACA

Cordillera Real

To La Paz

Tiwanaku

Achacachi

Laguna

Straits of Tiquina

Huañuimarca

Isla de la Luna

Islas Anapia and Yuspique

Yunguyo

Desaguadero

Zepita

Isla del Sol

Copacabana

Pomata

Lake   Titicaca

Escoma

Juli

To Tacna, Moquegua, and Chile

Puerto Acosta

BOLIVIA

INCA ANATAWI

PERU

Tilali

Isla Soto

Ilave

Moho

ISLA SUASI

Capachica

Isla Amantani

ISLAS AMANTANI AND TAQUILE

Isla Taquile

TITILAKA

Acora

KAYAKING LAKE TITICACA

Llachón

Chucuito Peninsula

Chucuito

CUTIMBO

Huancané

Islas de Uros

RN Titicaca

Taraco

Lago de Arapa

YAVARI

Puno

Saman

FOLKLORE FESTIVALS

Lago de Umayo

Juliaca

Sillustani

SILLUSTANI

To Pukara and Cusco

Lampa

To Arequipa

20 mi

20 km

0

0

CANYON COUNTRY

tótora rafts made on the floating Islas Uros outside of Puno

look almost like Viking ships with their huge dragon heads.

Many visitors find it disconcerting to walk upon the springy, waterlogged reeds, which have to be continually replenished as the bottom layers rot, creating the fermented odor that is peculiar to the islands. But the scenery is spectacular and the islands are unique—the largest even has a clinic, school, and Seventh Day Adventist church on it!

Tourism to the islands, which began in the late 1960s, has helped pull the Uros out of grinding poverty and maintain their population of several hundred. But it has also brought problems. Thousands of tourists each year arrive here with camcorders, creating a generation of begging children and adults who aggressively push miniature reed boats and other trinkets. Do not give money to begging children—give them fruit or school supplies, or buy something from them instead. The islanders also offer US$1 boat rides in their reed boats to neighboring islands. Most Puno agencies offer guided tours for the Uros Islands,

and cheap public boats to the islands leave frequently from the Puno public pier.

LLACHÓN

Villagers in Llachón, a charming village on a peninsula near Puno and Juliaca, may not wear traditional clothing anymore, but staying with families is every bit as interesting, and less touristy, than visiting Islas Amantaní and Taquile. Valentín Quispe, who lives outside of town near a cemetery, runs a rustic lodge with fabulous views over the lake for US$12 pp, room and board. The little cabins, with whitewashed walls and thatched roofs, are at the top of a hill and seem like stone huts in the sky. Nearby, an adobe arch supports nothing and leads nowhere—but it beautifully frames a piece of the lake itself. At night a billion stars come out, including the Southern Cross, pointing the way to Isla Amantaní.

Valentín also arranges homestays with other Llachón families, and his lodge serves as the point of departure for kayak trips to the islands. The kayaks can also be rented from Valentín for the day for a reasonable price, and there are the ruins of a pre-Inca temple at the top of a nearby hill.

Llachón can be reached by private boat from Puno in the Mercado Bellavista or by bus from Juliaca's Talara Street. Buses leave here every half hour for the village of Capachica (1.5 hours, US$1.50), from which the half-hour taxi ride to Llachón should be US$7–8. There is a nice beach at Llachón with free camping and a French-owned campground at one end that can rent tents or provide meals. Anglers are glad to take travelers to nearby Islas Taquile and Amantaní, only 11 kilometers away from here, by sailboat for US$6 or private motorboat for US$36.

◖ ISLAS AMANTANÍ AND TAQUILE

Staying for a night or two with a family on Isla Taquile, about 35 kilometers from Puno, or the slightly farther Isla Amantaní, has become a classic Lake Titicaca experience that some travelers may consider excessively touristy

LAKE TITICACA: FOLKLORE CAPITAL OF PERU

The festivals and celebrations in Lake Titicaca are some of the most vibrant and spirited in Peru. It's worth timing your visit to the region to coincide with one of the 300 annual festivities. PromPeru, the government promotion agency, keeps an updated list of festivals at www.peru.info.

- January, third Thursday: **Pacha Mama ceremony** on Isla Amantaní

- February 2-19: **Virgen de Candelaria** in Puno

- February, second Thursday: *Ispalla* **dance** to Pachamama at hilltop pre-Inca temple in Llachón

- All February: **Carnaval** in Puno and surrounding areas

- May 2-3: **Alasitas,** a festival featuring good luck charms to be hung on the Aymara Ekeko doll in Puno

- May 3-8: **Fiesta de la Cruz y de San Martín de Porras** in Ilave

- May, first week: **Fiesta de San Bartolomé** in Chucuito

- May 5-17: **Pentecostal celebration of San Isidro Labrador** on Isla Taquile

- May, fourth week: **Roundup** *(chacu)* **of vicuña** on Isla Umayo, near Sillustani; visitors are invited to join

- June 10-14: **Founders Day** celebration in Llachón with dances and bullfights

- June 23-25: **Festival de San Juan** in Puno

- July 2: **Founders Day** celebration in Capachica, en route to Llachón

- July 25 onward: **Fiesta de Santiago Apóstol** on Isla Taquile, in Chucuito, and in Lampa

- August 1-3: **Fiesta de la Octava de Santiago,** on Isla Taquile

- August 6: **Fiesta Niño de Praga** in Capachica, en route to Llachón

- August 10-17: **Fiesta de San Simon** on Isla Amantaní

- August 15: **Festividad de la Virgen de Cancharani** in Puno

- August 15-18: **Festividad de la Virgen de Asunción** in Chucuito

- September 15: **Fiesta de la Virgen de la Natividad** in Acora

- September 24: **Festividad de Nuestra Señora de las Mercedes** in Juliaca

- September 29: **Fiesta de San Miguel Arcangel** in Ilave

- October 2: **Fiesta de Nuestra Señora del Rosario** in Acora

- October 12-19: **Fiesta de Nuestra Señora del Rosario** in Chucuito

- October, third week: **National road rally** around Lake Titicaca, with dances in Puno

- November 1-7: **Puno Week** including the arrival by raft of the legendary founders of the Inca empire, Mamo Ocllo and Manco Cápac, on November 5

- November 1-2: **Fiesta de Todos los Santos** throughout the area

- December 5: **Fiesta de Santa Bárbara** in Chucuito, Ilave, and Puno

- December 6-8: **Fiesta de la Inmaculada Concepción** in Puno, Lampa, and other villages

CANYON COUNTRY

arch on the island of Taquile

high pass separating the two sides of the island. Everyone speaks Quechua, some speak Spanish, and almost no one speaks English. Taquile can receive as many as 500 overnighters during the high season (June–August), so during high season it can be hard to have a secluded experience. Restaurants have sprung up in recent years, locals pose for photos, and people hawk handicrafts in the village and along popular walks.

The slightly larger Isla Amantaní, about 40 kilometers from Puno, rarely hosted foreigners for overnight visits, but since 2000, travelers have begun to stay the night here and homestays have become an important means of making a living on the island. The quality of each homestay experience often depends largely on the family you are offered when you arrive.

Your host family might teach you how to weave blankets and farm potatoes at high altitude. Or you might join them for family meals, with guinea pig as the main course.

As tourism has become an increasingly important source of income for the islands, the local elders, or *varayocs,* have struggled to find a system to spread the new wealth evenly among all families or, as they say, ensure that *"todos comemos el mismo pan"* ("all of us eat the same bread"). Their solution, based on the communal *ayllu* system, is run by the *varayocs,* who meet boats at the docks and rotate visitors to nearly a hundred families. This equitable system has faltered somewhat in recent years because tourist agencies are allowed to do direct deals with certain families, which end up getting a disproportionate share of guests. These family homes can have as many as four guest homes, which seems to water down the homestay experience.

Taquile has a true guest lodge, TikaWasi (House of Flowers, in Quechua), which has been built by former *varayoc* Alejandro Flores. It clearly raises the bar of quality with wood floors, reed ceilings, comfortable foam beds, clean whitewashed walls, and a spectacular terrace with lake views. Because of its privileged access to one of the island's only springs, it is also the only home on the entire island with

nowadays. In these islands, visitors are picked up at the dock by a family member and led home to clean but rustic accommodations: a simple adobe room next to the family house, a lumpy mattress, and an outhouse without running water. With luck, visitors are invited to help herd the sheep, work in the terraced fields of potatoes and quinoa, or learn how to weave with backstrap looms. Evenings are spent watching the sunset, and usually there is music and dancing, arranged for the visitors, in the town square at night.

Taquile is closer to Puno and has been receiving increasing numbers of overnight visitors for nearly three decades. Because Taquile is just six kilometers long and one kilometer wide, it is possible to walk around the island in two hours on walled paths carved into the hillside that bob up and down along its contours. There are a few beaches, which can be nice on sunny days and conducive to a plunge in the lake's icy waters. There are pre-Inca ruins, though not very elaborate, on the tops of the hills, and an elegant stone arch at the

young girl on the island of Taquile

running water and solar-heated showers. On Amantaní, Hospedaje Kantuka (amantani_@ hotmail.com) has a similarly elaborate setup. Though comfortable, these kinds of lodges represent a critical challenge to islands' communal way of life.

If you go on a prepaid tour to one of the islands, go with a socially responsible agency and ask a few questions beforehand. Ensure, for instance, that the agency pays the islanders the going rate—US$6 pp per night for lodging, US$3 for breakfasts, and US$4 for lunches and dinners. Ensure also that no more than two people will stay with each family and preferably away from the touristy area. Otherwise, arrange your own homestay by simply hopping aboard the US$6 boat that leaves from Puno's public pier every morning between 7:30 and 8 A.M.—you will be assigned a family upon arrival and will need to pay an arrival fee.

Whether you stay with a family or eat at one of Taquile's restaurants, you are likely to be served the same delicious and wholesome food: quinoa soup, steamed or fried *pejerrey* (the local

fish), an omelet, or tortilla mixed with potatoes and vegetables. The main handicrafts are elaborately woven hats (*chullos*) and cloth belts, both of which play an important role in island culture. Travelers are advised to bring their own snacks and beverages—even a small bottle of beer can cost US$2 on Amantaní. Beds are likely to have a woolen blanket or two but it is a good idea to bring a sleeping bag to stay warm, as well as a water bottle, soap, and toilet paper.

PENÍNSULA DE CAPACHICA

Six indigenous communities situated in this peninsula, northeast of Puno (http://turismocapachica.wordpress.com), have organized themselves in tourism associations to offer the real thing: a genuine homestay experience, with no intervention of agencies, as it used to be decades ago on Taquile and Amantaní. Each community offers different tourist circuits and services, totally independent of each other, some of them quite isolated without phone or Internet access, but truly well organized and ready to host travelers in comfortable lodgings, with homemade meals and an extremely hospitable and friendly crowd of villagers that will surely make this an amazing and revealing experience.

The six communities are Paramis, Chifrón, Escallani, Ccotos, Isla Tikonata, and Ccollpa.

Paramis (tel. 051/950-949-705, contact: Balbino Quispe), 67 kilometers from Puno, offers a series of activities, including the P'utin–Canjarno trek, artisan fishing, adobe brick making, farming, and bonfires, for US$1–3 each. Meals cost US$3 each and lodgings range from US$5 s to US$9 d.

Chifrón offers three different experiences: **Flor de Lago** and **Casa Rural Inti Wasi** (tel. 051/950-936-611, contact: Walther Pancca Páucar, titikakaintiwasi@hotmail.com), and **Playa Chifró** (tel. 051/951-919-652, contact: Emiliano Pacompia). They all offer similar activities, ranging US$2–9, such as walking the Centilinayok circuit, with spectacular views of the lake, boat rides around Isañata island, storytelling of local myths and legends, and a ceremony to Pachamama, among other things.

CANYON COUNTRY

Meals cost US$3–4 each, and lodgings are US$5–12 s, US$11–23 d.

Escallani is the northernmost and remote community, grouped in **Munay Suyo** (contact: Rufino Paucar Pacompia), without phone or Internet access. This is probably the most interesting village; you could go and try your luck just dropping by and staying there for a night or two. You can join families to sail in the lake in traditional boats through the *tótora* wetlands where a wide variety of birds can be observed. Circuits to Apu Wiracochani or Kawayojapina cost US$4–7. Meals are US$3–5 and lodging US$5 pp.

On the eastern side of the peninsula, **Ccotos** also has two groups: **Inca Samana** (tel. 051/951-856-462, contact: Alfonso Quispe Acuña, incasamanatours@yahoo.es) and **Posada Ccotos** (tel. 051/951-620-826, contact: Santos Ramos, korythica@yahoo.es). This community offers walks, fishing and sailing in the lake, and the experience of milking cows or farming. Rates are US$1–3. Typical foods are served for US$3–5 each meal, and quite comfortable lodgings are US$5 s, US$10 d.

Isla Tikonata (tel. 051/951-664-881, contact: Marino Humpiri Charca) is an island off the coast of Ccotos and northwest of Amantaní. You can sail around the island, fish, and even shear sheep or participate in the building of a house. These activities cost US$2–4 each. Food is about US$4 each meal and lodgings US$5 pp. The transportation from the peninsula to the island costs US$3.

Ccollpa is down south of the peninsula and has two groups hosting travelers: **San Pedro Ccollpa** (tel. 051/951-637-382, contact: Richard Cahui Flores, ccollpallachon@hotmail.com) and **Pacha Ccollpa** (tel. 051/951-311-622, contact: Dorca Cahui Padillo) offer artisan fishing, learning to dye wool, and sailing in the lake. Rates are US$1–5. Food is served for US$2.50–5 per meal, and lodgings cost US$6 s and US$12 d.

◖ ISLA SUASI

If you are looking for a upscale Titicaca island experience, step onto the Isla Suasi and all the stresses of the real world will disappear. Antonio, the friendly manager of the new **Casa Andina Private Collection** (Ugarte 403, Lima tel. 01/213-9700, www.casa-andina. com, US$165 d for two days and one night) will hand you a lime-and-*muña refresco,* then you'll head off to a lunch of barbecued local meats and finally on to the elegant, rose petal–sprinkled rooms.

Suasi is the lake's only privately owned island, and the owner, Martha Giraldo, recently signed a 20-year contract with Peruvian hotel chain Casa Andina to give it exclusive managing rights of the island's only lodge. The result is an excellent hotel on a truly secluded island. Casa Andina, in its remodeling, has added a gourmet restaurant, a eucalyptus steam sauna, and a private suite that is actually a two-room, lakeside cottage with butler included. But in all the change, Martha's house, island trails, Andean cultural center, and gardens remain the same.

A walk or kayak around Suasi affords incredible views of distant, blue mountains, islands

cebiche **extravaganza on Isla Suasi**

© JORGE RIVEROS CAYO

in Bolivia, and orange-tinged sunsets. The dry air and the rustic smell of grasses remind you that, while you are in the lap of luxury, you are in the middle of nature.

The trip may be a splurge, considering that you have to hire a boat or car to make the 3–5-hour trip to the hotel, but it's completely worth it. All meals and activities are included in the price, and the lake's natural beauty is never as perceptible as it is here on the island. You'll return to the mainland with a spirit as clean as the Suasi air.

ISLAS ANAPIA AND YUSPIQUE

The trip to these islands begins with a two-hour drive along the Lake Titicaca's south shores, visiting the towns of Juli and Pomata, before passing through Yunguyo to the port of Punta Hermosa. Visitors than hop aboard a sailboat for a two-hour ride to Anapia's beach, where the father of each family leads each visitor to their new home. That afternoon families and guests go hiking on nearby Isla Yuspique, which has a large herd of vicuñas, and have a beach picnic to try *huatia,* which are potatoes cooked in a natural oven with pieces of hot soil.

The trips are not staged or overly planned, which seems like a good thing, so the activities vary: There is usually an evening meeting of neighbors, with conversation and music, or a chance to herd animals, fish, or help build a house. Depending on the time of the year, visitors also help plant or harvest crops.

All Ways Travel, managed by a father-and-daughter team in Puno, runs a socially responsible homestay program on Islas Anapia and Yuspique, in southern Lake Titicaca. All Ways Travel is introducing a new brand of sustainable tourism that gives back to, and helps preserve, the communities they work with. As a mark of its success, All Ways Travel recently won an award from the Ford Foundation for the **Best Community-Based Project in Peru.** Since the project began in 1997, All Ways participants have helped to build a library and a puppet theater and to paint the local school.

For a group of four, costs are US$65 pp for one night and US$75 pp for two nights (the latter is recommended). This trip also works well for travelers either coming from or continuing on to Bolivia and can be combined with a visit to Tiwanaku or the Islas del Sol y de la Luna. For budget travelers, Eliana at All Ways is also glad to explain how to do this trip independently, for about US$43 for two days, using public transportation and boats, which only run on Thursdays and Sundays. **Edgar Adventures** (Lima 328, tel. 051/35-3444, www.edgaradventures.com) also leads trips to the islands.

PUNO TO BOLIVIA

Travelers make a mistake when they breeze between Puno and the Bolivian border without stopping. The road passes through a string of quaint towns, with interesting colonial churches and a seemingly continuous schedule of festivities.

The south shores of Lake Titicaca are the center of Peru's Aymara population, a distinct language and cultural group. They have a historical reputation for repelling domination, be it the Inca 500 years ago or the Shining Path in the 1980s and 1990s. In 2004, several towns in this area rose in protests against allegedly corrupt leaders. In the worst instance, the mayor of the town of Ilave was dragged from a house and lynched by a mob of Aymara Indians. Before visiting these towns, inquire in Puno beforehand about the present situation.

Chucuito

Located 18 kilometers south of Puno, Chucuito is one of the oldest towns in the area and is surrounded by farming fields that slope gently down to Lake Titicaca. The town was once the capital of the whole province and has colonial churches on its two main squares. **Nuestra Señora de la Asunción** has a Renaissance facade from 1601 and sits near the upper Plaza de Armas. The second church, **Santo Domingo,** is L-shaped with beautifully painted stone arches, a wooden altar carved in *pan de oro,* and a single ancient stone tower.

Chucuito's lead attraction, however, is **Inca**

Uyo (7 A.M.–dark, free), a walled enclosure next to Santo Domingo that looks, at first glance, like a garden of giant mushrooms. But upon closer inspection, the mushrooms are carved stone penises, some pointing up at the sky (presumably toward Inti, the Inca sun god) and others rammed into the ground (toward Pachamama, mother earth goddess). At the center of this obvious fertility temple is the largest phallus of all, placed atop a platform carved with the outlines of a human figure. Village children, who work as the temple's very charming and dead-serious guides, claim that women still sneak into the temple at night, with coca leaves and *chicha,* to perform a ceremony designed to help them get pregnant. The essence of the ceremony, they contend, is that the women sit atop the head of the giant phallus for several hours. The origin of this temple is hotly debated; some say it was built by the Aymaras or the Inca. Others contend that cannot be possible, because the priests, who built the church next door, had a fondness for destroying idols that surely would have included phallus-shaped rocks. Whatever you believe, the site is still interesting.

ACCOMMODATIONS AND FOOD
There are two great options near Chucuito. The best place to stay in town is **Albergue Las Cabañas** (near Plaza de Armas at Tarapaca 538 or Bolognesi 334 in Puno, tel. 051/35-1276, www.chucuito.com, US$25 s, US$37 d with breakfast). Inside high adobe walls is a charming garden of yellow *retama* and *queñua* flowers surrounding bungalows with wood floors, hearths, exposed beams, and new bathrooms. The owner, Juan Palao Berastain, has authored the highly informative pamphlet to the area, *Titikaka Lake: Children of the Sacred Lake,* on sale at the hotel. Members of Hostelling International receive a discount.

A brand-new lodging option is **Titilaka** (US tel. 866/628-1777, www.andean-experience.com, rates tailored according to request) is one of a kind accommodation, situated on the shore of Lake Titicaca, on the Chucuito Peninsula. The hotel offers 18 lake-view suites

with heated floors and oversize tubs. The hotel also offers a series of half- and full-day excursions to surrounding villages. The best restaurant in town is at Titilaka. On the lower square, **Tío Juan** (10 A.M.–4 P.M. Mon.–Sat., US$2) is a locals' hole-in-the-wall that serves up trout, roasted pork, and *chairo,* a soup of beef or lamb, potatoes, beans, squash, cabbage, *chuño* (dried potato), wheat, and *chalona* (dried mutton).

Juli
The road from Chucuito to Juli, 84 kilometers from Puno, heads off from the meandering shores of Lake Titicaca through the town of Platería, a village once known for its silverwork, to Acora, and finally to Ilave, a crossroads town that has more commerce than colonial architecture. The road returns to the lake at Juli, which was once a stopping point for silver caravans between the coast and the Potosí mine in present-day Bolivia. This was also an important center for the Jesuits and Dominicans, who trained missionaries here to work with the native Guaraní in Paraguay. The town's principal

Iglesia de San Juan de Letrán in Juli

© JORGE RIVEROS CAYO

attractions today are its churches from the 16th and 17th centuries: **San Pedro Mártir** is on the plaza and has an interesting Renaissance facade, baroque altar, and paintings by Italian master Bernardo Bitti. Beautiful windows made of a translucent stone called *piedra de huamanga* can be found at **San Juan Bautista,** down the street, along with a carved altar, 80 paintings from the Cusco School, and beautiful carved sacristy door. **Santa Cruz de Jerusalén** has magnificent doors and excellent views of Lake Titicaca. **Iglesia de San Juan de Letrán,** in the Plaza San Juan, was restored in 2007 and has a stunning interior that is worth a look. **Nuestra Señora de la Asunción** offers an eerie glimpse at a church in ruins with a fine remaining door, tower, and arch outside in the atrium. There is a colorful fair in Juli every Thursday.

Pomata

The road continues to Pomata, 104 kilometers from Puno and the crossroads for the roads to Desaguadero and Copacabana. The town's 18th-century church, **Santiago Apóstol de**

Nuestra Señora del Rosario, is built of pink granite with a huge gold-covered altar and paintings from the Cusco School. Toward Desaguadero there is another fine colonial church, **San Pedro,** in the town of Zepita.

Crossing into Bolivia

From Puno, there are a few ways to make the **border crossing to Bolivia.** The first, and most popular, is to go from Puno to Yunguyo to Copacabana to La Paz, Bolivia, a route that leads through a series of interesting villages on the lake's south shore before a scenic ferry ride across the **Straits of Tiquina.** From Copacabana, it is easy to visit the **Isla del Sol** (Island of the Sun), a 20-kilometer boat ride from Copacabana. This island, covered in Inca ruins and graced by a sacred stone, was revered by the Inca as the place from where Manco Cápac emerged to found the empire. Nearby is the smaller but interesting **Isla de la Luna** (Island of the Moon), birthplace of Mama Ocllo.

Panamericano (Tacna 245, tel. 051/35-4001, tourpanamericano@hotmail.com) leaves

© JORGE RIVEROS CAYO

view from the drive from Puno to Bolivia

Puno daily for this seven-hour route at 7:30 A.M. **Tour Peru** (Tacna tel. 051/35-2191, tourperu@ mixmail.com) also has good buses going to Copacabana daily. Or explore the towns along the way by hopping on and off a local bus from Puno to Yunguyo (2.5 hours, US$3). These *colectivo* buses leave from the local bus station, two blocks from the main Terminal Terrestre (1 de Mayo 703, intersection with Bolívar). From Yunguyo, take a *colectivo* from the border to Copacabana (30 minutes, US$0.50). There are several buses daily from Copacabana to La Paz (5 hours, US$4).

A more direct, but less scenic, five-hour route to La Paz goes through **Desaguadero,** an ugly duckling of a town that straddles the border. Buses along this route pass **Tiwanaku,** the capital city of an empire whose deities and monumental architecture spread throughout Peru nearly a millennium before the Inca. Though ravaged by grave robbers and modern-day reconstructions, the ruins here were once so impressive that even the Inca thought them constructed by giants. What stands out today is the **Kalasasaya temple,** a rectangular temple surrounded by pillars, monolithic figures, and the renowned Gateway of the Sun, chipped from a single piece of andesite and adorned with a carved deity. **Ormeño** (tel. 051/36-8176) leaves from Puno at 5:45 A.M. (US$17), and **Panamericano** (tel. 051/35-4001) leaves at 8 A.M. Cheaper, slower buses run from Puno to Desaguadero (2.5 hours, US$2) frequently,

and the last bus from Desaguadero to La Paz (4 hours, US$3) is at 5 P.M. Bolivia time (4 P.M. Peru time). This border is open 8 A.M.–noon and 2 P.M.–7:30 P.M.

Crossing is usually a 20-minute, hassle-free process at either place—as long as you have your passport and a valid tourist visa and the border is open (Bolivia's border shut down for several weeks because of political unrest in 2001 and 2003). Peru gives tourists a 90-day tourist visa, while Bolivia gives only 30 days—always ask for more before having your passport stamped. Border officials occasionally try to charge unsuspecting travelers an *embarcación* tax, which is illegal. North Americans, Britons, New Zealanders, and Australians do not need visas to enter Bolivia at this time, while French travelers do. There is a Bolivian consulate in Yunguyo (8:30 A.M.–3 P.M.), although it is best to check updated requirements before you travel.

A longer way to Bolivia leads along the seldom-visited north shore of Lake Titicaca, a string of interesting towns that include Huancané and Moho. As there is no immigrations post at the border of Tilali, travelers must get their exit stamp a day before they depart in Puno at Peruvian Immigrations (Ayacucho 270, tel. 051/35-7103, 8 A.M.–2 P.M.). For this route travelers must hopscotch on frequent local buses from Juliaca onward. If you catch a 7 A.M. bus from Juliaca, it is possible to arrive by 3 P.M. that afternoon.

Between Puno and Cusco

SILLUSTANI

The most interesting ruins near Puno are surely Sillustani (6 A.M.–dark, US$4), which are halfway between Puno and Juliaca at the end of a 14-kilometer detour off the highway. The site consists of more than a dozen stone tombs, or *chulpas,* up on a bluff over Lago Umayo. They were mostly built by the Colla, a highland people conquered by the Inca in the 15th century and for whom this quarter of the Inca empire

(Collasuyo) was named. The Colla were stone craftsmen and built gravity-defying towers that widen as they go up. Whether they built the towers this way to show off their masonry virtuosity or to stymie grave robbers is unknown, but the Inca continued the tradition. Over time, even the perfectly fitted granite stones of the Inca have spilled onto the surrounding ground, exposing the tower's adobe-filled interior, which was long ago ransacked by looters.

The drive in passes the stone homes of llama herders, which are decorated with arches and stone bands. Near the *chulpas,* don't miss the *waru waru,* an ingenious farming technology that was developed around Lake Titicaca during the Tiwanaku empire. These raised earth platforms are surrounded by a thin pool of water that absorbs the sun's energy during the day and re-radiates it at night, protecting the potatoes and other crops from frost. To arrive, take any bus heading north from Juliaca (many leave from Simón Bolívar) and ask to be dropped off at the Sillustani turnoff (US$0.30, 20 km). Taxis wait at the turnoff and charge US$0.50 to take travelers the remaining 14 kilometers to the ruins.

JULIACA

Juliaca, 45 kilometers north of Puno and the teeming hub of Peru's southern highlands, is a unfortunate collection of ramshackle buildings. The slogan of this working people's paradise is *mientras Puno danza, Juliaca avanza* ("while Puno dances, Juliaca advances"). Travelers pass through here mainly because of the airport—the closest to Lake Titicaca—and the rail and highway connections to Puno, Arequipa, and Cusco. It is also the launching pad for the quaint towns of Llachón and Lampa and the backroads route into Bolivia along the north shores of Lake Titicaca. There is no reason to stay in Juliaca, and if you can skip it, you should. All Puno travel agencies run airport shuttles, and it is worth starting your day early so that you can pass through Juliaca on your way to Lampa or Bolivia.

The best hotels, restaurants, and services—as well as the train station—are near Plaza Bolognesi, which is graced by a colonial church, **Iglesia La Merced.** The Plaza de Armas, a few blocks to the northwest, has another colonial church, **Iglesia Santa Catalina.** There is a large **Sunday market** in the Plaza Melgar, several blocks from the center, where you can buy cheap alpaca wool sweaters. A more tourist-oriented daily market is held in the plaza outside the railway station. Beware of pickpockets in this area.

Accommodations

Hostal Luquini (Braceso 409 on Plaza Bolognesi, tel. 051/32-1510, US$7 s, US$10 d, shared bathroom) formerly Hostal Peru, is the best budget place to stay in Juliaca. The rooms are quiet, arranged around an open communal space, and are fairly clean with good beds. If you're lucky, you can get a TV, although it won't have cable, and there are some more expensive rooms (US$8 s, US$13 d) with private bathrooms. **La Maison Hotel** (7 de Junio 535, tel. 051/32-1763, www.lamaisonhotel.com, US$19 s, US$29 d with breakfast) is a quiet, friendly place with 30 comfortable rooms. Though the orange walls and red plastic furniture are a bit much, the rooms are comfortable with good beds, skylights, cable TV, and spotless bathrooms. At the **Royal Inn** (San Ramón 158, tel. 051/32-1561, hotel_royal_inn@latinmail.com, US$25 s, US$33 d with breakfast), ask for the interior rooms, which are quieter and face a small courtyard. Rooms are decked out with cable TV, refrigerators, and heaters, and some even have whirlpool tubs for US$3 extra.

Food

Good restaurants are few and far between in Juliaca and most are in the city's best hotels. **La Fonda del Royal Inn** (inside the Royal Inn, San Ramón 158, tel. 051/32-1561, 6:30 A.M.–10 P.M., US$4–5) has an excellent selection of entrées that range from ceviche (made from both local *pejerrey* and coastal sea bass), pepper steak, gnocchi with alfredo sauce, and *lomo al vino* (steak in wine sauce). The restaurant itself is a welcome respite from the street, and the waiters hustle. Across the street, **Trujillo Restaurant** (San Ramón 163, tel. 051/32-1945, US$5–9) has an endless menu of Andean and Creole food along with a full drink list that includes daiquiris. **Confitería Meli Melo** (Braceso 403) has good-looking pies and cakes.

Information and Services

Most services are within a block or two of the Plaza Bolognesi. The **Tourism Office** (Junín

638, tel. 051/32-1839, 7:30 A.M.–5:30 P.M. Mon.–Fri.), however, is not very conveniently located. The **police station** is at Ramón Castilla 722 (tel. 051/32-1591, 24 hours), and the best health care is at **Clínica Adventista** (Loreto 315, tel. 051/32-1001, emergency tel. 051/32-1071), run by the Seventh Day Adventists. For money matters, there is a **Banco de Crédito** on the plaza itself, and a **Banco Continental** on San Román and 2 de Mayo. The **post office** is on the corner of Salaverry and Sandía. For email, try **Internet Clic** (San Ramón 216, 7:30 A.M.–11:30 P.M. daily). For international calling, there is a **Telefónica office** on San Martín and Tumbes, but there are some closer private phone booths half a block from Plaza Bolognesi on Pasaje Santa Elisa.

Suri Tours Service (Jorge Chávez 133, tel. 051/32-1572, www.suritour.com) offers a half-day trip to Lampa for US$10 pp as well as a two-day trip in the high jungle around Sandia.

Getting There and Around

Buses for the 45-minute ride to **Puno** leave from a terminal in the Plaza Bolognesi (US$0.50, 45 minutes) when full. A private taxi to Puno is about US$15. A range of buses for **Cusco** (US$3–7, six hours) and to **Arequipa** (US$3–5, five hours) leave from a terminal on the 10th block of San Martín. Buses leave for **Lampa** daily from 2 de Mayo, near the Mercado Santa Bárbara (US$0.70, one hour).

The best way to get to Cusco, however, is aboard the tourist buses that leave Puno each morning and pick up passengers in Juliaca around 9 A.M.: **Inka Express** (Tacna 255, Puna, tel. 051/36-5654, www.inkaexpress.com, US$25) makes stops in Pukará and La Raya before having a buffet lunch in Sicuani. The bus then continues to see the extraordinary Inca ruins at Raqchi and the exquisite colonial church at Andahuaylillas. A similar service is offered by **First Class** (Lima 177, Puno, tel. 051/36-5192, or Sol 930 in Cusco, tel. 084/22-3102, firstclass@terra.com.pe, US$20).

Juliaca has the only airport for Lake Titicaca, **Aeropuerto Internacional Inca Manco Cápac** (Aviación s/n, Santa Adriana, tel. 051/32-8974). A taxi for the 10-minute drive between Juliaca and the airport is US$2; cheap buses and *colectivos* leave from the Plaza Bolognesi. Buses leave the airport regularly for the one-hour drive to Puno (US$1.50). The office of LAN (San Ramon 125, 8:30 A.M.–7 P.M. Mon.–Fri., 9 A.M.–1 P.M. Sat.) is a block from the Plaza Bolognesi.

PeruRail (www.perurail.com) has revamped the Cusco–Puno train service, which makes daily stops in Juliaca for either direction of travel. The rail station is across from the Plaza Bolognesi.

Because the lake-bottom land is so flat, Juliaca is overflowing with bicycle taxis that charge US$0.30 to take you anywhere in town.

LAMPA

Though a bit stranded, the charming village of Lampa was probably fortunate to have been bypassed by both the Cusco–Puno highway and the train line. Otherwise it would have become another Juliaca, a tangle of congestion and ramshackle buildings. Instead, Lampa, at 3,910 meters, is a clean-swept, hushed town with two large squares, a huge church from the 17th century, and *casonas* splashed in hues of ochre, maroon, and salmon—hence the town's nickname, La Ciudad Rosada. This entire village, an oasis of red tiles amid the yellow grass of the high plains, feels like a colonial time warp.

Sights

Lampa's huge church in the shape of a Latin cross reflects the fact that Lampa had many more inhabitants—as much as 50 times its current population, some historians say—when a dozen silver mines operated in the area. Construction on the **Iglesia Santiago Apóstol** began in 1675, the same year Lampa was founded. Like the bridge to the south of town, the church was built of *calicanto,* a combination of lime mortar (*cal*) with river stones (*canto rodado*). The church was immaculately

Iglesia Santiago Apóstol in Lampa

restored in the 1950s by a mining engineer and the town's favorite son, Enrigue Torres Belón (1887–1969), who even went to the Vatican to get a rare copy of Michelangelo's *Pietà*.

The interesting things about this church are its huge colonial paintings, a pulpit every bit as elaborate as that of San Blas in Cusco, and extensive catacombs that are crisscrossed with mysterious Inca tunnels from an earlier temple. In a side area of the church, the **Torres Belón mausoleum** offers an interesting comment on mortality and is proof of the slogan "He who lives longest laughs last." While Torres Belón and his wife rest comfortably beneath thick slabs of marble, the skeletons of hundreds of priests, hacienda owners, and Spanish miners hang on the walls of the round chamber above. The bones were transferred here after Torres Belón ordered the catacombs filled with cement to shore up the church's foundations. In this way, the last remains of generations of colonial nobility became mere adornment for the tomb of a modern-day mining engineer.

There are half a dozen homes worth visiting, including the **Casona Chukiwanka** in the Plaza Grau, from which Simón Bolívar addressed the town during the independence wars. A few homes have patios paved with the white and black stones from Lake Titicaca's Isla Amantaní, which are laid out to form huge game boards. One house features a chessboard, while others have popular colonial gambling games, including *juego de la oca,* a sort of craps table with odd animal figures. The rules have long since been forgotten.

A highly recommended bike or drive from Lampa leads south on good dirt roads for 76 kilometers before joining the road to Cusco at Ayavari. From Lampa, the attractions packed along this route include a forest of *queñua* (*Polylepis incana*)—the tree known as *lampaya* in Aymara and the probable origin of Lampa's name. Next along this route come three rough tombs, or *chullpas,* from the Colla culture; the well-preserved remains of two colonial mines; a huge forest of *Puya raimondii;* and bizarre geological formations at the **Tinajani Canyon.** Buses do not run this route, unfortunately. Another road leads six kilometers west of town to **Cueva de los Toros,** a cave with animal carvings and funerary towers similar to those at Sillustani.

Entertainment and Events

Lampa erupts into dance and colonial-style bullfights July 29–31 during the **Fiesta de Santiago Apóstol.** Masses and elaborate religious processions take place December 6–8 centering on **La Virgen de la Inmaculada,** which was brought to Lampa from Barcelona in the 17th century.

Accommodations

Hospedaje Milan (Juan José 513, US$4 s, US$6 d) has queen-size foam beds and plain, clean rooms with shared bathrooms. The owner is the hospitable, and extremely courteous, Edgardo Méndez. On the main square is a red **colonial home** (Plaza Grau, US$12 s, US$22 d) that has been well restored by owner Oscar Frisancho and converted into a charming two-star hostel. The rooms have high ceilings, brick floors, and loads of colonial charm.

Food

The best restaurant is **Las Delicias,** on the Plaza de Armas and operated by the charming Señora Delia. Lunch or dinner menu is US$1. The other good restaurant in the plaza, **El Pollón,** serves spit-roasted chicken and other food and is also open for breakfast.

Information and Services

The best source for information is the affable Edgardo Méndez at **Hospedaje Milan,** which also offers laundry service. The **police station** is two blocks north of the plaza, along with a nearby **Banco de la Nación** that does not have an ATM. There is a **phone center** on the plaza, and the **IPSS** clinic is one block west of the plaza.

Getting There and Around

The only way to reach Lampa with public transport is from Juliaca, where *combis* leave when full from 2 de Mayo near the Mercado Santa Bárbara (US$1, one hour). From Lampa, cars, when full, leave for Juliaca from the

© AMBER DAVIS COLLINS, WWW.LIFEUNSCRIPTEDPHOTOGRAPHY.COM

view out the window of the Cusco-to-Puno train, near La Raya Pass

intersection of Juan José and leave for Cusco four blocks south of square, starting at 5 A.M.

NORTH TO CUSCO
Pucará

This ceremonial center, 107 kilometers north of Puno, was built by the Pucará, one of Titicaca's earliest cultures (300 B.C.–A.D. 300). Though a bit difficult to visualize, the ruins (daylight hours, free admission) offer a glimpse into the shadowy origins of Lake Titicaca's civilized life and show clear links to the Chavín culture, which was flourishing at the same time in Peru's central mountains. The first temple is U shaped and was originally decorated with stelae, or carved stone slabs, showing a deity similar to the *degollador,* or decapitator deity, of the Chavín. The second, known as the Kalasaya Temple, is rectangular and has eight large niches along the main remaining wall. The stelae recovered from the site are interesting and are housed in a small INC museum near the plaza. Across the street is an exquisite colonial church, **Iglesia Piñon de Pucará,** which the museum caretaker can open upon request.

La Raya

At 4,321 meters, La Raya is the highest pass on the route, marks the divide between the Urubamba and Lake Titicaca watersheds, and is roughly the halfway point on the Puno–Cusco journey. Snowcapped mountains stretch out over a plateau that is barren except for one colonial chapel.

CANYON COUNTRY

THE AMAZON

Nearly 60 percent of Peru is jungle, whether it is the montane cloud forest or the deep, lowland rainforest known simply as *selva*. Peru's Amazon basin is quite accessible and is one of the most biodiverse spots on Earth with an ample variety of excellent lodges and activities. In as little as three hours after landing in Iquitos or Puerto Maldonado, travelers can be boating down a chocolate-brown, winding river with the endless jungle rising on both sides. Animals that you are most likely to see on any trip are monkeys, capybaras, turtles, caimans, pirañas, gray and pink river dolphins, hundreds of bird species, and many insects. Large mammals like anteaters, ocelots, and tapirs can be spotted at least a day's travel away into more remote areas. The jaguar, king of the Amazon, is stealthy and rarely seen. Seeing these animals through all the greenness of the rainforest is a serious challenge, but being on a river or lake with good binoculars and an experienced guide greatly increases the odds.

First-time jungle visitors usually are concerned about suffocating heat, malaria, mosquitoes, yellow fever, bugs, and other discomforts. But Peru's Amazon is mostly malaria free—at least the places travelers tend to roam. The mosquito issue can be minimized by wearing light-colored long clothing and a head net during outdoor walks in the evenings, and a yellow fever vaccination is strongly suggested before visiting the rainforest (see www.cdc.gov for full recommendations). Other than that, the new generation superb ecolodges and deluxe river cruises offer the experience of visiting Peru's Amazon in quite comfortable conditions.

HIGHLIGHTS

◖ **Wildlife:** Feel amazed by the Amazon's wildlife, whether you observe a giant otter, pink river dolphin, taricaya turtle, or the giant capybara rodent. Observe the brightly plumed macaws and the magnificence of a harpy eagle in flight (page 210).

◖ **Canopy Walks:** Climb up into the canopy, whether by ladder or ropes, to have a closer look at the amazing biodiversity a hundred feet off the ground in the rainforest (page 214).

◖ **Explorer's Inn:** The 5,500 hectares surrounding the lodge are home to 61 bird species and more than 1,235 types of butterflies, as well as howler monkeys, otters, and coral snakes (page 221).

◖ **The Tambopata Research Center:** On the Río Tambopata, visit the only lodge near the Parque Nacional Bahuaja Sonene, just 500 meters away from the world's largest macaw clay lick (page 222).

◖ **Reserva Amazónica:** Indulge yourself in the most luxurious and romantic lodge in the Peruvian Amazon, situated at the shores of the Río Madre de Dios (page 222).

◖ **Manu Expeditions:** Spend a two-week birding trip, high in the treetops, and observe Manu's speckled and cinnamon teal or the red-backed hawk, among hundreds of other species (page 228).

◖ **Aqua Expeditions:** Become a privileged observer of the Amazon rainforest through an unforgettable journey on Peru Amazon's top end river cruise, available in three-, four- and seven-night travel packages (page 264).

◖ **Tahuayo Lodge:** Visit one of the most renowned lodges of Peru's northeastern

Amazon, offering access to the Reserva Comunal Tamshiyacu Tahuayo, habitat of the rare red uakari monkey (page 267).

LOOK FOR ◖ TO FIND RECOMMENDED SIGHTS, ACTIVITIES, DINING, AND LODGING.

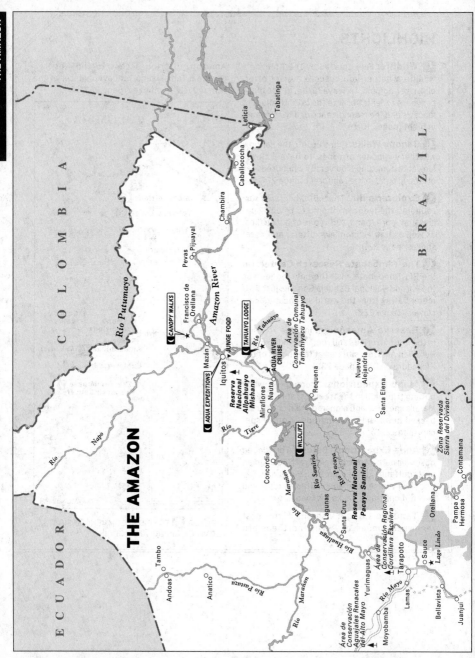

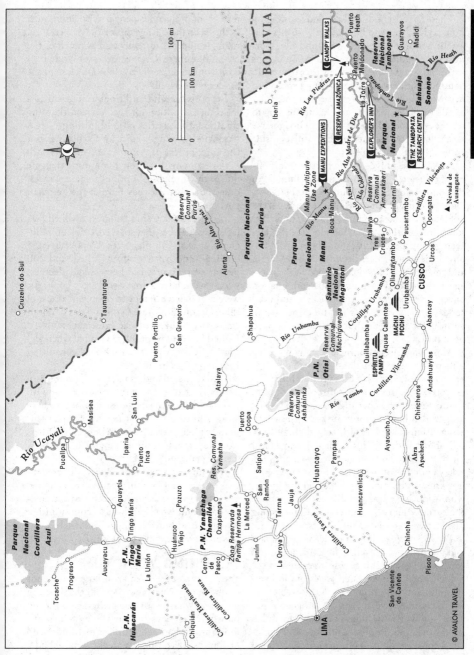

© AVALON TRAVEL

There are dozens of well-run lodges, ranging from stylish, top-end bungalows with electricity, air-conditioning, hot water, and tile floors to simple, more adventuresome wood cabins with cold water (which actually isn't that cold), hammocks, kerosene lamps, and a mosquito net over the bed. River cruises, on the other hand, are a comfortable and luxurious way to see the Amazon rainforest, with all imaginable amenities on board, including gourmet cuisine and savvy bilingual guides.

Most of the lodges in the northern rainforest are clustered in the area around Iquitos. In the southern patch of the jungle, east of Cusco, lodges are located in the **Reserva de Biósfera del Manu** (Manu Biosphere Reserve) or farther south in the Puerto Maldonado area. Lodges arrange transport such as motorboats with canopy shades, four-wheel-drive trucks (in Manu), and small canoes. Food is included in the package and normally is a nutritious combination of veggies, beans, rice, fish, chicken, and local foods such as *yuca frita* (manioc root fries), palm heart salad, and *cecina* (tender smoked pork meat).

Most lodge programs include early-morning bird-watching, a visit to an oxbow lake and/or macaw clay lick, day hikes through the forest, piraña fishing, and evening boat rides to spot caiman and other night creatures. Some lodges also have canopy walks, zip lines, or observation towers. A visit to a shaman for a talk about medicinal plants or a visit to a local farm or village crafts market is also common. A key component of any rainforest experience is a knowledgeable, English-speaking guide, whose job is to spot wildlife and introduce the extraordinary web of connections among plants, trees, animals, and insects.

Peru's Amazon, though under siege from oil and gas drilling, as well as illegal logging and small-scale gold mining, continues to host the planet's most concentrated levels of biodiversity. Humans have been part of this web of life for thousands of years, and 56 indigenous nations—of which the largest are the Asháninka, Aguaruna, and Shipibo-Conibo—still populate a considerable area of the rainforest. Small pockets of indigenous people in isolation, such as the Isconahua, Kugakapori, or Mashco-Piro, roam as nomads in remote areas north of the Manu Biosphere Reserve, the lower Urubamba basin, or the higher Ucayali basin, close to the border with Brazil.

Responsible and sustainable tourism is a much better option for the Amazon than the traditional industries of gold mining, illegal hardwood logging, and drug trafficking. But the integration of Amazonian nations into Peru's economy has been a long-time struggle due to the immense—and, in some instances, deserved—distrust they have of the Peruvian government.

In June 2009, Peru's congress revoked two legislative decrees that sparked a violent indigenous uprising. In the melee, 23 policemen, 5 civilians, and 5 natives were killed, and 200 people were injured. The revoked decrees, which were later reinstated Peru's congress, were a bungled attempt to open vast tracts of the Amazon rainforest to oil and gas developers as part of the free trade agreement with the United States. The problem resulted when legislative action was taken without consulting Indian nations in the area.

Unlike the oil and gas industry, ecotourism has expanded in the Peruvian Amazon with little conflict. Some lodges share profits or have as an aim to transfer ownership to the community after a certain number of years. Others work to provide local employment and fund local schools and clinics.

It is important to cross-check the credentials of the lodge or tour operator you choose. Choose a lodge that is respectful of the environment and works with local communities. By support sustainable lodges, you will be helping preserve the Amazon as well.

PLANNING YOUR TIME

Your visit to Peru's Amazon largely depends on the money you want to spend, the time you have, and what season you are traveling. If you only have 3–5 days and a few hundred dollars, look into lodges around Puerto Maldonado or Iquitos. If you have a week or more and a bigger budget, go to the Reserva de Biósfera del Manu or indulge yourself with a river cruise on the Amazon. There are exceptions to this rule, however. High levels of wildlife can also be found in the **Reserva Nacional Pacaya Samiria,** southwest of Iquitos, or the **Reserva Nacional Tambopata,** farther south of Puerto Maldonado. Either way, the best time to visit Peru's jungle is during the dry months May–October, though Iquitos can be visited year-round.

To figure out where to go, it helps to understand Peru's different jungle zones. The jet stream in the southern hemisphere moves west, not east as in the northern hemisphere. Amazon humidity cools and condenses as it is forced over the eastern slopes of the Andes. This gives rise to the damp and chilly montane cloud forests perched between 700 and 2,900 meters of elevation. This is the habitat of the **cock of the rock,** a crimson, chicken-shaped bird; the **Andean bear,** the only surviving bear species of South America; and a huge range of colorful orchids, bromeliads, and humming-birds. Peru's most accessible montane cloud forests are around Tarapoto, Tingo María, Machu Picchu, and the drive into the Reserva de Biósfera del Manu.

Lower down into the jungle, clear mountain streams cascade through steep mountain forests, giving way to broader, progressively muddier rivers that weave in through the increasingly flat landscape. This type of lowland rainforest occurs in Manu and Puerto Maldonado but reaches its greatest expression all the way downriver near Iquitos, where the Amazon reaches to be around two kilometers wide and the forest is perfectly flat.

The **Reserva de Biósfera del Manu,** which stretches from an altitude of 4,000 meters all the way down to 150 meters, protects one of the most pristine swaths of Peruvian Amazon, where a wide range of birds, primates, and mammals can be seen. The best time to visit is during the dry season May–November, though only sporadic rains occur starting November and December. There are only eight licensed tour operators in Manu, which charge between US$600 and US$2,250 for five- to nine-day tours ranging from beach camping to comfortable lodges. The Manu, like Puerto Maldonado, is in Peru's southeastern jungle and is reached by a full-day bus ride or via flights into Boca Manu, a small airport.

The advantages of the lodges around **Puerto Maldonado,** downriver from Reserva de Biósfera del Manu, are cost and access: Travelers arrive within 30 minutes of flying from Cusco, and a two-night stay costs anywhere from US$60 to US$350. This area, on the edge of the **Reserva Nacional Tambopata,** has a good variety of monkeys, birds, caimans, and small mammals. As at Manu, the best time to visit here is May–November. There are levels of wildlife comparable to Manu at the **Tambopata Research Center,** a 7–10 hour boat ride from Puerto Maldonado. This center is next to the remote **Parque Nacional Bahuaja Sonene** and the world's largest macaw clay lick or *collpa.*

The city of **Iquitos,** in Peru's northeastern Amazon, forged Peru's tourism industry back in the late 1960s but has grown so large that tourists have to go a long way to find interesting jungle. There is a wide variety of cost and quality in this area. If you don't mind traveling a bit longer, some of Peru's best lodges are upstream on the Marañón River, near the **Reserva Nacional Pacaya Samiria,** Peru's largest protected rainforest area. Endangered wildlife such as the rare Amazonian manatee or sea cow can be observed here. Close to the **Reserva Comunal Tamshiyacu Tahuayo,** a reserve self-managed by the local communities, there are some good lodges. An hour by car from Iquitos, on the Iquitos–Nauta highway, is the **Reserva Nacional Allpahuayo Mishana,** the only protected white-sand forest, where new bird species have recently been discovered.

Unlike Puerto Maldonado, Iquitos can be visited year-round. The Puerto Maldonado area, which is higher jungle, has an intense rainy season from January to April. Iquitos, which is much farther downstream, has more constant weather year-round. Although the weather is relatively constant, the river rises 7–15 meters during the November–May rainy months in the Andes. During these months, the forests around Iquitos flood and soils are replenished with silt. Animals can most easily be spotted on the mud banks after the river drops, between June and September. The cost of Iquitos lodges ranges US$60–200 per night, depending on the distance from Iquitos.

There are interesting access points to the Peruvian high jungle or *selva alta,* including **Chanchamayo Valley** in Peru's central jungle; **Tingo María,** a former drug trafficking zone that is rapidly becoming a safe and low-budget jungle destination with nearby **Parque Nacional Tingo María;** and **Tarapoto,** located upriver from Iquitos.

Lodges

The lodges in this book are recommended because, in our opinion, they all have a strong environmental commitment, a sustainable approach and design, and have forged strong and supportive relationships with surrounding communities. We also consider the amount of wildlife and primary forest that can be seen nearby, along with the quality of food and lodging. Finally, we evaluate whether lodges work with fully licensed and professional guides, who are essential for spotting wildlife and understanding how the rainforest works. A good guide should give the local, English, and scientific name for all birds, talk about a wide range of trees and medicinal plants, and boil down the complexity of symbiotic relationships and rainforest ecology.

Avoid private guides who will often promise trips down remote rivers for an unbelievably low price. There have been numerous reports of clients robbed at gunpoint and left stranded on a riverbank. But more common experiences include mediocre food, faulty equipment, and unfulfilled promises. If you must, use only private guides that come recommended from a trusted source. A better option is to use the agencies recommended in this book, which are professional, safe, and worth the money.

Packing for the Jungle

Yes, there are biting insects in the jungle, so bring plenty of repellent (20 percent DEET is what the Center for Disease Control recommends). The best defense, however, is to cover the body with light-colored, long clothing and, in the evenings, cover up with a mosquito head net. Apart from two or three pairs of long pants and shirts other items include T-shirts, lots of socks, a swimsuit, one pair of shorts, a sweater or fleece for chilly evenings, hiking or tennis shoes—rubber boots are normally supplied by the lodge or river cruise you choose—rain suit or poncho, toiletries, sunglasses, sunscreen, binoculars, headlamp, water bottle, photocopy of passport, camera, and one or two memory cards. Most agencies require that you keep your luggage to a minimum because of tight space on the planes and boats. You can usually store your extra luggage at the agency's main office. Better though, is to pack lightly!

HISTORY

There are 56 indigenous nations living at in the Peruvian Amazon basin, many of which can be traced back thousands of years. Still, it is largely a mystery as to when and exactly how human civilization fanned out through the waterways of the rainforest.

The **Inca** were aware of the geographic challenges and the skilled archers that were hidden in the **Antisuyo**—"land of the east," as they named the Amazon in Quechua. Garcilaso de la Vega, a mestizo chronicler of the 16th century, reports that Inca Túpac Yupanqui crushed an insurrection of the Manu tribes and ordered the construction of two fortresses that have yet to be discovered. From Pisac, an Inca road led to Paucartambo and on to coca plantations maintained in the high jungle at Pilcopata. This is still the main route to reach the Reserva de Biósfera del Manu.

Apart from Pilcopata, the Inca conquered, in some of the most bloodiest campaigns they waged, other jungle fringe areas including **Moyobamba** and the montane cloud forests where the **Chachapoya** flourished. As a result, the Inca had jungle archers in their army, as the

Spanish learned the hard way at the battles of Sacsayhuamán and Ollantaytambo. But even before the Inca, trade routes were established from the jungle to the coast to export exotic woods and animals, cacao, natural dyes, and medicinal plants, among other products.

The Spanish conquistadors explored the jungle recklessly and paid a heavy cost in their feverish search for fabled gold cities such as **Paititi** and **El Dorado.** One of these adventurous deeds was conducted by **Francisco de Orellana.** If Vicente Yañez Pinzón was the discoverer of the Amazon River in 1500, Orellana was immortalized as the first European to navigate the whole length of the "sea river," 41 years later.

A cousin of Francisco Pizarro according to some historians, Orellana accepted in 1541 to head an expedition in search of El Dorado. With a party of only 49 men, and under constant threat from the Omagua tribes, Orellana sailed down the Río Napo until he finally reached the confluence with the Amazon in 1542, not far away from present-day Iquitos.

According to the Spanish friar Gaspar de Carvajal, who traveled with Orellana's men, they were attacked by "women warriors." The Spanish Jesuit Cristóbal de Acuña wrote that the area close to the Amazon River, rich in gold, was dominated by Yacamiaba Indians, which in their language meant "women without husbands." The tribe of fierce women that battled against Orellana's expedition inspired the explorer to baptize the river as **Río de las Amazonas,** after the Greek myths of the mighty Amazons. Orellana never found any golden city, but managed to sail the complete length of the Amazon to the Atlantic, one of the great epic journeys of human history.

Orellana's report of vast uncivilized territory triggered what is perhaps the largest missionary effort ever. Jesuit and Franciscan missionaries hacked their way down into nearly all of the Amazon's important tributaries from Peruvian cities such as Cajamarca, Chachapoyas, Moyobamba, and Huancayo, which became important bases for these evangelical missions.

The suppression and expulsion of the **Jesuits** from Latin America in 1767 left not only an intellectual abyss but also large tracts of the Amazon nearly abandoned. At one point, much of what is now the Peruvian Amazon was attached to the Viceroyalty of Santa Fe (present-day Argentina). But because access to the Amazon was easier from Peru, a royal dictate of 1802 transferred much of the Amazon basin to the Viceroyalty of Peru.

In 1839, the U.S. citizen **Charles Goodyear** vulcanized rubber by heating natural rubber and sulphur to create an elastic, durable substance that could be fused into objects for real use. Suddenly *caucho,* as the gooey, white latex from the rubber tree was known, became a valuable commodity. First Brazil and later Peru became the center of the **rubber boom** (1879–1912), which caused Iquitos to explode in size and fortunes overnight. Within a decade, Iquitos became the second-richest city in Latin America after Manaus, another rubber boom town, in Brazil.

During the rubber boom, Iquitos's wealthiest families built elaborate mansions decorated with tiles imported from Seville and Portugal, and large public buildings were commissioned, such as Gustav Eiffel's **Casa de Fierro** or Iron House. Rubber barons, such as **Julio César Arana del Águila** and **Carlos Fermín Fitzcarrald,** headed a class of "new rich" that accumulated big fortunes, founded on slavery and extremely cruel treatment of indigenous populations. Extravagant stories from this time abound, such as families who sent their laundry each week to Paris, or the rubber baron who ordered a crate of expensive beaver skin hats from Europe and tossed all but the perfect-fitting hat into the river.

During the rubber boom, millions of Indians were coerced to collect *caucho* in the forest. These workers became some of the most abused, wretched workers in Peru's history, and their sufferings have not been sufficiently researched and studied. Enslaved by debt, malnourished, and diseased, the workers often faced the choice of perishing or attempting an oft-fatal escape through the jungle.

The rubber boom collapsed in 1912 as rapidly as it had begun. The Dutch and English smuggled *caucho* plants out of Peru and Brazil and successfully cultivated them in Malaysia. Thanks to a railroad network and orderly rows of trees, collecting latex became far easier in Southeast Asia than among the wild vegetation of the Amazon forest.

A decade after the rubber collapse, oil was discovered in the Amazon around the 1920s. Engineers from international petroleum companies, along with Mormon missionaries, were among the first outsiders to explore many remote headwaters of the Amazon. Since then, huge pipeline projects such as the **North Peruvian Oil Pipeline,** completed in 1996, and the **Camisea Pipeline,** operational since 2004, have brought foreign revenue to Peru but have also affected huge areas of virgin Amazon. Whenever a large pipe has to be filled with fossil fuel, a network of roads, platforms, testing paths, helicopter pads, and pumping stations springs up in front of it.

The future of Peru's Amazon is quite uncertain, trapped between an unstoppable exploitation of resources—a result of the country's modernization and need for foreign currency— and the urgent need to protect the most biodiverse rainforest on the planet.

Exploring the Jungle

The Amazon jungle, blanketed in a brilliant monoshade of green, depends on its inhabitants to give it color and noise. Strange, noisy, and even stinky, Amazon wildlife is often colorful—and loud. Birds squawk, beetles wiggle across the floor, and monkeys howl at sunrise. The wildlife is the energy of the rainforest.

Although the jungle is home to thousands of creatures, the ones discussed here are especially noteworthy. We recommend exploring the rainforest with a guide. His or her trained eye is likely to see double what your beginner vision will spot.

◖ WILDLIFE
Hoatzin

Known locally as *shansho,* few birds are more common and bizarre in the jungle than the hoatzin, a chickenlike bird with a spiky crest that can often be seen flapping noisily around bushes at water's edge. They make odd grunting noises and eat only leaves, which are digested by a system of three stomachs, or "crops." The leaves ferment inside their crops, thus giving these birds a bad odor. The hoatzin doesn't mind being smelly because its scent is its main protection from predators.

Hoatzin chicks are born with claws on their wings like the flying pterodactyl. When an anaconda or other predator comes to the nest to eat the chicks, they dive into the water. When the danger is past, they use their claws to climb back into their nest. Scientists once thought the hoatzin was a descendant of the prehistoric bird, but recent DNA analysis indicates the hoatzin is a strange member of the cuckoo family. Its claws are probably a relatively recent adaptation.

Macaws, Parrots, and Parakeets

There are few natural sights more remarkable than a *collpa,* or a macaw clay lick, covered very early in the morning with dozens of brightly colored macaws, parrots, and parakeets jostling with each other for access to the mineral-rich clay mud they eat. The world's largest *collpa* is near the Tambopata Research Center, on the Río Tambopata, about a seven-hour boat ride upstream from Puerto Maldonado. At dawn, as many as 600 birds perch on surrounding trees before they cautiously descend to the riverbank. By 7 a.m. the show is over. There are similar but smaller *collpas* spread throughout the Parque Nacional Manu and the Reserva Nacional Tambopata.

Why do these birds eat the clay? As scientists have recently discovered, the answer has to do with the fact that many jungle fruits contain

© BETH FUCHS

Macaws feed on clay early in the morning at this riverside clay lick in the Manu Biosphere Reserve. Ornithologists believe the clay allows macaws to properly digest green fruit.

toxins that give unripe fruit a sour taste. The toxins are designed to prevent predators from eating fruit until the seeds are fully developed. But the minerals contained in the clay eaten by macaws, parrots, and parakeets neutralize the toxins, allowing the birds to digest unripe fruit and giving them a competitive advantage over monkeys and other fruit-eating animals

The most common macaws found in the Peruvian Amazon are the **red-bellied macaw,** which is mostly green with a dullish yellow color on the underside of its wings and tail, and the **blue-and-yellow macaw,** which is bright blue on top and yellow underneath. Less common are the **chestnut-fronted macaw,** which is mostly green but with a reddish color in the underside of its wings and tail; the **scarlet macaw** with yellow median upper wing coverts; and the **red-and-green macaw,** which is deep scarlet with green median upper wing coverts.

Piraña

There are 20 species of piraña in a rainbow of colors, though the most common in Peru is the **red-belly piraña,** which is crimson on the bottom and silvery-green on the sides. This piraña hunts in schools and eats whatever it can: mollusks, crustaceans, insects, birds, lizards, amphibians, rodents, baby caiman, and other pirañas. During the Amazon's high-water months, they also eat submerged fruit.

Contrary to the pop culture image of pirañas devouring people in a bloody maul of frothy water, these fanged creatures rarely bother humans, as proven by troops of Amazon children that play each day in the river. Nobody remembers a human being killed by a piraña, although plenty have been viciously nipped. If you swim in a jungle river, avoid the warm, still waters favored by these fish. Pirañas, like sharks, are attracted by blood and splashing in the water. They can become especially aggressive when food is scarce, such as when trapped in a drying lake. They are most active at dawn and dusk and sleep at night.

A must-do activity at most jungle lodges in the Peruvian Amazon is **piraña fishing.**

You will be provided with a string, a hook, and a chunk of red meat. Just plunk the baited hook into the still waters of nearly any Amazon backwater and presto! Once you feel the aggressive tug of these palm-sized fish, the fun has just begun. Before you grab hold of your catch, ask your guide to do so instead. With a bulldog face, powerful lower jaw, and a set of razor-sharp teeth, these little creatures will nip at anything in reach and cause a nasty bite. So leave the fish handling to the guide.

Giant Otter

Once found throughout thousands of kilometers of Amazon waters, the populations of river otters have been reduced to only two species, found mainly in remote headwaters and oxbow lakes. The larger species, the giant otter, is most commonly seen in lakes in Parque Nacional Manu, Reserva Nacional Tambopata and in remotes areas of the Reserva Nacional Pacaya Samiria.

A family generally consists of a pair of adults plus a few juveniles. Their home is a mud cave in a lake bank marked by trampled vegetation and carefully placed boundaries of feces and urine. The giant otter has stubby feet, which makes it an awkward land traveler, but a powerful flat tail, which makes it an impressively fast and acrobatic swimmer. With luck, otters can be seen and heard chomping on their fish catch from their log perches or even taking sun baths. Otters hunt baby caimans, snakes, and young turtles. Though extremely inquisitive animals, they steer clear of predators such as adult black caimans and anaconda. If attacked, however, a group of otters can use their powerful jaws and swimming abilities to prevail over these much larger predators.

Because of intense hunting between the 1940s and 1970s, otter populations have plummeted and become declared an endangered species. Even though it is illegal to hunt otters and sell their pelts, river otter populations continue to decline in some areas. Because they are at the top of the food chain, many biologists consider their decline to be a worrisome sign of watershed contamination from the mercury used in gold mining.

Taricaya Turtle

Fossils indicate that earth's first turtles could not withdraw their heads into their shells. Instead they tucked their heads to one side, as the taricaya turtle still does. These creatures eat meat but also chomp on fruits and seeds, which they can reach during the high waters of rainy season. They are solitary nesters and lay approximately 30–50 eggs, which have been an important source of protein for Peru's Amazon natives. Thanks to programs in Reserva Nacional Pacaya Samiria, they have been brought back from the edge of extinction in some parts of Peru, though they remain common along the Madre de Dios and Manu Rivers. Look for groups of this aquatic turtle, stacked on top of each other like fallen dominos, on logs jutting from the water. They sun themselves in order to increase body temperature and probably also to eliminate the buildup of algae on their carapaces.

Caiman

This reptile is a crocodilian that can reach an astonishing six meters in length. Caimans live in the still waters of oxbow lakes and rivers and are very good swimmers, with long, slender bodies and powerful tails that propel them through the water. They crush their prey with their powerful jaws and, along with their staple diet of fish, will eat anything they can get their jaws on, including capybaras, juvenile otters, birds, insects, and mollusks. Caimans may be such fierce predators because they have such a hard time growing up. The eggs are eaten by snakes, fish, and hawks. After hatching, baby caimans hide in the water grass, coming out only at night to avoid being eaten by a turtle, otter, or wading bird. A very small percent of caimans survive the ordeal.

Caimans can be easily spotted by the red reflection of their eyes in a flashlight beam, a common night activity at many lodges. With a fast hand jab into the water, most Amazon guides are capable of pulling a juvenile

©TERRA INCOGNITA, PROMPERU

a Taricaya turtle in the Reserva Nacional Pacaya Samiria

caiman up to a half meter out of the water for inspection.

There are four species of caiman in Peru: the dwarf (1–5 meters), the smooth-fronted (two meters), the spectacled (five meters), and the black (up to six meters). This last, rarest of all, has black marks, a spiky tail, and a short snout. After being hunted relentlessly for their skins in the first half of the 20th century, the Amazon's caiman population is a fraction of what it was in 1900.

Capybara

The cuddly shape and peaceful demeanor of the capybara seems out of sync with the brutal, anaconda-eat-jaguar world of the Amazon. Troops of capybaras can be seen munching on the lush grasses and aquatic vegetation at the banks of most rivers. At the first whiff of danger, these timid animals scurry into the muddy water and sink like submarines out of sight. Though they are mammals, they can hold their breath underwater and even sleep underwater, their snouts barely protruding above the surface.

The capybara, which in Guaraní means "master of grasses," is the largest rodent in the world. It grows to about the size of a large pig and is covered with a thin layer of reddish brown hair. It has small ears and nose, and eyes that are perched at the top of its barrel-shaped snout for easy use while swimming. Though clumsy on land, capybaras are agile swimmers thanks to their webbed toes.

Capybaras are prized bush meat among Amazon natives and an food source for anacondas, big cats, harpy eagles, and caimans. Despite all the hunting, the capybara remains common thanks to its rapid reproduction. Females begin mating in the water a year after they are born and have 2–8 babies at a time. Capybaras can live up to 10 years.

Pink River Dolphin

One of the Amazon's most flabbergasting sights is the pink river dolphin rising above the waters of lakes or rivers. Unlike their ocean-going relatives, these dolphins have a strange dorsal hump that gives them an S-shape and a huge set of flippers. Their elastic vertebrae allows them to contort their pinkish bodies nearly in half in search of crustaceans and fish in the grassy waters and flooded forests of the Amazon. Their pink color comes mainly from capillaries near the surface of the skin.

Pink river dolphins occupy a special place in Amazon mythology. Some tribes consider it a sacred animal, while others regard them as an evil spirit that seduces young women. Regardless of its exact reputation, the pink river dolphin has never been hunted by Amazon indigenous people. As a result, it was extremely common in the lower waterways of the Amazon up until about 30 years ago. The biggest enemies of the dolphin these days are deforestation, which has damaged its aquatic home, and gill nets, which ensnare and drown dolphins.

Jaguar

Known as *otorongo* in Peru, derived from the Quechua word *uturunku,* the jaguar is the biggest spotted cat in the Americas and probably the hardest animal to spot in the rainforest. They are solitary and keen hunters, feeding chiefly on capybaras, deer and tapirs—their favorite—but also fish, caimans, and smaller mammals.

Jaguars are mostly spotted at night. But during the months of May and June, 30 percent of Manu visitors report seeing these felines stretching out on a river log under the morning sun. Most jaguars will flee quickly from human presence once spotted.

Considered a deity in pre-Hispanic cultures such as Chavín or Cupisnique, the jaguar has been overhunted by centuries for its fur and is listed as endangered.

◖ CANOPY WALKS

Visitors to the Amazon are often surprised by how dark, gloomy, and colorless the rainforest ground can be. The situation is completely different 30 meters or more up in the air, where a dazzling array of orchids, bromeliads, and mosses hang out on the treetops and soak in the scorching sunlight. The fragrant scents of these epiphytes and the succulent fruit of the

ubiquitous *matapalo* or strangler fig lure monkeys and a huge range of pollinators, including birds, bats, and insects.

Most of the Amazon's biodiversity is in the canopy, which U.S. biologist Bruce Rinker describes as a "leafy aerial continent, elevated on stilts, called the treetops." Biologists have come up with ingenious ways to explore this airy world with a combination of suspended cable walkways, tree house–like platforms, and rope-climbing techniques adapted from rock climbing.

In the early 1990s the nonprofit ACER organization funded the Amazon's longest canopy walkway, which was built 80 kilometers northeast of Iquitos at the **Explorama Lodge.** It is a cable bridge suspended between a series of giant rainforest trees that runs for nearly half a kilometer and reaches 35 meters above the ground. Visitors hang out for hours on the walkway, peering down the sides of trees to the jungle floor below or scanning over the treetops for hundreds of different birds.

The bridge is completely safe, even for children. There are safety cables at shoulder height to grab onto, a wooden floor, and thick mesh stretched between. The whole thing is like a giant channel of mesh out of which it would be hard to climb, much less fall. Visitors climb up a wooden tower with wide staircase to access the bridge, and no harnesses or other safety precautions are necessary. Guides usually let visitors wander wherever they want on the bridge.

Reserva Amazónica east of Puerto Maldonado area has built a similar canopy walkway. A dozen other lodges in Peru's rainforest offer observation platforms. These platforms, such as the one at **Manu Wildlife Center,** are up to 35 meters off the ground and are usually reached via a circular staircase that is made of steel and held upright via steel cables. Again, no safety harnesses are required and, as long as you are not terrified of heights, getting to the platform is easy.

There are plenty more adventurous canopy options in Peru's rainforest, including the wooden platforms at **Cocha Salvador** in the Parque Nacional Manu. To reach these airy tree houses, you must don a rock-climbing

Searching for bats as the sun sets on a canopy walkway near the Explorama Lodge, near Iquitos.

harness and climb the rope via a set of jumars, ascending devices used most commonly in rock climbing. It is a completely safe, though strenuous, experience that allows you to appreciate how high 35 meters off the ground really is. For those uncomfortable with climbing the rope, another option is to be pulled up into the tree house by a geared contraption that is cranked by the guide.

The **Tahuayo Lodge,** 145 kilometers upstream of Iquitos, has what it calls a zip line, which is essentially a harness that slides along a set of steel cables about 30 meters above the ground. From a wooden platform, visitors launch into space and can either zing through the canopy or stop and hang quietly in order to observe wildlife. Obviously, this is for those extremely comfortable with heights!

Puerto Maldonado and Vicinity

For the quality of the lodging and the amount of wildlife that visitors see, the jungle lodges around Puerto Maldonado represent an excellent Amazon value. Just a half-hour plane ride from Cusco, Puerto Maldonado is the place for people with a limited budget and limited time. In an action-packed stay of two or three nights, visitors are likely to see a few types of monkeys (there are seven species in the area), capybaras and other jungle rodents, a wide variety of water and forest birds, caimans, and turtles. Large mammals such as tapirs and jaguars are seldom seen, though chances become better farther into the jungle at the Tambopata Research Center, which is inside the **Parque Nacional Bahuaja Sonene.**

Though there are fewer species here than in Manu, getting to Puerto Maldonado's jungle is a heck of a lot easier. Visitors arrive at the airport, where they are picked up by their lodge and taken up a river in a motorboat. In as little as three hours after leaving Cusco, visitors can

PUERTO MALDONADO AND VICINITY

Map information courtesy of InkaNatura Travel

© AVALON TRAVEL

be in a comfortable jungle lodge surrounded by miles of Amazon rainforest. Standard features of most trips include early-morning bird-watching followed by a nature walk, piraña fishing, and a visit to a local community and/or medicinal plant talk by a local shaman. If guests have energy, guides lead night jungle walks or boat rides to spot baby caimans, a close relative of the alligator, along the river bank. Prices include airport transfer, boat transport, lodging, and food.

There are two main protected areas near Puerto Maldonado. The **Reserva Nacional Tambopata** (275,000 hectares) stretches east from Puerto Maldonado all the way to the Río Heath on the Bolivian border. It serves as a buffer zone around the **Parque Nacional Bahuaja Sonene** (1.1 million hectares). The whole area of 1.4 million hectares is across the Río Heath from the **Parque Nacional Maididi** in Bolivia, forming the largest patch of protected rainforest in South America.

The jungle lodges are clustered in two areas on the edge of the Reserva Nacional Tambopata. The first group is an hour's boat ride down the Río Madre de Dios. The lodges

© RENÉE DEL GAUDIO AND ROSS WEHNER

Bird guides can help you spot and identify jungle birds in a dense sea of green.

here include some of the most comfortable in the Amazon, including Reserva Amazónica and Lake Sandoval Lodge. There are lower-budget options in this area as well.

The other main group is 3–4 hours up the Río Tambopata, on the way to the Parque Nacional Bahuaja Sonene. In general, wildlife-spotting opportunities are about equal between these two groups of lodges—all of them are near the reserve's buffer zone and are mostly surrounded by secondary forest.

An exception is **Explorer's Inn,** built in 1976, which is the only lodge inside the Reserva Nacional Tambopata and seems to have more bird and animal species than the other lodges—including frequent sightings of the giant otter and world-record levels of birds and butterflies. The reserve also includes areas of virgin forest, unlike the other lodges, whose large mahogany and cedar trees were cut down years ago.

The world's largest macaw clay lick, which attracts nearly all the area's species of macaws,

parrots, and parakeets, is seven hours up the Río Tambopata near the **Tambopata Research Center.** Most Puerto Maldonado lodges offer two-day trips to the lick, which include a night of camping on a sandy beach, a guided hike through the forest, meals, and a morning visit to the lick.

HISTORY

Puerto Maldonado began as a rubber boom-town in 1902 after a mule road was built from the coast to the headwaters of the Río Tambopata. After the rubber craze ended, gold mining and logging took its place and continue today, though fortunately tourism and Brazil nuts are increasingly important. The wide avenues of Puerto, as locals call the city, quickly peter out into mud lanes and ramshackle rows of wooden buildings. Instead of cars, mostly scooters and three-wheeled *motocars* buzz the streets. Puerto Maldonado is smaller and infinitely more relaxed than the Amazon megalopolis of Iquitos. Most travelers fly into Puerto Maldonado and transfer immediately to one of two dozen lodges in the area. Avoid staying the night in Puerto, as the jungle is more interesting.

There were two explorers with the last name of Maldonado who explored the Madre de Dios. The first, Juan Álvarez Maldonado, was a Spanish explorer who came here in 1567 in search of gold. He was the first to make it all the way to the Río Heath, the present-day Bolivian border, but he lost 250 Spaniards to disease and Indian attacks in the process. He returned to Cusco months later, half-crazed and in rags, and claimed to have found a sophisticated, wealthy jungle city known as Paititi.

Though the legend of Paititi grew, the memory of Maldonado's hardships prevented the Spaniards from returning to the area for nearly three centuries. In the mid-19th century Colonel Faustino Maldonado returned to make the first map of the area. But he perished, along with his valuable journals, in a rapid on the Río Madre de Dios. He carved his name on a tree trunk at the junction of the Tambopata and

ILLEGAL MAHOGANY LOGGING: PROFIT AND LOSS

Second to gold mining, logging is the main industry that took off when roads were completed to Shintuya, near Manu, and Puerto Maldonado in the 1960s. By 2003, there were an estimated 20,000 loggers in the Río Madre de Dios. The industry has more than doubled since 1990 and exported a whopping 23 million board feet in 2003, though accurate figures are hard to come by.

Loggers cruise the rivers and floodplains searching for three trees in the mahogany family that are used in furniture making: cedar (locally called *cedro, Cedrela odorata*), mahogany (*caoba, Swietenia macrophylla*), and *tornillo (Cedrelinga catenaeformis*). Very few of these trees, which can grow to up to 60 meters high, are left, except in remote headwaters or inside one of the parks. As a result, the focus is being shifted now to new, less-valuable species such as *lupuna*, which is used for plywood, kapok, and ironwood. After cutting a tree, loggers use chainsaws to make thick planks that are tied together into a raft and floated into Puerto Maldonado.

The government's effort to control logging in the region has generated considerable resentment. Loggers have reached the borders of Parque Nacional Manu and other protected areas and are clamoring for the right to selectively cut trees inside. INRENA, the Peruvian natural resources authority, has rejected the request and gone further by handing out concessions only to large timber companies that are easier to monitor. These concessions are the result of a forestry law passed in 2003, but small loggers see it as another example of big

© JOSHUA PAUL

a Manu lumberjack in front of his Ford F600

business and government trading money back and forth for their own benefit.

In May 2003, thousands of small loggers, led by union activist Rafael Río López, rose up in anger in and burned offices belonging to INRENA and other conservation groups in Puerto Maldonado. Río Lopez eventually turned himself in and was jailed but, in a highly unusual example of popular sentiment, was elected president of the Madre de Dios region from his cell.

Madre de Dios Rivers, where the town named in his honor is located today.

SIGHTS

The **Inkahtterra Butterfly House** (near Puerto Maldonado airport, www.inkaterra. com, US$6) is a great first thing to do upon arrival in Puerto Maldonado. It's adjacent to the airport and doubles as a welcome center and an introduction to Peru's 3,700 species of recorded butterflies. The facility includes restrooms with showers, a coffee shop, baggage store, and Internet. Butterflies are raised in the laboratory, which is open for visits, and there is a large, netted garden with hundreds of butterflies flitting about.

ENTERTAINMENT AND EVENTS

There are two nice pubs with games and dart boards that are next to each other on the Plaza de Armas. **Boulevard** (Daniel Carrión 271, tel.

082/57-2082, 6 P.M.–midnight daily) is right behind Hornito's, the pizza spot. The similar **Amnesis** is next door on Daniel Carrión. Live music is available every Friday night at **Plaza Bar** (Loreto, block 3, opens at 8 P.M. Tues.–Sat.). Also on the third block of Loreto, but on the other side of the street, is the very popular **Snack Bar Tsaica,** which is also open Tuesday–Saturday and has live music every other Friday.

For a more hip atmosphere, head to **Coconut** (Daniel Carrión, block 2, 9 P.M.–2 A.M. daily). The disco-bar plays a variety of music and has an excellent selection of cocktails. You might also try **Teocas** (Loreto, block 2, 9 P.M.–2 A.M. daily), a better dance spot that gets swinging after 11 P.M.

ACCOMMODATIONS
US$10-25
The best of the budget options is **Royal Inn** (Dos de Mayo 333, mitsutake4@hotmail.com, tel. 082/57-3464, US$12 s, US$15 d), with shared baths and cold water. It can get noisy here, so ask for a room away from the street and the central courtyard. The other budget option is the rather crummy **Hotel Wilson** (Gonzáles Prada 355, tel. 082/57-1086, US$8 s, US$12 d).

Even for budget travelers, Puerto seems like a good place to upgrade to **Cabaña Quinta** (Cusco 535, tel. 082/57-1045, US$15 s, US$24 d with breakfast), with smallish, tile-floored rooms and nice gardens. Rooms have hot water, cable TV, and optional air-conditioning for twice the price. The setting is quiet, and the hotel restaurant is one of the better ones in town.

US$25-50
Don Carlos Hotel (León Velarde 1271, tel. 082/57-1029, www.hotelesdoncarlos.com, US$30 s, US$35 d with breakfast) is a pleasant hotel perched on a hilltop on the edge of town. There is a nice wood porch for having a drink, and a decent restaurant. The rooms have wood floors, nice beds, optional air-conditioning, and clean bathrooms with a limited hot water supply. Price includes airport transfer.

A better value is **Brombu's Lodge** (Carretera Maldonado Km 4.5, tel. 082/57-3230, brombuslodge@yahoo.es, US$23 s, US$30 d with breakfast), a 10-minute taxi ride outside of town on the way to the airport. The bungalows are large, sparsely decorated, but pleasant, and surrounded by plants and trees. There is a restaurant, probably Puerto's finest, with river views and a full bar. Avoid this place on weekends because of a neighboring *peña* that cranks loud music all night.

The most charming and expensive place in town is **Wasaí Maldonado Lodge** (Guillermo Billinghurst, tel. 01/436-8792, www.wasai.com, US$36 s, US$48 d with breakfast), a mini jungle lodge overlooking the Río Madre de Dios. Stilts and wooden ramps support and connect 16 wooden bungalows and rooms, which include minibar, cable TV, hot water, and a choice of air-conditioning or fan. Features include a tiny pool with a waterfall, Puerto's fanciest restaurant, and a gazebo bar with great views.

FOOD
A good place for breakfast, hamburgers, or a light lunch is **La Casa Nostra** (León Velarde 515, tel. 082/57-3833, 7 A.M.–1 P.M. and 5–11 P.M. Mon.–Sat., US$4), a small café with good service and good coffee.

The best food in town is at **Burgos's Restaurant** (corner of Billinghurst and Puno, tel. 082/57-3653, 7 A.M.–10 P.M. daily, US$4), which offers large portions of local cuisine made in its open kitchen. The dining room at **Brombu's Lodge** (Carretera Maldonado Km 4.5, tel. 082/57-3230, 7 A.M.–10 P.M. daily, US$4) looks over the river in a forest that is a surprisingly good place for bird-watching. The wide-ranging menu includes local dishes like *patarashka de pollo,* and the chicken brochettes with Brazil nut sauce are scrumptious. Other hotels like Wasaí, Don Carlos, and Cabaña Quinta also have good restaurants.

Another good option, and a local favorite, is **El Califa** (Piura 266, tel. 082/57-1119, 10 A.M.–10 P.M. daily), which serves local jungle cuisine and good Peruvian menus. Also for typical jungle food, try the no-frills **El Majas** (Tambopata with Dos de Mayo, 6–11 P.M. daily, US$2), where meats are barbecued in front of you. **El Paladar** (Gonzáles Prada, block 6) caters mostly to tourists, but its food is clean, reliable, and varied.

The best bet for pizza is **Hornito** (Daniel Carrión 271, Plaza de Armas, tel. 082/57-2082, 6 P.M.–midnight), with good music and a cozy, publike interior.

The best spit-roasted chicken is at **La Estrella** (León Velarde 474, tel. 082/57-3107, 5–10 P.M. daily, US$3 for half a chicken and fries).

INFORMATION AND SERVICES

The **Tourism Ministry** has an office in Puerto Maldonado at Fitzcarrald 252 (tel. 082/57-1164, 7 A.M.–3:30 P.M. Mon.–Fri.) and a small booth at the airport, but visitors should do their research before arriving in Puerto Maldonado.

The **police** are at Carrión 410 (tel. 082/57-1022) and can be called by dialing 105.

You'll find **Peruvian immigrations** at Ica at Plaza Bolognesi (tel. 082/57-1069, 9 A.M.–1 P.M. Mon.–Fri.). The **Bolivian consulate** is on the main square on Loreto.

Puerto's best medical care is at **Hospital Santa Rosa** (Cajamarca 171, at Velarde, tel. 082/57-1046, 24 hours). For medical emergencies, dial 117. **Es Salud** (Dos de Mayo, block 17, tel. 082/57-1230) is a relatively new hospital open 24 hours a day. A recommended private clinic is **Clínica Madre de Dios** (28 de Julio 702, tel. 082/57-1440).

The **Banco de la Nación** (Carrión 233, tel. 082/57-1064) and **Banco de Crédito** (Arequipa 334, tel. 082/57-1001) both have ATMs. There are several exchange houses on Puno. Few places in Puerto Maldonado accept credit cards, so bring cash.

The **post office** is at León Velarde 675 (tel. 082/57-1088, 8 A.M.–9 P.M. Mon.–Sat., 8 A.M.–3 P.M. Sun.), and there are pay phones on the main square.

Internet is available around the plaza and on León Velarde.

Laundry is available at **Lavandería Silán** on León Velarde 930 (closed Sun.) and several other places down the street.

GETTING THERE AND AROUND

As it is a short flight most travelers arrive via plane to Puerto Maldonado's airport (tel. 082/57-1531), which is eight kilometers from town, or about US$2 by taxi. Airlines fly Lima–Cusco–Puerto. **LAN** (Lima tel. 01/213-8200, www.lan.com) has regular flights and a local office at León Velarde 503 (tel. 082/57-3677, 8 A.M.–8 P.M. Mon.–Sat.). The cheaper option is **Star Perú** (Lima tel. 01/705-9000, www.starperu.com), with flights from Lima and Cusco.

The road between Cusco and Puerto Maldonado is now part of the Interoceanic Highway, the US$1.2 billion ongoing project to build a highway between Peru and Brazil. The highway was first proposed 30 years ago and is now nearly complete. Construction on the road has already made the bus journey to Puerto Maldonado far easier than it used to be—instead of a bumpy 20 hours, the journey is now a relatively smooth 12-hour trip past the high Andean villages of Ocongate, Tinqui, and the snow-covered peak of Ausangate before dropping into the Amazon.

The Bolivian border is six hours downstream from Puerto Maldonado, and boats sporadically leave from Puerto's port of Capitanía. Before you leave, however, you must get your passport stamped with an exit stamp at Peruvian immigrations. Visas are not required at this time for travelers from Britain, New Zealand, and Australia. North Americans need visas.

Motocars are everywhere and cost US$0.75 for a jaunt across town. *Colectivo* boats ferry passengers across the Tambopata and Río Madre de Dios and can be hired at the Capitanía port for local tours (US$20–25 per day).

There are a few places in town to rent **scooters** for US$2/hour, including Gonzáles Prada 321 and the intersection of Prada and Puno.

RÍO TAMBOPATA LODGES

There are lodges on two rivers around Puerto Maldonado: the Río Tambopata and the Río Madre de Díos. On both rivers, you will find a variety of accommodations, but for the most part, the jungle activities remain the same.

Posada Amazonas

Operated by Rainforest Expeditions, this lodge is a groundbreaking experiment in cooperation with the community of Infierno two hours upstream of Puerto Maldonado. The people of Infierno, mestizo descendants of Ese Eja Indians, receive training, jobs, and a share of the profits, while the lodge gets use of the land. The goal of the project is to return the land to the community in 2016 and integrate the community into ecotourism and the overall preservation of rainforest.

The elegant lodge has 30 thatched rooms, with the outside wall completely open to keep guests in contact with nature. They have private bathrooms (no hot water), beds with mosquito canopies, and candlelight only. There is a hammock lounge, library, open-air dining room, and a permanent snack/hot drink table. Tours include visits to an oxbow lake to see otters, an ethnobotanical center at Infierno, and a canopy tower 35 meters off the ground and walks in the effervescent jungle.

Rainforest Expeditions is a well-managed outfit with biologist guides, excellent boats, and reliable service. It has won a series of sustainable development awards and also operates the more rustic and remote Tambopata Research Center. Contact information for both lodges is the same (Lima tel. 01/421-8347, www.perunature.com, three days/two nights US$295–385 pp).

Libertador Tambopata Eco Lodge

This lodge is affiliated with the exclusive Libertador hotel chain and, as a result, is one of Peru's more luxurious jungle lodges. The older wooden bungalows are charming with porches, hammocks, and thatched roofs—plus the new comforts of hot water, tiled bathrooms, and electric lighting (though candles are still provided).

Tambopata Eco Lodge is also building a new generation of larger, luxurious bungalows made from cement, the new material of choice for ecolodges because it lasts longer than wood and does not require the felling of trees. These cement bungalows have the same comforts but with larger, newer rooms and queen-size beds (the only downside is that there are two units per bungalow, so you hear your neighbor through the open-air ceiling). The bungalows are spread out in a jungle clearing, with the cozy bar and dining room a short walk away along a wooden ramp.

The lodge is surrounded by 100 hectares of secondary forest, in which a few old trees remain. Highlights of a visit are the slide show, bird-watching at Lago Condenado, a medicinal plant talk at a local farm, and a bird-watching platform that is 24 meters high. An excursion to the macaw clay lick, several hours farther upstream, costs US$400–500 pp extra. The lodge is three hours upstream from Puerto Maldonado (Nueva Baja 432, Cusco, tel. 084/24-5695, www.tambopatalodge.com, three days/two nights US$301–509 pp).

◀ Explorer's Inn

Built in 1975, Explorer's Inn (Lima tel. 01/447-8888, www.explorersinn.com, three days/two nights US$198 pp in double room; US$238 pp in single room) is the oldest, most experienced ecolodge in Puerto Maldonado and has a comfortable, worn-in feel. The palm-thatched, wood-rich bungalows have foam mattresses, palm-wood walls, en suite bathrooms (but no hot water), and are romantically lit by candles at night. They are comfortable but not luxurious. The central dining room is made entirely of wood and has an upstairs library with a number of natural history exhibits left behind by biologists and other researchers who have worked here over the decades.

Compared to other Amazon lodges, Explorer's Inn has the best combination of convenience, prices, and biodiverse rainforest. It is one of few located within Tambopata National Reserve, and it carefully manages 5,500 hectares of pristine rainforest that began as a private reserve and has since been incorporated into the new Tambopata National Reserve (the private property of the lodge is 105 hectares). The owner, Max Gunther, speaks flawless English, as well as German, and has been a leading figure in Peruvian ecotourism and conservation for three decades.

Biologists have proclaimed the 5,500 hectares surrounding the lodge to be "the most biodiverse place on the planet" because of a number of Guinness World Records that have been set there for animal species, including 600 bird species and more than 1,235 types of butterfly. Beside the lodge is located the new Max Gunther Centre, a made to order research station built by Lima's Catolica University, which is used by many visiting biologists from around the world. The lodge also runs a volunteer resident naturalist program designed to appeal to graduates of the environmental sciences eager to gain experience in the Amazon rainforest.

There are 37 kilometers of well-marked trails that lead to huge tracts of virgin forest, a small macaw clay lick, and two lakes where giant otters live. In one two-hour walk, we saw 20 bird species, including macaws and toucans, howler monkeys, otters, and a meter-long coral snake. The guides are extremely knowledgeable, and most tours include a visit to a farm in the nearby community of La Torre. The lodge also arranges other trips, including a mystic adventure with an ayahuasca session, a trip to the macaw clay lick on the Río Tambopata, a six-night bird-watchers program, and a variety of camping trips with the chance of observing tapirs at a salt lick at night. The lodge is 1.5 hours upstream from the native community of Infierno.

◖ The Tambopata Research Center

Also operated by Rainforest Expeditions, the Tambopata Research Center offers five- to seven-day packages where guests will experience a huge range of biodiversity that is comparable to the Parque Nacional Manu or Reserva Nacional Pacaya Samiria. Compared to those areas, the seven-hour journey up the Río Tambopata is a relatively short trip with a one-night stop there and back in Posada Amazonas. It is the only lodge near the Parque Nacional Bahuaja Sonene, a rainforest wilderness the size of Connecticut. The lodge is also 500 meters away from the world's largest clay lick, where dozens of species of macaws, parrots, and parakeets come to ingest detoxifying mud. The clay lick is amazing and well worth the long trip by river.

The newly renovated and slightly relocated lodge has 18 double bedrooms with shared bathrooms (no hot water). As at Posada Amazonas, one wall is completely open to the forest. Although more rustic than Posadas it has the added advantage of generally being quieter (Lima tel. 01/421-8347, www.perunature.com, five days/four nights US$745–945 pp).

Inotawa

A good budget option, about 15 minutes before Explorer's Inn, is Inotawa, which has a main thatched building with open-air rooms and single beds with mosquito net covering. Bathrooms are shared, with flush toilets but no hot water. There is a small bar, a restaurant with vegetarian food, and an option to visit the clay lick near the Tambopata Research Center. Inotawa offers two- to five-night, lodge-based and expedition trips and is 3.5 hours upstream from Puerto Maldonado (tel. 082/57-2511, www.inotawaexpeditions.com, three days/two nights US$240–230 pp).

RÍO MADRE DE DIOS LODGES
◖ Reserva Amazónica

This fabulous lodge is the most luxurious, and most romantic, in the Peruvian Amazon. It was founded in 1975 and is the oldest lodge in the area. The hotel was the brainchild of José and Denise Koechlin, Peruvian ecopioneers, who also own the elegant Machu Picchu Pueblo Hotel.

Near the riverbank, a sophisticated round dining building sets the tone for this lodge. This is not the kind of place where guests sit around in mud-spattered rubbers. After long walks or boat rides, guests take hot showers,

THE ECOLOGICAL TOLL OF AMAZON GOLD

The endless carpet of green Amazon rainforest, seen from above, is violently interrupted by the view of thousands of hectares of denuded brownish-black sand and earth, with lifeless pools of water contaminated with mercury.

Tens of thousands of people involved in illegal gold mining in the last decade have destroyed 150,000 hectares in Madre de Dios, where 40,000 kilograms of mercury is dumped into the environment annually. Peruvian authorities seem to have lost control over large areas of land and the activities that take place where, ironically, more than 1,500 jungle mining concessions have been granted by the government, driven by the high price of gold – at the end of 2009 more than US$1,100 per ounce or US$36 a gram.

For every gram of gold extracted, up to three times more mercury is needed. The toxic metal is used to bind with the gold particles, forming an amalgam that makes them easier to extract. The process is cheap and efficient. But the leftovers are thrown into rivers and lagoons, poisoning flora and fauna and in turn passing into the food chain.

Despite the negative impacts, stopping the mining is impossible in the short-term, with an estimated 30,000 informal miners working the Amazon. Poverty and the lack of jobs in the highlands continue to send people down to the Amazon looking for work.

These small-time miners are often armed and go about their work without any restrictions, much as in the American Wild West of the mid-19th century. The Peruvian government recognizes the problems but does not have the power or staff to stop the thousands of miners operating illegally. Antonio Brack Egg, a respected Peruvian conservationist and Peru's Minister of Environment, warns of grave repercussions for the Madre de Dios, a swath of Amazon near Cusco that has recorded record numbers of birds, butterflies, and plants. "Within 20 years Madre de Dios will be an ecological disaster like mankind has never seen before," Egg warns.

get cleaned up, and take cocktails in the dining loft with hip lounge music. The elegant dinner buffet, served downstairs, features organic salads and gourmet jungle entrées like *paca*, which is *doncella* fish, tomatoes, and onions cooked inside a bamboo tube over an open fire. There are 41 private wooden bungalows, including three luxury suites, with wood porches and hammocks, beds with mosquito netting, hot showers, kerosene lamps, and interesting touches like wooden sinks and the hotel's own line of organic shampoo and conditioner.

The lodge has several unique attractions. First, it is surrounded by 200 hectares of private lands plus a 10,000-hectare reserve. Second, it is the only lodge with a hanging canopy walk: 344 meters of swinging bridges that, at 27 meters off the ground, connect six treetop platforms and two towers and truly allow for a bird's-eye view. Guests have the options of some 15 different activities while staying at the lodge, including trekking seven kilometers through the jungle, learning about the flora and fauna, piraña fishing on Lake Sandoval, and a nighttime caiman-spotting cruise (Lima tel. 01/610-0410 or U.S. tel. 800/442-5042, www.inkaterra.com, three days/two nights US$345–781 pp).

Just downstream from the lodge, InkaTerra maintains the **Fundo Concepción,** an environmental research and education center run jointly with the U.S.-based ACER. The main building is the restored home of Dr. Arturo Gonzáles del Rio, a beloved local doctor who bought a steamship from the Bolivian navy in the 1930s and used it as an ambulance for local native people. The rusty girders and boilers of the boat can be seen during the walk into the center, which also has the area's largest garden of medicinal plants.

Sandoval Lake Lodge

This comfortable lodge has a privileged location on Lago Sandoval, a crystal-clear lake fringed with muriti palms and teeming with aquatic birds. The lodge's operator, InkaNatura, often combines a trip to this lodge with a sister operation near the Bolivian border, the Heath River Wildlife Center.

The Sandoval Lake Lodge has clean rooms made of recycled cedar, with electricity and hot water. The lake itself is an enchanting place, especially when waters turn pink and orange with the sun's rising and setting, forming a perfect mirror for the elongated palms at the water's edge. About 30 bird species, mostly aquatic, can be seen on a typical boat ride, including several species of kingfisher, herons, and egrets. There are giant otters on the lake, but they are hard to see. Trails from the hotel's backyard lead into the Reserva Nacional Tambopata, which backs up against the property.

Reaching the lodge is the best part. Boats drop guests off at a dock, from where they walk three kilometers through a jungle lane flitting with butterflies. Then guests board a canoe, which is paddled across the lake to the lodge. Each leg of the journey—motorboat, walking, and canoe—takes about 45 minutes.

The lodge is the result of a deal struck in 1996 with the Mejía family, who homesteaded around the lake in the 1950s and now operate their own lodging nearby, Casa Hospedaje Mejía. A two-night program costs US$190 and can be booked through InkaNatura Travel (Lima tel. 01/440-2022, www.inkanatura.com, two days/one night US$178–198 pp) or in the United States through Tropical Nature Travel (tel. 877/827-8350, www.tropicalnaturetravel.com).

Casa Hospedaje Mejía

This option is extremely rustic, bordering on untidy, but we challenge you to find a cheaper Amazon alternative (US$10 s, US$12 d). It is run by the Mejía family, who settled here in the 1950s. There are a dozen rough huts with rusting screens and bamboo walls in a yard teeming with hens and dogs. Its main advantage is being on Lago Sandoval.

The Mejía family members lead canoe and walking tours, though they speak only Spanish and are not trained biologists. They do know this jungle better than anyone, however, and seem friendly.

The only way to contact this lodge is via a sporadically functioning cell phone (tel. 082/961-2346) or their address in Puerto Maldonado (León Velarde 420, tel. 082/57-3567). To reach the lodge, head to the port of Capitanía in Puerto Maldonado and hire a boat for the 45-minute trip to Lago Sandoval's dock (US$10 one-way). From there it is a 45-minute walk to the lake, plus a canoe ride, if they know you are coming. It is also possible to walk all the way to the lodge, about 1.5 hours.

Heath River Wildlife Center

Off the beaten path and in a seldom-visited part of the Amazon, the Heath River Wildlife Center is run by a local community of Ese Eja Indians. This community works closely with InkaNatura Travel, which guides the lodge's management. The lodge is a 4.5-hour boat journey from Puerto Maldonado and is sandwiched between Bolivia and Peru and in the middle of South America's largest patch of protected rainforest. The lodge has six bungalows with hot showers and a rustic communal space. The basic program is three nights, and longer programs often include the related Lake Sandoval Lodge. Trips can be booked through InkaNatura Travel (Lima tel. 01/440-2022, www.inkanatura.com, four days/three nights US$575 pp) or in the United States through Tropical Nature Travel (tel. 877/827-8350, www.tropicalnaturetravel.com).

Manu Biosphere Reserve

Sprawling across the eastern slope of the Andes, the Manu Biosphere Reserve (Reserva de Biósfera del Manu) is one of the most biodiverse corners of the planet. Roughly the size of New Hampshire, the park begins at high-altitude grasslands at 4,100 meters, drops through cloud forest and mountainous rainforest, and then fans across a huge swath of rainforest at around 350 meters. There are 13 species of monkeys here (more than anywhere else in the country), 15,000 plants, 1,300 butterflies, and more than a million insects that have not been even close to documented. In May and June, the beginning of the colder and dry season, the odds increase of seeing jaguars, which come out to sun themselves on river logs. From July to November, near the end of the dry season, macaws, parrots, and parakeets are especially abundant around the riverside clay licks. Other frequently seen megafauna include giant otters, black caimans, tapirs, armadillos, anteaters, sloths, wild pigs, and the endangered harpy eagle. As if that were not enough, Manu is one of world's top birding spots, with more than 1,022 confirmed species—almost 15 percent of the world's total!

The **Parque Nacional Manu** was created in 1973, but the area was deemed so biodiverse that UNESCO incorporated the whole surrounding area into a biosphere in 1977. Then Manu won the ultimate accolade when the International Union for the Conservation of Nature declared it a **World Heritage Site,** one of only 200 in the world.

These days the biosphere is classified into several areas. The section along the Río Alto Madre de Dios is the Multiple Use Zone (commonly referred to as the **Cultural Zone** or **Buffer Zone**), where there are a few villages and a variety of ecolodges. The more pristine section up the Río Manu is the Parque Nacional Manu, to which access is strictly

© BETH FUCHS

horned screamer, Manu Biosphere Reserve

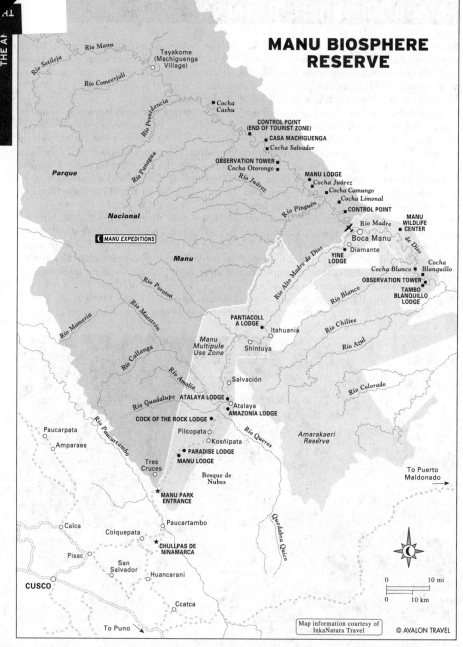

MANU BIOSPHERE RESERVE

Río Manu

Río Sotileja

Río Comeerjali

Tayakome
(Machiguenga
Village)

Río Providencia

Río Panagua

Cocha
Cashu

CONTROL POINT
(END OF TOURIST ZONE)

CASA MACHIGUENGA

Cocha Salvador

Parque

OBSERVATION TOWER
Cocha Otorongo

Río Juárez

MANU LODGE
Cocha Juárez

Cocha Camungo

Cocha Limonal

Nacional

Río Pinguén

CONTROL POINT

MANU
WILDLIFE
CENTER

Río Madre

[MANU EXPEDITIONS]

Boca Manu

de Dios

Manu

Diamante

YINE
LODGE

Cocha Blanco

Cocha
Blanquillo

Río Alto Madre de Dios

OBSERVATION TOWER

Río Porotoa

Río Maestron

Río Blanco

TAMBO
BLANQUILLO
LODGE

Río Mameria

Río Callanga

PANTIACOLL
A LODGE

Itahuania

Río Chilive

Río Azul

Manu
Multipule
Use Zone

Shintuya

Río Amalia

Salvación

Río Colorado

Río Guadalupe **ATALAYA LODGE**

Atalaya

AMAZONÍA LODGE

Río Paucartambo

COCK OF THE ROCK LODGE

Pilcopata

Kosñipata

Río Queros

Amarakaeri
Reserve

Paucarpata

Amparaes

Tres
Cruces

PARADISE LODGE
MANU LODGE

Bosque de
Nubes

To Puerto
Maldonado

MANU PARK
ENTRANCE

Calca

Paucartambo

Colquepata

CHULLPAS DE
NINAMARCA

Quebrada Quico

Pisac

San
Salvador

Huancarani

CUSCO

Ccatca

0   10 mi

0   10 km

To Puno

controlled. To enter the area, travelers must be with one of Manu's eight licensed operators, who have built comfortable safari camps (and one lodge) alongside oxbow lakes. The lower part of the Río Manu, formerly known as the Reserved Zone, is used for sustainable ecotourism and research.

The vast majority of the 1.5-million-hectare Parque Nacional Manu is closed off to everyone but licensed biologists and anthropologists. This chunk of rainforest shelters at least two ethnic groups who have had almost no contact with western civilization, the Kogapacori and the Mashco Piro. Other groups have only limited contact with the modern world.

Only a handful of companies are allowed to operate in Parque Nacional Manu. They offer trips from 5 to 10 days that range from US$600 for camping to US$2,250 for more comfortable, high-end tours that include lodges with cotton sheets, electricity, and hot water. Some of the agencies are offering new adventure options, from rafting and trekking to extreme mountain biking and even llamacart touring.

One of the best parts of Manu is getting there and dropping through the dizzying sequence of ecosystems along the way. The first day is spent either driving seven hours through the altiplano near Cusco or flying in a small-passenger plane over the Andes and down into the jungle. The driving option takes you to one of a handful of lodges perched in the cloud forest and surrounded with orchids, hummingbirds, butterflies, and the crimson Andean cock of the rock. From there, visitors descend to the lower jungle that same morning and take a several-hour boat ride down the Río Alto Madre de Dios.

The flying option skips the bus and boat rides, dropping passengers directly into the small town of **Boca Manu** and its tiny **Aerodrome** airport. The landing strip lies at the junction of the Madre de Dios and Manu Rivers. There are two lodges here, but the highlight for most people is heading up the slow-moving Río Manu into the park or cruising the Río Madre de Dios into the Cultural Zone. In the national park, guests commonly stay in safari camps, but in both national park and Cultural Zone trips, participants spend their days exploring oxbow lakes with floating platforms and spotting scopes.

Most companies return to Cusco by air. Air service into Boca Manu unfortunately continues to be irregular and unpredictable. Flights are often postponed because of rain, and passengers are sometimes bumped at the last minute because of overbooking and other issues. Check with your agency for information about how they will handle delayed or postponed flights from Boca Manu.

To avoid the potential complications of flying and to reduce costs, a few operators are backtracking all the way up the Río Madre de Dios to return to Cusco by road. Other agencies are continuing down the Río Madre de Dios to the gold rush town of Boca Colorado, which is an eight-hour drive to Puerto Maldonado's airport. Either of these overland options is a grueling one-day combination of boats and trucks. A shorter option, offered by Manu Expeditions, is a trip farther down the Río Madre de Dios by boat to Laberinto and then on to Puerto Maldonado via car. This latter option can take as little as eight hours. Regardless, these options are bundled with trips of seven days or more, or may be used if the flights are shut down for any reason.

Apart from the eight operators listed here, many other Cusco agencies sell Manu trips. Some of these agencies simply "endorse" their clients over to a licensed Manu operator at an additional cost. Others only take passengers through the Cultural Zone of the park, which is cheaper because there is no US$45 park fee and less gas is used. You will have better guides, see more wildlife, and be more comfortable if you stick with one of the eight operators listed here, who also offer budget options. It is not recommended to visit Manu on your own or with a private guide. Boat traffic is highly sporadic, and without one of the licensed agencies, the rangers absolutely will not allow you into the Parque Nacional Manu.

The best time to visit Manu is during the

dry season May–October, though rains only become unbearably heavy during January and February. Considering how hard Manu is to reach, it does not make sense to go for less than six days—except for those who fly in and out of Boca Manu and choose to bypass the cloud forest.

MANU AGENCIES AND LODGES

All the prices quoted are all-inclusive, covering food, lodging, US$45 park entrance, and airfare between Cusco and Boca Manu.

Manu Nature Tours

Manu Nature Tours (Pardo 1046, Cusco, tel. 084/25-2721, www.manuperu.com, five days/four nights US$1,628 pp) has the most comfortable and expensive trips and the only lodge inside the Parque Nacional Manu (except for the rustic Casa Machiguenga at the Cocha Salvador). The company was launched in 1985 by Boris Gomez with funding from American biologist Charlie Munn, who has been a key force behind preservation of the Manu and other rainforests. It has been repeatedly voted the best Manu operator by Peru's Ministry of Tourism.

The company was the first to build a lodge in the cloud forest, and all the other Manu agencies followed suit. **The Manu Cloud Forest Lodge** is a magnificent thatched structure with a glass atrium and view over a whitewater creek. Guests can try a half- or one-day **rafting trip** down two rivers in the area, the Kosñipata and Tono, which are Class III or IV depending on the season.

In 1987 Manu Nature Tours also built the first lodge inside the Parque Nacional Manu. **Manu Lodge** is built of salvaged mahogany next to a lake where guests can see black caimans, brown capuchins, and giant otters.

Another Manu Nature Tours innovation is the **Llama Taxi** project with the Jajahuana community, in the high grasslands on the way to Manu. Guests take a 15-minute ride on a cart pulled by a llama, after which the villagers explain their medicinal plants, weaving,

and natural dyes. The goal is to empower the Jajahuana people over the next several years to lead their own treks from the grasslands into the edge of the Manu rainforest.

In addition Manu Nature Tours offers **trekking** and **mountain biking trips** from the grasslands into the Manu, a brain-spinning descent of thousands of feet through the cloud forest.

🄲 Manu Expeditions

Manu Expeditions (Calle Clorinda Matto de Turner #330, Urbanización Magisterial Primero Etapa, Cusco, tel. 084/22-4135, www.manuexpeditions.com, five days/four nights US$1,489 pp) is run by English ornithologist Barry Walker and has a solid reputation for high-quality tours and world-class bird guides. On their way to Manu, guests first stay at the **Cock of the Rock Lodge,** a wood building in the cloud forest with cozy, simple rooms lit by candles and kerosene lamps. Once in the rainforest, guests typically stay nights at a Madre de Dios lodge near Boca Manu and the company's own safari camp near Cocha Salvador in the Parque Nacional Manu. Manu Expeditions is also owner of the new Manu Rainforest Lodge, which is about a 45-minute boat ride from Boca Manu at the old park station of Romero.

Manu Expeditions also sends guests to the **Manu Wildlife Center** (www.manuwildlifecenter.com), which it owns along with Peru Verde, a nonprofit Peruvian conservation group. The 44-bed wooden lodge is 90 minutes downriver from Boca Manu in a section of rainforest adjacent to the Manu Biosphere Reserve. There are 35 kilometers of trails through mature forest, two 35-meter-tall canopy platforms, and oxbow lakes with giant otters and floating observation platforms. A natural clay lick near the lodge offers the best chances in Manu for seeing the tapir, a 250-kilogram cousin of the hippopotamus. Because tapirs mainly forage at night, guests camp out in a comfortable nearby blind, which is outfitted with mosquito netting, snacks, and mattresses. The lodge is also 20 minutes from Manu's largest macaw lick.

In April 2008, Manu Expeditions opened the area's most upscale lodge, Manu Rainforest Lodge.

Barry personally leads private birding tours to Manu and all over Peru and Bolivia, which are described on the website www.birding-in-peru.com. An 18-day odyssey around the Marañón Valley, including Chiclayo, Jaén, Abra Patricia, Tarapoto, and Celendín costs US$3,600.

InkaNatura

The other high-end Manu operator is InkaNatura Travel (Lima tel. 01/440-2022, www.inkanatura.com, five days/four nights US$1,475 pp), which is one of Peru's leading ecotourism operators, with programs in Chachapoyas, Puerto Maldonado, and the jungle around Quillabamba as well.

InkaNatura is the profit-making arm of the Peru Verde conservation organization that owns Manu Wildlife Center. It offers a four-day trip to a tented camp at Cocha Salvador, with a round-trip flight between Cusco and Boca Manu and an optional two-day extension to the Manu Wildlife Center.

Early mornings will be spent in boats, birdwatching; afternoons are filled with jungle walks, where with binoculars in hand you are likely to see a variety of monkeys, butterflies, and even more birds; and evenings are spent looking for tapirs or other nocturnally active animals. With such full days, it is a good thing that InkaNatura provides for all your other needs: refreshing snacks, filling meals, comfortable bedding, and excellent guides.

InkaNatura is also involved with an innovative community-based lodge on the other side of the Manu Biosphere Reserve in the lower Urubamba basin.

InkaNatura is represented in the United States by Tropical Nature Travel (U.S. tel. 877/827-8350, www.tropicalnaturetravel.com).

Pantiacolla Tours

Pantiacolla Tours (Plateros 360, Cusco, tel. 084/23-8323, www.pantiacolla.com, five days/four nights US$1,295 pp) was started in 1991 by conservationist Gustavo Moscoso, who was born in Boca Manu, and his Dutch wife, biologist Marianne van Vlaardingen.

Pantiacolla offers a series of highly recommended camping trips into Parque Nacional Manu, which are broken up with stays in rustic lodges. Pantiacolla operates a wooden lodge with shared bunkrooms in the cloud forest and a similarly rustic tented camp near Cocha Salvador.

The couple also operates the nearby **Yine Project,** one of Peru's more successful community-based tourism efforts. Working with the Yine Indians in the community of Diamante, Pantiacolla has built an attractive and rustic wooden lodge that is a four-hour walk from Diamante. Guests spend time with villagers, participate in traditional art workshops, and learn how to canoe with the expert Yine boatsmen. Far from the staged village visits offered by Iquitos lodges, the Yine Project projects a realistic view of a people who are caught between their traditional ways and the encroachments of modern society. Pantiacolla also offers seven-day trips and nine-day trips, with an option to visit the large macaw clay lick downriver from Boca Manu.

Caiman Tours

Caiman Tours (Garcilaso 210, of. 207, Cusco, tel. 084/25-4041, www.manucaiman.com, five days/four nights US$850 pp) is run by Manu pioneer Hugo Pepper and is best known for custom-designed, creative adventure trips in and around the Manu. Hugo took the first tourists to the Manu in the early 1980s; they camped on beaches and boiled water from the river.

Caiman is famous for its five-day Cusco–Manu **mountain-biking trips,** which pass through Pisac and include a 3,100-meter descent from Tres Cruces, which overlooks the Amazon, to the edge of the Río Madre de Dios at Atalaya. These trips include a cook and a support vehicle that follows the bikers.

Upon request, Hugo can dream up an extraordinary range of Manu adventures. A recent brainstorm included a two-day hike from Salvación, on the banks of Río Madre de Dios, over the jungle into the headwaters of the remote Río Chilive. From here, a crew of expert native guides helped the adventurers assemble a flotilla of **balsa wood rafts,** held together with hardwood nails and tethered with bark fiber. The descent of the river ended up taking only eight days, thanks to a series of storms that dramatically quickened the river current! After reaching the Río Manu, the crew took a *peke-peke* boat to the gold-mining town of Colorado and a truck onward to Puerto Maldonado. Hugo is planning on offering these trips in the future, which can easily be combined with a night's stay at the Tambo Blanquillo Lodge and a visit to the large macaw clay lick.

Hugo has not lost sight of the original Manu experience—his most successful ventures are rugged camping trips throughout the Manu. Before venturing into the wild, however, groups stay at the brand-new and highly comfortable **Manu Paradise Lodge** (www.manuparadiselodge.com). The lodge has screened rooms, spring beds, full bathrooms, a gorgeous dining area, and a rooftop library with views over the jungle. Once in Manu's Reserved Zone, Caiman's groups stay at a safari camp on Cocha Salvador.

Other Agencies

Our readers rave about **Oropéndola** (Av. Circunvalación s/n Urb. Guadalupe, Cusco, tel. 084/24-1428, info@oropendolaperu.org, www.oropendolaperu.org, five days/four nights US$795 pp), a Manu operator with a socially conscious core. Proceeds from the five- to nine-day, fixed departure trips flow right back into the maintenance of the agency's protected reserve as well as community programs that teach Boca Manu kids to speak English and make books. The company's guides have been praised for their bird knowledge, which you will get to experience firsthand when exploring Manu, staying at the Amazon Manu Lodge, or camping at the Manu Camping Lodge.

There are budget operators to Manu that can

be booked at the last minute, often at sharply discounted prices, for travelers who don't mind waiting in Cusco for a few days. The prices quoted include trips into the Parque Nacional Manu but not airfare, and they can often be combined with Inca Trail trips at very little additional cost.

Manu Ecological Adventures (Plateros 356, Cusco, tel. 084/26-1640, www.manuadventures.com, five days/four nights US$880 pp plus entrance fees) has worked in Manu for nearly two decades and leads a great number of trips every year. It leads camping-and-lodge trips to Manu and now has a zip line for viewing the jungle canopy.

The final licensed Manu operator is **Expediciones Vilca** (Plateros 363, Cusco, tel. 084/24-4751, manuvilca@terra.com.pe, www.cbc.org.pe/manuvilca, five days/four nights US$819 plus entrance fees and flight), which offers Manu trips at the Casa Machiguenga and Tambo Blanquillo Lodge. It also offers Inca Trail and other adventure trips.

Independent Lodges

There are a few independent lodges that the licensed Manu operators often use in their packages. **Casa Machiguenga** is a lodge built and operated by Machiguenga natives in the communities near Yombebato and Tayakome, with financial assistance from a German nonprofit organization. Various agencies use the facilities they have on offer. The wooden lodge, with adequate bathrooms, is more rustic than other Manu lodges but offers a good chance to glimpse the lifestyles of Manu's true people.

Tambo Blanquillo Lodge (www.tamboblanquillo.com) is owned by one of the owners of the reputable ExplorAndes agency. It includes an observation tower and is a 10-minute boat ride from the largest of Manu's macaw clay licks.

PONGO DE MAINIQUE (LOWER URUBAMBA BASIN)

The Urubamba River flows 725 kilometers north from the Sacred Valley, passes Machu Picchu, and then enters some of the most pristine and remote forests of the Amazon. One of the most spectacular spots of the river is the **Pongo de Mainique,** a 50-meter wide, three-kilometer-long white-water gorge that is festooned with orchids and swarming with macaws. This is the portal to the afterlife of the Machiguengas. This is a wonderful opportunity to get off the beaten path and get a good sense of how people live in the Amazon. Because of this area's tremendous elevation changes, scientists have noted unusually high levels of bird and animal species, which include military macaws, wooly monkeys, black spider monkeys, and quetzals.

The only lodge in the area is **Sabeti Lodge** (tel. 01/420-4340, www.sabetilodge. com, US$60 pp per day), which is near the Machiguenga community of Timpia, at the confluence of the Urubamba and Timpia Rivers. The lodge began as a joint venture between Peru Verde, a Peruvian environmental organization, and the community of Timpia. The lodge is now 100 percent owned and controlled by the Machiguenga community of Timpia. It includes 10 screened rooms, flush toilets, and hot-water showers. There are 125 Machiguenga families in Timpia and they cooperate in showing guests the biodiverse jungle in the area, which includes a half-dozen clay licks and a chance to see a wide range of wildlife. This is a great opportunity to get off the beaten path, see unusual animals, and get a good sense of how people live in the Amazon. The lodge can be reached either by a 50-minute flight from Cusco to a nearby airstrip, or via a seven-hour bus ride from Cusco to Quillabamba, and then another eight-hour bus ride to Ivochote. From Ivochote, it's a three-hour bus ride to Timpia.

Chanchamayo and Vicinity

From Lima the closest shot of jungle warmth is Chanchamayo, an area that includes the towns of **San Ramón** and **La Merced** on the Río Chanchamayo. The paved highway has shortened the drive from Lima to 5–7 hours.

There are lots of interesting things to see and do around Chanchamayo, including 100-meter waterfalls in the nearby **Perené Valley,** virgin forest with colossal cedars in the **Zona Reservada Pampa Hermosa,** and visitor-friendly Asháninka villages. There are Class III–IV rafting rivers, great mountain biking, and a bizarre Austrian-German colony from the mid-19th century, where villagers still speak German and hold onto their Tyrolean customs. Via a network of roads and rivers, truly wild jungle on the Río Tambo can be reached in a day or two. The best time to visit is during the dry months April–October.

The **Franciscans** who came here in 1635 had to leave after Spaniards entered the area looking for gold and were slaughtered by local Indians. By 1750 a few plantations in the valley were growing sugarcane, cocoa, coffee, and coca leaves. But the settlers were massacred during the indigenous rebellion led by **Juan Santos Atahualpa,** a local and legendary Indian hero, raised by the Jesuits, who claimed kinship with Inca Atahualpa. Colonists entered the area for good after 1850 when a rough road from Tarma down into the valley was constructed. The area today is famous for its tropical fruits, avocado, *rocoto,* and high-octane coffee.

SIGHTS
Perene Valley
Several agencies have put together one-day tours into the valley below Chanchamayo that pack an extraordinary number of activities into one day. These include crossing a river on a wire trolley, sunbathing on a sandy beach, traveling by boat from the river port of Pichanaki to an Asháninka community, and swimming or even rappelling off a set of extraordinary 120-meter-high waterfalls known as Bayoz

and Velo de la Novia (Bride's Veil). The closest waterfall is Cascada El Tirol, just outside San Ramón.

San Miguel

This interesting Asháninka village in the Perene Valley has a lodge that has been recommended by Norwegian anthropologist Ole Steinert as an excellent way to understand the daily life of this indigenous group. **Ñapirori Lodge,** which means "strong man" in the Asháninka language, consists of three houses built in native style, each with a double bed and a balcony out front. Around the lodges are mango trees, coffee plants, tropical flowers, and spectacular views of the Perene Valley. The 40 families that live in San Miguel are very friendly and proud of their uncommercialized settlement. Men still hunt with bows and arrows and, during communal meetings, show up in traditional dress. This is a great place to stay for some days and be enriched with the Asháninka way of life.

Colectivos leave frequently from La Merced to Santa Ana, also called Villa Perené, and then from Santa Ana to San Miguel throughout the afternoon. The dirt road to San Miguel is about five or six kilometers up in the hills. From here it is a 500-meter walk farther to the village, where guests should ask for lodge owners.

Pozuzo-Oxapampa

In 1857, after a formal invitation from the Peruvian government, a group of German and Austrian immigrants from Prussia and Tyrol hacked their way into a remote jungle enclave northeast of the Chanchamayo Valley. They survived despite the odds, were largely forgotten, and over time developed a charming, and somewhat bizarre, Bavarian village in the Amazon that they christened **Pozuzo.**

Where else in the Amazon can you find three-story Tyrolean homes with carved wooden rafters, blonde damsels who speak German, and huge wheels of cheese? The blue-eyed villagers have built comfortable, Alpine guesthouses that charge as little as US$10 pp, including breakfast. There are also caves, ox-driven sugarcane mills known as *trapiches,* waterfalls, and German dancing contests during holidays.

Oxapampa, founded by Pozuzo settlers in 1891, is a two-hour 80-kilometer journey from Chanchamayo on a partly paved, partly rough dirt road. Pozuzo is another four hours (80 kilometers) farther on spectacular, bumpy roads that cross several streams. The best lodging in Oxapampa is **Albergue Turístico Böttger** (Mariscal Castilla, block 6, tel. 063/46-2377, www.oxapampaonline.com/bottger, US$21 s, US$36 d with breakfast), with six beautiful wooden-made rooms, hot water, laundry service, a small TV lounge, and a big backyard. The owner, Doris Böttger, is a very warm host and extremely resourceful woman, with information about what to see and what to do around the area.

Check www.oxapampaonline.com, in Spanish, which has good information about Oxapampa and Pozuzo, including other lodgings, restaurants, and places to visit.

Zona Reservada Pampa Hermosa

A two-hour drive, about 24 kilometers, along a rough road from San Ramón's Victoria Bridge, followed by a steep two-hour walk, leads to a stunning patch of high cloud forest known as Pampa Hermosa. This reserved zone with almost 10,000 hectares, protected since 2005 by the Peruvian government, contains primeval cedar, walnut, and strangler fig trees. It is oddly flat, like an island of jungle perched 1,600 meters in the air. Steep access has kept loggers away. Nearby communities are now protecting this last patch of virgin primary forest, which is filled with the noises of monkeys and the musky odor of the white-collared peccary.

On the hike up is a *lek,* a sort of sexual playground where up to a dozen male Andean cocks of the rock flit up and down every dawn and dusk to attract their mates. At the road head, the Signori family has built **Pampa Hermosa Lodge** (Lima tel. 01/225-1776, www.pampahermosalodge.com, US$70 pp with full pension and guide services), consisting of 11 wooden bungalows with thatched roofs, solar-heated water, and river-generated electricity.

RECREATION

Undisturbed jungle areas can be found within the **Parque Nacional Yanachaga Chemillén,** 3–4 hours from Chanchamayo. More remote jungle is a day's journey from Chanchamayo. A seven-hour *combi* ride leads to Puerto Bermúdez, a lazy settlement on the Río Pachitea. Both the river and the dirt road (not passable in rainy season Nov.–Mar.) lead all the way to Pucallpa, an adventurous journey that runs through the town of Puerto Inca. Another option is to head to **Satipo,** two hours along paved road from Chanchamayo, and then travel farther by *combi* to the riverside town of Puerto Ocopa. From here, boats can be hired to descend the Río Tambo, a remote corner of Peru's Amazon.

If you are driving, or not shy about hitch-hiking, there is a spectacular dirt road to Huancayo from Satipo, which leads up and over a 4,320-meter pass, **Abra Tortuga,** in the Huaytapallana range. No regular transport follows this route, a 10-hour journey between Satipo and Huancayo.

Tour Agencies and Guides

Agencies tend to come and go in Chanchamayo, but the friendly Rodolfo May, owner of **Hostal Golden Gate,** can give excellent information about activities in the area, and with advance notice can arrange trips.

Lucho Hurtado, the energetic owner of **Incas del Peru** in Huancayo (Av. Giráldez 652, tel. 064/22-3303, travelinfo@incasdelperu.org, www.incasdelperu.org) takes groups into the Chanchamayo area for a five-day, action-packed stay at his father's farm near Pozuzo.

SAN RAMÓN AND LA MERCED

The launching points into the Chanchamayo jungle are the nearby towns of San Ramón and La Merced. Although there are only 11 kilometers between both towns, they are drastically different. San Ramón is a sleepy town with a good restaurant and hostel. The bigger and much more hectic La Merced has more restaurants and agencies, and a collection of drab hostels. The best accommodations are the nice bungalows on the road between both towns.

Entertainment and Events

San Ramón has a lively **Founders Day** celebration in late August, with burro races and cooking contests. Oxapampa has a similar celebration in late August that includes an Asháninka archery competition. The two main German colonies have fascinating, beer-soaked celebrations that also include cockfighting championships and *torneo de cinta,* a jousting contest on fast horses where men lunge for bits of suspended embroidery.

Accommodations

La Merced is a rather unappealing town, and its lodging options are lackluster. San Ramón is cleaner but has few services. If at all possible, spring for the charming bungalows between the two towns.

La Merced has a few plain but clean budget hostels—the trick is avoiding street noise. **Hospedaje Cristina** (Tarma 582, tel. 064/53-1276, US$9 s, US$13 d) has parquet floors and peeling walls but the bathrooms are clean. It also has cable TV.

In La Merced, **Hostal El Rey** (Junín 103, tel. 064/53-1185, US$21 s, US$29 d) has been in business 30 years and has excellent service. It has retiled all of its rooms, which have private bathrooms, hot water, and WiFi.

In San Ramón, a highly recommended option is the peaceful, quiet, and friendly **Hospedaje El Parral** (Uriarte 355, tel. 064/33-1128, US$13 s, US$21 d). Just east of San Ramón, cheap bungalows are to be had at **Hospedaje El Rancho** (road to waterfall El Tirol, tel. 064/33-1076, US$27 d with breakfast). There are no luxuries here, but the river is nearby and the bungalows are nice and out of earshot from the road.

The oldest, and still the best, bungalow option in Chanchamayo is **Hostal Golden**

Gate (just west of Herrería Bridge outside La Merced, tel. 064/53-1483, US$22 s, US$39 d), named after a nearby bridge that resembles the San Francisco bridge in miniature. This place was opened in 1983 by longtime Chanchamayo residents Rodolfo and Divna May. Service is friendly and informal; there are several family bungalows lined with beautiful dark wood, between gardens against the hillside. Other services include table tennis, a bar, a communal barbecue, and swimming pool.

In San Ramón, **El Refugio** (El Ejército 490, tel. 064/33-1082, www.hotelelrefugio.com.pe, US$22 s, US$36 d) is a very good choice, with 21 bungalows, gardens, swimming pool, WiFi, and a good restaurant.

Food

La Merced has three safe and well-known restaurants, all lined up near the main square and specializing in jungle cooking, including *cebiche* made from *doncella* fish as well as deer or wild pig dishes. The first, **Los Koquis** (Tarma 376 interior, tel. 064/53-1536, 6:30 A.M.–11 P.M. Mon.–Sat., 8 A.M.–3 P.M. Sun., US$3–6), has excellent *comida criolla*. The second, **Shambari-Campa** (Tarma 389, tel. 064/53-2842, US$3–6), has an even more extensive menu and an interesting series of old historical photos on the wall. The third, **El Sabroso** is next door with a similar menu but a cleaner, less cluttered interior. For dessert, head to **Dulcería La Encantada** (Tarma 252), which serves delicious apple pie.

The quieter San Ramón also has two excellent options. If you are leery of the sketchy sanitary habits of most *chifas,* you can dive in head first at **Felipe Siu** (Progreso 440, tel. 064/33-

1078, 11:30 A.M.–3 P.M. and 6–11 P.M. daily, US$3–5). This charming, decades-old establishment is known for *pollo chijau kay* (fried chicken with ginger sauce) and *limón kay* (strips of chicken in lemon sauce). You would call it a hole-in-the-wall.

Meat eaters can find everything grilled to perfection at **El Parral** (Uriarte 355, tel. 064/33-1128, noon–4 P.M. and 6–11 P.M. daily), which also has a bar and the recommended Hospedaje El Parral next door.

Getting There and Around

La Merced's main bus station is on the eastern end of town, at the triangular intersection of Fitzgerald and Carmen. From here *combis* can be taken nearly anywhere: to Satipo (US$4, two hours, leave throughout day), Oxapampa (US$5, four hours, leave between 4–6 A.M.), Puerto Bermúdez (US$8, seven hours, leave between 3–5 A.M.), or Huancayo (US$5, three hours).

Double-deckers from **Empresa de Transportes Junín** (http://transjunin.com.pe) also leave from here to Lima for US$9 per seat, a seven-hour drive. Across the street is **Transmar** (Fitzgerald 572), which offers buses along the paved highway to Pucallpa on Sundays, an 18-hour journey with stops in Huánuco and Tingo María that costs US$15.

Mototaxis are everywhere in La Merced but are not really needed unless you want to take the US$1 ride to the hilltop cross, a fabulous lookout over the Chanchamayo Valley that is not safe at night. *Combis* are also frequent between La Merced and San Ramón and leave when full from the corner of Junín and Arica in La Merced, every 15 minutes.

From Lima to Pucallpa

Built on the shores of the Río Ucayali, Pucallpa is the east-central gateway to the Amazon jungle and the launching point for a four-day cargo boat journey down the Río Ucayali to Iquitos.

Pucallpa can be reached from Lima by daily flights or by bus. The area has become safer for travelers and the overland journey from Lima to Pucallpa is interesting. A good way break up the journey is to stay in Huánuco, with its ideal climate, and/or Tingo María, which is surrounded by gorgeous natural settings. Both towns are in the Huallaga Valley and were off the tourist circuit until the end of the 1990s, because of intense drug trafficking and terrorist violence. Since then the situation has changed slowly but dramatically for the better. Huánuco and Tingo María are becoming off-the-beaten-path destinations for bird-watchers, nature lovers, and adventure seekers.

HUÁNUCO

The 410 kilometers—about 10 hours on a bus—between coastal Lima, up the **Carretera Central** and all the way to Huánuco is a magnificent day trip and crosses at least five different geographic regions. After passing by Chosica and San Mateo, among other smaller towns, the highway makes a winding ascent on its way to Ticlio and the Anticona Pass at 4,820 meters. At the mining center of La Oroya (3,700 meters), the highway detours north to Huánuco. It crosses the high-altitude puna at 4,000 meters and runs next to the **Reserva Nacional Junín,** which protects wetlands and the highly endangered Junín grebe in Lake Junín. The Carretera Central passes by the detour road to Cerro de Pasco before descending the Huallaga River, which eventually broadens into a fertile valley where Huánuco is located.

Situated at 1,894 meters of altitude, the inhabitants of this small city on the Upper Río Huallaga Valley boast they have the best climate in Peru, due to its warm weather all year-round. Founded in 1541, the town itself has some churches and old historic buildings, but its major interesting sites are located in the surrounding area.

Sights

The **Temple of Kotosh,** known in Spanish as **Templo de la Manos Cruzadas** (9 A.M.–5 P.M., US$1 pp), is five kilometers west of the city and is one of Peru's oldest archaeological sites. It was intensely studied by Japanese archaeologists, led by Seichi Izumi, in the 1950s and 1960s. It can be easily visited hiring a taxi (US$8, including a 30-minute wait, and return).

South of the city lies a long and wide stretch of the fertile Upper Huallaga Valley where the **Cachigaga Hacienda** is located and which can be reached by taxi (US$5, one-way). It is well reputed for its *aguardiente* (distilled sugarcane alcohol), and rum, which are sold there. The owner, Honorato López (tel. 062/962-94-7140), is a friendly man who doesn't speak English, but he will gladly tour you around his small hacienda showing you the process to make his spiritous drinks, if he is around and you know some Spanish.

About 20 kilometers up from **Cachigaga** are the **Lagunas de Pichgacocha,** a beautiful set of five waterfalls and lagoons, which you can reach by trekking from Conchamarca (5–6 hours) or by driving if you hire a taxi (US$30 for a roundtrip). It is possible to camp, explore, and trek around the lagoons.

Accommodations

Huánuco has some backpacker hostels, such as **Hostal Huánuco** (Huánuco 777, tel. 062/51-2050), and a couple of midrange hotels, such as the centric **Grand Hotel Huánuco** (Dámaso Beraún 775, tel. 062/51-4222, www.grandhotelhuanuco.com, US$45 s, US$64 d). The best is **Hotel Trapiche Suites** (General Prado 636, tel. 062/51-7091, US$25 s, US$32 d), with extremely comfy beds (with lots of pillows!) in cozy rooms, impeccable private bathrooms, cable TV, WiFi, and minifridge.

Food

El Bambú (Av. Universitaria Km 2.2, tel. 062/51-6097, US$1.5–8), a bit outside the city, is an excellent place to try regional food such as fried or stewed *cuy* (guinea pig). **El Leñador** (28 de Julio 1233, tel. 062/50-3467, US$3–8) is ideal for meat-eaters or grilled chicken-lovers. If you prefer pizzas or pasta, **Pizzería Don Sancho** (General Prado 645, tel. 062/51-9606, US$3–6), just across Hotel Trapiche Suites, is your place.

Information and Services

Huánuco does not have an Iperú office, but **Dircetur** (Bolívar 381, tel. 062/51-2980) can offer some guidance about tourist destinations and services. The **police station** is at Constitución 621 (tel. 062/51-3117).

Scotiabank (28 de Julio 1016–1018), **Banco de Crédito** (Dos de Mayo 1005), **BBVA Banco Continental** (28 de Julio 1137), and **Banco del Trabajo** (28 de Julio 924), have ATMs 24 hours.

TINGO MARÍA

The 135 kilometers between Huánuco and Tingo María takes about two hours and ascends the **Cordillera Carpish** before plunging into the cloud forest. Tingo María is gradually shaking off its ill-fated reputation as one of Peru's biggest drug-trafficking hubs. Tourism started to pick up in the late 1990s due to this town's extraordinary natural surroundings, including waterfalls, an amazing population of birds, and the Parque Nacional Tingo María, which was established in 1965 and is Peru's second-oldest park. The whole Huallaga region still has its share of coca plantations, but tourism is growing quickly.

Sights

The main attraction is, without doubt, **Parque Nacional Tingo María,** 12 kilometers southeast of the city, with almost 4,800 hectares of protected montane cloud forest that lies around the mouth of the **Río Monzón,** a tributary of the Huallaga. The park has lots of caves, and the most popular to visit is the **Cueva de las Lechuzas** (US$3 park fee), or Owl Cave, which paradoxically is inhabited by oilbirds instead. The best time to visit the cave is early in the morning or in the afternoon. Taxis or *mototaxis* will take you for US$3–5. Additionally, Tingo María has, at least, a dozen waterfalls that can be visited and accessed by *mototaxis,* including **Cueva de las Pavas** (8 km south), **Santa Carmen** (30 meters high, 13 km south), and **Velo de las Ninfas** (15 km south). About 20 kilometers north of Tingo Marí, on the newly paved Carretera Marginal heading to Tocache, is **Laguna El Milagro,** a lagoon in the middle of a beautiful high jungle setting where you can either take a canoe ride or a paddle boat (US$1.50/30 minutes).

The **Market** in downtown Tingo María (between Alameda Perú and Tito Jaime Fernández) is an interesting place to observe (and buy) jungle products such as fruit, river fish, bush meat, and other exotic products.

Accommodation

Tingo María's downtown has a variety of low budget hostels, most of them clean, with private bathrooms and fans. **Hostal León** (Monzón 311, tel. 062/56-4223, www.hostal-leon.com, US$14 s, US$16 d) is a very good choice.

Eco Albergue Villa Jennifer (Km 3.4, Sector Monterrico, Castillo Grande, tel. 062/962-603-059, www.villajennifer.com, US$32 s, US$39 d with breakfast) is undoubtedly the best option in the outskirts. Owned by a friendly Peruvian-Danish couple, Graciela and Erlan Ohlsen, this place has a swimming pool, delicious food (try the banana lasagna!), and hectares of green to stroll and relax.

Food

If Tingo María is the first jungle town you go to, be ready for the explosion of fruits and fish you have as eating options. Explore your senses. **D'Tinto & Madero** (Alameda Perú 391, 2nd Fl., tel. 062/56-3012, US$3–10) has *picuro a la parrilla,* which is grilled *picuro* (also named *majás*), a medium-size rodent, or grilled deer, as well as beef, lamb, chicken, and pork. **El Viejo Madero** (Raimondi 599, tel. 062/56-2891, US$3–6) has very good pastas and pizzas.

© JORGE RIVEROS CAYO

Tingo María, once the center of Peru's drug trade, is slowly opening up to tourists. Tingo María produces some of country's best fruits, on display here at the local market.

Information and Services

The **Municipalidad de Tingo María** (Alameda Perú 225, tel. 062/56-2058) has a **Tourism Office** that can provide information and some brochures.

Banco de Crédito (Raimondi 249) and **BBVA Banco Continental** (Raimondi 555) both have ATMs.

The **public hospital** is at Ucayali 144 (tel. 062/56-2018). **Inkafarma** and **BTL** are both on Raimondi.

There are Internet cafés all over the town, with decent speed, charging US$0.60 per hour.

PUCALLPA AND VICINITY

From Tingo María to Pucallpa there are 282 kilometers—a five-hour drive. The highway, also known as **Carretera Federico Basadre,** is paved but with some sections that are constantly being repaired. Once you pass by **Boquerón del Padre Abad,** a river gorge that cuts through the southern tip of the **Cordillera Azul,** the jungle opens into a flat plain of endless vegetation, passing through the town of Aguaytía before reaching Pucallpa.

Sights

Pucallpa, which means "red dirt" in Quechua, was entitled as a city in 1883, during the rubber boom. Today, it still is underdeveloped despite being the Ucayali region's capital city. Tourist attractions are limited to **Yarinacocha,** an oxbow lake 10 kilometers northeast of the city, with boat rides available to go fishing or visit nearby Shipibo communities. Pucallpa is the last town where you can get provisions and money before embarking in a cargo boat to do a river cruise on the Río Ucayali and the Amazon River towards Iquitos. If you decide to stay for a day or two, there are comfortable lodgings and good restaurants.

Accommodations

The city has a wide range of hotels for all budgets. **Hotel Los Gavilanes** (Ipuatía 370, Yarinacocha, tel. 061/59-6741, www.losgavilaneshotel.com.pe, US$25 s, US$29 d with breakfast and airport transfer included) has rooms with fans and air-conditioning, cable TV, minifridge, swimming pool, bar, and restaurant in a relaxed atmosphere. Another good option is **Foresta Inn** (Av. Centenario Km 4800, tel. 061/57-7167, http://forestainn.com, US$28 s, US$32 d), which has comfortable rooms with air-conditioning, cable TV, flat screens, WiFi, and ample gardens. Bungalows with double rooms are available, too.

Food

On the Puerto Callao lakeside village in Yarinacocha there are some inexpensive restaurants. The better ones are **Anaconda** and **Puerto Rico** on the waterfront. In Pucallpa **Parrilladas Orlando** (Aguaytía y 28 de Julio, tel. 061/59-6577, US$3–8) has superb grilled meats including *majaás*. **Chez Maggy** (Inmaculada 643, tel. 061/57-4958, US$3–6) is a good option for pizzas and pasta. **Restaurante Golf** (Huáscar 545, tel. 061/57-4632, US$3–7) has delicious river fish dishes including *doncella* and *paiche*.

Information and Services

Banks with ATMs in Pucallpa are **Scotiabank** (Raimondi 466–468), **Banco de Créditto** (Raimondi 404), **Interbank** (Raimondi 569), and **BBVA Banco Continental** (Ucayali con Raimondi 699).

Clínica Monte Horeb (Inmaculada 529, tel. 061/57-1689, 24 hours daily), previously called Santa Rosa, is a good clinic for emergencies.

The **police station** is on Independencia (block 3, tel. 061/59-1433).

Getting There and Around

Pucallpa has daily flights from Lima, but the trip can also be done by bus. It takes around 17 hours, from desert coast to rainforest, on a nonstop bus directly to Pucallpa.

Boats from Pucallpa to Iquitos leave from the wharf. *Gilmer I, IV* and *V,* owned by **Transportes Eduardo,** and the *Baylón I* and *II* are recommended boats for this travel. There is no office or phone available to book a ticket. You need to approach the decks and talk to the captain or the second in command. Both companies sell tickets offering closed decks to hang your hammock on (US$29 pp); there are also cabins with a bunk bed, TV, and private bathroom in the *Baylón* boats (US$64 pp) and better cabins on the *Gilmer* boats (US$145 pp).

Moyobamba and Tarapoto

The less-visited area of northeastern Peru is a good stopover for tourists en route from the coast to Chachapoyas, or vice versa. The Moyobamba cloud forest, along with Tarapoto, is Peru's best off-the-beaten path jungle. While the cities themselves have only a mild draw, the surrounding areas are rich in activity and natural beauty.

MOYOBAMBA AND VICINITY

For travelers coming over the Andes from Peru's northern coast or Chachapoyas, Moyobamba is the first city with an unmistakable jungle feel. The air is warm and humid, cooled by rains that fall heaviest between January and March. Travelers also encounter exotic new fruits and an explosion of animals and plants. In the cloud forest surrounding Moyobamba there are more than 2,500 recorded types of orchids. The long riverboats common to the lower Amazon also navigate the lazy meanderings of the **Río Mayo,** fringed by alternating patches of fields and high jungle.

Moyobamba is one of the few jungle areas occupied by the Inca. Túpac Yupanqui conquered the local tribes of the **Motilones** and **Muyupampas** in the mid-15th century. The city of Moyobamba was founded by Spanish captain Juan Pérez de Guevara in 1540. In Quechua, Moyobamba means "circular plain," which makes sense because the city is situated on a flat area perched above the Río Mayo.

© RENÉE DEL GAUDIO AND ROSS WEHNER

footbridge over Río Mayo near Moyobamba

Various streets dead-end into spectacular views of the muddy, snaking river, which offers a good range of white-water rafting and kayaking. There are also thermal baths, caves, and waterfalls in the area, with relatively pristine patches of cloud forest that harbor orchids and endangered or extremely rare mammal species such as the yellow-tailed monkey.

Sights

The best of Moyobamba lies outside the city. In the town there is little to see besides the modern cathedral on the Plaza de Armas and a municipal museum with sporadic hours on Benavides 380.

For a pleasant view of the Río Mayo, and the tiny river port of Puerto Tahuishco, head to **Punta de Tahuishco,** 20 minutes northeast of the Plaza de Armas (US$1 by *mototaxi*). The municipality has built a variety of gardens and pleasant overlooks in this neighborhood, known as Zaragoza. Nearby is **Agroriente Viveros** (Reyes Guerra 900, tel. 042/56-2539, agroriente@terra.com.pe), a commercial greenhouse featuring a wide range of local orchids.

Entertainment and Events

Discos in Moyobamba come and go quickly, but a reliable place to go and play is Punta de Tahuishco, where there are a handful of discos open on the weekends.

The town erupts into a week of parties, local dances, beauty pageants, and processions that spans both the town's birthday (July 25) and Peru's independence celebration (July 28). Orchid lovers descend on Moyobamba in the first week of November for the annual Orchid Festival.

Recreation

The **Gera Waterfalls,** once a tourist favorite, have been reduced to a trickle due to the construction of Gera hydroelectric. But a good hike can be done all the way to the top of **Morro de Calzada,** an isolated, humpbacked mountain that rises above the landscape 12 kilometers from Moyobamba. There is a pleasant, two-hour walk through cloud forest to the top, past a few small waterfalls and a variety of orchids. There are caves at both the top and bottom of the hill and an incredible panoramic view from the summit. This overlook is a launching point for hang gliders and parapent aficionados. You can also camp on the top.

Selene Tours (Serafín Filomeno 150, tel. 042/56-4471, www.selenetours.com) offers tours to all the sites outside Moyobamba. Roxana Díaz, the manager, is extremely helpful and you can contact her at roxanadiaz8@hotmail.com.

Accommodations

The budget hotels are all pretty standard in Moyobamba, and the best options one can be found along Alonso de Alvarado. **Residencial Albricias** (Alonso de Alvarado 1066, tel. 042/56-1092, www.moyobambaperu.com/albricias, US$11 s, US$18 d) has hot water, clean rooms, gardens, cable TV, WiFi, and kitchen facilities. **Hostal Atlanta** (Alonso de Alvarado 865, tel. 042/56-2063, atlantainn@hotmail.com, US$11 s, US$16 d) is also safe, clean, and quiet with hot water, cable TV, and Internet. **La Cueva de Juan** (Alonso de Alvarado 870, tel. 042/56-2488, lacueva870@hotmail.com, US$11 s, US$18 d) is a third and good option with spartan but clean rooms, hot water, cable TV, garage, and a small café.

A mid-budget option is **Río Mayo Moyobamba Hotel** (Pedro Canga 415, tel. 042/56-4193, www.riomayo.com, US$29 s, US$39 d with buffet breakfast), a quite modern hotel with swimming pool, laundry service, garage, Internet, and a café/restaurant.

The resort option in Moyobamba is **Hotel Puerto Mirador** (Sucre s/n, tel. 042/56-2050, www.hotelpuertomirador.com, US$30 s, US$54 d with breakfast). In a peaceful setting on the outskirts of town, this hotel offers brick bungalows and a swimming pool overlooking the Río Mayo. Rooms are large with cable TV and private terraces surrounded by generous amounts of green. The main lodge has access to WiFi, a good restaurant, and a full bar. The hotel offers tours to various lakes, waterfalls, and thermal baths, as well as boat tours on the Río Mayo.

Food

La Olla de Barro (corner of Pedro Canga and Serafín Filomeno, tel. 042/56-1034, 8 A.M.–11 P.M. daily, US$3–7) serves traditional food as well as pizzas and pastas in a charming, jungle-themed atmosphere. **El Avispa Juane** (corner of Alonso de Alvarado and 25 de Mayo, tel. 064/56-3904, 9 A.M.–9 P.M. daily, US$2–7) is another good option for regional food, with a set menu (US$2) and a variety of dishes, including *juanes,* of course.

Chico's Burger Club (corner of Pedro Canga and Plaza de Armas, tel. 042/56-1222, 3 P.M.–2:30 A.M. daily, US$3–5) is a greasy spoon serving burgers, milk shakes, and pizzas.

The restaurant at **Hotel Puerto Mirador** (Sucre s/n, tel. 042/56-2050, 8 A.M.–11 P.M. daily, US$5–10), serves Peruvian dishes and international food in a peaceful setting. Juices are great and the fish is pretty good.

Information and Services

The **tourist police** office is at Pedro Canga 298 (tel. 042/56-2508).

Both **Banco de la Nación** (Plaza de Armas) and **Banco de Crédito** (Alonso de Alvarado 903) have ATMs.

For medical issues, **EsSalud** is in the first block of Grau (tel. 042/56-2524).

Serpost, the post office, is at Serafín Filomeno 501.

For a high-speed Internet connection, go to the corner of Alvarado and Benavides (9:30 A.M.–midnight, US$0.75/hour). Another good place for Internet is on Pedro Canga, across from Hotel Marcoantonio.

La Popular Lavandería (Alvarado 874, tel. 042/56-2440) does washing (US$1.50/kg). If you are in need of long pants or shirts for the jungle, try the **street market** around 25 de Mayo and Callao.

Getting There and Around

The nearest airport is at Tarapoto, 105 kilometers or 2.5 hours away by bus. All the buses between Chiclayo and Tarapoto pass through Moyobamba. **Movil Tours** (Grau 547, tel. 042/56-3720) has the best bus service from Moyobamba to Chiclayo (US$23).

Transportes Cajamarca (Serafín Filomeno

298, tel. 042/56-1496) has modern, reliable station wagons on their routes Tarapoto–Moyobamba (US$7) and Moyobamba–Nueva Cajamarca (US$2). From Nueva Cajamarca you can head on to Pedro Ruiz via **Transportes Etcaosa** for US$6.

Moyobamba is teeming with cheap *mototaxis* that cost US$0.75 for a local trip.

Tingana

About two hours away from Moyobamba, Tingana is in the heart of an amazing patch of flooded forest and swamps abundant with *aguaje* and *renaco* palm trees. Almost 3,500 hectares of this fragile and endangered ecosystem is currently protected in the **Área de Conservación Regional Municipal Aguajales Renacales del Alto Mayo,** a long name for an area with high numbers of flora and fauna, including orchids, bromeliads, river otters, monkeys, snakes, and a great variety of birds, which can be observed in canoe rides along the Río Avisado.

Tingana is a self-sustained joint venture between the German Cooperation Agency (GTZ) and Tingana's own nonprofit organizations (tel. 042/56-4000, www.tingana.org). Tours are available (full-day US$54 pp, two days/one night US$63), including transportation from Río Huascayacu to Tingana and back, all meals, lodging in cabins with mosquito net, guide, and boat trips. Tour prices do not include transportation from Moyobamba to Río Huascayacu, which can be done via *combi* (US$3) or private four-wheel-drive for four people (US$25).

TARAPOTO

Tarapoto is the main gateway to the northeastern high jungle, situated in the lower Río Mayo watershed, surrounded with pristine montane cloud forest that tumbles into the flat, steamy lowlands of the Amazon rainforest. This area, with daily flights to and from Lima, is well known for waterfalls, orchids, very good food, and unusual birds.

© JORGE RIVEROS CAYO

exploring the flooded rain forest of Área de Conservación Regional Municipal Aguajales Renacales del Alto Mayo, near Tingana in northern Peru

Tarapoto was founded in 1782 at the base of the Ríos Cumbaza and Shilcayo. It was named after the native palm tree *taraputus*. The surrounding valley has rich agricultural lands that yield corn, bananas, manioc, cocoa, tobacco, tea, coffee, palm oil, and tropical fruits. Its role as a commerce hub between the Amazon and the northern regions of Peru was cemented by the construction of the **Carretera Marginal** (Marginal Highway) to the northern coast, known today as **Carretera Fernando Belaunde Terry** in honor of the president who built it in the 1960s.

Coca cultivation began in the nearby upper Huallaga Valley in the 1970s, and much of the area's valuable lands were destroyed by slash-and-burn agriculture. Tarapoto became the place where all drug traffickers built their lavish homes and laundered their money in all kinds of real estate projects that dot the city. During the 1980s, Tarapoto was at the center of the territory dominated by the **Movimiento Revolucionario Túpac Amaru** (MRTA), a left-wing terrorist organization that occupied the cities and towns surrounding the city. Eventually, the MRTA developed close ties to the area's drug lords.

During the Fujimori regime, Tarapoto's prominent drug traffickers were jailed and the MRTA was completely defeated—a small remaining faction was wiped out after taking over the Japanese ambassador's residence in Lima in 1996.

Tarapoto is now a safe place to visit and is making a dramatic comeback as a tourist destination, especially for those who fly in from Lima with a few days on their hands. The leader of the tourist comeback in Tarapoto is **Puerto Palmeras** resort (Carretera Fernando Belaunde Terry, Km 614, tel. 042/52-3978, www.puertopalmeras.com.pe), which operates several excellent lodges in the region.

Sights

If you want to see the elusive cock of the rock, head out at dawn or dusk to **Aguashiyacu Waterfalls** (US$1 admission at trailhead hut), about 14 kilometers outside Tarapoto on the winding new highway to Yurimaguas. If you are quiet, you have a good chance of spotting these crimson birds flying in and out of their nests on the rock wall below the waterfall. If you have a bird guide, available at Puerto Palmeras, there is also excellent bird-watching on nearby ridges.

This area, along with **Huacamaillo Waterfalls,** is part of the **Área Regional de Conservación Cordillera Escalera,** which protects big patches of cloud forests, indigenous communities, flora, and fauna. The Huacamaillo falls can be reached after a two-hour walk from the village of San Antonio de Cumbaza, 18 kilometers north of Tarapoto. This waterfall jets forth from a stunning rock gorge and is well worth the walk.

An interesting destination is **Laguna Sauce,** a two-hour trip south from Tarapoto that involves crossing the Río Huallaga by steel barge. There are several hotels and restaurants around the town of Sauce and canoe rental is available. At the far end, accessible via narrow channel, is the more remote **Lago Lindo,** a 5,300-hectare private reserve, accessible only through Puerto Palmeras. The beautiful bungalows resembling an Amazon lodge are surrounded by 15,000 mahogany trees that have been planted in an effort to reintroduce this endangered species. The place is peaceful and ideal for bird-watching. There are rafting opportunities on the nearby Río Huallaga and Río Mayo.

Tarapoto is also home to two unusual sites. The first is the village of **Lamas,** 21 kilometers north of Tarapoto, an isolated village of people known as the Lamistas, who speak a mixture of Quechua and jungle dialects. They are grouped together in one half of the town, have their own museum, and have a sense of community and identity that never fails to impress visitors.

The second is the **Takiwasi Center** (Alerta 466, tel. 042/52-2818, www.takiwasi.com, call before visiting), a drug rehabilitation center that uses ayahuasca and other hallucinogenic jungle medicines as a central part of its treatment. The center also caters to the growing number of travelers interested in taking ayahuasca. Because of its highly experienced staff of authentic jungle *curanderos* (healers) and a serious philosophy that includes post-experience debriefing with a psychoanalyst, participants almost invariably have a safe, meaningful experience.

Outside of Tarapoto is the nationally renowned **Orquídea Chocolate Factory** (Santa Mónica 200, tel. 042/52-6573, mayo@aice.org.pe, hours vary). Here you can see demos and hear explanations of how cacao is processed into chocolate, melted into a bar, and eventually prepared for export. Most of the chocolates are organic.

Entertainment and Events

Tarapoto's most popular discotheques nowadays are **Makumba** and **Anaconda,** five kilometers outside of Tarapoto in the Morales district near the Río Cumbaza bridge on the highway to Moyobamba. There are several discotheques in the same neighborhood, including **Tropicana, Ovni,** and **Las Rocas.**

The whole intersection of Lamas and San Pablo de la Cruz has several lively bars and pubs. **Stonewasi** (Lamas 222, tel. 042/52-4681, 10 P.M.–close daily) is a Tarapoto institution and a great place to grab a beer and listen to 1980s music. **Musmuki** (Arias de Morey 173, 10 P.M.–close daily), on the other side of the Plaza de Armas, has cocktails mixed with *aguardiente* (sugarcane distilled alcohol). Drinks are good and strong. A few meters away is **Café d'Mundo** (Arias de Morey 179, tel. 042/52-4918, 10 P.M.–close daily), probably the smartest bar in Tarapoto, if not in the region. You ring a button to be let into a very relaxed setting. Thursday evenings seem to be the best.

Tarapoto's most festive day is its birthday, July 16, which comes in the middle of **Tourist Week.** Lama's **Fiesta de Santa Rosa** at the end of August is said to be spectacular.

Shopping

Few people associate Tarapoto with 21st-century art, but the truth is that there is a growing community of exceptionally talented painters and sculptors in and around the city.

Information about these artists is posted on the Puerto Palmeras website (www.puerto-palmeras.com).

Of the six most prominent painters, Juan Echenique stands out for his Picasso-like paintings, ranging from political satire to nudes, and Savrín has a well-known series of Dali-esque ayahuasca hallucinations. The paintings are exhibited at Puerto Palmeras and at Hostal La Patarashca, where contact information for the artists can be obtained. There are some handicraft stores at the corner of Delgado and Pimentel and at **Artesenía Riojas** (Rioja 357, tel. 042/52-2616, 10 A.M.–6 P.M. daily).

To buy high-quality cigars, head to **Tabacalera del Oriente** (Martínez de Compañón 1138, tel. 042/52-7911, www.tabacaleradeloriente.com, 10 A.M.–6 P.M. daily), a factory with a fancy shop that makes the best *puros* (cigars) in the region.

If you need inexpensive though high-quality clothing, the city is teeming with stores hawking jeans, surfing shorts, and shirts imported up the Amazon from Brazil. The best place to go bargain shopping is Jimenez Pimentel, near the southwest corner of the Plaza Mayor.

Recreation

A handful of agencies in Tarapoto offer excellent, reasonably priced tours to the area, which include lunch and have a three-passenger minimum.

Puerto Palmeras (Carretera Marginal Sur, Km 3, tel. 042/52-3978, www.puertopalmeras.com) has well-maintained Land Rovers that head to Lama, Huacamaillo, and Ahuashiyacu waterfalls; Lago Lindo; Yurimaguas; or as far as Chachapoyas and Kuélap. It can also arrange **rafting** trips down an eight-kilometer section of the Río Mayo, downstream of the town of San Miguel. From Puerto Pericos, its lodge in Yurimaguas, this company also offers trips to Reserva Nacional Pacaya Samiria (with a minimum of two people). An eight-day trip allows one full day at remote Lake Pastococha and includes all meals, camping, and shaded canoe. Check the website for current rates and customized travel packages.

Adventure options include guide César Reategui, owner of hostel and restaurant **La Patarashca** (Lamas 261, tel. 042/52-8810, www.lapatarashca.com). He is willing to go anywhere, including out-of-the-way river spots and visits to Tingana, near Moyobamba. He also leads backpacker treks to Pacaya Samiria.

The best rafting outfitter in town is **Los Chancas Expeditions** (Rioja 357, tel. 042/52-2616), which organizes day trips on the Río Mayo, which gets up to Class III during the rainy months of November–March. This agency also organizes trips into the Pacaya Samiria and longer, six-day trips down the Class IV waters of the lower Río Huallaga July–October.

Selva Tours Viajeros (Sofía Delgado 284, tel. 042/52-4562, www.selvatoursviajeros. com) also offers tours around Tarapoto and to Moyobamba, Rioja, and Janjuí.

Accommodations
US$10-25
Alojamiento Arévalo (Moyobamba 233, tel. 042/52-5265, US$11 s, US$16 d) is a classic backpackers' place. It has private bathrooms, fridge/bar, cable TV, and hot water. It also has laundry service.

La Patarashca Lodge (Lamas 261, tel. 042/52-7554, www.lapatarashca.com, US$21 s, US$30 d with breakfast) is a funky low-budget hangout with clean rooms painted in colorful and interesting jungle tones, good breakfasts, and WiFi but no air-conditioning. Owner César Reategui operates a restaurant next door and, in his spare time, works as a wilderness guide. This is definitely the nicest backpackers' hostel in Tarapoto and well worth the money, especially if you plan on contracting César for tours. Groups of two or more will enjoy the room with a loft.

US$25-50
◖ **Hostal Casa de Palos** (Leoncio Prado 155, tel. 042/52-0479, hostalcasadepalos@hotmail. com, US$25 s, US$32 d) is the best option for a midprice budget. Opened in 2009, this seven-room hostel has really nice and comfy

beds, impeccable bathrooms, hot water, WiFi, remote-control fans, 21-inch flat screens, and cable TV. It is conveniently situated two blocks away from the Plaza de Armas.

La Posada Inn (San Martín 146, tel. 042/52-2234, laposada_inn@hotmail.com, US$25 s, US$34 d) is a renovated colonial house a few meters from the Plaza de Armas. Off the busy street, guests enter a hushed atmosphere of orchids, stained wood floors, and comfortable rooms with hot water, refrigerators, TV, phone, WiFi, and air-conditioning or fans. The landings outside the rooms are a great place to relax and chat.

Plaza del Bosque (Av. Circunvalación 2449, tel. 042/52-3448, www.plazabosque. com.pe, US$36 s, US$50 d, with breakfast) is on the high part of town, five minutes away from the Plaza de Armas. It has 31 bungalow brick-built rooms surrounded by dense vegetation. Amenities include cable TV, WiFi, laundry, garage, swimming pool, and a restaurant. Rates also include free transfer to the airport. There are also cheaper rooms only with fans (US$29 s, US$43 d). Claudia Arévalo, who used to run Colonial Inn, is now the manager of this hotel. She is helpful, friendly, and resourceful.

Cordillera Escalera Lodge (Prolongación Alerta 1521, tel. 042/942-614-850, www.cordilleraescalera.com, US$30 s, US$36 d, breakfast and airport transfer included) is a good option if you want to be outside of the city, savoring nature, without spending loads of money in a lodge. Overlooking the Cordillera Escalera, on top of a small hill, this lodge is 15 minutes east of Tarapoto and can accommodate 14 people.

A relatively new hotel in town is **Hotel Río Cumbaza** (Pedro de Urzúa 515, tel. 042/52-1491, www.riocumbazahotel.com, US$39 s, US$57 d with breakfast), which has 50 rooms with air-conditioning, cable TV, minifridge, WiFi, garage, laundry service, a swimming pool, and 24-hour room service.

US$50-100
About 10 minutes outside the city is **Hotel Río**

Shilcayo (2 km outside Tarapoto, Pasaje las Flores 224, Banda de Shilcayo, tel. 042/52-2225, www.rioshilcayo.com, US$68 s, US$82 d, buffet breakfast and airport transfers included), with five hectares of green. Brick buildings surround a round pool with bar, thatch-shaded tables, and well-maintained palm groves and lawn. There are 22 rooms with all the modern services, including air-conditioning, cable TV, minifridge, and WiFi. Another option is one of the 15 more private bungalows, which sleep up to three and cost US$93. The hotel also offers 3–4-day packages, starting at US$150 pp, all-inclusive.

Puerto Palmeras (Carretera Fernando Belaunde Terry, Km 614, tel. 042/52-3978, www.puertopalmeras.com.pe, US$78 s, US$128 d, breakfast and airport transfer included) has a logo in Spanish, *el paraíso existe,* "paradise exists." When you reach this tasteful and relaxed resort, tucked into a river bend far from the hustle and bustle of Tarapoto, you will totally agree it is paradise. This resort is a perfect getaway for both couples in search of solitude and families looking for a range of well-organized activities.

Everything—riverside restaurant, poolside bar, elegant rooms, local tours—is done with the highest level of quality, making Puerto Palmeras one of the best resorts in the Peruvian Amazon. Rooms are spacious, with beautiful bathrooms, minifridge, cable TV, hot water, and private terraces that look out over either the pool or the river. You also have suites (starting at US$182) and duplex rooms for four or five people (starting at US$171). For moments of peace and quiet, there are stone courtyards and open-air sitting areas decorated with a mind-blowing collection of paintings from local artists. The sprawling grounds around the resort also include playing fields, a lake with canoes, and an island population of monkeys.

This resort, constructed during the strife-ridden 1990s by determined entrepreneur Carlos González Henríquez, is the crown jewel in a network of hotels that includes Puerto Patos, on the shore of Laguna Azul; Lago Lindo; Puerto Pericos, in Yurimaguas; and

© JORGE RIVEROS CAYO

canoes at Lago Lindo, outside of Tarapoto, where Puerto Palmeras operates a rustic lodge

Puerto Pumas, a stone's throw from Laguna Pomacocha. Check the website for programs and other travel options.

OVER US$100

PumaRinri Huallaga Lodge (tel. 042/52-2225, www.pumarinri.com) is 35 kilometers southeast of Tarapoto, on the road that leads to Chazuta. It is in the middle of a 62-hectare private reserve situated in the canyon stretch of the Río Huallaga. Surrounded by montane cloud forest, rivers, and streams, the lodge is very close to the **Área Regional de Conservación Cordillera Escalera** and **Parque Nacional Cordillera Azul,** both protecting unique ecosystems. PumaRinri offers two all-inclusive programs: Tarapoto Adventure, combining stays at Hotel Río Shilcayo with the lodge (starting at three days/two nights, US$189 pp), and Tarapoto Amazonía, exclusively at Puma Rinri, with a variety of outdoor activities, including rafting in the Huallaga (starting at three days/two nights, US$214 pp).

Food

If you like pork and *camarones* (freshwater prawns), this is definitely your town!

On Moyobamba Street, right on the Plaza de Armas, there are three good eatery options. **Las Terrazas** (10 A.M.–10 P.M. daily) is a small restaurant-café serving *lomo saltado, cecina* (smoked pork), salads, fish, and other dishes. **Real Grill** (Moyobamba 131, tel. 042/52-2714, 8 A.M.–11 P.M. daily, US$3.50–8) has a decent variety of food, including meats, seafood, salads, and pastas. The best option is **Doña Zully** (Moyobamba 253, tel. 042/53-0670, 8 A.M.–midnight daily, US$3–12), named after the owner, Zully Moreno Díaz, with large portions of delicious fish, pork and chicken dishes, salads, soups, and great juices.

Bello Horizonte (San Pablo de la Cruz 248, tel. 042/53-1720, 10 A.M.–11:30 P.M. daily, US$2–7) has daily setup menus (US$2.50) and also seafood and meat dishes.

A good option for meat eaters and from the same owner of Doña Zully is **Parillas El**

Rincón Sureño (Leguía 458, tel. 042/52-2785, 10 A.M.–10 P.M. daily), which serves Peruvian food and grilled meats.

La Pizzeria (corner of Lamas and San Pablo de la Cruz, 11 A.M.–11 P.M. daily) is a good spot for low-price pizzas. The best place for Italian food is **Café d'Mundo** (Arias de Morey 157, tel. 042/52-4918, 11 A.M.–11 P.M. daily, US$5–15), with a relaxed ambience, illuminated at night by candles. It has a good and varied option of starters, thin-crust pizzas, and pastas.

La Patarashca (Lamas 261, tel. 042/52-3899, 10 A.M.–11 P.M. daily, US$6–10) is next to the hostel of the same name, with an upstairs tree house–like space, decorated with paintings, that serves up delicious local food. The specialty is *patarashca,* a delicious seafood stew of fish and local prawns in a broth of cilantro and *bijao* leaves. There is also *paiche* served with *chonta* (palm heart salad).

Another good option for local dishes is **La Collpa** (Circunvalación 164, tel. 042/52-2644, 10 A.M.–11 P.M., US$2–12), strategically located over a balcony overlooking the Río Shilcayo and a patch of the Cordillera Escalera rainforest. The best dishes are made up of meat, freshwater prawns, and fish.

Great ice cream, delicious milk shakes, and refreshing juices can be found at **Heladería Cachete** (Ramírez de Hurtado 187), just aside LAN's office.

Information and Services

There is no Iperú office in Tarapoto, but most midrange hotels have general information about what to do and where to go. An excellent website about the whole San Martín region (Spanish only) is www.turismosanmartin.com, with facts, tips, photos, and maps.

Police are on Ramírez Hurtado (block 1, tel. 042/52-6112).

There is a **state hospital** (Delgado, block 3, tel. 042/52-2071), but the best option is the private **Clínica del Oriente** (Alonso de Alvarado 207, tel. 042/52-1250). On the Plaza de Armas, there are branches of pharmacy chains **InkaFarma** and **BTL.** Another good place to buy medicine is **Farmacia Guadalupe**

(Maynas 300, tel. 042/52-8154), which usually has a doctor on call.

The best supermarket is **La Inmaculada** (Martinez de Compagñon 126, tel. 042/52-3216).

Banks with ATMs are **Banco de Crédito** (San Martín 156), **Scotiabank** (corner of Ramírez Hurtado and Grau), and **Interbank** (Grau 119), which also has an ATM at the airport.

The best Internet is at **Ciber Nautas** (San Pablo de la Cruz 110, US$0.60/hr) or **Cabinas Internet** (Pimentel 134). The **Serpost** office is at San Martín 482 (tel. 042/52-2021, 8 A.M.–10 P.M. Mon.–Sat., 9 A.M.–1 P.M. Sun.).

Cheap international calls can be made from **Gama.Com** (Plaza Mayor, San Pablo de la Cruz 182).

Laundry service is available at **Tarapoto Express** (Lamas and Manco Cápac, tel. 042/53-1761) and the newer **Eco Clean** (Leguía 404).

Getting There

Tarapoto is connected by air to Lima and Iquitos, and the airport is a US$3 *mototaxi* or US$5 *taxi* ride from town. **LAN** (Ramírez de Hurtado, tel. 042/52-9318, Lima tel. 01/213-8200, www.lan. com) has at least two daily flights to Tarapoto. **Star Perú** (Lima tel. 01/705-9000 www.starperu.com) has a daily flight.

Buses move in and out of Tarapoto on a daily basis on a good highway. Most of the bus companies are lined up along Salaverry (blocks 6 and 7). **Movil Tours** (Salaverry 858, tel. 042/52-9193) is the best and safest bus service to Chiclayo (12–15 hours, US$23) and Lima (US$57), in three different schedules.

Transportes Gilmer (Alfonso Ugarte 1480, tel. 042/52-0464) has daily departures to Yurimaguas, 5 A.M.–6 P.M., every hour (US$5.50). The journey to Yurimaguas takes two hours through a excellent paved but winding 120-kilometer highway.

YURIMAGUAS AND VICINITY

At an elevation of 180 meters, Yurimaguas is the northeastern gateway to the Amazon rainforest, accessible from Tarapoto via a two-hour drive on a 120-kilometer, serpent-like highway that crosses the Cordillera Escalera.

Founded by the Jesuits in 1710, Yurimaguas is a sleepy town that still contains remnants from the golden rubber boom days on Avenida Arica. It is popularly known as La perla del Huallaga, "the pearl of the Huallaga River." Nevertheless, the main reason to go to Yurimaguas is to hop on a cargo ship and head towards Iquitos or the Reserva Nacional Pacaya Samiria, via Lagunas. Depending on what time you arrive from Tarapoto, you might have to sleep overnight to catch your boat.

Cargo boats from **Transportes Eduardo** (Elena Pardo 114–116, tel. 065/35-1270 or 065/35-2552) are recommended and depart Yurimaguas around noon, with accommodations ranging from covered decks for slinging hammocks (US$30 pp) to cabins with huge beds and private bathrooms (US$145 pp). The company has seven boats and different services available on each. Even if departures are confirmed boats get delayed quite often. Be prepared to stay overnight in this town.

Accommodations and Food

A budget place to stay is **Hospedaje Lucy** (Atanasio Jáuregui 305, tel. 065/35-2139, US$5 s, US$10 d), a block away from the market, with clean but spartan rooms, private bathrooms, TV, and a fan. **Posada Cumpanamá** (Progreso 403, tel. 065/35-2905, US$27 s, US$30 d, with a/c) is a nicer place with 13 rooms, swimming pool, and a very helpful manager named Nieves Romero. Internet costs US$1.50 an hour, and breakfasts range US$3–4.50. **Puerto Pericos** (San Miguel 720, Malecón Paranapura, tel. 065/35-2009, www. puertopalmeras.com.pe) is the top-end hotel in town; you will probably stay here if you hook up with a travel program at Puerto Palmeras in Tarapoto.

There are budget restaurants around the marketplace, but **El Dorado** (Aguirre 126, Barrio La Loma, tel. 065/35-1023) is worth visiting for a superb lunch if you want to try some of the exotic Amazon delicacies. The

THE AMAZON

© RENÉE DEL GAUDIO AND ROSS WEHNER

Yurimaguas is the launching point for a two-night boat ride to Iquitos.

decor is surreal, with stuffed *carachamas* (a prehistoric-looking armored catfish) hanging from the roofs. Specialties include *huevos de charapa* (turtle eggs), *guiso de majás* (a stew made out of a medium-sized rodent), *chilcano de carachama* (*carachama* soup). There is also fish, chicken, and pork for the less adventurous.

Information and Services

The **Municipalidad Provincial de Alto Amazonas** (town hall, Plaza de Armas 112–114, tel. 065/35-2323) can give tourist information during office hours.

BBVA Banco Continental (Sargento Lores 132) and **Banco de Crédito** (Julio C. Arana 143), both have ATMs.

Getting There and Around

Transportes Gilmer (Víctor Sifuentes 580, tel. 065/35-3361) has daily departures to Tarapoto, every hour 5 A.M.–6 P.M. (US$5.50). The journey to Tarapoto takes two hours along a 120-kilometer paved highway.

Iquitos

Iquitos is a swanky and sassy place to go, with around half a million inhabitants and hemmed in by muddy rivers and flooded rainforest on all sides. Being the largest city in the world that cannot be reached by road, Iquitos's only bridges to the outside world are planes and boats. It is the launching pad for exploring Peru's northern Amazon.

Because of its isolation, terrorism never reached the city during the 1980s and 1990s. Perhaps as a result, Iquitos has a relaxed, laid-back vibe that seems much closer to Bangkok than, say, Cusco. The air is thick and steamy, and the noisy buzzing of the *mototaxis* invades all your senses. Life revolves around the Amazon River, a couple of kilometers wide after collecting water from all of Peru's major rivers. People are descended from a dozen different Indian groups and waves of European and Chinese immigrants.

The weather in Iquitos, even during the October–May rainy season, is fairly predictable. The sky dawns blue most days but by late afternoon fills with the clouds of convection storms, which release sheets of cool rain. Between mid-December and June, the Amazon rises anywhere from 7 to 15 meters, carrying silt and fallen trees brought down from the Andes. The river floods hundreds of kilometers of forest around Iquitos. Oil supertankers and huge passenger cruisers make the 3,600-kilometer odyssey from the Atlantic.

The floods enrich the surrounding fields, which are planted with rice, peanuts, watermelon, and pumpkin, as soon as the water begins to recede in July. Fish leave the oxygen-poor oxbow lakes in the low season and concentrate in the river, prompting huge harvests of *corvina* (bass), *dorado*, catfish, and *paiche* (a prehistoric-looking fish, quite tasty, and the biggest in the Amazon).

After Francisco de Orellana's epic descent down the Amazon River in 1542, the Spaniards left the area to the Jesuits, who founded a settlement here in the 1750s before being expelled from Latin America shortly thereafter. Two hundred years later, the ramshackle settlement exploded into one of Peru's richest cities thanks to the rubber boom. The flip side of the opulence was the oppression and abject poverty of the Indian and mestizo rubber tappers, who lived in virtual enslavement and frequently died of malaria and other diseases. The floating city of **Belén,** which some call the Venice of South America and others a slum, is a leftover from that era.

Iquitos is the pioneer of Amazonian tourism, which began in the 1960s, and is the base for a variety of lodges, cruise ships, and adventure agencies. Other industries include lumber, agriculture, the export of exotic fish and birds and *barbasco,* a poisonous plant used by the natives to kill fish that is now being used as an insecticide.

SIGHTS
City Tour

In the center of the **Plaza de Armas** you will find the Obelisk, a monument to the Iquitos military heroes who fought in the War of the Pacific against Chile in 1879. The south side of the plaza is marked by the **Iglesia Matriz,** built in 1919. Inside you will find religious paintings by Américo Pinasco and César Calvo de Araujo. Across the plaza, on the corner of Putumayo and Próspero, is the **Casa de Fierro** (Iron House), designed by Gustav Eiffel for the 1889 Paris Exhibition. It was bought by wealthy rubber businessman Anselmo del Águila and shipped in pieces only to be reassembled on its current site. Around the corner at Napo and Raimondi is the **Casa de Barro,** the mud-and-wood house used as a warehouse by rubber baron Fermín Fitzcarrald.

A block from the Plaza de Armas along the **Río Itaya** is the hectic and busy pedestrian Malecón Tarapacá, also a prime viewpoint from which to view the river's landscape. The construction of this walkway began during the rubber boom in the late 19th century; it was

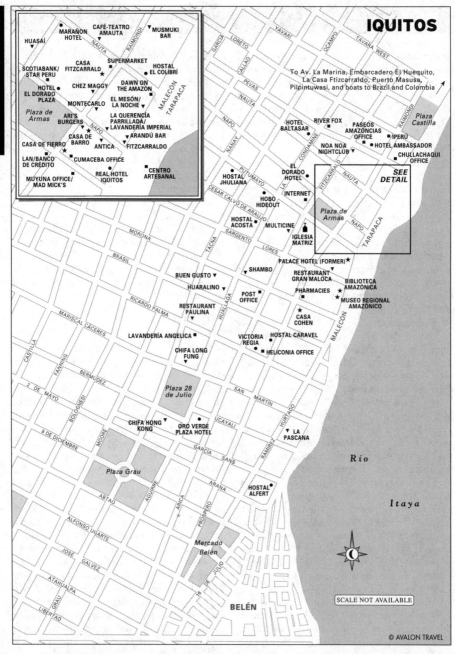

IQUITOS

To Av. La Marina, Embarcadero El Huequito,
La Casa Fitzcarraldo, Puerto Masusa,
Pilpintuwasi, and boats to Brazil and Colombia

DETAIL (inset)

- HUASAÍ
- MARAÑON HOTEL
- CAFÉ-TEATRO AMAUTA
- MUSMUKI BAR
- SCOTIABANK/ STAR PERU
- CASA FITZCARRALDO
- SUPERMARKET
- HOSTAL EL COLIBRÍ
- HOTEL EL DORADO PLAZA
- CHEZ MAGGY
- DAWN ON THE AMAZON
- MONTECARLO
- EL MESÓN/ LA NOCHE
- ARI'S BURGERS
- LA QUERENCÍA PARRILLADA/ LAVANDERÍA IMPERIAL
- CASA DE FIERRO
- CASA DE BARRO
- ARANDÚ BAR
- ANTICA
- FITZCARRALDO
- LAN/BANCO DE CRÉDITO
- CUMACEBA OFFICE
- MUYUNA OFFICE/ MAD MICK'S
- REAL HOTEL IQUITOS
- CENTRO ARTESANAL
- Plaza de Armas
- MALECÓN TARAPACA

Main map labels:

- Plaza Castilla
- SEE DETAIL
- HOTEL BALTASAR
- RIVER FOX
- PASEÓS AMAZÓNICAS OFFICE
- IPERÚ
- NOA NOA NIGHTCLUB
- HOTEL AMBASSADOR
- CHULLACHAQUI OFFICE
- EL DORADO HOTEL
- Plaza de Armas
- HOSTAL JHULIANA
- INTERNET
- HOBO HIDEOUT
- HOSTAL ACOSTA
- MULTICINE
- IGLESIA MATRIZ
- PALACE HOTEL (FORMER)
- SHAMBO
- RESTAURANT GRAN MALOCA
- BIBLIOTECA AMAZÓNICA
- BUEN GUSTO
- HUARALINO
- PHARMACIES
- MUSEO REGIONAL AMAZÓNICO
- POST OFFICE
- RESTAURANT PAULINA
- CASA COHEN
- LAVANDERÍA ANGELICA
- VICTORIA REGIA
- HOSTAL CARAVEL
- CHIFA LONG FUNG
- HELICONIA OFFICE
- Plaza 28 de Julio
- CHIFA HONG KONG
- ORO VERDE PLAZA HOTEL
- LA PASCANA
- Plaza Grau
- HOSTAL ALFERT
- Mercado Belén
- Río Itaya
- BELÉN
- SCALE NOT AVAILABLE

Street names:
GARCIA, LORETO, YAVARI, OCAMPO, TAVARA WEST, CALLAO, PEVAS, NAUTA, NAPO, NANAY, CONDAMINE, RAIMONDI, FITZCARRALDO, TARAPACA, PUTUMAYO, CESAR CALVO DE ARAUJO, MORONA, TACNA, SARGENTO, LORES, BRASIL, MARISCAL CACERES, RICARDO PALMA, HUALLAGA, CASTILLA, FANNING, BERMUDEZ, 2 DE MAYO, BOLOGNESI, 9 DE DICIEMBRE, MOORE, SAN MARTIN, UCAYALI, GARCIA, SANS, RAMIREZ, HURTADO, ARANA, ARICA, PROSPERO, AGUIRRE, ABTAO, ALFONSO UGARTE, JOSE GALVEZ, ATAHUALPA, GRAU, LIBERTAD, 16 DE JULIO, MALECÓN

© AVALON TRAVEL

© SERGIO SCHABEL MAN

a mother and child canoeing to pick *camu camu,* a local citrus fruit

recently improved with fountains, benches, and street lamps. The promenade is lined with 19th-century mansions built by rubber barons and decorated with *azulejos* (tiles imported from Spain and Portugal).

The most spectacular of these is the former **Palace Hotel** (Malecón Tarapacá 208). Built 1908–1912 in an art-nouveau style, this three-story building was the most luxurious in Peru's Amazon. Its iron balconies were imported from Hamburg, the marble from Carrara, and the multicolored mosaics from Seville. The building currently serves as a military base.

Along the Malecón is the **Biblioteca Amazónica** (Malecón Tarapacá 354, 7:30 A.M.–9 P.M. Mon.–Fri., 8 A.M.–noon and 3–8 P.M. Sat.), an excellent library containing a range of books, maps, old photographs, newspapers, and films.

The **Museo Regional Amazónico** (Malecón Tarapacá 386, 9 A.M.–1 P.M. and 3–7 P.M. Mon.–Fri., 9 A.M.–1 P.M. Sat., US$1.50) houses the **Sons of our Land,** a selection of 76 fiberglass statues out of approximately 300, of indigenous Indians from various tribes of Peru, Brazil, and Venezuela, created by the eccentric Peruvian-Swedish artist Felipe Lettersten in 1987 to preserve the memory of these rapidly vanishing cultures. The historic building was built in 1863 and restored in 1996 to be converted into a museum. It contains wall panels, doors, and ceilings of intricately carved old-growth mahogany.

There are elegant old rubber baron homes near the city center. **Casa Cohen** (Próspero 401) was built with Moroccan tiles and Parisian grates in 1905, and now houses a supermarket. Another is the neoclassic **Casa Morey** (Próspero 502).

Belén

This is a gigantic floating shantytown of homes built atop rafts of balsa wood that rise and fall with the river. It is an exotic sight, with children jumping into the water from their front porches and entire families

ADVENTUROUS RIVER TRAVEL TO IQUITOS

To reach Iquitos you have two options: travel by air or travel by water – there are no highways. There are plenty of direct flights from Lima, but if you are looking for adventure you can hop aboard a cargo boat from either **Yurimaguas** or **Pucallpa.** As you lounge in a hammock, the jungle will pass by while the ship meanders through the muddy waters of the Marañón or Ucayali River, flowing into the Amazon under a bright blue sky. Just when the heat and humidity become unbearable, a refreshing afternoon rain might fall to reveal a spectacular clear sky dominated at night by the Southern Cross. With a little preparation, the right attitude, and some patience, a river journey through the jungle can be a comfortable, safe, and a unique travel experience.

Yurimaguas is located in northeastern Peru, 2-3 days away from Iquitos down the Río Marañón. This small city is reached by a two-hour drive from Tarapoto. Comfy minivans and *colectivo* station wagons offer daily trips on a 120-kilometer highway that crosses the **Cordillera Escalera,** the last mountain range with cloud forests, before descending into the Amazon basin.

Cargo boats from **Transportes Eduardo** (Yurimaguas tel. 065/35-1270 or 065/35-2552) are highly recommended, departing Yurimaguas around noon, with accommodations ranging from covered decks for slinging hammocks (US$30 pp) to cabins with huge beds and private bathrooms (US$145 pp). The company has seven boats (*Eduardo I, II, III* and so on) and different services available in each. Be warned, however, that boats wait until their cargo deck is full, and confirmed departures can get delayed quite often.

The other option is Pucallpa, on the shores of the Río Ucayali, a commercial hub 4-5 days upstream of Iquitos. The city is unattractive but is the southern gateway to the northeastern Amazon jungle. The wharfs are always busy loading and unloading goods – bananas, cars, passengers to and from Iquitos and other small towns along the river.

From Lima, Pucallpa is reached by daily flights or by a gorgeous 17-hour bus journey from desert coast to Andes to rainforest, reaching an altitude of almost 5,000 meters crossing Ticlio. The bus ride can can be broken up in two parts with an overnight stop in Huánuco or Tingo María, which are opening up to travel after being shut down for years by drug trafficking in the area.

Gilmer I, IV, and *V* (also owned by Transportes Eduardo) and the *Baylón I* and *II* are the boats we recommend. Unlike in Yurimaguas, there is no office or phone available to book a ticket. You need to approach the decks and talk to the captain or the second in command. Both companies sell tickets offering closed decks to hang your hammock on (US$29 pp); there are also cabins with a bunk bed, TV, and private bathroom in the *Baylón* boats (US$64 pp) or better cabins on the *Gilmer* boats (US$145 pp).

Regardless of whether you travel from Yurimaguas or Pucallpa, the ticket includes three hot meals a day on any of these vessels, served up by the boat cooks and announced by a bell or a hammer blow on some metal surface. Passengers must bring their own spoon, bowl, and mug (US$2-3), available from the vendors roaming on the boat before departure. The food is pretty good: mostly stews with chicken, fish, and rice. If you need a special diet, do not rely on the boat food. Buy fruit or whatever you think you might want to eat during your journey. As long as you consume bottled water, you won't get sick aboard. The *Baylón II* has a small restaurant offering set-up dishes, cold beers, and other beverages.

Hammocks can be bought on board or around the wharf (US$11-21). The upper decks get less crowded than the lower ones. If you travel in a group you might consider the security of a locked cabin and alternate beds and hammocks to sleep.

paddling along the waterways in dugout canoes. Closer to the riverbank, other families live in thatched homes lifted above the water on rickety stilts. Because of the recent meandering of the Amazon away from Iquitos, the whole area becomes a gigantic mudflat during the dry months of July–December. Although the municipality does a good job with trash collecting, there are serious health problems during the dry months because of the open sewers.

To visit the floating city, head down Próspero south from the Plaza de Armas to Belén's raucous and colorful market, which begins around García Sanz. Along with plastic kitchen items and cheap clothing imported from Brazil, vendors sell every imaginable jungle fruit and vegetable, dried fish, medicinal herbs, chickens, and contraband meat of *sajino* (wild pig) and *venado* (deer). The smells of garbage, mud, and all of these foods baking in the sun can become overpowering at times, so visit in the morning when the market is cleanest and most active.

Once in the market, head left toward the waterfront along 9 de Diciembre and walk out on wooden walkways toward the water. Here, people with canoes will paddle you around Belén for US$3 a half hour. Make sure to bring sunscreen, glasses, and a hat because the sun on the river is powerful. The area is relatively safe but locals will insist that you should not go on your own. It is best to leave valuables and most of your money behind. Ask at your hotel about the latest updates on security in the Belén area.

Pilpintuwasi Butterfly Farm and Animal Orphanage

The best day trip from Iquitos is Pilpintuwasi (tel. 065/23-2665, pilpintuwasi@hotmail.com, www.amazonanimalorphanage.org, 9 A.M.–4 P.M. Tues.–Sun., US$5 adults, US$3 students), which means "butterfly's home" in Quechua. Huge mesh tents contain numerous butterfly species fluttering above the stone paths that lead through exotic gardens. The facility was founded by an Austrian-Peruvian couple, Gudrun Sperrer and Roblar Moreno,

Amazon boats with floating city of Belén in the background

who have designed the garden to contain all the fruits, flowers, and leaves that caterpillars and butterflies need for survival.

Apart from butterflies, the place also receives rescued wild animals, including Pedro Bello, a jaguar; Chavo, a red uakari monkey; Rosa, an anteater; and another dozen animals that Sperrer and Moreno adopted to save from being sold or killed. Pilpintuwasi is in Padre Cocha and always welcomes volunteers who want to work in the butterfly farm or help take care of the animals.

To reach the farm, head to the port of Bella Vista–Nanay, 15 minutes outside of town and accessible by *colectivos* along Próspero that read Bella Vista–Nanay. It is about a 20-minute boat ride from here, passing Bora and Yagua villages along the way, though in low-water months passengers have to disembark early and walk along a path for 15 minutes.

Amazon Golf Course

Located around 30 minutes by taxi from Iquitos's downtown, this amazing nine-hole course (tel. 065/965-943-267, www.amazon-golfcourse.com, 6 A.M.–6 P.M. daily) is probably the only golf course in the Peruvian Amazon. Started in 2004 by a group of expats, it offers almost 10 hectares of flat green where you can play 18 holes for US$25. There is a clubhouse, and a bar, restaurant, swimming pool, and tennis court are in the works.

Other Side Trips

There are a number of places to visit outside Iquitos, though frankly the surrounding jungle is far more interesting. About 15 minutes west of the city is the **Quistococha Tourist Center** (8 A.M.–5 P.M. dail) which has a lake with rowboats, a fish farm, and a small zoo. Iquiteños head here and to **Lago Moronacocha,** three kilometers east of the city, on the weekends to swim, sunbathe, and water-ski. There are a few bars at Moronacocha that offer bathroom services for guests. **Santo Tomás** is a lakeside village 15 kilometers northeast of Iquitos known for carved root and ceramics handicrafts.

ENTERTAINMENT AND EVENTS
Nightlife

All along the first block of Malecón Tarapacá there are small bars and restaurants with tables on the walkway where locals and travelers sit down, enjoying a beer and watching the people stroll by. **Arandú Bar** (Malecón Tarapacá 113, tel. 065/24-3434, 4 P.M.–2 A.M.) is a classic, decorated with kitsch-like, jungle-motif wall paintings by renowned artist Christian Bendayán. It has hip music, pretty good drinks, and a friendly crowd.

Another good place for drinks is **Nikoro Bar** (Pevas 100, 9 P.M.–close daily). At **Musmuki Bar** (Raymondi 382, tel. 065/24-2942, 5 P.M.–2 A.M. daily), all cocktails are mixed with *aguardiente,* sugarcane distilled alcohol. As strong as it can sound (and taste), drinks are good and the ambience quite hip. On Plaza Castilla, there are some small bars selling cheap beer to plenty of thirsty locals and backpackers.

For a night of dancing, **Noa Noa Nightclub** (Pevas 292, tel. 065/23-2902, 5 P.M.–2 A.M. daily) is quite an institution. A couple of blocks from the Plaza de Armas, this club plays salsa, *cumbia,* and other catchy Latin rhythms over a two-level dance floor. **El Pardo** is a local favorite if you want to dance to live music. It is actually a huge fenced open space where local salsa and *cumbia* bands play all night. Any *mototaxi* can take you there for US$1.50. Tickets go for US$1.50–6, depending which band plays.

Iquitos also has a big screen movie theater, **Cine Star Iquitos** (Arica 258, 3–10 P.M. daily, US$3), that shows the latest Hollywood blockbusters.

The Festival of San Juan

Celebrated on June 23–25, this festivity overlaps with the *friaje* during this time—winds that originate in the southern Atlantic and the Patagonia, sweeping northwest and across the Amazon basin with temperatures as low as 8°C. These cold spells or *friajes* can happen anytime from May to August but are most common around San Juan's birthday in late June. Don't expect to see many animals during a *friaje*—the monkeys huddle up together in balls to stay warm and the birds roost until it's all over.

The religious and meteorological coincidence has merged over the centuries into Iquitos's biggest party, celebrated these days at the Mercado Artesanal de San Juan on the way to the airport. Dance competitions from indigenous groups and rock concerts are enjoyed while eating *juanes,* rice tamale–like bundles of chicken, tomato, and onion wrapped in a *bijao* palm leaf, which imparts a delicious flavor to the concoction. A sweater or a windbreaker is quite handy, because *los vientos de San Juan* "the winds of San Juan" make the place feel more like Seattle or London than Iquitos.

Iquitos also has a Founders Day celebration on January 5 and a Carnaval in late February or early March. Santo Tomás has a handicraft fair on August 21 and a festival in honor of its patron saint September 23–25.

SHOPPING

Market stalls on stilts hovering above the Amazon make up the **Centro Artesanal Anaconda** (Malecón Tarapacá, 8 A.M.–8 P.M. daily). Vendors sell jewelry, sandals, paintings, beaded curtains, shoulder bags, and other souvenirs. There is also a line of crafts stores along Próspero south of the Plaza de Armas, though Iquitos's largest handicraft market is the **Mercado Artesanal de San Juan** (Av. Quiñones Km 4.5, 9 A.M.–10 P.M. daily), on the road to the airport. The colorful native jungle seeds sold by the kilogram are a notable find here. These can be used to make your own jewelry or for other artistic endeavors.

For books and drawing and writing materials, go to **Librería Tamara** (Próspero 268, tel. 065/22-1711, 8 A.M.–1 P.M. and 3:30–9 P.M. daily). Rubber boots, binoculars, and other jungle equipment can be purchased with a buyback guarantee at **Mad Mick's Trading Post** (Putumayo 163, 2nd Fl., tel. 065/975-4976, 8 A.M.–8 P.M. daily) near the Iron House. Locals do their food shopping at the colorful **Belén Market,** which is liveliest in the mornings. Much of Iquitos slows down, or shuts down, in this area during the afternoon,

1–4 P.M. There is a cluster of handicraft stores on the sixth block of Arica; they are generally open all day, 8 A.M.–9 P.M.

ACCOMMODATIONS

Most hotels in Iquitos will pick you up at the airport and save you the hassle of dealing with taxi drivers. In general the area north of the Plaza de Armas is safer and more attractive. There are dozens of hostels clustered around the Belén Market, south of the Plaza de Armas, but they are mostly grimy and filled with the drone of passing *mototaxis.*

Under US$10

Hostal Alfert (García Sanz 301, tel. 065/23-4105, reservacionalfert@yahoo.es, US$5 s, US$9 d) has stunning views over Belén and the Río Itaya. This 17-room establishment has been in operation for two decades by former riverboat captain Alfonso Fernández. Situated seven blocks south of the Plaza de Armas, it is probably the best place you can get for less than ten dollars. The upstairs rooms look out over the river toward a vast complex of thatched homes propped up off the water on stilts. The hostel's rooms are simple, mostly clean, and have spongy beds and a bit of hot water.

US$10-25

Hostal El Colibrí (Nauta 172, tel. 065/24-1737, hostalelcolibri@hotmail.com, US$14 s, US$21 d) is a long-time favorite. It has a homey feeling not found in many other Iquitos hotels. Rooms are small but have big windows and fans, but there are also nice rooms with air-conditioning (US$20 s, US$27 d) and nice writing desks. The hostel is small but clean and with a friendly staff. There are only a few rooms with hot water but all rooms have private baths and cable TV.

Hotel Baltazar (La Condamine 265, tel. 065/23-2240, US$13 s with fan, US$20 d with a/c) has clean rooms, cable TV, private baths with hot water, and rooms with fans or air-conditioning.

Hostal Caravel (Próspero 568, tel. 065/23-2176, hostalcaravel.blogspot.com, US$18 s,

© RENÉE DEL GAUDIO AND ROSS WEHNER

the Amazon River, near Iquitos, during the high-water months

US$25 d) has been upgraded and continues to be a well-managed place, four blocks from the main square. Rooms are comfy and all have air-conditioning, but double-check about the amenities they actually have since their blog page is not quite accurate.

For a more standard hotel, try **Hostal Jhuliana** (Putumayo 521, tel. 065/23-3154, hostaljhuliana@e-milio.com, US$20 s, US$25 d with breakfast). Carpeted rooms have comfortable beds, air-conditioning, refrigerators, and hot water. There is a full-service restaurant and bar.

US$25-50

Real Hotel Iquitos (Malecón Tarapacá and Napo, tel. 065/23-1011, realhoteliquitos@ hotmail.com, US$29 s, US$36 d). This former state-owned Hotel de Turistas is literally a grand dame of a hotel, though somewhat abandoned. It definitely is not the choice for its top-end service. But the historic hotel more than half a century old has an elegant though somewhat rundown interior. The rooms have unique touches, such as wood or black-and-

white tile floors, red curtains and green walls, and balconies. Rooms of the same price vary from small and cozy to absolutely enormous (especially room 218 or 312). This location on the pedestrian waterfront is wonderfully quiet. Amenities include private bath, TV, air-conditioning, and refrigerator.

Marañón Hotel (Nauta 285, tel. 065/24-2673, hotelmaranon@hotmail.com, US$35 s, US$46 d with breakfast) is quite centric. This hotel is somewhat of an oasis in this hot, sticky town. Large rooms with clean white walls are kept cool with tile floors and air-conditioning. Amenities include refrigerators, comfortable beds, hot water 24 hours daily, WiFi, and a nice outdoor pool with an adjoining Peruvian restaurant. Rooms on the fourth floor have a view of the Amazon. Make reservations ahead of time, as this hotel fills up frequently.

Oro Verde Plaza Hotel (Ucayali 315, tel. 065/22-1616, oroverdeplazahoteliqt@speedy. com, US$46 s, US$57 d with breakfast) is near the Plaza 28 de Julio. Situated a bit off the main drag, its big rooms, firm mattresses, and bright reading lamps are worth the extra walk. The hotel has some rooms that face the street, which are well lit but a bit noisier. Room rates include airport transfer.

Over US$50

La Casa Fitzcarraldo (Av. La Marina 2153, Punchana, tel. 065/60-1138, www. LaCasaFitzcarraldo.com, US$57 s, US$107 d with breakfast) is probably the most extravagant place to stay in Iquitos. It is owned by Walter Saxer, personal friend and former producer of Werner Herzog's most famous films, including *Fitzcarraldo* and *Aguirre, the Wrath of God*. Self-defined as a "jungle oasis," due to the intense vegetation that surrounds the house built in the 1960s, this swanky bed-and-breakfast hosted Mick Jagger (in the Blue Room), Klaus Kinski (in the Green Room), and Herzog himself (in the Bungalow).

The rooms are huge, with high ceilings, painted with pastel colors and soberly decorated with Shipibo and other Indian arts and crafts. The amenities include a swimming pool, satellite TV, WiFi, airport transfer, and a privileged peek into photos of the film shooting when Jagger and actor Jason Robards were still in the cast. If you stay in this place, with a bit of luck you might bump into Saxer. Then he might tell you a tale or two, if he is in the right mood.

Hotel Acosta (Huallaga 254, tel. 065/23-1761, www.hotelacosta.com, US$59 s, US$71 d with breakfast) is a modern and comfortable three-star hotel including air-conditioning, hot water, cable TV, phones, refrigerators, Internet, laundry, and safe deposit boxes. The price includes airport transfer.

Victoria Regia Hotel and Suites (Ricardo Palma 252, tel. 065/23-1983, www.victoriaregiahotel.com, US$75 s, US$86 d with breakfast), owned by the Acostas, one of the pioneering Peruvian families in tourism in the jungle, is an upgraded version of her sister, Hotel Acosta. In addition to all amenities imaginable, it has a swimming pool and comfy suites, making this place one of the best hotels in the city. The same owners manage

Heliconia Lodge, 80 kilometers downriver from Iquitos.

The five-star hotel of Iquitos is **El Dorado Plaza Hotel and Business** (Napo 258, Plaza de Armas, tel. 065/22-2555, www.eldoradoplazahotel.com, US$242 s or US$297 d with breakfast). Extremely overpriced for what it is, the 65 rooms are divided between the newly remodeled with huge windows and the older ones, which are not as nice. The upper floors have nice views toward the Amazon River. Additional services include gym with sauna, boutique, WiFi, air-conditioning, business center, a huge sun-filled atrium in the lobby, and an outdoor pool with bar and whirlpool.

FOOD

Iquitos's most famous dish is the *juane,* and restaurants serve a variety of exotic jungle juices made from the *cocona* and *camu camu* fruits. Main plates include *paiche con chonta* (fish with palm heart salad) and *tacacho con cecina* (fried banana mixed with smoked pork meat). *Inchicapi de gallina* is chicken soup with peanut, cilantro, and manioc root; it is quite good, as is *picuro* or *majás* rodent stew (which actually tastes more like pork).

Apart from these typical foods, many restaurants offer bush meat, including alligator, deer, turtle stew, and even grilled monkey. Eating these plates only encourages illegal hunting. There is a ban on fishing or serving *paiche* during its reproductive season October–February. If you order it during this time, ensure that it comes from one of the fish farms and not from the river.

Cafés, Bakeries, and Ice Cream

A main Iquitos hangout for both locals and gringos is **Ari's Burgers** (Próspero 127, tel. 065/23-1470, 7 A.M.–3 A.M. daily, US$1–7). This open-air establishment resembles a jungle version of a greasy spoon. It is strategically located on the Plaza de Armas with its fluorescent lights. The huge menu includes burgers and fries, milk shakes, vegetarian dishes, grilled meats, and a huge range of desserts.

Ice cream in Iquitos is ubiquitous. The hot, humid climate invites pushcart ice cream vendors, a number of gelato shops on the Plaza de Armas, and lots of popsicle stations. The best of these is **Shambo** (Morona 396, 9 A.M.–11 P.M. daily, US$0.30), which sells only natural, fruit juice popsicles. Your flavor choices range from grape to strawberry to *aguaje* to beer!

Peruvian

A block off the Plaza de Armas is **Huasaí** (Napo 326, tel. 065/24-2222, 7 A.M.–4:30 P.M., US$4), a family-owned bustling restaurant whose tables fill up very quickly at the lunch hour. Most people come for the US$2.50 lunch menu with fish, chicken, beef, and vegetarian options. It also serves tamales, *cebiche,* sandwiches, and juices.

There are two excellent places for Peruvian food on the south end of town. **Restaurant Paulina** (Tacna 591, tel. 065/23-1298, 10 A.M.–10 P.M., US$4–6) serves up a mouthwatering array of local food, including *cebiche* and *paiche a la loretana* with fried *yuca* and palm heart salad. The owner, Paulina Angulo, has operated here for more than a decade, attracting locals with a good-value US$2 lunch menu.

On the Malecón, there are a couple of good restaurants with outdoor seating. **La Noche** (Malecón Maldonado 177, tel. 065/22-2373, 7 A.M.–11 P.M. daily, US$5–7) opens early for breakfast, serves refreshing fruit drinks throughout the day, and draws its biggest crowd in the evening. **Restaurante Turístico El Mesón** (Malecón Maldonado 153, tel. 065/23-1857, 11 A.M.–1 A.M. daily, US$5–7) is the more traditional option, where you can try everything from *pescado a la cubana* (fish with bananas and eggs) to *tortuga al curry* (curried tortoise).

Despite the heat, the favorite evening option in Iquitos is grilled meat. The tiny **Buen Gusto** (Morona 441, tel. 065/22-3337, 7 P.M.–midnight Mon.–Sat., US$5–7) has *parilladas* of beef, chorizo, and *tacacho,* which are among the favorites. **La Querencía Parrillada** (Napo 138, tel. 065/22-5785, 6 P.M.–midnight daily, US$3–6) is a small corridor of a restaurant with bamboo ceilings and wooden tables. Locals claim this place has the best steak in Iquitos.

Fine Dining

Fitzcarraldo (Napo 100, on the Malecón, tel. 065/22-3298, 8 A.M.–11:30 P.M. daily, US$5–7) has become a classic, with its rubber boom days stylish decor. The restored colonial house has a pleasant, open-air atmosphere, and there are also tables outside on the Malecón. The menu includes brochettes of meat, fish, and chicken and *pescado en salsa de maracuya,* an Amazonian fish with passion fruit sauce.

Located in a grand, tile-covered 19th-century house, **Restaurant Gran Maloca** (Lores 178, tel. 065/23-3126, noon–11 P.M. Mon.–Sat., noon–8 P.M. Sun., US$4–10) serves a wide variety of jungle dishes. If bush meat does not appeal to you, there are also pastas, fish, and meat. The formal dining room is air-conditioned. The restaurant has a recommended and affordable three-course lunchtime menu.

For a true night on the Amazon, take a boat out to the extravagant floating restaurant/bar **Al Frío y al Fuego** (Embarcadero el Huequito, tel. 065/965-607-474, www.alfrioyalfuego.com, noon–4 P.M. and 7–11 P.M. Tues.–Sat., US$7–15). The place, built in 2006, also has a floating swimming pool. The specialties are regional fish, meat, and exotic drinks from the jungle. A good treat.

Pizza

Good wood-fired pizzas, lasagna, and ravioli are served in a cozy atmosphere at **Chez Maggy Pizzeria** (Raimondi 177, tel. 065/24-1816, 6 P.M.–midnight daily, US$3.50). Colorful art and a full bar make this a great place to have a leisurely dinner.

Antica Pizzeria (Napo 159, tel. 065/24-1988, www.anticapizzeria.com.pe, 7 A.M.–midnight daily, US$5–14) is the more hip pizza choice. They have delicious thin-crust pizza, great salads, fresh pasta, whole-wheat pasta, and more. Highly recommended.

Chifa

The best place for Peruvian-Chinese food is **Chifa Long Fung** (San Martin 454, in front of Plaza 28 de Julio, tel. 065/23-3649, noon–2:30 P.M. and 6:45 P.M.–midnight daily, US$4–6), claimed to be one of the best in the whole Amazon. Across the plaza is a solid budget choice, **Chifa Hong Kong** (Bermúdez 471, tel. 065/24-1691, 11 A.M.–2 P.M. and 7 P.M.–midnight daily, US$3–5).

Markets

The largest **supermarket** is at Próspero 401 (7 A.M.–11 P.M. daily), located in a 19th-century mansion called Los Portales that is covered in Portuguese tiles. Another good option is **Mini Market Marthita** (Arica and Ucayali, tel. 065/23-5734, 6:30 A.M.–1 A.M. daily). If you are looking for imported favorites, you might likely find them in **Autoservicio Saby** (Raimondi 195, 6 A.M.–midnight daily).

INFORMATION AND SERVICES

The **Iperú** office is across Plaza Castilla (Loreto 201 on the corner with Raimondi, tel. 065/23-6144, www.peru.info, 9 A.M.–6 P.M. daily). There can be updated tourist information and maps at the **Dircetur** office (La Condamine 173, tel. 065/23-3472, 8:30 A.M.–12:30 P.M. and 2:30–4:30 P.M. Mon.–Sat.).

A good English-language resource is the *Iquitos Times* (www.iquitostimes.com), a free newspaper that provides up-to-date information and is available at many cafés or Mad Mick's Trading Post (Putumayo 163, tel. 065/975-4976, 8 A.M.–8 P.M. daily). Mick, himself, is also an excellent source on activities around town, including his annual Longest Raft Race in the World.

In an emergency, call the **tourist police of Iquitos** (Lores 834, tel. 065/23-1852 or 065/24-2081).

For health care, the **Hospital Regional de Iquitos** (28 de Julio s/n, tel. 065/25-1882 or 065/25-2743) is open 24 hours. The **Ana Stahl** Adventist clinic (Av. La Marina 285, tel. 065/25-2535, www.caas-peru.org, 24 hours) offers the best care. There are reliable **pharmacies** at the corner of Morona and Próspero: InkaFarma (tel. 065/23-3867), Botica BTL (tel. 065/22-4789), and B y S (tel. 065/22-3825) are all open 7 A.M.–midnight daily and offer delivery.

Scotiabank and **Banco de Crédito** both have ATMs and are located on the Plaza de Armas. Farther south are the **BBVA Banco Continental** (Lores 171) and **Interbank** (Próspero 336). During the week, banks typically close at 1 P.M. and reopen at 4:30 P.M. On Saturday banks are open only in the morning.

Iquitos's **post office** is at Arica 402 (tel. 065/26-1915, 7:30 A.M.–6:30 P.M. Mon.–Fri., 7:30 A.M.–5:30 P.M. Sat.).

There are plenty of fast Internet cafés around town. The local and tourist favorite is on the Plaza de Armas at the intersection of Napo and Arica.

The **Peruvian immigrations** office, where tourist visas can be extended, is at Mariscal Cáceres 18 (tel. 065/23-5371).

For a choice of full-service or coin-operated laundry go to **Lavandería Imperial** (Putumayo 150, tel. 065/23-1768, 8 A.M.–7 P.M. Mon.–Sat.). For drop-off service, there is the friendly **Lavandería Angelica** (Ricardo Palma 429, tel. 065/23-3757, 8 A.M.–10 P.M. Mon.–Sat., 9 A.M.–noon Sun., US$1/kg).

GETTING THERE AND AROUND

Because Iquitos is water locked, nearly all visitors arrive by plane. Iquitos's airport is seven kilometers outside of town or a US$5, 20-minute cab ride.

Two airlines fly from Lima. **LAN** (Lima tel. 01/213-8200, Iquitos tel. 065/23-2421, www.lan.com) has four daily flights and **Star Perú** (Lima tel. 01/705-9000, Iquitos tel. 065/23-6208, www.starperu.com) has three daily flights. From Iquitos, Star Perú also flies to Tarapoto and Pucallpa (one daily flight each).

The only other way to enter or leave Iquitos is by boat. From Puerto Masusa, on the north end of Iquitos, boats leave for Pucallpa and Yurimaguas (US$25–110), and sporadically on the weekends for Puerto de Coca in Ecuador up the Río Napo (US$30, 15 days). Public *colectivo* boats head upstream to **Nauta** from the Puerto Bella Vista–Nanay, 15 minutes outside of town and reachable from buses that run along Próspero. Boat tickets should be bought the day of or the day before departure.

Covered passenger boats also go down the Amazon from here to Pevas and the border towns of Leticia, Colombia, and Tabatinga, Brazil. Most of these companies have their offices in the third block of Raimondi. Two recommended options are **Golfinho** (Raimondi 350, tel. 065/22-5118), with departures Tuesday, Thursday, and Saturday at 6 A.M.; and **Hover Amazon Express** (Raimondi 390, tel. 065/23-3201), with Tuesday and Friday 6 A.M. departures. The boats leave from a small dock on Marina Avenue across from the San Carlos gas station.

There are not many cars in this town but hundreds of noisy *mototaxis,* which provide cheap and quick transportation. A ride anywhere in the city costs US$0.50–2, depending where you go.

To rent a motorcycle or a four-wheel drive, head to **River Fox** (La Condamine 300, tel. 065/23-6469, 7 A.M.–11 P.M. daily, US$1.50–5/hr for a motorbike).

PEVAS SIDE TRIP

The best place to stop for a night or two for those traveling downstream to Brazil is Pevas, a laid-back village 145 kilometers downstream of Iquitos that was founded by missionaries in 1735. Pevas's main attraction is **La Casa del Arte,** a huge thatched structure on the banks of the Amazon that serves as studio and home of **Francisco Grippa,** a well-known painter in the Amazon. Born in Tumbes in the 1940s, Grippa attended art school in Los Angeles and somehow ended up in Pevas, where he paints the extreme beauty and destruction of the Amazon on canvases he makes himself from tree bark. His work ranges from the mystical to the abstract, although his best-known works portray Amazon natives, animals, or landscapes with explosions of color reminiscent of Jackson Pollock. A sampling of Grippa's work can be seen in the lobby of the El Dorado Plaza Hotel or at **Camu-Camu,** an art gallery at Trujillo 438 (tel. 065/25-3120). For more information about Grippa, see his website at www.art-and-soul.com.

© SERGIO SCHABELMAN

three-wheeled *mototaxis* in Iquitos

Iquitos Jungle

The jungle in the northeastern Amazon can be explored in a number of ways: by visiting a jungle lodge, cruising on a riverboat, or going on a camping trip. What you see depends in large part on how far you travel from Iquitos. The riverbanks that were mostly wilderness in the 1960s are now wall-to-wall farms and cow pastures. Most of the jungle within 80 kilometers of Iquitos is secondary forest, but dolphins, monkeys, and birds can still be seen. The jungle gets more interesting the farther away you travel. **Reserva Nacional Pacaya Samiria** (12 hours upstream) and the **Reserva Comunal Tamshiyacu Tahuayo** (4–6 hours) have wildlife and pristine jungle comparable to Parque Nacional Manu in Peru's southern Amazon.

One advantage that this jungle region has over Peru's southern Amazon is that even during the rainy season, it typically only rains in the afternoon, so lodges can be visited year-round. It's also the only place in Peru where pink river dolphins live. There is a high-water season, however, between January and June, when the Amazon rises 15 meters and floods much of the surrounding forest. Guides say there are more birds during these months, though mammals are easiest to see during the low-water months of July–December when they hang out on the muddy riverbanks. The number of monkeys seems to hold steady year-round.

The land that does not become flooded is called terra firma or *restinga* and has different animals. Typical birds in a flooded forest include flycatchers, tanagers, woodcreepers, kingfishers, finches, woodpeckers, parrots, macaws, and all species of cotingas. Because there is more food in a nonflooded forest, there is a greater variety of mammals and reptiles and different birds, including antbirds, manakins, curassows, guans, foliage cleaners, and all species of woodcreepers and woodpeckers. To see the greatest range of wildlife and birds, choose lodges that have access to both flooded forest and terra firma.

Competition is intense among the jungle outfits in Iquitos, and discounts are sometimes handed out to those who make their reservation in town, as opposed to over the Internet. If you come into town without a reservation, use the agencies, lodges, and guides recommended in this book and, when in doubt, consult the Iperú or Dircetur office listed.

RECREATION
Reserva Nacional Pacaya Samiria

One of the most pristine areas of Peru's northern Amazon is the Reserva Nacional Pacaya Samiria, an immense wedge of flooded rainforest between the Ucayali and Marañón Rivers. At just over two million hectares, it is still Peru's largest nature reserve. Its vast network of lakes, lagoons, swamps, and wetlands harbors many endangered animals, with big chances for spotting wildlife rivaling that in Parque Nacional Manu, though there are no lodges in the reserve.

Commonly seen animals in the reserve include huge Amazon manatees, tapirs, gray and pink river dolphins, black and white caimans, giant otters, at least 12 types of monkeys, the *paiche* fish, and hundreds of aquatic birds. The best times to visit the park are the low-water months July–December, when animals can often be spotted on the riverbanks. The reserve began in the 1940s in an effort to save the endangered *paiche*. After biologists realized its world-class biodiversity, the present reserve was officially established by the Peruvian government in 1972. More than 30,000 colonists and indigenous inhabitants live inside the reserve, including Cocama, Huitoto, Bora, and Yagua Indians.

Visitors to Pacaya Samiria require a guide, a US$33 entrance fee, and at least five days, whether you motor the 300 kilometers upriver from Iquitos (15–18 hours) or downriver from Yurimaguas (10 hours). Because there are no lodges in the reserve itself, options range from deluxe cruises to rustic camping trips. Trips usually travel up the Río Ucayali to the town

IQUITOS JUNGLE

of Requena and then enter the heart of the reserve through the Canal de Puinahua and the Río Pacaya. Generally speaking, this southern side of the reserve has more wildlife than the northern area along the Río Samiria.

A fast access point for the reserve is **Yurimaguas,** which lies two hours from Tarapoto. Cargo boats that leave here most afternoons chug down the northern border of the park for nearly two days. The fringes of the park, however, have been heavily impacted by colonists, and the more pristine areas can now

only be reached by a two- to three-day canoe journey inside the reserve. In the middle of the first night after leaving Yurimaguas, cargo boats stop in the small village of **Lagunas.** From here it is possible to contract a local guide and a canoe for about US$30 per day, though there are no guarantees on the quality of service. A surer bet is to set up a guide and transport in Tarapoto through either Puerto Palmeras resort or adventure guide César Reategui. From Lagunas, a half-hour *mototaxi* ride will take you to the headwaters of the Río

THE AMAZON

VISITING AMAZON VILLAGES

© SERGIO SCHABELMAN

the small village of Esperanza on the Tahuayo River

If your Iquitos tour operator says the package may include a visit to a native community, you should know what to expect. "Native" these days means a highly staged experience, where Yagua or Bora Indians emerge in grass skirts, explain a few aspects of village life, do a quick song and dance, and then try to sell their handicrafts. Some foreigners feel awkward with the situation. But before misjudging or making assumptions, here's a review of the pros and cons of such experiences.

There are few remote tribes left in the Amazon, and tourists, missionaries, and even anthropologists should frankly leave them alone. On the other hand, the indigenous communities who have chosen to contact the Western world are extremely glad to have the extra money that comes from tourism. For them, it is an important means of acquiring the cash to buy city items such as sugar, salt, gasoline, and medicine, which otherwise they simply could not afford.

The benefits of tourism for these people are even clearer with the visits to the mestizo or mixed-blood towns that have sprouted up along tributaries of the Amazon. Many of them began three or four decades ago with a few thatched huts but now boast soccer fields and schools. Many are close to lodges that employ villagers or have Indian markets that are visited by tourists. These new sources of tourism income have helped change local economies and lessen the prevalence of game hunting.

Amazon visitors should choose lodges that employ local villagers with fair wages and are actively involved in improving the quality of life for nearby villages. It is also a good idea to carry Peruvian *soles*, and not dollars, as the dollar has been dropping alongside the Peruvian *sol* in recent years. Dollars are also hard to exchange in the Amazon, and done so only at a steep discount in Iquitos or other cities.

© SERGIO SCHABELMAN

a village *shamana* (spiritual medicine healer) on the Tahuayo River

Samiria. From here, it is a three-day paddle to Laguna Pastococha, a huge oxbow lake teeming with wildlife. Fewer tourists enter the park via this route, so this is more of a wilderness experience. The farther you go, the more you are likely to see.

Camping and canoeing through the reserve is an amazing experience with the right equipment and a good operator. When combined with a stay at a community-based lodge, it is one of the best ways to understand the rhythms of life in a flooded forest.

Reserva Nacional Allpahuayo Mishana

Created in 2008, this national reserve encompasses 58,068 hectares of rainforest, protecting the scarce white-sand forests, exceedingly rare in Peru, and flooded forests by the Réo Nanay. Allpahuayo Mishana is famous for its variety of soil types, from white quartz sands to red clays, which makes it a very biodiverse spot in the Amazon.

Located 23 kilometers south of Iquitos, aside the highway to Nauta, this protected area has surprisingly high numbers of flora and fauna despite being surrounded by farms. At least four new species of birds have been discovered in the reserve, including the ancient antwren, mishana tyrannulet, allpahuayo antbird, and the northern chestnut-tailed antbird. Allpahuayo Mishana also contains other protected primate species, including the collared titi monkey and equatorial saki.

RIVER CRUISE AGENCIES

Cruises on the Amazon are a great option for those who are lured to the romance of traveling by boat on the world's largest river and want to indulge themselves in deluxe comfort. Some boats bear an uncanny resemblance to Mississippi paddleboats without the paddle but with air-conditioning, such as the Jungle Expedition boats, while others are more sophisticated vessels with a lounge-like atmosphere and a minimalist touch, such as the Aqua or Delfín boats. The most popular trips are up-river to the Reserva Nacional Pacaya Samiria, where passengers disembark for walks into the jungle and village visits. The smaller boats can enter shallow rivers where more wildlife can be seen. It is hard to see much wildlife from a boat deck, apart from dolphins and birds.

◖ Aqua Expeditions

The ultimate luxury cruise experience in the Amazon is only possible onboard the M/V *Aqua* (U.S. tel. 866/603-3687, www.aquaexpeditions.com, three nights starting at US$2,250, seven nights starting at US$5,250), a 12-suite vessel exquisitely designed by Peruvian architect and designer Jordi Puig. Minimalistic decor and a sober elegance made this river cruise a floating five-star boutique hotel. A second ship is currently being built, the M/V *Aria,* to be launched in April 2011.

The voyages on the *Aqua* depart year-round out of Iquitos, offering three-, four-, and seven-day itineraries to Reserva Nacional Pacaya Samiria. The suites feature large panoramic windows and en suite sitting areas, all with air-conditioning, and with available interconnection up to four—ideal for families. The Aria will be slightly larger, with 16 stylishly designed suites accommodating 32 passengers. It will also feature an outdoor Jacuzzi, an exercise room, and a reference library. All meals on board are highlighted by fresh, delicious Peruvian fare created in partnership with Pedro Miguel Schiaffino, one of Peru's top 10 chefs. Complimentary South American wines are paired with dinners each evening.

GreenTracks

After a 15-year partnership, GreenTracks, a Colorado-based ecotourism agency, has recently taken over the classic riverboat company Amazon Tours & Cruises. GreenTracks (U.S. tel. 800/423-2791, information@amazontours.net, www.amazontours.net, seven days/six nights US$1,995 pp) continues to maintain the quality of trips given by Amazon Tours & Cruises. It offers midlevel air-conditioned cruises, though its boats are not as luxurious as those of Jungle Expeditions. All-inclusive tours begin and end with an airport pickup and include good food, cabins with private baths, excellent guides, and a full program of activities.

GreenTracks constantly adapts its itinerary to take advantage of the activity of different wildlife, but the basic trip includes early-morning canoe trips to see monkeys, hoatzin viewing, a visit to a local village, and, of course, some lounging on the boat deck. Group size ranges 8–12, and cabins sleep 2–3 people. Basic GreenTracks cruises are led by a trained naturalist guide, and the company also offers zoologist-led trips for US$2,195. Reservations must be made from abroad.

Dawn on the Amazon

After a career in Indiana farming, Bill Grimes left the United States for a leisurely life on the Amazon, and he arrived in style with his new cruise boat company Dawn on the Amazon (Malecón Tarapacá 185, tel. 065/22-3730, www.dawnontheamazon.com, US$144–289 pp per day). Bill has built two tropical hardwood boats whose carved beams constantly catch the eye of travelers, and whose elegance even piqued the curiosity of a Peruvian reality TV show, which filmed a series on the boats. The simpler *Dawn I* is an open-air boat that can be contracted for day trips or adventure overnights. For the day trip, Bill sets up chairs in the boat's main hull. For the overnights, he strings up hammocks or lays down mattresses. The luxurious *Dawn III* boat is best for multiday excursions and has all the comforts of a modern hotel: private rooms, double beds, and lots of space to move around.

Bill contracts his boats to private parties and will arrange trip itineraries to the travelers' interests, be it freshwater fishing, the national reserves, or visiting local villages. All trips, regardless of their length, provide food and cover entrance fees. Bill accompanies most of his highly professional trips, and his enthusiasm for the Amazon is contagious.

Jungle Expeditions

Jungle Expeditions (Quiñones 1980, tel. 065/26-1583, www.junglex.com) cruises the Amazon with six elegant, five-star boats that look as if they were transported right out of the 19th century. Nine-day tours of the Pacaya Samiria reserve start at US$2,800 pp and include deluxe air-conditioned cabins, professional guides, and gourmet meals served in a grand dining room. During the evening, drinks are served on the upper canopy deck. The trips spend a night or two at La Posada Lodge, the company's upscale rest stop on Río Marañón, with the opportunity to visit both flooded and terra firma forest. The company offers a range of other trips as well to the south of Iquitos. Jungle Expeditions only accepts passengers through its Lima booking office or the U.S.-based International Expeditions (tel. 800/643-4734, www.internationalexpeditions.com).

JUNGLE LODGES

Though more expensive than Peru hotels of the same category, jungle lodges are an excellent deal when you consider that transport, English-speaking guide, food, lodging, and a full range of activities are included in the price.

THE AMAZON

© SERGIO SCHABELMAN

village woman doing laundry on the Tahuayo River

In general, you get what you pay for, and the better guides tend to work at the more expensive lodges. Because the main cost of any lodge is gasoline for the outboard motor, the lodges farther away from Iquitos become progressively more expensive but offer the chance to see a wider array of animals.

Explorama

Founded by U.S. anthropologists Peter Jenson and Marjorie Smith in 1964, Explorama (La Marina 340, tel. 065/25-2530 or 800/707-5275, www.explorama.com) has grown into a large, highly professional organization, with five lodges, great cooking, huge boats, and some of the Amazon's best guides. As a bonus, all of the lodges offer access to both flooded and terra firma forest. Explorama's claim to fame is one of the longest canopy walkways in the world, a half kilometer of continuous hanging bridges suspended between more than a dozen giant trees. At 35 meters off the ground, the walkway is an excellent way to spot birds and see tremendous jungle vistas.

Explorama's **Ceiba Tops Luxury Lodge** (two days/one night US$270 pp) is 40 kilometers downriver from Iquitos on the north shore of the Amazon. With modern, air-conditioned bungalows, WiFi access, a hammock house, swimming pool with a slide, and a huge dining room and full bar, it qualifies as the only resort along Peru's Amazon River. Activities include nature walks through the lodge's 40 hectares of old-growth forest, bird-watching, and village visits. This lodge is a good option for people who don't really want to rough it. With Explorama's fast boat, it can be reached in 45 minutes from Iquitos, but the preferred large group option is the *Amazon Queen,* a luxury riverboat with a bar and sightseeing deck.

Explorama Lodge (three days/two nights US$365 pp) is 80 kilometers downriver from Iquitos near the Amazon's junction with the Río Napo, surrounded by large portions of primary rainforest. It was built in 1964 and is the oldest of the lodges. After undergoing an upgrade, all 55 palm-thatched jungle rooms have private bathroom facilities. But the lodge has kept its genuine taste with covered walkways lit by kerosene lamps, the hammock house, great food, and the Tahuampa Bar with excellent cocktails.

ExplorNapo Lodge (five days/four nights

US$950 pp), with similar accommodations to those at Explorama Lodge, is 160 kilometers from Iquitos on a tributary of the Río Napo. It provides access to Explorama's Sucusari Reserve and is a 45-minute walk from the canopy walkway and the **ACTS Field Station** (one night/two days US$115 pp), where both scientists and travelers can stay. More than 85 species of birds can be spotted around here.

ExplorTambos Camp (one night/two days US$120 pp) is Explorama's most remote lodge, with a maximum capacity of 16 people, who sleep in individual shelters with mosquito netted beds. It's a two-hour hike into the rainforest from ExplorNapo Lodge, and due to its isolation offers the best possibilities for spotting wildlife.

◖ Tahuayo Lodge

Operated by Amazonia Expeditions, Tahuayo Lodge (10305 Riverburn Dr., Tampa, FL 33647, tel. 800/262-9669, www.perujungle.com, eight days/seven nights US$1,295) is 145 kilometers south from Iquitos on the Río Tahuayo, near the Área de Conservación Regional Comunal Tamshiyacu Tahuayo, where it has been operating since 1981, started by U.S. naturalist, Paul Beaver, author of the autobiographical book, *Diary of an Amazon Jungle Guide.*

Tamshiyacu Tahuayo is a communal reserve, created by the Peruvian government in 1991, to protect, among other species, the rare uakari monkey. Biologists have since recorded 500 bird species and exceptional levels of biodiversity in this area.

This lodge has 15 wooden rooms, some with private bathrooms. Amenities include a dining room where very good food is served, a hammock hall, a small library, and a laboratory with a terrarium that contains tarantulas and other creepy crawlies. There is access to both flooded and terra firma forest in the area, and a controlled zip line that allows guests to cruise safely through the canopy at 35 meters off the ground. With a good team of experienced guides, a wide variety of activities can be done upon request; they are listed on the website.

© SERGIO SCHABELMAN

view from the Tahuayo Lodge on the Tahuayo River

A stay in Tahuayo Lodge can also include one or two days at the **Amazon Research Center** (formerly Jacamara Lodge), 45 minutes upstream of the Río Tahuayo, a stone's throw away from the reserve. Here, a **trail grid** has been completed covering almost 84 kilometers over an area of 400 hectares, with at least four different rainforest ecosystems. A vast amount of fauna can be spotted exploring this trail grid, including primates, birds, and small mammals.

Muyuna Amazon Lodge

At 140 kilometers upriver from Iquitos on the Río Yanayacu, Muyuna Amazon Lodge (Putumayo 163, tel. 065/24-2858, www.muyuna.com, three days/two nights US$414 pp) was founded in 1999 by a Peruvian couple, Analía and Percy Sánchez. Since then this lodge has developed a solid reputation for excellent guides, simple but comfortable rooms, and affordable rates. The lodge is nestled in an interesting swath of flooded forest that has several types of monkeys, a large variety of birds, caimans, sloths, pink dolphins, and a good chance of seeing a giant otter, armadillo, or porcupine. There are 2–6-bed bungalows with private bathrooms, and food is served buffet-style. Guides are well spoken and energetic, willing to make late-night forays into the jungle or spend time visiting the local community of San Juan, with which Muyuna has forged an excellent relationship. The lodge also has equipment to listen to mother dolphins whistle to their young.

Amazon Yarapa River Lodge

One of the best Amazon options is the Amazon Yarapa River Lodge (La Marina 124, Iquitos tel. 065/993-1172, U.S. tel. 315/952-6771, www.yarapa.com, four days/three nights US$800 s, US$1,400 d). This lodge, around the corner from the Reserva Nacional Pacaya Samiria on the pristine Río Yarapa, is surrounded by world-class jungle and oxbow lakes teeming with exotic birds, pink dolphins, sloths, and monkeys.

© RENÉE DEL GAUDIO AND ROSS WEHNER

Amazon Yarapa River Lodge

Along with Explorama, Amazon Yarapa River Lodge probably has the most experienced and eloquent guides in the Amazon, and they are absolutely relentless in their efforts to pinpoint as many species as possible. In a single morning we saw 30 bird species, including the rare Amazonian umbrella bird, which has a crest of black hair that earns it the nickname "the Elvis bird."

The lodge itself is a magnificent structure with huge bungalows with private bathrooms and private rooms with shared baths. Solar-powered electricity heats the showers. The food is excellent, consisting of fresh fish and a large range of salads, and there are nice small details—like icy towels after each jungle outing. The lodge has a good relationship with villages in the vicinity, and has even acquired the titles of nearby villages so that it can help villagers stop poachers and illegal hunters. There is also a green system for everything from local building materials to flush compost toilets.

As a sign of its success, the lodge has partnered with Cornell University, which has built an adjacent research station for the professors and students who visit here each year, along with groups from The Nature Conservancy. The lodge is entirely surrounded by flooded rainforest, but guests who stay a few days often make trips to remote areas of terra firma upstream.

Paseo Amazónicos

Another well-managed outfit that has been around since 1975 is Paseos Amazónicos (Pevas 246, tel. 065/23-1618, www.paseosamazonicos. com). It has excellent guides and three lodges, built in native style and purposefully left rustic with simple rooms and kerosene lamps. The lodges are listed from most comfortable to most adventurous.

Amazonas Sinchicuy Lodge (two days/ one night US$212 pp; four days/three nights US$419 pp) is located on the Río Sinchicuy, about 30 kilometers from Iquitos. It has 32 pleasant wooden rooms with mosquito screens, thatched verandas, private bathrooms, and kerosene lamps.

The lodge organizes a visit to a local shaman, who gives a talk on medicinal plants and is recommended for those interested in ayahuasca experiences. There are also visits to Yagua villages close to the lodge. There isn't much wildlife in the area other than dolphins and birds.

Tambo Yanayacu Lodge (three days/two nights US$320 pp) is on the shores of the Río Yanayacu, about 60 kilometers from Iquitos in a patch of flooded rainforest. It has 10 wooden rooms with private bathrooms, kerosene lamps, and a simple dining room where all food is cooked over an open hearth. There are many birds here, and at night the stars are reflected in the black, still waters alongside the lodge. It is a magical place that can be visited as part of a joint package with Sinchicuy Lodge (four days/three nights US$400 pp).

Tambo Amazónico (four days/three nights US$383 pp) is upriver from Iquitos in flooded rainforest along the pristine Río Yarapa. It is a rustic campsite used as a stop for backpacker excursions into Reserva Nacional Pacaya Samiria. There are two bunkrooms, each with 10 beds covered with mosquito netting. The services are basic: cold-water showers, kerosene lamps, and outhouses.

Cumaceba Lodge

A good option for a one-night stay is **Cumaceba** (Putumayo 184, tel. 065/23-2229, www. cumaceba.com, two days/one night US$114 pp), which is 35 kilometers downstream of Iquitos. The thatched lodge has nice rooms with private bathrooms, cold water, and kerosene lamps, along with a dining area, hammock hall, and plans for a swimming pool. The lodge's packed, one-night, two-day tour includes a walk through a patch of primary rainforest, caiman spotting, bird-watching, piraña fishing, and a visit to a Yagua village. To make up for a general lack of wildlife, guests visit a nearby family that keeps monkeys, turtles, sloths, parrots, and a pet anaconda.

Heliconia Amazon River Lodge

Heliconia Amazon River Lodge (Ricardo

Palma 242, tel. 065/23-1959, www.amazon-riverexpeditions.com, three days/two nights US$180 pp) is owned by the same group that operates the Acosta and Victoria Regia Hotels in Iquitos. Heliconia, 80 kilometers downriver from Iquitos, is a good midrange resort with a comfortable lodge, rooms with private bath, and well-guided tours. Trips can be arranged and leave the same day.

Heliconia offers excellent river sportfishing programs that start from four days/three nights, at US$545 for 2–4 people, but can be extended as many days as you want. You are required to bring your fishing equipment, or else you can rent it for US$100 per person. One of the most valued river fish to catch is the *tucunaré* or peacock bass, but other catches include *pacaya* (giant wolf fish), silver arowana, and pike cichlid, among others.

Pacaya Samiria Amazon Lodge

The Pacaya Samiria Amazon Lodge (Raimondi 378, tel. 065/23-4128, www.pacayasamiria.com.pe, three days/two nights US$765 pp) is 190 kilometers southwest of Iquitos—one hour upriver from Nauta on the banks of the Río Marañón—just past the village of San Isidro, on the outskirts of the Reserva Nacional Pacaya Samiria. The lodge is surrounded by high-ground secondary forest, but a good hour-long walk will lead you into primary forest. Bungalows have a porch, private bathroom, shower, and hammocks, and there is electricity in the evenings. There is a small library with interesting books about birds, plants, and mammals of the rainforest. The lodge is clean and well run and offers recommended camping trips into the reserve.

The lodge offers Jungle Programs, such as a six-day/five-night visit into the Pacaya Samiria Reserve (US$980 pp, minimum two), which features exploring along the Río Yanayacu and camping for three days in tents along the river beaches. Other activities include trekking primary forest, bird-watching, swimming, piraña fishing, canoe rides, and nocturnal excursions. Bird-watching Programs are also available, starting at three days/two nights (US$765 pp), all the way to nine days/eight nights (US$2,770 pp), this last one combining a three-day visit to Pacaya Samiria and a two-day visit to Allpahuayo Mishana.

NASCA AND THE DESERT COAST

Peru's southern desert coast, sucked dry by the frigid Humboldt current, is drier and less populated than the north coast. Rivers here often disappear into the sand before reaching the Pacific Ocean. To solve their water problem, ancient cultures such as the Paracas, Nasca, and Chincha moved inland and built aqueducts from the mountains. The Panamerican Highway follows the ancient inland migration, veering away from the coast toward the towns of Ica and Nasca, and in the process isolates a huge chunk of spectacular, wild desert wedged against the Pacific. A handful of qualified guides with four-wheel-drive trucks are now leading travelers into this ochre lunar land. Dunes for sandboarding, star-filled nights, the spiritual stillness of the desert, and the world's greatest collection of marine fossils,

including giant teeth from a gigantic extinct shark known as megalodon, all can be unveiled in the sea of sand.

On the northern edge of this desert is the Reserva Nacional de Paracas, a series of cliff bluffs that drop to long desert beaches teeming with 200 bird species, sea lions, seals, and the endangered Humboldt penguin. Camping, hiking, or mountain biking here is an unforgettable and safe experience.

Just up the coast at El Carmen, thousands of slaves from Africa stumbled off boats in the 17th and 18th centuries to work in the sugarcane plantations. These days, El Carmen is a center of Afro-Peruvian dance and music. Down the road is Hacienda San José, severely destroyed during the 2007 earthquake and now being restored into a beautiful Private

© MICHAEL TWEDDLE, PROMPERU

THE DESERT COAST

HIGHLIGHTS

◖ Reserva Nacional de Paracas: This coastline of rugged cliffs and islands is a good place to see a wide array of birds and marine mammals and, in the process, camp or hike amid the spectacular surroundings (page 279).

◖ Islas Ballestas: Launching off the desert coast into the brilliant blue waters of Peru's Pacific, you wouldn't think you were off to see a vibrant population of sea lions, seals, and penguins. But the Islas Ballestas, protected by the national reserve, are full of dozens of sea animals and hundreds of birds (page 281).

◖ Pisco Bodegas: Ica's wineries welcome visitors with tours, followed by hearty home-cooked Peruvian food, port wines, and a shot of pisco to wash it all down (page 288).

◖ Ica Desert: This ancient ocean floor, heaved upward by tectonic activity, is littered with marine fossils, sculpted hills, and towering dunes. Those who venture into this remote sandscape return dazzled by the experience (page 290).

◖ Nasca Lines: There are certain mysteries, like huge astronauts and hummingbirds etched onto the desert plain, that you have to see to believe (page 299).

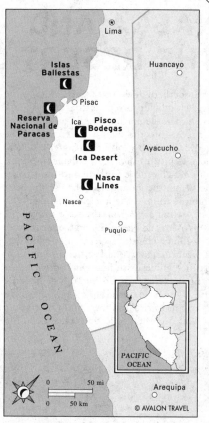

LOOK FOR ◖ TO FIND RECOMMENDED SIGHTS, ACTIVITIES, DINING, AND LODGING.

Collection hotel of the Casa Andina chain, opening in early 2011.

The highlight of the south coast, however, is the Nasca Lines, giant enigmatic drawings of hummingbirds, whales, and mythical beings etched onto the desert floor and surrounded by a maze of lines and triangles. Though theories range from extraterrestrial landing strips to sacred water symbols, the riddle of the Nasca Lines remains unsolved. The Nasca people,

who supposedly made the lines, produced some of the finest ceramics and textiles in pre-Columbian Peru, which are on display in excellent museums in Paracas, Ica, and Nasca.

PLANNING YOUR TIME

More travelers are hopping aboard a bus for at least one leg of this entertaining journey to and from Lima. If you have the time, and are interested by what you read here, points at the south

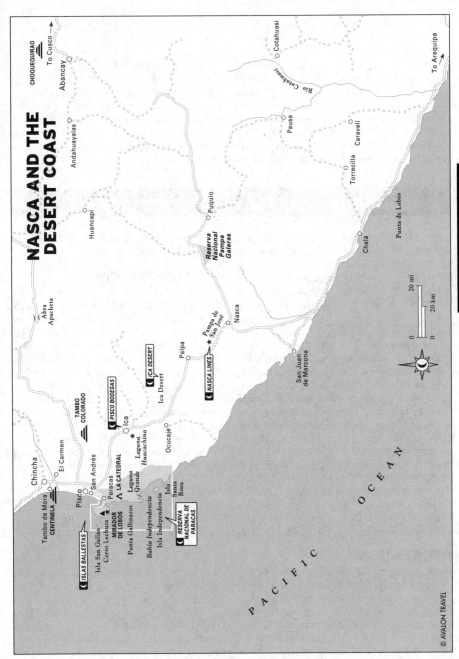

NASCA AND THE DESERT COAST

CHOQUEQUIRAO
To Cusco →
Abancay
Cotahuasi
To Arequipa

Río Cotahuasi

Andahuaylas

Pausa

Huancapi

Caravelí

Torrecilla

Puquio

Reserva
Nacional
Pampa
Galeras

Punta de Lobos

Abra
Apacheta

Chala

20 mil

20 km

Pampa de
San José

★ NASCA LINES

Nasca

Palpa

ICA DESERT

Ica Desert

San Juan
de Marcona

PISCO BODEGAS

TAMBO
COLORADO

○ Ica

LA CATEDRAL

Laguna
Huacachina ★

Chincha
El Carmen
Paracas
Ocucaje

Tambo de Mora
CENTINELA

Pisco
San Andrés

Laguna
Grande

Isla San Gallán
Cerro Lechuza
MIRADOR
DE LOBOS

Punta Gallinazos

Isla
Santa
Rosa

ISLAS BALLESTAS

Bahía Independencia

Isla Independencia

RESERVA
NACIONAL DE
PARACAS

PACIFIC   OCEAN

© AVALON TRAVEL

coast can make for quick, easy visits—with the exception of a four-wheel drive desert safari in the Ica desert, for which you need 3–5 days.

Lunahuaná is two hours from Lima and makes for a good escape with nearby rafting and hiking. Chincha is three hours away from Lima, boasting good food and pisco, with new hotels. Pisco, despite being still very much devastated by the 2007 earthquake, can still be a mid-budget place to stay in order to explore Ballestas Islands and the Reserva Nacional de Paracas. Ica's main attractions are its artisan-made pisco bodegas, which you can visit in a day or two.

Nasca is roughly the halfway point in the 20-hour journey between Lima and Cusco and is well worth the stop—there is no way to really comprehend the lines in the desert without flying over them. If you are short on time and prefer to fly, the Nasca Lines can also be seen in a one-day, round-trip package from Lima.

Lunahuaná

This relaxed town at the edge of the **Río Cañete** is an adventure sports center two hours (184 kilometers) from Lima. It's high enough up a desert canyon to enjoy fog-free, sunny days. Lunahuaná's claim to fame is its rafting and kayaking, which push Class III–IV during the high-water months December–April and are mellower but still fun the rest of the year. There are good trails for hiking and mountain biking in the area, and paragliders zip through the air during the town's annual sports festival, held the first week of March.

About 10 kilometers downriver from Cañete is **Incawasi,** a well-preserved Inca compound with two squares, storage spaces, and fine stone buildings that were probably elite residences. Archaeologists believe the compound was a military base for conquering Cañete, one of Peru's last coastal valleys to fall to the Inca. There are also about 10 wineries in the area that make pisco and *cachina,* a fortified wine. The best time to visit these is during the *vendimia,* or harvest, between January and March.

RECREATION
Agencies charge US$10–25 for a full day of rafting, including lunch, on the Río Cañete. There are some real hairball agencies operating on the river, so make sure that the rafts are in good shape and the guides experienced. A recommended local agency is **HemiRiver Rafting Co.** (Grau 255, tel. 01/534-2339 or cell 01/9965-8635, www.hemiriver.com), run by Michael Torres.

ACCOMMODATIONS
There are about 10 hostels in town, the best of which are **Hostal Casuarinas** (Grau 295, tel. 01/284-1045, US$15 s or d), **Hostal Los Andes** (Los Andes, tel. 01/284-1041, US$15 s or d), and **Garden Hotel** (a few km before Lunahuaná on main road, tel. 01/284-1308, US$18 s or d), which has a nice country setting. There are a few three-star hotels with pools in Lunahuaná that all cost around US$40 for a double, including **Rio Alto** (Cañete-Lunahuaná Hwy. Km 38.5, Lima tel. 01/463-5490, http://rioaltohotel.com), **Embassy** (Lima tel. 01/472-3525), and **Fortaleza del Inca** (Anexo de Paullo Km 31.5, www.fortalezainca.com).

FOOD
The best restaurants in town are **El Pueblo** (Grau 408, tel. 01/284-1195, 8:30 A.M.–11 P.M. daily, US$8–10) and **Incawasi** (in Hotel Embassy, tel. 01/472-3525, 7 A.M.–8 P.M. daily, US$6–8). In Cañete, recommended restaurants are **Muelle 56** (Bolognesi 156) and **El Piloto** (Panamericana Km 138, tel. 01/581-3184, US$5–7).

GETTING THERE
Lunahuaná is 42 kilometers off the Panamericana via a road that branches

inland at the village Cañete (Km 142 of the Panamericana), which sits at the foot of a valley famous for its surrounding fields of asparagus, cotton, and tangerines. *Colectivos* leave frequently from Cañete for the one-hour drive to Lunahuaná. The dirt road continues inland up and over the Andes, passing the snow-covered Cordillera Yauyos and spectacular emerald lakes en route to Huancayo. An **ETAS** bus leaves Cañete every morning for this 12- or 13-hour drive and picks up in Lunahuaná.

Most major bus companies headed south drop passengers in Cañete, from which *colectivos* run to Imperial, five kilometers up the dirt road. **ETTUSA** (Montevideo 752 in Lima, tel. 01/428-0025) has direct daily buses to Imperial, from which *colectivos* leave frequently for Lunahuaná (US$0.75, 45 minutes).

Chincha and El Carmen

Roughly three hours away from Lima stands Chincha, as the center of Afro-Peruvian culture. But then if that is true, El Carmen is its soul. Most travelers blow right by these two towns on their way south to Paracas, Ica, or Nasca. But El Carmen, 10 kilometers off the highway past Km 202, is worth a stop, because it is the cradle of Afro-Peruvian dance and music. This laid-back village was the birth town of Amador Ballumbrosio Mosquera (1933–2009), the talented dancer and musician who sparked the renaissance of this artistic expression in the 1970s with the help of Spanish-Peruvian rock musician, DJ, and guitarist Micky González.

Many of Ballumbrosio's children continue the tradition today with a variety of dancing including *zapateo* (tap dancing) and percussive music that involves seven instruments: *bongo* and *tumba* (two types of drums), *quijada* (a burro's jaw with rattling teeth), *cajón* (a box that is sat upon and drummed with the hands, now used also by flamenco musicians), *cincero* (a large bell), *castañuela* (castanets), and *cabaza* (a hand-held sheet metal drum with chains that rattle when twisted).

El Carmen, along with Chincha 15 kilometers away, erupts into all-night celebrations of music and dance several times a year, attracting Limeños for 24-hour partying and dancing. Lodging prices double or even triple during these parties—make reservations well in advance or, as many do, dance all night and take a bus onward in the morning. Outside the festivals in Chincha and El Carmen, the Ballumbrosio family puts on recommended shows of music and Afro-Peruvian dance, called *baile de los negritos* on most weekends (US$60 per group, plus home-cooked lunch for US$9 pp). You can also just stop by the home of this warm, generous family. Something is

African slaves were imported into Peru during the 17th and 18th centuries, and their music and dance legacy is alive and well in the towns of El Carmen and Chincha.

© RENÉE DEL GAUDIO AND ROSS WEHNER

Hacienda San José, one of Peru's best-preserved colonial plantations, was damaged in the 2007 earthquake, but will be restored and opened as a new Casa Andina hotel in 2011.

always going on, and the family even offers basic lodging to music students and inquisitive souls who simply want to linger longer.

There are plenty of other things to see in the area. At the top of the list used to be **Hacienda San José,** one of several plantations in the area that imported black slaves from Africa, via Spain, to work in the cotton and sugarcane fields. After the 2007 earthquake, the Cilloniz family, proprietors of this century-old hacienda, shut it down. **Casa Andina,** the Peruvian hotel chain, is restoring it and hopes to open it up as a Private Collection hotel in 2011.

Near the coast there are the ruins of **Huaca Centinela** and **Tambo de Mora,** which formed the capital of the Ica-Chincha culture, which was incorporated into the Inca empire in the late 14th century. The adobe ruins, once painted a dazzling white and covered with friezes of fish and birds, are badly deteriorated but offer commanding views over the Pacific Ocean on one side and Inca roads that wind up the valley on the other.

Grocio Prado, a small village just north from Chincha along the Panamericana, is a good place to see traditional basket weaving, and farther along there is the long wide beach at Jahuay. Finally, there are several pisco bodegas near Chincha, including **Tabernero,** right off the highway at Chincha, and **Naldo Navarro,** in Sunampe. All these places can be reached by inexpensive taxis from Chincha (US$20 for one day) or through tours offered by hotels in Chincha.

ENTERTAINMENT AND EVENTS

The biggest festivals in the Chincha–El Carmen area are **Verano Negro,** also known as **La Vendimia,** at the end of February/beginning of March; the festival of **Virgen del Carmen** in the middle of July; El Carmen's festival in late August; and an elaborate Christmas celebration that begins in mid-December and ends January 6. For more information, see www.perutravels.net.

THE FORGOTTEN CHINCHA

During the time of the Inca conquest, the most flourishing culture on the coast, apart from the Chimú in the north, was the Chincha. This kingdom rose out of two millennia of cultures that included the Paracas, Nasca, and Huari. The Chincha kingdom spread from Río Cañete at least as far south as Nasca, but its center was Tambo de Mora and Centinela, near present-day Chincha. These ceremonial centers were once painted dazzling white and covered with friezes of stylized birds, fish, and geometric designs. Though badly deteriorated, the huge adobe mounds still offer commanding views over the Pacific Ocean on one side and Inca roads that wind up the valley on the other.

There is an interesting legend, which seems to have some truth in it, about the Inca conquest of the Ica Valley, just south of Chincha. After peaceful overtures had been rejected by Chincha leader Aranvilca, Inca Pachacútec sent his son Inca Túpac Yupanqui to take the valley by force. Marching at the head of his troops, however, the young Inca was struck by the beauty of a daughter of Aranvilca's, named Chumbillalla. Túpac Yupanqui called off the invasion and began courting the princess, who explained her people's lack of water for farming. The Inca immediately threw his 40,000 soldiers at an ambitious scheme to build an aqueduct from the mountains through the desert, which, legend says, was completed in 10 days. This aqueduct, known as the Achirina del Inca, still serves as Ica's lifeline. It runs 30 kilometers through the desert from Molinos to Tate and irrigates 11,000 hectares of fields planted in asparagus, cotton, pecans, and grapes.

Though building a major canal in 10 days seems like a stretch, there is well-documented evidence of the grandeur of the Chincha. In his *Crónica* of 1533, Pedro de Cieza de León comments that "as soon as the Inca had finished their conquest, they took from [the Chincha] many customs and copied their clothing and imitated them in other things." The famous map made by Diego Rivero of Peru in 1529, three years before the conquest, marked the location of the Chincha kingdom but made no mention of the Inca. There were at least two litters carried into the square of Cajamarca on November 16, 1532, the date of the fateful first meeting between the Inca and the Spaniards. One litter held Inca Atahualpa and the other the lord of Chincha. The two litters were so luxurious that the Spaniards became momentarily confused as to who was the real Inca. In the ensuing slaughter, the lord of Chincha was killed, something that caused Atahualpa deep sadness.

The end of the Chincha kingdom is heartbreaking. By 1550, after Hernando Pizarro had been given Chincha as his *repartimiento,* the valley's population had plummeted five to one, according to Cieza de León. Because of the ravages of European diseases, enslavement by the Spaniards, and profound culture shock, the citizens of the Chincha kingdom, like coastal Indians across Peru, appear to have simply lost the will to live, as English historian John Hemming asserts in his *Conquest of the Incas.* Chincha was mentioned by Spanish Dominican priest Bartolomé de las Casas in *A Short Account of the Destruction of the Indies,* his long letter written in the 1560s to Spanish King Charles V about Spanish brutality. Las Casas estimated that the population in the Chincha Valley, estimated at 40,000 when the Spanish arrived, had dropped to a mere 1,000. By that time, the famous centers of Centinela and Tambo de Mora were already in ruins.

ACCOMMODATIONS

Chincha has dozens of hotels, but none of them seem a very good value for what they offer, especially considering the noise and confusion of the city itself. The three excellent options nowadays are outside the city, either La Estancia Sur, the newer Casa Andina Classic–Chincha Sausal opened in 2009, or the beachside Wakama Eco Playa.

US$10-25

In Chincha, **Hotel Princess** (Lima 109, tel. 056/26-1031, hphotelprincess@yahoo.com, US$20 s, US$27 d) has a pleasant brick interior with polished wood floors and prints of French impressionist paintings on the walls. Amenities include comfy beds, cable TV, WiFi, garage, restaurant, hot water, laundry, and nice furniture.

Hostal Condado (Santo Domingo 188, tel. 056/26-1216, hostalelcondado@speedy.com. pe, US$23 s, US$25 d with breakfast) is a good value for those who don't mind the sparkling white tiles running from floor to ceiling. The rooms include porches with skylights, cable TV, and bathrooms with plenty of hot water. Some even have a whirlpool tub, and guests are allowed to use the pool at a sister hostel near Sunampe, at Km 195 of the Panamericana Sur (tel. 056/26-1424).

US$25-50

One of the more pleasant lodging options, despite being a bit overpriced, is **Lega's Hostal** (Benavides 826, tel. 056/26-1984, legashostal-chincha@hotmail.com, US$34 s, US$41 d), a miniature walled compound with modern rooms, terrace, gardens, cozy bar, and small pool. The rooms are large, decorated with pastels and flowers, and include cable TV, WiFi, tables, and nice bathrooms. It is on the Panamericana Sur, next door to the Soyuz bus station and a five-minute walk from the center.

Five minutes before arriving to Chincha from Lima is **La Estancia Sur** (Panamericana Sur Km 192.5, tel. 056/26-6148, www.laestanciasur.com, US$43 s, US$64 d with breakfast), a beautiful hotel with five hectares of green areas. Despite the fact that the rooms are built with brick, they have been painted white and decorated with a rustic colonial style with comfy beds and bathrooms. Facilities include swimming pool, bar, outdoor terrace, pool, and a children's area with a trampoline, ping-pong tables, and a children's size pool. They also arrange tours around Chincha.

Over US$50

One of Casa Andina's newest hotels is **[Casa Andina Classic-Chincha Sausal** (Panamericana Sur Km 197.5, tel. 056/26-2451, www.casa-andina.com, US$98 s or d,

US$120 superior, with breakfast buffet), the old Hotel Sausal, which has been completely refurbished, keeping its ample gardens and swimming pool, plus a bar, billiards room, karaoke salon, and other amenities typical of this national hotel chain. There are 50 rooms, all with air-conditioning, WiFi, and minibars in the superior rooms. This is, without doubt, the best hotel in the city.

If you want a place, literally, on the beach, **Wakama Eco Playa** (Panamericana Sur Km 178.5, Lima tel. 01/998-386-154, www.wakamaecoplaya.com, US$310 four-person cabin, US$570 eight-person cabin, Fri.–Sat.) is about 20 kilometers before Chincha. Once you get there, you will never want to wear shoes. Let your toes wiggle in the sand as you trek back and forth to your beachside hammock, as you stop by the bodega, and even as you set the table for dinner. There are 21 brilliantly colored beach bungalows built meters away from the beach, where the floors of the sitting and dining rooms are sand, and the service is spectacular. The owners of this place are the amazingly laid-back Peruvian couple Beto and Anabel Cillóniz and their children. The family has developed a wonderfully long list of activities: horseback riding, sunset hikes, oceanside massages, afternoon volleyball games, and evening bonfires with Afro-Peruvian music. It's the perfect balance between relaxation and fun. You do have to bring your own sheets and towels and an ice cooler. There is electricity 6:30 P.M.–midnight.

FOOD

Aside from the lunches offered by the Ballumbrosio family, there are few eating options in El Carmen. The exception is during festival times.

In Chincha, **El Batán** (Panamericana Sur Km 200, tel. 056/26-1967, 6:30 A.M.–11 P.M. Mon.–Sat., 6:30 A.M.–6 P.M. Sun.) may be next to a gas station, but the food is gourmet. Try a *cebiche*, a *tacu tacu*, or grilled sole, and if you sit in the sunny, walled-in patio, you can almost forget the highway traffic. Another great option is **Restaurant Chicharronería Lorena**

(Panamericana Sur Km 196.5, tel. 056/27-1549, 7 A.M.–5:30 P.M. daily, US$7–10). You'd be silly not to try the house specialty—*chicharrones* of course—but don't forget to accompany them with excellent tamales or *seco de arroz,* the local specialty.

INFORMATION AND SERVICES

Banks in Chincha with ATMs include **Scotiabank** (Plaza de Armas 194), **Banco de Crédito** (Castilla 195–185), and Interbank (Benavides 288). The **Serpost** post office is on the Plaza de Armas, as is the **police station** (tel. 056/22-7673). Chincha has several fast Internet places. Simply walk around the Plaza de Armas to find one. The hospital is south of the center on the Panamericana.

GETTING THERE

Most of the major bus companies stop in Chincha en route to Ica and Nasca, though **Soyuz** and **Ormeños** have the best and most frequent service. *Combis* leave the Panamericana in Chincha frequently for the 30-minute drive to El Carmen (US$1).

The Paracas Peninsula

THE DESERT COAST

This sledgehammer-shaped chunk of desert coastline jutting into the Pacific Ocean is surrounded by frigid waters of the Humboldt current, causing a rich upwelling of mineral waters. The rich waters feed phytoplankton, which in turn feed huge schools of anchovies, which in turn feed one of the world's largest collection of seabirds—about 216 resident and migratory species including the Andean condor—two types of sea lions, and the endangered Humboldt penguin.

From 1000 B.C. onward the area's rich waters also sustained the Paracas culture, which inhabited the surrounding coastline before being subsumed by the Nasca culture in A.D. 200. In 1925, a Peruvian archaeologist, Julio C. Tello, discovered 400 mummy bundles in an ancient cemetery on the peninsula. The bodies were preserved in the bone-dry climate and hidden by wind-blown sands. The most extraordinary discovery was the textiles wrapping each mummy, woven from cotton or camelid fiber and decorated with birds, fish, and other designs. They remain today the finest, and most richly decorated, textiles produced in pre-Columbian Peru.

The Reserva Nacional de Paracas was set up in 1975 to protect 335,000 hectares of this spectacular area from the peninsula south to **Bahía de la Independencia,** or Independence Bay. It is Peru's largest chunk of continuous protected coastline, and its main attractions include the Museo Julio C. Tello, which contains Paracas textiles, and **El Candelabro,** a huge hillside etching of a candelabra that has a mysterious origin.

But the reserve's main attractions are its desolation and extraordinary rugged beauty. It's like the coast of Oregon or Northern California, but with no trees, no people, and 10 times the marine life. Southwesterly ocean winds blast the Paracas coastline each afternoon and, together with the surf, have sculpted promontories with tunnels and odd shapes. Cooled by the ocean, these winds are warmed when they hit the sunbaked land and their capacity to hold water rises. This is why no rain falls on Paracas and much of the Peruvian coastline, even though fog blankets the area July–October with *garúa* because of a winter temperature inversion.

Although the late-afternoon winds can be a challenge, camping or mountain biking along this coastline is a once-in-a-life experience, highly recommended. It is not difficult at all to find a deserted beach, and the controlled access to the reserve makes this a safe place to camp overnight on a beach.

◖ RESERVA NACIONAL DE PARACAS

There is a road junction right after the control booth of the Reserva Nacional de Paracas

THE DESERT COAST

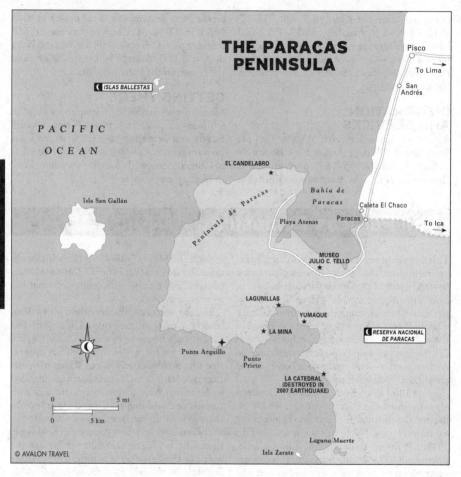

THE PARACAS PENINSULA

Pisco

To Lima

San Andrés

ISLAS BALLESTAS

PACIFIC

OCEAN

Isla San Gallán

EL CANDELABRO

Bahía de Paracas

Caleta El Chaco

Península de Paracas

Playa Atenas

Paracas

To Ica

MUSEO JULIO C. TELLO

LAGUNILLAS

YUMAQUE

LA MINA

RESERVA NACIONAL DE PARACAS

Punta Arquillo

Punto Prieto

LA CATEDRAL
(DESTROYED IN
2007 EARTHQUAKE)

Laguna Muerte

0   5 mi

0   5 km

© AVALON TRAVEL

Isla Zarate

(7 A.M.–6 P.M., US$2). The left road leads to the remote south coast beaches, which are anywhere from 30 minutes to three hours away on bumpy dirt roads. This road first passes a turnoff where there once used to be a rock formation known as **La Catedral** (The Cathedral), destroyed by the 2007 earthquake. The base of this million-year-old geological formation can still be seen. The road heads to Playón, the salt flats of Otuma, Mendieta, and **Bahía de la Independencia.** These are some of the more beautiful, less-visited beaches in the reserve and can be visited during a four-wheel expedition through the desert to Ica.

The paved road that leads straight from the control booth heads onto the peninsula. First stop is the museum, after a few kilometers, and, farther on, **Playa Atenas,** a combination of rocks and sand and a favorite windsurfing spot with its flat waters and strong afternoon winds. From Atenas a road leads to a huge etching in the hillsides, on the west side of the peninsula, similar at first glance to the Nasca Lines. Because it is of a candelabra, a rather European invention, archaeologists think pirates may have dug it into the hillside as a navigation aid. Visitors are prohibited from getting closer than 20 meters, and its huge shape, difficult to discern close up, can best be seen during a boat tour to Islas Ballestas.

At the museum an alternative dirt road leads to **Lagunillas,** which has a handful of restaurants—the best of which is **Tía Fela**—and two of Paracas's most beautiful (and, in the summer, crowded) beaches, **El Raspón** and **La Mina.** The road ends at **Punta Arquillo,** where there is a lookout over a rocky area crowded with sea lions, especially during mating season December–March.

MUSEO JULIO C. TELLO

The finest textiles produced in pre-Columbian Peru are on display at the Museo Julio C. Tello (7 A.M.–4 P.M. daily, US$2 in addition to park entrance). There are also ceramics, mummies, and an exhibit on how the Paracas people used boards and weights to change the shape of the skull according to a person's social status. The Paracas practiced trepanation, an early form of brain surgery whereby a disk was cut from the front of the cranium. Because of scar tissue, the trepanned skulls in the museum prove that patients survived this technique, which may have been used to treat mental disorders. Nearby are Cabezas Largas and Cerro Colorado, Paracas cemeteries that were excavated by Tello and are now covered with dirt to prevent looting.

◖ ISLAS BALLESTAS

These islands are finally protected under the newly created **Reserva Nacional de las Islas, Islotes y Puntas Guaneras,** a national reserve that protects all 33 islands and guano points along the Peruvian coast, including Ballestas. Though sea lions can be seen from Punta Arquillo lookout and other places around the reserve, visitors have a good chance of seeing dozens of sea lions, seals, and even a penguin or two during a four-hour boat tour of Islas Ballestas, the islands just to the north of the peninsula.

Hundreds of thousands of birds also roost on the islands, covering them with guano, which is another Quechuan word that's become commonly used by English speakers. These bird droppings contains 20 times more nitrogen than cow manure, and guano is a highly coveted fertilizer that sparked Peru's 1850–1870 guano rush. Nearly 10 million tons of the stuff was dug off the Islas Ballestas, along with the Islas Chincha seven kilometers to the north, lowering the islands' height by as much as 30 meters. These days the guano is removed in a sustainable fashion by the Peruvian government.

PISCO AND PARACAS

Paracas is also the name of what used to be a small village and now is pretty much a fancy middle-class beach town. A few meters north of Paracas is the small artisan fishing port of **El Chaco,** from where boats leave daily en route to Ballestas Islands.

Most travelers still end up staying in Pisco, a pushy little town near the highway that was almost completely destroyed during the earthquake of 2007. Three years later, pisqueños are learning to live with a city still in ruins that lives off tourism. Pisco's busiest evening spot is still Comercio, a pedestrian street that leads from the plaza and is lined with pizzerias and other restaurants. Pisco is 22 kilometers north from the reserve entrance.

Entertainment and Events

At Paracas, the only things happening at night are the lapping of waves and a few drinks being served at some beach restaurants. If you want something more classy and can afford it, simply buy alcohol from a bodega.

In Pisco, **As de Oro's** (San Martín 472, four blocks from the plaza, tel. 056/53-2010) is a classic. A restaurant with a pool by day, it transforms into a discotheque on weekend nights, staying open until 6 A.M. Catch a taxi at the door when you leave, because the surrounding neighborhood, though only four blocks from the plaza, is not safe at night.

On **June 29** fishermen in Pisco float the images of Saint Paul and Saint Peter into the Cove of San Andrés, as musicians perform

THE WHO'S WHO OF PARACAS BIRDS

Bird-watchers rightly flock to Peru's Amazon, home to 1,000 species of birds, or about 10 percent of the world total. Often overlooked, though, are Paracas's anchovy-rich waters, which attract nearly 200 species from around the world. Populations of these birds decline, or migrate south, during El Niño years, when coastal waters warm and anchovies move offshore. Here's a who's who:

- **Andean condor:** Sightings of the world's largest bird around Paracas are increasing, after guano workers nearly wiped the local population out for harassing local bird chicks. These massive vultures, with wing spans of up to 3.3 meters, descend from the highlands and feed mainly on sea lion carcasses.

- **Boobies:** Peru has six of the world's 10 booby species, including the blue-legged booby, but the most common in Paracas is the Peruvian booby. These chicken-sized birds have compact bodies and almost look like pelicans with smaller bills when they are sitting around. They are dramatic divers, like the cormorants, but eat only fish, so suffer huge declines in El Niño years.

- **Cormorants:** These long-billed diving birds

are found throughout the world but are so abundant in Paracas that up to four birds can nest in a single square meter. Along with the boobies and pelicans, they are Peru's main guano-producing birds. They are recognizable for the sleek bodies and long necks. They dive underwater, guiding themselves with their wings in order to catch anchovies, crabs, or whatever else is available. The two main species around Paracas both have red legs. But the guanay is black and white, whereas the red-legged *chuita*, in Spanish, is more grayish.

- **Flamingo:** This wading bird, with pink body, long neck, and baby-blue legs, uses its strangely bent bill to filter minute mollusks, algae, and diatoms found in Peru's brackish salt lakes. They summer in the altiplano near Ayacucho and winter in Paracas.

- **Frigate birds:** These large birds with forked tails, hooked bills, and long, slightly V-shaped wings are superb gliders. They are known as aerial pirates for harassing boobies, gulls, or terns until they drop their fish. The two species in Paracas, the magnificent and great frigate birds, are hard to distinguish: Both

on shore and cooks battle in a cooking contest of shellfish and fish dishes. Pisco's tourism week is the last week of September and includes **Peruvian *paso* horse shows, wine contests** and an **international sandboarding contest.**

Recreation

Camping at the Reserva Nacional de Paracas is possible and an extraordinary experience that can be combined with a four-wheel-drive safari through the Ica deserts. Buy all your groceries ahead of time in Lima or Pisco and make sure you pack plenty of water (3–4 liters pp, per day), sunscreen, clothes to protect from the wind and sun, and a camping stove—there is little driftwood on the

beach. Contract with a taxi either in Pisco or the beach town of Paracas to leave you at a beach and return the next day at a prearranged time (US$15–20 each way). The more remote beaches are on the south coast, past La Catedral, though if it is not a weekend La Mina is a beautiful, close beach that could be empty too.

The waters of the Paracas Bay, especially around Playa Atenas, remain flat even during stiff afternoon winds (over 30 knots). This makes for ideal **sailboating** and **windsurfing** conditions. There is a good **surfing** break off San Gallán, the large island south of Islas Ballestas that can only be reached via a private boat from El Chaco fishing port.

The standard four-hour agency tour of the

males have red necks and black bodies, while females have black bodies and white necks.

- **Humboldt penguin:** One of the best places in the world to see this endangered penguin is at Islas Ballestas. It is less than knee-high and wobbles along on its two webbed feet; its shrunken wings allow it to swim with amazing speeds underwater. It has a black body and face, with a white belly speckled with black dots. It nests in holes it digs in the guano.

- **Inca tern:** Terns, or *zarcillos* in Spanish, are known for migrating all over the world. They look like gulls, though they have smaller bodies, pointed wings, and a pointed bill and dive after shrimps and minnows. Out of the half-dozen tern species at Paracas, the Inca tern is unmistakable: red feet and bill, dark-gray body, and odd white feathers that curl downward from its eyes.

- **Oystercatchers:** These seagull-sized birds usually wade around rocky coastlines, where they use their long red bill to open oysters and clams with amazing speed. Paracas has two species, the blackish (all black) and the American (white chest, common in the United States).

- **Peruvian pelican:** One of the larger flying birds, the Peruvian pelican has a wingspan of up to 2.7 meters, a gray body, and streaks of light yellow on the neck. It is a superb glider, traveling up to 80 kilometers in a single day and just centimeters above rolling water. It scoops fish out of the water and stores them temporarily in its large pouch.

- **Seagulls:** Paracas has more than a half dozen gull species, but the most common is the band-tailed gull, which has a black band at the end of its white tail feathers. These birds cruise the beaches for fish, though they are not above eating other birds' chicks.

- **Whimbrel:** This sandpiper scurries in an erect posture along sandy beaches in search of mollusks. It has a mottled brown body, horizontal black stripes near its eyes, and light blue feet. It spends October through April along the South American coast before migrating back to North America for the rest of the year. It has a high-pitched scream when frightened, thus its name in Spanish, *zarapito trinador* (the whistling sandpiper).

Reserva Nacional de Paracas includes stops at the museum, La Catedral, Lagunillas, La Mina, and the sea lion lookout at Punta Arquillo. The best way to see the reserve, however, is to contract a car with a driver. This often ends up being cheaper for a group of two or more anyway, and allows for unscheduled stops such as lounging on the beach. For four hours, taxis from El Chaco or Paracas cost US$25, while drivers from Pisco can charge up to US$40. Taxis can also leave you at a beach and return for you later in the afternoon for an additional US$8.

The Islas Ballestas tours all leave from El Chaco. Before you buy your tour, inquire whether the agency has its own fast boat or you are likely to chug out of port on someone else's slow boat. Private tours are expensive and should not be done in the afternoon, when winds and seas pick up.

Most of the agencies are based in Pisco. The exception is **Zarcillo Connections,** which has an office at the entrance to the Paracas beach town on the left side of the road. It offers half-day tours to Islas Ballestas (US$15) and the reserve (US$10), as well as full-day excursions to the Inca ruins at Tambo Colorado (US$18).

Paracas Explore (tel. 056/54-5084, rogeraguilarr@hotmail.com) tours Islas Ballestas and the reserve via dune buggy. In El Chaco, the cheapest Islas Ballestas boats leave from the town pier every morning at 8 A.M. (US$10), and when there is demand, also at 10 A.M. Tickets should be bought the day before at a green control booth near the pier. The El Chaco taxi drivers' cooperative sells tickets in another booth nearby for a four-hour driving tour of the reserve (US$8).

In Pisco, all the agencies are lined up on San Francisco near the Plaza de Armas. The most reputable is **Ballestas Travel** (San Francisco 249, tel. 056/53-3095 or Lima tel. 01/257-0756, www.barrioperu.terra.com.pe/ballest), which charges US$16 for a full day including Islas Ballestas via speedboat plus a tour through the reserve. Also highly recommended is **Zarcillo Connections** (Callao Block 1, tel. 056/53-6543, www.barrioperu.terra.com.pe/zarcillo). A friendly, newer agency is **Amigos & Adventures** (Progreso, Plaza de Armas, tel. 056/970-2874, amigos_adventures@hotmail.com). The employees speak a bit of English, Hebrew, German, and Italian, and offer trips to Paracas, sandboarding in Ica, and Nasca flights. Ask a lot of questions beforehand: what type of airplane, where is the airport, how long is the flight, and which lines will you see.

ACCOMMODATIONS

Most low and mid-budget hotels are in Pisco. The upper-end hotels, mainly in Paracas, have low-season rates and also weekend packages on their websites.

US$10-25

Pisco's **Hostal San Isidro** (San Clemente 103, five blocks from the plaza, tel. 056/53-6471, www.sanisidrohostal.com, US$18 s, US$25 d) is a good backpacker style place to stay. Breakfast is not included except for free coffee in the morning, but you can get American (US$3) or Continental (US$2.5) upon request. There's a pool, ping pong and pool tables, as well as a kitchen and laundry machine for the guests to use. Internet is free, and there is a book exchange too. Big rooms are nice, but because of the location, you'll want to take taxis at nighttime.

Posada Hispana Hostal (Bolognesi 236, 1.5 blocks from the plaza, tel. 056/53-6363, www.posadahispana.com, US$21, US$29 d with breakfast) has been a favorite since it

opened in 1996, owned by a Peruvian-Catalan couple, Pilar and Joan Bericat. The hotel has a well-deserved reputation for friendly, reliable service. Their 24 rooms have cable TV, private bathrooms, and hot water. Amenities include a good restaurant with a cozy bistro atmosphere, free Internet and WiFi, laundry area, and even a barbecue pit. Apart from Spanish, the couple speak Italian, French, and Catalan. They are one of the best sources for information on the area.

A block away, the same couple also owns **La Hosteria del Monasterio** (Bolognesi 326, tel. 056/53-1383, reservaspisco@hotmail.com.com, US$25 s, US$29 d with breakfast). Still new, the stylish hotel is quieter than its sister hotel. There is a small garden, with tables perfect for breakfast and card playing. Rooms have cable TV, whitewashed brick walls, firm beds, and a small writing table.

US$25-50

In Paracas there is **Hostal Los Frayles** (Paracas Mz D5, tel. 056/54-5141, www.hostallosfrayles.com, US$25 d), which has clean rooms with great beds (some queen-size), private bathrooms, hot water 24 hours, free Internet, cable TV, and several rooms with ocean views. They will pick you up from Cruz del Sur's bus stop for an additional US$3.

A better option is **Hostal Residencial Santa María** (Av. Paracas s/n, Playa El Chaco, tel. 056/54-5045, www.santamariahostal.com, US$29 s, US$36 d with breakfast), right beside the Plaza Quiñonez. Rooms are simple but clean, with tile floors and ocean views, as well as private bathrooms, hot water, and cable TV. Ask about the tour packages the hotel offers to the reserve and the Ballestas Islands. It also has a seafood restaurant named El Chorito.

In Pisco **Villa Manuelita Hostal** (San Francisco 227, half a block from plaza, tel. 056/53-5218, www.villamanuelitahostal.com, US$21 s, US$30 d) is a good option. A restored colonial house—more than a century old—it miraculously survived the 2007 earthquake. Painted with pastel colors, this cozy hotel has large rooms with cable TV and nice baths, decorated with wooden tables and cabinets, and fresh flowers. There are rooms with windows and skylights, as well as a small patio with a fountain, elegant sitting areas, and a pizzeria.

Another option in town, a couple of blocks away from the Plaza de Armas, is **Hotel Embassy Beach** (San Martín 1119, tel. 056/53-2568, www.hotelesembassy.com.pe, US$40 s, US$60 d), a concrete-built, resort-like 70 room hotel with a tacky decor. Rooms are enormous, with fans, minifridge, and cable TV. There is a huge swimming pool and a restaurant with unexpectedly good seafood specialties.

Over US$50

In Paracas there are two top-notch hotels. The **Doubletree Guest Suites by Hilton Paracas** (Lote 30–34, Urb. Santo Domingo, tel. 01/617-1000, http://doubletree1.hilton.com, starting at US$189 king suite pool view) is on Santo Domingo beach, in the southern section of the Paracas village.

This U-shaped hotel has suites overlooking the pool and the ocean. These last ones are more expensive. Rooms are spacious, with a large balcony from which you have impressive views of the Paracas Bay and/or the hotel gardens.

There are super comfortable beds with plenty of hypoallergenic jumbo pillows, a luxurious linen package of a down-filled duvet wrapped in triple sheeting, and a specially designed plush-top mattress and box spring system. The bathroom features deluxe domestic bath products, curved shower rod, hair dryer, and modern fixtures and fittings.

The restaurant serves a buffet and also has a menu. Food is good but not spectacular. Since the hotel is pretty much isolated, surrounded by sand and the beach, be prepared to have all your meals there unless you have your own transportation to move around town or even outside. WiFi is available but not always reliable. There is an ATM in the hotel. Other than that, this hotel is a quite luxurious resort where you can spend a weekend indulging yourself.

Paracas Libertador Luxury Collection

Resort (Av. Paracas 173, tel. 056/58-1333, www.libertador.com.pe, US$225–252 double bed garden view, US$265–290 double bed ocean view, suites starting at US$348, with buffet breakfast) is, with no doubt, as of 2010 the most luxurious resort on the Peruvian coast, where celebrities such as supermodel Kate Moss have stayed. This is the latest and most splendid addition to the Libertador chain. There are 120 rooms with great views and all amenities imaginable. The superior rooms have bamboo-covered walls, iPod stations, and a king bed or two extra-long beds. There are three kinds of suites—balcony (US$374), solarium (US$406), and plunge pool (US$470)—with highlights such as 37-inch and 42-inch LCD flat screens, iPod stations, 440-thread cotton sheets, and luxury bathrooms.

The hotel has two restaurants, **Zarcillo** with Peruvian and Mediterranean cuisine, and **La Trattoria** with Italian food. Two bars and two swimming pools offer you both sides of excitement and relaxation. A travel agency called Tikariy (www.tikariy.com.pe) offers deluxe packages including anything from overflying the Nasca lines, four-wheel drives in the desert, tours to pisco bodegas, luxury sailing aboard the yacht *Garza,* and other options. There is free kayaking for all guests, and most important, there's an ATM to pull out any cash you might need.

Despite this being a chain hotel, the staff is extremely friendly and helpful, trying to make this place as personalized as possible.

FOOD

There are several inexpensive seafood restaurants along the waterfront in the beach town of Paracas or at El Chaco beach that have a reputation for causing traveler's diarrhea. Be cautious but not paranoid.

The best option in town is **El Chorito** (Av. Paracas s/n, Playa El Chaco, tel. 056/54-5045, 7 A.M.–9 P.M. daily, US$3–8), one block back from the beach, which has great grilled fish, delicious *pescado a la chorillana* or *sudado,* and good *cebiche.*

If you're willing to splurge on a good meal, you might consider one of the two restaurants at Paracas Libertador hotel (Av. Paracas 173, tel. 056/58-1333): **Zarcillo** with great Peruvian fish and seafood specialties and also Mediterranean cuisine, or **La Trattoria** with good pastas and pizzas.

In Pisco, **Panadería San Francisco** (Plaza de Armas, 6 A.M.–10 P.M. daily) is the best place for fresh bread, empanadas, espresso, fruit salads, or lemon pie and has US$2–3 breakfast menus. It has a second location with the same hours at San Francisco 111. Worth the walk away from the center, **La Viña de Huber** (Prolg. Cerro Azul, tel. 056/53-3199, 9 A.M.–7 P.M. daily, US$5–7) is a Pisco favorite with good prices. The lengthy menu offers plates, full enough for two, of *chicharrones,* fish, and *cebiche.* On the Plaza de Armas is **La Catedral** (San Juan de Dios 108, tel. 056/53-5611, 7 A.M.–11 P.M. daily), with good breakfast and lunch menus and a range of chicken, beef, and seafood plates. **Restaurante Catamarán** (Comercio 166, tel. 056/53-3547, 8 A.M.–midnight daily) serves up good-looking, large pizzas.

INFORMATION AND SERVICES

There is a medical post in Paracas. Internet, post office, small grocery stores, and a public phone are all within a block of the small main square.

Tourist information is available from Pisco's municipality on the main square (tel. 056/53-2525), though nearby agencies on San Francisco are a better bet. Candid advice is always available from Joan and Pilar at the **Posada Hispana Hostal** (Bolognesi 236, tel. 056/53-6363).

Pisco's **police station** is on the plaza (San Francisco, tel. 056/53-2165).

For medical issues in Pisco, go to **Clínica San Jorge** (Juan Osores 440, tel. 056/53-6100, 8 A.M.–8 P.M. Mon.–Sat., 8 A.M.–2 P.M. Sun.). Reliable pharmacies are **Botica Fasa** (www.boticasfasa.com) and **InkaFarma** (www.inkafarma.com.pe).

All the banks with ATMs are on Pisco's square, including **Banco Continental, Banco de Comercio, Interbank,** and **Scotiabank.**

The **post office** is on Pisco's main square (Bolognesi 173, 8 A.M.–6 P.M. Mon.–Sat.); there are private phone booths opposite the cathedral (Progreso 123A), and **email** places are a half block away on Comercio.

In Pisco, laundry is available at **El Pacífico** (Callao 274, tel. 056/53-2443, 9 A.M.–1 P.M. and 4–8 P.M. Mon.–Sat., US$1.50/kg).

GETTING THERE AND AROUND

To get to the Reserva Nacional de Paracas get off at Km 234 of the Panamericana and drive five kilometers to Pisco and then another three kilometers to the gate of the reserve itself. The town of Paracas is on the right a few kilometers before the reserve gate.

The best bus company to go to Paracas is **Cruz del Sur** (www.cruzdelsur.com.pe), offering Cruzero service on their Lima–Nasca route, with a stop in Paracas. **Ormeño** (San Francisco 259, one block from the plaza, tel. 056/53-2764, www.grupo-ormeno.com) has three buses a day between Pisco and Lima, ranging from economic (with stops in Chincha and Cañete) to the direct Royal Class. Ormeño also operates a Royal Class bus that heads south daily for Ica and Nasca.

A cheaper option, with frequent buses to and from Lima, is **Soyuz** (www.soyuz.com.pe), which has an office on the Plaza de Armas. From there, passengers are shuttled out to the highway to meet buses that are constantly rumbling north and south.

From Pisco, taxis charge US$5 for the 20-minute drive to Paracas. Buses marked El Chaco–Paracas leave every half hour from the market near Nicolas de Piérola and take about 30 minutes (6 A.M.–6 P.M., US$0.30). Buses return to Pisco every half hour from El Chaco's main, and only, entrance.

Ica

At 420 meters above sea level, sunny Ica is an oasis of palm trees and sand dunes. The town escapes the fog, or *garúa,* that blankets Lima much of the year. To the west, the Ica desert, a moonscape of sand dunes and eroded dirt formations, stretches to the Pacific Ocean. This wilderness is known primarily to a select group of paleontologists who come here to search for the fossilized bones of prehistoric sea lions and gigantic sharks. Recently the local guides of these paleontologists have begun showing travelers the paleontologists' route. On a desert safari, activities include hunting for gigantic fossilized teeth, examining the bones of marine animals scattered in the sand, and sleeping under a brilliant star-filled sky. No one who has gone on one of these trips has ever been disappointed—this desert, which extends from Paracas down to Nasca, is one of the most wild and spectacular in the world.

What Ica is most known for, though, is its **vineyards,** which were planted by the Spaniards in the 16th century. Ica's 80 surrounding bodegas produce the world's best pisco, or white grape brandy, and a variety of ports and wines. There is a huge range of bodegas, from the haciendas that have been outfitted with state-of-the-art technology, such as Tacama and Ocucaje, to more rustic mom-and-pop operations where grapes are crushed underfoot and pressed with the weight of a huge *huarango* trunk. Most visitors like to see one of each.

The city of Ica changed dramatically after a wave of highland settlers came here to escape terrorism in the 1990s. The city is more crowded now, and assaults on tourists have become common. When in Ica, walk in groups, stay near the plaza at night, and avoid the whole east side of the city between the plaza and the Río Ica. The best lodging options are now outside the city, including Hotel Hacienda Ocucaje, Lago Huacachina, or the quiet Angostura neighborhood on the edge of town.

Lago Huacachina, six kilometers outside of town, is a magical and incongruous sight, a lake of green waters fringed with palm trees and reed swamps and surrounded on all sides by huge sand dunes. There are excellent lodging options around the lake. During the day, the dunes are the best place in Peru to try sandboarding and dune buggy riding. For those who don't want to stay in Nasca, overflights of the nearby lines leave frequently from Ica, but the cost is slightly higher.

Ica has endured a series of natural disasters, from an earthquake that killed 500 people way back in 1664 to an El Niño flood in 1998. As a result, there are few colonial buildings or well-preserved ruins in the area, even though the valley has been home to a series of ancient cultures: the Paracas, Nasca, Huari, and Chincha. Inca Pachacútec conquered and integrated this valley into the Inca empire in the 15th century. A century later Luis Jerónimo de Cabrera founded the first city, Villa de Valverde, in 1563. The Spaniards, no doubt missing the *riojas* and *ribieros* of their

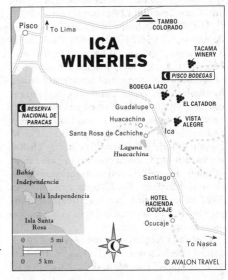

ICA WINERIES

Pisco — To Lima — TAMBO COLORADO

TACAMA WINERY

PISCO BODEGAS

BODEGA LAZO

RESERVA NACIONAL DE PARACAS

Guadalupe — EL CATADOR

Huacachina — VISTA ALEGRE

Santa Rosa de Cachiche — Ica

Laguna Huacachina

Bahía Independencia

Santiago

Isla Independencia

HOTEL HACIENDA OCUCAJE

Isla Santa Rosa

Ocucaje

To Nasca

0   5 mi
0   5 km

© AVALON TRAVEL

homeland, planted the first South American grapes in the 1540s.

SIGHTS
City Tour

There are a few churches to see in Ica, along with two recommended museums. The **Plaza de Armas** is lined with ancient trees and has been rebuilt with an obelisk and fountain since a 1998 flood sent a meter of water running through town. The 19th-century **cathedral** on the corner has a neoclassical facade and beautiful, though spooky, wood carvings inside. The biggest church in the city, **San Francisco,** is a block to the west of the cathedral and has a number of stained-glass windows illustrating the life of the patron saint. The most beautiful church, however, is **Señor de Luren,** which is reached by walking south on Lima for eight blocks and turning right on Cutervo. The church has a beautiful interior that holds an image that inspires a yearly October pilgrimage. There are a few colonial and republican *casonas* around town, which are not generally open for tours but are worth viewing from the outside, including **Casa de las Cornucopias** (Dos de Mayo 158), **Casa del Valle** (San Martín 159), **Edificio del Estanco** (Lima 390), and **Casa Colonial El Porton** (Loreto 233).

The **Museo Cabrera** (Bolívar 170, on Plaza de Armas, tel. 056/23-1933 or 056/21-3026 for a Sun. appt., 9:30 A.M.–1 P.M. and 4:30–7 P.M. Mon.–Fri., US$3) is an imaginative collection of thousands of stones and boulders collected by the late Dr. Javier Cabrera, a descendant of the town's founder. Carved on these stones are depictions of ancient hunts, brain surgery, and even dinosaurs. No one has been able to explain exactly who carved the nearly 11,000 stones that Dr. Cabrera claimed to have found in tombs around Ica, and archaeologists doubt their authenticity. Dr. Cabrera, who died in 2002, never revealed their exact origin. If nothing else, this idiosyncratic museum is a monument to one man's obsession.

El Museo Regional de Ica (Ayabaca, block 8, near intersection with J. J. Elias, tel. 056/23-4383, 8 A.M.–7 P.M. Mon.–Fri., 9 A.M.–6 P.M. Sat.–Sun., US$3) is 1.5 kilometers from the Plaza de Armas but definitely worth the visit. It is one of Peru's best small museums and offers a fascinating glimpse into the Paracas, Nasca, Huari, Chincha, and Inca cultures. Displays include textiles, ceramics, trepanned skulls, mummies, and *quipas* (bundles of knotted strings that served as memory devices). The museum presents a good historical overview of the area, along with photos and furniture from the 19th century and a full model of the Nasca Lines. To get there take a US$0.50 taxi or hop aboard any *combi* (US$0.15) that says Universidad at the cathedral in the Plaza de Armas.

◖ Pisco Bodegas

Most of Ica's bodegas welcome visitors with free tours and then wine and dine them with their own wines and piscos and heaps of home-cooked food. Ica's bodegas have a charming, down-home feel, and most visitors end up staying longer, and drinking more, than they had planned. The larger wineries are the best places to understand how pisco is made, though the smaller bodegas have a more charming atmosphere for eating and tasting. Taxis from Ica are cheap and easy to hire, even for non-Spanish speakers. For the return home, if there aren't taxis lined up outside the bodega, they can be called in a moment's notice. The most interesting time to visit is during harvest, or *vendimia,* January–March. Only Ocucaje and Tacama have English-speaking guides always on hand. The others can arrange for one with advance notice.

Hotel Hacienda Ocucaje (Panamericana Sur Km 334, Ocucaje, tel. 056/83-7049, www.hotelocucaje.com, 8 A.M.–6 P.M. daily) is a charming resort winery 36 kilometers south of Ica in the dusty village of Ocucaje. Unlike other large wineries, Ocucaje retains a look and feel that has changed little since the Jesuits produced wine here in the 16th century: hundreds of huge oak barrels stretch through cellars kept cool and musty via a combination of dirt floors, thick adobe walls, and cane-and-mud ceilings. A highlight of the Ocucaje winery tour is the

THE DESERT COAST

© RENÉE DEL GAUDIO AND ROSS WEHNER

Hotel Hacienda Ocucaje offers guests the chance to tour the distillery and sample locally produced pisco.

19th-century *alambique,* the bronze distillery where the pisco is made. Nearly 2,300 liters of fermented grape juice are heated in each boiler, and the evaporated pisco is cooled and collected in a series of tubes submerged in water. Wine-tasting is offered at the end of the tour—try the Moscatel port, sold under the Juana María label.

The Rubini family bought the 1,200-hectare hacienda in 1898 but was stripped of the property during the Agrarian Reform in the late 1960s. The family was able to buy back some of the land and eventually the buildings, but the colonial aqueduct leading from the mountains had fallen into disrepair. As a result, grapes are no longer grown at the hacienda itself. The family has converted the 1920s hacienda into a relaxed, hospitable resort with comfortable rooms, a sauna made from a wine barrel, whirlpool tub, horses, bikes, pools with slide, a discotheque, sandboarding, dune buggy riding, fossil tours—you name it! Taxis cost US$7 from Ica, and the hotel also picks guests up from Ica bus stations.

Just 11 kilometers northeast of Ica, **Tacama Winery** (Camino a La Tinguiña s/n, tel. 056/83-7030, www.tacama.com, 8:30 A.M.–noon and 3–4:30 P.M. daily) produces Peru's best (and only) dry wines and, along with Ocucaje, is a leading producer of pisco. There is a modern warehouse with state-of-the-art facilities, which backs up to the ochre walls of a colonial hacienda, a plaza of river stones, and a driveway lined with ancient trees. An old bell still rings every day from a tower, from which visitors can look out over 200 hectares planted with 20 different grape varieties.

The Olachea family bought the hacienda in 1898, lost much of the original 950 hectares in the Agrarian Reform, and is now producing about 1.5 million liters of wine and pisco per year—which is only half of the installed capacity. A tour of the winery includes a visit to an old grape press made from a *huarango* tree, a 19th-century *alambique,* and a full tour of the modern warehouse. There is an interesting museum of wine technology from the past few centuries and a wine-tasting room. The blended white wines—especially the Blanco de Blancos and the lighter Gran Blanco—are very good and sold at a 50 percent discount off retail. Taxis cost US$6 from Ica.

Another large winery even closer to Ica is **Vista Alegre** (Caminio a La Tinguiña Km 2.5, tel. 056/23-2919, www.vistaalegre.com, 9 A.M.–5 P.M. daily), which is only three kilometers from Ica across the Río Ica. Vista Alegra, like Ocucaje, was operated by the Jesuits in the 18th century. It was then purchased by the Picasso family in 1875, which continues to operate it today. Unfortunately, the half-hour walk to Vista Alegra—down Grau and across the Río Ica—takes you through the unsafe side of the city. Take a US$2 taxi instead.

Small Pisco Bodegas

Ica's best small bodegas—Lazo and El Catador—are just two kilometers apart along the dirt road that leads to Tacama. The more authentic of the two is **Bodega Lazo** (Camino de Reyes s/n, tel. 056/40-3430, bodegalazo_1809@hotmail.com, 7 A.M.–midnight daily). Locals come here to drink port and eat under the bougainvillea-covered bowers or inside the bodega itself, which is a charming and elegant space filled with wine barrels, presses, and other objects from the bodega's history, which began in 1809. There is a good tour here of the vines and winery, though you need to speak Spanish.

El Catador (Fundo Tres Esquinas 102, Subtanjalla, tel. 056/40-3427, josecarrasco50@hotmail.com, www.go.to/elcatador, 8 A.M.–6 P.M. daily) is a more established spot on the bodega circuit, run by the Carrasco family, which has large spaces for visitors to drink, eat, and dance. But first go on the excellent tour of the colonial wine and pisco process: The grapes are crushed underfoot and then pressed in a huge adobe platform with a 150-year-old *huarango* trunk as a weight. Then the juice is poured into clay containers, known as *botijas de barro,* which were used in this area long before the Inca. The pisco is distilled in huge brick boilers with copper basins known as *falcas.* In March, the height of the grape crushing, visitors are asked to roll up their pants and lend a foot. In the evenings, a disco even cranks. The food is good and reasonably priced, with entrées around US$4 and a full lunch menu for US$5. An alternative way to arrive at these wineries is via the Collazos buses (US$2.50) that leave from the first block of Loreto or third block of Moguegua from 3 P.M. onward.

◖ Ica Desert

Ica is the best launching point for tours through the desert, which apart from being beautiful also happens to be one of the world's richest hunting grounds for marine fossils. You need at least three days, preferably a week, to get there and back from the truly remote, wild desert, and make sure you have a hat, plenty of sunscreen, a gallon of water per day per person, and a desert-worthy vehicle with plenty of spare tires (protection against razor-sharp volcanic rocks). The two desert guides recommended here are intellectual but all self-taught, absolutely passionate about the desert, and safe. They make a living by guiding foreign paleontologists, and they know all the local *huaqueros* (grave robbers), who tip them off about new fossil areas.

The guide with the best transport, and most experience, is Roberto Penny Cabrera, alias **Desert Man** (tel. 056/962-4868, www.icadeserttrip.com). It is hard to miss Roberto, who hangs out most evenings in Ica's El Otro Peñoncito Restaurant. He is the one with the desert hat, military-style camo cargo pants, and huge bowie knife strapped to the waist. A former prospector for mining companies, he can show you detailed satellite imagery and geology maps of the whole area, and a quick glimpse of his truck is the best proof that you will not end up dying of thirst or crawling out of the desert on your hands and knees. His powerful diesel pickup has mattresses for three, a 22-gallon shower, and even an air pump for inflating his three spare tires. He speaks impeccable English, is a descendant of the town's founder, and lives to this day on the Plaza de Armas. He is intense, well organized, and endlessly entertaining.

THE SANDS OF AN ANCIENT BREEDING GROUND

Looking out over the endless sand dunes west of Ica, it is impossible to visualize the area as a huge ocean, with giant sharks, sea lions, penguins, dolphins, and whales all mating with each other. But that is what was going on here before the shifting of tectonic plates two million years ago heaved the ocean floor up into the hot, dry air where it is today.

After a paleontologist discovered a new dolphin species here in the 1980s, the Ica Desert has produced dozens more and become known as the best place in the world to hunt for marine fossils. There are so many, in fact, that bumpy points on the top of sand dunes are not usually rocks, but rather the perfect vertebrae of some long-extinct swimming animal. Experienced guides know where the most interesting fossils are, whether it's a sea sloth (oddly similar to a jungle sloth but with a beaverlike tail and hook hands for excavating soils), the delicate baleen of huge, plankton-eating whales, or a prehistoric pelican with a nine-meter wingspan.

Paleontologists believe that the whole area was once a shallow breeding ground for a variety of marine life, like the bays of Mexico's Baja California. The animals died, perhaps naturally or because of storms, and floated to the bottom where their carcasses were quickly covered with mud.

One of the more spectacular animals is the *Carcharocles megalodon*, the Tyrannosauruus rex of the sea. This gigantic, whale-eating shark was up to 14 meters (46 feet) long. Like sharks today, the megalodon had more than a hundred teeth, arranged in seven lines, which were constantly falling out and being replaced. These gigantic teeth, up to 20 cm long, are now fossils that can be picked right out of the dried mud.

Geological maps show the different formations around Ica and to which epoch they belong. The Pisco formation, a huge area of marine sediment that stretches from Arequipa to Pisco, contains mostly fossils from the Upper Miocene to the Lower Pliocene, or from about 16–2 million years ago. The huge bluff closer to the coast, which forces the Río Ica south on its way to the Pacific, is the Caballo Formation. It is far older, with fossils from the Triassic (230–145 million years ago) and even the Precambrian that goes back three billion years to the beginning of life on earth.

Other recommended guides include **Marco León Villarán** (Lima tel. 01/230-8316 or 01/230-8351, www.peruadventure.com), who leads trips in the Ica desert and works as a professional bone hunter throughout Peru's coast. He is a genuinely nice person who leads very professional expeditions and speaks Spanish only.

ENTERTAINMENT AND EVENTS

Nightlife in Ica is a weekend affair. At Lago Huacachina, head to the bar at **Hostal Rocha** (Balneario Huacachina s/n, tel. 056/22-2256). On the Panamericana and near the entrance to the Angostura neighborhood is **La Peña de Alamo,** which gets hopping Friday and Saturday nights around 11 P.M. with live creole music.

Otherwise most nightlife options are in the city of Ica itself. **Restaurant Chalán** (Callao 179, tel. 056/21-3722, 7:30–11 P.M. daily) is a republican-style patio with crumbling adobe walls that makes for a good place to have a shot of pisco and move on. A locals' favorite for beers and cocktails is the dark and swanky **Pekados** (Lima 261). The best disco is **La Who** (Av. Los Maestros 422, inside the Hotel Real Ica on Maestros, tel. 056/23-3330). The new **UVK Multicines** (Av. Ayabaca s/n, next to the INC Museum in the San Josí neighborhood, tel. 056/21-7261, www.uvkmultcines.com) shows international stars.

The best Ica festival is the **International Grape Harvest Festival,** which takes place during the height of the harvest in the first half of March. There are concerts, cockfighting, and beauty pageants. The girl chosen as the queen of the festival ends up wallowing in a vat of grapes.

Ica has been a center for **Peruvian *paso* horses** for centuries, and the **Sol de Oro horse competition** is held here every June, though the exact date varies. Peru's **national day of pisco** is July 25, and Iqueños celebrate with raucous parties. **Our Lord of Luren** takes place the third Sunday in October and includes processions of hundreds of people and streets covered with carpets of flowers.

RECREATION
Sandboarding the Dunes

Ica is the best place in Peru to try sandboarding and dune buggy riding. There is a thrill in speeding up and down the dunes, but simply being on the dunes lets you appreciate the magnitude of the desert geography. Dune buggies are available through Mario Vera, the dune buggy pioneer of Ica, inside the **Las Dunas** (La Angostura 400, tel. 056/25-6224) and Hacienda Ocucaje (Panamericana Sur Km 336, tel. 056/83-7049) hotels. Las Dunas and many of the Angostura hotels provide sandboards free of charge, though make sure they are waxed or they will not go very fast. The best places for these sports, however, are the huge, perfect dunes around Lago Huacachina. At the green control entrance to the lake there are dune buggies for rent—the best are available through Eduardo Barco, at El Huacachinero hostel (Perotti s/n, tel. 056/21-7435), but **Hotel El Huarango** (El Medano Y-5, tel. 056/25-6257) and Hostería Suiza (Balneario de Huacachina 264, tel. 056/23-8762) can also put you in touch with reliable operators. Dune buggy riding is like a roller coaster without a track, because the machines zip down 50-degree slopes at up to 80 kilometers per hour. Accidents do happen, so make sure you have seatbelts with chest harnesses and good roll bars—and don't hesitate to get out if your driver is reckless. The best times for both of these sports are early morning and late afternoon, to avoid heat and winds that pick up around midday.

LAGO HUACACHINA: LAKE OF TEARS

The name Huacachina is Quechua: *Wakay* means to cry and *china* means young woman. According to local legend, a young woman and her lover strolled most afternoons in the countryside around Ica. But just when the couple was to be married, he dropped dead. The woman was wracked with sorrow and spent the days afterwards wandering through the countryside and retracing her walks with her lover. As she walked, her tears formed a lake.

As she sat by the lake one day, an evil spirit in a man's form tried to rape her. She jumped into her lake's waters, imploring the water gods to protect her from evil spirits by covering her with a cloak of snow. Though she escaped the man, she drowned in the lake. Now, every full moon, she floats over Lago Huacachina, cloaked in sparkling white light. Locals say she drowns nighttime swimmers as a sacrifice to the lake gods who protect her.

Tour Agencies and Guides

If you are short on time, Ica can also be a good base for seeing the Nasca Lines, and 35-minute overflights from here cost around US$45 per person. Because the flight is longer from Ica, pilots occasionally try to save gas by skipping some of the lines. Have the agency write down a list of lines beforehand, and pay extra if necessary to get more flight minutes. Agencies also offer US$32 tours to the Reserva Nacional de Paracas that include a trip to the Islas Ballestas. This seems, however, like a very rushed way to see such a spectacular reserve.

Of the companies that offer these kinds of trips, the best option is **Lineas Completas** (Bolívar 255, 2nd Fl., tel. 056/21-0310, lineascompletas@hotmail.com). Other options are **Desert Travel** (Lima 171, tel. 056/23-4127, desert_travel@hotmail.com) and **Dolphin Travel** (Municipalidad 132, tel. 056/21-8920, av_dolphintravel@hotmail.com). Local tours

THE DESERT COAST

© RENÉE DEL GAUDIO AND ROSS WEHNER

Lago Huacachina, near Ica, offers world-class sandboarding down pristine sand dunes.

cost US$8 and include El Museo Regional de Ica, Lago Huacachina, Cachiche (a town known for its now-disappeared tradition of witchcraft), Señor de Luren church, and a bodega or two. One option would be to take this tour and then stay at the wineries and take a taxi home.

ACCOMMODATIONS

The best place to stay near Ica is Lago Huacachina (southwest of town, US$1 taxi). The best place for families and a completely relaxing spot is Hotel Hacienda Ocucaje, a half-hour drive south from Ica. Finally, Ica's Angostura neighborhood is quiet and safe and only a few minutes from town.

Under US$10

The main backpacker place on Lago Huacachina is **Hostal Rocha** (Balneario Huacachina s/n, tel. 056/22-2256, kikirocha@hotmail.com, US$4 s, US$8 d), with a friendly, family feel and an open-door policy for even the rowdiest of backpackers. The rooms have yellow tile or polished concrete floors, and some have balconies, private baths, and hot

water. A breakfast of fruit and eggs is served for US$2. The owner, Lucho Rocha, rents sandboards for US$1.50 per day. There are a few other hostels around the lake but the best, for the moment, is this one.

In Ica itself, the best budget lodging is **Hospedaje Callao** (Callao 128, tel. 056/22-7741, US$7 s, US$9 d), a half block from the Plaza de Armas and run by the kind Huamani family. Rooms are quiet, safe, and pleasant with 4.5-meter ceilings, pastel purple and green walls, red polished cement floors, and a few odd pieces of furniture. Private rooms have hot water, and the Huamani family runs a good Internet place next door.

A basic place that's not too noisy is **Hostal Antonio's** (Castrovirreyna 136, tel. 056/21-5565, US$7 s, US$11 d), sandwiched between the market and plaza. Returning at night, it is a good idea to take a taxi. Rooms have foam mattresses, TV, and hot water. The front of **Hostal Oasis** (Tacna 216, tel. 056/23-4767, US$8 s, US$11 d) is a colonial home a block from the plaza and close to most of the bus terminals. Rooms are plain, but some have queen-size beds with private bathrooms, cable TV, and hot water.

US$10-25

In the Angostura neighborhood, **Hotel El Huarango** (El Medano Y-5, tel. 056/25-6257, hotelelhuarango@hotmail.com, US$17 s, US$23 d) offers large rooms with parquet floors, TV, big bathrooms, and antique furniture. Deep roof eaves make the rooms a bit dark, but it's great for sleeping. There are Internet stands and a restaurant next to the pool that serves excellent Peruvian food, and there are sandboards for surfing the dunes right next to the hotel. The owner, Antonio Carrión, can also arrange dune buggy rides (US$13 for two hours) and bodega tours (US$10 pp).

In Huacachina, Eduardo Barco's **El Huacachinero** (Perotti s/n, tel. 056/21-7435, www.elhuacachinero.com, US$19 s, US$25 d) is an excellent option. Rooms are decorated with bright bed covers, the garden is full of hammocks, the pool is surrounded by lounge chairs, and the bar is never far away. Piña colada by the pool? The friendly Eduardo can arrange dune buggy rides.

US$25-50

Hotel Austria (La Angostura 367, tel. 056/25-6106, www.hotelaustria-peru.com, US$35 s or d), in Angostura, is a pleasant compound with red tile floors, large rooms with TV, and a nice pool run by an Austrian-Peruvian couple. *Criolla* food is served for a reasonable price. This is one of the cleanest hotels in Peru, though a bit rigid in its Austrian impeccability. You will not find a speck of dust here.

Another option, but on Lago Huacachina, is **Hostería Suiza** (Balneario de Huacachina 264, tel. 056/23-8762, www.hosteriasuiza.com, US$25 s, US$42 d). The Baumgartner family, which ran the Hotel Mossone in the heydays of the 1940s, bought this house five years ago and converted it into a peaceful, friendly family hotel. The 22 rooms have comfortable beds, fans, and big bathrooms, and some have views over the lake. Though the rooms aren't particularly luxurious, the pool

outside is very nice and this hostel runs like a fine-tuned Swiss watch; the staff can set you up with dune buggy riding.

In Ica, a rather ugly modern option is **Hotel Sol de Ica** (Lima 265, tel. 056/21-8931, www.hotelsoldeica.com, US$26 s, US$35 d), a huge building a block from the Plaza de Armas that has a pool and restaurant. The rooms are small and plain, with cable TV, clean bathrooms, and thin stucco walls that let in the street noise.

US$50-100

The old-world ambience of **Hotel Mossone** (Balneario de Huacachina s/n, tel. 056/21-3630, hmossone@derrama.org.pe, www.derrama.org.pe, US$68 s, US$86 d) is the pride and joy of every Iqueña and, after years of neglect, is undergoing somewhat of a Renaissance. This grand hotel was one of the country's most famous resorts from the 1920s to 1950s, when politicians and diplomats came here to relax on the elegant colonial porch overlooking the lake and sand dunes. Present management is restoring the hotel's fabulous grounds, which include a stone patio with huge ficus and *huarango* trees, a dining room and porch overlooking the lake, and an elegant pool across the street. The colonial rooms are simple with high ceilings, air-conditioning, TV, fridge, and bathtubs. Guests can use bikes and sandboards free of charge.

Just north of Ica, the luxury hotel **Las Dunas** (La Angostura 400, tel. 056/25-6224 or Lima tel. 01/241-8000, www.lasdunashotel.com, US$77 s, US$93 d, prices lower on weekdays) could easily be in Marrakech, with its sparkling white buildings and looming sand dunes overhead. Rooms are shaded and cool, with red tile floors and all the comforts of a three-star hotel, including TV, fridge, phone, and fans. Las Dunas feels at times like an American theme park, with tennis, golf, volleyball, sandboarding, horseback riding, three pools with a 37-meter waterslide and poolside bar, playground, bicycles, discotheque with karaoke, game room, and even a small golf course. An extraordinary buffet of international and regional cuisine is served on an outdoor dining terrace. Horseback riding in the desert (US$11 per hour with guide), sauna with massage (US$18), and the planetarium (US$5) all cost extra. The hotel offers a variety of packages that include lodging and tours to Paracas, Tambo Colorado, Ica wineries and churches, and overflights to the Nasca Lines.

Hotel Hacienda Ocucaje (Panamericana Sur Km 336, Ocucaje, tel. 056/40-8001, www.hotelocucaje.com, US$76 s or d, lower prices on weekdays) is a unique bodega resort a half hour south of Ica. This spacious hacienda from the 1920s is less expensive and fancy than Las Dunas and has a more down-home, relaxed feel. Amenities include a nice pool with a slide, a bar, a restaurant with excellent food, plain but comfortable rooms, sauna, whirlpool tub, horses, bikes, and sandboards, all included in the price. Three-day packages include lodging, elaborate meals served in the wine cellar, wine tour and tasting, horseback riding, and sandboarding for US$100 during the week and US$130 on weekends. Not surprisingly, this is a popular weekend getaway for families from Lima. The winery next door, Ocucaje, is one of Ica's most charming and historic large operations.

FOOD
Cafés, Bakeries, and Ice Cream
Most of the area's better restaurants are in Ica. **Anita's** (Libertad 133, on Plaza de Armas, tel. 056/21-8582, 8 A.M.–midnight daily, US$3–8) is an upscale, rather expensive café and restaurant with great service. The huge menu is good for breakfast and includes a wide range of Peruvian dishes and desserts. A locals' favorite for pies and empanadas is **Dulcería Pastelería Velasco** (Grau 199, tel. 056/23-2831, 9:30 A.M.–8:30 P.M. daily), which was founded in 1936 and serves up a staggering array of local sweets. The best-known sweets maker in Ica is **Helena Chocolates & Tejas** (Nicolas de Ribera 227, Urb. Luren, tel. 056/23-3308), which offers tours of its factory 11 blocks south of the Plaza de Armas. There is also a store near the plaza, at Cajamarca

139, which sells the local specialty *tejas,* or pecans and candied fruits—figs, lemons, grapes, oranges—filled with *manjar blanco,* a milk caramel, and bathed in sugar. The chocolate-covered version is called *chocotejas.*

Peruvian
First opened in 1968, **El Otro Peñoncito** (Bolívar 255, tel. 056/23-3921, 7 A.M.–midnight daily, US$5–7) has passed through several generations of the Hernández family. The current restaurant opened in 1992 and has a huge, classy menu of Peruvian concoctions including a dozen different salads, meats, pastas, fish, and vegetarian cuisine. Try *pollo a la Iqueñas,* grilled chicken with spinach covered in a pecan sauce. The Hernández family makes their own pisco, and bartender Hary is one of Peru's better-known bartenders. A larger branch of this restaurant is just down the street at Bolívar 422.

Plaza 125 (Lima 125, Plaza de Armas, tel. 056/21-1816, 7 A.M.–4 A.M. daily, US$3) serves salads, *adobos,* steaks, and US$2 pisco sours. The same owner runs the new **Caine y Pescao** (Elias 417), serving fish, shellfish, and creole food.

International
Restaurant Venezia (Lima 230, tel. 056/23-2241, 10 A.M.–3 P.M. and 6–11 P.M. daily, US$4) is the best place for pizza, and also serves gnocchi, homemade pasta, and ice cream. The best place for fish is **La Candela** (Túpac Amaru F-5, Urb. San Jose, around the corner from Museo Regional, US$3–6). The menu includes a range of mouthwatering ceviches, *tiraditos,* and other seafood plates.

Vegetarian
Try **Food Light** (Ayabaca 184, tel. 056/21-6929, 8 A.M.–8 P.M. Sun.–Thurs., 8 A.M.–5 P.M. Fri., US$1.50), which has a cheap lunch menu and is across from the hospital on the way to Lago Huacachina. A second location is on the third block of San Martin in the center. Another good vegetarian restaurant, near Ica

WHEN IN PERU, DRINK PISCO

Peruvians have a lot of national pride about pisco, a grape brandy distilled from sweet grapes cultivated in Peru's desert near Ica. Peruvians got all up in arms during the 1980s when Chile tried to patent the name pisco – in the same way the French laid sole claim to Champagne, leaving the rest of the world to make sparkling wine.

Experts agree that Peru makes a more delicate, aromatic pisco – though the Chileans might beg to differ. The key difference between the countries is that Peru's hot climate allows it to produce sweeter grapes.

With sweeter grapes, Peruvian bodegas can distill pisco from grape juice that has been fermented for 45 days. The less-sweet Chilean grapes, on the other hand, have to be made into wine first, distilled, and then cut with water to lower their alcohol content. The difference is noticeable. Fine Peruvian pisco, such as Biondi from Moguegua, or Castañeda or Bohorquez from Ica, has a delicate range of flavors that experienced pisco sippers recognize immediately.

Peru's pride in pisco goes back several centuries. The Spaniards first planted red grapes

© JORGE RIVEROS CAYO

Peru's leading brands of pisco are sipped like fine single malts and sold around the world, especially in Europe.

in the Ica Valley around 1547 and, within a decade, began exporting wine to Spain and its colonies. Sometime thereafter, someone came up with the idea of distilling the fermented juice of the dark-red Quebranta grape, and pisco was born. Peru's climate is too hot to compete with the fine, dry wines of Chile and Argentina, but its pisco was an immediate success around the world. Pisco became an important drink in Spanish salons and even in the saloons of 1849 gold rushers in San Francisco – after all, it was much cheaper to ship pisco up the Pacific Coast than to lug whiskey across the Panama Strait from the East Coast of the United States.

No one knows for sure how pisco got its name. The word means "bird" in Quechua, and apparently the Nasca and Paracas cultures used the word to describe the huge clay jugs they used for fermenting *chicha*. The Spaniards later used these same jugs for fermenting pisco. The port through which the brandy was exported to the world was also called, surprise, Pisco, and its first reference comes in a 1574 map made by Diego Méndez.

There are five different types of pisco: *Pisco puro* is made from nonaromatic grapes such as Mollar, Quebranta, and the black grape; *pisco promático* is made from Albilla, Torontel, Italian, and Moscatel grapes; *pisco aromatizado* gets its fruit bouquet from limes or cherries added during the distillation process; *pisco acholado* is a blend of many different grapes; and *pisco mosto verde* is made from partially fermented grapes.

Although fine pisco is chilled and sipped by itself, Peruvians have invented many pisco-based cocktails: They range from the *algarrobina*, a caramel-colored sweet drink prepared with the honey of the *algarroba* tree, to Peru's version of a Cuba libre, a simple mix of Coca-Cola and pisco. No doubt the favorite, however, is the pisco sour, which was invented in the early 20th century in the Maury Hotel's **Rojo Bar** in downtown Lima. The preparation is simple: fresh-squeezed lime juice, sugarcane syrup, egg white, and water are blended together, topped with Angostura bitters, and served in a tumbler. Drink as many as possible while in Peru. The small, bitter limes essential for pisco sour – known as *limón de pica* – are impossible to find outside of Peru.

PISCO SOUR – THE NATIONAL DRINK OF PERU

3 oz. pisco (white grape brandy)
1 oz. fresh-squeezed lime juice
½ oz. sugarcane syrup
1 egg white
4 ice cubes
Blend for 20 seconds. Drop 2 drops of Angostura bitters on top before serving in cocktail glass or, in the case of a double, in a short but wide tumbler.

ALGARROBINA

1.5 oz. pisco
1 tsp. sugar
¾ oz. *algarrobina* syrup
2 oz. evaporated milk
1 egg yolk
4 ice cubes
Blend for 1 minute. Serve in a champagne glass and garnish with nutmeg or cinnamon and two short straws.

Center, is **Mana** (San Martín 248, tel. 056/80-8366, 8 A.M.–8 P.M. Sun.–Fri.).

Markets
The best supermarket is **Ica Market** (Municipalidad 260, 7 A.M.–11 P.M. daily).

INFORMATION AND SERVICES
The **tourist office** (Grau 150, 8 A.M.–2:30 P.M. Mon.–Fri.) is helpful, and the **tourist police** (tel. 056/22-7673) are on the Plaza de Armas next to **Banco Continental** and also on the fourth block of Elias.

The best hospital is **Felix Torre Alba** (Cutervo 204, tel. 056/23-4798, 24 hours), and there is also a clinic in the Angostura neighborhood. There are several pharmacies on Calle Municipalidad. **Botica Arcangel** is the only 24-hour option.

Scotiabank, Continental, and **Banco de Crédito** are all on Plaza de Armas. Most are open 8 A.M.–5 P.M. Monday–Friday, mornings only on Saturdays, and travelers checks can be exchanged at the Banco de Crédito.

The **post office** is at San Martín 156 (tel. 056/23-4549, 8 A.M.–6:30 P.M. Mon.–Sat.), and the best **Internet** places are **Internet** (Municipalidad 247, 9 A.M.–11 P.M. daily, US$0.75/hr), **Cabin@sClub** (Grau 175, 9 A.M.–11 P.M. daily, US$0.50/hr), and the quiet **Internet Callao** (Callao 128, 8 A.M.–11 P.M. daily). The best option for international calls is **Datel** (Municipalidad 132, Plaza de Armas), which has private phone booths and crystal-clear service to the United States (US$0.15/min). There are private phone booths in the Telefónica office on Lima, in the Plaza de Armas.

La Opinion is a great regional newspaper run by the enterprising Isabel Tueros, who is a good source of information and available most evenings (Municipalidad 132, office #16).

There are several laundry services along San Martin, but the best is **Laundry** (Chiclayo, block 5, 8 A.M.–1 P.M. and 4–8 P.M. daily, tel. 056/21-5684).

GETTING THERE AND AROUND
There is no main bus station in Ica, but all of the main bus companies are clustered on the east end of town, a few blocks from the Plaza de Armas near the corner of Lambayeque and Salaverry. The best option to and from Lima is **Soyuz** (Matias Manzanilla 130, near Lambayeque, tel. 056/22-4138, www.soyuz.com.pe), which has comfortable buses leaving every 15 minutes for as little as US$4–6, though nicer buses cost more. The four-hour trip includes stops outside of Pisco (with a shuttle to the town center), Chincha, and Cañete. **Ormeño** (Lambayeque 180, tel. 056/21-5600, www.grupo-ormeno.com) has nicer, Royal buses that leave for Lima a couple of times a day. A similar bus leaves for Arequipa (10 hours) in the afternoon and evening. It also has a service between Ica, Nasca, and Paracas. A more affordable and recommended option for Arequipa and Nasca is **Flores** (Lambayeque and Salaverry, tel. 056/21-2266 or 056/21-2266, www.floreshnos.com). The only bus that goes directly to Pisco, the launching pad for exploring the Reserva Nacional de Paracas, is **SAKI** (Lambayeque 217, tel. 056/21-3143). Buses leave every half hour 6:15 A.M.–8 P.M. for the one-hour trip.

Ica is swimming with taxis but, for trips to the wineries or Lago Huacachina, it is probably best to go with a driver recommended by your hotel. A reliable taxi company is **Taxi Ya** (tel. 056/23-5361).

Nasca

Nasca would be just another dusty highway town were it not for its enigmatic lines in the desert, which have tormented scientists ever since they were spotted by planes in the 1920s. When seen from above, the stylized forms of hummingbirds, a killer whale, monkey, and other animals sprawl across the desert floor, surrounded by a maze of trapezoids and geometric figures and lines that recede to the horizon. The lines are so bizarre that many, spearheaded by Danish eccentric character Erik von Däniken, believed they are landing strips for extraterrestrials. That theory has somewhat faded, along with a dozen others, but the mystery of the Nasca Lines remains.

Despite the desolate surroundings, advanced cultures have occupied the Río Nasca Valley since the Paracas culture (800–200 B.C.), which probably made the area's first hillside etchings around 400 B.C. They also began work on

© RENÉE DEL GAUDIO AND ROSS WEHNER

rock formations along the remote Pacific coastline near Nasca

Cahuachi, a huge complex of pyramids 28 kilometers northwest of Nasca. The Nasca culture (A.D. 100–600) continued building Cahuachi and also built an ingenious aqueduct that pipes water under the desert floor and is still used by farmers today. The Nasca are world-famous for ceramics and, along with the Paracas, weavings, and excellent examples of both can be seen at the town's new Museo Antonini. After the Nasca, the area fell under the successive influences of the Huari, Chincha, and Inca. A small Spanish settlement was founded here in 1591 but has been destroyed so often by earthquakes—most recently in 1942 and 1996—that no colonial architecture remains.

Nasca today is a noisy hodgepodge of concrete buildings. The best places to stay, both budget and high-end, are in the surrounding countryside. Nasca has a particularly aggressive culture of *jaladores* (salespeople) that swarm tourists when they get off the bus. The city's tourism commission has passed laws making it illegal to sell tourist services on the street, because many travelers have been ripped off, or become pissed off, by this town's informal tourism racket.

SIGHTS
◖ Nasca Lines
The Spanish chronicler Pedro Cieza de León was the first European to comment on the hillside drawings that can be seen from ground level near Nasca and Paracas. Archaeologists had also studied similar hill drawings in Arequipa, Lima, Trujillo, and the mountains of Bolivia and Chile. But the profusion of lines etched onto the perfectly flat San José desert are the continent's fullest expression of this cryptic practice, and were not fully appreciated until the first planes flew over the area in the 1920s. When viewed from above, more than 70 giant plant and animal figures pop into view, etched impermeably onto the desert floor, along with hundreds of straight lines, trapezoids, and other figures as long as 10 kilometers. The shapes cover an astonishing 1,000

FROM UFO LANDING STRIPS TO RAIN CEREMONIES

The Nasca Lines first caught the world's attention in 1939, when American archaeologist Paul Kosok splashed their pictures across world newspapers. His translator, the German mathematician Maria Reiche, was so intrigued by Kosok's research that she moved to Nasca a year later. She spent the next six decades of her life living in austerity and spending her days measuring the lines under the broiling desert sun. By the time she died in 1998, she had developed an elaborate theory to support Kosok's original claim that the lines were "the biggest astronomy book in the world." In the process she had become a much-loved and venerated personality in Nasca, where her birthday remains the town's biggest celebration.

Many other researchers have wandered the deserts of Nasca and come up with theories that range from clever to crackpot. In 1947 Hans Horkheimer said they were tribal symbols, while George Von Breunig likened them to a giant running track in 1980, and Henri Stirlin claimed a few years later they represented huge weavings and strands of yarn. The International Explorers Club claimed that the Nasca people could in fact see the lines from the air. He attempted, unsuccessfully, to build a balloon from reed and cloth. The theory that struck the public imagination, however, was that proposed by Erich von Daniken in his book and movie *Chariots of the Gods*. He claimed the whole pampa was a giant landing strip for extraterrestrials and that one of the drawings, which shows a snowman-looking figure with large round eyes, was an astronaut (that name stuck, by the way).

But a broad consensus is emerging among Nasca experts that the lines are mainly about water. Unlike the broad coastal valleys of the north that supported huge cities of the Moche and Sicán, the valleys of the south are narrow and run with water only during the rainy season in the mountains. During a dry year, the Río Nasca may never even reach the town, much less the Pacific Ocean. In a valley where drought meant death, much of Nasca cosmography – as evidenced by their ceramics, textiles, and ceremonial architecture – is shaped by religious or magical practices to ensure a steady supply of water.

Researchers point out that the first drawings, made around 400 B.C., were of spirals, a water symbol that recurs throughout South America. These later morphed into other marine creatures such as sharks, orcas, and whales. Giuseppe Orefici, who has led excavations around Nasca since the early 1980s, says the subsequent phase of bird images is also water-related. The hummingbirds that suck life-giving nectar from flowers are fertility symbols, he says, and their fluttering wings are sacred dispensers of water. After studying lines in Chile and Bolivia, Dr. Johan Reinhard came to a similar conclusion – that the Nasca Lines are part of a pan-Andean fertility tradition.

After decades of gathering dust, the theory of the first-ever Nasca researcher, a Peruvian named Toribio Mejía Xesspe, is being picked up by modern-day researchers. Mejía Xesspe argued that the lines were sacred paths upon which hundreds of people walked during magical ceremonies. On close inspection, the lines that form the drawings do have an entrance and an exit, as if they were in fact made for walking. A recent documentary made by the Discovery

square kilometers, including a cluster of drawings farther north near Palpa.

The shapes were made thanks to the area's peculiar geography. A thin layer of manganese and iron oxides, called desert varnish, covers the rocky surface of the San José desert. The Nasca removed the dark rocks to expose the lighter-colored rocks beneath, in canals that average about 20 cm deep. They piled the rocks into walls about a meter high to enhance the canal's edge. The Nasca probably made the drawings in small scale and then used ropes and stakes to reproduce them larger on the desert floor.

The best way to see them is by airplane. Pilots bank sharply so that people on both sides of the plane can see the lines, and as a result, many people end up clutching barf bags.

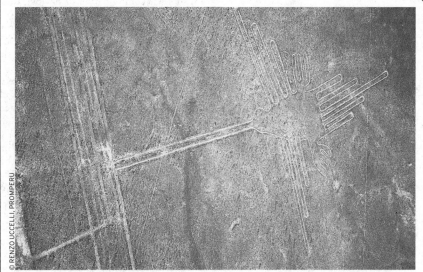

© RENZO UCCELLI, PROMPERU

The Nasca Lines continue to befuddle religious thinkers and archaeologists alike.

Channel showed what these ceremonies may have looked like. The swarms of humans tracing the drawings' edges seem to make these fertility symbols come alive, converting them into living icons for the gods above.

The last lines, a phase perhaps done as late as the Huari (A.D. 600-1000) or even the Chincha (A.D. 1000-1400) cultures, are the huge lines and intersecting plazas. There is evidence that huge masses of people also gathered here for ceremonies. There are stone constructions that appear to have been altars, and a number of clay flutes and arrowheads

were found nearby and were probably used in ceremonial dances.

There are aspects of the lines that have not been fully understood, though they all seem to involve water-producing, cosmic forces. Many of the lines point at sacred mountains, or *apus*, or at points on the horizon that mark important lunar or solar events. One leads to Cahuachi, the ceremonial complex of pyramids that faces the lines and is located on a sacred spot along the Río Nasca. Whatever relationship the pyramids had with the lines, archaeologists believe it too probably had to do with water.

Even those with a stomach of steel should avoid breakfast before flying and consider taking motion sickness medication beforehand. The best time to fly is in the morning before winds pick up, decreasing visibility and making the flight bumpier.

Another option for viewing the lines is a three-story observation tower 19 kilometers north of Nasca and on the way to the Casa-

Museo Maria Reiche. Three small lines can be seen from here, including a set of hands, a lizard, and a tree. A few hillsides offer good views during the clearest light of the morning, especially the giant sand dune of Cerro Blanco.

OVERFLIGHT AGENCIES

After recent plane crashes over the lines, only a few companies can thoroughly guarantee

PUERTO INCA

The nicest place to stop on the seven-hour drive between Nasca and Arequipa is the half-moon beach of Puerto Inca, at Km 603, 10 kilometers south of Chala. The Inca had a settlement here, thus the beach's name, where fish were caught for the Inca and run up to Cusco along Inca roads that can still be seen receding into the mountains. Today what's left is an area of ruins with other smaller ruins nearby – including a strange carved seat on a rocky cliff to the south. Located scandalously close to the ruins, **Hotel Puerto Inka** (Panamericana Sur Km 610, tel. 054/55-1055, www.puertoinka.com. pe, US$68 s, US$58 d with breakfast) has the beach all to itself, and all rooms have ocean views. Amenities include a video library, pool table, discotheque with karaoke, swimming pool, and playground; camping with showers costs US$4 pp. The hotel rents kayaks for US$10 an hour and Jet Skis for US$60 an hour.

flights. Nearly a dozen companies offer Nasca overflights, which range in price US$40–85 depending on the time of year and length of flight. Make advance reservations June–August, when entire days can be booked by gigantic package tours. Otherwise, travelers get the best price by negotiating directly at the overflight companies. This is especially true September–May, when even the top companies charge the low price of US$40.

While every agency offers the traditional 30-minute flight over the most enigmatic Nasca Lines, it is increasingly common to find a company that offers alternative flights. Preferential overflights, for example, last longer and see more lines, and there are flights over the Cantayoc Aqueduct or Palpa Lines. Even if you decide not to take one of these alternative flights, we recommend combining a typical overflight with a visit to the sites. This will greatly broaden your understanding of the cultures that created the lines.

Additionally, the three largest agencies in Nasca, have package deals that combine flights with hotel accommodation or daylong tours and lunch. We recommend Aerocondor's NC Travel, because it has the best service and the pleasant Nido del Condor hotel. Agency prices do not include the US$3 airport tax or the US$4 tourist ticket.

Aerocondor and its agency **NC Travel** (Lima 199, tel. 056/52-1168, www.nctravel-nasca.com) offers four basic tours in its three- and five-passenger Cessnas. A 30-minute flight cuts over the Nasca Lines for US$55; an US$85 45-minute flight does the same route adding on visits to Palpa and the aqueducts; and other flights combine the Nasca Lines with the aqueducts (US$63) or Palpa (US$85). Aerocondor also offers a round-trip package from Lima for around US$150 pp (minimum two people).

The reputable **Alegría Tours** (Lima 168, tel. 056/52-2444, www.alegriatoursperu. com) works with the highly professional Alas Peruanas airline. Its flights are similar to those of NC Travel but at slightly lower prices. The flights of **AeroIca** (Lima 103, tel. 056/52-2434, reservas@nazcagroup.com, www.aero-ica.net) are also recommended.

A smaller airplane company, with which you can directly contract your flight, is **AeroParacas** (tel. 056/52-2688, www.aeropa-racas.com).

Museo Antonini

This museum (Av. de la Cultura 600, tel. 056/52-3444, 9 A.M.–7 P.M. daily, US$5) is the labor of love of Giuseppe Orefici, whose excavations at Cahuachi continue to be funded by the Italian government. This museum has a small but exquisite collection that sheds light on the Nasca's religious way of thinking, including a ceremonial fishing net with embroidered crimson edges and a cotton coat fringed with supernatural dolls that look like tiny, cactus-like beings.

Other Nasca ceramics here portray a pantheon of seafaring creatures, pelicans, cats, birds, lizards, and snakes. These deities often have serpentine shapes emerging from their

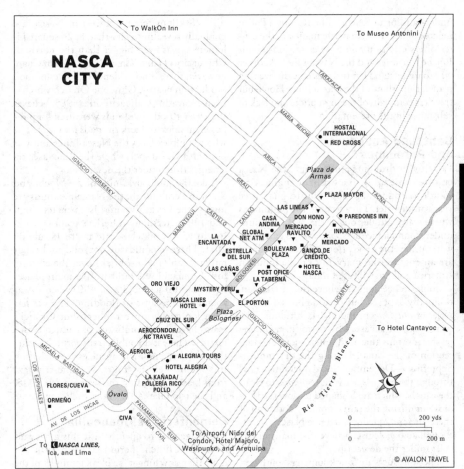

NASCA
CITY

To WalkOn Inn

To Museo Antonini

TARAPACA

MARIA REICHE

IGNACIO MORSESKY

ARICA

GRAU

CALLAO

CASTILLO

MARIATEGUI

Plaza de
Armas

HOSTAL
INTERNACIONAL
RED CROSS

PLAZA MAYOR

TACNA

LAS LINEAS

PAREDONES INN

CASA
ANDINA   DON HONO

GLOBAL   MERCADO
NET ATM   RAVLITO   INKAFARMA

LA   MERCADO
ENCANTADA

ESTRELLA   BOULEVARD   BANCO DE
DEL SUR   PLAZA   CRÉDITO

LAS CAÑAS   HOTEL
                                    NASCA

BOLOGNESI

POST OFICE
LA TABERNA

ORO VIEJO

MYSTERY PERU

NASCA LINES
HOTEL

BOLIVAR

EL PORTÓN

LIMA

Plaza
Bolognesi

IGNACIO MORSESKY

UGARTE

To Hotel Cantayoc

CRUZ DEL SUR

AEROCONDOR/
NC TRAVEL

SAN MARTIN

AEROICA

MICAELA BASTIDAS

ALEGRIA TOURS

HOTEL ALEGRIA

LA KAÑADA/
POLLERÍA RICO
POLLO

LOS ESPINALES

FLORES/CUEVA

ORMEÑO

Óvalo

AV DE LOS INCAS

PANAMERICANA SUR

GUARDIA CIVIL

CIVA

To Airport, Nido del
Condor, Hotel Majoro,
Wasipunko, and Arequipa

To **C**NASCA LINES,
Ica, and Lima

Río Tierras Blancas

0   200 yds
0   200 m

© AVALON TRAVEL

mouths, which archaeologists believe reflect the Nasca belief that blessings come from the nose and mouth. There are also elongated skulls, and others with trepanation holes, and a few well-preserved mummies. Out back there is a replication of a Nasca tomb, a Nasca irrigation canal, and a scale model of the Nasca Lines. Orefici has a spectacular collection of painted textiles that he hopes to put on display in the future.

Casa-Museo Maria Reiche and Maria Reiche Centre

During much of her six decades living in Nasca, German mathematician Maria Reiche lived in a simple room in the village of Pascana, about 27 kilometers south of Nasca. When she died in 1998 at the age of 95, she was buried here and her home converted into the Casa-Museo Maria Reiche (Panamericana Km 420, tel. 056/23-4383, 9 A.M.–7 P.M. Mon.–Fri., 8:30 A.M.–6:30 P.M. Sat., 9 A.M.–1 P.M. Sun.). The place now pays tribute to Reiche's life and her theories about the Nasca Lines.

The Maria Reiche Centre (Jose Fina de Mejía de Boca Negra and San Mauricio, 9 A.M.–9 P.M. daily, US$3) offers a similarly comprehensive understanding of Reiche's life. Run by a Polish mentee of the German mathematician, the center offers question and answer sessions about Reiche's theories and the Nasca Lines. Another way to understand her theories is at the evening planetarium show of the Nazca Lines Hotel, but travelers complain of the high prices and lack of substance in the presentation.

Cantayoc Aqueduct and Paredones

Faced with droughts and famine, the Nasca culture came up with a brilliant engineering solution around A.D. 300–500 to guarantee year-round water. They went to the mountains where water gurgles out of the rock and built underground aqueducts, *puquios,* to carry this water under the desert floor. These aqueducts are an engineering marvel of pre-Columbian America and are still used today.

Some archaeologists believe the canals were originally exposed but became buried after a series of *aluviones* or muddy flash floods. The canals can be accessed by periodic *respidores* or spiral ramps that lead down to an exposed section of the canal. During the dry months September–December, local farmers crawl through the tunnels between *respidores* to clean the canals, which are S-shaped to slow the flow of water during the rainy months. Today 36 of these ancient aqueducts irrigate Nasca's fields, though archaeologists believe that many others exist under the desert floor.

The aqueducts are four kilometers southwest of town near the Hotel Cantayo and reachable via taxi (US$5) or transport that runs along the nearby Abancay highway. Guards are now charging a US$4 entrance fee, which includes two other nearby sites: the Inca ruins of Paredones, a deteriorated *tambo,* or resting place, made of adobe walls atop stone foundations; and two lines, known as El Telar and Las Agujas (The Weaving and The Needles). This area is safe to walk around until the guards go home at 4:30 P.M.

Cahuachi

Excavations at Cahuachi, an area of low-lying hills 28 kilometers northwest of Nasca, are gradually revealing a city that, at 24 square kilometers, was even bigger than the northern Chimú city of Chan Chan. Unlike Chan Chan, however, there is no evidence of homes or food production nearby. Giuseppe Orefici, who has been excavating Cahuachi since 1985, believes the area's 40-odd pyramids were used for public ceremonies to thank the gods for water. The whole complex faces the Nasca Lines and was built on a sacred spot, where the Río Nasca reemerges from under the desert floor.

Like the adobe pyramids of the Moche and Sicán in Peru's north, the Nasca pyramids are huge—the Great Pyramid is 25 meters high and 100 meters long. Orefici's team is working to restore its elaborate north facade by 2011. These pyramids are not solid adobe, but rather a cap of adobe bricks over the existing hill. Cahuachi was built in five main phases between 400 B.C. and A.D. 400, when it was abandoned because of flooding. The site has been looted by grave robbers, but Orefici's teams have found tombs full of painted Nasca textiles. There is no public transport to the site, though more and more agencies are including this site in their day tours. A round-trip taxi from Nasca, including the wait, costs US$15, and the trip takes 40 minutes each way.

Cementerio de Chauchilla

Nasca agencies frequently visit this graveyard from the Chincha period (1000–1460), but more than anything it is a bleak reminder of the destructive force of grave robbers. Thousands of scraps of textiles, bones, and patches of human hair lay spread across the sands. A few of the clay tombs have been restored, and bleached skeletons, with huge dreadlocks, are on display inside. At other cemeteries, like the one near Lomas, locals have used bulldozers to unearth the cemeteries of their ancestors, leaving skulls strewn across the sand. The cemetery is about eight kilometers off the Panamerican Highway south of Nasca, or about a half-hour drive. There is no public transport to the site, though agencies visit here frequently and a round-trip taxi from Nasca costs US$17.

ENTERTAINMENT AND EVENTS

Discos get cranked up in Nasca only on the weekends. **Las Cañas** (Bolognesi 279, tel. 056/80-6891, 8 A.M.–8 P.M.) is a restaurant that transforms into a discotheque after 9 P.M. on weekends. If you are looking for a mellow environment, **Boulevard Plaza** (Bolognesi 388, tel. 056/52-3749, 2:30 P.M.–1 A.M. daily, US$4–7) has a long cocktail list and a good selection of accompanying appetizers.

The biggest party in Nasca is **Fiesta Yacu Raymi,** which kicks off with Maria Reiche's birthday on May 15 and includes dances, *pachamancas,* and other celebrations. Religious holidays include the **Virgen del Carmen** on September 19 and the **Virgen de Guadalupe,** patroness of Nasca, on October 8. During the low-water months between September and December, communities gather in the fields to clean the ancient aqueducts.

RECREATION
Trekking

Local trekking guide **Edmundo Watkin** (Wasipunko, Km 462, tel. 056/52-3212, www.nascawasipunko.com) has put together a range of interesting hikes, including an eight-hour jaunt from the altiplano to the summit of Cerro Blanco, one of the world's largest sand dunes, which rises 2,000 meters over the valley floor and offers good views of the Nasca Lines (US$40). He also has an interesting three-day package that includes an overflight of the Nasca Lines, a walking tour around the Cementerio de Chauchilla, and a full day of cultural tourism in a farming community near the former hacienda of the Benavides family. Although Edmundo speaks only Spanish, his brother Alan speaks English. Between the two, they can help you figure out travel plans.

Four-Wheel Safaris

Enzo Destro, the Italian owner and manager of **Hotel Cantayo Spa & Resort** (tel. 056/52-2264, www.hotelcantayo.com), offers a series of deluxe four-wheel-drive tours for up to four people at US$250 per day. Destinations include Pampa Galera, the high-altitude national reserve above Nasca with herds of vicuñas; Punta San Fernando, a remote Pacific point that offers reliable sightings of Humboldt penguins, sea lions, and Andean condors; and a descent along the rugged coastline between Nasca and Puerto Inca, including the quaint port of Lomas and a dozen unforgettable beaches.

Sandboarding and Biking

Alegría Tours (Lima 168, tel. 056/52-2444, www.alegriatoursperu.com) offers sandboarding on Cerro Blanco (six hours, US$25 pp) or a four-hour biking trip (US$20 pp) that drops 2,000 meters in 45 kilometers and whizzes past Cerro Blanco.

Tour Agencies and Guides

The agencies that organize Nasca overflights, **NC Travel** (Lima 199, tel. 056/52-1168, www.nctravelnasca.com) and **Alegría Tours** (Lima 168, tel. 056/52-2444, www.alegriatoursperu.com), can also arrange conventional day tours, which combine visits to the Museo Antonini, the aqueducts, and Cahuachi with a buffet lunch. **Mystery Peru** (Ignacio Morsesky 126, tel. 056/52-2379, www.mysteryperu.com) is an alternative option, whose tours include a bit more adventure. An excellent local guide and professor of tourism is **Perico Quiroz** (Bolognesi 592, 2nd Fl., tel. 056/52-2789, perico_tours@hotmail.com). Perico, who speaks Spanish, English, and Italian, has put together a US$20 one-day tour through the area, and we recommend his overnight on Cerro Blanco. If Perico is busy, try **Juan Valdivia** (tel. 056/52-3080 or 056/969-9335).

ACCOMMODATIONS
Under US$10

The hotel rooms of **Hostal Internacional** (Maria Reiche 112, tel. 056/52-2744, hostal-internacional@hotmail.com, US$9 s, US$12 d) are a good budget option. The whitewashed rooms have ceramic floors and decent beds. Bungalow rooms with bamboo ceilings, nice bathrooms, and cable TV are worth the slightly higher prices (US$14 s, US$19 d).

The concrete floors and shared baths of **Hotel Nasca** (Lima 438, tel. 056/52-2085, US$3 s, US$6 d) are a bit depressing, but the tiled rooms with private baths (US$9 s, US$12 d) are somewhat nicer. There is great camping with showers at **Wasipunko** (Panamericana Sur Km 462, tel. 056/52-3212, www.nascawasipunko.com, US$5 pp).

US$10-25

The family-run **Wasipunko** (Panamericana Sur Km 462, tel. 056/52-3212, www.nascawasipunko.com, US$22 s, US$38 d with breakfast), owned by Olivia Watkin, is a rustic country hostel 12 kilometers south of Nasca. Here, the Watkin family has eked out a paradise of palms, acacia, and *huarango* trees, which are scented by jacaranda blooms and filled with birds. The simple rooms have whitewashed adobe walls, bamboo roofs, antique furniture, clean bathrooms, and Olivia's own watercolors of local plants. The dining room is an adobe structure with large *huarango* beams, stained glass, and a telescope for stargazing. Because there is limited solar electricity, most spaces, including bedrooms, are illuminated with kerosene lamps. Phone calls must be made with a phone card, which Olivia keeps on hand. This is a great place to hang out for a day or two, hop aboard a horse (US$4, half day), and relax. There is a good US$8 lunch menu, and Olivia's sons, Alan and Edmundo, speak English and French, respectively. Edmundo also offers excellent local treks.

Recently overtaken by a Belgian-Dutch business team, **The WalkOn Inn** (José María Mejía 108, tel. 056/52-2566, www.walkoninn.com, US$10 pp), formerly Via Morburg, is undergoing wonderful transitions. All 11 rooms have firm mattresses and private baths, and the pool is heated. That means hours of evening stargazing. If you are taking the bus, give a call in advance, and one of the owners will meet you at the station.

The **Estrella del Sur** (Callao 568, tel. 056/52-2764, estrelladelsurhotel@yahoo.com.mx, US$12 s, US$22 d with breakfast) is on a quiet street three blocks from the Plaza

and across from the hospital. We liked this place because it was clean, fresh-smelling, and friendly and had big rooms with closets, cable TV, and fair bathrooms—some rooms even have a porch.

US$25-50

The charming **Oro Viejo** (Callao 483, tel. 056/52-2284, www.hoteloroviejo.com, US$28 s, US$35 d with breakfast) is a family-run place a few blocks from the plaza but away from the noise. Rooms, arranged around a flower garden, have nice furniture, big bathrooms, and fans. There is an outdoor bar and swimming pool. The tables in the indoor dining room are lit with candles.

The modern **Paredones Inn** (Lima 600, tel. 056/52-2181, paredoneshotel@terra.com, US$28 s, US$34 d with breakfast) is one of the best deals in town, with impeccable rooms, comfy beds, large bathrooms, cable TV, and 24-hour hot water. Breakfast can be taken on a rooftop terrace.

The major agencies own hotels that are typically bundled together in the overflight packages. We recommend two. Owned by Alegría Tours, **Hotel Alegría** (Lima 166, tel. 056/52-2702, hotelalegrianet, US$20 s, US$30 d) is a modern building near the bus stations with lots of light and a nice pool. The rooms are large and there is also laundry service, a book exchange, and a cafeteria in a quiet, grassy backyard. The other agency hotel, located across from the airport, is Aerocondor's **Nido del Condor** (Panamericana Sur Km 447, tel. 056/52-1168, nidodelcondornasca@terra.com.pe, US$30 s, US$45 d with breakfast). The TV, fans, phone, and clean bathrooms make up for the flowery bedspreads and tacky decorations. There are nice gardens outside with a small pool. Camping is possible for US$6.

US$50-100

A good hotel in the city itself is **Nazca Lines Hotel** (Bolognesi 147, tel. 056/52-2293, US$91 s, US$101 d with breakfast). Whitewashed arcades wrap around a luxurious patio with two pools, fountains, and tables shaded with palm trees and bougainvillea. The rooms are taste-fully decorated with *sautillo* tile floors, cable TV, and bathrooms with tubs. The restaurant (6 A.M.–10 P.M. daily, US$6–9) serves excellent food in the breezy dining room. The hotel's **Maria Reiche Planetarium** (7 P.M. daily, US$6, US$3 students) gives an evening presentation of the Nasca Lines and Reiche's theories. Travelers, however, give the planetarium a mediocre review.

Hotel Majoro (Panamericana Sur Km 452.8, tel. 056/52-2490, www.hotelmajoro.com, US$65 s, US$80 d with breakfast) is a charming country hotel whose gardens spill into pools, tennis courts, and horse corrals. The 40 comfortable, cool rooms with high ceilings have recently been remodeled. There are two nice pools, which have bougainvillea-covered rock islands shaded by fruit trees and gardens.

Casa Andina (Bolognesi 367, tel. 056/52-3563, www.casa-andina.com, US$65 s, US$75 d with breakfast), part of the national hotel chain, has an ideal location on the Bolognesi pedestrian mall. The modern rooms open on to a sunny, bougainvillea-lined patio, and a small circular pool is an essential stop after a morning of sightseeing. As always, the staff is friendly and can help you plan your sightseeing.

Over US$150

Our highest recommendation goes to **Hotel Cantayo Spa & Resort** (Hacienda Cantayo s/n, tel. 056/52-2264, www.hotelcantayo.com, US$180 s or d with breakfast). Every last detail of this place, which opened in 2001 as a sort of spiritual retreat, was cared for by owner and manager Enzo Destro, from Padua, Italy. From the ruins of a hacienda, Enzo managed to save original archways, floor tiles, a well, and a centuries-old ficus tree. Around these elements, he built a spacious and light-filled lobby graced with the old well and the contemporary art and Tibetan tapestries he collects.

The hotel succeeds in its goal of being a complete refuge from stress. Songbirds flit around the lawn, where the huge ficus tree rises alongside two elegantly shaped pools. There are grassy areas for yoga and meditation, a walkway with river stones for foot relaxation, and a dojo for Kyudo (an archery range for Japanese meditation). Other amenities include a whirlpool tub, hydromassages, both Turkish and herbal baths, and in the near future, a spa with sauna. You can also take a country ride on a Peruvian *paso* horse. Enzo also takes guests on four-wheel-drive safaris. For a midafternoon nap, guests stroll down shaded archways to the rooms, which have huge white walls and all the amenities: refrigerators, luxurious bathrooms with tubs, queen-size beds with hypoallergenic blankets, remote-controlled air-conditioning, and heat—but no television.

FOOD
Peruvian

Locals flock to the tasty and affordable **Don Hono** (Arica 254, tel. 056/52-3066, Sun.–Fri., US$2), which serves up a range of great local food prepared by an internationally trained cook. **La Kañada** (Lima 160, US$5–6) has been operated by the Benavides family for 40 years and serves excellent ostrich, vegetarian, and seafood dishes such as sea bass with prawns from the Río Palpa. Most nights there is live folkloric music at 8 P.M.

The very clean **Las Lineas** (Arica 299, tel. 056/52-2066, 7 A.M.–4 P.M. and 7–11 P.M. Mon.–Sat., 7 A.M.–4 P.M. Sun., US$4) serves appetizers such as avocado salad and *papas a la huancaina,* and entrées of meat, fish, and seafood. Located on a quiet street, **La Encantada** (Callao 592, tel. 056/52-2930, 7:30 A.M.–11 P.M. daily, US$3–8) also serves up Peruvian fare like ceviche, *salpicon de pollo,* and *camarones.*

For *pollo a la brasa,* your options are two-fold. **Plaza Mayor** (Call Bolognesi and Arica, tel. 056/52-3548, 7:30 A.M.–midnight daily, US$5–8), on the plaza, has great views and a more elegant atmosphere than **Polleria Rico Pollo** (Lima 190, tel. 056/52-1151, noon–1 A.M. daily, US$4–6). But they both serve up juicy, browned chicken, with piping hot fries.

International

Looking at its graffiti-covered walls, it's easy

to believe that **La Taberna** (Lima 321, tel. 056/80-6783) has been around for more than 20 years. The clean kitchen dishes up a wide-ranging menu that includes salads, pastas, ceviche, and local favorites such as *lomo saltado* and *arroz con mariscos.*

The best pizzeria in town is **Puquio** (Bolognesi 481, evenings only). For pastas, try **El Portón** (Ignacio Morsesky 120, tel. 056/52-3490, 11 A.M.11 P.M. daily, US$10–12), which also serves up local dishes like *aji de gallina* and *seco de cabrito,* along with *ensalada caprese,* seafood lasagna, and excellent pizzas. Stepping up a bit, the **Nazca Lines Hotel** (Bolognesi 147, tel. 056/52-2293, 6 A.M.–10 P.M. daily, US$6–9) has an excellent restaurant, which serves on a patio and in a breezy dining room, and specializes in seafood dishes and *brochetas.*

Fine Dining

Hotel Cantayo Spa & Resort (Hacienda Cantayo s/n, tel. 056/52-2264, www.hotelcantayo.com, 7 A.M.–10 P.M. daily) serves, without question, the best food in Nasca—and all of it is organic. Breakfast begins with fruit, toast, and eight types of gourmet marmalades, ranging from *membrillo* to *guanábana.* Lunch is tender chunks of lamb, chicken, veggies, and potatoes cooked in an underground *pachamanca* pit. For dinner, there are homemade pastas or lighter entrées such as sea bass steamed in a bamboo tube, along with organic salad and a bottle from the hotel's vast wine cellar. Much of the food here is imported from Italy, including large wheels of Parmesan cheese.

Markets

The *mercado central* is between Grau and Arica. **Mercado Ravlito** (Grau 245, 8 A.M.–10 P.M. daily) is the best-stocked grocery store.

INFORMATION AND SERVICES

Maps are available at the **tourist office** inside the municipality building (Plaza de Armas, tel. 056/52-2418, 8 A.M.–2 P.M.). **Iperú** has plans to open a Nasca office. Ask around to see if it is open yet.

Police are on the highway just outside of the center (Los Incas, block 1, tel. 056/52-2442).

The best health care is available from the **Red Cross clinic** on the Plaza de Armas (tel. 056/52-2607, 8 A.M.–1 P.M. and 4–8 P.M. Mon.–Fri., 8 A.M.–1 P.M. Sat.), which has good doctors, a pharmacy, and a laboratory, and a dentist works next door. They will also respond to emergencies 24 hours a day. Another 24-hour option is Nasca's **Hospital de Apoyo,** on the fifth block of Callao. The largest pharmacy is **InkaFarma** (Lima 596, tel. 056/52-3065, www.inkafarma.com.pe, 7:30 A.M.–11 P.M. daily), and a smaller option is **Boticas Universitarias** (Bolognesi and Grau).

For money matters, **Banco de la Nación** (Lima 431) and **Banco de Crédito** (Lima and Grau) both have ATMs. There is a **Global Net** ATM next to Casa Andina. Banks are generally open weekdays 8 A.M.–5:30 P.M. and Saturday mornings.

The **post office** is at Fermín del Castillo 379, between Bolognesi and Lima (9 A.M.–5 P.M. Mon.–Fri.). There are several Internet cafés with speedy connections; the most convenient way of finding these is by asking at your hotel which café is closest.

For overseas phone calls, the **Telefónica office** (Lima 525, tel. 056/52-3758, 7:30 A.M.–11 P.M. daily) has private phone booths.

GETTING THERE AND AROUND

Several agencies in Lima, including **Aeroica** (Lima 103, tel. 056/52-2434, reservas@nazca-group.com, www.aeroica.net), fly in tourists from Lima to have lunch and see the lines before returning the same day.

All of Nasca's bus companies are congregated around the roundabout at the end of Lima, where the Panamericana highway skirts around town. The bus trip between Lima and Nasca is 7–8 hours. **Ormeño** (Av. de los Incas 112, tel. 056/52-2058, www.grupo-ormeno.com) has Royal Class and economy buses to Lima. **Cruz del Sur** (Lima and San Martin, tel. 056/52-3713, www.cruzdelsur.com.pe) buses to and from Lima stop in Ica, Pisco, and

Paracas. Cheaper, less direct buses are available through **Flores** (Av. los Inca s/n, tel. 056/966-7202, www.floreshnos.com) or **Cueva** (Los Inca 108, tel. 056/52-2526), whose buses between Nasca and Ica leave approximately every half hour. Another recommended company is **Civa** (Lima 155, tel. 056/52-3960).

Because of highway improvements, buses now travel between Lima and Cusco in 20 hours and turn toward the mountains at Nasca. In 14 hours, the highway that leads uphill from Nasca passes the Reserva Nacional Pampa, crests over the Andes at 4,400 meters, and reaches Abancay before heading on to Cusco. Ormeño and Cruz del Sur travel this route, but the company with the most buses is **Expreso Wari** (tel. 056/22-9134, www.expresowari.com.pe). Cruz del Sur also runs Arequipa (9 hours) and Tacna (12 hours) buses.

Colectivos travel the Ica–Nasca route in two hours flat for US$4 per person. There are unfortunately no large taxi companies in Nasca. Recommended taxi drivers include Goyo (tel. 056/969-0020) and Bali (tel. 056/969-9464).

THE DESERT COAST

LIMA

Lima's taxi drivers tend to be educated, perceptive, and opinionated. When asked what they think about Lima, they will tick off a litany of complaints: The highways are congested with buses. The air is full of exhaust and noise. Slums have sprawled across all the desert hills around Lima and residents there lack regular plumbing, water, and sometimes even electricity. The city's politicians and business leaders create a daily circus of corruption, and there is a huge, and growing, separation between the rich and the poor. Then, as if that weren't enough, there's the *garúa*. The blanket of fog rolls in from the ocean and covers everything May–November, depositing a patina of grime that lends the city its gray, dismal appearance.

But, in the same breath, the taxi driver will extol the virtues of this once-opulent capital of the Spanish viceroyalty that stretched from present-day Ecuador to Chile. Limeños are an exotic cocktail, a bit of coast, sierra, and jungle blended with African, Chinese, and European to create an eclectic, never-before-seen blend. Heaps of tangy ceviche and succulent shellfish can be had for a few dollars, along with shredded chicken served in a creamy concoction of milk, mountain cheese, nuts, and *ají* pepper. Bars, clubs, and local music venues, called *peñas,* explode most nights with dance and the rhythms of *cumbia,* salsa, Afro-Peruvian pop, and a dozen forms of creole music. There are sandy beaches just a half hour south of the city. And despite all its griminess, the center of Lima shines forth with a wealth of colonial art and architecture, rivaled perhaps only by

© CARLOS SANTA MARIA/123RF.COM

HIGHLIGHTS

Catedral: After two decades of turbulence, the center of Lima is roaring back, and at the center of it all is a refurbished main square and the 16th-century cathedral, with elegantly carved choir stalls and a huge painting gallery (page 316).

Casa de Aliaga: This colonial mansion in the heart of Lima's old town is in pristine condition and offers a fascinating glimpse into domestic life during the opulent days of the viceroyalty (page 320).

San Francisco: This 16th-century convent has a brightly decorated patio and

painting gallery upstairs, and labyrinthian catacombs downstairs that served for centuries as Lima's general cemetery (page 321).

Museo Larco: With a huge collection of gold, textiles, and more than 40,000 ceramics, this museum offers a complete survey of all of Peru's archaeological treasures (page 323).

Museo Nacional de Arqueología: The best way to wrap your mind around Peru's complex succession of ancient cultures is by visiting this compact and concise museum (page 324).

LOOK FOR **(** TO FIND RECOMMENDED SIGHTS, ACTIVITIES, DINING, AND LODGING.

Mexico City, the other great center of Spanish power in the New World.

The bottom line: Lima is an extraordinary city, but it takes a little getting used to. The country's leading museums, churches, and restaurants are here, along with nearly eight million people, almost a third of Peru's population. It is the maximum expression of Peru's cultural diversity (and chaos). Whether you like it or not, you will come to Lima, because nearly all international flights land at this gateway. But do yourself a favor and see Lima at the end of your trip, not at the beginning. That way you

have a better chance of understanding what you see and not becoming overwhelmed in the process.

PLANNING YOUR TIME

Depending on your interests, Lima can be seen in a day's dash or several days to take in most of the museums, churches, and surrounding sights. Peru travelers tend to enjoy Lima more at the end of a trip than at the beginning. After visiting Puno, Cusco, and other Peruvian cities, travelers are more prepared to deal with the logistics of getting around this huge city. They

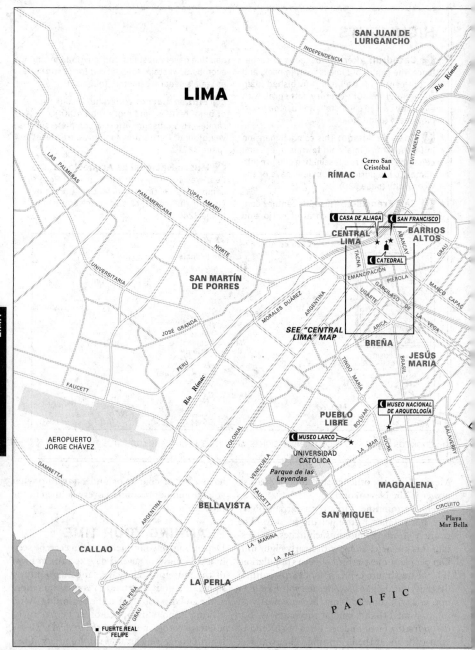

LA MOLINA

UNIVERSIDAD
AGRARIA

GOLF
LOS INCAS

0   1 mi
0   1 km

JOCKEY
PLAZA

HIPÓDROMO
MONTERRICO

MUSEO
DE ORO ★

MONTERRICO

CIRCUNVALACIÓN

SAN LUIS

PANAMERICANA SUR

MUSEO DE LA
NACIÓN ★

SAN
BORJA

SURCO

LA
VICTORIA

LINCE

SEE
"SAN ISIDRO"
MAP

CORPAC

SALVADOR ALLENDE

SURQUILLO

TOMÁS MARSANO

HEROES

PANAMERICANA SUR

SAN
ISIDRO

LIMA GOLF
CLUB

MIRAFLORES

SEE
"MIRAFLORES"
MAP

EJÉRCITO

PLAYAS

LARCOMAR

BARRANCO

SEE "BARRANCO" MAP

Playa
Costa Verde

Playa
Barranco

CHORILLOS

Playa Agua
Dulce

HUAYLAS

O C E A N

Playa La
Herradura

LIMA

have also seen enough of the country to make better sense of the vast, and often poorly explained, collections in Peru's museums. Things start making sense.

If you are short on time and are visiting Cusco, one headache-free option is to fly from Cusco to Lima early in the morning and spend the day touring Lima on an organized tour (if you are planning on seeing Lima on your own, plan on one day for just acclimatizing). Various good day tours include lunch at one of the better restaurants in the city. In the evening, you can head to the airport for your flight home.

This is also a good way to avoid a long layover at Lima's unpleasant airport. Because of afternoon winds, most flights leave Cusco in the morning. But from Lima, international flights tend to leave in the evening. So travelers coming from Cusco often end up spending several hours at Lima's airport on their way home.

HISTORY

Present-day Lima was never the center of any great empire but rather a verdant valley where a series of cultures flourished alongside the shrine of **Pachacámac,** which by the Inca's time housed one of the most respected, and feared, oracles in the Andes. Huaca Pucllana, in Lima's upscale Miraflores neighborhood, was a ceremonial center built out of adobe bricks by the seafaring **Lima culture** from around A.D. 200 onward. The valley later fell under the influence of the Ayacucho-based **Huari culture** and was integrated by 1300 into the **Ychma kingdom,** which built most of the monumental architecture at Pachacámac. Inca **Túpac Yupanqui** conquered the area in the mid-15th century and built an enclosure for holy women alongside Pachacámac's stepped pyramid.

The first Spaniard to arrive in the area was **Hernando Pizarro,** who rode with a group of soldiers from Cajamarca in 1533 to investigate reports of gold at Pachacámac. They found nothing, but his brother, Francisco, returned two years later to move the capital here from Cusco. **Francisco Pizarro** was drawn to the spot because of its fertile plains and the natural

port of Callao. (Both Pizarros had come here in January, in the middle of Lima's brief summer, and must have thought it was a sunny place!)

Pizarro laid the city out in typical checkerboard pattern, with the main square butting up against the **Río Rímac** ("talking river" in Quechua), a natural defensive line. He christened Lima **Ciudad de Los Reyes** (City of the Kings), and a decade later it was designated the capital of the Spanish viceroyalty in South America and eventually seat of the continent's archbishop. **Universidad San Marcos,** America's first university, was founded here in 1511, and the city was completely walled by the 17th century.

Most of the Catholic orders established themselves in Lima and built more than a dozen baroque churches and convents. Even the Spanish Inquisition for South America was based here (its headquarters is now an interesting museum). By royal decree all the commerce of the entire viceroyalty—essentially the entire west side of South America—had to pass through Lima, fueling a construction boom of elegant homes and promenades, such as the Paseo de Aguas on the far side of the Río Rímac (these days a downtrodden neighborhood).

The city was quickly rebuilt after a devastating 1746 earthquake that destroyed 80 percent of the city and slammed the port of **Callao** with a 12-meter tsunami. Lima's prominence began to fade after the independence wars of the 1820s, when it lost its monopoly over South American commerce.

Even in the early days of Lima, neighborhoods of black, mulatto, Indian, and mestizo workers began to crop up around the city, and the expansion continued after the city's walls were torn down by **President José Balta** (1868–1872). During the **War of the Pacific** (1879–1883), Lima was sacked by an invading Chilean army, which carted off church gold and most of the national library's books to Santiago de Chile.

There had always been a main avenue leading through the countryside to the port of Callao, but as the city expanded, other principal avenues were built outside the center, and

© ANIBAL SOLIMANO, PROMPERU

Balconies are for Limeños what the Eiffel Tower is for the French – an unequivocal stamp of national character.

the city's first electric train was inaugurated in 1906. For four centuries Lima had been a small city and even in 1919 only had 173,000 inhabitants. Over the rest of the 20th century, Lima's population would swell 44-fold to its current population of nearly eight million.

As in La Paz, Bolivia, and other South American capitals, Lima's population exploded as the country transitioned from a rural economy to one based on large industry. Impoverished campesinos immigrated here from the countryside and built ramshackle slums, called *pueblos jóvenes*. Since the mid-1990s, these slums have turned into full-fledged neighborhoods, albeit poor neighborhoods. Regardless, they no longer lack water and sewer service and have Internet and big grocery stores.

Lima's poverty became intense during the 1980s and 1990s, when a series of countryside massacres committed by both the **Shining Path** and the Peruvian army sparked a crushing migration to Lima. The new immigrants worked at whatever they could find, and many ended up becoming street vendors

(*ambulantes*), causing the center's main streets to become completely congested. After being elected in 1990, **President Alberto Fujimori** put an end—albeit through corrupt techniques which now have him exiled in Chile—to the rampant inflation, rolling blackouts, and car bombings that were terrorizing Lima residents. In 1992, he captured Shining Path leader **Abimael Guzmán. Túpac Amaru,** the country's other main guerilla group, staged a final stand in Lima in 1996 by taking 490 hostages during a gala at the Japanese ambassador's residence. The standoff ended four months later after a Peruvian special forces team freed the hostages, killing the 14 guerillas in the process (only one hostage died—of bleeding from a gunshot wound).

Even before the terrorism years, much of the commerce and most of the wealthy families had abandoned the center of Lima and established the upscale neighborhoods and corporate centers of Monterrico, Miraflores, and San Isidro, where nearly all of the city's best hotels and restaurants are now located.

Though still a bit grimy and unsafe to walk around in at night, the center of Lima is making a comeback. Street vendors were banned in the mid-1990s, and now the Plaza de Armas has been renovated with new riverside promenades and a spate of nice restaurants. Businesses like *Caretas,* the country's leading newsmagazine, have moved back to the center. Compared to the mid-1990s, the center of Lima feels pleasant and safe.

Sights

Lima can be thought of as a triangle, with the center at the apex. The base begins with the port of **Callao** and the nearby airport and runs along the coast through the neighborhoods of **Miraflores, Barranco,** and **Chorillos.** Other neighborhoods, such as **Pueblo Libre** and **San Isidro,** are in the middle of the triangle.

Lima is jam-packed with sights, but most interesting to many people are the colonial churches, convents, and homes in Lima's center, which is safe but warrants precautions nonetheless: Leave your passport and money in the hotel, and guard your camera.

Lima's best museums are spread out, set in neighborhoods that are sandwiched between the coast and the center. Excellent collections of pre-Columbian gold, textiles, and ceramics can be found at the Museo Larco in Pueblo Libre, Museo de la Nación in San Borja, and Museo de Oro in Monterrico. English- and sometimes French-speaking guides are usually available at these museums.

Most Lima visitors stay in San Isidro, Miraflores, and Barranco, neighborhoods near the coast with the best selection of hotels, restaurants, and nightlife. There is little to see here, however, except for giant adobe platforms that were built by the Lima culture (A.D. 200–700) and now rise above the upscale neighborhoods.

There are so many sights to see in downtown Lima that you would need a few days to see them all. The best idea is to start early with the big sights, be selective, and work your way down the list as energy allows. The old town is bordered by the Río Rímac to the north, Avenida Tacna to the west, and Avenida Abancay to the east. The center of Lima is perfectly safe, but it is a good idea not to stray too far outside these main streets—except for a lunchtime foray to Chinatown or a taxi ride to Museo de los Descalzos, on the other side of the river. Mornings are best reserved for visits to Lima's main churches, which are mostly open 8 A.M.–1 P.M. and 5–8 P.M. daily and have English-speaking guides who request a tip only. Taxis into the center from Miraflores cost US$5 (15–30 minutes), or on Arequipa Avenue catch a Todo Arequipa bus that runs to within walking distance of the center (US$0.50, 20–50 minutes).

CENTRAL LIMA AND PUEBLO LIBRE
C Catedral

Start on the **Plaza Mayor,** which is graced with a bronze fountain from 1650 and flanked on one side by the Catedral, which was built in the late 16th century. It contains the carved wooden sepulcher of Francisco Pizarro, who was murdered in 1541 by a mob of Almagristas, a rival political faction. As you enter, the first chapel on the right is dedicated to St. John the Baptist and contains a carving of Jesus that is considered to be among the most beautiful in the Americas. But the highlights of the cathedral are the choir stalls carved in the early 17th century by Pedro Noguera and the museum (9 A.M.–4:30 P.M. Mon.–Fri., 10 A.M.–4:30 P.M. Sat., US$5). Paintings here include a 1724 work by Alonso de la Cueva that paints the faces of the 13 Inca rulers alongside a lineup of Spanish kings from Carlos V to Felipe V. There is no clearer example of how art was used to put order on a turbulent, violent succession of kings. Other pieces include a series of allegorical paintings painted in the 17th century by the Bassano brothers in northern Italy (no one knows how or when this priceless art was imported) and chest altars, one from Ayacucho and the other from Cusco, with an astounding number of miniature painted figures made of potato flour.

Also on the Plaza Mayor are the magnificent **Archbishop's Palace** (not open to the public) and, on the corner, the **Casa del Oidor.** This 16th-century house is closed to the public but has Lima's signature wooden balconies on the outside, with carvings inspired by Moorish designs and wood slats from behind which women viewed the activity on the square. Next door is the **Palacio del Gobierno,** the president's palace, which forms the other side of the Plaza Mayor and was built by the Spanish on top of the home of Taulichusco, the ruler of the Rímac Valley at that time. It was at this spot that liberator Jose de San Martín proclaimed the symbolic independence of Peru on July 28, 1821. There is an interesting change of the guard at noon and a change of the flag at 5:45 P.M. Monday–Saturday.

Also on the Plaza Mayor is the **Club de la Unión,** a business club formed in 1868 that is a bit empty these days, are also on the Plaza Mayor. Between these buildings are the pedestrian streets of Pasaje Santa Rosa and Escribanos, which are lined with upscale restaurants, cafés, and bookstores. At the corner of the palace and the Municipality is Lima's antique post office, the **Casa de Correos**

COLONIAL VS. REPUBLICAN HOMES

The differences between colonial (1534-1822) and republican homes (1820-1900) are clear in theory but muddled in practice. Most of Peru's old homes were built in colonial times by Spaniards who received the prized plots on or near the Plaza de Armas. These houses, passed down from generation to generation, were often restored in the 19th or early 20th century with republican elements. So most houses, or casonas, are somewhat of a blend.

But all share in common the basic Spanish layout: a tunnel-like entry, or zaguán, leads into a central courtyard, or traspatio. The rooms are built with high ceilings and a second-story wood balcony around the courtyard. Rich homes have stone columns, instead of wood, and additional patios.

During the nearly three centuries of the Peruvian viceroyalty, homes went from the solid, fortified, construction of medieval times to the more intricate decorations of the baroque, which were often based on Mudejar, or Arabic, patterns brought from Spain. After independence, however, homes demonstrate neoclassic elegance and a more confident use of colors favored in the New World, such as bright blues, greens, and yellows.

COLONIAL HOMES

- Traspatios paved with canto rodado (river stones)
- Sparse interiors
- Heavy brown and green colors
- Simple ceilings, often made of plaster, cane, and tile
- Baroque or rococo decorations with Mudejar patterns
- Forged iron windows with intricate lace patterns
- Celosia balconies where women could observe but not be observed

REPUBLICAN HOMES

- Traspatios paved with polished stone slabs
- Elegant interior decorations and furniture
- Light yellow, white, and blue colors
- Elaborate, often carved, wooden ceilings
- Neoclassic decorations with ornate columns

LIMA

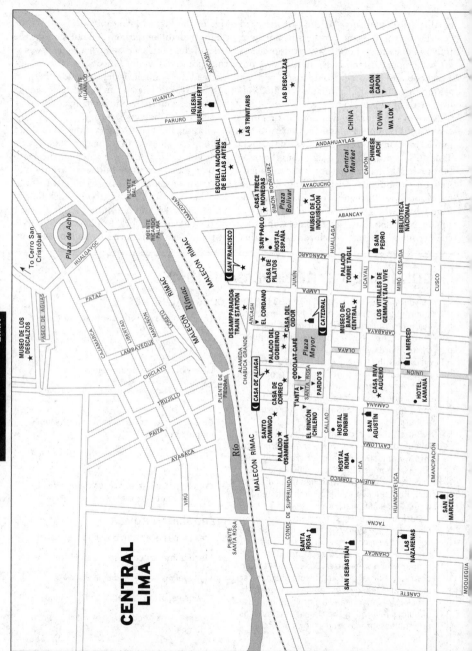

CENTRAL LIMA

To Cerro San Cristóbal

Plaza de Acho

MUSEO DE LOS DESCALZOS ★

PASEO DE AGUAS

Río Rímac

MALECÓN RÍMAC

MALECÓN RÍMAC

RÍMAC Rímac

PUENTE HUÁNUCO

PUENTE BALTA

PUENTE RICARDO PALMA

PUENTE DE PIEDRA

PUENTE SANTA ROSA

HUALGAYOC

PATAZ

LIBERTAD

MARAÑÓN

CAJAMARCA

LAMBAYEQUE

CHICLAYO

TRUJILLO

PAITA

AYABACA

VIRÚ

CONDE DE SUPERUNDA

ICA

HUANCAVELICA

TACNA

CHANCAY

CAÑETE

MOQUEGUA

EMANCIPACIÓN

RUFINO TORRICO

CAYLLOMA

CAMANÁ

UNIÓN

OLAYA

CARABAYA

MIRÓ QUESADA

CUSCO

BIBLIOTECA NACIONAL ★

LA MERCED ★

HOTEL KAMANA ●

CASA RIVA AGÜERO ★

LOS VITRALES DE GEMMA/L'EAU VIVE ●

PALACIO TORRE TAGLE ★

SAN PEDRO ★

MUSEO DEL BANCO CENTRAL ★

ABANCAY

UCAYALI

HUALLAGA

AZÁNGARO

LAMPA

JUNÍN

AYACUCHO

SIMÓN RODRÍGUEZ

ANDAHUAYLAS

CAPÓN

Central Market

CHINESE ARCH ★

CHINA

TOWN

WA LOK ▼

SALÓN CAPÓN ▼

LAS DESCALZAS ★

LAS TRINITARIS ★

ANCASH

HUANTA

PARURO

MÁRTIRES

MÁRTIRES

ANCASH

ESCUELA NACIONAL DE BELLAS ARTES ★

IGLESIA BUENAMUERTE ♦

CASA TRECE MONEDAS ★

Plaza Bolívar

MUSEO DE LA INQUISICIÓN ★

SAN PAOLO ●

HOSTAL ESPAÑA ●

CASA DE PILATOS ★

EL CORDANO ★

CASA DEL OIDOR ★

CATEDRAL ☾

Plaza Mayor

PALACIO DEL GOBIERNO ★

ALAMEDA CHABUCA GRANDE

DESAMPARADOS TRAIN STATION

CHOCOLAT CAFÉ

TANTA

SANTA ROSA

PARDO'S

SAN FRANCISCO ☾

CASA DE ALIAGA ☾

CASA DE CORREO ★

SANTO DOMINGO ★

PALACIO OSAMBELA ★

EL RINCÓN CHILENO ●

HOSTAL BONBINI ●

SAN AGUSTÍN ★

HOSTAL ROMA ●

CALLAO

SANTA ROSA ✝

SAN SEBASTIÁN ✝

LAS NAZARENAS ✝

SAN MARCELO ♦

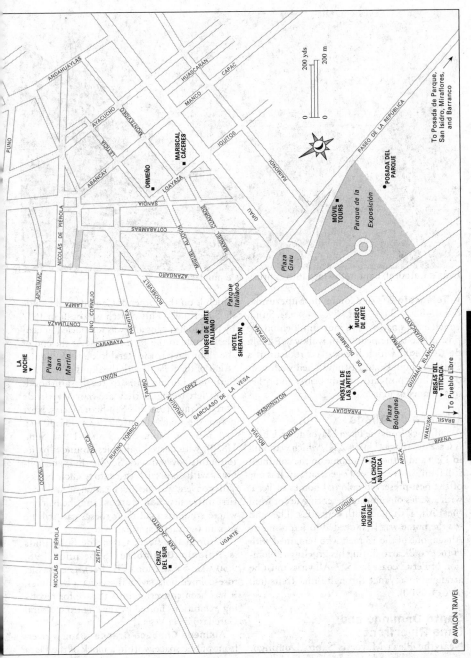

LIMA

200 yds
200 m

To Posada de Parque,
San Isidro, Miraflores,
and Barranco

ANDAHUAYLAS
HUASCARAN
CAPAC
MANCO
AVACUCHO
MONTEVIDEO
LETICIA
MARISCAL
CÁCERES
ABANCAY
ORMEÑO
LOAYAZA
IQUITOS
PUNO
SANDIA
NICOLAS DE PIÉROLA
COTABAMBAS
MIGUEL ALJOVIN
RAIMONDI
GRAU
PASEO DE LA REPÚBLICA
MOVIL
TOURS
POSADA DEL
PARQUE
AZANGARO
Parque de la
Exposición
APURIMAC
LINO CORNEJO
ROOSEVELT
LAMPA
PACHITEA
CONTUMAZA
CARABAYA
Plaza
Grau
LA
NOCHE
Plaza
San
Martín
MUSEO DE ARTE
ITALIANO
Parque
Italiano
HOTEL
SHERATON
ESPAÑA
MUSEO
DE ARTE
TARMA
HUANCAYO
UNIÓN
TAMBO
URUBISGA
LÓPEZ
GARCILASO DE LA VEGA
WASHINGTON
9 DE DICIEMBRE
HOSTAL DE
LAS ARTES
GUZMAN BLANCO
BRISAS DEL
TITICACA
To Pueblo Libre
QUILCA
RUFINO TORRICO
BOLIVIA
CHOTA
PARAGUAY
Plaza
Bolognesi
WAKULSKI
BRASIL
BREÑA
OCOÑA
ARICA
LA CHOZA
NAUTICA
IQUIQUE
HOSTAL
IQUIQUE
NICOLAS DE PIÉROLA
ZEPITA
SAN JACINTO
LLO
UGARTE
CRUZ
DEL SUR

© AVALON TRAVEL

Lima's Catedral, built in the late 16th century, is a must-see.

© PROMPERU

y Telégrafos (176 Conde de Superunda, 8 A.M.–8 P.M. Mon.–Sat., 8 A.M.–4 P.M. Sun.), which has a small stamps museum. Behind the post office is the pedestrian walkway **Pasaje de Correos,** which had a glass roof until a 1940 earthquake and is now lined with vendors selling postcards, teddy bears, and other miscellaneous items.

【 Casa de Aliaga

A half block from the Plaza Mayor down Unión is Casa de Aliaga (Unión 224), which was built in 1535 and is the oldest home on the continent still family owned after 17 generations. It is one of the best-preserved colonial homes in Peru, with a series of salons representing decor from the 16th, 17th, and 18th centuries. The land for the home was first deeded to Jerónimo de Aliaga, one of the 13 men who remained with Francisco Pizarro during his grueling exploration of Peru's coast in 1527. All visits must be arranged in advance through Lima Tours (tel. 01/619-6900).

Santo Domingo and Lima Riverfront

Near the Plaza Mayor is Santo Domingo, which is on the corner of Camaná and Conde de Superunda. This church was built in 1537 by the Dominicans and was remodeled in neoclassic style in the 19th century. At the end of the right nave is the Retablo de las Reliquias (Altar of the Relics), with the skulls of the three Peruvian Dominicans to reach sainthood. From left to right, they are San Martín de Porras, Santa Rosa, and San Juan Macias. Next door is the attached convent (9 A.M.–12:30 P.M. and 3–6 P.M. Mon.–Sat., 9 A.M.–1 P.M. Sun., US$3), with carved balconies around a patio, fountains covered with Seville tiles, and a library with colossal 17th-century choir books. This convent was the first location of America's first university, **San Marcos,** and the balcony where students read their theses can still be seen in the Sala Capitular.

Also on the street Conde de Superunda is **Palacio Osamblea** (Superunda 298, 9:30 A.M.–5 P.M. Mon.–Fri., free), a neoclassic, rose-colored home with five elegant balconies. It has been converted into a space for revolving exhibitions hosted by the Centro Cultural Garcilaso de la Vega.

Alameda Chabuca Grande is a new riverfront public space, within a block of the Plaza

DOMINGO GIRIBALDI, PROMPERU

the interior courtyard of Palacio Osamblea

Mayor, that is dedicated to one of Peru's best-known musicians, whose creole music is famous worldwide. This used to be the sprawling Polvos Azules market, which was shut down by the government in 2000 and moved to its present location along the Vía Expresa. The space is now used by musicians and artists and is generally safe to walk around until 9 P.M., when the security guards go home.

The Río Rímac, brown with mud and clogged with plastic, tumbles by here. Across the river, the Rímac neighborhood was populated by mestizos and mulattos during colonial times. The large hill on the other side is **Cerro San Cristóbal.** Walk upriver along Ancash to **Desamparados,** Lima's beautiful old station, which is being converted into a cultural center with revolving exhibits.

◖ San Francisco

San Francisco (Ancash and Lampa, 9:15 A.M.–5:45 P.M. daily, US$3.50, US$1.75 students) is a 16th-century convent featuring a patio lined with centuries-old *azulejos* (Sevillean tiles) and

roofed with *machimbrado,* perfectly fitted puzzle pieces of Nicaraguan mahogany. There are frescoes from the life of Saint Francis of Assisi, a 1656 painting of the Last Supper with the disciples eating guinea pig and drinking from gold Inca cups (*qeros*), and a series of paintings from Peter Paul Rubens's workshop depicting the passion of Christ. But the highlight is the catacombs, or public cemetery, where slaves, servants, and others without money were buried until 1821 (rich citizens were usually buried in their home chapels). The underground labyrinth is a series of wells, some 20 meters deep, where bodies were stacked and covered with lime to reduce odor and disease. After they decomposed, the bones were stacked elsewhere. Across the street from San Francisco is Casa de Pilatos (Ancash 390, closed to the public), a colonial home that is occupied by Peru's Constitutional Tribunal.

Museo de la Inquisición

Casa de las Trece Monedas (Ancash 536, closed to the public) was built in 1787 and gets its name from the 13 coins in the coat of arms on its facade. Nearby is **Plaza Bolívar,** flanked by Peru's congress building and graced with a bronze statue in honor of liberator Simón Bolívar. On the far side of the plaza is the interesting **Museo de la Inquisición** (www.congreso.gob.pe/museo.htm, 9 A.M.–5 P.M. daily, free), which served as the headquarters of the Spanish Inquisition from 1570 until it was abolished in 1820. The museum explains the harsh and bizarre punishments that the church doled out for crimes ranging from heresy and blasphemy to seduction and reading banned books. There are creepy dungeonlike spaces in the back where the punished were given 50 lashes and jailed while others were sent to work on slave ships or in public hospitals. This was also where autos-da-fé were ordered—public condemnation ceremonies in the Plaza de Armas where witches, bigamists, and heretics were hung to death or burned at the stake.

Chinatown

Chinatown is an excellent place to have lunch

LIMA

or late-afternoon tea, in the midst of a neighborhood founded by Chinese indentured workers, or coolies, who came here after finishing their contract on the train lines or coastal haciendas. The main street is **Capón,** which has three **Asian temples,** a **Chinese arch,** and a variety of stores and restaurants. The entire Chinatown area is adjacent to Lima's **central market.**

Historic Downtown

The 16th-century **San Pedro** (Azángaro and Ucayali, hours vary, free) has a drab mannerist facade but is one of the most spectacular church interiors in Peru. Huge white arching ceilings lead to a magnificent altar covered in gold leaf and designed by Matías Maestro, who is credited for bringing the neoclassic style to Peru. At the end of the right nave, ask permission to see the mind-blowing sacristy, decorated with tiles and graced with a magnificent painting of the coronation of the Virgin Mary by Peru's most famous painter, Bernardo Bitti. Painted on the ceiling boards above are scenes of the life from San Ignacio. If you come in the morning, it is possible to ask permission to see the cloisters and two interior chapels as well.

Palacio Torre Tagle (Ucayali 363) is a mansion built in 1735 that is, like Casa de Aliaga, in pristine condition. Visits can be arranged by popping into the Ministry of Foreign Affairs next door at Ucayali 318. At the **Museo del Banco Central** (tel. 01/613-2000, 10 A.M.–4:30 P.M. Tues. and Thurs.–Fri., 10 A.M.–7 P.M. Wed., free), the ground floor holds a colonial money exhibit, one flight up is a 19th- and 20th-century painting gallery, and the basement shines with pre-Columbian ceramics and textiles (including a range of intriguing Chanca pieces). The paintings include a good selection of watercolors from Pancho Fierro (1807–1879), paintings from 20th-century artist Enrique Polanco, and etchings by Cajamarca's indigenous artist José Sabogal (1888–1956).

The church of **San Agustín** (corner of Ica and Camaná, hours vary, free) has an 18th-century baroque facade that is one of the most

Palacio Torre Tagle

intricate in the Americas and looks almost as if it were carved from wood, not stone. **Casa Riva Agüero** (Camaná 459, 10 A.M.–1 P.M. and 2–8 P.M. Mon.–Sat., US$7, US$1.75 museum only), an 18th-century home with all original furniture, has an interesting museum of colonial handicrafts as well as ceramics and textiles from the Lima culture.

Other interesting churches, which are clustered together, are **La Merced** (Unión and Miró Quesada, hours vary, free), which was built in 1754 and holds a baroque retablo carved by San Pedro de Nolasco, and **San Marcelo** (Rufino Torrico and Emancipación, hours vary, free). Nearby there is a string of three 17th-century churches within four blocks of each other on the busy Avenida Tacna: **Las Nazarenas** (6 A.M.–noon and 5–8:30 P.M. daily), which holds the image of El Señor de los Milagros, the city's patron saint whose October festival draws as many as a half million celebrants; **San Sebastián** (hours vary, free); and **Santa Rosa** (9:30 A.M.–noon and 3:30–7 P.M. daily).

Art Museums

If you are taking a taxi from San Isidro or Miraflores into the center, you will travel along a sunken highway known as the **Vía Expresa** (also nicknamed "El Zanjón," or The Ditch). The highway emerges on ground level and passes along a series of public parks before entering old town. One of these is the **Parque de la Exposición,** which was built in the 19th century and is still thriving today. The park is ringed with a high fence and is best entered at the corner of 28 de Julio and Inca Garcilaso de la Vega. Nearby is an artificial lake with paddleboats and the **Kusi Kusi Puppet Theatre** (basement of the German-style gingerbread house, tel. 01/477-4249), which has Sunday performances listed in the cultural section of the *El Comercio* newspaper. Here too is the **Museo de Arte** (Paseo Colón 125, Parque de la Exposición, tel. 01/423-4732, http://museoarte.perucultural.org.pe, 10 A.M.–5 P.M. Thurs.–Tues., US$5.50 adult, US$3.75 students), which houses the best range of Peruvian paintings in the country, an espresso bar, and a cinema. The museum contains colonial furniture, some pre-Columbian ceramics, and a huge collection of paintings from the viceroyalty to the present. Another nearby park is the **Parque Italiano,** which contains the **Museo de Arte Italiano** (Paseo de la República 250, tel. 01/423-9932, 10 A.M.–5 P.M. Mon.–Fri., US$3), with a collection of European art mainly from the early 20th century.

Rímac

Right across the Río Rímac from Lima is the downtrodden Rímac neighborhood, which began as a mestizo and mulatto barrio during the viceroyalty and was refurbished in the 18th century by the Lima aristocracy. All the sights here are close to the Plaza de Armas—take a taxi, as assaults are common in this area.

The **Museo de los Descalzos** (end of Alameda Los Descalzos, tel. 01/482-3360, 10 A.M.–1 P.M. and 3–6 P.M. Tues.–Sat., 11:30 A.M.–6 P.M. Sun.) was a convent and spiritual retreat for the Franciscans. Today it contains interesting and elegant cloisters,

a chapel with a gold-covered baroque altar, an elegant refectory, and a gallery with more than 300 paintings from the 17th and 18th century—including a masterpiece by Esteban de Murillo. On the taxi ride home, ask your taxi driver to pass the nearby **Paseo de Aguas,** an 18th-century French-style promenade where Lima's elites strolled along its artificial waterways. All that remains today is a neoclassic arch, hidden next to a towering Cristal Beer factory. Nearby is the giant **Plaza de Acho,** Lima's bullring, where **bullfights** are held early October–early December. Inside is the **Museo Taurino** (Hualgayoc 332, tel. 01/481-1467, 9 A.M.–6 P.M. Mon.–Sat., US$1.50), which contains a wide range of bullfighting relics.

Towering above Rímac is **Cerro San Cristóbal,** where Francisco Pizarro placed a cross in thanks that Quizo Yupanqui and his Inca army did not succeed in crossing the Río Rímac into Lima during the Inca rebellion of 1536. Today the hill is encrusted with a dusty *pueblo jóven* named Barrios Altos. There is a lookout over Lima at the top, along with a small museum and a giant cross that is illuminated at night. To reach the top, take a taxi from the Plaza de Armas (US$6) or wait for buses with English-speaking guides that leave from the Municipality (US$3.50).

◖ Museo Larco

The charming neighborhood of **Pueblo Libre** is just south of central Lima and has a relaxed, small-town vibe. Its best-known sight is the Museo Larco (Bolívar 1515, tel. 01/461-1312, www.museolarco.org, 9 A.M.–6 P.M. daily, US$11), which rivals the Museo de Oro in terms of gold pieces and has far more ceramics and textiles. Founded in 1926 in an 18th-century mansion built atop a pre-Hispanic ruin, this museum has more than 40,000 ceramics and 5,000 pieces of gold and textiles. There are huge Mochica earrings and funerary masks, a Paracas textile with a world-record 398 threads per inch, and a jewelry vault filled with gold and silver objects. A back storage room holds thousands of pre-Hispanic ceramic vessels, including a Moche erotic collection that will cause even the most liberated to blush. There is an excellent on-site restaurant, and it is easy to reach by bus from Miraflores. Catch a bus at Arequipa Avenue that says Todo Bolívar and get off at the 15th block.

◖ Museo Nacional de Arqueología

A 15-minute walk away from Museo Larco is Pueblo Libre's laid-back Plaza Bolívar and the Museo Nacional de Arqueología, Antropología, e Historia (Plaza Bolívar s/n, Pueblo Libre, tel. 01/463-5070, http://museonacional.perucultural.org.pe, 9:30 A.M.–5 P.M. Tues.–Sat., US$5 including tour). Though smaller than the Museo de la Nación, this museum presents a clearer, certainly more condensed, view of Peruvian history, and linked with the Museo Larco it makes for a complete day in central Lima. Exhibits include Moche ceramics, Paracas tapestries, Chimú gold, and scale models for understanding sights of hard-to-see Chavín and Huari sites.

The museum's most important piece is the Estela Raimondi, a giant stone obelisk that once graced one of Peru's first ceremonial centers, Chavín de Huantár (1300–200 B.C.), near present-day Huaraz. It is carved with snakes, pumas, and the first appearance of the Dios de los Báculos (Staff-Bearing God), which would reappear, in different incarnations, throughout Peru's ancient history. The tour includes a walk through the adjacent colonial home where independence leaders José de San Martín and Simón Bolívar stayed.

Around the corner is the 16th-century Iglesia Magdalena (San Martín and Vivanco, 6:30–8 P.M. Fri.–Tues., 8 A.M.–8 P.M. Thurs.), which has attractive carved altars and a gold painting of Señor de los Tremblores (Lord of the Earthquakes). An excellent restaurant, café, and pisco-tasting bodega, all steeped in tradition, are down the street.

SAN ISIDRO AND MIRAFLORES

What appears to be a clay hill plunked down in the middle of Miraflores is actually a huge adobe pyramid from the Lima culture, which built a dozen major structures in and around what is now Lima A.D. 200–700. **Huaca Pucllana** (General Bolognesi 800, Miraflores, tel. 01/445-8695, http://pucllana.perucultural.org.pe, 9 A.M.–1 P.M. and 1:30–5 P.M. Wed.–Mon., free) has a small but excellent museum, which includes ceramics, textiles, reconstructed tombs, and artifacts from this culture that depended almost entirely on the sea for survival. A recently discovered pot shows a man carrying a shark on his back—proof that this culture somehow hunted 455-kilogram sharks. No free wandering is allowed, but guides lead tours every half hour around the ceremonial plazas and a few inner rooms. This is a good option for those who cannot see the larger Pachacámac, 31 kilometers south of Lima. There is an upscale and delicious restaurant on-site.

A similar, though completely restored, stepped pyramid in San Isidro is **Huaca Huallamarca** (Nicólas de Piérola 201, tel. 01/222-4124, 9 A.M.–5 P.M. Tues.–Sun., US$3.50), which offers a chance to understand what these temples once looked like. From the top, there is an interesting view over Lima's most upscale district.

Museo de Historia Natural (one block west of the 12th block of Arequipa, Arenales 1256, Lince, tel. 01/471-0117, http://museohn.unmsm.edu.pe, 9 A.M.–3 P.M. Mon.–Fri., 9 A.M.–5 P.M. Sat., 9 A.M.–1 P.M. Sun., US$3) is a severely underfunded museum with an aging taxidermy collection that nevertheless offers a good introduction to the fauna of Peru. Many of Peru's top biologists work from here. Ask for permission to see the storage area in the back, where thousands of stuffed birds are archived.

Museo Amano (Retiro 160 near the 11th block of Angamos Oeste, tel. 01/441-2909, tours at 3, 4, and 5 P.M. Mon.–Fri., donations appreciated) has a small but interesting collection of 200 pre-Columbian ceramics, including a Nasca piece with a scene of human sacrifice, and a range of textiles, which are the museum's specialty.

The **Museo Enrico Poli** (Lord Cochrane 466, tel. 01/422-2437 or 01/440-7100,

SAN ISIDRO

To Central Lima

Parque de las Americas

LIMA GOLF CLUB

SAN ISIDRO GOLF
LOS DELFINES
COUNTRY CLUB LIMA HOTEL/
EL PERROQUET

To Quattro D
and José
Antonio

LOFT
YOUTH HOSTAL
MALKA
MALABAR
SWISSÔTEL
COMO AGUA
PARA CHOCOLATE
TANTA
SONESTA EL OLIVAR
ICE CREAM FACTORY
SEGUNDO MUELLE
PLASCENIA
CASA ANDINA
SANTA ISABEL
SUPERMARKET
ASIA DE CUBA
DON MAMINO
AQUASPORT
CLINICA ANGLO-AMERICANA
PUNTA SAL
OSAKA
BRAVO RESTOBAR
LA BAGUETTE

LA BONBONNEIRE

ÓVALO GUTIÉRREZ ⭐ To Miraflores

0   400 yds
0   400 m

© AVALON TRAVEL

4–6 P.M., by appointment only, US$12) is one of Lima's more intriguing private collections, with a huge range of textiles, gold and silver objects, and other artifacts. The owner, Enrico Poli, gives the tours personally and speaks Spanish only. Agencies often visit here with their own interpreters.

BARRANCO

This bohemian barrio has a few small museums, the best of which is **Museo Pedro de Osma** (San Pedro de Osma 423, tel. 01/467-0141, www.museopedrodeosma.org, 10 A.M.–1:30 P.M. and 2:30–6 P.M. Tues.–Sun., US$5), which holds an exquisite private collection of colonial art and furniture. The museum itself is one of Barranco's oldest mansions and is worth a peek just for that reason. Down the street is a small exhibit on electricity in Lima at the **Museo de la Electricidad** (San Pedro de Osma 105, tel. 01/477-6577, http://museo-electri.perucultural.org.pe, 9 A.M.–1 P.M. and 2–5 P.M. Tues.–Sun., free). A restored electric tram, which used to connect Barranco to

LIMA

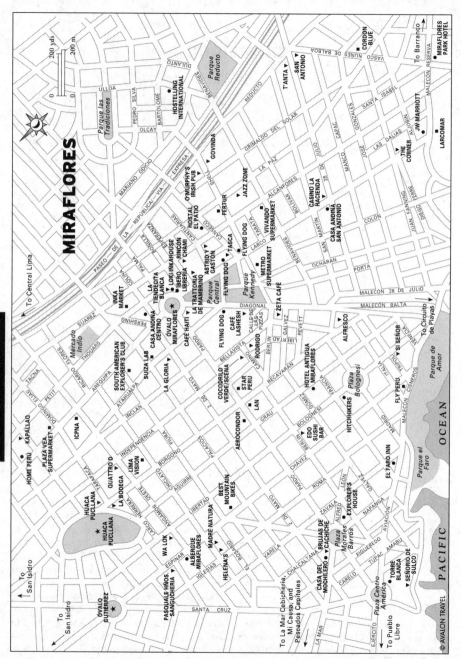

MIRAFLORES

200 yds
200 m

Parque las
Tradiciones

Parque
Reducto

ULLOA
PEDRO   SILVA
BARTOLOME
OLCAY

HOSTELLING
INTERNATIONAL

MARIANO ODICIO

EXPRESA

PALMA

BENAVIDES

REDUCTO

GRIMALDO   DEL   SOLAR

LA   PAZ

SNELL

FERTUR

GOVINDA

T'ANTA

SAN
ANTONIO

VASCO   NUÑES   DE   BALBOA

CORDON
BLUE

MIRAFLORES
PARK HOTEL

To Barranco

O'MURPHY'S
IRISH PUB

HOSTAL
EL PATIO

JAZZ ZONE

CASA LA
HACIENDA

SANTA   ISABEL

GONZALES

JOSE   LAS   DALIAS

JW MARRIOTT

THE
CORNER

LARCOMAR

MALECON   RESERVA

LA   REPÚBLICA   —   VÍA

PASEO   DE   LA

CONCHA

BONILLA

ESPERANZA

CANGALLO

CANTUARIAS

LA
TIENDECITA
BLANCA

LOKI INKA HOUSE
IBERO
RINCON
CHAMI
LIBRERIA

ASTRID Y
GASTON

VIVANDA
SUPERMARKET

ALCANFORES

BOLIVAR

CASA ANDINA
SAN ANTONIO

MARTIN

SAN   MARTIN

OCHARAN

PORTA

COLON

DIEGO   FERRE   ALOBIN

JUAN   FANNING

MANCO   28   DE   JULIO

CAPAC

CALLE DE
LAS
PIZZAS

LA TRATTORIA
DE MAMBRINO

Parque
Central

FLYING DOG

TASCA

FLYING DOG

Parque
Kennedy

METRO
SUPERMARKET

ZETA CAFÉ

BENAVIDES

LARCO   TARATA

LA REPÚBLICA

SUAREZ

PERSHING

INKA
MARKET

CASA ANDINA
CENTRO

ÓVALO
MIRAFLORES

CAFÉ HAITÍ

FLYING DOG

CAFÉ
LASHESH

DIAGONAL

BELLAVISTA

CALLE DE

RODRIGO

ALFRESCO

SI SEÑOR

To Circuito
de Playas

MALECON   28   DE   JULIO

MALECON   BALTA

Mercado
Indio

THOUARS

RICARDO   PALMA

SOUTH AMERICAN
EXPLORER'S CLUB

SUIZA LAB

LA GLORIA

ATAHUALPA

COCODRILO
VERDE/SCENA

STAR
PERU

LAN

HOTEL ANTIGUA
MIRAFLORES

Plaza
Bolognesi

HITCHHIKERS

FLY PERU

REYETT

GALVEZ

LIBERTAD

BERLIN

RECAVARAN

MADID

MALECON   CISNEROS

Parque de
Amor

OCEAN

TACNA

PETIT

DOMINGO   ELIAS

KAPALLAQ

HOME PERÚ

PLAZA VEA
SUPERMARKET

ICPNA

AREQUIPA

28   DE   JULIO

MAYO

AEROCONDOR

GRAU

BOLOGNESI

EDO
SUSHI
BAR

CHAVEZ

ROMA

BOLOGNESI

PANCO

PACIFIC

HUACA
PUCLLANA

LA BODEGA

QUATTRO D

LIMA
VISION

BEST
MOUNTAIN
BIKES

INCLAN

INDEPENDENCIA

BORGOÑO

CHICLAYO

PIURA

2   DE   MAYO

TARAPACA

LEON   ALFRED   ZAVALA

EL FARO INN

NAPANGA

AVIACION

Parque el
Faro

HERRERA

OESTE

AGUIRRE

CHALCALTANA

Plaza
Morales
Barros

TUPAC   AMARU

TORRE
BLANCA

SEÑORIO DE
SULCO

Plaza Centro
América

To
San Isidro

HUACA
PUCLLANA

WA LOK

PASQUALE HNOS.
SANGUCHERIA

ALBERGUE
MIRAFLORES

HELENA'S

ESPINAR

IGLESIAS

MADRE NATURA

ROSA

VARELA

CASA DEL
MOCHILERO

BRUJAS DE
CACHICHE

EXPLORER'S
HOUSE

FIGUEREDO

CARELO

ÓVALO
GUTIERREZ

To
San Isidro

SANTA   CRUZ

LA MAR

To La Mar Cebichería,
Mi Causa, and
Pescados Capitales

EJERCITO

To Pueblo
Libre

© AVALON TRAVEL

To Central Lima

ARICO

RAMOS

LIBERTAD

To
San Isidro

© BETH FUCHS AND JACK HOADLEY

Huaca Pucllana, Miraflores

LIMA

Miraflores and Lima, runs down the street on Sundays (US$2.75).

EASTERN LIMA
Museo de Oro

Monterrico, an upscale suburb in eastern Lima that is often sunny when the rest of the city is covered in fog, is known for its Museo de Oro (Molina 1110, Monterrico, tel. 01/345-1271, 11:30 A.M.–7 P.M. Mon.–Sun., US$11.50). This fabulous collection of gold pieces was one of Lima's must-see tourist attractions until 2001, when a scandal broke alleging that many of the prize pieces were fakes. Newspapers pointed the finger at the sons of museum founder Miguel Mujica Gallo, whom the newspapers accused of selling the originals and replacing them with imitations. The family countered, saying false pieces were bought by mistake and Mujica Gallo died of sadness in the process. Only true gold pieces are on display now at the museum, but the museum continues to suffer from a credibility problem. Gold pieces include spectacular funerary masks, ceremonial knives

(tumis), a huge set of golden arms, exquisite figurines, and crowns studded with turquoise. It is a huge potpourri of gold, with little explication in English, bought over decades from tomb raiders who work over Moche, Nasca, Sicán, and Chimú sites. Other objects of interest include a Nasca poncho made of parrot feathers and a Moche skull that was fitted, postmortem, with purple quartz teeth. Almost as impressive is the **Arms Museum** upstairs, which is a terrifying assemblage of thousands of weapons, ranging from samurai swords and medieval arquebuses to Hitler paraphernalia.

Museo de la Nación

Peru's largest museum, and cheaper to see than the private collections, is Museo de la Nación (Javier Prado Este 2465, tel. 01/476-9873, 9 A.M.–6 P.M. Tues.–Sun., US$4, US$3 students), in the east Lima suburb of San Borja. Though criticized for a rambling organization, this museum has a great chronological layout, which makes it perhaps Lima's most understandable and educational museum. There are

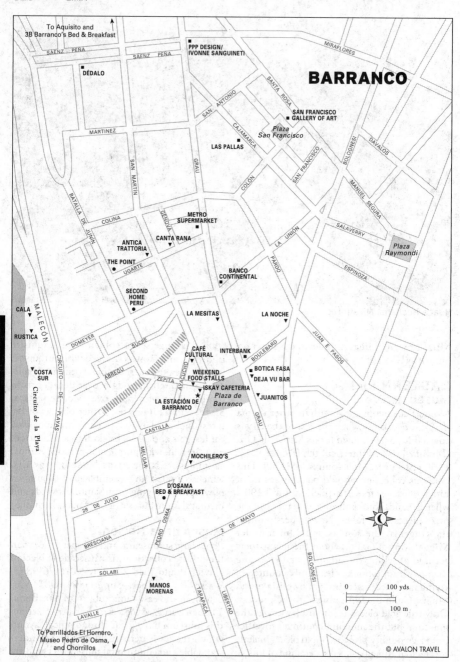

BARRANCO

To Aquisito and
3B Barranco's Bed & Breakfast

SÁENZ PEÑA

SÁENZ PEÑA

DÉDALO

MARTÍNEZ

SAN ANTONIO

SANTA ROSA

MIRAFLORES

PPP DESIGN/
IVONNE SANGUINETI

CAJAMARCA

SAN FRANCISCO
GALLERY OF ART

Plaza
San Francisco

BOLOGNESI

DÁVALOS

SAN MARTÍN

GRAU

LAS PALLAS

COLÓN

SAN FRANCISCO

MANUEL SEGURA

BATALLA DE JUNÍN

COLINA

GENOVA

METRO
SUPERMARKET

CANTA RANA

LA UNIÓN

SALAVERRY

Plaza
Raymondi

ANTICA
TRATTORIA

THE POINT

UGARTE

PARDO

ESPINOZA

SECOND
HOME
PERU

BANCO
CONTINENTAL

CALA

MALECÓN

RUSTICA

CIRCUITO DE PLAYAS

DOMEYER

SUCRE

LA MESITAS

LA NOCHE

JUAN E. PASOS

COSTA
SUR

Circuito de la Playa

ABREGÚ

ZEPITA

AYACUCHO

CAFÉ
CULTURAL

INTERBANK

BOULEVARD

WEEKEND
FOOD STALLS

BOTICA FASA

DEJA VU BAR

ISKAY CAFETERIA

Plaza de
Barranco

JUANITOS

LA ESTACIÓN DE
BARRANCO

GRAU

CASTILLA

MEIGAR

MOCHILERO'S

D'OSAMA
BED & BREAKFAST

PEDRO OSMA

28 DE JULIO

2 DE MAYO

BOLOGNESI

BRESCIANA

SOLARI

MANOS
MORENAS

TARAPACA

LIBERTAD

LAVALLE

To Parrillados El Hornero,
Museo Pedro de Osma,
and Chorrillos

0   100 yds

0   100 m

© AVALON TRAVEL

LIMA

© JORGE RIVEROS CAYO

colonial art in Lima's Museo de la Nación

LIMA

three levels of exhibits showcasing Peru's entire archaeological history, from Chavín stone carvings and Paracas weavings all the way to the Inca. There are good models of Machu Picchu, the Nasca Lines, and the Lords of Sipán tomb excavated near Chiclayo in 1987, one of the great finds of Latin American archaeology. This is a full-blown version of Peru's culture for the history hungry. A more condensed alternative is the Museo Nacional de Arqueología.

OUTSIDE LIMA
Pachacámac

This extensive complex of adobe pyramids, 31 kilometers south of Lima in the Lurín Valley, was the leading pilgrimage center on the central coast and home to the most feared, and respected, oracle in the Andes. The name of Pachacámac in Quechua translates to Lord of the World. Both the Huari and local Inca empires respected the oracle, adding to its prestige with additional buildings and consulting it for important decisions.

During his imprisonment at Cajamarca, Inca Atahualpa complained bitterly because the oracle had falsely predicted he would be victorious against the Spaniards. But Hernando Pizarro was so intrigued by Atahualpa's reports of gold at the oracle that he and a troop of Spanish soldiers rode here from Cajamarca in three weeks. Pushing aside the priests, Pizarro strode to the upmost level of the stepped pyramid. He describes a cane-and-mud house at the top, with a door strangely decorated with turquoise, crystals, and corals. Inside the dark space was a roughly shaped wooden idol. "Seeing the filth and mockery of the idol," Pizarro wrote, "we went out to ask why they thought highly of something so dirty and ugly."

What can be seen today is the idol itself (probably a replica) in the on-site museum and excavations of the main temples and huge pyramids, which have revealed ramps and entranceways. From the top of the Temple of the Sun there is an impressive view of Lima's well-organized shantytown, Villa El Salvador, and the Pacific Coast. The Palacio de Las Mamacuña, the enclosure for holy women built by the Inca, can be seen with

© JORGE RIVEROS CAYO

Pachacámac is an adobe ceromonial complex 31 kilometers south of Lima that was home to an oracle consulted by a series of pre-Colombian cultures in Peru, including the Inca.

a guide only (US$6 for an English-speaking tour of the entire site). On the way to the ruins, you will pass **Reserva Pantanos de Villa** at Km 18 of the Panamericana Sur. There is a surprisingly good range of ducks and other migratory aquatic birds here, luring bird-watchers.

The easiest way to see the ruins and the corresponding museum (http://pachacamac.perucultural.org.pe) is with an agency tour from Lima. Buses marked Pachacámac leave from Montevideo and Ayacucho in central Lima and can be picked up at the Primavera Bridge along the Panamericana Sur (US$4 taxi ride to the bridge from Miraflores). Ask to be dropped off at *las ruinas,* as the town of Pachacámac is farther along.

San Pedro de Casta and Marcahuasi

Marcahuasi is a strange set of rock formations on the high plains above Lima that have attracted a range of theories, from simple wind erosion to the work of UFOs or ancient cultures. The rocks are shaped like people and animals, inspiring names like the Frog, Indian, Three Virgins, and Turtle. Marcahuasi is set amid attractive country scenery and, along with the nearby charming town of San Pedro, makes for a great weekend outing from Lima. To arrive, catch a bus from Avenida Grau in Lima (near Plaza Grau in the center) and travel 1.5 hours to **Chosica,** a resort town 860 meters above sea level that is popular with those trying to escape Lima's fog belt. There are plenty of budget and nicer lodging options here. From Chosica's Parque Echenique, buses leave at 9 A.M. and 3 P.M. to San Pedro, a beautiful four- or five-hour trip that climbs to 3,750 meters above sea level. There is a hostel (US$5 pp) in the main square, along with two restaurants and a tourist information office. Marcahuasi, at 4,100 meters over sea level, is a three-kilometer, 1.5-hour hike; donkeys can be rented for US$6. Entry fee is US$5.

Entertainment and Events

NIGHTLIFE
Central Lima

There are a few night options in the center of Lima, though partakers should take a taxi to and from each one. On the Plaza San Martín is **El Estadio Futbol Club** (Nícolas de Piérola 926, tel. 01/428-8866, www.estadio.com.pe, noon–11 P.M. Mon.–Thurs., noon–3 A.M. Fri.–Sat., noon–5 P.M. Sun.), which is a soccer-lover's paradise bedecked with *fútbol* paraphernalia.

One of the largest and best *peñas* in Lima is **Brisas del Titicaca** (Wakulski 168, near block 1 of Brasil and Plaza Bolognesi, tel. 01/332-1901, www.brisasdeltiticaca.com, Tues.–Sat., US$18 cover). Foreigners come here on Thursday nights for an extraordinary exhibition of dance and music from around Peru that runs 9:30 P.M.–midnight. Those who want to see the same dances, and dance a lot themselves, should come on weekend nights when

mainly Peruvians party 10 P.M.–4 A.M. This is a safe neighborhood and is an easy taxi ride from Miraflores.

San Isidro

If you have come to Avenida Conquistadores for dinner, there are a few nightlife options (which also serve light dinner) along this strip. The moment's favorite spot is **Bravo Restobar** (Conquistadores 1005, tel. 01/221-5700, www.bravorestobar.com, noon–4 P.M. and 7 P.M.–midnight Mon.–Sat., US$15), a swanky wine bar that fills with Lima's hip, 30-something crowd most nights of the week. Another good choice is **Asia de Cuba** (Conquistadores 780, San Isidro, tel. 01/222-4940, www.asiadecubaperu.com), which has an upscale bar and an eclectic after-dinner nightlife scene, including a hookah and blackberry-flavored tobacco in the plush loft.

LIMA

© ANIBAL SOLIMANO, PROMPERU

Central Lima, long considered unsafe at night by Peruvians and foreigners alike, is making a comeback for travelers looking for affordable accommodations and diverse nightlife.

LIMA

GAY AND LESBIAN LIMA

Though smaller than that in other Latin American capitals, Lima's gay scene is growing, with a few great new discos and bars. There are a number of websites on gay Peru, but the best and most up-to-date information is on www.lima.queercity.info. This site, written in English, has travel tips, a chat room, links, and an opinionated listing of gay and lesbian bars, discos, saunas, cruising spots, and even retirement options. Other sites include www.peruesgay.com and www.gayperu.com.

A gay-friendly start to the evening is **La Sede** in Miraflores (28 de Julio 441, tel. 01/242-2462, www.publasede.com, 10 P.M.-late Wed.-Sat.).

Gay and lesbian discos do not start swinging until 1 A.M. and continue until the wee hours of the morning. Entry is typically free on weekday nights and goes up after midnight on weekends.

Miraflores's hippest, classiest gay and lesbian disco is **Legendaris** (Berlin 363, www.gayperu.com/legendaris, 11 P.M.-late Wed.-Sun., US$4.50 before midnight, US$6 after), which opened in January 2004 with an extravagant decor, great sound system, and room for 350.

The flamboyant **Downtown Vale Todo** (Pasaje Los Pinos, Miraflores, tel. 01/444-6433, www.peruesgay.com/downtownvaletodo, 10 P.M.-late Wed.-Sun., US$4 Fri.-Sat.) is still open despite some citizens' efforts to shut it down. This disco attracts a younger crowd, with drag queen performances and a cruising bar on an upper deck. The smaller gay disco **Splash** (Pasaje Los Pinos 181, Miraflores, 10:30 P.M. onward Thurs.-Sat.) is on the same street.

A late-2003 addition to San Isidro is **Mercury** (2 de Mayo 1545, tel. 01/592-2340, www.peruesgay.com/downtownvaletodo, 11 P.M.-late Fri.-Sat., US$4.50, US$6 for couples). This disco has two levels, a good music-and-light show, and is in the middle of one of Lima's most fashionable districts.

One of the only options in central Lima is **Sagitario** (Wilson 869, tel. 01/424-4383, www.gayperu.com/sagitariodisco, daily, free except after midnight on weekends), one of Lima's original gay-only bars. The neighborhood is sketchy at night, so travel by taxi.

Avenida 13 (Manuel Segura 270, off block 15 of Arequipa, tel. 01/265-3694) is a gay and lesbian dance club that is **women-only** on Fridays.

Gay-friendly hotels include **Hostal de las Artes** in the center, **Hostel Domeyer** in Barranco, **Aparthotel San Martín** in Miraflores, and **Loft** in San Isidro.

Miraflores

The nightlife in Miraflores is more spread out and harder to find than in the neighboring district of Barranco. And that is precisely why many a traveler ends up at **Calle de las Pizzas** (The Street of the Pizzas), a seedy row of pizza-and-sangria joints right in front of Parque Kennedy. But there are many other options.

If you want a more classic evening head across Parque Kennedy to **Jazz Zone** (La Paz 656, tel. 01/241-8139, http://jazzzoneperu.com, 10 P.M.-2 A.M. Mon.-Sat., free Mon.-Wed., US$7 Thurs., US$11 Fri.-Sat.). Mondays are Afro-Peruvian night, Tuesdays and Wednesdays are Latin jazz, Thursdays bossa nova, and weekends for all of the above.

For cocktails and music, swing around to Francisco de Paula Camino Street to **Cocodrilo Verde** (Francisco de Paula Camino 226, tel. 01/242-7583, www.cocodriloverde.com, 9 P.M.-1 A.M. Thurs.-Sat., free Thurs., US$18 Fri.-Sat.). Next door, **Scena Restaurante** (Francisco Paula de Camino 280, tel. 01/445-9688, www.scena.com.pe, 12:30-4 P.M. and 7:30 P.M.-12:30 A.M. Mon.-Sat., US$10-15) has a great wine list and a rotating art exhibit. **Huaringas** (Bolognesi 460, tel. 01/466-6536, www.brujasdecachiche.com.pe, noon-4:30 P.M. and 7 P.M.-midnight Mon.-Sat., 12:30-4:30 P.M. Sun.) is rumored to have the best pisco sours in town. Get there early, and try the strawberry, passion fruit, and grape sours.

There are several British-style pubs in Miraflores, good for drinking draft ales and playing darts, and the classic is **O'Murphy's Irish Pub** (Schell 627, 6 P.M.–2 A.M. daily), with Guinness on tap, darts, and a pool table.

To hang out with an international crowd, there's **Tasca** (Diez Canseco and Parque Kennedy, tel. 01/241-1832, www.flyingdogperu.com, noon–2 A.M. Mon.–Sat., 5 P.M.–midnight Sun., US$9), a small, tapas-like bar. Or there's **The Corner Sports Bar and Grill** (Larco 1207, tel. 01/444-0220, 11 A.M.–3 A.M. daily, US$8), whose 26 TVs broadcast international sports games.

There is always something happening at **Larcomar** (Malecón de la Reserva 610, www.larcomar.com), the oceanfront mall at the end of Avenida Larco. Even those who dislike malls are impressed with this public space, buried in the cliffside and overlooking the Pacific. Lima's hottest and most expensive new disco, **Aura** (Larcomar 236, tel. 01/242-5516, www.aura.com.pe, 9 P.M.–7 A.M. Thurs.–Sat., cover varies depending on event), is here.

Barranco

The most happening neighborhood for nightlife, any day of the week, is Barranco. **Juanito's** (Grau 274, 11 A.M.–3 A.M. daily, no cover) is a hole-in-the-wall bar that has been a gathering spot for intellectuals since the 1960s. The traditional fare at Juanito's, right on the main square, is malt beer and smoked ham sandwiches. **La Noche** (Bolognesi 307, tel. 01/477-4154, www.lanoche.com.pe, 7 P.M.–3 A.M. daily, US$6–9) is Barranco's best live music bar, with tables set on different levels to look down on a range of (mostly jazz) performances. Monday nights, when there is no cover charge, are especially crowded. **Mochileros** (San Pedro de Osma 135, tel. 01/274-1225, 6 P.M.–2 A.M. daily, no cover), in a 1903 house, has a great patio, with live rock bands and mind-blowing cocktails.

Located in one of Barranco's oldest colonial homes, **Deja Vu Bar** (Grau 294, tel. 01/247-3742, 7 P.M.–2 A.M. Mon.–Sat., no cover) is a dance club for the young and wild.

Barranco is full of *peñas* (live *criollo* music clubs) that make for a rowdy night out among locals. **La Candelaría** (Bolognesi 292, tel. 01/247-2941, www.lacandelariaperu.com, 9:30 P.M.–2 A.M. Fri.–Sat., US$10) is a new and comfortable *peña* where spectators do not stay seated for long. With a slightly older crowd, **La Estación de Barranco** (Pedro de Osma 112, tel. 01/247-0344, 7 P.M.–2 A.M. daily, no cover) is a nice place to hear *música criolla* in the digs of an old train station. The most upscale *peña* in Lima, and a good restaurant, is **Manos Morenas** (Pedro de Osma 409, Barranco, tel. 01/467-0421, www.manosmorenasperu.com, US$16). Shows start at 9 P.M. Tuesday–Thursday, and at 10:30 P.M. Friday–Saturday.

The hippest, but still authentic, *peña* is **Peña del Carajo** (Catalino Miranda 158, tel. 01/247-7023, www.del-carajo.com, 6 P.M.–2 A.M. Fri.–Sat., no cover). Cockfights are waged in the entrance arena and *música negra* plays inside.

CINEMAS

Lima has more cinemas than the rest of the country combined. Most foreign movies are shown in their original language with subtitles, except for children's movies, which are often dubbed. Film listings are posted in *El Comercio* (www.elcomercioperu.com.pe).

The **Centro Cultural PUCP** (Camino Real 1075, tel. 01/616-1616, http://cultural.pucp.edu.pe), in **San Isidro,** hosts several film festivals throughout the year. Its biggest show is in August with the increasingly well-known Lima Latin American Film Festival.

In **Miraflores** alone there are three multiplexes showing both Hollywood and Latin American movies: **Cineplanet Alcázar** (Santa Cruz 814, Óvalo Gutierrez, Miraflores, tel. 01/421-8208, www.cineplanet.com.pe, US$7), **El Pacífico 12** (Jose Pardo 121, Miraflores, tel. 01/445-6990, US$5.50), and **Multicines Larcomar** (in Larcomar mall at end of Larco, tel. 01/446-7336, www.uvkmulticines.com, US$3). A smaller recommended theater is **Cine Club Miraflores** (Larco 770, Miraflores, tel. 01/446-2649). In central Lima there is

Cineplanet Centro (Jr. de la Union 819, tel. 01/428-8460, www.cineplanet.com.pe, US$2, US$3.50 Mon.–Wed.).

For art and classic films, check out **El Cinematógrafo** (Pérez Roca 196, Barranco, tel. 01/477-1961, www.elcinematografo.com, US$4.50) in **Barranco.**

PERFORMING ARTS

For the most up-to-date listing of cultural events, pick up the monthly *Guía del Arte de Lima,* which is available free in most museums and cultural centers. Or view its website, http://guiadelarte.perucultural.org.pe. *El Comercio* (www.elcomercioperu.com.pe) newspaper also has complete listings.

Lima's performing arts received a body blow when the Teatro Municipal, the main venue for ballet, symphony, and opera, burnt to the ground in 1998. Some of these events have been transferred to the **Teatro Segura** (Huancavelica 265, central Lima, tel. 01/426-7189) or the **Museo de la Nación** (Javier Prado Este 2465, San Borja, tel. 01/476-9878).

Theater productions, always in Spanish, can be seen at **Centro Cultural de España** (Natalio Sánchez 181, Sta. Beatriz, www.ccelima.org), **Centro Cultural PUCP** (Camino Real 1075, San Isidro, tel. 01/616-1616, http://cultural.pucp.edu.pe), **Teatro Canout** (Petit Thouars 4550, Miraflores, tel. 01/422-5373), **Teatro Marsano** (General Suárez 409, Miraflores), **Teatro La Plaza Usil** in Larcomar (tel. 01/242-9266, www.larcomar.com), **Alianza Francesa** (Arequipa 4595, tel. 01/241-7014, www.alianzafrancesalima.edu.pe), and **Teatro Británico** (Bellavista 531, Miraflores, tel. 01/447-1135, www.britanico.edu.pe), which occasionally has plays in English. Tickets are normally purchased at the box office for only US$8–12.

Other frequent cultural events, such as films, concerts, and expositions, are held at the **Instituto Cultural Peruano Norteamericano** (tel. 01/706-7000, www.icpna.edu.pe), with a location in central Lima (Cusco 446) and Miraflores (Angamos Oeste 106); the **Centro Cultural Ricardo Palma** (Larco 770, Miraflores, tel. 01/446-3959); and the

Asociación Cultural Peruano Británica (Bellavista 531, Miraflores, tel. 01/447-1135, www.britanico.edu.pe).

CASINOS

Lima is overflowing with casinos, though the most reputable ones tend to be in the major hotels. Wherever you go, do not play the slot machines, as they tend to be rigged. Some casinos open in the evenings and close around dawn. Others are open 24 hours a day. Regardless, they usually offer free drinks, food, and cigarettes to those who are betting.

Better casinos include the **Hotel Sheraton** (Paseo de la República 170, tel. 01/315-5000) in central Lima. In **San Isidro** there's the upscale **Los Delfines Hotel** (Los Eucaliptos 555, tel. 01/215-7000), with minimum US$5 blackjack bets. And in **Miraflores,** the **Stellaris Casino** at the Marriott (Malecón de la Reserva 615, across the street from Larcomar, tel. 01/217-7000) has minimum US$3 bets at the blackjack tables, and Best Western's **Casino la Hacienda** (28 de Julio 511, tel. 01/213-1000) also has a minimum US$3 bet.

SPECTATOR SPORTS

Lima is a great place to catch a **soccer game,** either at the Estadio Nacional along the Vía Expresa and 28 de Julio or at the more modern Estadio Monumental Lolo Fernández in the Molina neighborhood. Games happen mostly on Wednesdays, Saturdays, and Sundays, and prices and locations are published two days beforehand in the newspaper. Tickets run US$5–9 and can usually be bought the same day for nonchampionship matches. Tickets are bought at the stadium, at Farmacia Deza (Conquistadores 1140, San Isidro, tel. 01/222-3195), and at TeleTicket counters at Wong and Metro supermarkets.

Bullfighting takes place at the Plaza de Acho (Hualgayoc 332, tel. 01/481-1467) near the center of Lima from the first week of October to the first week of December, a centuries-old tradition that coincides with Lima's biggest festival, El Señor de los Milagros. Tickets for the Sunday afternoon events range US$30–100 for a two-hour contest featuring world-class bull-fighters from Spain and Peru. Tickets are also sold at Farmacio Deza and at TeleTicket counters in Wong and Metro supermarkets.

Cockfights, traditionally part of *criollo* culture, are weekend events at various *peñas* and the **Coliseo de Gallos Sandia** in Surquillo.

Horse races can be seen at the **Jockey Club of Peru** (El Derby s/n, puerta 3, Hipódromo de Monterrico, tel. 01/610-3000), where betting races are held Tuesdays, Thursdays, and weekends.

To watch American football or European soccer, head to **The Corner Sports Bar and Grill** (Larco 1207, tel. 01/444-0220, 11 A.M.–3 A.M. daily). With TVs even in the bathrooms, you are unlikely to miss a moment of action.

FESTIVALS

Lima's biggest festival is **El Señor de los Milagros** (The Lord of Miracles), which draws as many as a half million people on its main days of October 18 and 28 and is accompanied by bullfights at Plaza de Acho. The processions begin in central Lima at **Iglesia Las Nazarenas** (Tacna and Huancavelica), which was built atop a wall where a black slave painted an image of Christ in the 17th century. The wall was the only thing left standing after a 1755 earthquake, prompting this annual festival in October, the month when Lima's worst earthquakes have traditionally struck. To this day a brotherhood of priests of mainly African descent care for the image, which some anthropologists say is related to the pre-Hispanic cult of Pachacámac.

Other good festivals include **Lima's anniversary** on January 18, the **Feast of the Crosses up San Cristóbal** on May 3, the **Feast of Santa Rosa de Lima** on August 30, and **Día de la Canción Criolla** (Creole Music Day) on October 30, when *peñas* hold a variety of concerts around the city.

Peruvian *paso* horse competitions are held in the Lurín Valley south of Lima and are highly recommended. These include the Peruvian Paso Horse Competition in February, a national competition in Mamacona in April, and the Amancaes competition, also in Mamacona, in July. For more information see the website www.yachay.com.pe/especiales/caballos (Spanish-only).

Shopping

Lima is the clearinghouse for handicrafts produced in places like Huancayo and Ayacucho and sold with a considerable markup. There is a huge range, from cheap tourist-oriented items to boutique shops, but bargaining is always an option. Several American-style malls have been built in Lima, most notably the cliffside Larcomar at the end of Avenida Larco and under the Parque Salazar.

HANDICRAFTS

In **Pueblo Libre,** an excellent crafts markets with a cause is **La Casa de la Mujer Artesana Manuela Ramos** (Juan Pablo Fernandini 1550, 15th block of Brasil, Pueblo Libre, tel. 01/423-8840, www.casadelamujerartesana.com, 9 A.M.–5 P.M. Mon.–Fri.). Proceeds from this market benefit women's programs across Peru.

The largest crafts markets are in **Miraflores** on blocks 52 and 54 on Petit Thouars. Market after market is filled with alpaca clothing, silver jewelry, ceramics, and textiles from all over the country. **Mercado Indio** (Petit Thouars 5245) and **Indian Market** (Petit Thouars 5321) are the best of the lot, with nicely presented stalls and wide selections. Nearby is a **Manos Peruanas** (Plaza Artesanal, Petit Thouars 5411, tel. 01/242-9726, 10:30 A.M.–7:30 P.M. daily), with a contemporary line of handcrafted silver earrings, necklaces, and bracelets. Other huge, cheap crafts markets are **Feria Artesanal** on Avenida Marina on the way to the airport (every taxi knows it) or in central Lima across from Iglesia Santo Domingo, at the intersection of Camaná and Superunda.

Miraflores's other main shopping strips are in the area next to Parque Kennedy that includes La Paz, Schell, and Diez Canseco Streets. The reasonably priced **Hecho a Mano** (Diez Canseco 298) has a high-quality selection of crafts from all parts of Peru, especially Ayacucho. Another plaza at Diez Canseco 380 is filled with jewelry shops, and a wide selection of baby alpaca sweaters can be found at Diez Canseco 378.

For a more upmarket shopping experience, visit the hugely popular **Larcomar** (Malecón de la Reserva 610, www.larcomar.com), an elegant open-air mall dug under Miraflores's Parque Salazar and perched over the ocean. Upscale alpaca clothing stores (the finest of which is **Alpaca 111,** www.alpaca111.com), cafés, a sushi restaurant, bars, a disco, and a 12-screen cinema are just a few of the businesses here. An excellent place for high-quality jewelry, alpaca clothing, textiles, and creative gifts is **Peru ArtCrafts** (Malecón de la Reserva 610, Larcomar, www.peruartcrafts.com).

The most sophisticated range of handicrafts in Lima can be found in **Barranco. Las Pallas** (Cajamarca 212, tel. 01/477-4629, 9 A.M.–7 P.M. Mon.–Sat.) is a high-end gallery with exquisite Amazon textiles, tapestries, and carved gourds from Huancayo, as well as colonial ceramics from Cusco. Prices run US$30–800. Another good option for high-end crafts and art is **Dédalo** (Saenz Pena 295, Barranco, tel. 01/477-0562, 11 A.M.–9 P.M. Tues.–Sun.). Unique art and antiques from all over the world can be found at **San Francisco Gallery of Art** (Plaza San Francisco 208, tel. 01/477-0537, 10:30 A.M.–1:30 P.M. and 3:30–7 P.M. Mon.–Sat.). Expensive gifts, including jewelry and purses, are sold in the courtyard. For Ayacucho crafts, try **Museo-Galería Popular de Ayacucho** (Pedro de Osma 116, tel. 01/246-0599).

Sáenz Peña is the street for contemporary art. There are numerous galleries, whose work is

Larcomar is a giant shopping and entertainment complex perched over Lima's coast and smack in the middle of Miraflores, one of the capital's most upscale neighborhoods.

mostly modern and anything from paintings to photography to sculpture. Check out **Lucía de la Puente Galería de Arte** (Sáenz Peña 206, tel. 01/477-9740, www.glucladelapuente.com), in a large, old mansion, **PPPP Design** (Grau 810, tel. 01/247-7976), or **Yvonne Sanguineti** (Grau 810, tel. 01/477-0519, 11 A.M.–8 P.M. Mon.–Sat.).

CAMPING EQUIPMENT

If you need to buy outdoor gear, you will pay a premium in Peru and your only options are Lima, Huaraz, and Cusco. Varying qualities of white gas, or *bencina blanca,* can be bought at hardware stores across Peru, so test your stove before you depart. Gas canisters are available only at specialty outdoor stores.

Miraflores has several stores: **Alpamayo** (Larco 345, tel. 01/445-1671, 10 A.M.–8 P.M. Mon.–Sat.) sells tents, backpacks, sleeping mats, boots, rock shoes, climbing gear, water filters, MSR stoves, and more. Similar items are found at **Camping Center** (Benavides 1620 Miraflores, tel. 01/242-1779, www. campingperu.com, 10 A.M.–7 P.M. Mon.–Fri., 10 A.M.–1 P.M. Sat.) and **Mountain Worker** (Centro Comercial Camino Real, A-17 in basement, tel. 01/421-2175). **Todo Camping E.I.R.L.** (Angamos Oeste 350, tel. 01/242-1318, 10 A.M.–8 P.M. Mon.–Sat.) also sells more technical equipment like crampons and higher-end fuel stoves.

BOOKSTORES

The best bookstore in central Lima is **El Virrey** (Paseo los Escribanos 115, tel. 01/427-5080, www.elvirrey.com, 10 A.M.–1 P.M. and 1:30–7 P.M. Mon.–Sat.). If you are looking for specialty books in science, history, or sociology, this is the place to find them. The store also has shops in **San Isidro** (Miguel Dasso 141, tel. 01/440-0607, 8 A.M.–8 P.M. daily) and at Larcomar in **Miraflores** (tel. 01/445-6883, noon–9 P.M. daily).

Additionally, there are several bookstores, or *librerías,* in Miraflores with good English and other foreign language sections. Despite its humble door, **SBS** (Angamos Oeste 301, tel. 01/241-8490, www.sbs.com.pe, 8 A.M.–7 P.M. Mon.–Sat.) has the best collection of English-language guidebooks. Its storefront on Parque Kennedy goes by the name **Ibero Librería** (Larco 199, 10 A.M.–8 P.M. daily) and it has an excellent selection of English-language books as well as a helpful staff. **Crisol** (Santa Cruz 816, Óvalo Gutierrez, tel. 01/221-1010, www.crisol. com.pe, 10 A.M.–8 P.M. daily) is a huge, glassy bookshop in the same mall as the Cineplant Alcázar. Other options are **Zeta** (Comandante Espinar 219, tel. 01/446-5139, www.zetabook. com, 10 A.M.–9 P.M. Mon.–Sat., also at Lima airport) and **Delta Bookstore Librería** (Larco 970, tel. 01/445-8825, 10 A.M.–9 P.M. Mon.–Sat., 11 A.M.–6 P.M. Sun.). International newspapers are available from Miraflores street vendors in front of Café Haiti by Parque Kennedy.

Recreation

BIKING

There are great places to go mountain biking within a few hours of Lima, including Pachacámac and the Reserva Nacional de Paracas. Good bike shops in **Miraflores** include **Best Mountainbikes** (Comandante Espinar 320, tel. 01/263-0964, bestint@ terra.com.pe) and **Rent-a-Bike** (Marquez de Torre Tagle 107, tel. 01/446-9682), for rentals. **BiciCentro** (Av. San Luis 2906, tel. 01/475-2645), in **San Borja,** is good for repairs and services. **BikeMavil** (Aviación 4021, tel. 01/449-8435, bikemavil@terra.com.pe), in **Surco,** rents bikes and leads excursions.

BIRD-WATCHING

With an early start, there are several doable bird-watching day trips from Lima. **Pantanos de Villa** is a 396-hectare, protected marsh within the Lima city limits. Here, you can see over 130 coastal marsh species, and the area is accessible by public transportation. For guaranteed sightings of the Humboldt penguin, your best option is the **Pucusana** fishing village. Public transportation also covers this route.

An absolutely excellent bird-watching guide and source is Princeton-trained biologist Thomas Valque's *Where to Watch Birds in Peru,* available through the American Audubon Society or www.granperu.com/bird-watchingbook. PromPeru's website (www.peru-birdingroutes.com) is also chock-full of good information.

To make your trip more efficient and learn more, you'll probably want to contact a guide. Thomas Valque's company **Gran Perú** (tel. 01/344-1701, www.granperu.com) leads a variety of scheduled tours and can also coordinate day and private trips. Swedish ornithologist Gunnar Engblom's agency **Kolibri Expeditions** (tel. 01/476-5016, www.kolibriexpeditions.com) offers regular weekend expeditions in the Lima area.

BOWLING

There are plenty of lanes at **Cosmic Bowling** (Larcomar, Malecón de la Reserva 610, Miraflores, tel. 01/445-7776, 10 A.M.–1 A.M., US$14/hour), which turns out the light, leaving patrons to aim in the "cosmic light." **Jockey Plaza** (tel. 01/435-9122, 10 A.M.–midnight, US$15 pp) on Javier Prado in Monterrico also has a huge alley.

COOKING

For those familiar with Lima's culinary delights, it should come as no surprise that it hosts a cooking school licensed by **Cordon Bleu** (Nuñez de Balboa 530, Miraflores, tel. 01/242-8222, www.cordonbleuperu.edu.pe, prices vary by course). The various classes include short-term seminars on Peruvian food, international food, and even desserts. Another option is the hotel and restaurant management school **Cenfotur** (Pedro Martinto 320, tel. 01/241-4726, www.cenfotur.com, US$200 per course), whose workshop classes also feature cocktail making and wine-tasting. At either of

© MICHAEL TWEDDLE

The thermal winds rising from the cold Pacific Ocean allow paragliders to spend hours cruising the coastline of Miraflores.

these institutions you will have to make special arrangements for English-speaking classes.

HORSEBACK RIDING

Check out **Cabalgatas** (tel. 01/9837-5813, www.cabalgatas.com.pe, US$45–65), an option for riding Peruvian *paso* horses near Mamacona, the town where the *paso* horse competitions are held each year. They lead interesting excursions around the ceremonial center of Pachacámac.

PARAGLIDING

First-time visitors to Miraflores, promenading the *malecón,* are sometimes surprised to find a paraglider just meters above their heads, zipping back and forth along the oceanfront bluffs. Although the thrill is short lived, paragliding does offer an excellent alternative viewpoint of Lima. One recommended operator is **Peru Fly** (Jorge Chávez 658, Miraflores, tel. 01/444-5004, www.perufly.com) organizes flights in Lima and Paracas and also offers six-day basic-training courses.

ROCK-CLIMBING WALLS

Available on Mondays, Wednesdays, and Fridays at 7:30 P.M., the rock wall at **Millennium Gym** (Jr. Independencia 145, Miraflores, tel. 01/242-8557) is good training for the boulders around Huaraz. You must become a member to climb. **Youth Hostal Malka** (Los Lirios 165, San Isidro, tel. 01/442-0162, www.youthhostelperu.com) in San Isidro also has a rock wall.

SCUBA

There are no coral reefs on Peru's Pacific coast, but agencies do offer interesting dives. **AguaSport** (Conquistadores 805, San Isidro, tel. 01/221-1548, www.aquasportperu.com) rents all equipment for snorkeling and scuba diving. Standard scuba day trips from Lima include a 30-meter wall dive at Pucusana, an 18-meter dive to a nearby sunken ship, or diving with sea lions at Islas Palomino off Lima. Two dives are US$95, or US$55 if you have your own equipment. This agency rents a range of aquatic and off-road equipment.

SEA KAYAKING

For those who like to get out on the water but aren't surfers, there's always sea kayaking. **Chingos** (tel. 01/9926-6363, www.chingos.com, around US$75 pp) is a professionally run operation, with new equipment, that takes passengers out on the Pacific anywhere between Ancón and Cerro Azul.

SURFING

Though the swells in front of Lima are dotted with dozens of surfers, we do not recommend surfing in these polluted waters. The better breaks are La Herradura in Chorrillos, Punta Hermosa, and Punta Rocas. Or head instead to the beaches north or south of Lima, and you will find some untouched. Keep an eye out for opportunities to surf at **San Gallán,** one of Peru's few right point breaks in the Paracas National Reserve; **Pepinos** and **Cerro Azul,** near the mouth of the Cañete River Valley; and **Playa Grande,** north of Lima, which is a challenging, hollow point break for expert surfers.

Good sources of surfing information are www.surfingperu.org and www.peruazul.com.

For surfing classes, call Rocio Larrañaga at **Surf School** (tel. 01/264-5100 or 01/9710-7345), who will pick you up at your hotel and lend you a wetsuit and board. **Luis Miguel de la Rosa** (tel. 01/9810-1988) offers a similar service. If you're just looking to rent, **Centro Comercial** (Caminos del Inca Tienda 158, Surco, tel. 01/372-5106) has both surfboards and skateboards. **Big Head** (Larcomar, Malecón de la Reserva 610, tel. 01/242-8123) sells new surfboards and body boards along with wetsuits. One of the better surf shops in Peru is **Focus** (Las Palmeras Block C, Playa Arica, Panamericana Sur Km 41, tel. 01/430-0444). The staff is knowledgeable about local surfing spots, rents boards at a good price, and even has a few hostel rooms.

OFF-THE-WALL FUN

Laser tag pickup battles are available at the Jockey Club's **Daytona Park** (El Derby s/n, Puerto 4, Hipódromo de Monterrico, Surco, tel. 01/435-6058, 10 A.M.–10 P.M. daily) and

LIMA

cost US$9 for 30 minutes. It is also possible to go-kart around a racetrack.

Bus Parrandero (Benavides 330, Of. 101, Miraflores, tel. 01/445-4755, www.elbusparrandero.com) operates an air-conditioned **party bus,** where people hop on board, drink as much as they want, and listen to live performers—all for US$25. The bus travels from Miraflores to Plaza Mayor in central Lima and then takes passengers to the popular Barranco *peña* La Candelaría (entry included).

TOUR AGENCIES AND GUIDES

Do not get hustled by agency reps at Lima's airport or bus stations. They will arrange travel packages that tend to be as expensive as, or more expensive than, if you were to do it on your own.

Sightseeing Agencies

Our favorite travel agency in Lima is **Fertur Peru** (www.fertur-travel.com, 8:30 A.M.–8 P.M. Mon.–Sat.), run by the enterprising Siduith Ferrer with offices in central Lima at the Plaza Mayor (Junín 211, tel. 01/427-2626) and Miraflores (Schell 485, tel. 01/242-1900). It can buy a variety of bus and plane tickets and set up tours around Lima and day tours to see Paracas or the Nasca Lines.

Peru's most reputable agency, with decades in business, is **Lima Tours,** with offices in central Lima (Belén 1040, tel. 01/619-6900, www.limatours.com.pe). Its city tours have exclusive access to the pristine 17th-century mansion Casa de Aliaga. Because the company works with large international groups, it is best to get in touch before arrival in Lima.

A good agency for booking flights and other logistics is **Nuevo Mundo,** with offices in the center (Camaná 782, tel. 01/427-0635), Miraflores (Jorge Chávez 225), and San Isidro (28 de Julio 1120, tel. 01/610-8080).

Reputable agencies in Miraflores include **Exprinter** (Pardo 384, tel. 01/444-5350, www.exprinterviajes.com.pe) and **Carlson Wagonlit Travel** (Ricardo Palma 355, tel. 01/610-1600, www.cwtvacaciones.com.pe).

A final option for day tours in Lima is **Peru Smile** (tel. 01/997-1349, perusmile@yahoo.com), which is run by Jorge Fernández and has tours and prices similar to Lima Vision (but without the large groups).

Many of the recommended agencies sell tours run by **Lima Vision** (Chiclayo 444, Miraflores, tel. 01/447-7710, 24 hours, www.limavision.com), the city's standard pool service, which offers three- to four-hour daily tours of Lima's center (US$25), museums (US$35), Pachacámac (US$35), Museo de Oro (US$25), or a full-day city tour with lunch (US$70). Whether you buy from Lima Vision or from an agency, the cost is the same. All of Peru's main agencies are based in Lima.

Specialized Agencies

For those who can't make it to Paracas, **Ecocruceros** (Arequipa 4960, tel. 01/9910-8396, www.ecocruceros.com) offers half-day boat tours from the port of Callao to see sea lions at the Islas Palomino.

Guides

Recommended and certified private tour guides are **Tino Guzmán Khan** (tel. 01/429-5779, tinogpc@yahoo.com), who speaks English, Chinese, and French, and **Cecilia Paredes** (tel. 01/475-3829), who speaks English, Spanish, and Italian.

Accommodations

When in Lima, our favorite places to stay are Barranco, with lots of nightlife, backpacker options, and bohemian energy, and Miraflores, which has Peru's best selection of hotels and restaurants in all categories. If you're in town for corporate work, or want the highest-end hotels Lima has to offer, San Isidro's financial district is your best bet. If you are comfortable in noisy, developing-world cities and interested in understanding the city's colonial center, you should stay in downtown Lima. The neighborhood of Breña is a more peaceful alternative to the center that is close to the Museo de Arte and a 10-minute walk to the edge of old town. Pueblo Libre, only a 10-minute taxi ride to the center, has a charming small-town feel for those who want to get off the beaten track.

CENTRAL LIMA AND PUEBLO LIBRE
US$10-25

In downtown Lima, the (**Hostal Roma** (Ica 326, tel. 01/427-7576, www.hostalroma.8m. com, US$16 s, US$25 d with breakfast and private bath) is a charming place catering to backpackers. With high ceilings, wood floors, and 10 different types of breakfast, Roma stands out from the rest. Internet, safety boxes, and airport transfers are available. A small, attached café serves espresso, beer, and cocktails. The 36 rooms here fill up fast, so make reservations early.

Another good budget option in downtown Lima is **Hostal España** (Azángaro 105, tel. 01/428-5546, www.hotelespanaperu.com, US$6 dorm, US$12–16 s, US$16–20 d, rooms with private baths US$5 extra). This backpacker classic is a labyrinth of tight halls and patios, decorated with hanging ivy, marble busts, and reproductions of colonial paintings. The rooms are small and basic with clean, shared bathrooms and hot water. Despite its location, the hostel manages to disconnect itself from the hustle and be a peaceful escape. With

LIMA

© JASON RUPP

One of the best lodging values in all of Lima is the elegant Hostal España, in central Lima.

a charming upstairs restaurant and neighboring Internet café, this place fills up quickly. Make reservations early.

In Breña, the friendly **Hostal Iquique** (Iquique 758, tel. 01/433-4724 or 01/423-3699, www.hostal-iquique-lima.com, US$17 s, US$26 d with breakfast) is a longtime backpackers' favorite with good service, kitchen, rooftop terrace, and hot water. Rooms with tiled floors are not too noisy and some even have TVs. Private baths cost an additional US$4–7.

Bordering Breña, **Hostal de Las Artes** (Chota 1460, tel. 01/433-0031, www.hostaldelasartes.net, US$5 for dorm bed, US$9 s, US$18 d) is a clean, well-managed, gay-friendly place with Dutch owners. Sevillean-style tiles line the entrance off a quiet street that is a 10-minute walk from Plaza San Martín. Rooms are simple with whitewashed walls, dark wood, comfy beds, and near silence. A book exchange, gardens, and two patios round out the hostel. There are good restaurants down the street.

Pueblo Libre's artist-owned **Guest House Marfil** (Parque Ayacucho 126, tel. 01/463-3161, casamarfil@yahoo.com, US$12 s, US$18 d) is a converted house with splashes of color, lots of paintings on the walls, and three resident cats. The bohemian rooms are private, making this a great value, and the shared baths are clean with plenty of hot water. There are two Internet stations and a group kitchen. Banks and supermarkets are nearby.

US$25-50

Sitting at the end of a quiet park, near the Museo de Arte, is the recommended **Posada del Parque** (Parque Hernán Velarde 60, block 1 Petit Thouars, tel. 01/433-2412, www.incacountry.com, US$31 s, US$41 d). This hotel in an old colonial house, filled with traditional art, is the perfect escape from central Lima. The Parque de la Exposición, just blocks away, makes for great strolling. Monica, the attentive owner, provides two Internet-ready computers, firm beds, great "what to do" advice, and a sitting room with a TV and DVD player.

Hostal Bonbini (Cailloma 209, tel. 01/427-

6477, http://bonbini.tripod.com.pe, US$30 s, US$40 d with breakfast) has large rooms with nice but dated furniture, cable TV, and big bathrooms. Avoid noisy rooms on the street front. **Hotel Kamana** (Camaná 547, tel. 01/427-7106, www.hotelkamana.com, US$43 s, US$58 d with breakfast) is overpriced, but safe and well operated. There is a 24-hour snack bar, and the back rooms are quiet. This is a safe and reliable option for a good night's sleep.

Over US$150

The only five-star hotel in central Lima is the **Hotel Sheraton** (Paseo de la República 170, tel. 01/315-5000, www.sheraton.com.pe, US$165 s, US$190 d), a square tower that rises at the entrance to old town. This business hotel has a huge open atrium rising 19 floors. The normal rooms have older furniture and feel four-starish. If you stay here, upgrade to the tower rooms on the upper floors, which have easy chairs, California king-size beds, elegant wood floors and paneling, and astounding views over Lima. Other services include whirlpool tub, sauna, gym, and ground-floor casino. If you bargain, prices at this hotel get as low as US$83.

SAN ISIDRO
US$10-25

The bulk of San Isidro's hotels are oriented toward high-class business travelers, but there is one great exception to this rule. **Youth Hostal Malka** (Los Lirios 165, San Isidro, tel. 01/442-0162, www.youthhostelperu.com, US$8 dorm, US$19 d) is a rare find with its own rock-climbing wall. This converted home has simple, clean rooms, Internet, laundry service, and a grassy yard with a table tennis table. The hostel is a block from a park, and a supermarket and a few restaurants are down the street. Rooms with private baths are US$2 more.

US$100-150

Like its sister hotels around the country, **Hotel Libertador San Isidro Golf** (Los Eucaliptos 550, San Isidro, tel. 01/421-6666 or U.S.

tel. 800/537-8483, www.libertador.com.pe, US$115 s or d with breakfast) is an elegant, classy act. These four-star rooms are a great value, with dark-stained furniture, elegant carpets, golf course views, and all the creature comforts, including luxurious bathrooms with tubs. There is an elegant pub downstairs with lots of wood, and the Ostrich House Restaurant serves up ostrich and other delicious steaks. Features include a sauna, whirlpool tub, and gymnasium.

Over US$150

At the top of El Olívar, a park shaded by ancient olive trees, **Sonesta Hotel El Olivar** (Pancho Fierro 194, San Isidro, tel. 01/712-6000, www.sonesta.com, US$230 s, US$260 d with breakfast) has spacious though quite ordinary rooms, a beautiful sitting area with bar, and a rooftop pool. Ask for a room with views over the olive grove.

Built in 1927, the **Country Club Lima Hotel** (Los Eucaliptos 590, San Isidro, www.hotelcountry.com, US$295 s, US$310 d) has a classic, turn-of-the-20th-century elegance. Couches fill a marble lobby decorated with Oriental rugs, dark wood, and high windows. Perks include an elegant restaurant, an English bar, a gymnasium, and an outdoor pool. Suites are decorated with museum pieces from Museo de Osma. Ask for a room with a balcony or a view over the golf course, which as a guest you'll be able to play.

Sandwiched between the Camino Real Mall and a glassy office park, **Swissôtel** (Via Central 150, San Isidro, tel. 01/421-4400 or U.S. tel. 800/637-9477, www.swissotel-lima.com, US$330 s or d with breakfast) is one of Peru's leading business hotels. All rooms have king-size beds, down comforters, large bathrooms with tubs, and wireless Internet. Each floor has its own security card. You have your choice of food: Swiss, Italian, or Peruvian. An elegant swimming pool surrounded by grassy lawn, a tennis court, a whirlpool tub, a sauna, and a gym make for a relaxing afternoon.

Los Delfines (Los Eucaliptos 555, tel. 01/215-7000, www.losdelfineshotel.com,

US$219 s or d, buffet breakfast included), with a pool full of leaping dolphins, was an extravagant concept from the go-go Fujimori years. But guests eating breakfast or having a drink at the bar seem to love the hotel pets: dolphins. The comfortable rooms feel new and are decked out with deep blue carpets, elegant tables, and bathrooms. Amenities include a casino, luxurious outdoor pool, spa with massages, aerobics room, sauna, and whirlpool tub, and the restaurant serves first-class Mediterranean food.

An upcoming luxury hotel, which will likely become Lima's most expensive hotel, is **Westin Libertador** (tel. 01/421-6666 or U.S. tel. 800/537-8483, www.libertador.com.pe, US$300 s or d with breakfast). This 301-room skyscraper, right in the middle of San Isidro's financial district, is set to open in 2011 with two restaurants, a bar-lounge, luxury spa, and conference facility.

Long-Term Stays

With a minimum stay of 15 days, **Loft** (Jorge Basadre 255, Of. 202, tel. 01/222-8983, www.loftapar.com), an apartment rental agency, offers travelers well-located, fully equipped apartments in San Isidro and Miraflores. Rates start at US$500 a month for the studio but there are also one-, two-, and three-bedroom apartments.

MIRAFLORES

Along with San Isidro, Miraflores is one of Lima's upscale districts. The shopping and restaurants are top-notch, and you're only a five-minute cab ride to nightlife action in Barranco.

US$10-25

One of the best places in town to meet other travelers is **Home Peru** (Arequipa 4501, tel. 01/241-9898, www.homeperu.com, US$9 dorm, US$12 pp s, US$24 d shared bath with breakfast), a restored colonial mansion five blocks from Miraflores's Parque Kennedy. Spacious, sunny wood-floored rooms have comfortable bunk beds and shared baths with hot water. There is a nice room on the ground

LIMA

floor with cable TV, as well as free Internet, in-expensive laundry, a shared kitchen (the super-market is just a block away!), and a charming open-air dining area for morning breakfasts.

A great place for budget travelers is **Explorer's House** (Alfredo León 158, tel. 01/241-5002, explorers_house@yahoo.es, US$8 dorm, US$12 s, US$20 d with break-fast). The house-cum-hostel has a common kitchen and TV room with a video library. The communal baths are clean, and laundry is US$1/kilogram. The friendly owners Maria Jesus and Victor give a remembrance gift upon departure!

Casa del Mochilero (Cesareo Chacaltana 130A, 2nd Fl., tel. 01/444-9089, juan_kalua@hotmail.com, US$8 pp dorm with shared bath) is a clean and plain backpackers' hang-out, about 10 minutes' walk from Parque Kennedy, with bunk rooms, shared bathrooms, and group kitchen. Mochilero's Inn is a lesser, though similarly priced, knockoff down the street, which we do not recommend.

Loki Inkahouse (Larco 189, tel. 01/242-4350, www.lokihostel.com, US$8 dorm, US$24 s, US$25 d with breakfast), on Parque Kennedy, couldn't be better located. Next door are some of the city's busiest restaurants and bars. But you may never need to visit them. Loki's Peruvian owners have converted this co-lonial house into a backpacker's haven, with everything you might want: a great rooftop patio, card-playing tables, three Internet sta-tions, a TV/DVD room, a communal kitchen, and even a bar.

It doesn't get more secure than at **Hitchhikers** (Bolognesi 400, tel. 01/242-3008, www.hhikersperu.com, US$10 dorm, US$25 s and d with breakfast), an old house tucked away behind fortress-like walls. There's no scrimping on space here. Shared rooms have tall ceilings, the communal kitchen has two rooms, and there's even a huge parking area, which doubles as a table tennis arena.

The cheerful **Flying Dog Hostels** (www.flyingdogperu.com, US$10 dorm, US$23 d with breakfast) have become an institution in central Miraflores, and there are locations in other parts of Peru. The three Lima locations (Diez Canseco 117, tel. 01/445-0940; Lima 457, tel. 01/444-5753; Martir Olaya 280, tel. 01/447-0673) are within a stone's throw of Parque Kennedy, and all guests eat breakfast at outdoor cafés on the park. The layout of each hostel is more or less the same: tight dormi-tory rooms, a few private rooms, sitting areas, clean bathrooms, and lots of hot water. If you make a reservation, be sure to know for which Flying Dog you've made it. They also have op-tions for longer stays.

Hostelling International (Casmiro Ulloa 328, tel. 01/446-5488, www.limahostell.com. pe, US$12 dorm, US$18 s, US$24 d) has a va-riety of rooms spread out in an old home with sunny courtyard that is a 10-minute walk to Parque Kennedy. There is a travel agency in the lobby.

US$25-50

The charming **Hostal El Patio** (Diez Canseco 341, tel. 01/444-2107, www.hostalelpatio.net, US$40 s, US$50 d with breakfast) is a memo-rable colonial home overflowing with plants and flowers and cheerfully painted walls. Large rooms have either tiled floors or carpet, as well as homey furnishings and large windows. Ask for a mini-suite for an additional US$5—you'll get your money's worth with a kitchenette. Rooms are interspersed with terraces, which are great places for reading or sunbathing.

Francis, the friendly owner of **Albergue Miraflores** (Espinar 611, tel. 01/447-7748, www.alberguemirafloreshouse.com, US$34 d or s with breakfast), claims that his second-floor staircase is practice for Machu Picchu. Then he laughs. It is the cheerful attitude that makes the small, dark rooms acceptable. Plus there are spacious common rooms, Internet, a patio with a barbecue, and third-floor rooms with nice lighting.

US$50-100

Our favorite upscale hotel in Lima is the charming **Hotel Antigua Miraflores** (Grau 350, tel. 01/241-6166, www.peru-hotels-inns. com, US$79 s, US$94 d with breakfast). This turn-of-the-20th-century mansion has all the comforts of a fine hotel and the warmth of a bed-and-breakfast. The rooms are large, cozy, and handsomely decorated with hand-carved furniture, local art, and warm colors. Plus, the remodeled bathrooms have big tubs. There are plush couches in the downstairs sitting room, and the six types of breakfast are served in a sunny, black-and-white-tiled café. It is worth paying another US$20 for a room in the old part of the house, and suites are also available with kitchens and whirlpool tubs.

Across the street from the handicrafts-haven Inka Market, the new, upscale **Casa Andina Centro** (Petit Thouars 5444, tel. 01/447-0263, www.casa-andina.com, US$65 s, US$80 d with breakfast) puts you in the middle of the action, but without the hustle. Rooms have everything for comfort: modern bathrooms, firm beds, down comforters, cable TV, minifridges, air-conditioning, and Internet in the lobby. The hotel chain has a second location slightly away from the center, **Casa Andina San Antonio** (Av. 28 de Julio 1088, tel. 01/241-4050), which is near some of Miraflores's best cafés, and another five-star version nearby as well.

Aparthotel San Martín (San Martín 598, tel. 01/242-0500, www.sanmartinhotel.com, US$110 s, US$130 d) offers spacious suites with living room, double bedroom, closet, bathroom, kitchen, cable TV, and phone. There are beds for two people and a pullout couch for two more. Floors 8–10 have wireless Internet.

The new **El Faro Inn** (Francia 857, tel. 01/242-0339, www.elfaroinn.com, US$40 s, US$60 d with breakfast) is a modern hotel one block from the oceanfront. Small rooms are carpeted, with cable TV and basic furnishings. Other amenities include cheap Internet, laundry, and a rooftop terrace. Also one block from the oceanfront is **Hostal Torre Blanca** (José Pardo 1453, tel. 01/242-1876, www.torreblancaperu.com, US$53 s, US$65 d with breakfast), which offers large carpeted rooms with cable TV and minifridge. There is free Internet and airport transfer.

Over US$150

Most of the five-star hotels are in San Isidro, but Lima's best is **Miraflores Park Hotel** (Malecón de la Reserva 1035, tel. 01/610-4000, www.mira-park.com, from US$230 s or d). This elegant glass high-rise, located on an old park overlooking the ocean, offers the best in service, comfort, and views in Lima. The grand marble entry is decorated with antique furnishings that are complemented by modern art. The luxurious rooms offer ocean views, elegant furnishings, cable TV with DVD player, fax machines, and wireless Internet. Other amenities include video library, massage (US$40), swimming pool, and squash court.

The oceanfront **JW Marriott** (Malecón de la Reserva 615, tel. 01/217-7000, www.marriotthotels.com, US$245 s, US$265 d) occupies prime real estate overlooking the Pacific Ocean and just across the street from the deluxe, full-service Larcomar mall. The rooms live up to five-star Marriott quality and are nearly silent despite the street below. For the best view, ask for a room on one of the upper floors with ocean view. Perks include glass-enclosed bars and restaurants, casino, pool, and tennis court.

BARRANCO
US$10-25

The Point (Malecón Junín 300, tel. 01/247-7997, www.thepointhostels.com, US$9–11 dorm, US$15 s, US$22 d with breakfast) is a backpacker option with everything a traveler needs: WiFi, long-distance calling, sitting room with cable TV, nice bunk beds with shared bathrooms, cheap lunches, pool table, sauna, book exchange, travel agency, a grassy lawn, and an outdoor bar. This 11-room, restored 19th-century house is just paces away from Barranco's best bars and sweeping ocean views. There are frequent barbecues and Monday night outings to the local jazz bar, La Noche.

US$25-50

D'Osma Bed & Breakfast (Pedro de Osma 240, tel. 01/251-4178, www.deosma.com,

US$22–40 s, US$30–50 d with breakfast) has upgraded its services and is a great option if you are looking for a tranquil, family-oriented environment.

Backpackers Inn (Malecón Castilla 260, tel. 01/247-3709, backpackersinnperu@hotmail.com, US$10–11 dorm, US$30 d with breakfast) is another option, less hectic and more quiet. Some rooms open onto the oceanfront, and a nearby path leads down to the beach. The inn has a communal kitchen, sofa lounge, dining room with board games, TV and DVD player, WiFi, and plenty of tourist information.

Aquisito (Centenario 114, tel. 01/247-0712, US$18 s, U$29 d) is a great bed-and-breakfast. The place is small and cozy, located on a noisy part of Barranco but incredibly quite inside. Rooms are comfortable and staff are quite friendly and helpful.

US$50-100

3B Barranco's Bed & Breakfast (Centenario 130, tel. 01/247-6915, www.3bhostal.com, US$55 s and d) is the newest addition to a group of comfy and well-equipped hostels and bed-and-breakfasts in Barranco. With a neat, minimalistic design and decor, the rooms are clean, bright, and spacious with very comfy beds and impeccable bathrooms. The hostel is on a very busy street but two blocks away from the ocean and a few more from all of Barranco's nightlife.

Second Home Peru (Domeyer 366, tel. 01/477-5021, www.secondhomeperu.com, US$75 s, US$85 d with breakfast) is inside the home of Víctor Delfin, a prominent Peruvian painter and sculptor, and his works fill the first floor of the house as well as the five elegant guest rooms. Lilian Delfin, his daughter, is a welcoming and helpful host who will lead you into a morning visit to Víctor's studio. A swim in the cool pool overlooking the ocean from a cliff, with a lion fountain spouting above, is an absolute must. The high ceilings, crisp white linens, and designer bathrooms make any visitor to Second Home feel simultaneously at ease and refined. All rooms have cable Internet connection. A night in this hotel should not be missed.

Food

Peruvian cuisine has an extraordinary range of flavors and ingredients, and nowhere is that more evident than Lima. The range of high-quality restaurants is extraordinary. The best lunch deal is always the fixed-price *menú*, which typically includes three well-prepared courses. Upscale restaurants tack on a 10 percent service charge and an 18 percent value-added tax.

The center has good budget eateries, including some of the best *chifa* (Chinese-Peruvian food) in town. San Isidro and Miraflores have the most interesting and refined restaurants, where dozens of Cordon Bleu–trained chefs busily cater to their refined Lima clientele.

CENTRAL LIMA AND PUEBLO LIBRE

Other than the cluster of restaurants around Pasaje Nicolás de Ribera El Viejo and Pasaje Santa Rosa, central Lima's restaurants are spread out. That said, it is worth taking a cab to some of them, especially the classics in Pueblo Libre.

Cafés, Bakeries, and Ice Cream

Antigua Taberna Queirolo (San Martín 1090, tel. 01/460-0441, www.antiguataberna queirolo.com, 10 A.M.–10 P.M. daily, US$8) is a charming Spanish-style café that has been open since 1880. This is a good place to come in the afternoon or evenings to sample pisco (fortified wine), made in the winery next door. There is a slim but good menu that includes salted ham sandwiches, plates of sausage, and steamed fish.

Opening onto the lawns of the Museo Larco is the tasteful **Café del Museo** (Bolívar 1515, tel. 01/462-4757, www.museolarco.org,

A baking contest in Lima features such delights as *budín de durazno* (peach pudding).

9 A.M.–6 P.M. daily, US$10). Renato Peralta leads the small kitchen and sends out precisely flavored, light plates of ceviche, *rocoto relleno,* and *chicharrones.*

Sandwiches and salads, as well as truffles, cakes, and mousses, are available at **Cocolat Café** (Pasaje Nicolas de Rivera el Viejo 121, tel. 01/427-4471, 8 A.M.–6:30 P.M. daily, US$4–7). Nearby is the historic **El Cordano** (Ancash 202, tel. 01/427-0181, 8 A.M.–9 P.M. daily, US$6–12), a century-old establishment that was a favored haunt of writers and intellectuals. Though its facade is a bit tattered, this is an excellent place to come for a US$3 pisco sour or a filling midday meal.

Peruvian

If you are staying in Pueblo Libre or visiting the Museo Larco, eat lunch in the neighborhood. **El Bolivariano** (Pasaje Santa Rosa 291, tel. 01/261-9565, www.elbolivariano.com, 10 A.M.–10 P.M. daily, US$10) is a time-honored Lima restaurant in an elegant republican-style home that is visited mainly by Peruvians. The menu includes Peruvian classics such as *seco de cabrito* (stewed goat) and *arroz con pato* (rice with duck). More intimate than its sister restaurant in Breña, **La Choza Náutica** (La Mar 635, tel. 01/261-5537, www.lachozanautica.com, 10 A.M.–8 P.M. daily) has excellent ceviche and seafood.

OK, it is a chain, but **Pardo's** (Pasaje Santa Rosa 153, tel. 01/427-2301, www.pardoschicken.com.pe, noon–11 P.M. daily, US$10–12) still serves the best spit-roasted chicken, with affordable lunch menus and open-air tables right off the Plaza Mayor. It also serves *anticuchos,* brochettes, and *chicharrones.*

In the same pedestrian walkway, **T'anta** (Pasaje Nicolás de Rivera el Viejo 142-148, tel. 01/428-3115, 9 A.M.–9 P.M. Mon.–Sat., 9 A.M.–6 P.M. Sun., US$7–14), a Gaston Acurio restaurant, serves up refined plates of Peruvian favorites *lomo saltado* and *recoto relleno,* as well as creative new inventions like *ají de gallina* ravioli.

A new and more upscale spot is **Los Virtrales de Gemma** (Ucayali 332, tel. 01/426-7796, 9 A.M.–7 P.M. Mon.–Sat., US$10), in a restored colonial home one block

© JORGE RIVEROS CAYO

A bartender at Malabar serves up a pisco sour.

from the Plaza Mayor. The hardworking owners have created an excellent and varied menu of Peruvian and international food.

Though a bit faded from its past glory, **L'Eau Vive** (Ucayali 370, tel. 01/427-5612, 12:30–3 P.M. and 7:30–9:30 P.M. Mon.–Sat., US$7) still serves up wholesome and delicious lunch *menús* prepared by a French order of nuns. Dinners feature cocktails, the singing of "Ave María," and an eclectic selection of international entrées.

In Breña, **La Choza Náutica** (Breña 204, off first block of Arica, tel. 01/423-8087, www.lachozanautica.com, 11 A.M.–1 A.M., US$9–11) is a former hole-in-the-wall *cebichería* that has become more upscale and successful over the years. It serves special ceviches (including an "erotic" version) and *tiraditos* in huge portions.

Chifa

When in central Lima, do not miss the opportunity to sample *chifa* (Chinese-Peruvian cuisine) at one of the largest Chinatowns in South America. There are at least a dozen places spread along the town's two main streets, Capón and Paruro. The best known of Lima's Chinatown is **Wa Lok** (Paruro 864, tel. 01/427-2750, 9 A.M.–11 P.M. daily, US$12–17), serving more than 20 types of dim sum. Try *ja kao dim sum,* a mixture of pork and shrimp with rice, or *siu mai de chanco,* shredded pork with mushroom and egg pasta. A good, less expensive alternative to Wa Lok, with a more elegant dining room, is **Salon Capon** (Paruro 819, tel. 01/426-9286, 9 A.M.–11 P.M. Mon.–Sat., US$8–10), serving Peking duck, *langostinos Szechuan* (sautéed shrimps with *ají*), and *chuleta kin tou* (grilled sweet pork). Both have lovely display cases of after-lunch desserts.

Vegetarian

The Hare Krishna–operated **Govinda** (Callao 480, tel. 01/426-1956, 9:30 A.M.–9 P.M. Mon.–Sat.), the country's tried-and-true vegetarian chain, has a varied, inventive menu with pizzas, sandwiches, yogurts, and veggie Chinese food.

SAN ISIDRO

San Isidro's restaurant and nightlife scene lives mostly on the Avenida de los Conquistadores.

Here, you will find some of Lima's newest and most upscale restaurants.

Cafés, Bakeries, and Ice Cream

For those who want a good place to read, **La Baguette** (Aliaga 456, 7 A.M.–11 P.M. Sun.–Wed., 7 A.M.–midnight Thurs.–Sat., US$7) has a nice second-story balcony and a long list of sandwiches on real baguettes. **Don Mamino** (Conquistadores 790, tel. 01/344-4004, 6:30 A.M.–11 P.M. daily) has gourmet desserts and fresh-baked breads. **The Ice Cream Factory** (Conquistadores 395, tel. 01/222-2633, 11 A.M.–10 P.M. daily) has a good range of ice creams and affordable sandwiches. The geranium-lined patio of **La Bonbonneire** (Burgos 415, tel. 01/421-2447, 8 A.M.–midnight Tues.–Sun., US$9) is straight out of France, as are the delicate sandwiches of cream cheese and smoked trout. The patio of **T'anta** (Pancho Fierro 117, tel. 01/421-9708, US$7–14) is an excellent place to linger over a cup of coffee, glass of wine, or a rich chocolate dessert. The very best ice cream in Peru is at **Quattro D** (Las Begonias 580). *Lúcuma* and chocolate make an unbeatable double scoop.

Peruvian

Punta Sal (Conquistadores 948, tel. 01/441-7431, www.puntasal.com, 11 A.M.–5 P.M. daily, US$10–14) is a large, casual place for good seafood and ceviche. The lunch-only **Segundo Muelle** (Conquistadores 490, tel. 01/421-1206, www.segundomuelle.com, noon–5 P.M. daily, US$8–12) successfully combines pastas with seafood and tasty ceviche. Try the ravioli stuffed with crabmeat or lasagna with shrimp and artichoke.

San Isidro's classic Peruvian restaurant, with 35 years in the business, is **José Antonio** (Bernardo Monteagudo 200, tel. 01/264-0188, www.joseantonio.com.pe, 12:30–4:30 P.M. and 7:30 P.M.–midnight daily, US$14–17). Said to have the best *lomo saltado* in town, the restaurant also offers *ají de gallina, cau cau,* and *causa* with *camarones.*

International

With a culture of ceviche, it isn't surprising

that Lima has latched on to sushi. **Osaka** (Conquistadores 999, tel. 01/222-0405, www.osakafusion.com, 12:30–4 P.M. and 7:30 P.M.–1 A.M. daily, US$9–12) is doing with Japanese food what many Peruvian restaurants have done with international cuisine: fusion. *Camote* (sweet potato) tempura and Inca rolls are dinner highlights. **Asia de Cuba** (Conquistadores 780, San Isidro, tel. 01/222-4940, www.asiadecubaperu.com, 7 P.M.–close Mon.–Sat., US$15) is a swanky sushi house with over-the-top decor. There are more than 30 types of martinis, a range of buttery sushi, and other Asian fusion cuisine.

A casual place for great Mexican and margaritas is **Como Agua Para Chocolate** (Pancho Fierro 108, tel. 01/222-0297, noon–midnight Mon.–Sat., noon–10 P.M. Sun., US$8), with brightly colored walls and friendly service. If you are in the mood for an Argentine grill, and an all-meat menu, head to **La Carreta** (Rivera Navarrete 740, tel. 01/442-2690, 11 A.M.–11 P.M. daily, US$20–30).

Fine Dining

Featured in many local cookbooks, the recipes of **Malabar** (Camino Real 101, tel. 01/440-5200, 12:30–3:30 P.M. and 7:30–11:30 P.M., US$15–20) have garnered national acclaim. The flavors are a mix of the Mediterranean (chef Pedro Miguel Schiaffino studied in Italy), Amazonia (then he lived in Iquitos), and finally classic Peruvian. The intimate restaurant, with clean white tablecloths, is the perfect fusion for a traveler who's been all over the country.

To live classic Lima's elegance, you can do nothing better than have a pisco sour on the wide open patio of **Perroquet** (Los Eucaliptos 590, tel. 01/611-9000, www.hotelcountry.com, 11 A.M.–11 P.M. daily, US$15–20), inside the Country Club Lima Hotel. Follow your sour with grilled chita fish, and finally top it off with a medley of Peruvian fruit sorbets.

With only 10 tables, the city's most intimate seafood restaurant is probably **El Kapallaq** (Petit Thouars 4844, tel. 01/444-4149, noon–5 P.M. daily, US$14–18). The owner, of Basque ancestry, throws in twists from his home country, dishing up favorites like *marmitako* (a seafood stew). But the Peruvian influence is just as strong, and classics like *arroz con conchas y langostinos* (rice with scallops and shrimp) and *chita* (Peruvian grunt fish) are also present. This classic restaurant is a lunch-only establishment. With a steel bed on its entrance patio and a dining room full of round mirrors, **Restaurante Rodrigo** (Francisco de Paula Camino 231, tel. 01/446-0985, www.restauranterodrigo.com, 1–4 P.M. and 8 P.M.–midnight, US$20–25) is Lima's chic and cosmopolitian, Basque-influenced restaurant. Here, the precursor to dinner is an appetizer sampler, each shot-glass-size, including spinach salad and pork mousse with applesauce. Dinner is calamari stuffed with rich risotto or halibut served over black rice.

MIRAFLORES

Even if you are on a limited budget, splurging on one of Miraflores's top restaurants will be a memorable experience you will not regret.

Cafés, Bakeries, and Ice Cream

One of Lima's classic cafés is surely **Haiti** (Diagonal 160, tel. 01/446-3816, 7 A.M.–2 A.M. Sun.–Thurs., 7 A.M.–3 A.M. Fri.–Sat., US$9), in operation for more than half a century on Parque Kennedy. Indoor and sidewalk tables are overflowing with Peruvians day and night. Haiti is less known for its food than its intellectual conversation, good coffee, and pisco sours. Right across the street is **La Tiendecita Blanca** (Larco 111, tel. 01/445-1412, 7 A.M.–midnight daily, US$11), an elegant Swiss-style café and deli that has been in business since 1937. Anything you eat here will be excellent. This is Miraflores's most happening business breakfast spot, and in the evenings, steamy fondues emerge from the kitchen.

The youthful, trendy **Café Zeta** (Oscar Benavides 598, tel. 01/444-5579, 7 A.M.–11:30 P.M. daily, US$6–10) is straight out of Chicago. Here you can sip mango tea while nibbling banana bread, or down a big sandwich and beer.

Ugo, the Italian owner of **La Bodega de la Trattoria** (General Borgoño 784, tel. 01/241-6899, 7:30 A.M.–2 A.M. daily, US$9–13), claims that sitting on his patio is almost like being on a European plaza. His Italian menu and strong espressos aid in the illusion, and the effect is the whiling away of a Lima afternoon. Meals are also served.

Try the *lomo saltado* sandwich at **Pasquale Hnos. Sangucheria** (Comandante Espinar 651, tel. 01/447-6390, noon–10 P.M. Mon.–Fri., 10 A.M.–1 A.M. Sat., 10 A.M.–midnight Sun., US$6). This sandwich joint makes fast food fancy and purely Peruvian, since all sandwiches are inspired by classic Peruvian plates.

San Antonio (Vasco Núñez de Balboa 762, tel. 01/241-3001, 7 A.M.–11 P.M. daily) is a bakery/café/deli with 35 gourmet sandwiches (including smoked salmon and Italian salami), huge salads with organic lettuce, and an extensive dessert case with an out-of-this-world *tortaleta de lúcuma*. Across the street, **T'anta** (28 de Julio 888, tel. 01/447-8377, 7 A.M.–midnight Mon.–Sat., 7 A.M.–10 P.M. Sun.) is similarly gourmet, but the menu is all Peruvian.

Your dessert choices are twofold, chocolate or ice cream. Limeños are right when they say that **Quattro D** (Angamos Oeste 408, tel. 01/447-1523, 6:30 A.M.–12:30 A.M. Sun.–Fri., 6:30 A.M.–1:30 A.M. Sat.) has the best ice cream and gelato in Lima, but at **Chocolates Helena** (Chiclayo 897, tel. 01/242-8899, www.chocolateshelena.com, 10:30 A.M.–7:30 P.M. daily) the *chocotejas* and truffles are hard to resist.

Ceviche

An upscale *cebichería,* **Alfresco** (Malecón Balta 790, tel. 01/444-7962, 9 A.M.–5 P.M. daily, US$12–14) serves grilled shrimp, clams, and a special *cebiche alfresco* with three sauces. This stylish place also serves tempting desserts, such as *crocante de lúcuma* and *suspiro de Limeña,* and international wines. At a more affordable price, **Punto Azul** (San Martin 395, tel. 01/445-8078, 11 A.M.–4 P.M. Mon.–Fri., 11 A.M.–5 P.M. Sat.–Sun. US$7–9) serves a similar menu. One plate is enough for two, but arrive early because after 1:30 P.M. you'll have to wait to get a seat.

Ceviche is elegantly served in martini glasses at Gaston Acurio's **La Mar Cebichería** (La Mar 770, tel. 01/421-3365, 11 A.M.–5 P.M., US$15–20). No reservations are accepted and lines can get long, so plan for a leisurely lunch over several types of ceviche, cold beer, grilled fish, and crisp white wine.

Peruvian

One of the greatest Peruvian comfort foods is the creamy potato-based *causa,* and now, there is an entire restaurant devoted to it. **Mi Causa** (La Mar 814, tel. 01/222-6258, www.micausaperu.com, noon–5:30 P.M. daily, US$10–12) has the classic tuna and avocado offerings, but why not try a *lomo saltado* or *cauchi de camarones* (crayfish stew) *causa?*

Budget eaters flock to **Rincón Chami** (Esperanza 154, tel. 01/444-4511, 9 A.M.–9 P.M. Mon.–Sat., 9 A.M.–5 P.M. Sun., US$7) for ceviche, tamales, *brochetas,* and *lomo saltados,* dished up in a dinerlike atmosphere. Each day there is a different special of the house (Sunday, for instance, it's *chupe de camarones,* a cream-based soup with sea shrimp).

International

La Trattoria di Mambrino (Manuel Bonilla 106, tel. 01/446-1192, 1–3:30 P.M. and 8:30–11:30 P.M. Mon.–Sat., 1–3:30 P.M. Sun., US$10–12) is owned by a Roman and may be Peru's best Italian restaurant. This cozy place serves authentic Italian dishes like gnocchi with pesto genovese, risotto with wild mushrooms, panfried shrimp with wine sauce, and porcini mushroom pizza.

For Middle Eastern food, stop in at **Tarboush** (Diagonal 358, tel. 01/242-6994, 9 A.M.–midnight Mon.–Thurs., 9 A.M.–1 A.M. Fri.–Sat., 10 A.M.–11 P.M. Sun., US$5–6), with sidewalk tables across from Parque Kennedy. Lamb kebabs, Greek salads, tabouli, and falafel are prepared fresh for incredibly cheap prices. Don't miss the *lúcuma* juice.

Located at Larcomar mall, **Makoto** (Malecón de la Reserva 610, tel. 01/444-5030, www.larcomar.com, 11 A.M.–7 P.M. Mon.–Sat., 11 A.M.–3 P.M. Sun., US$20) is an excellent, though touristy, sushi restaurant with high prices. **Edo Sushi Bar** (Berlin 601, tel. 01/243-2448, www.edosushibar.com, 12:30–3:30 P.M. and 7–11 P.M. Mon.–Sat., US$10) is a cool, quiet restaurant for authentic sushi.

Fine Dining

Our vote for best restaurant in Peru is **Astrid y Gastón** (Cantuarias 175, tel. 01/444-1496, 1–3 P.M. and 7:30–11:30 P.M. Mon.–Sat., US$35–40). This adventurous gourmet restaurant, set in an elegant republican-style home, is the labor of love of a Peruvian-German couple who met at the Cordon Bleu in Paris. The evening begins with creative pisco drinks such as the *aguaymanto* sour, made with *pisco puro* and the tangy juice of *aguaymanto* fruit. Then, as diners watch through a glass wall, chefs concoct never-before-sampled entrées such as kid goat basted in *algarroba* honey and marinated in *chicha de jora,* or river prawns served with red curry, coconut milk, and jasmine rice. Save room; the desserts are the best part: *blanco mousse* with a sauce of *sauco* and blackberries.

You will not regret the cab ride to **Pescados Capitales** (La Mar 1337, tel. 01/421-8808, 12:30–5 P.M. Tues.–Sun., US$10), a witty play on words (*pescados* means fish but rhymes with *pecados,* or sins) that makes sense when you see the menu. Each dish is named for a virtue or sin; Diligence will bring you a ceviche of tuna and *conchas negras,* while Patience will bring you a ceviche of shrimps with curry and mango chutney.

The elegant **Huaca Pucllana** (General Borgoño block 8, tel. 01/445-4042, noon–4 P.M. and 7 P.M.–midnight daily, US$10–22) has a magical feel when the ruins of the same name, only six meters away, are lit up at night. Guests sit at linen-covered tables on an open-air patio next to the ruins and enjoy dishes such as grilled portobello mushroom salad with goat cheese, rabbit stewed in a red wine, mushroom sauce over polenta, and grilled lamb chops.

If you're in the mood for Mediterranean, head to **La Gloria** (Atahualpa 201, tel. 01/446-6504, www.lagloriarestaurant.com, 1–4 P.M.

LIMA

and 8 P.M.–midnight Mon.–Sat., US$29). Especially good are the *carpaccio de pescado* with ginger and the seared tuna steaks.

Two restaurants are locked in battle for Lima's best place for *comida criolla*. **Brujas de Cachiche** (Bolognesi 460, tel. 01/446-6536, www.brujasdecachiche.com, noon–midnight Mon.–Sat., noon–4:30 P.M. Sun., US$25) has an extraordinary buffet every day of the week, except Sunday, that includes a tour de force of centuries of indigenous Peruvian cooking. **El Señorio de Sulco** (Malecón Cisneros 1470, tel. 01/441-0389, www.senoriodesulco.com, noon–midnight Mon.–Sat., noon–5 P.M. Sun., US$10–16) also has an extravagant daily lunch buffet and a range of seafood plates. Try the *chupe de camarones,* a cream-based soup full of sea shrimp, yellow potatoes, and *ají* pepper.

We think Lima's time-honored seaside gourmet restaurant, Rosa Naútica, is a bit faded. But a good contender, **Costanera 700** (El Ejército 421, tel. 01/421-4635, noon–5 P.M. and 7–11 P.M. Mon.–Sat., noon–5 P.M. Sun., US$30), is gaining ground and has been repeatedly voted one of the best restaurants in Lima. This is a good place to come for an elegant array of both Peruvian and international cuisine.

Chifa

Central Lima's time-honored *chifa* restaurant **Wa Lok** (Angamos Oeste 700, tel. 01/447-1314, noon–11:30 P.M. Mon.–Sat., noon–11 P.M. Sun., US$15–20) now has a Miraflores location. You'll have to ignore the charmless first-floor casino before you can settle down into your fish with corn sauce or steaming stir-fry.

Vegetarian

Miraflores's best vegetarian restaurant is **Govinda** (Schell 634, tel. 01/444-2871, 10:30 A.M.–8 P.M. Mon.–Sat., 11 A.M.–4:30 P.M. Sun., US$4). The creative dishes of this Hare Krishna–operated restaurant include pad thai, Asian tofu salad, and *lomo saltado* with soy meat.

When you walk through a health food store to get to the restaurant, you know lunch will be balanced and nutritious. **Madre Natura**

(Chiclayo 815, tel. 01/445-2522, 8 A.M.–9 P.M. Mon.–Sat., US$6) is all that, and well priced. Sit down for a soy-based hamburger, and leave with wheat bread in hand.

Markets

Plaza Vea (Arequipa 4651, 9 A.M.–10 P.M. daily), **Metro** (Schell 250, 9 A.M.–11 P.M. daily), and the upscale **Vivanda** (Benavides 495, 24 hours) have large selections of international and domestic foods.

BARRANCO AND THE SOUTH

Slow-paced Barranco has a number of romantic eateries and cafés, and on the weekends, outdoor food stalls fill a walkway near the central plaza.

Cafés, Bakeries, and Ice Cream

For an affordable lunch *menú*, head to **Iskay Cafeteria & Artensía** (Pedro de Osma 106, tel. 01/247-2102, 9 A.M.–midnight daily, US$6–8). Pastas, sandwiches, and *piqueos* are the specialties. Stop by **Café Cultural Restaurante** (San Martín 15-A, tel. 01/247-5131, 9 A.M.–2 A.M., US$4–8), in a 1920s English train car, for a drink, but skip the food. The best café is on the open-air patio of **Dédalo,** the artisan shop.

Ceviche

CantaRana (Génova 101, tel. 01/247-7274, 9 A.M.–11 P.M. Tues.–Sat., 11 A.M.–6 P.M. Sun., US$8–11), a no-frills lunch place with loads of history, serves up great *cebiche* and a range of seafood. The unassuming **Costa Sur** (Chorrillos 180, tel. 01/252-0150, 11:30 A.M.–5 P.M. Tues.–Sun., US$8–10), in Chorrillos, has fried shrimp and *conchas a la parmesana* worth a taxi ride.

Peruvian

With bow tie–clad waiters and an old piano, **Las Mesitas** (Grau 341, tel. 01/477-4199, noon–1 A.M. daily, US$5–7) has an old-timey feel. For those on a budget, this is a great place to sample Peruvian food, including *humitas,* tamales, *sopa criolla, ocopa arequipeña,* and *lomo saltado.*

Lunch buffets are popular in Lima, and

Barranco seems to have an especially high per capita number of restaurants serving up just that. In order of preference, we recommend: **Puro Perú** (República de Panamá 258, tel. 01/477-0111, 12:30–5 P.M. daily, US$15) and the oceanside **Rustica** (Playa Barranco, tel. 01/9403-4679, 12:30 P.M.–midnight daily, US$15).

Mi Perú (Av. Lima 861, Plaza Butters, tel. 01/247-7682, noon–5:30 P.M. daily, US$8–10) is what you call in Peru a *huarique,* a hole-in-the-wall with good food. In this case it's all about the *concentrado de cangrejo* (crab soup), the best you will try in all Peru. *Cebiches* are good here, too, but go for the soup. It's worth every penny.

For a steak and red wine fix, **C Parrillados El Hornero** (Malecón Grau 983, tel. 01/251-8109, noon–midnight Mon.–Sat., noon–6 P.M. Sun., US$8–10), in Chorrillos, is a must. The second-floor tables have impressive ocean views, and the grilled provolone and Argentine baby beef will do for your palate what it won't do for your cholesterol.

Fine Dining

Amor Amar (Jirón Garcia y García 175, tel. 01/651-1111, US$10–25) is the newest and smartest restaurant in town, and it happens to be in Barranco. Luis Alberto Sacilotto, the renowned chef of La Gloria, and the owners of Pescados Capitales decided to open this new culinary (ad)venture. The food is incredibly good, having on the menu *cebiches, tiraditos,* and grilled octopus, among other seafood specialties. Other options include risottos, duck, lamb, and beef. Cocktails are well done and the varied wine list is pretty impressive.

Pizza

The best pizzas are at the new **Antica Trattoria** (San Martín 201, tel. 01/247-3443, 12:30 P.M.–midnight daily, US$7–10), a charming Italian eatery with stucco walls, exposed beams, and rustic furniture. The lasagna here is excellent, as is the array of homemade pastas.

Markets

The large modern supermarket **Metro** (Grau 513, 9 A.M.–10:30 P.M. daily) is within walking distance from all Barranco hotels.

Information and Services

TOURIST INFORMATION

Free maps and tourist information are available at **Iperú** (Jorge Chávez Airport, main hall, tel. 01/574-8000, www.peru.info, 24 hours daily). There are other branches in San Isidro (Jorge Basadre 610, tel. 01/421-1627, 8:30 A.M.–6 P.M. Mon.–Fri.) and Miraflores (Larcomar, tel. 01/445-9400, noon–8 P.M. daily).

The best source of travel information in Peru, along with maps, advice, trip reports, restaurant and hotel discounts, and all-around friendly people, is the amazing, Miraflores-based **South American Explorers Club** (Piura 135, Miraflores, tel. 01/445-3306, www.saexplorers.org, 9:30 A.M.–5 P.M. Mon.–Fri., 9:30 A.M.–1 P.M. Sat.).

In Barranco, **Intej** (San Martín 240, tel. 01/247-3230, www.intej.org, 9:30 A.M.–12:45 P.M. daily) is the Lima base for all student travel organizations. Student travel cards can be acquired here with a letter on the appropriate stationery, and student flights can be changed.

MAPS

The easiest place to buy maps is in **Miraflores** at the **South American Explorers Club,** which has good maps of Lima, the Huaraz area, and Peru in general. It also sells the more popular of Peru's military topographic maps.

If you are planning on driving or biking through Peru, excellent driving maps and information are contained in *Inca Guide to Peru* (Peisa, 2002), which is available in most bookshops. Another recommended series is published by Lima 2000 and also available in bookshops.

© RENÉE DEL GAUDIO AND ROSS WEHNER

Giant teddy bears and other oddities are for sale in the street market behind Lima's main post office.

For hard-to-find topo maps, head to **Surquillo** and the **Instituto Geográfico Nacional** (Aramburu 1180, tel. 01/475-3085, www.ignperu.gob.pe, 8 A.M.–6 P.M. Mon.–Fri.), which also sells digital, geological, and departmental maps.

POLICE AND FIRE

Through **Iperú's** 24-hour stand (tel. 01/574-8000) in the main hall of the airport, you can report tourist-related crimes. The headquarters of the national police are in **Lince** (Pezet y Miel 1894, tel. 01/373-2423, www.pnp.gob.pe), and the tourist police have an office in **Magdalena** (Moore 268, tel. 01/460-0849, dipolture@hotmail.com). Dialing 105 also reaches police from a private phone, or dial 116 for the **fire department.**

IMMIGRATIONS OFFICE

Lima's **Migraciones** (immigrations office) is near the center (España 734, Breña, tel. 01/330-4144, 8 A.M.–1 P.M. Mon.–Fri.). Arrive early and with US$20 if you want to receive a new visa the same day.

HEALTH CARE

Lima has Peru's best hospitals, and it is easy, and quite inexpensive, to get parasite tests and yellow fever or tetanus shots.

Perhaps the easiest option, if you need a doctor, is to call **Doctor Más** (tel. 01/444-9377), a company that, for US$40, will send an English-speaking doctor to your hotel to check on you and write a prescription. Doctor Más physicians can also be reached directly on their cell phones. Try **Dr. Ana del Aguila** (tel. 01/9818-2561) or **Dr. Jorge Garmendia** (tel. 01/9818-2554). You can even pay with a credit card if you notify them while setting up the visit.

If you prefer a clinic, all of the places listed have English-speaking doctors. In central Lima, the **Clínica International** (Washington 1471, 8 A.M.–8 P.M. Mon.–Fri., 8 A.M.–2 P.M. Sat.) will see walk-in patients for about US$30. Doctor's visits at both places cost around US$30.

The best (and most expensive) medical care in Peru is in **San Isidro** at the **Clínica Anglo-**

Americana (Alfredo Salazar, block 3 s/n, tel. 01/712-3000, www.clinangloamericana.com. pe, 8 A.M.–8 P.M. Mon.–Fri., 9 A.M.–noon Sat.), which charges US$60 for a doctor's visit.

In **Miraflores,** a high-quality option is **Clínica Good Hope** (Malecón Balta 956, tel. 01/241-3256, www.goodhope.org.pe, 9 A.M.–midnight), which charges about US$40 for a doctor's visit. For lab testing and shots, **Suiza Lab** (Angamos Oeste 300, tel. 01/612-6666, www.suizalab.com.pe, 9 A.M.–midnight) is very professional, clean, and reasonably priced. With dental problems, call **Dr. Flavio Larrain** (Pasaje Sucre 154, tel. 01/445-2586, 8 A.M.–7 P.M. Mon.–Fri.), who charges US$50 for a checkup and cleaning.

Pharmacies

Most pharmacies are willing to deliver to your hotel. Near central Lima, the **Metro supermarket** in Breña (corner of Venezuela and Alfonso Ugarte) has a good pharmacy. In San Isidro, try **Deza** (Conquistadores 1144, San Isidro, tel. 01/442-9196, 24 hours). In Miraflores, try **InkaFarma** (tel. 01/314-2020, www.inkafarma.com.pe, delivery service), **Farmacias 24 Horas** (tel. 01/444-0568), **Botica Fasa** (Larco 135, www.boticasfasa. com.pe), **Superfarma** (Benavides 2849, tel. 01/222-1575, or Armendariz 215, tel. 01/440-9000).

BANKS AND MONEY EXCHANGE

For those just arriving in Peru, there are two exchange houses inside the Lima airport that change travelers checks for a 2.5 percent commission. In general, the best place to cash travelers checks is at any Banco de Crédito, which charges the lowest commission—1.8 percent. ATMs are now ubiquitous across Lima (and most of Peru). Almost all work with Visa, MasterCard, and Cirrus, and Interbank's Global Net and Banco de Crédito even handle American Express. Take care when getting money at night; it's a good idea to have a taxi waiting.

Money-change houses (*casas de cambio*) offer slightly better rates than banks and are mercifully free of the hour-long lines that snake inside most banks. There are a few change houses on Larco in Miraflores and on Ocoña in central Lima. Be careful changing money with people on the street, even if they do have the requisite badge and bright-yellow vest. Safe places for money-changing on the street are Parque Kennedy or Pardo and Comandante Espinar in Miraflores.

Here is an alphabetical listing of banks and money changers, by neighborhood. Banks are generally open 9 A.M.–6 P.M. Monday–Friday and 9 A.M.–12:30 P.M. Saturday. All banks are closed on Sunday.

In central Lima, there's **Banco Continental** (Abancay 260-262, tel. 01/427-4623), **Banco de Crédito** (Washington 1600, tel. 01/433-2785), **Interbank** (Jr. de la Unión tel. 01/536-544), **Scotiabank** (Camaná 623-627, tel. 01/211-6000), and **Western Union** (Carabaya 693, tel. 01/427-9845), for wiring money. A recommended change house is **Lac Dolar** (Camaná 779, tel. 01/428-8127).

San Isidro, Lima's financial district, has a **Banco Continental** (Camino Real 355, tel. 01/440-4553), **Banco de Crédito** (Jorge Basadre 301, tel. 01/440-7366), an **Interbank** (Jorge Basadre 391-395), **Scotiabank** (Carnaval y Moreyra 282, tel. 01/222-6567), and **Western Union** (Petit Thouars 3595, tel. 01/422-0014).

Miraflores's banks are generally clustered around the Parque Kennedy: **American Express** (Santa Cruz 621, Miraflores, tel. 01/221-8204, 9 A.M.–5:30 P.M. Mon.–Fri., 9 A.M.–1 P.M. Sat.), which will replace its traveler checks; **Banco Continental** (Pardo 791-795, tel. 01/241-5853); **Banco de Crédito** (Av. Larco 1085 tel. 01/447-1690); **Interbank** (Larco 690); **Scotiabank** (Av. Diagonal 176, tel. 01/242-3797); and a **Western Union** (Larco 826, tel. 01/241-1220). **Lac Dolar** (La Paz 211, tel. 01/242-4069) will change travelers checks for a 2 percent commission and is open 9:30 A.M.–6 P.M. Monday–Saturday.

Even quiet Barranco has a selection of financial institutions: **Banco Continental** (Grau

414, tel. 01/477-0280); **Banco de Crédito** (José M. Eguren 599, Ex-Grau), tel. 01/477-0101); **Interbank** (Grau 300); **Scotiabank** (Grau 422, tel. 01/477-0604); and **Western Union** (Grau 422, tel. 01/477-4337).

COMMUNICATIONS

The main **post office** (www.serpost.com.pe) is on the corner of **central Lima's** Plaza Mayor (Pasaje Piura, s/n, 8 A.M.–8 P.M. Mon.–Sat., 8 A.M.–3 P.M. Sun.). The **Miraflores** branch (Petit Thouars 5201, tel. 01/511-5018, 8 A.M.–8:45 P.M. Mon.–Sat., 8:45 A.M.–2 P.M. Sun.) has slightly different hours. There is also **FedEx** (Pasaje Olaya 260, Surco, tel. 01/242-2280) and **DHL** (Los Castaños 225, San Isidro, tel. 01/422-5232).

High-speed Internet is ubiquitous in Lima. In **central Lima,** try **Internet** (Pasaje Santa Rosa 165, Center, 7:30 A.M.–9 P.M. daily, US$0.75/hr). Recommended places in **Miraflores** are **@lf.net** (Manuel Bonilla 126, 9 A.M.–10 P.M. Mon.–Fri., 11 A.M.–8 P.M. Sat.–Sun., US$0.50/hour), **Refugio Internet** (Larco 1185, tel. 01/242-5910, 8:30 A.M.–11 P.M. Mon.–Fri., 9:30 A.M.–11 P.M. Sat., 10:30 A.M.–11 P.M. Sun., US$0.75/hour), and the helpful and cheap **Via Planet** (Diez Canseco 339, 9 A.M.–midnight daily, US$0.30/hour). These places do Internet calls as well.

For local calls or national calls, buy a 147 card and dial away from Telefónica booths on nearly every corner.

For international calls, put away those phone cards, because new generation cable and satellite shops offer crystal-clear communication for as low as US$0.15 per minute to the United States. **Call Center USA** (Junín 410, four blocks toward Vía Expresa from Arequipa and near the Home Peru hostel, 9 A.M.–midnight daily) offers cable calls to the United States (US$0.15/min), Europe (US$0.20/min.), or Asia (US$0.25/min.). This place also has high-speed Internet.

NEWSPAPERS

Lima's largest newspaper is *El Comercio* (www.elcomercioperu.com.pe), but we personally prefer the tabloid-format *La República* (www.larepublica.com.pe) for its daily **Mirko Lauer** political column and a more straightforward approach to news. Lima's best magazine for news, humor, and cultural information is, hands down, *Caretas. Etiqueta Negra* (www.etiquetanegra.com.pe) is a literary/social commentary magazine, and *Bocón* (www.elbocon.com.pe) is the soccer paper.

LANGUAGE SCHOOLS

There are many Spanish schools in Lima, though getting away from all the English speakers is a challenge. **San Isidro** language schools include **Instituto de Idiomas** (Camino Real 1037, tel. 01/442-8761, www.pucp.edu.pe, 11 A.M.–1 P.M. daily), which charges US$105 for 36 hours of lessons. **Asociación Cultural Peruano-Británico** (Arequipa 3495, tel. 01/221-7550, www.britanico.edu.pe) charges US$66 for 36 hours of lessons.

In **Miraflores, Instituto Cultural Peruano-Norteamericano** (Angamos Oeste 160, Miraflores, tel. 01/241-1940, www.icpna.edu.pe) charges US$54 for 40 hours of lessons plus US$82 in materials.

For a well-rounded Spanish school, try **El Sol** (Grimaldo de Solar 469, Miraflores, tel. 01/242-7763, www.idiomasperu.com), which has a Survival Spanish program for travelers that includes cooking and dancing classes, city walks, volunteer opportunities, conversation partners, and family homestays. El Sol charges US$15 per hour for small group lessons or US$110 for 10 hours of semi-intensive classes. The one-week program for beginners is US$50.

For one-on-one lessons, some recommended private tutors are **Lourdes Galvez** (tel. 01/435-3910, US$5/hour), **Llorgelina Savastaizagal** (tel. 01/275-6460, US$5/hour), and **Alex Boris** (tel. 01/423-0697, US$5/hour).

FILM AND CAMERAS

Lima's best developing and camera repair shop is **Taller de Fotografía Profesional** (Benavides 1171, tel. 01/241-1015). Other top-quality developing with one-day service is available from

Laboratorio Color Profesional (Benavides 1171, tel. 01/214-8430, 9 A.M.–7 P.M. Mon.–Fri., 9:30 A.M.–1 P.M. Sat.). A cheaper option is **Kodak Express** (9 A.M.–9 P.M. Mon.–Sat.), with offices in Miraflores (Larco 1005), San Isidro (Las Begonias), and central Lima (Unión 790, Centro). For camera repairs in the center, try **Reparación** (Cusco 592, central Lima, 4th Fl., tel. 01/426-7920, 10 A.M.–2 P.M. Mon.–Fri.). For digital camera technical glitches contact **Jorge Li Pun** (General Silva 496, Miraflores, tel. 01/447-7302, 10:30 A.M.–8 P.M. Mon.–Fri.).

LAUNDRY

In **Breña** try **Lavandería KIO** (España 481, tel. 01/332-9035, 7 A.M.–8 P.M. daily, US$1/kg). There's also a branch in **Pueblo Libre** (La Mar 1953, 2nd Fl., tel. 01/428-2776, delivery).

In **San Isidro, Lava Center** (Victor Maurtua 140, San Isidro, tel. 01/440-3600, 9:30 A.M.–8 P.M. Mon.–Fri., 9:30 A.M.–6 P.M. Sat., US$1/kg) is reliable.

Recommended places in **Miraflores** are **Servirap** (Schell 601, Miraflores, tel. 01/241-0759, 8 A.M.–10 P.M. Mon.–Sat., 10 A.M.–6 P.M. Sun., US$2.50/kg), which offers drop-off and self-service, and **Lavandería Cool Wash** (Diez Canseco 347, tel. 01/242-3882, 8:30 A.M.–7:30 P.M. Mon.–Sat.).

LUGGAGE STORAGE

Besides your hotel, you can also store bags at the airport for US$6 per day. **South American Explorers Club** members can store luggage at the clubhouse (Piura 135, Miraflores) free of charge.

Getting There and Around

AIR

Lima's international airport is **Jorge Chávez** (tel. 01/595-0606, www.lap.com.pe), 16 kilometers west of the city center at Callao.

The leading domestic airline, with international flights as well, is **LAN** (Pardo 513, Miraflores, tel. 01/213-8200, www.lan.com). It flys to all major Peruvian airports, including Trujillo, Chiclayo, Tumbes, Arequipa, Cusco, Puerto Maldonado, and Juliaca.

Useful for specific domestic routes are **Star Perú** (Pardo 269, Miraflores, tel. 01/705-9000, www.starperu.com.pe) for Trujillo, Chiclayo, Iquitos, Yurimaguas, and Tarapoto; **Aerocondor** (Juan de Aroma 781, San Isidro, tel. 01/614-6014, www.aerocondor.com.pe) for Cajamarca, Ayacucho, Talara, and Piura; **LC Busre** (Los Tulipanes 218, Lince, tel. 01/619-1313, www.lcbusre.com.pe) for Huaraz, Huánuco, and Pucallpa; and **TACA** (Comandante Espinar 331, tel. 01/511-8222, www.taca.com) for Cusco.

All of the international airlines that fly into Peru also have offices in Lima, including **Aerolíneas Argentinas** (Carnaval y Moreyra 370, San Isidro, tel. 01/513-6565, www.aerolineas.com.ar), **AeroMexico** (Pardo y Aliaga 699, of. 501, San Isidro, tel. 01/705-1111, www.aeromexico.com), **American Airlines** (Las Begonias 471, San Isidro, tel. 01/211-7000, www.aa.com.pe), **Avianca** (José Pardo 14, Miraflores, tel. 01/445-9902, www.avianca.com), **Continental Airlines** (Victor Andrés Belaúnde 147, of. 101, San Isidro, tel. 01/221-4340, www.continental.com), **Copa Airlines** (Carnaval y Moreyra and Los Halcones, San Isidro, tel. 01/610-0808, www.copaair.com), **Delta Air Lines** (Victor Andrés Belaúnde 147, of. 701, San Isidro, tel. 01/211-9211, www.delta.com), **KLM** (Alvarez Calderon 185, of. 601, San Isidro, tel. 01/213-0200, www.klm.com), **Lloyd Aero Boliviano** (José Pardo 231, Miraflores, tel. 01/241-5513, www.labairlines.com.bo), and **Taca Peru** (Comandante Espinar 331, Miraflores, tel. 01/231-7000, www.taca.com).

BUS

Highways in Peru have improved immensely over the last decade, making in-country bus travel not only cheap but efficient. From Lima,

LIMA

Lima's main highway, the Via Expresa, at night

buses head to every major city in Peru except water-locked Iquitos. The South American Explorers Club has an excellent Lima folder with a detailed rundown of bus companies and the schedules. Unfortunately, there is no main bus station in Lima. Instead, companies have their own terminals in the center and sometimes also on Javier Prado or Paseo de la República near San Isidro. All of these neighborhoods are rough, so take a taxi to and from the terminal and keep a hand on all your belongings.

The two classic and reputable bus companies in Lima are Cruz del Sur and Ormeño. Movil Tours and the new Oltursa, however, both get consistently strong reviews. **Cruz del Sur** has a terminal in the center (Quilca 531, tel. 01/451-5125) and near San Isidro (corner of Javier Prado Este 1100, tel. 01/225-5748). Though it does not go as many places as Ormeño, Cruz del Sur's Cruzero is the most comprehensive bus service in Peru. Best of all, tickets can be bought instantly online, from any agency in Lima, or at the TeleTicket counters at Wong and Metro supermarkets (in Miraflores there

is a Wong at Óvalo Gutierrez and a Metro at Schell 250, near Parque Kennedy). Spanish speakers can even call the Cruz del Sur call center (tel. 01/311-5050, have passport number ready) and have their tickets delivered free of charge. Payment is in cash upon receipt of tickets. Buses leave first from the central Lima terminal and pick up passengers a half hour later at the Javier Prado terminal. For complete route information, see the website www.cruzdelsur.com.pe.

Ormeño also has a terminal in the center (Carlos Zavala 177, tel. 01/427-5679, www.grupo-ormeno.com) and an international terminal near San Isidro (Javier Prado Este 1059, La Victoria, tel. 01/472-1710). Ormeño has better coverage and is slightly cheaper than Cruz del Sur. To buy an Ormeño ticket, visit a terminal, go through an agency (the agency will get the tickets a few hours later), or call the Spanish-only call center (tel. 01/472-5000). Again, have passport number when calling and cash in hand when the ticket is delivered.

The highly recommended **Movil Tours** (Paseo de la República 749, La Victoria, tel.

LIMA BUS SCHEDULE

The following is a thumbnail of bus trip duration and prices to/from Lima with a range from economical to luxury service. At the bottom end, buses stop frequently, are crowded, and lack bathrooms. The top-end buses are decked out with reclining semibeds, clean bathrooms, onboard food and beverage service, video, and a second story with great views. Prices increase 50 percent around holidays, including Christmas, Easter, and the July 28 Fiestas Patrias weekend.

CITY	PRICE	TIME
Arequipa	US$20-48	13-15 hours
Ayacucho	US$20-30	8-9 hours
Cajamarca	US$25-48	14 hours
Chachapoyas	US$16-35	25 hours
Chanchamayo	US$19-27	8 hours
Chiclayo	US$19-36	10 hours
Cusco	US$26-37	52 hours
Huancayo	US$17-26	7 hours
Huaraz	US$20-26	8 hours
Máncora	US$28-57	16-17 hours
Nasca	US$20-31	8 hours
Pisco	US$18-28	4 hours
Piura	US$25-38	14-15 hours
Puno	US$34-60	21-24 hours
Tacna	US$37-50	18-20 hours
(Chile border)		
Trujillo	US$16-34	8 hours
Tumbes	US$30-57	18 hours
(Ecuador border)		

recommended for its service (some claim that it's better than Cruz del Sur), and advance reservations can be made by telephone or online.

Phone reservations do not work well at the other companies. Your best bet is to buy tickets at the terminal.

Expreso Wari (Montevideo 809, central Lima, tel. 01/330-3518) goes to Nasca, Ayacucho, and Cusco.

Empresa Molina (Nicolas Arriola and San Luis, central Lima, tel. 01/342-2137) goes to Huancayo, Ayacucho, and Cusco.

Enlaces (Javier Prado Este 1093, La Victoria, tel. 01/265-9041) runs between Lima and Arequipa.

Flores has the best coverage of the small bus companies, lower prices, and a terminal in both central Lima (Montevideo 523) and near San Isidro (Paseo de la República 627, La Victoria). It has cheap buses for Arequipa, Cajamarca, Chiclayo, Máncora, Nasca, Piura, Puno, Tacna, Trujillo, and Tumbes. With questions, call 01/332-1212 or enter the company's website at www.floreshnos.com.

Mariscal Cáceres has offices both in central Lima (Carlos Zavala 211, tel. 01/427-2844) and near San Isidro (28 de Julio 2195, La Victoria, tel. 01/225-2532) and heads primarily to Huancayo.

Soyuz (Carlos Zavala 217, tel. 01/266-1515, www.soyuz.com.pe) has good frequency on the south coast.

Companies whose travelers report frequent delays, breakdowns, or other problems include **Tepsa** and **Civa.**

Recommended international companies are Caracol, Ormeño, and El Rápido.

Caracol (Brasil 425, Jesus María, tel. 01/431-1400, www.perucaracol.com) receives the best reviews and covers the entire continent. It partners with Cruz del Sur so you can buy tickets from either company's terminals. Among other places, Caracol travels to Santiago, Chile; Santa Cruz and La Paz, Bolivia; Asunción, Paraguay; Córdoba and Buenos Aires, Argentina; Montevideo, Uruguay; São Paulo and Rio de Janeiro, Brazil; and Quito and Guayaquil, Ecuador.

01/332-9000, www.moviltours.com.pe) has a station near San Isidro and runs mainly to the northern cities, including Huaraz, Chachapoyas, and Chiclayo, and is about the same price as Ormeño. Phone reservations are accepted for payment at terminal.

The local favorite, **Oltursa** (Av. Aramburu 1160, Surquillo, tel. 01/225-4499, www.oltursa.com.pe), runs primarily a coastal route, both north and south of Lima. The destinations of Arequipa and Chiclayo are the exceptions to that rule. The company comes highly

LIMA

Ormeño (Javier Prado Este 1059, tel. 01/472-1710) no longer travels to Brazil but does go to Bogatá, Colombia; Santiago, Chile; Buenos Aires, Argentina; and Guayaquil, Ecuador.

El Rápido (Rivera Navarrete 2650, Lince, tel. 01/425-1066) has cheaper fares to Santiago, Chile; and Buenos Aires, Argentina.

TRAIN

Between May and October, a passenger train still departs on Fridays from Lima's antique Desamparados train station downtown. After climbing the steep valley above Lima it crests the Andes at 4,751 meters (nearly 15,700 feet!) and continues to Huancayo. Trains return from Huancayo to Lima on Sunday evening, making for an interesting weekend outing.

Sunday excursion trains also leave the station for San Bartolomé, a country hamlet 1.5 hours by train outside Lima that is often sunny when the city is fogged in. These trains leave at 6 A.M. and return at 6 P.M. For tickets and exact departure information, contact the **Desamparados train station** (Ancash 201, tel. 01/361-2828, ext. 222).

LOCAL TRANSPORTATION
Taxi

If you want to make a spare buck in Lima, buy a taxi sticker from the market for US$0.50, plop it on your windshield, and start picking up passengers. Understandably, the vast majority of taxis in Lima are unofficial and unregulated, and assaults on passengers picked up at the airport occur occasionally.

The best way to take a taxi is to call a registered company and pay an additional 30–50 percent. Recommended taxi companies include **Taxi Lima** (tel. 01/213-5050, daily 24 hours), **Taxi Miraflores** (tel. 01/446-4336, daily 24 hours), and **Taxi Móvil** (tel. 01/422-6890, San Isidro, daily 24 hours).

If you feel comfortable, and have a smidgen of Spanish, stand on the street until a safe-looking, registered taxi passes by. These should be painted yellow and have the taxi sign on the hood of the car and a registration sticker on the windshield. Older taxi drivers

tend to be safer than young ones. Of course, avoid old cars with tinted windows and broken door handles. Bargain before you get in a taxi or you will get fleeced. Fares from the airport to Miraflores should be US$15–20, airport–center about US$15, Miraflores–center about US$6, and Miraflores–Barranco about US$4. Prices go up during rush hour and at night. Taxis can also be rented by the hour for US$12 (registered taxi) or US$8 (street taxi).

Bus and *Colectivo*

Buses and *colectivos,* or minibuses, are an interesting, economical way to travel around Lima. Bus fares are US$0.50 on weekdays and a fraction more on Sundays. *Colectivos* cost US$0.70 on weekdays and US$0.80 on Sundays. You can tell where buses and *combis* are going by the sticker on the front windshield (not by what's painted on the side). There are also slightly more expensive *colectivo* cars, which can take up to five passengers and are a bit faster than the van-style *colectivos,* which in turn are faster than buses. To get off a bus or *colectivo* simply say *"baja"* ("getting off") or *"esquina"* ("at the corner"). Have your change ready, as money is collected right before you get off.

To reach Miraflores from the center, head to Garcilaso de la Vega (formerly Wilson) and take one of the buses or *colectivos* marked Miraflores or Todo Arequipa, which go all the way to Parque Kennedy. To reach Barranco, take a bus marked Barranco/Chorrillos from the same place. Or head to Miraflores and change buses there.

From Miraflores, most buses and *colectivos* can be taken from Larco along Parque Kennedy. To reach central Lima, take the bus marked Tacna/Wilson and ask to be dropped off at the central street of Ica or Callao. To reach Barranco, take the bus marked Barranco/Chorrillos, and the airport is Faucett/Aeropuerto. However, buses for the airport aren't very reliable and at times only come within five blocks of the airport. Take a taxi and keep your luggage safe.

Car Rental

The major rental car agencies are **Hertz**

(Salaverry 2599, San Isidro, tel. 01/421-0282, airport tel. 01/517-2402, www.hertz.com.pe, 24 hours), **Budget** (Larco 998, Miraflores, tel. 01/444-4546, airport tel. 01/517-1880, www.budgetperu.com), and **Avis** (Grimaldo del Solar 236, Miraflores, tel. 01/446-3156, www.avisperu.com). There are many more options under *Automóviles-alquiler* in the yellow pages.

Private Car

Private drivers can also be hired for the hour, day, or for a trip like the Nasca Lines. Many travelers who are only in Lima for a single day would greatly benefit from a driver who recommends museums and restaurants and then drops them off at the airport in the evening. A highly recommended driver is **José Salinas Casanova** (tel. 01/9329-2614, casanovacab@hotmail.com, US$7/hr) based out of the Hotel Antigua Miraflores. **Miguel Vásquez Díaz** (Carlos Izaguirre 1353, central Lima, tel. 01/9809-2321, sumisein@latinmail.com) and English-speaking **Mónica Velasquez** (tel. 01/9943-0796 or 01/224-8608, www.monicatourism.da.ru) are also recommended. **Fidel Loayza Paredes** (tel. 01/533-1609, armandoloayza280671@hotmail.com) does not speak English but is trustworthy.

Southern Beaches

We notice with some dismay that many guidebooks give poor write-ups about the beaches just south of Lima. The general thought is that they are dirty, crowded, treacherous, and, in general, not worth visiting. Though it is true that the white sands and subtropical climate of Peru's north beaches are more alluring, they are also a 20-hour bus ride to the north of Lima. If you are in Lima and in need of a beach fix, head south for a half hour to Punta Hermosa or San Bartolo. You will find sandy beaches, world-class surfing waves, protected beaches for safe swimming, rocking nightlife, a few good hostels, and lots of *cebicherías*. The only time to visit these beaches is during the summer months from mid-December to the end of April—they are cloudy during the rest of the year. Make reservations well in advance, especially January–mid-March, when surfers from around the world flock here along with Peruvian students on summer break. The best time to go is Sunday–Thursday nights, when beaches are empty and hotel prices are often 30 percent lower than those listed.

There are other options besides Punta Hermosa and San Bartolo—check out the *Guia Inca de las Playas,* for sale at Lima bookstores, for more details. **Santa María,** at Km 48 of the Panamericana, is an upscale beach with a control point that admits only residents and respectable-looking day-trippers. If you want a fancier, clean, but fairly snobby beach experience, this is your place, though there are few or no lodging options here. **Pucusana** is a picturesque fishing town at Km 58 of the Panamericana. **Puerto Viejo,** at Km 72 of the Panamericana, is a long beach good for beginning surfers—including a left point break that ranges 1–2 meters. **Leon Dormido** (Sleeping Lion) at Km 80 has a calm beach that is often crowded. The best parties, however, are at **Asia,** Km 97, which becomes an explosion of discos, condos, private clubs, and even car dealerships in the summer. Teenagers here for the parties pack the beach and the discos at night. Near Asia's beaches, and close to shore, there are several islands with great sea kayaking and possibilities to see Humboldt penguins and sea lions. Finally, **Cerro Azul** at Km 128 is a forgotten port, with a small fishing community and pleasant beach with both pipeline and beginner waves for all levels of surfers.

PUNTA HERMOSA

A half hour south of Lima at Km 40 of the Panamericana, Punta Hermosa is a big-time surfing destination with a great range of beaches and services. It is here that **Pico Alto,**

LIMA

© RENÉE DEL GAUDIO AND ROSS WEHNER

Lima's coastline is known as the Costa Verde because of the green vegetation that clings to portions of the ocean bluffs.

LIMA

the largest wave in South America, forms in May and reaches heights of up to 12 meters. The town itself is on a rocky peninsula, called La Isla, which is surrounded by seven beaches. From north to south, these are El Silencio, Caballeros, Señoritas, Pico Alto, Playa Norte, La Isla, and Kontiki. When covered in rocks and not sand June–November, Playa Norte is a good place to get away from crowds, along with Kontiki. But wherever you stay in Punta Hermosa, these beaches are no more than a half-hour walk away.

Entertainment and Events

Every May or June, during the first big swell of the year, Punta Hermosa comes alive with Peru's annual big-wave competition. There is no fixed date for the competition and it is usually organized within a week or two—check out www.buoyweather.com (you have to pay) or www.stormsurf.com (free) for the right ocean conditions, or stayed tuned to www.peruazul.com, the country's premier **surfing** website.

Otherwise nightlife is clustered around the entry to Punta Hermosa and the few pubs on the waterfront.

Recreation

Punta Hermosa has several places to rent a board and wetsuit, get an instructor, and **surf** a variety of waves from gentle to suicidal. The best beginner beaches in Punta Hermosa are Caballeros, Pacharacas, and La Isla. Taxis and surfing camps can arrange transportation to beginner beaches farther south, such as Puerto Viejo and Cerro Azul.

The honest and straightforward **Marco León Villarán** (tel. 01/230-8316 or 01/230-8351, www.peruadventure.com), who runs a bed-and-breakfast in town, can arrange a variety of fabulous adventures in the area. His main passion is **spear fishing,** and if you have the snorkel, fins, and mask he can lead you to just about any fish you have ever dreamed of seeing—or spearing—including 1.2-meter yellowtail or gigantic flounder near Punta Hermosa. In his Zodiac with outboard motor, he also leads trips to nearby Isla Pachacamac (US$25 pp) for the rare opportunity to see Humboldt penguins, sea lions, and the occasional sea otter (known in Spanish as *gato de mar* because of its catlike appearance).

Marco is also a professional bone-and-fossil hunter who knows Peru's desert coastline very well—from the fossil-rich deserts of Ica to the pristine and remote surfing beaches north of Chiclayo. He owns a reliable four-wheel-drive van and is an excellent, affordable, and trustworthy option for getting into remote areas of the Ica desert. Like all fossil hunters, Marco keeps in touch with all the local *huaqeros,* or grave robbers, and can even arrange an opportunity to witness their ceremonies. Before they begin digging at midnight, they read coca leaves and drink *aguardiente* to protect themselves from evil spirits. He charges a US$50 daily guiding fee and then bills travelers for gas, food, and other expenses, probably another US$50 per day for a group of up to four people. He speaks Spanish only.

Accommodations

Punta Hermosa's better places are in La Planicie, a quiet neighborhood to the north of town that offers a nice respite from the rowdy surfer scene in town, a 10-minute walk away. A good restaurant and Internet access are nearby, along with Señoritas and Caballeros beaches. There are more hotels and nightlife, and the monster Pico Alto wave itself, near the center of Punta Hermosa—along with crowds of rowdy Brazilian and Argentinean surfers who are in town to test their mettle on waves that have made Punta Hermosa known as the Hawaii of South America. Nearly all of the hotels below offer full pension—for another US$10–15 per day, you can take all your meals at your hostel. This is an excellent deal and a good way to avoid stomach issues.

Finding a room for under US$15 a night is possible but not easy in Punta Hermosa's high season. The best bet is to simply walk around town and look for signs that say Se Alquilan Cuartos (Rooms Are Rented Here)—these can often be clean and as cheap as US$8 pp per night. Surfer hostels spring up in Punta Hermosa in the summer and are listed at www.peruazul. com. We found many of these to be noisy, so choose carefully. For a mere US$12, Cebichería Carmencita will set up a tent on the beach for up to seven people and make a campfire.

In the Planicie neighborhood, long-time Punta Hermosa resident Marco León Villarán offers something for everyone at the **Peru Adventure Lodge** (Block Ñ, Lote 1, La Planicie, tel. 01/230-8316 or 01/230-8351, www.peruadventure.com, US$20 pp). His rooms are quiet, large, and comfortable, with tons of hot water and two labrador retrievers who can lick you awake every morning for a bit extra. He and his wife, Gloria, prepare excellent meals and his sons, Daniel and Joaquín, are excellent, English-speaking surfing instructors (US$10 for two hours). The family rents out boards and also organizes surf and fossil tours all along the Peruvian coast.

A good friend of Marco's, right around the corner, is Flavio Solaria, a surfboard shaper and international surfing judge who runs **Señoritas Surf Camp** (Block Ñ, Lote 4, tel. 01/230-7578, srtsurfcamp@yahoo.com, US$20 pp, full board). "What I offer is a lifestyle," explains Flavio. "A surfer's pension." The wooden rooms are smaller and simpler than Marco's, with tapestries from Bali and nice lighting. Rooms range from simple bunks to a private room with queen-size beds. Flavio also sells his extraordinary boards (US$300 for short, US$620 for long) and rents both boards (US$10/day) and wetsuits (US$5/day). He happily takes guests to nearby beaches and teaches them to surf at no additional charge.

A final surf camp in Planicie is the **Punta Hermosa Surf Camp** (Block R, Lote 19, tel. 01/230-8357, puntasurfcamp@hotmail.com).

In Punta Hermosa, **Hostal La Isla** (Malecón Central 943, tel. 01/230-7146, sandrolaisla@ hotmail.com, US$16 s, US$30 d) is a relaxed guesthouse run by the family of longtime Punta Hermosa resident and surfer Sandro Testino. Though a bit more expensive than the rest, Hostal La Isla is on Punta Hermosa's beach promenade, has nice ocean views, and is close to town but still quiet at night. The rooms are simple but comfortable with nice shared terraces. Services include laundry, surfboard rental, transport to surfing areas, and Internet. Another camp is run by Oscar Morante, a surf guide who leads trips all around Peru for several international surfing agencies. His **Pico**

LIMA

Alto International Surf Camp (Block L, Lote 14, tel. 01/230-7297, www.picoalto.com.pe, US$25–35 pp, full board) is well worth it.

A final good hostel, also near the center, is **Hospedaje Nylamp Wasi** (Pacasmayo 167, tel. 01/230-8401, surfperu50@hotmail.com, US$10 s, US$20 d, including breakfast).

Hotel La Rotonda (Bolognesi 580, above the restaurant of the same name, tel. 01/230-7390, larotondasurfcamp@hotmail.com, US$20 s, US$40 d) has eight nice rooms with ocean views and cable TV. These are right near the bars, however, and probably get noisy at night.

One of the nicest places to stay on the Peruvian coast, and one of the better values, must be **Casa Barco** (Punta Hermosa 340, tel. 01/230-7081, www.casabarco.com, US$18 dorm, US$55–72 d with breakfast). A five-minute walk from the center, this small and friendly hostel has a great pool with whirlpool tub, a beautiful flower garden, and a classy bar/restaurant with a full, reasonably priced menu of ceviche and other fish dishes. The rooms have black-and-white floor tiles, luxurious beds, cable TV, wraparound porches with ocean views, and huge, beautiful showers. Shared rooms are much simpler, but clean with access to all the hotel's services. The best part, however, is the art. The owners, ceramic artist Teresa Carvallo and writer Felix Portocarrera, have assembled a mind-blowing collection of contemporary art from Peru's best painters and sculptors.

Food

There are many seafood restaurants, but probably the safest is **La Rotonda** (Bolognesi 592, tel. 01/230-7266, 8 A.M.–11 P.M. daily, US$5). Apart from ceviche, the restaurant also does *chicharron* and grilled fish, serving on a second-story deck with good views of surfers on Pico Alto. Another option is **Cebichería Carmencita** (Malecón de Punta Hermosa 821, tel. 01/9976-4792, 7 A.M.–10 P.M. daily, US$5), which serves a range of fish dishes; the owner will even set up a tent and campfire for you. At Señoritas beach, ask around for the ceviche stall run by Paco and Cecilia, which has a good reputation among locals.

For Italian check out **Donde Luis** on the Punta Hermosa waterfront or, in La Planicie, **Trattoria Don Ángelo** (near control gate, tel. 01/230-7104 or 01/9740-9982, 7 A.M.–midnight daily, US$5). This is a family-run store and restaurant that serves pizzas and homemade pastas, including lasagna, ravioli, cannelloni, and gnocchi.

Getting There and Around

Probably the easiest way to get to Punta Hermosa from Lima is to hire a taxi (US$10) or arrange a pickup through your hotel. **Flavio Solaria** (tel. 01/230-7578, srtsurfcamp@yahoo.com) picks up groups from the Lima airport for US$25. Buses for Mala—which stop outside of Punta Hermosa, San Bartolo, and Santa María—pick up passengers at the circle, or *trébol,* where Avenida Javier Prado intersects with the Panamericana in Monterrico. These buses, called Maleños, take 45 minutes to reach Punta Hermosa and charge US$0.75.

Three-wheeled *motocars* abound in Punta Hermosa and are a US$0.50 option for getting between La Planicie and the town center.

SAN BARTOLO

Farther down the Panamericana, past an exclusive area of homes perched on a seaside cliff and an exclusive beach club known as La Quebrada, lies the laid-back beach town of San Bartolo. The town itself is perched on a bluff above an attractive horseshoe-shaped beach, lined with hotels, condos, and a *malecón,* known as Playa Norte. San Bartolo is less of a surfer party spot than the center of Punta Hermosa, even with Peñascal, a right reef break that gets as high as four meters on the south end of the Playa Norte. There are gentler waves and a good place for swimming on the north end of Playa Norte, along with a few nice beachfront hotels. After entering from Km 48 of the Panamericana, the main drag into town is Avenida San Bartolo. Most hotels are along Mar Pacífico, a street that runs to the left (south). To the right, another road leads around to Kahunas Hostal and Playa Norte.

Entertainment and Events

San Bartolo's best disco, **Peñascal,** is near the town's highway entrance and is only open during the summer.

Accommodations

Prices in San Bartolo double on weekend nights, so if you are planning a budget trip, make sure to visit during weekdays. Prices listed are for weekdays.

On the bluff above town, **Playa Mar Hostal** (San Bartolo 211, tel. 01/430-7247, US$18 s or d) is a surfer's hangout with brick walls, bamboo ceilings, tile floors, and private bathrooms. Another good option, and much cleaner than a few other hostels nearby, is **Hostal La Marina** (San Martín 351, tel. 01/430-7601, US$15 s or d). About half the 20 rooms have ocean views; it also offers cable TV, restaurant, and all-you-can-drink potable water.

For what it is, **Hostal 800** (Malecón 800, tel. 01/430-7514, US$25 d, cheaper by the week) is a great value. This hotel, like the others on the beach, is built up onto the hillside, so all the rooms have great ocean views. But these apartments are huge and luxurious, each with a private porch and commodious bedroom. An extra US$5 buys you a separate kitchen with fridge and microwave. There are also slightly cheaper rooms without terraces for US$15 a night. The owners of Hostal 800 also have **Hostal 110** (Malecón 110, tel. 01/430-7559, US$30 d, cheaper by the week) on the south end of the beach, a similar setup with even larger two-bedroom apartments.

Great service and plush surroundings can be found at **Sol y Mar** (Malecón 930, tel. 01/892-1999, US$27 s, US$42 d), with white leather couches, huge tiled rooms, great bathrooms, cable TV, fridges, full kitchens in a few rooms, and terraces with great ocean-view rooms. The other nice place on Playa Norte is **La Posada del Mirador** (Malecón 105, tel. 01/430-7822, www.posadadelmirador.com, US$20 s, US$25 d with breakfast), with furnished apartments.

Peruvian surfing champion Makki Block rents surfboards and offers lessons from his **Kahunas Hostal** (tel. 01/430-7407, US$20 s, US$35 d with breakfast). The hostel is perched on a bluff at the north end of Playa Norte and overlooks the Peñascal surfing break. Perks include a secluded terrace, pool, hydromassage, and TVs in all the rooms, which are decorated with surf decor.

Food

Most of the eating options—except for the spit-roasted chicken at Mar Pacífico 495—revolve around seafood. **Restaurant Curazao** (San Bartolo 231, tel. 01/430-7787, 8 A.M.–5 P.M. daily, US$3–5) is known for its Peruvian seafood plates, but can also make Chilean dishes upon request. There's a line of restaurants down Mar Pacífico. The best of these include **El Arador del Mar** (Mar Pacífico, tel. 01/430-8215, US$3–5), with a good seafood lunch menu for US$3. But the next-door **El Rincón de Chelulo** (Mar Pacífico s/n, tel. 01/430-7170) wins out for a greater variety of fish and shellfish, unbelievable friendly service, and a larger US$3 lunch menu. These restaurants are in front of the plaza where the town's market opens up every morning. This square also holds a few ice cream shops and pizzerias, open in summer only.

Information and Services

The best place for local info is the town's chamber of commerce, which can respond to questions in Spanish via email at **sanbartoloperu@ yahoo.es.** Or check the surfers' website **www. peruazul.com.** Both the **police** and the **local clinic** are on Avenida San Bartolo near the highway entrance. There is Internet at **Mar Pacífico 495** (tel. 01/430-7137, US$0.60 per hour), which is also a surf shop.

Getting There and Around

Probably the easiest way to get to San Bartolo from Lima is to hire a taxi (US$15) or take the Cruz del Sur bus, which stops at the town entrance. Local buses for Mala—which stop outside of Punta Hermosa, San Bartolo, and Santa María—pick up passengers at the circle, or *trébol*, where Avenida Javier Prado intersects with the Panamericana in Barranco. These buses, called Maleños, take 50 minutes to reach San Bartolo and charge US$0.75.

LIMA

AYACUCHO AND THE CENTRAL HIGHLANDS

The villagers of Peru's central highlands were already hard-hit in the 1980s by bad roads, little or no phone communication, and a life that revolved around subsistence agriculture. Then came the Sendero Luminoso, the Shining Path, a terrorist movement based on Maoist ideals that tried to spark a nationwide revolution by destroying the state and "old oligarchy."

During the 1980s and early 1990s, a staggering 70,000 people were killed in the cross-fire between the Shining Path and the army. Sendero Luminoso began in Ayacucho and wreaked most havoc in the central highlands—more than 75 percent of those killed were Quechua-speaking villagers.

These days terrorism has disappeared and the highways are in fantastic shape—thanks to the national government, which is doing everything it can to connect this forgotten part of Peru to the rest of the country. The area is safe for travel—even the conservative U.S. Embassy says so. Families have moved back to their towns, and there is a sense of recovery, of wounds slowly healing.

But still, fewer than 500 travelers a month end up in Ayacucho, which is without question the least visited of Peru's Andean cities. There are 33 colonial churches in Ayacucho, a huge amount of colonial art, colorful markets, artisan studios on every corner, and one of Latin America's most famous Easter week celebrations.

Huancayo, farther north, is equally as interesting, but for its countryside, not its city. There are a dozen or more quaint adobe villages in the surrounding Mantaro Valley where artisans make a living by carving gourds or

HIGHLIGHTS

◖ **Festival de Apóstol Santiago:** This July 25 festival features dancing and a ritualistic branding of cattle that blurs Christian and pre-Hispanic religious beliefs. It is but one of hundreds of traditional celebrations throughout the year in Huancayo and the surrounding Mantaro Valley (page 374).

◖ **Hualhuas:** The authentic tapestries and rugs found in the Ayacucho market are produced here (page 379).

◖ **Cochas Grande:** Here artisans practicing gourd carving – which dates to pre-Inca times – are glad to invite visitors into their homes (page 379).

◖ **Ayacucho City Tour:** The streets of this hidden jewel include Renaissance and baroque churches and the friendliest and most interesting market in Peru, where bubbling pots of corn stews, dozens of *chichas*, and huge rocks of black salt are on display alongside a staggering array of countryside produce (page 386).

◖ **Huari:** Exploring the countryside around Ayacucho leads to the ruins of Huari, the empire that made the Inca possible. Just 15 kilometers up the road, you'll find Quinua, a charming adobe village known for its red-clay ceramics (page 388).

◖ **Barrio Santa Ana:** The winding streets of this charming Ayacucho neighborhood are lined with stone carvers and rug weavers and

graced with Iglesia Santa Ana de los Indios, a simple baroque church with an embossed silver altar (page 393).

LOOK FOR ◖ TO FIND RECOMMENDED SIGHTS, ACTIVITIES, DINING, AND LODGING.

making weavings from alpaca wool and natural dyes. There are more traditional festivals here than anywhere else in Peru, and outsiders are welcome. After such bitter years, they are overjoyed to have guests.

PLANNING YOUR TIME

Most travelers arrive to Huancayo via bus from Lima, a comfortable six-hour journey on 300 kilometers of paved roads. The Lima–Huancayo railroad, billed as the second highest train in the world, is once again running, though its schedule is much reduced and sporadic.

After visiting Huancayo, most travelers

return to Lima, but a growing number continue to Ayacucho (8–10 hours), to Andahuaylas (10 hours), and then Abancay and Cusco (10 hours). This is a fascinating bus journey well off the Gringo Trail and on steadily improving roads. If traveled by day, it is completely safe.

The most interesting town in the central highlands—in the whole of Peru's Andes—is Ayacucho, but for those short on time, it does not make sense to spend 20 hours on a bus to Cusco. Right now the quickest way on is to return to Lima and fly to Cusco, but watch for Ayacucho–Cusco flights in the future. Plan on spending at least three days in Ayacucho.

CENTRAL HIGHLANDS

Lima to Tarma

If you want a crash course in Peruvian geography, take a bus up the Carretera Central, the well-paved highway that connects Lima with the interior of the country. Even on the foggiest of Lima's winter days, blue skies and sun can usually be found after less than an hour's drive inland to the towns of Chaclacayo, Chosica, and Santa Eulalia. From here the Carretera Central follows the Río Rímac through the subtropical valleys outside Lima, sheer rock canyons, desolate expanses of puna (high plains), and down into the jungle on the other side.

This trip is not for the fainthearted: In two hours, or 126 kilometers, travelers head from sea level to the town of Ticlio and the Anticona Pass at 4,820 meters (15,080 feet)! One of Peru's greatest engineering achievements was building a railroad over this pass in the 19th century. When traveling this route, bring warm clothing and water, and travel quickly to avoid headaches, nausea, crabbiness, and the other effects of altitude sickness.

After passing snowcapped Nevado Anticona and Lago Huacracocha, the route drops through striking, pea-green puna and a string of grimy mountain towns that end with La Oroya, an industrial rust heap hemmed in by bare hillsides. The river that runs through it is choked with foundry runoff and crossed by a series of concrete bridges, over which miners with plastic helmets and sooty faces trudge to and from their shifts.

At La Oroya the highway branches toward two Lima weekend spots, both of which are about a two-hour drive away: to the south lies the highland countryside around Huancayo; to the east lie the towns of La Merced and San Ramón, or Chanchamayo as they are collectively known.

The Chanchamayo road winds gently to **Tarma,** a colonial city at 925 meters that is famous in Peru for its Easter celebration. Past Tarma the road plunges another 2,300 meters to Chanchamayo, a fertile region for growing coffee, yuca, and banana.

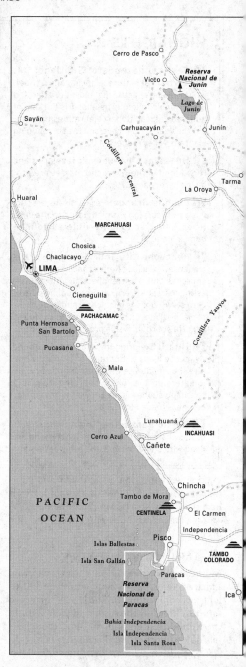

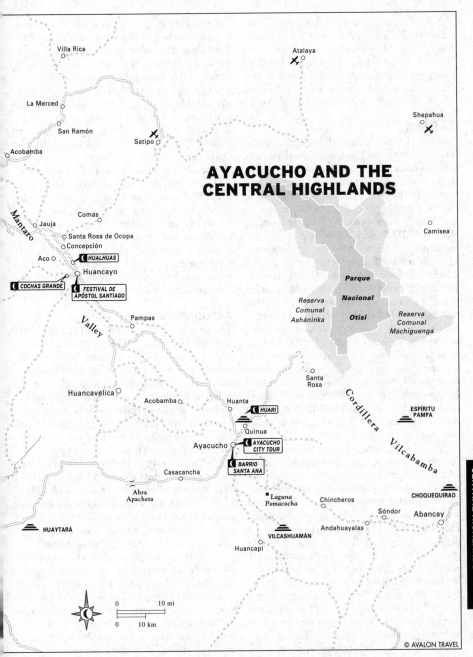

AYACUCHO AND THE CENTRAL HIGHLANDS

Villa Rica

Atalaya

La Merced

Shepahua

San Ramón

Acobamba

Satipo

Camisea

Comas

Jauja

Santa Rosa de Ocopa

Concepción

Aco

HUALHUAS

Huancayo

COCHAS GRANDE

FESTIVAL DE APÓSTOL SANTIAGO

Reserva Comunal Asháninka

Parque

Nacional

Otisi

Reserva Comunal Machiguenga

Valley

Pampas

Santa Rosa

Huancavelica

Acobamba

Huanta

HUARI

Cordillera

ESPÍRITU PAMPA

Quinua

Vilcabamba

Ayacucho

AYACUCHO CITY TOUR

BARRIO SANTA ANA

Casacancha

Laguna Pomacocha

Chincheros

CHOQUEQUIRAO

Abra Apacheta

Sóndor

Abancay

HUAYTARÁ

Andahuaylas

VILCASHUAMÁN

Huancapi

0   10 mi
0   10 km

© AVALON TRAVEL

A third route to the north leads past Junín, a battlefield from Peru's war for independence, Tingo María, and the low-jungle city of Pucallpa. Tingo María and the Upper Huallaga Valley north of it is Peru's prime cocaine-producing region and is not safe for travel. For that reason, the route is not included in this book.

TARMA

Tarma is the first decent lodging option on the long haul between Lima and Chanchamayo, and strolling townspeople crowd the streets in the evening, a warming sight after the barren landscape of the puna above. Because of its chilly weather and altitude (925 meters or 3,053 feet), people coming from Lima occasionally feel altitude sickness here.

Tarma was founded by the Spanish soon after the conquest, though narrow streets and a handful of old homes are the only clues to its colonial pedigree. There are two churches worth a visit on the main square. **La Capilla del Señor de la Cárcel** (Chapel of the Lord of the Prison) was built in 1800 and remodeled in 1954 by General Manuel Odría, Tarma's most famous son and a Peruvian dictator during the 1930s. The church receives its name from the Christ image painted on its left wall and the fact that it was built atop the town's prison. Across the plaza is **Catedral Santa Ana** (6–10 A.M. and 5–8 P.M. daily), which was also built by Odría.

What Tarma is most known for, however, is incredible festivals, starting with elaborate processions, singing contests, and water balloon–throwing during February's **Carnaval.** During Tarma's **Easter week,** millions of flowers and seeds are carefully arranged on and around the Plaza de Armas. The resulting flower carpet—depicting everything from landscapes to religious images—sets a new world record every year, covering every inch of street in an eight-block area around the main square, an estimated 3,400 square meters. At 5 A.M. on Easter Sunday, a religious procession walks over the carpet and through a number of decorated wooden arches on its way to and from the cathedral.

Other nearby attractions include **Tarmatambo,** a collection of Inca ruins nine kilometers to the south of Tarma. The **Santuario del Señor de Muruhuay** is a huge white modern church with an electric bell tower, visible from the highway nine kilometers east of Tarma at **Acobamba.** This is only the latest building to cover a rock carving of Christ reputed to have miraculous properties. Tradition maintains that it was etched on a boulder from a survivor of the Junín independence battle of August 6, 1824.

There is world-class **caving** near Palcamayo, 23 kilometers north of Acobamba along a dirt road. This town is the launching point for exploring one of Latin America's largest caves, the **Gruta de Huagapo.** Cavers using scuba equipment and oxygen tanks have descended as far as 2,800 meters into the cave. Guides can be contracted locally to help descend some distance into the cave, but unguided visitors with headlamps can enter to about 300 meters.

Accommodations

The best budget option in Tarma is **Hostal Dorado** (Huánuco 488, tel. 064/32-1914, US$11 s, US$15 d), a colonial home with a plant-filled courtyard and wooden second-story balcony. Rooms are simple, clean, and quiet, and cheaper rooms with shared bathrooms are available. **Hotel Galaxia** (Lima 262, tel. 064/32-1449, US$17 s, US$21 d) is clean and quiet, despite its location on the main square, but lacks charm.

The luxury option in Tarma is **Hotel Los Portales** (Ramón Castilla 512, tel. 064/32-1411, www.hotelportalestarma.com, US$67 s, US$92 d with breakfast), which was built (of course) by General Odría in the 1950s on the main road just west of town. Rooms are newly remodeled and there is a bar with karaoke.

A German-Swiss couple are running **Hacienda La Florida** (6 km outside Tarma, tel. 064/34-1041, www.haciendalaflorida. com, US$41–48 s, US$66–80 d with breakfast), a colonial hacienda that once belonged to Peruvian painter José Otero. There are 12 tasteful rooms, some decorated with antiques, and courtyards and gardens for strolling.

OVER THE ANDES BY TRAIN

One of Latin America's great engineering achievements of the 19th century was the completion of a train line across the Andes between Lima and Huancayo. The 12-hour journey begins in the desert coast around Lima and climbs through a subtropical river valley, into dozens of rock tunnels, onto the puna, and finally up and over the snow-covered *cordillera*. Needless to say, the 12-hour ride is a memorable experience.

The train was built between 1870 and 1908 and was the brainchild of American entrepreneur Henry Meiggs, who bragged that he could "get a train wherever a llama can walk." Polish engineer Ernest Malinowski designed most of the 61 bridges, 65 tunnels, and 21 switchbacks, built over four decades by 10,000 workers – more than half of whom were indentured workers, or coolies, from China.

The train, considered to serve the highest passenger station in the world, climbs nearly nine meters per minute until reaching Ticlio at 4,758 meters. Shortly afterwards it climbs to its highest point at La Galera, a tunnel through the Andes at 4,781 meters. Depending on the season, the snow line hovers a few hundred meters above.

The service was shut down in 1991, following attacks by Sendero Luminoso. It began again briefly in the late 1990s but once again fell out of service. Now, the recently upgraded service is running once or twice a month. The six cars have been remodeled and there is an onboard lookout station and bar.

If you're coming from Lima, there's really no way to acclimatize for this journey except by sipping plenty of water (or even better, *maté de coca*) and being well rested. Symptoms of altitude sickness include headaches and sometimes nausea – which usually pass once the train descends, though some passengers continue to suffer from *soroche*, or altitude sickness, even in Huancayo (3,240 meters).

Mountain guides swear the best medicine to take for altitude headaches is Excedrin. While adjusting to a higher altitude, it is always a good idea to avoid alcohol, heavy foods, and physical exertion. As the Bolivians say, *"Come poco, tome poco, y duerme solo"* ("Eat little, drink little, and sleep alone").

Food

For spit-roasted chicken, trout, meats, and meal-sized soups, head to **Restaurant Señorial** (Huánuco 140, 9 A.M.–2 P.M. and 4–11 P.M. daily, US$2–5). **Lo Mejorcito de Tarma** (Arequipa 501, tel. 064/32-3500, 7 A.M.–11 P.M. daily) has excellent Peruvian food. **Restaurante Midamar's** (Plaza de Armas, Arequipa 221, 9 A.M.–9 P.M.) serves breakfast and has a good lunch menu.

Information and Services

There is some tourist information, as well as guides for surrounding sights, at the **information office** on the main square next to the municipality, a local government building. A good local guide, who speaks only Spanish, is **Carlos Torres** (carlostours@latinmail.com), who is often found at the Librería XXI on the corner of Lima and Moguegua. The town's fastest Internet is **Infomedia,** on the corner of Paucartambo and Lima.

Getting There and Around

The two main transport companies, with terminals in Lima, have daily buses down to Chanchamayo and to Huancayo. **Empresa de Transporte Nuestra Señora de la Merced** (Vienrich 420, tel. 064/32-2937) has buses to Lima two times a day at 11:30 A.M. and 11 P.M. for US$15. The company also offers US$3.50 buses to Chanchamayo three times a day between noon and 5 P.M. **Empresa de Transportes Chanchamayo** (Callao 1002, tel. 064/32-1882) is another reputable bus company for the Lima–Chanchamayo journey. **Los Canarias** has frequent departures to Huancayo.

Huancayo and Vicinity

The Mantaro Valley in Peru's central highlands is one of the country's most productive agricultural areas, a giant swath of flat land famous for its potatoes, corn, barley, quinoa, artichokes, and many vegetables. The charming adobe villages of this valley are the best places in all of Peru to see a wide range of craftspeople at work (and acquire the highest quality artwork at a fair price that benefits the artist, not the merchant).

Artisans here produce the ceramics, weavings, carved gourds (*mates burilados*), and silver filigree that is sold, at a considerable markup, in the crafts markets of Cusco and Lima. Many of the artisans are national champions in their disciplines and produce works of staggering beauty that are impossible to find elsewhere in the country. The artisans are glad to work and chat at the same time and gladly invite in visitors who knock on their unmarked, wooden doors.

More so than residents in other more touristy areas of Peru, Mantaro Valley villagers do not behave differently in front of foreigners and go about their lives much as they have for centuries. They are proud and prosperous people. Depending on the time of the year, villagers are out in the fields planting or harvesting, threshing wheat with horses and donkeys, herding cows with colorful tassels tied to their ears, or building rammed-earth homes that are the same chocolate color as the surrounding fields. There is a festival nearly every day somewhere in the valley.

A good way to experience local culture is through one of the walking or mountain-bike routes mapped out by the energetic and affable Lucho Hurtado at Incas del Peru, the best source of information on the area (Giráldez 652, tel. 064/22-3303, www.incasdelperu. org). He has good contacts among local craftspeople and leads treks to the Cordillera Huaytapallana, a small but spectacular range 50 kilometers east of Huancayo that includes a number of glaciated peaks, including Mount Lasuntay (5,780 meters).

There are many local ruins from the Xauxa and later Huanca culture, which ran a lively coast–jungle trade from A.D. 900 onward until being conquered by the Inca in the 15th century. Like the Chachapoyans farther north, the Huanca resented Inca rule and sided with the Spanish, who followed the Inca roads through the Mantaro Valley en route to Cusco in 1533. The following year, Francisco Pizarro returned to the area to found Jauja, Peru's first, though short-lived, capital, and the land was divided up among the Spaniards (a source of dismay, no doubt, to Huanca elders).

During the independence struggle three centuries later, the Spanish troops based themselves in Huancayo for three years until they were defeated at nearby Junín and Ayacucho in 1824. During the War of the Pacific (1879–1883), several bloody battles were again fought in the Mantaro Valley between Chilean soldiers and the Peruvian army led by General Andrés Cáceres, who was dubbed the Wizard of the Andes for his ability to attack and quickly disappear into the mountains. During the 1980s and 1990s, Mantaro Valley villages were caught in the crossfire between the Shining Path and the Peruvian army. The area is recovering strongly, thanks in part to good farming lands, crafts production, and tourism.

The best base for touring the valley is Huancayo (3,240 meters), an unfortunate sprawl of cement buildings topped off by the exhaust of far too many old buses. The city's biggest attraction is the Sunday market, where fresh food is sold side by side with handicrafts. There are not many other sights, nor good lodging options, in the city itself—the best options are on the edge of town or in the nearby village of Concepción.

SIGHTS
City Tour

The best way to enjoy Huancayo is to take a taxi to the east end of Giráldez and walk up Cerrito de la Libertad, which offers nice views over the city and a few stands with *comida típica*. From

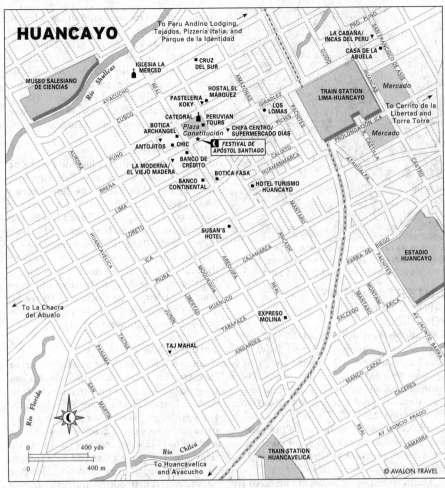

HUANCAYO

To Peru Andino Lodging,
Tejados, Pizzería Italia, and
Parque de la Identidad

LA CABAÑA/
INCAS DEL PERU

CASA DE LA
ABUELA

MUSEO SALESIANO
DE CIENCIAS

Río Shullcas

IGLESIA LA
MERCED

CRUZ
DEL SUR

HOSTAL EL
MÁRQUEZ

PASTELERIA
KOKY

CATEDRAL

BOTICA
ARCHANGEL

PERUVIAN
TOURS

Plaza
Constitución

CHIFA CENTRO/
SUPERMERCADO DÍAS

ANTOJITOS

CHIC

FESTIVAL DE
APÓSTOL SANTIAGO

LA MODERNA/
EL VIEJO MADERA

BANCO DE
CRÉDITO

BOTICA FASA

BANCO
CONTINENTAL

HOTEL TURISMO
HUANCAYO

TRAIN STATION
LIMA-HUANCAYO

Mercado

To Cerrito de la
Libertad and
Torre Torre

Mercado

LOS
LOMAS

ESTADIO
HUANCAYO

SUSAN'S
HOTEL

To La Chacra
del Abuelo

EXPRESO
MOLINA

TAJ MAHAL

Río Florida

0   400 yds

0   400 m

Río Chilca

TRAIN STATION
HUANCAVELICA

To Huancavelica
and Ayacucho

© AVALON TRAVEL

Streets labeled: PRO. PUNO, SAN FRANCISCO DE ASIS, GUIDO, HUANCAS, AMAZONAS, GIRÁLDEZ, PACHITES, PICHIS, CALIXTO, PROLONGACION ICA, CASTILLA, CASTRO, ATAHUALPA, REAL, CUSCO, PUNO, AURORA, BRENA, LIMA, HUANCAVELICA, ICA, PIURA, MOQUEGUA, LIBERTAD, HUANUCO, JUNIN, TACNA, PANAMA, SAN MARTIN, CORETO, AREQUIPA, CAJAMARCA, ANCASH, RUAMANMARCA, HUAMANMARCA, MANTARO, PARRA DEL RIEGO, MANTANO, ARICA, SALCEDO, TARAPACA, ANGARDES, MANCO CAPAC, CACERES, AV. JACINTO BAIRA, AV. LEONCIO PRADO, GAMARRA, REAL

there continue another two kilometers to an odd formation of sandstone towers known as **Torre Torre** and then traverse the hillside above the city for another few kilometers. The end point is the **Parque de la Identidad Huanca,** an interesting Gaudí-esque park with curving stone walls, sculptures, and native plants. It is a great evening hangout spot near a range of affordable Peruvian restaurants. A map of this walk, which takes a few hours, is available through Lucho Hurtado (Giráldez 652, tel. 064/22-3303, www.incasdelperu.org).

There is not much to see in Huancayo itself. The central plaza, Plaza Constitución de Armas, is nondescript, and Huancayo's churches are all modern, except for **La Merced,** on the first block of Real, where Peru's constitution was signed in 1839. **El Museo Salesiano de Ciencias Naturales** (Santa Rosa, El Tambo, tel. 064/24-7763, 9 A.M.–1 P.M. daily) has an amazing collection of more than 13,000 Amazon insects, jungle birds, butterflies, fossils, and archaeological artifacts.

© PILAR OLIVARES, PROMPERU

Parque de la Identidad Huanca, with its Gaudí-esque curves and meanderings, is Huancayo's best evening hangout spot.

ENTERTAINMENT AND EVENTS
Nightlife

La Cabaña (Giráldez 652, tel. 064/22-3303, www.incasdelperu.org, 5–11 P.M. daily) is an excellent drinking and dancing spot that is popular with both locals and travelers. Local bands crank out folkloric music Thursday–Saturday from 9 P.M. onward. **Antojitos** (Puno 599, tel. 064/23-7950, 7 A.M.–1 A.M. daily), on the corner of Arequipa and Puno, serves up light food in an atmosphere of classic rock and salsa, as does **Galileo** (Paseo La Breña 378, 6 P.M.–midnight Mon.–Sat.).

The three best discotheques of Huancayo are **Taj Mahal** (Huancavelica 1056, 7 P.M.–2 A.M. Mon.–Sat.), **La Noche** (San Antonio 241, 9 P.M.–3 A.M. Fri.–Sat.), and **El Molino** (Ugarte 503, 7 P.M.–2 A.M. Thurs.–Sat.). Cover charges hover around US$3, including a drink, and things get going around 11 P.M. There is a good karaoke spot on Plaza de Constitución called **Torre Torre** (Giraldez 137, 7 P.M.–2 A.M. Mon.–Sat.).

Festivals and Events
◖ FESTIVAL DE APÓSTOL SANTIAGO
Some of Peru's most interesting (and most frequent) festivals are found in the Mantaro Valley, which has more traditional festivals than there are days in the year. During the Festival de Apóstol Santiago on July 25, villagers throughout the Mantaro Valley brand their livestock amid much dancing and drinking of *chicha* (fermented corn beer). Though Christian on the surface, this pre-Hispanic ritual invokes the protection of Andean deities.

OTHER FESTIVALS
Other festival highlights include **Fiesta del Niño** in January, **Carnaval** in February, **Cruz del Mayo** in May, **Fiesta de San Pedro y San Pablo** on June 28 and 29, **La Fiesta de Santiago** on July 25, and **Todos los Santos** (Day of the Dead) on November 1. In **Jauja** there is **Jala Pato** (Pull the Duck) in late January, when horsemen compete to yank off the head of a suspended duck. The village of **Sapallanga** is known for the colorful processions of the Virgen de Cocharcas September 7–9. For a complete list of Mantaro Valley festivals, visit www.incasdelperu.org.

SHOPPING

Huancayo is famous for its Sunday market on Huancavelica Street, where fresh food is sold alongside handicrafts on three blocks from Puno to Loreto. The best time to go is around 4–5 P.M., when vendors are packing up and are eager to bargain. There are several small markets in Huancayo that sell mostly tourist items—the best place is **Casa de Artesano** on the Plaza de Constitución (Real 495). However, you will receive better prices and have a memorable experience if you buy directly from the artists in their homes.

Villages around the Mantaro Valley have markets where crafts are sold on different days of the week, including Wednesday in **San Jerónimo de Tunán,** Saturday in **Chupaca,** and Sunday in **Concepción** and **Jauja.**

RECREATION

The peaks and valleys around Huancayo invite all sorts of excuses to escape the city. Spend the day visiting Mantaro Valley towns, learning

© ANIBAL SOLIMANO, PROMPERU

The Mantaro Valley has more traditional festivals than there are days in the year.

about traditional weaving, or biking or even exploring the neighboring jungle.

Tour Guides and Agencies

The colorful, all-natural, traditional **weavings** from the Huancayo area draw textile experts from across the world to not only buy weavings but also to participate in hands-on classes. If you have a real curiosity in the subject, Sasha McInne's 22-day Textiles/Folk Art/Market Tour is the best option. Sasha's tours operate through her agency, **Puchka Peru Cultural Tours** (Canada tel. 250/360-1898, www.puchkaperu.com), traveling through Peru stopping in Lima, Cusco, the Sacred Valley, and Arequipa. In Arequipa, travelers meet up with traditional Huancayo weavers to learn from their techniques and experiences. The energetic and knowledgeable Sasha grew up in Peru, knows the lay of the land, and exposes trip participants to a variety of weaving techniques, including knitting, braiding, embroidery, and backstrap and tapestry weaving.

For closer-to-Huancayo weaving experience, contact Juana Sanabria of **Peru Andino Lodging** (Pasaje San Antonio 113, tel. 064/22-3956, www.geocities.com/peruandino_1). Juana is a passionate weaver and patient teacher. She organizes in-house weaving classes and demonstrations at Peru Andino. Contact her before your arrival so that she can gather the necessary plants and fiber to make the natural dyes, which you will in turn learn to make and mix with wools that will eventually be woven into textiles.

Juana's husband Luis is the mountain man of the family. As his contribution to Peru Andino, he leads a variety of organized **treks** into the surrounding hills and even into the nearby jungle. The treks can be contracted with as little as a day's notice.

True adventure, however, wears the name of Lucho Hurtado. Lucho operates **Incas del Peru** (Giráldez 652, tel. 064/22-3303, www.incasdelperu.org, 9 A.M.–1 P.M. and 4–7 P.M. Mon.–Sat.), from which he rents mountain bikes and hands out free walking and biking maps to those who rent bikes or stay in La Casa de la Abuela, his hostel across the street. The walks include the lake-to-lake circuit near

Jauja and the loop above Huancayo; ruins and hot mineral baths at Matachico, north of Jauja; and a ridge walk between the villages of Ahuac and Chupaca that passes through a line of Huanca granaries and offers views of the snow-covered Cordillera Huaytapallana and Lago Ñahuimpuquio. Lucho also knows the jungle around Chanchamayo and takes travelers out to his father's ranch on the way to Pozuzo. Although Lucho also offers cultural classes and tours, we recommend him only for his outdoor adventures.

The other tour agencies in Huancayo offer cheaper tours that do not include food, entry fees, or truly bilingual guides. They are, however, much more economical at about US$10 a day. Recommended agencies include **Peruvian Tours** (Plaza Constitución on the side of the cathedral, tel. 064/21-3069, perutours@hotmail.com) and **Darqui Tours** (Ancash 367, Plaza Constitución, tel. 064/23-3705).

ACCOMMODATIONS
US$10-25
La Casa de la Abuela (Giráldez 691, tel. 064/22-3303, www.incasdelperu.org, US$10 dorm, US$14 s or d with breakfast) is a charming 1930s house stuffed with art objects, maps, magazines, games, and books. La Casa de la Abuela is more like a forgetful household than an efficient hotel, but that is precisely its charm. The second floor's sporadic water, an early-rising, squawking parrot, and other blemishes are wiped away by a yummy breakfast of coffee, bread, fruit, and juice plus a welcoming *calentito*, a hot pisco drink. Having worked with backpackers for so long, the hotel is a beehive of traveler information and is only a 10-minute walk from downtown. Rooms without baths are slightly cheaper.

Peru Andino Lodging (Pasaje San Antonio 113, tel. 064/22-3956, www.geocities.com/peruandino_1, US$10 pp shared bath, US$12 pp with private bath) is a modern home in a quiet neighborhood run by Juana and Luis Sanabria. The beds are firm, bathrooms are clean, and the surrounding San Carlos neighborhood is absolutely quiet. There are two nice rooftop rooms with a bit more privacy, and staying with older Luis and Juana is a bit like visiting your grandmother's home. All the care and hot tea you'd ever want.

US$25-50
Susan's Hotel (Real 851, tel. 064/20-2251, www.susanshotel.com, US$22 s, US$29 d) is another modern hotel on the main street with clean bathrooms, firm beds (with kitschy lion bedspreads), and quiet back rooms.

Walking distance from the Plaza Constitución, **Retama Inn** (Ancash 1079, tel. 064/21-9193, retamainn73@hotmail.com, US$14 s, US$27 d with breakfast) is centrally located. The 20 clean rooms have all the basic amenities: comfy beds, carpet, cable TV, phones, room service, and private baths. The traditionally decorated café bar is great for evening drinks.

US$50-100
Hotel Turismo Huancayo (Ancash 729, tel. 064/23-1072, www.hoteles-del-centro.com, US$50 s, US$60 d) is an elegant 1930s colonial-style hotel, smack in the center of town, with good views over the Plaza Huamanmarca. The long tile hallways are a cool escape from the busy city, and rooms are genuinely comfortable: king-size beds, heater, cable TV, WiFi, and immaculate bathrooms. If you want to be in the city and need some comfort, this is your place.

Located 20 minutes north of Huancayo, the new **Hotel Loma Verde** (Leopoldo Peña, Concepción, tel. 064/58-1569 or Lima tel. 01/242-7599, www.lomaverdeperu.com, US$60 s, US$90 d full board) has plenty of country charm. The main lodge has sitting areas with fabulous views over the Mantaro Valley. Rooms are crafted from stone, plaster, and exposed beams and feature feather comforters, fireplaces, and porches with sunset views. The restaurant serves a wide variety of food on a veranda, and food is often cooked in the *pachamanca* pit or over open fire. It's an additional US$5 per day for lunch and dinner. There are horses and mountain bikes for rent.

The only drawback is audible truck traffic on the highway below.

Derrama Magisterial Huaychulo (Oriente s/n, Concepción, tel. 064/58-1001, cpijno@ derramajae.org.pe, US$39 s, US$75 d) is a country retreat with pleasant walks and good reading rooms—but it's not as charming as Hotel Loma Verde. Bedrooms are simple and clean with mediocre bathrooms.

For those willing to forgo charm for a firm bed, plenty of hot water, and a central location, there's the modern **Hostal El Marquéz** (Puno 294, tel. 064/21-9026, www.elmarquezhuancayo.com, US$43 s, US$57 d with breakfast). Rooms are large, carpeted, and quiet. There is cable TV and WiFi.

FOOD

Huancayo has some excellent places for *comida típica,* all of which are a taxi ride from the center. The region's most famous dish is *papas a la huancaína,* yellow potatoes smothered with a yellow sauce made from fresh cheese, oil, ground yellow chili pepper, lemon, and egg yolk—and topped off with black olives.

Cafés, Bakeries, and Ice Cream

The best place for a rich cappuccino, light snack, or dessert is **Pasteleria Koky** (Puno 296, tel. 064/23-4707, 7 A.M.–10 P.M. Mon.–Sat., 8 A.M.–1 P.M. and 4:30–9 P.M. Sun., US$2). It also makes homemade bread and sells good-for-picnics deli meats and cheeses.

A good place for hamburgers, pizzas, cake, or ice cream is **La Moderna** (Paseo la Breña 165, tel. 064/21-3288, 8 A.M.–midnight daily), though the best chocolate cake is at the tiny **Berisso** (Giráldez 258, tel. 064/22-5634). **Cafeteria Loredo** (Loreto 632, tel. 064/21-2853, 7:30 A.M.–noon and 3:30–10 P.M. daily) has been around for 40 years and is a cheap, unpretentious place to have coffee, oatmeal and milk, *biscocho,* and empanadas.

Peruvian

Huancahuasi (Mariscal Castilla 2222, El Tambo, tel. 064/24-4826, www.huancahuasi. com, 9 A.M.–8 P.M. daily, US$9) is a great place

for Sunday lunch, with live folkloric music and steaming chunks of pork, beef, and lamb from the *pachamanca* pit, followed by *humitas.* **La Tullpa** is also highly recommended and has one of the town's only chefs certified in Peruvian food.

La Chacra del Abuelo (behind the cemetery and near the corner of Daniel Carrión and Ica Nueva, tel. 064/23-7143, 11 A.M.–8 P.M. daily, US$4–7) has the town's best *tiradito de trucha* (strips of trout cooked in lemon juice), *cuy chactado* (pan-fried guinea pig with corn), and excellent cuts of meats.

Locals say the best *pachamanca* to be had is south of Huancayo along the road to Puno at **Doña Teófila,** a hole-in-the-wall hidden among a line of restaurants in the suburb of Asapampa.

After an evening's stroll around the Parque de la Identidad, wander over to **Restaurant Comida Wanka** (next to the park, 10 A.M.–9 P.M. daily), where 10 food stalls each sell yummy, safe local dishes, including *chicharrón colorado, picante de cuy,* and *pachamanca.*

On Parque Túpac Amaru, there is **Tejados** (Francisco Solano 220, tel. 064/22-2000, 5:30 P.M.–close daily, US$5–6), which has rich pasta alfredo and light lemon-marinated brochettes.

El Viejo Madero (Paseo a la Brena 125, tel. 064/21-7788, noon–11 P.M. daily, US$2) serves only one thing: huge chunks of juicy, spit-roasted chicken, topped off with french fries and a salad that is safe for foreigners. It's delicious.

Pizza

The welcoming **La Cabaña** (Giráldez 652, tel. 064/22-3303, www.incasdelperu.org, 5–11 P.M. daily, US$7) is a cozy place with a fireplace, art, and great pizza. Live folk music plays Thursday–Saturday from 8 P.M. It also serves grilled meats, sandwiches, and pitchers of sangria. Good pizza, sandwiches, and inexpensive lunch menus can be found at **Antojitos** (Puno 599, tel. 064/23-7950, 7 A.M.–1 A.M. daily, US$6–8), which has live rock music on the weekends.

CENTRAL HIGHLANDS

In the San Carlos neighborhood, try **Italia** (Leandra Torres 441, at Parque Túpac Amaru, tel. 064/23-3145, 6–11 P.M. daily), which delivers and has lasagna and a range of other pasta dishes.

Chifa

The quiet oriental music is the perfect background to the upscale cuisine of **Chifa Centro** (Giráldez 245, tel. 064/21-7575, 1–11:30 P.M. Mon.–Thurs., 1 P.M.–midnight Fri.–Sat., 1–10:30 P.M. Sun., US$4–6). Popular plates include grilled duck with pineapple and *arroz chaufa*. There is a second location in the San Carlos neighborhood at Leanda Torres 240.

Markets

The best small market is **Comercial Huaychulo** (Paseo a la Brena 174), with fruits, vegetables, deli meats, and cheeses. Grocery stores include the modern **Supermercado Días** (Giráldez 271, 8 A.M.–10:30 P.M. daily) and **Supermercado Casa Sueldo** (Real 696, corner of Loreto, 9 A.M.–10 P.M. Mon.–Sat., 9 A.M.–2 P.M. and 3:30–9 P.M. Sun.).

INFORMATION AND SERVICES

The best source of travel information in Huancayo is Lucho Hurtado at **Incas del Peru** (Giráldez 652, tel. 064/22-3303, www.incasdelperu.org, 9 A.M.–1 P.M. and 4–7 P.M. Mon.–Sat.).

The **tourist police** are at Ferrocarril 555 (tel. 064/21-9851).

The pharmacy with the widest selection is **Botica Arcangel** (Real 467, tel. 064/20-2200, 24 hours) on the Plaza de Armas, or try **Botica Fasa** (Real 703, tel. 064/21-7960, www.boticasfasa.com.pe, 7 A.M.–11 P.M. daily).

For health care, try the **Clínica Rhur** (Huancas 269, tel. 064/23-3051) or Dr. Jose Navarro (Abancay 580, tel. 064/22-4844), who charges US$11 for a consultation.

Most banks are located on blocks 5 and 6 of Real, including **Banco de Crédito, Interbanc, Banco Continental,** and **Scotiabank.** There is a **Western Union** (365 Ancash, tel. 064/23-3705) on the Plaza de Armas. Rigged calculators are a problem in Huancayo, so change bills in a bank or in a money exchange.

The **post office** (8 A.M.–8 P.M. Mon.–Sat.) is in the Plaza Huamanmarca, near the intersection of Real and Huamanmarca.

The Internet places around the Plaza de Armas are slightly expensive, and there are several faster places along Giráldez, including **Cibercentro** (Giráldez 275, US$0.50/hour, also does international calls) and a 24-hour place at Giráldez 288.

Telephone cabins at Real and Lima are open 7 A.M.–10 P.M. daily.

Incas del Peru (Giráldez 652, tel. 064/22-3303, www.incasdelperu.org) offers a Spanish for Travelers class with courses starting every Monday. The budget course for US$110 includes three hours of daily lessons, five days lodging at La Casa de la Abuela, and three meals a day. Additional options include homestays, weekend excursions, and field trips around town. The agency can also arrange classes for Quechua.

The best place to take your dirty laundry is **Chic** (Breña 154, tel. 064/23-1107, 8 A.M.–10 P.M. Mon.–Sat., 10 A.M.–6 P.M. Sun.).

GETTING THERE AND AROUND

A new train service now cuts from Lima up into the highlands onto Huancayo. **Ferrocarril Central Andina** (Paicheta and Giraldez, Lima tel. 01/226-6363, www.ferroviasperu.com.pe) operates a Sunday train that stops in all major tourist destinations. At 11 hours, the ride is a long one, but worth it for the scenic views and a once-in-a-lifetime experience. The coaches connect to a bar and lookout deck and have tourist (US$80) and economy (US$46) seats.

There are lots of options for bus service to and from Huancayo. The best include **Ormeño** (Mariscal Castilla 1379, www.grupo-ormeno. com), which has Royal and normal class buses to Lima. Other options include **Cruz del Sur** (Ayacucho 281, tel. 064/22-3367, www.cruzdelsur.com.pe), running buses at 8 A.M., 1:30 P.M., 11 P.M., and 11:45 P.M.; **Mariscal**

Cáceres (Real 1247); and **ETUCSA** (Puno 220, tel. 064/22-6524).

For Tarma and the jungle around Chanchamayo, try **Empresa Transporte San Juan** (Omaryali 159). Buses leave hourly for Tarma between 5 A.M. and 8 P.M. (US$5), with connections on to Merced (US$6) and Satipo (US$7).

For the rough and beautiful ride to the Cañete Valley on the coast, try **ETAS** (Loreto 744), which has buses leaving at 6 A.M. for the 13-hour journey on the dirt road through Yauricocha and past the Yauyos range (US$9).

For Ayacucho, try **Empresa Transporte Union Molina** at Angaraes and Real. The road has been improved and the trip now takes 8–10 hours. Buses leave in the morning and evening and cost US$12.

There are several options for reaching Huancavelica, the best and most comfortable of which is the train. The station is located at 1766 Leoncio Prado (no telephone), where an express train (US$5) leaves at 6:30 A.M. Monday–Saturday and arrives—assuming there are no breakdowns—five hours later. Offering basic seating compartments, the cargo train (US$2.50) leaves the same days at 1 P.M. and arrives at 7 P.M. On Sundays, there is a train with buffet lunch service (US$4) that leaves at 2 P.M. and arrives at 7 P.M. Buy tickets a day ahead as the trains are sometimes full.

There are bus companies that head to Huancavelica, but the roads are rough and the going is more comfortable in *colectivos,* which leave from Real between Tarapacá and Angaraes Streets. The 3.5-hour trip costs US$6. **Empresa Huáscar,** at Ancash and Angaraes, has several buses (US$4) a day for the 4.5-hour ride to Huancavelica.

With the Carretera Central running through Huancayo, finding transport around the Mantary Valley is easy. All transportation to the north (Hualhuas, San Jerónimo, Concepción, Jauja, Sicaya) passes the corner of Giráldez and Huancas. Transportation to the south passes the nearby corner of Ferrocarril and Giráldez.

THE MANTARO VALLEY

The Mantaro Valley is filled with ruins, churches, and, most important, entire villages that specialize in one type of handicraft. With an early start, it is easy to take public transportation and visit these towns on your own—many of the better artisans are now marked by yellow signs.

A spectacular way to walk between towns, and have a picnic lunch on the way, is to follow the out-of-the-way paths that have been mapped out by Lucho Hurtado. If you go on your own, get recommendations ahead of time and avoid the *artesanía* stores in the entrances of the towns. The easiest way to tour workshops is with an organized tour.

◧ Hualhuas

This **weaving** town 20 minutes north of Huancayo produces tapestries, rugs, and clothing—mostly from hand-spun wool and natural dyes. The highest quality is found at **Victor Hugo Ingaroca Tupac Yupanqui** (Huancayo 315, Hualhuas, tel. 064/967-0462). His weavings, based on pre-Columbian techniques used by the Nasca and Paracas cultures, are stunning. His rugs sell for close to US$400 at www. novica.com but can be bought for a better price at his home.

Antonio Cáceres (28 de Julio 888, Hualhuas) produces more affordable weavings and is an expert on the natural plants, bugs, and minerals used to make his bright, natural dyes.

To see a busy workshop of weavers at their looms, stop at **Taller Ecotextil** (Alfonso Ugarte 1175, Hualhuas, tel. 064/67-0353, ecotextil@ hotmail.com). Production here is high volume and of a wide variety, with purses, ponchos, and rugs of various sizes and styles.

A mother-and-daughter team sell their weavings at affordable prices at **Artesenia El Inca** (Parque Principal 1046, Hualhuas).

To reach Hualhuas, catch a *combi* at the corner of Giráldez and Huancas in Huancayo (US$0.50, 20 minutes).

◧ Cochas Grande

Carved gourds (*mates burilados*) are an art form

the Mantaro Valley

© ANIBAL SOLIMANO, PROMPERU

from pre-Inca times that continues to thrive in Cochas Grande and Cochas Chico, a pair of towns tucked behind the hills a half hour east of Huancayo. These gourds are carved in mind-boggling detail and usually tell a story about country life. Common stories include courtship, marriage, and childbirth; planting, harvest, and celebration; or the process of building a home. Some even include current political commentary, and gourds carved during the 1980s are rife with images of the Shining Path.

Delia Poma (Huancayo 797, Cochas Grande, tel. 064/993-7722, deliapoma58@latinmail.com) is a national champion and one of Cocha's most talented carvers. Her gourds are considered collectors' pieces and range in price US$25–100, though less expensive ones are made by her husband.

Alejandro Hurtado and Victoria Janampa, another award-winning couple, operate **Artesania Hurtado** (Loreto 326, Cochas Chico, tel. 064/24-5045). They have a series of fine gourds but also less expensive Christmas ornaments, boxes, and bowls. This is an excellent place to learn about the various engraving techniques and to watch Alejandro and Victoria at work.

Teodosio Poma (Huancayo 504, tel. 064/993-0170) specializes in large gourds, ranging in price US$80–500.

To reach Cochas, take a bus from the corner of Giráldez and Huancas in Huancayo (US$0.50, 30 minutes).

San Jerónimo de Tunán

This village 13 kilometers north of Huancayo is known for silver filigree. It is fascinating to watch **Jesús Suarez Vasquez** and his sister **Nelly Vasquez** (Arequipa 496, three blocks east of Plaza de Armas) make their delicate silver jewelry. A necklace that sells for US$16 in Lima can be bought here for US$6. Wednesday mornings are a good day to visit San Jerónimo, to catch the weekly market. There are many stores down the road and, on the main square, a beautiful 17th-century church with a baroque altar.

Other lesser crafts centers in the valley include **San Augustin de Cajas,** known for its

THE ART OF NATURAL DYES

Weavers in Hualhuas are keeping alive a tradition of making the unmistakably vibrant natural dyes that were pioneered by pre-Inca cultures such as Nasca and Paracas. The dyes are made by grinding up roots, leaves, flowers, fruits, vegetables, minerals, and even bugs. Some of these are seasonal, so certain dyes are only available during certain times of the year. After the dye is made, hand-spun wool is soaked in the color, then fixed with minerals and hung to dry. Here are a few of the sources for the natural dyes:

© RENÉE DEL GAUDIO AND ROSS WEHNER

- **Yellow:** crushed lichen

- **Reds and pinks:** extracted from *cochinilla,* a parasite that lives in the prickly pear cactus

- **Green:** chilca plant

- **Brown:** walnuts

- **Copper:** onion

wool hats; **Molinos,** near Jauja, which makes wood carvings including masks and stools decorated with animal shapes; and **Aco,** a center of ceramics. The best time to visit Aco is during its early Friday morning market, when ceramics wholesalers from all over the country snatch up pots and other goods for cheap.

Santa Rosa de Ocopa and Ingenio Trout Farm

There is a lot to see at Santa Rosa de Ocopa (9 A.M.–noon and 3–6 P.M. Wed.–Mon., US$1.25), a San Francisco convent founded in 1723 that is near Concepción, or about 25 kilometers northwest of Huancayo. As evangelical churches have grown, Santa Rosa has withered, and now only six monks are left. But the story behind Santa Rosa is fascinating. Franciscan missionaries embarked from here to proselytize in the Amazon jungle, and 86 were killed in the process, according to a commemorative plaque inside.

Baroque altars adorn the chapel, and it is

usually possible to descend into the catacombs. The newer convent building has a museum with stuffed jungle animals, paintings from the Cusco school, and gruesome paintings of missionaries being tortured by Amazon natives. The highlight of the convent, however, is a library that contains more than 25,000 volumes from the 15th century onward. The oldest book in the library, published in 1497, is St. Augustine's reflections on the Bible (the convent used to have a 1454 catechism in Aymara, Quechua, and Spanish, but it was stolen in a 2002 armed robbery, along with a painting from the Flemish School). The original adobe cloisters include a stone courtyard, a metal shop, and other rooms.

The best lunch spot nearby is Ingenio, home to Peru's largest fish farms, which produce approximately 50,000 kilograms of trout per year. Most visitors tour the state-owned trout farm before sitting down to lunch at either Ávila or Llao Llao, small restaurants that serve trout heaped with local artichokes. Afterwards there is a pleasant, hour-long walk up a dirt road alongside the river to a set of waterfalls.

Most Huancayo agencies visit Ingenio and Santa Rosa as part of a Mantaro Valley tour, though it is easy to arrive at both places via public transport. *Combis* for Concepción leave every 30–40 minutes (US$0.80) from Pachitea in Huancayo. In Concepción, there are nearby *colectivos* and *combis* that head to both Ingenio and Santa Rosa de Ocopa.

Jauja and Laguna Paca

Peru's first capital is 45 minutes, or 40 kilometers, northwest of Huancayo on the highway from Lima. It is an alternative base for exploring the valley but has few services. Few travelers come to this bustling, friendly town of old adobe homes and colonial churches. The main church, **Iglesia de Jauja,** was the first church Francisco Pizarro ordered to be built. Inside are a few finely carved wooden altars. Built in the 1920s, **La Iglesia del Cristo Pobre** is based on the chapel of France's Notre Dame. This church was the first building constructed of cement in the Mantaro Valley.

Lodging options include the excellent **Hostal Manco Cápac** (Manco Cápac 575, tel. 064/36-1620, www.hostal-mancoca-pac.com, US$15 s US$30 d), run by Bruno Bonierbale, and **Cabezon's Hostal** (Ayacucho 1027, tel. 064/36-2206, US$5 s), with shared bathrooms.

From Jauja there are US$0.50 *motocars* to Laguna Paca, the shores of which have been unfortunately marred by a line of cheap restaurants. A quick boat ride to the Isla de Amor, a tiny island in the middle of the lake, offers good views of Xauxa ruins on a nearby ridge and the mountains to the west. A good walk leads up from the lake to these and other Inca ruins in the area and passes through the villages of Acolla, Marco, and Tragadero. This is a good walk for those who want to spend the day walking through country and tracking down rarely visited ruins. The walk ends at a smaller, upper lake near a road where *combis* return to Jauja. A shorter hike is possible to Tunanmarca, the old city near Jauja. The trail starts in the town of Concho and takes about 2.5 hours. Maps of these walks are available from Lucho Hurtado. Cars to Jauja (US$0.90) and many other places leave from Calixto Street in Huancayo.

Huariwilca

These ruins from the Huanca and Huari cultures are six kilometers south of Huancayo. The ruins are located below the plaza of the village of Huari, which is next to Río Chancas. The ceremonial center includes a high wall, staircase, interior passageways, and two huge *molle* trees. Huariwilca means "sacred place of the Huari," the Ayacucho-based culture that spread throughout Peru's highlands between A.D. 700 and 1200. The nearby museum (8 A.M.–1 P.M. and 3–6 P.M. Tues.–Sun., US$0.50) includes many pre-Inca artifacts found at the site, including spondylus shells imported from Ecuador, ceramics, metalworks, and a female mummy, found at the site, known as **The Maiden of Huariwilca.** To get to the ruins, near the town of Huari, take a blue-and-white bus to Huari from the corner of Giráldez and Ferrocarril in Huancayo.

HUANCAVELICA

Huancavelica, at 3,680 meters, was a rich and world-famous mining town during colonial times. It withered into a ghost town during the last few centuries and was badly battered by the war against Sendero Luminoso. Though the town is trying to make a comeback, the chief reason for coming here these days is to wander around colonial churches and homes and get away from tourists.

The city was founded shortly after the nearby Santa Barbara mercury mine was opened in 1563. Mercury was invaluable for extracting purer grades of silver from the ore extracted at Potosí, Bolivia. As a result, Huancavelica and Ayacucho—where the owners of the Santa Barbara mine lived—exploded into the viceroyalty's richest mining towns. From here, caravans of mules and llamas carried the mercury in leather pouches to the Peruvian coast, where it was shipped to Arica, Chile, and transported into Bolivia.

Sights

There are eight colonial churches in tiny Huancavelica. The **Plaza de Armas,** bordered by the cathedral, town hall, and some colonial homes, features a granite fountain installed in the mid-19th century. The cathedral itself has a good collection of colonial paintings and a magnificent baroque altar and pulpit. The churches of **San Sebastían** (1662) and **San Francisco** (1774), in Plaza Bolognesi, are worth seeing for their collections of baroque art. The best time to find these churches open is during early-morning mass or on Sundays, when there is an excellent market along Torre Tagle that draws villagers from all over the surrounding countryside.

The **San Cristóbal Mineral Springs** (5 A.M.–5 P.M. daily, US$0.50), 10 minutes northwest of the city, have a great reputation for curing skin diseases, although they are more on the lukewarm side than hot. Ask at hotels for directions.

There are also good walks in the surrounding area, including the area around the Santa Barbara mine, which closed in the early 19th century.

Accommodations

Huancavelica's best hotel is **Hotel Presidente** (Plaza de Armas s/n, tel. 067/45-2760, www.hoteles-del-centro.com, US$42 s, US$56 d with breakfast), in a historic building on the Plaza de Armas. Prices quoted are for the executive rooms, which have been recently updated and have lots of hot water and cable TV. The hotel also has one of the city's better restaurants. Cheaper options include **Hotel Camacho** (Carabaya 481, tel. 067/45-3298, US$9 s, US$16 d), the town's best budget choice with clean rooms, decent mattresses, and lots of blankets. There is hot water in the morning only, and a few cheaper rooms with shared bathes. Another budget option is right on the Plaza de Armas: **Hotel Ascención** (Manco Cápac 481, tel. 067/45-3103, US$11 s, US$18 d). Check on hot water before paying for the room.

Food

Good restaurants are hard to find in Huancavelica. The best is probably in the **Hotel Presidente** (Plaza de Armas, tel. 067/45-2760, 7 A.M.–3 P.M. and 6–10 P.M. daily, US$4–6), which serves up *chifa,* trout, and a few chicken and beef dishes.

The best regional food is served at **Los Portales** (Virrey Toledo 158) and **Paquirri** (Arequipa 137).

Information and Services

The **national police** (tel. 067/45-2729) are on Huayna Cápac. For health emergencies, **Hospital Essalud** (Teresa Jornet s/n, tel. 064/45-3077) is in Barrio de Yananaco. The best pharmacies are **Salud** (Arequipa 145) and **Imaculada** (Virrey Toledo 276). For money matters, there is **Banco de la Nación** (Escalonada 127) and **Banco de Crédito** (Virrey Toledo 383). The post office, Serpost (Ferrúa 105), is in Barrio Santa Ana. Internet is available at **Ccoyllor** (Manchego Muñoz 488) and **Yomax** (Manchego Muñoz s/n). There are phone booths at Carabaya and Virrey Toledo.

Getting There and Around

Cargo trains travel daily between Huancavelica and Huancayo at 6:30 A.M. and sometimes at 12:30 P.M. as well. The five-hour ride is only US$4 and offers breathtaking views. Most locals travel the rough road to Huancayo via *colectivos* (US$6, 3.5 hours), which leave from the Plaza de Armas throughout the day. The best bus company for the route is **Empresa Ticllas** (US$4, 4.5 hours).

From Huancavelica buses from Empresa Ticllas and other companies also head west on dirt roads over the 4,800-meter Chonta pass, past a series of beautiful lakes and down to Pisco and the Paracas marine reserve on the Pacific coast.

Empresa Ticllas also runs buses on the complicated, rough route toward Ayacucho. An easier option is to take local transport to the town of Santa Inés, which is on the paved Pisco–Ayacucho highway. From there, wait for an Ayacucho-bound bus.

CENTRAL HIGHLANDS

Ayacucho and Vicinity

It is easy to understand why Peruvians are so fond of Ayacucho. This hidden jewel of Peru's southern Andes has Renaissance and baroque churches around every corner (33 in all!), its elaborate Easter week celebration is second only to that of Seville, and the one-of-a-kind Huari and Inca ruins are in the surrounding countryside. Ayacucho is colonial enough to seem like a time warp. At dawn, townsfolk stream into churches to listen to mass. In the nearby market, campesinas in big straw hats and colorful hand-knit skirts serve up lunch: *puca picante* (a spicy red stew of chili, pork cracklings, crushed peanuts, and potatoes), sheep's head soup, and about 10 varieties of *chicha*. Quechua is spoken everywhere in the soft, swishing sounds of the local dialect.

Ayacucho is known as one of Peru's most artistic towns. Some of the country's best *huayno* singers come from here, along with world-famous harp player Florencio Coronado and the guitarist Raúl García Zárate. Nearly every man knows how to play guitar—an essential skill for evening serenades—and artisans around the city produce ceramics, weavings, miniature altars, and stone carvings in alabaster, the local stone known as *piedra de huamanga*. At 2,761 meters above sea level, the city has one of the best climates in all of the country—the dry landscape, scattered with cactus and agave, receives only short, if hard, storms in the rainy season December–March. There are sunny skies and warm temperatures the rest of the year.

Ayacucho was a dangerous place to visit in the 1980s and early 1990s. The Shining Path, or Sendero Luminoso, was founded here by Abimael Guzmán, a philosophy professor from Arequipa who came to work at the local university. His movement, based on Maoist philosophy, fought an 11-year civil war that claimed the lives of 70,000 people across the country. The fighting was most intense around Ayacucho, where both guerillas and army soldiers terrorized local villages and caused a widespread migration to cities.

Ayacucho has been a safe place to visit since Guzmán's arrest in 1992 and the subsequent disintegration of the Shining Path. The U.S. Embassy has taken Ayacucho off its travel advisory. But, apart from April and Semana Santa, only 500 foreign travelers arrive in Ayacucho each month—as opposed to 45,000 per month in Cusco—mostly because Ayacucho is isolated by rough highways and lack of a plane connection to Cusco.

HISTORY

Ayacucho was the seat of the Huari empire, which spread across Peru A.D. 700–1200 and built many of the highways, cities, and fine stone buildings that made the Inca empire possible. Their capital, also named Huari, is 2,000 hectares of stone ruins that continue to yield clues about this mysterious empire. Between A.D. 900 and 1200 the Huari empire was probably conquered by the rebellious Chancas, who in turn yielded to the Inca in the mid-15th century.

After the Spaniards arrived, Inca forces retreated to the nearby jungle of Vilcabamba and would sporadically attack passengers on the main road that linked Lima, Cusco, and Potosí, in present-day Bolivia. Ayacucho was founded in 1539 (only three years after Lima) as a base for defending travelers on this route and soon thereafter became the home of Spanish families involved with the Santa Barbara mercury mine in Huancavelica. Money from this mine—which supplied the mercury critical for extracting silver in the mines of Potosi—financed a huge building campaign in the city, with rich families building entire churches and often competing for the most lavish altars.

Ayacucho, still referred to today by its more ancient name of Huamanga, is also known for a series of bloody battles in Spanish times—its name in Quechua means "corner of death." It was here that Peru's new viceroy, Cristobal Vaca de Castro, brought peace to the colony by defeating the rebel Almagrista forces at the Battle

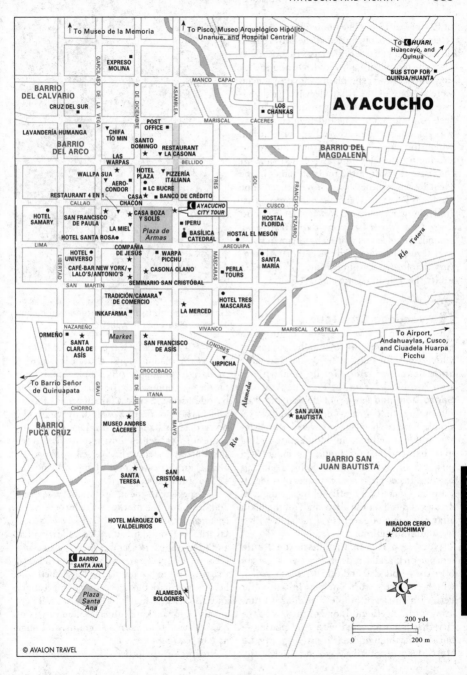

To Museo de la Memoria

To Pisco, Museo Arquelógico Hipólito Unanue, and Hospital Central

To CHUARI, Huancayo, and Quinua

BUS STOP FOR QUINUA/HUANTA

AYACUCHO

EXPRESO MOLINA

GARCILASO DE LA VEGA

9 DE DICIEMBRE

ASAMBLEA

MANCO CAPAC

LOS CHANKAS

BARRIO DEL CALVARIO

CRUZ DEL SUR

MARISCAL CÁCERES

LAVANDERÍA HUMANGA

BARRIO DEL ARCO

CHIFA TÍO MIN

POST OFFICE

SANTO DOMINGO

RESTAURANT LA CASONA

BARRIO DEL MAGDALENA

LAS WARPAS

BELLIDO

WALLPA SUA

HOTEL PLAZA

PIZZERÍA ITALIANA

TRES

SOL

FRANCISCO PIZARRO

AERO-CONDOR

LC BUCRE

RESTAURANT 4 EN 1

CASA CHACÓN

BANCO DE CRÉDITO

CALLAO

CUSCO

HOTEL SAMARY

SAN FRANCISCO DE PAULA

CASA BOZA Y SOLÍS

AYACUCHO CITY TOUR

HOSTAL FLORIDA

LA MIEL

Plaza de Armas

IPERU

BASÍLICA CATEDRAL

HOSTAL EL MESÓN

HOTEL SANTA ROSA

LIMA

COMPAÑÍA DE JESÚS

AREQUIPA

LIBERTAD

HOTEL UNIVERSO

WARPA PICCHU

MASCARAS

SANTA MARÍA

CAFÉ-BAR NEW YORK/ LALO'S/ANTONIO'S

CASONA OLANO

PERLA TOURS

SAN MARTÍN

SEMINARIO SAN CRISTÓBAL

TRADICIÓN/CAMARA DE COMERCIO

HOTEL TRES MASCARAS

INKAFARMA

LA MERCED

NAZAREÑO

VIVANCO

MARISCAL CASTILLA

ORMEÑO

Market

SAN FRANCISCO DE ASÍS

To Airport, Andahuaylas, Cusco, and Ciuadela Huarpa Picchu

SANTA CLARA DE ASÍS

LONDRES

GRAU

28 DE JULIO

CROCOBADO

URPICHA

2 DE MAYO

Alameda

To Barrio Señor de Quinuapata

ITANA

CHORRO

BARRIO PUCA CRUZ

MUSEO ANDRES CÁCERES

Río

SAN JUAN BAUTISTA

BARRIO SAN JUAN BAUTISTA

SANTA TERESA

SAN CRISTÓBAL

HOTEL MÁRQUEZ DE VALDELIRIOS

MIRADOR CERRO ACUCHIMAY

BARRIO SANTA ANA

Plaza Santa Ana

ALAMEDA BOLOGNESI

0   200 yds

0   200 m

© AVALON TRAVEL

of Chupas in 1542. The bodies of the slain officers were probably buried at the tiny Templo de San Cristobal, one of the city's first churches after the temple of La Merced. During the independence wars, the plains above Ayacucho were the site of the final, decisive battle between the Spanish and the patriot forces led by José Antonio Sucre. The independence treaty was signed in the nearby village of Quinua, which today is a Quechuan town known for producing the clay houses—called *casas de quinua*—that adorn the roofs of homes in the area. Recent studies have proven that Felipe Guamán Poma de Ayala, one of America's first Indian writers, was from Ayacucho. He is most known for *Nueva Crónica y Buen Gobierno,* a compilation of letters written by Guamán Poma over several years toward the end of 17th century that form a scathing critique of repression under the Toledo viceroyalty, 1569–1581.

SIGHTS
Ayacucho City Tour

An Ayacucho city walking tour begins with an early-morning visit to churches—most of which open for mass at 6:30 A.M. and close an hour or two later. Get up at dawn and start two blocks from the Plaza de Armas at **Santo Domingo** (corner of Bellido and 9 de Diciembre, 6:30–7 A.M. daily), which has a simple Renaissance facade covered with a bizarre column-and-balcony addition. According to local legend, Spanish Inquisition judges held public trials and hung their victims from this balcony. Inside are several examples of Andean-Catholic syncretism: Profiles of Inca with headdresses abound on the altars and, on the main altar, the eagle of San Juan is replaced with a local hummingbird.

Next stop is **San Francisco de Paula** (corner of Garcilaso de la Vega and Callao, 6:15 A.M.–7:30 A.M. and 6:15–7:30 P.M. daily), which competes with San Blas in Cusco for Peru's finest carved pulpit. The altar is brimming with angels and is one of the few in the city that is not covered with gold plating—but the Nicaraguan cedar is just as pretty. **La Merced** (corner of 2 de Mayo and San Martin,

© RENÉE DEL GAUDIO AND ROSS WEHNER

Santo Domingo is one of 33 Renaissance and baroque churches in Ayacucho.

6:15–7:30 A.M. daily) was constructed in 1542 and is the second oldest church in town. A mark of its antiquity is its simple Renaissance facade—as opposed to the later, more effusive baroque style. **Santa Clara** (corner of Grau and Nazareño, 6:30–8 A.M. daily) holds the revered Jesus of Nazareth image that is the center of Ayacucho's most important procession during Easter week. The ceiling above the altar is an intricate wood filigree of Mudejar, or Spanish-Arabic, design.

On the way to the next church, cross Grau and head into the **market,** which is clean, relaxed, and full of local foods. *Pan chapla,* a local favorite, is a round bread with a hollow center, and from August to October there is also *wawa* ("baby" in Quechua), an infant-shaped bread that is meant to be consolation for women who became pregnant during Carnaval in February and also used as a gift for godparents. There are also large rocks of mineral salt, a variety of *chichas* made from corn and grains, and huge pots of *puca picante.*

Emerge on the other side to a huge, rust-colored arch next to **San Francisco de Asís** (corner of 28 de Julio and Vivanco, 6:30 A.M.–8:30 A.M. Mon.–Sat., 6:30–10:30 A.M. Sun.), a Renaissance church built in 1552. Next door is the related convent, open to visitors only via prior arrangement, which contains one of the country's finest collections of colonial paintings.

The final stop is the **Compañía de Jesús** (28 de Julio between Lima and San Martin, 9:30 A.M.–12:30 P.M.), the Jesuit church built in 1605 with a facade of sculpted flowers. Next door was the Jesuit College, now the Seminario San Cristobal, where Indian children were taught music, Latin, painting, and wood carving until the Jesuits were kicked out of Latin America in 1767. A large international grant, interestingly, once again trained local kids to restore the building. Stop here to have breakfast at one of the cafés and shop at the stores, which are slowly paying back the costs of the restoration.

After breakfast, head down 28 de Julio to the **colonial home and museum of Andres Cáceres** (28 de Julio 508, tel. 066/83-6166, 9 A.M.–1 P.M. and 3–6 P.M. Mon.–Sat., US$0.75), Peru's top general during the War of the Pacific, who moved troops so quickly through the mountains that he was known as the Wizard of the Andes. The home, part of which is now a museum, contains his letters, photos, travel desk, weapons, etc., and has an excellent (and unrelated) collection of baroque paintings, alabaster stone carvings, and *petacas,* the elaborate burro satchels used by missionaries.

Go one block down from the Andres Cáceres home to **Santa Teresa** (28 de Julio, 6:30–7:30 A.M. daily), the church and Carmelite monastery where nuns remain cloistered today. The nuns make *mazapan, turrones,* and *agua de agráas* (a *chicha* made from local flowers), sold in the convent's foyer. By knocking on the door, visitors often gain admission here during the day to see the baroque altar and a painting of the Last Supper where Jesus is seated before a roasted guinea pig. If admitted after hours, visitors should leave a small donation as a courtesy.

Farther down the street is **San Cristóbal** (1540), the city's oldest chapel, which is rarely open, and the pleasant promenade known as **Alameda Bolognesi.** From here, walk uphill on steep streets to **Barrio Santa Ana,** a neighborhood with a small-town feel, and the **Iglesia Santa Ana,** referred to commonly as the Iglesia de los Indios because of the various ethnicities the Spanish brought here in the 16th century to serve as a buffer against the attacking Inca. Working in the streets around the plaza are some of Peru's most famous weavers, who have exhibited their work all over the world.

Ayacucho's elegant **Plaza de Armas** is bordered by the cathedral and university on one side and continuous stone arcades on the others. The best time to visit the cathedral, which was completed in 1672, is in the evening 5:30–7 P.M., when its huge interior is illuminated. There are two interesting examples of Andean-Spanish fusion: San Juan's eagle is replaced by a condor on top of the dome's columns, and the sacred half moon of Andean cosmology is at the foot of the Virgin Mary.

Next to the cathedral is **La Universidad San Cristóbal de Huamanga,** which was founded in 1677 but went bankrupt and closed two centuries later during the War of the Pacific with Chile. The university was reopened in 1959.

Around 1969 the Velasco government expropriated many of the colonial mansions around the main square, forcing their families to vacate, and resold them to banks. **Casa Boza y Solís** (Portal Constitución, Plaza de Armas, 8 A.M.–6 P.M. Mon.–Fri., free) today houses government offices and stands out for its massive stone arcade and Italian tiles decorating an original stone fountain, staircase, and second floor. The Banco de Crédito occupies the **Casona del Canonigo Frías** (Plaza de Armas, 10 A.M.–6 P.M. Mon.–Sat.). The rooms of this colonial mansion have been converted into the highly worthwhile **Museo de Arte Popular** (10:15 A.M.–5:30 P.M. Tues.–Fri., 9:45 A.M.–12:15 P.M. Sat., free), a showcase for the extraordinary range of art produced locally. The Banco de la Nación occupies the **Casona**

Olano (28 de Julio, a half block from Plaza de Armas, 9 A.M.–5 P.M. Mon.–Sat.).

The **Museo Arqueológico Hipólito Unanue** (Independencia, 1 km outside town, 8:30 A.M.–1 P.M. and 3–5 P.M. Mon.–Sat.) has a range of objects from the Warpa, Huari, and Chanca pre-Inca cultures: ceramics, weavings, turquoise jewelry, and seven priest monoliths carved out of volcanic stone. Plus, there is a botanical garden next door with more than 120 kinds of regional cacti.

Similarly on the outskirts of town is **El Museo de la Memoria** (Prolongación Libertad 1229, tel. 066/31-7170, 9 A.M.–1 P.M. and 3–6 P.M. Mon.–Sat.), which, although small and in Spanish, does a good job of showing the multisided issues of the terrorism era.

A beautiful view of Ayachucho can be had from the top of **Cerro Acuchimay,** which can be reached by taxi (US$2) and then descended via a long staircase that ends at the Plaza San Juan Bautista, near Londres Street. Do this walk during the day only.

C Huari

There are three worthwhile sites to the north of Ayacucho that can be seen in one (very full) day. Huari (22 km from Ayacucho, 8 A.M.–6 P.M. daily, US$0.75) is the sprawling capital of the same-named empire. Much of the city, which sprawled over 2,000 hectares (4,940 acres), has been buried by drifting sands. The ruins are badly deteriorated and largely unexcavated, but what can be seen today, about 10 percent of the original city, includes huge complexes of walls up to 12 meters high.

The best place to start a visit is at the onsite museum, which lies on the road between Ayacucho and Quinua and contains a stone monolith, ceramics, and a few useful historical charts. A short walk away lies the ceremonial center of Monqachayoc, which has an enigmatic half-moon shape. It appears to be a calendar, because it faces exactly north and contains 18 niches, which is a strange link to Mayan calendars in the Yucatán Peninsula of present-day Mexico. Holes, were stone cylinders once stood, were found nearby and were

probably used for casting shadows onto the niches. Nearby are a few unexcavated pyramids, covered with prickly pear cactus, and a huge stone table where sacrifices were probably made. Archaeologists believe the umbrella-shaped *paty* trees were used in a potion that prevented blood from coagulating during sacrifice ceremonies—a trick the Huari may have learned from the Moche in Peru's north.

A tunnel, closed to visitors, leads underground 50 meters from the ceremonial area to a labyrinth of funerary chambers that was excavated in 1997 and leads an astonishing 19 meters below ground—the hidden level underground is apparently built in the shape of a llama.

Another interesting area, called Cheqo Wasi, lies a half kilometer farther up the road and includes more funerary chambers, some of which are constructed of 1.5-ton rock slabs. The joints between the rocks are perfectly smooth and rival later Inca stonework. One theory holds that the Huari used these fortified chambers to store, and guard, both their own mummies and those of the cultures they conquered. Like the Inca, the Huari worshipped their ancestors' mummies as a source of power and displayed them in public during sacred festivals.

Quinua

Another 15 kilometers up the road lies Quinua, a pleasant Quechuan village 37 kilometers outside Ayacucho, which is known for its *iglesias de Quinua,* miniature clay churches that are placed on the roofs of homes to bring good luck. There are other hand-shaped ceramics as well, all in the region's red clay and bright mineral paint, ranging from religious images to more humorous depictions of musicians and drunken men. This remarkable town of cobblestone streets, adobe houses, and colonial church has a few good restaurants and a few basic rooms for rent at the Hotel Qenwa. The owner is Quinua's longtime, and somewhat controversial, leader, who headed up the town's militia against the Shining Path—an 11-year battle that forced much of the town's population to flee for Ayacucho or Lima.

THE HUARI: PERU'S FIRST EMPIRE BUILDERS

Partly because the Inca (and the Spanish) consolidated power by erasing past history, the Huari's role in Peruvian history has until recently been vastly underestimated. Archaeologists are still trying to explain the rise of the Huari, whose complex, polychromatic ceramics began to replace the simple, two-color pots of Ayacucho's Huarpa culture around A.D. 500. The Huarpa were one of southern Peru's early cultures, along with the Nasca on the coast and the Tiahuanaco at Lake Titicaca. The Huari appear to have grown out of all three, combining their different technologies and religious beliefs into a more powerful combination. But many of their beliefs stretch even further back in time – Huari ceramics repeatedly portray a staff-wielding warrior deity, apparently the same worshipped by the much earlier Chavín culture (1200–300 B.C.) in Peru's northern mountains.

Jokingly referred to as the Mormons of the Andes, the Huari built their empire by persistent evangelization, not by force. By A.D. 700 they had spread as far north as the Moche capital near present-day Trujillo, and images of the Moche decapitator god, Ai-Apaec, begin to appear on Huari ceramics. At the height of the Huari empire, around A.D. 900, the capital near present-day Ayacucho covered 300 hectares (740 acres) and sustained a population of anywhere from 10,000 to 70,000. The empire was connected by good roads and stretched from Arequipa in the south to Chiclayo in the north. The Huari did beautiful work in bronze, silver, lapis lazuli, and gold, made architectural models for all of their new buildings, and produced weavings with as many as 250 threads per square inch.

The Huari literally paved the way for the Inca. They were the first to base their empire on large cities – and not just ceremonial centers used during festival times. Their transnational roads and advanced stone-carving techniques formed the foundation upon which the Inca empire was built. Other traditions passed on to the Inca include mummy worship and the use of *quipus*, which were bundles of brightly colored strings with elaborate knots tied in them. Ethnohistorians will probably never decipher exactly what information was catalogued by the elaborate knots and different colors of thread.

Like the Huns invading Rome, a weakening Huari state was invaded by less civilized rebel groups, probably the fierce Chancas from the Huancavelica area. Sometime between A.D. 1000 and 1200 the empire collapsed – perhaps overnight. At the capital city of Huari, some of the tunnels leading into the underground funerary chambers appear to have been hastily blocked – an effort perhaps to protect the sacred mummies. Today the city of Huari, 22 kilometers outside of Ayacucho, remains largely unexcavated – most of the ruins have been literally covered by the sands of time.

Pampa de Ayacucho

A short walk uphill from Quinua is the Pampa de Ayacucho, the broad plain where Spanish and patriot troops clashed on December 9, 1824, in the final battle of South America's independence. This is one of Peru's three historical sanctuaries, along with Machu Picchu and the other independence battlefield at Junín. Above the plain rises Cerro Condorccuncca, where the Spanish force of 9,300 soldiers were led by Viceroy José de la Serna. On the plain below, 5,800 patriot soldiers from all over South America and Europe were led by General Antonio José de Sucre—not Simón Bolívar as is commonly believed (Bolívar was in Lima at the time). The battle began at 10 A.M. after relatives and friends on opposing sides were allowed to greet each other. After a series of tactical mistakes by the Spanish, the patriots pushed downhill and won the battle after three hours of grueling, mostly hand-to-hand fighting. By 1 P.M., the patriots had lost 300 men and the Spanish 1,700.

A post-battle peace treaty was signed in a room on Quinua's plaza—now glassed off for public viewing in the Casa de la

Capitulación—while the wounded were being treated in the town's church. Today the battlefield is marked with a stone obelisk, 44 meters tall in recognition of the 44 years between this battle and Túpac Amaru II's indigenous rebellion against the Spanish in 1780. There is a recommended two- to four-hour walk between Quinua and Huari that includes good views and interesting countryside. Ask in Quinua for the start of the well-marked path.

An agency day tour to Huari and Quinua usually includes the **Pikimachay Cave,** a few kilometers past the turnoff to Quinua on the road to Huanta. Some agencies also continue on through a striking desert valley, known for its production of avocados and *lúcuma* fruit, to visit villagers and take a hike up the nearby mirador of Huatuscalla.

Buses from Ayacucho to Quinua can be taken at Salvador Cavero 124, next to El Niño Restaurant on the northeast edge of town. *Combis* leave when full (US$1, 1.5 hours). If taking public transport, visit Huari on your trip out and then continue on to Quinua—*combis*

passing Huari in the afternoon on their way to Ayacucho are usually full, making it hard to get home.

Wilcashuamán and Laguna Pumaqocha

After Cusco, Peru's most important Inca city is Wilcashuamán, the administrative center founded by Inca Pachacútec after the defeat of the Chanca. The present village of Wilcashuamán, site of horrific massacres during the Shining Path revolution, is built entirely on Inca ruins. There are the ruins of a fine sun temple, on top of which is the colonial church of San Juan Bautista with its carvings of serpents, monkeys, and pumas. According to the chronicler Pedro Cieza de León, this three-level sun temple was decorated inside with sheets of silver and gold, along with another, now disappeared, moon temple.

A block away is an *ushno,* a four-level Inca pyramid that can be found nowhere else in Peru and is the main reason for making the Wilcashuamán trek. A trapezoidal doorway

© CARLOS SALA, PROMPERU

At Wilcashuamán, an Inca administrative center outside of Ayacucho, the Spanish leveled the Inca sun temple and used it as a foundation for a Catholic church.

and stairs lead to the upper platform, where the throne with two seats was probably used by the Inca administrator and his wife (*coya*). This *ushno* originally had a clear view of the temples through a single, gigantic plaza and is surrounded by three sacred mountains (*apus*). Consequently, it is not surprising perhaps that President Fujimori often brought TV cameras to this place to make important announcements. The festival of the sun, or **Vilcas Raymi,** is celebrated here during the July 28 weekend, but lodging is almost nonexistent.

On the way to Wilcashuamán, it is possible to see Laguna Pumaqocha, a spectacular lake located up a side road four kilometers before the town of **Vischongo.** The detour from the main road takes about 10 minutes by car or half an hour walking. There are semiburied Inca constructions around this sacred lake, fine walls, and a bath that features a seven-sided rock with twin water chutes.

Puya raimondii, a gigantic agave-like plant that shoots up a 15-meter flower stalk only once at the end of its life (at about 100 years old), can be seen on the high plains before Wilcashuamán. Titankayoq, the largest forest of these plants in the world, sprawls across 440 hectares, a two-hour uphill walk from the village of Vischongo. Between August and September there is always a *Puya raimondii* in bloom—a rare and beautiful sight.

Combis to Wilcashuamán leave from the main bus station for the bumpy five-hour ride. There is no lodging in Vischongo, but Wilcashuamán has several options, the best of which is **Willka Waman** (US$5 s, US$7 d, with private bath). A private car and driver to Wilcashuamán can be rented for US$100 for a one-day round-trip, but the best, and easiest, way is to go with an agency. This way you can visit Lago Pumaqocha and Wilcashuamán, along with the *Puya raimondii* along the way, in a single day.

ENTERTAINMENT AND EVENTS

Discotheques come and go quickly in Ayacucho, but **Puka's** (Cusco 246, evenings

Ayacucho's elaborate Danza de Tijeras (Dances of the Scissors)

© MICHAEL TWEDDLE, PROMPERU

only) is for the moment packed on weekends. The best *peña* is **Los Balcones** (Asamblea 187, 2nd Fl.), which is a disco Tuesday–Thursday and a *peña* on Fridays and Saturdays. **Los Warpas** (Mariscal Cáceres 1033, tel. 066/31-5559) has a good *peña* on Friday and Saturday nights (don't eat here, though). A good bar is **Magia Negra** (9 de Diciembre 293, tel. 066/960-5644, 7 P.M. onward Tues.–Sun.), and an evenings-only pool hall operates on the corner of Bellido and Garcilazo. A small cinema on the Plaza de Armas, near the corner of Cusco and Asamblea, shows movies and documentaries sporadically.

Ayacucho's **Easter week** is Peru's best-known religious festival. Other important festivals in Ayacucho include **Carnaval** (usually the last day of February), **Inti Raymi** in late June at Lago Pumaqocha, the **Virgin de Cocharcas** in Quinua September 8–11, the feast of **El Señor de Maynay** in Huanta in mid-September, and **Vilcas Raymi** at Wilcashuamán during the July 28 weekend.

EASTER WEEK IN AYACUCHO

© RENEE DEL GAUDIO AND ROSS WEHNER

Ayacucho's Semana Santa

Peruvians regard Ayacucho's Semana Santa, or Easter week, as Peru's most beautiful and intense religious festival. For the 10 days leading up to Easter Sunday, Ayacucho becomes a city of flower-carpeted streets, solemn processions, fireworks, and wild partying. Religious processions throughout the week depict the various passions of Christ, and there are also art shows, folk dancing, music concerts, sporting events, livestock fairs, and traditional food contests. During the festival, lodging and bus tickets triple in price and are often sold out, so book in advance. The tourist office publishes an annual brochure, and information may be available at www.ayacuchocompetitivo.org.pe.

The principal events begin on the Friday before Palm Sunday, when the first religious procession starts from the Iglesia Magdalena.

Palm Sunday itself has two important celebrations. At noon there is a huge caravan of mules and llamas carrying dried *retama* (broom) flowers and accompanied by several orchestras. After processing around the plaza twice, the *retama* is unloaded, to be burned during all important religious ceremonies. At 4 P.M., Christ, on a white mule, leaves from the Carmelite monastery of Santa Teresa, along with crowds of people carrying golden palm fronds, and proceeds around the plaza to the cathedral.

The most sacred, and intense, ceremony of the week occurs on Wednesday, when the Plaza de Armas becomes a stage for the allegorical meeting of Jesus of Nazareth and the Virgin Mary. During this mystic ceremony, the images are carried on their thrones as townspeople, many in tears, watch. Because most visitors arrive the following day, there are mostly Ayacuchanos at this event.

Friday night is a candlelit procession of the deceased Jesus and the Virgin Mary, during which all the lights in the city are turned off.

On Saturday morning, a bull is released every half hour from 11 A.M. onward from the Alameda Bolognesi. Surrounded by shouting kids, some of whom are injured each year, a total of six bulls run through a cordoned-off area of town. People party in the Plaza de Armas until late in the night with dancing and orchestras.

At 5 A.M. on Sunday, before dawn, El Señor de la Resurreción (the resurrected Christ) is carried out of the cathedral atop a huge white pyramid adorned with 3,000 candles. As many as 250 people carry the pyramid, which goes around the plaza until 7 A.M., amid ringing bells, fireworks, and smoke from the last bit of burning *retama*.

SHOPPING
(Barrio Santa Ana

A short walk above Ayacucho is the Barrio Santa Ana, a quirky neighborhood with cobblestone streets that is filled with an amazing variety of crafts workshops. At the center of it all is the Plazuela Santa Ana, which is graced with the colonial **Iglesia Santa Ana de los Indios** and lined with artisan studios.

At **Galería Latina** (Plazuela de Santa Ana 107 and Plazoleta 605-A, tel. 066/31-2516 or 066/31-1215, Huari39@hotmail.com), Alejandro and Alexander Gallardo are the third and fourth generation of weavers in their family and produce exquisite tapestries based on Huari designs. The Gallardo family makes its own natural dyes and produces only a few dozen rugs per year, which are mostly sold to galleries in Europe and the United States. Even if you are not buying (a 1.2-by-1.6-meter rug costs US$250–350 here, three times that overseas), the weaving demonstration is fascinating.

Locals also highly recommend the weavings of **Chrisantino Montes.** His production is small, and exclusively of naturally dyed pure alpaca wool. Prices are similar to those of the Gallardos. Ask around Barrio Santa Ana for directions to his workshop.

Alfonso Sulca Chavez (Plazuela de Santa Ana 83, tel. 066/31-2990) is another highly skilled weaver whose designs are a free interpretation of pre-Inca motifs in brilliant natural dyes. Next door is the Huaranca family, which focuses on animal and nature themes.

Though hard to transport, carvings in the local *piedra de huamanga* (alabaster) are made by **Julio Gálvez** (Jerusalén 12, Plazuela de Santa Ana, tel. 066/31-4278, edgard_galvez@yahoo.es).

For a good introduction of what crafts are produced in the Ayacucho area, visit the Museo de Arte Popular in the Banco de Crédito on Ayacucho's Plaza de Armas. Other crafts stores outside the Barrio Santa Ana include **Guitarras Flores** (Graud 676, Plaza Santa Teresa, 6 A.M.–8 P.M. daily), where the Lago family sells handmade guitars for US$70–115.

Brightly painted metal crosses, candelabras, and masks can be bought from **Ignacio and Victor Bautista,** a father-son team, at their store on Londres 235.

Especially beautiful are the brightly colored retablos, portable altars made of wood and plaster, which were once used by mule drivers to pray for a safe journey. The retablos usually have two opening doors that reveal a religious scene on top and a secular one on the bottom. Good places to buy these and other crafts are **Seminario San Cristobal** (Plaza Mayor), **Galeria Union** (Portal Union 25), **Galerias Artesanales Pascual** (corner of Cusco and Asamblea in Plazoleta San Agustín), and **Mercado Artesanal Shosaku Nagase** (Plazoleta María Parado de Bellido, Bellido and 9 de Diciembre).

The good place to buy ceramics is the town of Quinua, which is famous for miniature clay chapels known as *iglesias de Quinua* that are placed on the roofs of homes for good luck. Recommended ceramics workshops in Quinua include the Sánchez and Lima families and Galerias Limaco, all on the main street of Sucre.

RECREATION
Ayacucho has a variety of **mountain-biking** routes in the area, mapped out by Peruvian mountain bike champion George Scoffield and available from Warpa Picchu Eco-Aventura (Portal Independencia 65, Plaza de Armas, tel. 066/31-5191, verbist@terra.com.pe). There are also **river float** opportunities on the Río Pampa, although you need your own gear, as well as **treks** to waterfalls near Cangallo, a village reached by a branch highway on the Wilcashuamán route.

Tour Agencies and Guides
The best agency in Ayacucho is **Warpa Picchu Eco-Aventura** (Portal Independencia 65, Plaza de Armas, tel. 066/31-5191, verbist@terra.com.pe, 8 A.M.–8 P.M. Mon.–Sat.). Belgian owner Pierre Verbist conducts tours in French, English, and Dutch, and partner Carlos Altamirano is probably Ayacucho's most knowledgeable

CENTRAL HIGHLANDS

guide; he speaks Spanish and Quechua and has a good knowledge of English. For a group of two, the agency charges US$10 pp for a city tour, US$15 for Huari and Quinua, US$30 for Huari and Quinua plus a Huanta hike, US$33 for the waterfalls around Cangallo, and US$34 for Wilcashuamán. Verbist has also mapped out a series of interesting walks and mountain-biking routes in the area. His new pet project is four-wheel drive adventures in the surrounding hillsides.

Another recommended agency is **Perla Tours** (Tres Máscaras 200, tel. 066/31-4066, juan_perlacios@hotmail.com). Led by Professor Juan Perlacios, these Spanish-only tours are very well informed and visit the major tourist destinations, like Huari, Quinua, and Wilcashuamán. Juan is the author of the recent book *Huamanga: Tierra de Halcones,* a complete history of the Ayacucho area.

ACCOMMODATIONS

There are great hotel options in Ayacucho, for both the budget and upscale traveler—even the best hotels are relatively inexpensive. Rates triple for Easter week and rooms are booked months in advance.

Under US$10

An excellent budget option is **Hostal El Mesón** (Arequipa 273, tel. 066/31-2938, hselmeson@hotmail.com, US$8 s, US$12 d). Clean rooms with tile floors front a sunny courtyard and include cable TV. Some rooms have private bathrooms, and there is 24-hour hot water. The next best choice is **Hotel Samary** (Callao 329, tel. 066/31-2442, US$6 s, US$7 d), with communal and private bathrooms, bedrooms with tile floors, and hot water.

US$10-25

The best deal in town is **Hotel Tres Máscaras** (Tres Máscaras 194, tel. 066/31-4107, hotel-tresmascaras@yahoo.com, US$13 s, US$19 d). The gardens and cool sitting areas have great views of the surrounding hills. Large, carpeted rooms have good beds, cable TV, and lots of hot water. Another great deal is the quiet,

comfortable **Hostal Florida** (Cuzco 310, tel. 066/31-2565, US$14 s, US$21 d), with comfortable beds, hot water, cable TV, and even heating. The second-floor sunny terrace has great views over the city. **Hotel Marquez de Valdelirios** (28 de Julio 720, tel. 066/31-8944, US$16 s, US$22 d with breakfast) is a restored old home with large rooms, a sunny courtyard, and cable TV. The hotel is in front of a nice park and near the crafts workshops of Santa Ana.

The **Santa Maria** (Arequipa 320, tel. 066/31-4988, US$24 s, US$32 d) stands out for its modern architecture, interesting art, and luxurious furniture. The huge rooms are decorated with dark wood armoires and comfortable beds. Downstairs is a bar, with leather couches, for sipping cocktails.

A lesser option, but only a half block from the Plaza de Armas, is **Hostal Marcos** (9 de Diciembre 143, tel. 066/31-6867, US$14 s, US$21 d with breakfast), with large, clean though plain rooms and parquet floors.

US$25-50

The elegant courtyard of **Hotel Santa Rosa** (Lima 166, tel. 066/31-4614, hotel_santa_rosa@yahoo.es, US$27 s, US$43 d with breakfast) is a beautifully restored colonial building, but the rooms don't match up. From the outside, Ayacucho's most luxurious hotel is **Hotel Plaza** (9 de Diciembre 184, tel. 066/31-2202, hplaza@derramajae.org.pe, US$34 s, US$45 d with breakfast) but the rooms need an update. The best bet is a US$76 suite—two large rooms, queen-size bed, bathtub, and a balcony overlooking the Plaza de Armas. One block from the Plaza de Armas, **Hotel Universo** (Grau 101, hotel.universo@hotmail.com, US$31 s, US$58 d with breakfast) is another good option with all the amenities (telephone, cable TV, and Internet). Its blue walls and beds with crisp white sheets make for easy sleeping.

FOOD

Ayacucho has an excellent range of restaurants. Do not miss the local specialty *qapchi,* a delicious sauce of *queso fresco* and chives over boiled yellow potatoes.

Cafés, Bakeries, and Ice Cream

For breakfast or a light snack, **Cafe-Bar New York** (28 de Julio 178, tel. 066/80-2851, 9 A.M.–midnight Mon.–Sat., 4 P.M.–midnight Sun., US$1) has a peaceful, sun-filled colonial patio. The busy **Café La Miel** (Portal Constitución 11–12, Plaza de Armas, tel. 066/31-7183, 9:30 A.M.–10:30 P.M. daily) has good service, empanadas, and desserts. Or get a cone to go. **Lalo's Cafe** (Lima 169, tel. 066/31-9012, 7 A.M.–1 P.M. and 4–10 P.M. Mon.–Sat.) is a warm café, good for an evening espresso with a slice of cake or pie. Try the cherimoya mousse, *pie de lúcuma,* and empanadas.

Peruvian

Past its humble door, **Wallpa Sua** (Garcilaso de las Vega 240, tel. 066/40-3987, 6–11:30 P.M. Mon.–Sat., US$7–9) is a warmly lit republican house with great food ranging from spit-roasted chicken to tender steaks smothered in basil and garlic. Locals are met at the door by owner Mario Chahud, who joins them for a long, slow dinner, and on Friday and Saturday nights a bit of regional music.

The best place for *comida típica* is **Restaurant La Casona** (Bellido 463, tel. 066/31-2733, 9 A.M.–11:30 P.M. daily, US$5–6). Locals fill the tables for the daily lunch menu of *qapchi* or *puca picante*. Portions are huge and prices reasonable. **Urpicha** (Londres 272, tel. 066/31-3905, US$5–6) serves sectioned and pan-fried guinea pig, which is much easier to eat than the roasted, fuller-bodied version. **Los Álamos** (Cuzco 215, tel. 066/31-2782, 7 A.M.–10 P.M. daily, US$3) has a good US$2.50 menu, tasty grilled trout, and a pleasant colonial courtyard.

Tradición (San Martin 406, tel. 066/31-2595, 8 A.M.–10 P.M. Mon.–Sat., US$6) has a good US$2 lunch menu. **Cámara de Comercio** (San Martin 432, 9 A.M.–10 P.M. daily, US$2–3.50) serves spit-roasted chicken after 4 P.M., as well as fried trout, ceviche, and salads in a colonial courtyard. **Café Restaurant 4 en 1** (Callao 219, tel. 066/31-6822, 8 A.M.–10 P.M. Mon.–Sat., US$5) is a clean, rather plain place with a good reputation and a range of food from all over Peru.

Pizza

Next door to Café New York is the town's best pizzeria, **Antonino's** (tel. 066/31-5738, 5 P.M.–midnight daily, US$7 for big pizza). This is a hangout spot for the whole city. Locals come to drink beer and watch soccer games. **Pizzeria Italiana** (Bellido 486, 6 P.M.–midnight, US$6) serves pizzas from a wood-fired oven in a cozy atmosphere.

Chifa

The best, and safest, Chinese food in town is **Chifa Tio Min** (Mariscal Cáceres 1179, tel. 066/31-1274, 6–11 P.M. daily, US$2–4).

Markets

Maxi Market (28 de Julio 100) and its neighbor **Maxi's** (28 de Julio 236) have a reasonable selection of cold cuts, yogurts, and dry goods.

INFORMATION AND SERVICES

A new website chock-full of information about Ayacucho is www.ayacuchocompetitivo.org.

Tourist information is available at the helpful **Iperú** office (Portal Municipal, Plaza de Armas, tel. 066/31-8305, www.peru.info, 8:30 A.M.–7:30 P.M. Mon.–Sat., 8:30 A.M.–2:30 P.M. Sun.) on the Plaza de Armas and also at the airport.

The **tourist police** office is at 2 de Mayo 103, near the intersection with Arequipa (tel. 066/31-5845).

Health care is available at **Clínica de la Esperanza** (Independencia 355, tel. 066/31-7436, 8 A.M.–8 P.M. daily) or **Clínica el Nazareno** (Quinoa 428, tel. 066/31-4517, 7 A.M.–9 P.M. daily). The **Hospital Central** (Independencia 355, tel. 066/31-2180) is the only 24-hour option. **InkaFarma** (28 de Julio 262, tel. 066/31-8240, www.inkafarma.com.pe, 7 A.M.–10:30 P.M. daily) has the widest selection.

The **Banco de Crédito** (Portal Union 27 on the Plaza) and **Banco de la Nación** (half block from plaza on 28 de Julio) both have ATMs and are typically open 9 A.M.–6 P.M. weekdays and Saturday mornings.

The **post office** is at Asamblea 293 (tel. 066/31-2275, 8 A.M.–7 P.M. Mon.–Sat.).

Fast **Internet cafés** are at Cusco 136 (US$0.50/hr) and Bellido 532. There are private **telephone booths** for international calling at Bellido 364 and also on the plaza.

Lavandería Humanga (Marical Casceres 1252, tel. 066/31-9158, 9 A.M.–7 P.M. Mon.–Sat.) charges US$1/kg.

GETTING THERE AND AROUND

Flights back and forth to Lima are available through **LC BUSRE** (tel. 066/31-6012, www.lcbusre.com.pe) or **Aerocondor** (Lima tel. 01/614-6014, www.aerocondor.com.pe). The airport is four kilometers outside of town or a US$2.50 taxi ride.

With paved highway connecting Ayacucho to Pisco on the coast, bus times to Lima have shortened to as little as nine hours. The bus route from the coast crosses a 4,480-meter pass along the Ruta de los Libertadores, which José de San Martín traveled before proclaiming the independence of Peru in 1821 (the battles, and official independence, came over the next three years). The best companies on this route are **Cruz del Sur** (Mariscal Cáceres 1264, tel. 066/31-2813, www.cruzdelsur.com.pe), the only company with direct buses; **Ormeño** (Libertad 257, tel. 066/31-2495, www.grupo-ormeno.com); and **Expreso Union Molina** (9 de Diciembre 458, tel. 066/31-9989). There are both day and night buses to and from Lima with reclining seats that cost approximately US$18.

Before the terrorism of the 1980s, many travelers went from Lima to Huancayo and then on to Ayacucho and Cusco. This route is once again becoming popular. The best Huancayo–Ayacucho company is **Molina,** with both day and night buses for US$8 (US$10). As usual, we recommend traveling during the day. The views are incredible. There are actually two routes: The faster one goes low through the towns of Huacrapuquio, Imperial, Acostambo, Izcuchaca, and Mayocc, where it meets up with the high route before continuing to Huanta and Ayacucho. The higher route is 12 hours of dusty, bumpy driving, and unfortunately, it is used more frequently because it goes through more populated areas.

The best company for traveling south to Andahuaylas (10 hours), Abancay (15 hours), and Cusco (22 hours) is **Los Chancas** (Pasaje Mariscal Cáceres 150, tel. 066/31-2391). A private car and driver from Ayacucho to Andahuaylas can be rented for US$115, or US$330 for the one-way trip to Cusco.

The rough dirt roads between Ayacucho and Andahuaylas are the most spectacular part of the journey to Cusco. The route first heads up and over the frigid puna before descending to the Pampa Valley, a cobalt-blue river meandering through subtropical desert. On the other side lies the Apurímac department and the Quechuan town of Chinchero. The road then climbs to a series of stunning views and switchbacks along precipices that drop thousands of feet before arriving in the pleasant Andahuaylas valley.

After the dark years of terrorism, all the highways in and out of Ayacucho are safe now. By no means should travelers continue on the dirt road past Quinua into the Apurímac Valley, which is a fast-growing center of drug production.

Ayacucho is teeming with US$0.75 *motocars.*

ANDAHUAYLAS

Tourism has not yet reached Andahuaylas, a city of steep, narrow alleys that has one of the poorest demographics of the Peruvian sierra. The city sits on the banks of the Río Chumbau and is sandwiched between the smaller towns of San Jerónimo and Talavera. Most travelers stop here for the night only because Andahuaylas is midway in the Ayacucho–Cusco odyssey—it's roughly 10 hours by bus to either place. This is a good place to stretch the legs and walk through pleasant countryside and friendly villages.

Andahuaylas was once the region of the Chancas, a warrior tribe that may have toppled the Huari around A.D. 1000 and almost extinguished the Inca empire before it started. Despite overwhelming odds and panic in Cusco, the young Inca Yupanqui managed to rally the troops and turn back the Chancas. The event was so important in the Inca's mythological history that the young Inca afterwards changed his name to Pachacútec, meaning "He Who Moves the World." The Inca empire grew relentlessly from that point forward.

Andahuaylas's main colonial building is the cathedral, built of huge granite blocks in the 17th century. The best time to visit the cathedral is during early-morning mass, usually around 7 A.M.

Sights

The city's biggest attraction is the Chanca fortress of **Sondor,** 21 kilometers outside Andahuaylas on the way to Cusco. The fort itself is a rather unimpressive series of hilltop terraces, with a reconstructed garrison nearby, but the view is fabulous. The fort was obviously built to protect the rich valley bottomland around Lago Pacucha. On the other side of the fort, the valley drops thousands of feet toward the Pampa and Apurímac drainages. **Lago Pacucha** itself, 17 kilometers from Andahuaylas via a short cut off the main highway, has attractive marshlands, a few species of ducks, and dirt roads for walking. On the far side of the lake, *combis* from Andahuaylas arrive at the town of **Pacucha,** which has a few restaurants. The town is best known for its annual Yawar festival.

Entertainment and Events

The discotheques **Kusi Kusun** (Cáceres 361) and **Choza Inn** (next door), are open most nights after 9 P.M. **Ciné Antoon Spinoy** in the Plaza de Armas shows nightly movies.

Andahuaylas's best-known festival is **Fiesta de Yawar,** or the Festival of Blood, which takes place at the end of July in Pacucha. A week

before the event, men from the village head into the high sierra and capture several condors, using horsemeat as bait. During the festival, the condors are tied, one by one, onto the back of a bull. Anthropologists theorize that the ensuing struggle may represent a symbolic confrontation between the Inca (condor) and the Spanish (bull). The contest ends before either animal is killed and the condor is always released back into the wild.

El Niño Jesús de Praga takes place in Andahuaylas in late January. The **Virgen de la Candelaria** is celebrated in San Jerónimo in early February, and **Nuestra Señora de Cocharcas** is feted in Cocharcas on September 8.

Accommodations

Our favorite lodging in the whole city is **Hostal Delicias** (Juan Francisco Ramos 525, tel. 083/42-1104, US$6 s, US$9 d), a simple but clean place with pleasant *lúcuma*-colored walls, hot water, tile floors, and nice furniture. Considerably farther down on the food chain is **Hostal Cusco** (Pedro Casafranca 520, tel. 083/42-2148, US$4 s, US$7 d), offering simple, small rooms with electric shower heads. Rooms without private baths are even cheaper. Other, lesser budget options, such as **Hostal Los Libertadores Huari** and **Hostal Las Americas,** are down the street.

The most luxurious hotel is **El Encanto de Oro Hotel** (Pedro Casafranca 424, tel. 083/72-3066, US$14 s, US$18 d with breakfast), with great beds, tons of hot water, and cable TV. A generous breakfast is served in a fourth-story restaurant overlooking the city. Similar in quality is **Sol de Oro Hotel** (Juan Antonio Trelles 164, tel. 083/42-1152, US$14 s, US$18 d), with large, comfortable rooms and parquet floors.

Food

The best restaurant in town is **Pico Rico** (corner of Constitución and Andahuaylas, 5 P.M.–midnight daily, US$2.50), which serves one thing and does it well: *pollo a la brasa,* with soup, french fries, and salad. A recommended *chifa* is **Chun Yion** (corner of Antonio Trelles and Constitución, 3–11 P.M. daily). **Pizzería Napolitana** (Ramón Castilla 431, tel. 083/42-2196, 7 A.M.–1 P.M. and 3:30–9 P.M. daily) serves decent pizzas and juices, and is one of the few places in town that sells ice cream. Another locals' favorite for *comida típica* is **Club Social** (Juan Antonio Trelles 251, 7 A.M.–10 P.M. daily, US$2). House specialties are huge dishes of *caldo de gallina* and *adobo* stewed in corn *chicha*—best washed down with a shot of *anisado*. Basic cafés for breakfast, bread, desserts, or coffee are **El Pan Nuestro** (Ramón Castillo 599, tel. 083/42-1644, 6 A.M.–10 P.M. daily) and **Las Delicias** (Ramón Castillo 468).

Information and Services

There is no permanent source of tourism information, though an agency sporadically operates in front of the cathedral. **Police** are located on Avenida Peru.

Banco de la Nación on the Plaza de Armas and the **Banco de Crédito** on the second block of Peru both have ATMs.

The best **Internet cafés** are at Tres Sierra 322 (8 A.M.–11 P.M.) and at Andahuaylas 328 (9 A.M.–11 P.M.). There are private **phone booths** at Juan Francisco Ramos 317 (7 A.M.–9:30 P.M.).

The local laundry is **Lavandería Di-Li** (Cáceres 352, tel. 083/42-1978, 9 A.M.–7 P.M.).

Getting There and Around

From Andahuaylas, **Expreso Los Chankas** (Malecón Grau 474, tel. 083/42-2441, US$8) has buses to Cusco (10–11 hours) at 6:30 A.M., 6:30 P.M., and 7:10 P.M., and north to Ayacucho at 6:30 A.M. and 6:30 P.M. (10–11 hours). **Aerocondor** (Ricardo Palma 330, Plaza de Armas, tel. 083/42-2877, www.aerocondor.com.pe) has regular flights to Lima and, weather-permitting, to Ayacucho.

The route between Andahuaylas and Abancay takes around five hours and includes a climb to the Andean puna around Kishuara (3,450 meters) and a descent to the balmy climate of the Río Pachachaca Valley (2,000 meters), where sugarcane is cultivated. During

the drive, Abancay appears far in the distance with snow-covered Nevado Ampay looming overhead. From Abancay, there is another five hours of paved road to Cusco, passing through the balmy Apurímac Valley.

ABANCAY

Along with Andahuaylas, Abancay is mostly a resting stop for travelers along the Ayacucho–Cusco route. Most of the services are grouped along the busy streets of Arenas Arequipa. The Plaza de Armas, one block away, is quiet and graced by a colonial cathedral. **El Señor de la Caída,** on la Plazoleta la Victoria, is a very simple colonial church that has fine paintings from the Cusco School. These churches are mostly open during early-morning mass, with longer hours on Sunday.

Abancay is at the center of one of the purest Quechua-speaking zones in Peru, and even urbanites rant in a Quechua-Spanish hodgepodge. The road between Abancay and Cusco was paved in 2002, cutting travel time between the two cities down to four hours.

There is good trekking around the snow-covered **Ampay** (5,240 meters), center of a 364-hectare national sanctuary that preserves one of the last highland forests of *itimpa,* Peru's only indigenous conifer. Though rarely visited, this wilderness contains small lakes up high near the snowline. The entrance to the park is a mere six kilometers from Abancay itself.

Some trekkers also use Abancay as a launching point for reaching the ruins of Choquequirao, though nearly all of the trekking agencies are based in Cusco.

Entertainment and Events

Carnaval is a colorful tradition during February and March in Abancay and apparently includes a contest in which young men spar with whips. The **Yawar Fiesta** is celebrated in Antabamba on October 8. **Abancay Day,** a large town party, is November 3.

The main strip in Abancay is first called Arenas and then becomes Arequipa, and it's where all the discos, bus stations, cheap restaurants, and hostels are. A popular evening

THE SAYWITE STONE

On the road to Cusco 47 kilometers outside of Abancay lies the Saywite Stone (7 A.M.-dark, US$2.50), an immensely interesting half-egg-shaped boulder that was dragged down from the fields above and carved with what appears to be the Inca kingdom in miniature. Among other things, there are obvious architectural models of Machu Picchu, Choquequirao, Ollantaytambo, Pisac, and Tipón, all roughly geographically oriented. The four corners *(suyos)* of the Inca empire (Tawantinsuyo) are represented by four square indentations, or windows, on the blank side of the rock. Animals represent the three realms of Inca cosmology: a monkey and condor represent the heavens; puma and deer represent the earth; and frog and snake the area beneath the ground.

Perhaps most interesting, the different climates of the Inca kingdom are spread around the rock and conjured by their corresponding animals — octopus and lobster for the coast, llama for the mountains, and jaguar, wild pig, and tapir for the jungle. Finger-width channels lead from above to all these areas before draining off the rock through miniature tunnels. One theory is that priests poured llama

blood or *chicha* on the rock in order to control or predict rainfall. Crops would be good in whatever region of the rock was reached by the liquid. Unfortunately, some of the figures have been chipped away — by the Spanish, locals say — and are hard to distinguish. Ask the person collecting tickets for some of the harder-to-see details.

The rock was the center of a religious complex. A labyrinth of stone walls next to the rock was probably once a granary and home for the priests. A staircase leads down a ridge past a series of restored pools. At the bottom of the hill, a huge boulder has been split in half and is carved with steps leading nowhere, another set of four square windows, carved circles, and other mysterious geometric figures. In the fields above and on the other side of the Abancay-Cusco road, there is a boulder field with another half-carved stone that is similar in appearance. The Saywite Stone is about an hour outside of Abancay and three hours from Cusco. Bus drivers between the two cities can drop travelers at the site, which is well known and marked with signs. From Cusco, the trip to the Saywite Stone leads through the spectacular Apurímac Canyon.

hangout is the **Parque Micaela Bastidas,** on the second block of Arenas. *The* pub to hang out in is **Garabato** (Arenas 164, 7 P.M.–1 A.M. daily), with furry benches, full bar, and nice atmosphere. It has a sister pub in Cusco. There are several other pubs in this vicinity. The best disco is the nearby **Choza Inn** (Arequipa, block 3, weekends only).

Accommodations
A great budget option is **Hostal El Dorado** (Arenas 131-C, tel. 083/32-2005, US$8 s, US$11 d), with private baths, cable TV, and telephones in the rooms. The rooms are a bit musty, but there are banana and lemon trees in the patio, a swing set, and humorous stalactite formations in the eaves of the rooms.

The best place for a comfortable night's sleep is the quiet **Hostal El Imperial** (Díaz Bárcenas

517, tel. 083/32-1578, US$14 s, US$23 d), with great beds, cable TV, hot water, parking, and good service. Rooms without bath are about half the price. Across the street at **Hoteles y Turismo Abancay** (Díaz Bárcenas 500, tel. 083/32-1017, hotelturistas@yahoo.es, US$20 s, US$46 d with breakfast), the rooms are a bit stuffy and overpriced, but the restaurant is probably the best in town. Third-floor rooms are significantly more expensive. It has cheaper rooms without private bathrooms. **Hotel Flor de Amancaes** (Lima 840, tel. 083/32-3094, US$9 s, US$12 d) has simple, clean, tile-floored rooms.

Food
The Health Ministry did a sanitary inspection of all of Abancay's restaurants in 2003, and only the following three passed: The state-owned **Hoteles y Turismo Abancay** (Díaz Bárcenas

500, tel. 083/32-1017, 6:30 A.M.–10:30 P.M. daily, US$3–5) serves good salads and grilled meats in its dining room. **Mauri's** (Arenas 170, tel. 083/32-3042, 5 P.M.–12:30 A.M., US$2–4) is easily identifiable by its familiar golden arches sign and is popular for grilled meat and *pollo a la brasa*. It offers delivery. Finally, **Wachi** (Lima 862, 8 A.M.–3 P.M. daily) has the best *comida típica* in town.

Other safe places that were not evaluated because they are somehow not considered restaurants include these spots: **Focarela Pizza's** (Díaz Bárcenas 521, next to Hostal El Imperial, tel. 083/32-2036, 6 P.M.–midnight daily, US$3) serves above-average pizzas out of a wood-burning oven. Rumor has it that **Pizza Napolitana,** two blocks farther down the street, has better crust.

The best places for breakfast, cakes, and pies are **Café Heladería Dulce y Salado** (Arequipa 400, 8 A.M.–10 P.M.), **Café Heladería Mundial** (Arequipa 301, 8 A.M.–9:30 P.M.), and **Cafetine** (Arequipa one block from Hotel Flor de Amancaes).

The best supermarket is **Comercial Karina** (Arenas 156, 9 A.M.–11 P.M. daily).

Information and Services

The only recommended guide in Abancay is Carlos Pacheco with **Karlup Andean Trek** (tel. 083/32-1070, karlupandeantrek@terra.com).

The **state hospital** is at Venezuela 606 (tel. 083/32-1165). The best pharmacies are **El Olivo** (Arequipa 401, 8 A.M.–1 P.M. and 3–10 P.M.) and **Luren** at Diaz Bárcenas 519.

The **Banco de Crédito** on the third block of Arequipa changes money, with exchange houses along the street and private phone booths across the street.

The **post office** (www.serpost.com.pe) is at Arequipa 217.

Good **Internet cafés** are at Diaz Barrenas 539 (9 A.M.–11 P.M. daily), Cusco 377 (9 A.M.–1:30 P.M. and 3–11 P.M. daily), and Arenas 169 (8 A.M.–midnight daily, also private phone booths).

Getting There and Around

The route to Cusco is entirely paved and only takes four or five hours, including incredible scenery in the Apurímac Valley and a long ascent into the high plains around Anta before entering Cusco.

The best bus company is **Expreso Wari** (Arenas 200, tel. 083/32-2932), which runs buses to Cusco (US$5) at 3 A.M., 7 A.M., 10 A.M., and 2:30 A.M.

The company also runs buses over the dirt road that passes Puquio (and a 4,400-meter pass) to Nasca (US$13, US$23 with bed), where a different bus can be taken to Lima. These buses leave six times a day, around the clock, for this beautiful drive.

Turismo Ampay (corner of Arenas and Nuñez) runs buses for the five-hour trip to Cusco at 6 A.M., 1 P.M., and 11 P.M., and to Quillabamba in the jungle at 7 A.M., 1 P.M., 4 P.M., and 7 P.M. **Expreso Los Chankas** (Diaz Barcena 1033) has two buses a day leaving for Cusco and Andahuaylas–Ayacucho.

HUARAZ AND THE CORDILLERA BLANCA

The jagged peaks and crystalline glaciers of Peru's Andes sprout magically out of the pea-green high plains, a remarkable sight considering the country's subtropical latitude and the sunny, dry months May–August. Glaciers sprawl across more than a dozen ranges in southern and central Peru, where the Andes rise above 5,000 meters (16,400 feet) and freeze Amazon humidity carried west by the jet stream. Most of these ranges are rarely visited because they are very remote (such as the Cordillera Yauyos east of Lima), very small (the snowcapped volcanoes around Arequipa), or very technical (the Urubamba and Vilcanota ranges around Cusco).

The exception is the Cordillera Blanca, the highest mountain range in the world outside of the Himalaya. This extravagant collection of jagged pyramids, glacier domes, and knife-edge ridges runs north–south for 180 kilometers but is only 20 kilometers wide. To its west lies the Cordillera Negra, a humble, snowless range that reaches 5,200 meters before petering out onto the coast. Between the two ranges runs the Río Santa Valley, also known as the Callejón de Huaylas. The highway from the coast drops into this valley near Huaraz, at the top of the valley, and leads through a string of villages before reaching the city of Caraz. At this point the Río Santa jags toward the coast, and the road somehow follows it, through a spectacularly steep canyon known as the Cañón de Pato.

The Cordillera Blanca contains 34 peaks over 6,000 meters (19,685 feet), including the world-famous snow pyramids of Artesonraju,

HIGHLIGHTS

◖ Chavín de Huántar: Built more than 2,000 years before the Inca, this center of the Chavín culture includes underground tunnels that lead to the Lanzón, a carved rock pillar that was the focal point of the culture, which eventually spread across the Andes (page 421).

◖ Lagunas Llanganuco: These turquoise-blue, high-altitude lakes glow in the midday sun beneath the Cordillera Blanca snow pyramids (page 426).

◖ Cordillera Blanca: Two days is enough time for a quick jaunt through the mountain range and its corresponding Parque Nacional Huascarán, which includes Peru's tallest peak (page 430).

◖ Cordillera Huayhuash: Spend two weeks circumnavigating this stunning range, with some of the finest mountain scenery on earth (page 435).

◖ Cordillera Negra: This often-overlooked range, just west of the Cordillera Blanca, offers challenging mountain-bike routes with panoramas of glaciers and snow peaks (page 436).

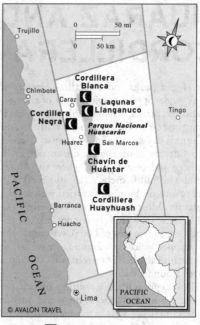

© AVALON TRAVEL

LOOK FOR ◖ TO FIND RECOMMENDED SIGHTS, ACTIVITIES, DINING, AND LODGING.

Chopicalqui, and Tocllaraju. Some of the peaks, such as Pisco and Ishinca, are accessible to first-time climbers with experienced guides, and there are even a few gentler trekker peaks, such as Urus and Maparaju. The area's most postcard-perfect peak is Alpamayo, a peak at 5,947 meters that lures climbers to its 70-degree face.

The mountain that dominates the entire valley, however, is Huascarán. At 6,768 meters (22,204 feet), Huascarán looms over Huaraz much like Mount Blanc towers over Chamonix, France. During the climbing season May–August, when the weather is dry and sunny, Huaraz's streets are flooded with rough-shaven adventurers in fluorescent parkas and trekking boots. The area is a world-

class mountain destination, in league with the Himalaya or the Alaska Range.

Farther south is the Cordillera Huayhuash, a stunning range that is an increasingly popular option for treks ranging from five days to two weeks. Whereas the gradual, glaciated valleys of the Cordillera Blanca allow trekkers to walk over the range, the Huayhuash is an odd island range fortified with jagged peaks and serrated ridges—your only choice is to circle. One of mountain climbing's most famous dramas was acted out on the Huayhuash peak Siulá Grande (6,356 meters) and is recounted by Joe Simpson in his memoir *Touching the Void*, which was made into a docudrama for the big screen in 2003.

Besides trekking and climbing, there are plenty of other adventure sports around

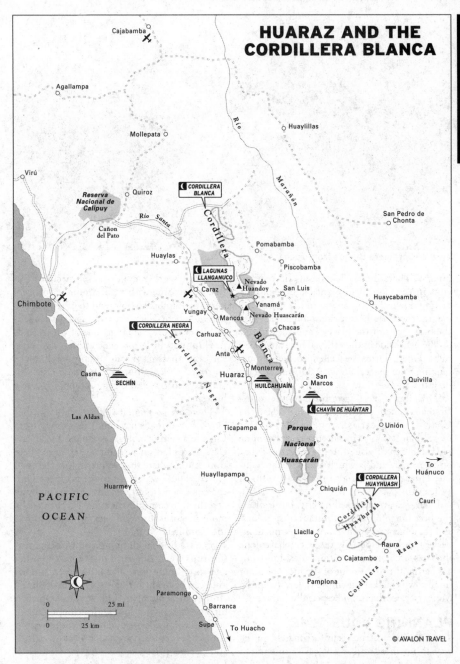

HUARAZ AND THE CORDILLERA BLANCA

Cajabamba

Agallampa

Mollepata

Huaylillas

Río

Virú

Reserva
Nacional de
Calipuy

Quiroz

Río Santa

Cañon
del Pato

Huaylas

Pomabamba

Marañón

San Pedro de
Chonta

CORDILLERA
BLANCA

Cordillera

Caraz

Piscobamba

LAGUNAS
LLANGANUCO

Nevado
Huandoy

San Luis

Huaycabamba

Chimbote

Yungay

Mancos

Yanamá

Nevado Huascarán

CORDILLERA NEGRA

Carhuaz

Chacas

Cordillera

Anta

Casma

SECHÍN

Huaraz

Monterrey

Blanca

San
Marcos

Quivilla

HUILCAHUAÍN

Negra

Las Aldas

CHAVÍN DE HUÁNTAR

Ticapampa

Parque

Unión

To
Huánuco

Nacional

Huascarán

PACIFIC

OCEAN

Huarmey

Huayllapampa

Chiquián

CORDILLERA
HUAYHUASH

Cauri

Cordillera
Huayhuash

Llacla

Raura
Raura

0   25 mi

Cajatambo

Cordillera

0   25 km

Paramonga

Pamplona

Barranca

Supe   To Huacho

© AVALON TRAVEL

© RENÉE DEL GAUDIO AND ROSS WEHNER

view of Cordillera Blanca from Tocllaraju

Huaraz. There are excellent mountain-bike circuits in the Cordillera Blanca and beginning rafting down the Río Santa. In the Cordillera Negra, there are hikes, rides, and treks with the best views of the glaciers and snow peaks on the other side of the valley. There are horses to be rented. There is excellent rock climbing, ranging from sport routes to 1,000-meter granite walls.

This area of Peru gave birth to one to the first advanced cultures of the Andes, the Chavín. Their carved stone capital of this more than 9,000-year-old empire, Chavín de Huántar, can be visited from Huaraz in a day, or overnight, and is worth a look. Right outside Huaraz there are also the Huari ruins of Wilcawaín.

Huaraz is an unappealing city, but it offers the best range of hostels, restaurants, guides, and equipment rental shops. An increasing number of travelers, especially those who have done their research and reservations ahead of time, are basing themselves out of the more pleasant small towns farther down the valley, including Monterrey, Carhuaz, and especially Caraz.

PLANNING YOUR TIME

The Cordillera Blanca is unfortunately on the way to nowhere and is not easily integrated into Peru's other major travel circuits. But that is just fine with a good number of trekkers and climbers who spend their entire Peru trip right here. There are two rugged dirt roads on either end of the range, one of which leads to **Huánuco** in Peru's central highlands and the other, passing through many small towns en route, to **Cajamarca.** But these take several days to travel and require hopping a few buses.

There are no regular flights to Huaraz, but newly paved roads have cut the journey from Lima to a comfortable seven hours. Most travelers who plan on visiting Cusco come here from Lima, where they return before flying to Cusco. Those who want to see northern Peru can come here from Lima on the main highway and then, to continue their journey, can take a more adventurous route back to the coast over the Cordillera Negra.

The traditional climbing and trekking season runs May–August, but the best weather and snow are in June and July. Ascents, however, can be made during the sometimes-sunny climate of September. And if you happen to hit Huaraz during low season (Sept.–Apr.), you can enjoy a series of day hikes, deep green landscapes (colored by the afternoon rains), and cheaper prices.

Huaraz and Vicinity

Under Huaraz's facade of sprawling cement-and-rebar buildings, muddy rivers, and haphazard produce markets, there is a thriving tourist town full of quaint hostels, coffeehouses, and delicious French restaurants. The city, at 3,028 meters (9,934 feet), is the heart of the adventure sports scene in the Cordillera Blanca—and all of Peru. It has the best range of guides, agencies, and equipment shops. With a bit of common sense, hustle, and moolah, it is possible to arrive in Huaraz with no equipment and, within a few days, leave for a trek, climb, or bike trip. But beware of hustlers, con artists, and phony guides; their services also abound.

People in Huaraz are friendly, gregarious, and especially festive. The Plaza de Armas is often blocked off by a stream of children's parades, *marinera* contests, and military formations. In the evenings, people stroll up and down **Luzuriaga,** the town's eyesore of a main drag, passing a variety of restaurants, gear shops, and travel agencies. To the north, the market stretches along the **Río Quilcay.**

Some final words of advice for Huaraz travelers: Keep an eye on your backpack, don't leave the bus station with an unknown guide, be careful where you eat, and take at least two days to acclimatize before heading up into the mountains.

SIGHTS
The sights mentioned are easy day trips in or around Huaraz. Often Huaraz agencies include Chavín de Huántar and Lagunas Llanganuco in this day-trip category, but we recommend giving these sights at least a day and overnight. Consequently, we describe them in their own sections later in this chapter.

City Tour
Huaraz's chief attraction is the **Museo Arqueológico de Áncash** (Luzuriaga 762 on the Plaza de Armas, tel. 043/42-1551, 8 a.m.–5 p.m. daily, US$3.50). It contains a well-organized collection of stone sculptures from the local Chavín (2000–200 b.c.) and Recuay (a.d. 200–700) cultures. Upstairs are displays of pottery, textiles, and metal objects from the later Huari, Chimú, and Inca cultures, which also passed through this valley.

The Plaza de Armas is a sprawl of concrete and tile that funnels onto Luzuriaga Street. Directly uphill from the plaza is the **Iglesia Soledad,** rebuilt after the 1970 earthquake and surrounded by a pleasant plaza. There are a few good hotels in the neighborhood and some of the best views of both the Cordillera Blanca and sunsets over the Cordillera Negra.

For a view of the city, head up to the **Mirador Rataquena,** a lookout marked with a giant cross. The safest way to get there is by taxi. The round-trip journey should cost US$5. To get there walking, head up Villón or Confraternidad Este to the cemetery and then head right, up a switchbacking gravel road. But travel in groups and during the day, as assaults have been reported.

ONE BIG PINEAPPLE

The *Puya raimondii,* common to Peru's high-altitude grasslands, is considered the largest bromeliad in the world and a cousin to the pineapple. In an adaptation aimed at casting its seeds as far as possible, this agave-looking plant with spiky, waxy leaves shoots up a 12-meter-high stalk only once during its 100-year life. When in bloom around May, the stalk erupts into as many as 20,000 flowers in the last three months before dispersing six million seeds. Even when not in bloom, these giant plants stand out on Peru's high-altitude grasslands and are worth seeing. In the Huaraz area, these plants can be seen on the way to the Pastoruri Glacier. Peru's biggest forest of these monsters, however, is outside Ayacucho.

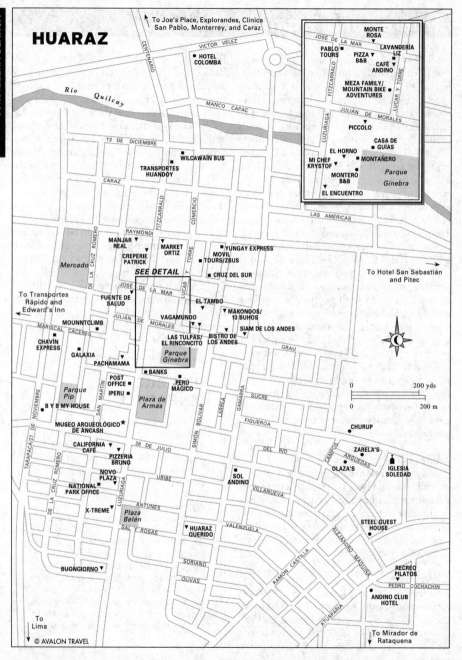

CORDILLERA BLANCA

HUARAZ

To Joe's Place, Explorandes, Clínica San Pablo, Monterrey, and Caraz

Río Quilcay

CENTENARIO

VICTOR VELEZ

HOTEL COLOMBA

MANCO CAPAC

13 DE DICIEMBRE

WILCAWAÍN BUS

TRANSPORTES HUANDOY

CARAZ

FITZCARRALD

COMERCIO

LAS AMERICAS

RAYMONDI

Mercado

DE LA CRUZ ROMERO

MANJAR REAL

CREPERIE PATRICK

MARKET ORTIZ

TORRE

YUNGAY EXPRESS

MOVIL TOURS/ZBUS

CRUZ DEL SUR

SEE DETAIL

To Transportes Rápido and Edward's Inn

FUENTE DE SALUD

JOSÉ DE LA MAR

LUCAR Y

EL TAMBO

To Hotel San Sebastián and Pitec

MOUNNTCLIMB

JULIAN DE MORALES

VAGAMUNDO

MAKONDOS/ 13 BUHOS

MARISCAL CACERES

CHAVÍN EXPRESS

GALAXIA

PACHAMAMA

LAS TULPAS/ EL RINCONCITO

Parque Ginebra

SIAM DE LOS ANDES

BISTRO DE LOS ANDES

GRAU

SAN MARTIN

POST OFFICE

IPERU

BANKS

PERÚ MÁGICO

Parque Pip

B Y B MY HOUSE

Plaza de Armas

SIMÓN BOLIVAR

LARREA

SUCRE

GAMARRA

CHURUP

DE LA CRUZ ROMERO

27 DE NOVIEMBRE

TARAPACA

MUSEO ARQUEOLÓGICO DE ANCASH ★

CALIFORNIA CAFÉ

PIZZERIA BRUNO

NOVO PLAZA

NATIONAL PARK OFFICE

X-TREME

28 DE JULIO

FIGUEROA

DEL RIO

SOL ANDINO

URIBE

VILLANUEVA

CAMPOS

ARGUEDAS

ZARELA'S

OLAZA'S

IGLESIA SOLEDAD

LUZURIAGA

Plaza Belén

ANTUNES

SAL Y ROSAS

HUARAZ QUERIDO

VALENZUELA

STEEL GUEST HOUSE

SORIANO

ALEJANDRO MAGUIÑA

RAMON CASTILLA

BUONGIORNO

OLIVAS

RECREO PILATOS

PEDRO COCHACHIN

ANDINO CLUB HOTEL

ATUSPARIA

To Lima

© AVALON TRAVEL

To Mirador de Rataquena

0   200 yds
0   200 m

Detail inset

JOSÉ DE LA MAR

FITZCARRALD

MONTE ROSA

PABLO TOURS

PIZZA B&B

LAVANDERÍA LIZ

CAFÉ ANDINO

LUCAR Y TORRE

MEZA FAMILY/ MOUNTAIN BIKE ADVENTURES

LUZURIAGA

JULIAN DE MORALES

PICCOLO

EL HORNO

CASA DE GUÍAS

MI CHEF KRYSTOF

MONTAÑERO

MONTERO B&B

Parque Ginebra

EL ENCUENTRO

Wilcahuaín

Monumento Arqueológico de Wilcahuaín (7 km north of Huaraz, 8 A.M.–5 P.M. daily, US$2) consists of two imposing stone buildings constructed around A.D. 600–900, when the Huari empire expanded north from the Ayacucho area and took over the local Recuay civilization. The main building has a gravity-defying roof of thick stone slabs and three floors of finely wrought, spooky stone chambers. These rooms once held the mummified bodies of prominent leaders, kept dry by ventilation ducts running throughout the complex. The outer walls were decorated with sculpted heads, one of which remains today in the shape of a mountain lion.

Wilcahuaín stands out from other ruins in Peru because it is an intact building that requires no imagination to understand. Bring your flashlight in case the electricity goes out, as it did when we were there. *Combis* marked Wilcahuaín cost US$0.60; ask your hotel for directions to the bus stop. Or take a cab (US$2). The two ruins are a few hundred meters apart along a dirt road. This makes for a pleasant two-hour walk back to town through countryside and villages.

Cooperativa Artesanal Don Bosco

Catholic priest Ugo de Censi began this non-profit organization (Catholic Parish in Jangus, tel. 043/44-5061, andesdbosco@hotmail.com, 8 A.M.–4:30 P.M. Mon.–Fri.) in 1970 as a way to give people working skills and an escape from poverty. The organization has blossomed from its roots in Chacas, a small town on the other side of the Cordillera Blanca, into a large workshop in Jangus, just north of Huaraz. Here, teenagers learn how to make contemporary furniture, ceramics, blown glass, weavings, and stone sculptures, which are then shipped throughout the world! Visitors tour through all the workshops and have a chance to see an interesting video. The organization also has offices in Lima (Av. Alejandro Tirado 158, Sta. Beatriz, tel. 01/471-0515) and Cusco (Primavera, 100 S. Jerónimo, tel. 084/27-7316).

ENTERTAINMENT AND EVENTS

One of the coolest bars in town is **Vagamundo Travelbar & Maps** (Julián de Morales 753, tel. 043/50-9063, 5 P.M.–close daily high season, 8 P.M.–close daily low season, US$5), with all kinds of music. Another popular backpacker spot is the legendary **X-Treme Bar** (Luzuriaga 1044, tel. 043/42-3150, 8 P.M.–late Mon.–Sat.), in its new site across Plaza Belén, with couches, dartboards, and great music as always, set up by Benquelo Morales, DJ and owner of the place.

The hot spot for dancing is the **El Tambo** (José de la Mar 776, tel. 043/42-3417, 8 P.M.–dawn Mon.–Sat., cover US$3), with top 40 pop, salsa, and techno spun by a DJ. It also has rooms for live music and mingling over cocktails. Several other nightlife options are nearby, including the popular **Makondos** (José de la Mar 812, 9 P.M. onward daily, cover varies), which blasts disco and Latin pop until the wee hours of the morning. For a mellow beer, try **Los 13 Buhos** (José de la Mar 812, 7 P.M.–close daily, US$3). This small bar is above Makondos and makes a good evening stop, featuring its coca-leaf homemade beer.

For an alternative evening, head to **Cine-Café Huaraz Stayricon** (Parque del Periodista, at the Restaurant Mi Chef Kristof, tel. 043/42-6765, www.huarazsatyricon.tripod.com, US$2). Kristof's place has a comfy, loungy area in the back of his restaurant where international films are shown. All food is available. Showtimes change weekly, and most hotels have schedules.

Huaraz's biggest celebration is **Semana Santa,** the week before Easter, when Huaraz natives and their friends return home from Lima. There are important religious processions on Good Friday and Easter Sunday, along with a lot of partying and a carnival-like spirit (think water balloons). During the **Fiesta de Mayo** (May 2–9), there are processions and dance festivals for Huaraz's earthquake-controlling patron saint, El Señor de la Soledad (Our Lord of Solitude).

SHOPPING

Tucked in the small store of **Perú Mágico** (Sucre 765, 9 A.M.–2 P.M. and 3–9 P.M. Mon.–Sat.) are high-quality textiles, ceramics, and jewelry. Another good souvenir shop is **Last Minute Gift Store** (Lucar y Torre 530, 2nd Fl., tel. 043/42-4259, 9 A.M.–12:30 P.M. and 4:30–8:30 P.M. Mon.–Sat., by appointment Sun.), which sells similar items as well as maps, T-shirts, and Andean music CDs. **Andean Expressions** (Julio Arguedas 1246, 10 A.M.–8 P.M. Mon.–Sat.) sells hand-printed T-shirts with contemporary designs.

For cheaper prices, and goods made by local communities, browse the two crafts markets off the Plaza de Armas and the shops along Luzuriaga south of Raimondi. Here, beautiful Andean rugs, sweaters, bags, and blankets are sold at affordable prices.

RECREATION

From trekking to biking to experiential tourism, the options for activity in Huaraz are diverse. And there are a number of ways to organize each activity. You can arrange details from abroad, which is preferable if you plan to do popular treks during peak season. Or you can arrive in Huaraz and make arrangements then. This option is more complicated during peak season.

Regardless, an invaluable resource, once in Huaraz, is the **Casa de Guías** (Parque Ginebra 28-G, tel. 043/42-7545, www.casadeguias. com.pe, 8 A.M.–1 P.M. and 4–8 P.M. Mon.–Sat., open Sun. during high season). As the Mountain Guide Association of Peru, the Casa de Guías trains and certifies guides according to international standards, provides contact to Huaraz's certified mountain guides, and helps with trip planning. In its office, you can find maps, route information, weather forecasts, and snow condition reports. Here, you can also make contacts with certified guides, who can lead almost any trip imaginable; less expensive guides-in-training (*aspirantes*), a good choice for nontechnical routes; and porters, *arrieros* (muleteers), and cooks.

For safety, and because of the technical demands of many of Huaraz's climbs, it is essential to work with a certified mountain guide and to give yourself a couple of days to acclimatize. Remember that Huaraz is at 3,050 meters (10,000 feet) and the mountains above are much, much higher; altitude sickness is a common problem. All the companies listed work with certified guides and can recommend acclimatization hikes. For trips during high season, these companies should be contacted a month or two in advance. If you are planning your trip independently, you can verify your guide's legitimacy by asking to see his official Mountain Guide Association identification card. Beware because there are many fly-by-night agencies.

Trekking and Climbing

Surrounded by three distinct and impressive mountain ranges, Huaraz offers access to a variety of multiday to multiweek treks and climbs. The majority of trekking and climbing trips use porters and muleteers to carry food and equipment. This leaves trekkers with a lighter load and better prepared to confront the area's high altitudes. Treks, because they usually do not reach altitudes over 5,000 meters, do not require previous training. Climbs, by contrast, summit high, glacier-covered peaks and demand the use of ice axes, crampons, and technical climbing knowledge, Some prior experience is often essential.

A Huaraz classic, **Montañero** (Parque Ginebra 30-B, tel. 043/42-6386, www.trek-kingperu.com) is the agency and shop of Selio, who founded the Casa de Guías, and his wife Ana. The Peruvian couple coordinates trips to the traditional circuits and is now offering multiday alternative trips around Alpamayo and to deep valleys near Huaraz. Out of their office, the couple also runs an excellent gear rental shop, where you can find everything from crampons to parkas. Between them, they speak English, French, and German.

MountClimb (Mariscal Caceres 421, tel. 043/42-6060, www.mountclimb.com.pe) is an equally good place to buy maps and rent cutting-edge gear. The owner, Alfredo Quintana, is a fully certified mountain guide, speaks English, and manages guides that speak French and Italian. Alfredo's climbs, treks, ice-climbing courses, and guided ski descents are highly recommended.

Managed by members of the same family, **Sol Andino** (Gamarra 815, tel. 043/42-2205, www.solandino.com) and **Explorandes** (Av. Centenario 489, tel. 043/42-1960, www.explorandes.com) both operate well-organized, high-quality trips. Sol Andino, known primarily for its climbing expertise, offers basic trips starting at US$65 pp per day and fully-outfitted group trips for US$80–120 pp per day. Explorandes has operated trekking trips for 30 years and was recently awarded for its environmental management. (The company uses bio-gas, composts, and packs out all inorganic trash.) New on its trip list is a Best of Cordillera Huayhuash trip.

A solid budget agency is **Galaxia Expedition** (Marsical Caceres 428, tel. 043/42-5355, www.galaxia-expeditions.com). The agency offers US$45 pp per day basic trekking trips and US$65 pp per day full service trips, as well as mountain-biking adventures, an indoor climbing wall, and rental of brand-name equipment.

A recommended, fully certified mountain and trekking guide who spends a third of her year in Huaraz, is **Val Pitkethly** (133 Rundle Crescent, Canmore, Alberta, Canada, T1W 2L6, tel. 403/678-6834, valpk@hotmail.com). Val leads a few trips in the Cordillera Huayhuash each year.

Richard Hidalgo (richard_hidalgo@yahoo.com) is a certified guide who speaks excellent English. Richard and a team of Peruvian climbers won headlines for the successful ascent of the Shisha Pangma, a notoriously difficult Himalayan peak that rises to 8,027 meters. Richard is now on a crusade to climb the world's 14 8,000 meters peak solo and without oxygen.

A knowledgeable trekking resource who has spent a lot of time in the Cordillera Huayhuash and runs logistical support for expeditions is

Chris Benway, owner of Café Andino. Chris is available at the café (Lúcar y Torre 530, 3rd Fl., tel. 084/42-1203, www.cafeandino.com) or through his company **La Cima Logistics** (lacima_peru@hotmail.com).

Rock and Ice Climbing

If you're coming to Huaraz to mountaineer, don't forget your quick draws and rock shoes. Local crags fill the valley and stretch 20–200 meters. The best crag near Huaraz is Chancos, which offers eight bolted routes on sedimentary rock with big, chunky holds ranging 5.6–5.9. To reach Chancos from Huaraz, head to the bridge area near Centenario and take a Carhuaz *combi* north for 11 kilometers to Marcará. From here, the crags are about a 30-minute walk up the road, on the left side. There is a nice river for bathing, and the Chancos hot springs are nearby.

A closer spot, though less developed, is Monterrey, seven kilometers north of Huaraz, which has a handful of sport routes about 12 meters long.

© RENÉE DEL GAUDIO AND ROSS WEHNER

ice climbing in the Cordillera Blanca

CLIMBING AROUND HUARAZ

The Cordillera Blanca, the second-highest mountain range in the world next to the Himalaya, is a world-class climbing destination. Here are a few pointers for organizing your climbing trip.

WHEN TO GO

The traditional climbing season is May–August, but the best snow conditions are usually found in June and July. The rain season ends in March, but heavy snows can still strike in April and May. By August, snow cover over the glaciers is relatively thin and route finding is more difficult.

GUIDES

To guarantee your safety, work only with a guide who is certified by the Huaraz's Casa de Guías, which represents the Mountain Guide Association of Peru. Accidents, and sometimes fatalities, happen each year in the Cordillera Blanca because trip leaders with insufficient training and experience try to guide trips. By law, all agencies are required to use certified guides.

Even if you are an experience climber, you have a much better chance to summit with a certified guide who has already climbed a route a few times *that season*. He or she will know the latest routes, the condition of the snow pack, and the right acclimatization schedules. The going day rates are US$80–100 for a mountain guide for moderate peaks like Pisco, Urus, and Ishinca, and US$100–140 for technical peaks such as Tocllaraju, Huascarán, Chopicalqui, Artesonraju, and Alpamayo.

Before you pay, make sure that your agency or guide understands and abides by **Leave No Trace** principles, which can be found at www. Int.org. Huaraz is filled with informal agencies and gear shops that can sell stolen gear. Avoid them.

ENTRY FEES

By Peruvian standards, visiting Parque Nacional Huascarán is not cheap. Climbers and trekkers must pay US$1.50 directly to the community of Chasapampa and then US$20 for a park pass that lasts one month. Day-trippers ante up US$2 for the same pass. The national park fee can be paid at the park's headquarters in Huaraz or at ticket booths at Laguna Llanganuco, Pastoruri Glacier, the village of Musho on the way to Huascarán, and in Quebrada Ishinca. This park, like most in Peru, is badly underfunded and needs all the money it can get for trail maintenance, trash removal, park rangers, rescue infrastructure, endangered species protection, and community-based programs.

Local communities throughout the Huaraz area have recently begun charging informal fees in an attempt to get their fair share from the local trekking traffic. Collón, for instance, charges US$5 to groups that enter the Quebrada Ishinca. In other areas, such as Quebrada Quilcayhuanca, there is a gate where climbers need to pay in order to pass through the territory (though trekkers without pack animals can just climb over). In the Cordillera Huayhuash, these village fees total up to about US$30.

MAPS, GUIDEBOOKS, AND INFORMATION

Agencies and cafés in Huaraz sell maps, which are also available at the South American Explorers Club in Lima.

For the Cordillera Blanca, the 1:100,000 map published by Carhuaz resident Felipe Díaz gives a good overview of basic trekking routes but does not give enough detail for climbers. The Austrian Alpine Club and Alcides Ames, the owner of B y B My House, have published a 1:100,000 topo map for the north and south ends of the Cordillera Blanca. For the Cordillera Huayhuash, the Alpine Mapping Guild has a 1:50,000 scale map, which is on sale in Huaraz for US$15.

The best climbing guide for the Cordillera Blanca is Brad Johnson's *Classic Climbs of the Cordillera Blanca*, which has up-to-date information on the area's rapidly changing snow and ice routes. Another good guide for the Huaraz area is Globetrotter's *Trekking and Climbing in the Andes*, coauthored by Val Pit-

© RENÉE DEL GAUDIO AND ROSS WEHNER

Quebrada Llaca is close to Huaraz and is a popular place for an acclimatization hike or overnight stay.

kethly. It has a good description of the 12- to 14-day Huayhuash circuit, the Llanganuco-Santa Cruz trek, a two-week loop around Alpamayo's remote north side, and an exploratory circuit through the less-crowded valleys near Huaraz.

The best sources of up-to-date information are climbers and guides returning from the areas where you are headed. Casa de Guías in Huaraz is the area's number one information center.

GEAR

High-quality equipment can be rented for affordable prices in Huaraz. You can request prices and make reservations ahead of time by emailing the agencies, which also sell gear but at a significant markup.

Most U.S. airlines no longer allow passengers to fly with used camping stoves, even in checked luggage. Your alternatives are to rent a stove in Huaraz (MSR Whisperlites and similar models are available) or to bring a new stove (in the box) and then sell it in Huaraz. Selling used gear, either to a shop or other climbers, is easy.

Pretty much all supplies, with the exception of freeze-dried food, are available in markets in Huaraz and Caraz. You'll find pasta, powdered soup, cheese, powdered milk, beef jerky, dried fruit, and more. White gas (bencina blanca) is sold at hardware stores and along Avenida Luzuriaga. Get a recommendation from an agency or gear store to ensure you find the highest quality gas, and fire up your stove before you go to make sure everything works.

ACCLIMATIZATION

Acclimatization in Peru is key. Even the first camps of many of the major climbs and trekking routes are high enough to make people seriously ill. As an example, if you are going to climb in the popular Quebrada Ishinca – launching pad for Ishinca, Urus, and

(continued on next page)

CLIMBING AROUND HUARAZ (continued)

Tocllaraju – the first day's walk to the lodge leads to 4,350 meters. The other major climbs are even worse: Pisco's refuge is at 4,665 meters and Huascarán's is at 4,700 meters! Most of the passes in the Cordillera Huayhuash are between 4,500 and 5,000 meters, and the second day of the popular Santa Cruz trek is at 4,700 meters.

Instead of falling ill and ruining your trip, spend your first day in Huaraz walking slowly up, through mountain villages, toward the Lazy Dog Inn or the Urbanización El Pinar. Another option from Huaraz is to hop aboard a *combi* heading east up over the Cordillera Negra and get off at **Callán Pass** (4,225 meters). If you have a group, a taxi will only cost around US$30. From here you can walk or mountain bike back to town on a network of dirt trails. That night, sleep in Huaraz.

For the second night, many trekkers camp at their trailhead. Climbers, however, take advantage of the other good acclimatization possibilities near Huaraz. A good second-day walk is **Laguna Churup** (4,485 meters), and a flat nearby option is **Quebrada Quilcay-huanca.** There is a place to camp at Pitec, the village near the Churup trailhead, at 3,850 meters.

Another second-day option, if you have your own transport, is a slightly longer drive up to the refuge in **Quebrada Llaca** (US$15 pp lodging, US$5 pp area admission). There is a lodge here and excellent camping spots. A knife-edge moraine trail has mind-blowing views of **Ranrapalca** (6,162 meters) and the near-vertical south face of the **Ocshapalca glacier** (5,888 meters). The lodges on the outskirts of Huaraz make good starting points.

HAZARDS AND PRECAUTIONS

While the vast majority of trekkers to the Huaraz area never encounter any threats on their personal safety, certain touristy areas have a history of theft or assault. Use cau-

tion in these areas. Robberies, sometimes at gunpoint or knifepoint, have been reported at Mirador Rataquena, the bouldering area at Huanchac, and Laguna Churup. When visiting these areas, you should not go alone and should avoid nightfall.

Base-camp theft has decreased in recent years. If you are organizing your own trek, hire a camp guardian (US$15/day), or strike a deal your *arriero*, so that there is someone in camp during the day to watch over your equipment and supplies.

The Cordillera Huayhuash route passes though several larger villages, such as Lla-mac, Pocpa, and Huayllapa. Here, trekkers can supplement their supplies with common items like cheese, potatoes, and beer. It is not a good idea, however, to rely on the availability of these products as supplies are limited and expensive. The long Huayhuash route also slows medical evacuation, delaying it as much as several days.

Accident risk in Peru's tropical glaciers has been increased by their rapid retreat. Huascarán's ice fall has become notably less stable in recent years. On July 21, 2003, at 9 a.m., huge blocks of ice fell down the 350-meter face of Alpamayo, killing eight climbers and leading the U.S. climber's magazine *Rock and Ice* to question whether accidents caused by unstable ice conditions are linked to human-induced climate change. Huascarán and Alpamayo are the two most popular and well-known peaks in the Cordillera Blanca, but plenty of other mountains exist of similar difficulty that do not involve such a level of objective danger.

In case of an accident, climbers should contact the **Casa de Guías** or Yungay's **High Mountain Rescue Unit.** Any rescue will cost hundreds of dollars, and if a helicopter is involved, it will be thousands. Consider buying an international insurance policy that covers high-risk sports.

Other recommended spots for all levels of climbing are Antacocha, one hour by bus from Huaraz, and Balcón de Judos, 20 minutes away. Huanchac near Huaraz is not recommended for bouldering.

Advanced climbers will have plenty to keep them busy in the polished granite walls that line many of the Cordillera Blanca valleys. Over the past several years, teams of climbers have put up both free and aid routes on the cliffs of Quebrada Llaca and Ishinca. The best-known, hard-core areas are in the Rurec Valley and the Torre de Parón, also known as the Sphinx.

There is an artificial climbing wall behind the municipality in Huaraz and a bouldering cave at **Andean Kingdom** (Luzuriaga 522). This climbing agency, however, has had a series of accidents and is not recommended.

Mountain Biking

In Huaraz, there is at least one agency that has well-maintained mountain bikes, Trek or better, with front suspension. The other agencies, mostly along Luzuriaga, have cheaper bikes and often do not supply helmets. The best day trips and views are to be had in the Cordillera Negra, which has single-tracks that lead a thousand meters back to Huaraz. Longer trips can take you up and over the Cordillera Negra to the Pacific Ocean or through the Cordillera Blanca, on valley single-track, and over 4,500-meter passes. The longer trips require support vehicles to carry gear.

Julio Olaza at **Mountain Bike Adventures** (Lúcar y Torre 530, tel. 043/42-4259, www.chakinaniperu.com) offers a range of guided mountain-bike trips and bike repairs. Julio is a longtime Huaraz resident who speaks perfect English. Rental rates, which include a guide, start at US$35 per day.

Day Hikes

In the dry hills of the Cordillera Negra and the steep valleys of the Cordillera Blanca, there are plenty of options for good day hikes. A 40-minute taxi drive will drop you at the start of the trail, and hikes can range 2–9 hours in length. In both ranges, the trails fade in and out of grasses, and can be a challenge to follow, but with a guide or an adventurous spirit and an early start, you can easily make it to your destination and back in one day. The Casa de Guías can provide good maps and trail information; Michel Burger, the French owner of **Pérou Voyages** (Julián Morales 823, tel. 043/42-6249, www.perouvoyages.com), has spent many weekend mornings scoping out trails. Michel, who speaks French, Spanish, and German, is happy to guide or give information about hikes.

Horseback Riding

Horseback riding is easy to set up and follows beautiful routes through the Cordillera Negra. A recommended outfit in Yungar, a village 20 minutes north of Huaraz, is **La Posada de Yungar** (Km 219 Huaraz-Caraz Highway, tel. 043/978-4732, edergirald@hotmail.com, US$8 per hour). Guide Eder Giraldo offers excellent day trips in the Cordillera Negra, as well as longer rides into the Cordillera Blanca's Quebrada Ishinca.

Skiing

The Cordillera Blanca is not the best place for ski mountaineering. Finding good snow often means climbing well above 5,000 meters. Because of rapid glacier retreat, even the most experienced guides cannot keep track of new crevasses from year to year. That said, if you are interested, the snow is best April–June, and you can hire both guides and reliable ski equipment in Huaraz. The most frequented skiing spot is Glacier Pastoruri, and other good options include moderate mountains such as Huálcan and Copa. A good contact is Alfredo Quintana at **MountClimb** (Mariscal Caceres 421, tel. 043/42-6060, www.mountclimb.com. pe). Skis can be rented here or from Enrique Bosshard at **Inka Pub Monte Rosa** (José de la Mar 661, tel. 043/42-1447, pmonterosa@ yahoo.com, 11 A.M.–midnight).

Rafting and Kayaking

Low water levels in Río Santa have made rafting

and kayaking less accessible in recent years. Water levels continue to be the highest between November and May, but year-round the water is murky. Consequently, Huaraz is a good option for the beginning kayaker or rafter.

During high season, **Ario Ferri** (arioferri@ naturevive.com, also available through Casa de Pocha, prices vary depending on group size and trip length) offers beginning kayaking classes, which start in the pool at Casa de Pocha, a guesthouse in Carhuaz, and finish with a day on Río Santa. Ario is also a proficient raft guide and can organize river trips.

Fishing

While you may not catch a fish large enough to inspire a tale, there are decent opportunities for fishing around Huaraz. Stocked lakes, such as Lago Querococha in the Cordillera Blanca, are the best option. According to the regulations of Parque Nacional Huascarán, it is illegal to keep fish below 25 centimeters (about 10 inches). In 2007, there was no rental fishing equipment in Huaraz, but Michel Burger of **Pérou Voyages** (Julián Morales 823, tel. 043/42-6249, www.perouvoyages.com) is an authority on local fishing and can fill you in on the most updated information.

Paragliding

Though the sport is common in the Cordillera Blanca, the unstable conditions and lack of equipment rental shops in Huaraz require that nearly all paragliders be experienced and bring their own equipment. The most common launching spots are Pan de Azúcar, a round hill near Yungay, and the Cordillera Negra, though European daredevils can often be seen chucking themselves off snow peaks as well. For assistance within Peru, contact **Peru Fly** (Jorge Chávez 658, Miraflores, tel. 01/444-5004, www.perufly.com) in Lima.

Experiential Tourism

As you head up to the hillsides around Huaraz, you pass through several traditional Andean communities. Here life revolves around family, agricultural work, and the Sunday soccer game. Many houses still do not have electricity, educational resources are limited, and poverty discourages people from investing many resources in their daily lives. To experience how these local communities live and to help them through volunteer work or by participating in their daily lives, you can contact two locally based organizations.

Respons Sustainable Tourism Center (28 de Julio 821, tel. 043/42-7949, www.respons.org) is the newest and, so far, the most complete center offering a wide variety of experiences in nearby indigenous communities, such as homestays in Vicos, Umacchuco, or Huaripampa, as well as treks to lakes and the Inka Naani, a well preserved segment of the Inca road between Áncash and Huánuco. Dutch-born Guido van Es and Pablo Tadeo of Vicos, who are co-heads at the center, will offer you options in order to design your travel experience exactly as you wish.

Andean Alliance (Km 3.1 Marian Cachipampa Road, tel. 043/978-9330, www.thelazydoginn.com), a nonprofit run by the Lazy Dog Inn's Canadian owners, tries to match your skills and availability with community projects. If you're gardener, for example, you might end up working in a community greenhouse. Diana can arrange a homestay or camping in local towns, but you should consider staying at the inn.

Tour Agencies and Guides

The conventional day tour leaves Huaraz at 9:30 A.M., returns at 7:30 or 8 P.M., costs between US$10 and US$12 pp, and includes transport and guide. Bring plenty of warm clothes, bag lunch, and sun protection, and make sure your guide speaks English well.

The most reliable tour operator is **Pablo Tours** (Luzuriaga 501, tel. 043/42-1145, www.pablotours.com). Other options are **Chavín Tours** (Luzuriaga 502, tel. 043/42-1578, www.chavintours.com.pe) and **Sechín Tours** (Julián de Morales 602, tel. 043/42-1419, www.sechintours.com). Although these agencies offer other trips, their services are only recommended for conventional tours.

ACCOMMODATIONS

A top destination for international trekkers and climbers, Huaraz is full of high quality hostels. Prices for lodging and transport double or even triple during high season and the national holidays July 25–August 5. To get into some hotels, you'll need to make reservations three months in advance.

Under US$10

Familia Meza Lodging (Lúcar y Torre 538, tel. 043/42-6763 familiameza_lodging@hotmail.com, US$8 pp) has private rooms with shared bath in a safe and pleasant building just a block from Luzuriaga. Features include a terrace with views, a fully-equipped, open-air kitchen, and laundry service. This hostel is run by one of Huaraz's most friendly families, which operates a plethora of recommended businesses out of an office downstairs: the Sierra Verde Spanish School, Mountain Bike Adventures, and the Last Minute Gift Shop.

US$10-25

Jo's Place (Daniel Villazón 276, tel. 043/42-5505, josplacehuaraz@hotmail.com, US$11 s, US$14 d) is north of the Río Quilcay and about a 15-minute walk from city center. Here Jo Parsons, a British expat, and his Peruvian wife have created a friendly and relaxed collection of rooms that ring a hammock-filled garden. All guests have access to a simple shared kitchen, WiFi, a TV and DVD room with books, laundry service, and long-term storage space. Rooms with shared baths are US$5.50 pp, and the newest rooms have mountain views.

Backed against the Cordillera Negra, **Edward's Inn** (Bolognesi 121, tel. 043/42-2692, www.edwardsinn.com, US$12.50 s, US$25 d) has the feeling of truly being near the mountains. The quiet hotel has gardens, a small café, and an excellent view into the soccer stadium. Breakfast is available for US$3 (Continental) or US$3.50 (American). Simple rooms have private bathrooms and solar-heated hot water. Cheaper dorm rooms cost US$7.50–10. The Peruvian owner, Eduardo Figueroa, is

a certified guide and resource for treks, climbs, and *arrieros*.

B y B My House (27 de Noviembre 773, tel. 043/42-3375, bmark@viabcp.com, US$11 pp with breakfast) is a charming home tucked away in a central, but tranquil, neighborhood. The six rooms spiral around a sunny courtyard. Beds are comfortable, and rooms have a writing desk and private baths. The hostel is in the home of Alcides Ames and his wife, Francisca. Alcides, who speaks mostly French, is a long-time Huaraz resident and one of the area's foremost glaciologists. He has climbed nearly every peak in the Cordillera Blanca.

The popular, family-run **C Churup Bed and Breakfast** (Amadeo Figueroa 1257, La Soledad, tel. 043/42-4200, www.churup.com, US$23 s, US$32 d with breakfast) has 16 simple rooms intermixed with nicely furnished sitting areas, a top floor lounge, and even a foosball table. The book exchange, laundry area, shared kitchen, equipment rental, and Spanish classes are likely to tempt you out of your room and into conversations with other travelers. Owners Nelly and Juan Quiros and their son Juan Manuel, a trekking guide, serve a fortifying breakfast and offer cheaper bunk rooms downstairs (US$6 pp) without breakfast.

US$25-50

A solid favorite among climbers is **C La Casa de Zarela** (Julio Arguedas 1263, tel. 043/42-1694, www.lacasadezarela.com, US$27 s or US$32 d). Spiral stairs lead up from a sunny courtyard to rooms and terraces with spectacular Cordillera Blanca views. The 17 rooms are simple but a good value. There is WiFi, and breakfast is served in the homey downstairs area, with very good coffee, the best burritos in town, and a great variety of herbs and teas. There is also a bar. A rooftop kitchen is available for the use of all guests.

Huaraz native Tito Olaza has guessed the traveler's every need, and answered it in his intimate, nine-room guesthouse **Olaza's Bed & Breakfast** (Julio Arguedas 1242, tel. 043/42-2529, www.olazas.com, US$29 s, US$32 d with breakfast). The water's hot, the shared kitchen is sparkling, and the fourth-floor lounge has a DVD player, fireplace, and fridge full of cold beers. Breakfast is served on the sunny rooftop patio, and views of the mountains are explained on a notecard that accompanies your hot coffee. Tito has plans to add a mellow, evening café.

US$50-100

Hotel Colomba (Francisco de Zela 278, tel. 043/42-1241, www.huarazhotel.com, US$68 s, US$86 d), once a hacienda, has been converted into a series of large rooms spread out through a labyrinth of gardens and grassy lawns. Lucho and Sylvana Maguiña, the Peruvian-Argentine owners, are extremely generous and kind. And with all the birds, peace, and quiet, you might think you were in the countryside. This hotel is north of the Río Quilcay and a few minutes' taxi ride into the center.

A bit out of the town center, **San Sebastian Hotel** (Italia 1124, tel. 043/42-6960, www.sansebastianhuaraz.com, US$52–58 s, US$66–70 d with breakfast) is a very relaxed, safe option. All rooms have been recently built or remodeled, so bathrooms are new and beds are plushly covered with duvets. The main lobby has Internet, WiFi, big sofas, and a TV with DVD player. The adjoining breakfast room doubles as a cozy pizzeria in the evening.

Over US$100

The distinctively Swiss **Andino Club Hotel** (Pedro Cochachín 357, tel. 043/42-1662, www.hotelandino.com, US$100 s, US$121 d) is the luxury hotel of Huaraz, with an elegant lobby, great views, and a very good international restaurant. Room styles vary according to location within the hotel, and it is worth asking in advance which services your room will have. More expensive rooms include terraces with views and bathtubs, and there are also accessible rooms and mini apartments with kitchen, DVD player, and whirlpool tubs. Additional services include laundry, mail, free Internet, and a travel agency that rents four-wheel drives and organizes horseback riding, canoeing, and

fishing adventures. Many international climbing and trekking agencies stay here with their groups, so make reservations ahead of time.

Outside Huaraz

Snowcapped peaks tower above **The Lazy Dog Inn** (Km 3.1 Marian Cachipampa Road, tel. 043/978-9330, www.thelazydoginn.com, US$40–80 depending on room type, with breakfast and dinner), which rests at the foot of the Cordillera Blanca. This unique bed-and-breakfast, 20 minutes outside of Huaraz, is the home of Diana Morris and Wayne Lamphier, a Canadian couple who open their stylish adobe lodge and two adobe cabins to guests. All the rooms are tastefully decorated and painted in warm colors. Amenities include WiFi access, on-site horses, and an outdoor sauna. If you coordinate your visit in advance, Diana will help you plan treks, day hikes, and horseback rides from the Inn.

The British owner of **The Way Inn Lodge** (15 km up the Pitec road, www.thewayinn.com, US$10 dorm, US$16 d) describes his retreat as a big playground. The eight-room lodge, 30 minutes from Huaraz, has spectacularly close mountain views, beds with cozy duvets and orthopedic mattresses, and plenty of board games to while away the hours. Horseback riding and other outdoor activities can be arranged with advance notice.

FOOD

Huaraz is filled with a variety of high-quality restaurants, comparable only to Cusco or Arequipa.

Cafés, Bakeries, and Ice Cream

Café Andino (Lúcar y Torre 530, 3rd Fl., tel. 084/42-1203, www.cafeandino.com, 8 A.M.–10 P.M. daily, US$3–8) is a great meeting spot for travelers, coffee lovers, and avid readers. The Peruvian-U.S. owners, Ysabel Meza and Chris Benway, are warm hosts and an endless gold mine of information about mountain climbing and trekking in the Cordillera Blanca and Huayhuash. Their café is filled with maps, books, and big tables, perfect for trip planning.

As you while away the day over books, magazines, WiFi, and board games, order up a strong cup of joe (Chris roasts his own beans), a salad, sandwich, or even *lomo saltado.* The menu is inventive and diverse.

California Café (28 de Julio 562, tel. 043/42-8354, http://huaylas.com/californiacafe, 7:30 A.M.–6 P.M. Mon.–Sat., 8 A.M.–3 P.M. Sun., US$3–5) feels as if it was lifted out of laid-back Berkeley, California. The strong espressos, tempting desserts, board games, WiFi, magazines, a big book exchange, and couches will keep you seated for hours. Breakfast and light meals are served.

Restaurant Encuentro Grill and Coffee (Luzuriaga block 6, Parque del Periodista, tel. 043/42-7971, 8 A.M.–midnight daily, US$3.50–5) has tables set in a sunny square and is a good place to sit and have a beer, lemonade, or coffee. It serves Peruvian food such as tamales, *trucha,* and roasted guinea pig as well as sandwiches, pastas, and grilled meats.

The cozy **Pizzeria Alpes Andes** (Parque Ginebra 28-G, tel. 043/42-1811, 6–11 A.M. and 5–11 P.M. daily, US$3) is next to the Casa de Guías and serves seriously strong coffee, yogurt, and muesli in the mornings, and great pizzas in the evening.

Piccolo Café and Pizzeria (Julián de Morales 632, tel. 043/50-9210, 7 A.M.–midnight daily, US$3.50–8) has outdoor tables on the park and is best for an afternoon drink.

It's worth a walk to the south end of Luzuriaga for the apple pie at **Buongiorno** (Luzuriaga 1190, tel. 043/42-7145, 6 A.M.–10 P.M. daily, US$0.50). The display case also holds tempting cheesecakes, mousses, and empanadas. **Manjar Real** (Raimondi 624, tel. 043/948-9118, 6 A.M.–10:30 P.M. daily) will cure your sweet tooth with ice cream, cakes, and pastries. Delicious gelato stands line Luzuriaga, but the best is **Buono** (Luzuriaga and Jose de la Mar, 10 A.M.–11 P.M. daily) with *manjar,* peanut, and coconut flavors.

Peruvian

Las Tulpas & Chimichurri Restaurant (Julián de Morales 759, maviqrojo@yahoo.

com, 8 A.M.–10 P.M. daily, US$4–9) has good Peruvian food. The daily menu is US$3.50, and à la carte items include *lomo al pesto, brochetas,* and *arroz con pato.* There are also several vegetarian options.

Next door is the cozy, and slightly more classic, **Café Restaurant Rinconcito Minero** (Julián de Morales 757, tel. 043/42-2875, 8 A.M.–11 P.M. daily, US$3–10). The restaurant may be known for its *tacu tacu* (a fried rice and bean patty), but the menu is extensive, including breakfast and fish.

For country-style Peruvian fare in a garden setting, head to one of the many *recreos* along the Huaraz–Caraz Highway. One we especially like is **La Colina** (100 meters from Essalud, tel. 043/42-8841, 11 A.M.–6 P.M. daily) just outside of Huaraz near the Es Salud Hospital. Lunch is flavorful and full of roasted guinea pig, rabbit, pisco sours, and *chicha de jora.* In Huaraz itself there is also ◖ **Recreo Pilatos** (Pedro Cochachin 146, tel. 043/42-2444, noon–6 P.M. daily, US$1–2). It serves steaming white-corn tamales and huge plates of *chicharrón.*

International

Pachamama (San Martín 687, tel. 043/42-1834, www.huaraz.net/pachamama, 4 P.M.–close daily, US$4–6) serves a variety of Italian and Peruvian dishes, as well as the house specialty, *raclette.* The indoor, glass-covered patio (great for stargazing) holds a fireplace, pool and table tennis tables, a giant chess board, a sapo table, occasional live music, and intriguing, purchasable paintings.

Filled with wooden tables, Swiss flags, and warm lighting, **Inka Pub Monte Rosa** (José de la Mar 661, tel. 043/42-1447, 11 A.M.–midnight daily, US$4–9) feels like a European mountain lodge. The bar, with its good beer and wine selection, is a perfect pub stop, and the tempting restaurant menu is likely to invite you to stay for more. Pizza, grilled meat, pasta, Peruvian food, and fondue are among the choices.

Acclaimed throughout Peru as the country's best Thai restaurant, **Siam de los Andes** (Julián de Morales and Gamarra, tel. 043/50-9173, 11 A.M.–3 P.M. and 6–10 P.M. daily,

US$5) is the creation of a native Thai chef who worked in the United States for 15 years. Elephants decorate the elegant dining room, and peanut, mint, coconut, and curry flavors fill the dishes.

☾ Mi Chef Kristof (Parque del Periodista, tel. 043/42-6765) has great salads, soups (try the Thai soup), fresh pasta—the spaghetti with chicken and curry sauce is the best—meat dishes, and excellent desserts, such as the chocolate mousse. The place is cozy, and it has a nice lounge area in the back where you can have a drink or two or see a movie.

☾ Chilli Heaven (Parque Ginebra, next to Casa de Guías, tel. 043/22-1313, chilliheaven@hotmail.com, US$5–10) is exactly that. You won't find any other eatery in Huaraz, actually in the country, with so many varieties of chili sauces. And all of them are good and spicy enough to go along with the Indian and Thai curries (with rice or noodles), Mexican food, or the pizzas.

Fine Dining

The quiet and cozy, French-owned **Bistro de los Andes** (Julián de Morales 823, tel. 043/42-6249, 7 A.M.–11 P.M. Mon.–Sat., 3–11 P.M. Sun., US$5–9) is *the* spot for a special meal. The menu includes red curry chicken, grilled trout, pesto pasta, a vegetable stir-fry, and beef bourguignonne. As you wait, there are fresh-baked French baguettes and an extensive wine list to enjoy. The restaurant has a less formal second location in Plaza de Armas, above the Serpost.

Creperie Patrick (Luzuriaga 422, tel. 043/42-6037, 5:30–10:30 P.M. Mon.–Sat., US$2–8), also French owned, invites a long and leisurely meal. The service is unhurried, and the flavorfully prepared crepes, fish, meat, and chicken dishes deserve to be enjoyed. The textured restaurant walls and dark wooden tables create an intimate setting, and the espresso and wine list are both good.

Pizza

Pizza B&B (José de la Mar 674, tel. 043/42-1719, 5 P.M.–midnight daily, US$3–5) is not simply an excellent pizza place. The French owners have a menu that offers fresh salads, very good pastas, lasagnas, trout, their famed wood-fired pizzas, and the real and genuine *flambée flammenkuche,* the house specialty. Additionally, this is the place to find an interesting and high-alcohol-content variety of Belgian, British, French, and German beers (US$8–12 each).

A good family option, **Pizza Bruno** (Luzuriaga 834, tel. 043/42-5689, 3–11 P.M. daily, US$5) has games for the kids and white tablecloths for the parents. The *pizza caprese* is highly recommended, but the French chef also serves salads, crepes, pastas, and steaks.

The busy, but cozy, **El Horno** (Luzuriaga block 6, Parque del Periodista, tel. 043/42-4617, www.elhornopizzeria.com, 5–11 P.M. Mon.–Sat., US$3–5) serves thin-crust pizzas, large salads, grilled meats, and sandwiches.

Vegetarian

The clean and well-kept **Fuente de Salud** (José de la Mar 562, tel. 043/42-7428, 8 A.M.–11:30 P.M. daily, US$1–6) serves natural yogurts, muesli, and fruit salads for breakfast, as well soy-based entrées, pastas, and even steaks throughout the day. It has an excellent set-price vegetarian menu.

Markets

Huaraz's market runs along Raimondi from Luzuriaga down to Cruz Romero and is generally open from dawn to dusk. The best selection is in a market building at the corner of San Martín and Raimondi. Inside are a few booths that supply a wide range of food for trekkers, including some imported products (although no freeze-dried food). Surrounding the market are stalls of fruits, vegetables, mountain cheese, and freshly slaughtered chickens. Anything you cannot find here, like fresh bread, will be in the minimarkets on San Martín.

The best grocery stores, which do not have a good section of produce, are **Market Ortiz** (Luzuriaga 401, tel. 043/42-1653, 8 A.M.–10 P.M. daily) or, on the opposite side of town, **Novoplaza** (Luzuriaga 882, tel. 043/42-2945,

7 A.M.–11 P.M. Mon.–Fri., 7 A.M.–midnight Sat., 8 A.M.–11 P.M. Sun.).

INFORMATION AND SERVICES

The best spot for trekking and climbing info is **Casa de Guías** (Parque Ginebra 28-G, tel. 043/42-7545, www.casadeguias.com.pe, 8 A.M.–1 P.M. and 4–8 P.M. Mon.–Sat., open Sun. during high season), but all the trekking and climbing agencies, along with **Vagamundo Travelbar & Maps** (Julián de Morales 753, tel. 043/50-9063) and **Café Andino** (Lúcar y Torre 530, 3rd Fl., tel. 084/42-1203, www.cafeandino.com) sell maps and books.

The government's **Iperú** on Plaza de Armas (Luzuriaga 734, 2nd Fl., Pasaje Atusparía, tel. 043/42-8812, www.peru.info/iperu, 8 A.M.–6:30 P.M. Mon.–Sat., 8:30 A.M.–2 P.M. Sun.) gives limited advice but can provide lists of official trekking agencies.

Parque Nacional Huascarán (Sal y Rosas 555, tel. 043/42-2086, 8:30 A.M.–1 P.M. and 2:30–5:30 P.M. Mon.–Fri., 8:30–11 A.M. Sat.) sells entry tickets to the park (US$20 for climbing and trekking, US$2 for day).

To plan a trip to the Callejón de Conchucos, including Chavín de Huántar, visit the valley's helpful information office (Julián de Morales 616, tel. 043/42-2313, ecastro@rainforest.com, 9 A.M.–1 P.M. and 3–7 P.M. Mon.–Sat.).

The best website on Huaraz is www.huaraz.com. Other good pages include www.andeanexplorer.com, www.huaraz.org, and www.huaylas.com. The outfits that maintain these websites also put out helpful brochures with good area maps. Weather information can be found at www.senamhi.gob.pe.

Police and Emergency

The 24-hour **tourist police** office is in a small passageway on the west side of the Plaza de Armas (Luzuriaga 734, 2nd Fl., Pasaje Atusparía, tel. 043/42-1330). There is also a 24-hour **national police** office (28 de Julio 701 tel. 043/72-1021). For mountain emergencies, call the **Casa de Guías** (tel. 043/42-7545) or the Yungay-based, 24-hour **Unidad de**

Salvamento de Alta Motaña (USAM, High Mountain Rescue Unit, tel. 043/39-3333, 043/39-3327, or 043/39-3291, www.huaraz.info/usam).

Health Care

The best clinic in town is **Clínica San Pablo** (Huaylas 172, tel. 043/42-8811, 24 hours). For attention at your hotel, call **Dr. Saul Benavides** (tel. 043/948-5425). For nonemergencies the public hospitals are much cheaper. The best is **Hospital Huaraz** (Luzuriaga, block 13, tel. 043/42-1861 or 043/42-4146, 24 hours).

On Luzuriaga, there are several big, well-stocked, brand-name **pharmacies** like Botica Fasa, InkaFarma, and Botica Arcangel. Most of these are open 7 A.M.–11 P.M. daily.

Banks and Money Exchange

Clustered around the Plaza de Armas are several banks with ATMs: **Banco de Crédito, Scotiabank, Banco Continental,** and **Interbank.** Banks are generally open 9 A.M.–1 P.M. and 4–6:30 P.M. Monday–Friday and 9:30 A.M.–noon Saturday. The exception is Banco de Crédito, which doesn't close midday.

Communications

The **Serpost** post office (702 Luzuriaga, tel. 043/42-1030, 8 A.M.–8:30 P.M. Mon.–Fri., 8 A.M.–8 P.M. Sat.) is on the main plaza.

There are many fast Internet cafés around town, and several are on Sucre, east of the Plaza de Armas. These cafés are open daily approximately 7 A.M.–11 P.M.

At the corner of Sucre and Simón Bolívar, a handful of call centers have phone booths and sell phone cards. Here, you can make local, national, and international calls 7 A.M.–10 P.M. daily.

Language Schools

The best language school in Huaraz is **Sierra Verde** (Lucar y Torres 538, tel. 043/42-1203, sierraverde_sp@hotmail.com), which offers both private classes and group lessons. Another good option is **Langway** (Luzuriaga 975, #203, tel. 043/42-4286, langwayhz@yahoo.com), which offers classes not only in Spanish, but also English, Italian, German, Japanese, and Quechua.

Volunteering

The best volunteering option in the Cordillera Blanca is undoubtedly **The Center for Social Well Being** (tel. 01/252-2947, www.social-wellbeing.org). The goal of this nonprofit organization, founded in 2000 by veteran anthropologist Patricia Hammer, is to improve the lives of Andean people. The organization is run through the delightful **Casa de Pocha,** a five-hectare highland ranch outside of Carhuaz, and offers many opportunities for both volunteering and academic field trips. The center also offers Quechua and Spanish language lessons, and health and healing workshops.

Laundry

The best laundries are the **Lavandería Liz** (José de la Mar 674, tel. 043/42-1719, 9 A.M.–1 P.M. and 3–8 P.M. Mon.–Sat., US$1/kg) and **Lavandería Denny's** (José de la Mar 561, tel. 043/42-9232, 8 A.M.–9 P.M. Mon.–Sat., US$1/kg).

Massage and Spa

The **Centro Holístico** (Av. Villon 756, tel. 043/42-8277, 8 A.M.–1 P.M. and 3–9 P.M. daily, www.centroholisticoperu.com), run by the professional Flor Figueroa, offers massages, chiropractic treatments, hypothermal baths, and psychotherapy. The center's facilities are simple, but the treatment prices are very reasonable (US$11–17). Make reservations in advance.

GETTING THERE AND AROUND

LC Busre (tel. 01/619-1313, www.lcbusre.net) has daily flights (US$130, one-way) to the area's airport, which is 32 kilometers north of Huaraz in Anta.

Huaraz is a comfortable 7–8-hour bus ride from Lima. The highway runs up to Lago Conococha at 4,000 meters before dropping into the Callejón de Huaylas and Huaraz.

Buses going back and forth to Lima often start and end in Caraz, passing Huaraz en route. In recent years, bus companies have begun to pay particular attention to safety, and it is common for all passengers to be videotaped before departure. These extra measures have made night travel safer.

The best option for Lima–Huaraz travel is **Movil Tours** (Simón Bolívar 452, tel. 043/42-2555, www.moviltours.com.pe, 7 A.M.–11 P.M.), which has a range of buses to Lima with a late-night, 180-degree reclinable seat service, just like in a first-class flight. Movil also goes to Chimbote and Trujillo.

A similar service, but not as comfortable, is provided by **Cruz del Sur** (Simón Bolívar 491, tel. 043/42-8726, www.cruzdelsur.com.pe, 5 A.M.–10 P.M. daily). The company has buses only to Lima.

The cheaper option is **ZBus** (Simón Bolívar 440, tel. 043/42-8327), which has two daily bus departures.

Yungay Express (Raimondi 930, tel. 043/42-4377, 6 A.M.–9 P.M. daily) has day buses that follow a gravel road through the Cañon de Pato to Chimbote (eight hours).

For reaching Chavín de Huántar and the cities east of the Cordillera Blanca in the Callejón de Conchucos, **Chavín Express** (Mariscal Cáceres 338, tel. 043/42-4652, 5 A.M.–10 P.M. daily) sends three buses per day.

For making the interesting journey across the high plains east of Huaraz to Huánuco, **Transportes El Rápido** (Bolognesi 261, tel. 043/42-2887, 5 A.M.–8 P.M. daily) will get you as far as the midway point of La Unión (five hours). The company also travels to Huallanca (four hours), a starting point for treks in the Cordillera Huayhuash.

For heading north to **Monterrey,** catch the green-and-white buses from the corner of Luzuriaga and 28 de Julio (US$0.30, 30 minutes). Or hop a *combi* or *colectivo,* which will take you as far Caraz. Departure points for these communal transports were scheduled to change. Ask at your hotel or the Iperú office for the current bus stop.

For reaching **Recuay** and points along

the highway south of Huaraz, head to the Transportes Zona Sur terminal at Gridilla and Tarapacá.

Taxis are cheap in Huaraz and cost US$1–1.50 for in-town travel. The Andino Club Hotel and Inka Pub Monte Rosa rent four-wheel drives and motorcycles.

C CHAVÍN DE HUÁNTAR

Chavín de Huántar (tel. 043/42-4042, 8 A.M.–5 P.M. daily, US$3.50), four hours east of Huaraz, was the capital of the Chavín culture, which spread across Peru's northern highlands 2000–200 B.C. The site includes a sunken plaza ringed with stylized carvings of pumas and priests holding the hallucinogenic San Pedro cactus. A broad stairway leads to a U-shaped stone temple, called the **Castillo,** which rises 13 meters off the ground in three levels of stone.

This site was visited by Italian explorer **Antonio Raymondi** in the 19th century and later excavated in the early 20th century by **Julio Tello.** Both men brought back elaborately carved pillars, which are now on display in Lima's museums. Tello developed an elaborate theory that Chavín de Huántar was the launching pad for all of Peru's advanced cultures. Recent excavations have revealed that the city was preceded by Caral and other important centers on the coast, but Chavín's importance is still irrefutable. During its peak from 400–200 B.C., the Chavín culture spread across Peru as far as Ayacucho in the south and Cajamarca in the north. Its exotic deities, which included the puma and a mythical deity with a staff in its hand, became central icons throughout Peru's ancient art and iconography.

The highlight of Chavín de Huántar is the series of underground chambers beneath the main temple. Illuminated by electric light, three of these passages converge underground

giant stone sculpture from Chavín de Huántar

© JORGE RIVEROS CAYO

at an extraordinary stone carving, known as the **Lanzón.** This granite pillar is carved with a frightening mythical being, which has thick, snarling lips and a pair of menacing, upward-arching canines. Heavy earrings hang from the ears and snakes appear to grow from the head. The notched top of the pillar extends upward into an upper gallery, where priests may once have performed rituals.

Its underground architecture gives Chavín de Huántar an entirely different feel than the other cultural ruins of northern Peru. The sensation is part-playful and part-terrifying. As you wind your way through impressive, ventilated tunnels that once led to dressing and ceremonial rooms, you can't help imagine the terrible existence of the prisoners who were also kept in the tight underground passageways.

Many of Huaraz's agencies offer a day tour to Chavín de Huántar, which leaves Huaraz at 9:30 A.M. and returns about 10 hours later. Although this is an efficient way to see the ruins, with a tour group, you are unlikely to perceive the true magnitude of the sight, because all agencies hit the ruins at the same hour (right after lunch). There's a bit of herding as people try to move in and out of tight spaces. It is advisable to go on your own, spend the night in Chavín, and head to the ruins early. At the entrance, you can contract a Spanish-speaking guide (US$8).

Shopping

You have to knock to be let into the **Centro Artesanal** (across from the Centro de Salud, 2–6:30 P.M. daily), but the co-op's sweaters, tablecloths, and hand-knit shawls are worth a heavy pounding. Made by local women, who study weaving at the center, the textiles are brightly colored and high quality. If you ask, you can usually see the women at work.

Accommodations

Hostal La Casona (Plaza de Armas 130, tel. 043/45-9004, lacasonachavin.peru.com, US$5 s without bath, US$10 d with bath) offers pleasant rooms circled around a stone patio. All rooms have good beds and TV. Bathrooms may

be private or shared. Once a busy house full of eight children, **Gran Hotel R'ickay** (17 de Enero 172, tel. 043/45-4068, informes@www. hotelrickay.com, US$22 s, US$38 d) is now a quiet and clean hotel. Rooms are a bit dark, but they are wrapped around sunny patios.

Food

Café Renato (Huayna Cápac 285, Plaza de Armas, tel. 043/50-4279, 7 A.M.–10 P.M. daily) makes its own yogurt, cheese, and *manjar,* which it serves up in a small corridor of a patio. The café can also arrange horseback riding trips. Close by is **La Portada** (17 de Enero 311, tel. 043/50-4292, 7 A.M.–8 P.M. daily, US$2–6), which has good food, including *cuy* and *conejo* (rabbit). Next door to the ruins, **Buongiorno** (17 de Enero 520, tel. 043/45-4112, 7 A.M.–8 P.M. daily, US$2–5) has a flavorful and interesting menu, which features local foods like trout, guinea pig, and *pachamanca.* Service can be slow. At lunchtime, **Restaurant Chavín** (17 de Enero 439, tel. 043/45-4051, 7 A.M.–10 P.M. daily) is full of tour groups filling up on trout, chicken, and rabbit. Word has it that the restaurant serves a mean *pastel de manzanas* (apple pie).

Information and Services

The Plaza de Armas has both call centers and Internet cafés. The Centro de Salud (24 hours) is on the main road, heading toward San Marco.

Getting There and Around

There is a spectacular trek that crosses the southern end of the Cordillera Blanca from **Olleros,** a village just south of Huaraz, to Chavín de Huántar. The trek, which is not crowded, heads along an ancient trade route up and over **Yanashallash Pass** at 4,700 meters.

From Huaraz, **Chavín Express** buses (Mariscal Cáceres 338, Huaraz, tel. 043/42-4652, 5 A.M.–10 P.M. daily) head to the town of Chavín, about one kilometer north of the ruins. Until 4 or 5 P.M., regular *combis* head through the valley toward San Marcos.

Callejón de Huaylas

Huaraz lies at the top of the Callejón de Huaylas, a river valley that cuts between the Cordilleras Blanca and Negra. As you descend into the valley, there are a handful of pleasant towns. Among them, Carhuaz, Yungay, and Caraz are reasonable base-town alternatives to Huaraz.

MONTERREY

Easygoing Monterrey is seven kilometers north of Huaraz. Reputed for its hot springs and saunas, the town also has a few worthwhile hotels and restaurants. The **hot springs** (7 A.M.–6 P.M. daily, US$1) include two large pools, of varying temperatures, along with private bathing rooms. Don't be put off by the water, which is simply stained brown by minerals. Slightly past Monterrey, **La Reserva** (Km 8 Huaraz–Caraz Highway, tel. 043/42-4865, 8 A.M.–6 P.M. Tues.–Sun.) offers Turkish baths, as well as steam and dry saunas. The facilities are clean and well-kept.

Accommodations

There are no good budget options in Monterrey, and prices rise during high season. The best lodging choice is the peaceful **El Patio de Monterrey** (Km 206 Huaraz–Caraz Highway, tel. 043/42-4965, www.elpatio.com.pe, US$59 s, US$69 d with breakfast). The colonial-style hotel, with tile roofs, a stone terrace, and water fountain, has rooms with nice furniture and all the modern amenities, minus cable TV. Many of the rooms look out over gardens, and meals are served in a dining area with fireplace.

Right next to the hot baths is the former state-owned **Real Hotel Baños Termales Monterrey** (Upper Av. Monterrey s/n, tel. 043/42-7690, US$22 s, US$30 d). This rather austere hotel has rooms with hot showers, temperamental service, a handful of more expensive bungalows, and free access to the hot baths.

Food

There are several small *recreos,* or country restaurants, near Monterrey. The best is **El Ollón**

de Barro (Km 7 Huaraz–Caraz Highway, tel. 043/42-3364, US$3–8), which serves up huge portions of *chicharrón,* huge red *rocoto* peppers stuffed with spiced meat, local trout, and grilled meats. Tables are spread around a grassy lawn, and there is a playground for kids. Owners Patrick and Adela also run Creperie Patrick in Huaraz. Another good option is **El Cortijo** (Huaraz–Caraz Highway s/n, tel. 043/42-3813, 8 A.M.7 P.M. daily, US$5–12), where tables spill out onto a grassy, bougainvillea-lined garden, and lunch is often a pisco sour, *papa a la huancaina, pachamanca,* and *humitas.*

Getting There and Around

From the south end of Huaraz, at the corner of Luzuriaga and 28 de Julio, catch the green-and-white buses to Monterrey (US$0.30, 30 minutes). Or from the north end, hop on any valley-bound *combi* or *colectivo.* Ask at your hotel or the Iperú office for the *combi* stop. A taxi costs US$2 from Huaraz to Carhuaz.

On the Huaraz–Caraz Highway in Monterrey, you can catch a *combi* back to Huaraz or on to the remaining towns in the Callejón de Huaylas.

CARHUAZ

Carhuaz is a quiet town with spectacular views of **Hualcán.** At 2,650 meters above sea level, the town is about 400 meters lower than Huaraz and about 32 kilometers farther down the valley. Carhuaz has just the right amount of tourist infrastructure to make it a comfortable place to stay without being a go-go tourist destination. It is pleasant relief from Huaraz. The relaxing Plaza de Armas is full of fragrant rose gardens and palm trees. The town's Wednesday and especially **Sunday markets** are busy and diverse. Colorfully dressed vendors hawk local fruits and vegetables, dried herbs, crafts, and even livestock.

The outskirts of Carhuaz stretch into the Cordilleras Negra and Blanca, which means the town has some great options for day trips. For US$3, you can hire a taxi to take you to **Mirador Ataquero** in the Cordillera Negra. Walk back following a trail that drops you on the edge of town. There are rustic hot baths above town at the **Baños de la Merced** (US$0.30). *Combis* heading that direction leave the Plaza de Armas once an hour, or hire a round-trip taxi (US$6). The **Cueva de Guitarreros,** a cave that was inhabited 12,000 years ago, is an hour's walk west of Tingua, the town north of Carhuaz.

Another highly recommended day excursion is hiking in the Cordillera Blanca. Take an early-morning *combi* heading east up the **Quebrada Ulta** to Chacas. Before the *combis* wind the final switchbacks to the high pass of **Punta Olímpica** (4,890 meters), there are starting points for two excellent day hikes. The first leads to **Laguna Auquiscocha** (4,320 meters), where there is a granite waterfall reminiscent of Yosemite Falls. The second leads to the stunning alpine cirque around **Lago Yanayacu** (4,600 meters). The last Carhuaz-bound *combi* leaves Chacas around 4 P.M.

Accommodations

The best budget option is the family-run **Casa Alojamiento Las Torrecitas** (Amazonas 412, tel. 043/39-4213, US$8 pp). Simple rooms face onto a long sofa-lined patio. Guests are allowed to use outdoor sinks for washing clothes and the family kitchen. **Las Bromelias Guesthouse** (Brasil 208, tel. 043/39-4014, US$6 s, US$12 d) features a garden with a *chirimoya* tree and roses. Rooms are clean with good beds, tile floors, and hot water.

A great country retreat is **Casa de Pocha** (1.5 kilometers east of town, tel. 043/961-3058, www.socialwellbeing.org, US$40–55 pp with breakfast and dinner). Perched in hills above Carhuaz with views of Hualcán, this hand-built home is surrounded by trees and a working organic farm. Peruvian Pocha and American Patricia live with a great consciousness of the natural world. Breakfast is cooked on solar stoves, showers are heated with solar energy, and dinner is made over an open flame.

Have in mind most meals are vegetarian. Both women speak fluent English and love engaging in political, environmental, and social justice conversations.

The retreat's adobe rooms are simple and rustic, and dinner is served outdoors or in a charming dining room. The grounds hold a sauna, a rec room with a pool table, and a sun-filled yoga studio. The lodge is 1.5 kilometers east out of town on a dirt road heading up the valley. Call or email ahead for reservations and directions.

More modern and centrally located is the immaculate **El Abuelo Hostal** (9 de Diciembre 257, tel. 043/39-4456, www.elabuelohostal. com, US$30 s, US$40 d with breakfast). The first-floor lobby opens onto a lovely garden full of local trees and plants. And upstairs, the rooms, decorated with Andean rugs, have comfortable beds and modern baths. There is also a terrace with great views of the Cordillera Negra.

Food

The best restaurant in town is **El Abuelo Café** (La Merced 727, Plaza de Armas, tel. 043/39-4149, 8 A.M.–9 P.M. daily, US$5–10). Operated by Felipe Diaz, the owner of El Abuelo Hostal, the clean restaurant looks on to the Plaza de Armas. For a midafternoon treat, have an espresso and a natural ice cream (flavors include pisco sour and beer!). And at mealtime, order up *ají de gallina, lomo saltado,* or a lighter sandwich and salad. The café also sells homemade marmalades of *sachatomate* (Andean tomato) and *sauco* (gooseberry), as well as local sheep wool weavings colored with natural dyes. **La Punta Olímpica** (La Merced 785, Plaza de Armas, tel. 043/39-4022, 8 A.M.–10 P.M., US$1.50) serves a cheaper but less reliably clean *comida típica*.

Information and Services

An extraordinary source of information, and an all-around nice guy, is local resident **Felipe Diaz,** who authored the Cordillera Blanca's most used trekking map. If you speak Spanish, he will talk your ears off about all the exciting trekking options in the area. Ask for him at El Abuelo Café or hostel. The newly opened **Puyas Expeditions** (Río Buin, Plaza de Armas, tel. 043/39-4472, puyasexpeditions@ yahoo.es) can provide helpful advice about day trips, but the quality of its guide services is uncertain. Carhuaz also has a small **tourist office** (Comercio 530, tel. 043/39-4294, 7:30 A.M.–12:30 P.M. and 1:30–4 P.M. Mon.–Fri.).

Several **pharmacies** ring the Plaza de Armas. Hours are typically 8 A.M.–1 P.M. and 3–10 P.M. daily.

Banco de la Nación has a branch on the Plaza de Armas, but there is no ATM in town.

The **post office,** also on the Plaza de Armas, is open 8 A.M.–noon and 2–5 P.M. Monday through Saturday. A few doors down, **St@rnet** (Río Buin 648, tel. 043/39-4332, 8 A.M.–midnight daily) has quick Internet as well as telephone booths for local, national, and international calls.

Getting There and Around

Carhuaz is a half hour north of Huaraz. For long-distance trips to Lima and Chimbote (both eight hours), **Movil Tours** (Plaza de Armas in Helados Huscarán, tel. 043/39-4141, 8 A.M.–9:30 P.M. daily) and **Yungay Express** (Progreso 672, tel. 043/39-4352, 7 A.M.–8 P.M. daily) are good options. The latter also has buses to Huallanca.

To get here from Huaraz, hop a Caraz-bound *combi* and get off in Carhuaz. From Carhuaz's Plaza de Armas, *combis* leave every 15 minutes heading south to Huaraz, north to Caraz, and, on market days, west toward the Mirador Ataquero and the Cordillera Negra.

YUNGAY

Yungay, 54 kilometers north of Huaraz, is a quiet town with minimal services, but it is the closest launching point for Lagunas Llanganuco and classic peaks such as Pisco and Huascarán.

The original village was the site of a horrific tragedy on May 31, 1970, when an earthquake

© RENÉE DEL GAUDIO AND ROSS WEHNER

The facade of Yungay's church was the only building left standing after the 1970 mudslide.

dislodged an immense chunk of mud and ice from Huascarán. The resulting *aluvión* destroyed the town in minutes and killed 18,000 people, nearly the entire village.

The few hundred survivors of the tragedy built a new settlement on a nearby, more protected, site. New Yungay is a mix of modern buildings and a hundred or so prefab wooden cabins that were donated by the former Soviet Union. The silt plain above the old village has been converted into the **Campo Santo Cemetery** (8 A.M.–6 P.M. daily, US$0.60) and remains a solemn place. The only evidence of the village is the tops of a few palm trees, which once ringed the town's square and now just barely stick out of the hardened mud, and the church's old facade.

In the floodplains nearby, huge boulders and a crumpled bus attest to the power of the mudslide. Miraculously, a huge white statue of Christ, which stands above the town's hilltop cemetery, survived the flooding. It was there that a few hundred people clambered to safety during the mudslide. From this statue, there are views over the entire valley up to the flanks of Huascarán, where the path of the mudslide can still be seen. There are two festivals here in October, including Virgen del Rosario in the first week of October and the town's anniversary, October 25–28.

◖ Lagunas Llanganuco

These two pristine lakes, surrounded by rare *polylepis* trees, are perched high in the glacial valley above Yungay at 3,850 meters. Between the tumbling glaciers of Huascarán's north summit (6,655 meters) and Huandoy (6,160 meters), the lake and its turquoise waters, a result of glacial silt, glow in the midday sun. The first lake is Chinacocha. Rowboats can be rented here 8 A.M.–3:30 P.M. The second lake is Orcon Cocha, and the best mountain views are a bit farther on.

The highway from Yungay passes these lakes en route to Portachuelo Llanganuco, a high pass at 4,767 meters, and leads to the towns of Vaquería, Colcabamba, and Yanama in the Callejón de Conchucos. Shortly before the lakes, there is a control booth of the Parque Nacional Huascarán, which charges day visitors US$2.50 and overnighters US$20.

These lakes are one of the starting points for the popular Santa Cruz trek. The base camp for climbing Pisco and the newly built Refugio Peru are a four-hour hike from the Lagunas Llanganuco. The best time to visit the Lagunas Llanganuco is at midday when the sun is brightest. In the afternoon, the lakes fall into shade and winds whip their waters.

Accommodations and Food

The only decent place to stay in Yungay is **Hostal Gledel** (Areas Graciani s/n, tel. 043/39-3048, US$5 pp). This very simple but clean hostel has solar-powered electricity and rooms with shared baths. The nicest rooms are upstairs.

While nothing fancy, **Chicken Progreso** (Areas Graciani s/n, tel. 043/58-4818, 7 A.M.–10 P.M. daily, US$2.50–5) serves up large portions of spit-roasted chicken with fries and salad, or *lomo saltado*.

© RENÉE DEL GAUDIO AND ROSS WEHNER

The waters of Lagunas Llanganuco are turquoise in the midday sun.

Restaurant Alpamayo (Km 255 of the highway, tel. 043/39-3090, 8 A.M.–10 P.M. daily, US$2–4) serves fortifying breakfasts of *chicharrón* and *tamal* and a range of Peruvian food throughout the day.

Information and Services

Yungay is headquarters of the national police **Unidad de Salvamento de Alta Montaña-USAM** (High Mountain Rescue Unit, tel. 043/79-3333, 043/39-3327, or 043/39-3291, www.pnp.gob.pe, 24 hours daily).

Getting There and Around

During high season (June–August) mini-buses take tourists from Yungay to Lagunas Llanganuco (26 kilometers). Early-morning buses for Yanama, on the other side of the Callejón de Huaylas, also leave from Yungay. The bus stop is at the intersection of Graziani and 28 de Julio. You can ask to be dropped off at the lakes. *Combi* transport heading north to Caraz or south to Huaraz is frequent.

CARAZ

Caraz, at the north end of the Callejón de Huaylas, is the valley's best option for those who are looking for a peaceful, less touristy option to Huaraz. It is a pretty town with a graceful plaza and colonial air. A market comes alive each day with fresh food, colorful basketry, gourd bowls, votive candles, and woven hats. Around the town are the brilliant glaciers of Huandoy, where the Río Santo begins to tumble toward the Pacific.

Despite its small size, Caraz offers good hotels and well-equipped, knowledgeable climbing and trekking agencies. At 2,285 meters, Caraz is 800 meters lower than Huaraz and enjoys much warmer weather. Its nickname, Caraz Dulzura (Sweet Caraz), denotes its reputation as a land of *manjar blanco,* a rich caramel spread.

Caraz is well positioned for the valley's major climbing and trekking endeavors. It is near a trailhead for the popular Santa Cruz trek and is close to Alpamayo. It is also the starting point for explorations into the rugged northern regions of the Cordillera Blanca. Carry cash since credit cards are not generally accepted in town.

Sights

There are a few excellent day excursions from Caraz. Just north of town, a road leads 32 kilometers up past towering granite walls to the spectacular **Laguna Parón,** the largest lake in the Cordillera Blanca. A dozen snow pyramids hem the lake in on all sides, including the perfect towers of Artesonraju (6,025 meters), Pirámide Garcilaso (5,885 meters), and Chacraraju (6,185 meters). This is a good spot for camping.

Just a few kilometers north of Caraz is **Tumshukaiko,** a huge archaeological site that looks like a fort and may have been built by the Chavín culture. To walk here from Caraz's main square, follow San Martín uphill, take a left on 28 de Julio, and continue to the bridge over the Río Llullan. The ruins are another 300 meters from here and before the road for Laguna Parón.

A rough dirt road heads west over the Cordillera Negra toward a gigantic stand of *Puya raimondii* plants at **Abra Huinchus** (4,300 meters). This road leads to the coast and, in the dry season, makes for a spectacular and fast mountain-bike descent.

Entertainment and Events

Turn off Daniel Villar Street, en route to Los Pinos Lodge, and you'll come across **La Taberna Tabasco** (8 P.M.–close Thurs.–Sat.), the only nightlife spot in Caraz. The rustic disco-pub is good for drinking, dancing, or both.

Recreation

Pony Expeditions (Jr. Sucre 1266, tel. 043/39-1642, www.ponyexpeditions.com) was founded in 1993 by Peruvian couple Aidé and Alberto Cafferata, and is the most solid adventure outfit in Caraz. It has top-rate equipment and offers a range of climbing, trekking, mountain biking, and fishing trips. Treks offered include the famous Santa Cruz loop (four days/three nights, starting from US$200 pp),

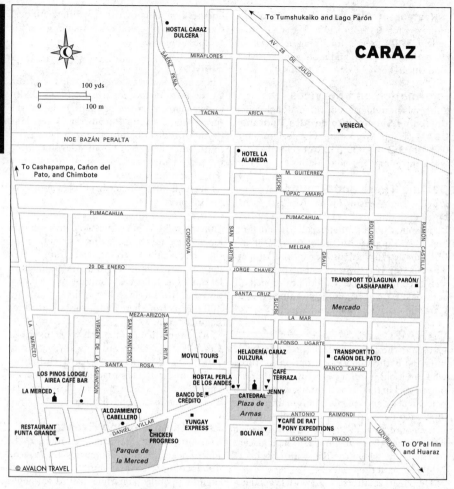

Alpamayo (12 days/11 nights, starting from US$600 pp), bike rentals to Cañó del Pato (US$18 pp), and guided climbs on nearly all of the technical peaks around Laguna Parón. English and French are spoken and there is a good gear shop where you can rent camping equipment and buy camping gas cartridges and very good maps.

Another good agency is **Summit Peru** (tel. 043/39-1958, www.summitperu.com). Because the company is primarily Web-based, it is a good idea to get in touch with Carlos Tinoco and Haren Montes, its operators, before you arrive in Caraz. Carlos and Haren organize a variety of trips and provide reliable equipment.

Accommodations

Both clean and safe, the eight-room **Alojamiento Caballero** (Daniel Villar 485, tel. 043/77-0919, US$4 pp) is a reliable budget option. The beds are droopy and bathrooms are shared, but there is a lovely little terrace, which looks out onto the street and the impressive peaks nearby.

The most tasteful option in town is **Los Pinos Lodge** (Parque San Martin 103, tel. 043/39-1130, www.apuaventura.com, US$11 s, US$20 d with breakfast). The lobby and 12 spacious rooms are filled with antiques, which give the house a colonial feel. Grassy gardens enclose the house and are perfect for post-trek sunbathing. Travel information, bike rental, book exchange, and a DVD library are available to all guests. The small restaurant is the town's best dinner option and serves a creative Novoandino menu.

Tucked away in a neighborhood above town is **Grand Hostal Caraz Dulzura** (Sáenz Peña 212, tel. 043/39-1523, www.hostalcarazdulcera.com, US$11 s, US$17 d with breakfast), a modern hotel with a friendly staff. The large rooms are plain but impeccably clean with comfortable beds. Downstairs, there is both a restaurant and a TV/DVD room. Knowledgeable owner Carlos Huaman enjoys helping travelers plan their adventure excursions.

For good service and a location on the main square, try **Hostal Perla de los Andes** (Daniel Villar 179, Plaza de Armas, tel. 043/39-2007, hostalperladelosandes@hotmail.com, US$11 s, US$17 d). Simple, unadorned rooms are clean, with cable TV and private baths, and there is a café downstairs.

Hotel La Alameda (Noe Bazán Peralta 262, tel. 043/39-1177, www.hotellaalameda.com, US$10–15 pp) is a maze of rooms, each one of surprisingly different quality. The primary distinction between the rooms is the comfort of the beds and shared versus private bathrooms. Regardless, all rooms are slightly overpriced.

Just one kilometer outside of town is the sprawling **O'Pal Inn** (Km 265.5 Huaraz–Caraz Highway, tel. 043/39-1015, www.opalsierraresort.com, US$14–20 pp). A series of rustic bungalows (some with kitchenettes) and spacious rooms, the inn is a good option for families or travelers looking for privacy. On the grounds, there are a playground, swimming pool, restaurant, and 60 hectares of orange groves.

Food

Café la Terraza (Jr. Sucre 1106, tel. 043/30-1226, 7 A.M.–11 P.M. daily, US$2–4) serves flavorful espresso, omelets, sandwiches, and main courses. It also makes box lunches for day hikers and has a great selection of homemade ice creams. Flavors include *lúcuma,* chocolate, and *manjar blanco.*

Café de Rat (Jr. Sucre 1266, tel. 043/39-1642, 8 A.M.–10 A.M. and 4–9 P.M. daily) is the most charming spot in Caraz, upstairs from Pony's Expeditions, serving breakfast, salads, pasta, pizzas and fondue upon request. The café has a cozy atmosphere, with a balcony from which there is a great view of the Plaza de Armas. Additionally there is WiFi and a book swap. Ask for crayons and sign the wall with an original drawing if you have the skills.

The best restaurant is **Airea Café Bar** (Parque San Martin 103, tel. 043/39-1130, US$6) inside Los Pinos Lodge. The tiny restaurant, packed with tables, serves breakfast and dinner. Andean cereals and fruit, trout with *sachatomate* (Andean tomato) sauce, and tofu are all on the menu.

For classic Peruvian food there's **Restaurant Punta Grande** (Daniel Villar 595, tel. 043/39-2101, 8 A.M.–7 P.M. daily, US$3). This pleasant garden restaurant serves fresh trout roasted over an open fire, grilled meats, and good corn tamales.

Stop at **Chicken Progreso** (Daniel Villar 326, US$3) for juicy *pollo a la brasa,* french fries, and a cold soft drink.

Information and Services

The **tourist office** (San Martín, tel. 043/39-1029, 7:45 A.M.–1 P.M. and 2:30–5 P.M. Mon.–Fri.) has city maps, though the best information is available from the agencies on the plaza.

Pharmacies, many of which are near the Plaza de Armas, are usually open 8 A.M.–1 P.M. and 4–10 P.M. daily.

Banco de Crédito (Daniel Villar 217, 10 A.M.–4 P.M. Mon.–Fri., 9:30 A.M.–12:30 P.M. Sat.) and **Banco de la Nación** are near the plaza, on Raimondi, both with ATMs.

Pony Expeditions will change U.S. dollars and euros.

Fast **Internet cafés,** some with telephone booths, can be found on just about every corner. Most locations are open 7 A.M.–10 P.M. daily.

Getting There and Around

Combis leave frequently along the highway south toward Yungay and Huaraz. When full, cars leave from the corner of Ramón Castilla and Santa Cruz at 5 A.M. and 1 P.M. for the 90-minute drive to Pueblo Parón, a village nine kilometers from Lago Parón. Cars from Pueblo Parón return to Caraz at 6 A.M. and 2 P.M. From Ramón Castilla and Santa Cruz, cars also leave for Cashapampa, a trailhead for the Santa Cruz trek. Trekkers can use these cars to get to and from Caraz.

Several bus companies travel to Lima from Caraz, with a stop in Huaraz along the way. **Movil Tours** (Córdoba block 1, tel. 043/39-1922, 7 A.M.–noon and 2–8:30 P.M. daily) is the best among the Lima-bound bus companies. **Yungay Express** (Daniel Villar 316, tel. 043/39-1888, 7 A.M.–7 P.M. daily) has a daily bus down the Cañon del Pato (US$6, nine hours) to Chimbote; from there same-day buses can be taken to Trujillo.

◖ CORDILLERA BLANCA

The spectacular wilderness of the **Parque Nacional Huascarán** includes Peru's tallest peak, Huascarán, and every bit of the Cordillera Blanca above 4,000 meters (except for Nevado Champará at the extreme northern end). The land drops away on all sides of this long but narrow range, creating an interesting island habitat for several endangered species. Among the park's 340,000 hectares (840,140 acres), there are *Puya raimondii,* the largest bromeliad in the world, and forests of endangered *polylepis,* the highest-altitude trees in the world. Andean condors can be seen here, as can populations of vicuñas, white-tailed deer, Andean dwarf deer, Andean lynx, foxes, pumas, and more than 100 species of birds.

© RENEE DEL GAUDIO AND ROSS WEHNER

Some of the Cordillera Blanca's hardest climbs, such as the Ocshapalca glacier, may only be climbed once every few years (if at all).

CLASSIC PEAKS OF THE CORDILLERA BLANCA

Peak	Altitude (meters)	Altitude (feet)	Time	Alpine Grade
Huascarán	6,768	22,204	6-8 days	PD/AD
Chopicalqui	6,354	20,847	4-6 days	AD
Tocllaraju	6,034	19,792	4-5 days	AD
Artesonraju	6,025	19,762	4-5 days	AD+
Alpamayo	5,947	19,511	6-8 days	AD+/D
Pisco	5,752	18,872	3-4 days	PD
Ishinca	5,534	18,151	3 days	PD
Urus	5,495	18,028	3 days	PD

Note: The alpine grading system is a French method for rating climbs according to their technical difficulty, number of belays, quality of rock, exposure to heights, objective dangers, etc. F = Easy (*Facile*), PD = Moderately difficult (*Peu difficile*), AD = Fairly difficult (*Assez difficile*), D = Difficult (*Difficile*), TD = Very difficult (*Très difficile*), ED = Extremely difficult (*Extrêmement difficile*), ABO = Horrible (*Abominable*).

The twin peaks of Huascarán are frequently covered by clouds in the afternoon.

ALUVIONES: MUDSLIDES IN THE CORDILLERA BLANCA

Huaraz's ramshackle appearance is due to a series of natural disasters that have, over the millennia, wrought havoc not only on this city but in the villages along the valley, which is known as the Callejón de Huaylas. The trouble is the hundreds of turquoise-colored lakes, which are perched thousands of feet above the valley. The lakes form behind push moraines, the huge hills of rock and dirt that an advancing glacier pushes like a bulldozer. When the glaciers retreat, as they have been doing for half a century, water collects behind these moraines to form lakes. After the lake fills, water trickles slowly over the top of the moraine and creates picturesque mountain streams. But trouble lies above, where the huge lakes are time bombs waiting to be sparked by the next earthquake, avalanche, or landslide – or sometimes a combination of all three.

Imagine holding a bucket filled with water and shaking it from side to side. Waves reverberate back and forth against the surface, banging and spilling over the sides of the bucket. When this happens to a glacial lake, the waves crash over the moraine again and again until it begins to erode. Then it goes altogether.

The result is a mass of boulders and mud that crashes and careens down the narrow mountain valleys at speeds over 100 miles per hour. Scientists believe the debris moves this quickly because it travels over a cushion of air, like a puck on an air hockey table. These mudslides, or aluviones, have carved the steep sides of the Cordillera Blanca's valleys for millions of years and leveled the plains with silt. Within the last few decades, they have also killed tens of thousands of people in the Huaraz area.

In 1941, an aluvión from Lago Palcacocha wiped out the northern third of Huaraz, killing more than 5,000 people. Similar aluviones struck the village of Chavín in 1945, Cañon de Pato in 1950, and the village of Ranrahirca in 1962. In 1970, an earthquake that measured 7.8 on the Richter scale leveled Huaraz and killed more than 70,000 people throughout the surrounding Ancash department. During the earthquake a huge avalanche fell from Huascarán and plunged into a lake above Yungay, just north of Huaraz along the highway. Within minutes the village was obliterated by a 10-meter-high wall of mud and boulders, which destroyed buildings and crushed school buses into balls of steel. When it was over, the only thing left of Yungay was the tops of a few palm trees sticking above the mud. The only survivors of the aluvión were children who had gone to a nearby circus and a few hundred villagers who managed to clamber in time up to a hilltop cemetery. The rest of the townspeople, an estimated 18,000 people, were buried alive.

After 1970 the Peruvian government got serious about reducing the risk of mudslides in the area and launched an effort to build control dams in the high mountains. More than 35 control dams, large cement blocks that prevent the moraines from eroding, have been built since then. Most important, these dams include a pipe that drains the lake and prevents it from becoming full.

In early 2003 a satellite operated by NASA, the U.S. space agency, detected a major crack in the glacier above Lago Palcacocha, the same lake that wiped out a third of Huaraz in 1941. Huaraz became world news for a moment as the Associated Press and other world

---

The Cordillera Blanca, when seen from afar, looks like a huge wall of glaciated peaks rising from the Río Santa Valley. Nevertheless, the range dips low enough in places to allow trekking routes, and a few roads, to cross it. The road to Chavín de Huántar, one of Peru's most enigmatic ancient ruins, tunnels through the lowest pass at 4,450 meters (14,596 feet). The valley on

the far side of the range, the western end of the Callejón de Conchucos, is an isolated and remote area of small towns linked only by rough dirt roads. Glaciers spread over much of the terrain, along with more than 300 lakes. Inside the Parque Nacional Huascarán, thousands of people continue their traditional ways of life. For the most part, the range's inhabitants live below the

media jumped on the threat of an imminent mudslide that could, according to NASA, reach Huaraz in 12 minutes. But when local glaciologists arrived at the scene, they realized that the "crack" NASA saw was not a crevasse in the glacier at all. Rather it was a band of rock that had melted through the glacier, which was only a few feet thick in some places. Far from being a menace, the glacier had receded to the extent that it was a pitiful reminder of what it was just two decades ago, another victim of what many feel is human-induced global warming.

Local glaciologists are, however, worried about Quebrada Shallap, another valley that feeds into Huaraz. Here a controversial dam has been built that some glaciologists say puts this city of 60,000 in danger. The dam was built by Duke Energy of Charlotte, North Carolina, which purchased the Cañon de Pato hydroelectric station from the Peruvian government during a 1995 privatization auction. Duke Energy has long complained of low water flows through the canyon, which drains the Cordillera Blanca, during the dry months June–October. Its solution was to create a huge summertime reservoir above Huaraz by plugging up the control dam that drains a lake at the top of Quebrada Shallap. Then it built another dam on top of it to form a huge reservoir to supplement the low-water months. The company conducted a survey of the surrounding glaciers, which have receded out of sight up the mountainside in recent years, and concluded there is no danger.

Many of Peru's scientists are not so sure. Benjamin Morales, the glaciologist who led Peru's drive to build the control dams in the Callejón de Huaylas, sharply criticized the project. "Avalanches are not a danger in Quebrada Shallap," agrees local glaciologist Alcides Ames. "But what about landslides?" If they are big enough, landslides can, like avalanches, cause a lake to wash over a dam. In 2003, such a landslide dumped into Huaraz's main reservoir, muddying water and shutting off the water supply for several days. Glaciologists are concerned the same could happen in Quebrada Shallap, but on a larger scale.

The problems that Duke Energy faces in getting year-round water to make electricity are probably going to get worse in the coming decades. Bernard Francou, a glaciologist with the French government's Institute of Research and Development, has spent the last two decades studying the retreat of tropical glaciers in Ecuador, Bolivia, and Peru. He predicts that all of South America's small glaciers – about 80 percent of the continent's total – will disappear in the next 15 years. Many of Peru's glaciers are retreating uphill by as fast as 35 meters a year, and one glacier Francou studies in Bolivia lost two-thirds of its volume in the mid-1990s alone. "The trend is so clear that you can't argue with the numbers," he says.

Retreating glaciers do not affect only hydroelectric companies. One of Francou's main backers is the city of Quito, Ecuador, which is worried about its water supply from the fast-disappearing Antizana Glacier. Farmers along Peru's desert coast, who supply a big chunk of Peru's gross domestic product, rely on mountain runoff to irrigate their fields. Even climbers and trekkers in the Huaraz area are affected, when ice routes disappear or gentle, snow-covered passes melt away to reveal loose scree and impassable cliffs.

poverty line, subsisting on maize, quinoa, and *kiwicha* grains, and a variety of potatoes and tubers. Their latest source of income is providing burros for the foreigners who pass through this world-class trekking and climbing paradise.

The roads that lead up and over the Cordillera Blanca provide good access for day hikes. To hike here, stay in any of the villages along the Callejón de Huaylas, including Huaraz, Carhuaz, and Caraz. Then contract a taxi or horse or hop aboard a *combi*—but make sure to plan for your return ride in the afternoon. Many agencies in Huaraz offer cheap day excursions to Lagunas Llanganuco or Pastoruri Glacier for US$8–10 and can pick you up at any of the towns along the way. Another option is to hike in to one of the refuges and use them as launching pads for day hikes.

Routes

SANTA CRUZ TREK

The most spectacular, and crowded, trekking route in the park is the four- to five-day, 40-kilometer Santa Cruz trek, which traditionally begins from the small settlements of **Vaquería** or **Colcabamba** and ends at **Cashapampa** near Caraz. The high point of the pass is **Punta Unión**, at 4,760 meters, and the rest of the trek is all downhill along the Quebrada Santa Cruz, which offers a series of emerald lakes and mesmerizing views of Taulliraju, Alpamayo, Quitaraju, Artesonraju, and other snow peaks. Two days can be added to the beginning of the trek by starting at Lagunas Llanganuco and heading over the **Portachuelo Llanganuco** pass at 4,767 meters. Acclimatized and fit trekkers can hike this route with a light backpack, and burros can be contracted at Vaquería or Colcabamba. This route can also be approached in the opposite direction, starting in Caraz and finishing near Huaraz.

NORTHERN CIRCUIT
AROUND ALPAMAYO

A two-week, 150-kilometer option starts in Cashapampa and involves a huge northern circuit around Alpamayo. The trek takes in pristine mountain scenery and a roller-coaster ride of high passes on Alpamayo's remote northern side, including Paso los Cedros at 4,900 meters. If you start from Cashapampa, the final days of the trek lead down the Quebrada Santa Cruz along the traditional route. This trek is operated by Pony Expeditions in Caraz and is almost always done with burros.

QUEBRADA QUILCAYHUANCA

Just above Huaraz, we recommend a two- or three-day hike up the Quebrada Quilcayhuanca, with a longer option to climb over a high pass and descend **Quebrada Cojup** on the return. Another option is a hike into **Quebrada Rajucolta,** two valleys over. All of these are pleasant two- or three-day hikes up

into the valleys to lakes. Because few tourists walk these routes, they are safe to do alone or with another person. No burros are required.

OLLEROS-CHAVÍN TREK

There are at least two highly recommend routes that cross the Cordillera Blanca south of Huaraz and end at the ruins of **Chavín de Huántar.** The best-known version starts from **Olleros,** a village just south of Huaraz, and heads up and over **Punta Yanashallash** at 4,700 meters along an ancient trade route. If you get a ride up the dirt road above Olleros, this 35-kilometer route should take 3–4 days and can be done with or without a burro.

QUEBRADA CAYESH CLIMB

The other route that takes you to Chavín is a 40-kilometer, four- or five-day route. It requires a bit of mountaineering and starts above the village of Pitec (above Huaraz) and climbs the Quebrada Quilcayhuanca and then forks south into the Quebrada Cayesh. At the end of the valley, a rough trail leads up and over a snowy pass next to **Nevado Maparaju** (5,326 meters). This peak can be climbed from the saddle before continuing down the pass on the other side to the village of **San Marcos,** eight kilometers from Chavín de Huántar. Because of the technical demands of this route, it is best done with a guide. Regardless, ask around about conditions before you try this route, as we have received reports that the far side of the pass is badly melted out and difficult to descend. You should bring all your own technical equipment, like crampons and ice axes, and inquire beforehand if there are snow-covered crevasses or other conditions that might merit a rope.

Accommodations

Three lodges have been built inside the park to accommodate visitors in the three most popular climbing areas. Built by **Operación Mato Grosso** (tel. 043/44-3061, www.huaraz.org/omg), an Italian relief organization based in Marcará, and associated with Don Bosco de los Andes (http://nuke.andesbosco.com, Italian only), the lodges are similar to what you might find in the European Alps. Each one has rooms of 60 bunks, and there is a large downstairs dining area with an amiable kitchen staff. Prices are reasonable: US$30, including lodging, breakfast, and dinner. Hot teas and other drinks average US$1.50–3. All profits go to aid projects.

The **Refugio Ishinca** (4,350 meters) is in the Quebrada Ishinca, a four-hour walk from the village of Collón and the launching point for Urus, Ishinca, and Tocllaraju. **Refugio Peru** (4,665 meters) is a three-hour walk from Llanganuco and at the base of Pisco. **Refugio Giordano Longoni** is a four-hour walk from the village of Musho and at the base of Huascarán. All these peaks except for Huascarán and Tocllaraju could be climbed directly from these *refugios,* eliminating the need for a tent, though climbers usually bring one in which to bivouac.

There's also a refuge in **Quebrada Llaca** (US$15 pp lodging, US$5 pp admission into the area) owned by the Mountain Guide Association of Peru, but it is run down and most people prefer to camp.

Getting There

Transport options for accessing different areas of the park range from public *combis* to private cars from Huaraz, Carhuaz, Yungay, and Caraz.

◖ CORDILLERA HUAYHUASH

Though only 30 kilometers long, the Cordillera Huayhuash packs in some incredibly dramatic mountain scenery. It is one continuous serrated ridge that falls away into fluted snow faces and glaciers. Seven peaks here top 6,000 meters, and another seven are over 5,500 meters. The highest peak, Yerupajá (6,634 meters), is the second-highest peak in Peru and is followed by Siulá Grande (6,356 meters). Here, Joe Simpson fell into a crevasse and lived to tell the story in *Touching the Void.*

The Huayhuash is 50 kilometers southeast of the Cordillera Blanca yet utterly different. First, there are no broad, U-shaped valleys in the Huayhuash that lead over high passes to the other side. Instead trekkers must walk around the outer edges of the range, climbing up and over passes between 4,500 and 5,000 meters. To manage these heights, nearly all trekkers use *arrieros* and burros, which can be contracted easily at the range's trailheads. The peaks here tend to be extremely technical, with the exception of Nevado Diablo Mudo, and require guided expertise, as well as previous experience. Because of Huayhuash's attitude, we recommend three days of acclimatization in Huaraz before a trip.

The other main attraction to the Cordillera Huayhuash is its raw wilderness feel. Although daily *colectivos* and buses have made the area easily accessible, the rocky ridges ceding to turquoise lakes and wide open rolling grasslands draining into the Amazon basin give the area a pristine feel. Condors are seen here frequently, along with a range of migratory birds, and small herds of vicuñas live up in the narrow valleys. A great website is www.huayhuash. org.

Routes

The time-honored trek in the Cordillera Huayhuash is a 12-day loop around the entire range that begins and ends in the village of **Chiquián.** These days, this route is somewhat shorter because new roads have been built onward from Chiquián, creating different trailheads. From Chiquián, *combis* now travel to Llamac via a new mining road, which shortens the route by a day. This trek continues clockwise around the entire range and crosses eight passes between 4,600 and 5,000 meters before completing the circle at Pacllón, where a new road returns to Chiquián.

A few groups are now entering through **Huallanca,** a village at 3,400 meters that lies along the dirt road between Huaraz and Huánuco. Huallanca was rarely used as an entry point in the past because it was a long one- or two-day slog to get to the Huayhuash. But *combis* now travel along a new road that goes as far as the village of Matacancha. Trekkers usually get off beforehand at the tiny village of **Ishpac** and head over the

4,700-meter Cacanpunta Pass en route to their first campsite at **Lago Mitacocha.** This trek essentially does half of the full circuit and skirts the range's eastern side. After a campsite at **Lago Carhuacocha,** the trail diverges, and trekkers have to decide between a 4,600-meter pass or a pass 200 meters higher with better views of the glaciers. The next camps are at the village of **Huayhuash** and then on to **Laguna Viconga,** where hot springs lie a mile to the southwest. The final day is a long walk over rolling hills out to **Cajatambo,** where a good road leads to Pativilca on the coast.

Because of the new Huallanca access, trekkers can now see a good bit of the Cordillera Huayhuash in five days. But there is a downside. Huallanca, at 3,400 meters, is the same altitude as Cusco and takes some getting used to. Those who come from the coast usually have to spend a day or two in Huaraz before trekking. Another issue is that each day of this five-day route includes a pass over 4,600 meters, which is a feat even for the acclimatized. The full circuit, on the other hand, has three days of acclimatization on rolling hills before hitting this string of knockout passes. Another problem is luggage: Five-day trekkers come in from the Huaraz side of the range and exit at the coast, so they have to carry everything with them. And of course this route misses the mountain views on the west side of the range. Val Pitkethly guides in the Huayhuash each year and has written the Globetrotter guide *Trekking and Climbing in the Andes.* She highly recommends the full circuit for all the above reasons, but also because "it's just too beautiful of a place to rush through."

Accommodations

There are hostels and restaurants in all the main access towns of the Cordillera Huayhuash. But if you choose to trek with an organized agency, you will probably never visit them. In **Chiquián,** try the **Hostal Nogales** (Comercio 1301, three blocks from main square, tel. 043/74-7121, hotel_nogales_chiquian@yahoo.com.p, US$6 s, US$12 d, cheaper rooms have shared bath). In **Cajatambo,** try **Tambomachay** (Bolognesi

140, Lima tel. 01/244-2046, US$10 s, US$15 d) or the upscale **International Inn** (Benavides, block 4, Lima tel. 01/244-2071, international. inn@hostal.net, US$40 s, US$50 d, prices negotiable). There are a few basic hostels in **Huallanca,** from where public transport leaves to Matacancha and Ishpac (90 minutes).

Getting There

Transportes El Rápido (Mariscal Cáceres and Tarapacá, tel. 043/72-2887) in Huaraz has a bus at 6 A.M. and 1 P.M. to Chiquián (US$3, three hours) and at 6 A.M. and 12:30 P.M. to Huallanca (US$4, four hours), continuing on to La Unión (10 hours). **Empresa Andia** in the main square of Cajatambo has buses every morning at 6 A.M. to Lima (US$8, nine hours).

◖ CORDILLERA NEGRA

Though overshadowed by the snowy summits of the Cordillera Blanca, the brown mountains of the Cordillera Negra on the other side of the valley offer some great day hiking and biking. Routes often begin up in high-altitude grasslands and follow trails that have been used for centuries, passing Andean villages, old bridges, creeks, and fields along the way. There is a range of difficulty for bikers, from broad traverses to dodgy, downslope single-track, and the views of the glaciers and snowy peaks are like something out of a fairy tale. **Caraz** has the best accessibility to the Cordillera Negra, and Felipe Diaz in **Carhuaz** or Pony Expeditions in Caraz can give good, up-to-date suggestions. But here are some hiking and biking routes in the Huaraz area used by mountain-bike guide Julio Olaza (www.chakinaniperu.com).

Routes

CALLÁN PASS TO HUARAZ

This pure downhill route begins with a *combi* ride to the high pass above Huaraz at 4,225 meters and makes for a good acclimatization day for climbers and trekkers. If you don't mind improvising your route a bit, this route can even be done without a guide.

A network of footpaths and mule tracks leads

downhill through russet fields of grains and potatoes, though the best route takes you through the villages of Culcururi and Atipallán. The bizarre rock formations along the way have earned the area the moniker Little Moab, and the route finishes down steep, hair-raising shortcuts through the hillside suburbs above Huaraz.

SHECTA TO HUARAZ

This route begins at 4,050 meters in the village of Shecta near Huaraz and follows a long traverse to the settlement of Huáscar before plunging 1,000 meters on dodgy single-track back to Huaraz. This strenuous, daylong route is best for the well acclimatized.

SUMMIT TO SEA

This phenomenal route leads not west to the Río Santa but east toward the Pacific Ocean and includes a mind-boggling descent through remote countryside. A truck from Catac, a village north of Huaraz, takes you up to the start of the route at Huancapeti Pass (4,680 meters). From here, nearly 40 kilometers of stone paths and steep single-track lead to the mountain village of Aija, where prearranged transport should await you for the ride back to Huaraz. The adventurous can continue another 80 kilometers all the way to the town of Huarmey on the coast.

Getting There

There are dirt roads leading into the Cordillera Negra from **Huaraz** and throughout the Río Santa Valley from **Yungay, Carhuaz, Caraz,** and **Huallanca.** Private transport can always be hired to ascend these roads and, because most trails lead downhill, it is almost impossible to get lost. You might consider arranging your transport through an agency.

TRUJILLO AND THE NORTH COAST

Depending on your perspective, it is either a terrible injustice or happy circumstance that most visitors never see the north coast, which holds much of Peru's best ruins, untrammeled wilderness, and world-class surf breaks. Because 9 out of 10 foreign tourists begin in Machu Picchu in the south, the average visitor simply runs out of time.

Peru's north coast, however, is one of the richest and most diverse archaeological zones in all of the Americas. An ocean teeming with fish and desert coastline punctuated by verdant river valleys formed a cradle of civilization comparable to Egypt or Babylon. The most important cultures were the Moche, Chimú, and Sicán empires, who built elaborate adobe cities over a millennia and a half before being conquered by the Inca around 1470.

Little was known about these cultures because the Inca carefully erased memory of them in order to consolidate their own power. But in the late 1980s, the world glimpsed the splendor of these forgotten civilizations when archaeologists unearthed royal tombs from the Moche and Sicán cultures. The tombs, somehow overlooked by 500 years of diligent grave robbers, were filled with exquisite works in gold and silver, including gigantic earrings, breastplates, and delicately worked spiders perched on webs of gold. The tombs gave archaeologists their first clear understanding of the complex social and religious structure of these northern empires. The objects found in the tombs are now on display in two fabulous new museums outside of Chiclayo: Museo Tumbas Reales de Sipán and Museo Sicán.

© FELIPE REBOLLEDO

HIGHLIGHTS

◖ Old Trujillo City Tour: After seeing Trujillo's Spanish homes and churches, there is no better way to soak in colonial elegance than having a drink on the Plaza de Armas at the bar of the stately Libertador Trujillo Hotel (page 446).

◖ Museo Cassinelli: The best collection of ceramics in Peru, including erotic Moche pieces, is housed in this odd but worthwhile museum in the basement of a Mobil gas station in Trujillo (page 450).

◖ Huaca de la Luna: This 10-story adobe pyramid is an impressive monument to the Moche culture, with recently uncovered murals of Ai-Apaec, the decapitator god, and commanding views of Trujillo and the surrounding valley (page 451).

◖ Museo Tumbas Reales de Sipán: This museum outside of Chiclayo is dedicated to the dazzling objects found in 1987 inside of a series of royal Moche tombs, which recall the splendor of King Tut's tombs in Egypt (page 466).

◖ Museo Sicán: Chiclayo's other must-see, modern museum contains an elaborate reconstruction of a royal Sicán tomb excavated in 1991, which contained 20 sacrificed women, two huge golden arms, and nearly a ton of metal objects (page 469).

◖ Máncora: What was once a small fishing town has become a surfing mecca, with a stunning coastline that attracts wave-riders from around the world (page 489).

LOOK FOR ◖ TO FIND RECOMMENDED SIGHTS, ACTIVITIES, DINING, AND LODGING.

The great cities of the north collapsed after being conquered by the Inca in the 1470s. By the time the Spaniards rode into the area six decades later, the Chimú city of Chan Chan had been reduced to ruins. The Huaca de la Luna, abandoned in A.D. 800 by the Moche, looked much as it does today—an eroding mountain of adobe bricks. Near this spot Gonzalo Pizarro founded Trujillo, an important colonial city that today contains Peru's best collection of colonial homes.

PLANNING YOUR TIME

It's a common dilemma: How can I see Machu Picchu, Cusco, *and* the ruins of the north coast? Even though Peru's two richest archaeological regions are at opposite ends of the country, it is possible to see both within two weeks. The logical start is to fly to colonial Trujillo, see Chan Chan and the Moche *huacas,* and then take a bus to Chiclayo for the Lords of Sipán treasures, Túcume, and the Museo Sicán.

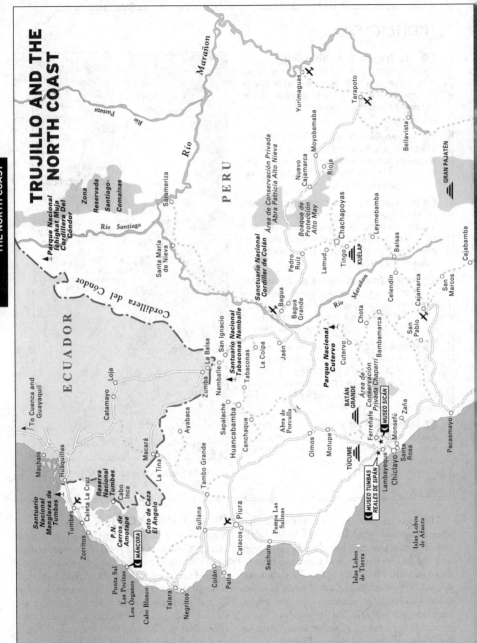

TRUJILLO AND THE NORTH COAST

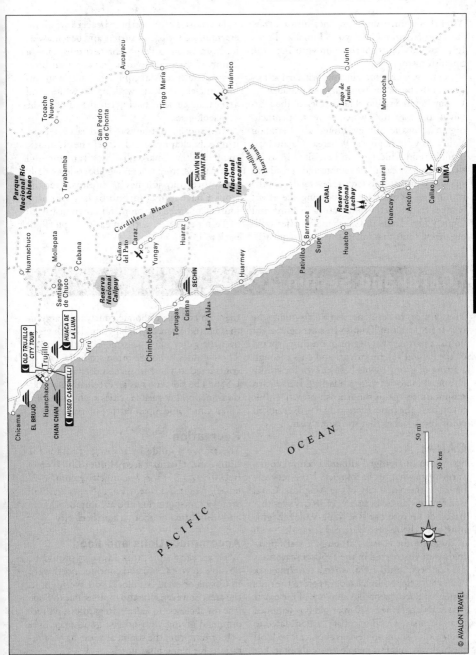

Aucayacu

Tocache Nuevo

San Pedro de Chonta

Tingo María

Huánuco

Junín

Lago de Junín

Morococha

Parque Nacional Río Abiseo

Tayabamba

CHAVÍN DE HUANTAR

Parque Nacional Huascarán

Cordillera Huayhuash

Huaral

LIMA

Callao

Huamachuco

Mollepata

Cabana

Cordillera Blanca

Caraz

Huaraz

CARAL

Reserva Nacional Lachay

Chancay

Ancón

Santiago de Chuco

Cañón del Pato

Yungay

Barranca

Supe

Huacho

Reserva Nacional Calipuy

SECHIN

Huarmey

Pativilca

OLD TRUJILLO CITY TOUR

HUACA DE LA LUNA

Trujillo

Virú

Casma

Tortugas

Las Aldas

Chimbote

Chicama

EL BRUJO

Huanchaco

CHAN CHAN

MUSEO CASSINELLI

OCEAN

PACIFIC

50 mi

50 km

0

0

© AVALON TRAVEL

After this immersion in pre-Inca history, travelers can fly from Chiclayo to Lima, and then Lima to Cusco, to continue on with Inca and Spanish history.

For those with more time, the principal attractions of the north can be thought of as a sideways U, starting in Trujillo. The first leg of the journey is to Cajamarca, which serves as a launching point for the journey through the Marañón Valley to Chachapoyas. Whereas Cajamarca, Trujillo, and Chiclayo can be visited in as little as two days each, the remote and spread-out ruins of Chachapoyas require several days at the minimum—especially considering the effort it takes to get there. InkaNatura in Lima and Gran Vilaya Tours in Chachapoyas offer well-organized tours that follow this basic sequence.

For most, Peru's northern beaches are an inessential side trip. But surfers and beach lovers jet from Lima to Peru's northernmost city of Tumbes, then take public transport an hour or two south to Máncora. After just a morning's travels, they are walking on white sand and eating ceviche, having left the ruins to the archaeologists.

Still another option is to head east after visiting Chachapoyas and travel the dramatic route into the Amazon basin to Tarapoto and Yurimaguas, from where cargo boats leave daily for a three-day journey to Iquitos. Getting from Chachapoyas to Iquitos is a stunning journey of a week or more, taking in nearly all of Peru's climates, with an easy escape flight back to Lima.

Caral and Sechín

Most visitors to Peru's northern coast make the trip from Lima to Trujillo in a straight eight hours, a journey that begins in the dusty sprawl of the capital's shantytowns and cuts through a string of grimy towns best known for stinky fishmeal factories and a bustling trade with mountain towns of the Ancash province. But if you have the time, there are a few overlooked ruins and beaches that warrant a visit.

CARAL
Six pyramids arranged around a central courtyard form what archaeologists have recently hailed as the oldest city of the Americas. Caral is in fact the largest of a series of 18 city sites that stretches up into the Río Supe Valley, beginning with the Aspero pyramid (near the town of **Supe** on the coast). Although Caral's pyramids were discovered in the 1950s, excavations did not begin until 1996, when a puzzling lack of ceramics tipped archaeologists off to the site's antiquity. Subsequent digs atop one of the oldest pyramids unearthed a 10-year-old boy wrapped in a cane mat, which scientists carbon-dated to 2900 B.C. Visitors are few, as the site is well off the highway and few people know about it. For the moment, the elaborate courtyards, amphitheater, and 12-meter-high pyramids with views over the valley must be explored with a guide. These guides, who are often students, can be contracted at the entrance and charge about US$6. The site serves as an excellent introduction to later, but related, cities such as Sechín, Chan Chan, and Sipán farther up the coast.

Recreation
To arrange a guide in advance, contact the Lima- and Huaraz-based **Miguel Chiri Valle** (tel. 01/423-2515, www.angelfire.com/mi2/tebac). Miguel, a fluent English speaker, will arrange transportation and accommodation to and from Lima or another northern city.

Accommodations and Food
With an early start from Lima, it should be possible to visit Caral and continue northward to Casma or even Trujillo. If you overnight in the area, however, **Huacho** is preferable to Supe (the town closest to Caral). Regardless, we recommend giving your hotel a good once over before accepting the room, as some have reputations for being hour hotels.

Once in Huacho, head 30 minutes west to the beach for **Fundo Centinela** (tel. 01/994-5813, www.surfsurvival.com/fundocentinela, US$55 s, US$65 d), a quaint farm nestled among sugarcane fields within walking distance of Playa Paraíso, one of the 10 most beautiful beaches in Peru (according to the *Guia Inca de Playas*). The owners, Americo and Ursula Debernardi, serve heaping plates of delicious Italian food.

In Supe, a safe though somewhat noisy option is **Hostel Las Palmeras** (Panamericana North Km 585, tel. 01/236-4037, US$8 s, US$12 d), on the highway one kilometer north of town on the left side. Major bus companies stop here when asked. Get coffee and breakfast at **Doña Lobatón's** on the main square. Right around the corner, **Charito** serves traditional *ceviche de pato*, a stew of duck, potatoes, and onions.

There is a wider selection of hotels and restaurants in **Barranca,** five kilometers north along the Panamericana from Supe but still within taxi distance of Caral. **Hostel Emilio** (Gálvez 651, tel. 01/235-5224, US$9 s, US$15 d) offers huge, comfortable rooms with TVs on the main drag. The rooms in the back are quieter, and whirlpool tubs are available for about twice the price. Slightly fancier, but considerably more expensive, is **Hotel El Chavín** (Gálvez 222, tel. 01/235-2358, US$20 s, US$25 d), which has rooms with cable TV and a pool. Recommended restaurants include **Restaurant Gitana** (near the intersection of Bolognesi and the Panamericana, US$4–6), known for its *ceviche mixto.* Also cheap and clean are **Los Tronkitos** (Gálvez 787, US$3–5) and **El Alaska** (Gálvez 564), which serves espresso and scrumptious desserts until midnight.

Getting There and Around

Caral is most easily reached via a dirt road that begins on the Panamericana about three kilometers north of Huacho. There is another bumpier though more scenic road up the Río Supe Valley that begins about three kilometers south of Supe. The latter road crosses the Río Supe at one point and becomes impassable during the mountain rainy season October–May.

The best way to reach Caral is to contract a round-trip taxi in Huacho or Supe for US$14, though cheaper *colectivos* also run from Huacho. It is about 45 minutes on either route. Allow 1–2 hours to see the ruins.

FORTALEZA DE PARAMONGA

Traveling north through Barranca and the nearby town of **Pativilca,** you'll find the Fortaleza de Paramonga (Panamericana Km 210, 8 A.M.–5 P.M. daily, US$1.50), a fascinating introduction to the Chimú empire. The massive adobe fortress, which may have had both religious and military functions, is composed of seven defensive walls constructed on a hill next to the highway. It is still possible to see remnants of the murals admired by Hernando Pizarro when he passed by the fortress in 1533, less than half a century after an invading Inca army overran the fort in its conquest of the Chimú empire. The top of the yellow fortress offers panoramic views of the surrounding sugarcane fields. The on-site museum is worth a visit. The fort will become visible after passing a hill about four kilometers north of the Huaraz turnoff on the Panamericana, or seven kilometers north of Barranca. If traveling from Barranca, go to the north end of town and take a *colectivo* or *combi* to travel four kilometers north to the village of Pativilca, where you can either walk the remaining three kilometers or take a taxi for US$2.

SECHÍN

While some of Peru's adobe ruins require a little imagination to understand, no such effort is required for Sechín (5 km southeast of Casma, 8 A.M.–5 P.M. daily, US$1.50), a temple complex built around 1500 B.C. Along the temple's base, hundreds of warriors with their mutilated prisoners are carved into the granite with startling and gruesome detail. Soldiers carved into stone columns march on both sides toward the temple entrance with decapitated heads of the defeated hanging from their bodies. The range of human cruelty exhibited at Sechín is

THE NORTH COAST

© RENÉE DEL GAUDIO AND ROSS WEHNER

carving of a decapitated head at Sechín

a prelude to the rituals of human sacrifice during the Moche and Chimú empires. The adjacent **Museo Max Uhle** contains reconstructed murals along with models of Sechín and other nearby ruins. Bilingual guides are available for the museum and the temple for US$4.

For archaeology buffs, Sechín is only one of several sites in the **Casma** area that can be visited in a daylong circuit. Nearby lies **Sechín Alto,** a deteriorated U-shaped complex. Farther south at Km 361 of the Panamericana, but only accessible with four-wheel drive, is the fortress of **Chanquillo,** a watchtower surrounded by three concentric walls.

Accommodations

Las Aldas is a long beach separated by a rocky point that lies at Km 347 of the Panamericana, 30 kilometers south of Casma at the fishing village of La Gramita. Clean, simple Italian-owned bungalows at the northern end of the beach, named **Las Aldas** (tel. 01/440-3241, US$22 pp), serve as a good base for exploring the nearby deserted beaches. There are a few ruins in the hills above the bungalows.

Casma's good budget option is **Hostel Ernesto's** (Garcilazo de la Vega, tel. 043/41-1475, US$6 s, US$9 d), with basic, clean, and quiet rooms.

The best value in Casma is the **Hostel El Farol** (Túpac Amaru 450, tel. 043/41-2183, hostelfarol@terra.com.pe, US$12 s, US$18 d), a spacious hotel laid out on landscaped grounds complete with caged monkeys and tropical birds. The bungalow rooms surround a courtyard with a pool and have cable TV and plenty of hot water. On the north edge of town is **Hotel Las Poncianas** (Km 376 of Panamericana, tel. 043/41-1599, ponciana@terra.com.pe, US$20 s, US$25 d), a large hotel with nice views from the second floor and similar amenities, plus a sauna, pool table, playground, restaurant, and a very friendly owner. Larger, more comfortable rooms are also available (US$30 s, US$35 d).

The best lodging option around Casma, however, is El Farol's sister hostel at **Tortugas,** a beach town 22 kilometers north of Casma that is marked by a huge blue arch at Km 391 of the Panamericana. **El Farol** (tel. 043/991-1693,

US$20 s, US$26 d) is perched on the hills at the southern end of Tortugas's stone-and-sand beach and offers breathtaking views of the surrounding desert hills and the clear blue waters. There is good snorkeling, safe swimming, a fine assortment of seafood restaurants, and a secluded beach that is a short walk over the hills to the south. Make reservations during summer and holidays. There are also several basic budget hostels in Tortugas, including **Hospedaje Pedro Pablo** (tel. 043/48-7593, US$6 s, US$9 d) near the road entrance to Tortugas.

Food

It's a long walk or a five-minute *mototaxi* ride through the fields to **Recreo Campestre Los Pacaes** (Prolongación Bolívar, tel. 043/71-1505, US$3–7), the place most recommended by locals. Musicians play while guests lunch under a flower-covered trellis. Local specialties include *chicharrón de pato* (deep-fried duck), *pepián de pavo* (rice and turkey casserole), and *cuy* (guinea pig). Camas's best in-town option is **Restaurant Tío Sam** (Huarmey 138, US$3–4), with excellent creole food, including a delectable *sopa criolla*.

In Tortugas, the best food is at **El Farol** (tel. 043/71-1064, US$5–9), where chefs prepare fresh *lenguado* (sole) with a mouthwatering garlic/tomato sauce. Huber, the manager, can prepare you a stiff Cuba libre as you admire the extraordinary views. For less expensive food, there are several good restaurants near the road entrance to Tortuga, the best of which is 30-year-old **Restaurant Costa Azul** (corner of road entrance to Tortuga, US$3–6).

Getting There and Around

All the major bus companies stop at Casma, which is a five- or six-hour drive from Lima. Recommended companies include **Cruz del Sur, Ormeño,** and **Flores,** which head to Trujillo and beyond. Casma, along with Chimbote farther north, is also the starting point for the dramatic, though bumpy, ride over the 2,800-meter Callán Pass to Huaraz, which offers excellent views of snow-covered mountains. Taxis charge US$5 for the 15-minute drive north to Tortugas. The cheaper, three-wheeled canopied motorcycles are not recommended for the exposed highway drive.

Trujillo and Vicinity

Modern-day Trujillo has one of Peru's greatest collections of colonial homes, but it is only the latest city over the last few millennia in the Moche Valley. A few kilometers on the other side of town is the **Huaca de la Luna,** where archaeologists continue to unearth pristine murals from the Moche civilization (A.D. 1–850). Then there is **Chan Chan,** a vast city of elaborately sculpted walls that served as the capital of the Chimú, the largest pre-Inca empire in Peru (A.D. 900–1470). When Inca Pachacútec and his son Túpac Yupanqui conquered the city in the 1470s, they were dazzled by the grandeur of the largest adobe city in the world. At the coastal village of **Huanchaco,** 14 kilometers west of Trujillo, fishermen launch their reed rafts into the surf as they have for thousands of years.

Trujillo thrived after the arrival of the Spaniards, who, like the Moche and Chimú before them, reaped tremendous wealth from the fertile Moche Valley and the nearby ocean. Shortly after conquering Peru, Pizarro came to Trujillo in 1534 and helped found the city named after his hometown in Spain, Trujillo de Extramadura. Large sugarcane haciendas flourished here and financed large homes, churches, and a way of life that included two icons of *criollo* culture, the Peruvian *paso* horse and the *marinera* dance.

Trujillo became a center of Peru's war of independence from Spain. It was the first Peruvian city to declare itself independent of Spain, in December 1820. Liberator Simón Bolívar later established himself here after moving his way down the coast from Ecuador. From the Casa Urquiaga on the Plaza de Armas, Bolívar planned the campaign that culminated in the battle of Ayacucho, where Spanish forces were turned back for good on December 9, 1824.

A century later, a bohemian movement flourished in Trujillo that produced Peru's best poet, César Vallejo; painter and musician Macedonio de la Torre; and one of Peru's most controversial political leaders, Victor Raúl Haya de la Torre. Vallejo eventually emigrated to France, but Haya de la Torre launched what would become one of Peru's most influential political parties: APRA, the Alianza Popular Revolucionaria Americana. With its call for worker rights, APRA was banned by the military governments of the time. As repression against the party continued, a crowd of angry Apristas attacked an army outpost in 1932 and killed 10 soldiers. In retaliation, the government rounded up nearly 1,000 Apristas, trucked them out to the sands near Chan Chan, and executed them by firing squad. Haya de la Torre was exiled to Mexico but returned and was elected president in 1962—only to have the victory voided as a fraud by the military government.

Great effort has been made to preserve Trujillo's colonial feel, including the burial of electrical and power lines. But at least one well-intentioned effort has backfired. The city government banned buses and *micros* from entering the city center in 1990, causing an explosion in the taxi pool. These days the air pollution and constant honking of *taxistas* as they troll for passengers is unbearable. If you prefer quiet and clean air, we suggest that you consider staying in nearby Huanchaco. Remember, in Trujillo and much of the north, people take their siesta seriously and most sights are closed 1–4 P.M.

SIGHTS
◖ Old Trujillo City Tour

Allow at least a half day on foot for seeing Trujillo's colonial core, which offers a dense cluster of well-preserved homes and churches to the north of Plaza de Armas. Start at the

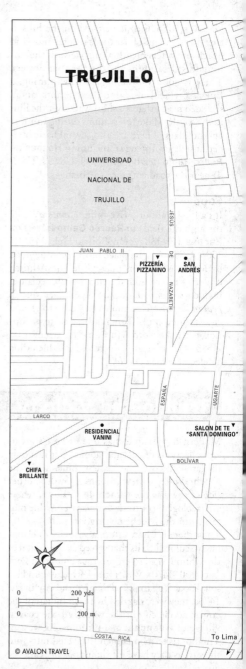

TRUJILLO

UNIVERSIDAD NACIONAL DE TRUJILLO

© AVALON TRAVEL

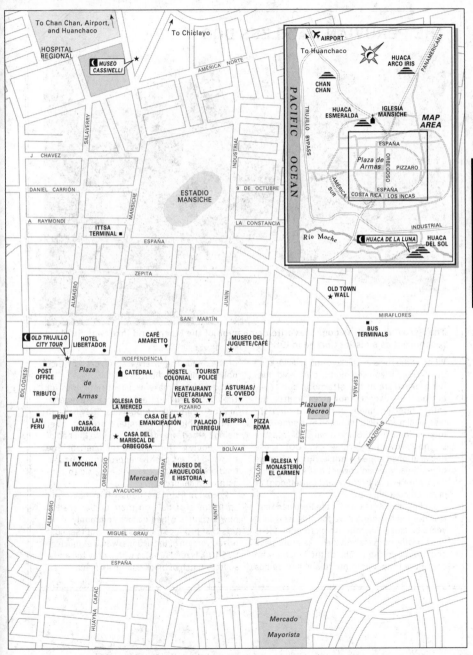

THE NORTH COAST

THE PERUVIAN HAIRLESS DOG

© JORGE RIVEROS CAYO

The Peruvian Hairless dog, a favorite companion of the Moche and Inca, was finally recognized as a distinct breed in 1986.

When at the ruins in Chiclayo and Trujillo, don't be alarmed if you see mud-brown, bald dogs lying prostrate in the afternoon sun. They are neither diseased nor street mutts, but rather fine specimens of the Peruvian Hairless, declared a distinct breed by Kennel Club International in 1986 and a national treasure by the Peruvian government in 2001. These declarations capped a modern-day struggle of legitimacy for an ancient dog known commonly in Peru as *perro calato* (naked dog) or *perro chino* (Chinese dog).

Archaeologists know that the Peruvian Hairless has been around Peru for at least 4,000 years because the dogs are pictured in Vicus and Chavín ceramics and their skeletons have been found in the tombs of the Moche, who considered them both guardians and guides of the dead. They were also favored by Inca nobles, who kept them as pets.

Though they make excellent sight dogs for the blind, Peruvian Hairless dogs are legendary for their healing properties. They have an unusually high body temperature and, after being bathed, are often tucked into the bed of sick people suffering from rheumatism. The dog also brings positive energy into a household and contact with its skin is said to cure asthma in children.

Peruvian Hairless dogs often have odd sprinklings of hair on their bodies (called powder puff), which occurs commonly in litters that produce hairless pups. But the most prized version of these dogs, worth as much as US$400, is medium size with a gray tail and a solitary patch of black hair on its head.

northern edge of town at Avenida España, the congested beltway that was once a six-meter wall built 1680–1685 to ward off pirate attacks. The crumbling military wall was knocked down in 1942, but a section has been preserved at the intersection of España and Estete. The waterworks for colonial Trujillo can be seen a few blocks away at Plazuela El Recreo (Estete and Pizarro), where the Spaniards extended Moche and Chimú irrigation channels in order to deliver river water to the aristocratic households of the city. The *plazuela* is graced with an elegant fountain, carved from local marble in 1750 and then relocated from the Plaza de Armas in 1828.

Knock on the Lazy Susan–like window of the **Iglesia y Monasterio El Carmen** (Bolívar 826, 9–11:40 A.M. and 4–5:20 P.M. Mon.–Sat., 9–11:20 A.M. Sun., US$1), a Carmelite monastery founded in 1724, to be let into the home of Trujillo's best collection of colonial art. The monastery has somehow withstood the earthquakes that have rocked Trujillo and houses the city's best-preserved gilded baroque altar.

Its *pinacoteca,* or painting gallery, contains 150 colonial works, including *The Last Supper* by Otto Van Veen (Peter Paul Rubens's mentor).

If you have extra time, the University of Trujillo's **Museo de Arqueología e Historia** (Junín 682, tel. 044/24-9322, 9 A.M.–4:45 P.M. Mon.–Fri., 9 A.M.–1 P.M. weekends, US$1.50) is nearby and traces Peruvian history from 12,000 B.C. to the arrival of the Spaniards. Because the university is directing the excavations at the Huaca de la Luna, the museum contains excellent artifacts from that site. Just a peek inside the courtyard will give you a sense of the grandeur of the **Palacio Itúrregui** (Pizarro 688, 8–10:30 A.M. Mon.–Sat., US$1.50), which now houses the Club Central. The house was built in 1855 in the Italian neo-Renaissance style by General Juan Manuel Itúrregui and has three plazas ringed with ornate columns.

Nearby is the headquarters of the APRA political party (Pizarro 672). Another nearby center of dissent is the **Casa de la Emancipación** (Pizarro 610, 9 A.M.–1 P.M. and 4–8 P.M. Mon.–Sat., free), a beautifully restored republican

La Casa Urquiaga

home where Marquis Torre Tagle signed a document declaring Trujillo's independence from Spain in 1820—long before the *libertadores* arrived. The house hosts cultural events and contains a small exhibit on César Vallejo, Peru's most famed poet, who was born in the nearby mountain town of Santiago de Chuco. Another block south on Pizarro is the **Iglesia de La Merced** (Pizarro 550, 8 A.M.–noon and 4–8 P.M. Mon.–Sat.). This 17th-century church was built by Portuguese artist Alonso de las Nieves and has an impressive rococo organ and cupola. When the order lacked the money for a traditional wood and gold-plated altar, they instead opted to paint one onto the wall in 1755—the only painted altar in the city. Near the altar is an interesting juxtaposition of the virgins that most embody the Old and New Worlds: Mexico's brown-skinned and dark-haired Virgen de Guadalupe and Spain's blue-eyed and blond Virgen Fátima.

Around the corner is the 17th-century **Casa del Mariscal de Orbegoso** (Orbegoso 505, 9 A.M.–8 P.M. Tues.–Sun.). The house is a showcase for the features of colonial homes: a plaza of *canto rodado* (river stones), brick and lime floors, simple ceilings, and enormous, sparsely decorated rooms. The house was originally the home of José Luis Orbegoso, who led troops during the War of Independence and served as president of Peru 1833–1838.

The **Plaza de Armas** is where Martin de Estete began to lay out the city grid in December 1534, in preparation for Francisco Pizarro's arrival the next year. At the center of the plaza is the Monumento de La Libertad, and the face of the winged figure holding a torch closely resembles that of Simón Bolívar. On the other side of the plaza is the Casa Bracamonte, occupied by the Ministerio de Salud and not open for tours. Its most famous features are a *balcón de celosia* (a wooden balcony from which women could see but not be seen) and finely wrought iron windows, an art form that flourished in 18th-century Trujillo.

Compare the colonial style of Casa Orbegoso with the more elegant republican design of **La Casa Urquiaga** (Pizarro 446, 9 A.M.–3 P.M. Mon.–Fri., 10 A.M.–1 P.M. weekends, free and includes an English- or Spanish-speaking guide). This house is one of the best preserved and most elegant republican houses in Trujillo. The original house was destroyed in the 1619 earthquake and was remodeled at least twice, most recently in the mid-19th century. Simón Bolívar lived here during his military campaign against Spain, and many of his personal possessions remain in the house, including his mahogany writing desk and personal china.

Construction of Trujillo's **Catedral** (Plaza de Armas, 7 A.M.–noon and 4–9 P.M. daily, free) began in 1610 but had to begin anew after the devastating earthquake on February 14, 1619, which destroyed the city and prompted townspeople to adopt Saint Valentine as their patron. A more recent earthquake, in 1970, partially destroyed the main altar, which contains an image of Saint Valentine, among other saints. The cathedral's **museum** (9 A.M.–1 P.M. and 4–7 P.M. Mon.–Fri., 9 A.M.–1 P.M. Sat., US$1.25 admission) contains the shadowy paintings of the baroque Quito School as well as access to catacombs.

Museo del Juguete

Opened in 2001 by Trujillo-born artist and painter Gerardo Chávez, the Museo del Juguete (Independencia 705, 10 A.M.–6 P.M. Mon.–Sat., US$1.50) exhibits an unusual collection of a thousand pieces, including toys as old as a 2,500-year-old Vicus whistle, Chanca rad-dolls, 18th-century French biscuit dolls, metal toy cars, and battalions of tin soldiers. Chávez aims to build the largest private toy collection in Latin America. He most likely will succeed.

◖ Museo Cassinelli

Buried deep within the basement of a grimy Mobil station on the edge of town is the Museo Cassinelli (Nicolas de Pierola 601, 9 A.M.–1 P.M. and 4–7 P.M. Mon.–Fri., 9 A.M.–12:30 P.M. Sat., US$2). This fabulous collection of ancient ceramics was assembled, piece by piece, over four decades of haggling between Señor Cassinelli and the local community of *huaqueros* (grave robbers). There are pieces here you won't see anywhere else in Peru: an enigmatic Moche pot of a bearded man (a Viking?) and a ceramic partridge from the Huari civilization that doubles as a bird whistle. Make sure to have the museum keeper open the locked erotic collection, which depicts masturbation, anal intercourse, necrophilia, and nearly every conceivable sexual practice from Moche and earlier cultures. There is even a penis-shaped *chicha* vase from which brides reportedly drank during Moche weddings!

(Huaca de la Luna

To see the latest discoveries of Peruvian archaeology, head eight kilometers south of Trujillo toward two massive, crumbling adobe mounds that rise from the desert. These were built during the Moche empire (A.D. 100–800). The farthest, Huaca del Sol (Temple of the Sun), was an administrative center, and the other, Huaca de la Luna, was a religious complex. This last *huaca* has been the focus of a well-funded archaeological campaign since 1991 and has produced some of the most dazzling and best-preserved murals in all of Peru.

The shape of the *huaca* mirrors that of **Cerro Blanco,** an adjacent mountain that has a curious arching dike of black rock near its summit. The Moche probably believed this arch represented the rainbow serpent, a fertility symbol that appears alongside Ai-Apaec, the deity that decorates the walls of Huaca de la Luna. Archaeologists believe the first single, compact platform of the *huaca* was built around A.D. 100. But every century, the Moche apparently sealed the bodies of deceased rulers into the *huaca* and then completely covered the platform with a new, stepped platform above it. In this way, over 700 years, the L-shaped temple evolved into a 100-meter-long stepped pyramid with as many as eight stepped levels. The overall shape is oddly similar to temples of the Maya, a culture that some say influenced the Moche.

Because of the gold buried here, the temple has been the target of relentless plundering by *huaqueros* since at least colonial times. A dozen caves penetrate the base of the *huaca*, and a massive house-sized hole is found up top, with an alley cut through the sides of the pyramid where the grave robbers cleared debris. Although much treasure and many murals have been lost, the *huaquero* holes have helped archaeologists examine cross sections of the temple's various platforms. On the north face, archaeologists have discovered a stairwell and a horizontal mural of soldiers performing a victory dance. Elaborate designs of Ai-Apaec in the form of a snake, crab, octopus, spider,

THE NORTH COAST

HUMAN SACRIFICE AT HUACA DE LA LUNA

Archaeologists believe Huaca de la Luna was a center for human sacrifice because murals often show Ai-Apaec, the fearsome Moche deity, with a crescent-shaped ceremonial knife (called a *tumi*) in one hand and a severed human head in the other. Additional proof came in 1996, when archaeologists discovered the skeletons of more than 40 men, age 15-32, buried in thick sediment near the back of the *huaca*. The men – many with their throats, hands, and legs cut or pelvic bones ripped out – were apparently sacrificed to stop the El Niño rains that partially destroyed the temple and forced the Moche to relocate farther north. Above the skeletons, there is the pyramid's upper throne, which appears in Moche ceramics depicting human sacrifice, and a sacred rock from which the victims were apparently thrown into the mud below. In a famous scene known as the Presentation, often painted on ceramic copies around Trujillo, a priest appears to cut open a prisoner's chest to either remove his heart or drain out blood. A cup of blood is then presented to the ruler, possibly to be drunk. High levels of uric acid found in the bones of Moche rulers in the Sipán tombs could, scientists say, indicate they drank blood – or that they ate a lot of shellfish.

and even a potato and a corn cob have also been found. In 1997, just a few inches from a *huaquero* hole, archaeologists discovered a cane basket filled with gold disks, textiles, and characteristic feline images, an indication that tombs remain hidden nearby and below, hidden in hundreds of feet of adobe bricks.

The top of Huaca de la Luna, nearly 10 stories high, offers an impressive view of Huaca del Sol, which was built with an estimated 100 million adobe bricks and is considered one of the largest adobe structures in the world. Few excavations have been done at Huaca del Sol, however, and there is little for visitors to see. Much of the *huaca* was eroded in the 17th century when the Spaniards diverted the Río Moche in a failed attempt to uncover hidden treasure. A Moche city with irrigation channels between the two *huacas* is being excavated and will be open for tours in the future, and a museum, featuring excavated objects, has been added to the visitor center complex.

The Huaca de la Luna (9 A.M.–4 P.M. daily, US$3.50, includes an English- or Spanish-speaking guide) can be reached via US$6 round-trip taxi or via the *combis* at Suárez and Los Incas near the Mercado Mayorista that say Campiña de Moche. Make sure the *combi* lets you off at the visitor center entrance. There have been reports of tourist muggings on the outskirts of the ruin site.

Huaca Arco Iris and Esmeralda

As a warm-up for Chan Chan, head first to the restored Huaca Arco Iris (Rainbow Temple), which was built by the Chimú around A.D. 1200 before being covered, and partially preserved, by desert sands. The temple is guarded by thick, six-meter clay walls, and there are two main platforms inside connected by a ramp. The first platform contains seven restored adobe panels that are carved with the namesake motif of the *huaca*, two lizardlike beings with an arching rainbow or serpent overhead. The ends of the rainbow/serpent connect to two human figures dancing below, and the relief is fringed with animal figures, which have been interpreted as both sea otters and squirrels. The

exact meaning of the mural has been lost, but many archaeologists believe the mural represents a kind of rain dance or fertility ritual. The rainbow/serpent and the sea otter are associated with rain and are a recurring fertility symbol of both Moche and Chimú art. The sea otter/squirrel, repeated endlessly at Chan Chan, is also a fertility symbol.

The second platform contains 14 niches that were probably used to store ritual objects such as textiles, shells, seed necklaces, and gold objects. Local legend has it that Huaca Arco Iris was also the home of Takaynamo, the mythical, bearded man who arrived by raft to found the city of Chan Chan. At the top of the *huaca*, there was probably a small temple where priests communicated with the gods. Nowadays there is a panoramic view of La Esperanza, a neighborhood of Trujillo founded in the 1960s by campesinos looking for work in a now-defunct industrial park. Because of combined effects of the 1970 earthquake, terrorism, and Peru's ongoing economic crisis, La Esperanza has exploded to its present population of 700,000, more than half of Trujillo's total population.

To get to Huaca Arco Iris, take a one-way taxi for US$1 and have it drop you off (there are plenty of taxis in the area). Or from in front of the Museo Cassinelli, take a blue-and-white *combi* that says La Esperanza and get off at the *quinto paradero* (fifth stop). You will see the *huaca* on the side of the highway, surrounded by walls.

Another *huaca* that is often mentioned in tourist literature but only worth visiting if you have extra time is Huaca Esmeralda. This partially restored *huaca* consists of two superimposed platforms with areas for storing foods and stylized carvings of nets with birds and fish. Unfortunately this *huaca* used to be a favorite hangout for drug addicts and has been mostly destroyed. To get there, take a *combi* toward Huanchaco and get off at Iglesia Mansiche and then walk four blocks. The best option, however, is to go with a guided tour from Trujillo or take a round-trip taxi for US$3, as the neighborhood is not safe. Make sure to buy a pass beforehand at Chan Chan or Huaca Arco Iris, because they are not sold at Huaca Esmeralda.

Chan Chan

The highly evolved Chimú civilization emerged in A.D. 900 after the decline of the Moche culture and stretched 1,300 kilometers from Chancay, near present-day Lima, to Tumbes. It was Peru's largest pre-Inca empire, and its capital was Chan Chan, now reduced to 20 square kilometers (4,940 acres) of eroded adobe. The city was abandoned in the 1470s, when Chan Chan was overrun by the army of Inca general Túpac Yupanqui.

In its heyday, Chan Chan was an elaborately sculpted and painted adobe city with nine-meter-high walls and an intricate complex of ramps, courtyards, passages, terraces, towers, gardens, palaces, and homes for an estimated 30,000–60,000 people. One of the most important archaeological sites in Peru, it was declared a UNESCO World Heritage Site in 1986, which has helped protect it somewhat from looting.

At the center of the ruined city are 10 royal compounds, or *ciudadelas,* built by successive Chimú dynasties, that cover six square kilometers (2.3 square miles). Only the upper strata of Chimú society was allowed to enter these palaces, through a single north entrance that breached massive walls. The palaces were used during the life of the king and then sealed and converted into a mausoleum upon his death, a custom also followed by the Inca in Cusco. The most often visited of these is Ciudadela Tschudi, which some say has been restored too much, but the signed pathway helps visitors make sense of it all.

From the entrance, the pathway leads into a vast walled plaza, where religious ceremonies were once held. The king sat on a throne near a ramp at the front of the square and was flanked by hundreds of priests and other court attendants, while human sacrifices were made on an altar in the center of the square. The walls are decorated with reliefs of sea otters/squirrels—a fertility symbol passed down from Moche times—and cormorants. The acoustics of the

© RENÉE DEL GAUDIO AND ROSS WEHNER

THE NORTH COAST

ceremonial Chan Chan figure with stylized sea otters in the background

plaza are stunning: the ocean, more than a kilometer away, roars on a windless day. From the plaza, the circuit continues down a corridor decorated with pelicans and zigzagging fish designs that probably represented the ocean tide and currents. On the opposite wall are diamond-shaped designs of fishing nets, a motif throughout Chan Chan. This passageway leads to a more intimate square with a ceremonial altar (now covered in adobe to preserve it) and U-shaped audience chamber.

One of the more surprising sights of Tschudi, given the desert surroundings, is a pool with a marsh reed at one end that was probably once a pleasure garden for Chimú royalty and a place for worshipping the moon. Unlike the Inca, the Chimú apparently valued the moon over the sun because it comes out during both day and night and controls the oceans. It was here that El Niño rains in 1983 uncovered two adolescent sacrifice victims, one with a mask of gold and another with a collar of jungle seeds used in shamanic rituals. At the back of the palace complex is the royal tomb surrounded by niches where human sacrifices were probably placed. Most of Chan Chan's tombs, once laden with gold and silver objects, were ransacked as early as Inca times, according to colonial documents. Near the end of the circuit, there are warehouses and a ceremonial hall with 24 niches that were probably used for idols. The nearby Museo Chan Chan does not have much of interest except for a collection of *tumi* knives and a display showing the evolution of Chimú pottery.

The US$3.50 admission to Chan Chan (9 A.M.–4:30 P.M. daily) includes Huaca Arco Iris, Huaca Esmerelda, and the museum. For US$8, a taxi will make the round-trip from Trujillo and wait while you are in the ruins. Or, if you are traveling with another person, take the Huanchaco *combi* or *colectivo* along España or, even safer, from the main stop at Óvalo Grau where the Museo Cassinelli is. Ask the driver to let you off at the **Cruce de Chan Chan** (7 km) and walk a few hundred meters down a dirt road that leads to the ruins, which is safe as long as you are accompanied by another person. Excellent guides wait daily in the Chan Chan parking lot. Guides generally charge US$6 for Chan Chan, or US$17, including transport, for the four Chimú sites covered in the ticket.

Wandering through the endless maze of ruins outside of Chan Chan's Tschudi Palace is not advised, as assaults on tourists have been reported—especially during the daily change of police guard between noon and 2 P.M. The neighborhood around Huaca Arco Iris and especially Huaca Esmeralda can also be dangerous. We recommend a guided tour that includes all of these sites plus the museum—you'll learn more and will be relaxed and safe.

ENTERTAINMENT AND EVENTS

Trujillo has a well-hidden but interesting nightlife, which gets going around 10:30 P.M. If you are looking for a lively atmosphere before midnight, shoot pool and mingle with university students at **The Bug Bunny Club Billiards & Pub** (Jesus de Nazareth 311, tel. 044/971-1045). The best pub in town is **Chelsea Pub Disco** (Estete 675, tel. 044/25-7032, open until 4 A.M.), which has a restaurant and different kinds of live music depending on the night. **Cañana's Peña y Disco** (San Martín 788, tel. 044/23-2503) is a good restaurant with an elegant courtyard that becomes a nightclub around midnight. For dancing, try the disco-pub **Tributo** (Almagro and Pizarro, 9 P.M.–close Thurs.–Sat.), just off the Plaza de Arms, or **Nuestro Bar** (Bolognesi and Pizarro, 9 P.M.–close daily). For a little bit newer, international scene on the edge of town, there's **Hop's** (Av. Húsares de Junín Mz. B-5, tel. 044/47-1013, open daily at 6 P.M., US$5.50), a microbrewery that brings wheat, Pilsen, or Munich beer to the table in special dispensers. If you have the late-night munchies, head to **Jano's Pub (Pizarro),** Trujillo's well-frequented, 24-hour hamburger shop a few blocks west of the Plaza de Armas. **Cine Primavera** (Orbegoso 554, www.cineprimavera.com) shows international hits.

Marinera dancers from up and down Peru's

© RENÉE DEL GAUDIO AND ROSS WEHNER

school children line up for a parade in Trujillo

coast flock to Trujillo in the last weeks of January and the first week of February for the **National Marinera Contest.** In between rounds of judged dancing, the city comes to life with cockfights, horse-riding championships, a multitude of parties, and even surfing contests at Huanchaco. The partying is especially intense during the last weekend when the dancing finals take place.

Trujillo has a similar fiesta called **Festival de la Primavera,** a celebration of the beginning of spring during the last week of September or the first weeks of October. The event is best known as a showcase for Trujillo's other icon of Peruvian *criolla* (coastal) culture, the *caballo de paso.* These graceful horses with tripping gait allow riders to float even during a full trot and are highly prized around the world. Because the best *caballos de paso* are bred in ranches around Trujillo, buyers from California, Texas, and other areas flock to this event. Year-round horse shows are given at **Fundo Palo Marino** (Via de Evitamiento Km 569, tel. 044/24-5935, 11 A.M.–1 P.M. Mon.–Fri., 11 A.M.–2 P.M. Sat.–Sun.).

RECREATION
Tour Agencies and Guides

Several tour companies in Trujillo cover the city, Huaca de la Luna y Sol, Chan Chan, and even El Brujo. The best of these are **Guia Tours** (Independencia 580, tel. 044/23-4856, guiatour@amauta.rcp.net.pe, US$8–12) and **Colonial Tours** (Independencia 616, tel. 044/25-8261, daily, US$5–8), which is based out of Hostal Colonial.

If you prefer a personal tour, **Benito Jáuregui Rosas** (Pizarro 318, tel. 044/957-6409, guiabenitojauregui@yahoo.es) gives thorough tours in Spanish; **Carmen Linares Santos** (tel. 044/930-7177, karmelinsa@hotmail.com) is fluent in English; and **Michael White** (Cahuide 495, tel. 044/966-2710, casadeclara@yahoo.com) tackles both of those languages, plus French, Italian, and German.

ACCOMMODATIONS
US$10–25

Hostal Colonial (Independencia 618, tel. 044/25-8261, www.hostalcolonial.com.pe, US$20 s, US$30 d, breakfast not included) is nowadays the best budget option in town. The charming hostel has simple and tasteful rooms, with cable TV and WiFi, arranged above a courtyard, adorned with Huanchaco's *caballitos de totora,* or totora-reed boats. There are nice reading areas downstairs and a restaurant with room service.

US$25-50

Hotel San Andrés (Juan Pablo II 157, tel. 044/25-3660, www.hotelsanandres.com, US$39 s, US$52 d, breakfast included) is a clean and comfortable modern hotel that is walking distance to Trujillo's center. It has restaurant, rooftop pool, and all the amenities. Rooms have telephones, WiFi, cable TV, and room service.

Another option is **Pullman Hotel** (Pizarro 879, tel. 044/22-3589, www.pullmanhoteltrujillo.com.pe, US$36 s, US$50 d, with buffet breakfast). The hotel has the basic amenities, including WiFi and room service.

US$50-100

Southwest of downtown Trujillo is **El Brujo Hotel** (Santa Teresa de Jesús 170, La Merced, tel. 044/22-3322, www.elbrujohotel.com, US$50 s, US$68 with buffet breakfast), a modern, three-star hotel located in the quiet and safe neighborhood of La Merced. Rooms are nice with comfortable beds and impeccable bathrooms. Amenities include 24-hour room service, WiFi, business center, auditorium, transport service, bar-restaurant, and laundry.

Hotel Paraíso-Trujillo (San Martín 240–246, tel. 044/20-0073, www.hotelesparaiso.com.pe, reservastru@hotelesparaiso.com.pe, US$53 s, US$66 d, with breakfast buffet) is situated two blocks away from the Plaza de Armas. This hotel offers very comfortable rooms with cable TV, WiFi, and room service. There are also rooms with optional air-conditioning and refrigerator (US$61 s, US$75 d). Other amenities include bar, restaurant, business center, 24-hour cafeteria, laundry, parking lot, and a rent-a-car service.

US$100-150

Gran Hotel El Golf-Centro de Convenciones

Truxillo (Los Cocoteros 505, Urbanización El Golf, tel. 044/48-4150, www.granhotel.pe, US$104 s or d, US$154 suites) is a five-star hotel classic in the city. The hotel has 120 spacious and comfortable rooms and nine suites arranged around gardens and a central pool. It is a 10-minute drive outside of town, but the relaxed setting and clean air are worth it. The facilities include two saunas, an indoor pool, and an excellent restaurant. Tee times can be arranged to the club's golf course across the street.

Hotel Gran Marqués (Díaz de Cienfuegos 145–151, Urbanización La Merced, tel. 044/48-1710, www.elgranmarques.com, US$136 s, US$160 d, US$200 junior suite, with buffet breakfast) is on a quiet side street about a five-minute drive from the city center. The hotel offers a modern spa (massages start at US$22 pp), well-equipped rooms including WiFi and air-conditioning, excellent service, and a good breakfast buffet. Transportation to and from the airport is included.

Over US$150

With its colonial facade and a sun-filled atrium, **Libertador Trujillo Hotel** (Independencia 485, Plaza de Armas, tel. 044/23-2741, www.libertador.com.pe, US$252 standard, US$284 junior suite) is *the* four-star hotel in town. A member of the Peruvian luxury hotel chain Libertador, it is located on the north side of the Plaza de Armas. All 79 rooms are large and modern, with touches of colonial decor, and are sheltered from outside noise. All the usual services are available, as well as WiFi, a sauna, buffet breakfast, gym, and jewelry shop. Las Bóvedas Restaurant, off the lobby, serves very good *comida criolla,* northern Peruvian specialties, and international cuisine. The elegant Malabrigo Bar, with dark wood, leather chairs, and windows looking over the square, is a good place for an evening cocktail.

FOOD
Cafés, Bakeries, and Ice Cream

Try **Café Amaretto** (Gamarra 368, tel. 044/22-1451, US$2–6) for delicious salads, sandwiches, and fruit drinks. The tuna salad is superb with grilled potatoes, tuna, olives, and fresh tomatoes. Stop back in the evening for a cappuccino and homemade *lúcuma* cake.

Owned by Trujillo-born artist and painter Gerardo Chávez, **Café Bar del Museo del Juguete** (Independencia 701 on the corner with Junín, tel. 044/29-7200, 9 A.M.–11 P.M. daily) is Trujillo's classiest café. The ambience has a touch of old-world Paris with an antique cash register, wood bar, and a piano in the back room. The walls are covered with photographs of Peruvian intellectuals and artists. Some specialties include *mistela,* the house drink, a *sánguche de pavo* (turkey sandwich), and delicious tamales. Part of the proceeds go to the Museo del Juguete, right above the café.

To try traditional breakfasts with tamales or *humitas de queso* stop by **Salon de Té Santo Domingo** (Pizarro 268, tel. 044/31-8766, 7:30 A.M.–1 P.M. and 4:30–9:30 P.M. daily, US$2–4).

Peruvian

The seventh block of Pizarro Street has three café-restaurants with great local food and better coffee: **Asturias** (Pizarro 739, tel. 044/25-8100, 8 A.M.–midnight daily, US$3–9) is a Trujillo classic. There are US$3 lunch menus and an à la carte menu with meat and fish dishes, pastas (including vegetarian options), and salads, as well as sandwiches, fruit juices, and desserts. **El Oviedo** (Pizarro 737, tel. 044/23-3305, 8 A.M.–midnight daily, US$3–9) has deliciously spiced *lomo saltado* and café foods. **El Romano** (Pizarro 747, tel. 044/25-2251, 8 A.M.–midnight daily, US$3–8), established more than 50 years ago, has a well-earned reputation of having the best espresso and cappuccino in town. Sandwiches, salads, Peruvian dishes, and desserts are all good here.

Open only during lunch hours, **Restaurant Romano Rincón Criollo** (Estados Unidos 162, Urbanización El Recreo, tel. 044/24-4207, 11:30 A.M.–5 P.M., US$5–12) is a great place to enjoy regional food, whether it is *cebiche,* fried fish, stewed duck, or other delicious plates.

A good spot for fish and seafood is **Squalo's**

(Calle Cienfuegos 250, Urbanización La Merced, tel. 044/29-5134, 11:30 A.M.–5 P.M. daily, US$3–12), a mid-priced restaurant with pretty good food. There are chicken, beef, and duck dishes too.

El Mochica (Bolívar 462, tel. 044/29-3441, www.elmochica.com.pe, 9 A.M.–11 P.M. daily, US$4–12) is, according to iconic Peruvian chef Gastón Acurio, "an ideal place to find the aromas and tastes of grandmother's cooking." It's open for breakfast, lunch, and even dinner; some highlights are *sopa shambar,* a tasty, thick soup of wheat, vegetables, and pork, served only on Mondays, or *tallarines con pichón,* spicy spaghetti served with stewed baby pigeons—a delicacy hardly found elsewhere. Situated two blocks away from the Plaza de Armas, this is the eatery to explore the spicy and intense flavors of Trujillo's regional food, whether it is fish or seafood, stewed goat or duck. After a meal in this place, it can finally be understood why Peruvians insist on the saying *barriga llena, corazón contento,* "a full stomach makes a happy heart."

Pizza

A very good pizza place in Trujillo is **Pizzería Pizza Roma** (Estete 443, tel. 044/58-1017, 6–11 P.M. daily, US$5–10). The chef is Italian and the pizzas are excellent. **Pizzanino** (Juan Pablo II 183, tel. 044/26-3105, 6 P.M.–midnight daily, US$5–12) is also a good option for pizzas with a more local flavor.

Chifa

Chifa Ah Chau (Gamarra 769, tel. 044/24-3351, noon–4 P.M. and 6–11 P.M. daily, US$3–10) might not be the fanciest restaurant in Trujillo, but it definitely has the best Chinese food in the city. A plain doorway will lead you to a long corridor with curtained eating booths. The portions are generous and the food is tasty.

On the western side of town, **Chifa Brillante** (Junín 269, tel. 044/20-2041, noon–4 P.M. and 6–11 P.M. daily, US$4–6) serves up wonton soup and chicken stir-fry in a spacious dining room decorated with fish tanks.

Vegetarian

Restaurant Vegetariano El Sol (Pizarro 660, tel. 044/58-3521, 8 A.M.–11 P.M. daily) doesn't offer much in the way of atmosphere, but the vegetarian plates here are yummy and reasonably priced.

Fine Dining

Fiesta (Av. Larco 954, Vista Alegre, tel. 044/42-1572, www.restaurantfiestagourmet. com, noon–11 P.M. Mon.–Fri., 8 A.M.–6 P.M. Sun. and holidays, US$10–25, without wine) is one of the best restaurants in northern Peru. **Héctor Solís,** chef and founder of this gourmet temple, inaugurated his first restaurant in Chiclayo. In 2008, he opened in Trujillo to immediate success. Specialties include *tiradito de mero en salsa de ají mochero* (grouper carpaccio garnished with *mochero* chili sauce), *pechuga de pato al grill con cama de puré de loche* (grilled duck breast served over a purée of *loche* pumpkin), or *canilla de cabrito asada con pasta fresco* (roasted goat shank with fresh pasta), among 50 other dishes. If you want to indulge yourself, this is the place to go.

Las BóVedas (Independencia 485, Plaza de Armas, tel. 044/23-2741, www.libertador.com. pe, 6–10:30 A.M., noon–3 P.M., and 7–11 P.M. Mon.–Sat., US$10–30, without wine) is the refined gourmet restaurant of the Libertador Trujillo Hotel. You can order anything from a mushroom and shrimp risotto with grilled loin to a delicious grouper ceviche. There is a good selection of Chilean, Argentine, and Spanish wines to accompany your lunch or dinner.

Markets

There's a good but small **fruit market** at España 584, **El Mercado Central** is at Ayacucho and San Augustín, and the modern **Merpisa supermarket** is at Pizarro and Junín.

INFORMATION AND SERVICES

The very helpful **Iperú** tourist information office (Pizarro 412, tel. 044/29-4561, iperutrujillo@promperu.gob.pe, 8 A.M.–7 P.M. Mon.–Sat., 8 A.M.–2 P.M. Sun.) is on the Plaza de Armas. The **tourist police** are located at Independencia 630 (tel. 044/29-1705, 8 A.M.–8 P.M. daily).

The best medical service in town is at **Clínica Peruano-Americana** (Mansiche 810, tel. 044/22-2493, 24 hours).

Banks, often in beautifully restored colonial buildings, are scattered around the center of town. **Banco de Crédito** (Gamarra 562) and **Banco Continental** (547 Gamarra) are across the street from one another. Both have 24-hour ATMs and are open weekdays approximately 9 A.M.–6 P.M. and Saturday mornings.

The Serpost **post office** is at Independencia 286. **Internet** is widely available in the streets surrounding the Plaza de Armas, and most cafés are open daily 9 A.M.–11 P.M.

Lavanderías Unidas is at Pizarro 683 (tel. 044/20-0505, 9 A.M.–8:30 P.M. Mon.–Sat., US$2.50/kg for same-day service). The **La Lavandería La Moderna** (Orbegoso 270) is also reliable.

Librería SBS (Bolívar 714, tel. 044/22-0308, 9 A.M.–1:30 P.M. and 4–8 P.M. daily) has books in English, and **Adriática S.A.** (Junín 555, tel. 044/29-1569, 9 A.M.–1:30 P.M. and 4–8 P.M. daily), in addition to carrying a few English titles, stocks the best selection of books in Spanish.

GETTING THERE AND AROUND

LAN (340 Pizarro, tel. 044/20-1859, www.lan. com, 9 A.M.–7 P.M. Mon.–Fri., 9 A.M.–6 P.M. Sat.) has one-hour daily flights between Trujillo and Lima. **Star Perú** (Lima tel. 01/705-9000, www.starperu.com) is the budget option for the same route.

All of these bus companies are recommended and have daily service, usually in the evenings, for the eight-hour haul to Lima: **Oltursa** (Ejército 342, tel. 044/26-3055, www.oltursa.com.pe), **Cruz del Sur** (Amazonas 438, tel. 044/26-1801, www.cruzdelsur.com. pe), **Ormeño** (Ejército 233, tel. 044/25-9782), **Linea** (América Sur 2855, tel. 044/28-6538, www.transporteslinea.com.pe), and **ITTSA Sur** (Mansiche 145, tel. 044/25-1415).

The recommended **Movil Tours** (América Sur 3959, tel. 044/28-6538) has comfortable buses to Huaraz and Chachapoyas, and **Linea** has frequent buses to Chiclayo (3 hours) and Cajamarca (6 hours). Most of the bus companies head north as well, and Ormeño offers service to Ecuador.

Taxis within the center of the city cost US$0.75; *combis* and *colectivos* are US$0.30 but only operate outside the center. The best place to pick up public transport headed north, including Chicama, Chan Chan, and Huanchaco, is Óvalo Grau opposite the Museo Cassinelli.

Rental cars are available at **Global Car** (Ecuador 122, Urb. El Recreo, tel. 044/29-5548 or 044/965-2913).

HUANCHACO

A considerably more laid-back base from which to independently visit the ruins around Trujillo is Huanchaco, an ancient fishing village that has exploded over the last few decades into a favorite resort for Peruvians and a well-worn destination on the Gringo Trail. Even as new adobe homes fill the 14-kilometer gap between Huanchaco and Trujillo, this beach town still maintains a good bit of its village charm. Huanchaco has an excellent assortment of inexpensive and well-run hostels and restaurants for a range of travelers.

Huanchaco is the mythical landing spot of Takaynamo, the bearded founder of the Chimú empire who reputedly ordered the construction of Chan Chan around A.D. 1200. Even before Takaynamo's arrival, however, Huanchaco's fishermen were using their exquisitely crafted *caballitos de tórtora,* reed rafts with gracefully curved bows that are depicted on 2,000-year-old Mochica ceramics. About 80 full-time fisherfolk straddle their *caballitos* each morning, legs dangling into the water on each side as they fish with line and hook or drop weighted gill nets. The anglers surf in on the waves in the afternoon and then stand their boats upright to dry. Called *patacho* in the native tongue spoken first by the Moche and later by Chimú, the boats are made of tied

bundles of reeds, which are cut from the marsh (*wachaque*) at the north end of town. A few residents still speak the nearly extinct native tongue, including one elderly woman who is known for singing Moche ballads.

Most visitors to Huanchaco come for a rest from the rigors of travel and enjoy a relaxed nightlife that includes occasional bonfires on the beach, roving musicians, and a few pubs. Brazilians cram into the hostels along the beach, sure proof of good surfing. This is a great place to learn how to surf, with gentle waves, surfboards for rent, and quality instructors.

There is an important historical site on the hill above the town: **Santuario de la Virgen del Socorro,** reputed to be the second-oldest church in Peru. The yellow church with colonial facade and large bell tower has served as a landmark for sailors ever since the Spaniards built it atop a Chimú temple in 1540. After a Spanish caravel sunk one late night in a storm off the coast, legend has it that a box floated

The traditional Huanchaco boats, *caballitos de tórtora,* are named after sea horses.

to shore containing the Virgen del Socorro (Virgin of Rescue). It sparked the conversion of Huanchaco's natives, so the story goes, and has been venerated ever since.

A word of caution: Any beach spot popular with foreigners will have its share of *bricheros,* delinquents who specialize in ripping off tourists. They will often befriend travelers by offering free surfing lessons, only to end up in a bar later that night where the gringo is left with the bill. Travelers who wander the streets of Huanchaco—or most other cities in Peru for that matter—late at night either drunk or on drugs are asking to be robbed.

Entertainment and Events

There are occasional beach bonfires, but for more of a party head to **El Kero Restaurant Pub** (La Ribera 115, tel. 044/46-1186, www.elkero.com, 9 A.M.–midnight daily, US$2.50–4). The softly lit pub with yellow walls doubles as a restaurant during the day, but at night, it's known for its long list of cocktails—Bloody Mary to pisco sour—and live music during the summertime.

One of Huanchaco's more famous celebrations happens in the last days of June when a flotilla of *caballitos de tótora,* including a gigantic one made especially for carrying the religious image of San Pedro, arrives on the beach in Huanchaco atop breaking waves. The two-day festival of **San Pedro,** patron saint of fishermen, also includes a religious procession and celebrations.

Shopping

To window-shop a mix of handicrafts, stroll into the **Galeria Artesanal** (Larco 520, tel. 044/46-1305, 9 A.M.–9 P.M. daily, US$1–10).

Recreation

The Wave International (Larco 525, tel. 044/58-7005, thewaveinhuanchaco@hotmail.com, 7 A.M.–3 A.M. daily, US$13 for 3 hours of instruction), right on the main drag and full of young bronzed surfers, offers surfing lessons, board rentals, and even surfing tours to the northern beaches. The surf shop also functions as a bar.

Accommodations

Huanchaco hotels and lodges might offer discounts outside holidays and the summer months (Christmas–March).

Hostal Naylamp (Victor Larco 1420, tel. 044/46-1022, www.hostalnaylamp.com, US$12–14 s, US$18–22 d) is an oceanfront hostel offering a safe, clean, friendly, and relaxed atmosphere, a garden full of hammocks, and an open kitchen. Its upstairs rooms have an ocean view, and camping, along with tent rental, is available for US$3.50 pp.

La Casa Suiza (Los Pinos 308, tel. 044/46-1285, www.casasuiza.com, albergue@lacasasuiza.com, US$18 s, US$7 pp in shared rooms with bath) is a few blocks from the beach. Started back in the 1980s by a Swiss woman, Heidi Stacher, the small hostel is now managed by Frenchman Philippe Faucon. The place has small but neat rooms (there are cheaper rooms with shared bathrooms; check the website for rates) that are integrated into a hip decor. Services are plentiful and include laundry, kitchen, surfboard rentals, book exchange, and WiFi. It also serves breakfasts and small lunches. Reserve with time since both places are always full.

Once you enter **Huanchaco Hostal** (Victor Larco 287, tel. 044/46-1688, www.huanchacohostal.com, US$25 s, US$38 d), you'll first note its large, circular staircase, then its antique furniture, and finally its classic dark wood interior. Sitting across Huanchaco's small Plaza de Armas, just a few blocks from the beach, the rooms of this hostel aren't anything special. But the refined atmosphere, plus a game room and a swimming pool, make this a reasonable place to stay if you value peace and quiet, and a little fun. **Hostal El Malecón** (Av. La Rivera 225, tel. 044/46-1275, www.hostalelmalecon.com, US$35 s, US$50 d with breakfast) has rooms with hot water, cable TV, and private bathrooms. The hostel is a few meters before Los Pinos Street, in front of the ocean. It is clean, safe, and has a friendly staff.

Las Palmeras de Huanchaco (Av. Larco 1150, Sector Los Tumbos, tel. 044/46-1199, www.laspalmerasdehuanchaco.com, US$36 s, US$46–61 d) is a good option with a wide variety of rooms, including doubles at three different levels facing the ocean or the pool. It's on the northern end of Huanchaco, and there are family rooms with kitchenettes (US$89) and semi-suites (US$71). Amenities include a café-restaurant, a swimming pool, laundry service, and Internet. Rooms are very nice, with cable TV and clean, impeccable bathrooms.

❰ Bracamonte Hotel (Los Olivos 503, tel. 044/46-1162, www.hotelbracamonte. com.pe, US$47 s, US$57 d) is owned by the Bracamonte family, which started renting small rooms in the early 1980s. Thirty years later, they have built a three-star hotel with comfortable bungalows and a dazzlingly clear pool, restaurant and bar, game room, and Internet service. This hotel is one of the best options in Huanchaco.

Food

Huanchaco offers many great budget eateries.

CAFÉS, BAKERIES, AND ICE CREAM

Off the Plaza de Armas, in a quiet bohemian setting, is **Casa Tere** (257 M Soane, tel. 044/46-1197, casaterehco@yahoo.es, 3–11 P.M. daily, US$1.50–2.50), which comes alive during the evening as it dishes up pizzas, sandwiches, and crepes. Casa Tere also has a breakfast location farther south on Larco.

PERUVIAN

Don Pepe (Av. Larco 502, US$3–5) offers *cangrejo reventado,* a local dish where crab shells are broken open and the crab meat cooked with eggs, sea algae, and *ají.* **El Mochica** (Av. Larco on the corner with Independencia, tel. 044/46-1963) has great seafood dishes in a location just across from the ocean.

VEGETARIAN

❰ Otra Cosa (Av. Larco 921, El Boquerón, tel. 044/46-1346, www.otracosa.info, 9 A.M.–8 P.M. Wed.–Sun.) has outstanding veggie food at very good prices, including fruit salads, healthy breakfasts and lunches, and the best coffee in Huanchaco. The restaurant is part of Otra Cosa Network, a Peruvian NGO,

and the restaurant is managed by locals with the support of European and North American volunteers.

FINE DINING

❰ Big Ben (Av. Larco 836, El Boquerón, tel. 044/46-1378, www.bigbenhuanchaco.com, 11:30 A.M.–5:30 P.M. daily, US$4–16) has delicious seafood and fish dishes including *cebiches, tiraditos,* crab, deep-fried calamari, chicken, and beef plates. Enjoy your meal sitting at a table on the terrace overlooking the beach.

Getting There

From Trujillo, US$0.75 *colectivos* run along Avenida España before heading to Huanchaco. A taxi for the 10-minute drive will cost US$4–5.

NORTH TO PACASMAYO

The Chicama Valley, just north of Trujillo and the Moche Valley, is a worthwhile location for those in search of the world's longest left-breaking wave, or who want to further explore Moche archaeology.

El Brujo

About 60 kilometers north of Trujillo, reachable only via unmarked dirt roads, is El Brujo (tel. 044/29-1894, 9 A.M.–4 P.M. daily, US$4). Out-of-the-way and unexplored, El Brujo is difficult to explore without a guide but is considered one of the more important ceremonial centers of the north coast, used from 3000 B.C. through colonial times. If you enjoyed seeing Chan Chan and the *huacas* outside of Trujillo, El Brujo is the logical next step: a complex blend of the ancient cultures of the Chicama Valley, but above all the Moche. The site is essentially three *huacas.*

Huaca Cortada contains reliefs of Moche warriors, *tumi* in one hand and decapitated head in the other. There is also Huaca Prieta, but the most excavated is the Huaca Cao, a huge platform with murals on five levels depicting figures of priests, sacrificial victims, and dancing warriors—similar to those recently unearthed at Huaca de la Luna. In 2005, on the northern side of the Huaca Cao, archaeologists unearthed the tomb of the mummy Señora del Cao. The second oldest female mummy to be discovered in Peru, the Señora del Cao is covered in tattoos that suggest that she was a political dignitary, not a religious leader. Directly west of the Huaca Cao stand the remains of a Jesuit cathedral that the Spaniards built to emphasize their dominance over the Moche culture. And to the east thousand-year-old bits of fabric pop out of the unexplored Lambaque cemetery from A.D. 800.

On your way out of El Brujo, stop at **Restaurant El Timbo** (Bolognesi 452, behind the municipal building) in Magdalena de Cao for fried fish and a glass of *chica del año*, a winelike *chica* that ages underground about 10 months, deepening in color and sweetness.

Although you can technically visit El Brujo without a guide, it is easier to navigate both the unmarked roads and the ruins with a personal guide (US$45) or with a Trujillo tour company (US$70 for a minimum of two people). The nearest public transport goes only to Magdalena de Cao, which is five kilometers away from El Brujo, and because there are only a few *mototaxis* in Magdalena de Cao, you will probably end up walking to the site. To get to Magdelena de Cao, take a bus from Trujillo's Avenida America Sur, headed for Chocope, and from Chocope, take a *colectivo* to Magdalena de Cao.

Chicama

Puerto Chicama is a plain beach near an ugly town with only a few run-down places to stay and eat. As Chicho, the Huanchaco surfing pro, explains, "the only good thing Chicama has is waves," which, March–June, form the longest-breaking surf in the world. The wave ranges in height 1–2.5 meters and runs a reputed 2.5 kilometers. Four separate waves that link together, the megawave is the result of a flat, sandy beach, steady crosswinds, and southern and western ocean currents. Locals joke that surfers need a spare set of legs to surf it and a *combi* ride to make it back up the beach afterwards.

Long before surfing was in vogue, Chicama was a major port for the sugar and cotton brought by railroad from the nearby Hacienda Chicama. As a result the town has an old pier with railroad tracks and a group of old, wooden *casonas* along the waterfront. Most surfers pitch in and rent a group car to visit here for the day from bases farther north, such as Órganos or Máncora.

From Trujillo, take a bus from Óvalo Grau near the Museo Cassinelli that says either Puerto Chicama or Paiján. *Colectivos* run to Puerto Chicama often from Paiján.

Pacasmayo

This early-20th-century port, 105 kilometers north of Trujillo, has a famous old pier where tobacco, cotton, and sugar were loaded onto large sailing ships and, later, steamers. Boat traffic is still concentrated on the northern side of the pier, while sunbathers and swimmers congregate on the south. Precisely because so few people ever visit here, Pacasmayo is imbued with memories of bygone times and a nostalgia augmented by an interesting railroad museum outside of town. Just before the village of Guadalupe are the ruins of Pacatnamú. This complex of pyramids, cemeteries, and homes, occupied before Moche times, is rarely visited even though it is comparable in size to Chan Chan.

There are several hostels but the best lodging is **Hotel Pakatnamú** (Malecón Grau 103, tel. 044/52-2368, www.actiweb.es/hotelpakatnamu, US$27 s, US$38 d including breakfast and free parking), which offers nice rooms, TVs, and a waterfront view. It also has a restaurant with a surprising variety of dishes—from seafood to pasta.

The best restaurant in town is **Aruba,** just a block and a half from Hotel Pakatnamú.

All the major north–south buses stop in Pacasmayo, from which buses depart regularly for Cajamarca. The turnoff for Cajamarca is just 15 kilometers north of Pacasmayo, a road junction famous among Peruvians for a cluster of seafood restaurants.

Chiclayo and Vicinity

Among Peru's large cities, Chiclayo stands out as an underdog with a humble beginning. The city began as a mule watering spot between the opulent cities of Ferreñafe, Lambayeque, and Zaña, which were founded by the Spanish between 1550 and 1565. But in a twist of history, these once-proud Spanish towns have withered while mestizo Chiclayo has boomed in recent years as the commercial hub of northern Peru. There is not much colonial architecture in Chiclayo, but there are a few things you will not find elsewhere: a crooked street layout based on winding farmers' lanes and a witches' market that sells potions and amulets.

Chiclayo is northern Peru's number-one travel destination because of the **Moche** and **Sicán** cultures, which built elaborate cities and tombs in the surrounding desert from A.D. 100 until the arrival of the Inca in 1470. The Moche tombs of the royal lord and priest of Sipán were unearthed in 1987 and 1991, respectively, stunning archaeologists with their complexity and beauty. They were finds as important in Latin American history as the unearthing of Tutankhamen's tomb in Egypt. After several world tours, the gold objects from these tombs and three other royal tombs are on display at the state-of-the-art **Museo Tumbas Reales de Sipán** in Lambayeque.

The Moche empire declined around A.D. 750 and a new culture known as the Sicán (or Lambayeque) emerged to build **Batán Grande,** a complex of pyramids 57 kilometers outside Chiclayo. In 1991 Japanese archaeologist Izumi Shimada discovered two royal Sicán tombs, filled with beautiful gold masks, jewelry, and solid-gold disk earrings that rival those of the Lords of Sipán. The objects are now on display at Museo Sicán in Ferreñafe, another fascinating, well-designed museum that is a must-see. Around A.D. 1050, the Sicán, frustrated by an El Niño-spurred drought, set fire to Batán Grande and built the even more elaborate city of **Túcume,** which is 33 kilometers north of present-day Chiclayo. Túcume's 26 adobe

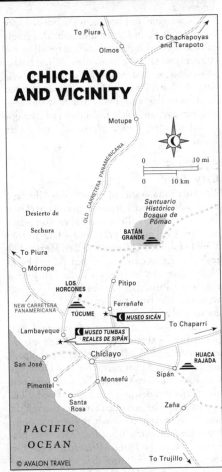

pyramids, reduced by time to dirt mountains, are spread through a dramatic desert at the base of Cerro Purgatorio.

Other sites of interest around Chiclayo include **Zaña,** an affluent colonial city that is now a ghost town of stone arches, columns, and church facades; **Huaca Rajada** (Cracked Pyramid), the twin adobe pyramids where the Lords of Sipán were found; **Monsefú,** a market town known for its woven straw and cotton goods; and **Santa Rosa,** a beach and fishing village with *caballitos de tótora* and a few good *cebicherías.*

It is possible, but not recommended, to see both the Sipán and Sicán museums in a single exhausting day. A better option is to follow the cultures and visit the Sicán sites—Gran Batán, Museo Sicán, and possibly Túcume—in one day; the Sipán sites—Huaca Rajada, Museo Tumbas Reales, and finally Museo Bruning—another day; and on a third day visit the optional sites of Zaña, Monsefú, and Santa Rosa.

SIGHTS
City Tour

The first inhabitants of present-day Chiclayo were Indians forced to settle here as part of a Spanish *reducción.* Religious conversion began here in 1559 when Franciscan friars from Trujillo founded **El Convenio San María.** The remains of this convent, all but ruined by El Niño rains, can be seen on Calle San José at the Parque Principal. Most of Chiclayo's streets were once dirt lanes that led to the convent and are named after saints.

Chiclayo does not have a Plaza de Armas but rather a **Parque Principal,** which was inaugurated in 1916. Historians believe this park once served as a goat corral for José Domingo Chiclayo, the town's namesake, who came here after Zaña was destroyed in a 1720 flood. (The city may have been named for him, though the word also means "place where there are green branches" in the all-but-lost Mochica language.) Near the Parque Principal is the historic municipal building that was set on fire September 4, 2006. Also on the main park is **La Catedral,** built in 1869 by José Balta, Chiclayo's most famous citizen, who launched a coup in the 1830s and briefly served as president of Peru. The other main churches in town are even more recent: **Iglesia La Verónica,** at Torres Paz and Alfonso Ugarte, was built in the late 19th century; and **Basílica San Antonio,** at the intersection of Luis Gonzáles and Torre Paz, was built in 1946.

Chiclayo has a highly interesting **Mercado de Brujos** (Arica, inside the Mercado Modelo, 7 A.M.–5 P.M. daily). Here are piles of all the materials used by Peru's *curanderos*—shark jaws, deer legs, snakeskins, potions, scents, amulets, and *huayruro* (jungle beads for warding off a hex). There are heaps of dried mountain herbs and San Pedro cacti, which, when sliced and reduced in boiling water, form a hallucinogenic drink used by shamans—and an increasing number of travelers. Shamans can be contracted here for fortune-telling or healing sessions. But beware of sham artists or shamans who dabble in the dark side—they are everywhere and can pose a real threat to your psychic health. It is always best to make *curandero* contacts through a trusted source.

If you have spare time in the evening, head to **Paseo Las Musas** (José Balta and Garcilazo de la Vega), an odd promenade with Greco-Roman statues and a triumphal arch sustained by armless Egyptian beauties. It is a charming Chiclayan invention, often filled with wedding parties emerging from the cathedral, five blocks away.

Huaca Rajada

Huaca Rajada (Cracked Pyramid, tel. 074/80-0048, 9 A.M.–5 P.M. daily, US$2.50), about 28 kilometers east of Chiclayo, is the original tomb site where the remains of the Señor de Sipán were discovered. The tombs have been decorated with replicas of the original findings and offer a comprehensive understanding of what archaeologist Walter Alva discovered when he excavated these 12 Moche tombs. Close by there is a small museum with photos from the 1987–1989 excavations.

South of the tombs there are two pyramids, built by the Moche around A.D. 300, that today look like clay mountains, along with a lower platform, about 120 meters long, where *huaqueros* plundered before they were caught. The pyramids are composed of *argamasa,* an adobe mixture that includes water, earth, seashells, ceramic fragments, llama dung, small stones, and *algarrobo* branches. This mixture sat for 20 days before being put in cane molds and baked in the sun. The pyramid itself was built

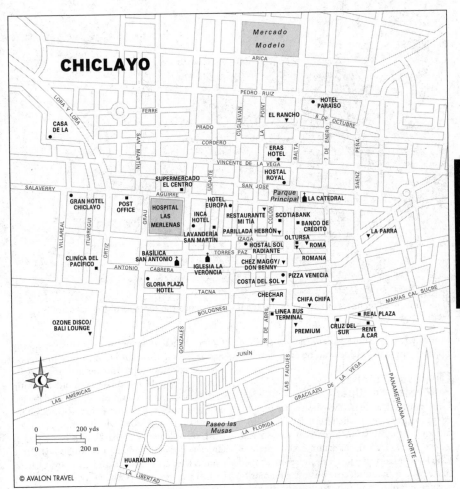

CHICLAYO

Mercado Modelo

ARICA

PEDRO RUIZ

LORA Y LORA

FERRE

EL RANCHO

HOTEL PARAÍSO

8 DE OCTUBRE

CASA DE LA

PRADO

CORDERO

ERAS HOTEL

7 DE ENERO

PEÑA

SAN MARTÍN

VINCENTE DE LA VEGA

SALAVERRY

SUPERMERCADO EL CENTRO

HOSTAL ROYAL

SAN JOSÉ

GRAN HOTEL CHICLAYO

POST OFFICE

AGUIRRE

HOTEL EUROPA

Parque Principal

LA CATEDRAL

THE NORTH COAST

VILLAREAL

ITURREGUI

GRAU

HOSPITAL LAS MERLENAS

INCA HOTEL

RESTAURANTE MI TÍA

SCOTIABANK

BANCO DE CRÉDITO

LA PARRA

PARILLADA HEBRÓN

LAVANDERÍA SAN MARTÍN

IZAGA

OLTURSA

HOSTAL SOL RADIANTE

ROMA

CLINÍCA DEL PACÍFICO

ORTIZ

BASÍLICA SAN ANTONIO

TORRES PAZ

CHEZ MAGGY/ DON BENNY

ROMANA

ANTONIO

CABRERA

IGLESIA LA VERÓNCIA

COSTA DEL SOL

PIZZA VENECIA

GLORIA PLAZA HOTEL

TACNA

CHECHAR

MARÍAS CAL SUCRE

BOLOGNESI

CHIFA CHIFA

REAL PLAZA

OZONE DISCO/ BALI LOUNGE

GONZALES

18 DE ABRIL

LINEA BUS TERMINAL

PREMIUM

CRUZ DEL SUR

RENT A CAR

JUNÍN

LAS AMÉRICAS

LAS FAIQUES

GRACILAZO DE LA VEGA

PANAMERICANA

NORTE

0   200 yds
0   200 m

Paseo las Musas

LA FLORIDA

HUARALINO

LA LIBERTAD

© AVALON TRAVEL

in huge, separate blocks of bricks in order to allow shifting, and prevent cracking, during an earthquake.

It is possible to climb to the top of the largest pyramid for a good view of the surrounding fields and the village of Sipán, a community of sugarcane workers who protested Alva's excavations and continue to feel resentful that their town has received so little financial benefit from all of Sipán's riches. The town received electricity only in 2001, and there is a long-delayed proposal to install running water

and sewerage. Five police and an archaeologist are stationed full time to protect the pyramids, which have not yet been excavated, and the platform, which, according to archaeologist Julio Chero is 75 percent excavated.

To efficiently include Huaca Rajada in a full day of sightseeing, it is best to take a guided tour from Chiclayo. If taking public transport, start early in the day, as there are no places to stay in Sipán. Buses to Sipán leave from the Terminal de Epsel at the corner of Avenida Oriente and Nicolás de Pierola in Chiclayo.

THE NORTH COAST

© RENÉE DEL GAUDIO AND ROSS WEHNER

Over time, erosion has worn away the Huaca Rajada, where the remains of the Lords of Sipán were discovered.

From there it is a short walk to the ruins, where Spanish-speaking guides can be contracted.

Museo Tumbas Reales de Sipán

Give yourself at least two hours to see this extraordinary museum (Juan P. Vizcardo y Guzmán s/n, tel. 074/28-3977, 9 A.M.–5 P.M. Tues.–Sun., US$3), 11 kilometers north of Chiclayo in Lambayeque. The museum, shaped like a Moche pyramid, contains the gold masks, scepters, jewelry, and other objects of the royal Moche tomb discovered by archaeologist Walter Alva in 1987. This museum succeeds in evoking the full grandeur and sophistication of the ancient Moche civilization (A.D. 100–850) in a way that adobe pyramids, now reduced to mud mountains, often do not. After nearly 500 years of continuous tomb looting up and down the coast of Peru, it is nothing short of a miracle that these tombs remained undisturbed. Their meticulous excavation has unlocked many of the mysteries of Moche society, built around a hierarchy of kings, priests, and military leaders.

Come with a guide (or hire a Spanish-speaking one at the museum for US$5) who can explain Moche cosmography and point out things a first-timer would miss. For example, the king and priest discovered in these tombs are depicted on the ceramics and murals found throughout the 600-kilometer-long Moche empire.

To reach Museo Tumbas Reales, hire a taxi in Chiclayo for US$5 or take a US$0.30 *combi* ride from Vicente de la Vega and Leonardo Ortiz, in front of the Otursa bus terminal. Slightly cheaper combination tickets are available at the Museo Tumbas Reales for those who plan on also visiting Huaca Rajada and Túcume.

Museo Arqueológico Nacional Bruning

Lambayeque is also home to the Museo Arqueológico Nacional Bruning (Huamachuco, block 7, tel. 074/28-2110, 9 A.M.–5 P.M. daily, US$2.50), an interesting museum founded in 1925 and remodeled in 2006. Museo Bruning has an eclectic collection: Sicán gold masks with the famous winged eyes and red patina of

KING TUT'S GOT NOTHING ON THE LORDS OF SIPÁN

Peruvian archaeologist Walter Alva knew he had found something big at Huaca Rajada in 1987 when he unearthed more than a thousand ceramic pots – with the food, apparently, for an afterlife journey. A bit deeper Alva found the skeleton of a sentry with the feet cut off – symbolizing eternal vigil – and the remains of wood beams that once supported a tomb. Below was a disintegrated sarcophagus with heavy copper fastenings, an array of gold covers and decorations, and, at the bottom, a Moche king in all his splendor. Around and on top of him were huge earrings of turquoise and gold, breastplates of delicately threaded shell beads, a necklace of gold spheres and another of huge peanut shells – 10 of which were in silver, 10 in gold. By his hand lay a scepter with an inverted gold pyramid decorated with scenes of human sacrifice. Gold balls were found in the king's mouth, abdomen, and right hand, and a silver ball was found in his left. There were seven sacrificial victims buried along with the king – the sentry, a general, a standard bearer, three young women, and a child – along with two llamas and a spotted dog.

After carbon-dating the tomb at A.D. 300, Alva's team found an earlier tomb nearby that may have belonged to the grandfather, referred to as El Viejo Señor de Sipán (The Old Lord of Sipán). This ruler was buried along with a woman and a decapitated llama, and although the tomb is smaller, the 53 gold objects found here show the highest level of craftsmanship. There are exquisite gold balls of spiders straddling their webs, necklaces with minute gold and silver filigree, and jewelry with the same octopus and crab motifs found in the recently uncovered murals at the Huaca de la Luna near Trujillo.

Alva's team discovered 10 other tombs, including that of a Moche priest – the mythical "bird man" who appears alongside the king in the human sacrifice ceremonies depicted on Moche ceramics and murals. The priest was found with a gold scepter capped with an *ullu-chu* – this sacred fruit, now extinct, is believed to have prevented blood from coagulating during ceremonies of human sacrifice. (It may also have had hallucinogenic properties as well, judging by the dazed looks on the faces of several flying priests.)

The excavation of these tombs began with a midnight call that local police made to Alva's home in 1987. Grave robbers digging at midnight near Huaca Rajada, the Moche Pyramid near the village of Sipán, had found a royal tomb and begun lugging rice sacks filled with gold objects. At one point, the robbers quarreled and one of them was killed in the ensuing fight. When police found out they called Alva and launched an international search for objects that had already been smuggled overseas. Police recovered a few objects, including a gold mask and a gold plate, called a *taparabos*, which the Moche elite hung behind their bodies. This last piece was recovered by the U.S. FBI, which arrested a Panamanian diplomat in Philadelphia in 1997 trying to sell the piece for $1.5 million. For a fascinating account of the Sipán heist and the worldwide network of antiquities smugglers, read American novelist Sidney Kirkpatrick's *Lords of Sipán*.

mercury ore found at Batán Grande; a variety of weapons and musical instruments found at Túcume; and a Moche ceramics collection that includes marine animals, an enigmatic vase of a man straddling what appears to be a torpedo, and other Moche vases depicting a range of human disease and sexual practices. This ceramics collection alone is worth the visit, especially if you missed Museo Cassinelli in Trujillo.

After the colonial center of Zaña was destroyed in a flood in 1720, Lambayeque flourished and several important colonial homes and churches were built. Now Lambayeque is a sleepy town with one new hotel and a handful of restaurants. Worth seeing if you have the time is **Iglesia San Pedro**, a large, yellow-and-white church on the main square that was completed by 1739. Inside are large murals and

10 altars, the oldest being the baroque Virgen de las Mercedes. One block away, at the intersection of Dos de Mayo and San Martín, is the **La Casa Montjoy,** with the largest balcony in Peru—over 65 meters long! It was from here that liberator San Martín gave the first shout of independence in 1820. To reach Lambayeque from Chiclayo, take a *combi* from Vicente de la Vega and Leonardo Ortiz, in front of the Otursa bus terminal.

Batán Grande

This sprawling pyramid complex, set amid a dry-forest nature reserve, was the first Sicán capital and the source for the majority of the plundered gold that was either sold to private collections or—before collecting became popular in the 1940s—simply melted down. Batán Grande (57 km northeast of Chiclayo, tel. 074/20-1470, 7 A.M.–6 P.M. daily, free) is about a half hour drive farther along the same road that leads to Museo Sicán. The royal tombs were discovered in front of Huaca de Oro (Pyramid of Gold), one of 34 adobe pyramids in the 300-hectare Reserva Bosque Pómac. The excavated tombs have been covered up to deter grave robbers, and there is little to see except for the pyramids, which look like huge dirt hills. They were badly eroded by the El Niño rains of 1982 and 1998, which did however boost the surrounding dry forest of *algarrobo,* ficus, *zapote,* and vichayo trees (one *algarobbo* tree, forced to the ground by its own weight, is reputed to be 800 years old and is the center of shamanic rituals). There is interesting wildlife in the reserve: 41 species of birds, numerous reptiles (iguanas, snakes, lizards), as well as foxes, deer, anteaters, and ferrets—though the spectacled bear and puma long ago disappeared from this forest.

More than anything, the reserve is a depressing case study of how Peruvians, driven by necessity, continue to plunder their cultural and natural treasures. Villagers frequently venture into the park at night to cut down trees for lumber or dig around the pyramids, though *huaqueros* are no longer finding the treasures they used to here. The punishments for these crimes are ridiculously low—US$60 for the first offense and US$120 for the second, with no jail time or confiscation of vehicles. The four guards in charge of patrolling the 5,800-hectare nature reserve have two motorcycles and one pickup truck between them. Because of the difficult conditions, local groups have taken it upon themselves to develop a volunteer ranger program to protect the trees in the forest as well as general ecotourism infrastructure. Locals have been trained to give tours of the cultural and natural resources in the park, and park rangers give tours, too. Both appreciate tips. To reach Batán Grande, take a *colectivo* from the Terminal de Epsel at the corner of Avenida Oriente and Nicolás de Pierola in Chiclayo. Be sure to designate that you are going to the archaeological site and not the town by the same name. Because the site is large and hard to find, it is best to see it on an organized tour.

Túcume

Túcume, the final capital of the Sicán culture, is 35 kilometers along the the old Panamericana from Chiclayo. Archaeologists believe that Túcume was built after the Sicán burnt and abandoned their former capital of Batán Grande around A.D. 1050. The most stunning thing about Túcume is the landscape, which can be best seen from a lookout on Cerro Purgatorio—a huge desert mountain rising in the midst of 26 eroded adobe pyramids scattered throughout 200 hectares of surrounding *bosque seco.* There is a powerful energy to the place, especially at dawn and dusk, which is probably why the Sicán chose it in the first place and why many shamanic rituals continue here today (notice all the makeshift hearths for ceremonies).

As at Bátan Grande, there is not much here in the way of murals or reliefs, though many have been found here. The last major excavation was undertaken here between 1989 and 1994 by the Norwegian adventurer **Thor Heyerdahl,** who spent much of his life in this area. What excavations continue are closed to the public. Walking around these huge

© RENÉE DEL GAUDIO AND ROSS WEHNER

Túcume

pyramids can make for interesting viewing—the Huaca Larga is an astonishing 700 meters long, 280 meters wide, and 30 meters tall. The area is commonly referred to as the **Valle de las Pirámides,** which is easy to understand from the lookout on Cerro Purgatorio, which offers a view over the entire complex.

Archaeologists believe the pyramids, like the Huacas de la Luna y Sol outside Trujillo, are superimposed structures built in phases. These pyramids were probably inhabited by priests and rulers even after waves of conquest (and new construction) by the Chimú in 1375 and the Inca in 1470. Atop Huaca Larga, for instance, archaeologists have uncovered a Chimú **Temple of the Mythical Bird** from around 1375 with an even newer Inca tomb, built of stone from Cerro Purgatorio, on top. The heavily adorned and scarred body inside the tomb was apparently a warrior who was buried with two other men and 19 women between the ages of 10 and 30. There is a small **site museum** (9 A.M.–4:30 P.M. daily, tel. 074/80-0052, US$2.50) that is uninteresting except for a series of outlandish, wall-sized cartoons that

trace Western history, somehow combining the medieval Crusades and the Gutenberg press with the winged disappearance of Naymlap. For those who want to linger and soak in the place—or use it as a base for visiting Chiclayo's surrounding ruins—there is an excellent hotel nearby, Los Horcones.

To get local transport to Túcume, you have to get to Lambayeque first by taking a *combi* at Vicente de la Vega and Leonardo Ortiz, in front of the Otursa bus terminal in Chiclayo. Frequent *combis* run to Túcume from in front of Lambayeque's market, 2.5 blocks from Museo Tumbas Reales. From the town of Túcume, it is another 3.5 kilometers to the ruins, either a 15-minute walk or a US$0.75 *motocar* ride.

Museo Sicán

This museum (Av. Batán Grande, block 9, tel. 074/28-6469, 9 A.M.–5 P.M. Tues.–Sun., US$5.50) is 18 kilometers outside of Chiclayo in Ferreñafe. Though unfairly overshadowed by the Museo Tumbas Reales, this modern museum has a fabulous collection of gold objects of the Sicán culture, which succeeded

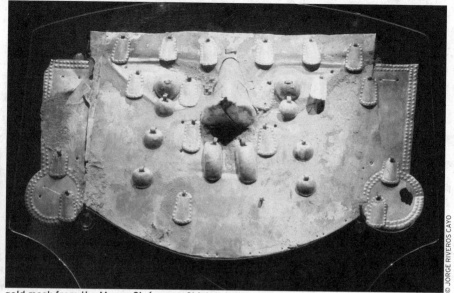

gold mask from the Museo Sicán near Chiclayo

© JORGE RIVEROS CAYO

the Moche in A.D. 850 and succumbed to the Chimú in 1375. The Sicán, also called the Lambayeque, were the first culture in Peru's north to discover bronze, which they made by mixing arsenic with copper—a technique learned from the Tiahuanaco and Huari cultures in southern Peru. The Sicán were at the hub of a great commercial network that moved emeralds and shells from Ecuador, gold nuggets from the Amazon, and mercury ore for their metallurgy from Peru's southern sierra.

As lifestyle dioramas in the museum show, the Sicán buried their kings in a unique way: deep within vertical shafts, sometimes accompanied by more than 20 sacrificed attendants and more than a ton of metal and other objects. Archaeologists believe that up to 90 percent of all gold plundered from tombs in Peru comes from Sicán sites in the Lambayeque Valley. Indeed, Sicán masks, with their characteristic *ojos alados* (winged eyes), are found in private collections all over the world. In 1936, renowned Peruvian archaeologist Julio Tello managed to track down a huge collection of gold artifacts looted from Huaca La Ventana in Batán Grande.

Fortunately, Tello was able to save many of these objects for Lima's Museo de Oro.

Yet little was known about the Sicán civilization until 1991, the year that Japanese archaeologist Izumi Shimada was able to carefully excavate two royal Sicán tombs at the first Sicán capital of Batán Grande. In the east tomb, the king was surrounded by sacrificed women and buried upside down, his decapitated head placed in front of him. The mass of objects in the tomb included two huge golden arms, sacred spondylus shells from Ecuador, a square copper-gold mask stained red with mercury ore, and several *cuentas* (massive heaps of shell beads). The west tomb is even larger, with similar gold masks and *cuentas* surrounding the king, along with niches containing women, sacrificed in pairs. DNA and dental tests have revealed that the two kings, and many of the women in both tombs, were close relatives. Spanish-speaking guides are available for US$6 outside of the museum. *Colectivos* to Ferreñafe can be taken from the Terminal de Epsel at the corner of Avenida Oriente and Nicolás de Pierola in Chiclayo.

THE MYTH OF NAYMLAP

The deepest mystery of the Sicán culture is the identity of a man with a beak-shaped nose and *ojos alados* ("winged" or almond-shaped eyes), who is depicted everywhere on Sicán masks, ceramics, and images. Like the Chimú's mythical Takaynamo, who landed at Huanchaco, the Sicán culture has a well-recorded legend of a mythical king who arrived by sea around A.D. 750 with a wife and full royal court. This king, named Naymlap, founded a temple and installed an idol known as Yampallec – the origin of the name Lambayeque. Upon his death, the relatives of Naymlap spread the rumor that the king grew wings and flew away, leaving his son to rule. The dynasty founded by Naymlap included 12 kings, according to historical evidence. According to legend, the last Naymlap king, Fempellec, committed a series of sins that caused a devastating flood and a period of crisis for the Sicán people. This is certainly possible: Nearly 1.5 meters of water coursed through Batán Grande during the El Niño floods of 1982 and a similar event might have caused the Sicán to abandon and burn the city in A.D. 1050. The Sicán then moved their capital to Túcume, where even larger pyramids were built.

Zaña

Connected to Sipán by dirt road, Zaña was an opulent town during the viceroyalty that might have been the capital of Peru if not for English pirate Edward Davis, who sacked the city in 1686. Many believed the subsequent decline of Zaña was due to the libertine ways of its inhabitants, earning it the moniker of *la ciudad malita* (the naughty city). That suspicion was confirmed in 1720 when an El Niño flood of biblical proportions destroyed what remained of the city and forced the citizens to move to Lambayeque. Today what is left is a fascinating ghost town of archways and columns. Most local tours include Zaña, which is 47 kilometers from Chiclayo. Buses also go there from Terminal de Epsel at the corner of Avenida Oriente and Nicolás de Pierola in Chiclayo.

Monsefú and Santa Rosa

Woven straw goods and embroidered cotton cloth are made by hand and sold in a daily market at Monsefú, eight kilometers from Chiclayo. Another five kilometers toward the coast is Santa Rosa, a fishing village of brightly painted boats where fishermen return from the sea late in the morning to mend their nets in the afternoon. Although not as beautiful as the beaches farther north of Piura, this is the best of several beaches around Chiclayo and a good place to relax and have a leisurely ceviche lunch. This circuit could be done with a tour agency, hired private car (US$30 per day), or via *combis* leaving Terminal de Epsel at the corner of Avenida Oriente and Nicolás de Pierola in Chiclayo.

Chaparrí

Peru's first private nature reserve, founded in 2001, **Area de Conservación Privada Chaparrí** (tel. 072/221-4092) is an extraordinary option for those interested in exploring a unique ecosystem. The 34,000-hectare reserve of dry forest is administered by the local campesino community and funded by Peruvian photographer Heinz Plenge with the support of several Peruvian corporations and large environmental organizations. The park's goal is to reintroduce and preserve endangered species such as the *pava aliblanca* (white-winged turkey), *el oso de anteojos* (the spectacled bear), the guanaco (a camelid), and the Andean condor, the world's largest flying bird.

ENTERTAINMENT AND EVENTS

The sleek and modern **Ozone Disco** and **Bali Lounge** (Av. Ortiz 490, tel. 074/23-5932, 7:30 P.M.–2 A.M. Thurs.–Sat.) are Chiclayo hot spots. The disco has three different atmospheres, which vary in price and VIP status. And the Bali Lounge is a narrow bar surrounded by sofa benches and is best for conversation, cocktails, and a *piqueo*.

Spanning nearly an entire block near the bus stations, **Premium** (Balta 94–98, tel. 074/20-4833, 7 P.M.–4 A.M. Mon.–Sat., 7 P.M.–close Sun., US$4–11) is part classic pub, part flashy karaoke stage, and part bright, modern café. On the outskirts of town is **Real Plaza** (Bolognese block 12, 11 A.M.–11 P.M. daily), a new shopping mall and local favorite that promises a mellow evening of creamy gelato from **D'Lara** (US$1–2) and a movie at **Cine Planet** (3 P.M.–midnight daily, US$1.25–2.50).

Monsefú, a town known for embroidered cotton and woven straw goods, is also famous for the procession of **El Señor Nazareno Cautivo in Monsefú.** According to legend, this effigy of Christ floated ashore one day and is chained inside the church because it has escaped before to perform miracles in other towns. The festival begins August 31 and involves fireworks, dances, and music, until the final and biggest party day September 14. Other important festivals include the **Purísima Concepción** in Túcume in February and the **Señor de la Justicia** on April 25 in Ferreñafe.

RECREATION
Tour Agencies and Guides
Guided tours are a good option for getting to Chiclayo's far-flung sites and having them explained by an informed guide. One of the most comprehensive operators in Peru's north is **InkaNatura Travel,** which has a Chiclayo office in the lobby of the Gran Hotel (Federico Villareal 115, tel. 074/20-9948, www.inkanatura.com). InkaNatura runs a range of local cultural tours that can be linked to longer excursions in Trujillo and Chachapoyas. InkaNatura also has an office in Lima (Manuel Bañon 461, San Isidro, tel. 01/440-2022, www.inkanatura.com) and an operator in the United States: **Tropical Nature** (www.tropicalnature.org).

Another recommended local agency is **Tumi Tours** (Colon 599, tel. 074/22-5371, www.tumitours.com, US$25 pp two person minimum), which has organized tours to the major

museums, Túcume, and even the southern beach towns like Santa Rosa.

For a private guide, call **Sysy Moreno** (tel. 074/20-6387, sysysilva@hotmail.com), a detail-oriented, Spanish-speaking guide. The friendly, English-speaking guide **José Jimenez** (tel. 074/22-1403, peko@viabcp.com) will go to any site you want for about US$9 pp, two-person minimum.

ACCOMMODATIONS
Chiclayo's lack of colonial history has resulted in a glut of modern, concrete hotels that are efficient but drab. A notable exception is Los Horcones, located outside of the city.

US$10-25
Palmira Hotel (Av. Belaunde 978, Urb. La Primavera, tel. 074/22-4115, www.palmira-hotelchiclayo.com.pe, US$14 s, US$21 d) is a low-budget hotel that is a five-minute taxi ride from Chiclayo's busy and noisy downtown. Rooms are clean and have wall-to-wall mirrors and nice bathrooms. There is WiFi, cable TV, 24-hour room service, laundry, parking, and a café-bar. Ask for the cheaper rooms (US$9) and the suites (US$29)! Definitely a good value.

US$25-50
The remodeled **Hotel Paraíso** (Pedro Ruiz 1064, tel. 074/22-8161, www.hotelesparaiso.com.pe, US$25–30 s, US$27–38 d) is on Parque Obrero, a few blocks away from Plaza de Armas. Rooms have modern baths, cable TV, and ceiling fans. Executive rooms include breakfast and WiFi. Amenities include a workout room, Internet stations, a 24-hour restaurant, parking, lockers, and a boutique store.

Eras Hotel (Vincent de la Vega 851, tel. 074/23-6333, www.erashotel.com, US$33 s, US$40 d with breakfast and airport transfer) has clean rooms painted in light colors. They have cable TV, minifridges, and phones. The hotel has laundry service, Internet, and a restaurant. There are executive rooms for US$45.

US$50-100

The design of **Hotel Casa de la Luna** (José Bernardo Alcedo 250, tel. 074/27-0156, www.hotelcasadelaluna.com.pe, US$53 s, US$68 d, breakfast and airport transfer included) is a modern and minimalist version of pre-Columbian Sicán decor. It has 26 colorful rooms, with WiFi and cable TV, arranged around a tiny garden. There is also a small restaurant and a rooftop pool. The suites are worth the money (US$100) and include hydro massage.

Gran Hotel Chiclayo (Federico Villarreal 115, tel. 074/23-4911, www.granhotelchiclayo.com.pe, US$84 s, US$98 d with breakfast) is a classic hotel in the city. Large rooms have baths, cable TV, WiFi, and telephones. Features include an excellent restaurant offering room service; a café serving cappuccinos, pizzas, pastas, and salads; a casino; and an elegant circular pool. Prices include a welcome cocktail, a morning newspaper, Internet, and airport transfer.

Inti Hotel (Av. Luis Gonzáles 622, tel. 074/23-5931, www.intihotel.com.pe, US$54 s, US$69 d with buffet breakfast) is the former Inca Hotel, a three-star lodging six blocks west of Chiclayo's Plaza de Armas. Rooms are carpeted with sound-proofed windows, cable TV, Wifi. There is a suite with Jacuzzi (US$80) and a good restaurant-bar-café called El Kero.

Garza Hotel & Casino (Av. Bolognesi 756, tel. 074/22-8172, www.garzahotel.com, US$80 s, US$101, US$171 suite) is situated halfway between the airport and the Plaza de Armas. There are 94 rooms, all with minifridges, air-conditioning, WiFi, cable TV and good bathrooms. Amenities include a swimming pool, restaurant, and casino.

Over US$100

Costa del Sol (Av. Balta 399, tel. 074/22-7272, www.costadelsolperu.com, US$101 s, US$118 d, US$180 suite, with buffet breakfast) is a couple of blocks from the Plaza de Armas. The intimate rooms are decorated in red and tan and have refrigerators, phones, cable TV, WiFi, and big bathrooms. Up on the roof, the whirlpool tub, dry sauna, and clear-paneled pool make for a relaxed afternoon. Facilities include a small gym, good bar, and restaurant.

Outside Chiclayo

If you enjoy natural beauty, we urge you to stay at the beautiful ◖ **Los Horcones de Túcume** (Lima tel. 01/241-1866, www.loshorconesdetucume.com, US$32 pp with breakfast) in **Túcume**. This rural lodge, built according to the building techniques of the ancient Moche culture, is in the backyard of the 26 massive pyramids of Túcume, which are 33 kilometers north from Chiclayo and 22 kilometers from the Museo Tumbas Reales. Twelve airy rooms, made of adobe and *algarrobo* beams, open up to covered terraces and views of the surrounding fields. Bamboo trellises drip with purple poinciana flowers that shade outdoor spaces from the hot sun. The hotel, designed by its Peruvian architect-owner, Rossana Correa, has a pleasant harmony that appeals to people from around the world who come here to be close to Túcume and enjoy starry nights. Los Horcones has horseback riding and a good, affordable restaurant. Not far away is the old town of Túcume Viejo, well known for its shamans and traditional medicine use. Don Víctor, a reputed shaman in the area, lives nearby the lodge and works with visitors upon request.

FOOD

There is a wide variety of restaurants in Chiclayo nowadays: from top-end gourmet place to bustling little eateries. Pleasant waiters shuffle between hungry diners, carrying plates of flavorful *seco de cabrito* (tender goat marinated in *chicha de jora* and vinegar) and *arroz con pato a la chiclayana* (rich duck meat cooked in dark beer, mint, and cilantro).

Cafés, Bakeries, and Ice Cream

Don Benny (Av. Balta 465, tel. 074/20-6452, 6 A.M.–midnight daily, US$1–5) scoops up *manjar* ice cream cones and towering *lúcuma* sundaes. But should you need something more filling, there is also a large selection of breads, cheeses, cold cuts, and empanadas.

THE NORTH COAST

Peruvian

Romana (Av. Balta 512, tel. 074/22-3598, 7 A.M.–1 A.M. daily, US$2–8) is the best mid-range restaurant in town. *Palta rellena* (stuffed avocado), spicy plates of *ají de gallina, arroz con pato, lomo saltado,* and flaky apple pie are served up on white-and-blue tables. The *chicha morada* here is excellent. Midday menus are US$2–3.

Around the corner is **Roma** (Manuel María Ízaga 710, tel. 074/20-4556, 7 A.M.–11 P.M. daily, US$2–3), which has a less expensive and varied menu but is a locals' favorite with 60 years in business. Apart from their restaurant menus, both Romana and Roma have a good selection of hot drinks, breakfasts, sandwiches, desserts, and milk shakes.

El Rancho (Av. Balta 1115, tel. 074/27-3687, 7:30 A.M.–12:30 A.M. daily, delivery available, US$2–5) serves *pollo a la brasa* (spit-roasted chicken) and has an extensive menu.

Meat lovers should head to **Restaurant La Parra** (Manuel María Ízaga 752, tel. 076/22-7471, 5 P.M.–1 A.M. daily, US$3–7, *menú* US$2), one of Chiclayo's best restaurants. The restaurant serves huge portions of grilled meats, roasted chicken, and *cebiche*. Have *brochetas de lomo* (beef skewers) washed down with a pitcher of sangria.

Fine Dining

The front door of **☾ Restaurant Fiesta Gourmet** (Salaverry 1820, tel. 074/20-1970, 9:30 A.M.–11 P.M. daily, US$8–20 without wine) is always closed. But if you ring the bell, a suited gentleman will lead you through the converted house, past white tablecloths and stately wine glasses, to a quiet patio. Peruvian couple Bertha and Alberto Solís opened this restaurant in 1983 and, with the help of their son and chef Héctor Solís, have since expanded with locations in Trujillo, Lima, and Tacnais—but here is where it all started. Try the classic *seco de cabrito* (roast goat), which falls off the bone, along with delicacies such as *tiradito de lenguado* (flounder carpaccio) or *cebiche de mero a la brasa* (grilled grouper cebiche).

Casa Blanca Restaurante (Av. Grau 823, Urb. Santa Victoria, tel. 074/22-9395, casablanca.rest@hotmail.com, 11:30 A.M.–5 P.M. Mon.–Sun., US$5–15) has a modern decor and great garden views. The food includes *cebiches,* shrimp rolls, grilled fish and seafood, stewed duck and goat. The *mousse de maracuyá* (passion fruit mousse) is amazing.

Páprika (Av. Balta 399, tel. 074/22-7272, 6 A.M.–midnight Mon.–Sun., US$15) is inside Costa de Sol Hotel. There is a classic peppersteak with baked potato filled with sour cream, ostrich *paupiette* with champagne sauce fettuccini, and the more Peruvian *loche* pumpkin mousse with tuna sauce. Highly recommended.

Restaurant El Huaralino (La Libertad 155, Urb. Santa Victoria, tel. 074/27-0330, noon–4 P.M. and 7–10:30 P.M. daily, US$10) used to be a four-fork restaurant. Now, while the food is still up to par, the restaurant's lacy tablecloths and chair covers give it a dated feel. The restaurant's famed dish is *pato en ají a lo huaralino* (slow-cooked duck in a three pepper sauce).

Pizza

At **Chez Maggy** (Av. Balta 413, tel. 074/20-9453, 6:30 P.M.–midnight daily, US$4–8), you'll have to first slip past the warm wood-fired oven before you can slide into your table and order up a large pizza and sangria. Delivery is also available. **Pizzeria Venecia** (Av. Balta 365, tel. 074/23-3384, pizzavenecia@yahoo.com, 6 P.M.–midnight daily, US$4–7) has a friendly staff and excellent variety of pizzas.

Chifa

Next door to the Chinese-English language school is the best *chifa* in town: **Chifa China** (Bolognesi 773, tel. 074/20-4201, 12:30–3 P.M. and 6:30–11:30 P.M. daily, US$3–6). The menu covers the basics—wonton soup to chicken stir fry—and on Saturday nights and Sunday midday, it offers an extensive *chifa, criollo,* and *parrilla* buffet. The menu is eclectic and good.

Markets

The **Mercado Modelo** (Av. Balta 961) is a huge and friendly produce market. Modern supermarkets are increasingly common. **El Centro** (Gonzáles 711, tel. 074/23-7710,

9 A.M.–11 P.M. daily), with its original location at Elías Aguirre and Gonzáles, has a number of markets throughout town, and **El Super** is just down the street (Gonzáles 881, tel. 074/23-7710, 9 A.M.–10:30 P.M. daily).

Outside Chiclayo

€ **El Cantaro** (Dos de Mayo 180, tel. 074/28-2196, 8 A.M.–5 P.M. daily, US$6) in **Lambayeque** is your best bet for great and delicious regional cuisine with regional favorites such as *pepián de pavo* (turkey breast garnished with a ground peanut and corn sauce), *pato arvejado* (stewed duck with peas), or the unusual but tasty *tortilla de raya* (ray omelet). At lunch the restaurant often fills up with national and international tour groups. A second option in Lambeyeque, just as good, is **El Rincón del Pato** (Av. Augusto B. Leguia 270, tel. 074/28-2751, 11 A.M.–5:30 P.M. daily, US$4–7). The restaurant serves duck in every imaginable way, as well as fish and other seafood.

INFORMATION AND SERVICES

The regional **tourism office** is at Sáenz Peña 838 (tel. 074/23-8112, 8 A.M.–1 P.M. and 2–4 P.M. Mon.–Fri.). The **tourist police** office (Saenz Peña 830, tel. 074/23-6700, ext. 311) is open 24 hours a day.

A recommended clinic for travelers is the **Clínica del Pacífico** (Ortiz 420, tel. 074/22-6378, 24 hours). Off the Parque Principal, at Balta and Aguirre, there are two reliable pharmacies: Boticas Arcangel and InkaFarma.

Banco Continental, Scotiabank, and **Banco de Crédito** all have offices and ATMs on Balta between Izaga and Aguirre. They are typically open weekdays 9 A.M.–6 P.M. and Saturday mornings. A handful of exchange houses are on the same block. If you're cashing travelers checks, rates vary, so shop around.

The Chiclayo **post office** (Elias Aguirre 140, tel. 074/23-7031, 8:30 A.M.–7 P.M. Mon.–Sat.) is about six blocks from the Parque Principal at the intersection with Grau. **Internet** is widely available around town and open from early in the morning to late in the evening.

With a morning drop-off, **Lavandería San Martín** (Alfonso Ugarte 606, tel. 074/27-3601, 9 A.M.–9 P.M. Mon.–Sat., US$2/kg) will wash and iron your clothes overnight. Make sure to check all your clothes for any bleach stains before paying.

In the Real Plaza shopping center, **Zeta Bookstore** (11 A.M.–10 P.M. daily) has a sizable selection of novels, travel books, and picture books, all in English.

GETTING THERE AND AROUND

Flights arrive at **Aeropuerto José Abelardo Quiñones Gonzáles** (Bolognesi s/n, tel. 074/23-3192, 7 A.M.–11 P.M. daily), which is two kilometers east of downtown. Taxis should not cost more than US$1.50.

Many buses to Chiclayo travel only at night. Bus terminals are spread out along Bolognesi, five blocks or more from the main park. For traveling to and from Lima, we recommend three companies: **Oltursa** (Balta 598, tel. 074/23-7789, www.oltursa.com.pe), whose terminal is outside of the center at Avenida Vicente de la Vega 101 (tel. 074/22-5611); **Cruz del Sur** (Bolognesi 888, tel. 074/22-5508, 6 A.M.–10 P.M. daily), which has one morning bus and four evening buses; and **Linea** (Bolognesi 638, tel. 074/23-3497, www.transporteslinea.com.pe, 4:30 A.M.–11 P.M. daily). Linea also has regular buses to Chimbote, Piura, Cajamarca, Huaraz, and Jaén. **Movil Tours** (Bolognesi 195, tel. 074/72-2555) has two buses a day to and from Chachapoyas (US$9, 10 hours) or Tarapoto (US$11, 13 hours).

Chiclayo is a nice city to walk around, but if you're in a hurry, in-town taxis cost US$0.75. And even longer trips, as far as Túcume, can be negotiated for surprisingly cheap. If you would like to hire a car for the day, **Juan Arrieta Huancas** (Peru 167, tel. 074/25-2128, movilidadarrieta@latinmail.com) is an honest and cautious taxi driver.

At **Rent a Car** (Bolognesi 1462, tel. 074/20-4948, www.rentacarperu.com) rates are about US$55 per day.

Piura

Piura was magically described in *Casa Verde,* Mario Vargas Llosa's masterful novel that divides this city into two main barrios: the Mangachería, a sprawling den north of the city center, known for beautiful women, gambling, and the novel's namesake brothel, and Gallinacera, south of present-day Sánchez Cerro Street, the respectable side of the city known for singers, *guitaristas,* and players of the *cajón.* The north–south boundary remains today. The farther south you walk toward Piura's laid-back and pleasant Plaza de Armas, the gentler the town becomes. Narrow colonial streets and classic, old homes conjure up what life was like in the 19th century when this town's population was only 5,000.

Historically, Piura had a tough time establishing its roots. Up until 1588, the year the cathedral was established, every attempt to build up a city was frustrated by the vagaries of pirate attacks and torrential flooding. The first Piura city, named San Miguel de Piura, was founded by Francisco Pizarro in 1532 before the conquest of the Inca. But that site, on the Río Chira near the present-day site of Sullana, was so hot and disease ridden that the settlers had to move. But the second city did not last either, so Piurans shifted to Paita. But in 1577—a decade before the English navy delivered a body blow to the Spanish empire by wiping out its armada—an English pirate by the name of Sir Thomas Cavendish pillaged and burned the city, including the convent of La Merced. That was the last straw for Piurans, who packed up their things and headed inland to the city's present-day location. Piura is safe, but being so far inland, it is the hottest of Peru's northern cities. Unfortunately, even its new location hasn't completely protected Piura. El Niño floods hit the city hard in 1983, 1992, and 1998.

Outside the city is the town of Catacaos, one of Peru's major arts and crafts markets, and the pleasant beach of Colán. Among Peruvians, Piura is famous as a center for *brujería,* or witchcraft. The heart and soul of this tradition is centered on the lakes region near the mountainous Huancabamba, seven hours from Piura.

SIGHTS

Inside the **cathedral** (7 A.M.–noon and 4–7 P.M. daily, free) is a gold-covered altar and paintings by **Ignacio Merino** (1817–1876), one of Peru's leading painters, who was born in Piura but spent most of his life in France. One of the cathedral's more venerated images is a replica of baby Jesus (usually buried under teddy bears). The original Jesus figure was made in Spain by a Carmelite nun who prayed nightly to see baby Jesus. One night, during her dreams, her wish was fulfilled. She awoke, molded the statue, and died shortly afterwards. The image, however, continued on, making its way to Czechoslovakia, when a Spanish princess married the prince of Prague. Over time,

Piura's Plaza de Armas

© KAZIA JANKOWSKI

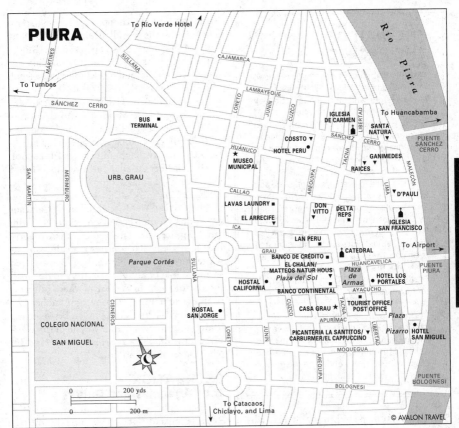

the image has become renowned for producing miracles.

The relaxing **Plaza de Armas** is ringed with tamarind trees and reigned over by a marble liberty statue given to the city in 1870 by then-president José Balta. A half block from the Plaza de Armas is the home of **Admiral Miguel Grau** (Tacna 662, erratic daytime hours, free), Peru's foremost naval hero. Grau's brilliant military maneuverings during Peru's disastrous War of the Pacific (1879–1883) continue to be a source of consolation for Peruvians.

Follow Tacna past the cathedral on your right before coming to Grau, the city's main commercial street. Farther north along Tacna—and the parallel streets of Arequipa, Libertad, and Lima—there are narrow streets with **colonial buildings** made of cane and adobe and fringed with fine woodworking.

Where Tacna hits Sánchez Cerro, you will find the 18th-century **Iglesia de Carmen,** which now houses the National Institute of Culture. In conjunction with the institute, there are museums of Puirian art, religious art, and industrial machines (9 A.M.–1 P.M. Mon.–Fri., US$0.75). The religious museum has a golden baroque altar and Cusco School–style paintings, but its pulpit was robbed of its carved angels and four evangelists. In the 1980s, crimes like this closed down the neighboring Benedictine convent.

Other lesser sites in Piura include **Iglesia**

THE WAR OF THE PACIFIC

With his British-built destroyer *Huascar*, Peruvian admiral Miguel Grau managed to elude a larger, and more modern, Chilean fleet during the War of the Pacific (1879-1883). He repeatedly broke the Chilean blockade, disrupted the enemy's communications, and even managed to bombard the Chilean city of Antofagasta. In the battle of Iquique, on March 21, 1879, Grau sunk the Chilean destroyer *Esmeralda* and killed Chile's top naval officer, Arturo Prat. In a show of magnanimity – not returned by Chileans when they later sacked and burned most of the country – Grau picked the surviving sailors out of the water and returned them to a Chilean beach. He even sent the objects he found alongside Prat's body, along with a consolatory letter he penned, to Prat's widow. Grau's end came in October of that same year when the entire Chilean fleet chased the *Huascar* down, exploding its control tower and killing Grau instantly. That battle marked a critical turning point in the war, allowing Chile to invade Peru and seize the port of Arica and nearby valuable nitrate fields.

San Francisco, near Lima and Ica, where Piurans announced their independence from Spain in 1821; and the **Museo Municipal** (Huánuco and Sullana), with a variety of ceramics and gold objects from the Vicus culture, which thrived nearly 2,000 years ago on Cerro Vicus, 27 kilometers east of Piura. Objects found on Vicus, and now on display at the museum, include a gold feline head with sharp teeth and extended tongue.

ENTERTAINMENT AND EVENTS

Piura is a peaceful town where nightlife is mellow and sometimes nothing more than a stroll through the plaza with an ice cream. But if you're hell-bent on finding some action, try block 5 of Ayacucho, where you'll find **Pepe's**

Pizzeria and **Alex Chopp,** popular nightspots. There is also the friendly **Raices Restaurant Pub** (443 Libertad, doors open at 8 P.M. Mon.–Sat.), which boasts US$1 drafts and Thursday night karaoke. Several blocks south, **Art Rock** (Apurímac 341, tel. 073/974-5870, 6:30 P.M. until close daily), owned by a young Peruvian-Swiss, has a dark wooden patio decorated with ceramic masks, live music, and a long list of cocktails. Art Rock also opens for breakfast. In the new shopping center **Plaza Sol,** catch a hit international movie at **Cine Planet** (Huancavelica and Arequipa, 3–11 P.M. daily, US$2–2.50).

The **Easter Week** celebration of Catacaos is famous around Peru—especially its Palm Sunday procession, a re-creation of Jesus's entry into Jerusalem that features a locally famous white burro. One of North Peru's most sacred shrines is that of **El Señor Cautivo** in the small mountain town of Ayabaca, where pilgrims from Ecuador and Peru converge October 12–13. During the first week of October there is a festival of *tondero,* a livelier version of the *marinera,* at the **Club Grau** (Av. Los Cocos Nr. 120, tel. 073/30-8020) in Piura.

RECREATION
Tour Agencies and Guides
The best sightseeing agency in town is **Delta Reps** (Libertad 640, tel. 073/32-1784, deltareps@terra.com.pe, 9 A.M.–1 P.M. and 4–8 P.M. Mon.–Sat.), which offers Catacaos and city tours and has free maps.

ACCOMMODATIONS
Lodging in Piura falls into two categories: basic or luxury. There's not a lot in between to recommend. So we suggest you either go big or tuck your money away for another time.

Under US$10
Hostal California (Junín 835, tel. 073/32-8789, US$5 pp) is a popular choice with backpackers because it's clean and safe.

US$10-25
Hostal Santa Lucía (Ayacucho 773, tel.

073/30-9464, US$12.50 s, US$18 d) is a good low-budget choice offering clean rooms with private bathrooms, cable TV, and WiFi.

Hotel San Miguel (Apurímac 1007, tel. 073/30-5122, US$16–23 s, US$27–35 d) is a great choice in this price range. Located in the southern end of town, on Plaza Las Tres Culturas, this is one of the few inexpensive hotels in Piura on a quiet street. Pricier rooms have air-conditioning. It also has telephones and cable TV in rooms, laundry service, a café, and a tour agency.

US$25-50
Four blocks off the Plaza de Armas is **Hotel Perú** (Arequipa 476, tel. 073/33-3421, US$18–43 s, US$32–46 d), which offers comfy and quiet rooms, cable TV, fans, or air-conditioning (hence the difference in the rates), and WiFi.

Hostal las Arenas (Av. Loreto 945, tel. 073/30-5554, www.hostallasarenas.com, US$25–32 s, US$36–43 d) is three blocks away from Óvalo Grau. The rooms are simple, clean, and comfy, with cable TV, fans or air-conditioning, and WiFi. The hotel also has a swimming pool with Jacuzzi, a café, private parking, and Internet.

US$50-100
Hotel Los Portales (Libertad 875, tel. 073/32-1161, www.hotelportalpiura.com, US$91 s, US$108 d with breakfast) is on the Plaza de Armas. Several of the hotel's rooms wrap around an elegant, sun-filled courtyard. The colonial house has large rooms with high ceilings, and modern remodeling projects have ensured that all rooms have air-conditioning, a fridge, cable TV, dial-out phones, WiFi, room service, and marble-made well-equipped bathrooms. The bar offers a complimentary welcome cocktail, and there's a restaurant by the pool.

Over US$100
Costa del Sol (Av. Loreto 649, tel. 073/30-2864, www.costadelsolperu.com, US$105 s, US$129 d, US$198 suite, with buffet breakfast) is two blocks away from Óvalo Grau, in a less noisy neighborhood than downtown Piura. Rooms are big and tastefully decorated, with minifridges, phones, cable TV, WiFi, and big bathrooms. Facilities include a swimming pool, a gym, and a casino. A good bar and restaurant are available too.

The four-star ◖ **Río Verde Hotel** (Ramón Mujica, Urb. San Eduardo el Chipe, tel. 073/32-8486, www.rioverde.com.pe, US$151 s, US$170 d with buffet breakfast and airport transfer included) might be confused for a Caribbean beach resort, with its coconut palms, shaded poolside dining areas, gardens, and gift shop. Rooms include phones, cable TV, WiFi, and air-conditioning. Golfing can be arranged through the hotel's connections to Piura's nearby country club. The hotel is a five-minute taxi ride from the center, but the peaceful neighborhood makes it the best luxury in town.

FOOD
Given the dry, hot climate of Piura, many budget restaurants close during siesta (1–4 P.M.), and others open only in the afternoons.

Cafés, Bakeries, and Ice Cream
For a quiet dessert stop, slip into the cozy, green-walled **D'Pauli** (Lima 541, 9 A.M.–2 P.M. and 4–10 P.M. Mon.–Sat., 4–10 P.M. Sun., US$4). This tiny café in a colonial building serves good coffee and tempting treats such as *crocante de lúcuma* and apple or pecan pie.

El Cappuccino (1014 Libertad, tel. 073/30-1111, 10 A.M.–2 P.M. and 5–11:30 P.M. Mon.–Sat., US$4–10), with its enclosed patio, has a simultaneously classic and modern feel. Start with a pisco sour, but follow it up with a Thai chicken salad or spinach ravioli.

The local favorite for burgers and shakes is **El Chalán** (Tacna 520, on Plaza de Armas, tel. 073/30-6483, 7 A.M.–11 P.M. daily). The restaurant's generous sundaes and megaburgers have garnered enough acclaim to merit several branch restaurants in the surrounding blocks.

Peruvian
Picantería La Santitos (Libertad 1001, tel. 073/30-9475, 10:30 A.M.–6 P.M. daily, US$3–7)

is extraordinary. Start with an *algarrobina* (a creamy cocktail made from pisco and *algarrobo* syrup or carob tree) and a powerful *cebiche de conchas negras* (black scallop cebiche).

Río Grande (Malecón Eguiguren 680, tel. 073/30-3886, 10 A.M.–11 P.M. daily, US$7–18) is a good option for fish and seafood. Recommended *cebiches* include *de lenguado* (flounder) and the popular *mixto* (fish, octopus, squid, and scallops).

Don Parce (Tacna 642, tel. 073/30-0842, 8 A.M.–10 P.M. daily) is one block away from the Plaza de Armas and offers breakfasts and lunch in a relaxed atmosphere with WiFi.

◖ **Casa de Tejas** (Av. Circunvalación Mz. G–2, Lote 4, Urb. Los Ficus, tel. 073/35-2654, noon–11 P.M. Sun.–Thurs., noon–midnight Fri.–Sat., US$7–15) is one of Piura's most reputable restaurants. The menu has an incredible variety of food—ceviches, deep-fried dishes, fish, soups, rices, regional dishes, and more—in abundant portions and good prices. They also set up a station in the food court of the Plaza del Sol.

Chifa

The best *chifa* is **Chifa Kin Tou** (Callao 828, tel. 073/30-5988, Mon.–Sat.) with cheap *combinados* (combined portions of fried rice, noodles, soup or chicken) for US$4.

Vegetarian

There are a couple of health food options near the intersection of Lima and Sánchez Cerro. Grab granola and all-natural yogurt takeout from **Santa Natura** (Lima 399, tel. 073/30-8103, 9:30 A.M.–2 P.M. and 4:30–9 P.M. daily), which also stocks vitamins and all-natural beauty products.

◖ **Ganimedes** (Lima 440, 7 A.M.–10 P.M. Mon.–Sat., 11 A.M.–10 P.M. Sun., US$3) offers a daily US$3 menu, a handful of soy-based starters, fresh juices, yogurt-and-fruit shakes (try *lúcuma*-strawberry), fruit salads, and vegetarian sandwiches. In the afternoons, baskets of fresh-baked, organic breads fill the café's countertops.

Markets

Shop for specialties such as chocolate, nuts,

wines, and liquors at **Cabo Blanco** (Sánchez 293). The big supermarkets in town are **Multiplaza** (Óvalo Grau, 10 A.M.–10 P.M. daily), **Don Vitto** (Arequipa 640, 8 A.M.–11 P.M. daily), and **Cossto** (Sánchez 525, 8:30 A.M.–10:30 P.M. daily).

INFORMATION AND SERVICES

The **tourist office** (Ayacucho on the Plaza de Armas, tel. 073/30-7775 ext. 124, 8 A.M.–1 P.M. and 5–8 P.M. Mon.–Sat.) is helpful with maps and city brochures. Driving maps may be available at **Touring y Automóvil Club de Peru** (Sánchez Cerro 1237). There is no tourism police station in Piura, but in an emergency call **Piura Police** (Sánchez Cerro block 12, tel. 073/30-7641, 24 hours).

Find health care at **Hospital Reátegui** (Grau 1150, tel. 073/33-1157, 24 hours) or **Hospital Cayetano Heredia** (Independencia and Castilla, tel. 073-34-2648, 24 hours).

There are many banks near the Plaza de Armas, including **Banco Continental,** corner of Ayacucho and Tacna, and **Banco de Crédito.** Both have 24-hour ATMs, and are open weekdays 9 A.M.–6 P.M. and Saturday mornings. *Cambistas* cluster around Grau and Arequipa.

The **post office** is at Libertad and Ayacucho (tel. 073/32-7031, 8 A.M.–4 P.M. Mon.–Sat.). There are several **Internet cafés** and call centers throughout town.

Take your dirty clothes to **Lavas** (tel. 073/58-4135, 9 A.M.–1 P.M. and 4–7:30 P.M. Mon.–Sat.) at the corner of Cusco and Callao.

Zeta Bookstore, on the first floor of the Plaza del Sol (Huancavelica and Arequipa, 11 A.M.–9:30 P.M.) has English editions of international best sellers, Peruvian novels, and guidebooks.

GETTING THERE AND AROUND

Most major carriers have daily flights into Piura's airport (tel. 073/32-7733), which is two kilometers out of town. A taxi costs

US$2–3. **LAN** Peru (Grau 540, tel. 073/30-5727, 9 A.M.–7 P.M. Mon.–Fri., 9 A.M.–4 P.M. Sat.) has an office near the Plaza de Armas.

Most bus companies are located on Sánchez Cerro, blocks 11–13. The best bus lines for getting back and forth to Lima are **Oltursa** (Bolognesi 801, tel. 073/33-5303) and **Cruz del Sur** (Libertad 1176, tel. 073/33-7094, www.cruzdelsur.com.pe). **Emtur Ximena** (Sánchez Cerro 1123) buses depart every 45 minutes for Paita. **El Dorado** (1119 Sánchez Cerro, 24 hours) has daily buses to Tumbes, with stops in Máncora for US$4.50. **Sertur** (Sánchez Cerro 1123, tel. 073/30-7317, four daily departures, US$8) drives upscale minivans directly to Máncora and Tumbes, but these vans are only worth their high price if they aren't crowded. Secure buses depart daily from the Linea station (Sánchez Cerro 1215, www.transporteslinea.com.pe) to Cajamarca, Lima, Jaén, Huaraz, Chimbote, Chiclayo, and Trujillo.

Unless you are going to a bus station or one of the outlying luxury hotels, Piura's colonial center is compact and best done on foot. Local *motocars,* however, cost US$0.75. Should you need a reliable taxi company, call 073/30-3999.

SIDE TRIPS
Catacaos

The village of Catacaos, a friendly, dusty little town 12 kilometers southwest of Piura, has the best arts and crafts market in northern Peru. The town is famous for a variety of **handicrafts** sold along four blocks of the old Calle Comercio, including panama hats, place mats, and other finely woven goods made of *toquilla* straw imported from Ecuador. Also watch for earrings and other jewelry wrought in gold and silver filigree, an art form that has flourished here since colonial times when gold was imported from the Amazon and Cajamarca. There are also painted ceramics in the shape of rotund campesinos, wood carvings and kitchen utensils made of *zapote* wood, colorful hammocks, wicker lampshades and baskets, and some leather goods.

As a bonus, this bustling town has some excellent restaurants, or *picanterías,* for northern cuisine: Here you can find *seco de chabelo, tamalitos verdes, majafo de yuca,* and other dishes that combine local foods like plantain and cassava with beef and pork. The market is biggest on the weekends, and stalls are set up around 10 A.M. and taken down as late as 7 P.M.

The town was first inhabited by the Tallán culture, which was eventually conquered by the Moche and later Chimú empires. The Tallán built some early pyramids at Narihualá, about five kilometers south of Catacaos. To reach Catacaos, hire a taxi for US$4 or take a US$0.30 *colectivo* at terminals on the third block of Sánchez Cerro or the intersection of Román Castilla and Tacna.

Colán

At 65 kilometers from Piura, this is the favorite local beach destination, a pleasant stretch of white sand with gentle waves perfect for swimming. The beach is fringed with stilted beach homes built during the 1950s, classic old wooden structures with long balconies facing west. There are few services (Internet, restaurants, etc.) outside of several resorts, which are all but dead in the off-season late March–early December. The beach is presided over by **Iglesia San Lucás de Colán,** the first church the Spanish built in Peru, near the small town of Esmeralda. This magnificent and unique stone church, recently restored to its original thatch-and-mud roof, has ancient wood columns and, with typical Spanish shrewdness, is built atop a Chimú *huaca*—inside you will find the coats of arms for the royal Spanish Hapsburg line.

Another 10 kilometers south along the coast is the picturesque fishing town of **Paita,** founded in the 16th century by the Spanish and the place where Manuela Saenz, Simón Bolívar's mistress, spent her final days ostracized from Lima society. This area's clear, starry skies at night and pastel clouds at sunset have given rise to the oft-repeated Peruvian saying: *"Nada como la luna de Paita y el sol de Colán"* ("There is nothing like the moon of Paita and the sun of Colán").

Good lodging options are: **Playa Colán Lodge** (Ayacucho 585, Piura tel. 073/32-6778, www.playacolanlodge.com.pe, US$45–65 bungalows for two; US$55–75 for four; US$65–85 for five) is on the southern tip of the beach town, with cozy bungalows right in front of the ocean. Amenities include a big swimming pool, hammocks, and tennis courts. The restaurant is probably the best deal in all of Colán.

Sol de Colán (Piura tel. 073/32-1784, www.elsoldecolanhotel.com, US$30–45 d, US$45–70 for six-person bungalow) includes brick bungalows and six rooms set back from the water along a stone walkway. Each tile-floored bungalow has a kitchen, separate sitting room, and covered terrace. Some of them have cable TV. The poolside restaurant serves excellent fish. Ocean water comes right up to the hotel, so no sandy beach here.

Transportes Dora, third block of Sánchez Cerro in Piura, has frequent US$0.75 taxis to Paita, where you can take another US$0.50 *combi* farther north to Colán.

Huancabamba

A truly adventurous journey that requires a minimum of four days and a lot of stamina leads to Huancabamba, a picturesque mountain town and the center of *brujería* (witchcraft and healing) for coastal Peru. The powers of the area's shamans and *curanderos* (healers) are legendary and are part of an ancient tradition in Peru that mixes natural medicine with spiritual beliefs. These healers play a major medical role in the country where people sometimes lack even rudimentary health services. People seek cures for a variety of problems such as infertility or psychological ailments. Shamans attribute those problems to *susto* (fear), whose symptoms resemble depression or post-traumatic stress syndrome because patients suffer from loss of appetite and insomnia. But probably the single largest group of seekers come for affairs of the heart: Jilted lovers place hexes on a competing suitor or bring a piece of clothing to lure back a departed lover. Others come to have a hex removed or to see into the future.

The physical center of all this work is **Huaringas,** a collection of 14 lakes over 3,900 meters (13,000 feet), where healing ceremonies *(mesas)* typically include dunkings in icy-cold lake water and the use of herbs and hallucinogenic substances such as the San Pedro cactus. The most famous of these lakes is Shimbe, which can be reached after a daylong mule ride. But there are also closer lakes.

A word of caution on Huaringas: If you come for healing, get a shaman suggestion ahead of time from a reliable travel agency or source. The tangibly magnetic energy of Huaringas can be used either for good or bad, and there are professionals who work *en el lado oscuro* (on the dark side) or as sham artists. It is also not a good idea to come if you are skeptical or merely curious. Shamans sense those attitudes immediately and often say it disrupts their work.

Huancabamba is also known as Resbalabamba, or "the city that walks," because the town's stratified, water-soaked foundation is causing the town to take an inexorable stroll downhill. In the area, there are excellent mountain-bike circuits and walks to Inca ruins. Guides are available in town.

The trip from Piura is a 215-kilometer, five- to seven-hour bus ride that passes through the scenic town of Chanchaque and over a bumpy mountain road before arriving at Huancabamba, around 1,950 meters (6,500 feet). In the town, there are several hostels and cheap restaurants. **ETIPSA** (first block of Av. Guardia Civil, near Primavera bridge) has buses leaving daily at 7 A.M. and 3:30 P.M. Once in Huancabamba, you still have a few hours of travel, first by *combi*, and finally on foot or mule.

The Northern Beaches

There is a secret about Peru that is jealously guarded by surfers around the world: The country has fabulous beaches, especially in the north, where the frigid Humboldt Current veers off into the Pacific and leaves behind a subtropical coastline bathed in balmy waters. Picture desert hills that ease into a winding, varied coastline of white sand and palm trees. There are many half-moon bays and beaches where odd volcanic formations break up the surf. These are safe for swimming: no currents and no sharks. But there are also many thundering point breaks and some of the best lefts in the world. Surfers flock here when waves are highest between January and March.

There is a lot of new development on these beaches, but the result, so far at least, is a pleasingly eclectic blend of mom-and-pop options—especially in the 25-kilometer stretch of spectacular coastline that includes the beaches of Órganos, Vichayito, Máncora,

and Punta Sal. You can find excellent value for food and lodging, ranging from US$5 surfer bungalows to exquisite bed-and-breakfasts for honeymooners. Unless you love huge parties, do not come here during the major Peruvian holidays (New Year's, Easter week, July 28 Independence Day weekend), when rates double and beaches overflow with Limeños. If you value empty beaches and deep discounts on lodging, try the off-season between April and mid-December (in October, whales pass here on their way to southern Chile). The sun still shines, even through the occasional overcast day, and the temperatures are plenty hot (80–90°F, or 27–32°C). For surfers, there is always a wave at Máncora, which ranges from gentle beginner waves to six-footers when the swell is up. And for other adventures, there are local tour operators who tackle any trip from fishing off the Máncora coast to rafting the Río Tumbes.

© RENÉE DEL GAUDIO AND ROSS WEHNER

fishing boats at high tide at Cabo Blanco

AN EL NIÑO WARNING

El Niño rains and floods along Peru's coast have been severe enough to spark the downfall of the Moche and Sicán empires, archaeologists say. But the El Niño cycles have become even more intense over the last half century, according to a recent United Nations report, because of global warming.

The warm, equatorial current is named after El Niño Jesús, or baby Jesus, because it arrives on the coast of Ecuador and Peru every year around Christmas. Some years, however, it extends far into the south Pacific and disrupts the Humboldt Current. The warm waters prevent the upwelling of deep, nutrient-rich waters, which causes anchovies to go elsewhere and ruins what is usually a world-class fishery. Winds across South America generally blow west to Asia, but during El Niño years they reverse and blow towards the continent, pushing up sea levels and sending huge systems of humid air toward Peru's desert coast.

One of the worst El Niño cycles of the century was 1983, when torrential rains began in Peru's north on January 4 and did not stop until the middle of July — the flooding alone destroyed 36 bridges and 1,685 kilometers of roads. Nine years later, in 1992, there was a similar El Niño. But both of these were dwarfed by the El Niño of 1998, which destroyed as much as 90 percent of the banana, rice, and cotton crops grown along Peru's northern coast. The floods killed several people in Piura when a bridge was swept away and created a huge, temporary lake in the middle of the Sechura desert between Chiclayo and Piura. The lake, known as Lago La Niña, forms after most El Niño years but had never been this big — 300 kilometers, stretching as far as the eye could see. While it lasted, anglers even began working on the lake and charter boats offered tourist excursions.

Travel becomes difficult and dangerous, or even impossible, during El Niño years. In early 1998, the 20-hour trip from Lima to the Ecuadorian border took over four days. Buses would drive until they reached a washed-out bridge, where passengers would then wade through water, slog through mud, or board a boat toward buses waiting on the other side. Many people became trapped for days on end, waiting for waters in both the south and north to subside before continuing their journey.

CABO BLANCO

Cabo Blanco is the point where the frigid Humboldt Current collides with the luke-warm El Niño Current from the equator. The result is a dazzling fishing ground and, for surfers, a welcome break from wet suits and chilly coastal waters. There are some beautiful, lonely beaches around Cabo Blanco, but the hillsides are unfortunately marred by pumping iron horses. It was once known internationally for the **Cabo Blanco Fishing Club,** which attracted a range of stars through the 1950s and 1960s, including Ernest Hemingway and Nelson Rockefeller. Now, it's a worldwide surfer destination. In June, and again October–January, Cabo Blanco has a monstrous, and dangerous, pipeline wave that reaches up to 3.5 meters (12 feet) and travels nearly 70 meters (240 feet) before closing out in a giant spray.

The Cabo Blanco wave forms over sand but crashes in front of large rocks, which have left many surfers badly scraped and broken.

The only place to stay is **Hotel El Merlín** (tel. 073/25-6188, US$36 d with ocean view, US$29 d without), a clean, white building on the oceanfront with stone floors and a cool, dark interior. The bathrooms have not been renovated since the hotel was built in the early 1980s, but the atmosphere is pleasant enough. The best restaurant in this one-street village is **Restaurant Cabo Blanco,** which is only open for lunch. While Cabo Blanco does have a few services (Internet and telephones), you'll find yourself going to the larger town of El Alto for ATMs, groceries, etc. To get to Cabo Blanco, take a *colectivo* or bus from Tumbes or Piura to El Alto. There you can catch a US$3 *mototaxi* for the 3-kilometer drive on dirt roads to Cabo

THE TRUTH BEHIND HEMINGWAY'S CABO BLANCO

The rocky, dusty coastline around Cabo Blanco was rarely visited until the 1940s, when the English-owned International Petroleum Corp., IPC, established itself in Talara and started setting up oil wells along the coast. That was the beginning of Peru's oil industry, which spread from here into the Amazon.

As far as Cabo Blanco is concerned, the story begins to get interesting around 1945 when foreign oil executives founded the Cabo Blanco Fishing Club, a simple building with a pool and a dozen rooms built atop a spectacular, remote, white-sand beach at Cabo Blanco. The club was not built to take advantage of the beach, however, but rather the world's richest marlin fishing ground, which lies off the coast here.

The size of the marlin caught here quickly attracted worldwide attention, beginning with a 465-kilogram (1,025-pound) black marlin caught by oil executive Alfred Glassell Jr. in 1952 – Glassell still holds the world record for a 709-kilogram (1,560-pound) marlin he caught here. Over the next two decades, American companies took over IPC, and sport fishers from around the world flocked to the humble digs of the Cabo Blanco Fishing Club. Among these were a range of luminaries and movie stars who arrived in Talara via direct flights from the United States. The list includes Ernest Hemingway, Bob Hope, Nelson Rockefeller, and Prince Philip of Edinburgh.

But the golden age of what became known as Marlin Boulevard ended in 1968 when the military government of Juan Velasco expropriated the oil wells. The hotel shut down soon after and is now a spectacularly sordid and peeling building that serves as home to a few hard-drinking local workers, along with a collection of chickens and dead seagulls. The beach in front of the club would still be spectacular were it not crisscrossed by pipes from nearby oil wells.

The stories from the fishing club are nonetheless still spectacular and fondly recounted by Pablo Córdoba, who owns Restaurant Cabo Blanco in town. John Wayne came here and met a woman from Paita whom he married and lived with until the end of his life. Many believe that Ernest Hemingway was inspired to write his *Old Man and the Sea* here, but the truth is he got the idea in Cuba. (He did, however, spend 45 days here in 1956, drinking whisky and pisco sours, as he and director John Sturges filmed the movie with the same name.)

The best-known story perhaps is that of the "million-dollar marlin." A wealthy New York City businessman arrived at the club in 1954 with his secretary. After a week of fishing, however, the fish weren't biting and, on the final day, the man had such a bad hangover that he decided to stay in bed. The secretary, however, ended up catching a 702-kilogram (1,545-pound) marlin, the woman's world record, which still stands. The catch was front-page news in the United States, which was unfortunate for the married man because his wife met him at the airport with divorce papers. The settlement, of course, was $1 million. "That was an expensive trip for that gentleman," chuckled one of the current residents of the fishing club.

Blanco. Most visitors, however, come for the day and make the 31-kilometer drive (about 30 minutes) from Máncora. To get to the Cabo Blanco Fishing Club, pass the dirt turnoff for the town of Cabo Blanco and look for a run-down, whitewashed building on the left.

LOS ÓRGANOS

Los Órganos, known locally as just Órganos, is an up-and-coming beach spot. Named after the wind, which makes an organ-like sound against the eroded rock walls of **Punta Veleros** (Sailboat Point), Órganos has a more remote feel than its neighboring towns. The town's accommodations are on the beach, slightly away from the center of town, and are good options for families and surfers wanting peace and quiet. A three- to eight-meter pipeline forms off Punta Veleros, slightly south of the main beach, November–March and a beginner's wave (July–February) a bit north.

Recreation

Órganos has one of the few **deep-water fishing** boats in the area, the *Cristina,* a 10-meter wooden fishing boat. The boat can handle up to four passengers and charges US$350 for six hours, US$450 for eight hours, and US$550 for 10–12 hours, though price is negotiable. All drinks and food are included, and *cebiche* is made on the spot. The best fishing is about 5–25 miles off the coast, where you can catch black and striped marlin, mahi mahi, and tuna. Reservations can be made by calling 073/85-7103 in Órganos, 01/368-1844 in Lima, or by email at prodexco@infonegocios. com. The best fishing is December–April and again in July and August.

Accommodations

Órganos's hippest lodging is **Las Pirámides Surf Point** (Km 1153, Panamericana Norte, tel. 073/969-968-166, www.vivamancora.com/ laspiramides). The owners are Peruvian national champion surfer César Aspíllaga and his wife, María Eugenia Vargas. Together with their daughter, Mohana, the couple has built a series of bamboo, pyramid-shaped bungalows high above the ocean on Punta Veleros. The bungalows feature an upstairs love nest for two with views of the stars. Downstairs there are beds for three more, along with kitchen and funky sitting area. There is no hot water, no TV, and precious little electricity, but these things aren't missed in the spacious, rustic surroundings. Each bungalow costs US$20 pp though prices vary. Rooms, with interesting adobe bathrooms and cloth curtains, are also available for US$15. Food is served only during high season, on a thatched patio in front of the ocean. Perhaps the best part is that César, who is a competitive surfer on the world circuit, offers lessons for US$10 per hour plus all-day board rentals for US$5. Of his famous point break, César says, "It's like Hawaii because it's a good reef base with a good tube that sucks air."

Hard-core surfers also congregate around **Bungalows Playa Blanca** (Playa Punta Velero, tel. 073/25-7487, www.bungalowsplayablanca. com, US$10 s, US$15 d without breakfast,

US$22 s, US$25 d with breakfast). Here, stone bungalows surround a central patio restaurant. The hammocks, wicker furniture, and beachfront view are charming, but the faded furniture and sometimes loud restaurant music make this a less formal option.

Next door is a good option, especially for families: **La Perla** (Playa Punta Velero, tel. 073/25-7389, www.elaperla.com.pe, US$30 pp with pension, half price for children 3–10, free for children under 3). The hotel, constructed by a Russian family, has Slavic touches—bright red, Baltic coast paint, paintings of windswept Russian landscapes, and a patio full of lacy hammocks. The rooms are immaculately clean, with sparkling tile floors, cable TV, and perfectly made beds in fair-sized rooms. The owners are very affable, but they speak more Spanish and German than they do English. If these are full, there are a few other lodging options, with more on the way, just north of Punta Veleros. Check the website www.vivamancora.com/english/dondedor.htm for other lodges and places to stay.

Food

Sitting at **Bambú** (Ribera del Mar, tel. 073/25-7038, 8 A.M.–7 P.M. daily, US$5–7), looking out over the ocean, *cebiche* is the logical lunch option. Customer favorites are striped marlin and *espada.* Vegetarians can get pasta dishes, and adventurous eaters should try the *timbal de mariscos,* a seafood casserole. Hidden behind the bus station, near the busy highway, **El Huequito** (Pasaje Olaya, 9 A.M.–6 P.M. Mon.–Sat., US$1–4) is pleasantly quiet and clean. The sea green walls, wooden tables, and thatched roof evoke the ocean, and the menu offers sandwiches, salads, and drinks, along with a US$3 midday *menú.* There is a friendly **Minimarket** in the first floor of Hospedaje Anyemarke.

Information and Services

Heading back toward the highway, you can find a variety of services. Órganos has a Banco de la Nación office and several Internet cafes with telephones.

Getting There and Around

The easiest way to arrive in Órganos is from Tumbes, either via airport taxi (US$25, 1.5 hours, 127 km) or via the frequent *colectivos* from Transportes Carrucho, at the intersection of Tumbes and Piura. The ride costs around US$3 and takes two hours with stops along the way. Once dropped off in town, take a US$0.75 *motocar* to the beaches on the south end of town.

VICHAYITO

South of Máncora, the exposed beaches of Vichayito can be accessed from either the Pan American Highway near Órganos or via a dirt road from Máncora. The sprawling bungalow complexes that populate Vichayito's beaches offer a quiet and remote beach vacation. Should you want access to the city life of Máncora, stay at one of Vichayito's northern resorts.

Accommodations and Food

Built in 1995, the **Vichayito Bungalows de Playa** (tel. 073/825-6942, www.vichayito.com, US$50–120) continues to feel well designed and modern, especially after the 2010 remodeling. The spectacular bungalows have five-meter-high thatched roofs, wood floors, and windows with soft muslin drapes. All bungalows face the ocean. Amenities include a large pool, bar, and restaurant. And for an extra US$25 a day, you can have breakfast, lunch, and dinner made for you. Located in south Vichayito, and best accessed from a point on the Panamericana near Órganos, **Villa Sirena** (tel. 01/9826-8072, www.villasirenaperu.com, US$25 pp with breakfast, US$65 pp with full pension) is simultaneously chic and ecoconscious. Bed frames are made of recycled wood, but covered with crisp white duvets; roofs don't quite meet the walls, allowing the passing of a constant ocean breeze; and showers are circled off by native tree trunks. Both the pool and the open-air restaurant are protected by grassy sand dunes, which makes for pleasant afternoons of reading or dining on delicious classic Peruvian dishes (US$10–15).

The Lima-born chef **Santiago Solari** (Vivero Palo Santo, cell 01/998-107-598, ssolaripe@gmail.com, US$10–20), who commanded the excellent Naylamp Restaurant in Barranco until a few years ago, now lives in Vichayito with his wife and two kids. He hosts travelers and friends in a pair of bungalows he has built. Most importantly, he cooks superb food in a family-like atmosphere. Born to a Welsh mother and Peruvian father, his command of English is perfect. Call him and ask, literally, what's cooking. It can be anything from a flounder *cebiche* to jumbo shrimp with curry sauce, among other delicious options.

There are several other bungalow hotels in the area, but they either lack access to the beach or are too steeply priced for their cramped and rustic accommodations. However, some of these hotels do offer camping, with bathrooms and showers. And for large families or groups, there are plenty of huge homes for rent in the area.

Getting There and Around

Without a private car, getting to Vichayito is a 15–30 minute *mototaxi* trip. From Órganos, the US$5 ride follows the Panamericana until Vichayito Sur, where it picks up the bumpy, El Niño–destroyed Ex-Panamerican. From Máncora, the price is the same, but the route is pure dirt road.

LAS POCITAS

At the bridge leading into Máncora, a rutted dirt road meets the new highway. This was the Panamericana, but El Niño rains washed away its paved surface, leaving it irregular and bumpy. That said, some very good accommodation lies down the road in Las Pocitas. Named after the sand pools that form around the beach rocks when the tide goes out, Las Pocitas is a string of compact hotel resorts. This area is only accessible via Máncora (10 minutes) or Vichayito (30 minutes).

Accommodations and Food

All the hotels in Las Pocitas have beachfront property and restaurants, but it's a good idea to check out both before you rent a room. Beaches tend to be rockier closer to Máncora, and restaurants vary from classic Peruvian to Italian. Most hotels have exceptionally good restaurants. Just as in the town of Máncora, room prices double during high season and may include different services.

US$10-25

On the border of Las Pocitas and Vichayito, **Peña Linda Bungalows** (tel. 073/25-8435, www.vivamancora.com/penalinda, US$25 pp) escapes the buzz of the hotel corridor. Its pleasant collection of bungalows is quiet, laid-back, and just off a sandy beach.

US$25-50

Los Corales (tel. 073/25-8309, www.loscoralesmancora.com, US$45 pp with breakfast) offers large, clean rooms with tile floors and thatched cane roofs. The rooms have private porches, but if you want to mingle, there is a playground, an open sitting area with coconut trees, and a mostly sandy beach. Services include Internet access and a TV room with DirecTV.

Near the southern tip of Las Pocitas is **Máncora Beach Bungalows** (tel. 073/25-8125, www.mancora-beach.com, US$30 s, US$68 d). American-owned, the hotel offers large, comfortable rooms in a pleasant two-story building. Each room has solar-heated water, a large modern and tiled bathroom, a telephone, TV with cable, and a private porch with a hammock and sweeping ocean views. There are two pools, a local fishing boat that has been converted into a bar, and an oceanside restaurant that specializes in fish and Mexican dishes. The staff here is a friendly and fun-loving family.

US$50-100

Honeymooners and couples looking for a romantic break should try **Sunset** (tel. 073/25-8111, www.hotelsunset.com.pe, US$58 s, US$66 d). The self-described "seafront boutique hotel" has only five rooms, which are intensely private and have spectacular second-story balconies. Inside, the large rooms are elegantly decorated with framed tapestries, elegant lighting, brush-painted walls, and vaulted bamboo ceilings. This hotel also has an excellent, if expensive, Italian restaurant, where an Italian chef rolls out authentic gnocchi and ravioli and then serves them with flavorful homemade sauces. Excursions include a US$120-per-person evening mud bath with wine, guided walks to nearby secluded beaches, horseback riding on the beach, and sportfishing on the *Cristina,* a yacht based in nearby Órganos.

Despite its ugly entryway, **Casa de Playa** (tel. 073/25-8005, www.hotelcasadeplaya.com, US$55 s, US$85 d with breakfast) has a nice pool, terrace, and restaurant and some excellent second-story rooms with private porches and hammocks. The other rooms here, however, are smaller, and the beach has quite a few rocks.

For a bit more space, and a sandy beach, try **Las Pocitas** (tel. 073/25-8432, www.laspocitasmancora.com, US$55 pp with breakfast). Constructed in 1987, this was the first hotel

beach at Hotel Las Arenas de Máncora

in Las Pocitas. It has a 1950s resort feel, but the rooms are large, with stucco walls and polished cement floors. There are table tennis and foosball tables. On the weekends, the quiet bougainvillea-filled gardens of **Playa Bonita** (tel. 073/25-8113, www.playabonitaperu.com, US$45 pp) fill with families. Rooms have tile floors, but some are stuffy from stale cigarette smoke.

The best of this group of hotels is the sophisticated **Hotel Las Arenas de Máncora** (tel. 073/25-8240, www.lasarenasdemancora.com, US$71 s or d with breakfast). Nineteen spacious bungalows spread across a grassy, palm-lined property. Each bungalow has a TV and DVD player, private patio, air-conditioning, and refrigerator. The hotel management provides a video library, evening bonfires, and helpful service. The open-air restaurant serves up fresh seafood and is a good place to watch semitropical birds flit between palm trees.

Getting There and Around

During the day, *mototaxis* constantly pass between Máncora and Las Poncitas. The ride is US$1.50. At night, however, the *mototaxis* concentrate in Máncora, making it easy to find transportation back to Las Pocitas but more difficult to find a *mototaxi* into town.

MÁNCORA

Over the last decade, Máncora has gone from a small fishing town with a few beach hotels to Peru's surfer mecca. During the summer late December–March, and during vacations such as Easter week and July 28, the town of Máncora overflows with surfers, hippies, Rastafarians, and young sun worshippers from both Lima and around the world. Máncora has become such a summer scene that it is hard to say which is its biggest attraction: the daytime waves or the parties at night. In response to the crowds, quite a few low-budget hostels, along with surf schools, restaurants, and bars (some of which are only open during the summer), have sprung up at the south end of town. During the off-season, Máncora is one of the few Peruvian beach towns that still receives a good flow of visitors and has

THE NORTH COAST

© AVALON TRAVEL

THE NORTH COAST

sunset at Máncora

a variety of restaurants to choose from. To get a better sense of the area, check out its fantastic website (www.vivamancora.com).

Entertainment and Events

Bars come and go in Máncora and many are closed during low season. But **Barracuda Bar** (Piura 269, 6 P.M.–close daily, except during off-season when the bar closes an unspecified night of the week, US$2–4) is a reliable bet. Before 10:30 P.M., the low light, twinkling candles, and sofas lend themselves to a drink and appetizer. But later, as the pisco, gin, and scotch make their mark, the crowds become more animated. **Iguana's Place** (Piura 245, 6 P.M.–close daily), a few doors south, turns up its pop music, and invites more of a party scene. **La Palma** (Piura just south of 318, 9 P.M.–close daily) is Máncora's only official discotheque, but during low season it's open only sporadically.

Shopping

Máncora's shopping options cater to hip surfer culture: bikinis, flip flops, and flowing dresses. In the back of the restaurant **Sirena** (Piura 316, 4 P.M.–close Mon.–Sat.), Argentine designer Mauvi has a small clothing boutique. Her designs are original and are sold both locally and in Lima. The beachfront **BirdHouse** (Pasaje Piura, 9 A.M.–9 P.M.), the project of a U.S. surfer turned businessman, is an upscale minimall. There, you will find casual-gourmet restaurants, Internet, clothing stores, and even a bar. But know that travelers frequently complain of slow and inattentive service. For athletic clothing and surf gear, check out **Soledad Surf Company** (BirdHouse, 9 A.M.–9 P.M. daily). And for handbags, bikinis, and even artistic paper lampshades, try **Maracuya** (10 A.M.–2 P.M. and 4:30–9 P.M. Mon.–Sun.).

Recreation

Run by an ecotourism specialist and her marine biologist husband, **Pacífico Adventures** (tel. 073/25-7686, www.pacificoadventures. com) offers a range of professional, nature-based trips. Spend the day snorkeling near Órganos or push off into deeper water and

© KAZIA JANKOWSKI

STINGRAY WARNING

Swimmers are not the only ones who love the warm, shallow waters of Peru's northern beaches. Stingrays occasionally bury themselves under a thin layer of sand and, when stepped on, will sting with a vengeance. Freshwater stingrays are also surprisingly common in many jungle areas in Peru, especially in areas with sandy or silty bottoms. Like their saltwater relatives, they have a poison-producing organ and a painful tail stinger. They can grow up to 70 centimeters (over two feet) in length and weigh up to 15 kilograms (33 pounds). Peru's stingray is not nearly as painful as those in Baja Mexico or other parts of Latin America, but still a few words of caution are in order.

When arriving at the beach, ask the locals if stingrays are around. They come and go for a variety of reasons and do not appear at all in certain places. If you suspect there are stingrays, shuffle and bang your feet against the sandy bottom as you enter in order to scare them away. Even surer bets are to wear running shoes — water shoes or sandals are not sufficient protection — or tap the sand in front of you with a stick. If you get stung, a bite extractor kit (Sawyer makes a good one) can remove much of the venom and reduce pain. The best treatment, however, is to place your foot in a pot of hot water for 10-20 minutes. Like boiling an egg, hot water coagulates the protein in the stingray poison, reducing the swelling and the fierce, radiating pain that can make even the most stoic jungle explorer burst into tears. If you are nowhere near hot water, you can always ask a friend to pee on your foot! (As unappealing as this particular pain reliever may sound, it really works.)

go fishing. Don't travel to Tumbes to arrange trips to the northern nature reserves. Either coordinate a trip with **Tumbes Tours** (tel. 072/968-3118, www.tumbestours.com), a long-term operator in the Tumbes area, or check out **Iguana's Trips** (Piura 245,, tel. 01/9853-5099, www.vivamancora.com/iguanastrips, 9 A.M.–close daily). Before starting Iguana's Trips, the energetic Ursula Behr was a Class V raft guide in the Cusco area. Now, she leads trips down the Río Tumbes (Class III) and hikes, horseback rides, or mountain-bike rides through the Parque Nacional Cerros de Amotape.

For private **surf** lessons, call Robby Munoz, **Surfing Lessons Máncora** (Grau 440, next to EPPO, tel. 073/957-6985, surfinglessons_1@ hotmail.com, US$18/hr including equipment). Born to Peruvian parents in North America, Munoz speaks perfect English. And he's lived in Máncora since 2001, so he knows the waves well. To rent surfboards or, if you are experienced, kiteboarding equipment, stop by **Hostal Las Olas** (Av. Pura s/n, tel. 073/25-8099, www.lasolasmancora.com).

Accommodations

During the summer months hotel prices are about 1.5 times more expensive than the rest of the year. And on the busiest weeks (New Year's, Carnaval, and July 28), tariffs double.

US$10-25

Our first budget recommendation is **Kimbas Bungalows** (Panamericana Km 1164, tel. 073/25-8373, www.vivamancora.com/kimbas, US$15 pp with hot water, US$12 pp without). The setting here is so peaceful that guests don't mind the five-minute walk to the beach. There are 12 bungalows along a stone walkway shaded with palm trees. Each bungalow has a private, open-air bathroom filled with tropical plants and a terrace with hammock. Decorations come from Indonesia and South Africa, where Lucho, the mellow Peruvian owner, has traveled widely. The cool blue pool and surrounding lounge chairs make for a quiet and secluded afternoon of sunbathing. There is also a nighttime guard.

Wedged between the most happening bars, you might think that the noisy location of **Casa

Blanca (Piura 229, tel. 073/25-8337, casablan-camancora@gmail.com, US$10 s, US$12 d) is the trade-off for its budget prices. But climb up to the spacious rooms on the third floor, catch the panoramic sunset view, and you might have another reason to stay. Not all rooms are the same, so check out a couple before deciding. Breakfast is included; mattresses are firm, but sheets are the only bedding. Some rooms have cable TV, and laundry service is available.

Hostal Las Olas (tel. 073/25-8099, www.lasolasmancora.com, US$15 pp) is a beach-side spot popular with surfers. Painted in cream and green, the hotel has 16 rooms each with a private balcony. Surfboard use is free for guests. Breakfast included.

US$25-50

Hotel Punta Ballenas (entrance just south of bridge, tel. 073/25-8136, www.puntaballenas.com, US$35 s, US$40 d), named after the pods of whales that head south along Peru's coastline August–October, is in a quiet location at the southern most end of town. Since the mid-1980s, Harry Schuler, whose Swiss father was a well-known hotelier and entrepreneur in Lima, has run the hotel. The 10 large rooms feel a bit dated, but the mattresses are firm, the nightstands hold literature about the area, and the walls display the paintings of regional artists. From the hotel bar, pisco sour in hand, you can watch the fiery sun set into the ocean.

Food

Inexpensive cafés intermixed with a few upscale restaurants line the Panamericana, which becomes Avenue Piura and then Grau as it passes through Máncora. On the north end of town, in the residential neighborhoods, are the local favorites: *cebicherías* and pizzerias. The most formal dining is in the elegant hotel restaurants in Las Poncitas and Vichayito.

CAFÉS, BAKERIES, AND ICE CREAM

In the evening, the quiet patio of **Café Restaurante La Bajadita** (Piura 424, tel. 073/25-8385, 10 A.M.–10 P.M. Tues.–Sun., US$6) is full of travelers and locals alike,

sipping sweetened passion fruit juice and snacking on sandwiches. Midday the restaurant offers several prix fixe menus, all of which include a delicious homemade dessert: apple crumble to *tres leches* cake to brownies. At the American-owned **C.S.I. Mancora** (Piura 261, tel. 073/407-8939, 7:30 A.M.–1 P.M. and 4–10 P.M. Wed.–Mon., US$3–4), you can be sure that your *café con leche* is just brewed, made from Peruvian beans, and finished off with real milk. The café also offers a small selection of international cheeses, homemade desserts, and wines. At nighttime, the TV and DVD collection can turn the café into an unofficial cinema.

Looking to escape the standard continental breakfast? **Head to Green Eggs and Ham** (BirdHouse Commercial Center, tel. 073/25-8004, 7 A.M.–1 P.M. daily, US$3) for waffles, French toast, pancakes, or omelets. Service can be slow.

CEVICHE

El Muelle (John Kennedy s/n, tel. 073/25-8319, 9 A.M.–9 P.M. daily, US$5) has two locations: a beachfront shack and a small neighborhood restaurant. Ceviches, *tiraditos,* and seafood rice are the house specialties, but the menu also lists meat options, like *lomo a lo pobre* (steak and eggs). If you head to **Cevicheria Meche** (John Kennedy s/n, tel. 073/25-8412, 7 A.M.–9 P.M. daily, US$3–7) for lunch, your tart lemon-cured octopus is likely to be accompanied by a noisy background of midday soap operas. Despite the lack of ambience, ceviche, grilled fish, *causas* (mashed potatoes filled with fish and vegetables), and seafood omelets are all reliably good.

PERUVIAN

Tucked behind a large, table-filled patio, the kitchen of **El Encuentro** (Pasaje Piura across from BirdHouse, tel. 073/25-8048, 7 A.M.–10 P.M. daily, US$1.50–7), or The Find, whips up everything from natural juices to tuna steaks to *lomo saltado.* **La Espada** (Piura 501, tel. 073/25-8338, 7:30 A.M.–11 P.M. daily, US$4–8) has two locations just blocks apart on Avenida Piura. Both restaurants have a big dining-hall feel, specialize in seafood, and offer a 2-for-US$13 lobster special.

FINE DINING
After studying Novoandino, new Andean, cuisine in Lima, chef Juan Seminario returned to Máncora and opened **Sirena** (Piura 316, tel. 01/9811-5737, 7:30–11 P.M. Mon.–Sat., US$8–10). Juan's cooking fuses local products with international ingredients and techniques. While the menu changes, you are likely to find Peruvian tamales spooned with an Asian curry sauce and a fresh tuna steak seasoned with the Argentine *chimichurri* sauce. Set in a small boutique clothing shop, the atmosphere is chic but intimate, and reservations during peak tourist season are recommended. Sirena has a less formal location in BirdHouse, where it serves up lunches (noon–5 P.M. daily) of tunaburgers and pasta dinners (7:30–11 P.M.) for about US$6.

In the evenings, light ocean breezes and classical music fill the Italian restaurant **Chan Chan** (Piura 384, tel. 073/25-8146, 6:30–11 P.M. Wed.–Mon., US$4–12). Best known for its pizzas, Chan Chan also offers mushroom pasta, rich lasagna, and classic antipasto plates.

PIZZA
On Sunday nights, when locals want authentic Italian and an escape from the rumbling main street, they sneak into **Pizzeria Ristorante Volentieri** (Talara 331, tel. 073/962-1575, www.vivamancora.com/volentieri, 7 P.M.–close daily, US$5). The pizza is wood fired, the pastas are made fresh, and the owner is 100 percent Italian. Pizza delivery in Máncora is free.

VEGETARIAN
Austrian Angela entered the restaurant business biking along the beach selling baked goods. Now, **Cafeteria de Angela** (Piura 396, tel. 073/25-8603, www.vivamancora.com/deangela, 8 A.M.–10 P.M. daily, US$2.50–3) has a quiet storefront and an almost entirely vegetarian menu. The whole-grain breads are dry and the passion fruit juice unsweetened, but the quinoa, garbanzo, and lentil dishes promise to be filling.

MARKETS
Small minimarkets, with sufficient dry goods selections and minimal produce options, are concentrated on Piura near the BCP ATM. Because of its competitive prices, **Roviluz** (Piura in the Oltursa bus stop, 8 A.M.–10:30 P.M. daily) gets the most local business. Closing hours are extended during high season.

Information and Services
Botica San José (Piura 520, tel. 073/25-8009, 24 hours) has the greatest variety of medications and will deliver, but its prices are more expensive than the other pharmacies. For lower prices, shop around.

Travelers can change money or use the 24-hour **Global Net ATM** near the **Banco de la Nación** (Piura 527, 8 A.M.–2:30 P.M. Mon.–Fri.). But Global Net charges a withdrawal fee, so the best ATM is the **BCP** across from Roviluz market. Because traffic through Máncora is high, its ATMs get a lot of use and over the weekends can run out of money. It is a good idea to withdraw enough money on Friday for the entire weekend.

Although Internet has yet to reach Las Pocitas or Vichayito, Máncora has quick connection and a plethora of Internet cafés.

Although most hotels offer laundry service, you may be able to get a better rate at one of the laundries on Piura at the southern end of town. The hostel **Costa Norte** (Piura 212) provides laundry service for both guests and nonguests.

Getting There
The closest airport to Máncora is Tumbes, reachable from Lima by a morning flight. Taxis can then be rented for US$29 for the 1.5-hour, 127-kilometer journey from Tumbes to Máncora. Once at the Tumbes airport, you can also take a US$2 taxi into Tumbes to **Transportes Carrucho,** at the intersection

of Tumbes and Piura, where US$2 buses leave every half hour for Máncora and nearby beaches.

High-quality overnight buses, with bathrooms and food service, travel from Máncora to Lima in 14 hours. **Oltursa** (inside Roviluz market, 8 A.M.–9 P.M. daily) runs one bus a day, with seats ranging US$26–43, and final drop-off is in the San Isidro neighborhood. **Cruz del Sur** (Grau 208, tel. 073/25-8232, www.cruzdelsur.com, 8 A.M.–7 P.M. daily) runs the same schedule, with slightly more expensive seats. **Cial** (Piura s/n) has three buses a day (US$15–30).

El Dorado (Grau 711, 8 A.M.–12:45 A.M. daily) has several daily departures to Tumbes (1.5 hours), Piura (2.5 hours), Chiclayo (6 hours, with connection), and Trujillo (8 hours, with connection).

PUNTA SAL

Like Cabo Blanco, Punta Sal was once a beach favored by the foreign execs at the International Petroleum Company. This long, half-moon beach of pure sand and lapping waves is better for bathing than surfing. The laid-back atmosphere and remote setting tend to attract more Peruvians than foreigners. There is only one restaurant outside of the resorts, and it is closed during low season. There are few services of any kind.

Accommodations and Food

Room prices can double or triple during high season. Be sure to confirm a price before accepting the room.

US$10-25

The pleasant backpackers' hostel **Hospedaje Hua Punta Sal** (tel. 073/960-8365, www.huapuntasal.com, US$10 pp) has only seven rooms, so make reservations ahead—especially if you want an ocean view. Though there is no pool or hot water, this hostel does offer two kayaks, body boards, a restaurant, and a bar that serves Cuba libres year-round. Across the street, and off the beach, is **El Bucanero** (tel. 073/38-1125, www.elbucaneropuntasal.

com, US$15 pp with breakfast). The cactus-lined walkways of this hotel will bring you to a 24-hour restaurant, a TV pavilion, and various rooms. All have good mattresses, but only some have patios with hammocks.

US$25-50

The best value in Punta Sal is ◖ **Hotel Caballito de Mar** (tel. 072/54-0058, www.hotelcaballito.com.pe, US$45–70 pp with breakfast). The rooms are fresh and spacious, with terraces, bamboo closets, and big bathrooms. Any activity you can name, the hotel can arrange: Jet Ski and dune buggy rentals, horseback riding, surfing lessons, massages, and mud bath tours. This hotel offers a US$25 Tumbes airport shuttle, Internet, and an incredible, two-night, US$170 (per couple) honeymoon special including a candlelit dinner on your private terrace.

US$50 AND UP

There are a few other resorts in this area, visited mainly by Peruvians. **Punta Sal Bungalows** (tel. 072/54-0044, www.puntasalbungalows.com, US$75 per bungalow) is a good family stop. The apartment-like bungalows accommodate up to six people and come with a fully equipped kitchen, DVDs, and even bicycles. **Club Hotel Punta Sal** (Km 1192 Panamericana, Lima tel. 01/442-5992, www.puntasal.com.pe, US$80 pp with all meals) is four kilometers farther north along the beach. While this resort offers a full array of activities including waterskiing, kayaking, tennis, and swimming, its most memorable feature is its replica pirate ship complete with an authentic masthead left by English pirates in Paita. The food is reputed to be excellent and plentiful, though the bungalows are a bit cramped.

Getting There

Punta Sal is several kilometers off a lonely stretch of Panamericana between Máncora and Tumbes. Frequent Máncora–Tumbes *combis* can drop you off at the main turnoff to Punta Sal, Km 1187, which is well marked with signs. Several *motocars* are usually waiting to bring you down to the beach. Do not do this at night. Club Hotel Punta Sal has a separate entrance farther north at Km 1192. From the Tumbes airport you can also take a US$2 taxi to Transportes Carrucho, at the intersection of Tumbes and Piura, where US$2 buses leave every half hour for the beaches. Have them drop you at Punta Sal and take a *motocar* to the beach.

TUMBES AND VICINITY

Tumbes is the main gateway for the cluster of excellent beaches near Máncora, one hour south (these beaches are, by comparison, 2.5 hours north of Piura). Tumbes is also the closest city to the astounding north–south ecological corridor of nature reserves, which includes ecosystems unique to Peru and a good variety of both mammals and birds. There are interesting mangrove swamps to visit, with the only crocodiles in Peru, from the small fishing town of Puerto Pizarro.

But that said, all of these reserves are serviced primarily by Máncora-based companies, and you shouldn't stay long (or at all) in Tumbes, a rough-and-tumble coastal town that has a history of hassling foreigners, since Pizarro arrived here for the third and final time in 1532. Up until then the resident Tumpis Indians, with their knowledge of the surrounding mangrove swamps, managed to turn back the Spanish army that later defeated the Inca. Pizarro left only a cross on the beach (at present-day Caleta La Cruz, Bay of the Cross) before moving his troops farther south, where he founded the city of San Miguel de Piura. Little has changed for foreigners in Tumbes, who continually complain of scamming money changers with rigged calculators, young pickpockets, and lousy service at local restaurants.

Sights

Tumbes's out-of-the-way location has kept visitors away from the country's only **mangrove swamps** and a fascinating chain of inland nature reserves—which all compose the **Reserva de Biósfera del Noroeste** (Northwestern Biosphere Reserve).

THE NORTH COAST

© ERASMO REBOLLEDO

touring mangrove swamps near Puerto Pizarro in Tumbes

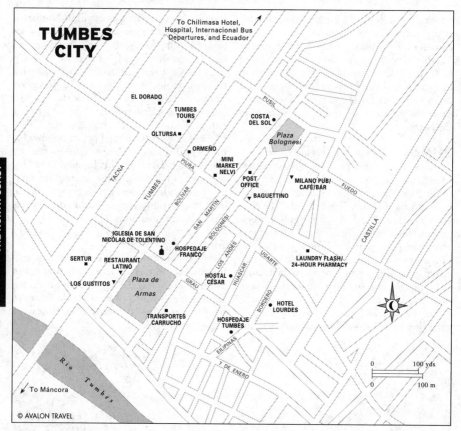

The mangrove swamps can be seen during an easy, three-hour boat tour from **Puerto Pizarro,** a fishing port 13 kilometers north of Tumbes. Things to see include Peru's only crocodiles, endangered because of hunting but now slowly reproducing in a nearby nursery. There are also interesting sediment islands in the area, including Isla de los Pájaros, a good birding ground, Isla Hueso de Ballena, and Isla de Amor, which has a good swimming beach. All the agencies in town arrange visits to this area and the more pristine mangroves at the **Santuario Nacional Manglares de Tumbes,** a nearly 3,000-hectare reserve that is an hour's drive from Tumbes and includes canoe, not motorboat, tours. Though there is no crocodile nursery at the Santuario, you are likely to see a greater variety of birds. Puerto Pizarro can be visited without an agency, by taking a US$0.75 *colectivo* along Tumbes Avenue to Puerto Pizarro. From there you can walk 15 kilometers northeast along the coast on a dirt road to reach the small town of El Bendito, where fishermen sometimes take visitors out in canoes. To see the sanctuary, however, you will need a guide, and most of the guided trips include stops at Puerto Pizarro and El Bendito.

Tumbes is also the starting point for three inland reserves, which form a north–south biological corridor critical for the conservation of the area's endangered species. Because roads into these parks are lousy, government

SHRIMP FARMING

© ERASMO REBOLLEDO

Puerto Pizarro, the main port in Tumbes, is a major center for commercial shrimp farming.

The biggest industry in Tumbes is shrimp farming, which has meant the destruction of 1,500 hectares of local mangroves around Puerto Pizarro to make room for the shrimp pools. The shrimp craze began in the 1980s in Ecuador, where shrimp farms spread across 200,000 hectares of mangrove swamps to become one of the country's most profitable, and important, exports. Peru's production began soon thereafter but peaked at about 5,000 hectares because of limited production areas. The industry has experienced severe ups and downs because of El Niño rains, which raise the water temperatures of the shrimp pens and cause die-offs and a disease called *la mancha blanca* ("white stain"). The virus spread from Asia to Central America in early 1999 and spread to Peru a few months later, where it devastated local production. From 1998 to 2001, Peru's shrimp exports dove from $50 billion to less than $4 billion. This has meant a huge economic loss for Tumbes, including the loss of 4,500 direct jobs. There is no known cure for the virus, which is named after white calcium deposits that form on the heads of infected shrimp. Scientists have developed strategies for living with the virus, however, which include using biosafe shrimp larvae and sticking to a strict production schedule. Many of Peru's shrimp farmers tend tiny, unregulated pools and have neither the access to, interest in, nor cash for this new technology.

(Information cited from *Tumbes: y los Bosques del Noroeste*, Walter Wust, 1998.)

permission is needed, and there is no visitor infrastructure whatsoever, the easiest way to visit is with Tumbes Tours or with a Máncora agency. Make sure to bring bug repellent, and don't plan to go during the rainy season January–mid-April, because often the roads are closed or impassable. If you have a four-wheel drive, camping equipment, and a sense of adventure, you could also explore these parks on your own. Permits and updated information can be arranged through SERNANP, which administers the area and is located at new offices on the Panamericana north of the soccer stadium.

Your best bet for seeing a range of wild animals, and the area we most recommend, is the eastern **El Caucho** sector of the **Parque Nacional Cerros de Amotape**. This 75,000-hectare section of the national park butts up against Ecuador and encompasses one of Peru's only chunks of Pacific tropical forest. Here you will find endangered species such as the Tumbes crocodile, a local howler monkey called the *mono coto*, and a local sea otter, *nutria del noroeste*. El Caucho is filled with orchids and gigantic trees such as the *ceibo*—a tree with bright-green bark and umbrella-shaped crown—and *pretino*, a related tree with gray bark that drops seed pods the size of soccer balls. Anteaters, cats (well, just their prints), and a wide variety of birds can be seen in the reserve.

The heart of the sector is the guard-point **El Caucho,** from which the area gets its name. It is 45 minutes from Tumbes on a rough dirt road, and the journey presently takes 2.5 hours in a four-wheel drive, plus one hour of walking. Most agencies that visit this park offer overnight trips with camping near El Caucho, which is a good idea so you can get up early in the morning to see wildlife. The hikes include swimming in rivers and spectacular scenery.

To the south and divided by the Río Tumbes lies the drier, hilly section of the national park. Sprawling across 91,300 hectares of equatorial dry forest, this sector has more sun exposure. Resident animals include pumas, gray and red deer, anteaters, and the Andean condor.

A royal Inca highway ran along the ridge of the Amotape hills, and a few interesting ruins can be visited along the way into the park. For those who prefer to ride through the park, burros can be rented for US$6 per day, including the guide.

Farther south is a hunting reserve called the **Coto de Caza El Angolo,** a 65,000-hectare chunk to the southwest of the Amotape Mountains.

Recreation

The best, and sometimes only, way to visit the natural attractions around Tumbes is with a travel agency. Prices are per person based on groups of two or more. The main tours are the mangrove swamps (US$25–35 pp), day trips to Amotape or the Zona Reservada (US$50–70 pp), and a day tour that includes nearby mud baths, beaches, and archaeological sites (US$25–35 pp). The well-informed **Tumbes Tours** is the only Tumbes-based agency (Tumbes 341, tel. 072/52-6086, www.tumbestours.com, 8 A.M.–1 P.M. and 2–7:30 P.M. Mon.–Sat.).

Accommodations

There are loads of cheap hotels in Tumbes to accommodate the border traffic to and from Ecuador. The very cheapest options, while clean, are unlikely to have hot water or toilet seats, and the mid- to higher-priced hotels have the amenities but not much charm.

Hospedaje Franco (San Martín 105, tel. 072/52-5295, US$6 s, US$9 d) and **Hospedaje Tumbes** (Grau 614, tel. 072/52-2203, US$5 s, US$8 d) are your best bets for a reasonably clean, quiet room with a private bath.

The plant-lined hallways of **Hotel Lourdes** (Bodero 118, tel. 072/52-2966, US$12 s, US$18 d) filter into a second-floor sitting room, which looks over the street. Rooms have firm mattresses and are quieter farther away from the street. If this place is full, try **Hostal César** (Huascar 311, tel. 072/52-2883, US$12 s, US$15 d), with hot water, cable TV, pleasant rooms, and big, clean bathrooms.

About four kilometers north on the

Panamericana, outside the city center, is **Chilimasa Hotel** (tel. 072/52-4555, chili@terra.com.pe, US$25 s, US$37 d with breakfast). This is a fairly upscale hotel, with a nice pool for sunbathing and large rooms with cable TV, fridge, and air-conditioning. The location makes it challenging to get back and forth from the center, but big families and tourist groups can make the hotel feel busier than the Plaza de Armas.

The more expensive option is **Hotel Costa del Sol** (San Martín 275, tel. 072/52-3991, www.costadelsolperu.com, US$61 s, US$72 d with breakfast), on the pleasant and quiet Plaza Bolognesi. The hotel itself is an oasis in this hot, dusty city, with a nice pool, excellent restaurant, and fully equipped rooms with air-conditioning.

Food

When in need of an empanada, swing by **Baguettino** (Piura 400, 6 A.M.–9:30 P.M. daily, US$1), where you can enjoy the flaky meat-and-raisin–stuffed pastry while peering onto the activity of Piura Street. **Milano Pub, Café, Bar** (Huáscar 514, 5:30 P.M.–3 A.M. daily) opens with a menu of snacks, light meals, and desserts, but by 10 P.M. when the discoteca is in swing, dancers forgo food for beer or cocktails. **Los Gustitos** (Bolívar 149, tel. 072/52-3198, 6:30 A.M.–11 P.M. daily, US$3.50) and **Restaurant Latino** (Bolívar 163, tel. 072/52-3198, 7 A.M.–10 P.M. daily US$3.50) are recommended for *conchas negras*—black clams with an aphrodisiac kick that local fishermen harvest from among the roots in the mangrove swamps.

For a finer dining experience and an international menu, try **El Manglar** (San Martín 275, tel. 072/52-3991, 7 A.M.–11:30 P.M. daily, US$4.50) inside the Hotel Costa del Sol. Among its 200 dishes, the restaurant offers ceviches, fajitas, pizzas, grilled meats, and an excellent fixed menu for US$5.50. The shelves of **Mini Market "Nelvi"** (Piura 501, 9 A.M.–11 P.M. Mon.–Sat., 9 A.M.–1 P.M. and 6–10 P.M. Sun.) are well stocked with everything from wine to cold cuts to cookies.

Information and Services

The **tourist information office** (Bolognesi 194, tel. 072/52-3699, tumbes@mitinci.gob.pe, 7 A.M.–noon and 1–4:30 P.M. Mon.–Fri.) on the second floor of the civic center—the ugly government complex on the Plaza de Armas—is friendly and helpful. The **Ecuadorian Consulate** is across the plaza next to Restaurant Gustitos (Bolívar, 123, 9 A.M.–1 P.M. and 4–6 P.M. Mon.–Fri.). Reach the local police at **San José District Police** (corner of Novoa and Zarumilia, tel. 072/52-2525, 24 hours).

Jamo Hospital (24 de Julio 565, tel. 072/52-4775, 24 hours) or **Zorritos Medical Post** (Grau s/n, tel. 072/54-4158, 8 A.M.–8 P.M. Mon.–Sat.) can be called in an emergency. There is a **24-hour pharmacy** on Bolognesi near the plaza, or try **Farma Rodrich** at Piura 1012, also open 24 hours.

Travelers can exchange money at **Banco de la Nación** on the corner of Grau and Bolívar at the Plaza de Armas. *Cambistas* hang out on the corner of Bolívar and Piura, but many ripoffs and rigged calculators have been reported. **ATMs** are located at Bolívar 123 or 209.

The **Tumbes Post Office** is at San Martín 208 (tel. 072/52-3868, 8 A.M.–8 P.M. Mon.–Sat.). All Internet and telephone needs can be met on the pedestrian malls leading off the Plaza de Armas. **Flash** (Piura 1006, 8:30 A.M.–1 P.M. and 3:30–8 P.M. Mon.–Sat.) offers same day service and washes and dries clothes by the kilogram.

Getting There and Around

For Máncora, taxis can be rented at the airport (US$29, 1.5 hours). Or take a US$2 taxi into Tumbes to **Transportes Carrucho** (Tumbes and Piura, 5 A.M.–8 P.M.), where US$2 buses leave every half hour for Máncora and nearby beaches.

For travel on to Ecuador, **Ormeño** (Piura 499, tel. 072/52-2288, 7:30 A.M.–1:30 P.M. and 3–7:30 P.M. daily, US$15–50) has Royal and business class buses to both Guayaquil and Quito. **Sertur** (Tumbes 253, tel. 072/52-5305) shuttles 12-seat modern vans to and from Piura. But these expensive *combis* are only worth their price if they aren't crammed full.

Cruz del Sur (Tumbes 319, tel. 072/52-6200, www.cruzdelsur.com.pe, 8 A.M.–6 P.M. daily, US$34–43) and **Oltursa** (Tumbes 307, tel. 072/52-6524, www.oltursa.com.pe, 8 A.M.–1 P.M. and 2–6 P.M. daily, US$26–43) have daily buses to Lima. The direct trip is about 16 hours.

To Máncora, Sullana, Piura, Chiclayo, and Trujillo, **El Dorado** (Av. Tacna 351, tel. 072/52-3480) provides less expensive service.

Tumbes is absolutely filled with *motocars,* which charge US$0.50 for an in-town trip, and *colectivos* that run north and south along the Panamericana.

CAJAMARCA AND THE NORTHERN HIGHLANDS

Though cartographers have penciled in the names of rivers and towns, Peru's northern highlands remain largely unexplored—and filled with extraordinary adventure. Here, the Andes are lower and the mighty Marañón Canyon, which slices through the mountain range, offers subtropical climates at its riverbed and high-altitude altiplano at its rim. East of the canyon, the land tumbles away into rugged rainforest, and here, covered in bromeliads, explorers continue to find lost cities and tombs built by the Chachapoya culture. An mind-bending bus journey cuts through this entire area en route to the jungle.

The first stop when traveling from the coast is Cajamarca, a hidden gem of Peru's Andes. Despite growing rapidly because of the gold mining industry, Cajamarca retains its historic charm with cobblestone streets, colonial houses, and baroque churches. Villagers roam the streets in colorful skirts or tall hats, learning to coexist with a growing tourism activity and expanding economy. This is the place where Francisco Pizarro's men captured Inca Atahualpa in 1532, marking the beginning of the end for the Inca empire.

Cajamarca is also the place where Inca and pre Hispanic trails intersect. Roads that are still in use by local peasants have been adapted in recent years into trekking routes. Exploring the remote villages and sprawling countryside through these ancient trails is one of the best ways to experience Peru's highland culture.

From Cajamarca, a winding highway heads east towards Celendín and then drops steeply into the Marañón Canyon, which at 3,000

© JORGE RIVEROS CAYO

NORTHERN HIGHLANDS

HIGHLIGHTS

◖ Complejo Belén: Admire this 17th-century religious complex built by the mysterious Bethlemites, who combined medieval medicine with Catholicism (page 508).

◖ Cuarto de Rescate: Contemplate this single stone room with perfect blocks and water channels. Historians believe Inca Atahualpa was imprisoned here for eight months – only to be executed in the end by Pizarro (page 509).

◖ Cumbemayo: Up in the magical *ichú* grasslands above Cajamarca, crystal-clear water flows along perfectly sculpted stone canals, which were built thousands of years ago and continue to befuddle archaeologists (page 511).

◖ Kunturwasi: Admire exquisitely crafted gold masks unearthed in the most important archaeological sanctuary of Peru's northern highlands (page 511).

◖ Qhapaq Ñan Treks: Walk along these Inca highways and experience the villages of Cajamarca's wide-open and majestic countryside (page 513).

◖ Gocta Falls: A two-hour trek from the small village of Cocachimba brings you to this impressive 771-meter waterfall, situated in the most extraordinary natural setting in the region (page 521).

◖ Museo Leymebamba: This excellent collection of archaeological artifacts and mummies, exhibited at this museum owned by the community of Leymebamba, is a wonderful introduction to the Chachapoya world (page 527).

◖ Kuélap: This stone citadel, perched on a limestone ridge thousands of feet above the Río Tingo, includes 420 round houses and a variety of bizarre buildings. It's no wonder that many visitors find it as impressive as Machu Picchu (page 528).

◖ Gran Vilaya: Visit the Belén Valley, trek an old Inca trail, and explore forgotten Chachapoya ruins. This once-populated montane cloud forest is full of stories yet to be revealed (page 530).

◖ Bird-Watching at Abra Patricia: Observe some of the most spectacular bird species in the pristine montane cloud forest of Abra Patricia, including the spatuletail hummingbird (page 533).

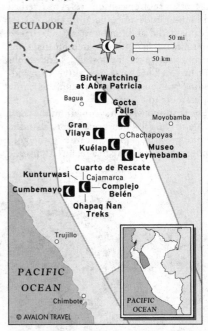

LOOK FOR ◖ TO FIND RECOMMENDED SIGHTS, ACTIVITIES, DINING, AND LODGING.

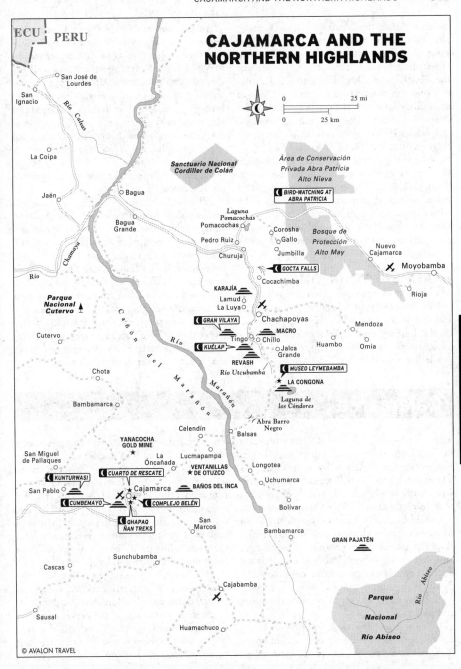

CAJAMARCA AND THE NORTHERN HIGHLANDS

ECU | PERU

San José de Lourdes
San Ignacio
Río Canchis
La Coipa
Jaén
Bagua
Bagua Grande
Chamaya
Río
Parque Nacional Cutervo
Cutervo
Chota
Bambamarca
San Miguel de Pallaques
San Pablo
KUNTURWASI
CUMBEMAYO
San Pablo
QHAPAQ ÑAN TREKS
Cascas
Sausal
Sunchubamba
Huamachuco

Sanctuario Nacional Cordiller de Colán
Área de Conservación Privada Abra Patricia Alto Nieva
BIRD-WATCHING AT ABRA PATRICIA
Laguna Pomacochas
Pomacochas
Pedro Ruiz
Churuja
Corosha
Gallo
Jumbilla
Bosque de Protección Alto May
Nuevo Cajamarca
Moyobamba
Rioja
GOCTA FALLS
Cocachimba
KARAJÍA
Lamud
La Luya
GRAN VILAYA
Chachapoyas
Mendoza
MACRO
Tingo
Chillo
Jalca Grande
Huambo
Omia
KUÉLAP
REVASH
Río Utcubamba
MUSEO LEYMEBAMBA
LA CONGONA
Laguna de los Cóndores
Cañón del Marañón
Río Marañón
Abra Barro Negro
Celendín
Balsas
YANACOCHA GOLD MINE
La Óncañada
Lucmapampa
Longotea
VENTANILLAS DE OTUZCO
Uchumarca
CUARTO DE RESCATE
Cajamarca
BAÑOS DEL INCA
COMPLEJO BELÉN
Bolívar
San Marcos
Bambamarca
GRAN PAJATÉN
Cajabamba
Parque Nacional Río Abiseo
Río Abiseo

0   25 mi
0   25 km

NORTHERN HIGHLANDS

© AVALON TRAVEL

meters is deeper than Arizona's Grand Canyon and even more spectacular. On the other shore of the river the mountains rise into an almost impenetrable cloud forest: the land of the Chachapoya. Once home to a federation of city-states that the Inca were never able to fully subdue, it's now the site of fascinating archaeological sites. The grandeur of Kuélap, a stone citadel floating in the air atop a limestone ridge, is often compared to Machu Picchu.

Most of the major ruins of the Chachapoya can be reached via horseback or day hikes. A multiday, mule-supported trek is clearly a better option, time permitting. Treks in the Chachapoya area offer an unforgettable combination of forest scenery and lost ruins and are a great alternative to the crowds on Cusco's Inca Trail.

PLANNING YOUR TIME

The best way to explore northern Peru is by land, not air. Start in Trujillo, head up to Cajamarca, and then brace yourself for the rough but spectacular journey into the Marañón Valley and Chachapoya area. The return journey, on the gentler highways, ends in Chiclayo.

Another option after visiting the Chachapoya region is to continue east on the good highway that crosses the **Área de Conservación Privada Abra Patricia-Alto Nieva** and the **Bosque de Protección Alto Mayo,** two protected montane cloud forests with stunning bird populations that attract hundreds of zealous bird-watchers each year. Tarapoto is reached after passing Moyobamba, and from there a two-hour drive on a paved highway will lead you to Yurimaguas, from where cargo boats leave daily for the three-day chug down the Río Marañón to Iquitos.

Whereas Cajamarca, Trujillo, and Chiclayo can be visited in as little as two days each, the ruins in the Chachapoya region require several days at a minimum, especially considering the effort it takes to get there. Depending on your interests and time availability, the whole route can take 7–14 days, though this could be shortened a bit by flying into either Cajamarca or Tarapoto. Flights into Chachapoyas, the city, are not available at this time. Cloudforest Expeditions, InkaNatura Travel, and Andes Tours offer a variety of well-organized treks that follow this northern circuit route.

Cajamarca

This is probably the most charming city of Peru's northern sierra, where despite the economic boom fueled by mines such as **Yanacocha,** you can still see campesinos with straw hats, bright shawls, and wool spindles scuffle along the city's cobblestone streets. This laid-back city revolves around its Plaza de Armas, flanked by two spectacular colonial churches and brimming with strolling couples and screaming schoolchildren. Cajamarca's quaint countryside produces a cornucopia of products, including *manjar blanco* (a type of gooey caramel), wheels of edam and gouda, and fresh yogurt.

One of the pivotal moments of Latin American history happened in Cajamarca's Plaza de Armas on November 16, 1532, when

a motley army of 160 Spanish conquistadores brought the entire Inca empire to its knees by capturing **Inca Atahualpa.** The Inca themselves had conquered the local **Caxamarca** culture six decades earlier and used this area as a staging ground for invading the Chachapoya and Chimú. In Cajamarca's square, the Inca built large stone warehouses where tribute from the surrounding territories was stored. All these buildings were destroyed by the Spaniards.

The Caxamarca people probably built the mysterious and perfectly sculpted aqueducts at **Cumbemayo,** 20 kilometers southwest of Cajamarca. They were at the center of a busy commerce between the coast and the jungle, as well as between southern Peru and Ecuador. The Inca later improved these routes

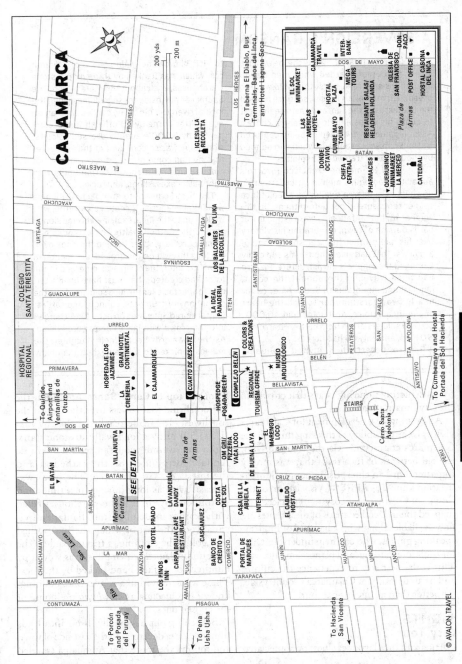

CAJAMARCA

NORTHERN HIGHLANDS

0 200 yds
0 200 m

© AVALON TRAVEL

Detail (inset):

CAJAMARCA TRAVEL
INTER-BANK
DON PACO
DOS DE MAYO
EL SOL MINIMARKET
HOSTAL PLAZA
MEGA TOURS
IGLESIA DE SAN FRANCISCO
POST OFFICE
HOSTAL CASONA DEL INCA
LAS AMERICAS HOTEL
CUMBE MAYO TOURS
RESTAURANT SALAS/ HELADERÍA HOLANDA
Plaza de Armas
BATÁN
DONDE OCTAVIO
CHIFA CENTRAL
PHARMACIES
QUERUBINO/ MINIMARKET LA MERCED
CATEDRAL

Main map labels:

To Taberna El Diablo, Bus Terminals, Baños del Inca, and Hotel Laguna Seca

LOS HEROES
PROGRESO
EL MAESTRO
IGLESIA LA RECOLETA

AMAZONAS
AYACUCHO
URTEAGA
COLEGIO SANTA TERESITA
GUADALUPE
URRELO
PRIMAVERA
HOSPITAL REGIONAL
To Quinde and Airport and Ventanillas de Otuzco
DOS DE MAYO
SAN MARTÍN
EL BATÁN
BATÁN
SABOGAL
Mercado Central
APURÍMAC
LA MAR
CHANCHAMAYO
BAMBAMARCA
CONTUMAZÁ

INCA
ESQUINAS
AMALIA PUGA
LOS BALCONES DE LA RECOLETA
D'LUKA
LA IDEAL PANADERÍA
ETEN
HOSPEDAJE LOS JAZMINES
GRAN HOTEL CONTINENTAL
LA CREMERÍA
EL CAJAMARQUÉS
CUARTO DE RESCATE
COLORS & CREATIONS
HOSPEDE POSADA BELÉN
COMPLEJO BELÉN
REGIONAL TOURISM OFFICE
MUSEO ARQUEOLÓGICO
VILLANUEVA
Plaza de Armas
SEE DETAIL
OM GRI/ PIZZERÍA VACA LOCA
DE BUENA LAYA
EL MARENGO LOCO
SAN MARTÍN
LAVANDERÍA DANDY
COSTA DEL SOL
CASA DE LA ABUELA
INTERNET
CRUZ DE PIEDRA
HOTEL PRADO
CARPA BRUJA CAFÉ RESTAURANT
CASCANUEZ
EL CABILDO HOSTAL
ATAHUALPA
LOS PINOS INN
BANCO DE CRÉDITO
PORTAL DE MARQUÉS
AMAZONAS
AMALIA PUGA
COMERCIO
TARAPACÁ
PISAGUA
To Porcón and Posada del Puruay
To Pena Usha Usha
To Hacienda San Vicente

SANTISTEBAN
SOLEDAD
AYACUCHO
DESAMPARADOS
HUÁNUCO
URRELO
BELÉN
BELLAVISTA
PABLO
PETATEROS
SAN
APURÍMAC
HUÁNUCO
UNIÓN
ANCÓN
JUNÍN
STA APOLONIA
ANTISUYO
STAIRS
Cerro Santa Apolonia
PERÚ
To Cumbemayo and Hostal Portada del Sol Hacienda

EL MAESTRO

A SOVEREIGN'S RANSOM

When Inca Atahualpa heard the news of a strange group of bearded white men traveling into his empire, his first thoughts were to breed their marvelous horses, sacrifice most of the Spaniards to the sun, and castrate the rest to guard his wives and do household chores. Atahualpa never dreamed of being captured by the Spanish – especially when surrounded by thousands of trained Inca soldiers.

It is hard to imagine Francisco Pizarro's audacity, leading his men in strict formation down into Cajamarca's valley as a sea of Inca soldier tents spread out before them. On November 16, 1532, Atahualpa was resting in hot baths outside of town, celebrating his victory over his half-brother Huáscar and the end of a civil war that had killed thousands and badly damaged the empire's infrastructure. Pizarro had been traveling throughout the coast, jungles, and mountains of South America for nearly two years in order to find the heart of the Inca empire. Atahualpa had 40,000-80,000 soldiers, fresh from battle. Pizarro had 170 men, and only 60 had horses.

Pizarro, nevertheless, invited Atahualpa

to visit him on the main square of Cajamarca, which was flanked by three empty stone warehouses, each about 180 meters long. The Spaniards hid inside these buildings when the Inca arrived the next day, carried atop an elegant litter borne by 80 officials and accompanied by 5,000 elegantly dressed soldiers. Atahualpa was so confident of the encounter that he had come dressed for ceremony, not combat, and his men were armed only with light battle axes, slings, and rocks.

The first Spaniard to approach Atahualpa was Dominican friar Vicente de Valverde, who walked up to the Inca, explained his mission to spread the Catholic faith, and extended him a small breviary. After looking the book over, the Inca threw it on the ground and spat on it. Moments later, the Spaniards emerged in full force and created what must have been a terrifying spectacle for the Inca soldiers. Amid the cacophony of trumpets, cannon, and rattles, fully armored Spaniards on horseback charged into the crowd with lances and swords flying. As the Spaniards began their slaughter, the Indians panicked to such an extent that many

---

by constructing stone highways that crossed in the city's main square.

An exciting new development for Cajamarca visitors is the possibility of trekking through the Cajamarca countryside via the **Qhapaq Ñan,** the old network of Inca trails that was mostly forgotten until an enterprising nonprofit organization known as **APREC** (Association for the Rescue of Cajamarca's Ecosystem) retraced and mapped them. Detailed maps of these routes are now available, along with a handful of English-speaking guides, who can help understand history, folklore, birding, and plants along the way. This is the best way to experience the culture and natural beauty of Cajamarca's countryside, far better than an agency car tour.

SIGHTS
City Tour
Cajamarca's Inca layout can best be appreciated

from the top of **Cerro Santa Apolonia,** the hilltop shrine that towers over the city to the southwest. It can be reached either by taxi (US$1.50) or by a long walk up stone stairs. From the summit, you can see the Plaza de Armas, surrounded by the cathedral and the Iglesia de San Francisco. The plaza was at least twice as long during Inca times and surrounded by three stone warehouses filled with textiles made of cotton, llama, and vicuña wool, the last of which the Inca valued over gold. The clothing, a tribute paid by the surrounding northern empires, was woven by hundreds of women hand-picked by the Inca. These women lived in a conventlike building, known in Quechua as *acllahuasi* or "house of the chosen ones."

Branching out diagonally, Jirón Inca leads from the Plaza de Armas to the east side of town and follows the route that Atahualpa traveled

suffocated in the rush. A wall nearly two meters thick was pushed over by the fleeing crowd.

But the Spaniards chased after them, lancing them down until well after dark, when an estimated 7,000 bodies lay littered across what is today downtown Cajamarca. Accounting for exaggeration and those killed by suffocation, English historian John Hemming estimates that each Spaniard killed an average of 15 Inca soldiers in those two gruesome hours. Pizarro, with a group of his soldiers, meanwhile had fought his way to Atahualpa's litter and dragged him inside one of the buildings. In just a few minutes, the New World's most powerful and best-organized empire had been brought to its knees.

Shortly thereafter, Atahualpa offered his infamous ransom: In exchange for his liberty, he would fill a large room – nearly 88 cubic meters – with gold and another two rooms with silver. Pizarro rapidly agreed and, as llama trains loaded with gold began to arrive in Cajamarca, he sent messengers back to the coast to call for reinforcements. Nine furnaces ran continuously between March 16 and July 9 to melt down nearly 10,000 kilograms of exquisite gold sculptures, chalices, and other priceless items into gold bars. The eventual result, according to Hemming, was 6,100 kilograms of 22-karat gold and 11,820 kilograms of good silver.

Though he met his ransom, Atahualpa was far from free. As rumors filtered to the Spaniards of a large army approaching, the Spaniards began to suspect that Atahualpa was plotting against them. Though Francisco Pizarro objected, and no trial was held, a majority of Spanish officers made the hasty decision to execute the Inca. As dusk fell on July 26, 1533, Atahualpa was led onto the main square. Atahualpa allowed himself to be baptized at the last minute, apparently to avoid being burnt at the stake – and probably to allow his body to be mummified and venerated after his death, according to Inca custom. Instead he was hung from a rope. When Emperor Charles V learned of the execution some months later, he condemned the conquistadores for their audacity in killing a sovereign prince.

NORTHERN HIGHLANDS

---

before his fateful meeting with Pizarro. The old Inca highway cuts through the fields to **Baños del Inca** and then switchbacks up between two hills on its way to Cusco. Following Jirón Inca west, the road leads up from the plaza, zigzags through the hills west of Cajamarca, and on to Quito. Ancient Inca highways also run northeast to the former Chachapoyas federation and southwest to the Chimú capital of Chan Chan.

The Caxamarca used Cerro Santa Apolonia as a shrine, the Inca carved their own altars at the lookout, and the Spanish worshipped at the hilltop Iglesia Santa Apolonia from 1571 until it was burnt down by invading Chileans during the War of the Pacific (1879–1883). The Santa Apolonia image can now be found in the museum at the Iglesia de San Francisco. Scanning the horizon to the left of Cerro Santa Apolonia, there is a triangular, earth-colored summit poking up above the other hills. This is **Cerro San José,** also known as Cerro Carachugo, a sacred mountain exactly north of the city that, throughout history, has stood as a reference point.

In the Plaza de Armas, the **cathedral** (open sporadically on weekdays and 9–11 A.M. and 6–8 P.M. Sun., free) contains the city's only original baroque altar, built in 1689. The construction of the cathedral dragged on for nearly a century (1682–1780) because the city's stonemasons constructed seven churches at once.

On the opposite side of the plaza, the **Iglesia de San Francisco** (8:30 A.M.–noon and 2:30–6 P.M. Mon.–Sat., 9–11 A.M. and 7–8 P.M. Sun., free) has a baroque facade that features two angels trumpeting the power of the pope, represented only by his papal hat or *mitra*. Inside are several interesting colonial religious images, including El Señor de la

Cajamarca has some of Peru's most important colonial architecture.

© JORGE RIVEROS CAYO

Caña, depicting Jesus in the hours before his crucifixion. The church's **religious museum** (8:30 A.M.–noon and 2:30–6 P.M. Mon.–Sat., 9–11 A.M. and 7–8 P.M. Sun., US$1.50, Fridays free) has a fabulous collection of 17th-century paintings that were made in serial fashion by Indian painters in the Franciscan workshop. Because Cajamarca is situated between Cusco and Quito, these paintings show traits of both schools of painting.

◖ Complejo Belén

This sprawling colonial religious monument (9 A.M.–1 P.M. and 3–5:45 P.M. Mon.–Sat., 9 A.M.–1 P.M. Sun., US$1.50) was built between 1627 and 1774. A Bethlemite religious order arrived from Nicaragua with the express purpose of building this hospital for the local Indians. The building, made of volcanic stone, is now a medical and archaeological museum.

Though the towers of the corresponding **Iglesia Belén** were never finished, the church has one of the most stunning baroque facades in all of Peru. Four angels float above swirling sculpted forms and guard a central window.

Through there, the souls of the dead entered before traveling down the nave onto the cupola, where more painted angels uphold the weight of heaven on their fingertips. The altar is neoclassical, from the late 19th century, and was replaced after the original was accidentally burnt down.

A quick tour of the adjacent men's hospital—which operated until 1965!—shows how miserable conditions were: patients stretched out in dark niches, watching mass so that the spirit of the devil would leave their bodies. They were bled nearly constantly, usually until they died, and families were not permitted to use either traditional medicines or burial rituals. After death, families paid dearly for masses that would elevate their loved one's status from hell to purgatory and finally to heaven.

Across the street is another hospital built for women. The startling facade is a sculpted woman with four breasts, carved by Indian artisans, that could be a fertility symbol. Inside is the **Museo Arqueológico** (9 A.M.–1 P.M. and 3–5:30 P.M. Mon.–Sat., 9 A.M.–12:30 P.M.

THE SACKINGS OF CAJAMARCA

Cajamarca has always been the center of gold production for Peru. Consequently, it's been the target of fierce sacking by different armies, first the Inca in 1470, then the Spaniards in 1532 – the year that a ransom of 18,660 kilograms of gold was paid by **Inca Atahualpa** and promptly exported to Spain.

After nearly three centuries of once again accumulating gold, silver, and precious gems, Spanish priests had to hand them over in 1822 as **Simón Bolívar** demanded donations for the independence cause. Because the Spanish controlled southern Peru, Bolívar relied on churches and wealthy families in Trujillo, Cajamarca, and Lambayeque to finance the entire campaign.

But the worst sacking of Cajamarca happened during the **War of the Pacific** (1879–1883), when marauding Chilean soldiers demanded that the city pay a certain amount of gold and silver. When the town paid only a portion, the enraged Chileans burned the Santa Apolonia church and the altars of every church in town except for the cathedral, which was saved by the frantic begging of a priest. Soldiers stripped the cathedral's altar of its gold plating, however, and removed all the precious ornaments from the town's religious images – see the dense clustering of precious religious charms on the Virgin de Dolores in Iglesia San Francisco to get an idea of the wealth this must have represented.

gold objects for his ransom. The existing white line, which the Inca supposedly drew to mark the level, is certainly not genuine. One of the chroniclers, Cristobal de Mena, wrote that the line was so tall that even the reach of the tallest of the Spaniards fell about a palm short, about two meters and four centimeters. John Hemming and other historians contend that this room is probably where Atahualpa was held captive instead.

Baños del Inca

Six kilometers east of downtown Cajamarca, Baños del Inca is suppose to be the original place where the Inca enjoyed his baths. The water is most pure at 5:30 or 6 A.M. because the nighttime coolness naturally reduces the water temperatures. Later in the day, to keep from scalding visitors, the thermal water must be mixed with cool, nonmineral water.

These thermal baths, known as the **Complejo Turístico Baños del Inca,** are managed by the local municipality and can receive more than a thousand visitors a day. Avoid the crowds during weekends and February Carnaval. There are different price schemes according to the quality of the tub, but the best is the restored *pabellón imperial* (royal pavilion), which offers 30-minute private baths for US$3 pp, 5 A.M.–8 P.M. daily. The complex also includes a public pool, sauna, and spa with a US$5 massage that lasts 20–30 minutes.

Getting to the Baños del Inca is an easy 10-minute trip, either via a US$2.50 taxi from Cajamarca downtown or via cheaper *colectivos* labeled Baños del Inca that leave from Calle Amazonas.

Ventanillas de Otuzco

About seven kilometers northeast of town, and often included in city tours, are the Ventanillas de Otuzco (highway to Otuzco, 9 A.M.–6 P.M. daily, US$1). What appear to be 200 small windows carved into volcanic rock are actually 600-year-old burial sites from the Cajamarca culture. The original tombs were sacked and destroyed by the Spanish but, nonetheless, the structure maintains a sense of history and magnitude.

Sun.), which displays an excellent collection of ceramics and implements of Andean life.

Cuarto de Rescate

The perfect Inca stonework at the Cuarto de Rescate (8:30 A.M.–12:45 P.M. and 3–5 P.M. Mon.–Fri., 8:30 A.M.–noon weekends, admission included with Complejo Belén) was probably part of the sun temple, destroyed long ago by the Spaniards. It is believed that Atahualpa ordered this room to be filled entirely with

NORTHERN HIGHLANDS

NORTHERN HIGHLANDS

THE PROBLEM WITH YANACOCHA

Given the fact that the conquistadores and Francisco Pizarro, Simón Bolívar, and even the Chileans have ransacked Cajamarca for its gold, it is perhaps not surprising that Cajamarca's citizens have mixed feelings about the Yanacocha gold mine. Yanacocha, which opened in the early 1990s, has brought unprecedented social mobility and progress to this sleepy mountain town. But there have been a lot of bumps along the way.

Yanacocha, 48 kilometers outside of Cajamarca, is visible from outer space. It sprawls across 9,720 hectares (24,000 acres) of countryside and is the world's second-largest gold mine. There are five giant open pits, four leach pads, and three gold recovery plants. In 2009 Yanacocha produced a staggering two million ounces of gold. The mine is majority-owned by Newmont Mining Corp. of Denver, Colorado, and has been a big factor behind Newmont's ascension into the largest gold producer in the world.

Yanacocha has created thousands of local jobs and pumped tens of millions of dollars into the local economy. It has launched widespread revegetation campaigns, enacted strict environmental controls, and invested in local communities. Local school attendance has soared with new teachers, some imported from as far away as Lima. Villagers, who have lacked potable water for centuries, now have their first-ever water well.

But for many citizens the influx of Yanacocha's money does not compensate for its negative effects on Cajamarca. Prostitutes stroll along the city's main square, catering to the mine workers who have come from all over Peru. Violent crime is on the rise, and hundreds of yellow Tico taxis and mining trucks clog the city's narrow streets.

The mine's bad relationship with locals started on June 2, 2000, when a truck driven by a Yanacocha contractor leaked mercury, a by-product of the extraction process, along a 30-mile stretch of road outside Cajamarca. Thinking it was silver, villagers rushed out to scoop up the shimmering substance with spoons, bowls, even their bare hands. They stored the mercury in their homes, and some even boiled it. Over the next few days, 800 people were treated for mercury poisoning and a few remain permanently disabled.

But for many Cajamarcans, the mine's worst transgression was Cerro Quilich. The pyramid-shaped mountain is revered by local campesinos as an *apu*, or a mountain with a sacred spirit. To make matters worse, Cerro Quilich also drains into the Río Grande, which supplies water to Cajamarca's 50,000 (and growing) residents.

Controversy erupted in 2004 shortly after Yanacocha moved to mine Cerro Quilich. City officials said the mine would destroy the grasslands that serve as a spongy reservoir for the area's drinking and irrigation water. And because the mine uses cyanide to dissolve gold from massive dirt piles, city officials worried about water pollution. But Yanacocha execs countered that Quilich accounts for only 4 percent of the city's water.

In the end, Yanacocha's legal arguments were overcome by the protesting power of thousands of villagers. Rock-slinging protestors blocked the road from Cajamarca to the mine, clashed with police, and forced the mine to temporarily shut down. The blockade was lifted only when Yanacocha promised never to exploit Cerro Quilich.

© RENEÉ DEL GAUDIO AND ROSS WEHNER

Yanacocha, near Cajamarca, is the second-largest gold mine in the world.

C Cumbemayo

Located 20 kilometers southwest of Cajamarca up a dirt switchback that climbs to 3,510 meters, Cumbemayo (8 A.M.–5 P.M. daily, US$2.50) is a shrine of pre-Hispanic **carved water canals** that still baffles archaeologists. The canals are at least 3,000 years old, but the exact date and the reason they were built is unknown.

The lines are so perfect and the rock ground so smooth that it is difficult to imagine these works of art being carved with obsidian hammers, the best technology of the time. If you arrive at this spot before 9 A.M., and before the tour groups ascend, the religious explanation of Cumbemayo becomes more plausible. The area is covered in *ichú* grass and punctuated by bizarre volcanic formations (known as a *bosque de piedras,* a rock forest), and power and energy of the place is palpable.

A marked trail from the parking lot descends to a rocky formation and a cave with several mysterious petroglyphs. Follow the narrow path through the cave (a headlamp really helps) until you emerge on the other side. Then head up a hill and down a drainage to a trail junction. Follow the canals to the right until you reach a carved chairlike stone, which served a ceremonial purpose. Return the same way and follow the canals downhill, where the road leads back to the parking lot.

The road to Cumbemayo passes through villages where campesinos produce everything they need to live except for salt, matches, and kerosene. They live in *casas de tapial* or rammed earth homes. Their diet is mostly vegetarian, consisting of oca and *olluco* (two types of tubers), corn, supergrains such as *kiwicha* and quinoa, and lentils—or *chocho,* the bean-like seeds of a purple-flowered, lupine plant, which are cooked, mixed with tomato and cilantro, and sold on Cajamarca street corners.

Monday, or market day, is the best day to visit Cumbemayo. It is the only day that you will find public transportation to the ruins. *Colectivos* that leave from behind Cerro Santa Apolonia at 5 or 6 A.M. will drop you within walking distance of Cumbemayo. A great walk

can be returning down to Cajamarca by a distinctly marked trail that goes back to pre Inca times and is still used today. Ask around for directions and beware of dogs (having a stick and small rocks helps to keep them away). To visit the site another day of the week, your options are a tour or a taxi.

Granja Porcón

This interesting, though somewhat controversial, tourism-oriented farming operation is 30 kilometers northeast of Cajamarca. Granja Porcón (www.granjaporcon.org.pe, tel. 076/36-5631 or 076/976-682-207) has around an 11,000-hectare plantation of coniferous forest, situated between 3,200 and 3,800 meters of altitude. In the middle of it, every aspect of local farm life, from milking cows to working with leather and wood, is on display. The farm is run like a well-oiled clock by an evangelical community under a co-op based system, with a rustic restaurant serving local trout and *cuy,* guinea pig. It also has a zoo with vicuñas, deer, lynxes, eagles, and even monkeys and jaguars.

Porcón seems to have thrived because of its disciplined community, the support of the Yanacocha gold mine, a venture with the European Union, and a lot of faith-backed hard labor. On the road in, billboards tout biblical quotes extolling hard work, prayer, and other values of Porcón's evangelical approach.

Porcón's lodgings include **Casa Histórica** (US$18 s, US$71 d), which has a living and dining room, shared bathrooms, and hot water 24 hours. The **Hostal Posada** (US$29 s, US$39 d) is a two-story building housing 10 rooms with private bathrooms, carpeted floors, a huge fireplace, and an upstairs loft. To get there, contact the farm's Cajamarca office (Chanchamayo 1355, tel. 076/36-5631) or a local travel agency. Porcón also offers private transportation for traveling groups, in a 14-passenger van (US$57) or a 32-passenger van (US$93) to and from the airport and/or the bus station.

C Kunturwasi

The oldest gold forged in the Americas—2,800 years old, a thousand older than Sipán—was

NORTHERN HIGHLANDS

discovered in 1989 by a group of Japanese archaeologists. The place, on top of the hill La Conga, near a small village named San Pablo, about 130 kilometers west of Cajamarca, has been known for decades as Kunturwasi ("the house of the condor"). Masks, crowns, chest plates, and other artifacts such as ceramics and stone jewelry with anthropomorphic designs—mainly jaguars, condors and snakes, unearthed from a series of tombs, confirmed that Kunturwasi was the most important ceremonial center in Peru's northern highlands during the Formative Period (2,500–50 B.C.).

Further explorations have uncovered ceremonial architecture that can be seen (US$1.60) in a day visit from Cajamarca. But the main attraction is obviously the gold. A modern museum (tel. 076/976-679-484, US$1.50) built with Japanese financial aid exhibits around 200 artifacts, including an exquisitely made crown with 14 human faces, showing a highly developed technique used by these ancient Peruvians.

Tour agencies offer a full-day trip to Kunturwasi (around US$110 with a two-person minimum) with transportation, lunch, a visit to both the museum and the ruins, and all tickets included. Independent travelers can also reach San Pablo on their own, in a two-hour trip, taking a *colectivo* (US$5) from Grifo Continental near downtown Cajamarca.

ENTERTAINMENT AND EVENTS

There is a long list of clubs and bars lined up on Amalia Puga Street, including **Bambolé, Orni,** and **Indio Bar.** The best disco is **Los Frailones** (Av. Perú 701, tel. 076/36-4113, 9 P.M.–5 A.M., US$5).

Peña Usha Usha (Amalia Pugia 142, tel. 076/997-4514, 9 P.M.–dawn Mon.–Sat., US$5) is the best place for local live music; musicians play *música criolla* until early hours of the morning. The bar is liveliest on the weekends. Ask at your hotel for updated information about other places in the city.

On the road from Cajamarca center to Los Baños del Inca is the restaurant-bar combination **Paskana** and **El Diablo Taberna** (Km 2, Av. Atahualpa, tel. 076/34-4217, 11 A.M.–3 P.M. and 7–11 P.M. daily at the restaurant, 8 P.M.–dawn Thurs.–Sat. at the *taberna*). For an upscale evening, enjoy a pisco sour and appetizer in the lounge of Paskana. And for more of a party, grab a beer and shoot darts in El Diablo.

For an international movie, head to El Quinde shopping mall. There, **Cinerama** (1–11 P.M. daily, US$1.50–2.50) shows the latest movies in four different theaters.

Every February or March, serene Cajamarca explodes in a riot of water balloons, paint, elaborate parades, and roaming bands of tipsy youths singing *coplas* or the rhymed couplets of colonial *carnavales*. If you do not want to get drenched in water, paint, or worse, avoid Cajamarca at this time. If you do go, have fun! This is Peru's wildest Carnaval—actually, it's called a *carnavalón* (a huge carnaval), and all hotels are booked.

Cajamarca also has a beautiful **Corpus Christi** celebration in May or June, which includes parades, live music, dancing, bullfights, and horse shows. The village of Porcón Bajo celebrates a colorful **Easter week** with traditional songs and the carrying of a heavy wooden cross on Palm Sunday.

SHOPPING

A few handicraft shops above the Plaza de Armas on Dos de Mayo sell leather goods, ceramics, alpaca wool sweaters, jewelry, and handwoven hats. **Colors & Creations** (Belén 628, tel. 076/34-3875, colors.creations@gmail. com, 9:30 A.M.–1:30 P.M. and 2:30–7 P.M. Mon.–Sat., 10 A.M.–6 P.M. Sun.), across from El Complejo Belén, has a small, but good quality, selection of unique and locally made jewelry, baskets, weavings, and ceramics.

A US$1 taxi ride from the Plaza de Armas to **El Quinde** shopping mall (10 A.M.–10 P.M.) will offer you anything you might need: medicine (Botica Fasa), ice cream (Helados Holanda), books in English (Zeta Bookstore), groceries (El Centro), and the cash to pay for it all (ATMs).

RECREATION
◖ Qhapaq Ñan Treks

Cajamarca's countryside is stunning and ranges from the high-altitude puna, where only the hardy *ichú* grass grows, to lush pastures where farmers lug around metal jugs of milk. Although there are only a few pockets left where people speak Quechua, the mountain folk maintain their centuries-old lifestyle. They live in *casas de tapial,* weave their clothes, grow native foods, and rely on herbs and natural medicines.

Interesting hiking routes around Cajamarca are offered by **APREC** (Civil Association for the Rescue of the Ecosystem of Cajamarca, at Hotel Laguna Seca, www.aprec.org, tel. 076/58-4300), a nonprofit dedicated to saving the natural beauty and cultural heritage of

Cajamarca's countryside. APREC's treks expose participants to the campesinos living along a considerable portion of the nearly 30,000-kilometer-long road network of the Qhapaq Ñan (Great Paths) that crossed Cajamarca. APREC's objective is that ecotourism will encourage local communities to preserve their traditional lifestyles and their ecosystem.

The routes often integrate existing natural wonders and archaeological sites that have been rediscovered in the tracing of the Inca highways. During the day, trekkers stop at villages to share a meal with locals, and then, at night, after a local dinner of trout and dried potato soup, they curl up on sheepskins inside rammed-earth houses. Trekkers should follow APREC's strict guidelines and be respectful of the land and people they encounter. As a

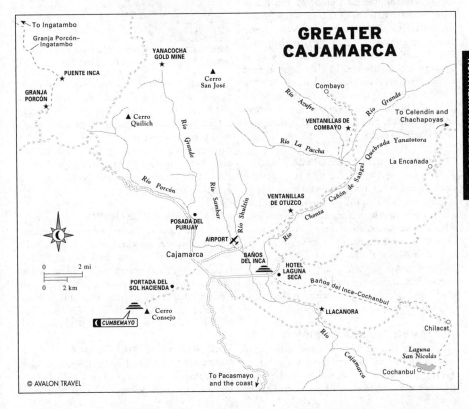

© AVALON TRAVEL

plus, APREC has published a series of excellent Qhapaq Ñan maps and guides that describe flora, fauna, birds, and folklore and include topographic maps (US$5). Ask about these booklets since some of them might be currently out of print.

At this time, there are four principal routes. Doing these treks can be quite expensive (around US$100 or even more per route) due to the low touristic demand. Ask around at recommended travel agencies or with APREC as costs vary.

COMBAYO-CAÑON SANGAL

The most popular of all treks takes you to the colonial town of Combayo, after a two-hour drive from Cajamarca. Along the best-preserved section of Inca highway, you will see the **Ventanillas de Combayo,** larger and more remote than the cliff tombs at Otuzco. The 10-kilometer day hike includes the Cañon Sangal, a canyon formed by two thin rock ridges punctured by the Río Chonta. The countryside in this area has not been altered by European cows imported in the 1940s. Thus, a staggering abundance of native plants, trees, and birds can be seen, starring the **grey-bellied comet,** an endemic and endangered hummingbird species.

COCHAMBUL-BAÑOS DEL INCA

This 20-kilometer, two-day hike begins in the small hacienda of Cochambul and leads first to Laguna San Nicolas, full of *pejerrey* (kingfish), which are caught with handmade nets and reed rafts. You set camp here and can visit the fort of Coyor, an unexcavated Inca-Caxamarca battle site. Next stop is the town of Chilacat, where everyone makes guitars. Along the way there is an excellent section of paved Inca highway with knee-high walls on each side. End at the Baños del Inca for a pleasant thermal bath.

INGATAMBO-GRANJA PORCÓN

This route begins in the tiny hamlet of Ingatambo 47 kilometers from Cajamarca, tracing a 20-kilometer section of the Inca highway that led from Cajamarca to Quito.

© RENÉE DEL GAUDIO AND ROSS WEHNER

Aqueducts at Cumbemayo were cut at right angles to slow the flow of water.

The walk, which usually takes around eight hours, can also be divided into an overnight trip. Start near the ruins of an Inca *tambo,* a resting place for *chasquis* (foot messengers who formed a sort of Pony Express) and visit campesino families along the way. Enter the pine forests of Granja Porcón and end at an Inca bridge. From here, it is possible to visit or stay overnight at Porcón.

CAJAMARCA-CUMBEMAYO

When you visit Cumbemayo, instead of returning in a bumpy car ride, why not walk back downhill? The three-hour walk follows a bit of Inca highway that connected the Chimú capital of Chan Chan with Cajamarca, passing through Andean villages and an Inca *huaca* or holy stone. The trail was used by horseback riders as late as 1940 to make the weeklong ride to the coast.

Tour Agencies and Guides

Cabalgata Los Alpes (cabalgatalosalpes@hotmail.com, tel. 076/34-1869 or 076/36-2287) organizes tailor-made horse rides to Cajamarca's countryside, including Tres Molinos, Otuzco, Porcón, Llacanora, and even Cumbemayo, among other destinations.

Recommended sightseeing agencies include **Cumbe Mayo Tours** (Amalia Puga 635, tel. 076/36-2938, 8 A.M.–9 P.M. daily) and **Destinos Viajes & Servicios** (Amalia Puga 633, tel. 076/34-1821, 8 A.M.–8 P.M. daily), owned by Carlos Mantilla, who also is an excellent guide. These companies are on Plaza de Armas and offer half- and full-day tours to sights around Cajamarca for about US$8–10.

For a personally guided tour **Manuel Portales** is the guide with the most detailed and sometimes controversial historical knowledge. He's a walking encyclopedia who can rattle off direct quotes from obscure Spanish chronicles and has an excellent command of English. Portales can be located at Cumbe Mayo Tours or contacted directly (manueljpc11@hotmail.com, tel. 076/996-8016). **Fany Ortiz Blanco** (tel. 076/976-861-949, fanyperu@yahoo.com) is also a friendly, well-informed, English-speaking guide.

ACCOMMODATIONS
Under US$10

The backpackers' choice is **Hostal Plaza** (Amalia Puga 669, tel. 076/36-2058, US$6 s, US$9 d shared bath, US$11 s, US$18 d private bath), a wooden colonial house on the plaza. Rooms are unadorned but big and clean. There is hot water in the mornings and evenings only.

US$10-25

Hostal Casona del Inca (2 de Mayo 458, tel. 076/36-7524, www.casonadelincaperu.com, US$22 s, US$32 d with breakfast) is conveniently situated across the Plaza de Armas and decorated with painted plates and masks in the interior. The yellow-and-red rooms have a simultaneously homey and artistic touch. The beds have been improved and the bathrooms are quite new.

The German-owned **Hospedaje Los Jazmines** (Amazonas 775, tel. 076/36-1812, hospedajelosjazmines@yahoo.com, US$17 s, US$29 d private bath) is a converted colonial house with six older and darker rooms around a front courtyard and seven lighter and bigger rooms in the back addition. It has WiFi and a quite good restaurant at the side. A percentage of the profits go to helping children with Down syndrome.

Los Balcones de la Recoleta (Amalia Puga 1050, tel. 076/36-3302, US$25 s, US$32 d) is a charming colonial house with vine-covered balconies and an overflowing garden. Nearby is the charming Iglesia La Recoleta, and the Plaza de Armas is only a five-minute walk. The rooms are quiet with cable TV, Internet, hot water, and telephones.

US$25-50

Las Americas Hotel (Amazonas 618, tel. 076/36-3951, www.lasamericashotel.com.pe, US$45 s, US$59 d) caters either to business travelers or tourists. As a result, there is a fast Internet connection, WiFi, a bar with a long drink menu, and a huge TV for watching soccer games. The rooms are comfortable, carpeted, and feature room service and cable TV.

Hostal Portada del Sol Hacienda (6 km outside Cajamarca on the road to Cumbemayo, tel. 076/36-3395, www.hostalportadadelsol.com, US$24 s, US$35 d) is a great value for a country hacienda. This converted weekend house has 15 large, simple rooms, many with views of the surrounding eucalyptus forest. Amenities include a restaurant and bar, walking trails, horseback riding, and—surprise—no TVs.

US$50-100

Hotel El Portal de Marqués (Comercio 644, tel. 076/36-8464, www.portaldelmarques. com, US$53 s, US$66 d with breakfast) has a quiet garden with a sitting area and fountain. The hotel's 33 rooms are small but their facilities have been renovated and the bedding is good.

Posada del Puruay (Carretera Porcón Km 4.5, tel. 076/36-7028, www.posadapuruay. com.pe, US$57 s, US$68 d) is a restored 1822 hacienda, with elegant rooms spread around a stone courtyard, in the middle of a country paradise about 15 minutes from Cajamarca. The grounds include horse stables, eucalyptus and pine forests, and a botanical garden with hundreds of labeled plants. During the day, you can take out Peruvian *paso* horses for circuits through the countryside, grab a mountain bike, or hike on one of the area's many trails. The restaurant is excellent with a wide variety of food including vegetables from the organic garden, homemade apple pie, and a *calientito cajamarquino*, a hot rum drink ideal for cold mountain nights. Rooms include cable TV, DVD player, access to a huge movie library, and minifridge.

The best spa and thermal baths in Peru are at the **Hotel Laguna Seca** (Manco Cápac 1098, Baños del Inca, tel. 076/58-4300, www.lagunaseca.com.pe, US$96 s, US$118 d with buffet breakfast). The hotel draws from the same hot springs that Atahualpa enjoyed in 1532, and which now run through the hotel grounds in steaming, open canals. Although the hotel's architectural style is true to the original 1930s hacienda—originally owned by the Puga family—all the rooms are outfitted with modern amenities: WiFi, cable TV, king-size beds, a minifridge, and terrycloth bathrobes. Guests truly feel in the lap of luxury when they slip into their personal and huge, thermal-water-filled tubs.

Facilities include a Turkish sauna, two heated pools, and a professional spa that offers clay treatments, herbal baths, and full-body massages. The restaurant is superb with a delicious variety of regional and international food. Next door is the hotel's *fundo,* a farm with an organic vegetable garden and an area for children to pet alpacas, parrots, rabbits, turkeys, cows, and a pair of monkeys. Rides on Peruvian *paso* horses are also offered, as are travel agency services and access to APREC, a nonprofit dedicated to the area's Inca trails.

Costa del Sol (Cruz de Piedra 707, tel. 076/36-2472, www.costadelsolperu.com, US$96 s, US$118 d with buffet breakfast) has prime real estate next to the cathedral on the Plaza de Armas. The sofa-filled lobby, where tea and coffee are always available, and the spacious rooms match its location. The service is mainly corporate but making changes to aim at a more tourist crowd. Rates include access to a small pool, one hour of free Internet, and rooms with cable TV, WiFi, and security boxes. The restaurant is quite good with excellent cappuccinos and is open 24 hours.

FOOD

Cajamarca is Peru's dairy center, and from its verdant countryside come fresh butter, yogurt, *manjar blanco* (a caramel spread made of milk, sugar, and egg whites) and rich, sharp-tasting cheeses. Other local specialties include *chicharrón con mote* (deep-fried chunks of pork with boiled corn) and *caldo verde* (a "green" broth prepared with herbs). Desserts include *quesillo con miel* (a nonfat, fresh cheese served with cane syrup) and *dulce de higos* (fig preserves).

Cafés, Bakeries, and Ice Cream

Cascanuez (Amalia Puga 554, tel. 076/36-6089, 8 A.M.–11 P.M. daily, US$1.50–6) is Cajamarca's traditional café; it serves the best sweet corn *humitas* in town, homemade pastries and pies, and decent coffee. It is the ideal spot for a sweet tooth after lunch or dinner.

The modern and softly lit **Panadería y Pastelería La Ideal** (Amalia Puga 966, tel. 076/34-5462, 7 A.M.–1 P.M. and 3–11 P.M. daily, US$3) is the ideal place to order fresh bread, good sandwiches, and freshly squeezed fruit juices. There is a second location near the Plaza de Armas.

The Dutch-Peruvian owned **Heladería Holanda** (Amalia Puga 657, Plaza de Armas, tel. 076/34-0113, 9 A.M.–10 P.M. daily, US$1.50–6) serves up the best homemade ice cream and gelato in the city, with flavors harvested from the surrounding countryside native fruits. Other locations exist in the Quinde Shopping Plaza and Baños del Inca.

Peruvian

At lunchtime locals take advantage of Wally's famous cooking and fill **Don Paco Restaurant** (Amalia Puga 726, tel. 076/36-2655, 8:30 A.M.–11 P.M. daily, US$2–5) for its multicourse *menú* (US$2). The small restaurant, packed tight with orange-cloth-covered tables, offers a small gourmet menu that ranges from a Cajamarquino breakfast to Andean vegetable ratatouille.

Probably one of the oldest restaurants in the city and hugely popular with old-time Cajamarquino diners, **Restaurant Salas** (Amalia Puga 637, tel. 076/36-2867, 7 A.M.–10 P.M. daily, US$3–10) still catches the spirit of the 1940s in its long-held spot on the Plaza de Armas. The food is good and abundant on your plate, whether it's *humitas, chicharrones,* guinea pig, trout, or a good pork chop with fries and salad. If you have a big appetite, this is your place.

Lanterns strung from ox yokes give **De Buena Laya** (Dos de Mayo 343, tel. 076/34-2789, 7 A.M.–10 P.M. daily, US$2.50–6) a rustic feel, but its thoughtful menu and soft yellow walls show that the restaurant knows style both in food and atmosphere. Try the beef in a Porcón mushroom sauce.

The family-operated **D'Iuka** (Amalia Puga 1050, 6 P.M.–close daily, US$3–5) serves up the best late-night *anticuchos,* skewers made of grilled chicken or beefheart.

International
They serve fresh fish and seafood during the day. At night it is all about meat on the grill. In either case **Restaurant El Pez Loco,** the "crazy fish" (San Martín 333, tel. 076/976-825 633, noon–11 P.M. daily, US$5–10), is surprisingly a good spot for either choice of food, with friendly personnel and generous portions on the plate.

The name **OM Gri** (San Martín 360, tel. 076/36-7619, 1–11 P.M. Mon.–Sat., 6–11 P.M. Sun., US$4–7) is derived from the pronunciation of the French "homme gris." Tito Carrera, the conversationalist owner, claims to spend eight hours prepping his pasta bolognese sauce. Whatever he does, it works. Both his meat and veggie lasagna are recognized as Cajamarca's best.

Fine Dining
Around the corner from the cathedral is **Querubino** (Amalia Puga 589, tel. 076/34-0900, 11:30 A.M.–11 P.M. daily, US$5–10), a classy restaurant with exquisite, superb food. The bar boasts at least 20 different pisco cocktails.

The sophisticated menu of **El Batán** (Batán 369, tel. 076/36-6025, 10 A.M.–midnight daily, US$4–10) includes Greek salad, tenderloin steak in cognac sauce, flambé-cooked meat with mashed potatoes, and martinis. Upstairs there is a gallery of local artists' works.

Pizza
The German-Peruvian owned **Pizzeria Vaca Loca** (San Martín 330, tel. 076/36-8230, 6–11 P.M. daily, US$2.50–10) is a charming restaurant that celebrates the cows and cheeses of Cajamarca. It's decorated with cowhide seat covers, paintings, and ceramics. The comfy cow booths are perfect for sipping sangria and eating pizza, spaghetti, or calzone.

Chifa
Don't expect the utmost Peruvian-Chinese food experience at **Chifa Central** (Batán 149, tel. 076/34-4182, noon–4 P.M. and 6–11 P.M. daily, US$4–6), but the food is good and with pretty big portions. Slide into a booth or settle in front of the huge screen TV and order up a menu of wonton soup and *arroz chaufa.*

Markets
Cajamarca's bustling **Mercado Central** stretches along Amazonas and sells everything from dairy products to guinea pig. For cheeses and other dairy products, stop by **Villanueva** (Dos de Mayo 615, tel. 076/34-0389, 8 A.M.–2:30 P.M. and 3–9 P.M. daily) or roam along the seventh and eighth blocks of Amazonas. The best place, though, to buy cheese (gouda, raclette, edam, you name it) is undoubtedly **Lacteos Los Alpes** (Junín 965, tel. 076/36-2287, 8 A.M.–10 P.M. Mon.–Sat., 9 A.M.–9 P.M. Sun.). The store can arrange tours to its factories.

For general groceries, try **Minimarket La Merced** (Amalia Puga 537, 8:30 A.M.–1:30 P.M. Mon.–Sat., 9:30 A.M.–2 P.M. Sun.), **El Sol Multimarket** (Amazonas 679, 8 A.M.–11 P.M.

daily), or **Supermercado Metro** at El Quinde Shopping Plaza (10 A.M.–10 P.M. daily).

INFORMATION AND SERVICES

Located inside the Complejo Belén, **Dircetur,** the regional tourism office (Belén 600, tel. 076/36-2997, 7:30 A.M.–1 P.M. and 2:30–6 P.M.), provides written guides and maps. The small **Oficina de Información Turística** (Batán 289, tel. 076/36-1546, 7:45 A.M.–2:45 P.M. Mon.–Fri.), managed by the Universidad Nacional de Cajamarca, in reality opens at irregular hours.

The **police station** is on Plaza Amalia Puga (tel. 076/36-2944 or 076/36-2832).

The best health care is at **Clínica Limatambo** (Puno 265, tel. 076/36-4241 or 0800-20-900). Fill prescriptions or pick up medicine at **Boticas Arcangel** (Batán 155 or Amazonas 693, 7 A.M.–midnight daily) or **Boticas Fasa** (Batán 137 or El Quinde Shopping Plaza, 7 A.M.–11 P.M. daily).

Near the Plaza de Armas are the large national banks with ATMs. Most are open weekdays 9 A.M.–6:30 P.M. (some close midday for lunch) and Saturday mornings. You'll find **Interbank** (Dos de Mayo, Plaza de Armas), **Banco de Crédito** (Apurímac 717), and **Scotiabank** (Amazonas 750). Many of these banks do not exchange travelers checks. For quick money transfers, there are **Western Union** services offered by the **Cajamarca Travel** agency (Dos de Mayo 574, tel. 076/36-8642).

Cajamarca's post office **Serpost** is at Amazonas 443 (tel. 076/36-4065, 8 A.M.–8:45 P.M. Mon.–Sat.).

Internet cafés are everywhere. Most locales are open from 8 or 9 A.M. to 10 or 11 P.M. and charge US$0.60 for the hour. For one-stop Internet and international calling, there's **@tajo Internet** (Comercio 716, tel. 076/36-2245, 8 A.M.–11 P.M. daily).

Lavandería Dandy (Amalia Puga 545, tel. 076/36-8067, 8 A.M.–7:30 P.M. Mon.–Sat., US$1.50/kg) is good and reasonably priced.

GETTING THERE AND AROUND

LAN, Star Perú, and **L.C. Busre** have daily flights to Cajamarca's airport, three kilometers east of the Plaza de Armas. Taxis to town cost US$3.

Cruz del Sur and **Movil Tours** have daily bus services direct and nonstop from Lima to Cajamarca. **Transportes Línea** (Av. Atahualpa 318, tel. 076/36-6100, www.transporteslinea.com.pe, 7 A.M.–11 P.M. daily) goes daily to Cajamarca from all major coastal cities, including Lima (14 hours), Trujillo (7 hours) and Chiclayo (6 hours); in Cajamarca the best buses are from **Turismo DIAS** (Sucre 422, tel. 076/36-8289), which goes to Trujillo.

To reach Celendín (4 hours), Leymebamba (10 hours), and Chachapoyas (12 hours) **Movil Tours** has daily departures at 6 A.M.

Transportes Royal Palace (Av. Atahualpa 339, tel. 076/36-5855) runs buses to Celendín at 9 A.M. on Thursdays, Saturdays, and Sundays, and also to Cajabamba and Bambamarca.

Taxis are ubiquitous and cheap in Cajamarca (US$1–4), though traffic can make walking faster.

Chachapoyas and Vicinity

The Chachapoya region (Chachapoyas is the name of the city; Chachapoya the name of the civilization) is a huge swath of cloud forest in northern Peru that stretches between the Marañón and Huallaga Rivers, containing some of Peru's most rugged and least explored terrain. Every decade or so explorers in this region discover a major archaeological site from the Chachapoya, a mysterious civilization that disappeared from Peru shortly before the Spanish arrived in the 16th-century.

Because of their geographical isolation from the rest of Peru, the Chachapoya developed unique forms of architecture and urban living that continue to baffle archaeologists. They also had a reputation for being feisty and independent, and the Inca spent more than a century trying to subdue this well-defended confederation. The Inca finally prevailed and wiped out every trace of this once-great culture just decades before the Spaniards arrived. What remain are hundreds of stone-built cities, funerary sites, and other ruins that are often covered by thick cloud forest. This same wilderness hosts endangered species such as the Andean bear and the marvelous spatuletail hummingbird.

Considering all there is to see and do, it is surprising how few travelers come to this area. The absence of visitors is due largely to difficult accessibility. Currently there are no

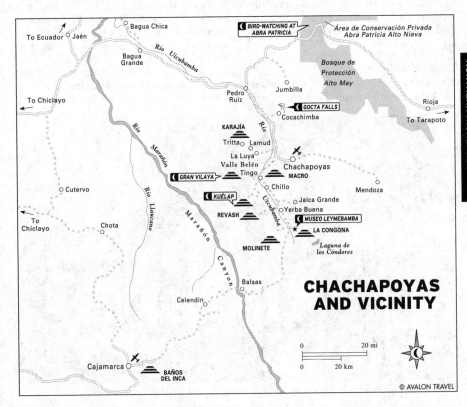

CHACHAPOYAS AND VICINITY

© AVALON TRAVEL

commercial flights to Chachapoyas, so travelers arrive via road from Cajamarca (12 hours), Chiclayo (10 hours), or Tarapoto (6 hours). Apart from Kuélap, most ruins must be accessed by a day or multiday hike.

Most tourists use the small city of Chachapoyas as their base for exploring the region. Although it is located hours from the ruins, it has the best services and transport options in the area. Chachapoyas, at 2,335 meters of altitude, is geographically closer to the Andes than to the Amazon, so its nights are chilly and its sunny days hot.

Besides Chachapoyas, a growing number of travelers are now staying at smaller villages along the Río Utcubamba road leading to Choctamal, Tingo, Chillo, and Leymebamba. These options are increasingly popular because of their comfortable lodges, shorter travel times to the ruins, the promise of peaceful evenings, and the beautiful surroundings.

SIGHTS
City Tour

Chachapoyas was founded in 1545 by conquistador Alonso de Alvarado. The location of the city was changed several times, but the present-day capital of the Amazonas region contains quite a few colonial homes with wooden balconies and large courtyards. Two of the best colonial homes, **Casona Monsante** (now a hotel) and **Casa de las Dos Rosas,** are on Amazonas Street and can be visited. At the side of the **Plaza de Armas,** almost facing the cathedral, is a monument to **Toribio Rodríguez de Mendoza,** a highly respected priest and one of the intellectual leaders of Peru's independence. He grew up in the large colonial building on Ayacucho Street, now the Archbishopric of Chachapoyas.

Religious buildings worth visiting include the **cathedral** (on the Plaza de Armas) and the **Capilla de la Virgen Asunta** (intersection of Asunción and Puno), where the image of the city's patron is kept. On the other side of town is the **Templo de Nuestra Señora de Belén,** at Triunfo and La Unión, beside what used to be the old city hospital controlled by the Bethlemites.

Also on the Plaza de Armas is the INC's **Museo Amazonas Arqueológico** (Ayacucho 908, 8 A.M.–1 P.M. and 2–5 P.M., free), which

Plaza de Armas in Chachapoyas

© JORGE RIVEROS CAYO

contains a range of Chachapoya artifacts, including mummies, ceramics, and utensils. The **Museo Étnico Religioso de Santa Ana** (Santa Ana 1054, 8 A.M.–6 P.M. daily, US$2.50) opened in 2008 and is located on the Plaza Santa Ana. The museum exhibits a wide variety of objects—from religious items dedicated to the cult of Santa Ana to archaeological artifacts.

You can walk around Chachapoyas in a few hours. Actually, if you stroll in any direction for about 10 or 12 blocks you will find yourself in the outskirts of the city. Catch a cab for US$1.50 and head to the **Mirador de Luya Urco** viewpoint, from where you can have a good panoramic view of the city and the mountains that surround it in a clear day.

Huancas

Just five kilometers north from Chachapoyas is this small village inhabited by a group of people with distinctive traditions. They descend from *mitimaes*, immigrants from the Inca period that were sent to colonize new territories. The town is situated at the edge of the impressive **Cañón del Sonche,** a very deep canyon with waterfalls and amazing geological formations that can be seen from a viewpoint. Take a *colectivo* (US$1.50) on your way there and come back on foot to Chachapoyas. It's a pleasant two-hour walk.

【 Gocta Falls

With a height of 771 meters, the existence of Gocta Falls was made public in 2006 by a German engineer, Stefan Ziemendorff, and a group of Peruvian explorers. Initially it was stated that Gocta was the third-tallest free-falling waterfall in the world, after Angel Falls in Venezuela and Tugela Falls in South Africa. Months later, after much global dispute about whether this was accurate or not, the World Waterfall Database ranked Gocta as the 14th-tallest.

The trip is two hours by car to Cocachimba, a small town from where you can already see the waterfall at a distance. You register (US$2), and then you (or your group) get assigned local guides (US$7), who carry plastic ponchos for

© JORGE RIVEROS CAYO

Gocta Falls

NORTHERN HIGHLANDS

guests in the event of rain. The hike is pretty straightforward and perhaps more strenuous on the way back to the village. Horses are available (US$9) for those who want to horse-back ride.

Either way the trek is great and the view of the waterfall quite spectacular once you reach the last leg of the trail. Gocta can appear either as a thin stream of water or a monstrous drop of roaring water, depending in what season you go, falling down from an impressive semicircular, steep escarpment covered with clouds and vegetation. Travel agencies around the Plaza de Armas offer this full-day tour with private transportation (usually a van), all tickets, and lunch for US$13–15, but rates can be negotiated depending on the number of people in the group.

If you have the spare time, **Gocta Lodge** (www.goctalodge.com, tel. 041/52-2225, US$53 s, US$68 d) is a great place to stay overnight. Located a few meters away from Cocachimba, the lodge has 10 rooms and suites, all with magnificent views of the waterfall at a distance, very comfortable beds, and amenities. The lodge offers transfers to Chachapoyas or Pedro Ruiz (US$18) and additional interesting travel packages, such as a Gocta–Kuélap combo (three days/two nights, US$162 pp, all-inclusive).

ENTERTAINMENT AND EVENTS

There is limited weekend nightlife in Chachapoyas, but it seems to be mostly concentrated around the intersection of Ayacucho and Dos de Mayo (a block away from the Plaza de Armas). The best disco-pubs are **Los Troncos** (Dos de Mayo 565) and **La Farra,** which is nearby, also on Dos de Mayo. A couple of bars on Ayacucho have good music and a laid-back atmosphere.

Towns around Chachapoyas have a lively February **Carnaval,** including the cutting down of *humishas* (gift-covered trees), in Luya. The festival for Chachapoyas's patron saint, **Virgen Asunta,** takes place the second week of August. **Patron saint festivities** take place in surrounding villages: Luya (June 24), Jalca Grande (June 28), and Lamud (second week of September).

SHOPPING

Etni-k (Grau 649, tel. 041/941-964-833) has the most interesting crafts, including ceramics from the village of Huancas, wood sculptures, and weavings and bags made from the local sheep wool.

Rusti-k (Ortiz Arrieta 672-676) sells textiles, ceramics, and other crafts made by community co-ops. **Kenkos** (Amazonas 1041) sells wood sculptures, T-shirts with native designs, and textiles.

Café Fusiones (Chincha Alta 445, tel. 041/47-9170, 8 A.M.–11 A.M. and 4–9 P.M. daily) sells not only the best organic coffee in town but also textiles and other crafts made by local communities as well as beautiful postcards from the surrounding areas.

RECREATION

The area surrounding Chachapoyas is a paradise for those who enjoy trekking in wild mountains, breathtaking geography, and montane cloud forest. Archaeological sites such as **Laguna de los Cóndores** and the vast area of **Gran Vilaya** can only be reached and explored by multiday treks made, most often, with horses and mules. Trekking, camping, or homestaying in villages is the best way to understand the life of the modern-day Chachapoya, whose fair skin and clear eyes have fueled much speculation as to their ancestry. The scenery includes plunging waterfalls, squawking parrots, and ridgetops blanketed in dense fog.

Unlike in other spots in Peru, contracting a guide or going with a guided tour is definitely a good idea in Chachapoyas. Travelers who forge out on their own can spend hours, even days, looking for ruins that blend perfectly into the lush landscape or, even worse, suffer an accident in a very desolate place. That said, be careful when contracting trekking guides. Either use the agencies listed or get recommendations from traveler reports in the South American Explorers Club.

Tour Agencies and Guides

Vilaya Tours (Grau 624, tel. 041/47-7506, www. vilayatours.com) is managed by Rob Dover, a friendly and knowledgeable Englishman who has lived in Chachapoyas since 1997. Vilaya Tours offers an extraordinary series of treks to out-of-the-way places. A two-week trek through the roadless mountains south of Leimebamba, along an old Inca Trail, includes a visit to the ruins of Cochabamba, a remote imperial Inca site with double-jambed doorways, fountains, and *kancha* enclosures. The agency also leads the best treks to Laguna de los Cóndores, regular trips to the Gocta waterfall, and excellent multiday, hotel-based tours.

InkaNatura Travel (Manuel Bañon 461, San Isidro, Lima tel. 01/440-2022, www.inkanatura.com) offers high-end, recommended multiday, culturally oriented trips. Nights are spent in cozy lodges, dining on generous meals, and days are filled visiting the major ruins and museums. Transportation is generally by car, although some trips include short hikes and horseback rides. The company can also be contacted through its U.S. agent, **Tropical Nature Travel** (www.tropicalnaturetravel.com).

Cloudforest Expeditions (Puno 368, www.kuelapnordperu.com, tel. 041/47-7610) is an English and German-speaking agency offering tours in the Chachapoya region and the rest of northern Peru. The owner, Oscar von Bischoffhausen, a Peruvian from German descent, is a very knowledgeable and friendly man who personally guides his groups.

Nuevos Caminos Travel (Chincha Alta 445, tel. 041/47-9170, www.nuevoscaminos-travel.com) offers an alternative way to explore the region. Trips are tailored to your needs, visiting Kuélap and other major sites, but keeping in mind a sustainable and responsible way to travel. Tours can last as many as 15 days, including a volunteering period of time in Huanchaco, near Trujillo, and working with farmers near Chachapoyas. For details and costs write to Marilyn Velásquez, an inspiring woman who owns this agency and sometimes leads the groups herself.

Andes Tours (Grau 517, tel. 041/47-7391, www.chachapoyaskuelap.com.pe) is a family-owned business headed by Carlos Burga, a seasoned guide and local tourism expert. This agency offers full-day tours to Gocta, Kuélap, and Karají and the highly recommended tour to Gran Vilaya (four days/three nights, US$170 pp) that includes Valle Belén, an Inca trail trek, La Pirquilla and Lanche ruins, homestays, all meals, mules, and Kuélap. They have an excellent guide, Augusto, extremely knowledgeable and fluent in French, German, Italian, and English.

ACCOMMODATIONS
Under US$10
Kuélap Hotel (Amazonas 1057, tel. 041/47-7136, US$7–11 s, US$11–18 d) is a low-budget hotel with a wide variety of rates, depending on room amenities.

Hostal Johumaji (Ayacucho 711, tel. 041/47-7279, hostaljohumaji@hotmail.com, US$8 s, US$15 d), two blocks from the plaza, is another economic choice offering private baths with hot water. Rooms vary in size but are clean and quiet.

US$10-25
The most charming budget option in town is the family-run **Hostal Revash** (Grau 517, tel. 041/47-7391, www.chachapoyaskuelap.com.pe, US$14–18 s, US$21–25 d with breakfast), a rambling colonial house with 14 huge rooms surrounding a plant-filled courtyard. The house has new wood floors, very comfy beds, cable TV, WiFi, and modern bathrooms with real hot water. It's amazingly quiet despite being right on the plaza. On the first floor is the office of **Andes Tours,** managed by the same family.

Hotel Puma Urco (Amazonas 833, tel. 041/47-7871, www.hotelpumaurco.com, US$21 s, US$32 d with breakfast) is a relatively new hotel, conveniently half a block away from the Plaza de Armas with comfy rooms, hot water, cable TV, WiFi, garage, and laundry service.

If you prefer to stay a bit away out of town **Villa de Paris** (Salida Carretera a Chiclayo Km 2, tel. 041/79-2332, www.hostalvillaparis.com, US$23 s, US$34 d) should be your choice. This place, not very far away from town, has a beautiful setting overlooking the Utcubamba valley. Comfortable bungalows for five people are also available (US$89).

US$25-50
La Casona Monsante (Amazonas 746, tel. 041/47-7702, www.lacasonamonsante.com, US$25 s, US$43 d) is the best-preserved colonial house in Chachapoyas. The rooms are huge and sparsely decorated to show off the ancient doors, high ceilings, and tile floors. Beds are comfortable, and all rooms have cable TV and WiFi. Breakfast is available for US$2–3 and heaters for an additional US$4 per day.

Gran Hotel Vilaya (Ayacucho 755, tel. 041/47-7664, www.hotelvilaya.com, US$25 s, US$32 d with breakfast) is a four-story modern hotel with 20 large, very corporate, carpeted rooms with comfortable beds, phones, cable TV, WiFi, and hot water. The café-bar is downstairs.

Casa Vieja (Chincha Alta 569, tel. 041/47-7353, www.casaviejaperu.com, US$32–45 s,

US$50–64 d with breakfast) is the top hotel in the city and worth the money. Carpeted rooms surround a stone courtyard and rose garden. The smell of burnt hickory wafts through the house and into the grand sitting room and dining area. Rooms have telephones, WiFi, and cable TV. The bigger rooms have a fireplace. Liliana Muñoz, the owner, is extremely helpful.

FOOD
Cafés, Bakeries, and Ice Cream

Café Fusiones (Chincha Alta 445, tel. 041/47-9170, 8 A.M.–11 A.M. and 4–9 P.M. daily, US$1–3) serves excellent organic coffee coming from the Rodríguez de Mendoza province, east of Chachapoyas, supporting fair trade in the region. Biscuits, homemade desserts, and delicious sandwiches are also available in the cozy coffee shop. Volunteers help out and offer information. This café also has a book exchange, board games, and WiFi.

For juices, cakes, and fruit salads, locals converge at **Café Ciomara** (Ortiz Arrieta, Plaza de Armas, 8 A.M.–10 P.M. Mon.–Sat.). One traveler even claims that this place produces *the best* chocolate cake in South America.

The front room of **Cafe San José** (Ayacucho 816, 6:30 A.M.–10 P.M. Mon.–Sat., 8 A.M.–1 P.M. and 4–9 P.M. Sun., US$1–3) bustles with bread-buyers, but the back room is full of quiet conversation and locals sipping coffee as they eat tamales. The café will specially prepare early-departure breakfasts.

Peruvian

Restaurant El Tejado (Santo Domingo 424, tel. 041/47-7592, 11 A.M.–9 P.M. daily, US$3–7) is by far the best eatery in Chachapoyas. Great menus (US$3) on weekdays and specialties as *tacu-tacu* (a fried bean and rice patty topped with beef or fried egg), as well as chicken, pork, and beef dishes, make this place a favorite.

Sabores del Perú (Dos de Mayo 321, tel. 041/47-9181, 11 A.M.–11 P.M. daily) has a wide variety of Peruvian meals, from a steamy *sopa criolla* to *pollo a la brasa*. Food is tasty and abundant.

Despite a cold, nondescript atmosphere, **La Tushpa** (Ortiz Arrieta 753, tel. 041/80-3634, 1–11 P.M. Mon.–Sat., 6–11 P.M. Sun., US$1–3) serves mouthwatering *brochetas, parrillas* (grilled meats), and *anticuchos* (grilled beef-heart skewers). The prices are dirt cheap and the kitchen immaculate.

Vegetarian

Restaurant Vegetariano El Eden (Grau 448, tel. 041/47-8664, 7:30 A.M.–9 P.M. Sun.–Fri., US$1–2) has the best and cheapest *menú* in town. It serves excellent yogurts, salads, soups, and large helpings of rice and soy-based dishes. Vegetarian or not, don't miss this place.

Markets

For the best selection of groceries, try **Mini-Market** (Ortiz Arrieta 528, Plaza Mayor, 7 A.M.–11 P.M. daily), with a café-bar on the second floor.

The **Mercado Central,** full of local fruits and vegetables, is on Libertad between Grau and Ortiz Arrieta, behind the Plaza de Armas.

INFORMATION AND SERVICES

There is an **Iperú** office at Ortiz Arrieta 590, Plaza de Armas (tel. 041/47-7292, iperuchachapoyas@promperu.gob.pe, 9 A.M.–6 P.M. daily). Above the **Institute of National Culture Museum** (Ayacucho 904, Plaza de Armas, 9 A.M.–1 P.M. and 3–5 P.M. Mon.–Fri.), there is a library and some tourist information.

The **national police** office is at Ayacucho 1040 (tel. 041/47-7176).

For health care, the two options are **Hospital Chachapoyas** (Triunfo, block 3, tel. 041/47-7016 or 041/47-7354, 24 hours) and **Hospital Higos Urco (Essalud)** (Ortiz Arrieta and Amazonas, tel. 041/47-7052, 24 hours). There are several pharmacies in town. **Botica del Pueblo** (Ortiz Arrieta and Amazonas, 7 A.M.–11 P.M. daily) is centrally located on the Plaza de Armas.

Banks with ATMs include **Banco de la**

Nación (Ayacucho, block 8) and **Banco de Crédito** (Ortiz Arrieta 580, on the plaza). Both banks are open weekdays 9 A.M.–6 P.M. (Banco de Crédito closes for lunch) and Saturday mornings.

Serpost, the post office (Ortiz Arrieta block 6, tel. 041/47-7019, 8 A.M.–8 P.M. Mon.–Sat.), is on the Plaza de Armas.

Chachapoyas has speedy **Internet,** and normal café hours are 8 A.M.–10 P.M. On the Plaza de Armas, there are several *locutorios* for local, national, or international calls. Prices are posted.

The best place for laundry is **Lavandería Clean** (Amazonas 813, tel. 041/47-7078, 8 A.M.–9 P.M. Mon.–Sat., US$1.50/kg), offering same-day service, one block from the plaza.

GETTING THERE AND AROUND

Most visitors arrive to Chachapoyas via either the 10-hour bus from Chiclayo or an 8-hour trip from Tarapoto. Intrepid and adventurous spirits who aren't afraid of heights continue south on dirt roads towards Leymebamba, and then up and out of the Utcubamba Valley to drop into the awe-inspiring Marañón Valley.

A private company owns the city airport, but flights have not been reestablished since a Fokker F–28 crashed in 2003. Check with a local travel agency to learn more about flights in the future to Chachapoyas.

Colectivos and taxis run the one-hour route on an excellent paved highway from Chachapoyas to **Pedro Ruiz,** a town on the Chiclayo–Tarapoto Marginal Highway where buses can be caught for either direction, including Movil Tours (Libertad 464, Chachapoyas, tel. 041/47-8545).

Etcaosa serves Bagua Grande, Pomacochas, and Nueva Cajamarca in modern sedan or station wagon cars from Pedro Ruiz (Av. Marginal 231, tel. 041/797-801, between 5 A.M. and 6 P.M.). From Nueva Cajamarca, **Transportes Cajamarca** (Av. Cajamarca Sur 650, tel. 041/55-6739, between 5 A.M. and 8 P.M.) goes to Moyobamba, Tarapoto, and Yurimaguas daily.

On weekdays *colectivos* serve the route Chachapoyas–Leymebamba, and all points in between, at noon, from Dos de Mayo (block 4, US$3), and every day from Grau 302 (US$4).

TINGO AND CHILLO

These two small villages along the Río Utcubamba are much closer to Kuélap, Revash, and Leymebamba. Despite lacking the services of Chachapoyas, they have a string of charming lodges worth considering.

From Tingo, it is possible to walk to Kuélap. Start the 10-kilometer hike early, with sunscreen, a hat, and with plenty of water.

Accommodations

In Tingo, accommodations are in the neighborhood of Tingo Bajo, by the river and just off the road, but away from the Plaza de Armas. Take a right after the bridge and follow a dirt road to **Hospedaje and Restaurante Tingo** (tel. 041/941-732-2515, US$4 s, US$6–9 d). Rooms share clean bathrooms, and some doubles have private bathrooms. The owner, Carmen Jiménez, also has a restaurant with set and quite delicious menus for US$2.

Just a few kilometers down the road in Chillo lies the family-run **Estancia Chillo** (Km 46 Carretera Chachapoyas–Leymebamba, tel. 01/991-661-552, www.estanciachillo.com, US$45 pp with all meals), a lodge in which nearly every detail—furniture, doors, and sculptures—was hand-built by the owner, Arce Cáceres. Rustic, stone-floored rooms are strung around a patio and various sitting rooms. The gardens are filled with fruit trees, bougainvillea, and the geometric stone sculptures of Oscar's son Peter. Though he speaks only Spanish, Oscar Arce, a long-time guide, is a good source of information and enjoys taking travelers to Kuélap (or anywhere else) on horseback.

Food

The favorite stop of travelers and truckers who pass through Tingo is **Restaurant Kuélap** (main road, 8 A.M.–9 P.M. daily). What the small restaurant lacks in atmosphere, it makes up for in bustle and generous plates of food.

NORTHERN HIGHLANDS

© JORGE RIVEROS CAYO

Estancia Chillo, on the road from Chachapoyas to Kuélap

Carmen Jiménez, the owner of **Restaurante Tingo** (6 A.M.–10 P.M. daily, US$2 menu), serves up safe *comida típica,* either hen, lamb, or pork in abundant portions.

Getting There and Around

Tingo and Chillo are an easy drop-off with any transport headed between Leymebamba and Chachapoyas. From Chachapoyas, *colectivos* leave for Tingo from Grau (block 3). There is no direct transport to these towns from Pedro Ruiz.

TINGO TO KUÉLAP

Choctamal is one of the villages along the bumpy road from Tingo to Kuélap. Very close by is **Choctamal Marvelous Spatuletail Lodge** (tel. 041/47-8838, U.S. tel. 866/396-9582, www.marvelousspatuletail.com, US$30 s, US$40 d), which is named after a local endemic hummingbird. The lodge sits high on a hilltop and has a direct view of Kuélap from its bedroom balconies. The rooms with wooden floors are elegant, though spartan, and there are plenty of blankets for the area's chilly

nights. The outdoor hot tub, sunset over the valley, and delicious breakfast are not to be missed.

In the nearby town of El Tambo is Robert Jiménez's restaurant **El Gran Shubit** (7 A.M.–8 P.M., US$4), which serves local dishes. A small hotel with the same name (US$3 s, US$5 d) has clean rooms with shared bathrooms and hot showers.

LEYMEBAMBA

Leymebamba, near the head of the Utcubamba Valley at 2,200 meters, is a quiet town with cobblestone streets and stone church. Situated 80 kilometers south of Chachapoyas, the road between towns is not paved but it is amazingly in quite good condition. En route to Celendín and Cajamarca, the road from Leymebamba climbs out of the Utcubamba watershed and plunges into the Marañón Canyon.

Leymebamba was one of the first Chachapoya towns that **Inca Túpac Yupanqui** encountered in 1472. Here, the sovereign celebrated the Inti-Raymi festival, a celebration of the summer solstice from which Leymebamba derives its name. The town celebrates its patron saint **Virgen del Carmen** in mid-July.

The ruins of **La Congona** are a three-hour walk above the city. Ask at the Museo Leymebamba or at one of the lodgings about how to get there.

◖ Museo Leymebamba

Open in 2000, the Museo Leymebamba (Av. Austria s/n, San Miguel, tel. 041/81-6803, http://museoleymebamba.org, 9:30 A.M.–4:30 P.M. Tues.–Sun., US$3.50), two kilometers southwest of Leymebamba on the highway leading to Cajamarca, is an extraordinary introduction to the Chachapoya culture.

The museum was opened after the 1997 discovery of approximately 200 mummies and 2,000 artifacts at **Laguna de los Cóndores,** which can only be reached via a 10-hour mule ride on muddy trails heading south from Leymebamba. A team led by bio-archaeologist Sonia Guillén carefully excavated the site and, in the process, revealed much of what we is known about the Chachapoya.

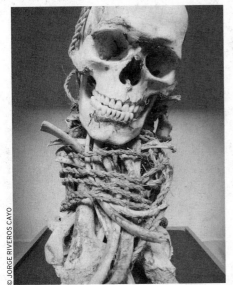

Chachapoyan mummy on display at the Museo Leymebamba

© JORGE RIVEROS CAYO

The mummies are housed and exhibited in a temperature-controlled chamber. They were found in cliff tombs above the lake, which perfectly preserved the mummies despite the high humidity of the montane cloud forest. DNA from these mummies helped scientists decipher the migration patterns, diseases, and genetic origins of the Chachapoya. Other artifacts include collections of colorful shawls, feathered headdresses, baskets, sandals, flutes, and artistic renderings found in Kuélap and other sites.

The museum was built using old Chachapoya construction techniques and local building traditions. Apart from the artifacts, the museum also contains scale models of Chachapoya cities and tombs and an ethnographic exhibition on the modern-day descendants of the Chachapoya.

The museum has a small shop with interesting books written by Guillén and Adriana von Hagen about the Chachapoya and the archaeological digs. Likewise, the artisan Miguel Huamán Revilla, sells his crafts. Across the road from the museum is **Kentikafé** "the hummingbird café," where you can observe at a very short distance these small creatures, including the marvelous spatuletail hummingbird. Coffee, sandwiches, and especially the hot chocolate are as marvelous as the hummingbirds.

Accommodations and Food

Hospedaje Laguna de los Cóndores (Amazonas 320, tel. 041/83-0104, www.loscondoreshostal.com, US$10 s, US$15 d) is one block away from Leymebamba's Plaza de Armas. It has several rooms, with private and shared bathrooms, and some with hot water. The rooms are arranged around a courtyard with hammocks perfect for an afternoon nap.

La Casona de Leymebamba (Amazonas 223, tel. 041/83-0106, www.casonadeleymebamba.com, US$12 s, US$15 d with breakfast) is by far the best place to stay in town. Features include large rooms with private baths and delicious breakfasts. The owner, Nelly Zumaeta, is welcoming and extremely helpful.

NORTHERN HIGHLANDS

La Tushpa (16 de Julio 612, Plaza de Armas, 7 A.M.–10 P.M. daily, US$2–4) is a good place to have lunch or dinner. Sitting on the back patio, you can watch as your trout is fried over an open, wood-burning stove.

The best eatery in town is **Cely** (La Verdad 530, 6 A.M.–10 P.M. daily, US$3–5), which offers a daily menu for US$1.50 and other dishes such as *lomo saltado,* soup, beans, and pizzas. Early breakfasts are also available.

Getting There

All buses from Cajamarca to Chachapoyas stop in Leymebamba. From Chachapoyas, Leymebamba *colectivos* leave weekdays, once full, from Grau 302 at noon.

Chachapoya Archaeological Sites

This section covers the most-visited archaeological sites in the Chachapoyas area, in order of traveler popularity, with rough instructions on how to get there. Remember that finding many of the lesser-known ruins is difficult and you run the risk of getting lost if you do not get a guide. The best place to get guides is Chachapoyas.

◖ KUÉLAP

Perched on a limestone ridge above the Utcubamba Valley and rediscovered by a local judge in 1843, Kuélap (8 A.M.–5 P.M. daily, US$5) must have been a nearly impenetrable fortress. This imposing stone citadel, 700 meters long and 110 meters at its widest, is surrounded by a huge wall reaching heights of 11 meters over sheer cliffs. Visitors enter from the east, via one of three funnel-shaped defensive entrances that penetrate the massive and remarkably intact walls.

Above are situated the remains of more than 400 circular stone houses, grain silolike homes. Peaked, conical thatch roofs top these two-story homes and their midsection is marked by protruding stones, which probably served as gutters to keep rain away from the foundations. Friezes with zigzag, rhomboid, or serpentine designs wrap many of the buildings. Cloud forest trees, like *nogal,* encircle the moss and bromeliad-covered ruins. Cool mountain breezes and buzzing hummingbirds sweep through the complex.

From the east entrance, there is a network of marked paths leading right to what was once the most fortified part of the citadel. At the top of a stone D-shaped lookout tower, archaeologists found a cache of 2,500 shaped rocks—sling ammunition.

Square buildings, which may have been built by the Inca, lie near the center of the platform. Nearby, Canadian anthropologist Morgan Davis and a team from Levanto have reconstructed a round house, complete with its thatched roof.

Canadian anthropologist Morgan Davis reconstructed a Chachapoyan round house with a mid-level rain gutter to protect the foundation.

© RENÉE DEL GAUDIO AND ROSS WEHNER

Kuélap's most famous building, however, is a stone tower whose walls widen as they go up as if it were an upside-down inkwell or *tintero*—its name in Spanish. Animal sacrifices were found inside, so archaeologists believe this building had a religious purpose. Others, though, say it was a solar observatory or cemetery.

Most visitors arrive to Kuélap via a day tour or three-hour *combi* ride from Chachapoyas. Backpackers, though, opt for a five-hour, 10-kilometer hike from the village of **Tingo.** The trail follows a path of stone slabs laid by the Chachapoya. The trail, best hiked in the cool of the morning, rises 1,210 meters from Tingo and is marked with red arrows. The National Institute of Culture operates **El Bebedero** (tel. 041/81-3172 or Lima tel. 01/349-9627, infokuelap@yahoo.es, US$3 pp) near the ruins, which is pleasant and has electricity though no running water. Ask about the hostel and meals when you sign in for the ruins. There are also a few *hospedajes* in Pueblo María with basic accommodations and meals.

From Chachapoyas, US$3 *combis* leave from the corner of Grau and Salamanca at 4 P.M. and 4 A.M. If you book your place on the morning bus the night before, it will pick you up at your hotel. Often the afternoon bus is full, so arrive ahead of time. The bus passes Tingo, Choctamal, Longuita, and María en route to Malcapampa, a 15-minute walk from Kuélap. There are no fixed return *combis*. In the case of Kuélap, it seems most sensible to go with a local Kuélap agency for as little as US$10. If you have a group, a private *combi* can be rented in Chachapoyas for the round-trip journey to Kuélap for about US$60.

KARAJÍA

At Karajía, clay tombs (sarcophagi) with human forms and eerie, oblong faces stand over dramatic cliff ledges. Made by the **Chipuric** subculture, the tombs were sacked and shattered long ago. But at least one group of six figures remains. Binoculars are a must to see the sculptural details and the skulls perched on top of them.

There are two ways to reach Karajía, which is

a 70-kilometer drive northwest of Chachapoyas. The shorter route is a half-hour walk from **Cruzpata,** a village at the end of a dirt road. Villagers charge a US$1 entrance fee. To reach Cruzpata from Chachapoyas, take a US$2 *combi* for the 1.5-hour trip to Luya. Luya *combis* depart a block from the Chachapoyas market at Ortiz Arrieta 364. From Luya, take US$7 *colectivos* in the main square to Cohechan. After he drops his other passengers, pay the driver a bit more to take you to Cruzpata. Guides can be hired at Cruzpata for US$5, though there are signs indicating the way.

The other route also starts in Luya, but it branches off to Lamud and Trita, the starting point for a 1.5-hour walk that crosses the valley and should be avoided in rainy season (December–March). For this walk, it is best to hire a guide in Trita, Lamud, or Luya for about US$12 per day. Consider a visit to Pueblo de los Muertos later in the same day. Public transport to Lamud and Trita leaves from Luya's main square.

REVASH

Revash is a collection of house-like tombs perched on cliff ledges. The hundreds of mummies were looted long ago, but what remains are several tombs in good condition, and red-and-white paintings of men, animals, and other abstract designs. Out of respect for the site and its preservation, visitors should not scramble onto the ledges but use binoculars to view them from a distance. Apart from the main site, there are 18 lesser sites spread through this Santo Tomás Valley.

To reach Revash, hop on a Chachapoyas–Leymebamba *combi* and get off at Yerba Buena, which is south of Ubilón and Tingo. At this point, a taxi can take you another half hour west on a dirt road that crosses the bridge. Proceed until you see a house built of sheet metal, where the trail begins. The walk up to the tombs takes three hours, and they are difficult to find without a guide. Guides can be contracted along the way at Estancia Chillo or in the nearby village of Yerba Buena. *Combis* leave regularly from the second block of Grau in Chachapoyas to Yerba Buena. Most days *combis* from Leymebamba to Chachapoyas pass Yerba Buena after 3 P.M.

LEVANTO, YALAPE, AND COLLA CRUZ

The picturesque village of Levanto (2,600 meters) and the Inca and Chachapoya ruins around it make for a pleasant day trip. Levanto is part of the popular three-day trek that begins in Chachapoyas, passes through Magdalena and Tingo, and ends at Kuélap. Accommodations and food can be obtained along the way. This trail follows the Inca highways that ran from Cusco to Quito, crossing the coast and the jungle.

Chachapoyas Tours (Grau 534, 2nd Fl., Plaza de Armas, tel. 041/77-8078 or U.S. tel. 800/743-0945, www.kuelapperu.com) has the best directions for this trek. It operates a **backpacker lodge** in Levanto (US$8 pp) whose construction mimics a thatched Chachapoyas home but which has flush toilets, electricity, and hot water. The lodge donated a ceramic kiln to the surrounding community to help generate new income. Another lodging option is the **Levanto Lodge** (main square, US$6 pp).

The hiking from Chachapoyas to Levanto is approximately five hours. The same is true from Levanto to Tingo, but it is six hours from Tingo to Kuélap. To shorten the hike, take a *colectivo* from Chachapoyas to Levanto. Departures are supposedly at 8 A.M. from the corner of Sosiego and Cuarto Centenario, but it is best to confirm beforehand. The return car leaves Levanto at 2 P.M. A private car charges US$14 one-way and US$17 both ways.

On the road between Chachapoyas and Levanto are the ruins of Yalape, a residential complex made of white limestone that sprawls a hill overlooking Levanto. There are fine defensive walls with diamond-shaped frieze patterns and numerous vine-covered walls and buildings. Nearby is an ancient Inca aqueduct.

U.S. archaeologist Morgan Davis restored an Inca garrison at the crossroads Colla Cruz, a 20-minute walk from Levanto. The round Chachapoya-style building, built atop an impeccable Inca stone foundation, has a reconstructed, three-story thatch roof. Ask for directions in Levanto.

◖ GRAN VILAYA

This is a vast area of a once-populated cloud forest that was "discovered" and publicized in 1985 by U.S. swashbuckler **Gene Savoy.** Starting from the Belén Valley, Savoy walked to the village of Vista Hermosa, clearing trail along the ridge above the town. In 10 days of constant work, he found ruins of several large urban settlements, which he somewhat absurdly called **Chacha Picchu.** Locals now call the ruins Pueblo Viejo and accuse Savoy of stealing gold and smuggling other objects from the sites.

There are about 150 sites in this area, of which 15 are considered exceptional. Visitors should plan a few days for exploring them and an additional three days of travel. Getting a guide in Chachapoyas is highly recommended. Spanish speakers, though, can also hike in on their own from Belén Valley and hire a local guide in Vista Hermosa. To avoid problems, independent travelers should get a letter from the National Institute of Culture (INC) in the main square of Chachapoyas.

Most trekkers start from the village of **Cohechan,** the beginning of a road that, despite controversy, may one day reach the remote town of Vista Hermosa. Locals want the road to transport coffee, but the animals, already threatened by heavy hunting, will suffer from smaller habitats. The area's fauna includes endangered species such as the **Andean spectacled bear.** In actuality, the road stops in the Belén Valley, which can also be reached by trail from the Quechua-speaking village of Colcamar.

Belén is a postcard-perfect valley with a river meandering through green pastures. It makes for a fine campsite but gets frosty in the evenings. The path to **Vista Hermosa** heads up and over a cloud forest pass and traces the Inca highway from Levanto to Cajamarca. On the other side of the pass, there is a stretch of

© JORGE RIVEROS CAYO

riding horseback through Gran Vilaya

Inca steps, known as **La Escalera,** which have amazingly survived centuries of mule hooves. Nearby is **La Pirquilla,** an area with dozens of well-made round buildings partially covered in the cloud forest.

The trail leads into the Sesuya Valley, passing through the village of Congón before climbing up into the village of **Vista Hermosa** on the other side of the river. There, the Bardales family welcomes trekkers with food and allows them to pitch tents in their front yard. Vista Hermosa makes an excellent base for exploring the area's ruins. The easiest ruins to visit from here are **Cacahuasha,** a large village perched on top of a mountain, about a two-hour, mostly uphill, walk from Vista Hermosa. The site is divided into two sections, separated by a saddle, and includes 10-meter walls similar to those found at Kuélap. This was probably a ceremonial center and has extraordinary views over the valley.

Pueblo Viejo, the city explored by Savoy, is even more impressive but is a hard day's hike or strenuous horseback ride from Vista Hermosa. This city is perched on a cloud forest ridge that stretches all the way to **Abra Yumal,** the high pass at 3,270 meters where the traditional Gran Vilaya trek ends at a newly built road. Some guides are avoiding Vista Hermosa by entering at Abra Yumal and staying in a new lodge along the path. It is also possible to reach Savoy's cities from this area, and there are other large ruins even closer, including **Tulupe** and **Lanche.**

Also recommended are the sites of **Macchu Llaqta** and **Paxamarca,** which are villages just to the west of Vista Hermosa. The first, an hour east of the village Pueblo Nuevo, was an important ceremonial center that has a ridge-top lookout tower and a large plaza with circular houses extending in all directions. Paxamarca, 1.5 hours east of the village of Pirca Pampa, covers about 20 hectares atop a ridge and includes ceremonial terraces, numerous circular buildings, and rectangular buildings with trapezoidal doorways, proof of Inca occupation following their invasion circa 1480.

After the grueling uphill hike from Vista Hermosa to Abra Yumal, trekkers can either hike or, if transport is waiting for them, ride down to **Choctamal** or **María,** where there are hostels. *Combis* head back to Chachapoyas a few times daily.

LA CONGONA

If you get to Leymebamba, take the three-hour hike up into the hills northwest of the town. There lies La Congona, a small site with some of the most beautiful ruins in the region. This five-hectare hilltop contains a few circular homes, in excellent condition. A few of these homes were built on unusual square platforms. Inside the homes are elaborate stone niches, probably ceremonial, and outside are wide walking balconies and highly elaborate stone friezes. A lookout tower boasts an extraordinary flight of curved switchback steps, from which it is possible to look across the Utcubamba Valley to the ruins of Cerro Olán. A guide is recommended for this trek; ask at the Museo Leymebamba. Tourists should register in the Leymebamba tourist office on the plaza and pay a US$1.75 archaeological tax before venturing into the hills or trek to La Congona.

OTHER ARCHAEOLOGICAL SITES

The region has a nearly limitless number of ruins to explore for those with the time and physical stamina—and there are plenty to be discovered as well. Here are more recommended ruins in the Utcubamba Valley, listed from north to south.

Pueblo de los Muertos

The site, which translates to Village of the Dead, groups funeral houses that were built onto a cliff ledge and plastered with mud. The round houses are decorated with serpents and other abstract anthropomorphic symbols. This necropolis, which treasure hunters looted after Gene Savoy publicized it in the 1960s, once contained hundreds of mummies housed in adobe statues like those found at Karajía. Hire a guide in Lamud for this hike, which is a strenuous one-hour walk. It is important to view the tombs from a distance only. By crossing to the main ledge, tourists put the buildings

and themselves in jeopardy. To reach Lamud, see directions for Karajía.

Macro

Macro's 60 circular buildings are wedged into a hillside along the Río Utcubamba, two kilometers north of the village of **Magdalena.** From this town, the walk is 40 minutes, and from Tingo it's 30. Macro is a small site; thorns and steep terrain make it hard to reach, but, with a little direction, it is easy to see from the main road. Most of the buildings stand on narrow platforms made on the cliff face. These ruins can be included as side trip on the Levanto–Kuélap trek.

Purumllacta

Purumllacta is very close to Chachapoyas and may have been one of the seven major cities of the Chachapoya confederation that Garcilaso de la Vega and Cieza de León recorded. The complex consists of white stone houses, agricultural terraces, and large temples or palaces scattered around hills. Near the center of the complex are stairways, plazas, and a few two-story buildings.

To reach Purumllacta, take a 3 P.M. bus to Cheto from Hermosura 319 in Chachapoyas. Purumllacta lies just a short distance beyond. If taking public transportation, try to leave early in the morning to make it back the same day. Accommodation can be found in the Municipalidad.

Jalca Grande and Ollape

Jalca Grande is a Quechua village with cobblestone streets and thatched roofs. The older generation still speaks Quechua, wears colorful wool clothing, and lives as it has for centuries. But sheet-metal roofs, cement roads, jeans, and Spanish are cropping up. This town has kept the area's best-known anthropologists busy over the years. One block west of the main square is a Chachapoyas home, known as **La Choza Redonda,** which was continuously occupied for centuries until 1964. The house, with a double zigzag frieze at the top, remains in nearly perfect condition and served as the model for Morgan Davis's reconstruction of Inca and Chachapoyas homes in Levanto and Kuélap.

A half hour walk to the west of the city is Ollape, a town that once numbered 150 buildings. It is now possible to see a number of platforms with rhomboidal and zigzag friezes that are different from friezes at other sites. About 2.5 hours north of Jalca Grande is **Moyuk Viejo,** a hilltop ruin considered to be the sixth city of the Chachapoya, mentioned by Inca Garcilaso de la Vega in his *Comentarios reales.* The site is larger, though more primitive, than Ollape, and many of buildings and balconies are in disrepair. To reach Jalca, take a *combi* from the city of Chachapoyas down the Utcubamba Valley and get off at the village of Ubilón. A dirt road leads up to Jalca Grande; the walk is three hours, but you have a good chance of getting a ride along the way. There is a small, very basic hostel near the Plaza de Armas. There are also US$2 *colectivos* for Jalca Grande leaving from Salamanca and Libertad in Chachapoyas every afternoon, a 3.5-hour trip.

Laguna de los Cóndores

Laguna de los Cóndores competes with Gran Vilaya as Chachapoyas's most popular trek. You reach this stunning lake after a one- or two-day hike from Leymebamba. The trail traces through remote cloud forest filled with Chachapoyas ruins, bromeliads, and birds, before arriving at a spectacular lakeside tomb site. Contact Chachapoyas's Vilaya Tours (Grau 624, tel. 041/47-7506, www.vilayatours.com) for treks in this area.

CHACHAPOYAS TO AND FROM CHICLAYO

The trip, by ground, from Chachapoyas to Chiclayo or vice versa is a bumpy, 10-hour bus ride. **Movil** (Libertad 464, Chachapoyas, tel. 041/47-8545; Bolognesi 195, Chiclayo, tel. 074/27-1940) has daily services for US$16 one-way.

CHACHAPOYAS TO AND FROM TARAPOTO
Lago Pomacochas

A good stop on the way to Tarapoto is Lago Pomacochas (2,200 meters), a miniature lake 31 kilometers east of Pedro Ruiz. The lake's blue-green waters and extensive *tótoras* (marshlands) are the last of the highlands before the highway follows the Cordillera Oriental and descends, along the Río Mayo watershed, toward the Amazon. Pomacochas is an excellent spot for bird-watchers.

There are a few basic restaurants and hotels, but **Puerto Pumas** (entrance marked by sign on south side of highway, Lima tel. 01/242-5550, www.puertopalmeras.com) is the place to stay. This former state-owned hotel is now operated by Puerto Palmeras resort in Tarapoto and, though the construction is a bit austere, the hotel has excellent views of the lake and a collection of paintings from Tarapoto artists. Often there are not many guests, so this is the perfect place for a peaceful retreat.

❰ Bird-Watching at Abra Patricia

Abra Patricia is a high pass (2,270 meters) on the highway between Pedro Ruiz and Tarapoto and is part of a great bicycle route. It is also the short name for the **Área de Conservación Privada Abra Patricia-Alto Nieva,** a private protected area created in 2007 and located within the buffer zone of the **Bosque de Protección Alto Mayo.** Both are protected areas with some of the highest bird counts on Earth. The area's bird list includes 317 species, of which 23 are considered globally threatened. These include the endangered long-whiskered owlet, the ochre-fronted antpitta, the royal sunangel, Johnson's tody-tyrant, and of course the marvelous spatuletail hummingbird.

The Owlet Lodge or **Estación Biológica Lechucita Bigotona** (tel. 041/47-8231, Chachapoyos, www.ecoanperu.org/lechucitabigotona/eblb.htm) is a lodge/biological station located around kilometer 364.5 on the highway between Pedro Ruiz and Moyobamba, owned by ECOAN (Asociació de Ecosistemas Andinos), which is funded and sponsored by a series of international nature and conservation organizations, including Bird Life International, IUCN, Conservation International, and 10 other institutions.

The lodge has three spacious and comfortable bungalows: Fenwick, Conoco, and Jeniam, each with two rooms, a double and a single, and a shared bathroom. There is hot water and electricity in the evenings. Internet access via satellite is available in the dining/lounge area. The lodge kitchen offers three meals per day, served in the spacious dining room.

CHACHAPOYAS TO AND FROM CAJAMARCA

On the bumpy, backroads route from Chachapoyas to Cajamarca, and even beyond, there are a couple of reliable stops. If you are driving, an overnight in Celedín will give you a flavor of northern, rural living.

Celendín

If you are making the Chachapoyas–Cajamarca overland journey renting a four-wheel drive, Celendín (2,648 meters) is a friendly place to stay for the night. The inhabitants of this area were once part of the Caxamarca culture.

Located near Celendín is Choctamalque, a central point in the trade route that connected the Chimú, Caxamarca, and Chachapoya cultures. In the colonial period, Celendín was a hacienda that had Spanish and Portuguese shareholders. The current city was founded in 1793.

There is an interesting market on Sundays and a good *artesanía* shop at Dos de Mayo 319. Like Leymebamba, Celendín celebrates the festival of its patron saint, **La Virgen de Carmen,** in July. The principal day of the celebration is usually July 30, the anniversary of Celendín, with a religious procession, dancing, orchestras, cockfights, and even a bullfight featuring matadors from Mexico and Spain.

ACCOMMODATIONS

Hostal Loyers (José Gálvez 410, tel. 076/55-5210, US$9 s, US$18 d) is Celendín's best budget option. Basic, quiet rooms with TV surround a large, pleasant courtyard. Water is lukewarm, and there are cheaper rooms with shared bathrooms.

The mind-blowing bus journey from Cajamarca to Chachapoyas descends 3,000 meters into the Maraíon Valley.

© RENÉE DEL GAUDIO AND ROSS WEHNER

NORTHERN HIGHLANDS

One of the best options in town is **Hostal Imperial** (Dos de Mayo 568, tel. 076/55-5492, US$9 s, US$13 d). It is a relatively new place with clean rooms (all with private bathrooms), hot water, and cable TV.

FOOD

There is good food in **La Reserva** (Dos de Mayo 549, tel. 076/55-5415, 8 A.M.–11 P.M., US$2–4). Locals watch TV movies in this cozy place while they dine next to a faux fireplace. The other option is **Jalisco** (Union 317, Plaza de Armas), next to Hostal Celendín, serving *comida típica,* but apparently not opening regularly. To cure a sweet tooth, visit **Heladería El Rosario** (Pardo 426, tel. 076/55-5109, 10 A.M.–11 P.M. daily, US$1–3) on the Plaza de Armas.

INFORMATION AND SERVICES

Banco de la Nación (Dos de Mayo 518) is the only bank in town and has an ATM that works exclusively with Visa debit cards. The website www.celendinperu.com has interesting information about the town and surroundings. The owners of the website, a Peruvian-Dutch couple, also own a bed-and-breakfast called Orange (Unión 333, tel. 076/77-0590) that will remain closed during 2010. Regardless, ask for Suzan van der Wielen, who has lived in the area for years and is quite helpful with information.

NORTHERN HIGHLANDS

BACKGROUND

The Land

Peru's foreboding terrain belies its extraordinary fertility. The country's arid coastal climate is caused by the frigid Humboldt Current, which sucks moisture away from the land. But these Antarctic waters also cause a rich upwelling of plankton, which in turn nourishes one of the world's richest fishing grounds. Peru's earliest cultures took root near the ocean and depended on mollusks and fish for their survival.

The snow-covered mountains and high passes of the **Cordillera de los Andes** would appear to be an impediment to the spread of advanced cultures. But the slow melting of the snowpack provides the desert coast with a vital source of year-round water. Once ancient

Peruvians developed irrigation technologies, Peru's early cultures began converting Peru's desert valleys into rich farming areas. The ingenious aqueducts at Nasca, which carry mountain water for miles underneath the desert floor, are still in use today.

In the more moderate topography of North America and Europe, temperature differences and climate zones are largely a question of latitude. Florida, for example, produces oranges, while Kansas produces wheat. But in Peru, climate zones are caused not by latitude, but by altitude. Peru's coast can rise from sea level to over 4,000 meters in less than 100 kilometers, creating a variety of climates apt for fruits,

vegetables, grains, and potatoes. The same phenomenon occurs to an even greater extent where the Andes plunge into the Amazon, a dizzying range of ecosystems that nourish a huge variety of fruits and medicinal plants such as the coca leaf.

Peru's cultural diversity has always been determined by its geography. Trade routes from the Amazon over the Andes to the desert coast were key to the flourishing of Peru's ancient cultures. The Chavín culture, based in the Andes south of the Cordillera Blanca, deified jaguars, snakes, caimans, and other Amazon animals in their enigmatic carvings. They traded their high-altitude grains and potatoes for fruits from the Amazon, dried fish and vegetables from the coast, and the highly valued spondylus seashells brought from Ecuador.

GEOGRAPHY

Peru's total land area is 1.29 million square kilometers, about three times the size of California. Peru's narrow strip of arid desert coast runs 2,400 kilometers between the borders of Ecuador and Chile. Some 50 rivers cascade from the Andes to the coast, though only about a third of these carry water year-round. In these areas, people are entirely dependent on the seasonal rains in the Andes. In Peru's extreme south, the coast forms part of the **Atacama Desert,** one of the driest places on earth.

The Andes rise so abruptly from the coast that they can be seen from the ocean on a clear day. They represent the highest mountain chain on earth next to the Himalaya. **Huascarán,** Peru's highest peak at 6,768 meters, is the world's highest tropical mountain. The Andes are divided into different ranges (called *cordilleras* in Spanish), which often run parallel to each other. In northern Peru, for instance, the Andes rise four separate times to form different *cordilleras* known as the Negra, Blanca, Central, and Oriental.

Between these mountain ranges lie fertile inter-Andean valleys and grasslands between 2,300 and 4,000 meters—the so-called breadbasket of Peru, where the majority of its indigenous highlanders live and produce about half the country's food supply. The Inca and other cultures terraced and irrigated this landscape to grow a range of crops, including maize, hardy grains such as *kiwicha* and quinoa, and indigenous tubers such as potatoes, *olluco,* and oca.

On the journey between Cusco and Lake Titicaca, travelers can appreciate the most extreme of Peru's mountain climates, the **puna** or **altiplano.** These rolling grasslands between 4,000 and 4,800 meters look bleak but form rich pasturelands for Peru's variety of camelids, including the wild guanacos, the domesticated llamas and alpacas and the highly prized vicuñas. These animals continue to provide wool, meat, and transport for Andean highlanders.

On the eastern side of Peru, the Andes mountains peter out into a series of ecosystems that cascade into the Amazon basin. Near the top of the eastern edge of the Andes is the montane cloud forest, a mist-drenched, inhospitable place that is one of Peru's most biodiverse habitats. Here live 90 varieties of hummingbirds and over 2,000 types of orchids and butterflies. Clear mountain streams cascade down these slopes, eventually merging to form the broad, muddy, and winding rivers of the lowland rainforest. This carpet of green is the largest jungle on the planet, making up almost 60 percent of Peru's territory, and stretches thousands of kilometers through present-day Brazil to the Atlantic Ocean.

CLIMATE

Peru's weather is a complex set of patterns caused by the Humboldt Current, the Andes, and the jet stream, which blows northwest (not southwest as in the Northern Hemisphere) and picks up the Amazon's moisture as it travels.

On the coast, the southwesterly trade winds that blow toward Peru are chilled as they pass over the frigid waters of the Humboldt Current. When these cold winds hit Peru's sun-baked coast, they gradually warm and rarely release rain because their ability to hold water increases. Clouds form only when the air begins to rise over the Andes, dropping rain over Peru's mountain valleys and high grasslands.

© RENÉE DEL GAUDIO AND ROSS WEHNER

Peru's southern coast near Nasca is an arid desert because of the frigid Humboldt Current from Antartica.

During much of the year, however, a curious temperature inversion occurs along much of Peru's coast. The rising air from the coast is trapped beneath the warm air over 1,000 meters, which is never cooled by ocean breezes. Fog blankets sections of the coast, and drizzle, known in Lima as *garúa,* falls lightly—mainly, but not only, between April and September.

The jet stream heads west over the Amazon basin toward the Andes, picking up transpiration from the Amazon basin. As this warm, humid air rises over the Andes it also condenses into a fine mist that nourishes the cloud forest. As it rises even higher over the puna, it falls as rain.

The heaviest periods of rain in the Peruvian Amazon and Andes occur between December and April, a time that Peruvians refer to as the *época de lluvia* (the rainy season). The first rains, however, begin in October, which is the beginning of the highland planting season. Soon after, rain from the Andes begins to cascade down on the coast, where desert farmers use it for irrigation, and into the Amazon, where rivers become swollen and muddy. The Amazon River can easily rise a staggering 7–14 meters during the brunt of the rainy season in the Andes, which is why most natives live in stilted homes.

EARTHQUAKES AND EL NIÑO

Peru is prone to a series of natural disasters caused by both its young geological formation and its peculiar climate. On the western edge of South America, the Nasca Plate is slowly sliding beneath the continent, and the resulting friction causes periodic earthquakes and volcanic eruptions. The area most affected by this is southern Peru, especially **Arequipa,** which was destroyed by earthquakes in 1582, 1600, and 1604 (and also covered in ash during periodic explosions of the nearby Huaynaputina volcano). The city averages roughly one major earthquake per century, most recently in 2001, when one of the cathedral towers collapsed across the Plaza de Armas.

The hardest-hit region, however, has been the **Callejón de Huaylas,** a river valley situated

A rescue worker builds temporary housing following the August 2007 earthquake in southern Peru, which killed 600 people and destroyed 16,000 homes.

between the Cordillera Negra and Cordillera Blanca ranges, where earthquakes cause glacial lakes to burst their dams and send huge mudslides (*aluviones*) to the valley below. In 1970, an earthquake measuring 7.8 on the Richter scale destroyed 90 percent of Huaraz and triggered a wall of mud and boulders that swept down the valley above the nearby town of **Yungay.** Within minutes, around 25,000 people were buried alive. The town has been rebuilt, and the only traces of old Yungay are the tops of a few palm trees poking out above the silt plain. These trees once graced the town's square.

El Niño, the periodic fluctuation in the water temperature of the Pacific Ocean, wreaks havoc across Peru and appears to be having increasingly dramatic highs and lows; some scientists think this is a result of global climatic change. In 1982 and 1998, El Niño events dumped torrential rains onto Peru's northern desert, causing floods that washed out bridges and stranded highway motorists for weeks. These natural phenomena also caused droughts in the southern Andes and a collapse in Peru's coastal fishery, as the plankton, anchovies, and larger fish moved deep into the ocean to follow the colder water.

ENVIRONMENTAL ISSUES

Peru suffers from a range of environmental problems that are caused in large part by the abuses of mines, fishmeal factories, oil and natural gas wells and pipelines and processing centers, illegal lumber operations, and other extractive industries. These industries have operated with little oversight in Peru for decades as a result of a weak political system that is cash-starved and corrupt. Legislation governing extractive industries, along with regulatory agencies, is improving in Peru but lags well behind other more developed nations.

Peru's zinc, copper, mercury, silver, and gold mines continue to pollute water supplies with mine tailings, especially in the areas of La Oroya in central Peru and the Cordillera Huayhuash. The U.S.-owned Yanacocha gold mine near Cajamarca has finally taken

ECOTOURISM: LEAVE NO TRACE

Travelers to Peru can either help or hurt the country's long-term survival depending on how they plan their trip and how they behave. A good ecotourism reference in the United States is **The International Ecotourism Society** or TIES (tel. 202/347-9203, www.ecotourism.org), which defines ecotourism as "responsible travel to natural areas that conserves the environment and improves the well-being of local people." A handful of Peru's jungle operators belong to this association. Find out whether the lodge or agency you have chosen lives up to these basic principles set forth by TIES:

· Minimize impact.

· Build environmental and cultural awareness and respect.

· Provide positive experiences for both visitors and hosts.

· Provide direct financial benefits for conservation.

· Provide financial benefits and empowerment for local people.

· Raise sensitivity to host countries' political, environmental, and social climate.

· Support international human rights and labor agreements.

A huge concern in Peru's main trekking areas, such as the Inca Trail and the Cordillera Blanca, is environmental degradation as a result of sloppy camping. A wonderful resource for traveling lightly through wilderness is Leave No Trace (www.lnt.org), which has pioneered a set of principles that are slowly being adopted by protected areas around the world. More information on these principles can be found on the LNT web page:

· Plan ahead and prepare.

· Travel and camp on durable surfaces.

· Dispose of waste properly.

· Leave what you find.

· Minimize campfire impacts.

· Respect wildlife.

· Be considerate of others.

Great pains have been made throughout this book to recommend only agencies and lodges that have a solid ethic of ecotourism. But the only way to truly evaluate a company's environmental and cultural practices is by experiencing them firsthand. Your feedback is tremendously valuable to us as we consider which businesses to recommend in the future.

Please send your experiences – both positive and negative – to us at feedback@moon.com (www.moon.com).

---

environmental measures, after being involved in numerous social conflicts with the nearby communities over the last 10 years.

Over the last three decades, gas and oil exploration in the Amazon has caused water pollution and deforestation and had a huge impact on native cultures. The most controversial recent project is the Camisea Gas Field, which is exporting 13 trillion cubic feet of natural gas from the lower Urubamba basin, one of the most remote and pristine areas of the Peruvian Amazon. The project also includes a pipeline over the biodiverse Cordillera Vilcabamba and a natural-gas processing plant next to Paracas, the country's only marine reserve.

Sewerage treatment is also seldom implemented in Peru, and water pollution and algae blooms in rivers are a serious problem. The situation is especially acute around Lima, where certain local beaches are often declared unsafe for swimming. Across the country, trash is dumped in landfills and burned. Because there is very little recycling in Peru, much of the plastic garbage ends up blowing across the land and floating down rivers. Even in the Sacred Valley near Cusco, plastic bottles can be stacked more than half a meter deep along the shores of the sacred Río Urubamba.

Population growth is also exerting tremendous pressure on Peru's resources, especially in the highlands. Overgrazing and the chopping of trees for firewood have caused the area's thin soils to wash away in many areas. The loss of vegetation combines with heavy rains to cause mudslides, known locally as *huaycos*. A series of floods and mudslides in the Cusco area in January 2010 swept away bridges, roads, and the railway that leads to Machu Picchu. The weeks of continuous rains also flooded large areas of fields of the Sacred Valley. As a result, 3,000 tourists were stranded for almost a week in Aguas Calientes, the town near Machu Picchu, and were finally evacuated with helicopters. Worse, thousands of peasants lost their crops and homes.

In the Amazon, conflict between the Peruvian government and the Amazon's native peoples reached a boiling point in 2009. Tensions had already been simmering, and occasionally flaring, because of government efforts over the last decade to regulate small-time gold panning, timber poaching, and illegal hunting in various parts of the Amazon. But a violent protest erupted in Bagua, northeastern Peru, in June 2009 when the Peruvian government suddenly opened up new areas of the Peruvian Amazon to oil and gas developers. The legislative move was made without the input of Amazon indigenous groups who resided in the area and was seen as a clumsy effort to comply with a recent U.S. free trade agreement. In the resulting protest, 33 people—both police officers and civilians—were killed and 200 were injured. Shortly after the protests, the Peruvian congress reversed the legislative change.

Natural Protected Areas

As of 2010, there were 68 natural areas protected by the Peruvian government, under the administration of **SERNANP** (Servicio Nacional de Áreas Naturales Protegidas por el Estado), which total more than 16 percent of the country's territory. There are twelve national parks, three of which have been classified internationally as Natural World Heritage Sites. These are Huascarán, Manu, and Río Abiseo, a huge swath of remote cloud forest in northern Peru that includes the Chachapoya archaeological site of Gran Pajatén.

Only tourism and scientific research are allowed inside national parks, which are meagerly funded by the government but luckily can count on private donations from international organizations. The other strict categories of protection in Peru are the historic sanctuaries—Machu Picchu and the Inca Trail are classified and protected under this designation—and the natural sanctuaries, such as the mangrove areas in Tumbes.

Other designations include national reserves or *reservas nacionales,* such as Paracas, Titicaca, and Pacaya Samiria, and reserved zones or *zonas reservadas* like the area surrounding the Cordillera Huayhuash or Sierra del Divisor on the Peru-Brazil border. Additionally, there are communal reserves or *reservas comunales* protecting large portions of land where the main Amazon groups live, and protected forests or *bosques de protección,* among other lesser classifications.

Since 2001, Peru's government has allowed protected areas that are administered privately or through regional, municipal, or community organizations. Currently there are five regional conservation areas or *áreas de conservación regional,* such as Tamshiyacu Tahuayo in the jungle, and 16 private conservation areas or *áreas de conservación privada,* with Chaparrí the first to be created in the northern coast. These areas have proven to be managed more effectively than the state-administered parks and reserves. There is a current tendency of protecting more and more forests and other ecosystems under this new system.

Flora and Fauna

If in case of a planet catastrophe we would have the choice to choose from one country to save and rebuild the planet from, undoubtedly I would choose Peru.

– English scientist David Bellamy

Peru is located in the heart of the richest and most diverse region in the world. Eleven eco-regions with a unique combination of climate and geography contain a sixth of all plant life in only 1 percent of the planet's land area. The country has 84 of the 114 Holdridge life zones. Few countries can rival Peru's biodiversity, which holds world records for highest diversity of birds (more than 1,800 species), butterflies (more than 3,500), and orchids (3,500). There are at least 6,300 species of endemic plants and animals, along with an estimated 30 million insects.

FLORA
Desert
Few plants can grow in the bone-dry conditions of Peru's southern and central coast, which is dominated by shifting sand dunes and arid desert. The irrigated valleys, however, are covered in cash crops, including olives, grapes, nuts, and a range of fruits and vegetables. In Peru's northern valleys, the hotter temperatures are ideal for the cultivation of cotton, rice, mangos, limes, and sugarcane.

As the Humboldt Current eases off Peru's coast at the tip of the Península de Illescas, west of Piura, trade winds bring humidity and even some rain to the coast. The coast northeast of Chiclayo is covered by vast tracts of *bosque seco,* a scraggly low-lying forest composed mainly of *algarrobo* (carob), a mesquite-like tree whose sweet pods are the base of the *algarrobina* cocktail. Other trees in these forest include ficus, *zapote,* and *vichayo.*

Even farther north, the climate turns subtropical and occasional patches of palm trees line up near the beaches along with the large **mangrove swamps** north of Tumbes. The swamps are protected as part of the Santuario Nacional Manglares de Tumbes, which includes Peru's only chunk of Pacific tropical forest. There are orchids and gigantic trees such as the ceibo, with its umbrella-shaped crown, and the *pretino,* which drops seed pods the size of basketballs.

Andes
The high grasslands region or **puna** is home to a collection of bizarre plants with endless adaptations for coping with the harsh climate. Many of them have thick, waxy leaves for surviving high levels of ultraviolet radiation and fine insulating hairs in order to cope with frequent frosts. They grow close to the ground for protection from wind and temperature variations. In Peru's north, wet grasslands known as *páramo* stretch along the northwestern edge of the Andes into Ecuador. The *páramo* has a soggy, springy feeling underfoot and serves as a sponge to absorb, and slowly release, the tremendous amounts of rain that fall in the area.

Peru's most famous highland plant, the **Puya raimondii**—baptized after Antonio Raimondi, the Italian naturalist who studied it—grows in the puna, from Huaraz all the way south to Bolivia. The rosette of spiky, waxy leaves grows to three meters in diameter and looks like a giant agave, even though the plant is in the bromeliad family along with the pineapple. The *Puya* lives for a century and, before it dies, sends a giant spike three stories into the air that eventually erupts into 20,000 blooms. Once pollinated, the plant's towering spike allows it to broadcast its seeds widely in the wind.

The spiky tussocks of grass known as *íchu* are the most ubiquitous feature of Peru's high plains. Highlanders use this hardy grass to thatch their roofs, start their fires, and feed their llamas and alpacas. Cattle, which were imported from Europe in the 16th century by the Spanish, are unable to digest it. Cows can only eat the *íchu* when it sprouts anew as a

MEDICINE PLANTS OF THE AMAZON

There are very few modern clinics in Peru's Amazon. Natives are not concerned, since they have relied for centuries on village **curanderos** (healers) and the abundant pharmacy of plants in the rainforest. Most of the medicines are based on the complex chemical defenses that plants produce to defend themselves from insects and other predators. North American and European pharmaceutical companies spend a lot of time and money to meet with *curanderos* and investigate the efficacy of various plants and herbs.

Here are the top 10 medicinal plants you are likely to see in the rainforest.

1. **Uña de gato,** or cat's claw, is a hairy vine named for its catlike tentacles. The bark is boiled for tea or soaked in alcohol and then consumed to treat prostate and lung cancer, rheumatism, and arthritis.

2. **Jergón sacha,** or fer-de-lance plant, is an understory herb with bark patterns identical to those of the poisonous Amazon's fer-de-lance snake. The plant's root is made into a tea as an effective remedy against this snake's bite. The root can also be applied directly to the wound.

3. **Hierba luisa,** or lemongrass, smells like citron and is a prime ingredient in both Inca Kola, the national soft drink, and citronella, the natural insect repellent. When boiled, it makes a stress-reducing tea.

4. **Bellaco caspi,** known in English as himatanthus, exudes a white latex when its bark is cut. The gooey substance can be used to heal cuts, set broken bones, and even suffocate the botfly larvae that burrow beneath the human skin.

5. **Ojé** grows 25 meters high, up to 1,000 meters above sea level. This tree also exudes a white latex, which is used in a variety of medical treatments: toothache, cleaning the digestive system, rheumatism, and snake bites.

6. **Pan de árbol,** or breadfruit, is a staple food in the Pacific islands and Southeast Asia. It was imported to Peru in the 19th century. In the Amazon, its leaves are used for cleaning and sterilizing a woman after she gives birth.

7. **Clavo huasca** is a pungent, clove-scented vine. It is a powerful aphrodisiac and is one of the ingredients used in Siete Raices, a tonic that serves as an energizer, reduces fever, and boosts the immune system.

8. **Achiote** is a shrublike tree with a red, spiky fruit from which the Yagua Indians extract a crimson dye for painting their bodies and palm-fiber skirts. It is also used to treat dysentery, venereal diseases, hepatitis, and skin rashes.

9. **Sangre de grado,** or dragon's blood, is a medium-sized tree that exudes a reddish latex used to stop vaginal hemorrhaging during childbirth. It is also used to decrease scarring and wrinkles. The sap is currently undergoing clinical trials in the United States.

10. **Cocona** is a tree that yields a tomato-like fruit that is high in vitamin C and often served as a juice. It is also taken to control nausea and to treat snake or insect bites.

(Information taken from *A Field Guide to Medicinal and Useful Plants of the Upper Amazon*, James Duke et al, Gainesville, Florida: Feline Press, 1998.)

tender green shoot. Hence, highlanders burn large tracts of hillside every year to make *ichu* palatable for cows.

The high deserts of southern Peru, such as those on the way to the Colca Canyon, are so dry that not even *ichu* can survive. Instead, green blob-like plants called **yareta** spread along the rocky, lunar surface. This plant's waxy surface and tightly bunched leaves allow it to trap condensation and survive freezing temperatures. It is currently considered an endangered species.

A few trees can be found in Peru's montane valleys. **Eucalyptus,** which was imported to Peru from New Zealand, is used widely by highlanders for firewood and ceiling beams. Eucalyptus is useful but also highly invasive; its rapid spread has greatly reduced the numbers of Peru's most famous highland tree, **queñual,** currently also endangered. This scraggly, high-altitude, onion skin–like tree can still be seen in abundance, however, in the Parque Nacional Huascarán, especially on a three-kilometer trail known as María Josefa that starts at the shores of Lake Llanganuco.

Amazon

The cloud forests that blanket the eastern escarpments of the Andes are a remarkable tumble of gnarled trees that cling to the steep, rocky soil. These trees have evolved to trap the thick blankets of mist that form when humid jungle air cools as it rises over the Andes. Aerial plants, such as ferns, mosses, orchids, cacti, and bromeliads, cover the trees and are collectively known as **epiphytes.** Because they have no roots to the soil, they must gather all of their water and nutrients from the passing mist. This forest has a dark, primeval feel and is seen in the surrounding areas of Moyobamba and Tarapoto, Machu Picchu, throughout the Chachapoya region, and on the road to Parque Nacional Manu. The Peruvians somewhat poetically call cloud forest the *ceja de selva* or the "eyebrow of the jungle."

The forest takes on a whole different feel farther downhill in the lowland tropical rainforest, where steep slopes give way to swampy soil and the rivers become slow and muddy. The trees are huge, often over 60 meters tall, and the understory is dark and curiously free of plants. Huge gray vines, as thick as the human body, descend from the highest branches into the ground. These are the **strangler figs** called *matapalo,* which begin life high in the canopy where birds and bats drop their seeds after gorging on the fig fruit. After dropping their vines to the forest floor, these vines merge together and form a sheath that envelops the tree, slowly choking off its nutrients. When the host tree dies, the parasite strangler fig remains in its place. They are often the largest, noblest trees in the forest, and it is hard to believe they began life as assassins.

Life in the rainforest is a battle for sunlight. This becomes readily apparent to those who climb up to the tree platforms or canopy walkways that have been built in the jungle lodges. Perched high in the canopy are an astounding number of epiphytes, far greater than in the cloud forest. Each of these plants has made adaptations to deal with the intense sunlight and evaporative breezes of the upper canopy. **Tank bromeliads** have long leaves that work as troughs to collect rain, while the orchids store water in their bulbous stems. All the plants, especially the cacti, have tough, waxy skins to retain moisture. These epiphytes are here not only for the sunlight, but also for the breezes that help disperse seeds and the vast number of bats, birds, and insects that forage in the canopy and serve as pollinators.

The fight for sunlight is evident on the forest floor when a large tree falls over, dragging its vines and smaller trees along with it. The sun-filled clearings created by falling trees are called "light gaps" and form fascinating mini-ecosystems for fast-growing pioneer trees, such as the **cecropia.** Its thin gray trunk, often marked with white rings, twists in odd shapes to catch the sunlight with its huge palm-shaped leaves. These clearings are wonderful places to examine the epiphytes, insect nests, and other forms of canopy life.

Large rainforest trees include mahogany (*caoba*), cedar (*cedro*), and *tornillo,* a highly

THE SUSTAINABLE BRAZIL NUT

Despite the severe depredation generated by the informal gold mining and the unorganized timber industry, the Amazon still has a hopeful model for rainforest development.

Though useful as lumber, the **Brazil nut tree,** locally known as *castaña,* is often the largest tree left standing in the forest because its nuts are more valuable than its wood. The tree's round seedpods look like the pod inside of a coconut and fall to the ground in December and January. Each pod contains between 12 and 24 Brazil nuts, and a single tree can produce as many as 500 kilograms in a year. The nuts are sold as food or for a burgeoning overseas organic products industry that uses its oil in lip balms and skin lotions.

The tough shells prevent birds from eating the seeds before they ripen and are used by natives as candle holders. Only one species of insect – the bee – is physiologically able to pollinate the Brazil nut tree's flowers. Once pollinated, the tree relies on only one animal for the dispersal of its seeds: the brown agouti, a rabbit-sized jungle rodent who collects the seeds and buries them in the ground for later eating. Luckily for the tree, the agouti either forgets where the hole is or returns after the seeds have already germinated. People have often tried to bury and germinate Brazil nut seeds, without success. Apparently the mild-mannered agouti has a few well-kept gardening secrets.

The base of a Brazil nut tree is also a good place to find the deadly bushmaster snake, which is perfectly camouflaged among the leaves as it waits for the agouti. For this reason, Brazil nut workers use a forked pole to pick up Brazil nut seeds off the ground. Otherwise, just imagine.

---

valuable wood for making furniture that can now be found only in Peru's stands of primary forest. You might also see the **Brazil nut tree,** which drops round pods containing seeds used to make organic oils and lip balms. There is also the **kapok,** also known as ceiba, which is readily identifiable by its huge red seed pods hanging from branches. When these pods open, they release seeds that are borne by the wind on cottonlike tufts, which Amazon natives use for making hunting darts. At the ground level, the kapok stands out for its huge buttress roots, which fan out in all directions and are often wider than the tree itself.

If you scuff the ground with your foot you will understand the reason for the roots. Jungle soil is amazingly poor because all the minerals are either sucked up by the voracious competition of plant life or leached away by the constant rains. As a result, even the roots of the largest trees run along the surface in a desperate search for minerals. Because rainforest trees lack the deep taproots of temperate-forest trees, they need buttress roots to help stay upright, especially during the violent windstorms that snap the tops of many trees right off.

Another surprising difference between temperate forests and rainforests is the age of the trees. In the United States, old-growth forests take centuries to develop. But rainforests are much more dynamic—the average life of a tree here is a mere 80 to 135 years.

For people used to the pines and oaks of temperate forests, the sheer variety of trees in the rainforest can be overwhelming. There are more than a thousand different tree species in Peru's Amazon, and even finding the same tree twice can be a challenge. There is no complete guide to rainforest trees; even if one existed, it would be the size of a telephone book.

Instead of trying to keep a mental catalog of the trees you see, it makes more sense to try to understand how different trees use common defenses to survive. The thorns and spikes on many rainforest trees serve as a protection against animals, while peeling bark prevents vines from climbing the trunk. Many leaves have thin hairs or contain a complex array of toxins that serve as protection from the predation of caterpillars and insects. Other trees have developed symbiotic relationships to survive. The **palo santo** (holy tree), for instance, has hollow chambers and a gooey nectar that provide food and lodging to fire ants. These ants are totally dependent on the tree for survival and will chase off any predator that would otherwise feast on the tree.

FAUNA
The Coast

The rich oceans off Peru's coast support a wide variety of marine mammals and seabirds. Sea lions, seals, and the endangered **Humboldt penguin** can be observed at the **Reserva Nacional de Paracas** and the new **Reserva Nacional de las Islas, Islotes y Puntas Guaneras** (this reserve, created in 2010, protects all islands and guano points along the Peruvian coast). Hundreds of thousands of birds also roost on these protected islands, which are covered in thick layers of guano or bird dung. There are more than 200 bird species at Paracas, including a variety of gulls, pelicans, boobies, cormorants, frigate birds, hawks, ospreys, and vultures. You are likely to see a pink Chilean flamingo or even an Andean condor.

The dry forests farther north begin to support a variety of mammals, such as gray and red deer, anteaters, foxes, pumas, and the endangered **oso de anteojos** (spectacled bear or Andean bear). A few dozen unique forest birds also live here, along with a range of iguanas, snakes, and lizards. Peru's small chunk of Pacific coastal forest near the border with Ecuador is home to the only crocodile in Latin America, the endangered **Tumbes crocodile.**

Andes

The most ubiquitous animals of Peru's Andes are the four species of native **camelids** that eat the high-altitude *íchu* grasses and produce wooly coats as protection from the rain and cold. Two of these, the llama and alpaca, were domesticated thousands of years ago by Peru's highlanders, who tie bright tassels of yarn onto the animals' ears. Herds of the much smaller

© JORGE RIVEROS CAYO

The endangered spectacled bear is the only bear species in South America and can be found in parts of Peru's cloud forest.

and finely haired vicuña can be seen in the sparse grasslands above Ayacucho, Arequipa, and Cusco. The fourth camelid, the guanaco, is harder to spot because its main range lies south in Chile and Argentina.

Other animals in the Peruvian Andes include white-tailed deer, foxes, and the puma. The only animal you are likely to see, however, is the vizcacha, which looks like a strange mix between a rabbit and a squirrel.

There is a huge range of **birds** in the Andes, the most famous of which is the **Andean condor,** the world's largest flying bird. Its range extends from the high jungle, including Machu Picchu, all the way to the coast. It can easily be seen in Colca Canyon, along with a variety of other raptors, including the impressive mountain caracara, which has a black body, red face, and brilliant yellow feet. There are also falcons, which have a russet belly and can often be seen hovering over grasslands in search of mice or birds.

A variety of water birds can be seen at Lake

Titicaca and in the cold, black lakes of the Andean puna. The Andean grasslands are one of the habitats for the Andean goose, a huge, rotund bird with a white belly and black back, and a variety of shimmering ducks, including the puna teal and crested duck. There are even flamingos and a few wading birds, such as the red-billed puna ibis. One of the most interesting birds, which can be seen in the river near Machu Picchu and in Colca Canyon, is the **torrent duck.** This amazing swimmer floats freely down white water that stymies even experienced rafters.

Amazon

The Amazon is a zoo without bars. Exotic birds flit through the air, turtles line up on riverside logs to sunbathe, and pig-sized aquatic rodents called capybaras submerge like submarines under the water's surface. Sloths clamber slowly through the trees along with noisy troops of monkeys. Just in the low jungle around Puerto Maldonado and Parque Nacional Manu, there are more than 600 bird species, 1,300 butterflies, an estimated 30 million insects and a range of animals including tapirs, armadillos, anteaters, caimans, otters, anaconda snakes, and the sovereign of all, the jaguar. Farther north in the Iquitos basin is a slightly different range of birds and animals, including the pink river dolphin and the mysterious and shy manatee.

The Amazon's lush greenery can make these animals hard to spot. To see much of anything, you need a good pair of binoculars and an experienced guide to spot them for you. As a result, the longer you stay in the jungle and the farther you are from cities, the more you will see.

A walk in the rainforest, however, will nearly always produce sightings of **monkeys.** Among the most common are troops of large playful squirrel monkeys, which shake the branches in search of sugary fruit. Accompanying them are black-fronted nunbirds, which eat the katydids that jump away from the commotion. You will also hear (and hopefully see) red howler monkeys and observe the pygmy marmoset, which

THE AMAZING LEAF-CUTTER ANT

They crawl, fly, hop, and sting. There is no way to avoid contact with tens of thousands of insect species in the Amazon, which are, so to speak, the real dominators of the rainforest grounds.

The most visible of these is the leaf-cutter ant, which clears neat paths from its colony to the areas where it collects its leaves. These paths are often littered with discarded leaf fragments and can surprisingly stretch a kilometer or more. There are many species of leaf cutters, but all make underground colonies that can reach the size of a living room. The red-colored colonies are made from earth, while black ones are made from partially chewed twig fragments.

Anywhere from 1 million to 2.5 million workers live inside a leaf-cutter colony, divided into five castes:

1. The queen, or egg-layer

2. Male reproducers, who fertilize the queen

3. Leaf-cutters, who chew and transport the leaves

4. Leaf travelers, who remove the waxy cuticle from the leaf and protect the treasure from parasitic *phoridae* flies

5. Cultivators, who tend and fertilize a fungus that grows on the leaves

Biologists believe these leaf-cutters are responsible for nearly half of all herbivore consumption in the neotropics, but the ants do not actually eat the leaves. Instead they pile them up inside their colony to cultivate a fungus, which occurs only in leaf-cutting colonies and is the ants' only food source. The ant and fungus rely on each other for survival, an example of how specific and complex rainforest symbiosis can be.

© JORGE RIVEROS CAYO

A guide in the Reserva Nacional Pacaya Samiria displays a *carachama* fish.

can survive on a few drops of sap per day and is the smallest monkey on earth.

There are various snakes, which is the reason jungle guides usually walk in front of visitors to inspect or "clean" the path. There are also plenty of iridescent **frogs,** some of which have elaborate chemical defenses on their skin that the Amazon natives use for their poison blowdarts. Colorful **butterflies** flit through the forest, and if you're sweating, one might land on your shirt to eat your salt. Most of all you will see **insects,** including long lines of leafcutter ants carrying bits of everything on their backs toward their huge ground nests. There are also smaller army ants and termites, which build tunnels toward their nests of mud built around tree branches. You may not see them but you will hear thousands of cicadas, which make a deafening chorus by vibrating a plate under their wings.

Macaw clay licks are one of the jungle's more extraordinary sights. They are found throughout the Amazon basin, generally on riverbanks where minerals are highly concentrated.

Assorted parrots, parakeets and macaws congregate at them every morning to eat the mineral-rich mud that helps neutralize the toxins in their stomachs, allowing them to eat a large variety of ripe and unripe fruit. The largest (and smartest) birds are the **macaws,** with the more common species being the chestnut-fronted, scarlet, and the blue-and-green. At the world's largest clay lick, near the Tambopata Research Center, dozens of these birds can be seen squawking and flying about as visitors use spotting scopes to watch them from a blind. There are also salt licks that attract mammals, including one at the Manu Wildlife Center that attracts reliable nighttime views of tapirs and brocket deer.

All Amazon jungle lodges offer an early-morning boat cruise to see **birds.** The ringed kingfisher darts above the river with its light blue body, russet belly, and white-ringed neck. Mealy, orange-winged, and festive parrots squawk noisily through air. You may see the Cuvier's toucan, which sometimes uses its huge tricolored beak for eating eggs and baby chicks from the nests of other birds. Smaller, colorful birds such as flycatchers, cotingas, and tanagers can often be observed perched on branches. Raptors perch on the dead branches above the river, including the slate-colored hawk and yellow-headed caracara. Rustling through lakeside bushes is the hoatzin, a chickenlike, stinky bird with a spiky crest and a grunting call. If you're lucky, you might see an Amazonian umbrella bird, nicknamed "the Elvis bird" for a crown of feathers that flops over its head, resembling The King himself.

History

Apart from natural diversity, Peru also is the cradle of human civilization in the ancient Americas. Its cultures were far more diverse, for example, than the Mesoamerican cultures that spread through present-day Central America and Mexico.

The first Peruvian states were worshipping at stepped adobe platforms on the coast 5,000 years ago, before the Egyptians were building their pyramids at Giza. And as the Roman empire spread across modern-day Europe, Peru's first empire states were moving like wildfire across the Andes. The **Chavín** and **Tiahuanaco** cultures established patterns of religion, commerce, and architecture that remain alive today among Peru's Quechuan-speaking highlanders.

Western notions of conquest and military-backed empires do not fit easily over Peruvian history. Peru's three large empires—the Chavín, the Huari, and the Inca—spread across Peru in three stages that historians call "horizons." Like the Aztec empire in Mesoamerica, these cultures spread more through commerce and cultural exchange than through military force. Even the Inca, who were capable of raising vast armies, preferred to subdue neighbors through gifts and offers of public works projects. The Inca used military force only when peaceful solutions had been exhausted.

Following the European arrival in the New World, Peru's history follows the same basic stages as other areas of North and South America. There was first a colonial period, which lasted longer and ended later than that of the United States; a war of independence; and then a period of rapid nation building and industrialization in the 19th and 20th centuries.

ORIGINS OF HUMAN CIVILIZATION

Human life in Peru, indeed all over the Americas, is a relatively recent event made possible when the last ice age allowed human settlers to cross the Bering land bridge that connected present-day Russia to Alaska between 20,000 and 40,000 years ago. Another theory, based on Norwegian explorer Thor Heyerdahl's raft expedition in the mid-20th century, suggests that early migration may also have been possible from the Polynesian Islands in the South Pacific. Either way, the first evidence of human civilization in Peru has been dated to as early as 20,000 B.C. at **Pikimachay Cave** outside of Ayacucho, where arrowheads, animal skeletons, and carbon remains were found.

These first human groups began domesticating Andean camelids and *cuys* (guinea pigs) as early as 7000 B.C., establishing small hunter-gatherer villages a thousand years later. The nomadic tribes followed animal migration patterns, exchanging mountain winter for the warmer coastal summers. Potatoes were first cultivated around 6000 B.C. in the Lake Titicaca region. Around 2900 B.C. humans began to plant crops such as manioc, quinoa, lima beans, and cotton, establishing Peru's long-standing agricultural tradition.

CARAL, THE OLDEST CITY

With the establishment of agriculture and the domestication of livestock, the first cities in

PERU TIMELINE

- **20,000 B.C.:** First humans arrive in Peru.
- **15,000 B.C.:** Earliest evidence of human life in Peru: Pikimachay Cave, Ayacucho.
- **7000 B.C.:** Andean camelids are domesticated.
- **2627 B.C.:** Sacred city of Caral is built on the coast north of Lima.
- **900-200 B.C.:** Chavín culture flourishes as the unifier of religious ideology from its ceremonial center in the Marañón basin.
- **900-200 B.C.:** Paracas emerges in the desert, producing vividly colored textiles.
- **A.D. 200-600:** Moche, Nasca, and Tiahuanaco flourish as regional civilizations in northern, central, and southern Peru.
- **A.D. 300:** Moche's Lord of Sipán is buried at Huaca Rajada, northeast of Chiclayo.
- **A.D. 450:** Moche's Lady of Cao dies at 25 and is buried in El Brujo complex, north of Trujillo.
- **A.D. 650:** Huari empire starts expanding across most of Peru.
- **A.D. 900:** Sicán culture builds 20 pyramids at Batan Grande.
- **A.D. 1200:** Mythical foundation of the Inca empire by Manco Cápac and Mama Ocllo.
- **A.D. 1400:** Chimú kingdom reaches its maximum expansion.
- **A.D. 1400:** Inca Pachacútec's 33-year reign begins.
- **A.D. 1450:** Chimú kingdom is conquered by the Inca empire. Chan Chan and Túcume are invaded.
- **1527-1532:** Huayna Cápac dies. His two sons Huáscar and Atahualpa plunge into a civil war.
- **1532:** Francisco Pizarro lands in Tumbes with 168 men, meets Atahualpa in Cajamarca, and takes him prisoner.
- **1533:** Atahualpa is tried and executed.

Manco Inca, a puppet leader, is installed. Cusco is invaded and sacked.

- **1535:** Pizarro founds Lima.
- **1536-1537:** Manco Inca rebels and subsequently retreats to Vilcabamba.
- **1538:** Diego de Almagro is executed after rebelling against Pizarro's authority.
- **1541:** Almagro's son murders Pizarro in Lima.
- **1542:** Spain's King Charles I establishes the Viceroyalty of Peru.
- **1542:** Potosí mines reach population peak with 160,000 people.
- **1572:** Túpac Amaru I is captured, tried, and executed.
- **1742:** Juan Santos Atahualpa proclaims himself Inca and rebels in the central jungles near Chanchamayo.
- **1767:** Jesuits are expelled from the Spanish empire.
- **1780-1782:** Túpac Amaru II leads a rebellion against the Spaniards but is captured, tried, and executed.
- **1814:** Revolution breaks out in Cusco.
- **1821:** José de San Martín proclaims Peru's independence.
- **1824:** Battle of Ayacucho. Antonio José de Sucre defeats the Spaniards.
- **1826-1866:** Simón Bolívar leaves Peru. A period of political turbulence starts with 35 presidents in 40 years.
- **1840:** Peru signs lucrative contract for exporting guano, or bird dung.
- **1849-1874:** Cotton and sugar plantations on Peru's north coast import 100,000 Chinese coolies to replace freed slaves.
- **1879-1883:** War of the Pacific. Peru loses the war against Chile.
- **1911:** Hiram Bingham discovers Machu Picchu.

- **1919-1930:** Augusto B. Leguía's 11-year civil dictatorship is marked by strong foreign investment and restriction of civil rights.

- **1927:** Víctor Raúl Haya de la Torre founds the Alianza Popular Revolucionaria Americana (APRA) from political exile in Mexico.

- **1941:** Peru enters a seven-week war over disputed border territories with Ecuador.

- **1955:** Women vote for the first time.

- **1963-1968:** President Fernando Belaúnde Terry begins land reform, heading a very unpopular administration.

- **1968:** Belaúnde is overthrown by socialist-leaning General Juan Velasco Alvarado.

- **1968-1980:** Twelve years of military dictatorship. Velasco nationalizes foreign-owned companies.

- **1970:** A 7.9 earthquake kills 70,000 in Áncash, including 18,000 covered by a landslide in Yungay.

- **1975:** General Francisco Morales Bermúdez, presumably supported by the CIA, overthrows Velasco Alvarado.

- **1980:** Belaúnde is reelected. Sendero Luminoso (Shining Path), a pro-Maoist terrorist organization, launches in Ayacucho a 20-year internal war that plunges Peru into violence and chaos.

- **1982-1983:** El Niño floods devastate northern Peru.

- **1985:** APRA candidate Alan García Pérez is elected president, pushing the country into hyperinflation and a downward economic spiral.

- **1985-1988:** The Accomarca massacre (1985); execution of 200 immates during prison riots in Lurigancho, El Frontón Island, and Santa Bárbara (1986); and Cayara massacre (1988) mark a period of constant human right violations under García's administration.

- **1990:** World-renown novelist Mario Vargas Llosa leads protests against García's intention of nationalizing the Peruvian bank system.

- **1990:** Outsider Alberto Fujimori defeats Vargas Llosa to become president of Peru. He applies a radical economic program tagged the "Fuji-shock."

- **1992:** Fujimori dissolves congress in his "self-coup." Shining Path bombs a building in middle-class Miraflores district. Abimael Guzmán, Shining Path's leader, is captured.

- **1993:** Peru's economy picks up and becomes the fastest-growing in the world.

- **1996-1997:** MRTA terrorist group assaults the Japanese ambassador's residence, taking 700 hostages, finally keeping 71 for four months. Peruvian military operation rescues all hostages but one, killing all MRTA members.

- **1998:** El Niño storms ravage the north coast.

- **2000:** Fujimori reelected president under allegations of electoral fraud. He leaves the country after scandal implications in extortion, corruption, and arms trafficking. Valentín Paniagua leads transition government.

- **2001:** Alejandro Toledo is elected president.

- **2003-2004:** Calls for Toledo's resignation heighten as Peru's largest union, the General Confederation of Workers, holds nationwide strikes.

- **2006:** Fujimori, en route to Peru to run for president, is detained and jailed in Chile with human rights violation charges. Alan García is reelected president.

- **2007:** An 8.0 earthquake hits the Ica region.

- **2009:** After being successfully extradited and taken to trial, Fujimori is sentenced to 25 years imprisonment.

all of the Americas were built in Peru. The most impressive example of monumental architecture during the Formative Period (2700–1000 B.C.) is Caral, considered the oldest city of the Americas. Situated 120 kilometers north of Lima, this complex urban center was built at the same time as similar ones in Egypt, Mesopotamia, India, and China. Radiocarbon dating of plant fibers indicate that Caral was built in 2627 B.C.—1,000 years before the Olmecs established settlements in Mesoamerica.

Excavations made from 1994 onward by Peruvian archaeologist Ruth Shady have unveiled 20 stone-built structures featuring six pyramids and many artifacts, including woven religious offerings known as *ojos de Dios,* "God's eyes." The varying sizes of the homes found suggest clear class distinctions within a hierarchical society, where religion was used as a means to ensure social cohesion and control. About 3,000 people probably lived in Caral at its height. Caral became a model for other religion-inspired urban centers in Peru.

CHAVÍN, THE UNIFIER

Considered the South American counterpart of China's Shang or Mesopotamia's Sumerian civilizations, Chavín flourished around 900 B.C. during the First or Early Horizon era (1000 B.C.–A.D. 200). Chavín managed to unite coastal, highland, and eastern lowland societies with its powerful religious ideology.

The Chavín built an elaborate stone temple at Chavín de Huántar, southeast of Huaraz, decorating it with finely carved stone sculptures and elaborate iconography. These figures depict their worship of a supreme feline deity—the jaguar—as well as other creatures such as snakes, caimans and natural spirits.

Chavín could have been an Andean oracle controlled by a powerful high-priest elite that relied on San Pedro cactus and other hallucinogens to interact with supernatural forces. This oracle presumably attracted thousands of travelers and pilgrims all the way from Ecuador in the north to the southern Andean region. The discovery of strombus shell trumpets and

the highly valued spondylus, which are only found off the coasts of Ecuador, strengthen this theory.

Despite being known for its brilliant and innovative metallurgists, builders, and strategists, Chavín's influence began to fade around 300 B.C. The influence, however, would resonate through Peru's civilizations for the next thousand years.

THE REGIONAL DEVELOPMENT

A variety of cultures sprang up to take the place of the Chavín. On the north coast, the **Moche** (220 B.C.–A.D. 600) began building the Huaca de la Luna, a stepped adobe pyramid south of present-day Trujillo. Highly militaristic and religious, the Moche spread throughout Peru's northern coast. They are best known for finely crafted metallurgy and ceramics, including artifacts recovered from the Lord of Sipán's intact tomb and the tomb of a tattooed priestess discovered at Huaca Cao Viejo in El Brujo, north of Trujillo.

On the south coast, the **Nasca** (100 B.C.–A.D. 700) began making elegant weavings from cotton and camelid fiber that are considered today the most advanced textiles produced in pre-Columbian America. Their complex cosmography is evident in the Nasca Lines, giant etchings in the desert floor that were likely once used for rain-inducing ceremonies. The Nasca also built Cahuachi, a large temple complex built around A.D. 100 that was probably a pilgrimage site.

In the southern Andean region, the **Tiahuanaco** (A.D. 200–1000) built an elaborate stone urban and ceremonial center on the southern shores of Lake Titicaca. They also developed a system of raised-bed farming that allowed them to cultivate crops despite the area's freezing temperatures. The perfect monumental architecture, witnessed at the Tiahuanaco archaeological site in present-day Bolivia, laid the base for Inca architecture nearly a thousand years later.

Though influences from the Chavín and Tiahuanaco had spread throughout Peru's highlands, the **Huari** culture (A.D. 600–1100) was the first in South America to establish a true empire. They also built the first well-populated cities, like their capital, Huari, north of Ayacucho. This capital covered nearly 300 hectares with aqueducts, warehouses, temples, and elaborate mausoleums for storing mummies. Archaeologists believe 70,000 people lived here comfortably.

Around A.D. 650 the Huari spread south toward the Tihuanaco culture near Lake Titicaca and Cusco, where they built the huge walled city of **Pikillacta.** The city spreads across 47 hectares of rolling grasslands and contains a maze of walled stone enclosures of the city and elaborate stone aqueducts. In the south, near Arequipa, the Huari built the remarkable stone fortress of **Cerro Baúi** atop a sheer-sided mesa. The Huari spread as far north as the edge of the Moche capital near present-day Trujillo and built a walled city near Huamachuco, in the highlands above Trujillo.

By the time the empire faded around A.D. 900, the Huari had left an indelible pattern of organization over Peru that would be repeated in larger scale by the Inca.

THE KINGDOMS OF THE LATE HORIZON

Once again, as happened after the Chavín culture, Peru splintered into various independent kingdoms after the fall of the Huari. The most important of these were spread along the coast and included the Chimú, Sicán, and Ica-Chincha cultures.

The **Chimú** built their mud city, Chan Chan, north of Trujillo and a short distance from the adobe stepped platforms built earlier by the Moche. Chan Chan is the largest city ever built by Peru's pre-Hispanic cultures, and its walled plazas, passageways, temples, and gardens spread over nearly 20 square kilometers. Over time, the kingdom would spread along the coast of Peru from Chancay, a valley north of Lima, to the present-day border with Ecuador.

As the Chimú were flourishing, other descendants of the Moche culture known as

the **Sicán** were building adobe pyramids at Batán Grande, farther north near Chiclayo. Discoveries of royal Sicán tombs there in 1991 revealed a wealth of gold masks, scepters, and ceremonial knives, along with elegant jewelry made from spondylus shell imported from Ecuador. After a devastating El Niño flood destroyed the center, the Sicán began building even larger pyramids a bit farther north at Túcume, which remains an enigmatic and largely unexcavated site today. By 1350, the Sicán culture was conquered by the Chimú.

Peru's south coast was dominated by the **Ica-Chincha** kingdom, which spread along Peru's southern desert valleys. This culture developed elaborate aqueducts for bringing water from the mountains under the desert floor. The ceremonial center of La Centinela, close to Chincha, was an adobe complex painted with sparkling white gypsum and decorated with ornamental friezes.

During this time, other cultures flourished throughout the highlands. The largest of these was the **Chachapoya,** a mysterious federation of city-states that spread across the cloud forests of northeastern Peru. The Chachapoya's most celebrated city is Kuélap, a stone citadel perched atop a sheer limestone bluff, but there are dozens of other major city sites.

Other cultures included the **Caxamarca** near present-day Cajamarca, the **Huanca** and **Chancas** in the central highlands, and the **Colla** and **Lupaca** near Lake Titicaca. One of these groups, almost too small to mention, was a diminutive tribe of highlanders in the Cusco area known as the **Inca.**

THE INCA EMPIRE

The Inca empire (referred to in Quechua as the Tahuantinsuyo, or "Four Corners") and its origins are obscured by myth. Historians believe that Manco Cápac, the first Inca leader, began his rule around A.D. 1200. For more than two centuries the Inca developed slowly in the Cusco area, until 1438, when the neighboring Chancas tribe threatened to overrun their city. Though Inca Viracocha fled the city, his son Inca Yupanqui beat back the Chancas, took over from his disgraced father, and changed his name to Pachacútec, the "Shaker of the Earth." He launched the meteoric rise of the Inca empire, which within a century would stretch for more than 4,000 kilometers from southern Chile to northern Ecuador and include huge chunks of Bolivia and Argentina as well. Pachacútec was also responsible for much of the Inca's monumental architecture, including the fortress of Sacsayhuamán and, in the Sacred Valley, Pisac and Ollantaytambo. Historians also believe he built Machu Picchu, which may have been a *llacta* or administrative center.

Though the Inca are known for their fine stonework, their greatest accomplishment was the organization of their empire. Cusco was actually smaller than other capitals of pre-Hispanic Peru, including Tiahuanaco, Huari, and Chan Chan. But the Inca imperial city was at the center of a paved road network that led throughout the empire. Inca runners known as *chasquis* would run along these roads carrying messages recorded in *quipus,* knotted bundles of string that store information. The *chasqui* would run at near-sprint speed until reaching a *tambo* or rest house, at which point a new Inca runner would continue. In this way, *quipus* recording harvests, weather, population data, and numerous other statistics could pass from Quito to Cusco in a few days.

As the Inca expanded they built a network of satellite centers that allowed them to support their far-flung conquests. Like most everything in the Inca world, these miniature cities were divided into *hanan* (upper) and *hurin* (lower) parts. The cookie-cutter pattern, which can be seen all over Peru, included one or two plazas; an *ushnu,* a stone-made platform where ceremonies took place; an *acllahuasi,* a compound for the chosen women of the Inca; a *kallanka,* a large hall; and *colcas,* or grain storehouses.

The Inca offered rich economic and cultural benefits to neighboring cultures that submitted peacefully to their rule. When the Ica and Chincha lordships were integrated into the empire, the Inca helped build a vast aqueduct near present-day Chincha that is still used. Though the Inca changed the names of places they conquered and encouraged the spread of their religion and language, they accepted a wide degree of cultural diversity. Spanish chroniclers such as Pedro Cieza de León were impressed with the tremendous variety of languages and native dress in Cusco at the time of the conquest. The Inca also behaved brutally to those who opposed them. After waging a long war against the Chachapoya, the Inca deported half the population to other parts of the empire as part of the forced-labor scheme known as *mita*.

Pachacútec's son and grandson, Túpac Yupanqui and Huayna Cápac, spent most of their lives abroad, extending the Inca empire to its farthest limits. Huayna Cápac, born in Tumipampa (present-day Cuenca, Ecuador) died in 1527 during a smallpox epidemic that devastated Peru's population and was probably spread by the Spaniards, who had set foot on the northernmost fringe of the Inca empire during a preliminary trip in 1526. His sudden death led to a devastating civil war between his two sons, Huáscar and Atahualpa, which had just ended when the Spaniards began their march from Tumbes.

SPANISH CONQUEST

Francisco Pizarro and his men rode through desert and into the Andes and found Atahualpa and an army of 80,000 Inca soldiers at Cajamarca. Atahualpa had just crushed the forces of his half-brother Huáscar and was returning, jubilant and victorious, to his home city of Quito.

The Spaniards invited Atahualpa to a meeting the next day in Cajamarca's square and planned a bold ambush. Firing their arquebuses and charging with their horses and lances, the Spaniards sparked a massive panic, killed at least 7,000 Inca soldiers, and took Atahualpa hostage. The Inca offered to pay a ransom that, when melted down six months later, amounted to an astounding 6,100 kilograms of 22-karat gold and 11,820 kilograms of good silver. The Spaniards executed Atahualpa anyway.

The Spaniards achieved their successes over far superior Inca forces not only because of their guns, dynamite, steel, and horses but also because Pizarro understood how to play Inca politics. After Atahualpa's death, the Spaniards befriended Manco Inca, another son of Huayna Cápac, and declared him the new leader of the Inca empire. Manco Inca did not remain a docile puppet for long, however, after the Spaniards sacked Cusco for all of its gold and raped the wives of Inca nobles. After the gold was gone, Francisco Pizarro left Cusco and headed for the coast to found Lima, which would soon become the capital of the newly declared Spanish Viceroyalty of Peru.

By 1536 Manco Inca had launched a rebellion and laid siege to Cusco with an estimated army of 100,000 soldiers. Against overwhelming odds, the Spaniards routed the Inca from their fortress of Sacsayhuamán during a week of constant fighting. Manco Inca repelled an army of Spaniards at Ollantaytambo in the Sacred Valley before retreating to the jungle of Vilcabamba. For the next 35 years, the Inca would use this jungle stronghold to continue their resistance against the Spaniards until the last Inca leader, Túpac Amaru, was captured and executed in 1572.

Just after the Inca rebellion, the Spaniards themselves erupted into civil war after differences arose between Francisco Pizarro and his junior partner, Diego de Almagro. After a series of bloody clashes, Pizarro's forces won out over the *almagrista* faction in 1538, and Pizarro shocked the king in Spain by executing Almagro. A few years later, Pizarro himself was murdered by a group of *almagristas* that included Almagro's son.

THREE CENTURIES OF VICEROYALTY

Cusco became a center of religious art during the viceroyalty but otherwise fell out of the spotlight after the conquest as the Spaniards turned their attention to mines. In a cynical use of Inca tradition for Spanish ends, Viceroy Francisco de Toledo in 1574 legalized the Inca's old labor scheme of *mita* in order to force huge numbers of Indians to work at the Potosí silver mine, in present-day Bolivia, and the Santa Bárbara mercury mine near Huancavelica. Far from home, thousands of Indians perished while working in virtual slavery at these mines.

Indians in other parts of Peru were not being treated much better. Some were forced to relocate to *reducciones* or new settlements that allowed the Spaniards to better tax the Indians and convert them to Christianity. Rich farmland was divided into *encomiendas* and all the Indians living on it became slaves to the Spanish owner, known as the *encomendero*. Other times Indians were herded into sweatshops (*obrajes*), where they made textiles and other objects for export under prisonlike conditions.

Given the abuse, it is not surprising that an uprising spread across Peru in the late 18th century. The leader of the 1780–1781 revolt was Túpac Amaru II, who claimed to be a direct descendant of the last Inca, Túpac Amaru. After a year-long rebellion, the Spaniards finished off Túpac Amaru II as they had his ancestor two centuries before: He was garroted in Cusco's main square, and then his body was ripped apart by teams of horses pulling in opposite directions.

INDEPENDENCE

After nearly three centuries of being administered from Spain, the native-born people of the Peruvian viceroyalty began to itch for independence. News of the American revolution in 1776 and French revolution in 1789 filtered to Peru and encouraged a groundswell of reform that was inspired by the European Enlightenment.

The descendants of Europeans born in Peru, known as *criollos,* were increasingly resentful of the privileges according to Spaniards, or *españoles,* who held all the powerful positions in the viceroyalty. Colonial society was rigidly classified into a hierarchy that attempted to make sense of, and control, the uncontrollable mixing between races in colonial Peru. The main categories included *mestizo* (European-Indian), *mulato* (European-African), *negro* (African), *zambo* (Indian-African), and *indio*

(Indian). Dozens of labels were applied to all the possible combinations and proportions of different ethnic mixtures, and some categories even included bizarre animal names such as *lobo* (wolf), which was used to describe certain types of *mulatos*. Despite the apparent rigidity, recent scholarly work has revealed that racial lines in the viceroyalty were surprisingly fluid and had more to do with wealth than skin color. Wealthy *mestizos* were usually considered *criollos*, for instance.

When Napoleon forced Spain's King Charles IV to abdicate in 1808, independence movements erupted across South America. By 1820, the last bastion of Spanish control was Peru, which for centuries had served as the main Spanish port and administrative center for South America. After liberating Chile, Argentine general José de San Martín routed the royalist forces from Lima in 1821 and proclaimed the symbolic independence of Peru. But he ceded control over the independence struggle to Venezuelan general Simón Bolívar, whose troops won two separate battles in Peru's central highlands in 1824 against the last strongholds of Spanish forces.

Bolívar envisioned a grand union of South American states known as Gran Colombia, which was modeled on the United States. After serving as Peru's first president for two years, he returned to Bogotá, Colombia, in a last-ditch attempt to hold the federation together. Bolívar's scheme fell apart as the former colonies bickered among themselves, and Peru plunged into a half century of chaos. During the four decades following Bolívar's departure, more than 35 presidents came and went.

Despite the chaos, Peru's rising class of merchants found new opportunities for making money besides mining. The biggest business was guano, the huge piles of bird droppings that covered the islands off Peru's coast. This natural fertilizer fetched exorbitant prices in Europe. The guano boom helped finance the ambitious project, spearheaded by American entrepreneur Henry Meiggs in 1870, to build a railroad line into the steep valleys above Lima to La Oroya mine. Following the abolishment of slavery in the mid-19th century, hacienda owners in the north began importing large numbers of Asian indentured workers, or coolies, to work on cotton and sugar plantations.

Despite all the abundance, Peru was devastated by the War of the Pacific against Chile (1879–1883), during which time Chilean armies sacked most of Peru's major cities. After surrendering, Peru was forced to cede an entire southern province to Chile—Tarapacá—which contained valuable fields of nitrate, used to make fertilizer. After the war, Peru plunged into bankruptcy and had to negotiate with its British creditors, who agreed to forgive the debt in exchange for 200 million tons of guano and a 66-year concession over the country's railroads. The British-owned Peruvian Corporation was set up in Arequipa in 1890 and built the current railroads that lead to Arequipa and Cusco. British families poured into Arequipa at this time to grab a share of the booming alpaca wool business. Following the completion of the Panama Canal in 1904, U.S. investors set up a series of mines and factories in Peru, including the Cerro de Pasco mine in the highlands above Lima.

THE 20TH CENTURY

As foreign investors increased their grip over Peru's main industries, worker dissent began to simmer following the October Revolution in Russia. In 1924, exiled political leader Víctor Raúl Haya de la Torre founded the Alianza Popular Revolucionaria Americana—APRA, a workers' party that continues to exert a tremendous influence over Peruvian politics. When Haya lost the 1931 elections, his supporters accused the government of fraud and attacked a military outpost in Trujillo, killing 10 soldiers. In response the Peruvian military trucked an estimated 1,000 APRA supporters out to the sands of Chan Chan and executed them in mass firing squads.

Peru's economic development in the mid-20th century was hampered by the hacienda system of land ownership inherited from the days of the viceroyalty. The independence movement had passed leadership from the *españoles* to the *criollos,* but otherwise Peru's economic structure remained the same—a minority of Peruvians, of direct European descent, still controlled the bulk of Peru's land and wealth. As Peru moved from an agricultural economy to an industrial one, campesinos flocked to Lima in search of a better life and built sprawling shantytowns, or *pueblos jóvenes,* around the city. Pressure for land reform began to grow.

Fernando Belaúnde, architect and politician, was president of Peru during much of the 1960s and instituted a few moderate reforms, but he was overthrown in 1968 by General Juan Velasco, who despite being a military man launched a series of radical, left-wing reforms that stunned Peru's white elite and transformed the Peruvian economy. He expropriated nearly all of Peru's haciendas and transferred the land to newly formed worker cooperatives. Velasco kicked foreign investors out of the country and nationalized their fish-meal factories, banks, oil companies, and mines. He introduced food subsidies for urban slum dwellers and, in a profound gesture of recognition to Peru's Indians, made Quechua the official second language of Peru.

Velasco's restructuring was so rapid and ill-planned that nearly all of Peru's major industries plunged to new lows and the country entered a severe economic crisis. Velasco was overthrown—some historians assure the CIA was behind the coup—and replaced by another pro-U.S. military leader, Francisco Morales Bermúdez, who attempted to control the economic chaos of the 1970s. Amid widespread strikes in the late 1970s, APRA politician Haya de la Torre headed a constituent assembly that finally secured full suffrage for all Peruvian citizens and the return to democracy.

TWENTY YEARS OF POLITICAL VIOLENCE

Peru's first full democratic election in 12 years, in 1980, coincided with the first actions of **Sendero Luminoso** (Shining Path), a terrorist group based on Maoist ideology that rose out of the country's economic chaos and social inequity. Shining Path rose alongside the smaller **Movimiento Revolucionario Túpac Amaru,** MRTA for short. Both organizations terrorized Peru's countryside over the next two decades and began receiving significant financial support from the cocaine business, which had just begun to grow rapidly in the upper Huallaga Valley.

Between 1980 and 2000, Andean villagers were frequently caught in the crossfire between these terrorist organizations and the Peruvian army. The Shining Path would force the villagers to give them food or supply information, and the army in retaliation would massacre the whole village, or vice versa. People in the city were largely uninterested and protected from the countryside war and were shocked to hear the official results of the Truth and Reconciliation Commission's report in 2003. More than 70,000 people were killed during the terrorism years, and 75 percent of them

© JORGE RIVEROS CAYO

a Shining Path terrorist, as depicted by art work in Arequipa's Museo de Arte Contemporáneo

were Quechua highlanders. Half were killed by Shining Path, a third by government forces (police and armed forces), and the rest are so far unattributed.

The worst massacres of the Shining Path were between 1983 and 1984, the same year that Latin American economies collapsed under a debt crisis and that Peru's north was devastated by El Niño rains. The APRA candidate, Alan García, at age 35, won the 1985 elections because he offered a jubilant, hopeful future for Peruvians. He promptly shocked the international finance community by announcing that Peru would only be making a small portion of its international debt payments. García's announcement sparked a two-year spending spree followed by Peru's worst economic collapse ever, with hyperinflation so extreme that restaurants were forced to increase their menu prices three times each day. Peru's struggling middle class saw their savings disappear overnight.

The García administration unsuccessfully sought a military solution to the growing terrorism, allegedly committing human rights violations that are still under investigation. The most important cases include the Accomarca massacre (1985), where 47 peasants were executed by the Peruvian armed forces; the Cayara massacre (1988) in which some 30 were killed and dozens disappeared; and the summary execution of around 200 inmates during prison riots in Lurigancho, El Frontón Island, and Santa Bárbara in 1986. An estimated 1,600 forced disappearances took place during García's presidency.

Peruvian novelist Mario Vargas Llosa led a series of middle- and upper-class protests against García's plan to nationalize Peru's banking system. Vargas Llosa appeared likely to win the 1990 election but was defeated at the last minute by Alberto Fujimori, a low-profile university rector of Japanese descent who appealed to Peru's mestizo and Indian voters mainly because he was not part of Lima's elitist white society. Former president García, meanwhile, fled Peru in 2002 under a cloud of allegations of extortion and corruption.

THE FUJIMORI REGIME

Soon after winning the elections, Fujimori reversed his campaign promises and implemented an economic austerity program that had been championed by his opponent, Vargas Llosa. His plan aimed to stimulate foreign investment by slashing trade tariffs and simplifying taxes. Fujimori also began the process of privatizing the state-owned companies that President Velasco had nationalized in the late 1960s–early 1970s. This program, which was nicknamed "Fuji-Shock," caused widespread misery among Peru's poor populations as food prices shot through the roof. Fortunately, the program also sparked an economic recovery. Inflation dropped from 7,650 percent in 1990 to 139 percent in 1991.

After struggling to convince Peru's congress to pass legislation in 1992, Fujimori strained international relations with the United States and other countries after he dissolved the congress in his famous *autogolpe* or "self-coup." That same year, Peru's level of terror reached a high point when Shining Path detonated two car bombs in Tarata street, right in the heart of the middle-class Miraflores neighborhood, killing 25 people and injuring more than 250.

That same year, Fujimori's popularity shot through the roof when the Peruvian military captured both Shining Path leader Abimael Guzmán and the main leaders of the MRTA. The economy began to pick up and, by 1993, was one of the fastest-growing in the world. Fujimori launched a new constitution and recovered international credibility by reopening Peru's congress.

Having tackled Peru's twin nightmares of terrorism and inflation, Fujimori was riding a wave of public support and easily beat former U.N. secretary-general Javier Pérez de Cuéllar in the 1995 elections. The following year, 14 MRTA terrorists led by Néstor Cerpa took 800 prominent hostages after storming a cocktail party at Lima's Japanese ambassador's residence. After releasing most of the hostages, the terrorists held 72 prisoners and maintained a tense standoff with the military for four months, until April 1997. As the situation grew desperate, Fujimori authorized Peruvian commandos to tunnel under the embassy and take it by surprise. The operation was an amazing success. One hostage died during the operation—of a heart attack—and one military commando was killed under fire. Except for human rights organizations, most Peruvians raised few objections to the fact that all 14 MRTA members were shot to death—including the ones who had surrendered.

Fujimori ran for a controversial third term in 2000, even though he himself had changed the constitution to allow presidents to run for only one reelection. Once again, Fujimori fell out of favor with the international community when he strong-armed his way into the elections against economist Alejandro Toledo. After alleging vote fraud in the main election, Toledo refused to run in the May 2000 runoff election, and the international community also threatened sanctions. Fujimori went ahead with the election anyway and was, despite the flawed process, elected president.

A huge scandal broke in September, when hundreds of videos were leaked to the media. The videos showed Fujimori's head of intelligence, Vladimiro Montesinos, bribing a huge cross-section of elite Peruvian society, including generals, journalists, politicians, and business executives. The resulting investigation uncovered more than *US$40 million* in bribes paid to subvert the three key institutions of democracy: the judiciary, the legislature, and the media.

Montesinos's grip on the media was so tight that he even held daily "news meetings" with their editors to formulate news headlines and decide which stories should be covered. In the judiciary branch, 21 top justices, including members of the Supreme Court, received bribes. Montesinos also bribed a range of politicians, even those within Fujimori's own party, for as much as US$10,000–20,000 per month. Others received cars or houses. To make matters worse, Peruvian investigators also concluded that both Fujimori and Montesinos amassed huge personal fortunes through extortion, arms trafficking, and the drug trade.

Fujimori conveniently resigned from the presidency, via fax, while on a state visit to Japan. Back in Peru, an international warrant for his arrest was issued because of his involvement in paramilitary massacres of leftwing political activists in the early 1990s. In 2005, when Fujimori left Japan to return to Peru and launch a campaign for the presidency, he was arrested in his stopover city of Santiago, Chile. He was held for six months in jail, on charges of corruption and human rights' violations, and was extradited to Peru. At the end of a 15-month trial, Fujimori was sentenced in April 2009 to 25 years in prison for ordering security forces to kill and kidnap civilians.

Montesinos was also arrested in Venezuela after being on the run for eight months and is in a high-security prison near Lima—one he helped design to house Peru's most feared criminals. About US$250 million in his funds have been recovered from bank accounts in the Cayman Islands, Panama, and Switzerland. Following Fujimori's departure, congressman Valentín Paniagua became interim president before Alejandro Toledo was elected in 2001.

RETURN TO DEMOCRACY

Toledo's political inexperience and lack of strong leadership caused his popularity to plunge among Peruvian voters, many of whom missed the dramatic results and bold programs of Fujimori. Strikes and civil unrest plagued the country in May 2003, which led Toledo to declare a temporary state of emergency to clear highways of protesters. After allegations of corruption, calls for Toledo to step down reached a fever pitch in early 2004. Peru's largest union, the General Confederation of Workers, held nationwide strikes in mid-2004, and thousands of coca farmers marched in Lima to demand an end to the U.S. sponsored eradication of their crops.

Toledo, however, did establish a stable and growing economy, which is precisely what newly elected President Alan García, with more charm and political experience than his predecessor, is out to maintain. García barely won the 2006 election against the populist Ollanta Humala, who was inspired if not financially supported by Venezuelan president Hugo Chávez. García's return to presidency was a result of "voting against" Ollanta, a turn of events not many Peruvians were happy with. Nevertheless, Peru's economic growth has favored him, despite the cases of corruption in his political party that have been exposed by the local media.

Government and Economy

GOVERNMENT

President Alan García, in office for a second time after serving as the nation's leader from 1985 to 1990, has continued to develop the political and economic policies of his predecessor Alejandro Toledo. The result has been a bursting economy and a relatively conservative but democratic and stable political atmosphere. This is quite a contrast to the authoritarian years of the Fujimori regime, 1990–2000.

Fujimori dissolved Peru's bicameral legislative system during his *autogolpe* in April 1992 and launched a new constitution with a single congress with 120 seats. Fujimori's new constitution allowed the president to run for two consecutive terms, a law that was changed after he resigned. In the current system, the president appoints a council of ministers, which is presided over by the prime minister. Apart from the president, Peruvian voters also elect two vice presidents. Voting is compulsory between the ages of 18 and 70, and those who do not vote can be fined. Members of the military were not allowed to vote in the past, but now they can.

The weak point of Peru's democracy is its judicial branch, which is rife with corruption. It is still common to read in the media about scandals involving judges who have been bribed to free prisoners or make a favorable ruling. The country's top courts include a 16-member supreme court and a constitutional tribunal. Each of Peru's regions also has a superior court that serves as a court of appeals for the lower courts. There is a huge backlog of cases in the Peruvian court system, and temporary courts have been set up.

During the Fujimori government, terrorist suspects were tried in secret military courts in order to protect judges from reprisals. Under such system, many were sent to jail with unfair trials. Under Toledo's government, some of these suspects have received new trials in civilian courts. The judicial branch is also currently prosecuting those accused of corruption under the Fujimori government. Nevertheless, the current administration controlled by the APRA party has also been under the spotlight due to cases of corruption within the government agencies. Additionally, people have accused García of shifting from his center-left ideological position to becoming a "neoliberal." The next presidential elections will take place in 2011.

ECONOMY

The investment-oriented reforms of the Fujimori years caused Peru to be one of the fastest-growing economies in the world between 1994 and 1997. Much of this growth was easy, however, because in many cases Peru's factories were simply returning to the level of production they had achieved before the chaotic 1980s.

Peru's stock market plummeted in early 1995 because of the "Tequila Effect" caused by Mexico's Zapatista revolution and the collapse of its economy. Peru's economy stagnated between 1998 and 2001 because of a variety of other factors, including the El Niño floods of 1998, global financial turmoil, and the collapse of the Fujimori government in 2001.

García maintained investment-friendly policies upon taking office in 2006, and Peru's economy continues to grow. In 2007, the predicted growth in the gross domestic product

© CAROLINE BOES

A typical elementary school classroom in Peru, such as this one in Ollantaytambo, has around 40 students per class.

(GDP) was 7.2 percent. This is up from 5.2 percent in 2002. The actual GDP hovers around $78.4 billion. García has continued to control the fiscal deficit; inflation, at 1.7 percent, is the lowest in South America, and Peru is second only to Chile, among South American countries, in the growth of its exportations. The key sectors of the Peruvian economy include manufacturing, agriculture, mining, retail services, and banking.

In the near term, foreign investment in mining, oil and gas, and tourism will play an important role in Peru's economy. Major players in the mining arena include the U.S.-owned Yanacocha gold mine in the Cajamarca area and the Canadian-owned Antamina mine southeast of Huaraz. The Camisea Gas Field Project, a $1.6 billion project led by U.S. and Argentine companies, is the major company pumping gas from the Amazon basin north of Cusco. A related $2 billion gas refinery has been built by the Kellogg Brown & Root unit of U.S.-owned Halliburton on the Peruvian coast near Paracas. President García, who is currently in negotiations with U.S.-based Hunt Oil and Brazilian PetroGas, is expected to encourage future oil growth.

More recently, the Inter-American Development Bank has estimated that Peru's GDP will grow 4 percent more than the rest of the world during 2010.

People and Culture

Even before the Spaniards arrived, Peru was covered by a patchwork of diverse cultures created by Peru's extreme geography. Valleys on the coast are separated by long stretches of barren desert. The canyons and peaks of the high Andes created such a degree of isolation that one anthropologist likened them to an archipelago. But the most culturally diverse area of Peru is the Amazon, where at least 65 different ethnic groups live today.

Peru's population, especially on the coast, is an exotic cocktail of world cultures that have

SACRED LEAF, WHITE GOLD

Peru continues to be the second-largest producer of cocaine worldwide, second only to neighboring Colombia. Peru's cocaine industry rakes in anywhere between US$300 and US$600 million per year in under-the-table money and employs an estimated 200,000 Peruvians, mainly in remote jungle areas of the country. And despite long-standing efforts of both the Peruvian government and the U.S. Drug Enforcement Agency (DEA), Peru's cocaine industry continues to grow. The 2009 report of the International Narcotics Control Board states that illicit coca bush cultivation increased in Peru for the third year in a row, especially in the Apurímac Valley area in southern Peru. In 2009, Peruvian authorities dismantled over 1,200 coca paste laboratories – the highest number since 2000 – and 19 laboratories manufacturing cocaine hydrochloride.

The truth is, coca – scientifically known as *Erythroxylum coca* – has not always been a curse for Peruvians. Probably best known in the world through cocaine, its most popular derived product, the plant has been used for thousands of years in the Andean world, mainly for its medicinal properties and religious significance. Archaeologists have found supplies of coca leaves in mummies 3,000 years old. The Moche might have been the first to chew the leaves, a custom spread widely afterwards by the Inca, who decided that planting coca should be a state monopoly, limiting the use of it to nobles. During the colonial period, Phillip II of Spain recognized the drug as an essential product for the wellbeing of the Andean inhabitants but urged missionaries to end its religious use.

Viewed as having a divine origin, coca has been an extremely important part of the religious cosmogony in the Andean world – from southern Colombia all the way down to northern Argentina and Chile – since pre-Hispanic times. Coca leaves play a crucial part in offerings made by shamans to the *apus* (mountain spirits), Inti (the sun god), and the Pachamama (mother earth). Leaves are also often read in a form of divination by *curanderos*, in similar ways to reading tea leaves in other cultures. They are also placed inside coffins at burials.

But coca is also used in various everyday activities. Men chew leaves as they work in the fields, and women use it to ease the pain while giving birth. When a young man is about to ask a woman to marry him, he first must present a bag of leaves to his future father-in-law. Coca leaves have been used for thousands of years as a stimulant to overcome fatigue, hunger, and thirst. Once you arrive at Cusco's airport, you will likely be greeted with a hot cup of *mate de coca,* an infusion made from the leaf, considered particularly effective against altitude sickness, known as *soroche*.

The effects of the coca leaf were discovered in Europe during the 19th century, when Albert Niemann (a promising PhD student of Friedrich Wöhler, one of the most celebrated chemists of the century) was able to isolate the active constituent of coca, which he baptized as "cocaine." But it was Paolo Mantegazza, an Italian doctor, who after experimenting with coca leaves in 1859 wrote, "one starts to become more and more isolated from the exterior world, and one is plunged into a consciousness

been mixing for nearly five centuries. The mixing of Peruvian culture began with the Inca's forced-labor scheme, *mita,* where rebellious tribes were moved to other parts of the empire where they would cause less trouble. The Spaniards continued *mita* and moved highlanders long distances to work in different mines.

The mixing between the Spanish and Peruvian cultures began the moment the conquistadores landed on the shores of Peru, giving rise to Peru's first mestizo population. The cocktail of racial mixes got richer when African slaves were imported to Peru during the viceroyalty. After slaves were freed in the mid-19th century, large numbers of Chinese and Japanese coolies were brought to work in plantations and on the railroad lines from 1850 to 1920. There were also waves of Italian

of blissful pleasure, feeling oneself animated with overabundant life." Angelo Mariani, a Corsican chemist who lived in Paris, saw coca's potential to make serious money, in 1863 making a wine with the coca leaves that he named Vin Mariani, a pleasant-tasting alcoholic brew with a real edge.

The success of the product inspired a number of wine imitations in the United States, including one that was converted into a carbonated soft drink known as Coca-Cola after the temperance movement hit Atlanta, Georgia, in 1885. By 1903 a public outcry over the ill effects of cocaine forced the company to remove cocaine from its beverage. What is not generally known is that Coca-Cola today continues to use flavoring from coca leaves, which have been "decocainized."

Making and taking cocaine today remains a nasty business. Villagers in the impoverished Huallaga Valley and other areas of Peru grow the plant because they can get as much as US$2 per kilo for the leaves, many times more than they would receive for selling wheat, potatoes, or corn. Cultivating coca takes a lot out of the soil, and fields therefore have to be changed constantly. The Huallaga Valley, once covered in cloud forest, is nearly denuded and covered with a patchwork of eroding fields.

The process of making cocaine is even worse. The leaves must first be crushed underfoot and soaked in water to remove their essence. This water is then mixed with kerosene and other toxic chemicals and stirred until a white substance floats to the top. This substance, known as *pasta básica* or *bruta,* is further refined to make pure cocaine, known officially as cocaine hydrochloride. About 400 kilograms of coca leaves produces one kilo of cocaine. The villagers who help stir the *pasta básica* can readily be identified by their scarred arms, which are burned pink by the toxic chemicals.

The cocaine industry has also wreaked havoc on Peru's cities. Though cocaine is widely available in Peru and used often by young Peruvians, the real problem lies in the dusty shantytowns, or *pueblos jóvenes,* on the outskirts of Lima. Because cocaine is too expensive, teenagers smoke cheap cigarettes made from the unrefined *pasta básica,* which is different from crack cocaine but equally as powerful. People become addicted immediately to the US$0.30 cigarettes, and, like crack smokers in the United States, their lives head downhill fast.

Experts say that the collapse of the Medellin and Calí cartels in the mid-1990s probably boosted Peru's cocaine business by fragmenting the industry and allowing players who were in the shadows to grab new market share. According to recent reports of the Peruvian army, one of the new leaders in the cocaine industry is the FARC, the Revolutionary Armed Forces of Colombia, which began cultivating coca in northern Peru near the Colombian border, and which is also behind a dramatic rise in Peru's cultivation of poppy, used to make opium and heroin. Remnants of the Shining Path, Peru's notorious terrorist group, which was crushed in the mid-1990s, are also reported to be involved in trafficking in the Apurímac Valley.

The Q'eros people, who live in the Cordillera Vilcanota outside of Cusco, are struggling to maintain the ancient ways of the Inca despite contact with tourism.

and Palestinian immigrants, and a pocket of German and Austrian colonists established themselves in the jungle at Oxapampa, in the Chanchamayo area. From the 1960s onward, huge waves of immigrants from the Andes settled in the shantytowns around Lima, especially during the height of Shining Path terrorism during the 1980s.

DEMOGRAPHICS

Peru's population today is around 28 million and growing about 1.6 percent each year. Nearly half the people, or 45 percent, are of indigenous blood and reside in the Peruvian highlands. Of the remaining population, 37 percent are mestizo and 15 percent are of European descent. The remaining 3 percent of the population comprises those of African, Japanese, and Chinese descent and also includes a tiny pocket of 250,000 Amazon natives who are divided into 65 ethnic groups. There remains a cultural and economic divide, passed down from colonial times, between the upper class of European descent and the middle

and lower classes of mestizos and Indians. But Peru's racial dividing lines have, even since the colonial times, been based more on economics than skin color. Marriage certificates from the 18th century, for instance, reveal that affluent mestizos were automatically considered *criollos* because of their wealth. In the same way, a full-blooded Indian in today's society goes from being an *indio* to a mestizo the moment he or she abandons native dress and puts on western clothing.

During Peru's economic growth of the mid-1990s the average wages of Peruvians also increased. The Fujimori government built new schools throughout Peru's impoverished regions, and the illiteracy rate has dropped below 10 percent (though it is still about 13 percent for women). Medical care also spread, dropping infant mortality rates from 57 per 1,000 births in 1991 to 31 in 2006. An estimated 98 percent of all infants in Peru now receive immunizations.

Despite these advances, Peru remains a crushingly poor country. More than half of

Peru's population, or 51 percent, live beneath the poverty line of US$54 per month, and 24 percent live in extreme poverty, earning under US$32 per month. Nearly 40 percent of the people live in the informal economy—that is, they live in isolated country hamlets or disenfranchised city slums and eke out a living outside of government taxes and services.

LANGUAGE

Peru's official language is Spanish, though about four million people in Peru's highland population speak Quechua, the language of the Inca, also known as *runa simi*. Among Quechua speakers, there is a huge range of variations depending where they are located. These mini dialects have grown as a result of the isolating effects of Peru's extreme geography. In the Lake Titicaca area, there is a smaller group of Peruvians who speak Aymara, the language of an ethnic group that spreads into Bolivia. In the Amazon lives 11 percent of Peru's population, divided into 65 ethnic groups and about 14 linguistic families.

RELIGION

The Spanish conquest dotted Peru with magnificent cathedrals, a plethora of churches, and a long-lasting and also certainly conflictive relationship with **Catholicism.** About 90 percent of the current population consider themselves Catholic. Although that number is far from the actual number of practicing parishioners, it does indicate the connection Peruvians feel toward the religion, more by tradition than by real practice. Festivals like Lima's day of Santa Rosa mean a citywide holiday, and the day of San Blas invites horns and processions in Cusco.

Catholicism, though, is a relatively recent addition to Peru's long list of religions. Peru's first civilization began around 2000 B.C., and it, along with the country's other major civilizations, was based on a set of unifying religious beliefs. These beliefs often incorporated **nature worship.** Deities like the sun, the ocean, the mountains, and mother earth appear in the imagery of several successive cultures. Representations of serpents, felines, and birds also make repeated appearances in pre-Hispanic religious iconography. Serpents symbolize the ground, felines the human life, and birds (often in the form of eagles) the air or gods. The religion of the **Chavín** culture, which existed 4000 years ago, incorporated that series of deities. Northern Peru's **Moche** culture did as well, but, unlike the Chavín, the Moche were clear to distinguish between the spiritual world and the everyday world. The **Chimú** worshipped the sun, moon, and ocean, and were clear to separate the secular and nonsecular worlds. In its pottery, the southern Nasca culture depicted felines, orcas, anthropomorphized birds, and serpentine creatures. And the **Inca** gave offerings to the surrounding mountains, the bright sun, and fortifying Pachamama, the mother earth.

In these pre-Hispanic cultures, there was also a strong tie between religion and medicine or religion and hallucinogenic experiences, which were usually performed for their curative

A *curandero*, or healer, prepares to make a *despacho*, or spiritual offering.

© FIONA CAMERON

properties. In the north, cultures like the Moche and the Chimú used *curanderos,* natural healers, to treat the "sicknesses of the gods," and in the southern Inca culture as well as the jungle **shamans** used a combination of natural herbs, chants, and calling to cure both physical and mental maladies. Often it was in these curative ceremonies that the *curanderos* or shamans used hallucinogens like the **San Pedro cactus** and **ayahuasca.** The drugs were meant to clear the vision of the ceremony participants.

As cultures rose and fell, and even when the Spanish conquered the Inca empire, Peru's religions tended to adapt, fluctuate, and blend. The Inca were known for allowing their conquered cultures to continue their own religious practices as long as they also followed Inca religion. When the Spanish arrived and imposed Catholicism, the Inca quietly integrated their imagery. A grand Last Supper painting in Cusco's cathedral shows Jesus eating a guinea pig.

Nearly 500 years after the Spanish conquest, this fusion of religious beliefs continues to define Peru's spiritual and religious customs, and the subject is a draw for many tourists. In areas like Cusco and Lake Titicaca, the traditional mountain cultures continue to use **shamans** to bless their homes and purify their spirits. In turn, travelers contract with shamans to perform offering or cleansing ceremonies. The Sacred Valley is known for its **energy centers,** and people come from around the world to meditate there. In the jungle, ayahuasca is an essential part of sacred ceremonies and again, curious travelers can contract with experts to help them experience it.

On the flip side, completely new religions are making headway. **Protestant groups, Jehovah's Witnesses, Mormons,** and **Adventist groups** have started small but vigilant communities throughout the country. If history holds true, these new groups should blend with the old to offer an increasingly diverse religious practice.

FOOD

One thing Peruvians are undeniably proud of is their food. Peru's biodiversity offers the country with a generous and varied amount of

© JORGE RIVEROS CAYO

Peru's world-famous cocktail is the pisco sour, a blend of lime juice, pisco, egg white, sugarcane syrup, and bitters.

fresh ingredients. These include a range of seafood, sweet corn, *ajíes* (peppers) and tubers—of the 3,000 varieties of potatoes documented in Peru, only 40 are eaten—exotic fruits, succulent river fish, palm hearts, and wild game.

The Spanish conquest of Peru brought together two great culinary cultures of the 16th century: the Mediterranean cooking techniques and the Andean ingredients. When Pizarro's men landed in Peru, they had their first taste of corn, tomatoes, avocados, potatoes, peanuts, alpaca meat, and blistering *ají* peppers. The Spaniards brought olive oil, lime, and garlic to the table and shortly thereafter created a local supply of lamb, beef, pork, wheat, rice, and sugar.

Things got even more complex with the arrival of Africans and North African Arabs during the viceroyalty, Chinese coolies in the mid-19th century, and successive waves of Italian and Japanese immigrants. Such a succulent mix in the pot created a bewildering range of dishes and entire subsets of Peruvian cuisine, such as *chifa,* a mixture of Cantonese and local *criollo* cooking.

Peruvian cuisine is still evolving and is difficult to classify into pat categories. Because Peruvian cooks work only with ingredients at hand, there do tend to be styles of Peruvian cooking separated by geography. Here are some highlights you should not miss.

Peru's coast is known for *comida criolla* or creole cuisine, which is based mainly on a huge range of seafood, including *corvina* (sea bass), *lenguado* (sole), *cangrejo* (crab), *camarones* (freshwater shrimp), *calamar* (squid), *choros* (mussels), and *conchas negras* (black scallops).

One of the more famous dishes is *cebiche*: chunks of raw fish marinated in lime juice, spiced with *ají*, and served with sliced red onions, slices of sweet potato, and *choclo* (boiled maize kernels) or *cancha* (roasted maize kernels). A delicious variation of *cebiche* is *tiradito*, which can be easily explained as a fish carpaccio topped with a *ají* and *rocoto* sauce over the cuts. Fish fillets can be served in a variety of ways, including *sudado* (steamed), *a la chorillana* (basted with onion, tomato, and white wine) or *a lo macho* (fried with yellow peppers or *ají amarillo*).

Other *comida criolla* favorites are *anticuchos*, grilled beef-heart brochettes served with a wonderful assortment of spicy sauces. *Papa rellena* is mashed potato stuffed with meat, vegetables, onions, olives, boiled eggs, and raisins and then fried. *Papa a la Huancaína* is a cold appetizer of potatoes smothered in a spicy sauce made from Andean cheese, milk, crackers, and *ají amarillo*. Another popular dish of Asian influence (some say now that it actually has French influence) is the richly-flavored *lomo saltado*, made with strips of beef stir-fried with tomatoes, onions, *ají amarillo*, and fries made of (preferably but not only) yellow potato. This dish can be found, literally, in any corner of Peru.

Sopa a la criolla is a cream soup made up of a mildly spicy concoction of noodles, beef, milk, and peppers with a fried egg on top. If you are in the mood for *chifa*, which you can have anywhere in Peru, try *tallarín saltado*, which is noodles spiced with ginger, soy sauce, green onions, bok choy, and any kind of meat, including beef or chicken or shrimp, depending on what kind you order. To drink, try a pitcher of *chicha morada*, a delicious juice made from purple corn mixed with clove, cinnamon, and lime juice.

Arequipa is well known for its robust, generous, and spicy food. *Chupe de camarones* is a cream-based soup with potatoes, milk, eggs, and lima beans, and laden with succulent sea shrimp. *Rocoto relleno* is another emblematic dish consisting of a a bell pepper–like chili, stuffed with meat, chopped onions, raisins, and black olives and then baked with a cheese topping. *Ocopa* is made of a spicy peanut sauce with *huacatay* (black mint) served over slices of boiled potatoes and garnished with eggs and black olives.

In the north, between Trujillo and Piura, some specialties are *seco de cabrito*, which is roasted goat marinated with *chicha de jora*, corn beer, and coriander, served with rice, and *arroz con pato*, which is duck stewed in black beer with spices and coriander, served with green rice.

Peru's Andean cuisine stands out for a range of meats, *choclos*, high-altitude grains such as *kiwicha* and quinoa, and a huge variety of more than 200 edible tubers, including potatoes, freeze-dried *chuño* (actually dehydrated potatoes), and tubers like *olluco* and oca. The high point of mountain cooking is *pachamanca*, which means "earth oven" in Quechua and consists of a variety of meats, tubers, corn, beans, and native herbs roasted underground with red-hot rocks. Andean restaurants often serve *trucha*, which is fried mountain trout, and *cuy* (guinea pig), either roasted (in Cusco), stewed (in Huaraz), or fried (in Arequipa).

Soups and broths are widely consumed in the highlands at any time of the day but especially during the early morning. Lamb, beef, hen, or certain parts of these animals are all good to make a tasty broth. For vegetarians a good option is *sopa de quinua*, made with potatoes and quinoa grains. Lastly, make sure to sample *choclo con queso*, which is an ear of steamed corn with a strip of Andean cheese. Gulp it all down with *chicha de jora*, corn beer that can be *fresco* (fresh) or fermented.

In the Amazon jungle, you will have a whole new type of cuisine to sample. At the top of the list are the roasted fillets of succulent jungle fish, including *paiche, doncella,* and *dorado. Patarashca* is fish fillets wrapped in banana leaves and seasoned with spices before being baked over coals. There is also *paca* fish steamed inside a bamboo tube. Iquitos is famous for *juanes,* a rice tamale stuffed with spices, chicken, and rice. A common game meat is *majá,* also called *picuro,* which is a medium-sized rodent that can be grilled, stewed, or fried.

If you tried *chicha* in the highlands, you have to try *masato* in the jungle, which is an alcoholic drink made from fermented yuca. Most of the jungle dishes are garnished with palm heart, which is often cut into piles of paper-thin ribbons, or *plátanos verdes* (green plantains).

Did we mention dessert? On the coast, you can try *suspiro a la limeña,* a sweet custard topped with meringue and vanilla, and *mazamorra morada,* a purple pudding made from corn and potato flour mixed with clove, cinnamon, and fresh fruit. Peru's exotic fruits make incredible desserts with flavors that can be shocking to a North American or European palate. *Lúcuma,* or eggfruit, is a small fruit with a dark peach color and a rich, smoky flavor, often made into pies or ice creams, as is *maracuyá* (passionfruit). *Chirimoya* (custard apple) is so exquisitely sweet that it is often served on its own as *chirimoya alegre.* Other delicious fruits such as granadilla (another type of passionfruit), *guayaba* (guava), tuna (prickly pear fruit from cacti), and *guanábana* are made into delicious juices—or try a few slices of papaya sprinkled with lime juice and powdered cinnamon.

MUSIC AND DANCE

Traditional Peruvian music can be easily divided between *música criolla,* music from the coast, and *música folklórica,* known as music from the mountains and the jungle. The best-known example of the latter is Simon & Garfunkel's 1970s hit "El Cóndor Pasa (If I Could)," arranged from an original song composed by **Daniel Alomía Robles** in 1913.

The *huayno* is the most popular dance form in Andean music. It originated in Peru as a combination of traditional rural folk music and popular urban dance music. High-pitched vocals are usually accompanied by a variety of instruments, including the *quena* (Andean flute), *charango* (a small mandolin), harp, saxophone, and percussion. In the last few decades *huayno* has undergone a huge change with the introduction of electronic instruments, including synthesizers and electric guitars. Nevertheless, the dance form utilizes a distinctive rhythm in which the first beat is stressed, followed by two short beats. The *huayno* is pop music for an audience of millions of listeners across the Andes. Despite constant evolution, its themes remain the pain of love lost and being far from home.

Andean music sounds different from Western music in part because it relies mainly on the pentatonic scale instead of the diatonic scale. The instruments include different types of *quenas, zampoñas* (double-row panpipes including the *sicus,* which can be as tall as the musician playing it), *tarkas* (squared flutes that produce an eerie sound), and *antaras* (single-row panpipes). There is also a huge range of rattles, bells, and drums, such as the *tambor* and *bombo,* which are made from stretched animal skins. Most of these instruments, as excavations prove, have been used at least 5,000 years.

In the last five centuries Peru's highlanders have incorporated a range of wind and brass instruments, including clarinets, saxophones, trumpets, euphoniums, and tubas. But the most important European contributions were stringed instruments like the violin, the guitar, and the harp, which was transformed into the Andean harp. This instrument looks like a western harp with 36 strings but has a half-conical, boatlike base that gives it a rich, deep sound. The 10-stringed *charango* is about the size of a mandolin and is made from wood or the shell of an armadillo.

Music evolved in a whole new way on Peru's coast, where African slaves were brought from western Africa over three centuries to work on

© MYLENE D'AURIOL, PROMPERU

Festival masks, such as this one from Paucartambo, are a complex fusion of Inca and Spanish influences.

Victoria Santa Cruz, Susana Baca, Eva Ayllón, and more recently **Novalima,** a band from Lima that blends Afro-Peruvian rhythms with electronic sounds. Novalima's second and third albums, *Afro* and *Coba Coba,* can be bought online from Amazon.

There is a wide range of percussive instruments used in Afro-Peruvian music. These include several types of drums, the rattling jawbone of a burro (known as a *quijada*), and a wooden box that is drummed with the hands (known as a *cajón*), among others.

The term *música criolla* refers directly to music played and danced by the *criollos.* The *vals,* which was inspired by the Viennese waltz, and the *marinera,* a very elegant dance from Lima and the northern coast similar to the Chilean *cueca,* both have unmistakable influences from Afro-Peruvian music as well. Major artists in this field include **Eva Ayllón** and **Chabuca Granda,** author of the popular *La flor de la canela.*

In these last 40 years, Peruvian music has evolved rapidly. In the late 1960s and 1970s, the traditional *huayno* fused with the tropical *cumbia.* As a result, *chicha* was born, the iconic music of highland immigrants living in Lima, having in **Chacalón y la Nueva Crema** the maximum exponent of this genre. Around the same period of time, hundreds of rock-based bands in the jungle were turning to *cumbia,* either *tropical* or *psicodélica.* Legendary bands such as **Juaneco y su Combo** and **Los Mirlos** have been revived in U.S. and European compilations and through local bands in Lima, such as **Bareto.**

HANDICRAFTS

A stroll through any of Miraflores's handicrafts markets will show you the depth and variety of handicrafts in Peru. Weavings, knittings, pottery, jewelry, and carved gourds have made the long haul from the provinces into Lima. Each piece is modern but carries with it a tradition that has existed for centuries.

World-renowned for its textiles, Peru's **weaving** tradition is over 4,000 years old. Using the wool of alpacas, llamas, and the

sugarcane and cotton plantations. Nowadays the Afro-Peruvian population—though small compared to that of other South American countries such as Colombia or Brazil—continues to exert a huge influence on Peru's music, food, and sports. The slaves brought with them African rhythms and combined them with Spanish and Andean music to create *festejo* and the *landó.* Dance forms sprung up alongside the music, including *zapateo*—a form of tap dancing—and *zamacueca.* In one frenetic dance known as El Alcatraz, women shake their hips furiously to avoid having their skirts lit on fire by men holding candles behind them.

The area of Afro-Peruvian music expands from Lima all the way south to the small town of El Carmen, including Mala, Cañete and Chincha. But it was in El Carmen where a renaissance began in the 1970s, mainly due to the **Ballumbrosio** family, which made Afro-Peruvian music famous around the world. Outstanding performers of this genre include

© JORGE RIVEROS CAYO

Peruvian woven baskets, such as this one from the Amazon, are made from natural fibers.

precious vicuñas, the pre-Columbian cultures wove their stories into textiles. Abstract figures, deities, and colors described the lifestyles of these people, who had no written language. In turn, the quality of the textile and the wool reflected one's social status and power. When the Spanish arrived, they introduced sheep's wool and silk into the custom. Now, contemporary weavers have the advantages of machine-spun yarn and even woven fabrics. While those are undeniably used, there are still plenty of traditional weavers who continue to use natural dyes, drop spindles, and handmade looms.

The weaving culture exists primarily in the mountainous regions of Cusco, Huancayo, and around Lake Titicaca. In these areas, you are likely to see women walking through the streets, toting a basket of wool that they are aptly dropping and spinning into yarn. Guided by memory and years of experience, women then dip the wool into dyes and then thread it into a weaving. The start-to-finish process can take anywhere from a month to several months and, consequently, the minimum going price for a cloth is about US$100.

Knitting is another important aspect of Peru's textile tradition. *Chullos* (hats), *mangas* (arm warmers), *polainas* (leggings), *medias* (socks), and *monederos* (change purses), are all typical products of the Quechua and Aymara cultures. As with weaving, the most prominent knitting cultures live in Lake Titicaca's Isla Taquile, Cusco, and Huancavelica. Although customs change between communities, knitting responsibilities are typically divided between men and women. Women spin the yarn and men knit it into clothing, most often hats.

Ceramics have also played an important historical role. Cultures as ancient as the Chavín left behind ceramic remains, and even later cultures like the Moche, Nasca, and Chimú were renowned for their craftsmanship and unique styles. The **Moche** perfected the skill of capturing human features and emotion; the **Chimú** pottery is recognized for its black surface; and **Nasca** ceramics are particularly prized because of their intricate paintings. When the Spanish arrived, they introduced a European form of pottery, which has been particularly influential in the designs of Urubamba-based ceramicist **Pablo Seminario.** Ceramics are best seen in the areas of Piura, Cusco, and Ayacucho.

Other important handicrafts, like carved gourds, jewelry, and even instrument-making, are best seen in the mountain areas. Again, Cusco, Ayacucho, and Huancayo make excellent bases to begin your exploring.

LITERATURE

Like the Greeks, the ancient Peruvians had a rich tradition of oral **poetry,** as there were no known writing systems at the time. It consisted of two main poetic forms: *harawis,* a form of lyrical poetry, and *hayllis,* a form of epic poetry. Both forms described the daily life and rituals of the time and were recited by a poet known as the *harawec.*

A variety of 16th-century Spanish chroniclers, most notably **Bernabé Cobo** and **Pedro Cieza de León,** attempted to describe the exotic conditions of the New World through the confining looking glass of the Spanish world-view and lexicon. An entirely different perspective was presented by indigenous writer **Felipe Guamán Poma de Ayala,** whose decision to write the king of Spain, Philip III, blossomed into a 1,179-page letter titled *Nueva Crónica y Buen Gobierno.* The letter was written between 1613 and 1615 but only discovered in the Royal Library of Copenhagen in 1908. Apart from a detailed view of Inca customs, what is most fascinating about this work is the blend of Spanish and Quechua juxtaposed with a series of 400 ink drawings that portray the bloodiest moments of the Spanish conquest, as well as Inca festivities and traditions.

Inca Garcilaso de la Vega (1539–1616) was educated in Cusco as the son of a Spanish conquistador and an Inca princess. He emigrated as a young man to Spain, where he spent the rest of his life writing histories and chronicles of his Inca homeland. His major work, *Comentarios Reales,* written in 1609, is a highly anecdotal and personal view of the Inca empire. Throughout the text Garcilaso employs a variety of rhetorical strategies to ennoble the Inca aristocracy—and in the process, himself—in the eyes of the royal Spanish court. It is the first example of a mestizo author from the New World grappling with the complexities of a torn identity.

During the viceroyalty, **theaters** in Lima and Cusco were at the center of the social life of the Peruvian aristocracy. Most of the productions were imported and written by Spain's Golden Age authors, who had no problem being approved by Peru's Catholic censors. Local playwrights were occasionally approved and their works, though innocuous on the surface, often contain subtle critiques of the viceroyalty's racial and political power structure. Scathing **poetic satire** was circulated secretly throughout upper-class Peruvian society and reflected the growing tensions as Peru's creole elite strained against the straitjacket of Spanish rule.

Following the 1821 independence, literary Romanticism took root in Peru, evolving in an entirely different direction from its European counterpart. Instead of a preoccupation with personal identity and freedom, Peru's Romantic writers fell into the task of nation-building and describing what it meant to be Peruvian. Some renowned authors of the period were **Carlos Augusto Salaverry** and **José Arnaldo Márquez.** At the same time, *Costumbrismo* developed as a literary or pictorial interpretation of local everyday life, mannerisms, and customs. Peru's best-known writer of this style is **Ricardo Palma** (1833–1919), whose most famous work is a descriptive collection of legends and personality sketches known as *Tradiciones peruanas.* Palma was a man of letters, a former liberal politician, and later the director of the National Library of Peru; he rebuilt the collection after it was sacked by the Chilean army during the War of the Pacific.

Peru's best-known female writer is **Clorinda Matto de Turner** (1852–1909), born in Cusco, who wrote both in Quechua and Spanish. She edited a series of acclaimed literary journals, including *Peru Ilustrado,* and wrote a trilogy of novels, the best known of which is *Aves sin nido* (*Torn from the Nest*), translated into English in 1904 and republished recently by Oxford Press and the University of Texas Press. Matto de Turner was forced into exile in Argentina after being excommunicated by the Catholic church and having her house burnt down. She died in 1909 and was forgotten for decades, though she is slowly gathering critical acclaim and recognition as one of the pioneers of Latin American feminism.

César Vallejo (1892–1938), poet, writer and journalist, is considered one of the great poetic innovators of the 20th century. His main works include *Los Heraldos Negros* (1918), the revolutionary *Trilce* (1922), and *Poemas Humanos* (published posthumously in 1939). Always a step ahead of the literary currents, each of Vallejo's books was distinct from the others and, in its own sense, revolutionary. Born in Santiago de Chuco in Peru's northern highlands, he moved to Paris in the 1920s, where he spent the rest of his life immersed in the vanguard movement and the rise of international communism. His complete poetry has been published in English by the University of California Press.

The growing industrialization of Peru in the 20th century and the continued oppression of the Indian population gave birth to a new genre of socially conscious literature known as *indigenismo*. **José María Arguedas** (1911–1969) was born to a white family but was raised by a Quechuan-speaking family in Andahuaylas, in Peru's southern Andes. He ended up in Lima, where he was educated at the prestigious University of San Marcos. His works of social realism portray the oppression of Indian communities and helped inspire the liberation theologies that continue to cause conflict in Peru's Catholic church. Two of his most famous novels, *Yawar Fiesta* and *Los Ríos Profundos* (Deep Rivers), are in English and have been published by the University of Texas Press.

Ciro Alegría (1909–1967) was a mestizo born in the Marañón Valley of northern Peru whose lyrical novels, like those of Arguedas, portray the suffering of Peru's Andean peoples. His best-known works are *La Serpiente de Oro* (*The Golden Serpent*) and *El Mundo Es Ancho y Ajeno* (*Broad and Alien Is the World*), which became widely known outside Peru in the mid-20th century and were translated into several languages.

Mario Vargas Llosa (born 1936) is one of Latin America's most significant novelists and essayists, and one of the leading authors of his generation. Some critics consider him to have had a larger international impact and worldwide audience than any other writer of the "Latin American Boom" of the 1960s. Latin America's boom writers dropped the regionalist, folkloric themes of their predecessors and experimented wildly with form and content. Nearly all of Vargos Llosa's novels, including his world-acclaimed *Conversación en la catedral* (*Conversation in the Cathedral*), *La guerra del fin del mundo* (*The War of the End of the World*), and *La fiesta del chivo* (*The Feast of the Goat*), have been translated into English and make an excellent introduction for those wishing to explore Peruvian literature. Once a supporter of Castro and communism during his youth,

Vargas Llosa led a middle- and upper-class revolt against President Alan García Pérez in the late 1980s and then ran for president in 1990. After being defeated by Alberto Fujimori, Vargas Llosa went to Spain. Nowadays he lives back in Lima's Barranco neighborhood and is actively involved in Peruvian politics and social issues. A prolific writer and columnist in newspapers around the world, Vargas Llosa is a die-hard defender of neo-liberalism and unquestionably a seeker of freedom through his writing.

Alfredo Bryce Echenique (born 1939) is Peru's other best-known novelist. He has produced a dozen novels and numerous collections of short stories. After spending much of his life in Europe, he now resides in Peru.

Several middle-aged and young Peruvians are making waves on the international literary scene. **Alonso Cueto** and **Santiago Roncagliolo** both won international prizes for their 2006 novels, *The Blue Hour* and *Red April,* respectively. The works deal with Peru's history of terrorism and war. More recently, **Daniel Alarcón** (born 1977), a promising Peruvian-born writer raised in the U.S., has published *War by Candlelight* and *Lost City Radio,* his debut novel.

SPORTS AND RECREATION

Peruvians go wild about *fútbol* or soccer, which is the main social activity in small towns across Peru. Matches, such as a *clásico* between Alianza Lima and Universitario de Deportes ("La U"), will fill stadiums throughout the year in major cities across Peru. Cienciano, an underdog team from Cusco, made world news when it defeated huge, internationally acclaimed teams such as River Plate in Argentina and Santos of Brazil—Pele's old team. In December 2003 Cienciano became the first Peruvian team ever to win the coveted Copa Sudamericana.

Despite the general lack of financial support from the Peruvian government to sports, surfing and, more recently, boxing have made headlines in recent years due to the world championships obtained. Kids in Lima and other parts of coastal Peru often grow up surfing, and it is no surprise that several Peruvians are among the world's top-ranked international surfers.

Volleyball is also a quite popular sport, especially among the female crowd. The Peruvian women's team was one of the dominant forces in the 1980s, culminating in the silver medal won at the Seoul 1988 Olympics. **Paragliding** has always been popular in Lima, where thermals rise along the ocean cliffs and allow hours of aerial acrobatics. Other adventure sports such as **rafting, kayaking, mountain biking, trekking,** and especially **mountain climbing** have lured a generation of young Peruvians who often make a living working as guides for foreigners.

Bullfighting is a long-running and nowadays controversial tradition that can be traced back to Peru's colonial days. Lima's bullfighting season begins with the Señor de los Milagros (Lord of the Miracles) religious festival in October. Limeños and fans in general pack the city's main bull ring, the historic **Plaza de Acho,** to see the Sunday-afternoon contests featuring internationally acclaimed bullfighters from Peru and Spain. Bullfighting is a standard part of many festivals celebrated in Peru's highland towns, despite animal rights organizations that have increasingly questioned and opposed this centuries-old tradition.

ESSENTIALS

Getting There

The most common way to arrive to Peru is by plane. That means you will fly into Lima and then, in all likelihood, wait for a plane to Cusco or another city. Because of flight patterns, most visitors end up spending at least a half day in Lima—so plan on spending some time there. It's a big and bustling city, and we recommend visiting at the end of a Peru trip once you have learned to navigate a smaller Peruvian city, such as Cusco. Though Lima takes some getting used to, Peru veterans linger in Lima for its food, unique cultural mix, museums, art scene—did we mention food?

AIR

Because Peru lies in the same time zone as the East Coast of the United States and Canada, North American travelers feel no jet lag after arriving in Peru. Depending on where you are flying from in North America, the flight can be anywhere from 6 to 10 hours, and many people fly in the evening in order to catch early-morning flights on to Cusco. The cheapest tickets to Lima in high season start around US$590 from Fort Lauderdale through Spirit, and around US$500 from Miami through American.

Most Europeans find it cheaper to travel to Peru via flights with stopovers in the United

HASSLE-FREE ROUTES INTO ECUADOR

Most travelers heading up the coast for Ecuador make the crossing on the coastal highway at **Aguas Verdes,** a dirty, loud town of vendors, border guards, and rip-off artists. This crossing has become easier as relations between Peru and Ecuador have simmered down thanks to the **Itamaraty Peace Treaty** signed in 1988 by both countries in Brazil. Passengers still have to disembark at least twice to get passports stamped on each side, but the process now takes less than one hour.

The easiest way to cross the border here and avoid the hassle of Aguas Verdes is to use a bus line, such as Ormeño or Cruz del Sur. These buses stop at the Peruvian immigration office (9 A.M.–noon and 2–5 P.M. daily), located three kilometers before Aguas Verdes. Then the buses roll through Aguas Verdes and military checkpoints at the bridge before stopping at the Ecuadorian immigrations office (8 A.M.–1 P.M. and 2–6 P.M. daily) in the border town of **Huaquillas.** The process is possible, but complicated, to do by a combination of taxis and walking. Watch your belongings. Remember too that Ecuadorian time is one hour behind Peruvian time.

But for a more scenic and a less hectic crossing, try the **La Tina-Macará** crossing, where Peruvian and Ecuadorian immigration offices have the same hours as those at the Aguas Verdes–Huaquillas crossing. The asphalted, though rough, road winds through carob, kapok, and mango trees, but the journey can be hot, so travel with water. Direct buses leave from Piura in the morning and arrive by evening in the Ecuadorian mountain town of Loja.

The best of these companies is Transportes Loja. It is also possible to catch *colectivos* to the border from Sullana, a town along the way. There is no good lodging in La Tina so, if you get stuck at the border, try to stay in Macará, Ecuador. The best place to stay in this pleasant, laid-back town is the **Hotel Paradero Turístico** (tel. 07/694-099, US$9 d), which is about 500 meters before the town on the road leading from the border. The international telephone code for Ecuador is 593.

Finally, there is the **Jaén-Loja** crossing, the option for the truly adventurous cross-country traveler who is looking for a break from the Gringo Trail and a shortcut between Chachapoyas and Ecuador's Vilcabamba. This two- or three-day trip involves lots of mountain scenery, and travelers who have done it say it's not nearly as difficult as it looks. This crossing starts in Jaén, a pleasant town with great lodging and restaurants, where you take a US$3 *combi* for the three-hour, 104-kilometer trip to San Ignacio. From there, take another US$3.50 *combi* for 44 kilometers to Namballe, then you cross Río Calvas.

Once in the Ecuadorian town of La Balsa on the other side, catch a *combi* to nearby Zumba, where lots of buses run to Loja. Travelers say the route is safe, with decent lodging options and very friendly, inquisitive people along the way. With an early start, travelers can go from Jaén to Zumba in one day, and then Zumba to Loja in another.

States or the Caribbean, though there are direct flights from Madrid and Amsterdam. The cheapest flights from major European cities start around US$1,000. Travelers from Asia, Africa, New Zealand, and Australia will also need to make at least one layover en route to Lima.

The most expensive times to fly to Peru are the Christmas vacations and the high tourist months from June to August. Prices begin to drop around May and September and are at their lowest during the shoulder seasons from October to December and January to April.

Lima Airport

All overseas flights from Europe and North America arrive in Lima at **Jorge Chávez International Airport** (tel. 01/511-6055 24-hour flight info, www.lap.com.pe). From here flights continue on to Cusco and other cities. Most planes from overseas arrive in the middle of the night, and flights to Cusco begin from about 5 A.M. onward. Some travelers wait in the airport for connecting flights, while the majority head to Miraflores, San Isidro, Barranco, or even Lima's historic center, where there is a good selection of hotels.

If you'd rather stay in the airport area overnight, the **Costa del Sol-Ramada** (Av. Elmer Faucett s/n, Aeropuerto Internacional Jorge Chávez, tel. 01/711-2000, www.costadelsolperu.com, US$250 s, US$265 d with buffet breakfast included) has a good restaurant, sushi bar, and all imaginable amenities. The hotel is literally right across the taxi lanes in the airport.

On the return, most flights from Cusco arrive here midday and leave for the U.S. at night—so many visitors have at least a half day in Lima.

Jorge Chávez has come a long way and is actually a pretty modern airport. It has a range of services, including banks, money exchange booths, ATMs, a post office, stores, café, two food courts, duty-free shops, a rent-a-cell service, and a recommended Quattro D ice cream shop with playground, among other services. There is even the **Sumaq VIP Lounge,** voted as the Lounge of the Year 2009 by Priority Pass. If you want to store your luggage, go to **Left Luggage** (tel. 01/517-3217, at the side of Domestic Arrivals, US$1.25 per piece of luggage per hour, US$7.5 per piece of luggage per 24 hours).

Pushy taxi drivers will be waiting for you outside the airport. The best thing to do is contract a taxi through **Taxi Green** (tel. 01/9826-7148), a private company that has stands just outside luggage claim. Have your destination address written down. Taxi prices from the airport to the center should be around US$12, to Miraflores about US$15. You may be able to get a cheaper taxi if you negotiate with a driver in the airport parking lot, but be sure to know where you are going. Hard-core budget travelers will walk outside the gate of the airport and save a few dollars by taking a taxi, *combi,* or *colectivo* on the street. Be very careful with your luggage if you do this!

There is a US$6.82 tax on all domestic flights leaving Lima and a US$31 tax on all departing international flights. Both taxes can be paid in either U.S. or Peruvian currency, according to the exchange rate of the day, which is normally posted outside the cashier's window. On your way home, arrive at the airport 2–3 hours in advance for international flights and 1–2 hours for domestic flights.

Velasco Astete International Airport in Cusco has flights arriving from Santa Cruz and La Paz, Bolivia, with **Aerosur** (www.aerosur.com), and **Benigno Ballón Farfán International Airport** in Arequipa has flights from Arica, Chile, with **Sky Airline** (www.skyairline.cl).

Cheap Fares

The best way to get a cheap fare to Peru is to travel outside the high season months of June through August. Within Peru's three-month high season, it will be difficult to find a discount fare to Peru and onward to Cusco and other main destinations.

The easiest way to start a search for airfare is to use an airfare price comparison website like **Kayak** (www.kayak.com), which compiles the best prices from hundreds of sources, including online travel engines like Travelocity, Expedia, CheapTickets, and Orbitz. Other options include **FareChase** (www.farechase.com), **SideStep** (www.sidestep.com), **Mobissimo** (www.mobissimo.com), and **Bookingbuddy** (www.bookingbuddy.com).

A slightly more difficult option is to find an agency with consolidator fares. Consolidators commit to selling huge blocks of tickets for airlines in exchange for preferred bulk rates. Most consolidators do not deal with the public, so the best way to get your hands on consolidated tickets is to call an agency that works with a consolidator. You can find one of these agencies by typing "Peru consolidator" or similar keywords into Google.

Consolidators sell out their cheap tickets early, especially during Peru's high season, so purchase well in advance. Be careful of fraud with online airline consolidator agencies. Before you purchase, call and make sure the company is legitimate. Always use a credit card so that you can protest a charge, if necessary.

Students and teachers can buy discounted airfare from **STA Travel** (www.sta.com). This web page links to STA representatives in nearly 75 countries and has a search engine for cheap fares. Students under 26 can purchase a US$22 student ISIC card that entitles them to trip insurance, student airfares, and a range of discounts for everything from bus fare to museum admission. Student discounts are very common in Peru—get this card if at all possible.

From North America

Direct flights from Miami are available, on a daily basis, through **LAN** (www.lan.com) and **American Airlines** (www.aa.com). Airlines with flights from Miami with one layover to Lima include **Avianca** (www.avianca.com), with a stop in Bogotá, Colombia; **Copa** (www.copaair.com), with a stop in Panama City, Panama; and **Taca** (www.taca.com), with a stop in San José, Costa Rica.

From Fort Lauderdale direct flights are available on **Spirit Airlines** (www.spiritair.com), from Los Angeles and New York on LAN, from Dallas–Fort Worth on American, from Houston and Newark on **Continental** (www.continental.com), and from Atlanta through **Delta** (www.delta.com).

From Toronto **Air Canada** (www.aircanada.com) offers direct flights to Lima.

Recommended U.S. agencies that deal with a number of consolidators include **World Class Travel** (U.S. tel. 800/771-3100, www.peruperu.com), **eXito Latin American Travel Specialists** (U.S. tel. 800/665-4053, www.exitotravel.com), and **Big Sky Travel** (tel. 800/284-9809, info@bigskytvl.com).

There are also several courier companies from the United States from which travelers may be able to find even cheaper fares in exchange for carrying packages to and from Peru. These fares come with heavy restrictions on flying times and luggage limits. The bigger companies are **Air Courier.org** (U.S. tel. 877/303-4258, www.aircourier.org) and **International Association of Air Travel Couriers** (U.S. tel. 515/292-2458, www.courier.org).

From Mexico, Central America, and the Caribbean

Direct flights from Mexico City are available through **Aeromexico** (www.aeromexico.com). Taca, Copa, Avianca, and other airlines operate a range of direct and layover Lima flights from Cancún, Mexico; Santo Domingo, Dominican Republic; La Havana, Cuba; Panama City, Panama; San José, Costa Rica; and San Salvador, El Salvador.

From Europe

The only direct flights to Lima from Europe are from Amsterdam through **KLM** (www.klm.com), and from Madrid though LAN, **Iberia** (www.iberia.com), and **Air Europa** (www.aireuropa.com). Carriers that make one stopover en route to Lima also include LAN, American, Delta, and Continental.

In the United Kingdom, good consolidators include **North-South Travel** (U.K. tel. 01245/608291, www.northsouthtravel.co.uk), which gives part of its proceeds to an international development trust it has set up. Others include **Travel Bag** (U.K. tel. 0800/804-8911, www.travelbag.co.uk) and **Quest Travel** (U.K. tel. 0871/423-0135, www.questtravel.com). **Flight Centre International** (U.K. tel. 0870/499-0040, www.flightcentre.co.uk) is good for tickets between the United Kingdom and the United States only.

From France, good consolidators include **Last Minute** (France tel. 0899/78-5000, www.fr.lastminute.com), **Nouvelles Frontiéres** (France tel. 0825/00-0747, www.nouvelles-frontieres.fr), and **Voyageurs de Monde** (France tel. 0892/23-5656, www.vdm.com).

From Germany, a good option is **Last Minute** (Germany tel. 01805/77-7257, www.de.lastminute.com) or **Just Travel** (Germany tel. 089/747-3330, www.justtravel.de). In the Netherlands, try **Airfair** (Netherlands tel. 0900/771-7717, www.airfair.nl), and in Spain, there is **Barcelo Viajes** (Spain tel. 902/116-226, www.barceloviajes.com).

From Asia, Africa, and the Pacific

From Asia there are no direct flights at this time to Lima. All flights from Hong Kong, Tokyo, and other Asian cities first stop in the United States. Good Asian consolidators include **Japan's No 1 Travel** (Japan tel. 03/3200-8977, www.no1-travel.com), Hong Kong's **Four Seas Tours** (Hong Kong tel. 2200-7777, www.fourseastravel.com), and India's **STIC Travels** (India tel. 79/2642-3518, www.stictravel.com).

From New Zealand and Australia, flights usually have stopovers in Los Angeles or Miami, or in Santiago or Buenos Aires, before heading to Lima. A good agency for flights to the United States is **Flight Centre International** (tel. 0870/499-0040, www. flightcentre.co.uk).

From Africa, travelers to Lima head to Europe first, though **South African Airways** (South Africa tel. 0861/359-722, www.fly-saa.com) has a flight from Johannesburg to São Paolo, Brazil. A good African agency is **Rennies Travel** (South Africa tel. 0861/100-155, www.renniestravel.com).

Within South America

More than a dozen South American cities have daily flights through **LAN** and **Taca,** to and from Lima, the regional hub for both airlines. Taca flies from/to Quayaquil and Quito in Ecuador; Bogotá, Cali, and Medellín in Colombia; Caracas in Venezuela; La Paz and Santa Cruz in Bolivia; Montevideo in Uruguay; Santiago in Chile; Buenos Aires in Argentina; São Paulo and Rio de Janeiro in Brazil. LAN also flies to/from Lima to all cities mentioned for TACA. **Aerolineas Argentinas** (www.aerolineas.com) flies from Buenos Aires. **Avianca** (www.avianca.com) flies from Bogotá, and **TAM** (www.tam.com.br) from Rio de Janeiro.

BUS

It is possible to reach Peru by international bus service from the surrounding countries of Paraguay, Uruguay, Ecuador, Bolivia, Chile, Brazil, and Argentina. The major buses that run these routes can be quite comfortable, with reclining seats, movies, and meals. The longest international bus trips leave from Lima. Some major neighboring cities from which buses travel to Lima are: Santa Cruz in Bolivia, Asunción in Paraguay, Córdoba and Buenos Aires in Argentina, Montevideo in Uruguay, São Paulo and Rio de Janeiro in Brazil, and Santiago in Chile. Buses leave frequently from/ to La Paz, Bolivia, for the five-hour direct journey to/from Puno and on to Cusco. The main international bus companies are **Cruz del Sur** (Lima tel. 01/311-5050, www.cruzdelsur.com. pe), **Ormeño** (Lima tel. 01/472-1710, www. grupo-ormeno.com), **Caracol** (tel. 01/431-1400, www.perucaracol.com), and **El Rápido** (Lima tel. 01/425-1066, www.elrapidoint.com.ar).

BOAT

Some shipping lines offer regular departures from the United States or Europe to Lima's port of Callao. Some cruises include Peru in their itineraries, arriving in Callao or Pisco. **Mediterranean Cruises** (www.royal-olympic-cruises.com), departing from San Francisco, and **Affordable Cruises** (www.affordable-cruisesweb.com) are some reputable companies to check out.

A variety of vessels, ranging from banana boats to luxury cruisers, chug up the Amazon River. **Golfinho** (Raimondi 350, tel. 065/22-5118, US$54 one-way) goes to the Peruvian-Brazilian-Colombian border every other day.

Getting Around

Peru's diverse landscape includes long stretches of desert, high Andean passes, and endless tracts of swampy jungle. Not surprisingly, Peru can be a complicated country to navigate. Nearly all of Peru's major jungle destinations require a flight unless you want to spend a few days on a cargo boat or one day, sometimes three, riding in a bumpy bus. Train service is limited, except in the Cusco area, but new highways have made traveling by bus much faster and more comfortable than it was a decade ago.

AIR

If you are on a tight schedule and want to see a range of places, flying is the best way to go. In Peru, a round-trip fare can be less expensive than one-way, but that depends on the season and the airline. The best way to buy tickets or reconfirm them is through the airline's local office or website, where you can buy tickets online for almost all domestic flights. Finding tickets around Christmas, Easter, and the national holiday of Fiestas Patrias in the last weekend of July is expensive and difficult.

The major Peru airlines are **LAN** (www. lan.com); **Star Perú** (www.starperu.com), **Peruvian Airlines** (www.peruvianairlines.pe), and **LC Busre** (www.lcbusre.com.pe).

BUS

Because most Peruvians travel by bus, the country has an incredible network of frequent, high-quality buses—much better, in fact, than in the U.S. or Europe. You will be safer if you avoid the dirt-cheap bus companies that pick up passengers along the way. Some of these buses have been adapted (stretched) to the point where they are structurally unsound.

Bus companies in Peru have a confusing variety of labels for their deluxe services, which include Imperial, Royal Class, Cruzero, Ejecutivo, Especial, and Dorado. The absolute best services, comparable to traveling business class on an airplane, are Cruz del Sur's Cruzero or Cruzero Suite class and Movil's better service 180° Bus-Cama class, which unfortunately only serves Huaraz. Deluxe bus service means nonstop (only for driver shifts), more legroom, reclining seats, onboard food and beverage service, videos, safe drivers, and clean bathrooms.

Reputable bus companies in Lima are **Cruz del Sur** (Lima tel. 01/311-5050, www.cruzdel-sur.com.pe), **Ormeño** (tel. 01/472-1710, www.grupo-ormeno.com), **Movil Tours** (tel. 01/332-9000, www.moviltours.com.pe), and **Oltursa** (tel. 01/225-4499, www.oltursa.com.pe).

Bus travel is easier in cities like Arequipa, Puno, and Cusco, where all the bus companies are consolidated in a main bus station, which is usually known as the *terminal terrestre*. Travelers can arrive there, shop around, and usually be on a bus in an hour or two. In other cities, such as Lima, each bus company has its own bus terminal, some even with VIP lounges, and travelers can save time by buying a ticket through an agency or at a Wong or Metro supermarket through **Teleticket.**

Luggage theft can still be a problem for bus travelers, especially for those who travel on the cheap bus lines. Always keep your hand on your luggage at a bus station. Once on the bus, the luggage that is checked underneath is usually safe because passengers can only retrieve bags with a ticket. The big problem is carry-on luggage. Place it on a rack where you can see it. Some people bring oversized locks to chain their luggage to a rack, but thieves will just razor through your bag and take what they want.

Assaults on night buses are still a problem in Peru, especially on less expensive buses. Highway bandits either hold the bus up by force or sometimes board as normal passengers and hijack it en route. Passengers are not hurt, but are shaken down for their money and passports. Though some companies use a camcorder to film all passengers getting on board, no company can eliminate the risk entirely.

TRAIN

The decade-long monopoly enjoyed by Orient-Express–owned **PeruRail** (www.perurail.com) is finally breaking up. New entrants into the market to provide train service from Cusco to Machu Picchu include **Machu Picchu Train,** owned by Andean Railways (www.machupic-chutrain.com) and **Inca Rail** (www.incarail.com). Check the websites for expected competitive fares, fancier coaches, and better service.

During high season, it is best to reserve tickets online ahead of time to travel to Machu Picchu. Buying tickets once you arrive in Cusco is a hassle, but many of Cusco's nicer hotels will purchase them for their guests. PeruRail and Inca Rail have online ticket purchase. There are several classes of services to Machu Picchu with a tremendous variance in price; Inca Rail is a bit cheaper.

The world's second-highest railway runs from Lima to Huancayo through the Central Andes at a high elevation point of 4,751 meters. The service is managed by **Ferrocarril Central Andino** (www.fcca.com.pe) with two different types of service. Tickets can be bought online. Departures are about once or twice per month for this 12-hour ride with stunning views.

Because of a new highway between Arequipa and Puno, passenger trains run on a charter-only basis between these two cities. PeruRail also operates trains from Cusco to Puno.

COMBIS AND COLECTIVOS

The cheapest way to move around a major city like Lima, Cusco, Iquitos, Trujillo, Arequipa, or Chiclayo is by public transportation. There are buses, *combis* (imported Asian vans that dart along the roads), and *colectivos* (station wagons with room for five passengers). The buses are cheap but slow, *combis* are a bit faster but tend to be very cramped, and *colectivos* are the fastest of all.

Bus fares usually hover around US$0.40–0.60; *colectivos* are about twice that, but fares go up on weekends and evenings. You can tell where buses and *combis* are going by the sticker on the front windshield, *not* by what is painted on the side. Before you take public transportation, ask a local for specific directions to where you are going. It can be a fun, inexpensive way to travel around. To get off a bus or *colectivo* simply say *"baja"* ("getting off") or *"esquina"* ("at the corner"). Fares are collected during the ride or right before you get off, by the *cobrador* or the man (seldom a woman) who also shouts out the route or destination the bus or *combi* is leading to, practically hanging out the bus door.

TAXI

The fastest but still not too expensive way to get around Peru's cities is via taxi or *mo-tocar,* the three-wheeled canopied bikes that buzz around cities in the jungle and the coast (not Lima, though). The typical fare for in-city travel is US$0.40–1 for a *motocar* and US$1.50–5 for a taxi.

Assaults on taxi passengers can be a problem in Cusco, Lima, and Peru's other tourist hot spots. The best way to avoid this is to have your hostel call for a taxi or to flag down only registered taxis on the street. Avoid young, suspicious-looking drivers and beat-up cars with tinted windows and broken door handles. When traveling, sit on the backseat diagonally opposite the driver's.

Bargaining is an essential skill for anyone taking a taxi, because taxis in Peru do not use meters. Know approximately what the fare should be and stand somewhere where your taxi driver can pull over without holding up traffic. Always negotiate the fare before getting in the car. A typical bargaining conversation would start with you asking *"¿Cuánto cuesta a Barranco?"* (or wherever you're going); the taxi driver replies, *"Ocho soles."* You bargain with, *"No, seis pues,"* and so on. You get the picture. If you can't get the fare you want, wave the driver on and wait for the next taxi. Have in mind that rates can rise during rush hours and the evenings.

Private drivers can also be hired for the hour or day, or for a long-distance trip. The fee can often start at US$7 per hour and go up to US$60–70 for all day. Ask at your hotel for recommended drivers.

© SERGIO SCHABELMAN

villagers on the Tahuayo River returning from a Sunday market on a river taxi

RENTING A CAR OR MOTORCYCLE

Renting a car does not usually make sense cost-wise in Peru because taking taxis or hiring a private car can be cheaper. Also, gas is expensive (about US$4–5 per gallon, depending on the grade), and distances between cities are considerable. Your best bet is to get to your destination and then rent a car to get around.

The phone book of any major Peruvian city is filled with rental car options, which are usually around US$70 per day once you factor in extra mileage, insurance, and other hidden costs. Four-wheel-drive cars are usually US$100–120 per day. Major rental companies include **Hertz** (www.inkasrac.com), **Avis** (www.avisperu.com), and **Budget** (www.budgetperu.com). All these companies have offices in Jorge Chávez International Airport, Lima, Arequipa, and Cusco. Smaller companies operate in many other cities. To rent a car, drivers usually need to be at least 18 years of age, have a driver's license from their country, and have a credit card.

BUYING A CAR

Second-hand cars can be purchased for low prices in **Tacna,** the duty-free port that supplies the country with Asian imports. If you are staying in Peru for more than a month and have a traveling companion or two, this may not be much more expensive than taking high-quality buses. Traveling along Peru's remote dirt roads with a four-wheel-drive vehicle is an exhilarating, wild experience.

Peru's highway system is much better than it was a decade ago, though gasoline is expensive and the road hazards are extreme. They include open manhole covers, herds of sheep or llamas, and rocks that have either rolled from the cliffs or been left by drivers after working on their cars. Night is even more dangerous, with speeding buses and slow-moving trucks. Gas stations are far apart, and the only option on dirt roads is low-quality fuel siphoned from a rusting steel drum. So fill up frequently and consider carrying spare gallons of gasoline. Drivers should also be prepared with spare tires, tools, food, water, and sleeping bags.

Speeding or running yellow lights is a bad idea, as police will certainly pull you over, especially in Lima and other big cities. Because you are a foreigner, some police officers will threaten jail time and thousands of dollars in fines and loads of paperwork, right before hauling you off to the *comisaría* (police station). Many drivers pay just to move along, while others adamantly refuse. It's up to you if you pay or not, but if money is requested we strongly recommend against bribing, and especially do not offer a bribe on your own initiative. You might not get away with it, being a foreigner. Women police officers have a reputation of being quite tough to deal with, being tagged as *las incorruptibles,* "the incorruptibles." In general terms, the problem of crooked police is less common now than in the past.

A Peru driver's worst nightmare is getting in an accident. The general rule is *quien pega, paga* (whoever hits, pays), but foreigners are going to be hard-pressed to get any money off a Peruvian taxi or truck driver. The best way to protect yourself, if you have a car worth anything, is to buy **car insurance** (about US$15 per day or US$35–70 per month depending on the car). Even now that many cars in Peru are insured, it's usually less of a hassle to resolve the situation by both drivers heading together to a mechanic to get a repair estimate. In the case of a serious accident, let the courts decide whose fault it was or you will end up paying for everyone's damage and medical bills.

U.S. and European licenses are valid for one month in Peru, and thereafter **international driving licenses,** available in the United States from **AAA** (www.aaa.com), are required. Drivers should also have the car's registration and their passports with them at all times or police will offer to *llevarle a la comisaría* (haul you down to the police station).

BOAT

There is no better way to experience Peru's Amazon than sitting in a hammock and watching the jungle go by. This experience is easy to

river boat on the Amazon carrying cargo and passengers between Iquitos and Pucallpa

have on an Amazon cargo boat, which offer bathrooms, plenty of deck space to sling a hammock, and kitchens that serve palatable meals. You need to be flexible on time, however, because boats wait until they are filled with cargo and rarely depart on the day they say they will.

The most popular routes start from **Yurimaguas** or **Pucallpa** and float toward **Iquitos** on chocolate-colored, torpid rivers. An even longer and more adventurous option is the **Río Urubamba** from **Quillabamba** all the way to Pucallpa. This journey includes incredible stretches of jungle and passes through the **Pongo de Mainique**, an infamous whitewater gorge that cuts through the Vilcabamba mountain range.

It is much faster to head downstream, and some routes become dangerous during high-water months between January and June. Some rivers are unsafe due to drug trafficking or conflicts with native groups. These include the **Río Huallaga** above Tarapoto, the **Río Marañón** from Bagua to where it joins with the Río Huallaga, and any of the small rivers around Chanchamayo that drain into the **Río Urubamba.** Because of its big rapids, the **Río Apurímac** can also be dangerous. Raft it only with a skilled guide.

A more upscale option in the Iquitos area is a deluxe river cruise. These comfortable journeys will take you down the Amazon River toward Brazil or into the Reserva Nacional Pacaya Samiria.

The preferred mode of local travel in the jungle is by **dugout canoe** or *peke-peke*, a name that perfectly describes the sound of the boat's engine. These boats, also used in parts of Asia, have a long propeller shaft that can be lifted out of the water for maneuvering or avoiding obstacles.

Boats also ply the waters of **Lake Titicaca,** which are inspected and carry life jackets for everyone. The captain even carries a cell phone for emergencies. Other boat options in Peru include **deep-sea fishing boats** that can be contracted in places like Órganos and Punta Sal on the north coast, though there is no transport service along Peru's Pacific coast.

BIKE

Biking is a great way to explore Peru's back roads and get to know local people along the way. Many of Peru's adventure agencies, especially those that offer rafting trips, rent **mountain bikes** starting at US$15 per day and up, though quality varies tremendously and the bikes are generally meant for local use only. Adventure agencies in Lima, Arequipa, Huaraz, Cusco, and Puno offer multiday bike expeditions with tents, a support vehicle, and a cook. These trips follow fabulous single-track routes up and over the mountains with mind-boggling descents on the other side.

Dozens of cyclists pass through Peru each year, during their epic Alaska–Patagonia pilgrimage. Those who want to start their tour from Peru will have to box their bike up and fly it with them, as good bicycles are extremely expensive in Peru. Some airlines provide a box in which your bike will fit once you take the handlebars off. If your bike is or looks new, smear mud on it so you can get through customs without having to pay duty taxes. Most people use mountain bikes to travel on dirt roads, often with slicks for road and highway travel.

When planning your route, keep in mind that the Pan-American Highway (Carretera Panamericana) is a dangerous bike route because buses pass at high speeds and the shoulder is cluttered with debris. The same applies for major routes into the mountains, including the Cañon de Pato near Huaraz. The best trips are on remote back roads, which are invariably spectacular and much safer. Keep in mind altitude, weather extremes, drinking water, and the complete lack of repair parts outside of major cities.

Good sources of information include the Adventure Cycling Association in the United States (www.adventurecycling.org) and the loads of trip journals from people who have biked in Peru, which can be found at www.geocities.com/thetropics/island/6810/. One of Peru's best known bikers, **Omar Zarzar Casis** (www.aventurarse.com), has written a book in Spanish, called *Por los camino de Perú en* *bicicleta,* describing 10 of Peru's most beautiful mountain-bike circuits, available in many Peruvian bookstores.

HITCHHIKING

People in Peru are not afraid to flag down whatever transport happens to pass by, and drivers usually charge them a bit of money for gas. Instead of sticking a thumb up, Peruvians in the countryside swish a handkerchief up and down in front of them to attract drivers' attention. We think hitchhiking is fairly safe on country roads where there are no other options. When near cities or large highways, though, always take buses. If you hitchhike, do it with a companion, and make sure your driver is sober before getting in.

TOURS

Organized tour groups are a good idea for travelers leery of traveling on their own or who long for a hassle-free, action-packed tour. A range of excellent, though often expensive agencies operate in Peru and offer anything from general tours with a bit of soft adventure to well-tailored adventures for trekkers, climbers, birdwatchers, spiritual seekers, or just about any other group.

With the right company, tours can be safe and enlightening, and a great way to make new friends. Common complaints include a lack of flexibility on meals and lodging options, a go-go schedule that allows no time for relaxation, and a large up-front payment.

Before booking, read the fine print and ask a lot of questions. Find out what hotels you are staying in and then check them with this book. Look for hidden expenses like airport transfers, meals, and single rooms if you are traveling alone. Find out who your guide will be and what his or her experience and language skills are. Ask about the size of the group, the average age of the other passengers, and the cancellation policy. Get everything in writing and add up what all the costs would be using this book. Peru is a relatively inexpensive place to travel in and you may be able to do it cheaper on your own.

hiking on a remote tributary of the Río Azul, just outside the Manu Biosphere Reserve

© JOSHUA PAUL

Day-Tour Operators

Because of all the public transport in Peru, independent travelers can usually find their way even to the country's most remote sites, if they don't mind waiting around for an hour or two, walking, and sometimes hitchhiking.

No one likes to be in a group of obvious tourists, but taking a day tour is the fastest, easiest, and sometimes cheapest way to see a given area's sights, like taking a group taxi. In most cities, tour agencies are clustered together on the main square or along a principal street. Before paying, confirm how good your guide's English is and get tour details confirmed in writing, including sites visited, how many people maximum will be in the group, and whether the cost includes lunch and admission fees. If your guide does a good job, make sure to give him or her a reasonable tip.

Package Tours

Package tours typically include airfare, hotels, and some meals—but you choose what to do and where to eat. Many Peru-bound airlines offer package tours, including **American Airlines Vacations** (tel. 800/321-2121, www. aavacations.com), **Delta Vacations** (tel. 800/654-6559, www.deltavacations.com), and Continental **Airlines Vacations** (tel. 800/301-3800, www.covacations.com, operated by Solar Tours). The web page of the **United States Tour Operators Association** (www.ustoa. com) has a search engine to find package tours and specialty tour operators.

Many of the package operators are based in Miami, including **Analie Tours** (tel. 800/811-6027, www.analietours.com), which offers rock-bottom prices. To get these rates, however, you have to travel on a specific date and stay in the hotels they have reserved—otherwise expect add-on costs. Resort hotels including Ica, Tarapoto, Puno, Cusco, Máncora, and Cajamarca often promote specials for Lima weekenders on their web pages. These all-inclusive packages can be an excellent value for foreign travelers.

Overland Journeys

Many companies in the United States and the United Kingdom offer overland backpacking trips for large groups. You and 39 others hop on a retrofitted Mercedes bus for a one- or two-month tour that could begin in Santiago, Chile, or São Paolo and end in Lima, visiting Cusco, Machu Picchu, and all the other sites along the way. These companies strike bargains with hotels ahead of time and take care of all food, lodging, and transport.

These trips move like an army, camp on beaches, advance along the Inca Trail and leave behind a litter of soap opera romances. With a two-month trip costing around US$3,000 these trips are about as good of a value as you are likely to find. A pair of budget-minded travelers could, however, do the same trip for the same cost or less. Last-minute web specials often offer 25 percent discounts on these trips.

The best agencies to look at are **Kumuka** (www.kumuka.co.uk), **Bukima Adventure Travel** (www.bukima.com), **Dragoman Overland** (www.dragoman.com), and **South**

American Safaris (www.southamericansafaris.com). A final highly recommended option is Australia-based **Tucan Travel** (www.tucantravel.com), which offers a range of trips including language schools and custom packages for independent travelers.

International Tour Agencies

Peru has a huge range of good tour operators with overseas agents, who can work with you regardless of what country you are calling from. The operators in Peru will be the ones you meet when you arrive there. The local operators are listed throughout this book. Contacting these operators directly can sometimes be cheaper, though they are officially supposed to offer the same price to you as their agent overseas does. Many of the agencies listed will organize a tour for as few as two people, with options for trip extensions. In the Cusco area, for instance, tour operators generally offer trip extensions to Lake Titicaca or the jungle.

Adventure tourism is growing fast in Peru, and new tour operators appear every year. To keep abreast of the latest operators, watch the classified ads sections of adventure magazines such as *Outside* and *National Geographic Adventure* or online resources such as www. andeantravelweb.com.

World Class Travel Services (U.S. tel. 800/771-3100, www.peruperu.com) is a leading seller of consolidated tickets and arranges professional, organized tours. It works with the best operators in Peru, such as **Amazons Explorer** and **InkaNatura**. World Class offers tours all over Peru, including a US$672 four-day package that includes all but a few meals for visiting Cusco, Sacred Valley, and Machu Picchu. World Class owner Bob Todd personally inspects all the hotels to which he sends clients and is willing to work with groups as small as two people.

CULTURE AND SOFT ADVENTURE

The Seattle-based nonprofit travel organization **Crooked Trails** (U.S. tel. 206/383-9828, www.crookedtrails.com) offers excellent travel programs, culturally sensitive and with exciting off-the-beaten-path destinations around Peru for families, schools, universities, and almost any type of group. There are at least 10 different packages, such as The Andes and the Sacred Valley, a 15-day tour including Cusco and Machu Picchu, along with homestays with villagers and their families in Vicos (Cordillera Blanca) or Chinchero (Cusco). La Gran Ruta Inca is a seven-day trek extension on one of the Inca highway's best preserved segments southeast of the Cordillera Blanca.

Far Horizons Archaeological & Cultural Trips (U.S. tel. 800/552-4575, www.farhorizon.com), a California-based agency, is the right choice for those with a passion for archaeology. Tours hit all of Peru's major ruins and are guided by an American university professor. Along the way, guests attend lectures by Peru's most noted archaeologists, including Walter Alva, who excavated the Lord of Sipán tombs. Their tours often include a complete tour of the north coast, Chavín ruins in the Cordillera Blanca, Cusco, Machu Picchu, and Lima's main museums.

Nature Expeditions International (U.S. tel. 800/869-0639, www.naturexp.com) has been in business for more than three decades and runs a range of upscale trips throughout Peru. Its 12-day Peru Discovery trip passes through Lima, Arequipa, and the whole Cusco area and includes stays in top-notch hotels like the Hotel Libertador in Cusco and the Machu Picchu Pueblo Hotel. It works with groups of just two people and can arrange lectures on a range of topics, from natural healing to Peruvian cuisine.

For a more luxurious trip, **Abercrombie & Kent** (U.S. tel. 800/554-7016, www.abercrombiekent.com) pampers its travelers with small groups, the top hotels of the country, and luxury train travel. The trips are expensive, but there are occasional discounts available on its website.

Seattle-based **Wildland Adventures** (tel. 800/345-4453, www.wildland.com) is renowned worldwide for its diverse international trips. In Peru alone, it offers 16 distinct trips that cover the three major geographic zones:

coast, mountains, and jungle. In addition to the more traditional Inca Trail and Cordillera Blanca treks, the company also offers trips designed especially for families. On a trip like the lodge-based Andes & Amazon Odyssey, kids and their parents visit and interact with local schools and markets.

Guerba Adventure & Discovery Holidays (U.K. tel. 01373/82-6611, www.guerba.co.uk) is a long-established U.K. operator that offers a good range of hotel-based culture tours and gentle treks. Its tours range from one week to four months and have won international awards for environmentally responsible tourism.

ADVENTURE AND NATURE TOUR OPERATORS IN NORTH AMERICA

Our top choice for treks anywhere in Peru is **Andean Treks** (U.S. tel. 800/683-8148, www.andeantreks.com). It is affiliated with the highly recommended Peruvian Andean Treks in Cusco, and its treks range from a six-day/five-night Inca Trail trek, to a Salcantay trip (US$920), to an 18-day Vilcabamba expedition. It has been around since the 1970s and has been a leader in taking care of the environment and porters—it's probably the only agency in Peru that pays retirement to its porters!

Adventure Specialists (U.S. tel. 719/783-2076, www.adventurespecialists.org) is based out of a spectacular ranch in Westcliffe, Colorado, and has operated quality educational and creative adventure programs in Peru since 1971. Founder and co-owner Gary Ziegler, a fellow of the Royal Geographical Society and Explorers Club, is a true adventurer, archaeologist and noted Inca expert. His expeditions have rediscovered and surveyed the important Inca sites Corihuayrachina, Cota Coca, and Llaqtapata. The company specializes in archaeology-focused horse trips around Cusco, but Ziegler and his crew can custom-design nearly any adventure you are looking for.

Adventure Life International (406/541-2677, U.S. tel. 800/344-6118, www.adventure-life.com) is a company based in Missoula, Montana, that is a good bet for budget-minded trekkers. Its 10-day Machu Picchu Pilgrimage includes Cusco, Machu Picchu, and a well-run Inca Trail trek for US$1,775. It also offers affordable trips to the fabulous Tambopata Research Center. It uses three-star, family-run hostels and local guides, and gives independent travelers flexibility on where they eat. Maximum group size is 12, though it often sends off groups as small as two people. It has recently set up a fund (www.earthfamilyfund. org) to give back to the countries it visits.

South Winds (U.S. tel. 800/377-9463, www.southwindadventures.com) is based in Littleton, Colorado, and offers a range of eco-adventures from the jungle to the high Andes. It comes highly recommended from people who have done the trips and from *Condé Nast Traveler* magazine.

The Miami-based **Tropical Nature Travel** (U.S. tel. 877/827-8350, www.tropicalnature-travel.com) works with a variety of conservation organizations across Latin American to plan jungle trips. In Peru it works with InkaNatura, the owner of some of Peru's best jungle lodges. Your choices range from the Manu Wildlife Center and Cock of the Rock Lodge in the Manu area, or the Sandoval Lake and Heath River lodges around Puerto Maldonado.

KE Adventure Travel (U.S. tel. 800/497-9675, www.keadventure.com) is based in Avon, Colorado, and offers a range of high-quality climbs and treks—at considerably lower prices than its competitor, Mountain Travel Sobek. It works with top international trekking guides and is best known for treks around the Cordillera Huayhuash and Nevado Ausangate near Cusco. It also guides peaks in the Cordillera Blanca and leads multi-sport trips that combine rafting, trekking, and mountain biking.

GAP Adventures (U.S./Canada tel. 800/708-7761, www.gapadventures.com) stands for Great Adventure People and is one of Canada's lead tour outfits. It is a good choice for independent-minded travelers who prefer small groups. Groups stay in locally owned hotels, and GAP is known for socially responsible tourism that includes a good deal of interaction with communities.

Our vote for best international climbing agency in Peru goes to Seattle-based **Alpine Ascents** (U.S. tel. 206/378-1927, www.alpin-eascents.com). The company's Peru guide, José Luis Peralvo, splits his time between Everest, his home in Ecuador, and Peru and has been guiding the world's toughest peaks for about two decades. Alpine Ascents is extremely responsible about acclimatization and small rope teams.

Other Peru adventure options can be found through the **Adventure Center** (U.S. tel. 800/277-8747, www.adventurecenter.com), which sells the packages of various operators from its offices in Emeryville, California.

For esoteric tours and ayahuasca sessions, check out **El Tigre Journeys** (U.S. tel. 303/449-5479, www.biopark.org/peru.html). This for-profit company has been in business since 1997 and is associated with the nonprofit **International Biopark Foundation** in Tucson, Arizona. It leads ayahuasca ceremonies in the Amazon, spirit journeys, and solstice celebrations throughout the year.

ADVENTURE AND NATURE TOUR OPERATORS IN THE UNITED KINGDOM

Amazonas Explorer (U.K. tel. 01437/89-1743, www.amazonas-explorer.com) has tons of local experience in Peru and an unmatched array of adventure trips that integrate kayaking, rafting, mountain biking, and trekking. It is constantly innovating new trips, with a team full-time in Cusco.

Based in Edinburgh, Scotland, **Andean Trails** (U.K. tel. 0131/467-7086, www.andean-trails.co.uk) was cofounded in 1999 by a former South American adventure guide. The company leads interesting, small-group mountain-bike and trekking adventures throughout Peru.

Journey Latin America (U.K. tel. 020/8747-8315, www.journeylatinamerica. co.uk) is the United Kingdom's largest operator of specialty tours and has been in business for more than 25 years. It does rafting, kayaking, trekking, and cultural tours that can either be escorted groups or tailored for two people. It also sets up homestays and language classes.

Exodus (U.K. tel. 0870/950-0039, www. exodus.co.uk) is one of the United Kingdom's larger adventure tour operators, with more than 25 years of experience and trips in countless countries. Its 28 Peru trips often include visits to Bolivia or Ecuador.

World Challenge Expeditions (U.K. tel. 0208/728-7200, www.world-challenge.co.uk) is a London-based adventure company for student groups in Peru. Its coordinator in Peru, Richard Cunyus, is a full-time resident, takes great care of the students, and tracks down excellent adventures such as trekking in the Cordillera Huayhuash or paddling a dugout in the Reserva Nacional Pacaya Samiria. The company also works with many students from the United States.

ADVENTURE AND NATURE TOUR OPERATORS IN AUSTRALIA

World Expeditions (Australia tel. 1300/720-000, www.worldexpeditions.com.au) is Australia's leader in adventure tours and treks to Peru. It works with Tambo Treks, a small and reputable trekking outfit in Cusco. In Peru, trips include treks through the Lake Titicaca grasslands, forays into Colca Canyon, and longer trips that take in Peru, Bolivia, and the Amazon jungle. It has representatives in the United Kingdom (enquiries@worldexpeditions.co.uk), the United States (contactus@worldexpeditions.com), and Canada (info@worldexpeditions.ca).

Visas and Officialdom

VISAS AND PASSPORTS

Citizens of the United States, Canada, United Kingdom, South Africa, New Zealand, and Australia do not require visas to enter Peru as tourists at the present time, nor do residents of any other European or Latin American country. When visitors enter the country, you can get anything from 30 to 180 days stamped into both a passport and an embarkation card that travelers must keep until they exit the country. If you require more than 30 days, be ready to support your argument by explaining your travel plans and showing your return ticket.

Extensions can be arranged at Peru's immigration offices in Lima, Arequipa, Cusco, Iquitos, Puno, and Trujillo for US$21. There are also immigration offices on the border checkpoints with Chile, Bolivia (Desaguadero and Yunguyo), and Ecuador, though at this point it is easier just to leave the country, stay the night, and reenter on a fresh visa.

Always make a photocopy of your passport and your return ticket and store it in a separate place. Carry yours in a money belt underneath your clothing, or leave it in a security box at your hotel. If your passport is lost or stolen, your only recourse is to head to your embassy in Lima. If you have lost or had your passport stolen before, it may take up to a week while your embassy runs an international check on your identity.

PERUVIAN EMBASSIES AND CONSULATES ABROAD

If you are applying for a work visa or other type of special visa for Peru in the United States, contact the consular section of the Peruvian embassy (tel. 202/833-9860, www.peruvianembassy.us), located in **Washington D.C.** Additionally, there are consulates in Atlanta, Boston, Chicago, Dallas, Denver, Hartford, Honolulu, Houston, Los Angeles, Miami, New Orleans, New York, Paterson, Phoenix, Sacramento, Salt Lake City, San Francisco, San Juan, Seattle, St. Louis, and Tulsa.

The Peruvian embassy in **Canada** is in Ottawa (tel. 613/238-1777, www.embassyofperu.ca), with consulates in Calgary, Montreal, Toronto, Vancouver, and Winnipeg. In the United Kingdom the embassy and consular section are both in **London** (tel. 020/7235-1917, www.peruembassy-uk.com). In **South Africa,** the Peruvian embassy and consulate are in Pretoria (tel. 27-12/348-8744, embaperu6@telkomsa.net).

In **Australia** the embassy is in Barton,

the flag of Peru

Canberra (tel. 612/6273-7351, www.embaperu. org.au), with consulate offices in Brisbane, Melbourne, Sydney. In **New Zealand** the embassy is in Wellington (tel. 64-4/499-8087, embassy.peru@xtra.co.nz), and there are two honorary consulates in Auckland and Christchurch. There is a complete list of Peruvian embassies and consulates around the world (www.rree.gob.pe/portal/misrree. nsf/webdiremb?OpenForm) on the Foreign Relations Ministry website.

FOREIGN EMBASSIES IN PERU

Many foreign travelers are surprised by how little help their own embassy will provide during an emergency or a tight situation abroad. If you have been robbed and have no money, expect no help from your embassy, apart from replacing your passport. The same applies if you have broken Peruvian law, even by doing something that would be legal in your own country. Go ahead and contact your embassy in an emergency, but don't wait for them to call back.

These embassies are all in Lima: **United States** (Av. La Encalada, Block 17, Surco, tel. 01/434-3000, http://lima.usembassy.gov/, 8 A.M.–5 P.M. Mon.–Fri.), **Canada** (Libertad 130, Miraflores, tel. 01/444-4015, www.canadainternational.gc.ca/peru-perou/, 8–11 A.M. and 2–4 P.M. Mon.–Fri.), **United Kingdom** (Av. Larco 1301, 22nd Fl., Miraflores, tel. 01/617-3000, http://ukinperu.fco.gov.uk/, 8 A.M.–1 P.M. Mon.–Fri.), and **South Africa** (tel. 612/4848, www.dfa.gov.za/foreign/sa_abroad/sap.htm). **Australia** does not have an embassy in Lima—the closest is in Santiago, Chile (www.chile.embassy.gov.au), but it does have a consulate (tel. 01/222-8281, www.australia.org.pe).

If you find yourself in trouble, your best hope for finding a lawyer, good doctor, or a bit of moral support may not be with your embassy, but with the **South American Explorers Club (SAE)** (www.saexplorers.org), which has offices in Cusco (Choquechaca 188, #4, tel. 084/24-5484, cuscoclub@saexplorers.org, 9:30 A.M.–5 P.M. Mon.–Fri., 10 A.M.–1 P.M.

Sat.) and Lima (Piura 135, Miraflores, tel. 01/445-3306, limaclub@saexplorers.org, 9:30 A.M.–5 P.M. Mon.–Fri., 9:30 A.M.–1 P.M. Sat.).

TAXES

Foreign travelers are required to pay a US$31 exit tax before boarding an international flight and US$6.82 for all domestic flights.

As of 2001, foreigners no longer have to pay a 19 percent value-added tax, commonly known as **IGV** or *impuesto general a las ventas* on rooms or meals purchased at hotels. When you check into a nice hotel, the receptionist will require to photocopy your passport. Check your bill upon leaving.

Foreigners still have to pay the 19 percent IGV at upscale restaurants that are not affiliated with hotels. These restaurants often tack on a 10 percent service charge as well.

CUSTOMS

Peru's customs office (*aduana*) is notorious for being strict with travelers coming back from Miami with loads of imported goodies. That is why you will see a line of Limeños nervously waiting to pass through the stoplight at the Peruvian customs checkpoint. If you get the unlucky red light, you should know the rules. Travelers are allowed to bring three liters of alcohol and 20 packs of cigarettes into Peru duty-free. You can also bring in US$300 worth of gifts, but not to trade or sell.

On your way home, it is illegal to leave Peru with genuine archaeological artifacts, historic art, or animal products from endangered species. If you're caught you will surely be arrested and prosecuted. Your home country will not let you bring in coca leaves but rarely do they hassle you about coca teabags.

BORDER CROSSINGS

Peru has around 10 official border crossings with Chile, Ecuador, Brazil, and Colombia. They are open year-round and are not usually a hassle as long as one's passport and tourist card are in order.

POLICE

Peruvian police officers are incredibly helpful and, for the most part, honest. Always carry your passport with you or a photocopy of it if you decide to leave your passport where you are staying. Other means of identification are pretty much worthless, unless you're renting a car and need to show your international driver's license. If you are stopped on the street, the only thing police are allowed to do is check your Peruvian visa or passport. If police hassle you for a bribe for whatever reason, politely refuse and offer to go to the police station or just act like you don't understand. Police will usually just give up and let you go.

Police corruption is much less common now in Peru than it was a decade ago. If you have an encounter with a crooked cop, get the officer's name and badge number and call Peru's 24-hour, English-speaking tourist police hotline (tel. 01/574-8000).

Peru has set up tourist police offices in Arequipa, Ayacucho, Cajamarca, Chiclayo, Cusco, Huancayo, Huaraz, Ica, Iquitos, Lima, Nasca, Puno, Tacna, and Trujillo. In Lima, the emergency number for the police is **tel. 105,** but English-speaking operators are usually not available. Your best bet is to call the 24-hour hotline.

Conduct and Customs

ETIQUETTE

Peruvians invariably exchange a *buenos días* or good morning, a *buenas tardes* or good afternoon, or a *buenas noches* or good evening. Women and men greet each other with a single kiss on the right cheek, though highland Indians generally just offer a hand—sometimes just a wrist if they have been working.

The title *señora* is reserved for older or married women with children and can be quite insulting if addressed to a younger girl. *Señorita* is for younger, usually unmarried women. *Señor* is used to address men, and *don* or *doña* is used for elder men or women as a sign of respect.

Machismo in rural areas especially is very much a part of Peruvian culture. Men will often direct dinner conversation only toward other men. Women can handle this situation by directing conversation at both the men and women alike at the table.

Peruvians typically dress nicely and conservatively, especially when dealing with official business or entering a church. Women in these cases should consider wearing pants or a skirt that is longer than knee length, and men should avoid shorts or casual T-shirts. Despite that, fashion in Lima and Amazon towns is more relaxed. You are likely to see men in shorts and women in shorts or short skirts. You should feel comfortable doing the same. Away from Lima or the jungle, shorts can be worn when participating in an athletic activity that requires them: trekking, beach volleyball, or even running. Foreigners will call less attention to themselves if they wear generally inconspicuous clothing.

CULTURE

Family is still the center of Peruvian society. Extended families often live in neighboring houses, and young cousins can be raised together as if they were brothers and sisters,

© FIONA CAMERON

A Peruvian family prepares to serve *chicha*, a fermented corn beverage, outside of Cusco.

especially in rural areas and small cities and towns. Women travelers over the age of 20 might be asked whether or not they are married or have children.

Many Peruvians seem to not be bothered with high noise levels, a cultural difference that most Western foreigners find grating. Shops will blare merengue, *tecnocumbia,* and other Latin pop music to the point where conversation becomes impossible but commerce goes on as usual. Radios tend to be turned up at the first sign of morning light, and workmen start hammering at dawn, so sleeping in is often out of the question. Ear plugs can be handy under these circumstances.

Most Peruvians are also used to crowded spaces and don't mind sitting close to one another on buses and *colectivos.* While at the bank, they will stand just inches away from one another even though there is plenty of space around. In the highlands, houses tend to be small, often with many family members sleeping in the same room. Women travelers often think that men are pressing in on them, when actually they just have a different sense of space.

Peruvians also have a very different relationship toward time, taking things relaxed and slow without the hectic attitude of Westerners. If you agree to meet somebody at noon, expect to wait at least 15–30 minutes. You will inevitably sit in a restaurant longer than anticipated, waiting for your food, waiting for your bill, and then waiting some more for your change. You are never going to change this, so just sit back, be patient, and smile.

PANHANDLING

Whether or not to give money to those asking for it on the street is a personal decision. The hardest to turn down are the street kids with rosy, dirt-covered cheeks and an outstretched hand. In the countryside, children will frequently ask for money in exchange for having their picture taken. Remember that when you give them money, you are encouraging the practice in the future. Also, know that parents often have their children working as teams to collect money in the street. Instead of money, the best-prepared travelers give pens, notebooks, or other useful items.

Tips for Travelers

ACCOMMODATIONS

Choosing the right place to stay is key to having a relaxed, enjoyable trip to Peru. The quality of lodging ranges dramatically in most Peruvian cities and often has no correlation whatsoever with price. If you plan well, you should usually be able to find a safe and quiet room, with a charming environment and a helpful staff.

Because where you stay makes a huge difference in the quality of your experience, we recommend making advance reservations by email—especially in hot spots like Lima, Arequipa, Huaraz, Cusco, and Puno and especially between the busy months May–September. Rates can increase as much as 50 percent during local festivals or national holidays such as the July 28 Fiestas Patrias weekend.

Walk-in travelers often get better rates than those who make reservations over email, but those with a reservation often get the corner room with a view, the quieter space off the street, or the room with a writing desk—especially if you ask for it in advance.

Lodging rates can be negotiated at budget hotels. That said, most hotels except for the top-end ones will probably have a low-season rate posted October–April, considerably lower than the usual rate posted year-round. But this depends on the city and can actually vary month to month.

Before you pay for a room, ask to see one or two rooms to get a sense of the quality standard at the hotel. Look carefully at how safe a hotel is, especially what neighborhood it is in, and avoid lodging around discos, bars, bus stations,

WHAT TO TAKE

Travel light and have a carefree vacation – drop-off laundry is common in Peru, so bring five days' clothing and put it all in a medium-sized backpack.

For Peru's hot jungle and coastal climates, we recommend light, fast-drying **clothing** that protects your arms and legs from sun and mosquitoes. Protect yourself from the sun with a wide-brimmed hat, bandannas, sunscreen, and sunglasses. These same clothes can be worn in the Andes, though you will want to add a lightweight rain jacket, fleece jacket, and silk-weight long underwear.

Miscellaneous items include a Leatherman-style folding knife, small roll of duct tape for repairs, mending kit, hand sanitizer, headlamp with extra batteries, camera, voltage adapter, water bottle, roll of toilet paper (Peru's public bathrooms are always out), binoculars, pocket English-Spanish dictionary, book, journal, and a tiny calculator for confirming money exchanges. Don't forget your **medical kit** with standard medicines, insect repellent, water purification tablets, and antimalarials.

Paperwork should include valid passport, plane ticket, student card if you have one, a yellow vaccinations card, travelers checks, ATM card and credit card, and a copy of your travel insurance details. Email yourself numbers for travelers checks, passport, and credit cards in case these things get stolen. Photocopies of the first few pages of your passport and your plane ticket are also a good idea.

or other places nearby that might make your room noisy at night. Inspect the bathrooms carefully and turn on the hot water to make sure it exists. If you are in a cold area, like Puno or Cusco, ask if the hotel provides electric heaters. If you are in a jungle city, ask if there are fans. If you are planning to make calls from your room, ask if there is direct-dial service that allows the use of phone cards—otherwise you will have to wait for the receptionist to make your call at a hefty rate that can be as much as US$0.50 per minute for local calls.

Budget Hotels

The cheaper establishments are called *hospedajes,* and the *hostales* are usually a bit fancier. There are government rules that define the difference between both and a hotel. Key things to look for with a budget place are the quality of the beds, nifty perks like shared kitchen or free Internet, or even WiFi nowadays, the cleanliness of the bathroom, and how the water is heated. A few hotels use water heaters with a limited supply of hot water. A few others use electric showerheads, which heat water with an electrical current like that of a toaster oven. Often the device needs to be turned on at the showerhead or via a circuit breaker in the bathroom. The whole concept is unnerving, but the devices are surprisingly safe. The problem is they often only make the water lukewarm. Fortunately, the majority have switched to gas water heaters.

Midrange Hotels

This category of lodging tends to encompass modern, charmless buildings with a fancy reception area and average rooms with tacky decorations. But they are usually a sure bet for hot water, safe rooms, phones, WiFi Internet, and refrigerators.

High-End Hotels

Nearly all major Peruvian cities have high-end hotels with the full range of international creature comforts, including swimming pools, WiFi Internet, spring mattresses, alarm clocks, refrigerators, loads of hot water, bathtubs, and direct-dial phones. The fancier establishments often have kitchenettes, slippers, bathrobes, and complimentary toiletries. Often suites are just a bit more expensive but much more luxurious. These hotels invariably charge a 19 percent value-added tax, which by law must be refunded to travelers as long you require so and the hotel has a copy of your passport.

DINING

Nowadays, a traveler's experience of Peruvian food can be a unique experience, considering that Peru has the best, most interesting and varied food offer in Latin America. It can also be a double-edged sword, especially if you have a sensitive stomach. Many travelers return with fond memories of the exquisite and surprising range of flavors, while others return with their stomachs crawling with bacteria or parasites. Choose where you eat carefully and work from the recommendations in this book or from fellow travelers. Peruvians often recommend *huariques,* or hole-in-the-wall restaurants that work well for their hardy stomachs, but not necessarily for yours.

Service at Peruvian restaurants is broken down into various steps, which include receiving the menu, ordering, waiting for food, waiting for the bill, and then waiting for change. If you are eating lunch, you can order from the *menú,* the fixed menu of the day, usually a list of prepared entrées and main courses that can be served quickly. À la carte items are more expensive than the *menú.* Many travelers choose to make their own breakfasts by buying yogurt, cereal, and some fruit if they have the facilities at the hostel. If you get good service it is encouraged to leave around 10 percent of the bill as a gratuity.

EMPLOYMENT

Jobs teaching English in Peru are easy to find and can often be arranged in-country without a work visa (which doesn't mean you will be legal). You should first scan expatriate bulletin boards in Lima, where language schools often advertise jobs for around US$8 per hour. One of Lima's better language schools is **El Sol** (http://elsol.idiomasperu.com).

International organizations that help find teaching positions include **Amerispan** (www.amerispan.com) and **TEFL** (www.tefl.com). These organizations are also worth contacting: **International Schools Services** (U.S. tel. 609/452-0990, www.iss.edu), **Británico** (Lima tel. 01/447-1192, www.britanico.edu. pe), **American Language Institute** (alisac@

terra.com.pe, contact Joseph Phrower in Lima), **Teaching Abroad in the U.K.** (www.teaching-abroad.co.uk), or **EFL** (efl.institute@terra.com.pe) in Lima. Wherever you work, make sure you get a contract in writing.

Other paid employment can be found through the **International Jobs Center** (www.internationaljobs.org). This organization collects information on current international job openings with governments, government contractors, United Nations agencies, private voluntary organizations, and student exchange organizations. Membership, including posting your credentials in its database and access to profiles of major employers, is US$26 for six weeks.

For tips on living in Peru see **Living In Peru** (www.livinginperu.com) or **Expat Peru** (www.expatperu.com); both webpages have resourceful information for expatriates with everything from apartments to tips on how to deal with cultural differences.

VOLUNTEERING

There are hundreds of volunteer opportunities in Peru, involving art and culture, community development, disability and addiction services, ecotourism and the environment, education, health care, and services for children and women. Although these organizations do not pay salaries, they often provide food or accommodation in exchange for your time.

The most common complaint with volunteer work is that the organization is disorganized, there is not enough meaningful work, or that organizations are exploiting eager beavers for their own bottom line. For that reason, do research and try to speak with people who have worked with the organization in the past.

One source for volunteer information in Peru is the Lima office of the **South American Explorers Club** (Piura 135, Miraflores, tel. 01/445-3306, www.saexplorers.com, 9:30 A.M.–5 P.M. Mon.–Fri., 9:30 A.M.–1 P.M. Sat.). If you're a member, you can even access the volunteer database online. If you're not, you can send an email or buy a phone card and talk to someone in person. Another organization

© CRAIG GEMMELL

High school and college students are increasingly participating in volunteer experiences in the Sacred Valley and other areas of Peru.

in Lima that hooks up volunteers with organizations is **Trabajo Voluntario** (www.trabajovoluntario.org). A good global resource for finding volunteer organizations is www.idealist.org.

There are many Spanish-language schools that combine teaching with volunteering. If you take morning language lessons, the school will often set you up with volunteer work for a minimal administration fee.

There are also many Peru-based volunteer organizations. Check out **Lucho Hurtado's** programs in Huancayo (www.incasdelperu.org); the organization **Center for Social Well Being** (www.socialwellbeing.org) in Carhuaz in the Cordillera Blanca; and **Awamaki** in Ollantaytambo (www.awamaki.org).

Crooked Trails (U.S. tel. 206/383-9828, www.crookedtrails.com) is a nonprofit, community-based travel organization with excellent 3–4 week volunteer travel programs in communities located in countries such as Peru, Ecuador, Guatemala, India, Nepal, Thailand, Bhutan, and Kenya, creating true cultural exchange bonds that make positive contributions to host countries and achieving lasting effects on their travelers.

Cross-Cultural Solutions Peru (U.S. tel. 800/330-4777, U.K. tel. 01237/66-6392, www.crossculturalsolutions.org) runs highly professional volunteer programs mainly for students from the United Kingdom and the United States in Lima, Trujillo, and Ayacucho. In Lima, the company works in Villa El Salvador, the shantytown that was a Nobel Peace Prize nominee for its community organization. The program is quite expensive but recommended for its professional staff. Costs are US$2,489 for two weeks with every additional week costing US$272.

World Leadership School (U.S. tel. 303/679-3412, www.worldleadershipschool.com) helps middle and high schools in the U.S. create global programs with schools in Peru. During the 3–4 week programs, volunteers focus on a single global issue, such as climate change, education, or public health. Volunteers understand and develop competence with each issue by working on solutions at the community level. The programs include a leadership curriculum and mentorship from local leaders, who share their perspective and wisdom.

ProWorld (U.S. tel. 877/429-6753, U.K. tel. 870/750-7202, www.myproworld.org) has locations in Peru, Belize, and Mexico. In Peru, ProWorld is based out of Urubamba, where, since 2000, it has built schools, irrigation systems, and bridges; replanted forests; helped developed sustainable industries like agro-tourism; and sent volunteers to work with countless local nonprofits. They have programs ranging from two weeks to a semester in length and they offer academic credit. Prices begin at US$1,795 for two weeks.

World Youth International (www.worldyouth.com.au) organizes volunteer programs in Cusco such as the Clínica San Juan de Dios, which is a well-organized resident program for children with disabilities.

Kiya Survivors (U.K. tel. 01273/72-1092, www.kiyasurvivors.org) works with special-needs children, abandoned women, and young single mothers. It is run by British citizen Suzy Butler out of Cusco and offers volunteer placements of 2–6 months. A standard six-month placement includes in-country tours, accommodations, and a tax-deductible donation to the organization.

The highly recommended nonprofit **Mundo Azul** (Lima tel. 01/447-5190, www.mundoazul.org/english) is dedicated to conserving natural biodiversity, and its volunteers play a first-hand role in helping that mission happen. The two-week to month-long volunteer programs take participants to the ocean to research dolphin populations or dive into open water to collect marine species. (Only experienced divers can apply for the latter option.) A rainforest trip to Manu involves researching tapirs, macaws, and giant river otters.

Ania (Lima tel. 01/628-7948, www.mundodeania.org) is an innovative nonprofit founded by Peruvian Joaquín Leguía in 1995. The nonprofit has focused mainly on helping children across Peru, and the world, connect with their love for nature through a creative, grass-roots effort that includes Ania, a cartoon character, and a series of Tierra de Niños natural areas. These "Children's Lands" are owned, designed, and maintained by children and range from only a few meters squared to a giant nature reserve near Puerto Maldonado. Leguía, who has been awarded the prestigious Ashoka fellowship, plans to begin working with volunteers, so check for available placements.

OPPORTUNITIES FOR STUDY

Peru has a variety of great Spanish-language programs in Lima, Huaraz, Cusco, Urubamba, Arequipa, Huancayo, and Puerto Maldonado. These programs offer either private instruction for US$7–15 per hour or much cheaper group classes that last between a week and a month. Many of these programs will also set up homestays, hikes, classes, and other activities. The schools vary in quality, so we recommend asking the school for email addresses of former students in order to contact them. Many of the schools also engage in volunteer projects, which is a great way to immerse into Spanish. When choosing a school, think carefully about what situation will provide the most immersion. We recommend a homestay where you will not be able to speak English and a city where there are few foreigners.

Council on International Educational Exchange (www.ciee.org) organizes study-abroad programs and has links to a variety of programs.

BSES Expeditions (U.K. tel. 0207/591-3141, www.bses.org.uk) runs annual science expeditions for British teenagers, though Americans also sign up. The trips usually include science "base camps" in unusual areas of Peru, along with trekking, rafting, and other adventure activities.

WOMEN TRAVELING ALONE

Machismo is alive and well in Peru, so women traveling in Peru should know what to expect. Most Latin men assume that a woman traveling on her own, especially a blonde, must be promiscuous. So you have to set the record straight.

At some level, there is the larger issue that some men feel threatened by women who travel abroad, study, work, and are generally independent because it conflicts with their perceptions of how women should be.

How you interact with men makes a huge difference. Speak with men you do not know in public places only. Treat them neutrally and avoid intimate conversation and behaviors, like friendly touches that might be misinterpreted. Wear modest clothing. Some say a fake wedding ring or a reference to a nonexistent husband or boyfriend helps, but that can also result in the reply *"no soy celoso"* ("I'm not jealous").

Peruvian men, and often teenagers, will ingratiate themselves with a group of female gringas and tag along for hours, even if they are completely ignored. The best way to deal with this is by telling them early on that you want to be alone: *"quiero estar sola, por favor."* The next step would be a loud and clear request to be left alone: *"déjeme, por favor."* The final step would be to ask passersby for help" *"por favor, ayúdeme."* The bad side of machismo is harassment, but the flip side is protection.

Be especially careful at night. Choose a hotel in a safe, well-lit part of town. Take care when flagging down a taxi and do not walk around alone at night, especially in tourist towns like Cusco. Walk with confidence and purpose, even if you do not know where you are going. Women who look lost are inevitably approached by strangers. Peruvian women ignore catcalls, aggressive come-ons, and flirtatious lines called *piropos,* which are almost a form of poetry among men. You should do the same.

Do not walk alone in out-of-the-way places in the countryside. We have heard reports of women who have been assaulted while walking alone on popular travelers' routes. Trek or hike in the daylight and with at least one other person. If you are robbed, surrender your purse rather than risk physical harm. Mace, whistles, alarms, and self-defense skills are effective tools that are likely to catch most assailants off-guard.

GAY AND LESBIAN TRAVELERS

Peru is far from progressive for gay and lesbian travelers, and Lima's gay scene is considerably smaller than that in other major South American capitals. There are a variety of well-hidden and exclusively gay bars, restaurants, and clubs in cities like Lima, and a growing number in Iquitos and Cusco—though none cater exclusively to lesbians. Most gay men in Peru's *machista* society are still in the closet and maintain heterosexual relationships as well as homosexual ones.

The only way to find about gay and lesbian establishments is online. The concept of gay rights is still relatively new in Peru, so gay and lesbian travelers are advised to be discreet and exercise caution. The best resource is the bilingual website **Gay Lima** (http://lima.queercity.info), written by a U.S. citizen living in Lima. It gives a good overview of gay and lesbian life in Peru and is updated constantly with the latest bars, nightclubs, and hotels, and also includes chat rooms and links. Another good online resource is **Gay Peru** (www.gayperu.com), a great site on gay travel, including gay-oriented package tours, although it is in Spanish only.

For those interested in learning about gay rights in Peru, check the website in Spanish of the **Movimiento Homosexual de Lima** (www.mhol.org.pe), one of the oldest gay movements in Peru.

The San Francisco–based **Now Voyager** (www.nowvoyager.com) is a worldwide gay-owned, gay-operated full-service travel agency, as is **Purple Roofs** (www.purpleroofs.com). The **International Gay and Lesbian Travel Association** (www.iglta.org) has an extensive directory of travel agents, tour operators, and accommodations that are gay and lesbian friendly. **Above Beyond Tours** (www.abovebeyondtours.com) is a California-based gay travel specialist offering independent and group travel packages.

ACCESSIBILITY

Facilities for people with disabilities are improving in Peru but are far from adequate. Most bathrooms are impossible to enter in a wheelchair. Hotel stairways are usually narrow and steep, and ramps are few and far between.

Peru's sidewalks are hard to navigate with a wheelchair because they are frequently narrow, potholed, and lack ramps. Cars usually do not respect pedestrians, so cross streets with extreme caution.

The exceptions to the above are airports and high-end hotels. Peruvian hotel chains such as **Libertador** (www.libertador.com.pe) and **Casa Andina** (www.casa-andina.com) stand out for providing accessible rooms in hotels in Trujillo, Lima, Cusco, the Sacred Valley, the Colca Canyon, Arequipa, and Nasca.

PromPeru, the government tourism commission, has launched a major accessibility campaign and now claims that more than a hundred tourist facilities in Aguas Calientes, Cusco, Iquitos, Lima, and Trujillo have been approved for travelers with disabilities. PromPeru lists these wheelchair-accessible places on its web page (www.promperu.gob.pe). Other resources for disabled travelers include **Access-Able Travel Source** (www.access-able.com) and **Society for Accessible Travel and Hospitality** (U.S. tel. 212/447-7284, www.sath.org).

SENIORS

Many organized tours of Peru cater to senior travelers. The major airlines offer discounts for seniors, as do international chain hotels, but other than that, senior discounts in Peru are nonexistent. For visiting the jungle, Amazon cruise boats are an excellent option for people with limited walking abilities.

Good senior agencies include **SAGA Holidays** (www.saga.co.uk), which offers all-inclusive tours and cruises for those 50 and older. **Elderhostel** (U.S. tel. 800/454-5768, www.elderhostel.org) arranges study programs for people 55 and over in countries worldwide, including Peru.

TRAVELING WITH YOUNG CHILDREN

With the right planning, traveling with kids through Peru can be a blast. Kids tend to attract lots of attention from passersby and can cause interesting cultural interactions. By traveling through Peru, children learn a great deal and gain an understanding of how different life can be for people across the world.

Experts suggest that children should be involved in the early stages of a trip in order to get the most out of it. Children's books and movies that deal with the history of the Inca and the Spaniards will help your kids better relate to the ruins they will see later on. Parents should explain to children what they will encounter, prep them for the day's activities, and then hear from them how it went afterwards.

Keeping your children healthy means taking precautions. Make sure your children get the right vaccinations, and watch what they eat while they are in Peru, because the major threat to their health is dehydration caused by diarrhea. Bacterial infection can be prevented by washing children's hands frequently with soap or using hand sanitizer.

For very young children, don't bother bringing your own baby food, as it is cheaper in the country. You will have a hard time, however, finding specialty items like sugar-free foods, which should be brought from home. Outside of Peru's major cities, there is not much selection in supermarkets, so stock up while you can. Always carry a good supply of snacks and bottled water with you, as there can be long stretches where nothing to eat or drink is available.

Pack your **medical kit** with everything you will need for basic first aid: bandages and gauze pads, antibacterial ointment, thermometer, child mosquito repellent (vitamin B acts as a natural mosquito repellent), envelopes of hydrating salts, and strong sunscreen. Items like Tylenol (*paracetamol infantil*), can easily be found in the local pharmacies, though quality varies. Medical services are very good in Lima and often quite good in the countryside, where city-trained, English-speaking medical students perform residency. Medical care is so cheap in Peru that parents should never hesitate about seeing a doctor. Bring photocopies of your children's medical records.

Your embassy may be of some help, but the best place to contact for advice or help is probably the **South American Explorers Club** (Piura 135, Miraflores, tel. 01/445-3306, www.saexplorers.com, 9:30 A.M.–5 P.M. Mon.–Fri., 9:30 A.M.–1 P.M. Sat.).

Think carefully about your travel arrangements. Kids are likely to enjoy a sensory-rich environment like the Amazon jungle much more than back-to-back tours of archaeological ruins. Buses generally allow children to travel for free until 5 years old and/or if they sit on your lap, but choose flights over long bus rides that could make kids crabby. Choose family-oriented hotels, which offer playgrounds and lots of space for children to run around unsupervised. If you ask for a room with three beds you generally won't have to pay extra. If you have toddlers, avoid hotels with pools, because they are rarely fenced off. Children's rates for anything from movies to museums are common and, even if they are not official, can often be negotiated.

Because parents are often distracted by their children, families can be prime targets for thieves in public spaces like bus stations and markets. Even if you have taught your children to be extra careful about traffic at home, you will have to teach them a whole new level of awareness in Peru. Time moves slower in Peru, and families spend a lot of time waiting for buses, tours, or meals. Be prepared with coloring books and other activities.

Health and Safety

It pays to think ahead about your health before traveling to Peru. With the right vaccinations, a little bit of education, and a lot of common sense, the worst that happens to most visitors is a bit of traveler's diarrhea.

Things get more complicated if you decide to visit the jungle, because Peru, like parts of Africa and Asia, lies in the tropical zone. Travelers who visit the Amazon should be vaccinated against yellow fever, be taking malarial medicine, and take full precautions against mosquitoes.

VACCINATIONS

Vaccination recommendations can be obtained from the **Centers for Disease Control (CDC)** (U.S. tel. 877/394-8747, www.cdc.gov/travel), which recommends the following vaccinations for Peru: **hepatitis A** and **typhoid. Yellow fever** is recommended for people traveling into the jungle below 2,300 meters. Rabies is recommended if you are going to be trekking through areas where the disease is endemic. **Hepatitis B** is recommended if you might be exposed to blood (for instance, health-care workers), plan on staying for more than six months, or may have sex with a local. Travelers should also be vaccinated against **measles** and **chicken pox** (those who have had these diseases are already immune) and have had a **tetanus/diphtheria** shot within the last 10 years.

Unless you are coming from a region in the Americas or Africa where yellow fever is a problem, you are not required by Peruvian law to have any vaccinations before entering the country. The yellow immunizations pamphlet, which doctors tell you to guard ever so carefully, is rarely checked, but you should carry it with your passport. The shots can be quite expensive, in the United States at least, and many of the shots require second or even third visits. Hepatitis A, for instance, requires a booster shot 6–18 months after the initial shot, which most people get after returning from Peru. Hepatitis B is generally received in three doses, and there are new vaccines now that combine both hep A and hep B in a series of three shots. Rabies is also given in three shots, though both yellow fever and typhoid are single shots.

Most vaccinations do not take effect for at least two weeks, so schedule your shots well in advance. If you are taking multishot vaccinations such as hep B, you will need to receive your first shot five weeks before departing, even under the most accelerated schedule.

PACKING A MEDICAL KIT

Having a small medical kit will come in handy over and over again in Peru, especially in remote areas. Here's a checklist of what should be included:

- antacid tablets (Tums)
- antihistamine (Benadryl)
- diarrhea medication (Imodium)
- motion-sickness medication (Dramamine)
- lots of ibuprofen (Advil)
- lots of acetaminophen (Tylenol)
- Pepto-Bismol (liquid is better)
- insect repellent (12-35 percent DEET or above)
- insect clothing spray (permethrin)
- water purification tablets
- bandages, gauze pads, and cloth tape
- butterfly bandages or Superglue (for sealing gashes)
- Ace bandage
- decongestant spray (Afrin)
- packages of rehydration salts
- antibacterial ointment (Neosporin)
- fungus cream (Tinactin)
- hydrocortisone cream for bug bites
- Moleskin, both thin and foam
- tweezers
- scissors or knife
- syringe and needles
- thermometer
- CPR shield (if you are CPR-certified)
- latex gloves

Your doctor might suggest the following: Advil for pain (no more than 2,000 milligrams per day), Tylenol for fevers over 101.5°F (38.6°C), and Pepto-Bismol for stomach upset and diarrhea (it apparently has a slight antibiotic effect too).

The following antibiotics can be prescribed by your doctor before traveling as well: Keflex (cephalexin) works for systemic infections, like when a cut causes your foot to swell; Zithromax or erythromycin for respiratory infections; and ciprofloxacin for gastrointestinal issues — though it is better to consult a local doctor before taking any of these medicines. Acetazaolamide, commonly known as Diamox, is effective for altitude sickness. If you want to be super-cautious, an Epi-Pen or Ana-Kit that contains epinephrine is the best safeguard against severe allergic reaction to insect stings.

Travelers should also put in their medical kit their brief medical history, including recent allergies and illness. If you take prescription drugs, include written instructions for how you take them and the doctor's prescription as well, just in case you get stopped in customs.

The medical kit only works at the level of the person who is using it. If you can't take a first-aid course, a backcountry wilderness guide like that published by Wilderness Medicine Institute (www.nols.edu/wmi/) will come in handy. Nearly all these medicines, including the antibiotics, can be bought in a pharmacy in Peru without a prescription — either generic or high-quality brands.

Getting shots in Peru is easy and a lot cheaper than in the United States, but you will not be protected for the first 2–4 weeks. Places to get shots include **Suiza Lab** (Atahualpa 308, Miraflores, tel. 01/612-6666, www. suizalab.com.pe, 7:30 A.M.–6 P.M. Mon.–Sat., 8 A.M.–2 P.M. daily), **Oficinas de Vacunación** (Independencia 121, Breña, 8 A.M.–12:30 P.M. Mon.–Sat.), and **International Vaccination Center** (Parque de la Medicina s/n, Dos de Mayo National Hospital, 7:30 A.M.–1:30 P.M. Mon.–Sat.).

TRAVELER'S DIARRHEA

Traveler's diarrhea pulls down even the stoutest of Peru travelers eventually and can be very unpleasant. It can be caused by parasites or viruses, but most often it is caused by bacteria carried in food or water. Plenty of other diseases in Peru are spread this way, including cholera, hepatitis A, and typhoid. Nothing is more important for you health-wise than thinking carefully about everything you eat and drink.

Only drink bottled water or water that has been previously boiled. Instead of buying an endless succession of plastic bottles, which will end up in a landfill, travel with a few reusable hard plastic bottles and ask your hotel to fill them with boiling water every morning. Refilling bottles is especially easy at hotels that have water tanks, or *bidones,* of purified water. Order drinks without ice unless you can be assured it is bagged ice or previously boiled water in order to make ice. Wipe the edges of cans and bottles before drinking or carry straws.

Avoid street vendors and buffets served under the hot sun. Instead, choose restaurants that come well recommended for taking precautions for foreigners. If the kitchen looks clean and the restaurant is full, it is probably all right. Before and after you eat, wash your hands with soap where available. Carry an antibacterial hand sanitizer as a backup.

The safest foods in restaurants are those that are served piping hot. Soups, well-cooked vegetables, rice, and pastas are usually fine. Eat salads and raw vegetables with extreme caution

and confirm beforehand that they have been previously soaked in a chlorine solution. Better yet, prepare your own salads with food disinfectants for sale in most Peruvian supermarkets if you have the facilities to cook your own meals.

An exception to the no-raw-foods rule is *cebiche,* which is raw fish marinated in bacteria-killing lime juice. As long as you are in a reputable restaurant, *cebiche* is a safe bet.

Market foods that are safe include all fruits and vegetables that can be peeled, like bananas, oranges, avocados, and apples. Many local fruits are okay as well, including *chirimoya,* tuna (the prickly cactus fruit), and *granadilla.* Dangerous items include everything that hangs close to the ground and could have become infected with feces in irrigation water. These include strawberries, mushrooms, lettuce, and tomatoes. There are plenty of safe things to buy in the market and, when combined with other safe items like bread and packaged cheese, make for a great lunch.

ALTITUDE SICKNESS

Cusco sits at 3,400 meters, and your main health concern should be altitude sickness. You will know if you're suffering from this illness very soon after your arrival. Symptoms include shortness of breath, quickened heartbeats, fatigue, loss of appetite, headaches, and nausea. There is no way to prevent it, but you can minimize the effect by avoiding heavy exercise until you get acclimatized and drinking plenty of water and liquids in general.

Many travelers carry acetazolamide, commonly known as Diamox, usually prescribed by a doctor in doses of 125–250 milligrams, taken during the morning and evening with meals. In Cusco everybody will say that coca leaf tea or *mate de coca,* taken in plentiful amounts, is the best remedy for *soroche,* the Quechua word for altitude sickness. And it works. A 100-milligram dose of the Chinese herb ginkgo billoba, taken twice a day, seems to work efficiently, too.

If you feel sick, it's good to know that all hospitals and clinics in Cusco have bottled oxygen. If you happen to be in a five-star hotel like Monasterio, Libertador, or Casa Andina Private Collection, they will provide oxygen in the rooms upon request. Have in mind that altitude sickness, if not taken care off appropriately, can develop into **high-altitude pulmonary edema,** with acute chest pain, coughs, and fluid buildup in the lungs, or **high-altitude cerebral edema,** involving severe headaches coupled with bizarre changes of personality. In both cases, these illnesses can lead to death if not treated immediately and adequately.

Hospital Regional (Av. de la Cultura, tel. 084/24-3240) and the **Hospital Lorena** (Plazoleta Belén 1358, Santiago district, tel. 084/22-1581) are the main health centers in Cusco. A bit more expensive, but faster and more reliable, is **Clínica Pardo** (Av. de la Cultura 710, tel. 084/24-0387). In an emergency situation try going to the hospital with a local if you're not fluent in Spanish.

MALARIA

Malaria is a concern for travelers who venture where the Andes slope into the Amazon below about 1,500 meters. There is a much greater chance of getting malaria in the jungle of northern Peru, such as in the surroundings of **Tarapoto,** the **Reserva Nacional Pacaya Samiria,** or **Iquitos,** than there is in the southern jungle of **Parque Nacional Manu** and **Puerto Maldonado** area.

The four species of parasite that cause malaria are all transmitted by a female mosquito, which bites most frequently at dawn and dusk. Symptoms include chills, sweats, headaches, nausea, diarrhea, and especially spiking fevers. We recommend that travelers heading to the Amazon protect themselves from mosquito bites and take antimalarial medicines.

Peru's mosquitoes, affectionately known as the Bolivian air force, have developed a resistance to **chloroquine,** the traditional malaria medicine. So that leaves three medicines available to travelers: **Mefloquine** is taken weekly both before and after leaving the jungle, but it has a host of side effects. **Malarone** is a new drug that is taken daily and has few side effects but is very expensive. And then there is **doxycycline,** which is also taken daily but is very cheap. Doxycycline's side effects can cause upset stomach and make your skin sensitive to sunlight.

Unfortunately, none of these medicines are completely effective, and many have contraindications. Consult your doctor about which is most appropriate for you. After returning from the jungle, finish your malarial meds completely. Malaria symptoms can take months to appear, and you should see your doctor if you experience fevers after your return from Peru. More information is available in the United States through the CDC's hotline (tel. 877/394-8747).

AVOIDING MOSQUITO BITES

Apart from malaria, mosquitoes in Peru also transmit **yellow fever** and **dengue,** a flu-like disease that is usually not life-threatening. Ticks and smaller insects can also transmit **Chagas' disease.** With a few simple precautions against insects, Amazon visitors greatly reduce their risk of exposure to these diseases.

Begin by wearing long pants, long-sleeved shirts, good shoes, and a hat with a bandanna covering the neck. Clothes should preferably be thick enough to prevent mosquitoes from biting through, but that is hard to do in the jungle. Lighter colors, especially white, for some reason, seem to keep mosquitoes away.

Spray your clothes with a **permethrin**-based spray, especially cuffs and sleeves. When arriving at the lodge, spray the mosquito net over your bed with the spray as well and let it dry before sleeping. Studies show that permethrin lasts up to several weeks on clothes, even after having been washed five or six times.

Apply a **DEET**-based solution when mosquitoes are present. Studies have shown that 20–33 percent DEET lasts for 6–12 hours (less if you are perspiring) and that anything over that strength produces only marginal improvements in protection. DEET is a highly toxic substance, so wash it off the skin as soon as possible. Use only 10 percent DEET on kids and none at all on infants. DEET will melt any plastic bag you store it in and will also ruin jewelry.

Many lodges provide a coil that can be lit and then smokes throughout the night, releasing a mild insecticide. These seem to work quite well. Make sure your mosquito bed net is wide enough so that you don't lie against it as you sleep—otherwise the mosquitoes will bite you right through it.

Peruvian mosquitoes, unfortunately, seem to pay no attention to natural repellents such as citronella or oils made from soybean and eucalyptus. Bring DEET-based lotion at least as a backup.

DOGS AND RABIES

There are lots of wild (or at least surly) dogs in Peru, as trekkers in places like the Cordillera Huayhuash soon find out. If you are planning to spend a lot of time trekking in Peru, you should consult with your doctor about getting a rabies vaccine.

There are lots of things you can do to avoid being bitten by a dog. As cute or as hungry as a dog may look, be careful about petting a dog in Peru unless you know the owner. Many street dogs have been mistreated and have highly unpredictable behavior.

If you are walking into an area with dogs, collect a few stones. All Peruvian dogs are acutely aware of how much a well-aimed stone can hurt, and they will usually scatter even if you pretend to pick up a stone, or pretend to throw one. This is by far the best way to stop a dog, or a pack of them, from bothering you.

If you do get bitten, wash the wound with soap and water and rinse it with alcohol or iodine. If possible, test the animal for rabies. Rabies is a fatal disease. If there is any doubt about whether the animal was rabid, you should receive rabies shots immediately.

HYPOTHERMIA

Peru's snow-covered mountains, highlands, and even cloud forests have plenty of cold, rainy days, conditions in which hypothermia is most likely to occur. Watch yourself and those around you for early signs of hypothermia, which include shivering, crankiness, exhaustion, clammy skin, and loss of fine coordination. In more advanced hypothermia the person stumbles, slurs his or her speech, acts irrationally, and eventually becomes unconscious, a state doctors refer to as the "metabolic ice box."

The key to preventing hypothermia is being prepared for the elements, and that starts with clothing. When you go for a hike, pack plenty of different layers in a plastic bag. Remember that cotton is great for evaporating sweat and cooling down on a hot day, but actually works against you in wet, cold weather. Artificial fibers like fleece or polypropylene work when wet because they wick water away from your body. Wool is another good choice because it insulates even when wet. And a waterproof poncho or a Gore-Tex jacket will help keep you dry. Having a lot of food and water is also important, and in demanding conditions you and everyone you are with should be fueling up constantly.

The key to avoiding hypothermia is catching it early. If you or someone in your group is shivering or having a hard time zipping up a jacket, take action immediately. In mild hypothermia, the body is still trying to warm itself, and all you have to do is support that process. Feed the person water and a variety of foods, from fast-burning chocolate to bread and cheese. Have them do vigorous exercises like squatting and standing over and over, or swinging their arms around like a windmill. If the person remains cold, set up a tent and put him or her in a sleeping bag with hot-water bottles. Monitor the person carefully until body temperature returns to normal. A person who was on the edge of hypothermia one day is more susceptible the next, so allow for at least a day or two of rest and recuperation.

HEAT EXHAUSTION

Peru's tropical sun and its climate extremes, from searing desert to steamy jungle, can be dangerous for those who are unaccustomed to them. Like hypothermia, heat exhaustion is caused by environmental conditions that knock the body temperature out of whack. And like hypothermia, heat-related illnesses can be deadly if not treated in time.

People suffering from heat exhaustion usually have been sweating profusely and have become dehydrated, which causes the person to have a headache. The skin appears pale and the person may vomit or feel dizzy after standing. The heart rate is elevated and, at first glance, the person appears to have the flu.

It is vital to take care of the problem before it gets worse. Find a shady spot—or create one with clothing—and give the person plenty of water, preferably mixed with electrolytes or at least a pinch or two of salt. Place damp, cool cloths on the person's face and back. Allow them to sleep if they feel drowsy. Another side effect of dehydration is painful heat cramps, which can be relieved by hydration and massage.

People are more prone to heat exhaustion when they are dehydrated, overweight, unaccustomed to a sunny or humid climate, and either very young or old. Taking it easy and drinking plenty of water is the best way to avoid heat exhaustion. Wearing a wide-brimmed hat and loose cotton clothing that covers the body is also important, along with applying plenty of sunscreen. If you exert yourself on a hot day, remember that you should be drinking 2–4 liters of water per day.

SEXUALLY TRANSMITTED DISEASES

HIV/AIDS is a worldwide health problem that is spreading in Peru along with **hepatitis B** and other sexually transmitted diseases. The United Nations officially classifies Peru's AIDS epidemic as low-level and estimated in 2005 that there were between 89,000 and 93,000 people in Peru living with HIV/AIDS. About 74 percent of the adults were men, more than half of whom identified themselves as heterosexual. The number of infected women and children is rising.

Despite state-promoted campaigns that have increased the concept of safe sex in public's

mind in Peru, many men still refuse to use condoms. HIV/AIDS and other sexually transmitted diseases may be transmitted just as often in homosexual sex as in heterosexual sex. Travelers should take full precautions before engaging in sex, beginning with the use of condoms.

MEDICAL CARE IN PERU

Peru's health-care system is excellent considering the fact that many Peruvians live in poverty. Even small villages usually have a medical post, or *posta médica,* which is often staffed with a university-trained medical student completing his or her residency. Midsize cities like Huaraz have a range of health options, including a few government hospitals and a few private clinics. In general, the clinics provide more personalized, high-tech service, but plenty of state hospitals offer in general better health care than what you could ever get in the United States. A country doctor in Peru is probably going to identify your particular stomach ailment faster than a specialist in the United States, simply because the Peruvian doctor has seen your condition many times before.

For serious medical problems or accidents, we recommend that people travel to Lima. The best hospitals are there, and insurance companies abroad are often able to handle payments directly with them (elsewhere the patient is expected to shell out the cash and hopefully be reimbursed later).

Nearly all international medical policies will cover a speedy evacuation to your country if necessary, which is one of the main reasons for getting insurance in the first place. A good resource for advice in medical situations is the **South American Explorers Club** in Lima (Piura 135, Miraflores, tel. 01/445-3306, www. saexplorers.org).

MEDICAL TRAVEL INSURANCE

Most medical insurance will not cover you while traveling abroad, so most Peru travelers buy overseas medical insurance. Go with a reputable insurance company, or you will have trouble collecting claims. Nearly all Peru hospitals will make you pay up front, and then it's up to you to submit your claim.

Some U.S.-based companies that have been recommended by travelers include **Medex Assistance** (tel. 800/732-5309, www.medexassist.com), **Travel Assistance International** (tel. 800/237-2828, www.travelassistance.com), **Health Care Global** by Wallach and Company Inc. (tel. 800/237-6615, www.wallach.com), and **International Medical Group** (tel. 800/628-4664, www.imglobal.com). Students can get insurance through the **STA** (tel. 800/226-8624, www.statravel.com).

Some companies sell additional riders to cover high-risk sports such as mountain climbing with a rope, paragliding, and bungee jumping. One good company is **Specialty Risk International** (tel. 800/335-0611, www.specialtyrisk.com), which insures for as little as three months. Membership with the **American Alpine Club** (tel. 303/384-0111, www.americanalpineclub.org) is open to anyone who has climbed in the last two years and includes rescue and evacuation for mountain climbers around the world.

PRESCRIPTION DRUGS

Generic medicines are easy to buy in Peru, much cheaper than in the U.S. or Europe, though quality might not always be the same. Travelers used to stock up their medical kit in Peru, but nowadays there are more restrictions with prescribed medicine, especially if you want to purchase it in big pharmacies, hospitals, or clinics. Specific birth control or allergy pills can be hard to find in Peru, unless you go to a private clinic pharmacy.

Though it's tempting, avoid self-medicating. Visiting a Peruvian doctor is inexpensive compared to U.S. and European rates. They are the world's leading experts on bacteria and parasite conditions specific to Peru, anyway, so it's worth it. You can waste a lot of time and money, and negatively affect your health, taking ciprofloxacin, for instance, when another medicine would have been better.

ILLEGAL DRUGS

According to the present Peruvian Criminal Code, the use and possession of drugs for personal consumption is not punished if the quantities are under the amounts stipulated by law (Art. 299: 2 grams of cocaine, 7 grams of marijuana). The problem is that almost no travelers and even very few police know this, and the police will probably still take you to the *comisaría* and charge you until a judge defines the amounts you carry. So to keep it safe, it is highly recommended not to take drugs while in Peru.

The penalties for smuggling out drugs are very strict for **cocaine,** which is common and of very high purity in Peru, and not as cut with all kinds of dangerous chemicals as in the United States and Europe. There is no bail for drug trafficking cases, and the legal process can drag on for up to two years. Your embassy will most likely decline to get involved.

Peru is well known for confidence scams that involve drugs. A typical one generally targets men and can start with a random meeting in the street with an attractive young woman. After conversation and moving to a bar or discotheque the woman will offer up some drugs. Suddenly and unexpectedly, police appear from nowhere and the attractive gal disappears.

What follows is extortion in exchange for not being arrested. The so-called "police" will explain that you could spend the next five years or more in jail unless you give them money. If you don't react, they will take you to the police station. If you decide to offer them money, the police will drive you to a series of ATMs in order to take as much money as possible from your accounts. Several hours later, and after having your bank account cleaned out, you will probably be dropped off in some remote area of Lima. The worst part is that the perpetrators probably are not even real police.

CRIME

Peru is generally a safe country, so travelers should not feel paranoid. But as in any other place in the world, follow common-sense rules and realize that thieves target travelers because they have cash and valuable electronics on them. You will be easy prey for thieves only if you are distracted.

Be alert and organized and watch your valuables at all times. Your money and passport should be carried under your clothes in a pouch or locked in a safety box at your hotel. Keep a constant eye on your luggage in bus stations. When in markets, place your backpack in front of you so that it cannot be slit open. When in restaurants or buses, keep your purse or bag close to you.

Make yourself less of a target. Do not wear jewelry or fancy watches, and keep your camera in a beat-up hip bag that is unlikely to draw attention. Be alert when in crowded places like markets or bus stations, where pickpockets abound. Go only to nightspots that have been recommended. Walk with a sense of purpose, like you belong exactly where you are. When withdrawing money from an ATM, be with a friend or have a taxi waiting.

Experienced travelers can sense a scam or theft right before it happens and, nine times out of ten, it involves momentary distraction or misplaced trust. If someone spits on you, latch onto your camera instead of cleaning yourself. If someone falls in the street in front of you or drops something, move away quickly. If an old man asks for your help in reading a lottery ticket, say no. If a stranger motions you over or offers a piece of candy, keep going. Be distrusting of people you do not know.

At nightspots, do not accept alcohol from strangers, as it might be laced with a sleeping drug. Do not do drugs. If you have been drinking, take a taxi home instead of walking.

Be careful when taking taxis and when changing money. When riding to the Jorge Chávez International Airport in Lima, lock your luggage in the trunk and hold onto your valuables. When traffic becomes heavy on Avenida La Marina, teams of delinquents often break windows and snatch bags before speeding away on a motorcycle.

Information and Services

MONEY

Thanks to ATMs, getting cash all over Peru is about as simple, easy, and cheap as it is in your own country. U.S. banks usually charge a US$3 fee per transaction, but the benefits of using bank cards outweigh the risk of carrying loads of cash. Banks usually charge hefty commissions for cashing travelers checks, but a modest supply is nice to have along in case your bank cards are stolen (check with your bank before you go to find out if it is even possible to replace your bank cards overseas). Credit cards are useful and it's increasingly common to use them to purchase almost everything in big cities. Throughout the country Visa cards are easiest to use in restaurants and hotels, but also ask if establishments accept MasterCard or American Express. If your bank cards get stolen and you spend all your travelers checks, you can always get a cash withdrawal off your credit card. Bottom line: Rely on your ATM card and bring some travelers checks and a credit card or two.

Peruvian Money

The official Peruvian currency is the *nuevo sol* (S/.), which for the last several years has hovered around 2.80 per US$1. Peruvian bills come in denominations of 10, 20, 50, 100, and 200 *soles.* The *sol* is divided into 100 smaller units, called *céntimos,* which come in coins of 1, 5, 10, 20, and 50 *céntimos.* There are also heavier coins for 1, 2, and 5 *soles.* Beware that 2- and 5-*sol* coins look very much alike, the only difference being the size (5-*sol* coins are slightly bigger). Currency calculations with today's rate can be made with online currency converters such as **XE.Com** (www.xe.com). Exchange rates are commonly listed on signs in front of banks and exchange houses and are also posted in daily newspapers.

AVOIDING COUNTERFEIT MONEY

Counterfeit money prevails in Peru. It includes both U.S. bills and Peruvian bills and coins. No counterfeit euros have been detected so far in these last years. Peruvians can recognize counterfeit *nuevos soles* quite easily, either in bills – mostly 100 and 50 notes, but also the 2- and 5-*sol* coins, which are very similar in design but a bit different in diameter. Getting money from an ATM or a bank reduces the risk but not totally. You will know when you have been scammed with a fake note. Depending on the value, it might be easier or harder to pass it on.

Here are a few tips for avoiding counterfeit bills:

· **Feel and scratch the paper.** Counterfeit bills are usually smooth and glossy, while real bills are crisp and coarse and have a low reflective surface. For U.S. dollar bills, many Peruvians scratch the neck area of the person pictured on the bill. The lapel should have a bumpy quality, unless it is an old bill. Hold both ends and snap the bill – it should have a strong feel.

· **Reject old bills.** This includes ones that are faded, tattered, ripped, or taped, especially if they are U.S. notes. You will never get rid of these bills unless you trade them on the street at a lesser rate. Banks will not change them, unless they are Peruvian notes. Counterfeit bills are made of inferior paper and often rip.

· **Hold the bill up to a light.** In both Peruvian and American bills there should be watermarks and thin ribbons that only show up when put against a light source. In the new U.S. $10 and $20 bills, the watermark is a smaller, though fuzzy, replica of the person pictured on the bill. These bills also have thin lines that run across the bill and say "US TEN" or "US TWENTY."

· **With Peruvian bills, look for reflective ink.** When you tilt a Peruvian bill from side to side, the ink on the number denomination should change color, like a heliogram. So far, Peruvian counterfeiters have been unable to reproduce this ink.

Changing Money

The U.S. dollar, despite being the most common foreign currency to exchange, is far from being the strongest. Nowadays, it is fairly easy to exchange euros in most Peruvian towns and other currencies only in big cities.

Inspect your dollar bills carefully before leaving your country and treat them with care. Even slight rips will cause them to be rejected everywhere you go. In the best case, you might be able to cash a tattered bill on the street for a lower rate, but regardless, US$50 and US$100 bills are difficult to exchange. There are a few banks and money exchange houses in almost all big airports in Peru. Generally speaking, most Peruvians exchange their dollars at exchange houses, called *casas de cambio,* because they give a slightly higher rate than banks. These are usually clustered around the Plaza de Armas or main commercial streets in every

city and town. In major cities, representatives of these *casas de cambio* will even come to your hotel to exchange money, depending on the amount.

In major cities, there are also money changers on the street who wear colored vests and an ID card. These people are generally safe and honest, though they will sometimes take advantage of you if you don't know the daily exchange rate. Never change money with unlicensed money changers, who will sometimes have rigged calculators. Whenever you change money on the street, check the amount with your own calculator.

When you change money, check each bill carefully to see that it is not counterfeit. Hand back all bills that have slight rips, have been repaired with tape, or have other imperfections. Insist on cash in 20- and 50-*soles* bills. Unless you are at a supermarket or a restaurant, the 100-*soles* bills are hard to change and you will end up waiting as someone runs across the street to find change for you.

Money Machines

ATMs, known as *cajeros automáticos,* are now commonplace in tourist towns, even small ones. The most secure ATMs are in glass rooms that you unlock by swiping your card at the door. Most ATMs accept cards with Visa/Plus or MasterCard/Cirrus logos. Banco de Crédito and Global Net are the only machines that accept American Express cards, and Global Net is the only machine that charges a commission to withdraw money. Other ATMs let you off scot-free! Interbank (available in most big cities in Peru) is the only bank with special ATMs that deliver coins. Unlike in Europe or the U.S., ATMs deliver the cash you requested first and then will give your card back. If you forget to pull it out, it will be eaten by the machine and be quite difficult to get back. Thieves sometimes wait for people to take cash out of their ATM and then follow them, sometimes on a motorcycle, to a secluded spot. For this reason, use ATMs during the day.

Banks and Wire Transfers

Banks are generally open 9 A.M.–5 P.M. Monday–Friday, mornings only on Saturday, and are closed on Sunday. Banks are useful for cashing travelers checks, receiving wire transfers, and getting cash advances on credit cards (Visa works best, but MasterCard and American Express are also accepted). Bank commissions for all these transactions vary US$20–30, so it is worth shopping around.

A cheaper option for wire transfers is often **Western Union,** which has offices in many Peruvian cities. Call the person you want to wire money to and give them an address and phone number where Western Union can contact you. Once your money has arrived, you just go to the Western Union office with your passport to pick it up.

Travelers Checks

American Express is the most widely accepted travelers check and can easily be exchanged in banks. From the United States these checks can be ordered over the phone by calling toll-free 800/721-9768. The best place to change travelers checks in Peru is at **Banco de Crédito,** also known as BCP, which often charges no fee at all. The other banks charge a 2.5 percent commission or a flat fee that can be as much as US$10. *Casas de cambio* charge even higher fees.

Remember to record the numbers of your travelers checks and keep them in a separate place. Some travelers email these numbers to themselves so that they are always available when needed. If you end up not using your travelers checks, they can always be converted into cash back home for their face value.

If your American Express travelers checks get stolen, you can call the company collect either in Peru at 0800/51-531 or in the U.S. at 801/964-6665. You can also go online to www.americanexpress.com to find the nearest office. American Express maintains representatives in Peru in Chiclayo, Trujillo, Lima, and Arequipa. In Lima its representative is Viajes Falabella, which has a half dozen offices in the city, including in Miraflores (Larco 747, tel. 01/444-4239, 9 A.M.–6 P.M. Sun.–Fri.).

Credit Cards

In recent times the use of credit cards has expanded to almost all big cities in Peru for even the smallest purchases. Be sure you ask, though. Not all cards are accepted everywhere. By far, the best card to have in Peru is Visa or MasterCard, though Diners Club and to a lesser extent American Express are increasingly accepted. Apart from their in-country toll-free numbers, most credit cards list a number you can call collect from overseas. Carry this number in a safe place or email it to yourself so that you have it in an emergency.

For Visa cards, you can also look online at www.visa.com or call collect in the United States to 410/902-8022. For MasterCard, see www.mastercard.com or call its collect, 24-hour emergency number in the United States at 636/722-7111. For American Express, see www.americanexpress.com or call the company in the U.S. at 336/393-1111. To contact Diners Club (www.dinersclub.com) while in Peru call 01/615-1111.

Bargaining

Bargaining is common practice in Peru, especially at markets and shops, and to a minor extent in mid-budget hotels. Bargaining can be fun, but don't go overboard. Have a good sense of what an item should cost beforehand. Ask them how much it costs (*"¿Cuánto cuesta?"*) and then offer 20 percent less, depending on how outlandish the asking price is. Usually vendors and shoppers meet somewhere in the middle. Some people bargain ruthlessly and pretend to walk out the door to get the best deal. On the other hand, a smile, humor, and some friendly conversation works better.

If you have a reasonable price, accept it graciously. There is nothing worse than seeing a gringo bargaining a campesino into the ground over a pair of woven mittens. We might go and have a coffee with the money we save, while the vendor might use it to buy shoes for his daughter!

Discounts

Student discounts are ubiquitous in Peru, so get an **ISIC card** (International Student Identity Card) if you can, and flash it wherever you go. If you are in Peru for a week or two it is usually possible to make up the money you spent on that **South American Explorers Club** membership just in the discounts you are entitled to at hotels, restaurants, and agencies—the hardest part is remembering to ask for it before you pay. The SAE in Lima and Cusco has lists of establishments that accept their discounts.

Tipping

Tipping is a great way for foreign travelers to get money to the people who need it the most—the guides, waiters, hotel staff, drivers, porters, burro drivers, and other front-line workers of the tourism industry. Though not required, even the smallest tip is immensely appreciated. It's also a good way of letting people

© SERGIO SCHABELMAN

fruit-and-vegetable market in Iquitos

know they are doing a great job. Tipping is an ethic that varies from person to person.

In restaurants a tip of 10 percent is ideal but not enforced. Try to give the tip to the waiter personally, especially when the table is outdoors or you pay with a credit card. It is not necessary to tip taxi drivers in Peru, but you should give a few *soles* to anyone who helps you carry your bags, including hotel staff or an airport shuttle driver. Assuming you were pleased with their service, you should tip guides, porters, and mule drivers at least one day's wage for every week worked. If they did a great job, tip more. Tipping in U.S. dollars or other foreign currency is not necessarily a good deal for these people, especially if they live away from big cities where they can't exchange the money. Tip in local currency.

MAPS AND TOURIST INFORMATION
Maps
You can buy a range of maps in Arequipa, Cusco, and Huaraz, but the best maps are to be found in Lima. **South American Explorers Club** in Lima and Cusco sells the leading country maps, plus a good selection of military topographic maps. To find topographic maps for remote areas you will have to make a trip down to Lima's **Instituto Geográfico Nacional** (tel. 01/475-3030, www.ign.gob.pe).

Good bookstores generally sell the better national maps, and we especially liked the maps in the back of the *Inca Guide to Peru* and the *Lima 2000* series (scale 1:2,200,00). Many hotels and Iperú offices give out free city maps. If you want to purchase maps before arriving in Peru, the *Lima 2000* map is sold for US$8.95 at www.gonetomorrow.com. Another online map store is www.omnimap.com.

Tourist Offices
The Peruvian government has set up tourist offices—known as **Iperú**—in most major cities, including Tumbes, Chiclayo, Trujillo, Chachapoyas, Iquitos, Huaraz, Lima, Ayacucho, Cusco, Arequipa, Puno, and Tacna. They receive questions and have a website in English, French,

German, Portuguese, Italian, and Spanish (tel. 01/574-8000, www.peru.info). They can give you brochures, maps, and basic info.

The Iperú office is also the place to go if you want to file a complaint or need to solve a problem. These can include a bus company not taking responsibility for lost luggage, a tour company that did not deliver what it promised, or an independent guide who is not honest. In an emergency, you should contact the police and also call Iperú's 24-hour hotline (tel. 01/574-8000).

FILM AND PHOTOGRAPHY
Peru is a very photogenic country, and don't be surprised if you shoot twice as much as you were expecting. In Peru, photographing soldiers or military installations is against the law.

Digital Cameras
Memory cards and other accessories are increasingly available in Lima and other large Peruvian cities. These same outfits will usually take a full memory card and burn it onto a compact disc for about US$5—but that requires the toggle cable that comes with your camera. Bring a few large-capacity cards and an extra battery. Unless you have your own laptop, there will be long stretches where you will not be able to download.

Film Processing
When it comes to conventional cameras, nearly every Peruvian city has a photo-processing lab, which is usually affiliated with Kodak. Quality varies, however, and if you are looking for highly professional quality, wait until you return home or get to a big city like Lima, Trujillo, Cusco, Arequipa, or Puno. Developing black-and-white or slide film is limited to big cities too.

Photo Tips
The main issue for photography on the coast and in the highlands is the intense sunlight. The ideal times to photograph are in the warm-color hours of early morning or late afternoon. Use filters that knock down UV radiation and

increase saturation of colors. In the jungle, the main problem is lack of light, so a higher ASA is recommended whether using conventional or digital cameras. If you want to take pictures of wildlife, you will have to bring a hefty zoom and have a lot of time to wait for the shots to materialize. A good source of information on travel photography is **Tribal Eye Images** (www.tribaleye.co.uk). The author offers free tips on choosing equipment and film, general techniques and composition, photographing people, and selling your work. Other sites include www.photo.net/travel and the members-only www.photographytips.com.

Photographing Locals

Photographing locals poses a real dilemma. On one hand, their colorful clothing and expressions make the best travel photos. But many Peruvians feel uncomfortable with having their picture taken, and foreigners need to respect that. They might even ask you, with all right, *¿Porqué me tomas una foto?*, "Why are you shooting a photo of me?" Before you take a picture of people, take the time to meet them and establish a relationship. Then ask permission to take their photo.

The most compliant subjects are market vendors, especially those from whom you have just bought something. Children in the highlands will ask for money in order to have their picture taken. Adults will even ask if you will be making business selling their portraits.

COMMUNICATIONS AND MEDIA
Mail

Peru's national post office service is **Serpost** (www.serpost.com.pe), and there is an office in nearly every village, or at the very least a *buzón* or mailbox. Postal service in Peru is fairly reliable and surprisingly expensive. Postcards and letters cost US$2–4 to the United States and Europe, and more if you want them certified. Letters sent from Peru take around two weeks to arrive in the United States, but less time if sent from Lima. If you know Spanish, check for a complete list of post offices by region and

provinces in Serpost's website (www.serpost.com.pe) under Red de Oficinas. To ship packages out of Peru use **DHL, FedEx** or some other courier service.

If you become a member of South American Explorers, you can receive personal mail at its offices in Lima or Cusco. You can also receive mail at your respective embassy in Lima.

Telephone Calls

International rates continue to drop both from overseas into Peru, and from Peru overseas. Our favorite option for calling Peru is Skype (www.skype.com), as most Peruvians have a Skype account. Even if they don't you can charge your Skype account with money and, via a service called "Skype Out," use Skype to call a Peruvian land line or cell phone. A number of calling cards, which can be purchased online, also make calling Peru incredibly cheap. **Alosmart** (www.alosmart.com) has a search engine for finding the best card depending on the type of calls you are going to make.

If you would like someone from home to be able to reach you, you should consider renting or buying a **cell phone.** In the baggage claim area of the airport, there are cell phone agents who rent phones from Peru's major carriers: Telefónica, Claro, and Nextel. Claro gets the widest service. Buying a cell phone will cost you a minimum of US$30. If you take your cell phone from home with you and it is unlocked, you can buy instead just the sim card for about US$5–10 and have a local number. A new phone comes with a standard number of minutes. Once you expend these minutes, you will need to buy a recharge card, which comes in denominations of US$3.50, US$7, or US$11. You can also charge your phone online. These cards allow callers to call both nationally and internationally—receiving calls is free once you have the phone.

Most towns have public phones on the main square and usually an office of **Telefónica,** Peru's main phone company. The phones are coin-operated, but most people buy telephone cards.

The most popular prepaid card is called 147 and can be bought in denominations of

US$3–30 at most pharmacies, supermarkets, and from the Telefónica offices themselves. Also available are HolaPerú cards for international calls. In either case, dialing the United States is more or less about US$0.80 per minute, and a local call, with 147, is about US$0.15 per minute. Surcharges are applied to all calls made from pay phones, so use your hotel phone or walk into any small store in Peru with the green-and-blue phone symbol above it.

All major **international phone cards** can be used in Peru, as long as you know the access code: AT&T is 0800-5000, MCI is 0800-50010, TRT is 0800-50030, and Sprint is 0800-50020. Worldlink has no direct access in Peru.

The cheapest way to make long-distance calls from Peru, however, is via the **net-to-phone** systems available at many Internet places for as low as US$0.17 per minute calling to the United States or Europe. There can be a lag when calling with most of these services, though Internet cafés that have cable service are usually crystal clear—often even better than a phone!

All long-distance calls in Peru are preceded by a 0 and the area code of that particular region, or department, of Peru. For instance, for calling Cusco all numbers are preceded by 084—these preceding numbers are listed whenever a number is listed in this book. All home phones in Lima have seven-digit numbers, and numbers are six digits in other towns and cities in the rest of the country. All cell phones have nine-digit numbers in all of Peru.

Peru's country code is **51,** and each of the 23 regions in Peru has a different code. Cusco, for instance, is 84. So dialing a Cusco number from the United States would be 011 (used for all international calls) + 51 (country code) + 84 (city code) and then the number. All cities in Peru have two-digit city codes when dialing from overseas, except Lima. When calling Lima from the United States dial 011-51-1 and then the number. When dialing Lima from within Peru, however, you must first dial 01.

To place a direct international phone call from Peru, dial 00 + country code + city code + number. The country code for Argentina is 54,

PERU'S AREA CODES

Abancay	83
Aguas Calientes	84
Arequipa	54
Ayacucho	66
Cajamarca	76
Chachapoyas	41
Chiclayo	74
Chincha	56
Cusco	84
Huancayo	64
Huánuco	62
Huaraz	43
Ica	56
Iquitos	65
Lima	01
Máncora	73
Nasca	56
Piura	73
Pucallpa	61
Puerto Maldonado	82
Puno	51
Tacna	52
Tarapoto	42
Trujillo	44
Tumbes	72

Australia is 61, Canada is 1, Chile is 56, Denmark is 45, France is 33, Germany is 49, Netherlands is 31, Israel is 972, Japan is 81, New Zealand is 64, Norway is 47, Spain is 34, Switzerland is 41, the United Kingdom is 44, and the United States is 1. So for calling the United Kingdom from Peru, callers should dial 0044 before any number, and for the United States 001.

Collect calls are possible from many Telefónica offices, or you can dial the international operator (108) for assistance. The correct way to ask for a collect call is: *"Quisiera hacer una llamada de cobro revertido, por favor."*

The following codes can be called for help: directory assistance 103, emergency assistance in Lima 105, international operator assistance 108, national operator assistance 109, fire 116, and urgent medical assistance 117. The chance of finding an English-speaking operator at these numbers is slim. However, Iperú maintains a 24-hour English-speaking operator at Jorge Chávez International Airport in Lima for emergencies (tel. 01/574-8000).

Fax

Sending a fax from Peru to the United States is expensive, ranging US$2–9 per page to the United States or Europe. Instead of a fax, scan your document and send it as an email attachment. Fax machines are available at most hotels, photocopy stores, and Telefónica offices.

Internet Access

Using a computer is by far the cheapest and most convenient way to communicate in Peru. Internet cafés are everywhere and are popping up in even tiny towns. Using the Internet is cheap (US$0.40–0.70 per hour), and often you can also make cheap net-to-phone overseas calls through **Skype.**

There is a lot that goes into choosing an Internet café, however. First off, make sure it is a high-speed connection, which in Peru is generally referred to as "speedy." Some speedy connections, however, are much faster than others. If your email takes more than a minute or two to open up, we suggest you head elsewhere. Another huge factor is noise, especially with Internet places that cater to schoolkids, who show up each afternoon and shout and scream and wrestle with each other over who gets to use what machine.

Besides speedy, which is a DSL line, Lima and the bigger cities now have faster connections with cable modems and—most important—crystal-clear, dirt-cheap international calls. Sometimes a remote jungle town can have a satellite Internet center, which is also amazingly fast.

Nowadays most upscale and medium-range hotels will have free WiFi access for guests traveling with laptops. In Lima and other touristy cities like Cusco, Arequipa, Trujillo, Puno, or Huaraz, you will find cafés with free WiFi access.

Printed and Online News

Publications in Spanish are headed by *El Comercio* (http://elcomercio.pe/), the largest and oldest standard daily newspaper with major credibility in Peru. It has a variety of supplements and magazines with good information on cultural activities and performing arts, including *Somos,* a weekly magazine published every Saturday. Among a dozen tabloids, two are worth checking out: *Perú21* (http://peru21.pe), with a moderate center political standing, and *La República* (http://larepublica.pe), traditionally left-oriented.

Caretas (www.caretas.com.pe) is a weekly magazine that has been around for more than half a century, founded by the Gibson/Zileri family. It is published every Thursday and contains a good deal of local political content, as well as sections devoted to art, humorous essays, interesting letters to the editor, jokes, crossword puzzles, and great photographs.

DedoMedio (www.dedomedio.com), with its slogan *"la verdad aunque te duela"* (the truth even if it hurts you), is a brilliant monthly publication full of satire, highly acidic content material, great caricatures, and very good written articles about almost any topic you can think of including domestic politics, art, music, etc.

Some useful news websites in English include **Living In Peru** (www.livinginperu.com), which also has classified ads and vast information on cultural activities, tourism, and gastronomy, among other subjects. One of the oldest English-written newspapers in South America, **The Andean Air Mail & Peruvian Times** (www.peruviantimes.com) resurfaced some years ago in the Internet, offering feature articles, op-ed columns, and good overall coverage of what is going on in Peru. The **Expat Peru Network** (www.expatperu.com) also offers local news coverage—actually linked to *The Peruvian Times*— but focuses more on service information such as legal aspects, traveling to Peru, and several discussion forums by topic.

WEIGHTS AND MEASURES

Peru uses the metric system for everything except gallons of gasoline. For conversion information, see the back of this book.

Electricity

The electrical system of Peru is 220 volts and 60 cycles. If you absent-mindedly plug in a 110-volt appliance from the United States into a 220-volt Peruvian outlet, you will start a small fire. All high-end hotels (such as Casa Andina or Libertador, for example) have additional outlets of 110 volts.

You can use 110-volt appliances in Peru with a converter, which can be quite heavy. You can buy one in an electronics shop, though they are cheaper in Peru. Make sure you get the right type, as a hair dryer needs a more robust converter than, say, a digital camera battery charger.

Voltage surges are common in Peru, so it is also a good idea to bring a surge protector from home that can be plugged between your appliance and the converter. Most laptops and digital cameras these days can take either 110 or 220 volts, so check on this before you buy a converter.

TIME ZONES

Peru is in the same time zone as New York, Miami, Bogotá, and Quito. Peru does not use daylight saving time, meaning that its time remains constant throughout the year. The entire country is in the same time zone (GMT -5:00).

RESOURCES

Glossary

abra high pass

aguaymanto an Inca fruit, also known as *capulí*, from which delicious jams, deserts, and other delicacies are made

ají any chili pepper; yellow peppers are *ají amarillo*

ají de gallina creamy chicken stew with yellow chili served over boiled potatoes, garnished with hard-boiled eggs and black olives

aluvión mudslide

anticuchos beef heart grilled brochettes served with an assortment of spicy sauces

arroz con pato duck with rice, originally from the north coast but now found everywhere

biscocho butter cookie

bodega storehouse for maturing wine or small grocery store

brochetas chunks of marinated chicken or beef skewered on wooden sticks and grilled

café (con leche) coffee (with milk)

camarones freshwater prawns/crawfish

camote sweet potato

cancha roasted corn kernels, a popular snack to nibble with beer, usually served with *cebiche*

canela cinnamon

cañón canyon

causa cold mashed potatoes mixed with yellow chili peppers and a dash of lime juice, layered with chicken, tuna fish, shrimp, or veggies mixed with mayonnaise, avocado, and diced onions

cebiche the trademark of Peruvian cuisine: fish, shrimp, scallops, or squid, or a mixture of all four, marinated in lime juice and chili peppers for five minutes, traditionally served with corn, sweet potatoes, and onions

cebiche mixto *cebiche* with fish and shellfish

cerveza beer; also *chela*

chacana a sacred symbol, also known as the Andean Cross, with varied and complex links to Inca cosmology; a common motif at Inca temples and other sacred sites

chancho/cerdo pig/pork

chela slang word for beer

chicha or chicha de jora drink made from different kinds of fermented corn or peanuts, quinoa, or fruit

chicha morada sweet, refreshing drink made from boiled purple corn and fruit, with clove and cinnamon, served chilled with a dash of lime juice

chicharrón deep-fried pork, chicken, or fish

chifa Peruvian-Chinese food/Chinese restaurant

chilcano a refreshing drink with pisco, ginger ale, lime juice, and a dash of Angostura bitters

chilcano de pescado a fish broth good for hangovers

chirimoya a sweet and pulpy, juicy white fruit with a mushy texture and a bitter dark green skin

choclo fresh Andean corn

choclo con queso steamy hot corn on the cob with slices of cheese and *ají* sauce

chupe Quechua word for a highly concentrated soup with beef, fish, or seafood with potatoes, corn, vegetables, and sometimes milk

cocha lake in Quechua

conchitas negras black scallop delicacy common in northern Peru

cordillera mountain range

crocante de lúcuma a meringue desert made with a fruit called *lúcuma*

culantro cilantro/coriander

cuy guinea pig; stewed, fried, or spit-roasted

granadilla sweet, pulpy passion fruit with a hard shell

guanabana indescribably delicious jungle fruit

guayaba guava

huaca in Quechua, *huaca* is a sacred object that is revered, such as a rock

huacatay black mint

humita fresh corn tamale that can be either sweet or salty

Inca Kola a unique and quite sweet Peruvian pop soda originally made out of lemongrass

juanes tamale stuffed with chicken and rice

jugo juice

kiwicha purple-flowered grain high in protein, which is folded into breads, cookies, and soups

lago lake

laguna lagoon

langostino river or sea shrimp

limón key lime or just lime

lomo saltado popular and inexpensive dish of stir-fried beef loin, with strips of *ají amarillo*, onions, tomatoes, and french fries, served with rice

lúcuma a small brown fruit recognizable by its dark peach color and smoky flavor; a popular ice cream, yogurt, and milk shake flavor

manjar caramel

manzanilla chamomile or chamomile tea

maracuyá passion fruit, served as a juice, in a pisco sour, or in cheesecake

masato alcoholic drink made from fermented yuca or manioc

mate de coca coca leaf tea

mazamorra morada pudding-like dessert made from purple corn

mirador lookout point

nevado mountain

ocopa a spicy peanut-based sauce, served over boiled potatoes and garnished with hard-boiled eggs and black olives

pachamanca the utmost Andean meal, made up of beef, pork, alpaca, *cuy*, and chicken cooked together with potatoes, sweet potatoes, and lima beans inside heated stones in a hole in the ground, covered with herbs

paiche Amazon fish; the largest freshwater fish in the world

palmito ribbons of palm heart that look like pasta when served

palta avocado

Panamericana Panamerican Highway

papa potato; Andean tuber originally from Peru and generic name for more than 3,000 different types of potatoes

papa a la huancaina cold appetizer of potatoes in a spicy light cheese sauce with *ají amarillo*

papa rellena fried oblong of mashed potatoes stuffed with meat, onions, olives, boiled eggs, and raisins

peña a bar with late-night, often folkloric, musical performances

pescado fish

piqueos finger food

pirañas small, vicious, sharp-fanged fish found in oxbow lakes and rivers

pisco grape brandy; distilled spirit

pisco sour cocktail made with three parts of pisco, two parts of lime juice, one part of sugar syrup, mixed with ice, a bit of egg white, and a dash of Angostura bitters

plátano frito fried bananas

playa beach

pollo chicken

pollo a la brasa rotisserie chicken

pomelo grapefruit; also *toronja*

pongo river gorge that is often dangerous in high water

puna high plains, often grasslands

quebrada narrow valley, ravine

quinoa golden brown, round grain, rich in protein

quipu a system of knotted, multi-colored cords that the Inca used to keep record and transmit data, such as weather forecasts, crop production, and accounting

río river

rocoto a red, bell pepper-shaped chili consumed in Arequipa

rocoto relleno red bell pepper stuffed with meat and spices

sachatomate a red fruit, also known as a *tamarillo*, that has an egg shape, an inside like a tomato, and a sweet, tangy taste

seco de cabrito roasted goat marinated with *chicha*, served with beans and rice

tacu tacu bean and rice patty, fried in a pan and topped with a fried egg, beef or fish stew, or any other kind of garnish

tiradito sashimi-like fish cuts with a chili sauce on top

toronja grapefruit; also *pomelo*

tumbo banana passion fruit

tuna prickly pear from desert cactus

valle valley

volcán volcano

yuca cassava root

Spanish Phrasebook

Even a beginner's grasp of the Spanish language will make your travels more enjoyable. Study the basics before your trip so you will be ready to practice once you arrive in Peru.

Spanish commonly uses 30 letters − the familiar English 26, plus four straightforward additions: ch, ll, ñ, and rr.

PRONUNCIATION

Unlike English, Spanish is a phonetic language. In other words, words are always pronounced exactly as they are spelled. As long as you know how to pronounce the vowels and consonants, you should be able to read Spanish and pronounce it correctly.

Vowels

a like ah, as in "hah": *agua* AH-gooah (water), *pan* PAHN (bread), and *casa* CAH-sah (house)

e like ay, as in "may": *mesa* MAY-sah (table), *tela* TAY-lah (cloth), and *de* DAY (of, from)

i like ee, as in "need": *diez* dee-AYZ (ten), *comida* ko-MEE-dah (meal), and *fin* FEEN (end)

o like oh, as in "go": *peso* PAY-soh (weight), *ocho* OH-choh (eight), and *poco* POH-koh (a bit)

u like oo, as in "cool": *uno* OO-noh (one), *cuarto* KOOAHR-toh (room), and *usted* oos-TAYD (you); when it follows a "q" the **u** is silent; when it follows an "h" or has an umlaut, it's pronounced like "w"

Consonants

b, d, f, k, l, m, n, p, q, s, t, v, w, x, y, z, and ch
pronounced almost as in English; **h** occurs, but is silent, not pronounced at all

c like k as in "keep": *cuarto* KOOAR-toh (room); when it precedes "e" or "i," pronounce **c** like s, as in "sit": *cerveza* sayr-VAY-sah (beer), *encima* ayn-SEE-mah (atop)

g like g as in "gift" when it precedes "a," "o," "u," or a consonant: *gato* GAH-toh (cat), *hago* AH-goh (I do, make); otherwise, pronounce **g** like h as in "hat": *giro* HEE-roh (money order), *gente* HAYN-tay (people)

j like h, as in "has": *jueves* HOOAY-vays (Thursday), *mejor* may-HOR (better)

ll like y, as in "yes": *toalla* toh-AH-yah (towel), *ellos* AY-yohs (they, them)

ñ like ny, as in "canyon": *año* AH-nyo (year), *señor* SAY-nyor (Mr., sir)

r is lightly trilled, with tongue at the roof of your mouth like a very light English d, as in "ready": *pero* PAY-doh (but), *tres* TDAYS (three), *cuatro* KOOAH-tdoh (four)

rr like a Spanish r, but with much more emphasis and trill. Let your tongue flap. Practice with *burro* (donkey), *carretera* (highway), and Carrillo (proper name), then really let go with *ferrocarril* (railroad).

Accent

The rule for accent, the relative stress given to syllables within a given word, is straightforward: If a word ends in a vowel, an n, or an s, accent the next-to-last syllable; otherwise, accent the last syllable.

Pronounce *gracias* GRAH-seeahs (thank you), *orden* OHR-dayn (order), and *carretera* kah-ray-TAY-rah (highway) with stress on the next-to-last syllable.

Otherwise, accent the last syllable: *venir*

vay-NEER (to come), *ferrocarril* fay-roh-cah-REEL (railroad), and *edad* ay-DAHD (age).

Exceptions to the accent rule are always marked with an accent sign: (á, é, í, ó, or ú), such as *teléfono* tay-LAY-foh-noh (telephone), *jabón* hah-BON (soap), and *rápido* RAH-pee-doh (rapid).

BASIC AND COURTEOUS EXPRESSIONS

Most Spanish-speaking people consider formalities important. Whenever approaching anyone for information or some other reason, do not forget the appropriate salutation – good morning, good evening, etc. Standing alone, the greeting *hola* (hello) can sound brusque.

Hello. *Hola.*
Good morning. *Buenos días.*
Good afternoon. *Buenas tardes.*
Good evening. *Buenas noches.*
How are you? *¿Cómo está usted?*
Very well, thank you. *Muy bien, gracias.*
Okay; good. *Bien.*
Not okay; bad. *Mal or no muy bien.*
So-so. *Más o menos.*
And you? *¿Y usted?*
Thank you. *Gracias.*
Thank you very much. *Muchas gracias.*
You're very kind. *Muy amable.*
You're welcome. *De nada.*
Goodbye. *Adios.*
See you later. *Hasta luego.*
please *por favor*
yes *sí*
no *no*
I don't know. *No sé.*
Just a moment, please. *Un momento, por favor.*
Excuse me, please (when you're trying to get attention). *Disculpe or Con permiso* (when you're trying to get through).
Excuse me (when you've made a boo-boo). *Lo siento.*
Pleased to meet you. *Mucho gusto.*
What is your name? *¿Cómo se llama usted?*
Do you speak English? *¿Habla usted inglés?*

I don't speak Spanish well. *No hablo bien el español.*
I don't understand. *No entiendo.*
How do you say...in Spanish? *¿Cómo se dice...en español?*
My name is . . . *Me llamo...*
Let's go to . . . *Vamos a...*

TERMS OF ADDRESS

When speaking with someone of respect, or someone you do not know, use *Usted* for you (formal). Otherwise use *tú* for you (informal).

I *yo*
you (formal) *usted*
you (familiar) *tú*
he/him *él*
she/her *ella*
we/us *nosotros*
you (plural) *ustedes*
they/them *ellos* (all males or mixed gender); *ellas* (all females)
Mr., sir *señor*
Mrs., madam *señora*
Miss, young lady *señorita*
wife *esposa*
husband *esposo*
friend *amigo* (male); *amiga* (female)
boyfriend/girlfriend *enamorado* or *novio* (male); *enamorada* or *novia* (female)
son; daughter *hijo; hija*
brother; sister *hermano; hermana*
father; mother *padre; madre*
grandfather; grandmother *abuelo; abuela*

TRANSPORTATION

Where is . . .? *¿Dónde está . . .?*
How far is it to . . .? *¿A qué distancia está . . .?*
From...to . . . *de...a . . .*
How many blocks? *¿Cuántas cuadras?*
Where (Which) is the way to . . .? *¿Por dónde es el camino a . . .?*
the bus station *el terminal de autobuses*
the bus stop *el paradero de autobuses*
Where is this bus going? *¿Adónde va este autobús?*
taxi *taxi*

public taxi *colectivo*
public van *combi*
three-wheeled motorized bike-taxi *mototaxi*
jungle boat with raised propeller *peke-peke*
mule driver *arriero*
mule, donkey *mula, burro*
the airport *el aeropuerto*
I'd like a ticket to . . . *Quisiera un boleto a . . .*
round-trip *ida y vuelta*
reservation *reserva*
baggage *equipaje*
Stop here, please. *Pare aquí, por favor.*
the entrance *la entrada*
the exit *la salida*
the ticket office *la boletería*
is (very) near; far *está (muy) cerca; lejos*
to; toward *a*
by; through *por*
from *de; desde*
the right *la derecha*
the left *la izquierda*
straight ahead *de frente*
in front *en frente*
beside *al lado; al costado*
behind *atrás; detrá*
the corner *la esquina*
the stoplight *el semáforo*
a turn *una vuelta*
right here *aquí*
somewhere around here *por aquí*
right there *allí; ahí*
somewhere around there *por allá; por ahí*
street *calle; jirón*
avenida *avenida*
highway *carretera*
bridge *puente*
address *dirección*
north; south *norte; sur*
east; west *este; oeste*

ACCOMMODATIONS

Hotel *hotel*
Is there a room? *¿Hay habitación?*
May I (may we) see it? *¿Puedo (podemos) verlo?*
What is the rate? *¿Cuál es la tarifa?*

Is there something cheaper? *¿Hay algo más barato?*
a single room *una habitación simple*
a double room *una habitación doble*
double bed room *una habitación matrimonial*
twin beds *camas dobles*
with private bath *con baño privado*
hot water *agua caliente*
shower *ducha*
bathtub *tina*
towels *toallas*
soap *jabón*
hair dryer *secador de cabello*
toilet paper *papel higiénico*
blanket *frazada; manta*
sheets *sábanas*
air-conditioned or a/c *aire acondicionado*
fan *ventilador*
key *llave*
manager *gerente; administrador*

FOOD

I'm hungry *Tengo hambre.*
I'm thirsty. *Tengo sed.*
menu *carta*
glass *vaso*
cup *tasa*
fork *tenedor*
knife *cuchillo*
spoon *cuchara*
tea spoon *cucharita*
napkin *servilleta*
soft drink *gaseosa*
coffee *café*
tea *té*
boiled water for drinking *agua hervida para tomar*
bottled carbonated water *agua mineral con gas*
bottled uncarbonated water *agua mineral sin gas*
wine *vino*
milk *leche*
cream *crema*
sugar *azúcar*
salt *sal*
black pepper *pimienta*
chili pepper *ají*
cheese *queso*

breakfast *desayuno*
lunch *almuerzo*
fixed lunch menu *menú del día*
dinner *cena*
the check please *la cuenta por favor*
eggs *huevos*
bread *pan*
salad *ensalada*
lettuce *lechuga*
onion *cebolla*
tomato *tomate*
fruit *fruta*
mango *mango*
papaya *papaya*
banana *plátano*
apple *manzana*
orange *naranja*
beans *frijoles*
shellfish *mariscos*
crab *cangrejo*
lobster *langosta*
mussels *choros*
scallops *conchas*
sea bass *corvina*
flounder *lenguado*
squid *calamares*
octopus *pulpo*
trout *trucha*
(without) meat *(sin) carne*
beef; steak *res; bistec*
bacon; ham *tocino; jamón*
fried *frito*
roasted *asada*
grilled *a la parrilla*

SHOPPING

money *dinero*
money-exchange bureau *casa de cambio*
money changer *cambista*
I would like to exchange travelers checks. *Quisiera cambiar cheques de viajero.*
What is the exchange rate? *¿Cuál es el tipo de cambio?*
How much is the commission? *¿Cuánto es la comisión?*
Do you accept credit cards? *¿Aceptan tarjetas de crédito?*
money order *giro*

How much does it cost? *¿Cuánto cuesta?*
What is your final price? *¿Cuál es su último precio?*
expensive *caro*
cheap *barato*
more *más*
less *menos*
a little *un poco*
too much *demasiado*

HEALTH

Help me please. *Ayúdeme por favor.*
I am ill. *Estoy enfermo.*
Call a doctor. *Llame un doctor.*
Take me to . . . *Lléveme a . . .*
hospital; clinic *hospital; clínica*
drugstore *farmacia*
pain *dolor*
fever *fiebre*
headache *dolor de cabeza*
stomachache *dolor de estómago*
burn *quemadura*
cramp *calambre*
altitude sickness *soroche*
nausea *náusea*
vomit; vomiting *vómito; vomitar*
medicine *medicina*
antibiotic *antibiótico*
pill; tablet *pastilla; tableta*
aspirin *aspirina*
ointment; cream *pomada; crema*
bandage *venda*
cotton *algodón*
sanitary napkins *toallas higiénicas*
tampons *tampons*
birth control pills *pastillas anticonceptivas*
condoms *preservativos; condones*
toothbrush *cepillo dental*
dental floss *hilo dental*
toothpaste *crema dental*
dentist *dentista*
toothache *dolor de muelas*

COMMUNICATIONS

long-distance telephone *teléfono de larga distancia*
I would like to call . . . *Quisiera llamar a . . .*
collect *por cobrar*

credit card *tarjeta de crédito*
post office *correo*
general delivery *lista de correo*
letter *carta*
stamp *estampilla*
postcard *postal*
air mail *correo aéreo*
registered *registrado*
package; box *paquete; caja*
string; tape *cuerda; cinta*

AT THE BORDER

border *frontera*
customs *aduana*
immigration *migración*
tourist card *tarjeta de turista*
inspection *inspección; revisión*
passport *pasaporte*
profession *profesión*
marital status *estado civil*
single *soltero*
married; divorced *casado; divorciado*
insurance *seguros*
title *título*
driver's license *brevete; licencia de manejar*

GAS STATION

gas station *grifo, gasolinera*
gasoline *gasolina*
unleaded *sin plomo*
full, please *lleno, por favor*
tire *llanta*
tire repair shop *llantero*
air *aire*
water *agua*
oil change *cambio de aceite*
My...doesn't work. *Mi...no sirve.*
battery *batería*
radiator *radiador*
alternator *alternador*
generator *generador*
tow truck *grúa*
repair shop *taller mecánico*

VERBS

Verbs are the key to getting along in Peru because Spanish is verb-driven. There are three classes of verbs, which end in *ar, er,* and *ir.*

to buy *comprar*
I buy, you (he, she, it) buys *compro, compra*
we buy, you (they) buy *compramos, compran*
to eat *comer*
I eat, you (he, she, it) eats *como, come*
we eat, you (they) eat *comemos, comen*
to climb *subir*
I climb, you (he, she, it) climbs *subo, sube*
we climb, you (they) climb *subimos, suben*

Got the idea? Here are more:
to do or make *hacer*
I do or make, you (he she, it) does or make *hago, hace*
we do or make, you (they) do or make *hacemos, hacen*
to go *ir*
I go, you (he, she, it) goes *voy, va*
we go, you (they) go *vamos, van*
to go (walk) *andar*
to love *amar*
to work *trabajar*
to want *desear, querer*
to need *necesitar*
to read *leer*
to write *escribir*
to repair *reparar*
to stop *parar*
to get off (the bus) *bajar*
to arrive *llegar*
to stay (remain) *quedar*
to stay (lodge) *hospedar*
to leave *salir* (regular except for **salgo,** I leave)
to look at *mirar*
to look for *buscar*
to give *dar* (regular except for **doy,** I give)
to carry *llevar*
to have *tener* (irregular but important: **tengo, tiene, tenemos, tienen**)
to come *venir* (similarly irregular: **vengo, viene, venimos, vienen**)

Spanish has two forms of "to be." Use *estar* when speaking of location or a temporary state of being: "I am at home." *"Estoy en casa."* "I'm sick." *"Estoy enfermo."* Use *ser* for a permanent state of being: "I am a doctor." *"Soy doctora."*

Estar is regular except for *estoy*, I am. *Ser* is very irregular:
to be *ser*
I am, you (he, she, it) is *soy, es*
we are, you (they) are *somos, son*

NUMBERS

0 *cero*
1 *uno*
2 *dos*
3 *tres*
4 *cuatro*
5 *cinco*
6 *seis*
7 *siete*
8 *ocho*
9 *nueve*
10 *diez*
11 *once*
12 *doce*
13 *trece*
14 *catorce*
15 *quince*
16 *dieciseis*
17 *diecisiete*
18 *dieciocho*
19 *diecinueve*
20 *veinte*
21 *veintiuno*
30 *treinta*
40 *cuarenta*
50 *cincuenta*
60 *sesenta*
70 *setenta*
80 *ochenta*
90 *noventa*
100 *cien*
101 *ciento uno*
200 *doscientos*
500 *quinientos*
1,000 *mil*
10,000 *diez mil*
100,000 *cien mil*
1,000,000 *un millón*

one-half *medio*
one-third *un tercio*
one-fourth *un cuarto*

TIME

What time is it? *¿Qué hora es?*
It's 1 o'clock. *Es la una.*
It's 3 in the afternoon. *Son las tres de la tarde.*
It's 4 A.M. *Son las cuatro de la mañana.*
6:30 *seis y media*
a quarter till 11 *un cuarto para las once*
a quarter past 5 *las cinco y cuarto*
an hour *una hora*

DAYS AND MONTHS

Monday *lunes*
Tuesday *martes*
Wednesday *miércoles*
Thursday *jueves*
Friday *viernes*
Saturday *sábado*
Sunday *domingo*
today *hoy*
tomorrow *mañana*
yesterday *ayer*
January *enero*
February *febrero*
March *marzo*
April *abril*
May *mayo*
June *junio*
July *julio*
August *agosto*
September *septiembre*
October *octubre*
November *noviembre*
December *diciembre*
a week *una semana*
a month *un mes*
after *después*
before *antes*

~ Spanish phrasebook adapted from *Moon Pacific Mexico* by Bruce Whipperman.

Quechua Phrasebook

Quechua is spoken throughout Peru's highlands, but especially in the area including Ayacucho, Cusco, and Lake Titicaca. Highlanders in the rural areas of southern Peru tend to speak only Quechua; in areas near major towns and roads, most locals speak both Quechua and some Spanish.

Quechua, or Runasimi as it is referred to by native spakers, is spoken by almost five million people in Peru and eight million throughout Peru, Ecuador, Bolivia, and Argentina. Because the Inca did not have writing, Quechua has only developed a written form in modern times. Quechua is currently receiving a revival in Peru because basic Quechua has become compulsory for all university graduates.

PRONUNCIATION

Quechua has a mixture of occlusive consonants that are separated in simple, glottal, and aspirate. The aspirate consonants are pronounced with a long soft sounds. The simple consonants are much less sharp than the glottal, which are emphasized (as indicated by the apostrophes next to them).

aspirate: ph th chh kh qh
simple: p t ch k q
glottal: p' t' ch' k' q'

NUMBERS

1 *hoq*
2 *iskay*
3 *qinsa*
4 *tawa*
5 *pisqa*
6 *soqta*
7 *qanchis*
8 *pusaq*
9 *isqon*
10 *chunka*
11 *chunka hoq ni yoq*
12 *chunka iskay ni yoq*
13 *chunka qinsa ni yoq*
20 *iskay chunka*
50 *pisqa chunka*
100 *pachaq*

INTERROGATIONS

Who? *Pi?*
What? *Ima?*
Which? *Mayqin?*
Where? *May?*
How much? *Hayk'a?*
When? *Hayk'aq?*
What for? *Imapaq?*

SOME BASIC SENTENCES

How are you? *Imaynallan kashanki?* or *Allianchu?*
I am fine. *Allillanmi kashani?*
What is your name? *Iman sutyki?*
My name is Maria. *Sutiyqa Maria.*
Where are you from? *Maymantan kanki?*
I am from Cusco. *Qosqomantan kani.*
. . . and you? *qanri?*
Where are you going? *Mayman rinki?*

BASIC AND COURTEOUS EXPRESSIONS

hello *napaykullayki*
yes *ari*
no *manan; manan kanchu*
please *allichu*
thank you *añay*
It's freezing! *Alalaw!*
It's really hot! *Akakaw!*
That's really scary! *Atakaw!*
That hurts! *Achakaw!*

QUECHUA-SPANISH CROSSOVER WORDS

As Quechua is spoken thoughout southern Peru, many words have made their way into the Spanish lexicon. Here are some examples:

baby *wawa*
cold *chiri*
no thanks *manan kanchu*
guinea pig *cuy*
brother (slang) *wayqi*
mother earth Pachamama
river *mayu*
old, ancient *macchu*

peak *picchu;* also means wad of coca leaves
star *chaska*
woman *warmi*
house *wasi*

The Quechua words for colors are often heard, especially if you have an interest in local naturally dyed textiles.

white *yurak*
black *yana*
red *puka*
blue *anqas*
yellow *q'ello*
green *qomer*

FAMILY

father or sir *tayta*
mother or madame *mama*
sister *panay*
brother *wayqi*
wife *warmi*
husband *qosa*
child *sullk'a wawa*

OTHER USEFUL QUECHUA WORDS

mountain god *apu*
Inca messenger runners *chasquis*
rest place for *chasquis tambo*
lake *cocha*
dried llama meat (jerky) *charqui*
until tomorrow *pakarinkama*
come here *hamuy*
big *hatun*
small *huchuy*
sun *inti*
moon *quilla*
sea *mamacocha*

VERBS

to speak *rimay*
to do *ruway*
to learn *yachay*
to eat *mihuy*
to rest *samay*
to walk *puriy*
to play *pukllay*

Suggested Reading

HISTORY

Burger, Richard. *Chavín and the Origins of Andean Civilization.* London: Thames and Hudson, 1995. A groundbreaking investigation of the Chavín culture, which spread across Peru's highlands 2,000 years before the Inca.

Hemming, John. *Conquest of the Incas.* New York: Harcourt Brace & Company, 1970. This is a masterpiece of both prose and history, in which famed Peru historian John Hemming lays out a gripping, blow-by-blow account of the Spanish conquest of Peru. Hemming, who was only 35 when *Conquest* was published, has written nearly a dozen books about Inca architecture and the native people of the Amazon.

Heyerdahl, Thor, and Daniel Sandweiss. *The Quest for Peru's Forgotten City.* London: Thames and Hudson, 1995. Norwegian explorer Thor Heyerdahl was most famous for piloting the *Kon-Tiki* balsa-wood raft from Callao, Peru, to the Polynesian Islands in 1947. From 1988 until he died in 2002, Heyerdahl's obsession with early ocean travel focused on the inhabitants of Túcume, a complex of 26 pyramids north of present-day Trujillo that was built by the Sicán culture around A.D. 1050. This remains the best work on Túcume.

Kirkpatrick, Sidney. *Lords of Sipán: A True Story of Pre-Inca Tombs, Archaeology, and Crime.* New York: William Morrow, 1992. Shortly after grave robbers unearthed a royal tomb of the Sipán culture near present-day Trujillo, Sydney Kirkpatrick documented the underworld of artifact smugglers and their Hollywood clients. At the center of this real-life drama is Peruvian archaeologist Walter Alva, who struggles against an entire town as he fights to preserve his country's heritage.

MacQuarrie, Kim. *The Last Days of the Incas.* New York: Simon & Schuster, 2007. Peru travelers with time to read just one book should read *The Last Days of the Incas,* written by an Emmy Award–winning author and filmmaker with years of life experience in Peru. MacQuarrie has produced what is, beyond a doubt, the most readable, fast-moving, and factual account of Peru's Spanish conquest. He describes the conquest and its aftermath in detail and integrates both 16th century Spanish chronicles and recent historical research. Unlike the more scholarly *Conquest of the Incas* by John Hemming, *The Last Days* does not end with the collapse of the Inca empire—the final chapters are devoted to 20th-century explorers such as Hiram Bingham, who identified Machu Picchu as the center of the Inca empire, and Gene Savoy, who discovered the real "lost city" of the Inca—Vilcabamba.

Mosley, Michael. *The Incas and Their Ancestors.* London: Thames and Hudson, 1993. This masterly work is still the best best general introduction to the history of Peru's early cultures, including the Nasca, Moche, Huari, and Tiahuanaco.

Muscutt, Keith. *Warriors of the Clouds: A Lost Civilization in the Upper Amazon of Peru.* Albuquerque: University of New Mexico, 1998. This book provides a good overview of what archaeologists know of the Chachapoya, a cantankerous cloud-forest empire that was never dominated by the Inca, and is replete with beautiful images of ruins in the remote cloud forest of northeastern Peru.

Protzen, Jean-Pierre. *Inka Architecture and Construction at Ollantaytambo.* Oxford, United Kingdom: Oxford University Press, 1993. Jean-Pierre Protzen spent years at the Inca site of Ollantaytambo in order to understand its historical significance and construction. This hard-to-find book is the best single work on Ollantaytambo, the most important Inca ruin next to Machu Picchu.

Savoy, Gene. *Antisuyo: The Search for the Lost Cities of the Amazon.* New York: Simon & Schuster, 1970. Gene Savoy, who is second only to Hiram Bingham in his knack for sniffing out lost cities, describes in somewhat stilted prose his search for Espíritu Pampa, the last stronghold of the Inca.

Starn, Orin, ed., Carlos Iván Degregori, and Rob Kirk. *The Peru Reader.* Durham, North Carolina: Duke University Press, 1995. This is a great paperback to bring on the airplane or a long train ride, stuffed with an endlessly entertaining and eclectic collection of short stories, anthropological essays, translated chronicles, and a bit of poetry.

Von Hagen, Adriana, and Craig Morris. *The Cities of the Ancient Andes.* London: Thames and Hudson, 1998. Writer Adriana von Hagen, daughter of the renowned German-born Peruvianist Victor von Hagen, and a curator of New York's America Museum of Natural History teamed up for this highly recommended introduction to Peru's major archaeological sites. This is the most concise and accessible history of Peru's ancient cultures, written around the centers and cities they left behind.

CHRONICLES

Cieza de León, Pedro. *The Discovery and Conquest of Peru: The New World Encounter.* Durham, North Carolina: Duke University Press, 1999. Pedro Cieza de León arrived in Peru in 1547, wide-eyed at the age of 27, and proceeded to explore every nook and cranny, describing everything as he went. He is the first Spaniard to describe Spanish mistreatment of Peru's natives. His reliable voice paints the Spanish-Inca encounter in simple and clear language.

Garcilaso de la Vega, Inca, and Harold Livermore, translator. *Royal Commentaries of the Inca and General History of Peru.* Austin, Texas: University of Texas Press, 1966. Inca Garcilaso was the son of a conquistador and an Inca princess who moved to Spain in his youth and spent the rest of his life documenting the myths, culture, and history of the Inca. Though criticized for historical inaccuracies and exaggeration, Inca Garcilaso's 1,000-page *Royal Commentaries* contains subtitles that make this work easy to thumb through.

Poma de Ayala, Felipe Guamán. *Nueva Crónica y Buen Gobierno.* Madrid: Siglo XXI, 1992. This magnificent 16th-century manuscript has become the New World's best known indigenous chronicle since it was discovered in the Royal Library of Copenhagen in 1908. It is a 1,200-page history of the Spanish conquest, told from the Andean point of view in an eclectic mixture of Quechua and Spanish. Its harangues against Spanish injustice are complemented by 400 drawings made by Poma de Ayala, which accompany the text. Parts of this text, which was intended as a letter to Spanish King Phillip III, have been translated into English and are published on the Internet at www.personal.umich. edu/~dfrye/guaman.htm.

LITERATURE

Alarcón, Daniel. *War by Candlelight. Story Collection* New York: Harper Perennial, 2006. Born in Peru and raised in Birmingham, Alabama, Alarcón returned to Peru on a Fulbright. As a result he wrote a series of short stories that evoke the sorrows and beauty of a ravaged land with a precision and steadiness that stand in inverse proportion to the magnitude of the losses he so powerfully dramatizes. Floods and earthquakes destroy what little equilibrium remains in a relentlessly violent world in which the authorities and the rebels are equally vicious and corrupt.

Alegria, Ciro. *Broad and Alien Is the World.* Chester Spring, Pennsylvania: Dufour Editions. This award-winning, lyric novel (*El Mundo Es Ancho y Ajeno,* 1941) was written by a celebrated Peruvian novelist who spent his career documenting the oppression of Peru's indigenous peoples. Look also for Alegría's other classic, *The Golden Serpent (La Serpiente de Oro).* The Spanish versions of these works are available in most bookstores in Peru.

Bryce Echenique, Alfredo. *A World for Julius.* University of Wisconsin Press, 2004. Bryce Echenique explores Peruvian society while describing a world of illusion created for little Julius, who eventually will have to fit perfectly in this society. A true masterpiece from one of Peru's top novelists.

Vargas Llosa, Mario. *Aunt Julia and the Scriptwriter.* New York: Penguin, 1995. This autobiographical tale of taboo mixes radio scripts with the steamy romance that a young radio writer carries on with his aunt—this is Vargas Llosa with Julia Urquidi, who became his first wife. This was one of Vargas Llosa's first novels revealing a glimpse into highbrow Lima society.

Vargas Llosa, Mario. *Captain Pantoja and the Secret Service.* New York: Harper Collins, 1978. This is the funny and ludicrous story of a faithful soldier, Pantaleón Pantoja, and his mission to begin a top-secret prostitution service for Peru's military in Iquitos, Peru. His problem is that he is too successful.

Vargas Llosa, Mario. *Conversation in the Cathedral.* New York: Harper Perennial, 2005. This is one of Vargas Llosa's masterworks. *Conversation in the Cathedral* takes place in 1950s Peru during the dictatorship of Manuel A. Odría. Over beers and a sea of freely spoken words, the conversation flows between Santiago and Ambrosio, who talk of their tormented lives and of the overall degradation and frustration that has slowly taken over their city. Through a complicated web of secrets and historical references, Vargas Llosa analyzes the mental and moral mechanisms that govern power and the people behind it. It is a groundbreaking novel that tackles identity as well as the role of a citizen and how a lack of personal freedom can forever scar people and a nation.

Vargas Llosa, Mario. *The Green House*. New York: Harper Perennial, 2005. Vargas Llosa's classic early novel takes place in a Peruvian town, between desert and jungle, where Don Anselmo, a stranger in a black coat, builds a brothel, bringing together the innocent and the corrupt: Bonificia, a young Indian girl saved by the nuns, who becomes a prostitute; Father García, struggling for the church; and four best friends drawn to both excitement and escape.

TRAVEL AND EXPLORATION

Bingham, Hiram. *Phoenix: Lost City of the Incas*. Edited by Hugh Thomson. London: Phoenix Press, 2003. Bingham's classic description of how he discovered Machu Picchu lends historical detail to Peru's stand-out attraction and also explains why Bingham went on to become the leading inspiration for movie character Indiana Jones.

Kane, Joe. *Running the Amazon*. New York: Vintage, 1990. Starting from a glacier at 17,000 feet, Joe Kane and a team of adventurers attempted the never-before-done feat of navigating the entire length of the Amazon River from source to mouth. The story begins as an accurate description of life in Peru's highlands and ends with the difficulties of managing personalities in a modern-day expedition.

Lee, Vincent. *Sixpac Manco: Travels Among the Incas* (1985). This self-published book is a must-read for Vilcabamba explorers and is available at the South American Explorers Club in Lima. It is out of print, but used copies can be found at Amazon.com or other Internet sites that sell used books. The book comes with highly accurate maps of the area around Espíritu Pampa and Lee's amusing, shoot-from-the-hip adventurer's attitude.

Mathiessen, Peter. *At Play in the Fields of the Lord*. New York: Vintage, 1991. Set in a malarial jungle outpost, this Mathiessen classic depicts the clash of development and indigenous peoples in the Amazon jungle. It was made into a motion picture as well.

Muller, Karin. *Along the Inca Road, A Woman's Journey into an Ancient Empire*. Washington, D.C.: National Geographic, 2000. The author traces her 6,000-mile journey along Inca roads in Ecuador, Peru, Bolivia, and Chile. Along the way she shares her insights about modern exploration and Inca history.

Schneebaum, Tobias. *Keep the River on Your Right*. New York: Grove Press, 1998. In 1955, New York intellectual Tobias Schneebaum spent eight years living with the Akarama tribe in the remote Madre de Dios jungle. His book describes his participation in homosexual and cannibalistic rituals and became an immediate jungle classic when it was published in 1969.

Shah, Tahir. *Trail of Feathers: In Search of the Birdmen of Peru*. London: Orion Publishing, 2002. A 16th-century mention of Inca who "flew like birds" over the jungle leads one journalist on a quest to unlock the secret of Peru's so-called birdmen. His journey takes him to Machu Picchu, the Nasca Lines, and finally into the Amazon itself.

Simpson, Joe. *Touching the Void*. New York: Harper Perennial, 2004. In 1985, Joe Simpson and Simon Yates attempted a first ascent of Siulá Grande, a forbidding peak in Peru's Cordillera Huayhuash. Simpson's subsequent fall into a crevasse, and his struggle to survive, will grip even nonclimbers. This book was recently made into a motion picture of the same name.

Thomson, Hugh. *The White Rock, An Exploration of the Inca Heartland*. New York: Overlook Press, 2001. British documentary filmmaker Hugh Thomson returns to

Vilcabamba, where he explored in his early 20s, to weave a recollection of his travels together with an alluring blend of Spanish chronicles and Inca history. It contains vivid, sometimes scathing, depictions of local personalities and makes for a fast, exciting way to read up for a Peru trip.

TRAVEL GUIDES

Frost, Peter. *Exploring Cusco,* 5th ed. Lima: Nuevas Imágenes, 1999. This book continues to be the best-written, most readable historical and archaeological approach to the Cusco area, written by longtime Cusco resident Peter Frost.

Johnson, Brad. *Classic Climbs of the Cordillera Blanca.* Montrose, Colorado: Western Reflections, 2003. Johnson has been guiding in the Cordillera Blanca for nearly two decades and presents detailed descriptions of the area's major climbing routes, together with three-dimensional maps and vibrant color photos. This is an award-winning guide to one of the world's top mountaineering destinations.

Wagner, Steven, and Matias Guzman. *Peru Surfing Travel Guide.* Buenos Aires: Gráficas Boschi, 2002. The authors had a tremendous time searching out Peru's breaks and writing the first book in English to South America's surfing mecca. This book can be found in Lima bookstores and ordered online in the United States.

Wust, Walter, et al. *Inca Guide to Peru.* Lima: Peisa, 2003. This excellent highway guide, sponsored by Mitsubishi, contains the country's best road maps and detailed descriptions of all the driving routes. There is also some historical and cultural information on each of Peru's main destinations, though little information on hotels and restaurants. This company has also published *Guia Inca de Playas,* which runs down all the remote camping and surfing spots along Peru's coast from Tumbes to Tacna. These books are for sale in Ripley department stores and most Lima bookstores.

Zarzar, Omar. *Por los Caminos de Peru en Bicicleta.* Lima: Editor SA, 2001. This is a guide to Peru's best mountain-biking routes. Though written in Spanish, the maps and itineraries are useful even for non-Spanish speakers.

NATURE AND THE ENVIRONMENT

Beaver, Paul. *Diary of an Amazon Guide: Amazing Encounters with Tropical Nature and Culture.* New York: AE Publications, 2001. Paul Beaver, owner of the Tahuayo Lodge near Iquitos, holds a PhD from the University of Chicago and has spent two decades exploring the upper Amazon. He provides a fast-moving, insightful, and humorous glimpse into both the nature and people of the area.

Forsyth, Adrian, and Ken Miyata. *Tropical Nature, Life and Death in the Rain Forests of Central and South America.* New York: Simon & Schuster, 1987. This well-written and at times humorous book lays out the principles of rainforest ecology in easy-to-read, entertaining prose. First-time jungle visitors will understand much more of what they see in the Amazon after reading this book.

Kricher, John. *A Neotropical Companion,* 2nd ed. Princeton, NJ: Princeton University Press, 1999. Compared to *Tropical Nature,* this book offers a more detailed, scientific look at rainforest ecology, though it is still designed for nonbiologists. This is the bible for the Amazon enthusiast, with a good listing of animals, plants, and ecosystems and theoretical discussions of evolutionary biology and other advanced topics.

MacQuarrie, Kim, and André Bärtschi, photographer. *Peru's Amazonian Eden: Manu National Park and Biosphere Reserve,* 2nd ed. Barcelona, Spain: Francis O. Patthe, 1998. This book of stunning photos is more than just a coffee-table book. Kim MacQuarrie spent six months living with a previously uncontacted tribe in the Manu and writes an eloquent evocation of the people and wildlife of Peru's most pristine patch of Amazon.

MacQuarrie, Kim, with Jorge Flores Ochoa and Javier Portós. Photos by Jaume and Jordi Blassi. *Gold of the Andes: The Llamas, Alpacas, Vicuñas, and Guanacos of South America*. Barcelona, Spain: Francis O. Patthe, 1994. This is another well-written book with large-format pictures of Peru's highlanders and the animals on which they depend.

Stap, Don. *A Parrot Without a Name*. Austin, Texas: University of Texas Press, 1991. Poet-naturalist Don Stap accompanied two of Latin America's more renowned ornithologists, Ted Parker and John O'Neil, on birding expeditions into unexplored corners of the Amazon. The book blends Amazon adventure with a close look at the odd, obsessive life of ornithologists.

BIRDING

Clements, James, and Noam Shany. *A Field Guide to the Birds of Peru*. Temecula, California: Ibis Publishing Company, 2001. Though much criticized by bird-watchers for its faulty pictures of certain birds, this US$60 tome catalogs nearly 1,800 birds known to reside in, or migrate to, Peru. This is the best alternative for birders unable to afford *Birds of Peru*.

Krabbe, Nils, and John Fjeldsa. *Birds of the High Andes*. Copenhagen: Denmark Zoological Museum of the University of Copenhagen, 1990. Real birders consider this such a must-have masterpiece that they are willing to shell out US$150 for it. It includes all the birds you are likely to encounter in the temperate and alpine zones of Peru.

Schulenberg, Thomas, and Douglas Stotz, Daniel Lane, and John O'Neill. *Birds of Peru (Princeton Field Guides)*. Sanibel Island, Florida: Ralph Curtis Books, 2007. This long-awaited bible of Peru birding is coveted by every professional bird guide in Peru. It represents a huge step forward and

was a colossal undertaking, as reflected by its beautiful color renderings of birds and its US$300-plus price tag.

Valqui, Thomas. *Where to Watch Birds in Peru*, 1st ed. Peru, 2004. This comprehensive self-published guide to birding in Peru explains not only what birds you'll see where, but how to get there and where you might stay along the way. This is an excellent resource, and there's nothing else like it on the market. More information about this book may be found at www.granperu.com/birdwatchingbook.

Walker, Barry, and Jon Fjeldsa, illustrations. *Field Guide to the Birds of Machu Picchu*. Lima: Peruvian National Trust for Parks and Protected Areas. This portable guide, written by Cusco's foremost bird expert and owner of Manu Expeditions, is widely available in Cusco. At US$30 it is an excellent value, with 31 superb color plates and descriptions of 420 species.

PHOTOGRAPHY

Milligan, Max. *Realm of the Incas*. New York: Universe Publishing, 2001. English photographer Max Milligan spent years trekking to the remote corners of Peru to capture images that range from the sacred snows of Nevado Ausangate to the torpid meanderings of the Río Manu.

Weintraub, Adam L. *Vista Andina. A Photographic Perspective on Contemporary Life in the Andes*. PhotoExperience.net, 2010. Seattle-based photographer Adam Weintraub explores Cusco and surroundings through his lens, attempting a journalistic and zealous look into the intimate world of the city's inhabitants.

Wust, Walter, and Marie Isabel Musselman, ed., *Land of a Thousand Colors*. Lima: Peisa, 2002. This coffee-table book sparkles with the prose of Peruvian writer Antonio Cisneros and painter Fernando de Szyslo. It captures Peru's diversity in large-format, color prints that are organized not by content, but by their color.

FOOD

Acurio, Gastón. *Peru: Una Aventura Culinaria.* Lima: Quebecor World Peru, 2002. This large-format photo book profiles Peru's array of foods in chapters titled Water, Land, and Air. It includes a range of recipes and profiles of Peru's leading chefs and is available in Lima bookshops.

Custer, Tony. *The Art of Peruvian Cuisine.* Lima: Cimino Publishing Group, 2003. This book has high-quality photos and an excellent selection of Peruvian recipes in both Spanish and English.

Morales, Edmund. *The Guinea Pig: Healing, Food, and Ritual in the Andes.* Tucson, Arizona: University of Arizona Press, 1995. This is the first major study, with good pictures, of how Andean highlanders not only eat guinea pig but also use it for medicinal and religious purposes.

PromPeru. *Peru Mucho Gusto.* Lima: Comisión de Promoción del Peru, 2006. This Spanish-English book is the latest of Peru's glamorous large-format cookbooks. Starting with the history of the country's cooking, the book gives a general overview of Peru's traditional cooking. The last chapter is dedicated to the creative chefs who will lead Peru's cooking into the future. Available in Lima bookstores.

SPIRITUAL AND ESOTERIC

Milla, Carlos. *Genesis de la Cultura Andina,* 4th ed. Cusco: Amaru Wayra, 2006. If you can read Spanish, this book presents esoteric theories based on many of Peru's ancient ceremonial centers. Milla's latest book, 2003's *Ayni: Semiotica Andina de los Espacios Sagrados,* from the same publisher, focuses on astrology. Carlos Milla can be reached in Cusco at cmilla@viabcp.com.

Villoldo, Alberto, and Erik Jendresen. *The Four Winds: A Shaman's Odyssey into the Amazon.* New York: Harper Collins, 1991. Even Peru's shamans respect this work, which documents the author's spiritual initiation into Amazon rituals.

WEAVING

Heckman, Andrea. *Woven Stories: Andean Textiles and Rituals.* Albuquerque: University of New Mexico Press, 2003. A series of ethnographic essays on Andean life and weaving by a researcher with two decades in the field.

Pollard Rowe, Anne, and John Cohen. *Hidden Threads of Peru: Q'ero Textiles.* London: Merrell Publishers, 2002. In vibrant pictures and concise prose, this book documents the extraordinary weavings of Q'ero, a remote town in south Peru where the authors have been researching for nearly four decades.

CHILDREN

Hergé, *The Adventures of Tintin: Prisoners of the Sun,* 1949. Copenhagen: Egmont Books Ltd., 2002. In this Hergé classic, a sequel to *The Seven Crystal Balls,* Tintin, Captain Haddock, and Milou catch a steamer to Peru to rescue a kidnapped professor. The adventure leads them through the Andes and the Amazon, which are depicted in fascinating detail and through the romanticized lens of the mid-20th century.

Internet Resources

TRAVEL INFORMATION
Andean Travel Web
www.andeantravelweb.com
This is the best of several websites in Peru that evaluate hotels, restaurants, and agencies.

The Latin American Network Information Center
http://lanic.utexas.edu/la/peru
The largest single list of links on Peru has been compiled by the University of Texas.

Living in Peru
www.livinginperu.com
This, along with www.expatperu.com, is a directory of resources for foreigners living and traveling in Peru.

Peru Links
www.perulinks.com
This huge website of links lists tons of hard-to-find Peru websites, including gay and lesbian clubs, alternative medicine, chat rooms, etc.

The Peruvian Times
www.peruviantimes.com
Lima's oldest English-language publishing house, which until recently published the *Lima Times,* has an interesting website with tips on arriving in Lima, photos, links, and a directory of expatriate associations.

South American Explorers
www.saexplorers.org
This web page for the South American Explorers Club has books for sale, information on insurance providers, an online bulletin board with cars for sale and apartments for rent, and interesting links.

FLIGHT INFORMATION
Lima Airport
www.lap.com.pe
This is the home page of the Jorge Chávez International airport in Lima.

Tráfico
www.traficoperu.com
This agency newsletter is an updated list of all international and domestic flights in Peru.

ECOTOURISM
GORP
www.gorp.com
This joint production of Away.com, Gorp, and Outside Online has hundreds of travel stories on Peru, a list of top 20 travel destinations, and links to tour operators.

Planeta
www.planeta.com/peru.html
This ecotourism site includes articles, essays, and links to responsible tour operators.

SURFING
Peru Azul
www.peruazul.com
Peru's most popular website for surfing and ocean conditions along the coast is for Spanish speakers only.

ANDEAN CULTURE
Culture of the Andes
www.andes.org
A labor of love from Peru fanatics Russ and Ada Gibbons, this site focusing on Andean culture includes short stories, jokes, music, songs in Quechua, poetry, and riddles.

Index

UV

List of Maps

Acknowledgments

In preparing the third edition of *Moon Peru,* we relied on a team of updaters located in various locations in Peru. Cusco residents Gabriela Holland and Fiona Cameron tackled Cusco, Sacred Valley and Machu Picchu content, with the invaluable help of the very capable Celine Wald. Jorge Riveros Cayo trekked across the rest of the country, and in the process, sampled Peru's finest cuisine, visited hundreds of hotels, and rode on a river boat for a week in the Amazon jungle. This book was possible because of these hard-working updaters and the extraordinary people they met along the way. For this edition, many of our old friends stepped forward to help again, but many new faces contributed their invaluable knowledge, resources, and enthusiasm. We thank them all.

In Lima, the Casa Andina team, lead by Peter Vicich and including Analida Marisca and Carla González del Riego, helped with travel arrangements around Cusco, Puno, Arequipa, and Nasca. César Torres Bazán is a wonderfully warm and kind host and helped debunk the mysteries of Colca Canyon. In Nasca, we will never forget the red wines and homemade pastas enjoyed with Enzo Destro.

In the north of Peru, Claudia Blanco was invaluable for helping update Piura. We also want to thank Santiago Solari, a talented chef and host in Vichayito, and Manuel Aguirre and Michelle Accolti Gil-Morey, good friends full of knowledge about surfing, delicious food, and convenient lodgings.

In Cajamarca, John Herdin was once again very helpful and generous with his time. In Chachapoyas, we want to thank Sonia Guillén and Adriana von Hagen, respected authorities on the Chachapoya culture, as well as Peter Lerche, the German major of Chachapoyas who has a Peruvian heart after living there for more than 30 years. The Tarapato content came to life because of the incredibly patient work of César Reategui and María Luisa Trigoso.

In the Huaraz area, where we once again spent considerable time and effort, we owe eternal gratitude to Isabel and Chris Benway, owners of a marvelous café. Also Benquelo Morales and Marcello Cafiero, owners of the best bars in Huaraz, made dozens of suggestions about hotels, restaurants, and new places where to go.

In the Cusco area, we also want to thank Raül Montes, Richard Webb, Wendy Weeks, Joaquín Randall, Kennedy Leavens, Adela Arenas, Marcela Zúñiga Sáenz, Carlos Zevallos from Casa Andina, Rafael Casabonne, and Ulrike and Josip Orlovac in Pisac, along with her next-door neighbors Fielding and Roman Vizcarra. Nicholas Asheshov is one of the great experts on Peru, and, along with his wife María del Carmen, contributed immeasurably as always.

We gained a new perspective on Lake Titicaca thanks to Martha Giraldo and her sister Consuelo. In Arequipa, the invaluable help of Angela Delgado and Miguel Barreda was crucial. Edmundo and Patricia from Wasipunko provided information, friendship, and their warmth.

The most difficult area in all of Peru to explore, and to write about, is the rain forest. This section was greatly improved thanks to the insight and guidance of a series of Amazon readers including Noam Shany, Paul Beaver, Rodrigo Custodio, Barry Walker, Max Gunther, and Kurt Holle. José Koechlin von Stein, a gentle but powerful voice in Peru's fight to conserve the Amazon, and his staff were a huge help as always.

We also want to thank the kind and professional staff at Avalon Travel. Publisher Bill Newlin and Associate Publisher Donna Galassi placed their complete trust in us. Our Editor, Erin Raber, guided us expertly and was exceedingly patient and professional. Thanks also to Cartography Director Mike Morgenfeld, Map Editor Albert Angulo, Graphics Coordinators Lucie Ericksen and Darren Alessi, Editorial Director Kevin McLain, Acquisitions Director Grace Fujimoto, and Production Director Jane Musser.

www.moon.com

DESTINATIONS | ACTIVITIES | BLOGS | MAPS | BOOKS

MOON.COM is ready to help plan your next trip! Filled with fresh trip ideas and strategies, author interviews, informative travel blogs, a detailed map library, and descriptions of all the Moon guidebooks, Moon.com is all you need to get out and explore the world—or even places in your own backyard. While at Moon.com, sign up for our monthly e-newsletter for updates on new releases, travel tips, and expert advice from our on-the-go Moon authors. As always, when you travel with Moon, expect an experience that is uncommon and truly unique.

MOON IS ON FACEBOOK—BECOME A FAN!
JOIN THE MOON PHOTO GROUP ON FLICKR

MAP SYMBOLS

▦	Expressway	◖	Highlight	✕	Airfield	✈	Winery
—	Primary Road	○	City/Town	✕	Airport	P	Parking Area
—	Secondary Road	◉	State Capital	▲	Mountain	≡	Archaeological Site
∷∷∷	Unpaved Road	⊛	National Capital	✛	Unique Natural Feature	♠	Church
- - - -	Trail	★	Point of Interest			▯	Gas Station
⋯⋯⋯	Ferry	•	Accommodation	⟋	Waterfall	▨	Glacier
▬▬▬	Railroad	▼	Restaurant/Bar	♠	Park	▨	Mangrove
▨	Pedestrian Walkway	▪	Other Location	▯	Trailhead	▨	Reef
∷∷∷	Stairs	▵	Campground	✗	Skiing Area	▨	Swamp

CONVERSION TABLES

°C = (°F - 32) / 1.8
°F = (°C x 1.8) + 32
1 inch = 2.54 centimeters (cm)
1 foot = 0.304 meters (m)
1 yard = 0.914 meters
1 mile = 1.6093 kilometers (km)
1 km = 0.6214 miles
1 fathom = 1.8288 m
1 chain = 20.1168 m
1 furlong = 201.168 m
1 acre = 0.4047 hectares
1 sq km = 100 hectares
1 sq mile = 2.59 square km
1 ounce = 28.35 grams
1 pound = 0.4536 kilograms
1 short ton = 0.90718 metric ton
1 short ton = 2,000 pounds
1 long ton = 1.016 metric tons
1 long ton = 2,240 pounds
1 metric ton = 1,000 kilograms
1 quart = 0.94635 liters
1 US gallon = 3.7854 liters
1 Imperial gallon = 4.5459 liters
1 nautical mile = 1.852 km

MOON PERU
Avalon Travel
a member of the Perseus Books Group
1700 Fourth Street
Berkeley, CA 94710, USA
www.moon.com

Editor: Erin Raber
Series Manager: Kathryn Ettinger
Copy Editor: Deana Shields
Graphics and Production Coordinator: Darren Alessi
Cover Designer: Darren Alessi
Map Editor: Albert Angulo
Cartographers: Kat Bennett, Mike Morgenfeld,
  Chris L. Henrick, Allison Rawley
Proofreader: Jamie Andrade
Indexer: Deana Shields

ISBN-13: 978-1-59880-600-7
ISSN: 1549-7445

Printing History
1st Edition – 2004
3rd Edition – January 2011

5 4 3 2 1

Front cover photo: Machu Picchu © Frank Siteman/
  Science Faction/Corbis
Title page photo: © Domingo Giribaldi, PromPeru
Interior color photos: page 4 © Renée del Gaudio and
Ross Wehner; page 5 (left) © José Alvarez, PromPeru,
(center) © Mylene D'Auriol, PromPeru, (right) © Renée
del Gaudio and Ross Wehner; page 6 (inset) © Gabriela
Holland, (bottom) © Renée del Gaudio and Ross Wehner;
page 7 (top left) © Renée del Gaudio and Ross Wehner,
(top right) © Dave Jankowski and Nancy Connick,
(bottom left) © Jorge Riveros Cayo, (bottom right) ©
Scott Collins, www.lifeunscriptedphotography.com;
page 9 © Gabriela Holland; page 10 (top) © Jeff Trebac,
(bottom) © Renée del Gaudio and Ross Wehner; page 11
© Jorge Riveros Cayo; page 12 © Alejandro Balaguer,
PromPeru; page 14 © Craig Gemmell; page 15 (top) ©
Amber Davis Collins, www.lifeunscriptedphotography.
com, (bottom) © Renée del Gaudio and Ross Wehner;
page 16 (top) © Carlos Sala, PromPeru, (bottom) ©
Renée del Gaudio and Ross Wehner; page 17 © Jorge
Riveros Cayo; page 18 © Renée del Gaudio and Ross
Wehner; page 19 © Renzo Uccelli, PromPeru; page 20
(top) © Sergio Schabelman, (bottom) © Beth Fuchs; page
21 © Renée del Gaudio and Ross Wehner; page 22 © Beth
Fuchs; page 23 © Jorge Riveros Cayo; page 24 (top) ©
Jorge Riveros Cayo, (bottom) © Renée del Gaudio and
Ross Wehner

Printed in Canada by Friesens

KEEPING CURRENT

If you have a favorite gem you'd like to see included in the next edition, or see anything
that needs updating, clarification, or correction, please drop us a line. Send your
comments via email to feedback@moon.com, or use the address above.